Service-Oriented Architecture

Personal Management Thoughts - A SOA P Opera

SOA (and Technology) Management Discussion

(Storytelling Format)

By
H. Howell-Barber

\\\✸///

Service-Oriented Architecture

Personal Management Thoughts - A SOA P Opera

Published by HBiNK, LLC

5900 Arlington Avenue

Riverdale, NY 10471

writers@HBiNK.com

ISBN-13: 978-0-6152-0157-3

Dedication

To my daughter, Cynthia Barber-Mingo - she helps me to remain technically and managerially sharp (with a "p") through discussions of her continuing work adventures. Read the book to find out about Sharf with an "f".

To my son-in-law Eric Barber-Mingo who helped me to keep things legal.

To my dinner partner and co-author of a prior book, Dr. James Lawler - he reinforced the value of determination.

To my friends Annette (also my sister), Rosemary, Marcia, and Murie who provided encouragement.

To my sister Rachel who helped me to verify that the "SOA P" people were probably not too far from real world people

About the Author

H. Howell-Barber has a total of 38 years of experience with computer technology and technology management, including 25 years of hands-on technical experience overlapping with 20 years as a hands-on manager, spanning 33 years. This came after spending two years as a statistical typist and general office worker in one of the original technical consulting firms.

H. worked with marketing, publishing, and utilities systems before spending 25 years with a financial services organization installing databases and trading systems, among dozens of other assignments. The last corporate assignment involved consulting on the implementation of a Web-based portfolio reporting application that provided information from DB2, Oracle, and SQL Server databases to users in North America, Europe, and Asia-Pacific regions.

Since official retirement as a Director of Technology (one level above vice president), H has co-authored several articles and a textbook on Service-Oriented Architecture, <u>Service-Oriented Architecture: SOA Strategy, Methodology, and Technology.</u>

H. has a BS degree in psychology with minors in chemistry, mathematics, and German (there were no computer science degrees then) and post-graduate studies in Learning Theory and Management Science. H is also the middle rung of three generations of people working with computers.

H. enjoys travel, photography, languages and linguistics (having collected books and reference works in 119 different languages before the Internet), astrophysics (a 54-year hobby), and collecting glass art and crystal (over 1,000 sandy items and counting).

H has a brown belt in Judo, and lives on a hill in Riverdale, New York, that commands a view of the Palisades.

Note: Fifty-fours (54) years with astrophysics is not a typo. It started with astronomy in 4th grade science and never stopped.

PROLOGUE

A New Way of Seeing Things

You are about to participate in an information presentation experiment. It discusses the effects that personal issues may have on management, business, and technology while providing serious recommendations about one of the hottest current business/technology paradigms (Service-Oriented Architecture (SOA)).

SOA P (P is for Personal) is three books in one - the management, business, and technology issues are presented from **inside the heads** of the SOA participants, using a SOA P opera format.

- You may skip the personal parts and read the management, business, and technology recommendations.
- You may read the background material and then go to the personal issues.
- You may choose to read the entire document.

You will have a wry look at people that you may find familiar, whether you work in business or technology (in management or in the trenches). I suggest that you look at Table A.16 in the Appendix as soon as you finish with the introduction. It contains comments from people in 36 SOA-related roles in Daxiao, nine of whom appear in the body of the book. Daxiao is a large composite organization that provides the backdrop for all "three" books of the SOA P opera.

** 38 Years of Serious Business/Technology **

The serious material in this book summarizes 38 years of experience with business and technology.

****** Revision #(Many) ******

If you show enough interest, there will be multiple revisions to this document and the second one in the set. It is likely that I will fix one thing and unfix something else. However, this is LULU, and I am persistent. This is Revision #2 already.

"Apollo gees": I am very (I say VARY) clever at getting around speling and gramar chequers.

****** Terminology ******

1. **SOA P** (this book) alludes to SOAP (with no space); a technical standard for connecting Web services (the processing components of SOA).
2. Explanations of other terms in SOA P are in Table A.5 in the Appendix.

****** Thank you in advance for your participation. ******

PS: I almost forgot to mention that there will be a SOAP (2), SOA Planning. It will use the roles and organizational structures presented in the SOA P opera to organize over 10,000 activities and tasks that you may use in business, technology, and start-up planning for SOA.

CONTENTS

Processes, Communications, Planning, Roles
For
Cross-Organizational SOA

Merged with

Personal Reasons for Being Stuck in SOA

Delivered as a

SOA P Opera

------------- -------------

Service-Oriented Architecture

Personal Management Thoughts - A SOA P Opera

SOA (and Technology) Management Discussion (Storytelling Format)

List of Figures

List of Tables in the Body of the SOA P Opera

List of Tables in the Appendix of the SOA P Opera

CHAPTER I - INTRODUCTION

ABOUT THIS BOOK

Service-Oriented Architecture (SOA) Personal: SOA P

SOA could be the ultimate business/technology **miracle**. If done properly, it can correct half the problems that we created over the last 50 years at the business-technology interface. While providing **HUGE return on investment**, SOA may also seriously affect the people in organizations that implement SOA.

SOA P is the first book that emphasizes SOA's effects on **people** - it presents **personal** concerns merged with business and technology issues from **inside the heads** of managers, their families and friends, and SOA advisors in a company attempting an organization-wide SOA.

Stuck in SOA

The company found itself stalled by intrigues, (character) assassinations, angst, passion, and general life problems associated SOA-related changes. These threatened to **override the benefits** of excellent SOA management, organizational, and technology skills and cause the loss of $ (000,000) s.

SOA Resistance Summary - Why

Notice the difference between Fig. 1.1 - "MINE" and Fig. 1.2 - "OURS!" on the next pages. Redundant structures in "MY" business and technology silos are replaced by "OUR" structures where everyone shares the best of everything?

Many individuals and business units do not wish to share. More critically, the transition from **"MY" system** to **"OUR" SOA** will require creation, change, rearrangement, or elimination of power bases, business/technology units, management structures, and jobs.

Major resistance occurs, resulting in situations that are best described in the first **SOA P opera**.

Serious SOA

SOA P also discusses serious management, business, and technology topics, including:

- An SOA Program methodology (WFSOA).
- SOA evolution and corporate strategy.
- SOA initiation and synergies with SOX, CMMI, ITIL, Six Sigma, etc.
- SOA processes (emphasizing SOA communications, planning, and maturity assessment).
- SOA-related roles and comments from role incumbents.
- SOA training recommendations.
- SOA lessons learned.

WHO SHOULD READ THIS BOOK

1. Anyone who wants a high-level view of Service-Oriented Architecture.
2. Anyone who is stuck trying to achieve "BIG SOA" and would like a list of 150 reasons for why they may be stuck (lessons learned and resistance factors).
3. Anyone interested in a recommendation for establishing an SOA Program.
4. Anyone interested in the synergies between SOA and Sarbanes Oxley (SOX).
5. Anyone who is interested in an alternative view of SOA evolution and risk management.
6. Anyone who wants to understand how a successful implementation may have major effects on people in both business and technology.
7. Anyone who ever looked at executive technology decisions and wondered, "Why in the heck would they do that?"
8. Anyone who wants to know how I could possibly come up with 110 roles and 130 alternate role names.
9. Any adult with a moderate understanding of technology who may appreciate a fun look at the

types of things that put the sizzle in technology stakeholders.

10. Anyone who likes word play, starting with **SOA P**. Consider translating the names of some of the characters (Gunnar/Gunther and Piccolo, for example).

HOW TO READ THIS BOOK

Read the section on presentation format (a few pages down) and then follow the **Readers** (notes) and the **STOP/SKIP** signs. Use **SKIP** to get around the extremely personal parts if you only want SOA management, processes, and planning.

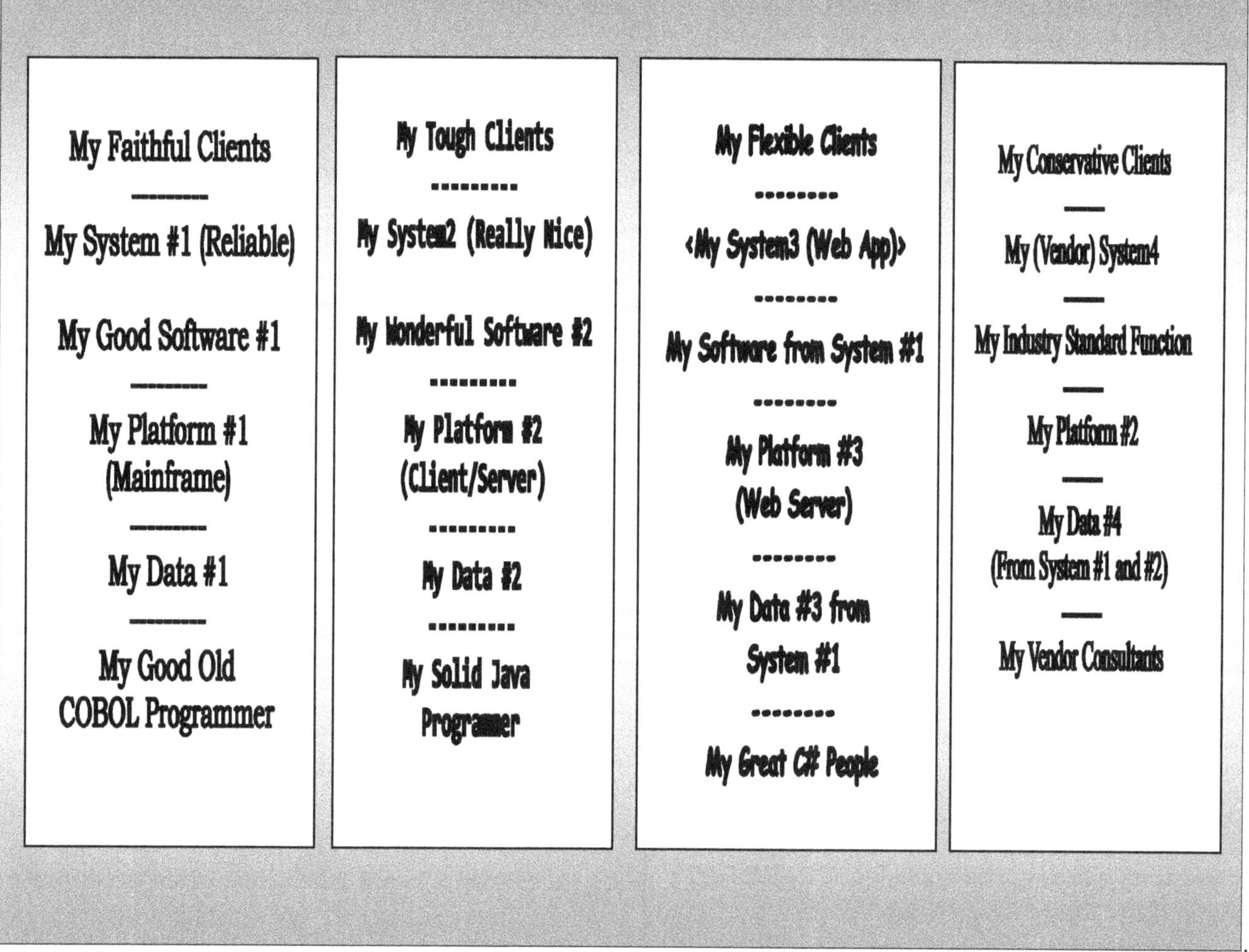

Fig. 1.1 - MINE, MINE! (Business/Technology Silos before SOA)

BACKGROUND - MIXING BUSINESS, TECHNOLOGY, AND SOA PERSONAL

Two years ago, I had assembled over 1,000 pages of information covering 36 years of my career. SOA was at the apex. The full document contained everything listed on the prior pages as well as:

- 10,000+ SOA planning hints (role + action + action object + Program methodology domain) that could be extracted, mixed, and matched to form SOA plans.
- 10,000+ tips for SOA communications (who talks to whom about SOA and how often).
- Recommendations for SOA security and access control.
- SOA standards and standards management
- A huge glossary of terms

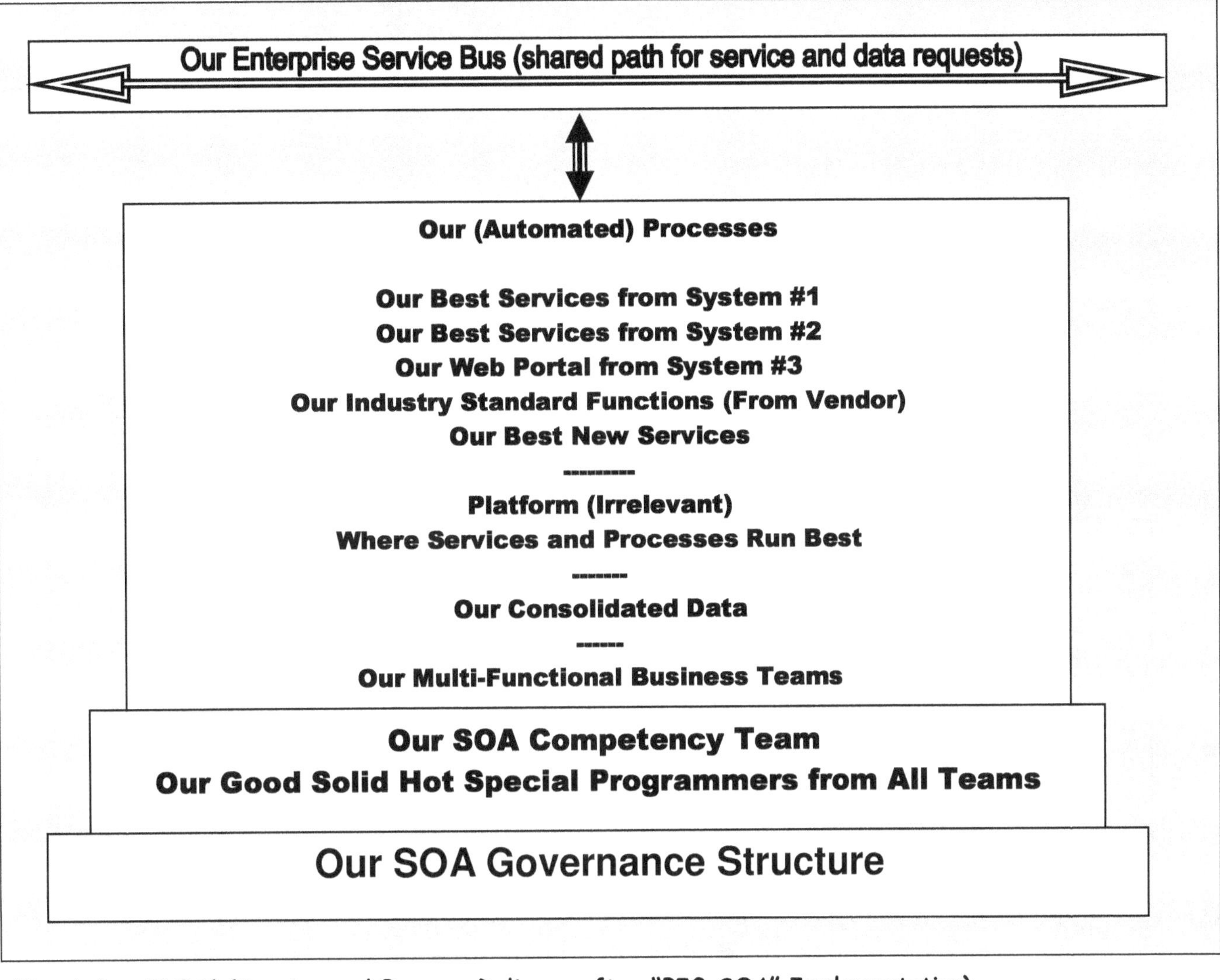

Fig. 1.2 - OURS! (Service and Process Delivery after "BIG SOA" Implementation)

I showed excerpts of a few of the sections to a friend. To my dismay, he referred to it as a "yada-yada" document. I came to realize that the presentation was unbelievably dry. It was **as interesting as watching grass grow**. It needed **context**, and the context had to be different from the hundreds of books and articles that had already been written about Web Services, SOA, and Business Process Management.

At the same time, I started noticing two trends in the industry. They were:

1. Companies were declaring SOA success, but the successes were seldom cross-organizational implementations.
2. Companies were getting stuck when they tried to initiate cross-organizational SOA. Their implementations looked like Fig. 1.3.

The organization in Fig. 1.3 below is stuck in the middle of an SOA evolution. The governance structure is not as solid as it needs to be. The environment will be more confusing until a critical mass of services runs on Service-Oriented Architecture and the silos are eliminated.

When that happens, you have Fig. 1.2. Creating a business system will be equivalent to choosing an outfit from a carefully coordinated professional wardrobe. The organization will be a Service-Oriented Enterprise (SOE). Strong SOA governance is required to coordinate the SOA transition, promote sharing, and provide ongoing coordination.

Technology Walls (More Resistance)

Since Bell Labs created the UNIX operating system in 1969, each successful technology platform has contributed to the creation of expensive technology platform silos. UNIX and DEC operating system silos were isolated from the big mainframe computers. UNIX became isolated from UNIX (Sun, Berkley, AIX, SCO, and Linux). The Windows platform was isolated from everyone else. Until the Internet, most connections between these platforms were proprietary. When people began to realize the benefits of Internet-based Web services, they began to build platform-specific Web service silos. The industry was still clinging to "MY".

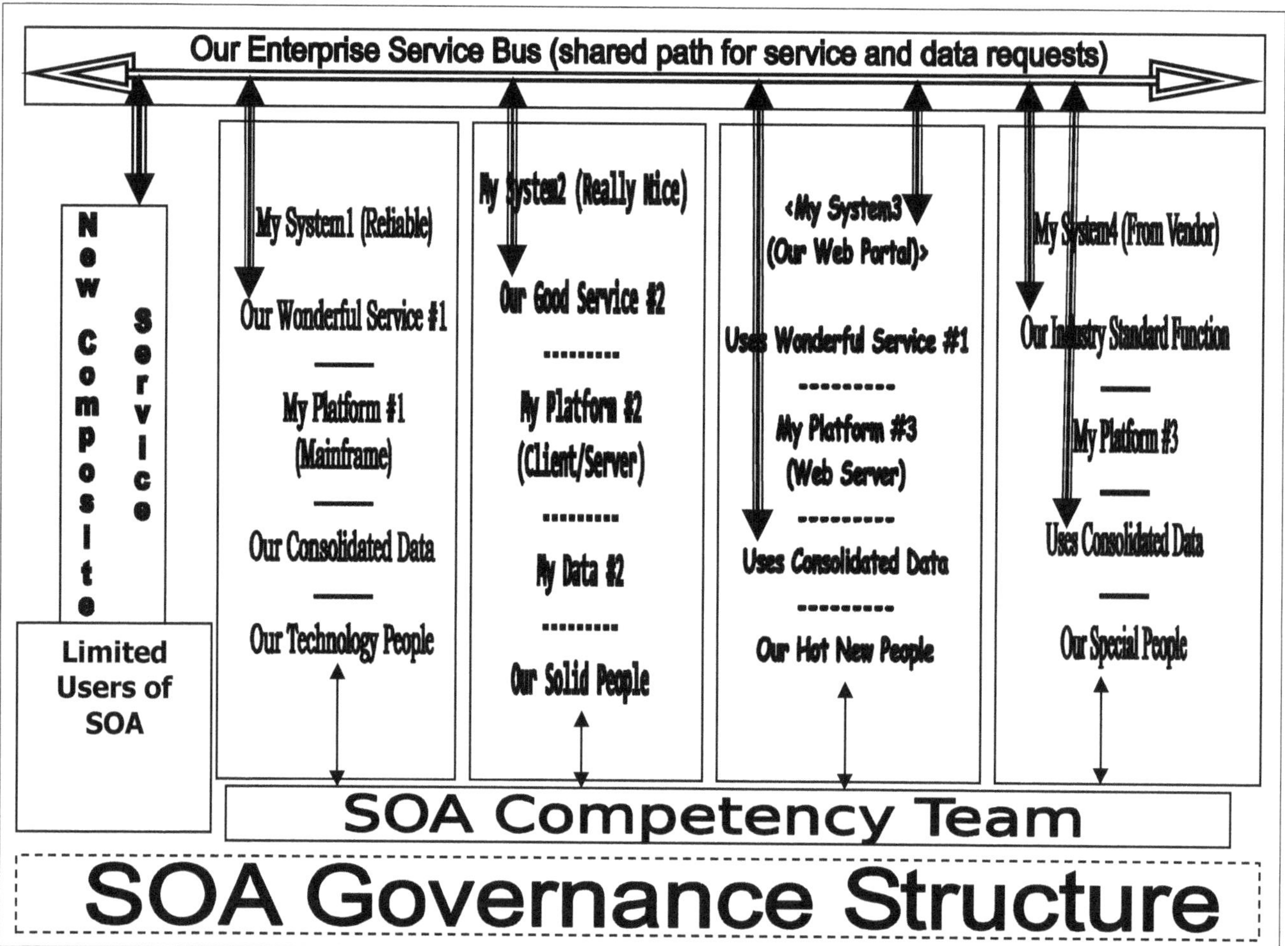

Fig. 1.3 - Stuck in SOA - Some Shared Services and Technology Participants

What Is Different This Time? - Scaling Walls for "BIG SOA"

SOA does not care about technology walls.

Internet-based standards (HTTP and SOAP) allow communication through, over, or under walls. Any service consumer who is willing to adhere to the standards may use (with appropriate security) processing from any service provider on any platform, as long as the provider software is adapted to the industry standards.

It is possible to build business systems using the best processing functions and the best quality data with fewer concerns about the technology barriers. Redundant functions and data may be eliminated. ***That statement gets people stuck.***

When an organization has overcome these artificially imposed boundaries and adapted its business structure accordingly, it will have "**BIG SOA**".

The next question is, "What happens to the people who spent so many years maintaining the walls?" You have resistance worthy of the most interesting SOA P opera.

> **Readers:** No one was likely to write a white paper explaining that their company knew all the right things that should be done, but they were stuck dealing with organizational and personal concerns.
>
> Therefore, you now have **SOA Personal** to drive the point home.

HOW WOULD YOU? - SOA ADVISORS

Before attempting to write SOA P, I decided that it would be a good idea to examine progress in one final area, large business/technology consulting organizations. I discovered that they were adding chapters to their training manuals to deal with SOA as quickly as they could.

But, in the chapters before they reach SOA, there are chapters that concentrate on how to keep customers and avoid consulting gauntlets. SOA may cause problems for consulting organizations too, as you will see later.

SOA advisors create ways to avoid SOA personal obstacles for themselves. They **do not** begin by telling organizations how to deal with SOA people issues.

They suggest that a few critical people (who turn out to be the ones "between assignments") should attend management classes dealing with the critical issues surrounding SOA. During the classes, they conduct breakout sessions that address a list of questions:

1. How would you define your SOA strategy?
2. How would you implement SOA governance?
3. How would you define the organizational structures necessary for SOA?
4. How would you implement SOA technology?
5. How would you manage your SOA evolution?
6. How would you define the new roles associated with SOA implementation?
7. How would you quantify benefits that accrue from SOA?
8. How would you mitigate risks associated with SOA?

After the "critical" managers provide answers that are politically or technically acceptable, the advisors work diligently to achieve what the organizations say they want to do. The advisors insert new concepts and guidance, but only to the level of sophistication that they perceive in the respective organizations. The result is that the most rigid organizations make limited progress toward "**BIG SOA**", and the flexible ones will be more flexible, but only if it does not hurt too much.

The senior advisor in SOA P is different, also for **personal** reasons. He asks, "How did you [...], and then explains how whatever the company did was wrong.

WHO IS "YOU"? - A MOST SIGNIFICANT OVERSIGHT

Another realization was that most sources did not clearly identify the "YOU" that would figure out the "HOW", and then perform the SOA activities. The longest list that I found contained 19 SOA-related entries, and they were primarily technical.

SOA P and SOA P (2) correct that. Both discuss 110+ roles, and suggest how they will fit within an innovative organizational structure.

If you do not like the 110+ primary role names, SOA P provides 140 alternates that you may be using in your organizations. If you believe 110 is too many, you may collapse them. SOA P provides recommendations for how that might be done in Table A.14.1 and A.14.2.

SOA P (2) will provide over 10,000 tasks that the 110 roles could perform. If you do not need 10,000 activities and tasks, decide which ones you need, and make sure they are preformed. If you perform more than 10,000 activities, let me know what they are. I am prepared to submit corrections and upgrades for the next several years (while I edit the editing).

DAXIAO - A COMPOSITE ORGANIZATION AND "BIG SOA"

I spent months looking for a real-world organization that had made sufficient progress with SOA that I could use it to place **SOA** Personal issues into a meaningful context.

I found "good" SOA implementations, and others that had more problems the companies would admit. There were bad points in all the good implementations, and there were good points in all the bad ones.

While reviewing Business Process Management (BPM), the latest SOA must-have, and discussing the creation of composite services from granular services, it occurred to me that it would be possible to create a composite organization that included the best features of hundreds of SOA "success stories". It would also be possible to illustrate **"failure points" and resistance points** within the success stories.

It could demonstrate a major attempt to ***Thunk*** to BIG SOA, the sticking points, and ideas for getting **unstuck**. Thus, Daxiao was born.

Daxiao means "big" (da) and "small" (xiao) in Pinyin (Mandarin Chinese written in western characters). Daxiao in the SOA P opera is a large organization that specializes in small electronics. The composite organization would be well formed. There is a well-formed discussion later in SOA P.

Daxiao would be:

- On the verge of implementing "BIG SOA" and already reaping the benefits of "agility, flexibility, and competitive advantage" (the SOA buzzwords).
- An organization that ran into personal icebergs that could ***destroy the SOA program***, and cause the company to lose place in the industry.
- A canvas for the hopes, fears, jealousies, and passions of the people working in SOA.

Daxiao's Products - the Beginning of Context

Readers: I will now step aside and allow SOA P characters to continue the narrative. We will start with the SOA architect, Hank Yu. His name is presented within XML tags (<angle brackets>), as are the names of all the characters that appear in the SOA P opera.

SOAP (no space) uses XML to format the messages that move between service providers and service users.

---------- ----------

I will drop in from time to time to provide reader tips and occasional clarification.

---------- ----------

Whial I'm at it, I apolojizes agane far eny speling an gramaticle errars.

<Hank Yu>: Daxiao makes electronic widgets - the insides and the connectors for electronics devices. Few of the things that we manufacture are larger than the motherboard of a desktop computer. We also produce very small products. Our digital recording devices have spaces between the recording layers of 1 nanometer (about 900 million nanometers fit on a yardstick). You will find parts that we built inside computers and network equipment, telephones, medical equipment, top secret research components, and communications satellites, but you will never see our name on the outside of anything. We write programs for some of the units that we build.

We perform electronics research, and we prototype designs for companies that wish to understand how a product will work before they set up to manufacture it themselves.

We had $28 billion dollars in revenue last year and $4 billion in profit. Our earnings per share were twice as much as our competitors. Nanotechnology and research support have large profit margins.

Service-Oriented Architecture allows us to maintain alignment between the rapidly changing business strategy and technology that Daxiao needs to achieve its results. I am one of the two senior technical contributors to the success of Daxiao's SOA Program. Maja Johanssen is the other one. We have many other talented SOA managers that you will meet as you continue through SOA P.

The head of Human Resources will provide more organizational context.

Daxiao Staffing

<Dr. Emery-Baldwin>: Since so few people have heard of Daxiao, the first question is often, "How large could it possibly be?"

Daxiao employs approximately 90,000 people, but its products affect the livelihood of about 5,000,000 people on four continents through our supply chain relationships. Fig. 2.1 provides a staffing overview.

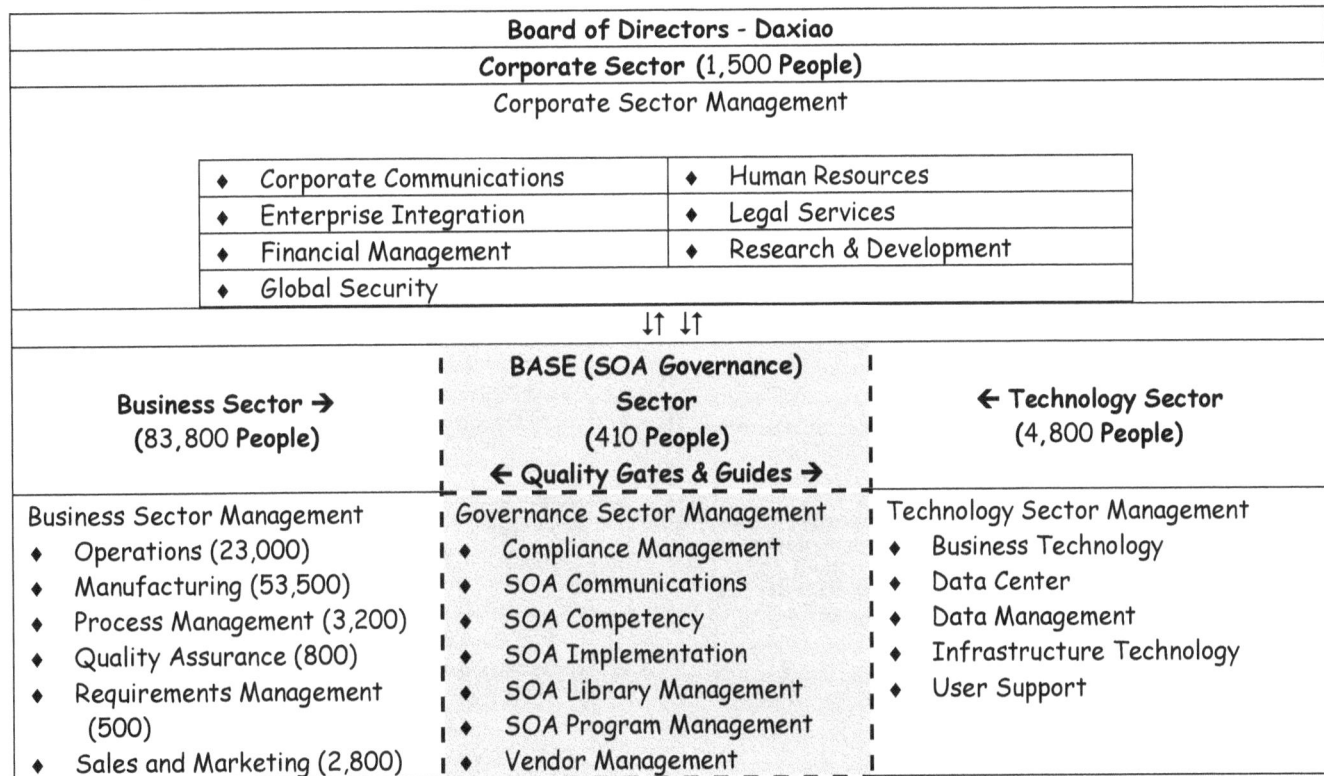

Board of Directors - Daxiao

Corporate Sector (1,500 **People**)

Corporate Sector Management

♦ Corporate Communications	♦ Human Resources
♦ Enterprise Integration	♦ Legal Services
♦ Financial Management	♦ Research & Development
♦ Global Security	

⇅ ⇅

Business Sector → (83,800 **People**)	**BASE (SOA Governance) Sector** (410 **People**) **← Quality Gates & Guides →**	**← Technology Sector** (4,800 **People**)
Business Sector Management ♦ Operations (23,000) ♦ Manufacturing (53,500) ♦ Process Management (3,200) ♦ Quality Assurance (800) ♦ Requirements Management (500) ♦ Sales and Marketing (2,800)	Governance Sector Management ♦ Compliance Management ♦ SOA Communications ♦ SOA Competency ♦ SOA Implementation ♦ SOA Library Management ♦ SOA Program Management ♦ Vendor Management	Technology Sector Management ♦ Business Technology ♦ Data Center ♦ Data Management ♦ Infrastructure Technology ♦ User Support

Fig. 2.1 - Daxiao Organizational Structure (Sectors, Teams, and Staffing)

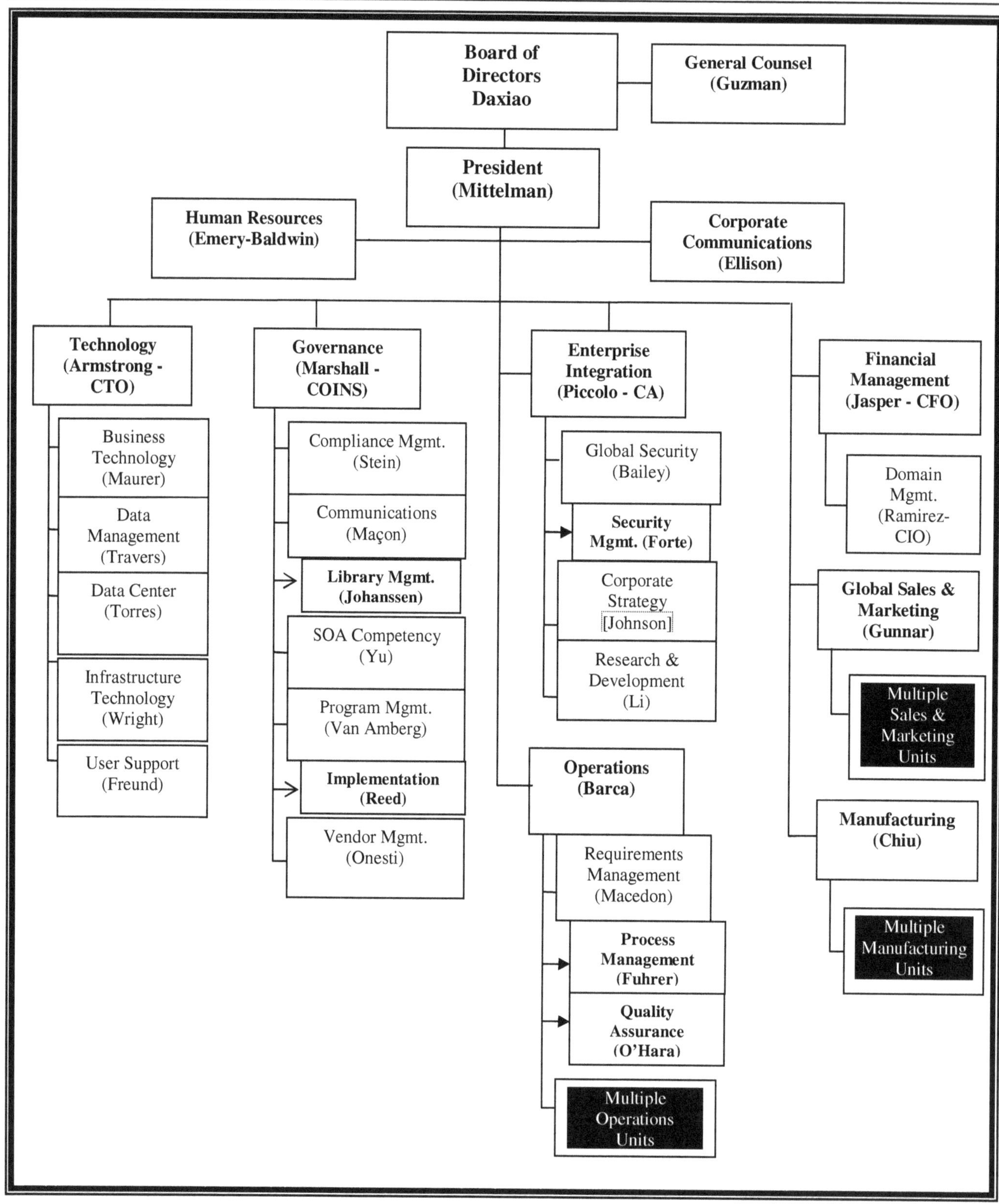

Fig. 2.2 - View of Daxiao Organizational Hierarchy

We have people in units in seven countries, including:

- 21,000 in the United States (administration, logistics, marketing, operational support, research, and information technology).
- 28,000 in Taiwan (administration, customer support, logistics, manufacturing, marketing, operational support, research, information technology).
- 14,500 in Mexico (customer support, logistics, manufacturing, operational support).
- 15,000 in Ireland (customer support, logistics, manufacturing, operational support, information technology).
- 10,000 in Canada (customer support, logistics, manufacturing and operational support).
- 1,000 in Belgium (logistics, security, and marketing).
- 500 in Switzerland (research).

Fig 2.2 above is a view of our organizational structure from the perspective of SOA.

Corporate History for Daxiao (Formerly Goodsand Electronics)

1. Goodsand Electronics was started in the early 1960's by a team of researchers who were not happy with the quality of the products their former employer manufactured. Goodsand thrived by building a reputation as producers of reliable components for products that had to last, usually in extreme conditions of temperature or pressure.
2. In 1970, they purchased Raycroft Labs to supplement their research capabilities. Raycroft held many international patents and had offices in Bern, Switzerland.
3. In the 1980s, we built manufacturing facilities in Canada and purchased a troubled assembly plant in Mexico in the early 1990s to supplement manufacturing and assembly capabilities.
4. The combination of talented research personnel and an aggressive sales force made it necessary for Goodsand to develop a presence in Ireland and Brussels in the mid 90s. They handled the European market. The Brussels office handles our international (computer) security issues.
5. Also in the mid-90s, while Goodsand Electronics' competitors improved their techniques for building reliable and durable niche products, Goodsand began to focus its research on nanotechnology. We wanted to build reliable miniature devices.
6. In the late-90s, Goodsand began to develop sophisticated supply chain relationships. This is where we had our first serious interactions with Daxiao. Daxiao manufactured excellent nanotechnology products, but they had reached the limits of what they could produce with their technology modeling capabilities. Goodsand had extensive modeling capabilities and production-ready patents, but we needed extremely high quality manufacturing facilities.
7. We agreed to a merger that is still in progress after six years. The name change shows that Goodsand believed that nanotechnology would be the wave of the future.

I leave the politics to the politicians. You should listen to the person whose job is Chief Risk Analyst for Politics. His official role is corporate architect, but he likes the acronym. That is a relatively new and very powerful role in Daxiao. He has survived four years in Daxiao, and he has interesting perspectives.

Political Context - the Organization and the Executive Team

<Dr. Daniel Piccolo, Esq.>: It is difficult to remain politically neutral in Daxiao, but I will try. We will start at the top of the organization chart in Fig. 2.2. It includes the:

Board of Directors: This group is split approximately down the middle. On one side are people who believe that sales and niche marketing determine Daxiao's success, while on the other side are the people who wish to continue emphasis on delivering the highest quality products. They believe that the company should only sell what it has demonstrated the ability to deliver.

We do not have a:

Chief Executive Officer: The responsibilities are split between the Board of Directors, the president, and the General Counsel.

Now comes:

Justin Mittelman: Daxiao hired the current president from the outside after the former president died in office, literally. Mr. Mittelman is committed to resolving conflicts without harming either faction. He successfully guided the company through its expansion into Europe and the Daxiao merger. He has a reputation for displaying robot-like stoicism in the face of adversity, and he has an uncanny knack for finding the root cause of an issue while appearing to be confused or not paying attention. His stated goal is to ensure that the company maintains year-over-year earnings gains of at least 8%. He has not requested the CEO title, and he simultaneously works to ensure that we do not offer it to anyone else.

Joseph Guzman, Esq.: The corporate counsel came to Daxiao with the acquisition of the assembly plant in Mexico. He and his family owned 15% of the factory. To upgrade his legal credentials, he took courses in Strafford's international program and at the University of Chicago. He passed bar examinations in California, Delaware, and New York. His stated goal is to keep Daxiao's reputation "pure white". If Daxiao considered appointing a CEO, he would be second in line for the spot.

Dr. T. Emery-Baldwin: We perceive the head of Human Resources as the president's right-hand person. She balances his robotic tendencies. She also brings corporate history and culture, as she has the second longest continuous tenure of any of Daxiao's senior staff. She was credited with keeping the company afloat for almost two years while the previous president battled a major illness. Her stated goal is to ensure that the current president succeeds.

Austin Ellison: The head of corporate communications is the newest member of the executive team. He looks good, and he ensures that the company will look good in their chosen niches. He is an Internet marketing specialist that we hired based on a recommendation from the president. Since Daxiao never sells directly to the public, large media campaigns are not necessary. His current objective is to ensure that Daxiao receives maximum beneficial exposure in the industry press, as determined by the niches chosen in the corporate strategy.

Weldon Armstrong: The head of information technology was the first senior executive hired by Justin Mittelman. He was hired to pursue technology innovation aggressively while holding the line on the company's technology budget.

He is an excellent visionary and his implementation skills are improving rapidly. After a moderately successful foray into the Internet, he lost stature when he handled the situation poorly after 9/11 and again after a highly visible overrun on his first major SOA implementation. In both cases, he was saved by the man he was hired to replace, Hamilton Marshall. By accepting assistance and guidance from Enterprise Integration (my team), the head of Requirements Management, and the head of the SOA governance (Hamilton Marshall) for the last four years, his success rate significantly exceeds that of the industry. With our assistance, he held the line on costs during those four years. He will be able to maintain his position, but he is out of the running for further advancement within Daxiao.

We will leave Hamilton Marshall and me for last.

Carson Barca: The head of business operations was hired to bring operations processes "out of the dark" and to expand the program for continuous process improvement that allows Daxiao to maintain leading positions in its chosen niches. As such, he has been a strong promoter of business modeling, (non-manufacturing) process automation, and business process management. He is working with the corporate architecture team to define a top-down process model and with compliance specialists and business analysts on the governance team to create a bottom-up model. His three-year plan promised a 33% increase in the number of automated functions each year. That is a trick number. When he started, 25% of the functions were automated. If his meets his objectives, 59% of the functions will be automated.

After quick wins during his first year, he ran into significant resistance from people who had "always done it that way". They maintained their secret techniques, and hopefully their job security by asserting that their jobs were too complicated to be automated. Barca's response, with support from my area, was that the complicated processes are the ones that require automated assistance. Areas that continued to resist found themselves in the middle of intense process audits after crises that were usually precipitated by the head of Sales and Marketing. Barca's career is stalled because of the resistance that he encounters.

Lorraine Jasper: The head of finance is building a reputation as being the tortoise that offsets the hares on the senior management team. She received the EVP appointment after guiding the company through several situations that could have been financially embarrassing. Each was associated with expansions or acquisitions.

With assistance from the compliance management team and the General Counsel, she has done increasingly well on SEC/SOX and international government audits. She allowed us to avoid approval conflicts for shared resources by accepting responsibility for shared services and data. Though she is one of the most powerful women in the electronics industry, she seems content on consolidating her position and staying in place.

A. Niklas Gunnar: Many people perceive the head of Sales and Marketing as the most powerful person in the company. After receiving an MD from a major medical school, he switched to selling medical equipment after a traumatic personal experience. He had 15 years of sales experience when Daxiao hired him as an SVP to lead a major niche initiative in diagnostic equipment. Clients perceive him as being simultaneously knowledgeable about the field, compassionate to them, and aggressive in assuring that Daxiao delivers what he sells. He has aspirations of becoming the president or the CEO, but the company needs him doing what he does.

Shen Chiu: The head of manufacturing is also well positioned in the organization. He was the president of Daxiao, Asia before the merger, and he assumed responsibility for manufacturing activities in four countries on three continents with ease. He aspires to become the president of Daxiao, Intl. He is perceived as being in line behind the head of Sales and Marketing.

Alexander Macedon: The most significant shift in the way that IT services are delivered is controlled by the Requirements Management Team. With this organizational adjustment, business areas have absolute control over the definition of all their work requirements up through detailed analysis and the initial project plan. The leader of this team (a project initiation manager) is a retired U.S. government logistics specialist who could not understand why it took programmers so long to respond to "two liners". He is four years into a one-year assignment where he volunteered to show that there was a better way to do things. He brokered techniques that improved the technology project success rate from a low of 37% to the current rate of almost 60%. That is considered miraculous for a company of our size.

The first thing he realized was the trouble with "two liners". He promotes the use of rules management and report management software that allows clients to take care of their own two-line changes, if they are indeed two-line changes. For the remainder of the changes, he works with my team and with the technology and governance sectors. We provide Macedon's people with the information they need to show business units how to define what they need to an ***appropriate level of detail***, guided by prior project experience.

Notice that Macedon is the only person on this list who does not report directly to the president. However, there is speculation that he is a strong contender to replace the EVP of governance, and he is occasionally mentioned as a presidential contender.

Dr. Daniel Piccolo, Esq.: The president hired me synchronize internal corporate strategy while he deals with external issues. They let me referee the politics because, currently, I have no further political aspirations. My goal is to ensure Daxiao's success while establishing an empirical environment for my theories of (a) organizational collaboration and (b) cross-functional learning. Because of my educational credentials (PhDs from both Strafford and MTC and a law degree from Horward), I lobbied for and took responsibility for the company's research and development efforts.

Hamilton Marshall: The last member of the senior management team may be the most powerful, though he is perceived as a politically inept, handicapped older person on the way to retirement.

He manages BASE, the smallest sector with only 410 people out of 90,000. His power is based upon a 38-year record for delivering what he promised when he promised (***he is obsessed with planning***). His dominion is supported by a network of "super efficient middle managers" that he and the former head of compliance placed in positions across Daxiao over a 35-year period.

One of my secrets of success is Marshall's underground network. I can handle strategy more effectively because it gives us the inside track on what is really happening within the business units while the senior managers tell us what they believe will be politically correct at any given moment.

Marshall's people, the official staff and the underground network, help the other senior executives deliver upon their "adjusted" promises. He encourages his peers to take most of the credit for these deliverables. Fig. 18 shows critical SOA-related functions that he initiated and/or delivered and the areas that took responsibility for the efforts. The dashed arrow pointing to communications indicates that significantly more work needs to be done.

SOA governance and planning responsibilities evolved as follows:

1. As head of compliance, he inherited the Capability Maturity Model Integration (CMMI) and Infrastructure Technology Infrastructure Library (ITIL) initiatives.
2. He inherited responsibility for technology planning from the technology executive in 2001 after showing the company how to survive serious planning gaps discovered during the crisis of 9/11 and after defending Goodsand's planning capabilities during post-merger consolidations. This provided him with a mandate for creating and maintaining ***a planning base*** within Daxiao and an excuse for aggressive pursuit of planning initiatives.
3. In early 2002, he assumed responsibility for technology procurement. His compliance team already coordinated procurement and provisioning for other areas of the company.
4. In late 2002, he was assigned responsibility for the Sarbanes-Oxley (SOX) initiative.
5. In 2003, he inherited responsibility for SOA in a final effort to save the troubled SOA implementation mentioned earlier. By building upon the knowledge ***bases*** and processes that he had salvaged from end-of-century efforts and then supplemented with CMMI, ITIL, and SOX, he succeeded in delivering the failing project.
6. Through collaboration with the head of Requirements Management and with my team, he devised an evolutionary plan that was designed to deliver a "BIG SOA" implementation with five years.
7. As head of compliance, he can enforce his SOA process and planning recommendations, though there has never been an official SOA mandate.

His officially stated goal is to position SOA so that its benefits cannot be reversed when he decides to retire. He is also determined to pass along what it took him 38 years to build to the people he has handpicked, groomed, and positioned. He will not say when. He is dealing with health issues that may affect the timing of his decision.

Acton: They are not on the chart, but they are critical. As Daxiao's external auditing firm, they perform SEC/SOX and international audits. They also provide management advisors or technology assistance when it is required. They work closely with the General Counsel (José Guzman).

SOA Managers and Responsibilities

The entries in Table 1 correspond to the organizational hierarchy in Fig. 2.2. It provides the names, titles, teams, roles, years in the company and years in the current title for the senior people who have a continuing role in the success (or failure) of SOA in Daxiao. The people in the BASE (governance) organization are presented in bold italics.

Table 1 - BASE-Related Teams and Managers

Manager and Title	Team	Role	Reports to	Years in Co./Title
Weldon Armstrong, EVP and Chief Technology Officer	Technology Management	Executive - technology	President	9/8
Vincent Bailey, SVP - Global Security	Global Security	Security specialist - corporate	SVP - Corporate Architecture	3/3
Carson Barca, EVP - Global Operations	Business Management	Executive - operations	President	2/2
Shen Chiu, EVP - Global Manufacturing	Business management	Executive - manufacturing	President	13/5
Paul Docente, VP and Managing Director of Training	Human Resources	Training specialist	SVP - Human Services	3/2
Austin Ellison, SVP - Corporate Communications	Corporate Communications	Communications specialist - corporate	President	2/1
T. Emery-Baldwin, SVP - Human Services	Human Resources	Personnel specialist	President	38/8
Aaron Forte, VP and Director of Security	Global Security	Security specialist - technology	SVP - Technology ------ SVP - Global Security	7/3
Amanda Freund, VP and Manager of Client Services	User Support	User support specialist	SVP - Technology Operations	3/1
Evangeline Fuhrer, VP and Managing Director of Process Control	Process Management	Process coordinator - business	SVP - Information Logistics	17/5
A. Niklas Gunnar, EVP - Sales and Marketing	Business Management	Executive - sales and marketing	President	8/5
Joseph Guzman, EVP and General Counsel	Legal Services	Corporate lawyer	Board of Directors and the President	33/5
Lorraine Jasper, EVP - Corporate Finance	Financial Management	Financial specialist - corporate	President	19/6
Maja Johanssen, VP and Director - Knowledge Cooperative	***SOA Library Management***	***Knowledge consolidator***	***SVP - Communications***	8/4
J. Stanley Johnson	Enterprise Integration	Strategist - corporate	SVP - Corporate Architecture	-/4
Wen Li, SVP - Research and New Product Development	Research & Development	Research scientist	SVP - Corporate Architecture	7/3
Alexander Macedon, SVP - Information Logistics	Requirements Management	Project initiation manager	President	6/4
Lisse Maçon, SVP and Managing Director - SOA Communications	***BASE Communications***	***Communications specialist - BASE***	***EVP - BASE (Governance)***	11/4
Hamilton Marshall, EVP and Coordinator of Information Services (COINS)	***BASE Management (Governance)***	***Executive - BASE***	***President***	38/5
Arnold Maurer, SVP - Enterprise Applications	Business Technology	Project manager - business technology	EVP - Technology	10/9

Justin Mittelman, President	Corporate Management	Executive - corporate	Board of Directors	10/9
Aine O'hara, VP and Director - Quality Assurance	Quality Assurance	Quality management coordinator	SVP - Information Logistics	26/7
Rafael Onesti, SVP and Director - Purchasing	***Vendor Management***	***Procurement specialist***	***EVP - BASE (Governance)***	18/5
Daniel Piccolo, SVP - Corporate Architecture	Enterprise Integration	Architect - corporate	President	5/5
George Ramirez, SVP and Coordinator of Information Optimization (CIO)	Financial Management	Domain specialist - service	SVP - Corporate Finance	7/3
Olivia Reed, VP and Director - SOA Development	***SOA Implementation***	***Project manager - SOA***	***SVP - Program management***	24/4
Hugo Stein, SVP and Director of Compliance	***Compliance Management***	***Compliance specialist - technology***	***EVP - BASE (Governance)***	21/4
Leonard Torres, SVP - Technology Operations	Data center Operations	Project manager - infrastructure technology	EVP - Technology	3/3
Dennis Travers, SVP - Information Architecture	Data Management	Data specialist	EVP - Technology	12/6
Valery Van Amberg, SVP and Director - SOA Program Relations	***BASE Program Management***	***BASE Program coordinator***	***EVP - BASE (Governance)***	37/4 *(Spanning 39 years)*
Wayne Wright, SVP - Technology	Infrastructure Technology Management	Architect - enterprise technology	EVP - Technology	8/7
Hank Yu, VP and Director - SOA Technology	***SOA Competency***	***Architect - SOA***	***EVP - BASE (Governance)***	9/5

Now I will introduce my wife. She was one of our highest earning sales people before we decided to start a family. Requirements on a high-powered salesperson make parenting difficult, so she agreed to work with Hamilton Marshall on BASE (SOA) communications.

Read This!

It introduces the remainder of the characters and discusses the presentation format

PRESENTATION FORMAT AND FLOW OF THE FIRST SOA P OPERA

<Lisse Maçon>: I am responsible for SOA communications. I travel less than I did in sales, but the job is much harder than selling physical things that people can see and feel. You will hear about my successes and failures throughout this book, but let us first discuss SOA P presentation and flow (the format for this book).

SOA People - Looking Inside Their Heads

Reading Minds (and Hands): The higher up in an organization that people climb, the less likely they are to say what is on their minds. Since personal agendas almost derailed our SOA Program, we let you know what the SOA P characters are thinking, especially when they are thinking something that does not agree with what they are saying or something that is totally unrelated to what they are saying. Personal thoughts and asides appear in *Times New Roman.*

Sign language and scribbled notes will appear in Alba (as in this example). You will have to keep reading to discover how sign language helps the SOA P to bubble.

More Mind Reading: Table A.16 - Comments from Role Incumbents contains additional information about the thought processes of BASE participants and about the evolution of the BASE Program.

> **Readers**: Please consider reading comments from incumbents now to gather valuable information about SOA P opera characters.

Flow of SOA P - Start with an Audit That Isn't an Audit

The next character in SOA P is Niklas Gunnar, the EVP and Board member who recommended another external auditing firm to review the SOX and SOA functions for Daxiao. He was my boss before I moved to SOA.

Gunnar wants to assist Daxiao, but more importantly, he wants to find advantages for Gunnar. He wants to convince the Board that he should become the next president, and he needs to understand more about what he is inheriting. He understands something about everything except SOA.

After Gunnar, you will meet William Sharf (with an "f"), a management advisor that Niklas Gunnar selected (and convinced the Board to approve). He will perform the review of Daxiao's SOX and SOA functions. The advisor has a personal agenda. He wants to find things wrong with SOX and SOA at Daxiao, whether there is anything wrong or not. Then he will convince Daxiao to pay him and his company to "fix" the problems. His ultimate goal is to displace the auditing firm that currently performs SEC/SOX audits.

The third character to be introduced is Hamilton Marshall. He is preparing for interviews with the advisor. After that, the SOA P opera events determine the sequence of appearance.

Tagged Character Names: Each change of speaker will be presented with XML tags as in the follow example: **<Character Name>**. XML is the language used to format SOAP (SOA messages) in the real world. The tags provide an easy way to identify character transitions.

Main Characters (in Order of Appearance)

<Henry Yu (Hank)> VP and SOA Architect reporting to Hamilton Marshall.
<Dr. T. Emery-Baldwin (Doc)> SVP and Board member, responsible for Human Resources at Daxiao.
<Dr. Daniel Piccolo, Esq. (Dan)> SVP, Corporate Architect, and Board member.
<Lisse Maçon (Liz)> SVP and SOA communications specialist reporting to Hamilton Marshall (also wife of Dan Piccolo and younger sister of Justin Mittelman).
<A. Niklas Gunnar (Gunnar)> EVP of Sales and Marketing and Board member.

<**William Sharf, CPA (Sharf)**> Junior Partner in Belvedere, LLP, a professional services firm specializing in SOX auditing and SOA Guidance.
<**Hamilton Marshall (HM)**> Referred to as H by his friends, is a LESSER EVP responsible for the SOA governance organization (BASE).
<**Renata Vitale (Rennie)**> Technology Associate from Belvedere working with William Sharf.
<**Ernest Dawson (Ernest)**> Administrative assistant to Hamilton Marshall and orthopedic nurse.
<**Valery Van Amberg, Esq. (Val or Frack)**> SVP of SOA Program Management reporting to Hamilton Marshall.
<**Indira Simone Frey-Marshall Winslow, CPA (Indy)**> Referred to as "Baby Girl" by his father and his older friends, is the older daughter of Hamilton Marshall and Nicola Frey and co-owner of Frey-Marshall Associates, a family business that supports technology start-ups.
<**Jonas Hugh Frey-Marshall (Huey)**> The older son of Hamilton Marshall and Nicola Frey and founder of Frey-Marshall Associates. He is also referred to as (Silicone) Huey.
<**Matthew Reese (Reese)**> Security Guard at Daxiao's New York Office reporting to Vincent Bailey.
<**Dr. Douglas Church (Church)**> Surgeon at the Hospital for Orthopaedic Surgery.
<**Kerstin Gunnar-Palatino**> Daughter of Niklas Gunnar. Referred to as Kerry.
<**Nicola Frey, Esq. (Machi)**> "Friend for Life" of Hamilton Marshall, mother of his children, technology litigator, and co-owner of Frey-Marshall Associates. She is also referred to as Nicky.
<**Lewis Barker (Nurse #1)**> A nurse practitioner at the Hospital for Orthopaedic Surgery.
<**Justin Mittelman (Justin)**> President of Daxiao.
<**Joseph Guzman, Esq. (Joe)**> EVP and General Counsel of Daxiao, reporting to the Board of Directors and the President.
<**Marybeth Higgins (Higgs)**> Administrative assistant to Justin Mittelman.
<**Lorraine Jasper, CPA (Lorrie)**> EVP and CFO of Daxiao reporting to Justin Mittelman.
<**Austin Ellison (Ellison)**> SVP and Manager of Corporate Communications.
<**Dr. J. Stanley Johnson (Jay)**> Strategy consultant and academician engaged by Daniel Piccolo.
<**Annika Maja Johanssen (Maja)**> Referred to as AJ, she is the VP and Director of the Knowledge Cooperative and reports to the manager of SOA communications.
<**Aaron Forte (Aaron)**> VP and Director of Security reporting to the director of Global Security.
<**Lillian Simpson (Lillian)**> Senior Corporate Librarian reporting to Daniel Piccolo.
<**John Laufer (Laufer)**> SVP of Regional Sales (U.S. Northeast Region) at Daxiao.
<**Margaret Gunther Sharf (Mags)**> Sister of Niklas Gunnar and wife of William Sharf.
<**Frederick Chase (Fred)**> A private duty nurse for Hamilton Marshall.
<**Patrick Frey-Marshall (Pat)**> The younger son of Hamilton Marshall and Nicola Frey.
<**Alexander Macedon (Macedon or Frick)**>: SVP reporting to the EVPs of Operations and Manufacturing and a retired military logistics specialist.
<**Isaiah Cane, CPA (Izzy)**> Partner at Belvedere, LLP, former tax accountant, and godfather to Hamilton Marshall's grandchildren

Supporting Characters

<**Kenneth Chase (Ken)**> Technology Librarian reporting to Maja Johanssen.
<**Gary Augen (Gary)**> Security specialist on the SOA Competency team reporting to Henry Yu.
<**George Miller**> The driver and personal assistant to Hamilton Marshall.
<**Gomez (Policeman Officer #1)**> Part of an emergency escort.
<**Policeman Officer #2**> Part of an emergency escort.
<**Reporter #1**> A freelance reporter.

<Reporter #2> A freelance reporter and cameraman.
<Nurse #2> Emergency room supervisor.
<Phillip Miles (Miles)>: The driver for Ms. Nicola Frey.
<Dr. Janice Gaines (Gaines)> Triage doctor in emergency room.
<Marcella Haines (Marcella)> Assistant to Niklas Gunnar.
<Doorman/guard> Employee at Niklas Gunnar's favorite New York hotel.
<Gerome Oswald (Oswald)> The driver, bodyguard, and personal assistant to Justin Mittelman.
<James Grady> The driver and personal assistant to Niklas Gunnar.
<Weldon Armstrong (Weldon)> EVP and CTO of Daxiao reporting to Justin Mittelman.
<Ryan Winslow (Ryan)> Ex-husband of Indira Frey-Marshall and father of her twin teenagers.
<Dr. Rebecca Vincent (Becky)> Wife of Jonas Frey-Marshall, inventor, and co-founder of Frey Associates.
<Patricia Frey-Marshall (Patty)> The younger daughter of Hamilton Marshall and Nicola Frey, she is also referred to as Queen 2.
<Helena Styles (Helena)> Former "Friend for the Season" of Nicolas Gunnar.
<Clarence Forester, CPA (Forester)> Former accountant for Justin Mittelman is currently an employee of Frey-Marshall Associates.
<Desmond Grayson (Grayson)> Junior Partner and Manager of Technology Consulting at Belvedere, LLP.
<Evan Hovland>: EVP of the Bateman financial conglomerate, and a classmate of Indira Marshall.
<Gerthe Gunther (Gerthe)>: Mother of Niklas Gunnar and Margaret Gunther Sharf.
<Leonardo Palatino (Len)>: Husband of Kerstin Gunnar and son-in-law of Niklas Gunnar.

How to Fail While Doing the Right Things 95% of the Time

A NEARLY PERFECT NEAR FAILURE - SOA P OVERVIEW

I am learning from my husband (Dan Piccolo) and his associate (Hamilton Marshall) that it is possible to do 95% of the things correctly in SOA (or any technology) and still have to deal with the possibility of failure due to personal issues. Van Amberg estimates that we have approximately a 55% chance of succeeding. We dealt with:

1. **Interpersonal Problems:** Personal fears, personal agendas, and emotional problems are about to derail SOA in Daxiao. The emotional situations may be unique to Daxiao, but the personal fears and personal agendas are not. These were the **most significant contributors** to SOA communications problems, and, therefore, the most significant contributors to BASE Program (SOA) problems. Because the problems were hidden, they were even more dangerous.
2. **Methodology:** Daxiao has a well-structured, well documented, and flexible Program methodology (WFSOA) that provided organizing principles for Daxiao's SOA-related processes. They are divided among three domains (Enabling, Delivery, and Support), with three process categories each. The 10,000+ planning hints in SOA P (2) are divided between Program activities and Project activities. Some activities appear in both groupings.
3. **Shared Goals and Objectives:** The act of linking SOA objectives with SOX, CMMI, ITIL,

and Six Sigma (unofficially) contributes to WFSOA survival and expansion.

4. **Financial Benefit:** Daxiao's SOA Program is helping the company make money and save money. It contributed approximately 25% of the bottom line in the last fiscal year. This level of contribution could allow the Program to overcome stakeholder resistance, but it also generates jealously and conflict.
5. **Common Terminology:** This subset of Communications makes it easier for business units to collaborate among themselves and with business technology (the computer people).
6. **Planning:** Planning processes in the business technology area allow the company to achieve the desired technical results within expected time frames. Though not directly initiated due to SOA, they contributed to SOA success.
7. **Continuous Process Improvement:** Daxiao has a program for continuous process improvement, and it is working. The more successful the improvements, the higher the level of anxiety became for people who were more comfortable complaining about problems in a stable (improperly functioning) environment. The Program will improve communications in this area through formal training and mentoring.
8. **Cultural Change Management:** Daxiao has a moderately successful cultural change management program (resistance mitigation) in place, but it missed critical individuals. Complete SOA success requires having all critical individuals actively involved.
9. **Governance:** Daxiao has good SOA governance and good corporate governance. However, **excellent** governance requires **excellent** communications.
10. **Information and Knowledge Sharing:** Daxiao is a learning organization that provides excellent training. This will support WFSOA survival, even if the existing organization (BASE) that promotes the SOA Program is disbanded.
11. **Lessons Learned:** Daxiao tracks SOA lessons learned, and makes them available to interested individuals. The problem is that not enough people were interested. Understanding lessons learned needs to become mandatory.
12. **Organizational Restructuring:** Significant organizational changes were implemented that brought Daxiao to the threshold of SOA success, even though Daxiao backed into the changes. These included:
    - Creating a Requirements Management Program that allowed the business to control their requirements with assistance from technology, rather than the reverse.
    - Moving service and data domain ownership away from silos to the corporate level.
    - Developing an SOA Competency Team.
    - Separating availability management from the regular architecture teams and placing it under Data Center Management.
13. **Quality Management:** Daxiao's technology improved from good to excellent during the initial stages of SOA evolution, even though Daxiao backed into this too. A more directed approach will sustain the level of excellence while the technology continues to change.
14. **Requirements Management:** Change management processes (business and technology) improved exponentially. This financial boon made people uncomfortable. Daxiao had to learn that making money has to be balanced with alleviating individual fears, or there may be bigger long-term problems.
15. **SOA Technology:** Daxiao became better at technology after the SOA Program was initiated. The changes put in place to make the technology work annoyed people inside and outside technology.
16. **Program Communications**: Daxiao has a robust SOA communications program in place, but it needs to be enhanced to ensure that it reaches the right people.
    - The president of the company was aware of Program communications, but he believed it was a sales pitch.
    - The SOA Program executive communicated selectively with senior management.
    - The company "rain maker" ignored all Program communications.
    - Massive amounts of information were available, but important information was either ignored or not understood by

powerful individuals who could make a difference in the Program.

GOOD NEWS ABOUT DAXIAO'S SOA

17. The BASE Program management team knew they had communications problems, though they were not aware of the (personal) root cause. They were taking steps to resolve the problem when this SOA P opera began. Knowing about a problem does not guarantee that it can be corrected, but awareness is a start.
18. Daxiao's SOA Program will continue for at least another year, and it has a chance of cross-organizational and worldwide success if the right people begin to communicate with each other, openly and effectively.

CONTEXT FOR SOA P CHARACTERS - INSIDE GUNNAR'S HEAD

SOA Self-Preservation Observations

<A. Niklas Gunnar>: *It took a tremendous effort to get on the short list of people who may become the next president of Daxiao because I contributed indirectly to a prior blip that nearly caused us to go out of business.*

SOA is something that I must understand if I am going to remain on in the short list. Everywhere I look inside Daxiao, SOA pops up. It also comes up in conversations with our industry partners (customers and suppliers). When I realized it was time to evaluate what SOA meant to me, I had already missed a few moves.

My peer in technology, Weldon Armstrong, says he used SOA to keep our information technology budget flat the first full year of implementation, and to save over $100 million dollars the second full year of implementation. He claims that he (with assistance from Hamilton Marshall and Daniel Piccolo) has already established the technical foundation and the organizational structure for across-the-board SOA implementation. He tells everyone who will listen in the trade press that we are reaching a critical mass, and when we do, we will be the largest company to have succeeded in becoming a Service-Oriented Enterprise. This will result in savings (and some earnings) that could reach more than $1 billion each year. While this is good for the company, I intend to discover specifically how SOA will affect my career and me.

Accidental EVP for an Accidental SOA

The person who seems to be the driving force behind SOA is Hamilton Marshall (HM or simply "H" to his friends). If he is running things, I have a problem. The blip that I mentioned occurred when I tried to help the president clean out some old wood - Marshall had been here for 30 years. Mittelman never used those exact words, though he is often not politically correct when he refers to Marshall. That is the impression that he gave me.

Soon after Marshall had been given responsibility for SOX (Sarbanes Oxley) compliance, one of my people produced preliminary research indicating that Daxiao's purchasing department (controlled by Marshall) was buying hundreds of millions of dollars worth of components from companies associated with Marshall's son. The Board discovered the contents of that research and immediately demanded that Marshall should take a sabbatical, during the investigation. With the WorldCom angst, he could have ended up in jail.

It turned out that Marshall never personally recommended any product associated with his son, that Daxiao never purchased anything from a company while his son was actively involved, and that Marshall forced additional quality checks on products from companies where his son had a prior relationship.

Meanwhile, in Marshall's absence, purchase procedures were loosened and one of our subsidiaries bought substandard products for an important new line from the company owned by a relative of the subsidiary's manager. The new product failed, customers lost confidence, and Daxiao had net earnings of about $100 million that year. That is insubstantial. Daxiao had $18 billion in revenue that year.

The Board went to Marshall, groveled, and convinced him to come back and fix what they let somebody else break, in return for major public apologies and the promise of a promotion if he fixed the problem. When he delivered what he promised, he became the Accidental EVP.

Though he had the title, I had never considered him as my peer. Now I get the strange feeling that he is my superior. I must determine how an organization with 410 out of 90,000 can have the effect that is becoming obvious. He has tentacles everywhere.

The next logical move would be for him to become a member of the Board. He does not seem to care that he is not. He says he has so much work that something would slip if he spent time running to all the meetings he would have to attend if he was on the Board, especially since he hasn't been able to run for 42 years.

SOX, SOA, and CMMI

Our company continually ranks among the top 5% on the SOX audit, even during the year that we forced Marshall out for five months. This year we hit the 99th percentile. I need to know how Lorraine Jasper (our CFO) fits into the equation or if Marshall is actually making a difference.

The company moved from Level 3 to Level 4 on last year's CMMI (Capability Maturity Model Integrated) assessment of process quality. HM shares the credit with Armstrong, although we know that Armstrong favors speed over quality and Armstrong's end game is often sloppy.

Marshall kept the credit for conformance to the new CMMI Acquisition Module. It appears that he is rubbing our noses in the purchasing fiasco.

The industry seems to agree with the progress we are making with SOA, even though the first major implementation was failing until Armstrong figured how to dump it on Marshall. Marshall is good at organizing sloppiness. Armstrong and Daniel Piccolo (both of whom sit on the Board of directors) take most of the credit for SOA, and Marshall does not protest. In fact, Marshall and Piccolo seem to be joined at the hip.

Marshall and Piccolo somehow positioned themselves to affect nearly everything that happens in the company. They are invisible back seat drivers, and they are good.

SOA Wake-Up Call

I received my SOA wake-up call two months ago when my business unit was evaluated for SOA maturity. The report says that I am performing "adequately" with room for improvement. It was signed by Piccolo, but the people who contacted us to follow up on the recommendations are on a compliance team that is controlled by Marshall. The idea of having either one of them in a position to assess my performance on something for which I see no obvious benefit was an unpleasant surprise. Besides, why would you evaluate a sales team for technical readiness?

Armstrong agrees with Marshall/Piccolo on this. He responded that the way I phrased the question was a major indicator that I had room for SOA growth. He also indicated that if my R&D (which now belongs to Piccolo) did not work so closely with Marshall's people, we would have fared less well on the assessment. That is preposterous. Except for the earlier Marshall fiasco, Niklas Gunnar has not failed anything in almost 21 years.

I have to decide:

- *(a) Do we really need SOA, or is there something else that is contributing to IT savings, while Armstrong uses SOA because it is a good buzzword this year?*
- *(b) If SOA is contributing significantly to Daxiao's success, how do I take credit for something that I have forcefully ignored?*
- *(c) If I cannot control the current SOA structure, what changes must be made so that I can control it.*
- *(d) Will it be beneficial to me if I try to convince Marshall to stay, or should I try to accelerate his departure?*
- *(e) Whenever he leaves, whom should I support as his replacement?*
- *(f) Can Armstrong survive without HM?*
- *(g) Is Piccolo really a management genius or simply a front man for HM?*
- *(h) Exactly what does Marshall do, theoretically, that causes CMMI to give us good ratings.*

Since my SOA "Immaturity" assessment, my associates on the Board and I have observed Marshall (and Piccolo) from the outside. We casually extract as much information from his people as we can, and it seems that there is little to extract. They answer our questions and then send us to the Knowledge Center for more detailed information.

SOA Financial Implications

One interesting aspect of SOA in Daxiao is that it did not cost the organization any extra money. He uses his SOX budget to pay for the core information structures and Armstrong, Marshall and Piccolo shifted around about 200 people that their peers didn't want anyhow.

HM purchased about $10,000,000 worth of new software and spent $5,000,000 on hardware and facilities upgrades after SOA was dropped on him. HM justified the expenditures by promising to cover headcount for Armstrong and the business units. Armstrong approved the purchases with reservations. Now, Armstrong is reaping more benefits from the expenditures than Marshall is. Together, they have replaced half of our line retirees and almost a third of our technology resignations with new software and updated processes.

Marshall is proud that he contributes significantly to Armstrong's ability to keep the technology budget flat. He says he is also helping the business save money. He lets the business quantify their savings.

Marshall's budget is low, considering that he manages the compliance organization. He has high-end lawyers (including intellectual property), CPAs, and international business experts.

His entire team, fully loaded, costs less than $35.5 million each year. He jokes that as long as his entire staff costs less than twice what the president makes in a single year, he should be OK. Last year the president received a $5.75 million salary and a $13 million bonus.

Last year HM's Partner Network started to receive pay for consulting with our business partners. They brought $3,000,000 in real money to the bottom line. It is a small amount, but few technology teams ever earn money. He expects to increase that amount by as much as 100% next year. I pointed out that he may be providing too much assistance to our partners, and some information is leaking back to our competitors. He says, and Mittelman agrees, that happy partners make it worth the risk.

HM is a very low-paid executive vice president. His annual salary is $600,000 and his last bonus was $350,000. We pay his driver but he uses a car that his son gave him. We also pay the maintenance on his place in Manhattan ($36,000). The last item is unusual, but I suspect that his wife told him to request the housing allowance as a test to see how much Daxiao needed HM.

That is still the lowest salary among our sector managers ($350,000 lower than the CTO).

Piccolo earns two thirds as much as Marshall does. He receives no residential allowance, and he shares the car pool with the other SVPs.

Mixed Reactions to the SOA Program

The business people have mixed feelings about HM (or them). Under SOA, the business has 100% control of the requests that are turned over to development. The business (with assistance from Piccolo's minions) also ensures that the work conforms to business strategy. We should like that, but I feel ambivalent. It is harder for me to blame Armstrong or Marshall when my people cannot decide what they want. On the other hand, they give us more time up front to evaluate options.

We believe that Armstrong hates having HM looking over his shoulder. Armstrong cannot buy a pencil without HM knowing about it. That is not directly related to SOA, but Marshall tends to place the SOA label on everything that he does. Armstrong hates it even more that HM shares everything with the Technology Sector Teams. Weldon was hired to replace Marshall. Therefore, his people should be better than Marshall's people are.

1. *Since Service-Oriented Architecture was approved (not mandated) for future development, 45% of our applications are SOA compliant, and Marshall promised to have another 20% under SOA control before his contract is up. HM lets Armstrong have most of the credit for that.*
2. *Technology realized a 25% improvement in work throughput and a 40% reduction in errors (in three years). HM lets Armstrong share the credit for that.*
3. *Manufacturing units deliver products that are more sophisticated and there is a 50% reduction in rejected products and a further 50% reduction in returned products. Mittelman takes the credit for that.*

The business people no longer have to pay for systems maintenance directly. That is good. In return, the business people share "their technology teams". They do not like that.

SOA and Project Visibility

HM arranged it so that everyone sees what everyone else is requesting (programming work requests or procurement requests) unless it is a secret strategic initiative. He is eliminating the walls that surrounded our isolated systems. We do not especially like that. He and Macedon also shut the side doors for sneaking changes to requirements. He does not stop them. They have to knock to enter.

He and Jasper provide visibility into the algorithms that Macedon uses to attach relatively accurate price tags to work requests. Not everyone agrees with the algorithms, but everyone is happy that the algorithms are applied consistently.

SOA Management Replacement - Who?

Justin understands that he will need to replace HM eventually, but he does not know what to replace. Marshall and Justin have maintained a cordial standoff due to our faulty investigation a few years ago.

Dan Piccolo may be able to handle HM's responsibility, but Piccolo wants someone to handle the details. Otherwise, he complains the job would detract from his ability to perform other critical functions. He wants to hire or promote someone with HM's understanding of the company, the industry, and technology. I cannot tell whether he is being sarcastic, or if he is bluffing.

To resolve Mittelman's problem, I created a problem. It appears that even though Marshall is an EVP, he never bothered to file a succession plan. All Justin's other direct reports have one. I scared the Board by reminding them that at least half of us do not understand Marshall's scope of influence. I suggested that when Marshall retires, we risk having another crisis similar to the one that occurred when they forced him to take the sabbatical. That made them pay attention.

I also noted that HM may be auditing members of the BASE team. He has 150 of the technical people that Armstrong dropped on him. HM reminds us that these people spend most of their time in matrix relationships with Armstrong's teams. Any development that his team actually performs goes through the same review processes as everyone else. Acton audits all BASE activities, including any development.

I suggested quietly, that because Acton and the General Counsel tacitly approve the unusual compliance arrangement, and because Acton cannot provide us with SOA clarification in a way that is effective, perhaps we should request a third opinion.

Personal Data on Hamilton Marshall (What I Think We Know)

I even spent my own money to hire people to investigate Marshall and Piccolo. We found nothing damaging on Marshall:

1. *They have four children. His eldest daughter is a CPA, and the CFO for the family business. His eldest son is the brains in the family. He helps to establish start-up electronics companies. Their babies (young adults actually) have significantly less conventional lifestyles than their parents and older siblings. Though they may have experimented with things that their parents would not like, neither of them seems to be hooked on anything. Nor are they doing anything illegal at this time.*
2. *Their family business earns about 150 to 250 times as much each year as Daxiao pays Marshall. His older*

son owns 50% of the business, and his wife and older daughter each have 25%. They pay Marshall an exorbitant amount as a planning advisor. It is hypothetically his part-time job.

3. *He and his wife have been married for more than forty years, but she never used his name. She is Ms. Frey. They refer to each other as friends or mates, and often give the impression that they were never married.*
4. *Ms. Frey is a lawyer and legal advisor for the family business.*
5. *Marshall and his wife/friend/mate still have an active relationship, as reported by the people who maintain their condo in Manhattan.*
6. *They support single-parent organizations and his mate does pro bono work for single mothers in distress.*
7. *Marshall spends an unbelievable amount of his spare time in Rands, a second-hand bookstore on lower Broadway. There is no one in the bookstore that appears to hold special interest for him.*
8. *Ms. Frey enjoys dance recitals, often with Marshall. She doesn't seem to have unusual interest in any of the dancers, producers, or directors.*

Personal Data on Daniel Piccolo (What I Think We Know)

We could not find anything significant that I can use on Piccolo either:

1. *Piccolo has income sources other than Daxiao (input from household assistant). Though he is nowhere near as rich as Marshall is, he could live on his outside income.*
2. *Aside from Strafford, MTC, and Horward, he has a few others that he does not bother mentioning. Until he met Liz in his late thirties, he had spent 2/3's of his adult life in school, and 1/3 consulting, usually with the U.S. Government.*
3. *He and Lisse Maçon maintain separate residences, but they are married, and he is probably the father of her second child.*
4. *Piccolo, his wife, and Justin Mittelman, the company president, have an interesting three-way relationship. She was a nun before she became involved with Justin Mittelman! I can't imagine what Mittelman did to attract one of the most exotic women I've ever seen away from one of the most prosperous charitable orders in the world, but there is a possibility that he is the father of her first child.*
5. *No one has caught Piccolo with anyone extraneous when he goes on his speaking tours.*

Quarterly SOA Updates

About half of us only see Marshall once every quarter when he comes to a Board meeting with the prescribed 12 slides to report on his SOA progress. He delivers his reports in English, but I can never understand what he is saying. If you ask HM for a single detail, he takes off on a 30-minute very slow harangue where he tells us what he is doing, why he is doing it, and how he is doing it. He stops when he sees the first person beginning to nod. That person is usually Mittelman. If there are no problems, they shut down after he explains how much money he saved for us this year (with Piccolo's help) or how many potentially painful issues he avoided before they became problems.

The Right Man for the Job

I recommended Belvedere for the Marshall/Piccolo assessment because my brother-in-law, William Scharf, works there. They are excellent financial auditors and above average management advisors with a fledgling practice focused specifically on SOA. William was once their top PCAOB certified (SOX) auditor, and now he is trying to build the SOA consulting subsidiary. He believes that SOA consulting will be profitable for the next few years, and he wants to have an opportunity to become a senior partner. Belvedere agreed to let him try as long as he handles a few their toughest financial audits for them.

He barely held it together last year, but he still had enough influence that they let him hire a top-tier SOA specialist from one of the standards groups.

Due to my efforts, William bubbled to the top of the selection process - Acton, our regular auditors, did not participate for obvious reasons, and the General Counsel could not make the evaluation meetings, unfortunately. Piccolo was somewhere singing the praises of SOA, and the head of personnel area was at an educational conference. Armstrong, Jasper, and Barca sat quietly and watched the proceedings. Everyone agreed to evaluate William's effectiveness two weeks after he started here. He would have met the important senior people by then.

William promises that in addition to providing us with a clearer view of our SOX compliance processes, he will show our SOA team how to clarify their mission while simultaneously evaluating aggressive new SOA options. Every one of those alternative options will benefit me in some way.

I am a little worried about how Sharf will handle the assignment, but I cannot trust someone that I do not control. Being forceful and occasionally abrasive are good traits for a successful auditor; he could cut through chaotic situations and find the major source of any financial problems. There are no financial problems with Marshall. If there were, we would have found them.

I have provided William with almost as much coaching as I can. He recorded everything, but I'm not sure that he was really listening. Nevertheless, I have set aside three hours to work with him on Friday afternoon and over the weekend if he needs it.

How Did You? *William provided us with a list of questions that his team will be asking. It was the same list* *he used to try to capture business for his practice last year, except that he changed the wording to "How did you?" from "How would you?" The Board agreed that the answers will provide input to a reorganization proposal (whenever HM actually leaves).*

A Place to Start - Roles, Responsibilities, and Activity Lists

William suggested that we would understand what Marshall does if we understood the roles and the processes in the SOA program. We have more than 110 role definitions for the SOA methodology and several appear to repeat. For instance, there are seven (7) different architecture roles, and five (5) different developer roles. HR doesn't have a problem with it. The Security Teams says the granularity is good, and so does Acton, but William is convinced that we should start there.

Approximately 40% of the roles are in the business or the corporate sector. Piccolo and Marshall agree that more of the roles will eventually move to the Business teams. This makes hard-line technology people nervous.

Process Flows - a Slight Slip Already

William agreed to provide us with process flows for the critical SOA functions. That should allow us to understand how Marshall does what he does. I mentioned the process flows in a note that I sent to business unit managers to let them know that I would be heading up that effort and to introduce Sharf.

HM reminded us that we already have flow diagrams for all his processes, as well as for the processes of all business teams that participate in SOA. He also says his processes are automated, more so than anyone else. That is how the process team learned to complete process flows.

I suspect that we had not noticed because none of the new processes or process upgrades made it to a Board meeting. I am lying. Most of the Board members recalled the addendum to Marshall's quarterly presentation after he sent the following to every SVP or above in Daxiao.

To: "Embarrassingly Long List"

From: Hamilton Marshall, BASE

Re: Process Documentation and Automation

I was recently informed that you require a status update regarding our progress you on process automation and continuous process improvement. The work you have helped us to complete is summarized in the following communications:

- Line 13 of page 39 of our report to the SEC.
- Line 4 of page 3 of the last SOX audit report.
- Line 23 of page 5 of the CMMI assessment.
- Line 42 of page 10 of the ITIL status update.
- Line 1 of page 52 of our annual report.
- WFSOA communications PRCS0002 through PRCS0015 (quarterly communications).

Click this link to access process documentation in the Knowledge Cooperative. Daxiao and partner processes that the corporate business analyst identified as critical are discussed here. All SOA processes are on the critical list. Several of the processes have animated flows along with text and illustrations. Some have video presentations or Web casts. Training sessions are available for 30% of the processes. If your staff is interested, they may follow the "Training Available" links.

If necessary, click the box labeled "Information Access Request" to update your access privileges.

We are working to refine our communications and outreach programs. We would welcome your suggestions for ways to avoid situations such as this in the future. Thanks in advance for your assistance and guidance.

HM, COINS

I cannot tell whether he was apologizing for insufficient communications, bragging about the degree of communications, bragging about the degree of process automation, or grabbing an opportunity to promote his communications team. Either way, I should have done my homework before I let that one flow through. It cannot appear that I am attacking Marshall when all I want to do comprehend what he does.

More Notes on the SOA Players

I cannot find a handle on Marshall and that has me annoyed. Reading people is required for an expert salesperson. Sharf and his assistant are supposed to find things that HM will not let me see. Here is more of the background information that I provided to Sharf.

(a) *Other than the quarterly meetings, we seldom see him. However, if I ask for a meeting he will come to me in New Jersey. There is no friendly banter. I ask business questions, and he gives extraordinarily precise answers. If I need more information, he asks how much detail I want, and he gives me precisely what I request. He asks very precise questions, and he will not let anything pass until he has a precise answer.*

We know that HM is different with his people. He has a laugh that shakes the walls when he is comfortable in his environment. He also sings when he believes that he is alone.

(b) *I was recently informed that Marshall has total recall and freakish techniques for deductive reasoning and mathematical calculations. Sharf is a good match, except that he may be slower with deductive reasoning. Marshall seldom loses arguments that are controlled by raw logic. I asked him if he was ever wrong. His answer was, of course. But, he never argues unless he is 98% sure of his facts, which is about 70% of the situations he encounters. He is also excellent at diagnosing situations where the facts are irrelevant, a skill he says he learned too late in his career.*

(c) *He expressed his opinions much more openly and inappropriately when he was younger. He was usually right, which annoyed people beyond reason. When he was in his early 40s, he had to have work done on his knee. He returned three months later with the stuttering and his opinions under control. His wife sent him to a Guru for advice on dealing with the pain. This improved his self-control and his speech. He still had the problem that he speaks very slowly, like some of the most boring professors that I ever ignored.*

(d) *When Marshall is annoyed, when he doesn't agree with you, or when he thinks you're being dumb, he clamps his jaws into a fake smile, and nods ever so slightly. I must remind William to watch out for the illogical nod. When he is enraged, he stops smiling, his eyes change color, and he stares straight through you. I saw that look once five years ago when I was trying to explain how I had saved his career. I never want to see it again.*

(e) *His people tend to be loyal to him. A disproportionate number of HM's people had painful experiences in other parts of the before working with him. They say they wish to avoid difficult situations they may have encountered in the past (a delicate translation).*

(f) *Piccolo and Marshall have developed a symbiotic relationship that we need to understand. Piccolo seems to have a strange hold on HM. For example, the Board started discussing whether HM should begin a Six Sigma effort before he leaves, if he leaves. Piccolo is adamantly against Six Sigma (rumor has it that he lost an embarrassing confrontation with Sean Wales). HM seemed neutral when he heard the suggestion, but he backed away two days later. He says his SOA processes are laying a foundation for a Six Sigma initiative.*

(g) *Marshall and Piccolo are physically mismatched. Piccolo is 5'4" and in his mid forties. HM is 6'5" and is near his mid sixties. Piccolo is blond with thinning hair (descended from northern Italians, he tells us). Marshall has thick dark hair with gray streaks that women love. He says that he is descended from people who came over on all the ships. Piccolo trots around as if he is a proud little rooster with gym-built shoulders, while HM works at disappearing into the woodwork, a difficult feat for a giant in custom-tailored shirts who is built like an inflated Marine poster.*

(h) *Piccolo has one other inconsistent trait. Immediately after he's spent a while trying to baffle you with his brilliance, he invariably does or says something which is stunningly stupid and occasionally funny, like the time he delivered a summary at one of his Board presentations while standing on his head on the boardroom table. He said he was doing what it took to drive a point home.*

(i) *Piccolo would not lift a pencil without evaluating the theoretical basis of pencil lifting. HM has been seen working with technicians to set up equipment in his "Star Wars" conference room. This is more difficult than you might imagine because one leg does not bend properly.*

(j) *His ultra high tech conference room seems to be his only concession to vanity. My team members who have seen the area joke that he could coordinate the campaign against global warming without leaving that space. HM is still in the vice president's office where they stashed him the first time he was on the way out the door.*

(k) *Piccolo tricked the president into letting him have two offices. One is the biggest office in the company, and the second one was the most elegant. I made sure he had to give up the second one.*

THE WINNING HAND - AT LAST

<William Sharf>: *I cannot believe my good luck. My pompous "better than thou" brother-in-law handed me an opportunity to destroy what is left of Hamilton Marshall's* *career. I will make sure that he ends up in worse shape than I was when his crazy daughter and her mother caused me to lose my fellowship and a chance to earn my PhD. After this assignment, I will finally be able to provide Mags with the things she deserves.*

If Gunnar's information is correct, enough people are confused about what Marshall does, that I will be in a position to report anything I want to report. He will have to spend energy trying to prove that I am wrong, and I will have the next president or CEO backing me up. If I displace Marshall, I will be able to show Gunnar how to stop the partner consulting. He is tired of showing up at sales calls and listening to customer raves about the wonders of Marshall's SOA team. I am tired of losing consulting contracts to Marshall's SOA team.

If Marshall talks to his women, he must know I am not happy with the way they set me up with the dean or the way Indy and her gorilla attacked me when I was begging her to be honest with me about her sessions with the dean.

Marshall did not try to block me, even when I made him rearrange everything to meet with me earlier. The element of surprise is always good. Maybe it is because he is as powerless or spineless as Gunnar says he is.

Maybe Marshall's daughter believes I should have forgiven her by now. After all, I did steal a few juicy contracts from under her nose when she was at Acton. Actually, it was only one, but I did such a good job that we have received millions of dollars in follow-up business.

The gorilla finally found out what she was really like (aggressive and frigid, and she is a tease) and moved on to greener pastures. Indy walks around in widow's garb. That is not good enough. I want her to know what she missed, and I want her to know that I am the one that hurt her father the way she hurt me.

My technology associate is due to meet me in the lobby of the Daxiao building in New York in a few minutes. She better not be late. I am about to shift my life into high gear, and I want a witness.

BASE - INQUIRY OR INQUISITION

Auditing the Auditors - the Wrong Man for the Job

<Hamilton Marshall>: *I am waiting for yet another study team. This is not one of Piccolo's staged events. We must be more careful than usual. The Audit Committee of the Board of Directors says they are sending an SOA/SOX Advisor from Belvedere to show me how to clarify my SOX and SOA processes and procedures, even though I'm already in the top 99 percentile in SOX compliance, and I suspect that I would be rated in the 99.9 percentile in SOA effectiveness. They want yet another opinion on how I do what I do in case I leave at the end of next year. They will not listen to Acton, CMMI, or Piccolo.*

They are in an awkward position, and Gunnar is the only one who sees a problem. Gunnar's Board buddies (Doc refers to them as Gooner's goons) do not seem to understand what they are looking for either, but they were happy to see a different approach.

The problem with Gunnar's approach to finding out what I do is that William Sharf, the person he selected to discover my secrets, has been competing with me for business for the last couple of years.

A more accurate statement would be that I have been taking business from Sharf (and Belvedere) and passing it on to Acton. Acton estimates that my team channeled over $7 million worth of contracts to Acton that Belvedere wanted. Acton adjusted our bill in proportion to the business that we helped them to find.

I had never paid much attention to Belvedere. It never occurred to me that I had external competition.

I do not believe Gunnar would be recommending this person if he understood that he was forcing me to give away techniques that would aid the competition. He is focusing on Sharf's supposed SOA knowledge without realizing that Sharf could aggressively use our techniques to eliminate some of our competitive advantages.

Acton says Sharf's people have handled fewer SOA engagements than we have, made less money than we have, and are not terribly sophisticated in either the business management or technology required to achieve "BIG SOA". Acton emphasized the dearth of SOA management sophistication. Grayson, a peer of Sharf's and another junior partner, is supposed to be a much better technology advisor.

Acton suggests that we should not mention the conflict of interest until we can determine whether Sharf may be useful. Acton will ensure that information is planted in the proper locations at the proper time.

Good News and Bad News about Gunnar

The good news is that Gunnar is paying attention to SOA and WFSOA finally. He sees that something important is happening. The bad news is that Gunnar is paying attention.

Gunnar is becoming powerful enough to cause difficulties in more critical areas of SOA. On the other hand, the same power could be used for beneficial results. Sharf may provide insights into Gunnar's true intentions.

I would really like it if we could use this opportunity to begin a positive dialog with Gunnar. If he actually begins to support SOA and WFSOA, it would almost guarantee the success of the SOA Program.

If we can use this opportunity get Gunnar to stop fighting us, at least for a while, that would be a boon for SOA, WFSOA, and for Daxiao.

Another option is to coerce Gunnar into leaving us alone by explaining that causing problems for SOA would be equivalent to the harm he caused Daxiao five years ago when he pushed me to the side and one of his associates caused major problems.

Preparation

My daughter (Indy), Nicky (the other 55% of me), and I created a family plan for dealing with Gunnar and Sharf. We will guide Belvedere's people toward creating a very large crisis of misinformation. In the process of clearing up the misinformation, we would show a limited number of people, again, how important my work is to Daxiao.

I believe we should do something more extreme. We can get Gunnar to back off by encouraging Sharf to do something that would backfire on Gunnar. Then I offer to help him if he helps me. I'm not sure how we would do that yet, so I didn't mention that angle to anyone.

Indy says Sharf is a brilliant number cruncher, but he is less than moderately competent when it comes to technology. Until two years ago, he let Belvedere's technology consultants handle the "bits and nits" while he followed the money. She says Sharf would not recognize an effective SOA Program if it was glued to his vital parts.

Indy met Sharf when she was a junior in college and he was a graduate teaching assistant. They disagreed over the interpretation of some of her test results, but apparently, it did not affect her grades. She and Nicky dealt with the situation and neither of them bothered to mention it until this weekend.

Surprise Rescheduling - Early Arrival

Sharf called and rescheduled his original meeting with my team three days earlier than expected - five days if you count the weekend. He was supposed to be here on Monday. He said he is really looking forward to working with us, and he would like to get started.

There is something wrong with that. Nobody schedules an audit, and then makes it earlier. The preparation process is too involved. I decided not to resist, because I am equally interested in discovering Sharf's intentions.

My major problem with starting today is that my BASE Program coordinator, Valery Van Amberg, may not be able to attend today's sessions. I need Val because he has mastered the art of slipping things past people by telling them the truth. If the first meeting was held on Monday, as we had originally scheduled, it would have been perfect.

He has been in the Asia for the last three weeks. He had planned to be stateside by tomorrow, prepare for the meeting on Friday, and recharge over the weekend. He is trying to make it before the day is over. He is probably crossing the Mississippi at this moment.

If we did not keep our ducks in a row, we would be in the middle of a mad scramble. However, the senior SOA architect, Hank Yu, and the Knowledge Consolidator, Maja Johansson, had copies of all the information Belvedere requested, except succession planning, by three o'clock yesterday. The topics Sharf recommended for the assessment (or the audit, or the inquisition) appear to be lifted directly from a SOX overview (the left side of Table 3. He also requested that we complete an SOA maturity self-assessment form (Table 9).

Acton says there is a list of more detailed questions circulating around the Board, but only Gooner's goons have that information. Sharf says the contents of the list are proprietary.

Hank Yu will be filling in for Val, as he has done several times before. Val preps him well. He is the smoothest super technologist that I have on staff, but he still thinks technology and translates it into business speak, a limitation that I understand because it has plagued me all my life.

Business Background of the head of SOA Governance

I am the SVP (I mean EVP) of BASE (Business Assurance through Service Excellence). That's better than SOA Governance. No one wants to be governed by me. The acronym explains the second major objective of the Program. We provide a foundation (base) from which everyone may achieve improved business results.

BASE evolved a Well-Formed Service-Oriented Architecture (WFSOA) methodology. WFSOA is the hardest job that I have done during all the years that I worked in this racket, and I am pleased with our results.

We are flying in a jumbo stealth bomber, and we are changing the engines while the plane is in flight. I am modest in some things, but this is not one of them. What I am about to say is verified in industry publications and vendor inside scoops. Our WFSOA only exists in Daxiao. We are among the largest and most effective SOA organizations in the world. Other large companies tend to be where we were two years ago.

BASE provides the tools and the processes to ensure that business and technology to work well with each other, and to ensure that none of us break any government rules.

Executive Titles in Daxiao

My job title is Coordinator of Information Systems (COINS). The reference to money in the title is descriptive. We are saving the company money, and we are making money.

The Board suggested that I could become the Chief Technology Officer (CTO) after they dumped Service-Oriented Architecture on me. I would be responsible for research into the hottest new technology (that was supposed to be the carrot in the deal). I rejected the title due to the "T". If SOA was supposed to promote synergy between business and technology, it was going to be hard enough without having the "Technology" staring the business people in the face.

Daxiao has a CIO, but it is not Armstrong. He wanted the CIO title, and that explains why he was willing to be so generous with the CTO moniker. The CIO (Coordinator of Information Optimization) reports to the finance organization, and Finance did not want "technology" staring them in the face either. Therefore, the technology EVP is stuck with "Technology", as he naturally should be.

The CTO has the Technology Sector with 4,800 people, and I have 410 people. That is fine with me. I manage 9% as many people as he does, but I earn 60% of his salary, and I affect 100% of what he does. My people and I pursue technical excellence at the expense of political expertise. We are good at tying up Armstrong's loose ends.

Professional History

I started here as a key punch operator and technical gopher after I finished college 38 years ago with financial assistance from the Marine Corp. I call it a degree for a knee. I have an undergraduate degree from the Courant Institute. I majored in mathematics and took some of the first computer courses that they offered. I decided that I would not have time to earn a law degree like my mate and our best friends. That almost became a deal killer when I was recommended for the job as head of compliance.

By 1996, I was responsible data management and part of application development (primarily mainframe, but with about 30% distributed systems). Travers and I built data warehouse applications that ran on client/server platforms. I let my people tinker with HTML and Web front-ends to the data marts. This kept them from becoming bored. Daxiao tossed in the end-of-century rollover event in 1997.

While I was working on "Y", .COM became the rage, and Mittelman hired the CTO and made him my boss. He said he needed someone who was forward looking, while my job required that I look backward. That is when I first considered changing jobs. Unfortunately, I had become a creature of habit. I was annoyed, but I was also fat and comfortable.

For a year after the beginning of 2000, they gave me responsibility for Compliance with the added responsibility of helping the new CTO along. Armstrong decided that he did not need me in the summer of 2001.

Guzman said I was doing well in compliance, and that I was beginning to make a difference. However, having other people get mad at me for noticing their dumb mistakes was not how I wanted to end my days.

About a third of them could have avoided the dumb mistakes if they had listened to me in the first place. Nicky and the Doc said I shouldn't even think that too loud, because people could see it in my eyes.

Meanwhile, Jonas (my son) and his wife said they had enough work to keep me busy for two lifetimes. I was sure that Mittelman would be happy to get rid of me, but I was having a hard time negotiating a severance package, even with Nicky's advice. My papers kept getting lost. Then the airplanes hit.

9/11 and Backward Lookers: *Daxiao discovered that the CTO may be a wunderkind with new ideas, but he was not as good in a crisis. He had also initiated processes that made the crisis worse than it needed to be. He was trying to save money by running 35% of our client/server production applications and 90% of the newer Web applications in the hot backup site. Our hot backup data center went away when #7 World Trade Center collapsed. The test environments in the main data center in New Jersey could not handle the load. He had been cutting back on the full test sites that I insisted upon to prove that I was wasteful.*

Thus, we needed to revive dozens of manual procedures to handle the applications that wouldn't fit into the test machines, and we had to enlist people who had been displaced by automation to make the manual processes work. The CTO could not imagine having to work that way. Rather than train his imagination, they gave me responsibility for recovery, and they made him responsible for making assuring statements to the stockholders.

My Secret Network, 9/11, and SOA

Val Van Amberg had been the head of compliance before he recommended me for the job. Over the last 35 years he and I have built a network of about 2,500 people (1,500 inside Daxiao) by saving the best people from the areas that were automated, "promoting" them to the compliance team, and training them in whatever was newest at the time.

Then Val sent them back out to critical areas. It was easy. If a unit was having trouble with an audit, Val would lend them the recycled auditor (most loans became permanent). The compliance network is my best-kept secret.

Due to those pockets of information and old-timer skill, we stabilized our environment a month ahead of other companies in the area. Daxiao convinced me to change my mind about leaving. I wore the hero hat that they denied me in 2000. They added responsibility for redoing the disaster recovery plan and rebuilding distributed systems (client/server) capacity to my compliance responsibilities.

My secret networks still helps me do the right things for Daxiao, and I don't want it dismantled, even after I leave. The network is more important than BASE, and in many ways it is more effective. No one can block what he or she can't see.

The First SOA: *In 2002, the first SOA happened. I am talking about the Sarbanes Oxley Act that you know as SOX. Enron and WorldCom mismanagement had caused major upheavals in the regulatory arena and everyone was suddenly in a compliance scurry.*

I was still responsible for compliance, my "Belt and Suspenders" reputation fit what they needed, I was only 58 years old, and I saw this as an opportunity to keep another outsider from dismantling the useful things that I had worked years to build.

Then Daxiao almost sent me to jail because I was assisting my son (Jonas) with his start-ups. It nearly made me lose my mind, upon which I have a tenuous grip anyhow.

While I was on sabbatical waiting for judgment, they found that someone else was doing what they accused me of doing.

They needed me again. Nicky, my friend for life, said it was time for me to leave, but both of us hesitated a bit after the profuse apologies, a big bonus increase (at least for me), and the promise that I would become an EVP. They let me make up a new title for myself, they gave me my own (very small) sector, and they set me up in a place that was hobbling distance from the office in New York.

Jonas was starting to make enough money that my pay package was a pittance, but my ego got in the way, and I came back. I did not want to leave under a cloud.

To Leave or Not to Leave - Again

I could tell Daxiao if I intend to retire at the end of next year. The truth is that if I knew whether I was planning to leave, I would not tell them. I need as much time as possible to take care of my people. In addition, I really enjoy annoying the hell out of Armstrong and Mittelman while I save their hides.

SOA Architect - Audit Coordinator

I mentioned my co-pilot earlier. Hank was the head of Daxiao's Emerging Technology Team (all 11 of them) before the merger between Goodsand and Daxiao. Armstrong already had people performing that function, and he circulated Hank's paper before they evaluated his capabilities. Stein (my current head of compliance) was responsible for technology compliance at the time, and he needed someone with experience in Daxiao to help him audit Daxiao technology "before" and "after". Stein asked me participate in Hank's interview the day after Hank's father called to see if I would "look out" for his son.

I would have recommended Hank five times over, even if his father had not left the keypunch room open at school, so I would have time to complete my assignments, after attending two or three classes each night and on Saturday mornings.

Hank has a degree in computer science from the Computer Laboratory at Cambridge and a master's degree in corporate communications from NYU. He speaks two dialects of Chinese, and they tell me that he speaks Spanish with a Chinese accent.

He has a peculiarity that his mind is so literal that he uses idioms almost as badly as I use puns. We both keep trying, and the results range from slightly annoying to positively hilarious. Fortunately, he restrains himself with people he does not know. I am less restrained than he is.

The SOA/SOX Advisors - Introduction

Sharf is a bit taller than I am which is very tall. Consulting firms do this too often for it to be an accident, but he is the tallest person so far. At least I don't have to worry that my height will intimidate him. On the other hand, maybe Gunnar ordered someone who could intimidate me.

To level the playing field, because he had heard so much about me already, he gave us copies of the résumés that Belvedere submitted when they were competing for the assignment. We may call him William or perhaps Will - not Bill. The resume says that he is a CFO-level CPA who has been doing SEC audits for 21 years and has been successfully growing an SOA practice for the last two years. He was trained at the Wheaton School (which Indy told me already).

His Technology Associate is Renata Vitale (Rennie). She worked with the WS-I (Web Services Interoperability) Basic Profile Working Group, before Belvedere wooed her away from a technology company. She contributed to two of the registry standards before that. She has a master's degree in computer science from MUDD (the engineering school at Columbia University). She provides technology backup for William while she takes notes. She looks like an older version of Val's daughter or a younger version of Paula (his wife), except that I have never seen either of them dressed like that.

Hank distributed the information packets. William synchronized his mannerisms with mine. Rennie did not flirt with either Hank or me. That's a twist. The ones in the short skirts usually do. The inquisition (oops, I meant to say assessment) started.

CHAPTER II -SOA ORGANIZATIONAL AND GOVERNANCE STRUCTURE

William Sharf>: We know enough about each other that we can skip the small talk. You have the Topics for Investigation on the Engagement Checklist that we created with guidance from your Board. Mr. Gunther already provided me with information about your staff counts (see Fig. 2.1), your organizational hierarchy, and the list of people he believes are important to SOA (Table 1). After we finish a high-level view of your structures and processes for handling SOX and SOA, we will set up interviews with your people to develop a more complete picture.

Reader's Note: Remember that:

- Each change of speaker is shown by a **<Name>** inside XML tags.
- Personal thoughts appear in ***Times New Roman.***
- Sign language appears in **Alba, · like this.**

<Renata Vitale>: ***This is crude, even for Sharf. Mr. Cane thought he would be bending over backwards to ensure that we make a good impression at Daxiao.***

<HM>: Do you mean Gunnar or Gunther?

<Sharf>: Gunnar. ***He is Gunther to his family, and he is Gunnar here. I will try to remember that.***

<HM>: Do you have an agenda for the session?

<Renata Vitale>: ***This isn't the boardroom, but it's a good set-up.***

<Sharf>: This will be more of a fact-finding event than an audit, so we do not have to be so formal. Agendas limit serendipity. I promise we will not discuss anything that is not on the topic list. Today's discussion will allow us to discover areas where agendas will be necessary. We will be more structured with the people who are lower down the totem pole. ***If you do not know what I am going to ask, I can keep you off balance.***

<HM>: ***Wrong answer. You are trying to catch us off guard.*** This isn't how the government auditors, Acton, or my compliance people approach audits, but I am always willing to try something new.

<Sharf>: Flexibility is a good way to start. How did you define the relationships among the units required for your SOA success?

He does not seem to know me. How is that possible? Maybe his women do not tell him about all their mischief.

It doesn't matter. They hurt me before, and now Marshall is hurting me. They all have to pay.

SOX ≈ SOA

<HM>: In Fig. 2.1, BASE sits in the middle of Daxiao's organizational structure and assists everyone.

<Sharf>: Which SOA do you mean?

<HM>: Both. Most of what we do for SOX assists with SOA, and everything we do for the new SOA assists with SOX. We practice reuse recommendations of the Service-Oriented Architecture version of SOA.

<Sharf>: How would you explain how your 410 people can assist almost 90,000 people for both Sarbanes-Oxley and Service-Oriented Architecture?

<HM>: We build the paths and recommend how participants should use them. We guide the work. We minimize the use of manual processes.

<Sharf>: How would you handle the bottlenecks?

<HM>: I am not aware of bottlenecks. Did the "BOARD" mention any?

<Sharf>: Some projects have difficulty moving through the requirements process.

<HM>: We do not control that, but we can look. Hank, what do you see?

<Hank>: What level do you want to see?

<HM>: Start at the business unit level, and use a two-week window.

<Rennie>: What are you doing?

<Hank>: I am checking in ReMain, our request management system, to see how many requests have not moved in the last two weeks.

<Sharf>: Make it one week.

<Hank>: There are 143 requests with yellow lights, and 52 are red.

<Sharf>: Show me the list for Mr. Gunther - I mean Gunnar.

<Hank>: He has 55 that are yellow and 22 that are red.

<Sharf>: That is a bottleneck. Why does that area have a disproportionate number of the problems?

<Hank>: Business analysts are waiting for requirements on 38 yellows and 18 reds. They are waiting for someone is Gunnar's organization to approve the funding on the remainder. Let me see what the problem is.

[...] This is a good one.

<Sharf>: What is it?

<HM>: Let me guess. Marcella took two vacation days, all his digital signatures expired at once, and the only other person who knew how to request authorization quit, or he fired them. *I goofed already.*

<Hank>: This one is different. The people on these requests moved in next door before all their equipment arrived, and they were tripling up on terminals for the first two weeks. *Planning is not their good clothes.*

<HM>: **Behave.** *I have to keep reminding myself.*

<Hank>: Getting the sales out was more important than approving change requests. The equipment came in last week, and the queue is now half as large as it was three weeks ago.

<HM>: When is the last time you discussed this with Gunnar?

<Rennie>: How did you do that?

<Hank>: I checked the user support queues. That is the first thing we do when he starts to bounce the walls. He is always exploding washers.

<HM>: **Be nice.** Mr. Sharf, are there any other bottlenecks that you would like to discuss? *Hank as is angry about this Gunnar silliness as I am, He's about to pop his own gaskets, but I can't laugh.*

<Sharf>: *That is where she got the smug look. She looks just like her father.* Let's move on.

<Rennie>: Why do you call your team BASE?

<HM>: "Business Achievement through Service Excellence" was always the motto of the Compliance Management Team. Business teams and the technology team resist being "GOVERNED" by BASE *(especially since we employ several castoffs from their teams).* We use BASE to minimize the allusion to governing as often as we can.

Similarly, we avoid association with titles that contain "technology anything". BASE fits very well in both contexts. If these illustrations were circulated among internal clients and partners, they would only see BASE.

<Sharf>: It also means that you are below the people that you support.

<HM>: We emphasize that we provide a firm foundation for both SOAs. At the same time, we must be strong, or the entire structure could fall.

<Rennie>: That is clever!

SOA Governance

<Sharf>: *I decide what is clever.* You are still governing something. What do you do?

<HM>: Governance in Daxiao takes four forms. This is illustrated in Fig. 3.1. BASE interacts with Corporate Governance through my Compliance teams. A fifth area, Data Governance, is tied closely to SOA Governance. SOA Data Governance is as important as governance of services and processes. That is my most "Critical Success Factor".

<Sharf>: Who runs Data Governance?

<HM>: We have a separate oversight committee for that. The CFO, the head of Data Management, and I share responsibility.

<Sharf>: How would you justify having the CFO involved with data governance?

<HM>: The data domain owners report to the CFO. Thus, the chair for that committee reports to Lorraine Jasper. See Table 2 for a list of the committees that affect both SOAs.

<Sharf>: How would you explain that Guzman give up the larger audit committee and kept SOX?

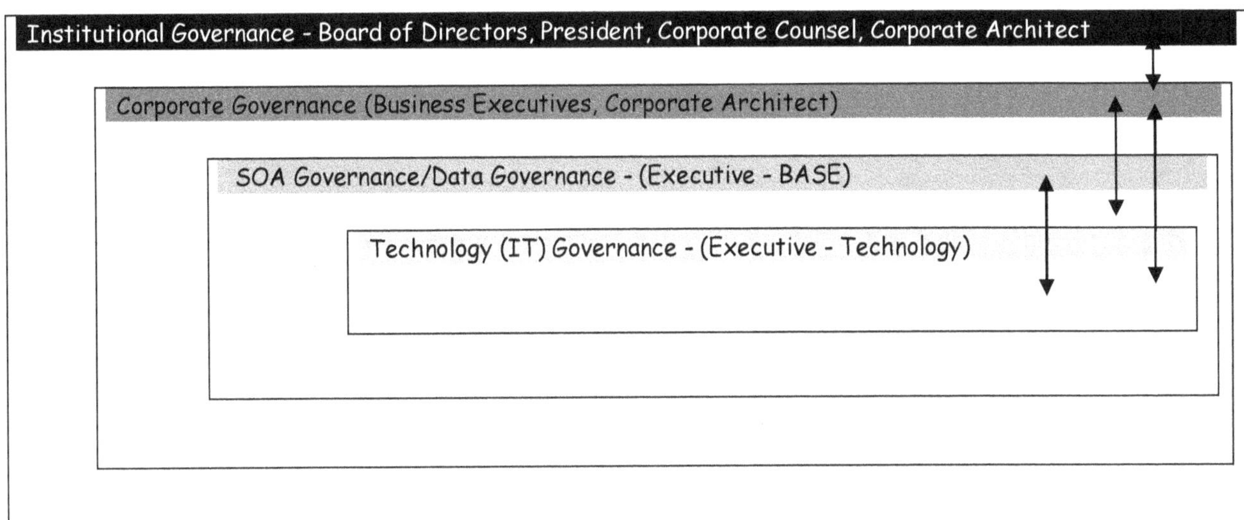

Fig. 3.1 - **Daxiao Layers of Governance**

<HM>: Daxiao has become very attractive to organizations all over the world. Guzman will use the time he saves on dealing with less important audit issues to deal with takeover attempts.

He hoped that Lorrie could keep Gunnar under control. We missed something between Gunnar and Mittelman, which doesn't make sense because Gunnar is going after Mittelman's job.

<Sharf>: Why did he keep SOX?

<HM>: ***That must be a trick question.*** If we messed up on SOX, we would be totally unattractive.

<Sharf>: Isn't Mr. Gunnar the head of the Audit Committee?

<HM>: That is an interim assignment. ***The results of our interactions will help decide whether it will become permanent, and this is not going well already.***

Table 2 - **Daxiao Committees Affecting BASE**

Committee Name	**Committee Chair**	**Charter**
Audit Committee	*A. Niklas Gunnar	A subset of Corporate Governance - responsible for ensuring performance of internal and external audits, and for follow-up on to audit recommendations. Seat vacated by Joseph Guzman.
Change Advisory Board	Alex Macedon	Prioritizes and synchronizes projects involving new or changed infrastructure, services, processes, and applications (business and technology).
Corporate Advisory Board	Emery-Baldwin and Daniel Piccolo, Co-chairs	Evaluates internal and external business trends, identifies intra-organizational directional conflicts, recommends resolutions, and coordinates cultural change management programs.
Corporate Governance	Joseph Guzman	Provides guidance to the Board of Directors and business executives on performance of duties.
Data Governance	George Ramirez	Identifies financial consequences of poor data quality, availability, and performance issues, and of unnecessary data redundancy, data overlaps, gaps, and conflicts. Gathers consensus on appropriate solutions and submits recommendations for problem solutions.
IT Governance	Weldon Armstrong	Manages delivery of infrastructure and business technology in a timely and cost- effective manner.
Service/Process Governance	Alex Macedon	Defines business rules, resolves conflicting rules, and supports automation of rules.

SOX Monitoring	Joseph Guzman	Focuses on interpretation of and conformance to PCAOB requirements.
BASE Governance	Valery Van Amberg	Defines and implements processes and procedures for synchronizing all the above.
* Interim assignment		

<Hank>: The functions of BASE are summarized in Fig.3.2 (Governance Relationships) and Fig. 3.3 shows the three components of SOA (BASE) Governance.

<Sharf>: I don't see your name in Fig. 3.3.

<HM>: Van Amberg is on our team.

<Hank>: Notice that the arrows take up more area than the circle. SOA governance gathers information from everyone, distributes information to everyone, monitors the information flow, and facilitates conversion of information to knowledge.

<Sharf>: You seem to view yourself as central to everything.

<HM>: We are central to everything. If we were not, the company would not be paying your rates to discover what we do.

<Sharf>: Our rates are conservative, given the quality of service that we provide!

<HM>: ***The rates comment annoyed him. H, you are not handling this correctly. Everybody agreed that we would let him put a few cards on the table first. You should appear humbled and a bit intimidated.***

<Sharf>: What do you have to do with research? That belongs to Piccolo.

<Hank>: Piccolo does more structured scientific research. That is something that a person with degrees from Strafford and MTC would be expected to do, and that is primarily with external partners. Our organization provides foundational (BASE) elements for internal areas of the company. We support corporate research, operational research, manufacturing research, and customer research. We also provide guidance and mentoring for technology research.

<HM>: ***Gunnar took Li from me, and we took him back.***

<Sharf>: Are you implying that your people are more technical than the technologists are? How could that be?

<HM>: My people are more familiar with both historical and emerging information sources. As a result, they can respond in innovative ways. ***That wasn't humble.***

<Sharf>: How would you explain what makes you tick?

<HM>: I enjoy delivering results in situations where others have failed. That balances my need for day-to-day order and structure. It is difficult to achieve both. ***There's a tiny bit of humility.***

<Sharf>: How do you balance this need?

<HM>: I have a question, if you don't mind. ***I need to understand what the Board (actually Gunnar) told him to do, and what he wants for himself.***

<Sharf>: Be brief.

<HM>: ***It feels like we started at the bottom, and we're going downhill.*** Are you here to find out what I do, to show me how to do a better job of what I do, both, or other? ***He couldn't show me how to tie my shoelaces, but I implied that he has something to offer.***

<Sharf>: I will be perfectly honest with you.

<HM>: ***BOHICA ...Here it comes again.***

<Sharf>: Your senior people see a result. They want to know the secrets of how you do what you do.

<HM>: ***I detect a glimmer of honesty here.*** All my "secrets" are in the details. When I try to explain the details, they say they don't want to be bogged down in the details.

<Sharf>: They hired my team because we are excellent at understanding, filtering, and organizing details to discover the essence of a situation. ***I am going to discover how you deliver, and what you deliver at half of what Belvedere charges.***

<HM>: That is extremely good, because I have more details for you than most people realized existed. Where shall we start? ***Nicky said that variable reinforcement consisting of information overload***

and information gaps will allow me to understand his motives.

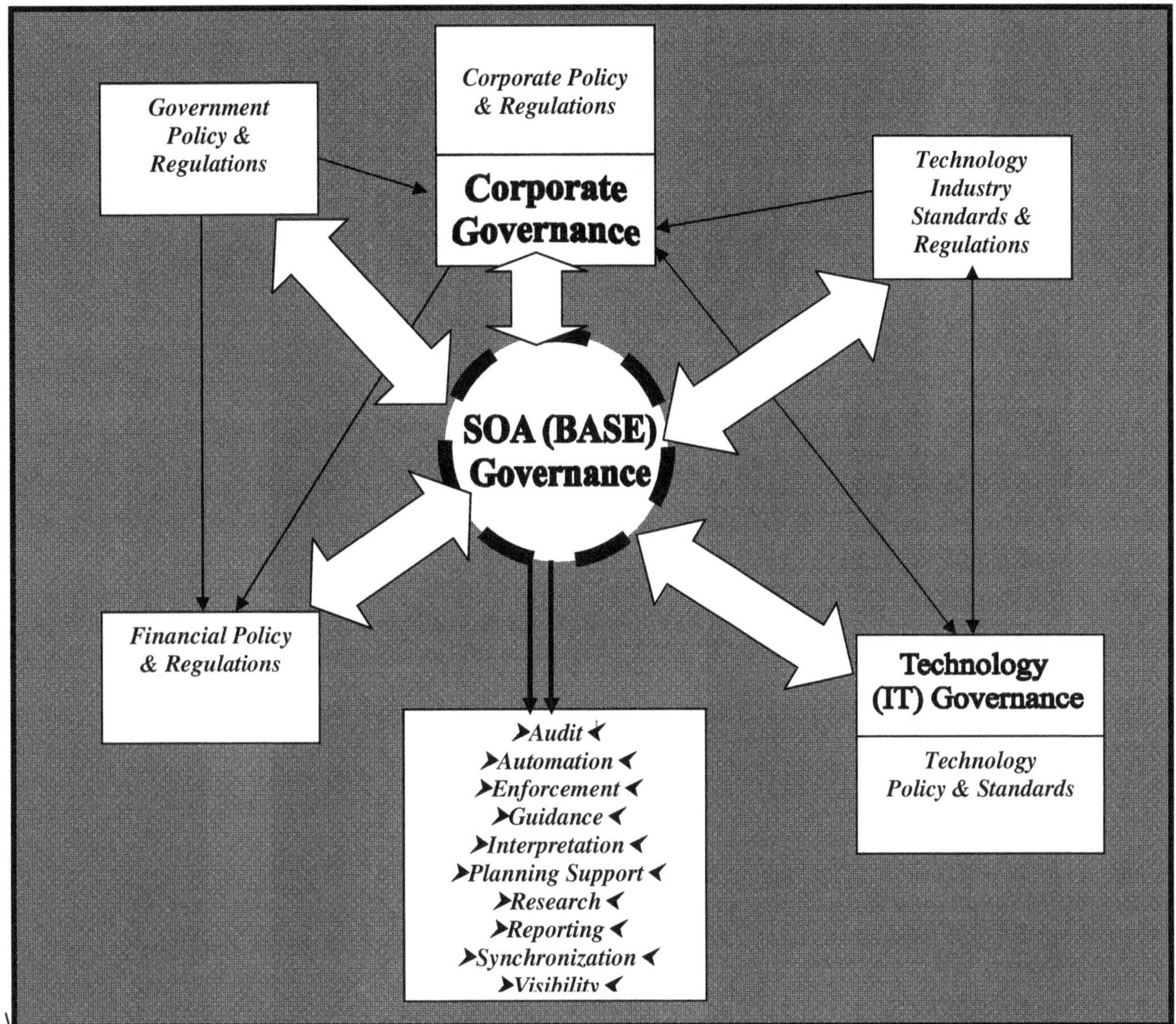

Fig. 3.2 - SOA Governance Relationships and Functions

SOA Organizational Structure

<Sharf>: I noticed in Fig. 2.2 and Table 1 that you have the right number of people, but you have too many SVPs for such a small organization.

<HM>: Our people need the authority to make decisions without coming to me. The titles are necessary for their approval levels. Remember those bottlenecks I told you that we do not have.

<Sharf>: Why didn't you print Table 1 in hierarchical order?

<HM>: Maja doesn't think that way, and we don't either. This is sufficient for our needs.

<Hank>: The Human Resources Team maintains rankings. I believe you will see them tomorrow. But, if it matters, you have a hierarchy in Fig. 2.2.

<Sharf>: Nevertheless, you might want to tell Maja to fix it. It's easier to anchor when it's in rank order.

<HM>: *He's doing memory tricks!* I understand. I will forward your suggestion.

<Sharf>: You forgot the title for Johnson.

<Hank>: Jay doesn't have a title. He's a consultant working on a post-doctoral research study, and we don't give him time to finish.

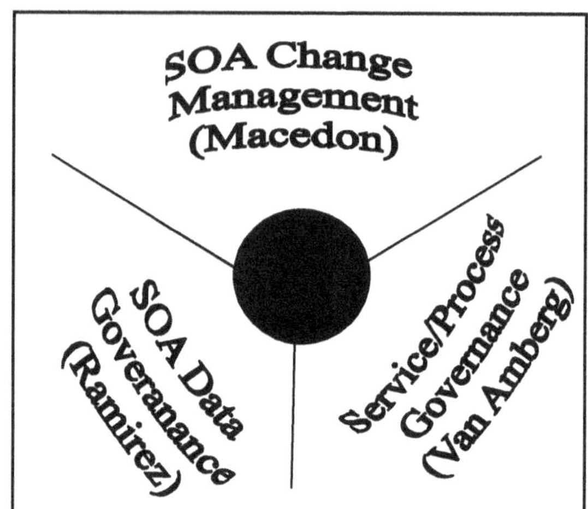

Fig. 3.3 - SOA (BASE) Governance Components

<HM>: Notice that the average experience in Daxiao of my people is almost twice as much for the rest of the people associated with SOA.

<Sharf>: How would you avoid stagnation in a situation such as that?

<Rennie>: *Will has lost his mind. That was totally inappropriate.*

<HM>: Listen closely. Come closer. I want you to hear this.

<Hank>: *He shot H's athlete's heel. H believes that maturity allows us to apply new concepts more effectively, as long as we are willing to keep trying. He only associates with people who are willing to keep trying.*

<Rennie>: *I saw William flinch.*

<HM>: I j- just put $100 in your p- pocket. After you understand our environment, you may pick anyone outside my organization for a head-to-head contest with anyone inside my organization based on knowledge and innovative skills. That includes the secretaries and administrative assistants. We will do a blind test, and we will let someone from your organization, perhaps Grayson, be the judge. If my people don't win at least 7 times out of 10, you keep the $100. If I win, you return the $100 bill, and you pay me $50. Is that fair?

<Sharf>: How do you know about [...]

<HM>: I did the background check on Belvedere. Here it is. *One of the things I want to know is why you are here and not Grayson. I'd also like to know what it is about your boss that seems so familiar.*

<Sharf>: I see where you're going. Keep your money and let's move along. We have many things to cover and not much time. *He circled Grayson's name. He'll pay for that.*

<Hank>: *Waltz of the Giants. The dance floor is dangerous.*

<Rennie>: What shall we cover next?

SOX, COBIT and COSO Overview

<Sharf>: Where is your SOX team? *We should finish SOX quickly. I really need to concentrate on SOA.*

<HM>: That is the SOX team.

<Sharf>: *Andy said this is where everything would become confusing.*

<Hank>: There is a 90% overlap between SOX and SOA teams and functions. That means that 90% of what we do satisfies two sets of requirements simultaneously. We said that before.

<Sharf>: It doesn't look like COBIT (Control Objectives for Information and related Technology) or COSO (Committee of Sponsoring Organizations)? How would you explain the missing COBIT frameworks or the COSO requirements? *This is why Andy's people are confused. Marshall keeps things jumbled together.*

<HM>: When I inherited SOX (*when they dumped it on me because everyone else was annoyed by it*), we mapped the COBIT frameworks and COSO requirements against or organizational structure.

<Hank>: The control groups were spread across multiple sectors, but they were fairly well covered. No one was willing to reorganize just for SOX. Instead, we split the COBIT frameworks and spread the control groups among the teams that were in place at the time.

Table 3 - Comparison of Critical Requirements for SOX and SOA		
Board/Belvedere Topic	Required in. Sarbanes-Oxley	Required in Service-Oriented Architecture
Areas for improvement	X	X
Business continuity planning	X	X
Business process evaluation	X	X
Business system acquisition	X	X
Business system development	X	X
Communications	X	X
Critical success factors	X	X
Industry Standards		X
Management structure	X	X
Methodology	X	X
Organizational structure	X	X
Planning processes	X	X
Policies	X	X
Risk management	X	X
Roles & responsibility	X	X
Security and Information Asset Protection	X	X
Strategy	X	X
Succession planning	X	X
Technical infrastructure	X	X

<Sharf>: How many people did you have then?

<HM>: We had approximately 230 people, but we were called Compliance.

<Sharf>: They gave you 180 people to set up your SOA team when you received your own sector?

<HM>: I already had more than half of the SOA team.

<Sharf>: *This confusion is rehearsed.*

<Hank>: They were doing SOX. We compared the list of SOA topics that you and the Board agreed upon to Sarbanes-Oxley (See Table 3). As an expert in both SOA-1 (SOX) and SOA-2, what do you believe that we should add?

<Sharf>: I will get back to you. However, at this high level, I don't expect that anything needs to be added. *This is logical, and too simple.*

<Rennie>: *I mentioned this in my interview, but this makes it clear. Maybe Belvedere will listen to me now?*

<HM>: When we inherited SOA, we noticed this nearly perfect alignment and determined that we could use one organizational structure to handle both functions with a bit of tweaking.

<Sharf>: Where is the current SOX mapping?

<HM>: That's in Table 4-Daxiao Teams and SOX Responsibility.

<Sharf>: It's good to see that you are addressing the guidelines. However, because it is spread across several areas, I can't tell who is ultimately responsible. Someone must be or nothing gets done.

<HM>: I have responsibility for collecting information for audits and for continuous monitoring. Joseph Guzman and Lorraine Jasper verify that I do it correctly. *Attack them if you're feeling frisky.*

Table 4 - Daxiao Teams and SOX Responsibility

Key:

- AI: Acquire and Implement.
- COBIT: Control Objectives for Information and related Technology.
- COSO: Committee of Sponsoring Organizations of the Treadway Commission.
- DS: Deliver and Support.
- ERM: Enterprise Risk Management.
- ME: Monitor and Evaluate.
- PO: Plan and Organize

Corporate Sector Teams	Have Primary Responsibility for COBIT Control Group
Corporate Communications	1. Communicate Management Aims and Direction(PO) 2. Information and Communication (COSO)
Corporate Sector Management	1. Define Strategic IT Plan (PO) 2. Objective Setting (COSO) 3. Information and Communication (COSO)
Global Security	Ensure Systems Security (DS)
Enterprise Integration	1. Conformity to the organization's strategy (ERM) 2. Internal Environment (COSO)
Financial Management	Reliability of financial reporting (ERM)
Human Resources	1. Educate and Train Users (DS) 2. Manage Human Resources (PO)
Legal Services	1. Compliance with applicable laws and regulations (ERM) 2. Control Activities (COSO) 3. Risk Response (COSO) 4. Ensure compliance with external requirements (COSO) 5. Obtain Independent Assurance (COSO) 6. Provide for Independent Audit (COSO)
Business Sector Teams	**Have Primary Responsibility for COBIT Control Group**
Business Sector Management	Effectiveness and efficiency of operations (ERM)
Clients	Define and Manage Service Levels (DS)
Quality Assurance	Manage Quality (PO)
Process Management	Develop and Maintain Procedures (AI)
Requirements Management	1. Acquire and Maintain Application Software (AI) 2. Identify Automated Solutions (AI) 3. Manage Changes (AI)
BASE (Governance) Teams	**Have Primary Responsibility for COBIT Control Group**
Compliance Management	1. Assess Internal Control Adequacy (ME) 2. Assess Risks (PO) 3. Ensure Compliance with External Requirements (PO) 4. Monitor Processes (ME) 5. Obtain Independent Assurance (ME) 6. Provide for Independent Audit (ME)

	7. Event Identification (COSO) 8. Monitoring (COSO) 9. Risk Assessment (COSO)
SOA Program Management	1. Determine Technological Direction (PO) 2. Identify and Allocate Costs (DS)
Technology Sector Teams	**Have Primary Responsibility for COBIT Control Group**
Data Center	1. Ensure Continuous Service (DS) 2. Manage Operations (DS) 3. Manage Performance and Capacity (DS)
Data Management	1. Define Information Architecture (PO) 2. Manage Data (DS)
Infrastructure Technology.	1. Acquire and Maintain Technology Infrastructure (AI) 2. Install and Accredit Systems (AI) 3. Manage Configuration (DS)
Business Technology	1. Manage Projects (PO) 2. Manage Third-Party Services (DS)
Technology Sector Management	1. Define IT Organization and Relationships (PO) 2. Manage Facilities (DS) 3. Manage IT Investment (PO)
User Support	1. Assist and Advise Customers (DS) 2. Manage Problems and Incidents (DS)

<HM>: This arrangement ensures that the entire management team shares responsibility for SOX. Acton rates us highly for shared SOX responsibility, and in high compliance with PCAOB guidelines.

<Sharf>: Daxiao may find that Belvedere has improved interpretations of the guidelines. We may wish to revisit Acton's interpretation.

<Rennie>: ***He's doing this all wrong.***

<HM>: I can understand your view. ***He hates Acton.***

<Sharf>: How often do you accumulate and report results?

<HM>: We officially update the results every month. They are available on the executive scorecard at all times.

<Rennie>: I'm familiar with COBIT and COSO, but when did ERM enter the picture.

<Hank>: COSO began promoting the Enterprise Risk Management framework in 2004. Our Compliance Team found it useful for handling the risks associated with SOA.

<Sharf>: How long will it take you to put together the list of roles associated with SOX responsibilities?

> **Readers**: Please don't confuse Table N.N with Table **A**.N.N. (The second set is in the APPENDIX). They are generally too large to fit into the body of SOA P.

<Hank>: Table A.1.1 is on the screen now. It shows teams in the Corporate Sector, roles that deal with COBIT, COSO, or ERM, and which roles have primary and secondary responsibility. Three other parts of Table A.1 deal with the other sectors. Notice that while there is only one primary for each control objective, multiple roles may share secondary responsibility for an objective.

<Sharf>: How many roles is that?

<Hank>: I believe there are between 65 and 70 on this list. I can give you the exact [...]

<Sharf>: Those are more roles than I have ever seen! How would you explain that?

<Hank>: The definition of **"BIG SOA"** requires involvement of people outside the traditional technology areas. We proved that:

- Every set of responsibilities is sufficiently different, or
- Each role's view of the requirement is sufficiently different that our SOX compliance efforts benefit from the granular role definitions.

<Sharf>: The list is long, but some roles seem to be missing. Show me the internal auditors.

<HM>: That would be the two compliance specialist roles.

<Sharf>: You have your own financial specialist. What does he do?

<HM>: She focuses on project estimation and the SOA budget, and she works with the planning specialists in Requirements Management while she (the CFO) controls all allocations and manages our financial position in relation to external situations.

<Sharf>: I may suggest a few improvements.

<Rennie>: I will add my comments to William's list.

<Sharf>: Do you believe that SOX is a burden or a benefit?

<HM>: Is that a trick question?

<Sharf>: One typically asks such a question.

<HM>: It's a major benefit. It gave us an opportunity to formalize many of the things that I have been trying to put in place for years. It gave me a mandate to document both business and technology processes. We consolidated the company's information base.

It also ensured that we had the money to widen the foundation (BASE) for everything we do that is related to compliance and technology.

<Hank>: We have:

1. One master client list.
2. One master parts list.
3. One master database designation for every piece of information.
4. A single business vocabulary for the entire company (with translations into 7 different languages).
5. A single technical vocabulary (also translated).
6. A single list of approved processes.
7. Consistent approval processes.
8. A process for process improvement and process exceptions.
9. A consistent risk management process (we mentioned ERM) above.
10. One purchasing department and one vendor list.

<Sharf>: *On which you forgot to consider Belvedere* [...]

<HM>: We could continue for days [...]

<Sharf>: That is enough about SOX for the time being. Let's set the stage for Service-Oriented Architecture, and then take a break. Where is your list of SOA roles?

<HM>: There's a lot more that we need to tell you about SOX.

<Sharf>: I've done enough SOX audits that I can tell you have an acceptable knowledge in that area. Except that the ultimate responsibility is not as clear as I would like it to be, I would leave it running the way that you have it. We can return to that after we clear up the fog surrounding SOA. *I will be able to tease the functions apart after I hear what he has to say about SOA.*

<HM>: *Note to self - Fog is in the eye of the beholder.* How would you like us to set the stage for SOA?

<Sharf>: Begin by explaining why you believe Daxiao is more successful with SOA than firms of similar size are.

<Hank>: Our success is due to a beneficial confluence of favorable circumstances. Hard work allowed us to take advantage of these circumstances.

<Sharf>: Be more specific.

<HM>: Serendipity, to use your term. *Sarcasm is not good, but I couldn't help myself.*

<Hank>: He means serendipity within the context of a Well-Formed Service-Oriented Architecture.

BASE (Governance) Critical Objectives and Goals

<Sharf>: Start by defining SOA and how your WFSOA is different.

<HM>: Daxiao supports four views of SOA (See Table 5-SOA Definitions). WFSOA pulls them together.

<Hank>: We emphasize **need.** Clients often ask for things that they don't need, and we still deliver things that they don't necessarily need, but now we all know the difference.

<Sharf>: What are the most important requirements for SOA success?

Table 5 - SOA Definitions	
Business Executive View	Service-Oriented Architecture is a cross-organizational management strategy for aligning business and technology ("BIG SOA"). It will change the way technology has been delivering service to business for the last 40 to 50 years. **It will** help **us to accomplish more with our technology dollars.**
Corporate Architecture View	BASE is the Daxiao implementation of SOA that supports business, governance, and technology views of SOA. It defines organizational structures, roles and responsibilities, actions, process flows, information flows, and supporting technology (**"BIG SOA")** and allows clients to receive the services and processes they ***need*** (as long as the services confirm to the most current business strategy). Daxiao reuses as much of what we have as possible. Daxiao conforms to and guides appropriate industry standards. It will change the way technology has been delivering service to business for the last 40 to 50 years. ← That is not a typo. The statement was repeated for emphasis. **It will allow Daxiao to achieve its goals based on its business strategy.**
SOA BASE (Governance) View	1. Service-Oriented Architecture is a business strategy that allows finer definition of business requirements and successively better alignment of technical support with business requirements. 2. Service-Oriented Architecture is the technical framework, supported by industry standards, that supports modularized computing functions (services) for easier alignment with business requirements. It also includes policies and practices to ensure the quality of services provided. 3. SOA: ♦ Changes the relationships between people, processing, and data. ♦ Drives and requires centralization. ♦ Promotes elimination of application and data silos. ♦ Identifies resistance reasons and removes them. **It will improve organizational and technology structure and processes to save money while achieving Daxiao's goals.**
SOA Technology View	Service-Oriented Architecture supports loosely coupled and interoperable services or processes and definition of techniques for integrating interoperable components. It includes mechanisms for describing services, advertising and discovering services, and communicating with services. It will change the relationships between technology and business units and between factions within technology. **It provides the technology that allows Daxiao to mix and match system components for delivery of flexible technology on time.**

Table 6 - SOA Critical Requirements

Key:
>>> BASE will fail without these.
>> BASE would struggle to survive without these.
> BASE effectiveness would be reduced by at least 25% each year without these.
Blank BASE effectiveness would be reduced by an amount that is not yet determined.

Criticality	Contributors to BASE Effectiveness - Corporate Sector
>>>	Executive support
>>>	Security management and monitoring (including role-based security)
>>	Business process management with continuous process improvement as critical components of Corporate Architecture
>>	Common terminology
>>	Corporate governance and architecture acceptance of SOA
>>	Cultural change management program
>>	Educational program with just-in-time training
>>	Organizational restructuring
>>	Risk Management (formalized)
>>	Service level agreements
>>	Stakeholder acceptance
>>	Strategy planning and oversight
>>	Support for clear definition and assignment of Roles and responsibilities
Criticality	**Contributors to BASE Effectiveness - Business Sector**
>>>	Executive support
>>	Business process coordination
>>	Business rules management
>>	Client participation and increased control through Centralized Requirements Management
>>	Common terminology
>>	Costing algorithms, metering, and billing
>>	ReMain - Request Maintenance application linking the best of vendor products with Daxiao extensions
>>	Understanding of company, industry, government, and international regulations
>	Automated approval processes for work promotion and funding
>	Extra costs for assumptions and outstanding issues
>	Test processes and procedures including WS-I Basic Profile
	Job Rotation
	Rewards for participation
Criticality	**Contributors to BASE Effectiveness - BASE (Governance) Sector**
>>>	Knowledge Cooperative
>>>	SOA governance (including service and data governance)
>>	BASE ***Thunk*** database (roles/activity) planning support
>>	Common terminology
>>	Problem prevention processes and procedures (best practices)
>>	Research and development (ongoing)
>>	Reusability objectives and reward structure
>>	Service development support structure
>>	Service management (catalog and life cycle)
>>	SOA Communications
>>	Technology process coordination (methodology including internal and external standards)
>	Compliance monitoring
>	Mapping dependencies (what affects services, what services affect)
>	Mapping of relationships between processing artifacts and between artifacts and owners.

Table 6 - SOA Critical Requirements	
>	Procurement processes and procedures
>	Service categories and hierarchy
	Job rotation
	Vendor training and information exchange
Criticality	**Contributors to BASE Effectiveness - Technology Sector**
>>>	Data management processes and procedures
>>>	Executive support
>>	Architectural processes and procedures
>>	Common terminology
>>	Discovery mechanism (for services)
>>	Middleware (ESB, messaging)
>>	Naming conventions
>>	Product delivery support
>>	Service development support structure
>>	Service monitoring and reporting
>>	Tool administrator
>>	Understanding of WS-* standards
>>	Understanding of WS-I (Interoperability)
>>	Use of core standards (XML, SOAP, WSDL, UDDI)
>>	Version control

Table 6 shows what we consider SOA critical requirements within each sector.

Table 7 defines the Program's objectives and our goals against those objectives in 18- and 36-month windows. The items are in order by probability of success within the 18-month timeframe.

<Sharf>: Armstrong is in better shape.

Table 7 - WFSOA Objectives and Goals		
Description of BASE objective	**% of Goal in. 18 Months**	**% of Goal in 36 Months**
Corporate Objectives		
Security architecture supports full SOA implementation	≈100	100
Corporate governance processes and procedures are institutionalized and support full SOA implementation	95	100
Education and training are available to enable BASE success	95	95
SOA communications model is institutionalized	80	100
Senior managers understand and acknowledge financial benefits of BASE	75	100
Program participants understand and use common terminology (business and technology)	60	90
Senior managers champion BASE	60	80
Cultural change management program supports institutional adjustments	60	80
Business Objectives		
Business decides when and how services and processes are implemented	100	100
Business organizational structure can support full SOA implementation (services and Business Process Management)	60	85
Appropriate business staff is experienced in SOA	60	80
Business processes are automated	50	75
Business understands benefits of lessons learned	40	80
Continuous (business) process improvement is institutionalized	40	65

Table 7 - WFSOA Objectives and Goals		
Business areas can create successful on-demand services	<10	25
BASE Objectives		
WFSOA information loaded into Knowledge Cooperative	95+	99+
Governance organizational structure will support full SOA implementation	95+	100
Service architecture is institutionalized	95	100
SOA governance processes and procedures for methodology and data will be institutionalized and support full SOA implementation	90+	100
WFSOA processes have appropriate automation	99	99+
Continuous (Governance) process improvement is institutionalized	95	95
Core services are available to support all business processes	80	95
Services are managed in domains	80	95+
Application and data silos are eliminated	65	90
Redundant data sources are eliminated	50	80
Services are reused	45	75
Partners participate in service automation	40	70
Data managed in domains	40	55
Processes are reused	15	25
Technology Objectives		
IT Governance structures are ready to support full SOA implementation	90	100
Infrastructure architecture is ready to support appropriate processes or services	80	100
Technology staff is experience in SOA	80	95+
Data center operations is ready to support appropriate processes or services	80	100
Technology understands benefits of lessons learned	70	95
New development uses services or processes	65	95
Data architecture ready to support full SOA implementation	60	95+
Appropriate applications are converted to services	55	90

<HM>: The technical parts of SOA are less difficult than the structural and interpersonal considerations. Go to a bookstore and count the number of books that tell you how to do XML. Check online and see how many vendors have registries and enterprise service buses (ESBs). Then tell me how many books tell you how to deal with the personnel fallout from the successful implementation of 49 services/processes that caused modification of (not elimination of) the jobs of 7,500 business people and 1,500 technology people. *Damn! I forgot to act intimidated again.*

<Hank>: Meanwhile, BASE is doing well because:

1. We have an evolutionary strategy that works.
2. We have a Program methodology that works.
3. We contribute to the success of Armstrong's technology implementations.
4. We constantly look for lessons that may benefit successive Program phases and projects, and we maintain in an extensive list of lessons learned.
5. We are willing and able to reinvent our wheels when there are significant changes in the terrain over which we are traveling.

<Rennie>: This covers about everything you could imagine. I assume that you borrowed the Well-Formed concept from XML.

<Sharf>: Why is that important? *I have special interest in this show, and I don't want her in the way.*

<Rennie>: Well-formed in XML means the code will pass an editor. It doesn't mean that it does what it's supposed to do. How do you know that BASE is doing the right things?

<HM>: *She is good, but he stands in her way, as he tried to do with Indy.* Our BASE Program coordinator, the auditors, and clients make us ask ourselves that question every day. They validate and revalidate what we do. Our results prove that we are better in maturity and coverage than the next best company our size and significantly better than the typical company our size.

<Sharf>: I will repeat the original question. Where are the critical success factors?

<HM>: You are looking at them in Table 6.

<Sharf>: Change the title to Critical Success Factors.

<HM>: Acton approved this title. ***That annoyed him, and I am happy that it did.***

<Sharf>: If you created Table 7 when you started your last contract, it proposes where you will be right before your contract runs out. You haven't reached the 18-month point. Where are you now?

<HM>: We will report that information to the Board next Tuesday. We will send you a copy then.

<Sharf>: Show me your prior figures.

<HM>: They would be 3 - 7% lower than where we are now. It is important that we accurately reflect our progress.

<Sharf>: ***I shouldn't say anything about withholding information if new information will be available in four business days.*** Let's discuss lessons learned.

<HM>: ***That is backwards.*** Wouldn't it be appropriate to discuss what we did to learn the lessons first?

Lessons Learned

<Sharf>: Show me what you think you learned, and I will tell you which lessons require clarification.

<Hank>: There are many of them. This is the first big dose of **DETAIL!**

<HM>: Give the man what he thinks he wants.

<Hank>: OOKAAY? Focus your attention on Table A.2.

> **Readers**: The contents of Table A.2 are critical for the success of any Service-Oriented Architecture. It is worth a look.

<Sharf>: I need a copy of that.

<Hank>: There is a copy in your package. We worry that it would not make sense until we discuss Program strategy, methodology, and data.

<Rennie>: This is the most comprehensive list I have ever seen.

Lessons Not Learned

<Sharf>: It looks like a glossary. It also repeats things that are common sense for any program or project.

<HM>: I repeat basic lessons because we, as an industry and within Daxiao, have not yet learned many of the basic lessons. I'm going to "run it 'til it runs good".

Meanwhile, until you have access to the Knowledge Cooperative, you may use this to enhance the common terminology found in Table A.5.

<Sharf>: Give me a minute. I will let you know whether you need to split out the resistance factors. ***There can't possibly be this many lessons to learn.***

<Hank>: We split out the resistance factors in Table A.3. They are in Table A.2 because resistance topics are an important component of lessons learned.

<HM>: ***He's speed-reading. I wonder how much he retains and how well he integrates what he retains.***

<Sharf>: Tell me how you started with SOA.

<HM>: Do you have any comments about the Knowledge Cooperative?

<Sharf>: Four hundred groupings of information seem to be excessive, but that should be placed on the list for later.

<HM>: We're upset that our planning success rate was only 40%. Do you believe you could provide guidance on how to achieve that?

<Sharf>: You said 50% in there. We don't have time for that now, but you should fix that number.

<Hank>: ***There are two of them! That is impossible.***

<HM>: ***He has total recall. That would be very intimidating to some people.*** You asked for lessons learned. I thought you might want to discuss them.

<Sharf>: You've proven that you have something. We will discuss them when the time is right. Lesson learned #1 should be that timing is everything.

What was your first significant SOA project?

SOA Implementation - Recovering Benefits from Failure

<HM>: The work that kick-started SOA was a highly visible project that was failing for the second time. The compliance people started paying attention because we had to figure out how to audit what he was doing.

<Hank>: I was working in technology compliance. The first project failure occurred because the CTO was trying to push everyone into Web services and agile development without a clear understanding of the cultural motivators. He brought in his own people and teams of vendor consultants to lead the projects. Business and technology forced them into isolation. Even if they had created a decent product, there was emotional resistance to the outsiders. They were stepping on highly critical pre-existing applications.

Next, he turned the project over to insiders, but he released the vendors before he ensured vendor knowledge transfer.

There were also major organizational changes in both manufacturing and operations that made 50% of the requirements fuzzy. We inherited the failing project, the fuzziness, and the resistance.

<HM>: ***Weldon dumped the project to save himself and put a noose around my neck. I used it as an opportunity to show what we could do, while Piccolo used it to change the organizational framework.***

<Sharf>: You obviously succeeded. What were your secrets?

<Hank>: There is no secret. Weldon's people hadn't done vendor knowledge capture, but we did.

<HM>: I had written it into their contracts. We forced the vendors to return and provide the training that we needed in return for the extreme sums of money that they earned. We set up 37 new topics in the Knowledge Center, and we changed the name to Knowledge Cooperative because the vendors knew they needed to cooperate. My people handle procurement, as everyone knows.

<Sharf>: What consulting organizations did you use?

<Hank>: It will take a few seconds to retrieve that information from the archives.

...This is what you want.

<Sharf>: ***Acton isn't on the list.*** That appears to be primarily technology firms.

<HM>: Weldon let the vendors sell him too much software and not enough skill.

<Sharf>: If you were responsible for purchasing, why didn't you stop him?

<HM>: All the firms were on our list of approved vendors at the time. Weldon convinced Justin that this was a technology problem. Justin said, "Show me". I was outvoted. We went to our corner and started subtracting vendor points.

<Hank>: There was a short learning curve for our people. My team monitored the project and gave recommendations that Weldon ignored.

We had also tested SOA methodology processes which we couldn't convince them to use. When the staff came to work for us, they had no choice. When things started working, the people who wanted to redeem themselves were very thankful.

<HM>: We had the entire SOA business information foundation in place. We still call it SOX, as I mentioned earlier.

<Hank>: The project was larger than it should have been. That was a lemon. However, because it was oversized, it required so many services that we had to define service strategy and service categories. That was the lemonade.

Initial Strategy - Only Fix That Which Is Broken

<Hank>: We decided that we would not try to force BASE on anything that was working. We waited until there was trouble, and we offered assistance. We worked in that mode for over 18 months. The teams had to agree to support us if we solved a problem for them. Since, on the average, 25 - 35% of the projects in any give year begin to slip, and 15% have big problems, we had a broad spectrum of projects to pull out of trouble.

<Rennie>: The slippage numbers are higher than that.

<HM>: Either way, because of BASE, about 1,500 people look better than they might have over the last five years. Approximately 45% of our processing uses Service-Oriented Architecture.

<Sharf>: How is that? You've only been doing SOA for four years.

<HM>: We've been building the BASE officially since 1997 when they gave me the "Y" project. I loaded the Asset List Library (ALL) into Travers's original Knowledge Center, and I brought it with me when I came to Compliance. After every compliance audit, I linked technical information to business requirements.

<Sharf>: ***He's mixing things up again.*** What else is there?

<HM>: Even considering the emotional backlash, we have a culture that is accustomed to change.

<Sharf>: How is that?

<Hank>: We build products that change every year. Model 432 begets Model 432 Mega and 432 Super Mega. Design specifications change. Components change. Suppliers change. Assembly processes change. Anything that we could do to allow those changes to happen more smoothly was appreciated.

<HM>: Manufacturing was begging for process improvement, and we have been able to deliver in controlled increments.

> **Readers**: Please note that in SOA P:
> - **Clients** are groups within Daxiao or within partner organizations who request services delivered through WFSOA. Clients may work in business units or business technology units.
> - **Consumers** are pieces of software that request processing services from provider software.
> - **Customers** are people or organizations that purchase Daxiao's finished products.
> - **Users** are the clients inside Daxiao or partner organizations who actually work with delivered software products.

<Hank>: Our clients are very much accustomed to the concepts of reuse, even while products change. If a new product contains 50 sub-widgets, 20 may be different, but 30 remain the same. For instance, they continually reuse the form factor for a DIMM. The pin outs on 8P8C connectors haven't changed significantly for the last 6 years, and neither have Type A and Type B USB connectors. The idea of a component signature was simple to them.

<HM>: ***Hank just had a technology attack.***

<Sharf>: This is not a discussion of physical components.

<HM>: Manufacturing clients embarrassed many people in Weldon's silos into accepting reuse concepts. They showed how a physical signature was similar to a software signature. If the lowly client could understand it, why couldn't a genius programmer?

> **Readers**: A software signature describes what a service expects to receive from a consumer (including the format), and what it will provide to a consumer (including the format).

<Rennie>: That is brilliant.

<HM>: Thank you, but we didn't feel particularly brilliant. We had to use what worked.

<Sharf>: That was arm-twisting. It is equivalent to making them beg you for help.

<HM>: We don't make them beg. They only have to ask.

<Sharf>: What happens if they don't ask?

<HM>: We continue to track and report their progress.

<Sharf>: How is the information reported?

<HM>: We perform management reporting as specified in COBIT A.4. It appears on the dashboards of work in progress. If the project has a 15% overrun, it is highlighted in yellow. After a 30% overrun, it is highlighted in red.

<Sharf>: You force them to do it your way?

<HM>: We have four options, and they are:

1. Let the teams fail miserably and hide the failure.
2. Show management what is happening, and let them choose to accept the risk.
3. Shove the teams out of the way and take over.

4. Work with them when they request assistance.

As a financially responsible manager, what would you do?

<Sharf>: You could offer assistance before they fail.

<HM>: We do. We reject input to ReMain (requirements, analysis, and design) and we explain why. We perform compliance evaluations with best practices recommendations. We follow up to see whether the recommendations are being accepted. You know the drill.

<Sharf>: They are still backed into a corner.

<HM>: Is this Torquemada defending the poor technology teams, or are you verifying a technique that you use regularly yourself? ***That wasn't humble or intimidated. I am annoyed to the point of losing control.***

<Sharf>: ***He knows my nickname, and he knows Grayson. He must know about Indy and me.***

<Hank>: H needs a snack break to help him remain humane.

<HM>: We're not ready yet, and I do apologize. I expected that you would show us ways to explain how we achieve beneficial results. It seemed to be turning into an Inquisition.

<Sharf>: We will show Daxiao better ways, ***after I destroy you***. I was simply concerned that you might have made enemies for yourself using those approaches. ***I certainly do, but when you have enough clout, enemies don't matter.***

<HM>: When we can save a project, about 10% of the people who were neutral begin to hate us. Thirty or 40% are forever grateful. There is usually a net gain. It's worth the risk.

<Sharf>: How often are you successful?

<HM>: In the last three years, we've been able to save 29 projects. We missed on two.

<Sharf>: You were successful 93.5% of the time.

<HM>: Give or take .04%.

<Hank>: ***I wonder why H is baiting him.***

<Rennie>: ***They are both insane.***

<Sharf>: What made you fail?

<HM>: In both cases, the specifications were inadequate, the technology was wrong, and business and technology had stopped talking to each other.

<Hank>: On one project, there wasn't enough to salvage. We replaced it with a new project, starting with requirements gathering. On the second, we realized that we already had 90% of what they needed after we found out what they really wanted. We taught them how to use services they had been ignoring. That gave SOA and reuse concepts a major boost.

<HM>: The first project was great for negative lessons learned. The second was one of our biggest wins. I guess that makes our success rate closer to 96.6%. Success breeds success. Many areas began using our processes before anything was broken.

<Sharf>: ***That smug look is driving me crazy.*** Make a note to check their project recovery rate with Armstrong.

<HM>: **Discuss the Knowledge Cooperative.**

<Rennie>: ***It is hard to type and watch them simultaneously, but I could swear that I just saw him using sign language.***

Knowledge Cooperative

<Hank>: We would like to discuss one more critical success factor before the break.

<Sharf>: You have my permission.

<Hank>: We have one of the most sophisticated Knowledge Cooperative databases anywhere. We track everything that affects or could be affected by BASE.

1. We have reduced the number of people sitting in corners with keys to organizational success hidden in the bottom of their desk drawers.
2. We reduced the time needed to find information by 95%. Business and technology teams have more time to develop a deeper understanding of issues and to devise better solutions to problems.
3. We ensure that most information is only entered once, and we automate parsing, storage, and presentation based on user preferences.

<Sharf>: You have knowledge management. Everybody does, to a degree.

<HM>: BASE participates in the corporate knowledge management program and provides a major part of the foundation for it. However, we don't own it.

<Hank>: We use the Knowledge Cooperative to encourage sharing and refinement of the subset of information related to BASE. We focus on the need to avoid repetition of mistakes and redoing things that have been done well already.

<Sharf>: That sounds like a sales pitch.

<HM>: It is, but it is also true.

<Sharf>: I suggest a different topic - how many development projects are active at this moment?

<HM>: *This is hopeless. Maybe it isn't.*

<Hank>: We must use the Knowledge Cooperative to answer the question. I can play it or read it?

<HM>: Play it.

<Animated Voice Response>:

- Daxiao technology is working on [...] 213 [...] small software projects. Small requires less than one year of effort and is typically less than 3 months in duration.
- Daxiao technology is working on [...] 87 [...] medium software projects. Medium requires between one and three years of effort and is typically less than 9 months in duration.
- Daxiao technology is working on [...] 42 [...] large software projects. Large requires greater than three years of effort and is typically greater than 6 months in duration, but less than 2 years.
- Daxiao technology is working on [...] 14 [...] umbrella software projects. Umbrella projects are combinations of 2 or more small or medium projects.

<HM>: Please note that this is only development duration. It does not include the time between the initial request and the time it is turned over to technology. Would you like to see those numbers?

<Sharf>: Why is nothing longer than two years?

<Hank>: We don't allow anything longer. Anything that takes that long is guaranteed to be misaligned with business strategy before it is installed.

<Sharf>: How many of those are SOA?

<Hank>: Notice the left side of the screen. Eighty-four small projects are SOA, as are 27 of the medium projects.

<Rennie>: Why does the proportion of SOA projects decrease as the projects become larger?

<Hank>: We break the big SOA projects into smaller projects.

<Sharf>: What's the technology platform for Project #2008-413?

<Hank>: I'll click this notes icon. The services will be provided by wrapped CICS transactions that read an IMS bill of materials database running on the mainframe. When the services are ready, they will be used in Project #2008-425. That composite service will run on BizTalk. The same services will be used in Project #2008-428 that is an equivalent composite service is running on a WebSphere BPEL server. Both 425 and 428 are research projects. We will use the results as the basis for platform recommendations on future projects.

<Rennie>: I don't see any mention of a research project.

<Hank>: The research box is checked.

<Sharf>: That wasn't obvious. It should be easier to see.

<Hank>: The work request was submitted, and it is backlogged. The request is REQMN2007040294. They backlogged Macedon's team backlogged their own request. They knew that insiders have other ways to locate the information.

<Sharf>: Why is the project listed under "Business Development Projects"?

<Hank>: One of the operations clients has agreed to pay for the one that turns out to be the most efficient. The other one will be deducted from our research budget.

<Rennie>: What are you using to organize the information?

<Hank>: We use the Knowledge Cooperative as a portal to our catalog/registry product. It uses ebXML and it has lots of slots - I love saying that. Our knowledge consolidator is responsible for the Knowledge Cooperative and for the catalog.

> **Readers:**
> **ebXML** is an industry standard that describes a consistent way to catalog information about business processes.
> **UDDI** is an industry standard that describes Web services that support the business processes. It is more concerned with the technical aspects of service creation and location.

<Rennie>: Does this mean that you don't use UDDI?

<Hank>: We test against WS-Interoperability (WS-I) standards, so we must have UDDI. We use both and our knowledge consolidator consolidated found a way to use both standards. One of the vendors is using our implementation as a model for their registry/catalog consolidation product. We will switch to a vendor product when it is ready.

<Rennie>: I've seldom seen it done, but it makes sense. How do you keep them synchronized?

<Hank>: Maja Johanssen created data virtualization services and treats each as an extension of the other.

<Rennie>: Does your consolidated catalog run in production?

<Hank>: Yes. It goes through the most rigorous testing possible every time she touches it.

<Rennie>: When are we scheduled with her?

<Sharf>: Their Human Resources Department will help us with the scheduling. We need the list of SOA roles first.

Let's take 15-minutes. When we return, we should talk about:

1. Success factors in the list of lessons learned. Focus (and I do mean focus) on:
   - SOA Maturity.
   - Resistance and Organizational Change Management.
   - Technology Fragmentation.
   - Alignment of Business and Technology.
   - Accelerated Information Capture.
   - Selling Services and Processes.
2. Well-Formed Service-Oriented Architecture Methodology (Processes and Procedures).
3. SOA Roles and Responsibilities Supporting WFSOA.

<HM>: What about the other lessons learned? That is a summarization of 1,400 staff years of work.

<Sharf>: The topics that I suggested will be most valuable at this point. I will verify the other lessons with your peers and their subordinates.

<HM>: I am sorry. We do tend to get carried away.

I must appear to be humble and intimidated. I will use the remainder of the day to figure out how to use you to my benefit, squash you, or both.

<Hank>: ***He's pretending to be self-effacing and humble. Extreme suffering will occur.***

<Sharf>: Where can I get some privacy? I have urgent calls.

<HM>: The office motel (the third door past the elevator) should be empty today. Pick any room that's labeled as open. There is a conference/snack area on the right side. I'll see you in 15 minutes.

---------- -----------

<Hank>: Why didn't you send them next door?

<HM>: Everything next door is new. Indy wouldn't want it contaminated. You will excuse me.

<Hank>: ***Another planet would be a nice place for Mr. Sharf to consider at this moment.***

----------**Office Motel**-----------

<Rennie>: What is wrong with you? He's an EVP, some of their ideas border on genius, and you are talking to him as if he was a school kid.

<Sharf>: I am controlling the situation. It's good to keep people like him a little off balance. He may be an EVP, but he's the least important one. I report to the Board, and they will not let him join.

<Rennie>: ***Mr. Cane told me to watch out for William, but he's hurting himself more in the last two hours than I've ever seen him do.*** I am certain that something happened a few minutes ago that we will regret. You are playing this wrong. Marshall is doing an excellent job.

<Sharf>: Only if I say he is.

I'll meet you back in the conference room.

----------13 **Minutes Later**----------

<Hank>: Did you find everything you needed?

<Sharf>: This is a nice little setup. Are all your people here?

<HM>: ***Little*** is the operant term. Space is at a premium, but I live with it because I can limp to work. We managed to make space for 175 permanent spots and 25 motel spaces. We have smaller spaces in our foreign locations. The project management and competency team members are usually on assignment.

<Rennie>: I have never seen a staff refrigerator with gourmet snacks.

<HM>: Healthy is better, so they say. I'm still trying to get over my Twinkies addiction.

<Rennie>: Twinkies?

<Hank>: Give him Twinkies and Kona coffee and he's in heaven.

<Sharf>: Let's get started.

<HM>: Where shall we start? ***He almost gave us an agenda before the break.***

SOA Maturity

<Sharf>: Start with SOA maturity. How mature are you?

<Hank>: The corporate architect defined a process for assessing WFSOA maturity. It includes process maturity (for which we receive excellent ratings) along with information asset maturity, and organizational acceptance. There are over 100 different positions on the maturity matrix. Our risk management team uses it for risk assessment of individual projects. ***We share it with Acton, and they use it to bring in consulting dollar.***

<HM>: On the other hand, we measure the entire organization in relation to a set of **evolutionary stages**.

<Sharf>: Please answer the question.

<HM>: Dan and I agree that most of Daxiao's business units have evolved to SOA Level #3 with limited areas at Level #4. If we look at the process categories first, the assessment of evolutionary level will make more sense?

Table 8 - SOA Maturity Self-Evaluation - Belvedere Format

Description of SOA Level	Maturity Level	Date Achieved
Level 1 - **Isolated Web Services**		
♦ Simple Web services in application silos	1	1999 - 2003
Level 2 -**Start-up**		
♦ Initiation of SOA Program	2.A	2002
♦ Investigation of implementation options	2.B	2002 - 2003
♦ Service reuse	2.C	2002 - ongoing
Level 3 - **Stabilization**		
♦ Strategy, vision, and mission defined	3.A	2003
♦ Centralized governance established	3.B	2003
♦ Business architecture, reference data, and service models available	3.C	1997 - 2003
Level 4 - **Expansion**		
♦ Alignment with strategic plans (business and technology)	4.A	2002
♦ Centralized shared service team created	4.B	2003
♦ Acceptance for cross-division implementation	4.C	2004
♦ Composite services delivered. ♦ External partner services implemented	4.D	2003 2001
Level 5 - **SOA Optimization**		
♦ Continuous process improvement	5.A	2002 - ongoing

♦ Re-engineering of legacy applications	5.C	2003 - ongoing
♦ Client-self service	5.B	2007 - ongoing

<Sharf>: We sent you a simplified SOA maturity assessment, based on the CMMI format. You were supposed to have it ready for this meeting.

<HM>: *You mean encounter.* Refer to Table 8, but it doesn't provide a true picture of where we are.

<Sharf>: I can make that determination.

<HM>: *I will not lose my temper!*

<Sharf>: According to this, you have reached the maximum level of maturity.

<HM>: Before you ask, we can provide proof for all those dates. That is why we are officially rated at CMMI Level IV. However, we believe that Daxiao will require at least three more years to achieve maximum SOA effectiveness.

<Sharf>: You performed some of these steps out of order.

<HM>: We performed them according to Daxiao business requirements, Daxiao evolutionary strategy, and Daxiao's maturity model. As you already know, we did them more successfully than our peers did. Our bottom line proves it. One year may be an accident, but we are consistent. *We have more experience than you have.*

<Hank>: First, we proposed how the environment would look in five stages and Dan showed them how to restructure Daxiao to support our evolution through the stages. Table A.4 shows the contents of each of the stages.

<Sharf>: Let me hear what Piccolo has to say about maturity first.

<HM>: That is smart. He explains it better than I do. *He can spend hours and tell you absolutely nothing.*

BASE, Resistance, and Organizational Change Management

<Sharf>: The next topic is SOA resistance.

<HM>: That was an excellent selection. Effective involvement of personnel resources is more important than the three sectors of "pure" governance.

<Sharf>: *I keep running into that soft stuff.* Explain as clearly as you can.

<Rennie>: *Why is he talking like that?*

<HM>: *If I ignore him, I can concentrate on how to make him go away.* SOA changes the way people work more than anything has done in the last 50 years. By nature, most people resist change. If we cannot help to deal with change, the Program is guaranteed to fail.

<Sharf>: Your entire organization must deal with change frequently. You said earlier that there is always a new gadget coming out.

<HM>: The lead-time on an entirely new gadget is 2 years. Some areas install significant process changes every five or six months.

<Sharf>: You are talking about manufacturing. What about your technical people.

<HM>: All employees in BASE have been trained to have a healthy attitude toward change (the right amount of change at the right time, but not change for the sake of change).

<Hank>: However, we are 410 people out of 5,000. You would be surprised at how resistant to change some C# programmers may be, and the language is only seven years old.

<Sharf>: Concentrate on dealing with resistance from firmly entrenched senior personnel. *This will do be good! Resistance is the biggest problem our consultants are running into. It hadn't occurred to me to merge everything into one list.*

<HM>: As part of the corporate change management program, the Human Resources area has established a process for dealing with resistance from critical employees. I'm sure they will explain it to you when you talk to them. *We cannot persuade Gunnar to attend.*

<Hank>: Table A.2-Lessons Learned shows the types of resistance which we encounter and the measures we take to deal with it. Table A.3 provides further comments and a success rating. Topics are presented in alphabetical order. If you

have anything to add to the list, we would appreciate it.

<Sharf>: Rennie, make a note to request Belvedere's list from our technology team. ***We should show them something.***

<Rennie>: ***You mean you want me to work all night and dig something out of our Engagement database.***

<Sharf>: The information may be classified, but we may declassify it for Daxiao. We cannot give the success ratings though. That information is subjective and private. ***We can use the "declassify" angle to postpone it for a couple of days.***

<HM>: That is actually a good thing. Our ratings are subjective too.

<Sharf>: I'm moderately impressed. However, you should emphasize:

<Rennie>: ***He wants me to take this list, and change a few words and the presentation order.***

<Sharf>: Provide more detail on:

1. Another wild goose chase.
2. No immediate benefit.
3. The reward structure - you mention reward often in lessons learned.

<HM>: "Another wild goose chase" will be covered under your next topic (Technology Fragmentation) and "no immediate benefit" is discussed under the subsequent one (Alignment).

<Hank>: The reward part was easy. It was merged with our usual bonus structure. A person who does something good for SOA earns SOA points. Resistance contributes to the loss of SOA points. You can get negative points. At the end of the year, we count the points and divide 25% of the bonus pool according to SOA contribution or SOA resistance.

Last year 87,000 on the regular staff shared $50,000,000 dollars.

<Sharf>: You pay that much for SOA each year.

<HM>: That is not exactly true. When earning increased, they added $50 million to the bonus pool. They always had rules for shuffling bonuses around, and they put SOA into the shuffle. With this shuffle, company's overall productivity is up 10% with nearly 5,000 fewer staff members.

Transition from LITTLE SOA to BIG SOA

<Sharf>: Are you ready to explain "another wild goose chase?"

<HM>: Hank, the corporate architect, and the corporate strategist worked with me to structure the framework of WFSOA.

<Sharf>: That would be Daniel Piccolo and J. Stanley Johnson.

<HM>: ***He has a photographic memory or Gunnar did an excellent prep job.*** Yes. They provide the resident brilliance. They provide words for concepts that should have been obvious to all of us.

<Sharf>: Piccolo is high on the list of people I need to see. If most of the ideas came from Piccolo, how did you grab it?

<HM>: I explained that before the break.

<Sharf>: Tell me again.

<HM>: Armstrong was trying to "reposition" his biggest and most problematic Web services project up to that time (he was still thinking "LITTLE SOA"). Every new miracle service caused critical existing functions to crash. They repositioned the project and the technology teams to me because, as the head of compliance, I had been the most vocal commenter on what they were doing wrong.

<Sharf>: I find it unusual to have so many developers in a compliance organization?

<HM>: I believe it was meant to be temporary.

<Sharf>: Why didn't you fight it?

<HM>: "Resistance is futile."

<Sharf>: I can't imagine you giving in that easily.

<HM>: The president tolerates resistance only as long as there is benefit for him. Armstrong was Mittelman's right-hand man. I could dig him out of his problem, or I could leave. ***I leaped at the opportunity to roll up my sleeves again. It was like tossing a rabbit into a briar patch.***

<Sharf>: Why didn't you leave?

<HM>: SOA resolved two issues for me. I had time to do one more thing before I left and 25 of my people could have been hurt if they had been dumped in the wrong place or released.

<Sharf>: What do you mean "your people"?

<HM>: I hired them.

<Sharf>: How did you turn a failed Web services project into SOA?

<HM>: Dan had, and still has, a pet project. He wanted a tighter bond between management theory and corporate reality. He couldn't call his project the "Grand Unified Management Theory". We rejected GUMT, GUT, and GUM.

Piccolo stumbled across SOA during his "junk" reading. He began to theorize that SOA, if done correctly, would provide "Grand Unified Management".

I knew that with minor adjustments, I could realize all my dreams about how technology should support the business. Rather than call it "BIG SOA", Hank added "Well-Formed". Piccolo liked "service" and "architecture". We agreed to work together, and Piccolo sold the ideas to the Board.

Technology Fragmentation before WFSOA (a Plane with too Many Engines)

<Rennie>: How did he do that?

<HM>: Piccolo used the airplanes (Fig. 4 and Fig. 5) and the related story (Why Bother with SOA) to show the Board and the senior management team how SOA is different from other technology wild goose chases.

Why Bother with SOA? Hundreds of organizations have completed Web services projects, several organizations have already claimed SOA success, and many others have successful implementations that use proprietary technologies. Few have gone through the complicated restructuring that I recommend.

Why would this be necessary? The answer is that Web services, after delivering initial successes, are starting to add complications to the technology environment. Companies that have declared SOA success may have achieved technology success without reaping the cross-organizational advantages.

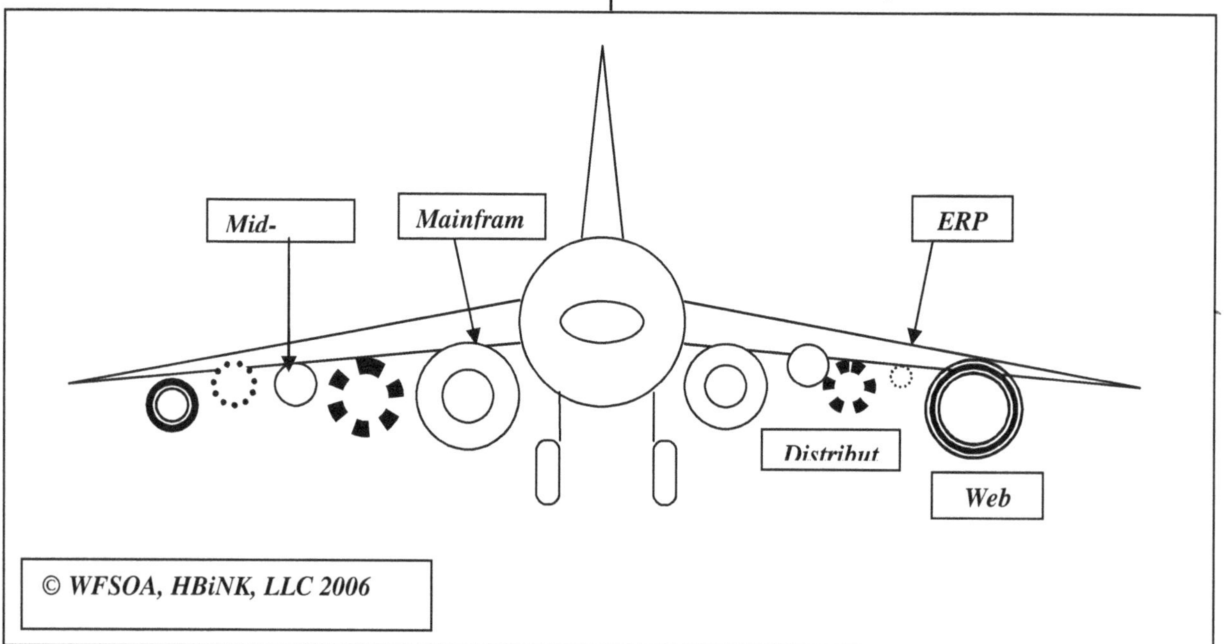

Fig. 4 - Before BASE - A Plane with Many Engines

Without SOA - An Airplane with Many Engines: To understand the state of most large organizations today, imagine that you are a pilot (executive management) trying to fly airplanes with 11 different engines (business units and closely aligned IT organizations). In Fig. 4 that the engines are different sizes, different ages, and built by different manufacturers (application platforms and IT vendors). The engines were added as the planes needed to fly for distances or carry heavier loads (new business functions). The engines were positioned along the wings in the order that they were built (new applications), with attempts to balance the load on the wing structures as the engines were being added (data center operations).

Some engines have their own fuel tanks, and some share with others (sponsors). Each engine type has its own repair crew. Some repair crews were trained on the equipment they repair (original developers), and some worked on similar products (new hires) for different manufacturers. Fuel trucks must switch nozzles to refuel different engines (infrastructure support).

The engines are controlled by different co-pilots (technology teams). Some co-pilots control more than one engine. The co-pilots speak different languages, usually the language of the country where the engine was built (sales, marketing, research, legal, manufacturing, subsidiaries, partner organizations). Some speak different dialects of the same languages (corporate sales, government sales, consumer sales). Each co-pilot has some control over the navigation system, in proportion to the power of the engine he or she controls. Each co-pilot has the option of giving up control to the pilot. A flight coordination system can funnel power from each of the engines into one power stream (organizational structure). This is a continuing challenge because not all the engines work consistently (application failures). The extra space required for power delivery and navigational controls reduces passenger and cargo space.

The most recently added engine (Web services) has great power potential; however, it is so far out on the wing that the plane occasionally goes around in circles (fixing one problem, but creating several others). None of the other co-pilots will give up their position on the wing (people and politics) to the Web services engine.

Flying a Plane with Many Engines - the Traditional Organizational Structure: The flight communications system has recordings of flight instructions in 20 major languages Most of the time it is adequate, but it presents a problem if a co-pilot speaks one of the dialects. To start the plane, the pilot plays 20 simultaneous recordings that say "power up" (tactical plans). The pilot then waits while each co-pilot starts his or her individual engine. When enough engines on each side of the plane are online, the pilot issues "transfer control" instructions in 20 languages. After enough of the left side and right side co-pilots have transferred navigational control, the pilot may begin to move the airplane.

After the plane is airborne, it flies slower than it needs to due to inefficient fuel utilization. It flies at a lower altitude than it could due to the extra weight of the multiple engines. Because it is flying at a low altitude, it has to fly around geographic features (infrastructure and facilities limitations), taking even longer to reach its destination. Because it is flying at a low altitude, it has to worry about visibility (seeing changing business patterns too late), poor weather (entanglement in business problems that might have been avoided), and bird migrations (changing government rules and regulations).

Because, the pilot has to communicate the reasons for changes of speed or direction using only the messages recorded in the communications system (lack of effective communications), he has trouble relaying information about unusual situations, resulting in bumpy rides or crashes if the pilot cannot change the plane's direction in time. Changing speed takes longer because the pilot has to negotiate with every co-pilot to increase or decrease power input. Changing directions causes problems because the navigation controls have to be synchronized. If a co-pilot disagrees with the pilot's request, either he may retract his power contribution, or she may retract a portion of the navigational controls.

If passengers (business sponsors) wish to know how far they are into a flight, flight stewards can give rough estimates of arrival time (project plans). They are usually off by significant amounts.

Missed Opportunities: Occasionally, the pilot may be asked to make unexpected deviations to pick up lucrative passengers (new business opportunities). She often misses these opportunities because the trouble of changing direction, landing, and taking off again is not worth the effort. Recently, the pilot has been asked to make longer flights (international markets), which he tries to avoid because there is no room to add another engine, and there is no capacity to carry more fuel. The airline is losing passengers to competitors who fly two engine jets.

BASE Aircraft - Evolutionary Product that Works: This intercontinental cruiser actually exists. It demonstrates the potential benefits of an SOA. This model was announced in 1994, and its test flight was in 1997. There were more than 120 of these planes flying as of 2007. It was chosen because it was the first plane to be completely modeled on a computer, Model-Driven Architecture (MDA).

It has two engines, one pilot, and one co-pilot. Cruising speed is 560 miles per hour, cruising altitude is 7 miles (it flies over business turbulence), and the flight range is 8,300 miles (one third of the way around the world to handle international markets). It is a block wide, but the wing tips fold up to fit in smaller airports. It takes advantage of the features of stealth technology. It is 30% more fuel-efficient than earlier models (return-on-investment), it can carry 386 passengers in three-class arrangements (multiple users and user requirements), and as of early 2008, there had been no fatal accidents.

The features of the airplane are evolving. It is fifth in a series that began flying in 1964 (evolutionary model). If the engineers of the first model had known what to build, the materials would not have been available to build the plane (standards and tools). The two engines are perfectly balanced on the wings (business and technology). Either engine may keep the plane aloft in an emergency. The plane is lighter because two powerful engines weigh less than 11 less powerful ones. When the pilot flips a switch, both engines come online simultaneously - business and technology are synchronized. The primary and backup navigational systems are both controlled by the pilot (strategic and tactical plans). The plane has fly-by-wire capability (allowing it to adapt quickly to changing business conditions). Every system on the plane goes through hundreds, sometimes thousands of tests, before the plane ever takes off (quality assurance).

The pilot speaks to his co-pilot in a maximum of two languages (common terminology). One is their native tongue and the other is the international language of the airline industry (business industry terminology and technical terminology). They have enough fluency in both languages to avoid communications delays.

The pilot has to worry about bad weather only during take-off and landing (SOA initiation and full implementation). The plan flies over geographic features, bad weather, and migrating birds (industry turbulence and regulatory changes). However, because migrating birds (regulations or absence of regulations) have caused crashes in other planes, the plane's engineers learned from the flight of birds and incorporated lessons into the plane's design (guidelines from Committee of Sponsoring Organizations (COSO) and their extension for technology in the Control OBjectives for Information and related Technology (COBIT)).

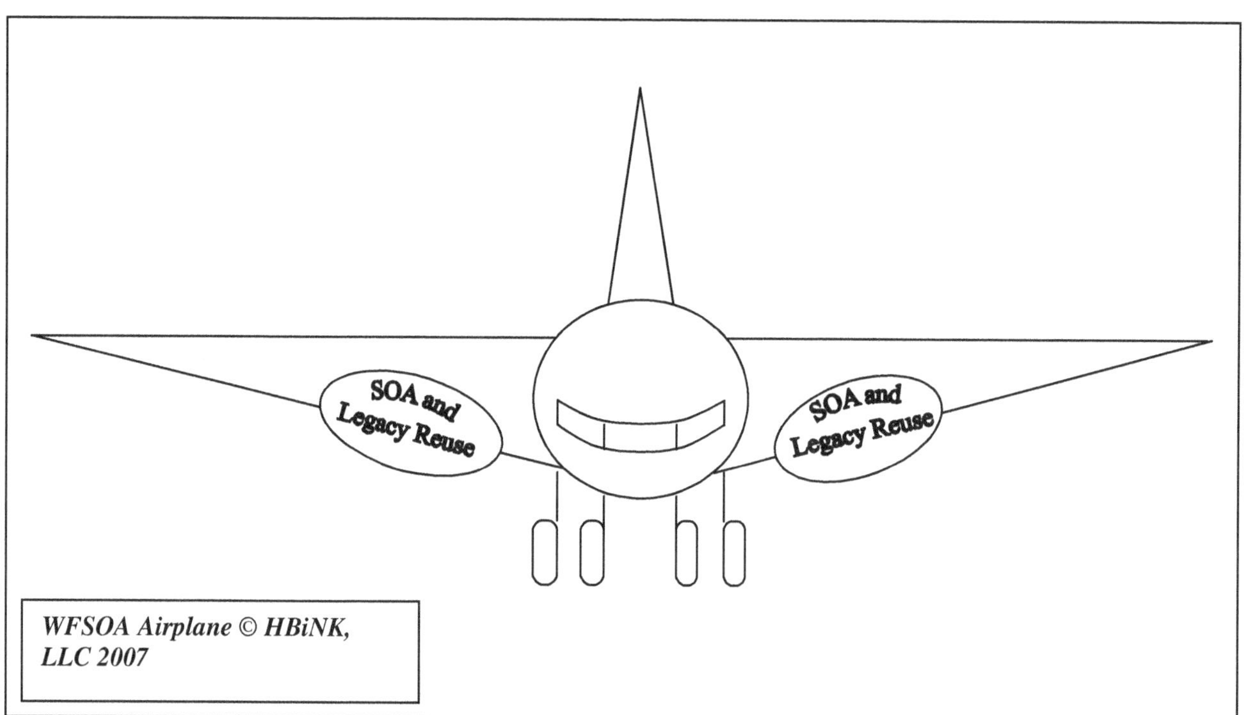

Fig. 5 - After BASE - SOA Airplane

If the pilot receives orders to change direction (take advantage of a new business opportunity, or avoid business problems), he and his co-pilot hear and understand simultaneously. The plane responds immediately to directional changes. Passengers (business sponsors) know where they are going and how fast because they can see it on televisions mounted on the seats in front of them (SOA Communications - dashboards and scorecards).

SOA Challenges - Harder than Building an Airplane: Airplanes have thousands of parts, including computers with millions of lines of code, but it is easier to assemble 180 tons of metal and plastic into a product that will carry another 110 tons than it is to arrive at the full realization an SOA. Witness the difference between the number of planes in the air, and the number of true Service-Oriented Architecture implementations - there are periods every day when airplanes land at major airports (e.g., Heathrow or Newark) every two minutes. The most evolved SOAs (BIG SOA) are still taking their test flights.

The Demise of "Too Many Engines" Airline

That airline went out of business after most of the customers moved to the two-engine planes. The flexible co-pilots learned to speak the common language of the industry. Some of them went to work for TWO ENGINE AIRLINES, and others became consultants to the airline's manufacturers. They were experts at what a company should not do. The inflexible ones are grounded.

Correction of Business Alignment Problems

<Hank>: After Dan had their attention, he used the alignment example below (Figs. 6.1 to 7.2) to explain how it is that we spend a major portion of our budget on IT every year, and our systems are often not synchronized with the business.

<HM>: After this example, they asked Acton to map strategic applications to business units. The alignment was a little better than 65%.

<Sharf>: It must have worked. They let you do SOA.

<HM>: They were not convinced. The real problem was that they were anxious to re-organize the failed project away from Armstrong, and they were willing to let us put any label on it that we wanted.

<Hank>: They let us perform "temporary reorganizations" in return for our commitment to deliver the Web services that they still needed. They thought we would fail too.

- The technology people let the business people try to handle change management because they were tired of the business people attacking technology's work priorities. Technology was sure it would never work.
- Since most of the new services had never existed, no one minded when Lorraine Jasper (the CTO) agreed to manage them and the related data on behalf of everybody. It was definitely verboten for us to own business applications (services and processes in the new terminology).

<Sharf>: What change management are you talking about. I didn't see it on your organization chart.

<HM>: Dan suggested that we call the organization Requirements Management. He felt that change management was overworked, and that it was often confused with data center change management.

<Sharf>: How much money were you asking for?

<HM>: They gave us the people, the tools they were using, and the lead boots.

<Sharf>: What was the project supposed to do?

<HM>: They wanted to improve the automation for new (electronic) product assembly. It was our first cross-unit Web services project. I mentioned that they had a major reorganization, but I didn't mention that they had a major strategy change.

We delivered the first iterations of the failed project in five months, Requirements Management started managing changes better than they have ever been managed, and the rest is history.

<Sharf>: Not quite. You didn't cover "no immediate benefit".

<HM>: Yes I did. I told you we delivered the first iteration in five months, and we delivered something every month after that.

<Hank>: When the project was over, I started lending the people back to Armstrong's teams for his other Web projects. I kept them by giving them away. The ones that were "on the SOA beach" started creating services that addressed functions that were repeated between three and 11 times within and across environments. When we finished, we transferred services to Jasper's service domain owners. Domain owners also inherited services from the projects that we saved, and many previously existing services.

Before SOA: Figs. 6.1 through 6.3 demonstrate how Daxiao could spend hundreds of millions of dollars more than necessary on computer technology each year because they are neither agile enough nor flexible enough to respond to changing requirements. Every market adjustment could create an IT emergency.

Definitions:

- Agility: A measure of how quickly the company could move from Fig. 6.1 to Fig. 6.3 if a change was necessary.
- Efficiency: A measure of the ability to make the adjustment with a minimum expenditure of time and effort.
- Flexibility: A measure of the ease with which the company may adapt to change without severe modification to existing structures.

Fig. 6.1 shows a hypothetical state of perfect alignment between business clients, operations, and the traditional applications that support them.

Business Client #1	Business Client #2
Operations Support #1	Operations Support #2
Mainframe Application #1 *(Functions 1a, 1b, 1c, 1d)* Web Service #2 *(Function 2a)*	Client Server Application #3 *(Functions 3a, 3b, 3c, 3d)* Web Service #4 *(Function 4a)*

Fig. 6.1 - Business and Application Alignment

Business requirements may change exponentially faster than it is possible to make changes to the traditional applications that support them. Fig. 6.2 demonstrates the misalignment that could occur if the organization changed its market focus within three months of the initial implementation.

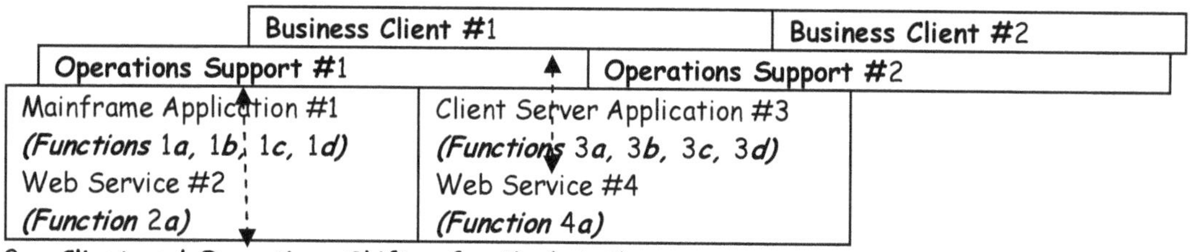

	Business Client #1		Business Client #2
Operations Support #1		Operations Support #2	
Mainframe Application #1 *(Functions 1a, 1b, 1c, 1d)* Web Service #2 *(Function 2a)*	Client Server Application #3 *(Functions 3a, 3b, 3c, 3d)* Web Service #4 *(Function 4a)*		

Fig. 6.2 - Client and Operations Shift - for Market Changes

Notice that:

- Half the functionality in Application #1 is no longer needed.
- Application #3 has functionality that Client #1 needs, but cannot access.

Fig. 6.3 demonstrates the work that would be done pre-SOA to provide support for the changing business environment.

Business Client #1	Business Client #2
Operations Support #1	Operations Support #2
Mainframe Application #1 **(Functions 1a, 1b, 1c, 1d)** Mainframe Application #3' **(Functions 3a', 3b', 3c')** Web Service #2 **(Function 2a)** Web Service #4' **(Function 4a')**	Client Server Application #3 **(Functions 3a, 3b, 3c, 3d)** Web Service #4 **(Function 4a)** Web Service #5 **(Function 5a)** Web Service #6 **(Function 1c)**

Fig. 6.3 - Application changes required before SOA

Client #1 would:

- Pay for reproduction of most of Application #3 on the mainframe.
- Pay for the rewrite of Service #4 to run on the mainframe.

Client #2 would:

- Pay for conversion of Function #1c into a service.
- Pay for the development of Service #5.

Operations would:

- Fill the functionality gaps by expanding manual procedures (and staff).
- Adjust staff again after new functions are implemented.
- Spend $60,000 for temporary staff and training on the use of old and new technology.

Technology would:

- Require three months to develop, test, and deploy the new functions.
- Spend $120,000 on staff salaries for development and modification of functions.
- Maintain two versions of functions Function 4a.
- Manage an uneasy relationship between the owners of Function 1c who support Client #1 and the consumers of 1c in the second client area.

After SOA: Service orientation would make it easier to meet client requirements. Fig. 7.1 and Fig. 7.2 show the improvements that would be possible if the company had accepted SOA.

All functions supporting the two clients would have been implemented as services.

Business Client #1					Business Client #2				
Combined Operational Support - Unified Service Domain									
Service #1a	*Service #1b*	*Service #1c*	*Service #1d*	*Service #2a*	*Service #3a*	*Service #3b*	*Service #3c*	*Service #3d*	*Service #4a*

Fig. 7.1 - Services Before Market Change - SOA

The effort required to adapt to the changing requirements in an SOA environment is illustrated in Fig. 7.2.

Client #1 **would not pay for any functional development**. They would:

- Assert intention to use Functions 3a, 3b, and 3c.
- Share the cost of running 1c and 4a.
- Officially, discontinue use of 1a and 1b.

Client #2 would:

- Sponsor creation of one new service (5a).
- Share the cost of running 1c and 4a.
- Officially, discontinue use of Functions 3a, 3b, and 3c.

Operations would:

- Reassign staff to business clients.
- Spend $3,000 to train staff to support the new service.

Technology would:

- Approve new users for access to five services.
- Spend $20,000 on staff salaries for development of the new service.
- Require six weeks to develop, test, and deploy one new service.
- Add Functions 1a and 1b to the list of deprecated services.

usiness Client #1							Business Client #2	
Combined Operational Support - Unified Service Domain								
Service #1d	*Service #2a*	*Service #3a*	*Service #3b*	*Service 3c*	*Service #1c (Shared)*	*Service #4a (Shared)*	*Service #3d*	*Service #5a (New)*

Retirement Candidates	
Service #1a	*Service #1b*

Fig. 7.2 - Services After Market Change - SOA

<Sharf>: The CFO inherited technology.

<HM>: She inherited responsibility for shared services.

<Sharf>: Who maintains them?

<HM>: Armstrong and I both provide managers. Armstrong's people do most of the development. We handle everything that occurs during user acceptance testing.

<Sharf>: You do make mistakes.

<HM>: There will always be mistakes. But, all our numbers are decreasing.

<Sharf>: Where do you keep track of this?

<Hank>: I'm ahead of you this time.

<Automated Voice Response>:

- 10 [...] new components installed by [...] SOA Competency [...] are associated with [...] 1 [...] problem reports in the [...] fourth quarter.
- 3 [...] modifications installed by [...] SOA Competency [...] are associated with [...] 0 [...] problem reports in the [...] fourth quarter.
- 184 [...] new components installed by [...] Global Technology [...] are associated with [...] 28 [...] problem reports in the [...] fourth quarter.
- 287 [...] modifications installed by [...] Global Technology [...] are associated with [...] 41 [...] problem reports in the [...] fourth quarter.

<Sharf>: He does 36.2 times as much work as you do.

<HM>: He has 40.1 times as many developers as I do, and he made 67 times as many mistakes as I did. The last number will change by the end of the quarter. Typically, he only has proportionately only four times as many problem reports as I do.

<Sharf>: He only has 11.7 times as many people as you do.

<HM>: Not all his people are developers and only 30% of mine are developers. Also, remember that at any given time, 50 - 75% of my people are working with his teams.

<Sharf>: I'd know that if I had you list of roles and responsibilities. ***This is taking longer than I had expected.***

<HM>: According to your list, we start dealing with roles at the end of this morning's session. We can't allow ourselves to keep getting sidetracked.

<Sharf>: Your people could be contributing to his mistakes.

<HM>: We make less than 1% of his mistakes. The teams that my people work with are proven to produce fewer errors. If not, I would have lost this whole thing after the first year. My team is the best thing that ever happened to Armstrong and Mittelman.

<Sharf>: You are modest. ***I intend to squash that confidence.***

<HM>: ***This annoys him, so I will rub it in.*** We are truthful. You like numbers, and we don't dare to let our numbers lie. If anything, I understate my success. Do you want any more figures?

<Sharf>: I will look at them later.

Tell me how you persuade people to use new services. I imagine there was a great deal of resistance. ***My people could benefit from that.***

<HM>: That comes under "Selling Services and Processes", the last of the success factors you wanted to discuss.

Selling Services and Processes

<HM>: There were fewer problems than we expected.

<Hank>:

- We worked with Piccolo and set up a WFSOA storefront.
- We showed how each service supported Business Strategy.
- Analysts, software architects, business people, and developers may perform keyword searches for service features and policies.
- Both business and technology people may practice using the services online. My people make sure the user proxies are very robust.
- Developers can discover code samples that they need and drop them into applications.
- We make sure that the test samples work.
- We keep the test databases synchronized with production.
- We have algorithms for securing data content, so you don't have to ask the data security question.
- Service performance, policies, runtime costs, and costing algorithms are provided.
- Change history and error rates are provided.
- The name of the original developers and the maintenance teams are provided.
- We provide test scripts and testing harnesses.

<Rennie>: Is this information in UDDI or ebXML?

<Hank>: We're using one of the virtualizations.

<Rennie>: Can you tell me which one?

<Hank>: Look at the "Page Source". It's there in the description. That is required in the development standard for Intranet and Extranet applications.

<Sharf>: Tell me again how you convince them to accept the services that they don't own.

<HM>: If someone went to the Requirements Management team to ask for yet another version of one of the converted services, or a revision to an existing function, we knew about it because the request was registered in the Request Maintenance system (ReMain), which is linked to our Knowledge Cooperative.

<Hank>: The requirements analyst offers an existing service in place of an update to their old functions or the price of creating a new function. If they insist on a new one, the project initiation manager tells them how much it cost us to develop the one we have. Even the areas that are floating in money seldom try to justify wasting money on something we already have, and which is proven to work.

<Rennie>: What if they want a simple modification to existing legacy functions.

<Hank>: It varies. We have found that the "spaghetti plate" delivers the message very effectively.

<Rennie>: You show them pictures of their code.

<Hank>: Yes! Furthermore, we allow them to see change history going back to 2002 along with the names of their people who requested the changes. It's wonderful when we show the number of conflicting requests that may occur in a relatively short period for code that may be 20 - 25 years old.

<Rennie>: What do you do if the new area has different business rules?

<Hank>: We show them how to use the business rules engine to customize rules for their individual requirements.

<Sharf>: That could increase development time and slow performance?

<Hank>: Development time is no longer a factor. If the specifications require a business rules engine, we can automatically generate the code to access the rules engine. Maja found the skinniest rules engine on the market.

<Rennie>: What is your definition of skinny?

<Hank>: We requested the shortest processing path and the highest performance rate.

<Rennie>: How does that limit the sophistication of the rules that you can apply?

<Hank>: *She understands this stuff!* Maja says they are not related. One of the database people was pushing his favorite product; they challenged each other and came out equal from the business viewpoint.

<Rennie>: How did Maja win?

<Hank>: Her product returned results in .037 seconds, and the other one required .068 seconds when they were both running in the same box and using the same database.

<Sharf>: You're off track again.

<HM>: She pinpointed one of the most significant contributors to our service reuse (sales) success.

Accelerated Information and Thought Capture (Secret SOA Benefit)

<HM>: This topic is not directly related to SOA, and I guarantee that you will think it is insane. Nevertheless, the BASE staff has mastered techniques that allow them to digitize their thoughts at least twice as quickly as the average teams within Daxiao, excluding Call Center representatives, of course. More than a thousand of Armstrong's people have taken training to master these techniques for accelerated information and thought capture.

<Sharf>: You have sophisticated voice recognition software.

<HM>: Yes, but it is difficult to train the programs to understand the dialects and pronunciation idiosyncrasies of our staff, or to train the staff to speak so that the programs understand them. After they speak slowly and carefully into the machine, many people spend a surprising amount of time editing what the software produces.

<Sharf>: It beats typing everything.

<HM>: We demonstrated that poor keyboarders using voice recognition software for technology topics take about the same time to produce acceptable results as average keyboarders who do not use voice recognition software.

<Rennie>: ***You're slipping Rennie. Giggling during an engagement is inappropriate.***

<Sharf>: So what are you saying?

<HM>: Before I give you the answer that you must suspect (Rennie figured it out already), think about this for a moment. What would a cab driver do if he or she could only drive 10 miles per hour? What would happen if a surgeon couldn't handle sutures? What would happen if every carpenter needed an assistant to hammer nails?

<Sharf>: TYPING! You intend to waste my time on a discussion of typing?

<HM>: The proper term is keyboarding. I'm showing you how we save time and perform more work. Most of the people in BASE keyboard at least 60 words per minute. About 25 of them do over 90 words per minute, as you have seen if you were noticing Hank.

<Sharf>: You cannot possibly be serious.

<HM>: ***This is not a joke.*** The keyboard is a major tool of our trade. Would it not be logical that people who keyboard well have an advantage over people of equal skill who do not keyboard well?

<Sharf>: How can you change it? These are highly trained professionals.

<HM>: If I hire or inherit someone who has limited keyboarding skills, training specialists point them to our keyboarding site, and I give them grunge typing assignments until they reach the minimum speed that an entry-level Call Center operator must demonstrate - which is 35 accurate words-per-minute. When they reach this initial level, they earn a $300 bonus. They receive an additional bonus of $300 when they prove they can sustain 45 words per minute and another $400 at 55 words per minute. Anyone who can demonstrate 55 words per minute coming in the door receives a $1,000 bonus. The speed parameters are different in China, but the concept is the same.

<Sharf>: How would you give typing tests to network engineers?

<HM>: Part of the interview process requires using a keyboard to provide information. We allow for interview jitters, and discomfort with the keyboards in the interview area (some people hate the ergonomic design), and we can still get an idea of their keyboarding skill.

<Sharf>: Do you force them to take the course, and the tests?

<HM>: Of course, we DO NOT. We rank people within their peer groups according to the quality and quantity of work produced. Non-keyboarders will tend to perform less well in comparison to equally experienced people who keyboard well.

Either that or they will have to work longer hours to perform the same amount of work.

<Sharf>: You penalize people for not being able to type.

<HM>: We reward the best performers. The ranking tends to look like this:

- #1 - Superior knowledge and skills - Good information capture skill.
- #2 - Good knowledge and skills - Good information capture skill.
- #3 - Superior knowledge and skills - Poor information capture skill.
- #4 - Good knowledge and skills - Poor information capture skill.
- #5 - Limited knowledge and skills - Good information capture skill.
- #6 - Limited knowledge and skills - Limited information capture skill.

<Sharf>: How much of your company's money is squandered like this?

<HM>: The head of training and I have been through this many times, and the answer as of the last quarter was that Daxiao has wasted NEGATIVE $18,750,000 (or alternatively a $18.750,000 in savings) on a $1,3000,000 investment. It's the best ROI in the company.

<Sharf>: How do you explain that?

<Hank>: In the beginning, H examined problem logs and could prove that almost 1/3 of the problems were related to input errors, not lack of knowledge. On the average, those errors were costing the company about $20,000,000 each year.

He also demonstrated that 50% of the errors were caused by 20% of the people. After the Program started, every one of these "problem" people achieved performance improvements.

<Sharf>: Do you have numbers for this?

<Hank>: Of course we do.

- If the average poor keyboarder improved 50% in speed and accuracy, and they work at their terminals 20% of the time, the maximum output improvement would be about 10%.
- Assume that 600 people actually achieved improvements.
- Those 600 people are doing the work of 60 extra staff each year. At a fully loaded rate of $84,000 per person, my typing silliness is saving the company $6.25 million each year.

The program has been in place for three years.

Additional benefits include more detail on critical documents because people don't mind typing and improved clarity because people don't lose their thoughts while hunting around the keyboard.

<HM>: We also have a research challenge every month. This is touted as a way to evangelize the Knowledge Cooperative. Participants are given 50 questions and one hour to find the answers. The top 10 people each month receive a day off. A person may only win twice a year. Managers may play, but they can't win. We invite their participation to take the stigma off keyboarding. Weldon is the fastest person on his team. Docente, the head of training, is among the fastest people in the company, but a man in Ireland is gaining on him.

<Sharf>: How many of your top people do not type? I meant to say keyboard.

<HM>: Gunnar and Chiu are proud that they do not find it necessary. I'm not sure about Barca.

<Sharf>: What about Mittelman? What about you?

<HM>: I try. I was tested at 70 words per minute recently. I was a little faster when I needed it to earn my living. My problem is that my fingers are too big for most keyboards. I get in my own way. However, Armstrong and I together have convinced some people that maybe they should perk up.

Mittelman does what he must, when he must. That may include keyboarding.

<Rennie>: The fastest people are all men.

<Hank>: In our experience, the fastest keyboarders for short sprints are men. Women are the most accurate in the long run. They tend to dominate the research challenges.

<HM>: The head of the Human Resources Department has never taken a speed test, but she finishes half of the challenges first. ***Marcella, Gunnar's assistant, wins her two days in the first quarter, and then doesn't compete for the remainder of the year.***

<Sharf>: It's time to move on.

<HM>: ***He wants Rennie to shut up and be a good carpenter's assistant.***

CHAPTER III: WELL-FORMED SERVICE-ORIENTED ARCHITECTURE (WFSOA) METHODOLOGY

<Sharf>: It's time for WFSOA.

<HM>: We mentioned earlier that the corporate architect accepted Hank's suggestion to place "Well-Formed" in front of SOA. It refers to strategic management style that enforces principles for organizing and guiding the interaction of business and technology.

<Hank>: Well-Formed was borrowed from the eXtensible Markup Language (XML), which you know is used to format the communications between SOA technology components. Both "well-formed" and "SOA" have strictly defined technical meanings, but I reiterate that within Daxiao, the term applies primarily to business and organizational issues. Because, as Rennie pointed out, "well-formed" **does not mean valid**, constant monitoring is necessary to ensure timely SOA course corrections.

We perform constant validation of processes, roles, responsibilities, and interactions and have devised mechanisms for implementing rapid change if necessary (when the strategy needs to change, for example). Everyone works the same way and speaks the same language until we realize that the roles need to be changed, or the terminology is wrong.

<Sharf>: *Piccolo isn't the only song and dance man.* Tell me more about why you keep emphasizing "Well-Formed" for business support when it is a technical term.

<HM>: The Well-Formed emblem (Fig. 8) shows how we organized WFSOA processes and procedures into the WFSOA Business/Technology Methodology. Note that this is only one of the possible alignments of the 9 process categories. The alignment is controlled by the project initiation manager, or the project manager.
<Sharf>: *Ho-Hum.*

WFSOA METHODOLOGY PROCESSES - HOW WE DO WHAT WE DO

WFSOA Process Categories

<Hank>: There are three groups (domains) of three process categories within WFSOA. They are the:

Program Enabling Process Domain - includes:

1. SOA Governance processes (including WFSOA Security Management).
2. SOA Communications processes.
3. Human Resources Support processes.

Product Delivery Process Domain - includes:

1. Requirements Coordination (requirements gathering, analysis, project initiation, and testing).
2. Product Creation (design, development, integration, and deployment).
3. Project Management.

Program Support Process Domain - includes:

1. Architecture.
2. Data Management.
3. Environment Management (supports the data center and production versions of products).

These nine sets of related processes support evolution toward a sophisticated Service-Oriented Architecture. The ultimate goal is to have clients create their own composite services and processes (with assistance from technology) rather than the other way around.

<Sharf>: *I know the drill.* Where in this evolution does the SOA become Well-Formed?

<HM>: We became well formed at the junction between the second and third evolutionary stages. At that point, the organization was aligned to support the nine process categories.

<Sharf>: What do you mean when you refer to maturity levels?

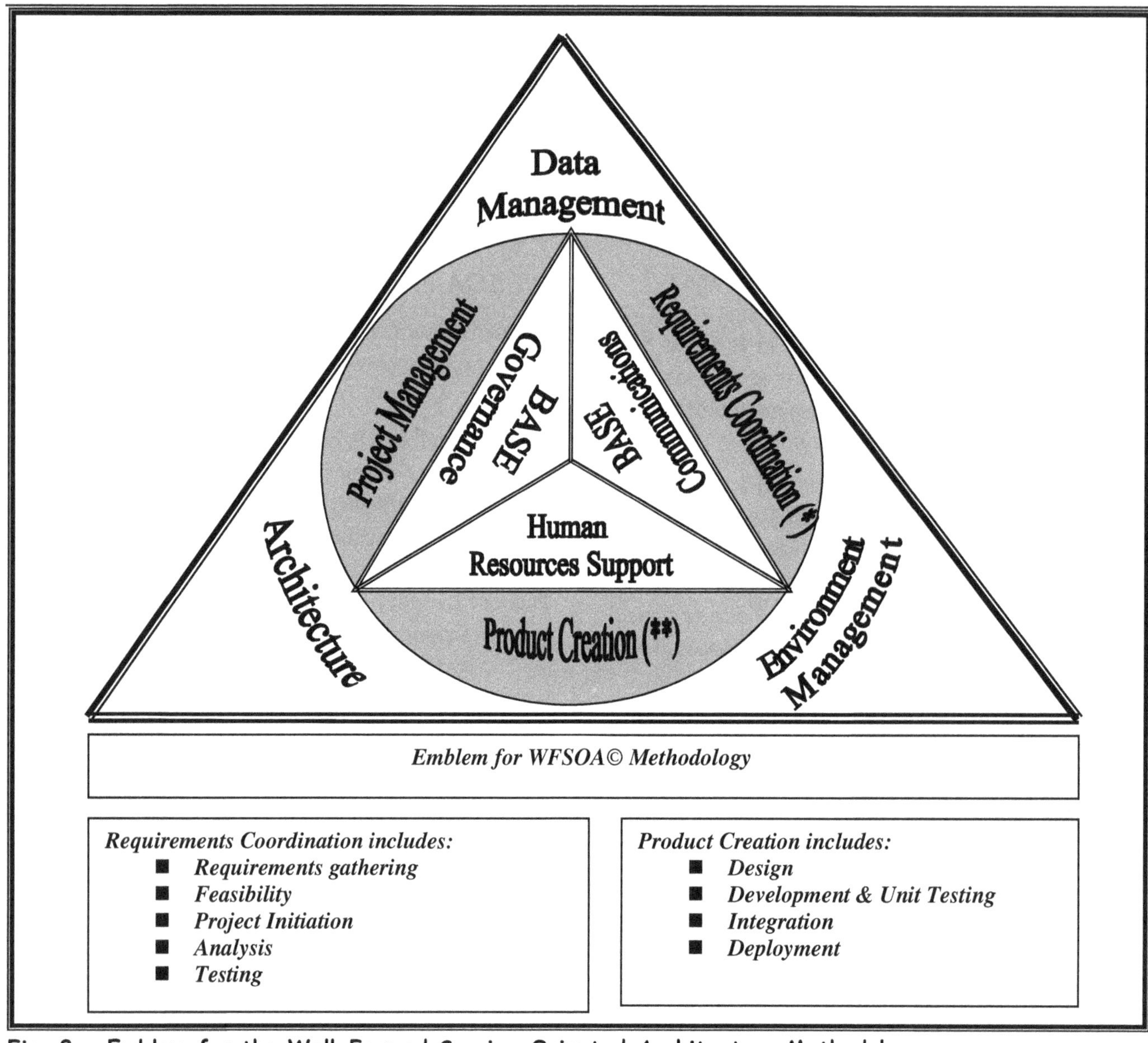

Fig. 8 - Emblem for the Well-Formed Service-Oriented Architecture Methodology

<HM>: That is a different view. Within Daxiao, evolution is a continuing process that does not have an end, analogous to continuous process improvement. Maturity, as Dan may show in intimate detail, is an indication of the probability of success at a specific point in time.

<Rennie>: Can you be well formed and not mature?

<HM>: Yes. A few areas have the organizational, technical, and process structures in place without pursuing SOA maturity.

<Rennie>: Can you be Well-Formed and not evolved?

<HM>: Well-formed is built into our definition of evolved.

<Sharf>: *This is taking too long. I need that roles information.* Do you have a Process Domain emblem with the roles plugged in? That would provide an understanding of the process categories.

<HM>: After we discuss the process categories and associated processes, we will relate the roles to the processes in several ways.

<Rennie>: William let them do this for me. It will give me a foundation upon which we can anchor the rest of the information, including the roles and responsibilities.

<HM>: You said you want clarification for the Board, didn't you?

<Sharf>: *I will when I have more time.* Project Methodology it is. Proceed.

<HM>: This is a Program Methodology, not a project methodology. If the Program succeeds, it will never end, while we try to finish projects as quickly as we can.

<Sharf>: We cannot overlook project methodologies.

<Hank>: You will discuss project methodologies with a technology process coordinator who will provide a theoretical justification for the selection of a project methodology for a specific project, or you may speak with a project initiation manager or a software architect. All three roles can demonstrate our automated processes.

<Rennie>: What is a technology process coordinator?

<Hank>: You would call them methodology specialists. We know that technology processes need to be coordinated just as business processes need to be coordinated.

Looking at the emblem again, you see that the top pyramid contains the enabling process categories, Human Resources Support, SOA Communications, and Governance. We picked the pyramid because it is nature's most stable geometric structure.

Furthermore, the top pyramid is anchored to the bottom pyramid, until a manager changes the alignment (loose coupling), and then it anchors again.

<HM>: We are convinced that if we do a poor job at **any one of the first three**, our Program will fail, even if the other six categories are perfect.

I'm thinking of communications, Gunnar pretends not to understand, and I don't know why.

<Hank>: The other six categories have pre-ordained limits to their effectiveness without good communications, good governance, and excellent personnel support. Because we believe that Human Resources Support is responsible for us being where we are, we will begin by discussing their contribution.

<Sharf>: Who defines the roles?

<HM>: We all do. ***Why is he obsessed with roles? Something is not making sense. I have to do more research.***

See how time flies. It's lunchtime already.

<Sharf>: That would be an early lunch?

<HM>: We should have time lunch on time. The shortest discussion of process domains would take us into the early afternoon.

Let's meet at the restaurant across the street in 30 minutes. They serve decent food, and I have a standing reservation.

<Sharf>: *Oh no!* It will be better to order in. That way we won't lose the momentum. We can work and eat.

<Hank>: ***There are the nod and the smile again!*** Let's do Chinese. I know a gourmet Chinese place that specializes in low fat dishes. Here a menu with pictures. ***I love doing that.***

<Sharf>: Why is the menu in your SOA system?

<HM>: The menu is in Knowledge Cooperative. Part of his job is to make things work more efficiently. We saved 10 minutes of restaurant discussion. What would you like?

<Sharf>: How long will that take?

<Hank>: Food should be here in less than 30 minutes.

<Sharf>: We will meet you here between 12:10 and 12:15. You will continue with the process categories as you suggested. Meanwhile, I will get my people started on declassifying our list of resistance factors.

<HM>: Place the order and I will have Ernest cancel the reservation at the grill.

----------- -----------

<Hank>: We gave them all the roles except about five when we discussed SOX. Why is he pushing this?

<HM>: That requires further evaluation.

<Hank>: ***You know, but you won't tell me.*** What shall we do to enable this evaluation?

<HM>: Gather a roles package. It should contain:

1. The organization chart with roles.
2. The alphabetical lists of role names and alternate role names.
3. The staffing numbers.
4. The Process Domains with primary role assignments.
5. BASE staff within the process categories.
6. The roles interaction cross-reference.
7. WFSOA catalog access rights.

I need approvals from the usual bunch before we distribute the role descriptions. If we don't hear from Human Resources in time, the roles interaction chart will provide over 12,000 explicit data points of information. He can plug it into a spreadsheet and derive hundreds of implicit concepts.

<Hank>: I'm on it.

----- **Lunchtime Phone Break (Staff Motel)** ------

<Sharf>: Our people really do have a list of 35 resistance factors. They started assembling them yesterday for Ādaemoa. They believe there may be 20 additional entries that must be vetted.

<Rennie>: That is shorter than Daxiao's list. Do we have anything that Daxiao doesn't have?

<Sharf>: We must ask Daxiao to print their list, so we can do a comparison.

<Rennie>: They did print the list. You're so busy pushing for the roles and responsibilities that you haven't taken time to look at the handout. What is the big deal? They gave us 67 out of 72 this morning.

<Sharf>: That information was for Sarbanes-Oxley.

<Rennie>: They say the same people work on both programs.

<Sharf>: I require exact specifications, and I want them before we leave this evening. Yesterday at Ādaemoa, we provided your list of 25 SOA roles. They said they already had a list that was much longer. I am convinced that they received it from Daxiao. Ādaemoa is still testing us. Daxiao doesn't want to deal with Ādaemoa, but they are still hindering us.

<Rennie>: Tell them my list is focused more specifically on SOA technology.

<Sharf>: We did. They said they wanted to see the big picture.

<Rennie>: Why didn't our team get a copy of the list from them? I'd like to see it.

<Sharf>: Ādaemoa said it was copyrighted as part of someone's consulting practice.

<Rennie>: Daxiao is a tough act to follow.

<Sharf>: That is a reason for us to move in front of them.

<Rennie>: How do you propose to do that?

<Sharf>: We start by extracting enough information from Daxiao to nail down the Ādaemoa contract. When we land that, I will receive 10% ($50,000), and you may have $10,000 of that.

<Rennie>: That's a nice addition to the sign-on bonus, but why are we going crazy over a $500,000 contract?

<Sharf>: Daxiao says they can do it for $200,000 as part of a partner project. Last year they made $3 million on SOA consulting which means that they could have made $7.5 million at our usual rates. Three million of that could have gone to Belvedere.

<Rennie>: That's still peanuts.

<Sharf>: Not for me it isn't. That $300,000 could have gone into my pocket.

<Rennie>: Where are you going with this? ***Clean up your act, and your practice will be in better shape.***

<Sharf>: There's a $50 million SOA pot in the tri-state area. We would be the best after Acton, of course, if Daxiao was not in the picture. When projects become too large for Daxiao, Daxiao routes them to Acton for the real action. When you and I figure out what they are doing, we will level the playing field with Acton.

<Rennie>: Why do they select Acton for the follow-up business?

<Sharf>: Acton performed Daxiao's SEC audits for the last 10 years. I'm not sure whether Piccolo and HM are teaching Acton, learning from Acton, or both, but they have a good thing going.

<Rennie>: Piccolo's name keeps popping up. Suppose you find that Piccolo is pulling the strings.

<Sharf>: Piccolo has a reputation for being an over-educated song and dance man. HM is the muscle.

<Rennie>: If Daxiao doesn't like HM, how did he become so powerful?

<Sharf>: We have to answer that question for Daxiao and Gunnar, *and for me. I'm tired of having Marshalls trip me up.*

<Rennie>: Do you believe Acton has any unusual dealings with HM?

<Sharf>: He annoys enough people that if they could have nailed him for that he'd have been gone 9 years ago. He doesn't need the money. They pay him close to a million a year, and his family figures out how to earn many times his salary with electronics start-ups.

<Rennie>: Are you saying that this family makes money because HM has the inside track on what Daxiao is doing, or will do?

<Sharf>: They say that Daxiao makes money by following HM.

<Rennie>: Isn't there a conflict of interest in there somewhere?

<Sharf>: No one has been able to find one, and many people tried. His son, an electronics genius, can smell silicone cooking in garages where his misfit friends from Strafford are playing. He nudges them along with assistance from lawyer Mom (her nickname is Machiavella) and "Big sister", an accountant. She worked for Acton until there was a potential conflict of interest. HM and Machi Mom keep Silicon Huey in the middle of the road. His real name is Jonas.

<Rennie>: Jonas Frey!

<Sharf>: You've heard of him too.

<Rennie>: Every tech type I know has heard of him. He is very handsome when he takes off the thick glasses, and he is a very rich nerd.

Why didn't you mention his wife? She worked in the first garage. I know at least three women who are annoyed that Jonas married her while they were still in college, and he's too absent-minded to have an affair.

<Sharf>: Gunnar didn't mention her. Do you know her name?

<Rennie>: Rebecca Vincent. Her family owns [...]

<Sharf>: Vincent Holdings - that's where they found money for the first two start-ups! Gunnar couldn't figure out how Huey overcame the snob barrier. Vincent buys patents and sells them to Huey's start-ups at very reasonable prices. *Even Marshall's daughter-in-law is sitting on millions of dollars. I must destroy them!*

<Rennie>: That would be Becky. They say she really enjoyed chasing him until he caught her.

<Sharf>: Get back to business. Would it ever have occurred to you that there was a connection between them and Marshall?

<Rennie>: Now that you mention it, he was blonder and fuzzier, but he looked like Mr. Marshall - a little.

<Sharf>: How do you know him?

<Rennie>: I didn't really know him. I was behind him in Science. I tried to say hello to him a few times, but he ignored me. I don't know a single person who claims to have been his friend.

<Sharf>: The Board didn't know they were connected until SOX. *They could have been multi-millionaires with cushy jail cells. I was ecstatic until he managed to wiggle out of the trap he set for himself.*

<Rennie>: How do Jonas and his family manage what they do without being in trouble?

<Sharf>: In every instance they can trace, Jonas Partners or Frey Associates sells their part in the start-ups just as a product is picked up by a manufacturer. If, 14 months later, there's a purchase recommendation (never from Marshall), the Frey organization no longer has an official financial connection.

<Rennie>: What else should I know about Marshall?

<Sharf>: There are a few other things:

- New Board members don't believe Marshall could be as good as Acton and CMMI indicate. Otherwise, he'd be asking for more money.

- The Board is ashamed to admit that they don't know what to do if he leaves.
- He has no air cover that they can discover.
- Many important Board members, especially the external members do not know him. He only attends mandatory company events.
- No one knows his family. Until a moment ago, I doubt that anyone knew that Marshall's daughter-in-law is in line to inherit almost $100 million of her own.
- They have three proposals from insiders for ways to unwind the emergency organizational changes that he forced on them for SOA, but they don't know which thread to pull.
- Operations and manufacturing people want to slow him down. When he creates processes at the requested speed, it also creates structural unemployment and an aura of unease while the company makes more money.
- The Sales and Marketing units wants to stop Partner Networks because Marshall steps on their territory.

There is today's craziness. No one at my level should be helping to take notes.

<Rennie>: ***Why does the typing bother him?***

I just figured it out! You want his job, ***but the typing alone would force you to perform less well than he does.***

- You show them the thread to unravel HM.
- You could sit in the Marshall's big chair, bring along a new governance manager, and earn a few million for Belvedere over the next few years (***enough bonuses to pay off the college loans***).
- You convince them that Daxiao should stop doing SOA consulting, and you earn money there too.

<Sharf>: Who says you tech types don't understand politics?

<Rennie>: Is Acton going to sit around and do nothing while we yank this away from them?

<Sharf>: They will fight us, but we can give the Board options if the head of the audit committee is on our side.

<Rennie>: What if Marshall contributes as much as he appears to contribute? What would happen if Daxiao does not perform as well after Marshall departs? They won't have the money to pay you. If Marshall's people leave, they won't have a competency team.

<Sharf>: First, no one can be as good as he appears to be. Second, we're cheaper than Acton is. Third, Grayson will be working for me, and I'll use his people to replace anyone who deserts from the competency team.

We've had enough of this. Go fix whatever women fix. When we return to the room, let them finish with the emblem, but we won't allow ourselves to become bogged down in the details. The next item on the list is SOA roles and responsibilities. When we see a list of SOA roles like the one they gave for SOX, we will have completed our assignment for today very successfully.

- **Lunchtime Phone Break (SOA Command Center)** -

<Hank>: The food will be here in 5 minutes, Maja printed out the roles documents for us, and she figured out what they are doing.

<HM>: Did someone hear them talking in the motel?

<Hank>: No, Maja was listening this morning, and then she signed off and went to do some research.

<HM>: Why didn't you tell me she was there?

<Hank>: Her phone number was in the "Meeting Attendants" box.

<HM>: Why was she listening?

<Hank>: Liz has Maja obsessed with learning how to communicate more effectively. She wanted to learn the consulting style of an organization other than Acton.

<HM>: Tell her to stick with her knitting. Above all, tell her not to imitate this nitwit.

<Hank>: When did she take up knitting?

<HM>: Tell her not to waste time on this fool. Belvedere couldn't survive if they had more like him.

<Hank>: She put him on her slippery list already. Don't you want to know what we found out?

<HM>: They're working with Ādaemoa. They believe they're taking business from us.

<Hank>: How did you know?

<HM>: Acton told me last week. I didn't mention it because you would have given them the short versions of everything, and the first line on their report would have been that we are being "difficult".

<Hank>: What are you going to do?

<HM>: I still need to discover how much of what he's doing is controlled by Gunnar or Mittelman and how much he's doing for himself.

<Hank>: Are you still going to give them so much information about roles?

<HM>: Of course, after we check with Human Resources. We must remember not to appear that we are defining the roles for Armstrong's people, even though we often define the roles for Armstrong's people.

Furthermore, we are going to give them:

1. ALL the action lists.
2. All the SOA maturity options.
3. The common terminology lists.
4. The list of catalog contents.
5. The asset inventory.

<Hank>: Confuse them with facts.

<HM>: If they want, they may have:

1. The entire product list.
2. All our reused components.
3. All the processes and procedures.

We will provide every bit of information that they could possibly imagine that they want.

I figured out step #1. We will accuse Gunnar of forcing me to give away the shop.

Verify that we have the necessary information before Maja starts her backup. We wouldn't want the system to slow down while we need information for Belvedere.

--- Advisors Returning to Command Center---

<Sharf>: That sounds like a great idea. Do we get food too?

<Hank>: My phone just buzzed. It's coming up behind you.

<HM>: Talk to Maja.

<Hank>: Of course. I will see if I can convince her to delay the backup.

<HM>: Hurry.

<Sharf>: Is something wrong?

<HM>: Not really.

<Sharf>: What are you backing up?

<HM>: Maja is taking a backup of the R&D section of the Knowledge Cooperative.

<Sharf>: At midday? Why?

<HM>: We go to lunch every day at this time.

<Sharf>: Why is she taking a backup?

<HM>: She wanted to create special extracts for you. It required a challenging merger of multiple sources, but she needs the backup first.

<Sharf>: Why can't take backups after we leave?

<HM>: She had it scheduled during my lunch break two days before you arrived, but you moved everything up a few days. As it is, she's working while she's on vacation.

<Sharf>: ***The better to keep you off balance.*** She could schedule that activity at night.

<HM>: ***How would he dare to suggest when my people should work late while they are on vacation!***

<Sharf>: Won't if affect the rest of the staff?

<HM>: My experimental dashboards and scorecards may be offline. Oops. They just went offline. There will be zero problems in the production environments.

<Sharf>: ***He's trying to stonewall us.*** One would imagine that your people would know how to keep the system up while you take backups. Don't you have non-stop requirements?

<HM>: Critical production databases must be non-stop. We have people working in six time zones on three continents. This is a research/experimental database. I haven't been able to justify the funding to move it into production. You don't have to worry. If Hank doesn't have printed versions of everything we will need, we can let the local librarian create copies.

--Hank returning to the SOA Command Center--

<Hank>: I have good news, bad news, and more good news. Here's the food, Maja had already started the back up, and Maja's people extracted everything we requested before the system slowed down. They'll bring the information to us in a few minutes.

<Sharf>: That was fast. Where is Maja?

<Hank>: She was physically on vacation in the Canadian Rockies, but she is logically here. Her second in command is on the other side of that wall. That's where we keep the onsite version of the digital library.

<HM>: Let's start on the food. You know I become irritable when I'm hungry.

<Sharf>: Keep going with the presentation. Before the break, you wanted to talk about your methodology, process domains, and process groups.

<HM>: The WFSOA methodology defines "HOW WE DO WHAT WE DO". We identified more than 140 processes, and we cross-referenced them to the nine process categories. If we spend the next three days providing you with the overviews of important processes, it would accelerate your ability to select the areas you wish to interview. It will also prove that our processes are documented.

<Sharf>: Three days! You must have a shorter version.

<Hank>: We have the version that we present at middle management seminars. That takes two to three hours, depending on how many questions you have. I will talk while you eat. You can tell us what you want to skip.

<Sharf>: *I don't have three hours either.* Let's see what we can do over lunch.

<HM>: *This is not going to work. He is here to discover what we do, and we have an hour to tell him while we are eating. I am wasting my time.*

<Hank>: As I mentioned earlier, the three process clusters in the Enabling Process Domain are in the top triangle of Fig. 8 above.

ENABLING PROCESS DOMAIN

Human Resources Support

"Support" is the operant concept. Their extraordinarily unique training and education program is necessary for our success. Look at Lessons Learned and the resistance list again to see how critical their Cultural Change management program is to the success of our program.

You will hear more about their Program when we discuss roles and responsibilities.

SOA COMMUNICATIONS

<Hank>: We already understand the importance of the SOA communications team, and we believe that it will acquire even more importance as we approach a critical mass. You are here, and that is a major indication that we still have work to do.

<HM>: *We never told anyone everything that we were planning though. If we did, they would want to stop us.*

<Hank>: We persuaded one of our top sales people to spend time with us while she's expanding her family unit (*with the assistance of papa Piccolo*). Lisse Maçon can sell sand to a Tuareg.

<HM>: *She and Dan promote the theoretical benefits of purchased sand versus the natural windblown type.*

She even sold Justin on the idea that having a high-powered husband and wife team would be a good idea, as long as they don't work in the same sector.

<Hank>: We engage in a continuing multi-pronged attack on our communications issues. It is more than evangelizing the benefits of SOA.

Multi-lingual Communications

<Hank>: Lisse promotes the benefits SOA in three major languages, English, Spanish, and Mandarin Chinese. She has a group that specializes in the Shengen languages of the European Community.

Our people have assured us that she speaks (and writes) excellent Mandarin and French. Everyone on her staff is fluent in at least two languages. She ensures that critical documents are translated either from English into the language(s) of project participants or from the language(s) of project participants into English for our cross-cultural teams.

<Sharf>: Why? If people work for an English-speaking company, wouldn't it save time if they learned to speak English? Look at Hank. I had a few East Asians on my accounting team, and they were as good as he is.

<HM>: Hank was born in the United States and spent a third of his adult life in England.

<Hank>: Fifty-five percent of our people were not hired into English-speaking companies. They were acquired.

<Sharf>: How much do you spend on the translations?

<Hank>: Maja's people spend a third of their time translating back and forth. Lisse worked out agreements with the Corporate Communications team, and they do about 75% of the work.

<Sharf>: You didn't say how much.

<HM>: The money is spread among the responsibilities of Lisse, Maja, Macedon, and Ellison. We can find the information when the system comes back.

<Sharf>: Whatever the number may be, you could spend the time and the money to teach everyone to speak English.

<HM>: We do spend time and money to teach them English. However, it takes 12 years of total immersion for the average human to develop enough fluency in their native language to function at the level of professionalism that we require. Some never do, even in their native tongues. I'm sure you know intelligent people who handle the language poorly.

<Rennie>: *You're looking at a tall lanky mean one. His wife was on the sauce when she told me he made 800 on his math GRE's and 525 in English, even with intense coaching. He made 500 on his SAT. He barely made it into Wheaton, and he wouldn't have made it out if his girlfriend/wife wasn't majoring in English.*

<Sharf>: That is why we have assistants. One of us does the thinking, and the other one does the writing.

<HM>: We cannot wait for everyone to become fluent, nor can we provide everyone with assistants, so we translate the important information.

If I call the guardians of political correctness, I could remove of this xenophobe, but I could end up with people who never had Asians on their accounting teams. I'm developing a tolerance for this poison.

Meanwhile, we provide basic cross-language and cross-cultural training. We teach Spanish and Chinese to the English speakers, Chinese and English to the Spanish speakers, and Spanish and English to the Chinese speakers. We hired an external team to provide special assistance with the Shengen languages. We provide some of the best ESL (English as a Second Language) writing support products. We have tried to handle every angle of the language issue.

¿Está de acuerdo usted?

<Sharf>: What?

<Rennie>: He asked whether you agree.

<HM>: *I'm wasting time on my soapbox again.*

- Will: cān fàn.
- Hank: huà. jì shí.

Did I say it correctly?

<Sharf>: Huh?

<Hank>: He said (approximately), "You eat while I talk. We have a schedule". *What he wanted to say is "the foot in the mouth does not taste good".*

<Sharf>: We agree about the schedule.

Resistance Reduction (Sales Training)

Lisse and her people work closely with Human Resources to identify areas of resistance, which is what salespeople must do well. Then she works to create messages that reduce the level of resistance.

Each member of the SOA Communications, Program Management, and Competency teams has received between two weeks and a month of sales training.

<Sharf>: Why? I never took a single minute of sales training in my life.

<HM and Rennie>: *It shows.*

<Hank>: They learn how to deal with the usual levels of resistance that they encounter in the process of performing their normal roles.

Facilitation Training

<Hank>: Similarly, each member of the SOA Communications, Program Management, and Competency teams has received at least two weeks of training in facilitation.

<Sharf>: When do these people do real work?

<Hank>: Facilitation is part of their real work.

<Sharf>: How did you manage that?

<Hank>: We only have 8 official facilitators, but we have more than 300 people working on SOA. We estimate that each of them saves at least two hours a week in meetings attended by at least 10 people, either by **not disturbing** the flow of the meetings or by enabling smoother information flow.

If a person can do that in any 6 weeks after two weeks of training, the company saves 80 hours of the time of people whose salary ranges from $1,000 a week to $6,000 per week. If the average savings is $2,000 per week, they save the price of their training and the salaries earned during training.

They are also trained to identify resistance.

<Sharf>: You train them to expose their coworkers.

<HM>: Resistance generates risk. We train them to identify patterns of risk and recommend techniques for risk mitigation. They address our COSO and ERM responsibilities.

<Sharf>: We are talking about SOA, not SOX. Don't allow yourself to be sidetracked again.

<HM>: For us, SOA resistance causes problems with SOX effectiveness. Fixing one set of problems improves our performance with the other.

<Rennie>: Hank, have you taken sales and facilitation training.

<Hank>: I took both in school and again when we merged with Goodsand. HM says I am 20 - 30% more effective, even with the same level of technical skill.

<Sharf>: You overran the place with a bunch of manipulators.

<HM>: We consider our SOA team to be closer to expert pilots or Chunnel builders.

<Sharf>: I was kidding.

<HM>: *When you blast Liz in your report, both Dan and Mittelman will have you hide. The game is afoot.*

Common Terminology

<Hank>: Devising common terminology was extremely difficult. But, before we could communicate across cultures, the business units had to learn to communicate within their own sectors.

<Sharf>: Teach business to the technology people. That's SOA yada-yada.

<Hank>: We found that the problem was much bigger than that. We must:

1. Teach business to the technology teams.
2. Teach technology teams to communicate across technology silos.
3. Teach technology to the business areas.
4. Teach business teams to communicate across business silos.

What learned what few people seemed to notice before - many processes had not been working due to problem #4 on the list above. We will provide more information on problem #4 in a moment.

Teaching business to the technology areas was easiest. It has been happening with varying degrees of success for years.

The second most difficult area was to teach technology people to communicate across and within technology silos. We were surprised at how many complications arose because technology teams were describing similar activities using different terminology. One person said she was developing C++ objects, and another was coding a program. One team tested their scripts while another submitted their JCL (Job Control Language).

H volunteered his management team to devise a common technology vocabulary, and he challenged the business teams and technology teams to do the same.

The third most challenging terminology issue was to teach technology to the business areas.

<HM>: William, before you sidetrack yourself, the reason this was necessary was that it allowed business people to understand when they were making totally unreasonable requests. They were becoming informed consumers. They could begin to make sense of the hundreds of actions associated with even the simplest request. It doesn't mean that they stopped making impractical requests. At least they know when they are being impractical.

It is successful in bursts. It revs up during every major new project and then drops off again until there is a major problem.

Common Terminology Sources

<Rennie>: What did you use as the foundation for common terminology?

<Hank>: We started with the Information Technology Infrastructure Library (ITIL). We merged IBM, Microsoft, and Hewlett Packard adaptations when we incorporated it into our management structure. The methodology mavens (technology process coordinators) will tell you exactly how they did that. ITIL overlapped with COBIT and CMMI, but there were gaps. The standards people produced variations, which were effective in some areas, and added confusion in others.

<Sharf>: I would think that the standards organizations would solve that problem.

<HM>: Rennie, you must have mentioned to William how successful the Organization for the Advancement of Structured Information Standards (OASIS) was with SOA Framework.

<Rennie>: They got nailed for trying to nail down SOA terminology?

<HM>: That is exactly the point.

<Hank>: Whenever most of the industry agreed, we used the commonly accepted definition. If there was a conflict, we let the area, standard, person, or the system that appears to be most critical determine the definition. We used ISO to fill some of the gaps. We used ISO 11179 Metadata registry standards and Universal Data Element Framework (UDEF) to complete the metadata circle. If there was no tiebreaker inside Daxiao, we used the Internet.

We also encourage Program participants to improve the definitions and add new ones.

We have people assigned to "Wiki Watch and Blog Watch". They pay attention to internal and external sources.

We provide definitions, historical derivations, illustrations, and demonstrations for areas that seem particularly difficult. We provide the sources for definitions and "who knows" (the names of people who are familiar with special topic areas).

<Sharf>: *Who cares?*

<Rennie>: These are your subject matter experts.

<HM>: You are correct. There will be more on that topic when we discuss roles and responsibilities.

<Hank>: If our subject matter experts, the Intranet, Extranet, or Internet were neutral, Maja and Liz's people make suggestions, and H selects one of the suggestions.

<Sharf>: How do you presume to be qualified for this review? Why don't the data people control this?

<HM>: I've been associated with this racket for 40 years. I have at least 5 more years of database experience than anyone who still does hands-on work. I have been a manager of something related to computers for at least 33 years. I kept a few fingers in the new technology all the years that I was a manager, which means I could maintain a 30,000-foot view and an up-to-date grass-top view. Who do you believe would be more qualified?

<Sharf>: *I will make him choke on his arrogance.* How much of the terminology is included in the documentation you gave us?

BASE Glossary - Technology and BASE History

Readers: Table A.5 is an extract of SOA P preparatory notes. It should be used in conjunction with Lessons Learned - Table A.2.

<Hank>: You have a condensed version of the glossary and notes in Table A.5. The full version is over 300 pages long. It contains illustrations and animations. Table 9 contains a list of the jargon files that we monitor and use as input to the glossary. The glossary facilitates cultural changes

<Sharf>: Do you claim that everyone in your organization uses the same terminology?

Table 9 - Common Terminology Jargon Lists

Terminology/Controlled Vocabulary	Provided By
Acronyms & abbreviations	Business & Technology Units
Advertising	Corporate Communications
Analysis and design processes	Technology process coordinators
Architecture	Technology Teams
Business unit jargon	Business Units
Change management	Requirements Management
Communications	Corporate Communications
Compliance and audit	Compliance teams
Configuration management (data center)	Technology Teams
Continuity planning	Enterprise Integration, BASE Program Management
Corporate architecture	Enterprise Integration
Cross-language translations	Communications Teams
Cultural change management	Human Resources
Customer service/relations	User Support Team
Data & database administration	Data Specialists
Data center operations	Technology
Deployment & release management	Infrastructure Technology
Development (services, processes, business systems)	SOA Competency & Software Architects
Distribution (business products)	Business Operations
Enterprise resource planning	Enterprise Integration & Technology
Financial management & accounting	Financial Management
Government regulations	Corporate Counsel
Import/export	Business Operations
Incident & problem management	User Support Team
Industry regulations and standards	Business & Technology Units
Integration & integration software	Infrastructure Technology
International business terminology	Business & Technology Units
International technology terminology	Technology Units & Vendors
Knowledge management	SOA Library management
Legal and Regulatory	Corporate Counsel & Compliance
Logistics	Business Operations
Manufacturing systems	Manufacturing
Marketing and market research	Communications teams
Measurements & conversion factors	Manufacturing
Methodology	Compliance
Modeling languages	Requirements Management
Negotiation	Business & Technology
Operations (business)	Business
Operations (data center)	Technology
Planning, corporate	Enterprise Integration
Planning, project	Requirements Management & BASE Program Management
Platform specific terminology	Technology
Policy and procedures	Business & Technology Units
Process management & reengineering	Business & Technology and Process Management
Process modeling	Process Management Team
Procurement	Vendor Management Team
Product specific terminology (including new product development)	Business Units
Quality management	Quality Assurance Team

Table 9 - Common Terminology Jargon Lists

Terminology/Controlled Vocabulary	Provided By
Requirements Management (business technology change management)	Requirements Management
Research & development	Enterprise Integration
Risk management	Compliance
Sales	Communications teams
Security & security management	Global Security
Service catalogs (registry or repository)	SOA Library Management
Service level management	Data Center Operations, Business Units, SOA Competency
SOA (includes Web services)	SOA Competency Team
Software asset management	Asset Librarian
Strategy, tactics, planning (business)	Enterprise Integration
Supply chain	Business Operations
Vendor products	Technology Teams and Vendor Management

<Hank>: We cannot guarantee that everyone uses it, but we are certain that everyone knows it exists. An icon was placed on the tool bar of every desktop, laptop, or PDA.

<Rennie>: Why does the Communications team provide the information on sales and marketing?

<HM>: *Because Gunnar is an arrogant fool.*

<Hank>: The sales people are very busy. They must talk with Corporate Communications, and they tend not to want to repeat themselves for us. Plus, the head of SOA communications was once in Sales.

Business Confusion Causes SOA Problems

Staying on track, we mentioned earlier that problem #4 was the most difficult. Teaching the business people to communicate with each other is more difficult than teaching them to communicate with technology.

<Sharf>: That is somewhat radical. How would you justify that statement?

<HM>: As one simple example, Maja showed them the 9 different definitions that they have for account, the supporting database requirements, and the conflicting definitions that they have for "customer" and "client".

<Sharf>: I have heard that a dozen times before. Major corporations use data virtualization services to solve the problems. Others learn to live with it.

<HM>: Our corporate architect says we differentiate ourselves by realizing that virtualization causes its own problems. He refused to believe that the inconsistencies cannot be resolved.

<Hank>: He says technology has taken the heat for a business problem for the last 50 years. When technology tries to please multiple masters, no one was satisfied. If business people do not understand what their peers are saying, they seldom admit it.

He showed how the communications breakdowns among the business teams may be more harmful than the ones between technology and business.

<HM>: He calculated that communication failure among the business units increases our operating budget by as much as 20%.

<Sharf>: *That is absurd.* You have details to support this assertion, of course.

<HM>: Dan speaks eloquently for hours on this topic. Keep your "on track" card ready when you start him on this one. He and the communications specialist work closely in this area. *They work closely in all areas.*

<Rennie>: I know. It's on the list of the topics for further discussion.

<HM>: Try KC again.

BASE Program Knowledge Cooperative

<Hank>: We have an aggressive approach to knowledge consolidation and organization. The result is that the BASE Knowledge Cooperative is now a major component of the corporate Knowledge Cooperative.

<Sharf>: Must you go back to this?

<HM>: It is an important part of how we do what we do. *This is where we keep the information on roles.*

<Sharf>: Continue if you insist.

<Hank>: Fig. 9 is a side view of Fig. 8-The WFSOA Emblem. Notice that the volume of information supporting BASE in the Knowledge Cooperative is equal to the total of all the knowledge associated with all the Program's processes.

We retrieved information that was crammed in old binders and bottom drawers and placed it online. We index and cross-reference e-mail messages as well as the text in images. Dublin Core Tags (See Table A.5.1) simplify indexing of data types.

Aggressive Notification: Maja maintains data or pointers to data in over 450 information categories. After we acquire the information, we establish security requirements and enforce sharing. We maintain notification lists, we tell people where to find new and necessary information related to their roles and responsibilities, and we send information along with the notifications when we don't want them to have an excuse for missing it. The Knowledge Cooperative can access the phone system to send the most critical notices.

<Rennie>: Where do you keep index information?

<Hank>: Knowledge Cooperative content (all 450 information categories) is indexed by one of the most complicated hierarchical databases in existence.

<Sharf>: I understand that. You are talking about a product that is over 40 years old.

> **Readers:** I wish to remain vendor-neutral. Technical people can guess the name of the product. I personally used it for some very fancy indexing. It won't matter to non-technical people.

<HM>: Yes, and that means that they had 40 years to get is indexing right. You may program the indexes as relational databases, it has excellent security algorithms, you can optimize performance in critical access areas, and the hierarchical structure supports native XML structures at least as well as any other available product.

<Sharf>: Other products must be as good or better by now.

<HM>: Perhaps there are, but I have worked with this one for 35 of those 40 years, and it was among Maja's top three favorites. We stayed with what works.

<Rennie>: How do you know about databases?

<HM>: I am Maja's main back up.

<Sharf>: Your team backs up the database team?

<HM>: I, H, am Maja's back up. The database people believe we are insane, and we are having trouble getting them take responsibility for some of our databases. We are insane, but what we do works. ***I don't really want them to have my research database, but I must act as if I do.***

<Rennie>: When the system recovers, will you show us the types of information that you indexed?

<Hank>: If you would like, we could go next door and show you our B2E Portal. In Daxiao, B2E also means BASE-to-Employee.

<HM>: Let's go. We have an animated demonstration that will clarify how the most critical information segments excelerate "How We Do What We Do". "Excelerate" is a word that Dan created to describe the Knowledge Cooperative. It runs for 17 minutes, and it could save hours of explanations.

<Rennie>: William, I think it would be helpful for everyone concerned.

<Sharf>: It would be helpful if we stuck with the agenda - the things that are immediately important,

Support for Human Interaction

<Sharf>: For instance, are you using the Knowledge Center to eliminate face-to-face interaction?

<Hank>: The opposite is true. Our Program participants have the ability to handle face-to-face interactions **more intelligently** because they have done their research in advance.

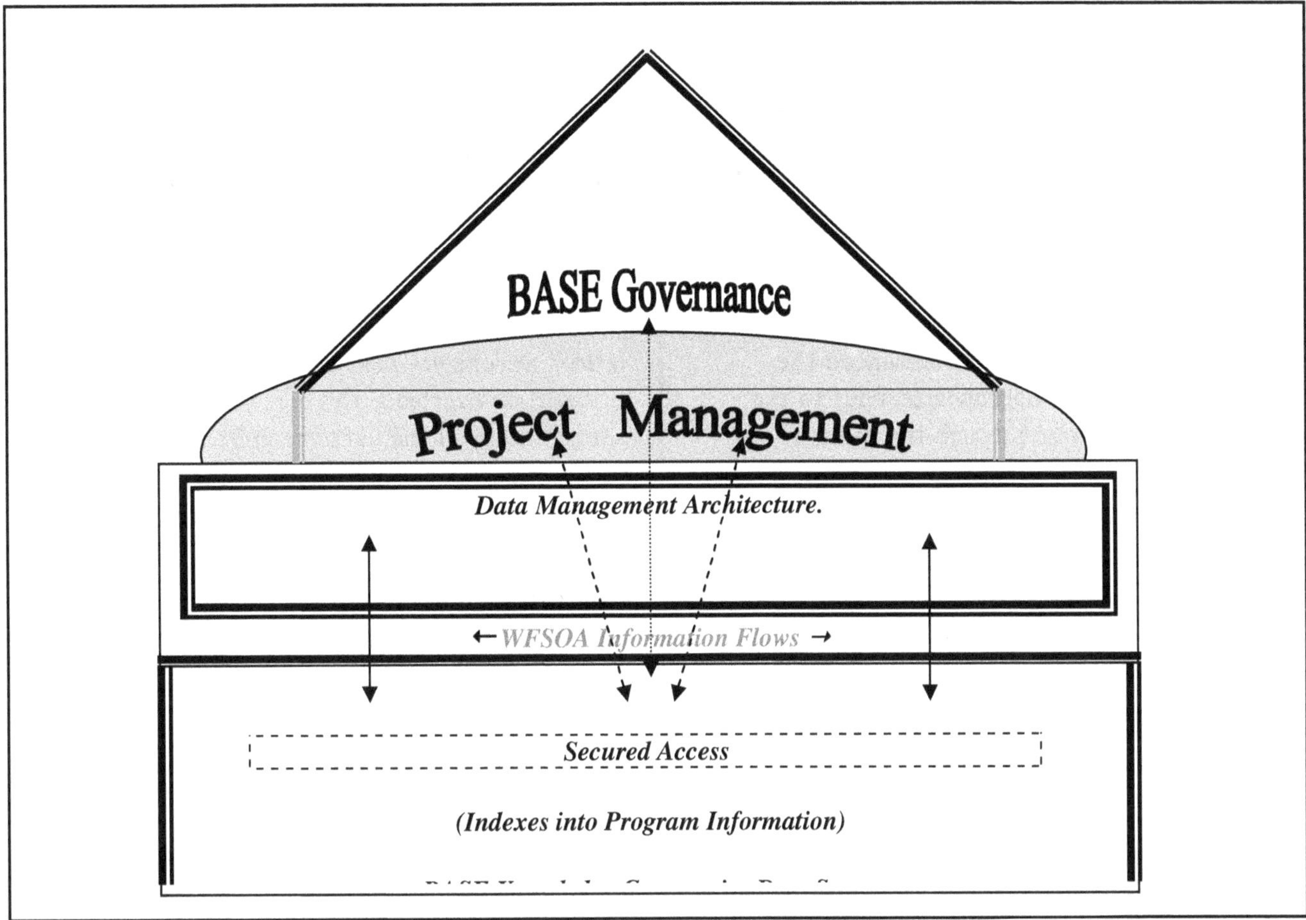

Fig. 9 - WFSOA Emblem with Knowledge Cooperative Information Flows

<HM>: To take it to its extreme, Dan, Lorrie (the CFO), Maja/Lisse and I have knowledge goals:

1. Our aim is to have 99+% of our SOA-related intellectual property is in the Knowledge Cooperative (with properly secured access).
2. We teach search techniques. The master index of topics is available to everyone in three languages (English, Spanish, and Mandarin). If the information is available in the Knowledge Cooperative, 90% of requests in the language of native speakers will be answered in fewer than four queries.
3. A second level help desk with rotating subject matter experts handles another five percent. One of our most popular information endpoints is SME.com.
4. The final five percent goes onto a research list. If the requestor's manager approves the work, it goes on our priority queue.
5. If people can prove a need, they will receive access to additional Knowledge Cooperative content within one hour.

The results are that people can deal with issues that are more substantial during their face-to-face interactions.

<Sharf>: Why would the CFO care?

<HM>: Before she would accept the service domains, she insisted that her people should have immediate access to all existing information?

<Sharf>: *She would do something like that*. How do you discover if people are hiding information?

<HM>: We track requests for information to determine why some projects were delayed longer than others were. We noticed when specific people and teams appeared in "reason for delay" often.

<Rennie>: You built a list of gatekeepers.

<Hank>: Fortunately, people on my team and I have been here longer than 95% of the information hoarders, and we know how things should work. That's a benefit of paying for tenure.

If necessary, we automate around them, and take our hits.

There have been instances where we simulated crises to force people to dust off their secret techniques list.

<HM>: At the same time, Dan convinced the company to encourage appropriate input to the Knowledge Cooperative through the reward structure.

<Sharf>: What will Daxiao do if something happens to you? ***What happens after I do something to promote your departure?***

<HM>: I have at least 30 people who have been associated with compliance for more than 20 years. Meanwhile, I'm dumping things out of my head as quickly as I can.

<Sharf>: Does that mean you are leaving?

<HM>: It means I'm developing half-heimers, and I need to deliver information before it is no longer accessible.

<Hank>: It means that he takes downloads of information faster than he can upload the new concepts that he derives from the information.

<Sharf>: ***He also has wings and a heavenly glow. This is sickening.*** What happens if you find conflicts?

<HM>: We maintain both sets of information and flag them. That becomes a higher priority research item. Resolution of conflicting information often provides updates to multiple sections in the Cooperative.

<Sharf>: Do you perceive that any effort is wasted on the Knowledge Cooperative?

<HM>: NO!

<Hank>: We established the foundation for most of the information when we began working on SOX.

<HM>: Don't forget to mention that the compliance people had the information before SOX.

<Hank>: I should have said that SOX provided justification for making that information available to everyone. Now we have tools and official processes for automated and incremental updates.

Before we create new information content for the Knowledge Cooperative, the requests must pass through the same Requirements Coordination pathways as requests for any other new data sources.

For the record, SOA library entries were a major source of new information.

<HM>: Before you ask, we have techniques to avoid information overload. The only people who are interested in all the lists are in BASE, Requirements Management, or Enterprise Integration. We may add Rennie to the group of interested persons.

<Hank>: We prevent information overload by maintaining minimal notification lists of critical topics associated with each Program role. People may request notification on additional topics, subscribe to RSS feeds, or access additional topics directly, assuming that they have security clearance. We send notifications when new information is added to a topic on a role's critical information list.

<Sharf>: How would you calculate the ROI?

<HM>: The time required for requirements gathering, analysis, and design has been reduced by 30%, and that is a conservative estimate. We are saving $20 - 25 million each year in these areas alone.

<Sharf>: Run your magic calculator.

<Rennie>: ***William believed he could frighten them with his number's ability, and now he is jealous of Mr. Marshall's ability.***

<HM>: Armstrong has about 3,600 developers, and I have over a 100. The average developer salary, worldwide, is $60,000. That is $186 million a year in development salaries. Forty percent of product delivery funding is spent on analysis and design - a little over $74 million. Reduce that by 30% and you have a $22.3 million savings in Requirements Management and Product creation.

We save time in the business area. Use the example where a subject matter expert earning $150,000/year spends 4 hours providing information on a critical topic and a KC specialist spends 8 hours (perhaps less) indexing and organizing that information. For the next 10 times that anyone needs the same information, they retrieve it in 10 minutes and spend 50 minutes of that expert's time to clarify what they don't understand. Before the Knowledge Cooperative, that expert might have spent 3 hours with each analysis team over the period of a year. Technology, Requirements Management, or my team used less than 13 hours of her time ($1,000), rather than 30 ($2,200). I paid my person $350 to index the information. The company is ahead of the game by $850 on the expert's time alone. Give me a moment to calculate how much our other teams save.

<Sharf>: I can do it later. *Maybe he is good. It doesn't matter. I'll eliminate him and use what he learned to my advantage.*

<Rennie>: How do you do handle numbers like that?

<HM>: *This will not be humble.*

The gods have an unusual sense of humor. By the time I was six, I could add a page-long column of numbers in my head. I majored in mathematics, attended school at night, while I kept a full-time job, and supported my family. My grade point average was 3.9 out of 4.

None of my math instructors were women either. That's a little risqué. I'm sorry.

Now I only get to use it when I'm showing off.

While I'm showing off, my daughter has the gift too, and she puts it to much better use than I do. William, you may remember my daughter. She's a few years younger than you are, but she was one of the tallest women that every majored in accounting at Wheaton. She was on the basketball team too.

<Rennie>: She sounds like someone I would like to know.

<Sharf>: *Never. I have to keep them apart.*

I know she wasn't cheating, but I don't care. With her body, she didn't need the grades. She was interfering with my plans, she was a show-off (just as you are), and her gorilla attacked me.

I tutored a tall g-, woman, but her name Frey.

<HM>: Maybe she was using Frey-Marshall. Many people stop at the hyphen. *I have to talk to Indy. This is more than a little problem with grades.*

<Rennie>: *William looks funny.*

<Sharf>: *He's toying with me. Perhaps he isn't. He's actually curious.* I seldom forget anything, but it takes me longer to remember things that happened half a lifetime ago. We can discuss that when it comes to me.

<Rennie>: *He's lying.*

Let's get back on track. If the system was up, could you show us real numbers?

<Hank>: We can find a terminal that is linked to production and show you now?

<Sharf>: If the system was up, we would be getting off track again.

<Hank>: *H was doing something. Maybe I can get him to explain it to me later.*

The next topic is Governance.

GOVERNANCE AND SOA EVOLUTION

<Hank>: BASE Governance:

1. Includes service, data, and methodology governance.
2. Guides the WFSOA methodology evolution.
3. Gathers, synchronizes, organizes, and presents the information necessary to ensure that governance structures work within Daxiao.
4. Reports on the progress of the BASE Program.
5. Promotes continuous process improvement, using incremental changes, rebel guidance, and grumble files.
6. Promotes reuse of everything that may be reused.
7. Supports compliance and audit requirements, by:
   - Providing guidance and mentoring.
   - Performing corporate audits.
   - Performing technology audits to ensure global application of technical standards and processes.
   - Performing self-audits.
   - Coordinating external audit procedures.
8. Automates processes and procedures for all areas of governance.

9. Applies value chain concepts to product development and ensures availability of information that supports value-added concepts.
10. Provides rebel guidance.
11. Delivers enabling products at the best possible cost.

<Sharf>: Why isn't data governance under Armstrong?

<HM>: Our work requires that we resolve business data conflicts more often than technology issues. Lorrie has the data domain owners, and I have governance experience and compliance.

<Rennie>: What is rebel guidance?

<HM>: It is impossible to maintain a staff with as many hyper-talented people as we have without having people who resist the status quo. Many rebels are visionaries. We monitor rebellion and use it as input to continuous process improvement.

<Sharf>: Add that to questions for later.

<Hank>: If you are willing to look at our SOA methodology evolutionary stages in Tables A.4, which we tried to show you a while ago, you will see how BASE works with the other governance areas to promote our evolutionary methodology. You will also see where the six process clusters in the other two domains fit.

<Sharf>: Proceed if it will save time.

<Rennie>: Don't skim over your standards process.

<Hank>: Notice in Table A.4 that SOA governance first assumed its role in 2003. We mentioned that most of Daxiao has evolved to Stage 3.

<Sharf>: I don't see your team in Stage #1. What were you doing then?

<HM>: We were part of corporate governance.

<Rennie>: What did your emblem look like then?

<HM>: We didn't have an emblem, but if we had, it would probably have looked like Fig. 10 on the next page.

<Rennie>: It was sloppy, unbalanced, and lopsided.

<HM>: The notes provide a kinder description. Except for Human Resources Support, many processes were in place. I knew exactly what was wrong, in excruciating detail, but I could only make recommendations. I didn't have the authority or the funding to fix it. We didn't have a sufficient mandate for enforcement until SOX. For the record, we still don't have an SOA mandate.

<Sharf>: Why? *I have to consider whether I want a mandate. The looser things are the more money I can make helping them to fix it.*

<HM>: Once we achieve a critical mass for WFSOA, it will be mandated.

Furthermore, SOA caught on across the industry last year. If Justin hears more about it at the club, it may become a mandate and that will accelerate reaching a critical mass.

If I wanted to fight for a mandate, I'd show them everything I'm doing and more people than Gunnar would know what we've achieved. I'd waste energy on stupid battles.

<Sharf>: *I could shut it down and make them pay me to start over my way. It would never happen, but the idea is extraordinarily tempting.*

<Rennie>: When do you achieve the service-oriented enterprise (SOE)?

<HM>: We will have achieved SOE at the end of Evolutionary Stage 4. We have two areas experimenting with on-demand processes, but it is still in the realm of research and development.

<Hank>: Rennie, you mentioned standards. That happens to be one of my team's specialties. William, should we address that topic?

Standards Management

<Sharf>: Give the high level. Rennie's people may come back for the details. *If they know anything that we don't, it will be good for my people. If they don't, we can emphasize Daxiao's standards problems.*

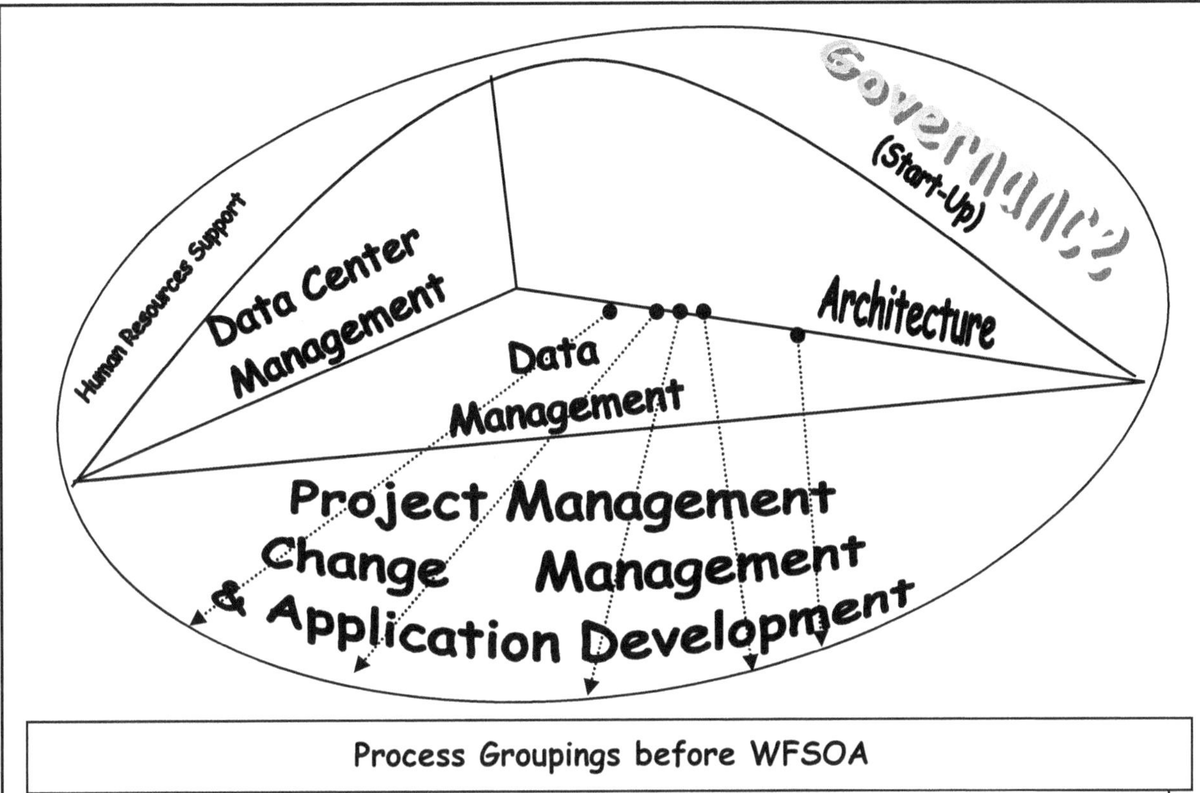

Process Groupings before WFSOA

Notes:

- Formal governance was beginning to take shape.
- The process groups were fluid, and depended on the personal preferences of business and technology managers.
- Architecture had disproportionate influence on application decisions.
- The quality of project management, change management, and application development varied across technology teams.
- Data management support varied across development teams.

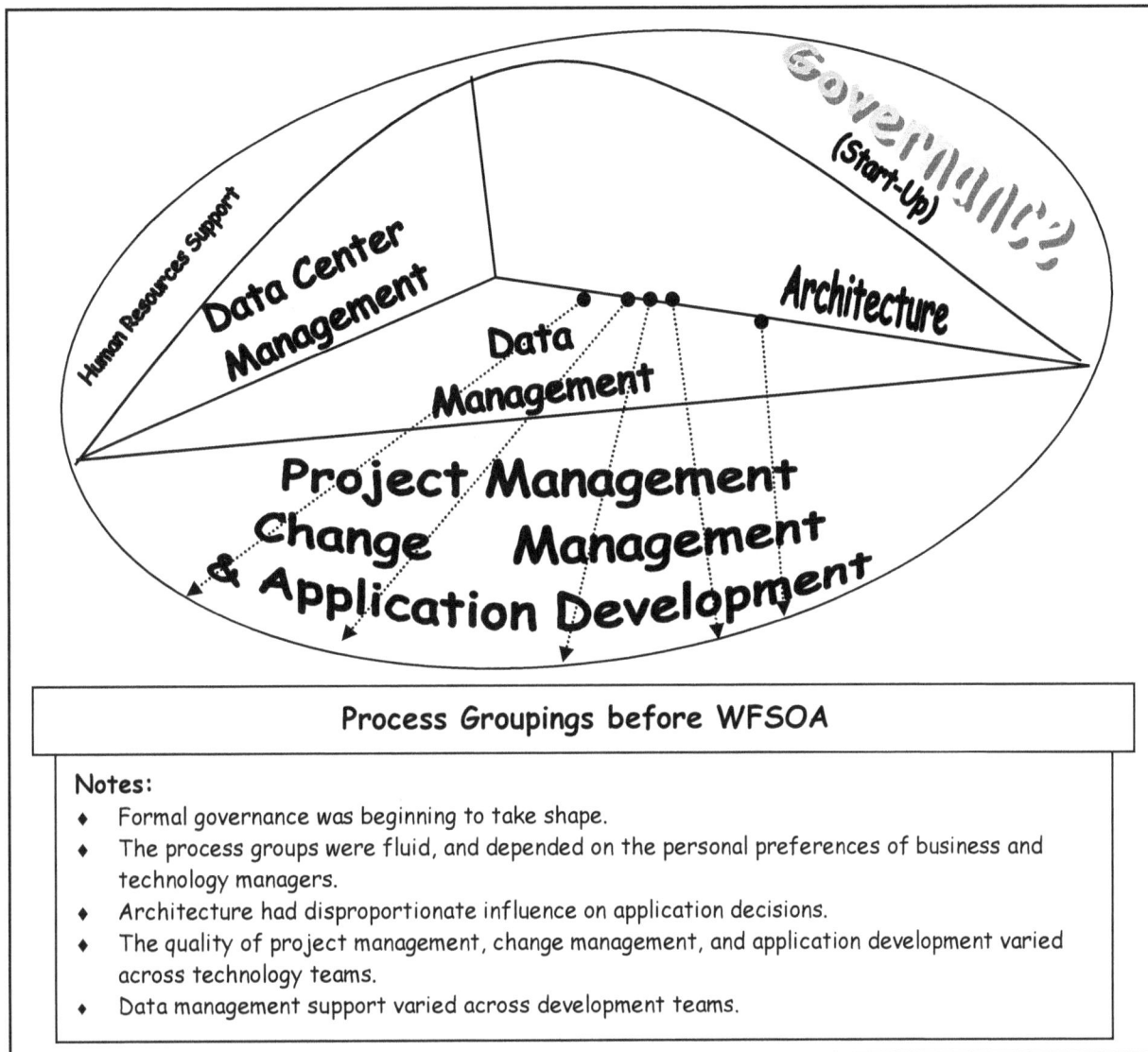

Fig. 10 - **Daxiao Process Groupings until 2003 (Pre-SOA)**

<Hank>: The three primary groupings of activities for standards management are:

1. Implementation.
2. Compliance Monitoring.
3. External Oversight:
   - Watch list (overlaps, gaps, evolving standards).
   - Committee participation.
   - Vendor watch.

We track standards in the following categories:

1. Business Processes.
2. Description and Discovery.
3. Interoperability.
4. Messaging.
5. Reliability.
6. Security (major emphasis).
7. Service management.
8. Transactions.
9. Transport.

<Rennie>: That's great.

<Sharf>: *Ho-Hum.*

<Hank>: We track standards from the Internet Engineering Task Force (IETF), International Standards Organization/International Electrotechnical Commission (ISO/IEC), OASIS, the Object Management Group (OMG), and the

World Wide Web (W3C). Lists of the standards that we monitor are presented in Tables A.6.1 through A.6.5. We also interact with the Liberty Alliance.

<Sharf>: *Overdone, as they tend to do. My people seldom mention ISO standards except for ISO 9000.* Do you adhere to all those ISO standards?

<Hank>: We need to keep up with what is happening around the world, not just here in the U.S. ISO/IEC supports that requirement. Furthermore, security and privacy standards are stricter outside the U.S. Some of our European partners are legally forbidden to let us have access to their customer information. ISO/IEC helps us to understand their concerns.

<Sharf>: Which ones affect you now?

<Hank>: The roles/training disciplines table (Table A.15.1) lists the standards applicable to each role.

<Sharf>: With all this, you left out the Java standards. *Ādaemoa tried to catch us on that one too.*

<Hank>: Java standards are for a specific platform. We participate in the Java Community Process, and I'll make a note to forward a list to Dr. Piccolo or Dr. Emery-Baldwin for you.

<Rennie>: How do you work with open source?

<Hank>: That would be a diversion from a diversion. We use open source because our partners use open source. It is a major part of our research effort. Selected products have been rolled into the Daxiao internal environment.

<HM>: He's trying to restrain himself. That is one of his personal obsessions. It allows us to save millions in procurement dollars. We spend some of that money on "OOPS" and "ALMOST", but we are ahead of the game. Please talk to Hank about it during your follow-up interviews. It would be a good idea to bring someone to take notes for Rennie.

Table 10 - WS-Interoperability Roles and Responsibilities

Role	WS-I Responsibility
Architect - availability	♦ Contribute WS-I test cases ♦ Support WS-I testing and review test results
Architect - enterprise technology	♦ Ensure environments conform to SOA reference architecture
Architect - infrastructure	♦ Assist with environment for WS-I testing
Architect - network	♦ Build/ensure network requirements for WS-I testing
Architect - SOA	♦ Contribute WS-I test cases ♦ Review interoperability test plans ♦ Verify interoperability testing
Client - partner	♦ Collaborate in interoperability testing
Compliance specialist - technology	♦ Review WS-I test results
Developer - SOA	♦ Contribute WS-I test cases
Domain owner - service	♦ Ensure interoperability testing is completed
Project initiation manager	♦ Include estimates for interoperability testing
Project manager - SOA	♦ Ensure interoperability testing is completed
Quality management coordinator	♦ Enable interoperability testing ♦ Track problems and their resolutions
Risk analyst - technology	♦ Review WS-I test results
Security administrator	♦ Support WS-I security testing
Security specialist	♦ Define requirements for WS-I security testing ♦ Contribute WS-I security test cases ♦ Review test results
SOA technology specialist	♦ Contribute test cases ♦ Review test results
Technology process coordinator	♦ Include WS-I test processes in Program Methodology
Testing specialist - technology	♦ Create test cases, scripts, and plans ♦ Automate where possible ♦ Execute tests and capture results

<**Hank**>: That is his way of saying that we should move on. I will send information about our participation in the Open Source Initiative (OSI)

WS-Interoperability (WS-I)

<**Hank**>: The WS-Interoperability Basic and Security Profiles are critical in WFSOA. Because WS-I was originally closed to non-IT firms, we tracked them differently, and we continue to do so. H assigned a technology compliance person who focuses only on this.

The activities span the roles/activity list. They are sufficiently important that we extracted them for our presentation (Table 10) on the prior page.

Standards Overlaps and Gaps

<**Sharf**>: I'm sure you had clever ways of dealing with standards. ***My customers are always asking Rennie about this. Now Marshall must mention proprietary implementations.***

<**Hank**>: With hundreds of standards, overlaps are understandable.

It is time-consuming, but dealing with overlaps is relatively straightforward. We pick the one or portions of two or three that work for us. If necessary, we create artifacts to bridge the standards and carefully document our implementations. We use a watch list to monitor our internal results, vendor implementations, industry trends, and standards adjustments. Our use of UDDI and ebXML standards is an example of that.

<**Hank**>: We manage five variations of "gaps" that are increasingly more difficult to handle.

1. Corrections to existing standards (in committee).
2. Additions to existing standards (in committee).
3. New standards -- (areas not previously addressed that are now in committee).
4. Missing portions of existing standards (not in committee).
5. Missing standards (not in committee).

We handle standards through assiduous participation in committee processes.

<**Sharf**>: Why don't you let the vendors handle it?

<**Hank**>: We work on a committee ourselves when we can, and we partner with software vendors who have good ideas and good salespeople. Some may have political or technical constraints in areas of implementation. We contribute to vendors' implementations if they are moving in the directions that we were going in the first place.

Sixty percent of the recommendations that we support become standards. It allows us to minimize proprietary components. At worst, we say that our implementation was in committee, but could not garner enough votes.

<**Rennie**>: Tell him the advantages.

<**Hank**>: Our primary advantage is that we are faster than most people are. Armstrong justified one of the biggest standing research facilities in the industry after 9/11, and we use it to demonstrate the standards that we approve.

We seldom have to buy anything to support standards testing. My people work with infrastructure teams to design plug and play SOA configurations. HM specializes in saving (or attracting) and polishing troubled super nerds with the intelligence that allows us to implement standards recommendations quickly.

<**Rennie**>: How does it work?

<**Hank**>: Suppose we have a knowledgeable person (who coincidentally keyboards well) who is willing to let her- or himself be squeezed into a standards mold from time to time. Our person delivers documented, positive, end-to-end results to a vendor representative who is sitting on a standards committee. That person knows how to promote what we have delivered.

Meanwhile, our favored vendors' peers are trying to convince their companies to cough up the funding for the testing. Given those circumstances, the versions of the standards that we recommend are often approved. We are also ahead of the pack because we know the standard and the vendor's product. We worked with James Daley.

<**Sharf**>: Who is that?

<**Rennie**>: He was my boss when I worked on the WS-I team.

Wow! You're Mister(y) Henry. You did half the work. You were with Goodsand.

<Hank>: I was with the Goodsand division of Daxiao.

<Rennie>: In exchange for the effort that you spend assisting committees, could minimize proprietary implementations.

<Sharf>: How would you handle the situation where a standard is missing?

<Hank>: We find a vendor who will submit a proposal for us.

<Sharf>: What if you can't "influence" a committee to your way of thinking. You're a long way from ISO.

<Hank>: We evaluate the vendor and committee preferences, adapt our direction, and then offer our assistance to a proposal that has a chance of winning.

<HM>: Every new product that we install conforms to a standard, if a standard (or standards) exists. When clients make requests that require non-conforming products, we educated them regarding the risks before we spend money. The price goes up significantly if they wish to sponsor non-standard activities. They must be willing to pay to migrate to a standardized product if there is one in the foreseeable future.

<Sharf>: Why don't you stop them?

<HM>: I am often outvoted. If Armstrong is willing to take the risk, I may do nothing other than monitor their progress and apply necessary (legal) controls.

Procurement

<Sharf>: Talk about procurement and the evolutionary process.

<HM>: ***He must have a customer that wants to buy something. That is not anywhere on his original list.***

Hank, eat something. I'll take is from here. It was part of SOA Preparation under Evolutionary Stage #2.

<Sharf>: You were talking about products for SOA software development. ***He's going to slow us down.***

<HM>: I'm talking about hardware, services, and software (whether developed in-house, offshore, or purchased from a vendor). All of them enable the business.

<Sharf>: Hank, add that before he does the presentation again. Clarity is of the essence.

<Hank>: *Gulp!* I'll mention it to Lisse. She normally formats our presentations. ***HM is nodding and smiling again, and he's doing it more than I've ever seen in a single session.***

<Rennie>: ***I saw William become livid when Mr. Cane used similar words with us. Why can't he see that HM is neither off balance nor afraid, and the smile is not real?***

<HM>: Table A.7.1 contains a list of procurement activities in (approximate) sequence. The procurement objective is to obtain reliable products and services from sources we believe to be reliable. Bells and whistles are optional.

Table A.7.2 contains a generic list of the products that our procurement team handles. Notice that we show which ones are specifically for SOA and which ones were improved for either SOX or SOA.

> **Readers:** Business Process Execution Language (BPEL) is a standard for organizing Web services and manual steps in an automated business process.

The procurement process is fully automated.

1. It was modeled using BPEL, and it runs in a BPEL engine.
2. All information required for the procurement process is captured online as close to the point of discovery as possible.
3. Process notifications are automated.
4. Approval requests and approvals are automated.

<Rennie>: Who automated the procurement process?

<HM>: People from each of Daxiao's sectors and most of the units participated in one or both of the following phases.

Phase #1:

1. The procurement specialists provided the initial requirements.
2. The corporate finance specialist dictated the approval process.

3. The corporate architect, the enterprise architect, the compliance specialist (who happened to be a lawyer), the legal department, and the financial specialist (a CPA) reviewed the requirements.
4. Mittelman, Armstrong, Jasper (the CFO), and I funded the development.
5. The software architect designed it.
6. The security specialist applied rigorous security, especially with automated approvals.
7. Distributed systems developers used Enterprise Application Integration (EAI) to link features of products we already had (including ERP purchase functions).
8. The knowledge consolidator and the data specialist designed databases that we needed to maintain state between products.
9. Quality assurance tested the processes.
10. Compliance, procurement, and the CFO's office performed user acceptance testing.
11. Users in each of the business units participated in a second round of user acceptance tests. That was a technique for publicizing the availability of the processes. They provided ease of use recommendations.
12. The deployment specialist and the process coordinators ensured that everyone understood how the processes affected their roles.
13. We provided online training for users and classroom training for critical roles.

Phase #2 - Replacement of EAI links with services.

14. SOA competency team members wrapped ERP functions as services.
15. SOA developers created the services to fill the processing gaps.
16. The process developer coded the BPEL.
17. The data people expanded the state maintenance databases.
18. Then we repeated steps #9 through #13.

<Sharf>: Why didn't you simply buy a product?

<HM>: We have very complicated and very rigorous purchase requirements. We could not find a single product that provided everything that we needed.

<Sharf>: Why didn't you use Web services in the first place?

<HM>: We did not have enough Web services expertise five years ago, and I was not responsible for SOA.

<Sharf>: Why is the knowledge consolidator in the middle of you being in the middle of everything?

<HM>: Data is in the middle of everything, and she is the best data person we have.

<Sharf>: Why isn't she responsible for a Data Management?

<HM>: She is more suited to Information Management.

<Sharf>: How long did it take to finish the first phase?

<HM>: We had a working prototype in two months. We fine-tuned it for a year. In 2003, we used the process to assist WS-BPEL implementation.

<Sharf>: How do you maintain the list of preferred vendors?

<HM>: We maintain a vendor list with positive and negative points. Negative points may cancel positive points. Organizations are ranked according to the net number of points.

<Sharf>: How do you assign negative points?

<HM>: Organizations where we find the biggest gaps between promise and delivery receive large numbers of negative points. *They do what you are doing now.*

<Sharf>: How would you measure the gaps?

<HM>: The criteria vary. For example:

- Consulting organizations that mismanaged a failed project earns hundreds of negative points in proportion to the resources we spent to employ them.
- Organizations that provided "specialists" whose only experience is equivalent to Cram Exams earn negative points in proportion to the time we spend training them or the time that we spend before we allow them to leave.
- Vendors of software products that fail in-house evaluation of documented features earn negative points. If we find the problem before purchase, they receive fewer negative points than if problems are discovered after installation. The more Armstrong or I are

embarrassed or our people are inconvenienced, the more negative points they tend to receive.

- Vendors of hardware that requires service calls and replacement outside an acceptable range receive negative points.

<Sharf>: Can an organization reduce its number of negative points?

<HM>: Points age. We have to allow for vendor learning (especially learning to be honest with us), or product improvements.

<Sharf>: What if an area has the money, they refuse to use your process, and they have the clout to go around you?

<HM>: We removed every valid excuse that they have for doing that? We are fast, our processes are transparent, we have expert and responsive contract negotiators in Legal Services, Armstrong provides excellent testing and installation support, and our selections perform as recommended.

<Sharf>: Has it ever been done? *I'm thinking about somebody like my very persistent brother-in-law.*

<HM>: If happened more often immediately after I assumed the procurement function from Armstrong than it does now. Armstrong was showing people how to avoid the recommended process. Procurement wasn't fully automated, so it was easier for him to justify providing "timely support to critical business requirements".

Half the products were acceptable. Half delivered uncomfortable results, including negative ROI.

If a business unit missed a market opportunity, they blamed Armstrong, and adjusted their contribution to his bonus accordingly. Mittelman's bonus and the business unit bonuses were also adjusted. Armstrong learned the disadvantages of supporting that type of rebellion.

<Sharf>: How would you deal with a situation where clients are going around you?

<HM>: I explain the risks, I monitor, I enforce legal requirements, I report, I provide guidance, and I provide assistance if they request it.

<Sharf>: How good is your procurement rate?

<HM>: The numbers are on the screen.

- 15% exceed expectations.
- 70% meet expectations.
- 10% have unexpected problems that we work around until the vendor fixes them.
- 5% were canceled at the first available opportunity, either because something slipped by, or because something better became available immediately after our purchase.

<Sharf>: *I'll figure out how to spin that so that it sounds bad.* What do you want to discuss next? Notice that I am giving you the option.

Automation of Processes

<HM>: An overview of process automation would logically be next. We firmly believe in using technology for technologist. We give foot coverings to the offspring of the shoemakers.

<Rennie>: The cobbler's children have shoes.

<Hank>: That's what I said. We have automated:

- Approval processes.
- Business reporting (dashboards and scorecards).
- Development methodology and processes.
- Planning (there will be an entire section on this later).
- Quality assurance processes and procedures.
- Requirements gathering.
- Standards compliance monitoring.
- Strategy management and maintenance.

It is less important to remember minute details of every process. The system provides recommendations. We have significantly more automated processes than organizations of equivalent size.

<Sharf>: *Thank goodness, this is moving again. Marshall was putting me to sleep.*

Reuse

Reuse would be next. In addition to software reuse, we promote reusing:

- Data (minimizing data redundancy).
- Quality assurance artifacts.
- Documentation.
- Requirements definitions.
- Plans (we attempt to commoditize planning).

<Sharf>: How do you reuse documentation?

<HM>: The more we standardize and modularize, the easier it is to reuse documentation. If we have settled on a standard definition (or two or three) of an account, and each definition is documented in a central location, no one has to rewrite a definition for account.

People use the centralized common terminology list to discover meanings that are relevant to their areas of interest. The metadata repository and the SOA catalog have the same meanings and the same relationship in every one of our development areas. Users may also enter requests in Spanish or Chinese, and find equivalent definitions.

Continuous Process Improvement

<Hank>: Process improvement techniques vary according to the situation. The first set supports incremental process improvement.

<HM>: These people are not very aggressive about change. They have good ideas, but they are not interested in rocking the boat. They regularly produce results that are a little better or deliver results bit faster. Some of them understand features or benefits of the technology that their peers don't understand and we missed. Some find holes in the processes we deliver and produced work-around processes. Whenever Macedon and I find them, we bring the people into the lab, and we encourage them to tell us what needs to be fixed. Then they work with us to deliver improvements.

Support and Guidance for Rebels (a.k.a. Visionaries)

<HM>: We are back to this again. Hank, finish your meal.

We call the next group of people rebels. Many people believe they have better ideas in an organization with as many talented people as Daxiao. They strongly resist prescribed processes and procedures and about 15% of the time, they have a better idea, but they need to make the idea fit into the overall picture.

We also bring them to the lab and give them an opportunity to create new or improved processes. They provide input to process modeling and testing. We've found many good ideas from new hires using that technique.

<Sharf>: What about the other 85% of the time.

<HM>: We provide training and guidance in the recommended processes. We explain why every internal standard was implemented and the consequences to the Program of non-compliance.

<Rennie>: What happens if they continue to resist.

<HM>: If they cannot show us how their way is better, they must comply with standards. They may also seek employment at a company with standards that they like, or they may start their own companies.

<Sharf>: You could be losing good people. ***I have on several occasions.***

<HM>: No matter how good they are, if their actions cause inconvenience for too many other people, they eventually have a net negative value. For instance, the most compact routine in the world will have no value if at least two other people do not know where to find it, or cannot figure out how to maintain it.

<Sharf>: How can you always be certain that your ways are better? ***Most of them seem ridiculous.***

<HM>: Our ways are not always better. However, in our game, we reserve the right to make the rules.

<Sharf>: You resist beneficial change.

<HM>: We balance innovation with effectiveness. Daxiao technologists, as a group, have seen more things that worked incorrectly than a single person would see. Our people are more likely to know what works here.

<Hank>: The most important thing is that we never toss out a recommendation. If we discover that a suggestion was ahead of its time, we re-evaluate it, and we try to ensure that the appropriate individual is rewarded for the suggestion.

The Grumble Application

<HM>: Though some people have perpetually negative personalities, we have also learned that grumblers:

1. Provide the first indications when a project is starting to have troubles.
2. Provide real-time input when a process is not working, technically or due to staff resistance.

To garner maximum benefit from grumblers, we have created a "Grumble Application". It supports formatted input to grumble files. Every grumble is recorded, indexed, and archived.

The "Grumble" application may capture problems when they occur in any production processes (corporate, manufacturing, or IT).

We decide, more quickly than our competitors can, whether a problem is cause by process installation, the process, the documentation of the process, or the skill level of the process participant.

The Grumble process includes:

1. The Grumble application where we capture formatted input.
2. For people who do not have dedicated input devices, there is a station that runs Grumble within 30 feet of everyone's work location.
3. E-mail: individuals may send messages to grumbledetail@Daxiao.com.
4. Snail mail: They mail complaints to the Grumble Department here in New York.
5. Grumble boxes: People may drop messages into grumble boxes located in camera-free locations in all our facilities.
6. Telephone: People may call in a grumble.
7. Handheld devices and PDAs.
8. Formal problem discussion meetings.

<Sharf>: You organized whistle blowing.

<Hank>: We make COSO very happy by collecting and acting upon positive recommendations.

<HM>: Some people use it to try to get revenge for real or imagined slights. We discourage that. It is difficult to maintain a balance, but we try.

<Rennie>: You must protect the integrity of the process, or no one would use it.

<HM>: I insist on protecting the integrity of BASE. Wouldn't you do the same Mr. Sharf?

<Sharf>: Definitely. ***The dean said something very similar to that. Those broads made him signal me out. Everyone assisted his or her favorites. It was easier to hide when you graded essays or team projects.***

<Hank>: ***William flinched again. I wonder why that's happening.***

PLANNING, ACTION LISTS, REUSE, AND COMMON TERMINOLOGY

<HM>: The planning-related processes I am about to discuss are among the things we do best. We enable light and effective planning with feedback loops that promote continuous process improvement.

Van Amberg will discuss the BASE Program Plan later.

<Sharf>: If Jasper controls the money and Armstrong has more people, how is it that you control SOA Program and project planning?

<HM>: After putting my size 14 foot in my mouth, I used the results of a life-long hobby remove it. It is an extreme example of reuse.

<Sharf>: ***He admits to playing at work.*** That should be interesting.

<HM>: Stay with me while we discuss Planning History. Plans must include work assignments, and we do role-based planning.

<Sharf>: It sounds like serious "How Did You". Proceed.

<Hank>: There was an apparent problem after Goodsand and Daxiao merged. Daxiao had a simpler technology environment than we did, a less expensive work force, and manufactured high volumes of simpler products. The Board pretended they wanted to decide whether to upgrade Daxiao or simplify Goodsand.

Both groups wanted to know why Goodsand spent $1.6 billion on technology, and we had 62,000 people, and Daxiao was spending $400 million on technology and supporting 28,000 people. I showed that 7,000 of their people (who became our people) were doing work that we did with computers. If each of those people earned only $20,000 each year, that would have evened the technology ratio.

<HM>: However, with the computing services available in the original Daxiao, it would have been impossible to hire enough people to produce products at the level of sophistication that we had in Goodsand. They needed our computing capabilities, and we needed extra workers and manufacturing capacity.

The logic was sound, but Daxiao was offended.

1. They wanted to see details to explain the disparities.
2. We received a SOX mandate soon afterward, so the requirement had more weight.
3. They wanted to treat technology as an assembly line, just as Web services were making it more complicated, and before Armstrong could demonstrate the proposed benefits.
4. Armstrong was promoting agile techniques with minimal planning.
5. The manufacturing people on both sides suggested that if the technology teams had to plan as accurately as they did, there would be fewer disparities.
6. All future funding would be connected to a plan. Because our estimates always came in higher, they wanted any historical documentation to justify how we planned.

<Sharf>: That must have annoyed the technology types.

<HM>: It certainly did. However, we caught our technology people in that one. They were less ready than I was. When I provided the numbers to justify our expenditures, they decided I was the logical one to provide planning support for everyone. They put me in the position to become everyone's salvation or everybody's bottleneck.

<Sharf>: How did you survive? ***He is made of Teflon. I will find better glue.***

<HM>: I am proud to say that my quirky obsession, the Grand Master Planning History and Action List for All IT Related Activities, provided a foundation for resolution of the problem. The Grand Master Plan was the hobby that I had been working on for 35 years at the time.

In addition to saving my hide, it improved technology and financial planning, facilitated role descriptions, supported ROI calculations, assisted skill assessments, training, and performance reviews. It identified best practices, and promoted common terminology. It is impossible to get more reuse out of noxious planning activities than we have.

So far, it has 78% success in the U.S., Canada, and Ireland, 54% success in Mexico, and 41% (and growing) success in Asia, with an overall average of 55%.

<Rennie>: ***Now it looks like HM is trying to annoy Will.***

<Sharf>: Are you saying that you merged a hobby with the SOA Program?

<Hank>: This occurred before SOA and provided part of the foundation for SOA.

<Sharf>: Prove it.

<HM>: I will start with a sidetrack, which is not actually a sidetrack. Before I joined Goodsand, I worked at what is now called technical writing for a group of unbundled IBM employees. They pooled their resources and started a company whose mission was to plan the installations of their first computer systems. My job was to prepare the proposals after my bosses returned from meetings with corporate executives.

Every proposal included a plan. Every plan had the same basic features, whether they were automating banks, cable manufacturers, or tobacco companies.

I never saw their master plan, but I could guess how it must have looked because of the documents I had to prepare. The version that I pieced together became the first Marshall (***technology***) plan. I took it with me when I left and went to the Northeast Telephone Company.

I was still primarily a technical writer, but my job was to produce a PERT chart for their first IMS database project. It was a customer records system. That plan was extremely detailed. It had 1000 lines in the work breakdown structure, and the PERT chart covered a table that was about 12 feet long. I fished a copy out of the garbage every time they printed a new one.

[...] Please, be patient. I am trying to answer questions about my ridiculous hobby before you ask them.

I merged the original Marshall plan and the customer records plan, and I called it "THE" plan. Since then, at least in my mind, there has been **ONLY ONE COMPUTER-RELATED PLAN IN THE ENTIRE WORLD,** just as there is only one basic plan for a tree. Depending upon the environment where the tree evolved, the roots and the branching structure may be different, but a tree is a tree.

I learned enough from NTC AND their plan enhancements to convince the grandparent company of Daxiao to let me have a job as a keypunch operator/junior database programmer and general gopher (*Val's recommendation definitely helped*). From the vantage point of a data entry clerk, I knew when a project was in trouble. If senior people were using a version of "THE" plan, the project felt right. If they didn't, I tried to sneak in plan steps while they weren't looking. I would ask questions about who was responsible for items in "THE" plan. I became the person who asked embarrassing questions in meetings. I was often in political trouble, but a few projects succeeded that may not have otherwise.

<Sharf>: How long did it take you to move from gopher to golden plan retriever?

<HM>: *I will ignore the allusion.* It took me five years (allowing for my political ineptitude) before I reached the point where I was responsible for my own planning within Goodsand.

<Sharf>: What was in this magic plan? Speed it up. This is the same as watching grass growing.

<HM>: *I can't let this upset me. I've been dealing with his type from the first time the Queen left me in a room alone with Richard. He bit me and I banged him on the temple with the corner of a block. When the Queen returned, we were both crying. I'll arrange a political block for Sharf.*

<Sharf>: *I hit a sore spot. Good!*

<Hank>: *That was the wrong thing to say. H is already in a bad mood.*

<Rennie>: *That was rude. I feel so sorry for HM and for Belvedere. We are in trouble!*

"THE" Plan

<HM>: "The" plan has the critical activities of every good plan that you have ever seen, *if you have ever seen any good plans*. The difference is that it always has extra steps supporting project communications, as my first bosses emphasized. I didn't realize that until Lisse pointed it out to me. Table 11 contains anglicized versions of "THE" project plan

I promised you roles. This version has been updated with Daxiao role names.

The activities without which the project will be most likely to fail are presented in bold.

Table 11 - The Only Plan (Business Systems Planning, Management, and Communications)

Activity	Responsible Role(s) in Daxiao
1. Propose work	Client
2. Determine whether something already exists that will do the work	Project initiation manager
3. Publish the first plan (Table 11 is a skeleton)	**Project initiation manager**
4. Make sure the proposed work has a sponsor	Project initiation manager
5. Find stakeholders	**Business analyst, project initiation manager**
6. Discover approvers (start with business and compliance people)	Project initiation manager
7. Ensure that everyone understands and agrees to what they must do to ensure success	**Project initiation manager**
8. Find out what the clients/users/sponsors want	Business analyst(s)
9. Educate (or train) everyone that needs education or training	**Training specialist, SOA technology specialist, subject matter experts**
10. Make sure everybody understands what they are asking for	Requirements analyst
11. Make sure everyone understands the potential impact of what is wanted.	Requirements analyst
12. Make sure everyone agrees on what they want	Project initiation manager

13. Agree that the proposed work may be secured	Security specialist
14. Agree that the proposed work may be tested	Client(s), business analyst(s), testing specialist(s)
15. Agree that the proposed work may be run in production	Architect(s)
16. Make sure it agrees with business and technology strategy	Requirements analyst, corporate strategist
17. Agree on what you will call the project	Clients, project initiation manager
18. Tell everyone	BASE communications specialist
19. Handle political situations and resistance	**Project initiation manager, clients, stakeholders**
20. Find out who will use it, how often, and where	Business analyst(s)
21. Identify external interface requirements (to other projects and to support teams)	Business analyst(s), Requirements analyst, planning specialist
22. Find out what information (data) is required	Business analyst(s), data specialist, data domain owner
23. Agree upon information quality requirements	Clients, business analyst(s), data specialist
24. Find out what will be necessary to acquire the necessary information (data)	Clients, business analyst(s), data specialist
25. Find out how secure the system needs to be (this was less of a problem when data was locked in the mainframe)	Security specialist - technology, compliance specialist - technology
26. Agree on how everyone will know if the (application, program, service, process, etc., is correct)	**Requirements analyst**
27. Decide whether you will build or buy the software to do the work	Architect(s)
28. Agree to reliability, availability, and performance requirements	Client(s), sponsor(s), availability architect
29. Decide if you will need new hardware, software, or skills - networking was added later	Requirements analyst, architect(s)
30. Agree on who will do the work	Project initiation manager, client(s), project manager(s)
31. Agree on where it will run (platform)	Architect(s), team leader
32. Agree on what you are going to use to build software	Architect(s)
33. Agree upon the development methodology	Software architect, technology process specialist
34. Buy what you need	Procurement specialist, tool administrator
35. Recommend reuse of processing components (services or legacy components)	Requirements analyst
36. Prototype to verify client requirements and tool performance	SOA technology specialist
37. Define plan dependencies	Planning specialist, project initiation manager, requirements analyst
38. Estimate the cost for plan implementation	Planning specialist, project initiation manager, requirements analyst
39. Identify and communicate risks and risk handling techniques	Risk analyst(s), security specialist
40. Find other stakeholders	**Business analyst, project initiation manager**
41. Ensure that everyone understands and agrees to what they must do to ensure success	**Project initiation manager**
42. Monitor political climate (handle resistance)	**Client(s), sponsor(s), project initiation manager, stakeholders**
43. Get financial approvals	Project initiation manager, client(s)
44. Discover additional approvers (add technology and process coordinators to the group)	Project initiation manager, BASE Program coordinator

45. Assign technology project manager	Executive - technology, executive - governance
46. Update the plan and plan dependencies	**Project initiation manager, planning specialist**
47. Agree that there is agreement on all the above	**Client(s), sponsor(s), project initiation manager, stakeholders, BASE Program coordinator, project manager**
48. Educate (or train) everyone that needs education or training	**Training specialist, SOA technology specialist, subject matter experts**
Handover to Technology	
49. Move project to "Development" phases	Project initiation manager, project managers
50. Find a team to do the work	Project manager, executives (technology & base), Human Resources Support, procurement specialist
51. Update the plan - emphasize business dependencies	**Project manager, business process coordinator, SOA financial specialist**
52. Update the plan	**SOA financial specialist**
53. Ensure that everyone understands and agrees to what they must do to ensure success	**Project manager**
54. Verify reuse recommendations	Software architect
55. Agree on how the users will use the system (input and output).	User interface specialist
56. Understand how automation will affect existing processes	Business process coordinator
57. Agree (again) on information/data requirements.	**Client(s), software architect, data specialist, data domain owner (if applicable), data administrator**
58. Approve iterations (if appropriate)	Client(s), sponsor(s), project initiation manager, Software architect, project manager(s)
59. Validate that support teams will be available	Project manager(s)
60. Track and report progress and expenses	Project manager(s), SOA financial specialist
61. Maintain plan	**Project manager(s), SOA financial specialist**
62. Tell everyone about the updated plan.	Project manager(s), BASE communications specialist
63. Maintain political support	**Client(s), sponsor(s), Project initiation manager, stakeholders, project managers, BASE Program coordinator**
64. Tell everyone what you agreed upon	**BASE communications specialist**
65. Update the plan	**Project manager, business process coordinator, SOA financial specialist**
66. Agree that there is agreement on all the above	**Client(s), sponsor(s), Project initiation manager, stakeholders, BASE Program coordinator, project manager(s)**
67. Track and report progress	Project manager(s)
68. Discover more approvers (add testers to the group)	Project initiation manager, project manager(s)
69. Educate (or train) everyone that needs education or training	**Training specialist, SOA technology specialist, subject matter experts**
70. Maintain plan	Project manager(s), SOA financial specialist
71. Maintain political support (handle resistance)	**Client(s), sponsor(s), Project initiation manager, stakeholders, project managers, BASE Program coordinator**
72. Discover approvers (add process coordinators)	Project initiation manager, client(s), project managers
73. Buy whatever additional things you may need	Procurement specialist, tool administrator
74. Hire if you must	Personnel specialist, project manager(s)
75. Ensure that everyone understands and agrees to what they must do to ensure success	**Business process coordinator, project manager, deployment specialist**
76. Create processing artifacts	Developer(s), SOA technology specialist, Developer -

	process, tool specialist
77. Glue the pieces together	Integration specialist, infrastructure architect
78. Notify data center of support requirements	Project manager
79. Make sure you have the data that you need.	Team leader, data specialist, data domain owner (if applicable), data administrator
80. Test the business processing requirements	Developer(s), SOA technology specialist, quality management coordinator, testing specialist - business
81. Expand the test environment	Infrastructure architect, quality management coordinator
82. Test to see whether the pieces work together (process and information)	Integration specialist, technology testing specialist
83. Test to see whether the pieces work in the place where they are supposed to run.	Technology testing specialist, infrastructure architect
84. Prepare a production environment	Infrastructure architect
85. Let users try the new system	Deployment specialist, process coordinator, user support specialist
86. Cycle through approvers until they agree	**Project manager(s), quality management coordinator, user support specialist**
87. Maintain political support (handle resistance)	**Client(s), sponsor(s), Project initiation manager, project managers, BASE Program coordinator**
88. Prepare for deployment	Deployment specialist
89. Agree that the proposed work is ready for delivery	**Client(s), sponsor(s), stakeholders, Project initiation manager, BASE Program coordinator, project manager**
90. Update the plan	**Project manager, business process coordinator, SOA financial specialist**
91. Agree that there is agreement on all the above	**Client(s), sponsor(s), Project initiation manager, stakeholders, BASE Program coordinator, project manager**
92. Tell everyone what you agreed upon	BASE communications specialist
93. Educate (or train) everyone that needs education or training	**Training specialist, SOA technology specialist, subject matter experts**
94. Schedule data center support	Infrastructure project manager, service assurance
Move to Production	
95. Ensure that everyone understands and agrees to what they must do to ensure success	**Business process coordinator, project manager, deployment specialist**
96. Place the proposed work where it will run	Deployment specialist
97. Let people know they can get to what they need from the system	Deployment specialist, process coordinator, user support specialist
98. Make sure the right people can access what they need.	Security administrator
99. Help people use what they need.	User support specialist
100. Track problems and solutions.	Availability architect, help desk, project managers, service assurance
101. Agree that all the above are completed	**Client(s), sponsor(s), project initiation manager, project manager, BASE Program coordinator**
102. Finish (post-implementation review and turnover)	Project Manager(s), domain owner(s)
103. Iterate	If iterations were recommended when the project was assigned to the product creation team

<Rennie>: The deliverables are missing.

<Hank>: The Role/Activity List will have hundreds of deliverables.

<Sharf>: You reworded PMI (Project Management Institute) concepts, except that the line where you turn over to development is in the wrong place, and security and testing are much too early.

We can show you how to you fix that. Some of the names of the roles are a little strange too. Otherwise, why did you bother?

<HM>: It was always necessary for me to perform ahead of PMI. For example, we have been managing SOA projects four years.

Yet, PMI ideas always seemed very similar to the ideas of the people who taught me. That is why Daxiao has sent hundreds of managers to PMI training. Every manager on my team is certified.

<Sharf>: They are the standard!

<HM>: I have not finished answering your question. I saw my first technology plan in 1967. I began working on PERT charts in 1969, which is when PMI started. PMI appeared on my radar in 1978. By then, I had already implemented successful plans for transaction processing systems using CICS on IMS databases.

By 1978, I had loaded all the roles and actions for "THE" plan into my own experimental database where I could sort them and mix and match any way that I wanted to. VisiCalc came out a year later and Lotus 1-2-3 in 1983. I changed the names of tasks and roles to fit the environment (as I had learned to do five years earlier). I was golden enough that they overlooked a few rough edges.

Every successive plan helped me to become better at planning (*so did my Nicky plans*). Eventually, I could put together a basic plan for some of the most complicated projects with less than a week of effort. After 15 years, my planning involved removal of sections of the work breakdown structure from "THE" master plan, changing the names of the roles to conform as well as possible to the roles (or missing roles) du jour, changing the terminology to accommodate the most recent technology, and adding or removing side branches as necessary. It's easier to drop unnecessary steps from a plan than it is to add them back later.

<Sharf>: It sounds like you were overdoing it.

<HM>: I was often accused of over planning, but I am happy to say that no project that I managed from the beginning ever failed. *That hurt me because they left me in the pits for another 15 years. My job was usually to fix the projects that were failing.*

Entire programs such as SOA are more difficult, but you are here, and you will help us to get it right. *I hope I didn't sound too sarcastic.*

Planning (*Thunking*) to BIG SOA

<Rennie>: How large is "The" Plan now?

<HM>: It is huge. In the last 35 years, I have created, been responsible for, or audited more than 1,000 plans. I kept copies of them all. The maximum number of combinations of **role/activity verb/action object** expanded from 1,000 to 1,500 when we started transaction processing. It doubled when we added client/server and the corresponding network and security requirements. Web services added a few hundred.

When I gave it to Daxiao, there were approximately 4,000 role/action verb/action object combinations and there were approximately 40 technical roles.

The biggest jump in the number of combinations occurred with SOA. It requires a higher-level organizational view and detailed requirements simultaneously.

<Hank>: When it hit 7,000 lines, we started calling it the ***THUNK*** list because it allowed us to run SOA in a much larger business space, and across diverse technical platforms.

<Sharf>: What is thunk?

<Rennie>: As with converting from 16-bit to 32-bit operating systems, you had to address a lot more issues.

<HM>: *I really like her. If Gunnar wasn't trying to set me up, they could have sent her without Sharf.* BASE planning requires selection of necessary and sufficient actions from a list of over 8,000 combinations and ensuring that there are people who have accepted responsibility for all these assignments. The list you will receive has 10,000+ planning entries. Be aware that it is inflated due to the approvals that Lorrie made us insert.

> **Readers**: The list is in SOA P (2), SOA Planning. A sample appears in Table A.7.1 that deals with

procurement.

<Sharf>: How did you expect people to deal with a list of 8,000 actions (not counting the approvals)?

<HM>: Only my people or Macedon's people have to understand all 8,000 combinations of role, action verb, and action object. However, the information is available to everyone who wishes to see it.

<Sharf>: It is available only when Maja is not playing.

<Hank>: *HM stopped nodding and raised his left eyebrow. I must keep him from saying something that will get us in a worse situation than we have already.*

The production version is available on the production system. Daxiao managers and planners know how to use virtual queries to link older roles to current task descriptions. You will not have to do that.

<HM>: Finish your lunch and don't worry about William's friendly barbs. He wishes to keep control of the situation while tricking me into providing more information than I normally would. I'm beginning to develop special feelings for him.

<Rennie>: *He heard the fool talking about him.*

<Hank>: *You want to bury him alive.*

<Sharf>: *I wonder if he has the motel rooms bugged.* I am sorry if I'm being a little rough. One does what one must do to reach the bottom of difficult situations.

<HM>: There is nothing to fathom. We will provide you with a list such as you have never seen before - something that you did not know you would receive, three days earlier than the original plan (five if you count weekends), and she rescheduled while she was on vacation.

Project Size Fallacy!

<Sharf>: *I have you off balance. Good.*

You haven't mentioned project size yet?

<HM>: I wanted to see if you would notice. This is one of the critical lessons that most our people have accepted. I will pass it along to you because I want you to make it stick after I leave, whenever I leave. *You can see his heart pumping through his shirt.*

<Sharf>: Let me hear it.

<HM>: Our planning people **tried to create** 21 generic software development plans and a lesser number of infrastructure plans. The software development plans included:

- Small, medium, and large mainframe plans.
- Small, medium, and large distributed systems plans.
- Small, medium, and large cross-platform plans (mainly Enterprise Application Integration at first).
- Small, medium, and large Web plans.
- Small, medium, and large Infrastructure plans.
- Small, medium, and large data plans.
- Small and medium SOA plans.
- Umbrella (synchronization plans).

<Sharf>: Where is the large SOA plan?

<HM>: There was no large SOA plan. We mentioned that earlier.

<Sharf>: What do you mean when you said **they tried**?

<HM>: It didn't work because they were trying to repeat what we have **done wrong** during the entire history of data processing (I mean IT). They were allowing business and IT management to decide how long an effort should take before they decided what they were going to do.

The 21-plan structure perpetuated that **erroneous** approach to planning. If the size of a plan is determined by duration and resource utilization, there was no way to know the size of a plan until after the plan is completed.

<Sharf>: You must be able to estimate.

<HM>: We do. We start out with the Daxiao modification of the Grand Master Plan for Almost Everything. All our new plans are **large** until a planning specialist or a financial specialist can prove otherwise.

It includes the management/communications module, and it contains the technology branches. Then the business and technology people tell us what to delete. Alternatively, they may select a plan for a similar **successful** project from the archive, and adapt it to project requirements. If there is no similar **successful** plan, they all start as big plans.

<Sharf>: That takes extra time. How do you justify that?

<HM>: It saves time. We have the right-sizing process refined so that we can customize complicated manual plans using only a person-week of effort. The automated ones require less than two days.

<Sharf>: Where did you secure the funding for the extra planning time?

<HM>: Though we were in better shape than most of the industry, about 50% of our projects were overspending their budgets by an average of 25%. Jasper and the Board had an IT contingency budget exactly for that purpose.

We showed them that they were using more of the contingency funds than was necessary. We suggested that they should:

1. Allocate 10% of the contingency money for additional planning.
2. Move half of the contingency into the official project budgets.

<Hank>: Using this technique, projects tend to overrun by 10% or less. Consider these numbers:

1. Suppose each project which is estimated to require one year of effort (2 months planned duration with six people) actually takes 1.25 years of effort (an overran of two weeks per person.
2. Suppose we added six (6) weeks (one week per person) into the original plan, and the project came in on time.
3. Suppose we spent a week right sizing the master plan and guaranteeing resources with the appropriate skill levels (*that would be excessive*).
4. That saves five (5) weeks of effort for one project.
   - This is time developers spent ensuring users agreed to the content of prototype screens before the entire team spent time supporting extra builds.
   - This is time that QA people did not spend waiting for test cases to be loaded into the database.
   - This is time that the user acceptance team did not spend waiting for system access.
   - This is time that people did not spend pointing fingers at each other.
5. If each individual worked on five such projects each year, that would be a give back of a month per person each year.
6. Since a little more than half of our people use this planning process, we save 171+ staff-years.

<HM>: Of the ones that use the new planning processes, some projects come in under the estimate, and an equal number come in a little over, often because the business people are not ready to use what Armstrong is ready to deliver. **We spend time to save time.** I will repeat what I said **s-l-o-w-l-y.**

<Hank>: *He's acting calm, but he is livid, worse than I've ever seen.*

<HM>: It is cheaper, on the average, for the business to say, "That's dumb, and we will not pay you to waste time on that", or "maybe we should add it back in", than it is to say, "OOPS, if you had mentioned it, you wouldn't have to squeeze it in."

You don't have to believe me. Acton uses our planning processes with any customer who is willing to take the up-front hit on the time estimates. Those projects tend to hit the date estimates 90% of the time. *That increased his pulse rate.*

The Way It (Planning) Works

<Sharf>: *Here's a chance to learn one of Acton's secrets. Take from Marshall, shut him down, and then use his techniques to gain ground on Acton. This is sweet.*

<Rennie>: How detailed are the plans?

<HM>: Larger activities are divided into a moderate number of tasks. Teams are allowed to report time at the task level if they feel it is important, but project estimation and time reporting were kept at the activity level.

<Sharf>: I should not have reacted the way I did. The numbers are so impressive that they have a startle effect. Please give us more information on how it works.

<**Hank**>: The clients guide the planning, and they use the same terms as the technology people use. We were able to provide information for improved estimation based in technology skill sets, skill levels, and best practices, all using the same terms.

As a result, clients understand the amount of time required to perform standard tasks. The clients' program-related activities are also included in the activity/task lists, so they understand what is expected of them. All participants see when they are not delivering necessary input for a work request or project.

<**HM**>: Usually when anyone goes to Macedon for help, his planning staff sets them up with samples of segments from successful plans that delivered functions similar to those mentioned in the specifications, the common terminology planning vocabulary, and the planning rules. He provides default time estimates for the most frequent types of activities and a set of estimation rules. Teams are allowed to delete activities that do not apply and add activities they believe are important at planning iteration points. They are asked to use the common vocabulary when they customize their plans.

When project managers accept projects from project initiation, they refine the plans using the identical process.

<**Sharf**>: You don't control it?

<**HM**>: I told you I gave it away.

<**Rennie**>: What type of rules?

<**HM**>: Here's a short list:

1. **Fuzzy requirements increase project costs exponentially!**
2. **Conflicting requirements increase project costs exponentially!**
3. Reuse of software saves money.
4. Reuse of data saves money.
5. Poor data quality costs money.
6. Assumptions cost money.
7. Open issues cost money.
8. Scope creep costs money.
9. 24-hour availability costs money.
10. High transaction volume costs money.
11. New technology costs money.
12. Use of external consultants costs money.
13. Cross-division projects cost money.

<**Sharf**>: Wouldn't item #13 encourage them to stay within their silos?

<**HM**>: Not if the sum of two silo projects is more than the cost of one cross-division project, and that is usually the case.

<**Rennie**>: Rules #1 and #2 seem more interesting. What effect did they have?

<**HM**>: Piccolo showed both Armstrong and I the benefits of removing ourselves from family feuds. I learned to highlight the conflicts and put a price tag on them. I have good figures due to the many times that I was caught before we figured this out.

I also explain to Armstrong that if he chooses to ignore BASE, multiple clients could be unhappy with the results and will complain about spending extra money on something with which they are not satisfied. It's better for them to reach a consensus before the project is approved.

When clients realize that three or four hours of effort on their part may save them $50 - $100 thousand dollars on a six-month project, requirements tend to be defined and conflicts resolved with miraculous speed.

<**Rennie**>: Sometimes it is impossible to know in advance.

<**HM**>: We know, and uncertainty has a price.

<**Sharf**>: How does this work with outsourcing?

<**HM**>: We outsource to ourselves. We are beginning to realize savings by using our international teams for SOA development and testing.

<**Rennie**>: What is in the planning vocabulary?

<**HM**>: Planning terminology (task, activities, dependencies, co-requisites, etc.), a list of planning action verbs, and the SOA Personal Notes/Glossary. The list of verbs is in Table A.8. You'll receive the definitions when Maja has finished creating the Role/Activity List.

Readers: The list of action verbs ***with definitions*** is in SOA P (2) along with the ***THUNK***

Role/Activity List.

If a team doesn't like our verb list, they petitioned us for changes when they are inclined to be cooperative, or they use the ones they like better. We understand that a plan with exotic action verbs is better than no plan at all.

<Sharf>: How do you resolve the inconsistencies?

<HM>: If the planning people can't figure out what the plan is requesting, they call us to negotiate clarification.

<Sharf>: How would you define the difference between a work request and a project?

<Hank>: It's a work request when it's in the hands of the Requirements team. They may mix them, match them, split them, and glue them together. When they are turned over to a creation team (business to technology), they become projects.

<HM>: With the procedural adjustment and organizational repositioning, most of our clients avoid asking for undefined deliverables in impossible time frames.

The rest of the clients know when they are asking for unreasonable deliverables in impossible time frames.

<Rennie>: Which ones continue to make impractical requests?

<HM>: Let's hold that until later. William is in a hurry. ***There is no need to pick on his patron unnecessarily.***

<Hank>: Now it is time for the wonderful planning news.

For the last nine months, we have been able to generate customized plans using the ReMain templates for automation of requirements definition. A Project Initiation Manager can push a button and generate a right-sized plan with funding estimates. If critical requirements are missing, related work activities are highlighted and cost estimates are inflated in proportion to the vagueness of the requirements specification. We use a rules engine for that.

If they don't use our automated requirements process, Macedon still provides them with standard planning process and information packets.

<Sharf>: You act like you still own it, but you say you gave it away.

<HM>: You caught me. They are my financial specialists, on long-term loan to Macedon. I rotate them in and out.

<Sharf>: Does everyone funnel his or her funding requests through you?

<HM>: Of course, they DO NOT. They file funding requests with Finance. When requests make sense, the client receives the funding. If the plans don't make sense, finance pulls us into the loop (as I mentioned previously). We show client/technology teams how to fix the plans, and then they receive the funding. In either case, we maintain a planning history. It becomes input to several other processes.

<Sharf>: Are the plans properly maintained?

<HM>: They have to do a semblance of plan maintenance if they want to want to keep their funding.

<Sharf>: What level of validation do you perform?

<HM>: We pay more attention to the high profile projects. In some cases, we do the planning for them, especially when they are using new technology with which we have no historical frame of reference.

After that, the most we can do is ensure that everyone has a plan; we don't have enough people to deal with everybody's details. Corporate finance provides the major point of enforcement. Jasper likes her job, and she doesn't intend to lose it because of somebody's sloppiness. Her people will delay an allocation until they have a plan that makes sense to them.

<Rennie>: What planning product do they use?

<HM>: In the beginning, we received faxes, snail mail copies of memos, e-mails, spreadsheets if we were lucky, and input from planning products if we were extremely lucky. Maja's people acquired very intelligent parsers, and enhanced them. The people who enhance the parsers usually have English as their second language. The catch things that Dan, Val, or I would not know were problems.

We manually entered information from the sticky notes taped to craft paper and the one from the woman who sent us pictures of two walls of her cubical with index cards held on by magnets. As activities were completed, she signed the cards, moved them to the opposite wall, and sent us new pictures.

[...] It is not funny. Her process worked and her projects were delivered on time and within budget. We used those pictures to secure funding for planning tools and training.

Everyone has been required to use a planning tool for the last 14 months, although we cannot convince the units to use the same tool. We can require that they use common versions of their preferred product. All plans are translated into English before we receive them. Common terminology and the action verb list are important for that.

<Sharf>: You mentioned performance reviews, roles, and skill assessments among your list of planning wonders a few minutes ago. I'm sure you know that we are expected to evaluate your list of roles and responsibilities and associated skill requirements. It would be important to address those issues.

<HM>: ***He's obsessing about roles. I will use this carrot to determine his true intentions.***

We can use ***THUNK*** (Role/Activity/objects) to itemize at least 95% of the work completed by everyone on the BASE team from the time that we started working on SOX. It contains information about most of the people who worked for Armstrong during the same period. It is how we justified the staffing difference after the merger.

<Sharf>: Do you mean that you maintain job descriptions?

<HM>: No, the action list shows what a person actually did, is doing, or was assigned to do. Job descriptions outline what you believe a person with a given title and position in the hierarchy should do.

<Sharf>: How would you ensure proper documentation?

Planning Information Flows

<HM>: ***I will control myself. I will control the content and the tone of what I say.***

Fig. 11 (BASE Planning, Roles, and Activities) shows how planning information and action lists fit together. We will focus on the **highlighted entities**. My hobby was the foundation for all four of these. Table A.9 describes the ***Thunk*** information relationships. It was extracted from training materials that we provide with the ***Thunk*** list.

<Sharf>: How would you use this ***Thunk,*** and for what, when you could simply look at the plans?

<HM>: The question one usually asks first is "Which plan(s)?" The Action List helps Program participants to discover appropriate plans for further examination.

<Sharf>: If you have the role descriptions, why do you need action lists?

<HM>: Role descriptions outline what the role is expected to do. Action lists identify what the role actually did. They provide more detail. They also capture actions that are not usually assigned to specific roles.

<Sharf>: That would occur due to inadequate role definitions.

<HM>: New business challenges, new vendor products, improved understanding of methodology, or changing business processes may require role changes. The action list assists identification of role change requirements, and it contributes to process improvement.

<Rennie>: You left off the cardinality.

<Hank>: Ask Maja for the actual Entity-Relationship Diagram. We lifted this piece out of the Daxiao business data model and modified it for people who don't care about data models.

<Rennie>: Do you have a list of users for the action lists?

<HM>: At your leisure, you may refer to Table 12.

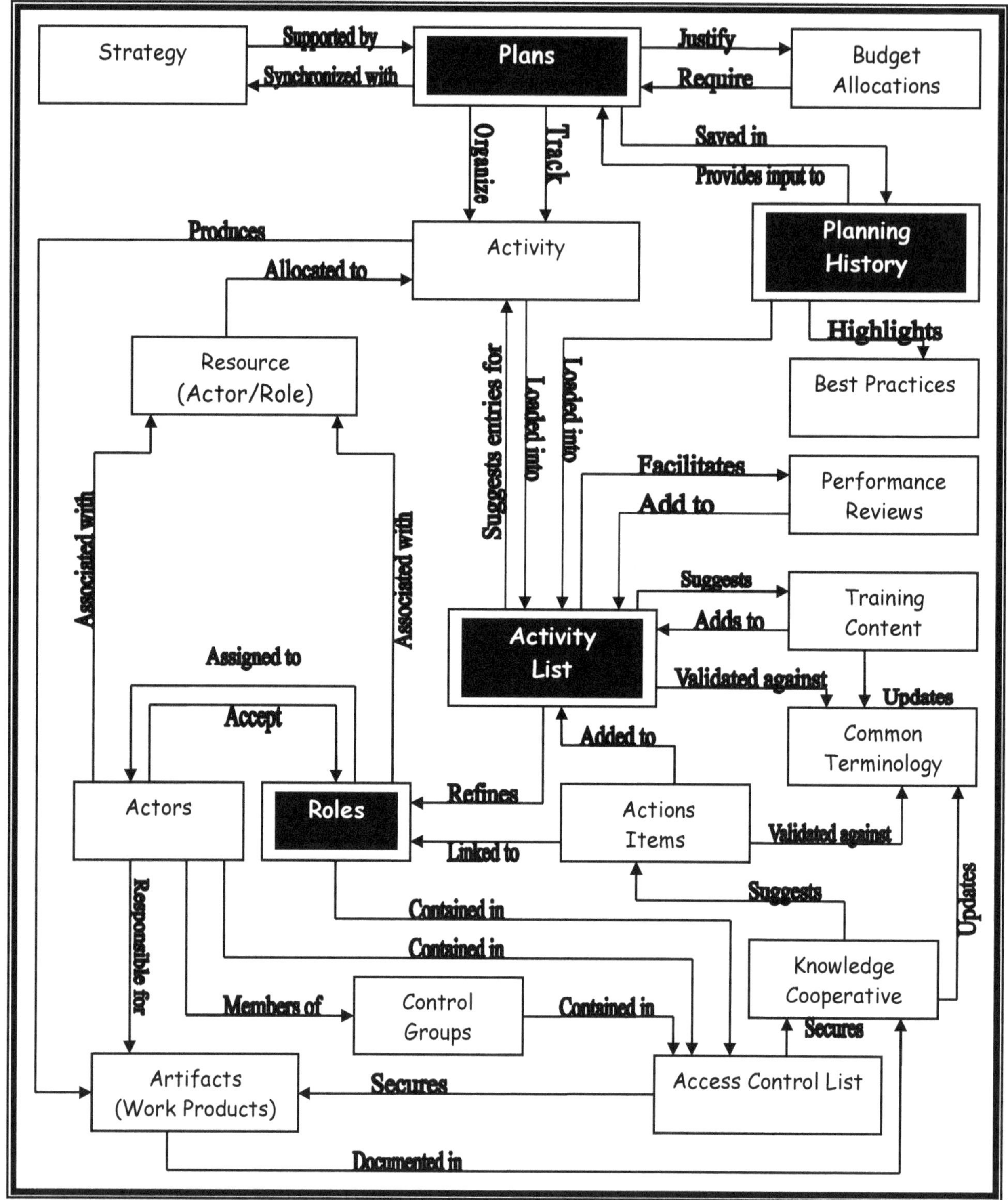

Fig. 11 - BASE Planning, Roles, and Activities (*Thunk*) Information Relationships

<HM>: *He's about to start drooling.* First, how can you need something that you never knew existed?

Second, giving you our list would not be in our best interest. The information is currently formatted for insiders. *I have decided that you should never be an insider.*

<Sharf>: Tell me again how my action list will differ from yours.

Table 12 - Users of *Thunk* Activity and Planning List		
Role	**Reason for Use**	**# of Users**
Acton	♦ To support WFSOA audit and compliance requirements	9
Business Analyst(s)	♦ To discover WFSOA subject matter experts	74
Client(s)	♦ To understand complications associated with WFSOA project delivery	843
	♦ To understand the expenses associated with WFSOA project delivery	
	♦ To understand the effort business participants must spend on WFSOA project delivery.	
Compliance specialist(s)	♦ To determine which roles are performing WFSOA work activities	34
	♦ To determine which roles may need to be audited	
Developer(s)	♦ To see the list of actions performed by individuals in their WFSOA roles	1,593
Domain owner(s)	♦ To discover who has prior experience with specific types of artifacts.	47
Executive - BASE	♦ To check on the state of BASE planning	1
Financial specialist(s)	♦ To discover the resources typically required to complete a WFSOA task	18
Process coordinator(s)	♦ To verify the actions and roles typically associated with WFSOA activities	55
	♦ To verify the list of processes and procedures maintained for WFSOA	
Personnel specialist	♦ To discover the individuals associated with specific roles	22
	♦ To discover new WFSOA actions that may need to be associated with roles	
	♦ To discover action items that may be associated with the wrong role	
	♦ To understand which plans have activities for which no WFSOA-trained resources are available	
Planning specialist	♦ To discover WFSOA plans with desired characteristics	33
	♦ To derive WFSOA estimation guidelines	
Procurement	♦ To identify individuals who may provide assistance with product evaluations	8
Project Initiation Manager	♦ To verify the actions and roles typically associated with planned activities	42
	♦ To discover participants on related projects	
	♦ To discover subject matter experts for related projects	
Project Manager(s)	♦ To verify the actions and roles typically associated with planned activities	67
	♦ To discover individuals/teams associated with successful WFSOA projects	
Security	♦ To verify which actions are normally associated with a role	32
Training	♦ To discover new action items associated with new products	9
	♦ To discover ideas for course content	
	Total - Frequent users (At least once per week)	2,887
Intermediate. Users. (10 - 51 times each year)	♦ To verify work performed during an evaluation period. ♦ To follow links into the Knowledge Cooperative.	7,593
Casual Users. (Less than 10 times each year)	♦ To verify work performed during an evaluation period. ♦ To follow links into the Knowledge Cooperative.	31,792

Readers: This is blatant promotion of SOA P (2) - The roles/activity list is the result a lifetime of planning. I am the person who moved the planning index cards from one wall to the other in 1983 and 1984.

<HM>: We are making it shorter by combining roles with similar functions.

<Sharf>: We need the version that Acton sees.

It would be confusing to you, and your report would suggest that the information needs clarification. Acton people do not require clarification. They contributed to use cases, database content, and data flows.

Furthermore, there are security restrictions on some of the information. Notice that the corporate auditors (compliance specialists) are on the list of users. *That was a good Gotcha! I have to find out what it is about Acton that sets him off.*

<Rennie>: How big is it?

<HM>: There are hundreds of thousands in the full database.

<Sharf>: How would you clarify that?

<HM>: *We already clarified.* Look at entry #12 in Table A.9.

<Ernest Dawson>: Excuse me Mr. Marshall. I have the information you needed.

<HM>: Thank you Mr. Dawson. *Ouch!*

<Hank>: **Are you all right? You made a loud sound.**

<HM>: That was the brace, not me.

<Rennie>: What's wrong?

<HM>: The t- table leg is roaming around again.

<Hank>: **You are not careful. You are worried.**

<Sharf>: *That really is his Achilles tendon. I wonder if I can pursue "unsuitable for health reasons".*

<Ernest>: **Let me check.**

<HM>: **No need. It's padded.** Did Mr. Chase have a message for me?

<Ernest>: He said I should bring these envelopes to you quickly. It contains information from Dr. Emery-Baldwin that you requested. Mr. Chase said he can make glossy versions of everything if you want, but it will take another 20 minutes. That will delay the action, and it is heavy stuff. I'm not sure I heard that right.

<HM>: You were close. He probably said action items. Show me.

[...] Tell him thanks. This is good enough for us to decorate with soy sauce.

Tell people not to worry. We are all right.

<Ernest>: **Okay.**

<Rennie>: *They are definitely talking with their hands!*

<HM>: Hank, we have the materials. Hurry up, so we can start with roles and responsibilities. Ken will do use the high-speed printer for the ***THUNK*** list. I'm happy to report that in spite of the rush, we will provide you with more than you ever imagined about roles and responsibilities within the next couple of hours.

<Hank>: **Emergency! FIRE!**

<Rennie>: Don't be silly.

<Hank>: **Rennie saw us.**

<Sharf>: What's silly about roles and responsibilities?

<Rennie>: **Why did you do that?**

<HM>: **Now we know that you know. How?**

<Rennie>: **Summer camp. Are you deaf?**

<HM>: **My son is deaf.**

<Rennie>: **I am sorry.**

<Sharf>: Why are you all fidgeting?

<Rennie>: We're learning more ways to communicate. I will explain later.

<Sharf>: *That may be a waste of your time.* Are you going to distribute that material now?

<HM>: Let me look at it first.

He's so anxious to see what's in this package that he ignored what Rennie said. I should put it back in the envelope before he reaches over and grabs them from me.

<Sharf>: In the ***Thunk*** list, how would you separate the tasks between SOX and SOA?

<HM>: Why do you insist that they should be separated? We may separate the tasks that are specific to SOA development (Product Creation Processes), but because SOA development comes under COBIT "Acquire and Implement Systems", that's still not a true separation.

<Sharf>: The main reason is budgeting. ***I can find a problem with any budget that was ever created. Theirs will be more difficult, but I'm up to the challenge.***

Also, I don't want Gunnar to get in trouble for messing with SOX. I will reassemble SOA and do it the way I want it done.

<HM>: We do not have an SOA budget. I'm sure Gunnar told you that.

<Sharf>: He told me that you hide your SOA funding under compliance. What about Armstrong?

<HM>: SOA is part of the corporate strategy that guides spending for all our projects. The BASE budget pays for compliance (with emphasis on SOX) and a new technology research budget. Armstrong has a business support budget and a new technology research budget. Piccolo has a budget for corporate architecture, corporate security, and corporate strategy. Jasper has a budget for corporate information optimization. Macedon has a budget for managing technology requirements.

<Sharf>: How would you justify the extra funding? Someone had to pay for the typing bonus and facilitation training.

<HM>: Due to our unique training, we save money in other areas. Everyone may do more work, make fewer mistakes, or instigate fewer conflicts. That means that when people leave, though our turnover rate is low, we don't need to replace about half of them. We also save money on:

1. Procurement (centralized software licensing and hardware purchases).
2. Reductions in data redundancy.
3. Reductions in the size of our application portfolio.
4. Reduction in planning resources.

<Sharf>: Prove it.

<HM>: Technology and BASE budgets combined were the same in 2003 as they were in 2002, and for each of the last three years, we spent less than the year before. Lorrie can show you the numbers.

<Sharf>: You have rambled around planning for too long. Hank, start the timer. Try to finish everything else 30 minutes.

<HM>: ***This makes no sense. I know he wants to start with the roles, but this is blatant oversight.***

<Hank>: How we achieve what we achieve is covered (explicitly or implicitly) in the 180 + processes in the three WFSOA domains. Table A.10 lists the processes and roles with primary responsibilities associated with the Enabling Process Domain. Tables A.11 and A.12 itemize processes in the Product Delivery and Support domains respectively.

Life Cycle Management

<HM>: Notice that life cycle management is highlighted in the table. It is also one of the longest lists of items in Lessons Learned. We save the company millions of dollars each year because we get rid of the things that no longer apply, and things that we no longer need. We must ensure that processes are completed. Thus, the list of assumptions and outstanding issues is much shorter. We transition staff and artifacts wherever possible. Thus, we "grandfather" as few things as we are legally allowed to do. That includes retirement of data, applications, and standards.

<Sharf>: That should be a job for a process owner.

<Hank>: HM is the senior process coordinator in Daxiao, followed by Van Amberg, Stern, Barca, Maurer, Wright, Piccolo and Macedon. HM ensures that process owners across the organization follow up on their processes.

[...] Remember, it is possible for an individual to have multiple roles.

<Sharf>: ***He's sneakier than I thought! They do the work and he gets the credit whenever they finish something. Maybe I can figure out a way to use that against him.***

<Hank>: That leads smoothly into the next topic.

BUSINESS PROCESS MANAGEMENT - MORE OF HOW WE DO WHAT WE DO

<HM>: In parallel, we resolve the non-issue related to WFSOA process automation and documentation.

<Sharf>: ***He should let Hank talk. He'll slow us down again.***

<HM>: Always remember that WFSOA processes support both SOX and SOA.

1. Processes requirements are derived from use cases provided by subject matter experts.
2. All processes associated with WFSOA have clearly defined guidelines that are captured in a production-level business rules engine.
3. All the processes may be accessed through a single well-advertised portal.
4. Within the portal, the processes may be accessed by keyword, by role, by domain, by category, by process function, or by team.

GOVERNANCE PROCESSES - VERY QUICKLY

5. Seventy-one (71) of the processes in Table A.10 are associated with WFSOA governance.

If you don't have time to listen to me, at do us a favor and look at the list.

BUSINESS PROCESS MANAGEMENT (Cont'd.)

6. The documentation and process models are maintained in the Knowledge Cooperative. The more complicated ones have special guidance files and tool mentors.
7. The portal and processes were sufficiently robust that CMMI upgraded our process maturity rating.
8. A major portion of our communications program is devoted to evangelizing the processes.
9. Each time a process is added or changed, a pre-defined list of critical individuals is notified. That list includes Mr. Gunnar.
10. Processes have key performance indicators and are monitored by an availability architect. Ninety-five percent of the automated processes currently meet performance requirements.
11. Process and service statistics are reported in online dashboards or scorecards.
12. Mr. Guzman, Mr. Ellison, and Ms. Jasper believed it was sufficiently impressive that it was mentioned in our SEC filing.

<Sharf>: I understand. Let's proceed.

<HM>: I'm not half done yet. ***I have to try to straighten out my leg. I banged it harder than I realized.***

13. All process documentation uses common terminology.
14. Formal training is available for 30% of them. You will see more about that when we show you the role descriptions and responsibilities.

<Rennie>: ***He's limping really badly. I wonder why he doesn't sit down.***

<HM>:

15. A few of the processes are represented in multiple categories, but these are the primary categories. You will see that as Hank advances through the descriptions of the categories.
16. S- Several of the larger processes have sub-processes. It is one of the mappings in the Knowledge Cooperative.

[...] D- Don't interrupt me.

17. The ***Thunk*** Roles/Activity database tells us which roles participate in which processes. You will see that several roles other than the primary may participate in a process.
18. On any given day, as many business people access WFSOA processes as do people in technology or BASE. We have the numbers to prove it. The usage figures are included in the executive sc- scorecard.

[...] Wait.

19. Several pr- processes combine automated and manual tasks.
20. The 180+ WFSOA processes are under Business Process Management, conform to WS-BPEL, and run on a production BPEL engine.
21. They are being managed in an SOA catalog using WSDL.
22. All the process flows have models created using Business Process Modeling Notation (BPMN) and some have associated animations or Webinars.
23. All our processes have clearly defined metadata schema maintained in a metadata catalog, whether they are automated or not. With the metadata, we will be ahead of the game when we are ready to automate additional processes.

Therefore, there is no need for you to either show us how to identify or document our WFSOA processes.

If you had trouble following me because I bore people to death, Hank will be glad to repeat what I said for you. I want to make sure it is in your notes.

<Rennie>: I captured most of it. *He's two separate people. I have seldom seen anyone look that angry.*

<Hank>: **You forget to breathe. You are not all right!**

<Rennie>: **William is different today. Sorry.**

<HM>: **Silly. We waste time.** Where's my cane?

<Sharf>: Stop flailing around. *Gunnar didn't mention that Marshall may be unstable. That's why his daughter is so explosive. Daxiao probably knows it already, but the instability should be emphasized.*

<Rennie>: Is that it leaning against the closet?

<HM>: I'm sorry I became a little agitated. *I must see Church today. This brace is practically useless.*

<Sharf>: Start with the next categories.

PRODUCT DELIVERY PROCESS DOMAIN

<Hank>: *H is meditating, thankfully.* Here we go. This will be the quickest coverage of 90 processes that ever occurred.

The circle in the emblem in Fig. 8 illustrates the three product delivery categories. They are:

1. Requirements Coordination.
2. Product Creation.
3. Project Management.

Requirements Coordination - an Exercise in Complicated Logistics

The **most important** difference in WFSOA is related to what you would call change management. Requirements gathering, validation, and prioritization for all business systems, business services, or business processes have moved into the business sector and are handled by the Requirements Management Team. Detailed analysis, prototyping, and testing are also handled by Requirements Management with assistance from Technology and our SOA Competency Team.

The SVP in this area has a matrix relationship with EVPs in the operations and manufacturing areas.

<HM>: *No one fits into a matrix with Gunnar.*

<Hank>:

1. Anyone who wishes to request a change or something new in technology may enter that request into the ReMain (requirements maintenance product), the primary support product for requirements coordination. Macedon ordered us to connect ReMain to everything, while simultaneously making it idiot-proof. We have made the connections, but we have very clever idiots.
2. Requirements Management approves requirements and changes to requirements based on a set of well-publicized prioritization guidelines.
3. If clients wish to know why a given task is necessary for product delivery, Macedon ensured that we created animations that allow the client to click an icon to see where the task fits in a product delivery flow, the role that normally performs the task, the individual who actually performed, is performing, or is scheduled to perform the task, and the consequences to the work request if the task is delayed or omitted.
4. If the Requirements Management team discovers problems, they stop the project before we assemble a technical project team.
5. If requirements change, Macedon's team reviews the nature of the changes and determines whether they are necessary.

<Sharf>: Why did I have to listen to that?

<HM>: We want you to understand how Alex Macedon does what he does.

<Rennie>: How successful is Requirements Management?

<Hank>: They achieve excellent results. They treat project delivery as complicated exercises in logistics. The head of Requirements Management says this is more difficult than regular logistics, and he would know. He was formerly responsible for Logistics in Daxiao. Before that, he was a Lieutenant General with responsibility for logistics in the U.S. Marines.

<Sharf>: Why do you have a Marine general approving title changes on reports?

<HM>: He does not. Armstrong provided the business units with a product that they use to control their report headings. They fight among themselves, and Macedon can stay out of it.

<Rennie>: Why does he believe delivery of technology is more difficult?

<Hank>: He didn't always believe it was more difficult.

Now he believes that the difference is that humans can see aircraft carriers, a supply of food or medicine, and a gun. People in manufacturing can see a processing chip and a power supply. They can see where the pins fit into the memory slots. On the other hand, no one has seen a bit or a byte since IBM stopped building metal cores for mainframes.

In technology, we deal with visual representation of concepts that reside in the heads of people who have different foundations for creating those concepts. He says that if you don't believe it, you should ask the next 10 expert SOA programmers/developers you see to draw a picture of a service interface. He tried it and he was amazed by the results.

He makes us animate everything so that you can see it.

<Rennie>: That is fascinating. I'll use that in my next Introduction to Software Integration course.

<HM>: *She teaches mortals. I wish I knew how to do that.*

<Sharf>: *Who says you needed to think of that?*

<Hank>: Another reason that Requirements Management is doing well is that each of the business areas contributed some of their best people, in self-defense. Operations didn't want manufacturing to have an unfair advantage when it came to setting work priorities. H contributed some of our best compliance people. Armstrong gave them the business Quality Assurance Team. Technology testers rotate into and out of the Quality Assurance Team.

Jasper and Piccolo also provided expert permanent staff. Macedon is Justin's contribution.

<Sharf>: You stacked the deck.

<HM>: Every area stacked the deck until the people developed affiliations to their new team.

<Hank>: Based on plans created for each work request, Armstrong provides database, security, and architecture support while H provides SOA competency people for analysis and prototyping.

We have 23 minutes to go. Please hold your questions to the end if you want to get to the roles.

Project Management

The BASE evolution requires the proper positioning of management talent at all times. We cannot succeed if agile managers who enjoy new challenges are tied to completed projects, while change-verse individuals are forced into areas where they are not comfortable.

No amount of training will change the basic preferences. People burn out from the stress or quit from boredom.

The result is that a significant change in project management was implemented for WFSOA. We have **loose coupling of the Project Management processes.**

We created two new management roles (SOA project managers and domain owners). Our most talented change-tolerant managers move from one new SOA challenge to the next one. It's similar to an internal consulting organization and SOA project managers are similar to engagement managers. SOA project managers have the option of picking teams from Weldon's organization or from BASE to work with people assigned by Macedon and the business for the duration of a project.

Our most talented change-averse managers become domain owners who remain in place. They don't mind promoting the reuse of the same service to seven or eight different development teams. They love bringing new users onto consolidated databases.

Domain owners have their own small teams composed of developers who have ventured into SOA, but would rather not have frequent major changes. They are in a pool that reports to Armstrong, but works for Ramirez.

SOA project managers deliver the results of service creation projects to service domain owners along with a few members of the service creation team when the projects are completed (after the official post mortem). When the service domain owners feel comfortable that the new services are stable, rotating team members are returned to the work pool. We shorten transition time by having domain SOA developers work with new project developers during deployment and user acceptance testing. (19 minutes).

<Sharf>: Why don't they report to Ramirez?

<HM>: Mrs. Jasper does not wish to appear greedy. It also keeps individual domain owners from snapping up the best developers. It guarantees rotation.

<Rennie>: Where do they find team leaders?

<HM>: Domain owners lead their teams. They tend to be more hands-on.

<Sharf>: If they are change-averse, how do you get them to accept new confrontational roles?

<HM>: First, we run them through the cultural change management program. Then we provide ongoing mentoring and support. Finally, clients have usually dealt with Macedon's people before they get to Ramirez's people. Macedon will confront a tornado, but even he is mellower than he was before. He took sales and facilitation training again (the corporate version).

<Hank>: SOA project managers are our internal versions of what you would call engagement managers. They learn quickly. They know the people, they know who knows what, and they understand the organizational politics and the existing technology. They are excellent facilitators and salespeople.

<Sharf>: Do they work on assignments with your partners?

<HM>: No. We don't dare to increase the risk of losing them. We have specially trained business analysts who coordinate between our internal project managers and our partner's project managers.

Product Creation

<Hank>: We have been rotating teams, just as we have been rotating managers. To build comfort levels, we let core teams and team leaders stay together. Armstrong plays well in this area, and he is building teams that are as talented as the competency team members that he gave away.

He and I both have tool specialists who move among teams and perform specialized functions. Examples include developing specialized Perl parsers to analyze service logs or developing specialized COBOL routines to secure the information extracted for test database creation.

My technology specialists are assigned to the SOA Competency team when they don't have business projects. They work on development of SOA core services, legacy service refactoring, database consolidation, or retirement projects.

People on the competency team receive cross-platform training, allowing them to respond to service and process emergencies, but we try to leave them on their platform of choice. We hire teams from vendors if we must, and we are doing successively more "in-house" offshore projects.

We have cross-platform races when we need to develop expertise with a different SOA design pattern, a different agile methodology, a new product, or new standards. (16 minutes).

<HM>: Please remember what I said about WFSOA processes and business process management. Table A.11 lists over 45 processes that support the three Product Delivery Domains. Would you be kind enough to take a fraction of a minute to look at the list? Here's another copy if you need it.

SUPPORT PROCESS DOMAIN

<Hank>: The three Program Support domains are in the outer triangle of Fig. 8. They are:

1. Data Management.
2. Architecture.
3. Environment Management (you would refer to it as the data center).

<HM>: The Support Domain processes are listed in Table A.12. Please remember to point out in your notes that we have 40+ documented processes in the Support Domain. I mentioned earlier that several of the processes have sub-processes. For example, XML includes sub-processes for translation, transformation, schema definition, and storage and retrieval.

Data Management

<Hank>: Data management processes are handled by data teams that report to Armstrong (for data in application silos) or by data domain owners: they are responsible for the databases after we separate them from application silos. Most data domain owners were very senior database administrators.

After full implementation of WFSOA, most application data will become joint property of the entire organization. We will have **loosely coupled data.**

We have a tremendous track record for data consolidation, data clean up, and retirement. However, several of the non-SOA participants absolutely refuse to give up "their data".

When one of our sales managers threatened to leave and take his customer base with him rather than share his data, we established the Data Governance organization. It will coordinate data sharing and data consolidation efforts. It is a way to ensure visibility for data issues and greater management support.

We have 13 minutes.

Environment Management

<Hank>: Environment Management was on the front line of a major cultural transition. An irony of SOA is that we had to ensure that the data center SOA processes worked early in WFSOA, or they would never have allowed us to advance to the next levels.

1. They had to build confidence in users for services that they do not own, using data that they do not own.
2. They had to understand the new architecture and the new terminology and be able to guide users through real problems and minor uncertainties.
3. They dealt with situations where major successes generated major problems, such as popular new services that affected the performance of moneymaking legacy applications.
4. They had to develop an understanding of the complicated relationships among service and process components.
5. They had to acquire and learn new service management and monitoring tools and capture different types of metrics. They provided the information foundation that was used to establish costing algorithms.
6. They contribute to service level agreements (SLAs), and then monitored the agreements.

Armstrong shifted some of his strongest architects into data center operations. We call them availability architects. They concentrate on specific sets of services and processes rather than the entire infrastructure. There isn't a one-to-one match with service domain owners, but the concept is similar. (10 minutes).

Architecture

<Rennie>: How would you visualize your architecture hierarchy?

<Sharf>: *That will cost her. She was not supposed to interrupt him.*

<Hank>: This is an area where we had conflicts before we went upscale and hired a corporate architect. Fig. 12 shows how Dr. Piccolo resolved it.

He says that corporate architecture manages entire cities while software architecture handles the construction of individual buildings. He says it's a lowbrow, but it works. He will provide you with the management theory behind this arrangement.

<HM>: We finished the quickest WFSOA process review ever delivered, and we are finished with lunch. Let's take a 10-minute break while we remove the leftover food.

<Sharf>: NO! Rennie can put everything into these bags while you start with roles and responsibilities.

<HM>: We will do it together. A few minutes won't hurt anything. If we had followed my plan, I would be deciding whether to embarrass myself by requesting the dessert menu, and you would have no idea of which processes are supported by the roles and responsibilities.

<Rennie>: Should we toss out the leftovers?

<HM>: We certainly will not. I'll carry them to the motel. Val will be in no later than tomorrow, and he loves this stuff. I will meet you back here in 10 minutes. Maybe we need 15 minutes. Something has come up. My phone needs me.

<Sharf>: Who ever hear of an EVP carrying leftover Chinese food to the staff? *He can't even walk.*

<Hank>: He takes care of his people in any way that he can.

<Sharf>: That's absurd. Hank, find that envelope. We can start without him.

<Hank>: The envelope is not here.

<Sharf>: Look on those piles.

<Hank>: Those are training materials.

<Sharf>: Let's look and see.

<Rennie>: You may look, or you can wait for HM to come back. I'm going for a walk.

<Hank>: *He didn't even hear her.* I hope you find our training materials informative and carefully thought out. You can check that off your list. I'll see you in a few minutes.

----------HM's Office----------

<Hank>: Ernest grabbed me in the hall and said you wanted to see me.

<HM>: Yes. I wanted to bring you up-to-date on my most recent research, but first, I want to know what William did immediately after I left.

<Hank>: Are you feeling OK?

<HM>: I was having trouble breathing in the room with Sharf. I'm better now. What did he do?

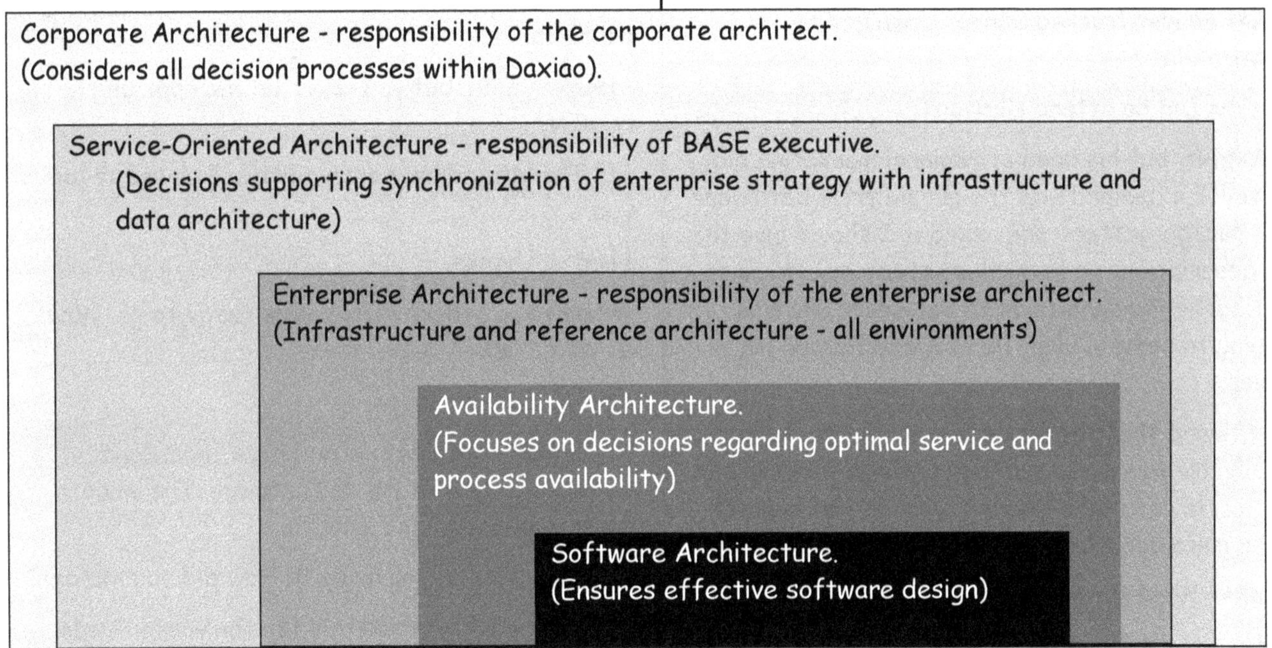

Corporate Architecture - responsibility of the corporate architect.
(Considers all decision processes within Daxiao).
Service-Oriented Architecture - responsibility of BASE executive.
(Decisions supporting synchronization of enterprise strategy with infrastructure and data architecture)
Enterprise Architecture - responsibility of the enterprise architect.
(Infrastructure and reference architecture - all environments)
Availability Architecture.
(Focuses on decisions regarding optimal service and process availability)
Software Architecture.
(Ensures effective software design)

Fig. 12 - **Architectures and Scopes within Daxiao**

<Hank>: He was extremely upset because he couldn't find the envelope with the roles information. He was rummaging through the training materials on the credenza.

<HM>: He's looking extremely annoyed now. It appears that he received a couple upsetting messages.

<Hank>: I've never seen a consultant who was that blatantly hostile before. He's setting fire to his path prematurely. What does he know that we don't?

<HM>: He's burning his bridges. He was probably bluffing, and we may modify our approach when we return.

<Hank>: What do you know that we didn't know before?

<HM>: I don't know anything more, but my theories are stronger. Before lunch, I decided it would be a good idea to call Human Resources to ask them to accelerate an official version of the role descriptions.

Dr. Emery-Baldwin wanted to know the reason for the rush. She said Gunnar called and asked for the updated SOA roles too. She had sent copies to Gunnar, Armstrong, Piccolo, and us.

I told her they were all right, and that I planned to give them to the people from Belvedere. She said that Gunnar needed them for a preparatory meeting on Friday afternoon. She suggested that I should check with Gunnar since Dan and Weldon had already responded.

<Hank>: Why didn't Gunnar prepare Belvedere before they came?

<HM>: Ernest tracked Gunnar down at the Horward Club.

<Hank>: Did he attend Horward?

<HM>: No, but his head of regional marketing did. Anyway, I explained how the people from Belvedere were real go-getters, and asked if I should give the role descriptions to them this afternoon? He said don't bother to send them to Belvedere. He was planning to bring William up to speed before he arrives.

I mentioned that the Belvedere people are here already. He was surprised, and perhaps it upset him a little. He covered by saying "yes, yes, of course" to the roles question.

<Hank>: What do you make of this?

<HM>: Let me finish. I tossed a little oil on the fire by mentioning that we hadn't finished investigating Belvedere or Sharf, and that I was worried about the types of details Sharf was requesting, especially without official clearance, and especially since the Ādaemoa fiasco and his vigorous objection to Partner Networks (I know he knows about Ādaemoa because one of the Acton people accidentally let it slip).

When he asked what Sharf had to do with Ādaemoa, I explained that I was still checking the rumor mill, but there's a possibility that Belvedere/Sharf is consulting with Ādaemoa currently. He said he would personally vouch for Sharf. He thanked me for being so meticulous, and then he had to run because the people at the table were waiting for him.

<Hank>: That means William is what you would call a rolling gun.

<HM>: Loose cannon.

<Hank>: What do we do now?

<HM>: We remove the rolling gun from the deck of our ship and put him on Gunnar's ship. Tell Maja to bring the command center back online. I bet she needed seven minutes for the backup.

<Hank>: I took it offline, and I can bring it back. Hand me your keyboard.

<HM>: Don't you keep one of those folding things with you?

<Hank>: I do, but you never let me hook up the receiver.

[...] This drawer was open a little. I closed it for you.

<HM>: Thanks.

<Hank>: [...] there it is. You're ready to go. What do we do next?

<HM>: Just a minute.

[...] Ernest, call Gaetano and have them send someone to look at my desk drawer. The smooth runners are a bit too smooth.

<Hank>: Val [...] you made it! How did you manage?

<Val>: I wouldn't miss this for the world. I was going to rent a bird, but Mittelman's was there for him, and he dropped me off on the West Side.

<Hank>: I have never been so happy to see anyone. I had to restrain myself to keep from leaping over the desk and hugging you.

<Val>: Leaping and hugging!

It's time for me to start working.

<HM>: Are you up to this? Hank is doing fine with the inquisitors, but he's not as good at controlling me.

<Val>: Asia became easier after I started following Hank's advice. It's time to return the favor. Give me 10 minutes to shave and change and 15 minutes to review the notes.

<Hank>: It's going to be rough, even for you.

<Val>: Where are the notes for these people?

<Hank>: I will enter the information into the system while I tell you about them.

Engagement Manager: Title - SOX/SOA Examiner.

1. Name: William Sharf (with an "f").
2. Stated Goal: Examine SOX and SOA Program to contribute to succession planning processes.
3. Issue #1: Obsessed with roles and responsibilities.
4. Issue #2: He has a strong desire to separate SOX and SOA roles and responsibilities.
5. Issue #3: He rescheduled meetings three days earlier without notifying Niklas Gunnar or the Board.
6. Neutral to hostile response to new ideas and approaches.
7. Negativity rating (-9 of -10). Among the worst that I have ever seen from a C-level consultant. He seems to know something that we don't.
8. Business understanding (9 on a scale of 1 - 10).
9. Technical familiarity (6 on a scale of 1 - 10).
10. 90% probability of causing unpleasantness.
11. 40% probability of causing damage.
12. Hostile (negative ally potential).
13. Ulterior motives:
    - #1: Gather information to help his fledgling SOA consulting practice (90% probability) - including an undefined relationship with Ādaemoa.
    - #2: Develop long-term consulting relationship with Daxiao (80% probability).
    - #3: Replace HM (50% probability).

Personal data:

1. BA Neudorf and MS Finance, Wheaton, '86.
2. Male.
3. Accounting genius.
4. Absorbs information quickly (integration ability not yet determined).
5. Structured to the point of rigidity, and he is reactionary.
6. Bully tendencies, masking insecurity.
7. Moderately xenophobic.

Engagement assistant: Title - Technology Associate.

1. Name: Renata Vitale.
2. Stated Goal: Support for engagement manager. Note: Not happy working with engagement manager.
3. Ulterior motive: None.
4. Working member of three industry standards teams.
5. Negativity rating (None).
6. Business understanding (not yet determined).
7. Expert technologist (9.5 - 9.8).
8. 10% probability of causing unpleasantness.
9. No probability of causing damage unless forced to do so.
10. 50% - Ally potential.

Personal data:

1. MS Engineering (computer science), Columbia, '93.
2. Female.
3. Excellent integration ability.
4. Appropriate emotional stability and flexibility.
5. Accepting of new ideas and approaches.
6. ***Fluent in American Sign Language*** and ***familiar with Spanish.***
7. Inconsistency between appearance and behavior.

- BASE Strategy: Tentative: Take advantage of Sharf's emotional limitations.
- BASE Tactics: 100% honesty, maximum information delivery.
- Note file: Belvedere\Day1. --- There are three sections out there already.

<Val>: Do you have anything to add?

<HM>: You trained him well.

<Val>: The sign language part will do be tricky. How did you find out?

<HM>: I was giving an "all OK" to Ernest, and she noticed. Hank noticed and he tricked her into acknowledging her skill.

<Val>: How did she react to that?

<HM>: She is proud of herself, I suspect.

<Val>: What about the behavior inconsistency?

<HM>: Discussion would be inappropriate. You'll have to see for yourself.

<Val>: How will you use his limitations?

<HM>: I'm still thinking, but I am certain that we will frustrate him enough to make him misbehave.

<Hank>: What are we going to do about Rennie?

<HM>: We will dazzle her with our brilliance and try to separate her from William.

<Val>: I'm going to get ready. Keep filling in the notes and behave until I make it down there.

<HM>: Bring this envelop to the command center in five minutes. Ernest can handle the food.

<Hank>: Should I leave when Val shows up?

<HM>: You may leave the room if you wish. The appearance of two-on-two is better. Tune in to the session. Stay here until we are finished. There are things we will need to discuss with you.

<Hank>: Wishing commands me.

--------In the Command Center -------

<Sharf>: *Why the hell does everything have to come apart at once? I should have let those messages wait.*

Our people just sent a message saying that Ādaemoa seems to be ready to decide today.

Grayson called to say that he has work for my team if we don't land Ādaemoa. He also has several openings for Rennie doing "real work" if we don't land Daxiao.

Cane says that if I don't hit it off with Gunnar, Piccolo, or Marshall, I don't have to worry. He has enough work in financial compliance to keep me busy until I'm 98.

Gunther is also trying to reach me. He will have to wait.

<Rennie>: Why are you looking so gloomy? You should step out for some fresh air too.

<Sharf>: We don't have time. Their monitors came back online. Get on the system and see if you can find anything about roles while we're waiting.

<Rennie>: I'm not sure we should be doing that.

<Sharf>: Before this is over, we will know everything about Daxiao. We may as well start.

WFSOA ROLES, COMPETITIVE DIFFERENTIAL, AGILITY AND FLEXIBILITY

<HM>: William, Rennie. What are you doing?

<Sharf>: The monitor came back online. We were checking to see if you have adequate security.

<HM>: The government hacker failed last month. Show me what you can do.

<Sharf>: I see that you handled the basics. I will send my security team to do a thorough evaluation. Let's return to what is most important.

<Rennie>: *Grayson has the security team*. The interface seems very intuitive. The way you handle the selective lockout is clever.

<HM>: Maja and the security team worked that out. Mention it when you see them. They always appreciate input from external sources, especially someone as knowledgeable as you are.

If you like, we set up two consultant logons for you.

<Sharf>: Why didn't you tell us that before?

<HM>: I didn't know you'd be interested before. If you were like many of the senior level people that we deal with, you would have accused us of wasting your time, as you are accusing us of wasting your time.

<Sharf>: We have to learn to understand what is important. Where are our IDs?

<HM>: They're on the backs of your badges. You would be Goodview1 and Rennie is Goodview2. The passwords are there too.

<Rennie>: How did you come up with this? Sorry, that would be a secret.

<HM>: Yes it is, even from me. They change it every 1 to 4 days, and there are over 100 algorithms from which to choose. I don't know that number either.

<Rennie>: How long is the ID valid?

<HM>: Until you leave the building or until 6:00 P.M. Today, whichever one is earlier.

<Sharf>: Gotcha! I could text this to anyone I wanted.

<HM>: They only work on the terminals in here. I told you that we passed a security audit a little while ago.

<Sharf>: Where are the materials for the remainder of the session?

<HM>: Which would you like to see first, roles and responsibilities or roles and responsibilities?

<Sharf>: You told us that plans, roles, and action lists are central to your SOA success, yet you have not shown us examples of any of them. I am willing to adjust my focus to what you feel is important.

<HM>: *Good response.* Thank you. In response to your generosity, we can provide you with a diagram containing both WFSOA roles and Daxiao team structures in a single image, but you must be willing to read the fine print.

<Sharf>: Show me. ***The timing is perfect. My people should be returning from lunch, and they will have the entire afternoon to impress Ādaemoa with their extensive knowledge of roles and organizational structure.***

<HM>: It will take me a minute to put it on the screen.

<Sharf>: Where's the printed information?

<HM>: It's right here. Sorry, let me call Ernest and tell him to bring us another set. Meanwhile look at screen #1 and screen #2.

<Sharf>: ***He's playing with me! Nobody plays with William Sharf.***

<HM>: ***He looks crazed. I wonder if Indy and Machi were hiding something from me.***

<Hank>: Were you looking for this?

<HM>: Yes. Where was it?

<Hank>: On the way to the refrigerator with the leftover rolls.

<HM>: I'm getting too old for this. Hand out the top sheet.

INTELLECTUAL PROPERTY NOTICE

Daxiao Roles and Responsibilities Information Packet

Our implementation of roles and responsibilities provides us with competitive advantage. They define and support an SOA management philosophy that we know is unique to Daxiao. They are the core of our copyrighted WFSOA processes and procedures (as well as SOX).

Only organizations that have shared WFSOA risks with Daxiao should benefit from WFSOA information.

Therefore, the package of information you are about to receive is proprietary and is covered by any intellectual property agreements that you signed with appropriate representatives of Daxiao.

<Rennie>: Why do we need a note about proprietary information? Roles are roles. An architect is an architect. You can't possibly have anything on that list that has not been used by millions of people millions of times.

<Sharf>: ***Good points Rennie.***

<HM>: The individual roles are not as important as the entire package. You will receive:

1. Roles within Daxiao teams.
2. Preferred and deprecated roles.
3. BASE Roles within process Categories.
4. BASE Teams and headcount.
5. BASE (Governance) staff allocation across process categories.
6. Roles and WFSOA project phases.
7. Role descriptions - short form.
8. The BASE Communications Model showing how role incumbents report that they communicate, as of the last survey. That was about 2 months ago.

9. Role-based access charts that provide insights into methodology process flow.

Role Flexibility

<Sharf>: Is it possible that having everything tied together so tightly limits your flexibility?

<HM>: *There is no way to win, or even to break even with this idiot.* If it wasn't tied together, you would be telling me to tie it together.

<Sharf>: We must find a middle ground.

<HM>: You have to listen to this no matter how long it takes me to say it. ***The roles are flexible.***

You have to listen to this, even if I am repeating some of what I said in the Action List/Roles discussion.

We have built-in processes for **ensuring role flexibility.**

Subject matter experts define the role's responsibilities, according to their areas of expertise. After an accelerated approval process, we assign the roles, ensure acceptance, provide training if necessary, and monitor what incumbents actually do. We keep track of that in the Roles/Activity list.

If there is enough of a discrepancy between the role descriptions and the activities performed by role incumbents, we adjust the descriptions, or we create new roles.

If we see that a role is not being used, we discontinue the role, and we merge related activities with similar roles.

We synchronize our role changes with the SOA strategy changes, which are in turn synchronized with Corporate and Technology strategy. As a result, the number of roles changes regularly. The longest we have gone without changing the number of roles is 10 months. The longest we have gone without changing a role description is four months. The biggest change occurred, of course, when we established BASE as a separate sector.

Therefore, though this seems counter-intuitive, clearly defined roles improve organizational flexibility. When Program participants know what we expect from them:

1. It is easier to change a role (en masse) if it needs to be changed.
2. It is easier to define or change process flows (for us, every process is the essence of a plan).
3. It is easier to figure out whether a person is performing as expected.
4. It is easier to figure out whether the expected actions are achieving the desired result.
5. It is easier to figure out whether we have gaps or overlaps. This is especially true when legislation changes, when new manufacturing components are being used, when IT standards change, or when new products come online.
6. It is easier to determine training requirements for new or changed roles.
7. It is easier to adapt training content.
8. It is easier to perform project planning (as previously discussed).
9. It is easier to monitor process effectiveness.
10. It is easier to control security and approval processes.

All the above translate into tremendous efficiencies. Furthermore, this is a major contributor to common terminology (for Daxiao - business and technology).

<Sharf>: On the other hand, it gives people the opportunity to say, "I didn't do it because it was not my job."

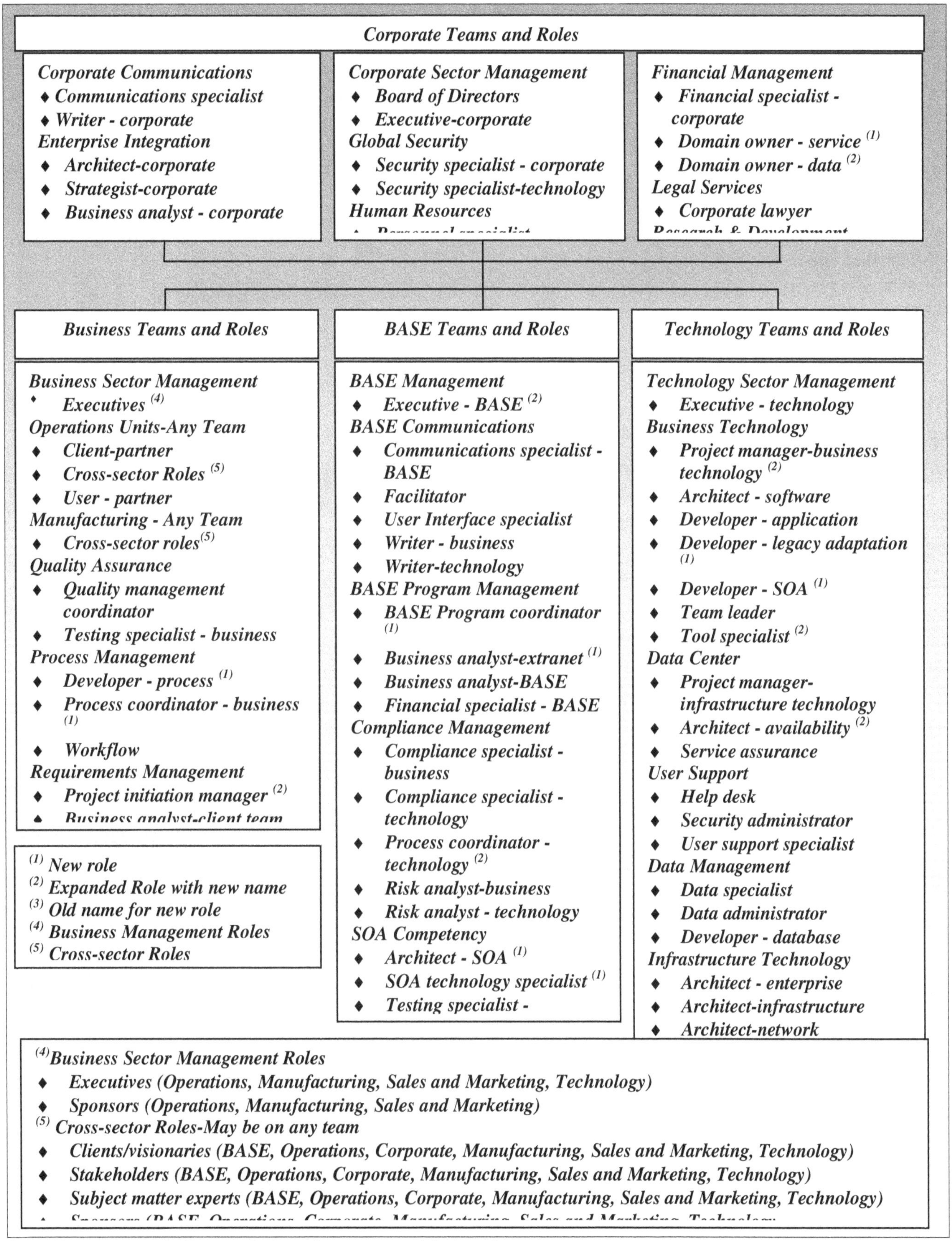

Corporate Teams and Roles

Corporate Communications
- *Communications specialist*
- *Writer - corporate*

Enterprise Integration
- *Architect-corporate*
- *Strategist-corporate*
- *Business analyst - corporate*

Corporate Sector Management
- *Board of Directors*
- *Executive-corporate*

Global Security
- *Security specialist - corporate*
- *Security specialist-technology*

Human Resources
- *Personnel specialist*

Financial Management
- *Financial specialist - corporate*
- *Domain owner - service* [1]
- *Domain owner - data* [2]

Legal Services
- *Corporate lawyer*

Research & Development

Business Teams and Roles

Business Sector Management
- *Executives* [4]

Operations Units-Any Team
- *Client-partner*
- *Cross-sector Roles* [5]
- *User - partner*

Manufacturing - Any Team
- *Cross-sector roles*[5]

Quality Assurance
- *Quality management coordinator*
- *Testing specialist - business*

Process Management
- *Developer - process* [1]
- *Process coordinator - business* [1]
- *Workflow*

Requirements Management
- *Project initiation manager* [2]
- *Business analyst-client team*

[1] *New role*
[2] *Expanded Role with new name*
[3] *Old name for new role*
[4] *Business Management Roles*
[5] *Cross-sector Roles*

BASE Teams and Roles

BASE Management
- *Executive - BASE* [2]

BASE Communications
- *Communications specialist - BASE*
- *Facilitator*
- *User Interface specialist*
- *Writer - business*
- *Writer-technology*

BASE Program Management
- *BASE Program coordinator* [1]
- *Business analyst-extranet* [1]
- *Business analyst-BASE*
- *Financial specialist - BASE*

Compliance Management
- *Compliance specialist - business*
- *Compliance specialist - technology*
- *Process coordinator - technology* [2]
- *Risk analyst-business*
- *Risk analyst - technology*

SOA Competency
- *Architect - SOA* [1]
- *SOA technology specialist* [1]
- *Testing specialist -*

Technology Teams and Roles

Technology Sector Management
- *Executive - technology*

Business Technology
- *Project manager-business technology* [2]
- *Architect - software*
- *Developer - application*
- *Developer - legacy adaptation* [1]
- *Developer - SOA* [1]
- *Team leader*
- *Tool specialist* [2]

Data Center
- *Project manager-infrastructure technology*
- *Architect - availability* [2]
- *Service assurance*

User Support
- *Help desk*
- *Security administrator*
- *User support specialist*

Data Management
- *Data specialist*
- *Data administrator*
- *Developer - database*

Infrastructure Technology
- *Architect - enterprise*
- *Architect-infrastructure*
- *Architect-network*

[4]*Business Sector Management Roles*
- *Executives (Operations, Manufacturing, Sales and Marketing, Technology)*
- *Sponsors (Operations, Manufacturing, Sales and Marketing)*

[5] *Cross-sector Roles-May be on any team*
- *Clients/visionaries (BASE, Operations, Corporate, Manufacturing, Sales and Marketing, Technology)*
- *Stakeholders (BASE, Operations, Corporate, Manufacturing, Sales and Marketing, Technology)*
- *Subject matter experts (BASE, Operations, Corporate, Manufacturing, Sales and Marketing, Technology)*
- *Sponsors (BASE, Operations, Corporate, Manufacturing, Sales and Marketing, Technology)*

Fig. 13 - Daxiao WFSOA-Related Teams and Roles ©

<HM>: We reward those who ensure that the right things are done at the right time, especially if they are going beyond the call of duty.

Their efforts appear in the planning history.

<Sharf>: Then they end up stepping on each other's toes.

<HM>: It is possible to see what everyone is planning to do. If there are visible conflicts, there are conflict resolution processes. If there is not time to correct the process, we recommend doing what is right.

<Sharf>: *I must stop this. I'm holding myself up.* Show us how it works.

<Hank>: Fig. 13 above contains a list of the roles that our people fill and the roles with which we interact to make WFSOA work. Notice that the roles are associated with the teams where their primary SOA activities are performed. That gives you a good idea of their major responsibilities.

<Sharf>: Whoa! After that build-up, those are the same teams and roles that you showed us this morning in the four parts of Table A.1, but the writers, facilitators, SOA technology specialists, and the research scientist are missing.

<Hank>: ***OOKAAY! I see why he's accustomed to people being afraid of him. His memory may be as good as H's or Maja's, and he's a walking calculator.***

<Sharf>: I'm looking for the SOA roles and responsibilities.

<Hank>: They are the same roles. The SOA technologists overlap with most of the technology roles. The research scientist also overlaps many other roles. SOA equals SOX, which equals SOA.

<Sharf>: That cannot be right.

<HM>: Let us phrase the apparent irregularity in a different light. What can you imagine that we could be doing in "BIG SOA" that shouldn't be covered by SOX guidelines?

<Sharf>: We will return to this until we can show you how it can be clarified. It seems that you have forgotten several critical roles. Off the top of my head, I see that you have omitted:

- BPEL specialist.
- Change management.
- Interoperability tester.
- SOAP specialist.
- UDDI administrator.
- WSDL specialist.
- XML specialist [...]

Rennie, tell me what I'm missing.

<Rennie>: You're doing just fine.

<Hank>: Those are **LITTLE SOA** roles.

<Rennie>: They cannot be omitted.

<HM>: We did not forget anything that William mentioned. You found our Catch-22. We are often accused of having too many roles, even when we present the short list that you see here.

<Hank>: With that in mind, focus your attention on Tables A.13.1 and A.13.2. They are extracted from the information we placed in the rules engine for verifying activity list contents. They are also the lists that the Human Resources Department uses when they are interpreting résumés.

Table A.13.1 lists SOA-related role names, process categories associated with each role, and the Team and the Sector where the roles discharge their primary responsibilities. You may also infer responsibilities from Fig. 14 below. It shows the roles within the process categories. We will verify the primary roles in Fig. 14 with Table A.13.1 as soon as we have an opportunity.

Alternate role names in Table A.13.2 are referenced back to preferred Daxiao role names in Table A.13.1. If the two Tables are combined, they provide the most comprehensive list of roles you will see associated with SOA, even though the client and user roles have been collapsed down to 15 or 16. Physical facility roles are not there. SOA support for desktops and handheld devices is under "User support specialist".

<Sharf>: This makes more sense, except that there are almost 250 roles between the two tables.

<Hank>: The combined tables contain every one of the roles you believed that we had missed.

Roles in Enabling Process Domain	Roles in Support Process Categories
Governance Process Category Architect - corporate Architect - SOA BASE Program coordinator Board of Directors Business analyst - corporate Compliance specialist - business Compliance specialist - technology Corporate lawyer Executives (all sectors and units) Financial specialist(s) Process coordinator - technology Procurement specialist Risk analyst - business Risk analyst - technology Security specialist - corporate Security specialist - technology SOA librarian Strategist - corporate **BASE communications Process Category** Communications specialist - BASE Communications specialist - corporate Facilitator Knowledge Consolidator Writer - business Writer - technology **Human Resources Support Process Category** Training specialist Personnel specialist	**Architecture Process Category** Architect-enterprise Architect - infrastructure Architect - network Asset librarian Deployment specialist Integration specialist Network services specialist Security administrator Tool administrator **Data Management Process Category** Data specialist Data administrator Developer - database Domain owner - data **Environment Management Process Category** Architect - Availability Help desk Service assurance Security administrator User - business operations Users - (all sectors and units) User - partner User support specialist

Roles in Delivery Process Domain	
Requirements Coordination Process Category Business analyst - BASE Business analyst - client team Business analyst - Extranet Clients (all sectors and units) Client - partner Process coordinator - business Project initiation manager Quality management coordinator Requirements analyst Research scientist Sponsors (all sectors and units) Stakeholders (all sectors and units) Subject matter experts (all sectors and units) Testing specialist - business Testing specialist - technology Writer - requirements Workflow analyst	**Product Creation Process Category** Architect - software Developer - application Developer - legacy adaptation Developer - process Developer - SOA SOA technology specialist Team leader Tool specialist User interface specialist **Project Management Process Category** Domain owner - service Planning specialist Project manager - infrastructure technology Project manager - SOA Project manager - business technology

Fig. 14 - **Roles within Process Domains and Process Categories**

<HM>: If you wish to reduce the size of the first list, 114 may be adjusted as shown in Table A.14.1. *That was Armstrong's idea.*

<Sharf>: Why didn't you start with 71 in the first place?

<HM>: This gave us an opportunity to show how the list evolved and how the roles are related.

<Sharf>: It is possible to tell which roles are SOA roles. All I have to do is count (1) new, and (2) expanded with new name.

<HM>: Every one of those other roles affects or is affected by WFSOA.

<Sharf>: Are you saying that you need at least 71 people to do SOA? How would smaller companies handle the requirement?

<HM>: *That is a question from the SOX audit. I'm sure he knows that.* These are roles, not individual jobs. Some people perform multiple roles, and most roles are assigned to more than one person. In a smaller company, several of the roles could be collapsed.

<Sharf>: If you were in a smaller company, what would you collapse?

Role Rotation Candidates

<HM>: Table A.14.2 shows roles with responsibilities in similar areas. We leave them separated because of different access rights, approval authority, or responsibilities. If we merged them using this scheme *(also suggested by Armstrong)*, the number is fewer than 50.

Notice that Table A.14.2 may also be used to identify possible rotation candidates. We mentioned rotation in relation to project management, but we also rotate people in other roles.

<Rennie>: Seventy-one is still a very high number. Why don't you implement role clusters?

<HM>: I may have agreed with that suggestion, but Human Resources, my own risk analysts, and the security people believe that 114 is a better number. They say it assists with skills tracking, role-based security, and separation of responsibilities.

They also say that if you have multiple roles allow both coarse-grained and fine-grained control. If we collapse the roles, the security people would have to work at the individual level to achieve the control that we need.

It would not have been astute to argue with any of those reasons.

<Sharf>: Some of the roles have levels, but most do not. Why is that the case?

<HM>: For us, roles don't have levels. Job descriptions are associated with levels. Senior people on the organization chart are related to these roles. However, Macedon, who is very senior, has recent college graduates who are also project initiation managers. An executive, a sponsor, or a client may be an EVP, an SVP, or a VP.

<Sharf>: Where are the responsibilities for the 71 roles?

<HM>: Human Resources just sent over a set of updated and approved role descriptions. They were approved by Dr. Emery-Baldwin, Dr. Daniel Piccolo, Weldon Armstrong, and me. Gunnar hasn't seen this set, but he gave me permission to show them to you.

<Sharf>: *They really are serious about this. I have to figure out a legitimate way to avoid it.* When did you talk to Gunther? I had trouble reaching him.

<HM>: *Gunther?* I spoke to him before lunch.

<Sharf>: *That means Andy knows I'm here. He acted as if they had never had a civil conversation.* Show me the descriptions.

<HM>: You will see them after we review numbers. We thought we would show you the smaller charts first. Table 13-BASE Teams and Headcount and Table 14-BASE Role Participation in WFSOA Process Categories show that BASE is associated with 21 roles. Six overlap with other roles (client, sponsor, stakeholder, subject matter expert, user, and visionary).

Table 13 - BASE (Governance) Teams and Headcount			
Teams, Roles (BASE), Headcount	SOA Staff	Staff Total	Discussion
BASE Management			Sector management reports to the president
♦ Executive - BASE	2	2	
Team Total	2	2	
BASE Communications			Everyone on this team works on knowledge coordination for SOX and SOA when they do not have other official assignments. Seven business writers work with procurement to prepare proposals and with Armstrong's technology teams.
♦ Communication specialist - BASE	10	10	
♦ Facilitator	8	8	
♦ User interface specialist	7	7	
♦ Writer - business (BASE)	6	13	
♦ Writer - technology (BASE)	9	9	
Team Total	40	47	
BASE Program Management			This team coordinates activities within the BASE team and between our team and the other sectors. They also monitor the status of the SOX, CMMI, and ITIL.
♦ BASE Program coordinator	8	15	
♦ Financial specialist - BASE	8	8	
♦ Business analyst - Extranet	8	8	
♦ Business analyst - BASE	11	11	
Team Total	35	42	
Compliance Management			These roles handle compliance and risk management for the entire company. Process coordinators (methodologists) concentrate on processes and procedures associated with program- and technology-related process development. Forty-two people deal with non-IT compliance and risk in manufacturing, intellectual property, etc.
♦ Compliance specialist - business	20	42	
♦ Compliance specialist - technology	14	20	
♦ Process coordinator - technology	11	11	
♦ Risk analyst - business	9	19	
♦ Risk analyst - technology	10	14	
Team Total	64	106	
SOA Implementation			These are rotating managers who specialize in SOA project delivery.
♦ Project Manager - SOA	20	20	
Team Total	20	20	
SOA Competency			The technology specialists on this team have varied specialties that mirror roles in the technology and business sectors, except that they are the foremost experts on Web services, business process management, and service- oriented architecture. They organize as project teams for research and quick-hit projects.
♦ Architect - SOA	10	10	
♦ Testing specialist - technology	12	14	
♦ SOA technology specialist	102	102	
Team Total	124	126	
SOA Library Management			Most of the people on this team formerly worked in the configuration section of the technology team or in corporate communications.
♦ Knowledge consolidator	20	20	
♦ SOA librarian	5	5	
Team Total	25	25	
Vendor Management			This team handles procurement for the entire company. Thirty-two people handle non-IT procurement (e.g., manufacturing, facilities, etc.).
♦ Procurement specialist	10	42	
Team Total	10	42	
Sector Total	320	410	

Table 14 - BASE (Governance) Role Participation in WFSOA Process Categories

Enabling Process Categories

Governance Processes

Role	Count
Architect - SOA	10
Compliance specialist - business	20
Compliance specialist - technology	14
Executive - BASE	2
Financial specialist - Base	8
Process coordinator - technology	11
Procurement specialist	10
Risk analyst - business	9
Risk analyst - technology	10
SOA librarian	5
BASE Program coordinator	8
Process Total	107

BASE Communications Processes

Role	Count
Communication specialist - BASE	10
Facilitator	8
Knowledge consolidator	20
Writer - business (BASE)	6
Writer - technology (BASE)	9
Process Total	53

Delivery Process Categories

Requirements Coordination Processes

Role	Count
Business analyst - Extranet	8
Business analysts - BASE	11
Testing specialist - technology	12
Process Total	31

Product Creation Processes

Role	Count
SOA technology specialist	102
User interface specialist	7
Process Total	109

Project Management Processes

Role	Count
Project management - SOA	20
Process Total	20

<Sharf>: How much of this is SOX.

<HM>: ***I will try this again.*** All my people work on SOX. Seventy-eight percent of my people (78.05% to be more precise) work on SOA. Everyone who is doing SOA is doing SOA-1 (SOX) by default. The differences, as you can see, are in compliance and procurement. My compliance and risk people handle areas that are not yet absorbed under SOA. The procurement people handle purchases for manufacturing and assembly areas that come under SOX, but are not directly related to SOA.

<Sharf>: You don't have numbers for the other roles!

<HM>: I just told you that I only had 21 roles that are unique to BASE. No one in those other roles works for me. Therefore, the numbers are outside my purview. Furthermore, we are the only ones who maintain counts by primary role. Everyone else counts by title.

<Sharf>: Somebody must be keeping track of that information. Where are your audit figures?

<HM>: I am not authorized to give you audit information.

<Sharf>: It would be better if you made every effort to cooperate.

<Rennie>: Will!

<HM>: ***Val will be here soon.*** I will check to see what I can do. I would not wish to get in trouble for giving away the wrong information.

<Sharf>: Don't bother. I will get it from someone who has fewer restrictions. You are still shell-shocked. Make a note Rennie.

WFSOA Roles and Process Categories

<Hank>: We'll skip the other counts.

<Rennie>: No. We want to see them.

<Hank>: Table 14 shows how the roles are distributed among the nine process categories. You may compare that to the information in Fig. 14.

- We have approximately an equal number of participants in Governance and Product Creation.
- The next heaviest concentration is in the Communications Team, as it needs to be, given the huge number of communication barriers we must still overcome. We have seen many examples today.
- We have no one in the Support categories. However, BASE has a person (we will not mention the name) who is internationally recognized as being among the best in security and data areas.

<Rennie>: Hank, why aren't you and your people listed under architecture?

<Hank>: We are enablers. The work we do is more in the area of research and guidance. We build and break down dozens of environments each month, our work may serve as models for production, but no environment that we create is used in production. While we prototype and demonstrate the SOA reference model, the final architecture responsibility belongs to Technology Infrastructure.

BASE-Related Roles and Generic WFSOA Project Methodology

<Rennie>: We are finally ready for the role descriptions, right?

<Hank>: Not quite.

<Sharf>: What is the hold-up now?

<Hank>: We must eliminate any confusion about whether we had documented process flows. Table 15.1 summarizes WFSOA Product Delivery processes. It shows the phases when BASE-related roles typically begin participation in SOA work activities. They are divided according to the primary reporting sectors of participating roles.

This is an overview of our ***generic WFSOA project methodology***. The phases are lengthened, shortened, or merged, depending upon the methodology recommended by SOA and software architects on individual projects.

Notice the alignment across the columns. Interpret that to mean "no later than". If a role starts later than recommended, the project could have problems. Roles may work in any phase after they begin participating in a project. Notice, for example, that domain owners enter the process at the same time as sponsors. The corporate strategist starts at the same time as the compliance specialist and the requirements analysts.

Notice that:

1. ***Just-in-time participation by clients is most critical to the success in ALL phases.***
2. Requirements gathering and analysis are controlled by the business with guidance from BASE and Technology.
3. Design, construction, testing, and deployment are controlled by technology with guidance from the business and assistance from BASE.
4. SOA project managers report to technology when they are managing a business technology project or a data upgrade project.
5. All the critical roles are involved before deployment.
6. Though deployment specialists report to technology managers, they work closely with the business process coordinators.

<Sharf>: Why is the user interface specialist in Communications and not in technology?

<Hank>: They facilitate verbal, visual, and audio communication with people. If they stay with us, they provide the company with the maximum benefit from the training we've given them.

If they were in technology, they'd be trying to figure out the technology behind our animation software. That's a better job for the tool specialist.

Project Roles for LITTLE SOA

<Sharf>: There are about 46 roles here. This proves that you don't need over a hundred.

<HM>: First, this is what you need for LITTLE SOA, i.e., individual Web Services projects. For instance, the corporate architect would not need to be here. Second, there may be 45 entries in the table, but there are more than 45 roles. Hank, show him how to count again.

Table 15 - Sequence of Role Participation in BASE Work Request and Project Phases				
Creation Phase	Order of Business Role Participation	Order of BASE Role Participation	Order of Technology Role Participation	Order of Corporate Role Participation
Controlled by Business with assistance from BASE and Technology				
Requirements	♦ Clients/visionaries/ users	↓	↓	↓
	♦ Sponsor(s)	----------------------->	----------------------->	♦ Corporate financial specialist ♦ Domain owners
	♦ Project initiation manager	♦ BASE Program coordinator	♦ Enterprise Architect	↓
	♦ Business analyst(s)	♦ BASE Business analyst(s)	♦ Security administrator	♦ Security specialist
	♦ Stakeholder(s)	♦ SOA Competency Team	♦ Network architect	↓
	♦ Workflow analyst	♦ SOA librarian ♦ Knowledge consolidator	♦ Asset librarian	↓
	♦ Testing specialist - business	♦ Testing specialist - technology	♦ Data specialist	↓
	♦ Requirements analyst	♦ Compliance Team members	--------------------->	♦ Corporate strategist
Analysis	♦ Process coordinator - business	♦ Process coordinator - technology	♦ Software Architect	♦ Training specialist
	♦ Subject matter experts	----------------------->	♦ Availability architect	↓
	♦ Planning specialist	♦ Project manager - SOA	♦ Project Manager - business technology	♦ Personnel specialist
Controlled by Technology with Guidance from Business and from BASE				
Design	↓	♦ User interface specialist	♦ Development team	↓
	↓	♦ Financial specialist	♦ Infrastructure architect	↓
	↓	♦ Procurement specialist	♦ Security administrator	↓
	↓	↓	♦ Data administrator	↓
	♦ Quality management coordinator	↓	♦ Integration specialist	↓
Construction	↓	↓	♦ Service assurance	↓
Testing	↓	↓	♦ Deployment specialist ♦ User support specialist	↓
Controlled by Business with Guidance from BASE and Technology				
Deployment				

<Hank>: Inflate the role counts in Table 15.1 as follows:

- Add 24. Reversing the calculations in Table A.14.1 gives you 24 more clients/sponsors/visionaries/users. Include the research scientist as a visionary.
- Add 15 - Reversing A.14.1 gives five more sponsors, stakeholders, and subject matter experts.
- Add 6 - There are as many as 5 different types of developers on the development team in addition to the team leader. There may also be a tool specialist.
- Add 3 - Two different writers and a facilitator may be used to ensure smooth project processes.
- Add 2 - For a BASE business analyst and a domain specialist.
- Add 1 - If they purchase anything, the tool administrator will get involved.
- Add 3 - There are four roles on the Compliance team.

This adds 53, giving 98.

<Sharf>: Fifty-four.

<Hank>: Ninety-nine is even better. It is easy to get from there to 114 when you toss in the executives who may be sponsors, corporate lawyers, and the corporate architect. The infrastructure project manager may be missing too.

<Sharf>: That would be easier to understand if I had the role descriptions.

<Hank>: We often spend days on role descriptions. Because you are in a hurry, you will receive Tables A.15.1 - Education and Training Disciplines, A.15.2 (three parts) containing roles cross-referenced to disciplines, and A.16 short descriptions of the responsibilities of each role.

> **Readers**: Your Table A.16 contains comments from role incumbents - more SOA P (SOA PERSONAL INSIGHTS). William **will never see those.**
>
> The short descriptions that he receives will be available in SOA P (2). There they are associated with the list of roles/actions and deliverables.
>
> You may derive most of the contents of William's version of Table A.16 by looking at the titles in Table 1 and the roles associated specific processes in Tables A.10 through A.12. William is avoiding those, because he tried to tell Daxiao that they did not exist.

<Sharf>: Why would you give us the short descriptions? *They are still withholding information!*

<HM>: Trust me when I tell you that you want the short form [...]

<Val>: Hello. I made it just in time to clarify some of the more important items.

<Sharf>: Who are you?

<Val>: I'm Valery Van Amberg, the BASE Program coordinator. Here's my card. I'm delighted to meet you. Mr. Sharf and Ms., or is it Mrs., Vitale? Don't bother to get up. Sorry I couldn't make it this morning. I see I'm in time for some fun.

All these educational requirements must be mind-boggling.

<Sharf>: I demand to know why we would not receive all the information regarding roles and responsibilities if they are so critical to what you do. Where are the long form descriptions?

<Val>: Why didn't you explain everything to him?

<HM>: If you had not interrupted, I would have told him that Table A.15.1, Table A.15.2 (three parts), and Table A.16 come to a total of 50 to 60 pages, while individual long form descriptions may range from 2 to 100 pages.

<Sharf>: What could you possibly put in a role description to make it 100 pages long?

<Val>: The long role descriptions are used when we need to bring new hires up to speed and to allow individuals to become comfortable in new roles. They include:

1. Detailed descriptions (long form) and expected interactions with other roles.
2. Roles cross-referenced to processes (automated and manual).

3. Role deliverables (links to sample content) - this is what produces large printed documents.
4. Frequently used contact information.
5. Frequently used information sources (Knowledge Cooperative endpoints).
6. Location(s) where roles are performed.
7. Role history and evolution.
8. Skill, education, and training requirements.

<Sharf>: *Van Amberg will be harder to handle. He's more like the executive types that I'm accustomed to dealing with.* What is included in the three tables that you are giving us?

WFSOA Education and Training

<Val>: A.15.1 includes the 35 education and training disciplines associated with BASE success. Software and hardware products associated with those disciplines are listed in Table A.7.2 (the Procurement Product List).

We consider ourselves a learning organization. A glance at Table A.15.2 - Mandatory, Optional, and Required Disciplines (cross-referenced with roles) will help you to understand why.

Table A.16 contains in one place, role names, alternate role names, titles of senior role incumbents (if applicable), usual reporting relationship, and a 2 - 25 line itemization of responsibilities. Here they are.

<Sharf>: We will let you know if the short descriptions are adequate. We may require complete sets of the long descriptions.

<HM>: *He never quits.* The "Board" gave us permission to give you the short descriptions and Dr. Emery-Baldwin sent the short descriptions.

<Sharf>: What does the corporate auditor use?

<HM>: They use the one that suits their purpose at the time.

<Val>: They tend to use long-form versions for new or changed roles as part of their audit.

<HM>: But, if you insist on the long ones, I can send a justification request to Gunnar immediately. After he secures approvals from the right people, I would estimate that Dr. Emery-Baldwin could prepare an entire set by early next week. If you would rather wait, we can reschedule.

<Sharf>: *I DO NOT want him to contact Gunnar again today, and I need as much information as I can get within the next hour.* This may be satisfactory for starters. I will get what I need from Human Resources.

<HM>: That is good. Do you wish to ask any preliminary questions, or we can take a 14-minute break while you memorize all 60 pages? I'm sure we need to be energized to deal with the dozens of questions you will have for us. I really hope that you will find it worth the wait.

We want that break to give you time to place your delicate anatomical parts where we can apply the most pressure. You are going to be in so much trouble that you won't be able get information from 411.

<Sharf>: *I won't need to make any excuses for leaving the room. I will ask a few questions, so I won't appear too anxious to get down the hall.* How would you provide training on all these topics? Why would you try to provide training in all those topics?

<Rennie>: The notes in the brackets show you how to make sense of it. I'd love to be able to do something like that.

<HM>: Dr. Piccolo convinced the Board that having an exceptionally talented organization is a competitive advantage. He says that knowledge or practical experience in each of those topics has contributed to BASE successes. Gaps in knowledge or experience in the listed topics may have contributed to BASE problems.

<Rennie>: How does it work?

<Hank>: On a regular schedule, the training area evaluates the knowledge and experiences of role incumbents. They also identify Program problems that are related to lack of skills. We perform queries against *Thunk* to discover that information. They update the table of disciplines (A.15.1) and update the cross-reference of disciplines to roles (A.15.2) every quarter. Training and education are synchronized with Strategy Management. The staff must have the skills to support the updated strategy.

<Sharf>: How do avoid getting in trouble for spending excess time and money on training?

<Val>: We haven't yet. If we had, I wouldn't be talking to you.

<Sharf>: Nobody could possibly know all the things you suggest for some of those roles.

<HM>: True, but everyone has to show progress against training goals that are tied to annual salary increases and to bonuses for their managers.

<Val>: H is not being quite truthful. A few people keep up with the courses, though they may not have hands on experience.

<Sharf>: Who!

<Val>: H is good enough to vet course content for everything technical that Docente produces, although he hasn't created training modules in more than five years.

He admits that he is weak in communications because he cannot understand what people don't understand. That's why we hired Lisse Maçon. It is most likely the main reason that you are here.

<Rennie>: How do you do that?

<HM>: Knowing something about everything is a good hobby for someone with an enforced sedentary lifestyle. I never go to sleep without ensuring that I know something that I didn't know when I woke up. My mother started it and my surrogate mother and my wife still enforce it. In fact, that is how I hooked my wife in the first place. [...] I'm sorry. That wasn't related.

<Val>: *Your "Zeusness" is what hooked her. Your smarts helped you to keep her hooked.*

<HM>: I have been to sleep more nights than 90% of the people on earth. The more you know, the easier it is to learn more.

<Sharf>: *Your women didn't teach you modesty. That is why your daughter was such an arrogant* [...] *I cannot allow myself to get distracted.*

<Val>: Maja is equally good, but with a greater communications problem. That is why she reports to Ms. Maçon. Stein (the head of compliance) is extraordinarily knowledgeable, and his communications skills have improved significantly. *Many people say he needs a wardrobe upgrade, but that is not a training topic.* Four people in Requirements Management understand something about most things. They let Alex Macedon do the talking.

[...] Darn. I figured it out after all these years!

<Rennie>: This sounds exciting. What did you figure out?

<Val>: They are so busy getting information into their heads, that they don't have enough time to get it out of their heads.

<HM>: It's worth exploring with the communications team.

<Rennie>: *He may be right! Sharf is an example.*

<Sharf>: *I never had a problem.* When do your people find time to do work? They're always taking courses. We must discuss the ROI issue later.

<HM>: They don't have to take all those courses. The ones that do often use personal time, or they use some of the time that they no longer waste fixing problems. I explained that the number of reported defects has been significantly reduced.

<Val>: Let me summarize.

1. Nobody needs everything. Doc and Docente work with Program participants to formulate customized training tracks.
2. Our training classes are tuned to the learning styles of most of the people who are assigned to a given role. Thus, they learn faster.
3. New hires come in with the "mandatory" requirements, except for the parts that are Daxiao specific.
4. We support follow-up mentoring for most of the technical courses. Much of it is provided by our SOA technology specialists, while SMEs from technology and compliance areas contribute.
5. Business units provide subject matter experts for follow-up mentoring on business topics.
6. We provide stipends for people who prove that they completed "self-directed" training. That has been particularly effective.
7. Maja worked with Docente to set up knowledge competitions. Individuals and teams may play. Winners receive token awards and plaques.
8. Our training budget is 14% percent more than the industry average, but we believe it generates 30% better results. It is good ROI.

Who Knows - Subject Matter Experts

<Rennie>: What does "Who Knows" refer to?

<Hank>: That's another way into SME.COM. We discussed that when we spoke about the Knowledge Cooperative. Notice the [m] in square brackets. Users may follow links to the designated subject matter expert (SME) "Who Knows" how to answer many of their questions.

<Sharf>: *Who cares? I want to get to roles.*

<Hank>: If an individual needs a quicker update, they can click on the [f] to get to FAQs. This ensures that role incumbents can access the information they need in the shortest amount of time.

1. Subject matter experts maintain lists of frequently asked questions, which may provide helpful information before people actually talk to the subject matter expert.
2. The next level after the FAQs is to contact the subject matter expert.
3. If a subject matter expert decides that a person needs additional training, he or she may recommend a course.
4. Most people (about 70%) find what they need without taking a course.

<Sharf>: The number 70% here and it was 90% when you were discussing the Knowledge Center?

<Val>: That number referred to general queries into the Knowledge Cooperative. Seventy percent refers to the number of people who are seeking training, but their needs are addressed by FAQs or a subject matter expert.

<Hank>: SMEs also create training snippets that accelerate responses to subsequent queries. The training snippets provide input to course creation or course updates. Ultimately, it saves time and money for everyone.

<Rennie>: You have Six Sigma among the topics, but I haven't heard you mention a Six Sigma program.

<Val>: Without our hidden Sigmas, Daxiao would not be in business. Components that control windows on billion-dollar satellites cannot fail. Since Raycroft, we had the foundation for a Six Sigma program, but we don't call it Six Sigma.

Macedon feels that we will soon be ready to add Sigmas to Product Delivery.

<Sharf>: How could you have a program if you haven't told anyone about it?

<Val>: The same way he worked on Service-Oriented Architecture foundations for years before it had a name. When we have reached a critical mass on Service-Oriented Architecture, our successors will be positioned for Six Sigma.

Extensive use of reliable services will position us to achieve the desired quality numbers. At this point, the most we can achieve is Five Sigma, and that is during two quarters in each year. Armstrong floats between three and four.

<Sharf>: When did he achieve Six Sigmas in all four quarters?

<Hank>: We mean Three Sigma or Four Sigma.

<Rennie>: If you don't have a program, how do you know what your quality numbers are?

<HM>: Acton and Mellon [...]

<Sharf>: Skip it. That is not on the list. We can show Daxiao how to proceed with Six Sigma after we improve their understanding SOA.

<Val>: *I think he just eliminated H.*

<Hank>: *I wonder if William knows what he just did.*

<Sharf>: Why are PMI and ISACA associated with so many roles? This list implies that you have hundreds of people who are certified to perform audits and hundreds of certified project managers.

<Val>: Abso-doggone-lutely. BASE has 300 people who passed the ISACA certification test. Every person on Piccolo's team is certified. Every one of the service and data domain owners is certified. Weldon is about to catch us. He already has over 200 people with certifications. Four hundred people are spread across the business units.

Approximately five percent of the entire Daxiao staff and 50% of our managers have PMI certification.

<Sharf>: Why would you pay for PMI certifications if they do not have the SOA modules that you need?

<HM>: When people understand project management fundamentals, it is easier to add SOA requirements.

<Rennie>: How did you secure approval for all of this?

<HM>: It was Dan's idea to spread the wealth outside BASE. He believes eXtreme education is a competitive advantage, as we said before. ISACA test preparation provides a wonderful technology overview. When you hear this from him, act as if you are surprised and in awe.

<Rennie>: I am awed.

<Sharf>: I am surprised. How did you keep this a secret? ***No ordinary company has a thousand trained auditors. Nobody! That is almost as many as we have in Belvedere.***

<HM>: It is not a secret. It is something we mention selectively due to the competitive advantage it provides. People who are certified to perform audits are only a bit **over one percent** of our employees, but it gives us a big boost. Fewer people have to learn lessons the hard way.

Acton helped us with the arrangements because they say it makes us informed consumers of their services.

<Sharf>: ***They are taking this learning thing to extremes. The first thing that I will recommend is to recover project time by letting people focus on the training that is relevant to their roles.*** How many people take all this training and then leave?

<Val>: About half as many people as leave other companies of equivalent size. Our pay scale is very competitive. Some people will leave a company where they have a 95% probability of being successful to take a 15% raise in a company where they have a 50 - 60% chance of succeeding. About half of the people who leave Daxiao try to return.

<Sharf>: ***He is as arrogant as Marshall is.***

<Rennie>: Does Acton worry that you will compete with them?

<HM>: Why would they worry? Of the people who are certified, 90% do not perform regular audits, though they become more effective in their other roles. Therefore, fewer than 100 of us are as good as average Acton auditors, and only 20 of us are as good as their best auditors.

<Sharf>: That means you are cheating on the experience requirement.

<HM>: Everyone who passed the test has at least three years of experience controlling something related to IT or business. Dan's people qualify due to their academic credentials.

<Sharf>: Are all three of you in the top 20?

<Val>: Yes, and I'm probably the best. I was doing it longer. ***He's checking to see if that annoyed H.***

<HM>: I had to take a crash course when they moved me over.

<Sharf>: Would you be the person who would replace H when he leaves?

<Val>: If they wanted someone older than he is to keep things working the way they are, there is no one in Daxiao who could do it better. If they needed someone who could see the future and make it happen, then they must fish in other parts of the ocean.

<Sharf>: We will show Daxiao how to find the person or people that they need, internally or externally. Meanwhile, tell us how many of your people work on SOX and how many work on Service-Oriented Architecture.

<Val>: ***You couldn't show us how to drink from a straw!*** All our people work in SOX. Seventy-eight percent of our people (plus or minus a few hundredths of a percent) work in SOA. Everyone who is doing SOA is doing SOA-1 (SOX) by default. The differences, as you see, are in compliance and procurement. My (our) compliance and risk people handle areas that are not yet absorbed under SOA. The procurement people handle purchases for our manufacturing and assembly teams that come under SOX, but they are not directly related to SOA. I know H told you that already.

<Sharf>: ***They both have the same lines. I have to find out who wrote the play***. Are any of your people consultants?

<Val>: We engage a few consultants, especially when we purchase or upgrade products. But, most of our consulting occurs in reverse. We provide consulting services to our partner organizations (***you know that already***).

<Sharf>: Why did you enter the consulting business?

<**Val**>: We did it in self-defense. We realized that if we assisted our partners, our external SOA implementations would be smoother. When we realized they were taking up more and more of our time, we tried to pull our people back. When 11 out of 20 partners who were working with us at the time offered to pay for our services, we went to the Board, and they approved our ability to earn money.

<**Sharf**>: What types of partners are included in this group?

<**HM**>: There are the partners from whom we receive parts, the partners to whom we provide assembled components, and the partners with whom we do research.

<**Sharf**>: How does the process work? I imagine that your saleswoman turned communications specialist makes the contacts, and then hands them over to your business analysts.

<**Val**>: No. It's the other way around. BASE business analysts for partner networks usually have the contacts, and they call in Lisse when they need the heavy artillery.

<**Sharf**>: How are they different from regular business analysts?

<**Val**>: Business analysts for partner networks are more politically aware. *They can stay ahead of the likes of you*. Several of them were in compliance before they took on these roles.

They have wider knowledge bases than analysts on the business team have. They need to understand networking protocols (ANSI X.12 especially), ebXML, security, and supply chain management well enough to understand when to ask for support from our network, compliance, risk, or security people. After that, they must understand the basics of the technology our partners use.

<**HM**>: They are our true engagement managers. I doubt that we have anyone as good as Rennie, but several people are close.

<**Rennie**>: Thank you. *Why did he say that?*

<**Sharf**>: *He meant to annoy me. He knows that I'm the engagement manager.*

<**HM**>: *That got him hot under the collar. It's good to know that he can't take what he dishes out.*

<**Sharf**>: How much do you have to cut back on your internal work requests?

<**Val**>: That is ridiculous. These business analysts only consulted on the external part of projects where we had internal teams working on high-priority SOA-approved assignments. Things progressed more quickly because we had our people in the partner sites making things happen faster. We were pitching to our own batters. We hit several things out of the ballpark. Nobody can touch us.

<**Sharf**>: We will need to see your partner list. *This will be another fight.*

<**Val**>: You don't need to see it, but I will give you clearance. *You've already made a fool of yourself with 25% of them.* Maja, are you there?

<**Kenneth Chase**>: This is Ken. Welcome back.

<**Sharf**>: Where are you?

<**Ken**>: I'm in the library.

<**Sharf**>: *What the hell?* Why do you have people listening to our conversations?

<**HM**>: Maja was embarrassed about needing to take the system down, especially today. She insisted on having someone listen in. She is testing our paper backup process. Notice his number in the call window.

<**Rennie**>: I noticed that this morning. William, we should discuss their collaboration products.

<**Sharf**>: I agree. When do we cover that?

<**HM**>: Lisse will cover collaboration products when you talk to her about communications.

<**Val**>: Ken, bring us a printout of the partner list. Highlight the ones where we're getting hard dollars. You may leave Ādaemoa on the list.

<**Hank**>: We were also going to discuss the BASE communications model.

<**Val**>: That is an excellent idea. It contains over 10,000+ information points that suggest how the roles interact (or do not interact) within Daxiao. It will allow you to discern primary, secondary, and tertiary interactions among the roles. It should cut the number of questions in half.

Readers: The complete communications matrix is in SOA P (2) with the ***Thunk*** List. A sample of the matrix appears in Table 17 later in the book.

<Sharf>: Would they cover that in Communications?

<Val>: It is equally beneficial to cover it with the roles. It provides the maximum possible amount of information without giving you the long, long, really long descriptions.

<Hank>: We have the catalog access information too. We were going to do that after the break.

<Val>: It is excellent that we are doing full disclosure.

William, I'm sure that we will have a beneficial relationship and you too.

[...] Ms. Vitale is very formal.

<Rennie>: Rennie.

<Val>: William and Rennie it is. Call me Val. Valery is a good Russian name for a man, but it doesn't fly well over here. Hank, do you want to keep going, or do you trust me to handle it?

<Hank>: Be my visitor. I have to prepare for an assignment with Armstrong's people tomorrow.

<Sharf>: We should move on to the roles.

<Val>: This is what you have been leading up to all morning. Here is Table A.16. It contains the short descriptions of approximately 90 roles.

<Sharf>: Why 90 and not 71?

<HM>: We show the difference between the corporate and technology security specialist, for example, but not necessarily the difference among clients in internal Daxiao units.

Read Comments from Role Incumbents in Table A.16 (Really get to know SOA Program Participants)

Readers: This is repetitive, but **you really should look at "Comments from Role Incumbents" in** the version of Table A.16 in this book. ***Belvedere will not see this information.*** It contains SOA Personal inside views from 30 Daxiao employees who will NOT actively participate in the assessment/audit/inquisition, and it contains added thoughts from nine people who will participate. If the terminology is not quite "common" to you, ***feel the personal moods and emotions.***

<Rennie>: What is the difference between a requirements analyst and a business analyst?

<Val>: *She is quick.* You've hit upon the role about which we receive the most frequent questions. A requirements analyst is a business analyst extraordinaire. ***They validate requirements that are produced by the business analysts.*** They are among the smartest people in Daxiao. They must understand everything that runs in production, everything on the wait list - it is much shorter than it was before they started - all the work in progress, and technical nuances associated with business strategy.

<Rennie>: Isn't that the same thing as the project initiation manager?

<Val>: Requirements analysts provide the information that the project initiation manager uses as input to prioritization of work requests.

Requirements analysts perform evaluations as objectively as possible, and every one of them flunked Politics 101. The project initiation manager handles the politics.

<Sharf>: How did you let that get away from you?

<HM>: I never wanted it. The way it's set up, the business people fight with each other before Daxiao spends money on two (three, five, or 10 of the same things).

<Sharf>: We should take that break. I could use some coffee.

<Hank>: Don't forget that Val has these other things for you.

<HM>: A break would be good. Should we order afternoon snacks, or do you believe the products in the vendor machine are adequate?

<Sharf>: The stuff in the consultant motel will be fine. We will meet you back here in 15 minutes. ***I saw a FAX machine in the vendor room.*** Rennie, I'm sure you need a caffeine fix too.

<Rennie>: ***He knows I don't drink coffee.*** I'm OK. I would like to ask more questions about their training program. This is obviously an important part of how they do what they do.

<Sharf>: That can wait. I want to clarify some of this information for you before it becomes too complicated.

<Rennie>: If I have questions, I will ask them. That will provide more information for our offline conversations. ***I do not want to be anywhere around when you do what we know you shouldn't be doing.***

<Sharf>: ***You will pay for this.***

----------- -----------

<HM>: That's' what happens when you have long legs that work. Rennie is that coffee or nicotine. ***I'm glad we didn't have to make up reasons to keep her away from the FAX machine.***

<Val>: It's not our problem. We have to prepare for the remainder of the day.

<Hank>: Rennie. What questions did you have about training?

<Rennie>: Let me see your training FAQs. Then I can ask questions that you haven't answered already, and you can go and do whatever you needed to do.

<Hank>: Here they are on the screen. The training list is also here. You may click in the brackets and follow the links.

<Rennie>: Thanks.

<Val>: Where are you going?

<HM>: Come with me. I need to walk off some of this stiffness.

<Hank>: I'll be in my office or otherwise reachable. I need some fresh air first. I'll sign on when I return.

<HM>: Before you go, walk with us down the hall. I need your input on something.

<Val>: We need your input on something. When are you going to let them fix whatever needs to be fixed?

<Hank>: I've been meaning to ask you that too.

<HM>: Jonas and Indy are coming over later today. They will go with me to get a brace that fits my new leg size. That should last me another couple of years.

<Hank>: Are you sure? These last few months have been rough.

<HM>: With less weight and the right support, I should be fine. ***I am not ready for them to replace my entire thigh.***

<Val>: Will you still need the cane?

<HM>: Later. I need you to help me to decide how to manage this situation now. Did you find the dumplings?

<Val>: No. I came right down.

<HM>: Let's grab a **few and enjoy the new décor.**

----------**Piccolo's Palace**----------

<Hank>: What input did you need? Everything is in the notes.

<HM>: Good. That is why you have the afternoon off. I need you here early in the morning to start saving Armstrong's backside with the Becton fiasco.

<Hank>: When I pull that out, will I have earned that promotion?

<HM>: Nope [...]

<Hank>: Why are you smiling? That will be the eighth major project that I have saved since I became a vice president. I've already saved this company millions of dollars.

<HM>: You have it already. Read this. Congratulations Mr. Managing Director.

<Hank>: This is from yesterday morning. Why didn't you tell me?

<HM>: When is the last time you checked your e-mail?

<Hank>: Thank you, thank you. Thank you. I must get home and tell Gin.

<HM>: [...] and only Gin.

<Hank>: Why? Is it a secret?

<HM>: It's not a secret. However, it may be a good idea to know where we are with Belvedere before we make an official announcement.

<Hank>: Are we really in that much trouble?

<HM>: Release my hand, and I will explain.

<Hank>: Sorry.

<HM>: You've been developing well lately, and this means you will have to grow up even faster. Listen carefully.

<Hank>: My whole body is ears.

<Val>: You mean you are all ears.

<Hank>: That's what I said.

<HM>: Let's return to the issue at hand. It is bigger than what's going to happen with BASE. Sharf is here because Gunnar had enough clout to hire him, without considering that he has a reputation for being a "Bill in a China shop".

<Hank>: Isn't that "Bull in a China store?"

<HM>: Please listen. Gunnar is trying to split the board between the newcomers and the old-timers. If he manages to do that, Mittelman will have to come down off the fence and start protecting himself. I'm not sure what that means for us. What I do know is that if we make it appear that Gunnar is not a good judge of character, he will be neutralized for some time, Mittelman can stay neutral, and that gives us time to push Piccolo's management theories past the point of no return.

<Hank>: You're doing all this for Piccolo.

<HM>: No. I'm doing it for me and us. It's a good idea to let Piccolo share the heat.

<Hank>: He also takes the credit.

<HM>: It's still a fair trade. Whom do you suppose rammed that promotion through so quickly?

<Hank>: That's good to know. Do you have a plan yet?

<HM>: We will let you know. Give Gin my regards.

<Hank>: Thanks again. I will see you early tomorrow.

<Val>: How did Piccolo pull this off in three weeks?

<HM>: It took two months to get the promotion approved.

<Val>: I mean the complete renovation of the Palace.

<HM>: Piccolo has hidden talents, especially when he is working with his family. They are as good with wood and wiring as Jonas is with electronics.

<Val>: How did he do an end run around Gunnar?

<HM>: He had to get it past Indy, and Lorrie is quite tickled by the turn of events. Don't choke on your dumplings. We will discuss décor later.

<Val>: We will discuss it now, so I can start to figure out how to get your rump and Lorrie's rump out of a Guzman sling.

<HM>: We own it. Actually, Indy owns it, as well as the space occupied by Gunnar's people. Daxiao is renting from a subsidiary of Frey Associates, which is owned by Simone Winslow, an aging fashion Model who ran out of funds before she could establish her own fashion line.

<Val>: Why would you omit to tell me that you intended to do that?

<HM>: At first, Nicky and Indy didn't know whether we could pull it off. When it came through, you were busy keeping things going, while I was in the hospital relaxing after my last tumble *(and getting measured for a new thigh).* After I came back, we were both tied up with Asia.

<Val>: *I wonder if anybody on earth can keep track of the machinations of Nicola and Piccolo.*

<HM>: It never came up in conversation because it didn't affect anything related to you, except that you'll have to learn how to use the new espresso machine. I believe it's a torture apparatus.

<Val>: Does Gunnar know?

<HM>: I doubt that he would have forced Lorrie to take the space back if he knew. He accepted the 10% increase per square foot, considering the fine quality of the renovations. This Simone person kept Piccolo's palace for herself, and she allows unlimited access to a limited number of people.

<Dan>: Indira Simone Frey-Marshall Winslow. Move the panel, so I can see you, and use the headphones. You don't want squeals and Tomaso tantrums flowing out into the hall.

<Val>: *We get used to it when Liz has them here.* How is it that Monsignor Tomaso is with you today?

<Dan>: Stop grinning. Liz is at the doctor's office with Octavia, the nanny has whatever Octavia is spreading, and I have a chance to play executive daddy.

<HM>: How is Viola handling the situation?

<Dan>: Mrs. Johnson just found the immediate need to run out and purchase a box of crayons with all the colors. She may have run out if he didn't need the crayons.

Viola and I are drinking gallons of Machi's ginger and chamomile tea today. The combination allows us to maintain an even keel.

<HM>: Let me contact Ernest first, and then we will discuss the 6'6" calamity that we must handle.

<Ernest>: Where are you?

<HM>: Page me in the Command Center in five minutes, and do it every five minutes until Sharf shows up. Rennie is probably still there. Call me in Piccolo's Palace as soon as they are both there.

<Ernest>: Who's Rennie?

<HM>: That's the young woman from Belvedere.

<Ernest>: How can you answer from the command center if you are in the palace? Are you sure that everything is all right?

<HM>: Ernest, my knee is a long way from my head. Say, "OK Boss".

<Ernest>: OK Boss.

<Val>: You both know that William is not the problem. He is the symptom of a problem.

<HM>: You are correct. We want to focus Gunnar's attention on something else long enough for us to be able to position our people effectively.

<Val>: Cut the people crap. Your worst person could find an equivalent job within two months (before the shortest package ran out). Your best people could find a better job within a week. Dan's learning organization is working for them.

<Dan>: You like me after all.

[...] Put that down. [...] Mommy is not here, and I am.

<Val>: Don't get carried away. Occasionally, you have a good idea.

<Val>: Gunnar is a bigger symptom, but not the problem. No matter how fast Piccolo dances, your handiwork is becoming glaring. Making SOA work is the easy part. Dealing with the power you sneaked while no one was looking will be more difficult. Gunnar wants to control that power and so will other people when they discover that it exists.

<HM>: Maybe you're right.

<Val>: This is not the time to act naïve. You have hidden the Marshall/Piccolo power grid for almost four years. I repeat. Gunnar or someone else had to figure it out sooner rather than later.

<HM>: Why isn't he satisfied with the damage he did the last time?

<Val>: My heart bleeds. You had anxiety attacks, and you received full salary for five months while you used the time to help Baby Huey earn millions, which he shares generously with his family.

Unless they figure out how to control you this time, and they don't even know what they are trying to control, what Gunnar did before was like swatting a gnat. Play their game, or get out of the game.

<HM>: Gunnar can't even control his own man. We were discussing loose cannons when you arrived.

<Dan>: What loose cannon?

<HM>: Gunnar didn't know Sharf was going to show up three days earlier than originally planned.

<Val>: What does Machi have to say about this?

<HM>: Ironically, she recommended a passive approach. She says we could encourage William to cause a lot of confusion, and then we could run in and clear up the confusion. Dan could sugarcoat what we're doing with his classic theories of everything.

<Val>: Thereby clarifying exactly how much clout you have.

<HM>: There was also Plan Aria. That one is also passive.

<Val>: What am I missing? You know I sleep through opera.

<Dan>: Did you sleep through freshman biology?

<HM>: It's a bad pun. We're discussing a carefully orchestrated version of what worries the entire team. We split the team and I leave the game.

<Val>: OOKAAY. I understand now. You're you referring to the flat worm.

<HM>: I'm talking about an organism that one can cut into dozens of pieces, and then the pieces regenerate. Lately, they have proven that the larger pieces remember most of the conditioning that the original worm experienced.

<Val>: Finally, the cross training makes sense, and it actually provided the skills we need to do a better job.

<Dan>: With two acclamations that close upon one another, I can hardly breathe.

[...] You need a time out, three minutes in the corner.

<Val>: Let me think about it a minute: OOKAAY. We will begin by expansion and enforcement of the role-based communications model. That will provide the invisible food supply for the regenerating organism.

<Dan>: My wife is truly brilliant, don't you think?

<Val>: We divide the BASE worm so that:

- Hank reports to Piccolo. His Cambridge degree would allow him to gain acceptance with your "egg nuts".

<Dan>: That is almost as good as having HM.

<Val>:

- Liz goes to Ellison. She'll be able to monitor what Gunnar's doing over there without putting herself in the line of fire.
- Jasper takes Onesti. Armstrong messed up too much to take that back.
- We split the competency team. The ones that Armstrong tried to dump will work for Macedon or Piccolo. Armstrong will have the remainder, especially the ones that have proven to Armstrong's managers how indispensable they are.
- We stop rotating the SOA project managers, give them to Jasper, and let them manage the biggest service domains we can cobble together.
- Maja becomes a data domain owner for all those strange databases that no one wants to bother with anyhow. That means she reports to Jasper. They're each tough enough for the other.
- Stein reports to Justin, just as H did before all this started, and as I did before I left. Either that or he reports to Guzman.
- Barca gets Partner Networks officially, although Macedon will run it for him. Gunnar will want it, but Macedon can make a case that it is related to logistics.
- If you want to work after your knee heals, you consult for Acton. You should be fine by the time Daxiao starts hiccupping.
- I retire again. We [...] I still have the place on Paradise Island. They have an AA chapter in Nassau.

[...] What are you doing to the little fellow?

<Dan>: I'm making him serve his time.

That is especially perceptive analysis, considering the source. You must have been talking to Machi lately.

<Val>: That's two in the same breath.

<HM>: Play nice. We implement Plan Aria and effectively eliminate his Gunnary target.

<Val>: It's obvious, once you think about it. It's also the wimp's way out, if I may speak honestly. These people have been kicking you in the teeth for 35 years. You finally found Mr. Glib to support you while you get what you have earned, and you're not willing to fight for it.

<Dan>: I'm glad Val said it instead of me.

<HM>: You are tired, Dan is frazzled, and neither one of you is thinking straight.

Do you agree that there is a 90% probability that Gunnar, or some other cabal, will be willing to destroy that which they do not understand or control?

<Val>: I just said that.

<HM>: Whom do I have as an ally?

<Val>: Maybe Lorrie, definitely Macedon, and the Doc. Dan must appear neutral or totally in favor of Piccolo. That is how he will provide benefit to us. Guzman/Acton finds our work more than acceptable. At least Guzman thinks you're too naïve to be dishonest.

<HM>: Lorrie and Alex are not enemies. Nor can we afford to let them hurt themselves for us. The Doc is a very effective "yes madam" for Justin, and we need her on Mittelman's side, just as we need Dan, Alex, and Lorrie on Dan's, Alex's, and Lorrie's sides. Therefore, I have one and four halves out of approximately 10 internal people.

In addition, Guzman is busy fighting take-over bids. That is how they slipped Belvedere past him.

On the other hand, how many people do you believe Gunnar has?

<Val>: He has Chiu in his pocket. I think. Armstrong acts as if he's learning from you, but he would be equally happy to get rid of you. Your automated process creation is starting to frighten Barca. He's suddenly discovering that he can't keep up you, and when your processes work, he loses people.

One third of the Board is solidly in favor of Gunnar, one third is solidly against him, but not necessarily in favor of you - they don't know you, and a third of them are not sure. They don't understand why you are not interested in joining their exclusive club. Mittelman seems to have fallen off the fence in Gunnar's direction.

<HM>: That means I'm outnumbered. I won't finish the pun. I could spend the next few months strengthening our communications and moving us closer to a critical mass, or I could fight with Gunnar. We would most likely get scraped and battered before we lost. It is a waste of corporate resources.

Alternatively, we can concede with elegance, and I can limp out gracefully.

<Val>: I hope you are not contemplating murder as a going away present. That look is scary.

<HM>: I'm sorry. I forget sometimes. *My leg is killing me. All of this from a little whack on the brace makes no sense.*

Career assassination is more like it. We strap political explosives to Sharf, and point him at Gunnar. That should soften him up while we figure out if he will be useful to you. Machi will be proud of me.

<Val>: If you know anything about Gunnar or Sharf that we don't know, talk fast. [...] You know what I mean.

<HM>:

1. First, Sharf tangled with Indy in school, Nicky showed her how to deal with it, and it is not likely that he forgot the experience.

<Val>: What type of tangle?

<HM>: Sharf was a teaching assistant who played favorites, and Indy was not one of his favorites.

<Dan>: Why would he be angry with you if he was the one that was picking on Indy?

<Val>: Why are you just telling me now?

<HM>: It happened during a time when I was worried about losing my leg (*just as I am now*), so they didn't bother to tell me until Sharf's name came up again last week. He's upset because he lost the fight that he started and ended up dropping out of a PhD program.

<Dan>: We should look into that further.

<HM>: We can look later. He was near the bottom of Machi's hate list, so I'm not worried. He makes more money doing what he does.

<Val>: *We should still look into it.* Keep going.

<HM>:

2. Sharf applied at Acton, and they turned him down. Acton hired Indy three years later. He knows because they competed for the same business a few times.
3. Probability 70%. He scheduled three days early because he needed information to help him get a contract with Ādaemoa.
4. Probability 90%. William is faxing the roles list to his people now. Thanks for backing me up on the intellectual property thing. That is why we have time. The paper Ken used was selected to ensure that it would get jammed in the fax machine.
5. Probability less than 10%. Sharf will ever be able to view our Program objectively.
6. Probability 100%. If he sees anything positive, he will pretend he has already implemented ways of improving on it.
7. Probability 80%. Rennie would fit with us.

<Val>: Henrietta?

<HM>: It pays to have options. All our people are a bit scared. Hank would be easiest to lose and hardest to replace.

<Val>: Hiring her could pose some contractual difficulties.

<HM>: It is also tied into the roles silliness. Wait just a moment.

[...] Gary, this is Marshall.

<Gary Augen>: Yes Mr. Boss, I know who you are.

<HM>: Pull the log for any transmission attempts from the fax machine in the motel that occurred in the last 10 minutes. Bring it to me in the command center in about thirty-five minutes. Rush in. Act as if you found a major security breach that you must report immediately.

<Gary>: Yes Mr. Boss. Your wish is my command.

<Val>: What's with the "Boss" business?

<HM>: I told them they must be respectful when C-level auditors are in the building.

<Dan>: It's about time.

<Val>: Why bother hiding information about the roles? Even with full disclosure:

- He wouldn't be able to explain it to anyone - our own people don't understand.
- Few people would have the guts to do it.
- The one's who are closest to us are still a couple of years behind us.

<HM>: But, they wouldn't remain behind us if Sharf does something to give Gunnar a reason to stop everything until they figure out how to replace me. Nor would they remain behind us if I am replaced and the replacement stops everything until a new manager reaches his or her stride.

<Val>: That still doesn't explain why you did the "secret roles" gambit.

<HM>: We created leverage. Ādaemoa is treating the roles list as a tiebreaker. If William did indeed rush down the hall to fax information to his people at Ādaemoa, when we show him the security report on the transmission, embarrassment of the highest order will occur. That will put him and Gunnar off balance, especially since Gunnar has been trying to use Ādaemoa to pull us out of Partner Networks.

<Val>: He could say he was sending information that would allow his team to assist with the Daxiao assignment.

<HM>: But, if he sent it to his team at Ādaemoa, it will be touchy, especially after I specifically mentioned the intellectual property issue. Belvedere might accidentally leave it where a competitor could see it.

<Val>: Ādaemoa has roles information from us already. I still don't see how this will aid us?

<HM>: Gunnar will be embarrassed. He wants power at Daxiao. He would not want it to appear that he engaged and outsider who does, in a negative way, that which he fights so vigorously when our people do it, even when projects benefit Daxiao (and Gunnar) more than our partners.

<Val>: He fought it because it was not his idea, and he hasn't figured out how to steal if from you yet. We need more than that.

<**HM**>: We have a huge lemon with which we must make the best lemonade possible. I want Sharf to leave here today, embarrassed, frustrated, livid, misguided, and with a wedge building between him and Rennie. The last part shouldn't be too difficult. I started that already.

<**Dan**>: You have two hours to manage as many of those as possible. I'm sure Tomaso could handle it, but I can't get him there in time. What rabbit will you pull out of the hat this time?

<**HM**>: Redirection is in order. We will point him at everyone who has taken our ideas for themselves.

<**Ernest**>: Mr. Marshall. Call Maja right away. She says it's extremely important. Sorry Mr. Val [...]

<**HM**>: I told you to relax. Neither of you is following my very specific instructions.

<**Dan**>: You'd better call her. If you don't, she'll have one of her robots banging on your knee.

<**HM**>: Half a ring. What is sufficiently important that you would risk giving Ernest an anxiety attack?

[...] Being you is fine. I am a bit off center today.

[...] While I have you on the phone, tell Ken to drop of the year-to-date SOA participation counts in the Command Center along with the partner list.

[...] Give the list for the entire company.

[...] Do it immediately. Tell him to put a big note on top that says BASE counts and leave them where Hank was sitting, whether I'm there are not. In fact, if the consultants are in the room, he should as them to remind me of the counts when I return.

[...] No. Do not cut your vacation short. We will talk later.

<**Val**>: This crisis is [...]

<**HM**>: We have a better understanding of the original crisis.

- Will is married to Gunnar's sister.
- Will lives beyond his means, trying to keep up with his brother-in-law.
- Will bid on projects with seven of the eleven partners we worked with last year. He believes I caused him personally to lose at least $200,000 last year.

<**Val**>: Are you sure Maja left the agency?

<**HM**>: I'm not sure. But, the information about Gunnar's relationship to Sharf has nothing to do with the agency. She found them in the white pages. She'll be submitting a voucher for $29.97 for three reports.

<**Val**>: Losing $200,000 is enough to upset him. Let's return to the part about livid, misguided, frustrated, and isolated.

<**HM**>:

- Livid is easy. At some time before he leaves, we will tell him what we know, and the things we believe with 70% or higher probability, even if he decides to send fuzzy photos using his cell phone.
- Frustrated and misguided is easy. He insists that we divide headcounts between SOX and SOA. The next thing you and I are going to do is have a strenuous disagreement about whether you should explain the BASE participation report. If you did, he might be able to figure out our secret.

<**Val**>: Which secret would that be?

<**HM**>: The one where he finds out that this is really Mittelman's, Armstrong's, and Jasper's show, while Gunnar and the other managers on our SOA list are providing the critical SOA guidance. We've spent the last few years implementing other people's ideas, and they don't realize it because they still don't communicate with each other as much as they should. **We have to work on communications. That part is no joke.**

He finds out that I've been left in position to take the flack all this time if something blew up; they get the credit whenever things are successful, and now they feel it's time to take back what's rightfully theirs. Mittelman's bonus and the gap between Armstrong's and my salaries prove it.

<**Val**>: How long will it take Maja to produce the participation report?

<**HM**>: Dan makes them keep copies of that one in case we have a spur of the moment "Razzle and Dazzle" opportunity. Ken should be dropping them in the room about now.

<Dan>: Sharf will ask the question which we are always asked, and that is, "how could we possibly convince that many people to cooperate with BASE", especially since there was never an official SOA mandate?

<Val>: How about blackmail and bribery?

<HM>: Would so many people have approved the bonus plans if they weren't leading the SOA effort in the first place?

<Val>: What about the times that you saved Armstrong from his own stupidity?

<HM>: In this respect, Armstrong is brilliant. He has grown a creative and inventive organization. He allows us into the loop at the right time to provide the appropriate structure. If it wasn't for Armstrong, Daxiao would be back in the mainframe stone age.

<Val>: That's Armstrong's line anyhow.

<HM>: You should:

1. Tell them how Armstrong wanted to move forward to **"BIG SOA"**, and we were stuck in Little SOA.
2. Reiterate the Communications Model and tell them how Ellison helped Lisse with that.
3. Go into excruciating detail about the catalog access rights, and how hard the security teams worked to put that together. Rennie will enjoy the information about the catalog.
4. When you talk to Rennie, slip and call her Mags, at least once, and then apologize profusely.
5. You are being her friend, and you are telling her versions of the truth that I won't even let myself believe. You get in trouble for trying to keep me honest.
6. At some time, I will send you an obvious sign that says stop with the sarcasm. You will not stop.
7. She will tell him later that you were being sarcastic.

Val>: Anticipated result:

HM>:

1. Sharf will get annoyed because you are paying attention to Rennie.
2. He will not listen to her because he will be annoyed that you were paying attention to her.
3. Even if she already told him about the sign language (I give that a 50/50), he will be annoyed that we could communicate with her in ways that he does not understand.
4. He will report to the people across the river and tell them their own lies, with a new twist. He will say, "They should speak more frequently about SOA."
5. They will get annoyed because they will not be able to deny the lies, after telling them so often.
6. He will charge them between $4,000 and $5,000 per day for delivering those elegant lies, and he will ask for more time (and money) to discover the details behind these elegant ideas, making himself appear both gullible and greedy.
7. If we manage the livid part carefully, he might be induced to deliver his first report quickly, assuring them that he is really on the case, gullible, and greedy.

<Dan>: Labyrinthine.

<HM>: Do either of you have anything better?

<Dan>: I've spent the last four years building us up. I'd need a couple of hours to figure out how to tear you down.

<Val>: There's a 70 - 75% probability that I could deliver the results you requested. Who's Mags?

<HM>: That's a little extra for agitation value. Maja says Margaret Sharf's nickname is Mags. When you apologize, you should say she reminds you of your daughter.

<Val>: That's why I like her! She looks like an older version of my daughter.

<HM>: *She also looks like a younger version of Paula.* To summarize, we will have embarrassment, misguidance that will lead to frustration, some agitation, and livid.

<Val>: He's going to be interviewing other people. We can't trust them to deliver the wrong information.

<HM>: I want them to deliver the right information. He will record what they say (perhaps literally) and deliver it with caveats as to whether they might actually be telling the truth.

<Dan>: I will see him tomorrow. Do you have any pointers?

<Val>: You could bore him to death with your theories. Make it look like he died of natural causes.

<HM>: I promised you'd let him see your version of the maturity model.

<Dan>: That is related to strategy and tactics. Jay was coming in tomorrow afternoon. I may be able to get him to come in earlier.

<Ernest>: Mr. Marshall, they are both in the Command Center.

<HM>: Thanks Mr. Dawson. Fellows, it is time to rock and roll, as Mr. Johanssen used to say.

<Val>: Does any of this mean that you're planning on staying around?

<HM>: It means that I have decided that William Sharf is not the person who should tell them how to replace me if I leave. By the way, Hanks promotion came through.

<Dan>: I still have the touch. He may thank me profusely later.

----------**Back in the Command Center**-----------

<HM>: We've been checking to see if you were back. Did we run out of coffee again?

<Sharf>: I had a call that lasted longer than I expected. ***My people were as confused about the roles list as I was.***

<HM>: ***You mean you had to figure out how to use the FAX machine.*** I see that your passwords work. What do you have on the screen?

<Sharf>: We found SOA participant numbers. Your librarian left a package for you with this URL on top. When we typed it in, it worked. I just mailed a copy to myself.

<Rennie>: I found the Resistance List too. I was about to send it to myself. Do you mind?

<HM>: Not as long as you keep your promise to send us yours.

<Sharf>: We will.

<Val>: Here's the partner list too.

<Sharf>: I don't believe it.

<Val>: What don't you believe?

<Sharf>: ***That you're actually showing me this.***

[...] There are over 400 companies on this list. You have automated links with 235, but you only did consulting with 11.

<HM>: It will increase next year. We have repeat business and about 17 more will be coming online. Make that 16.

<Val>: Maja told you to stay away from Ādaemoa, but you didn't listen. You almost blew the whole consulting thing. If you had given them one more piece of information, Gunnar would have blown you out of the water.

<HM>: We have guests. ***William is turning red. This is working.***

<Rennie>: Where's Hank? ***Will is turning red. I wonder if they notice.***

<Val>: ***She's turning white. I will let her divert me.*** We sent him home. After working especially hard to pull this information together ahead of schedule, he needs to rest.

I will facilitate the remainder of the meeting. Let me summarize where we are, using your engagement objectives, so that we can use the remaining time to maximum benefit.

<Sharf>: We got a bit off track, but we still covered many things. ***He's tougher than Marshall is. I wonder why he's not the boss.***

<Val>: We will get off track less often. Table A.17 (Belvedere Topics) positions the information we provided this morning in relation to the topics you suggested that we should cover in the engagement notice.

One added figure and a table with many parts will be discussed during this segment. We added we added contact names, whether we touched upon the topic or not.

Discussion of questions related to role descriptions.	20 minutes
Role-based communications model	30 minutes
Role-based access control.	30 minutes
Summary of lessons learned	30 minutes

<Sharf>: *How did he do this, and he wasn't here?* This is adequate.

<Val>: Here is a proposed agenda for the remainder of the day:

<Sharf>: No. *I have to regain control of the situation.*

<Val>: What would you like to change?

<Sharf>: You missed the part about not having an agenda. You could hide things behind an agenda. I must be free to determine what's important for this examination.

<Val>: An audit without an agenda! How in the hell did you convince H to accept that?

<Sharf>: I showed him the importance of being flexible.

<HM>: *A bully to the end.* He has the Board's ear, and we don't.

<Val>: OOKAAY. What would you like to discuss, Sir William?

<Sharf>: I wish to discuss SOA participant counts. Make this Table 16 or whatever comes next, being sure not to confuse it with Table A.16. *Half of Gunnar's people use this.*

Table 16 - SOA Participation

Daxiao Teams	Reported SOA Participants	Daxiao Teams	Reported SOA Participants
BASE Management	2	Legal Services	22
BASE Program Management	38	Manufacturing	28,778
Business Technology	1394	Operations	14,599
Business Sector Management	392	Quality Assurance	193
Compliance Management	59	Requirements Management	409
Corporate Communications	33	Sales and Marketing	1316
Corporate Sector Management	44	SOA Communications	40
Data Center	213	SOA Competency	124
Data Management	154	SOA Implementation	20
Enterprise Integration	97	SOA Library Management	25
Financial Management	57	Technology Sector Management	98
Global Security	83	User Support	65
Human Resources	53	Vendor Management	10
Infrastructure Technology	237		
		Total	47,453

I need to understand why these numbers don't agree with numbers from this morning. They are much too high. Then explain why you didn't show this to me an hour ago when I asked you about role counts in the other business units.

<HM>: Those counts are related to people, not roles.

<Val>: Those numbers were not meant for this discussion. That is preparatory work for this month's SOA scorecard, and they need to be reviewed.

<Sharf>: You were either under-reporting your success this morning, or you are over-reporting here.

<HM>: We are doing neither. This morning, I was reporting on the percentage of applications that run on SOA. This report shows the number of people who have reported work against SOA-related tasks. It is occasionally exaggerated.

<Sharf>: Why would they do that?

<Val>: They want their part of the SOA bonus, and their bosses want their part of the SOA bonus.

<HM>: I make their stupid ideas work, and they take most of the credit for the work that I do. ***I believe that sounded hostile enough.***

<Sharf>: ***Found it! I really am brilliant!*** Who approved the SOA bonus allocations?

<Val>: Everyone one the Board, including a man named Laufer who attended on Gunnar's behalf. SOA was helping them to make money and to save money. They wanted to continue making money and saving money.

<Sharf>: Whose idea was it to start SOA in the first place?

<HM>: Armstrong. I told you that this morning.

<Sharf>: Who started SOA Governance?

<HM>: Piccolo convinced Mittelman to let us start.

<Sharf>: Who gave the business control of their own change management processes?

<HM>: Piccolo, Armstrong, Mittelman, Barca, and Chiu. Gunnar ignored us.

<Sharf>: What about the roles?

<HM>: Human Resources and Security, as I mentioned earlier. That's why I can't change them.

<Sharf>: What about the Roles/Activity List?

<HM>: I collected the plans. Ta- Dr. Emery-Baldwin promoted the ***Thunk*** database for us.

<Sharf>: Whose idea was it to set up the Service Mart?

<HM>: Piccolo and Armstrong.

<Sharf>: Who structured organizational change management and resistance management?

<HM>: Piccolo, D- Doc, and Docente.

<Val>: **STOP BEING SARCASTIC!**

<HM>: I can't help myself.

<Sharf>: Who did the wonders of communications?

<HM>: Ellison, Maçon, Ch- Chiu, and Ramirez.

<Sharf>: Typing.

<Val>: Docente helped me push that, ***after H set the challenge for him.***

<Sharf>: Where did the Knowledge Center originate?

<Val>: Travers barely survived being the chief knowledge officer, but he kept the ideas alive. ***That is actually the truth, except it took Maja to make the databases work with the collaboration products.***

CHAPTER IV - POLITICS AND PERSONAL - LOADING A POLITICAL GUN

<Sharf>: You're nothing but an order taker! The real brains in this outfit come up with the ideas. You install the tools and make them run so they don't bump into each other. They handle the processes and you take credit when the finish what they have done.

<HM>: The best ideas are worthless without someone to pull them together.

<Sharf>: I know what was wrong with this picture. Those numbers are high because everyone here is supporting the implementation of their own ideas.

<HM>: I take the risk. If anything fails, I am blamed. ***It sounds paranoid, but it's also true.***

<Sharf>: Marshall the genius. When is the last time you had an original thought? You're an overpaid tool jockey.

<HM>: I ca- can't take this. You handle him. ***I don't believe that he could be hoodwinked this easily. I have to leave before I bust something.***

<Rennie>: Mr. Marshall! I'm sorry.

<Sharf>: Don't be sorry.

<Val>: Where are you going?

<HM>: To find something f- for [...] L- Later.

<Val>: William, do not believe most of what he just said. He was being sarcastic because you were nastier than any engagement manager that we have ever seen.

Is he always like that Mags? ***It worked. He nearly choked.***

<Sharf and Rennie>: Who?

<Val>: What did I just say?

<Rennie>: You called me Mags.

<Val>: I'm sorry. You remind me of my daughter. I meant to say Rennie. Mr. Sharf, you still haven't explained why you have such a negative attitude?

<Sharf>: ***He was trying to rattle me.*** The quicker I get to the bottom of a situation, the less a company pays Belvedere. The company saves money immediately, and they tend to remember how I saved them money when they are looking for a company to solve other problems quickly. How close was I to the truth?

<Val>: Your observations would be viewed as acceptable in some quarters, ***such as Gunnar's quarters.***

<Sharf>: Good. All I need to understand is what he did to implement other people's ideas. Nobody could comprehend what he was doing, because it's hidden in so many places.

<Val>: Nothing is hidden, ***except the people that make things work.*** He's upset because after he completes something that appeared to be impossible, people take it from him and take credit for themselves. It's been happening for 38 years, and it's happening with SOA.

<Sharf>: Give it a break. I saw what I saw, and I heard what I heard.

<Val>: You hit a sore spot.

Now I have to stop him from doing something foolish. We can reschedule next week, according to the original plan.

<Gary>: Mr. Van Amberg. Where's the Boss?

<Val>: He stepped away. What's this?

<Gary>: He told me to pull this transmission report for him. He said it was urgent.

<Val>: Let me have it. I'll give it to him when I find him.

<Gary>: That was weird. He's usually friendly.

<Rennie>: What kind of report was it?

<Gary>: I have to go.

---------- ----------

<Rennie>: What is there to be so happy about? Aren't you worried about what's in that report?

<Sharf>: No. Whatever it is, Gunnar can fix it.

<Rennie>: How can you be so sure? ***I'm in trouble too. I should have warned Mr. Cane.***

<Sharf>: I just realized that they don't need Marshall. They could stick anyone in the middle and make this work.

<Rennie>: Did you hear what Val said? HM was being sarcastic. You are reading this incorrectly.

<Sharf>: I did it. I finally have the Marshalls where I want them.

<Rennie>: ***He's snapped.*** Please listen to me. Something is wrong. I don't know what it is, but they are doing something to trip you up.

<Sharf>: Stop worrying. We need to put together a convincing summary of what just happened.

<Rennie>: OK, but not here. I'm going back to the office. I will be there until 5:00 o'clock.

<Sharf>: [...] ***Andy.*** What do you want?

<Gunnar>: Are you with HM?

<Sharf>: Not at this moment. He is taking a breather.

<Gunnar>: You were not supposed to be there today? I had not finished explaining the situation.

<Sharf>: You've been fiddling around with this for months, and I figured out your entire problem in less than a day. Wait until you and your buddies see how elegant the solution will be. You'll have my report soon.

<Gunnar>: Did you upset HM?

<Sharf>: Only so far as being forced to tell the truth is upsetting. I found out what you mean about the stuttering.

<Gunnar>: ***This requires damage control.*** Do you have people at Ādaemoa?

<Sharf>: Yes. We're handling a deal that Marshall botched. What does that have to do with this conversation?

<Gunnar>: ***This requires major damage control.*** Why didn't you tell me? Ādaemoa is close to the top of the Daxiao list of unacceptable firms. You must avoid conflict of interest.

<Sharf>: I don't tell you where to push your sandy widgets. You can't tell me how to run my business.

<Gunnar>: Stop whatever you are doing, apologize to HM, excuse yourself, and I will meet you at my New York apartment in 45 minutes.

If you have done anything that could harm Daxiao in any way, and that includes giving assistance to nasty competitors using information you receive from us [...]

<Sharf>: I can't hear you. What did you say? My battery needs recharging. [...]

----------Piccolo's Palace----------

<HM>: Shut the door.

<Val>: What do we do now?

<HM>: Hold on a minute. It's Gunnar.

<Gunnar>: Marshall, we have to talk.

<HM>: I'm so glad you called.

<Gunnar>: I'm in the middle of something. Quick answer - why did you bring Sharf in early?

<HM>: Slow answer. He told me you wanted him to start earlier because there would be a lot to cover.

<Gunnar>: Do you believe he can handle the job?

<HM>: Definitely. He absorbs information like a sponge. ***He's about to explode all over you.***

<Gunnar>: That is what his boss said. He also says he has a few rough edges.

<HM>: Dealing with him could be difficult, but I have a brother who acts very much as he does.

<Gunnar>: I could talk to Belvedere about bringing in someone else.

<HM>: Except for what's happening with Ādaemoa, he may be well intentioned. ***He has good intentions for himself.***

<Gunnar>: What is happening at Ādaemoa?

<HM>: We are still investigating.

<Gunnar>: We should discuss this in person. I will be there in an hour to check out my new space. Make time for me.

<HM>: M- make it 45 minutes. Goodbye. *I got him. This is going to work.*

<Val>: What does he want?

<HM>: He has to come by and see his people, and he wonders if we could spend a few minutes together. I believe it's related to the fact that Sharf just hung up on him.

<Val>: When did that happen?

<HM>: While you were on your potty run.

<Val>: Here's the FAXTrax report. There was a transmission from the motel to a machine at Ādaemoa during the expected period.

<HM>: The timing is perfect. Let me make a call.

[...] Gary, it's Marshall again.

[...] Yes, I received the report and thank you very much. How long will it take you to pull the video for the same period?

[...] That is good. Ship it to the archives first, and then mail it to me this time, as well as to Bailey, Forte, Guzman, and Armstrong (for full coverage). Put a full trace on Sharf. Monitor anything he sends or receives.

[...] Goodview1. The name is William B. Sharf, with an "f".

<Val>: Where is he now?

<HM>: He is still down there scribbling furiously. He is so happy that he discovered my "secret" that he's oblivious to almost anything else.

<Val>: What happened to Rennie?

<HM>: By the time I could check, she was leaving.

<Val>: Good. It's not fair to have her caught in the middle. She seems like a nice lady - woman.

<HM>: She looks like your daughter.

<Val>: [...] except that she dresses differently.

<HM>: Your corporate and legal detection skills are overwhelming.

<Val>: What's that?

<HM>: Tylanoll.

<Val>: In a gilded pencil case.

<HM>: Nicky thinks I'm overly sentimental about my Kristie's auction coup. Pass me a bottle of Nicky's Nutrients.

<Val>: Are you finally admitting that meditation isn't all it's cracked up to be?

<HM>: I'm admitting that meditation plus over-the-counter assistance is keeping me from developing a dependence on Perposet.

<Val>: Why would you start hiding things from Nicky? She's going to find out anyhow.

<HM>: I'm not hiding anything. I avoid mentioning it. She's not dealing well with the last round of problems.

<Val>: Give me an example.

<HM>: She won't even talk to Church. She acts as if the situation is something that he made up.

<Val>: That knee lasted 20 years. It's time for a tune-up. Stop trying to crawl in here every day. Take the six or eight weeks and do what needs to be done. You've been in the hospital a month already in the last year.

<HM>: *He's not dealing with it either.* We have a more immediate problem.

<Val>: [...] or two. I'm thirsty. What's in here?

<HM>: We're still doing ginger tea. Everyone agrees that it's good for the digestion and for the nerves. I can suppress the urge to do bodily harm.

<Val>: [...] I guess I was thirsty. The new fridge keeps them very cold. You changed bottles too. This reminds me of my chugging days.

<HM>: Nicky bought a supply from one of our breweries that didn't make it. The colored glass prevents extraneous photons from disturbing the delicate balance of whatever new balance she's discovered.

<Val>: Plan C started well, even if we had to switch roles. But, we missed the chance to do adequate wedge driving.

<HM>: Rennie left hurriedly. Perhaps the wedge was already there.

<Val>: How will we deal with the garbage that he produces?

<HM>: We should guide the product. Then we could prepare for what he delivers more effectively.

Go down there and tell him how you agree that it's time that we finally got everything out into the open, and you would like to work with him to do what's best for Daxiao. Tell him that if Gunnar doesn't pay for it, you could pay out of our secret research fund. He loves discovering financial misdoings.

<Val>: Your slush fund is the world's most widely known secret. It's in the 10 K Report.

<HM>: Try it and see if he bites. If he does, he'll earn more stupid points.

<Val>: You're destroying your own reputation. Why don't you talk to him and Gunnar, man to man?

<HM>: Does William seem like a reasonable man to you?

[...] I made my point. Tell him that I am in no shape to continue this meeting. I am having severe pains somewhere, which is true. Indy and Jonas will be here later to escort me to Dr. Church.

<Val>: Why?

<HM>: I missed two appointments, and today Indy will ensure that I do not miss the third one. I lost more weight (which is good), and now the brace doesn't fit (not good). Thus, I have a net negative knee situation. She also likes her new office.

<Val>: There's also the pain you had in your side when you were trying not to laugh.

<HM>: *He's ignoring me again. Maybe that is good.* Let's keep Sharf and Gunnar separated a while longer. Hustle Sharf over to the grill, and come back after you provide input to his thought formulation. You'll still have time to go home and rest.

<Val>: If we sit at your table, he'll see Gunnar coming in.

<HM>: Gunnar has people here. He can drop by whenever it suits him.

<Val>: What are you going to say to Gunnar?

<HM>: First, I must discover what he says he really wants. Then I will deliver an unexpected volley of truth. If I promote tearing the group apart, he will definitely consider trying to keep it together. That will help us.

A specially crafted version of Plan Aria with proposals for further collaboration will definitely keep him befuddled while we arm Mr. Sharf with structured befuddlement.

Don't forget the numbers. That will help him to relax while you slip in the truth. If we do this right, we could make it a win-win.

<Val>: Why would you want Gunnar to win anything?

<HM>: I am referring to a win for WFSOA and a win for Daxiao.

<Val>: Gunnar is accustomed to getting what he wants.

<HM>: I am too, in my backwards clumsy sort of way. *I need Gunnar to make this work, even if I would rather throttle him for what he did to me.*

Cut that out. Nicky would not approve.

<Val>: There must be a way that is less convoluted.

<HM>: If you found a better way in the last few minutes, tell me what you believe that should be.

<Val>: I'm on my way.

<HM>: Save your steps. He's going to check on his kill, or to discuss the FAX. Close the door. I have cogitation and meditation to do.

---------- ----------

<Sharf>: Val. I'm glad I found one of you. We still have more than an hour left. How should we use it?

<Val>: We will reschedule.

<Sharf>: What is that area?

<Val>: It is space that we borrow from the new landlords if they don't need it for themselves.

<Sharf>: H sent me to the motel, and this was right next door.

<Val>: You rushed them. They probably didn't remember to book it.

<Sharf>: Ernie says H is probably here. I'd like to apologize for being a little rough a few minutes ago.

<Val>: He is here, but he is dealing with other issues at this moment.

<Sharf>: Where are you going?

<Val>: Those leftovers left already. If you want, we can eat and talk about what happened today.

<Sharf>: Are you going to tell me the whole truth and nothing but the truth?

<Val>: I'm not sure what you mean.

<Sharf>: Are you going to tell me how Marshall and Piccolo, or perhaps the other way around, have kept this magic show going?

<Val>: I had considered the possibility (*though it's extremely remote*) that you and Gunnar could show me how to do what's best for Daxiao.

<Sharf>: What will HM have to say about this?

<Val>: I can almost guarantee that he would cooperate. This is a lot for someone with his other issues.

<Sharf>: What are you holding?

<Val>: It's an empty bottle. It's surprising how fast they disappear. We must leave.

<Sharf>: Let me talk to him.

<Val>: NO! He doesn't want to be disturbed.

[...] Sharf, don't go in there.

<Sharf>: What's wrong with him? Should we call a doctor?

<Val>: Why would he need a doctor? Indy and Jonas will take care of him as they always do. They're on their way over. We should leave. He needs a few minutes to pull himself together.

<Sharf>: What are those pills?

<Val>: HM's secret painkillers. Let's go.

<Sharf>: *Pills with booze straight from the bottle.* This could be very expensive. I don't believe Gunnar would be willing to pay for what we need here.

<Val>: HM has money. He's been hoarding it since 9/11.

<Sharf>: How? *This is becoming more interesting.*

<Val>: *He's falling for it.* Indy showed him how we can create mutually beneficial relationships where the vendors pay for a portion of our research in return for us helping them to test new products. He and Lorrie found a way to redirect a portion of the savings into a Research and Development slush fund. He also gets the half of the 10% overrun allotment for any project that comes in ahead of time. He's saving for a rainy day that never came.

<Sharf>: How do you do that?

<Val>: Vendors acknowledge when we are acting as their primary quality assurance organization. They adapt their pricing model to conform to our mutual reality. It avoids negative vendor points.

<Sharf>: How do you hide this?

<Val>: In plain sight. The daughter genius accountant helped the father who is head of compliance and purchasing convince Lorrie that this was a good idea. Lorraine is no match for Indy. *Lorrie and Indy are about even, but I need to see how he responds to Baby Girl.*

<Sharf>: Are you talking about Indira Marshall?

<Val>: Yes. Do you know her?

<Sharf>: *I will never forget her.* We were in school together. I ran into her again when she was at Acton. She was all right, but I doubt that she is as good as you say. I won a few deals from her.

I must find out what she told them.

<Val>: I'm surprised at that assessment. Most people say that she is unbelievably good. She had almost a perfect average in school, she was the top scorer on the girls - I mean women's - basketball team, she's a super mom, and the only time she didn't make the top rating at Acton was the year she was pregnant with the twins.

<Sharf>: *If she knew how to walk on water backwards in high heels, I would still hate the broad.*

That was long ago. We have to deal with the immediate situation. Do you have approval authority?

<Val>: *He's more agitated than he should be. H is missing something.* Of course I do. I sign when H is unavailable.

<Sharf>: When do we do whatever we are going to do?

<Val>: I must upgrade my network security. They make us do it every week now.

Then we go across the street to the grill where we will not be disturbed, and I give you what you need to assist us. In fact, you should go ahead? Tell them I said we will sit at Mr. Marshall's table.

<Sharf>: *Sitting in Marshall's seat is a good place to start.* Why not somewhere else?

<Val>: I want to be close enough to come back and clean up a few things. I've been out of the country for almost a month.

<Sharf>: *You're working double time to take up the slack for Marshall.* I'll meet you across the street.

----------At the Elevator-----------

<Jonas Frey-Marshall>: Val, how long have you been home?

<Val>: About two and a half hours.

<Indira Frey-Marshall>: Welcome back. Why didn't you go home and recuperate instead of coming in here? I put some of Mama's soup in the refrigerator. I cleaned it out too.

<Val>: Your father and I must tie some loose ends.

<Indy>: Where's Daddy? We saw the anaconda crawling across the street. I've been worried about Daddy all day.

<Val>: He just went into his office.

<Huey>: How is he?

<Val>: His leg is misbehaving, and his side hurts from trying not to laugh. Nevertheless, he was humming his happy song when he hobbled past. I'd give him 85%.

<Indy>: Which song?

<Val>: I believe it was "How to Roll Over", the steamroller song that Clara taught him.

<Indy>: "How I Got Over"?

<Val>: OOOKAY, only H is not over until I back over Sharf again. I have to put on some finishing touches. He should be at the grill waiting for me.

<Indy>: Is it Plan A or Planaria?

<Val>: It's Plan "C."

<Indy>: I don't know about Plan C.

<Val>: He intends to make Gunnar look stupid because Sharf is stupid.

<Indy>: Sharf is also vicious. Does Mama agree?

<Val>: Talk to your father, I have to run.

<Indy>: Tell Mama if he tries to bite.

<Huey>: *Val doesn't like the plan.* We need to talk to Daddy.

----------HM's Office----------

<Huey>: You look funny.

<Indy>: Val said you were 85%. What happened?

<HM>: I've been laughing myself to death.

<Huey>: What is funny about these insane plans?

<Indy>: [...] or dealing with Sharf?

<HM>: Val agrees that Plan A would show too many people how much clout I have, and that would cause more trouble. We will do Plan Aria instead, except that we need time to put more things in place.

<Indy>: *Good. Daddy is finally going to get some real rest. He worked 60 years in the last 40.*

<Huey>: You didn't answer the question.

<HM>: Plan C involves helping William make a fool of himself and sloshing over on Gunnar. That may soften him up a bit, and I can try to bring him around.

<Indy>: What dumb thing have you conjured up? Do I need to call Machi?

<HM>: Why didn't you mention that Sharf is married to Gunnar's sister?

<Huey>: *He sidestepped her. I wonder why.*

<Indy>: I didn't know!

<HM>: Furthermore:

- William thinks he discovered the big secret of how I've lost my edge, if I ever had one.
- William thinks Val is now in charge.
- Val is, as we speak, helping William put together a plan where he charges Daxiao $500,000 to document the abundance of brilliant SOA ideas that our executive team contributed.

<Indy>: Except for Dan and perhaps Alex, your executive team doesn't have SOA ideas.

<HM>: I told him that, but he would rather believe, especially because I am having so much trouble lately, that the process works the other way around. He called me an overpaid tool jockey.

<Huey>: He's too tall. I can fix that.

<HM>: Calm down. We are not violent, as much as I've contemplated it today.

<Indy>: I don't see what's funny.

<HM>: It would take too long to explain. Let's say that I practiced Machi redirection, and it was easier than I thought. They will look so ridiculous that I should have room to finish in grand style.

<Indy>: Why don't you just come home and start enjoying your life?

<HM>: Is your name Nicky, or is it Indy?

<Indy>: Never mind. This is your life.

<Ernest>: Boss. Mr. Gunnar is here to see you.

<HM>: Send him in.

[...] I'll call you in your new digs when I'm ready. This won't take long.

<Indy>: I'll be checking on you.

<Huey>: We need extra time to get across town.

<HM>: Don't worry, this first meeting will be quick, but we have to do this.

---------- ----------

<HM>: Gunnar, I'm over here.

<Gunnar>: They are both extremely tall. *I wonder why the investigators never mentioned that she's a panther.*

That's not PC, but Wow!

<HM>: I could consider beating you over the head with this cane, but I will be kind and let you catch your breath. Besides, she's not your type. She would be too strong-willed and not needy enough.

<Gunnar>: How tall are they? *How does he know my preferences in women?*

<HM>: Jonas is two inches taller than I am, and Indy is two inches shorter, except when she is feeling risqué, and she ventures into her two-inch heels.

<Gunnar>: Are they as smart as I have heard?

<HM>: You did not come here to discuss the stature of my children. This is only the second occasion that you've been in my space the whole five years that you've been with us.

<Gunnar>: *When I had to apologize for Montgomery.* As of six weeks ago, your space is my space. I hope you don't mind. We will be seeing more of each other.

<HM>: *He's trying to bait me.* It's a much more effective use of resources.

<Gunnar>: I'm glad you agree, and speaking of space, your office isn't nearly as small as it was the last time I was here.

<HM>: Since most of my staff is parked with Armstrong's teams, I had enough space to use 60% of my allotment and build an effective command center too. You knew that.

<Gunnar>: The burl is unique and so are the trapezoids? Who did the décor?

<HM>: The same organization that super-sized everything. I have a wood fetish and my son is very generous. The trapezoids are supposed to keep sharp corners away from my knee, but I still manage to find them.

<Gunnar>: The clarity on that photo is extraordinary, given its size. Do you mind if I look?

<HM>: My best friend has a 50-year photography obsession. *What is he up to?*

<Gunnar>: What did he use? That's your spring picnic, right?

<HM>: ***She*** did it with a Hasselblad 33 something. She's the midget in the family shot.

<Gunnar>: *She passed along the curvature gene.* She's a very pretty midget. How many children do you have?

<HM>: Thank you. I have four [...] three of those are my grandchildren. Randall and Cassandra are standing with their mother. Michael belongs to Jonas. Pat decided not to fly from Rome for burned hot dogs, and Patricia was preparing for a dance recital.

<Gunnar>: They all appear to be the same age.

<HM>: They grow fast in my family. The trick is the gray hair count. The young ones have none, you cannot tell with Jonas due to his hair color, and

Indy showed her first shiny sprinkles five years ago. She started when she was 35, as did her mother, who is now 100% gray, as you can see.

<Gunnar>: Forty! *She's not too young for me.* Your friend must be at least [...]

<HM>: She's old enough for Medicare.

<Gunnar>: There are two parents missing.

<HM>: *Ryan was tired of hearing people whispering about how stupid he was to - never mind that.* It was Indy's weekend with the kids and Jonas's wife had a stomach virus. *She still has it, and we're going to name her Rachel.*

<Gunnar>: *The dossier said his daughter was married, but that was five years ago.* Give me a couple more minutes. I need to look at the big picture.

<HM>: That is not going to tell you a darn thing about SOX or SOA.

<Gunnar>: You never know. *On the front row, they have Guzman (and Mrs. G., and she is not looking happy), Macedon, Piccolo, Liz and the terror tots, Doc and Jay (looking "together"?), Mr. & Mrs. Lorraine, Li and Marcella (I told them to check it out for me), Armstrong!, Higgs!@?, Van Amberg, two of Barca's people, one from Chiu (plus the two in the second row), Silicone Huey, her in a basketball jersey, Ellison acting chummy with Marshall, and about 20 people that I don't know. I missed all of this! He was supposed to be a hermit.* That is almost as many people as I have at a sales gathering.

<HM>: There are about 800 in the picture, but more came after they finished their Saturday chores. You'd have been in the front row if you had condescended to attend. You've been missing a lot of fun.

<Gunnar>: Your friend must have been standing in the next state to take that picture.

<HM>: She was in the middle of the soccer field.

<Gunnar>: *I wonder why nobody seems to be paying much attention to his daughter.* I suppose your friend is good at organizing things.

<HM>: Nicky's good, but Macedon arranged that. His military efficiency is often useful, and that was one of the times.

<Gunnar>: *Macedon is annoying as hell.* Look at the babies. *That always loosens them up a bit.*

<HM>: *Why is he stalling?* That is the entire Frey-Marshall line-up. My friend (the oldest) is at the top and Michael (the youngest grandchild) is at the bottom. My babies make me the luckiest unlucky man you will ever meet.

I'd mention that we're about to need more space, but I don't want to jinx it.

<Gunnar>: *Guntur! Somebody is holding my baby!*

<HM>: Could we focus on the reasons why you are here? I have some place else to be.

[...] Gunnar? ***GUNNAR!***

<Gunnar>: What a beautiful baby, but he's so little.

<HM>: Pipsqueak, I mean Patrick. He was the prettiest one, even though I could hold him in one hand with room left over. He almost didn't make it.

<Gunnar>: What was wrong with him?

<HM>: Do you really want to know this?

<Gunnar>: I asked didn't I, and hand me a tissue. My allergies are acting up.

<HM>: That's his twin sister right below him.

<Gunnar>: *She looks like Kerstin.* She's pretty too.

<HM>: They were late-life babies, they were distressed, and they were killing Nicky. They had to take them at eight months to try and save everybody's life. They weighed eleven pounds together, but he only weighed 4-1/2. He needed surgery two times in the first week.

<Gunnar>: *They took Guntur from Amal, but they both died. Too many things were crushed.*

His sister is dancing. How did he turn out?

<HM>: He's almost as tall as you are, and he's still the best looking one. He does every extreme thing that he can to prove that he's not a weakling.

<Gunnar>: *I can understand extreme.*

<HM>: He's also my language freak. They had to build a roof for his mouth, and he started studying multiple languages to exercise the man made apparatus. Now he speaks the languages of all his great grandparents. That includes Yiddish, Hebrew, and Russian on Nicky's side and Telugu, Urdu, and English on my side. He tossed in Spanish and Italian for kicks.

<Gunnar>: *Telugu? I'll leave that alone.* Is he more attractive than the ones I just saw?

<HM>: Indy is a close second, but I'd say Pat wins most days.

Ally or Negative Stakeholder?

<Gunnar>: *I just wasted five minutes of my time, and I don't need to be thinking about Guntur.* I dropped by because I wanted to clear the air about the Belvedere engagement before they arrived. However, it seems that you ran ahead of yourself.

<HM>: *Whoa! I just saw Jekyll and Hyde up close, exactly as everybody describes him.*

Give me the montage, and we can start clearing. Tell me exactly why you and Justin believe we need Belvedere, and exactly what do you want from me?

<Gunnar>: *Offense is appropriate.* Would you concede that if more of what you do was out in the open, and understandable by humans, no one would have given me approval to hire Belvedere?

<HM>: *He's picking on my weakest point.* Because of my well-known communications issues, I have placed effective communicators in front of me for 30 years. Few humans don't understand. Unfortunately, you are acting as if you are one of them.

<Gunnar>: *I will try another approach.* Talk to me about the team from Belvedere. How do you like them?

<HM>: *That was a quick change-up.* Sharf is annoying, arrogant, and a bully, but I've dealt with his type since I was 13 months old. He has a brilliant assistant who is also quite likeable.

<Gunnar>: I asked Belvedere for the best they had, and they told me Sharf was the best in both SOX and SOA. I suppose that being good contributes to arrogance.

<HM>: The only thing that worries me is the business with Ādaemoa. *I have to do this quickly and get to the doctor. Something is wrong.*

<Gunnar>: *He doesn't waste time as usual.* You were supposed to be finished with Ādaemoa.

<HM>: My team plugged the leak. However:

1. Your handpicked SOA man may have unplugged it. [...] 95% probability.
2. This FAXTrax report documents a transmission to Ādaemoa from the consultant motel today. The transmission contained our materials. Only Belvedere people used the motel today.
3. I will know whether one of my people slipped in and did the deed after I see the video clip.

<Gunnar>: You're not wasting time. *This is what happens when you try to help family.*

<HM>: You hate to watch paint dry, and I'm not good at subtleties.

<Gunnar>: *Who told him I said that? The situation is disintegrating.* I may have said that the topic you were discussing was as boring as watching paint dry. It's unfortunate that you heard it the wrong way.

<HM>: *I was looking straight at you when you said it.* Your assessment of my communications capabilities is accurate. The problem is that whatever bored you then is likely to be within the range of things we need to discuss. Give me a hint. Think about it while I check the report on the video.

<Gunnar>: You don't have to do that. If it was the person from Belvedere, he wasn't necessarily sending our information to Ādaemoa. He may have a team of people there.

<HM>: You would check if you were sitting here, would you not?

<Gunnar>: *He sets traps, and then pushes you in.*

<HM>: I will answer for you. This could bite me two ways. As the person responsible for compliance, I have sworn to work with Bailey to minimize further information leaks. Besides that, you still have your strong aversion to Partner Networks. You could use this to cause me trouble.

[...] Hmmm. I can't see his face.

<Gunnar>: *Good. We can let this go.* I've heard that if you don't reset those things regularly, they shift due to normal vibrations in the building.

<HM>: Nothing shifted. What it shows is the back of the neck and the Adonis-like chin of a very tall person. You may look if you like.

<Gunnar>: He's blocking the reference points. How do you know that he is tall?

<HM>: That is how it looked when they tested the camera with me, except this individual has a slimmer neck, and my not quite Adonis-like chin was fat. The security people will verify it. ***Let him know he's trapped, but don't scare him too much.***

<Gunnar>: That won't be necessary. Perhaps I didn't mention that I'm beginning to see the benefits of these partner relationships. It is obvious to us that Daxiao benefits from your work, and that you know when to pull the plug with difficult organizations, as you did with Ādaemoa. I could easily see myself supporting your partner initiatives.

Chiu was right. You have to be cautious with Marshall. I provided the cage for the trap that he set for me! William could say he didn't know there was a conflict of interest, but this could still be challenging.

<HM>: Thank you. But, I still need to keep an eye on this. I nearly took another nasty hit due to Ādaemoa.

<Gunnar>: I assure you that you no longer need to worry about that hit.

<HM>: Would you trust Gunnar's assurances if you were sitting here?

<Gunnar>: Where is the consulting team? We should deal with the situation immediately.

<HM>: Let me see if I can find them on the security monitor. This winking and blinking makes me a little crazy. ***I'll let him check to verify that I don't have cameras in his area.***

<Gunnar>: ***He has the entire place wired. I wonder if that includes my people.*** My man says there are buttons that you can push to stop that. May I try?

<HM>: Be my guest. ***We monitor Indy's property from the setup in the palace.***

<Gunnar>: That's a good set up, but I don't see them. ***I also don't see my people. Good.***

<HM>: I guess they cut out early. I'll call the front desk.

<Gunnar>: Don't bother. ***I'm glad they are gone. I need to wring Sharp's neck in private.***

<HM>: You would demand clarification. [...] Security, this is Marshall.

<Matthew Reese>: Hello sir, this is Reese. How may I be of assistance?

<HM>: Two new consultants from Belvedere came in this morning. Do you remember seeing them?

<Reese>: Of course I do. They were a bit of an odd couple.

<HM>: Have they left the building?

<Reese>: Quite definitely sir.

<HM>: How long ago did they leave?

<Reese>: Ms. Renata Vitale left alone [...] 50 minutes ago. She seemed to be upset. On the other hand, the tall gentleman (Mr. William Sharf, with an "f") seemed to be quite elated at some turn of events. He says we will be seeing a lot of him soon. His card was deactivated at exactly 15:45. Is there a problem sir?

<HM>: No. One of our people was asking about them. It can wait until tomorrow.

<Reese>: Is your new monitor functioning correctly?

<HM>: Yes. I see that you changed ties today. Where's the Union Jack?

<Reese>: There was an unfortunate encounter with pea soup at lunch. The one that you gave me is more appropriate. Mr. Gunnar commented on it.

<HM>: Thank you. I'll see you later.

<Gunnar>: It is unfortunate that they left. What do you make of them leaving separately?

<HM>: In addition to his arrogance, he's a bit of a chauvinist. He may have done something to annoy her.

<Gunnar>: There is something positive? If he left happy, he was satisfied with the contents of your presentation.

<HM>: The contents of my presentation are the reason I made time for you. Except for his obsession with our list of roles and responsibilities, he will not tell us where to focus just as you will not tell me where to focus.

He keeps talking about serendipity. Having been the auditor or the one being audited on more than 500 occasions, I have never heard of a serendipitous audit. ***What do you want him to look for?***

<Gunnar>: *He's agitated, but not the least bit frightened, as many people are who deal with me. He's close to intimidating The Intimidator. What am I missing?*

This is not an audit. It's an opportunity for you to share the benefits of 38 years of experience with the people who, for reasons we hope to determine, find themselves outside the Marshall/Piccolo fold.

<HM>: *What is happening? First, he tried to have me arrested, then he spent five years ignoring me, and now he's complaining that I'm excluding him from something.*

Let us approach this differently. I will give you this pile that represents the contents of our presentation and a few items that we intend to share during subsequent sessions. Tell me if what makes Mr. Sharf happy makes you happy.

<Gunnar>: I don't need that now.

<HM>: Oh yes you do. Don't worry. We created a very precise summary, but the copies are in the command center. Wait while I print one for you.

<Gunnar>: If you are in a hurry, it can wait.

<HM>: It should not wait. The summary will serve as an index to this felled forest.

[...] Ernest, I'm out of paper.

<Ernest>: My supply is low too. Hank and Ken used up a month's supply while preparing for those consultants. I can get some from the palace.

<HM>: Take your time. I keep a backup supply in here somewhere.

[...] Found it! *The drawer opened for me!*

<Gunnar>: Why spend the time? *I have to make Ādaemoa go away. I wonder who's in security that owes me.*

<HM>: It's a fast printer. Don't circle-file this before you tell me what you want.

<Gunnar>: *Say something positive.* Wasn't Val on the plane with Justin this morning?

<HM>: Yes, Why?

<Gunnar>: If Val he was on the plane, how did he produce this? It says he created it at 3:00 o'clock today.

<HM>: That's part of how we do what we do. We don't let information get lost.

<Gunnar>: Docente's keyboarding is paying off.

<HM>: William also had some opinions about the typing silliness, but he took his entire pile with him. Many people like the results without acknowledging the means.

<Gunnar>: What do you mean? *I'll tell Sharf to turn up the heat in other areas, but first I have to find out why Sharf did whatever it was that he did.*

<HM>: You and many other people are much richer than you might be without me. Good business sense says that unless you suspect something untoward, you would show me how to help you find what you want for the $500,000 you will pay Belvedere.

I know we could find a way to focus on what's good for Gunnar, because only what is good for Gunnar is important. Sharf may be focusing on what is good for Sharf. Did that ever occur to you?

<Gunnar>: *He can read your mind when he's looking through you!* Are you begging or threatening?

<HM>: I'm begging. I don't understand what you are pretending not to understand. As you see, everything that I do is archived, attested, authenticated, documented, confirmed, factual, legitimate, reliable, scholarly (thanks to Dan), validated, and verified. It must be, or you'd have been all over my case before now.

<Gunnar>: Someone must watch the watcher. The Board thinks I can help.

<HM>: Guzman watches the watcher, and Guzman tells me what he needs to see.

<Gunnar>: His view may be overly influenced by Acton. Sometimes a second opinion is useful.

<HM>: Second opinion about what?

<Gunnar>: We wish to understand what must be done to maintain the beneficial portions of your Program in case you choose to execute your retirement option.

<HM>: I discussed that at the last quarterly inquisition. Look at Tables 6 and 7 **please!** Here they are, side by side. The first lists what we believe are the necessary components of a successful Service-Oriented Architecture. Table 7 lists the portions of the Program, and it shows what I believe Daxiao could achieve before my contract is up.

What is on those lists that you believe will be beneficial to Gunnar and what may be detrimental to your personal objectives?

<Gunnar>: ***The whole thing may be detrimental to my personal objectives.*** Does this mean that you are leaving in 21 months, as one might infer from those projections and the huge exit plan?

Don't you understand that your problem is that nobody who counts knows a damned thing about you?

That was almost begging.

<HM>: The responses are:

1. If you know my work, you don't need to know me. Sit back and enjoy the benefits.
2. Mittelman could find what he needs to know from Piccolo.
3. I don't know whether I'm leaving. My leg makes me take one day at a time.

<Gunnar>: Who would replace you? ***I never knew what was wrong with his leg - birth defect, polio, accident (I had enough of those). I'll ask later.***

Loose Coupling of BASE

<HM>: No one. You (the generic you) would split up the team. Val, Hank, Lisse, Dan, and Macedon would help ensure an effective transition.

I call it ***loose coupling***. The parts will exist and they will work together if you help ensure that the communications linkages remain effective.

<Gunnar>: ***What?*** You worked to build this team all your life. Now you talk about splitting it up as if it was a cake that you just finished baking. ***I want it whole and working until I figure out what to do.***

<HM>: ***Take it slowly. Wind the reel a little at a time. I'll show Nicky that I can do this.***

My people cannot fight you and remain effective. If we break the group up, they could remain effective, and most of them will have jobs.

<Gunnar>: Who inherits the pieces?

<HM>: Primarily the people who have already taken credit for working with BASE. After we resolve the Sharf issue, I will review my exit recommendations with Dr. Emery-Baldwin.

<Gunnar>: I have never taken credit for anything that you did. ***He's insane! He'd rather destroy his life's work than let me have it.***

<HM>: Until now, you seldom noticed what I did, and you strongly resisted what you noticed. If you have recently found something that you would like to reserve for yourself, we could start there.

<Gunnar>: This clarification is not merely for me. It will ultimately benefit Daxiao and you. You won't have to spend so much energy hiding what you do.

<HM>: ***He heard about the mythical (but real) network.*** I hide nothing that you need? Everything that each of my people does is documented dozens of times over. Look at the bottom of that pile. As of this moment, you have something that William does not.

Readers: The ***Thunk*** Roles/Activity information forms the core of the SOA P (2) publication. A planner, manager, or technician might find it beneficial. Of course, if you want to see what I've been working on for 35 years, you may wish to peek.

1. It lists activities that 38,243 people who worked in Daxiao, Goodsand, Raycroft, or (gag) our partners have performed in the last 35 years.
2. It lists 2,500+ activities that my people and me do or have done, in excruciating detail, for the last five years.
3. Eight out of ten of the underlying entries have names and dates, while 9.5 out of 10 of mine have names and dates.
4. Your activities are there under executive - sales and marketing, sponsor(s), stakeholders, and Board of Directors.
5. If you check the approver links, I guarantee you will find dozens of people that you delegated to perform some of those activities.
6. You may also follow several million links to the details.

<Gunnar>: ***The baby moved! It was probably a reflection from the monitor. I'm about to lose it again.***

<HM>: Gunnar, what is so fascinating about those baby pictures? There are no SOA explanations in that montage.

<Gunnar>: The details are overwhelming.

Communications Ups and Downs

<HM>: First, you say I'm hiding something. ***Then I show you every business-related thing that I have done in the last 35 years, and you won't even look at it.***

<Gunnar>: *He is livid. There's something in this somewhere.* The government calls this hiding in plain sight.

<HM>: *I lost it. I must breathe slowly and deeply. One* [...] *two* [...] *three* [...]

<Gunnar>: What are you doing?

<HM>: We have some grass to grow.

<Gunnar>: What in the heck does this have to do with grass?

<HM>: That's how William describes my communications style. You will immediately shut your mouth, listen, and then tell me what you believe I could be hiding. *I have to go with option #2 - back him up and go around him.*

<Gunnar>: Nobody talks to Gunnar like that, *except Gerthe. She stopped when she realized she needed me to maintain her lifestyle.*

<HM>: *This is bad.* You are right. I am wasting my breath. In the line of full disclosure, here is a copy of my exit plan. Tell Marcella to call me, and I will tell her where to find the supporting notes. Notice that I'm giving you time to plan you're your political moves.

Please keep this quiet. Daxiao technology (and you) could take very nasty hits if a few critical people got wind of this at the wrong time and started bailing on us.

<Gunnar>: *He isn't bluffing.* This is 49 pages!

<HM>: *He's backing up.*

<Gunnar>: It looks like you're trying to separate the eggs from the flour. When does it start?

<HM>: As soon as I clear it with Mittelman and the Doc.

<Gunnar>: Are you doing this because you are afraid of me, or because you are angry with me?

<HM>: A bit of both.

<Gunnar>: I don't think you're afraid. *He was afraid five years ago, but he isn't now. The hundreds of millions of dollars that his family has in the bank would make a difference.*

Why are you so angry? *I need more information to bracket this "customer". I'm not good at handling people who are not afraid of losing something. I learned to use subtle intimidation with my customers.*

<HM>: If you want to hear this [...]

<Gunnar>: I definitely do.

<HM>: File it under new experiences and sl-o-o-o-w lessons learned:

1. Ms. Maçon gave you a dashboard that you may tune to exactly seven degrees of executive high-levelness. She scheduled personal demonstrations six times, and you canceled six times.

<Gunnar>: *He sounds like low rumbling thunder! He definitely is not the wimp that I believed he was.*

<HM>:

2. The highest level of detail says, essentially, "Gunnar got what Gunnar wanted", whether he needed it or not.
3. You could use the online version of this to extract information to the level of detail that Gunnar finds comfortable.
4. We gave you a graphics service that draws VERY PRETTY, VERY SIMPLE PICTURES for any of you who wish to make multi-million decisions without knowing more than 10% of what you need to know.

<Gunnar>: This level of emotionalism is peculiar. This justifies having Sharf as an intermediary.

<HM>: ***Qu- Quiet! You're slowing me down.***

5. Marcella uses it every time you get a bee in your boxers, and you want your damned "quick answers". Consider how quickly she answers your questions recently. She stopped coming to me and crying because she was afraid that you would fire her. Now she asks how to format queries where only Maja can provide assistance.

By the way, I was hoping that you would include her in one of your talent adjustments. I would have matched her with Stein, and she would have people calling us and reminding us when an audit was due.

<Gunnar>: *What would I do without Marcella? I never intended to frighten her, merely to keep her under control.*

6. Your sales people use it often. Check with Laufer, Houlihan, Powell, Huang, and Worthington.
7. This ***Thunk*** extract is not detail. It is an index into the details.
8. It has 9.7 million physical links (we keep count). Billions may be derived.

<Gunnar>: If you communicated that information properly, I would have known it too. You should have hired a communications specialist to do communications. *He is much tougher than I realized. Maybe we are not ready for him to unbake this cake.*

<HM>: Ms. Maçon communicates effectively (in three languages, as you well know) with everyone except the people that you decide shouldn't understand her.

1. Liz did 50% of the writing in sales during the year that she worked for your predecessor.
2. Almost every document that she delivers to Ellison is distributed without changes except that he replaces her name with his.
3. About 50% of his executive briefings were created by her.

Ch- Chew on that for a while. How much of what you believe came from Mittelman was created by me? *I'm talking too much. Let me change the topic.*

4. In addition to the dashboard that she created for you (that everyone uses except you) she and Doc created Webinars and animations for BASE everything, including vision, scope, and status.

[...] Don't look so surprised. Liz's babies could tell you what BASE does.

<Gunnar>: Liz is wasting her career on communications, and she's wasting her life with that stunted clown! *Now I'm displaying peculiar emotionalism.*

<HM>: *He knows about Liz and Dan! How could we have missed this? Gunnar ignores BASE and BASE communications because he's angry with Liz for slowing down to have a family.*

Could it be that you ignored Liz, and then you became upset because the Government and Mellon noticed what she was communicating, and they told the world about it?

<Gunnar>: Though she may be wasting her talent, I also understand that a lot of people burn out early. Her timing was probably right for her. *Why am I still upset because she chose a life with that muscle-bound runt?*

<HM>: Now that let's get back to the main topic.

Pay attention! B- Be c- careful what you use to try to control what you believe you want. You may end with absolute control of absolutely nothing.

You do not listen to Liz, you won't tell me what you want, and you force me to give Sharf information that he could use to help competitors harm Daxiao, starting with Ādaemoa.

This is more important than a list of roles. Ādaemoa could start bragging about how easy it was to get information from us that we did not intend to give. We need that B2 rating to do business. Bailey, Forte, and Johanssen could explain what that means.

<Gunnar>: I understand the importance of security. *Len is always bragging about how good he is at breaking people's security. Sharf is dangerous. Why didn't I see that?*

<HM>: I have your attention. T- Talk to me.

<Gunnar>: *Let me stall him while I think.* Since I started paying attention again, I noticed that hardly anyone goes to the bathroom without checking with you or Piccolo first.

<HM>: You exaggerate. It may be true that Stein keeps track of toilet flushes to ensure that we are environmentally compliant, and Maja handles grumbles about low water pressure in some of our facilities. However, few people outside BASE need or request my permission to do anything.

<Gunnar>: The space outside of SOA grows increasingly smaller.

<HM>: It's not shrinking nearly as fast as one might like. We've converted the "Low Hanging Business Units" and several of the middle ones. The tough ones are next, like you. You are limiting my ability to help you make money and save money.

<Gunnar>: Your modesty and passive acceptance of what you claim is inevitable are out of synchronization with my observations.

<HM>: What is there to observe about the g- gimp that couldn't sell a life raft to a dr- drowning man?

<Gunnar>: *Who told him I said that?* Perhaps an erroneous translation of that statement is why I suddenly find my organization coming up short on your SOA maturity evaluation.

<HM>: *That tickled a couple of your overused parts.* Piccolo does the WFSOA maturity evaluation.

<Gunnar>: Furthermore, Piccolo's research person (who was once was my research person) and who continues to provide me with excellent results in a very timely fashion will not change a single item on a new product specification without checking with Yi first. *You're like an octopus! Your arms are everywhere.*

<HM>: That would be Yu.

<Gunnar>: Not me, your man Yi.

<HM>: I love Abbot and Costello, but Hank Yu supports the research environments. It is through him that your people interact with Maja Johanssen, our consolidator of specification documents.

<Gunnar>: My marketing managers walk around reading RSS feeds from your Knowledge Center.

<HM>: Cooperative. Maja is responsible for that too. On the other hand, she has trouble persuading your people to provide input to the Cooperative. It is a very one-sided arrangement.

<Gunnar>: I keep them on the go.

<HM>: You still haven't told me what you want.

<Gunnar>: How do you explain that I can't do a project plan without your people helping us ***Thunk** it?*

<HM>: ***Thunk*** is the "detailed" extract that I wanted you to look at. You create plans without it, but it takes your people longer than it takes the rest of us.

Eventually, Sharf will help our competitors build what you had two years ago, but you will not use, and your sales hotshots would begin to look sluggish compared to our competitors.

At some time, your excuses for yelling at everybody else's teams would sound ridiculous, especially since you and your inside group would be the only ones perceiving certain types of problems.

<Gunnar>: How are you associated with so much of the planning? We only gave you Weldon's part.

<HM>: After Weldon stopped laughing at me, his people started planning more effectively, with Macedon's help, of course. The people that he supports began to notice. During compliance audits, more effective planning comes up conversation.

<Gunnar>: Some of our partners have voluntarily increased their business with us due to your Partner Consulting.

<HM>: I'm helping you make money, and that m- makes you angry. Wh- Why? You are g- g- receiving credit for something that I do, whether you want it or not. *Now it's time to pay up. You owe me.*

<Gunnar>: HM giveth, and HM could taketh away. *I would!*

<HM>: Why must you control everything, *as I try to do? If you wish to imitate me, you need assistance from Nicky, Indy, Jonas, Val, Doc, Maja, Hank, Dan, and Macedon.*

<Gunnar>: I am not trying to control everything. I wish to have an understanding, including an understanding of the game you are playing now. There is no way that you were planning on walking away from this. *Octopuses (-pi, whatever) all die within five years, and I need to know where you left your brood of eggs. Octopus babies have beaks too.*

<HM>: I have chosen people who perform the best work possible at the expense of political savvy. People who keep their heads down tend to leave their rear ends sticking out. My team would be broken up sooner rather than later because they don't know how to sell well, not even things that work perfectly as specified, and even though they received significant sales training.

[...] Listen until I finish saying this. *Why does he keep staring at Pipsqueak and Patty?*

The only one with enough savvy to play the games necessary to keep things together would be Valery

Van Amberg. The downside is that he focuses on structure, at the expense of flexibility. Though he is a great physical specimen, he's actually older than I am. Therefore, we will try to save the Program by giving away the pieces. ***Macedon is still under deep cover, but he and Val are the same age.***

[...] This is calming to me, but it is distracting to you. Let me move it out of your way.

<Gunnar>: Piccolo could sell sand to a Saudi prince. Could he replace you? Does he agree with you?

<HM>: It is sometimes hard to know exactly what Piccolo thinks, but I believe he will accept my recommendations. He could show people how to achieve many things theoretically and politically, but he has a technical gap that he cannot fill while simultaneously performing the other things that he does well.

<Gunnar>: I hate to repeat myself, but you have not told me how you would break this up.

<HM>: I would propose an effective non-organization that could survive the politics and keep Daxiao as far ahead of the industry as we are now. You have the plan in your hand.

<Gunnar>: ***That must be a Piccolo line. He just said absolutely nothing.*** What's in this for you?

<HM>: If my people do not fight you, I could continue to influence Daxiao's success in many areas while I'm sipping tea on an island in the Caribbean. Furthermore, you are sitting here talking to me as if you consider me an equal. ***He would believe that I worried about that.*** That would have been impossible four years ago, and improbable two years ago.

<Gunnar>: ***The dead octopus would leave hundreds of offspring to continue his work.*** Give me a summary of this plan.

<HM>: We will emphasize communications and lessons learned, as well as learning lessons through more communications. Which would you rather discuss?

<Gunnar>: Start with communications. ***Maybe I am a little less than professional when it comes to Liz.***

<HM>: Ms. Maçon has been working on that for four months. ***Something about Liz really bothers him.***

- You already support ***(in the most limited way possible)*** an SOA communications program. It is a critical part of our plan. At least you don't put much effort into resisting.
- With optimized communications, the organizational structure becomes less relevant.

<Gunnar>: How will you optimize communications?

<HM>: We are evolving a BASE communications model. This expands the contact sheets that Liz kept when she worked for you. ***He controlled his annoyance that time, except for the twitchy finger.***

William didn't receive that yet, but your people know about it. It contains over 12,000 data points regarding how we may be communicating in BASE. We know it is somewhat less than accurate, but it's a beginning.

Sample of Collaboration Matrix

> **Readers**: Table 17 below contains an extract of the table that appears in SOA P (2). In this sample, the shaded box indicates that data domain owners initiate communications with the availability architect frequently.

Your part of the survey listed SOA-related roles and asked you to report how frequently you initiated interaction with these roles. It also asked how often they initiated interaction with you. It would not be surprising that the contact rate was low.

In the completed online version, a person could click a cell and see the type of information that is exchanged between the two roles or the content. Liz gave your salespeople a version to track exchanges between salesmen and Daxiao clients.

<Gunnar>: I'm sure I would remember seeing something like this.

<HM>: I'm equally sure that you delegated the survey and refused to have time in your calendar to see the prototype matrix, even when Ellison tried to demonstrate it for you.

<Gunnar>: You can't dictate all these interactions.

<HM>: We dictate nothing. This summarizes what participants reported. The next program steps are:

1. Verify critical information that is delivered or expected at each communication intersection.
2. Devise ways to improve information quality.
3. Link collaboration nodes to Knowledge Cooperative content (including ReMain and the WFSOA catalog).
4. Identify communication problem areas, and add them to the resistance list.
5. Eliminate communication problems.

I just had an interesting thought. If I have trouble communicating, how do you think that Sharf would be an improvement?

<Gunnar>: We will deal with that in a moment. For the time being, explain why I don't I know about the Communications program?

<HM>: You were talking to Lorraine in order to ignore Lisse Maçon when she delivered the 15-minute presentation, and you left your handout on the boardroom table.

I believe you were discussing funding for your newest campaign in the United Kingdom.

I must talk to Dan and Liz about this. It is definitely a major part of the problem. You were ignoring a deserter.

<Gunnar>: How do you know that? You never sit within 15 feet of me. *I try to ignore Liz, whether it's relevant or not. I try to stay away from women who are already attached to someone else. Liz chose to attach herself to everyone except me.*

Table 17 - Extract of WFSOA Collaboration Matrix ©							
Role to the right responds to collaboration ➥ Role below initiates collaboration with high, medium, or low frequency ➘	Architect - availability	Architect - corporate	Architect - enterprise technology	Architect - infrastructure	Architect - network	Architect - SOA	Architect - software
Domain owner - data	H	L	M	H	M	H	H
Domain owner - service	H	M	M	M	M	H	H
Executive - BASE	M	H	M	H	M	H	M
Executive - corporate	L	H	-	L	-	M	-
Executive - manufacturing	L	H	L	L	M	M	-
Executive - operations	L	H	M	L	M	M	-
Executive - sales and marketing	-	-	-	-	-	-	-
Executive - technology	M	H	H	H	H	H	L
Facilitator	L	-	L	M	L	M	M
Financial specialist - corporate	-	H	-	-	-	L	-
Financial specialist - BASE	M	M	M	L	L	H	H
Help desk	H	H	H	H	H	H	-
Integration specialist	H	-	H	H	H	H	H
Knowledge consolidator	H	M	H	H	H	H	H

<HM>: I have 20/20 vision, with help, I read lips very well, and I sit where I can see you. *I am going from dumb to dumber.*

<Gunnar>: Why are you telling me now? *You're not a lummox!*

<HM>: This is the longest conversation we have ever had. *It is because I am furious and in pain, and the combination is making me have an attack of stupidity.*

<Gunnar>: It could make me feel tricked or trapped. Most people understand that it is not a good idea try to corner Gunnar.

<HM>: Your Intimidator act doesn't work with somebody who has already lost everything, repeatedly. The Intimidator pinky started twitching when we mentioned Partner Networks.

<Gunnar>: What do you know about that?

<HM>: *I built a dossier on you as you did on me. Three of your ex-girlfriends also mentioned it.* I was involved in saving 58 people that were affected by your talent adjustments. Four reported to you directly, and they remembered seeing your finger twitching when you were deciding how to control them or a situation related to them.

<Gunnar>: *Have I always been that obvious?*

<HM>: Since I am now being honest far past the point of stupidity, I suggest that you should stop hurting Liz, and you should not take another shot at me. Your aim is almost as bad as it was five years ago, Sharf could be as bad for Daxiao as Montgomery, and I will not come back to clean up the mess you made. *I waited five years for that.*

[...] *I messed up. Nicky will have me on punishment for at least a month - maybe three or four days. She'd be punishing herself.*

<Gunnar>: ***What "last time" are you talking about?*** *If he knew the truth about the investigation, and now he has me tied to the Ādaemoa situation, he could have been laying trip wires for me all these years, and I didn't know it.*

<HM>: *I'm talking too much.* I'm saying that unless you control Sharf, you could lose more than I will.

<Gunnar>: *I'd better go out and come in another door.* This was supposed to be an open collaboration effort, not a reversed vendetta. I explained before how Montgomery was trying to displace you before I knew him.

I'm the one that showed how he and Ling were connected, and how Ling wanted you out of the way because you were interfering with family interests. I cleared your name. Meanwhile, you may have benefited from the incident in the long run.

<HM>: It was very p- painful in the short run. They took my p- passport and put me under h- house arrest. My friend, who was formerly as assistant district attorney, was ashamed to show her face with her former associates.

<Gunnar>: No one found out. Justin was always obsessed Daxiao's image. [...] What are you doing?

He is one scary yeti when he starts to look like that.

<HM>: I am breathing. *I am also trying to remove my size 14 foot from my mouth.* We were getting of track. Ms. Maçon will appoint someone to work with whomever you select to work on the communications issue.

Let me cover lessons learned while I have your attention. It is important to discuss how we (you, Piccolo, and I) could ensure that the company continues to benefit from lessons I learned the hard way.

<Gunnar>: Let's return to communication. If we start now, it would give me a chance to explain and apologize properly.

The rabbit eats the snake. It may be better to have him as a friend than to have him as an enemy, especially if he had that hidden network. However, the first option may be impossible, given the circumstances.

<HM>: *Listening to you lie about that will certainly make me say more things that I shouldn't.* That will not be necessary. Table A.2 contains over 150 things that we've learned over the past few years. The industry may be aware of at least half of them by now, though many do not understand the implications. Eventually, some will become invalid. You'll need to monitor that. I believe you could save the company millions if you ensured that nobody accidentally wondered around any loops that I investigated already. *I'm asking for his help again.*

<Gunnar>: We seem to have learned a lot.

<HM>: You may keep it, or you may toss it. If you toss it, and the profits remain strong, you will have found a better way and my bonus options will become more valuable. If you toss it, and things start slipping, you could pull out the list, rename the lessons, and take credit for thinking of them yourself. *Seeing Church today is a good idea.*

<Gunnar>: *He just grimaced. There's something wrong with him that is not related to this conversation.*

This time I will try dropping in from the ceiling. Could we discuss these and the exit plan when we have more time?

<HM>: A spark of interest.

<Gunnar>: I would like to call a truce. Watching paint dry might be relaxing. I believe lessons learned would be more effective if I heard them from you. *If I make you angry enough again, maybe you'll tell me what you've been doing to punish me for the last five years.*

<Indy>: Pardon me, Daddy [...]

<Gunnar>: *I didn't hear her come in. She's as quiet as a panther too.* Hello. Let me introduce myself. My name is Gunnar. Anderssen Niklas Gunnar. My friends call me Andy.

<Indy>: *Randy Andy doesn't have friends. You have victims or co-conspirators, but you're mean enough to do things that Daddy wouldn't.*

Daddy, you are supposed to be at the doctor's office in 50 minutes. If you miss this appointment, Dr. Church will be very upset.

<HM>: I do not intend to miss this appointment. *Ernest may have to help me get to the car.*

<Gunnar>: *She acts as if I'm not here. She knows what I did too.*

<HM>: What are you looking for?

<Indy>: Jonas needs batteries.

<HM>: He used the ones I had here. There's a set in the car.

<Gunnar>: *That outfit is designed to camouflage, but she couldn't hide what she has in a barrel.*

<Indy>: That is more reason to hurry. I shut the drawer. We don't want you to trip over it.

<HM>: I shut it too, and Ernest called someone to look at it. I will remember to be careful.

<Gunnar>: *I wonder if she's going to stand there and watch us.* We were about to talk about how we could arrange for me to learn the lessons you have learned directly from you. *She smells good too - like Amal!*

<HM>: Baby Girl, you don't have to do that. The trip takes 35 minutes. If the traffic is bad, we can call Doug. I'm sure he'll wait a few extra minutes for his Guinea pig du jour. Gunnar won't bite while we're paying attention.

<Indy>: I'll check again in a few minutes.

<Gunnar>: *That can't be my Doug Church! How could I be so lucky? Maybe he could show me where to find out more about this mystery man.* She doesn't like me.

<HM>: Maybe she heard you threaten me. The women in my family are very protective of their men.

<Gunnar>: She heard our mutual threats.

<HM>: As one of my more challenging associates, your name may have come up in conversations.

<Gunnar>: About what?

<HM>: About anything unpleasant.

<Gunnar>: We absolutely must clear this up. If we do not, the next 21 months and the cake unbaking will be a living hell for both of us. What is it about the purchasing fiasco that makes your daughter pretend that I don't exist?

<HM>: *He's right about how rough this could be.* Perhaps, she and her mother have trouble understanding the sequence of events.

<Gunnar>: What do you believe the sequence was?

<HM>: I was a thorn in Armstrong's side, and I was getting closer to Ling than he wanted me to be. I didn't know he was connected to Montgomery. Mittelman was using the new bully on the block to figure out how to control me, and Montgomery leaped at the chance to help his new boss impress the boss and move me out of the way simultaneously.

<Gunnar>: Upon what do you base this series of deductions?

<HM>: Did it occur to you that if Montgomery was on the up and up, you wouldn't have needed to whisper in elevators? You would have been discussing a clean excision in Justin's spacious quarters.

<Gunnar>: What elevators? *What does he know about elevators?*

<HM>: You were in elevator #4 in the old building on John Street when he asked how his findings had been received. You reported that the head robot was pleased that you had found this so quickly and the "revelation" had been approved. You said, "Call Stokes at this number by 3:00 P.M. Tell him to keep it quiet. The robot doesn't like publicity."

<Gunnar>: *That is an exact quote! The world just turned upside down! He intimidated the Intimidator.*

<HM>: Don't look so amazed. That was not a particularly safe building. The only deterrents were the signs that said these premises are being monitored at all times. Daxiao makes excellent security products, and -

<Gunnar>: - You read lips! How do you know it was related to you? *I can't believe this is happening.*

<HM>: They ushered me out two days later. No other revelations that month were related to both you and Montgomery. Stokes is still with the PCAOB - he led the team that did our last SOX review. Stokes taketh away, and he giveth back.

<Gunnar>: Who gave you the tape?

<HM>: When I returned, many people were quick to give me access everything that was allowed for my role as compliance manager. They wanted to make me know that I was trusted 100%. That included access to the video archives. That is the original reason that I came back.

Some people who owed me for favors paid off their debts by spending hours watching replays looking for encounters between you and Montgomery that were recorded anywhere from the time you arrived until the time I came back. It was a needle in a haystack, but it was worth it.

<Gunnar>: Justin needed to make sure we were clean. I didn't know Montgomery was crooked. He acted as if he was eager to right the wrongs of the corporate world.

<HM>: I believe you. I was a big nothing, you were gunning for the top position, and you wouldn't have given me the time of day otherwise.

<Gunnar>: How many people know this?

<HM>: Many people may have found out "accidentally" during my morbid moments. I had lots of morbid moments around that time.

<Gunnar>: Why didn't I know that you knew? *Justin should have warned me. He's cozier with Macedon lately. Maybe he wanted me to look bad.*

<HM>: The information served no useful purpose except to clarify what I could have done that would make anyone want to destroy me.

<Gunnar>: Are you saying that you did nothing with it?

<HM>: My only ammunition was to show the company that I was still valuable. Vendettas often hurt the people on both sides.

Besides, Montgomery can't find a job selling pencils. Ling's family is using sand to make inexpensive paperweights, not sloppy electronic components.

I also took Liz from you as quickly as I could - that helped her family planning and my revenge.

<Gunnar>: **NFW!** Nobody is that passive! I gave you a chance to aim one big blast at me before you go.

<HM>: Keep your voice down. I was the victim. Why are you upset?

<Gunnar>: You plotted five years to repay me for an accident from which you received disproportionate benefit. Thanks to Montgomery, you and your family become unstoppable.

<HM>: Paranoia is unbecoming a man of your importance.

I don't know whether it's a coincidence, but you were divorced within six months after we found the tape.

<Gunnar>: Where does this leave us now? *I'm half way to hell, and I hired Sharf to pave the road.*

<HM>: I repeat that you should consider whether William may be causing a similar problem, *as big a problem as we can manage.*

<Gunnar>: *He's reminding me how well the road is paved.*

<HM>: What if you annoyed me, I left and didn't come back this time, and there are a few thousand more links in plain sight that either Val, Dan, Hank, or Stein did not pay attention to? *Maja has the whole picture, but nobody listens to her, and so does Liz, but she doesn't know what she's looking at. If she did, you wouldn't listen to her.*

- I was collecting this stuff while Dan and Stein were in kindergarten and before Hank was born. It takes time to give it away.
- What would happen if they were still piecing things together because the communications program wasn't finished yet?
- What if that piecing together was stalled because you and your cronies or Sharf tried to force Val and Dan to do things your way, when you have no clue what that way should be?
- What if Macedon dropped off your tail pipe and moved to the golf course at Milton Head, as he often threatens to do.

I will repeat what I said earlier. D- Daxiao would slip, but your bonus and your stature could slip more.

<Gunnar>: That just upped the threat level? *He intimidated the Intimidator. That's not difficult. Half of what I do is designed to control or intimidate people so they won't know that I am scared.*

I need time to think. He could be the toughest thing I've had to deal with since Amal died. What made me think about Amal?

<HM>: We are finally communicating. I will further communicate that I know my mean streak is showing. Now will you tell me what you want?

<Gunnar>: Why is this important to you? You could have spent this time helping your family make a couple of hundred million more. *I don't know whether to run or fight. I wouldn't know how to fight. Anything I do to Marshall could explode in my face.*

<HM>: I contributed to a couple of hundred million more. However, this is my day job. This oversized closet and the things that you believe that I am hiding belong to me, at least for the next 21 months. Jonas Associates belongs to Frey-Marshall.

<Gunnar>: You are one strange man. *This is the second time I remember being afraid like this since I started over, and they are both related to Marshall.*

<HM>: You know exactly where I am, and I know exactly nothing about you except that you carry a bigger grudge for a smaller reason than I do.

<Gunnar>: *The woman I was developing feelings for went to bed with everyone but me, and you gave her a spot to build a cozy nest where I couldn't avoid her. It's a good reason for a grudge I think.*

You know that I am the only one outside your massive underground who understands who is running this company, and you know you gave me several reasons to be worried, the least of which is the Ādaemoa embarrassment.

<HM>: *I guess that I always wanted Plan A.* Why do you keep ignoring the fact that Piccolo and I are helping both you and Mittelman make a lot more money than you might be making otherwise?

<Gunnar>: *That makes no sense either. Why?* What should we do next?

<HM>: This air clearing made me thirsty. Let us toast to Gunnar helping Marshall to help Gunnar. *Then Ernest can walk downstairs with me. This is not good.*

<Gunnar>: What's in the bottles?

<HM>: It's my friend's special brew of the season. I have a chilled bottle for you.

<Gunnar>: I'd prefer coffee, black.

<HM>: Kona coffee.

<Gunnar>: How do you know that?

<HM>: I mentioned it to make you wonder how much of your life I have wired.

<Gunnar>: *He's the toughest bastard in Daxiao and the most dangerous because everybody underestimates him.*

<HM>: Don't worry. I don't have anyone wired. I know because my assistant carried a welcome present to Laufer, and he mentioned that we have this in common.

<Gunnar>: *You have the key to everything that I want, and you hate me. How do I change that?*

<HM>: However, I didn't make coffee today. I was spending exciting moments with Mr. Sharf. By now, the pot outside must be gooey.

Try the brew. We can celebrate our newfound one-sided "clarity", or maybe that we're having a conversation with more than two sentences, even if it is extremely unpleasant.

<Gunnar>: It's not good to mix business with pleasure.

<HM>: It is ginger and chamomile with just a taste of honey for a sweetener.

<Gunnar>: Spiked with rat poison maybe. *This has turned around backwards! I don't know what land mines Mr. Mild and Meek who isn't mild and meek may have prepared for me.*

<HM>: Forget it. I'll drink yours.

[...] Ernest, bring Mr. Gunnar a cup of tar Macadam.

<Ernest>: Mr. Van Amberg took the last cup. Should I make more?

<HM>: We don't have time.

<Gunnar>: I'll try a swig of whatever it is.

<HM>: Pick one. [...] Glass, cup, or bottle?

<Gunnar>: Cup. Appearances

[...] *I have to figure out the new rules for this game.*

<HM>: Do you actually wish to pursue or exchange of information? *I'll settle for stalling while I nail down a few more things and hide a few more people.*

<Gunnar>: Pursuit is good. I doubt that I have many other options. ***It would look better if it appeared that this inquiry lead to the creation of a positive relationship.***

WFSOA Political Options

<HM>: You have multiple options. They are:

1. Let me be your personal tutor, and you can catch up on the things you ignored when Liz was trying to tell them to you. ***Keep your friends close, and your enemies closer.***
2. Let me tutor you long enough that you will see how this will make even more money for you, Mittelman, and the company, and you may eventually become an SOA advocate. You can afford to work with me, because as soon as I get it right, I'll be leaving.
3. Let me tell Sharf everything that you need to know. Meanwhile he could use the information to ensure more business for himself, at the expense of Daxiao and you.
4. Stop me before WFSOA is firmly anchored and take your chances.
5. Trust that I will ensure that Daxiao will do well when I am gone by positioning people that I have groomed with the people who will replace me. It's all in the plan. We need someone tough enough to make them play nicely together, and that person could be you, if you understood the importance of WFSOA.
6. Slow things down until you understand what it took me 35 years to build. Meanwhile our competition takes advantage of any openings with William's help.
7. Bring in someone(s) from the outside to replace me, perhaps brother-in-law and company, and see how long you'll be treading water. Go to #6.

I know about Margaret Gunther (originally Gunnar) Sharf, but I don't understand why you're willing to take your chances with him. He seems to be a few left turns away from a padded room.

<Gunnar>: ***He is acting stranger than his usual strange, and I don't know why.*** He was one of the few people I could find with both SOX and SOA experience. He just happens to be married to my sister.

Why am I answering to you?

<HM>: It's a characteristic of all that clear air. Say what, and say when.

<Gunnar>: Let's start with option #1. We could start next Tuesday at noon. Come to my place.

<HM>: The "make him come to me" game. You are not comfortable in my closet, and you want me to walk to the other end of the hall? Their closets are smaller.

<Gunnar>: We can meet in New Jersey. We have big rooms for offices.

<HM>: I must "squeeze it into my schedule." ***Traveling becomes more problematic for me.***

<Gunnar>: We have the quarterly inquisition that morning, so you have to be in Far Hills anyhow. We'll have lunch on the top floor. We could lock ourselves in a room for the rest of the day and discover how we might continue our search for clarity. ***I have to find out how to keep you here and under my control until you tell me what I need.***

<HM>: I had nearly forgotten. ***I would rather beat him with my cane. However, I can buy more time if I play this correctly. Then I'll have to work with Piccolo and Macedon to gum up his works, with Liz showing them the inside track.***

<Gunnar>: What about Sharf?

<HM>: You have the key to Mr. Sharf but no understanding? Here's a hint. He is technically incompetent and we helped Armstrong spoil Daxiao with quality. After I'm gone and after they stop blaming his mistakes on what I left, Daxiao's technology will slip faster than Macedon and Piccolo can glue it together. Many people may notice, including Mittelman, especially since they will receive copies of historical scorecards, which will show the difference. You have a noose around your neck. ***That should short-circuit a few conquests.***

<Indy>: Daddy. George is waiting for us. Move it.

SOA Personal - Pure Soapiness

Pure SOA P starts here. You could ** Skip to ** DAXIAO RESPONSE TO PRELIMINARY SOA ASSESSMENT

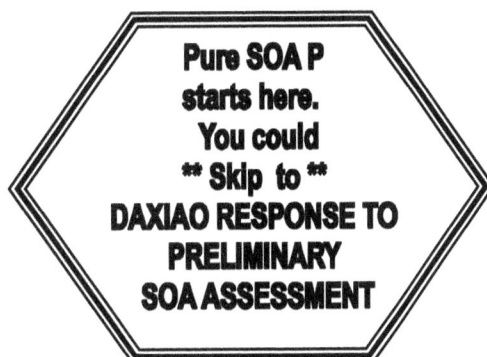

<Gunnar>: *He intimidated The Intimidator. I need her on Tuesday to protect me from HM.*

<HM>: [...] It's in my calendar.

It's time to go. *I can stand up. That's good. I'll walk him to the door and then ask Ernest for help.*

<Gunnar>: *The drawer!*

<HM>: *Hell, what did I do now?*

<Gunnar>: *I heard something snap.* Marshall. Are you all right?

<HM>: N- no! [...] *I would scream if I could catch my breath!*

<Gunnar>: Don't try to move.

Ernest! Get in here and help me with Marshall!

He hit the angle of credenza. I definitely heard something snap. Dozens of people know what I did before. The worse he looks, the worse I am going to look!

<HM>: G- [...] *I can't talk!*

<Ernest>: Not again!

<Indy>: What did you do to daddy?

<Gunnar>: The drawer came open again. I tried to [...]

<Indy>: Shut it, and shut up. Ernest, get Jonas in here **NOW**!

<Gunnar>: Let me look at him.

<Indy>: You want to check your own skeet? NO! Get the hell out of here.

<Gunnar>: Not yet. *He has the scorecards.*

<Huey>: The doctor was right and Mama was wrong.

<Indy>: You shut up too!

<Ernest>: We can handle this. Hold the chair. I'll help him up.

<HM>: *I AM NOT drowning in a swamp! I'm in Daxiao. Daxiao is a swamp!*

<Indy>: You're in the way. Sit.

<Gunnar>: Sitting on this desk is exactly what I had in mind. *She's the strongest woman I've ever seen, but she looks soft. I will sit and watch her until she asks for help.*

<Ernest>: He's not helping. We will have to lift him.

<Indy>: Move over there and hold the chair. Push that button and this one. Never mind, I'll do it.

<Gunnar>: *Move, or fall over!* I was going that way anyhow. *The arms slide out of the way, and that is a Marshall sized footrest.*

<Indy>: Jonas, LOOK AT ME. Help Ernest. I'll hold his legs. Gunnar will push the chair under him. JONAS! On three [...]

<HM>: *This is worse than ever before. I hurt all over.*

[...] *I have to try to concentrate. Mind over matter. Breathe.*

[...] *I can't breathe. This must be what it feels like to have a knife in the ribs. Try tiny breaths.*

<Ernest>: It's a good thing he lost that weight. That one reclines. Push the chair forward. Hand me a pair the scissors.

<Gunnar>: *The chair is a rolling cot!* Do you know what you're doing?

<Indy>: Of course he does. He's a nurse practitioner.

<Gunnar>: *Marshall has plans for everything.*

<Indy>: Jonas. ***Get the scissors.*** They're in the drawer beside you.

<Huey>: Daddy. What's wrong with your mouth?

<Gunnar>: He's not listening.

<Indy>: JONAS!

<Huey>: Daddy doesn't look right.

<Gunnar>: I found them. Here they are [...] umph!

<Ernest>: Are you all right?

<Indy>: Of course I am. Take the scissors, and look after Daddy.

<Huey>: That's a pair of his new slim slacks. He'll be annoyed.

<Indy>: Ernest. Cut the slacks. Gunnar, you can move now. Gunnar! Get the hell off of me.

<Gunnar>: [...] Don't try to move. ***I will get it right this time.***

<Huey>: NOBODY MOVES! Let me shut the drawer first. That should fix it, but we should move away from this corner.

<Gunnar>: ***He just picked me up too! I feel like a rag doll.*** Ms. Marshall. This is extremely embarrassing. Let me help you get up. ***She smells like lotus blossoms*** [...] ***And Amal. I almost killed her! Again!***

<Indy>: I will get myself up if you move back. ***Gunnar looks like he may need help for himself or maybe he is OK.***

Ernest how is Daddy?

<Ernest>: I'll know in a minute.

<Gunnar>: ***She rolled onto her feet. How did she do that?***

<Ernest>: It's the worst that we've seen. The appliance probably detached as the doctor said it could. The bone might have splintered too. I have to immobilize it, and it is really going to hurt.

<Gunnar>: ***What a mess! He's scarred from his calf to his groin! Something came very close to making him a eunuch. He was lucky that he could limp.***

<Indy>: That must be hurting already. Where does he keep the painkillers?

<HM>: ***I could deal with that, if I could breathe! Get a grip Marshall. This is another anxiety attack.***

<Gunnar>: Could we all move away from the man-eating drawer first? ***Whoa. The floor is uneven!***

<Huey>: Let me [...]

<Gunnar>: Tend to your father. I'm all right.

<Ernest>: All we have is Tylanoll.

<Indy>: That's ridiculous. I was there when the doctor gave him a prescription.

<Ernest>: They're in that drawer. He meditates, as he's trying to do now.

<Huey>: Where does he keep the painkillers? There is nothing in his first aid kit.

<Indy>: JONAS! **Pay attention.**

<Gunnar>: That looks like a field medical unit.

<Ernest>: It is, but there is nothing for pain.

<Indy>: Daddy, what's that in your pocket?

<Huey>: Look in his pocket.

<Gunnar>: ***Why does he keep repeating what she says?*** It's a fancy pencil case and Tylanoll.

[...] His shirt is wet. ***He sounds like Amal sounded, and my head is killing me.***

<Indy>: Daddy sweats when he hurts.

<Ernest>: He's going to have to do it the hard way. Jonas, hand me the splints.

<Indy>: Can't we just tighten the brace and carry him downstairs?

<Gunnar>: [...] I will prescribe regimen for the good of my patients according to my ability and my judgment and never do harm to anyone. ***Where is that coming from?***

<Ernest>: What did you say?

<Gunnar>: The brace isn't long enough, and it bends. You need longer splints. ***What is the hell am I saying? I should leave.***

<Indy>: They're in the truck.

<Gunnar>: Hand me the easel pad. Take the easel apart. NOW! Please. ***I can't keep my mouth shut.***

<Ernest>: That's a good idea.

<Indy>: The screws are too tight.

<Huey>: I can do that. [...] Here they are. I'll put this surgeon's tape over the rough parts.

<Gunnar>: *Like toothpicks.* It will be easier on HM if we worked together. Ernest, you and Jonas should hold his leg as still as possible and Indy, you slide the brace out from under. Fold the pants leg over it, wrap the easel pad around it, and the use the easel legs for splints. [...] *He's making that noise again.*

<Indy>: Who are you giving orders?

<Gunnar>: *I must remember to say please* [...] *PLEASE!*

<Ernest>: Ms. Indy, it's a good idea. **JONAS. We must hold your father's leg still.**

<Indy>: Gunnar, keep your claws off him.

<Ernest>: Indy, we need your help.

<Gunnar>: *If I keep this oath faithfully, may I enjoy my life and practice my art, respected by all men and in all times; but if I swerve from it, or violate it, may the reverse be my lot.* You have to sit him up before you do that. We have to call 911. *I may need 911 too.*

<Indy>: Ridiculous. George has the truck downstairs. As soon as we immobilize his leg, we'll roll him out. The doctor is waiting for him anyhow.

<Gunnar>: *Amal died and my little boy died, and* I couldn't make them hear me.

<Indy>: What are you mumbling?

<Gunnar>: *This is not Amal. If he dies, I lose nothing, or I could lose everything. I don't know what traps he's set.*

<Huey>: Here are bandages to hold everything together.

<Gunnar>: *Hold yourself together Gunnar. Move slowly to keep from falling over, and speak with moderate authority.* His leg is not your top priority. Jonas, you were right about his mouth. Look! *Maybe they'll hear me this time.*

<Huey>: The kit has extras of those magic cold things. Put that one your forehead.

<Gunnar>: Both of you. **Listen to me!** Your father is not breathing properly.

[...] Ernest, look at how he's holding his side.

<Indy>: *Gunnar, back off!* We're not your frightened lackeys. Daddy, you listened to Mama. Start meditating.

<Gunnar>: *Fools! He can't meditate if he can't breathe.*

<Ernest>: What did you do to him?

<Gunnar>: Nothing! The drawer tripped him as it tripped me, except that he landed on the edge of the credenza, and not on her. *What if I annoyed him, and he left, and we messed up something?* [...]

<Indy>: Where's the blood coming from? *He must have bitten his lip.*

<Ernest>: I'll sit him up. Call 911.

<Gunnar>: I'm at 18 West 40th Street in Manhattan, 10th floor. Tell Mike MacDonald that Gunnar called.

[...] All you need to say is *Gunnar.* I need an ambulance and a police escort immediately for Hamilton Marshall. He's an older man, he took a nasty fall, and he may already be going into shock. He has multiple traumas, including possible collapsed lung and internal bleeding. His pulse is racing, and he is sweating profusely. If we don't get him to the [...]

<Indy>: *He's exaggerating to make them get here faster.*

<Ernest>: Hospital for Orthopaedic Surgery.

<Gunnar>: Hospital for Orthopaedic Surgery in 30 minutes, you will have one final unpleasant conversation with Mike.

[...] Tell Mike that Andy Gunnar is collecting on favor. Send the best you have. NOW!

[...] Repeat what I said.

[...] Repeat the address. You're looking at the phone number. I know what you use.

[...] I know what to do. Get the unit here! You have 29 minutes.

<HM>: *I can't control the pain.* **Help me, Baby Girl. Please** [...]

<Indy>: Daddy, I don't know what to do.

<Gunnar>: Quiet! Mike, this is Gunnar. I know you're listening. I just put in a call to 911. The address is 18 West 40th Street. We have 28 minutes. This is for Huxley and Smithers. Make it good!

<Indy>: Why did you do that?

<Gunnar>: It was necessary. *He was running the whole damned company and nobody knew it except*

perhaps Piccolo. I need to know how they were doing what they did, and I don't expect to get straight answers from a man whose wife I was trying to court.

Ernest>: He did the right thing. We should tape his chest first.

<Indy>: He could lose his leg!

<Gunnar>: It won't matter if he's not breathing. Hand me the neck brace, two ace bandages, and two tong suppressors.

<Huey>: What can I do? ***Look at me!***

<Gunnar>: Let him bite on these. I'm going to put this collar over his rib cage, and you will hold his shoulders while I tape his arm to his body.

<Ernest>: He's doing it right Ms. Indy. *I'm sure he didn't learn that in sales training?*

<HM>: *Why is he helping me? Oh dear God! Maybe he isn't helping* [...]

<Indy>: He's hurting him.

<Ernest>: It can't be avoided. You have to work with me.

<Gunnar>: [...] That's the best we can do for now. Where's a blanket?

<Ernest>: Pay attention to what we're doing. Slide the brace from around his leg while we hold it steady.

<Huey>: Please help Ernest. Indy's moving in slow motion again. I'll find a blanket for Daddy.

<Gunnar>: Careful. You don't want to puncture anything more than he already did.

Now Call the doctor and explain your father's condition. **Now**! Please.

<Huey>: Stop staring and talk to the doctor. I believe I remembered which options to push.

<Gunnar>: *She looks like a sick wet kitten. I need to sit down.*

<Indy>: Hello, this is Dr. Church, isn't it?

[...] Good. I'm Simone [...]

[...] Indira Frey-Marshall.

<Dr. Douglas Church>: When does he want to reschedule this time?

<Indy>: Not this time. He's tripped again, his leg is in terrible shape, and he bruised his side.

<Church>: How does his leg look?

<Gunnar>: Tell him about the rib cage. *They are still not paying attention!*

<Ernest>: His whole thigh is swelling and changing color, and he hurt his side.

<Indy>: It's swelling [...]

<Church>: I heard him. Did he have the brace on? *Who's that in the background?*

<Indy>: Yes, but it was loose, so it may have done more harm than good.

<Huey>: It hurt a lot when we taped his side, and he hurt his mouth too.

<Church>: How bad is his side?

<Indy>: It's really hurting him.

<Gunnar>: ***It's a pneumothorax or a hemothorax!*** *They heard me that time.*

<Ernest>: WHAT? How do you [...]

<Church>: You should have told me that first! Call 911. Protect his chest first, and then take care of the leg. Tell the paramedics about his side. I'll meet you in Emergency with a trauma team.

[...] *I know that other voice!*

<Indy>: *There's an echo in here.* We called already. What's the problem? He knows how to take a fall.

<Church>: His luck ran out. Hang up now. Get him here.

<Huey>: He's sleep.

<Ernest>: He's better off "asleep". Let's finish what we have to do.

<Gunnar>: *He is a man of many surprises. Those definitely are "not your father's usual jockey shorts". Concentrate Andy. This is no time for dirty old man musings.*

<HM>: *Indy and Jonas look so worried. They stopped yelling at each other. That's good.*

[...] *Everything stopped hurting. I wonder why that is. I'll have to tell them that I'm OK.*

[...] *I wonder why I can't move my arm.*

[...] *What are they doing to my leg?*

[...] *They cut my new pants. Nicky said I looked almost as good in these as the day when I met her. I should have ordered two pairs in each color. It's going to take another six weeks to make another pair that fit me that good.*

[...] *I'll be darn. Gunnar definitely has a bald spot, but it's in the wrong place. You can see it when his hair is not perfectly coifed. He keeps his stylist busy.*

<Gunnar>: He's ready to go. Hand me another blanket.

<Ernest>: The easel pad was really a good idea. Where did you learn that?

<Gunnar>: We should wake him up now. Hand me some smelling salts. *What if I annoyed him, and he was distracted, and he dies from a freak accident before I figure out where he hid hundreds of baby octopuses, or is it octopi?*

<Huey>: ***Daddy! Wake up. Daddy!***

<HM>: *Why is Jonas yelling at me? He is loud enough to wake the dead.*

<Huey>: He's moving. Stop staring and call Mama. Daddy needs her.

<Gunnar>: You're scary, but it worked. *Now that I've touched him, he has to live, or I'll be in worse trouble.*

<Indy>: **Call Mama later. Get to hospital first.**

<Huey>: Look at me carefully! **Tell Mama you made me wait, as she made Daddy wait.**

<Indy>: **We skip last part. You talk to Mama.**

<Huey>: **Need batteries.**

<Indy>: **Good excuse. Not work for me.**

<Gunnar>: What are they doing?

<Ernest>: Talking. Jonas's hearing aids must not be working.

<Gunnar>: *That's why she wanted the batteries! She wasn't making excuses to stand and protect "Daddy".*

<Ernest>: Sit and put this on your head as Jonas suggested. You banged your head on the chair before you before you landed on Ms. Indy. The spot is turning black and blue.

<Gunnar>: Tend to Marshall. The chair arm has better padding than a lot of body parts that I run into on a soccer field, *and so does she. She is lotus over stone.*

<Ernest>: I cracked the cooling pack already. You may as well use it.

<Huey>: Now that he's awake, it will hurt again.

<HM>: *Going to hurt! I'd be roaring if I could catch my breath. I feel my heart pumping in my leg.*

I can't do that. It would scare the babies. I must remember that Clara always said, "Mind over Matter, control your mind and nothing else matters."

<Indy>: I have women's pills in my tote. These should help?

<Gunnar>: No!

<Indy>: You really are a vicious bastard. Give me that bottle.

<Gunnar>: Do you want to guarantee that he will lose that leg, or bleed to death? *She's an angry sick kitten. She nearly broke my wrist.*

<Ernest>: He's right. Aspirin makes bleeding worse, and he's allergic to aspirin.

<Indy>: It doesn't say aspirin.

<Gunnar>: Does it say acetylsalicylic acid?

<Indy>: Yes.

<Gunnar>: That means he can't have them, and you shouldn't be taking them for the reason that you mentioned.

<Huey>: She's sorry about your wrist. It will only be numb for a few minutes.

<Indy>: Daddy, try the mind tricks. Remember the baby girl with the big laughs - just like Daddy, Butchart Gardens, the Sierra Nevadas in the full moon, Mama swimming. [...] I know. You're working on it. Help is on the way. I hope.

<HM>: *Nicky, you're even prettier when you're wet. The fellows envy the old gimp when they see you at the pool. You're so graceful when you swim. Don't look at me like that. I'm trying, to be calm, but it's not working. They should have let me relax. That's dumb. I can't go to sleep.* Nicky! *Come back!*

<Huey>: Did he ask for Mama?

<Indy>: Let's take care of Daddy first. We should start by moving him downstairs in case the emergency response is sluggish.

<Ernest>: Unlock the pedestal, here, and move it. The drawer is open again!

<Gunnar>: I'll be more careful this time. [...] I did it. Now what?

<Ernest>: Unlock the table and move it.

[...] Don't ask. Dr. Piccolo put in special levers and bearings. Otherwise, I need a furniture jack to move it.

<Gunnar>: *Piccolo!* He should have fixed the drawer. ***My head doesn't hurt as bad as it did the last time, but it's still bad.***

<Ernest>: This is the first time that ever happened. I already called [...]

<Huey>: Let's straighten him up. He's leaning over too far.

<Ernest and Gunnar>: No! Let him lean.

<Ernest>: I'll make sure he doesn't fall.

<Indy>: George, come up here immediately with Daddy's medical case. We may need help with Daddy too.

<George Miller>: Mrs. Winslow, I was about to call to tell you that some policemen pulled up and made both James and me move the cars. We're going around the block.

<Indy>: WHY? We need you here!

<George>: They say they need the spots for an emergency medical unit. What is going on up there?

<Gunnar>: That would be your escort. ***Thank goodness! I hope this turns out to be worth a McDonald chit.***

Indira Marshall Winslow Frey Simone. She has more names than a Brussels street sign.

I've heard of Simone Winslow before. I didn't date her (that I'd remember), and I didn't sell her anything. I'll figure it out, but first, I must show Marshall and his family why they should be nice to me, and try to forgive any "accidental" skeet shootings. Mittelman gave me the gun the last time, and he helped me to aim it this time. Why?

<Indy>: I'll explain when I see you. Come back around as fast as you can.

<Ernest>: That's security calling on the other line.

<Reese>: Who is this please?

<Indy>: Indira Marshall.

<Reese>: Ms. Indy, there are police in the lobby. The say Mr. Marshall is quite ill. Is that right?

[...] An ambulance will be here in three or four minutes.

[...] I'll bring them up in the freight elevator.

<Ernest>: We'll meet you there.

<Gunnar>: It's a Gucci wheel chair/gurney!

<Ernest>: We should hurry. It's a Gaetano multi-use relaxation unit. Dr. Piccolo is very clever with these things.

<Gunnar>: ***Piccolo again!***

<HM>: Nicky [...] ***I'm trying so hard. When I get one more raise, we won't need Ike's help. I can pay for what Jonas needs. Then I'm going to repay every penny to Ike and Clara too. Where did Ike come from? He's dead.***

<Indy>: We're going to the hospital. Mama will see you there.

<Huey>: He's crying?

<Indy>: He's sweating, and I forgot his cane. Hospitals always run out of long canes. I'll be back.

<Ernest>: He won't need it for some time.

<Indy>: I always bring Daddy his cane. Jonas is too little.

<Huey>: Where's she going?

<Ernest>: She's going to find your father's cane. ***She's losing it?***

<Huey>: Right. That's her job. It was too heavy for me. My job was to hold his hand. ***She needs to scream, and she doesn't want to scare me. I couldn't hear her anyhow.***

<Ernest>: ***They're both losing it.***

<Gunnar>: ***I'm sure I'm missing something, but she definitely moves like a cat.*** Let me check his pulse first.

<Ernest>: What are you getting?

<Gunnar>: 140. It could be worse, but not by much. ***You're also tougher than I thought, Mr. Mystery Man. Stay with us. I'm not finished with you yet.***

<Ernest>: Same here. How do you know what you know?

<Gunnar>: I sell Daxiao's medical electronics among other things. You pick things up.

<Ernest>: I understand. ***You're better than the people that trained me. I must put this in the pipeline.***

<HM>: *How could all this happen to one person? If it hits 150, I'll be as dead as Ike is, and Nicky needs me?*

[...] *Stop being silly Marshall. You bruised a couple of ribs. It's a little better when you take tiny breaths.*

[...] *It wasn't supposed to happen like this. Forty years of work gone up in smoke, unless they listen to Maja. Liz and I are the only ones who understood Maja, and Gunnar won't listen to Liz.*

[...] *I need to rest.* [...] *No! Stay awake.*

[...] *My babies are here, but I have to explain to Nicky why my new brace plan and my new slim slacks plan will be late. I can't even remember the number for the slim slacks plan. I never forget numbers.*

[...] *Why can't I concentrate?*

<Huey>: He is definitely crying. I need a tissue.

<HM>: *I'm being morbid. I have to snap out of it before I scare the babies.*

<Gunnar>: This handkerchief is clean. *My headache is up to level 8, but at least my vision isn't blurred.*

<Huey>: I don't believe you're as mean as they say you are.

<Gunnar>: Yes I am. I am currently having a lapse. *I'm mean so they won't know I'm afraid, and I haven't been this afraid since Amal and Guntur died.*

<Huey>: We should be glad it happened now.

<Gunnar>: *Don't be too glad yet.*

I know people who sell appliances such as the type that he may need, and I am curious. Who operated on him before? They did a terrible job.

<Ernest>: Dr. Church should do so well. It was more than 20 years after his original injury before anyone had the nerve to try the surgery. They had to reroute several blood vessels.

<Gunnar>: What was the original trauma?

<Ernest>: Misguided projectiles in Southeast Asia.

<Gunnar>: They did a lot of damage.

<Ernest>: He's still lucky. If any of those projectiles had been an inch to the left or right, either he'd be dead, or he'd have lost the leg, which would be the same for him. The one in the middle almost punctured his femoral artery.

<Gunnar>: I understand what you mean. *His "friend" has a good reason to be happy that the one higher up missed by an inch too. Gunnar, you're jealous of an old man.*

<Indy>: Why are you still here?

<Gunnar>: I've been asking myself the same question. *She's definitely a cat. I wonder if she purrs.*

<Indy>: Tell yourself it's a bad idea to be here, and then leave.

<Huey>: Indy. You look like you're being inconsiderate. Leave him alone. He's hurt too.

<Gunnar>: *I'd stay if I wasn't hurting. I'm happy that projectile missed too. Otherwise, there wouldn't be an Indy to look at. I bet she's prettier when she's happy.*

[...] *The bump on the head rattled something again.*

<Huey>: See, he's still groggy.

<Gunnar>: *He's defending me! I must have banged my head a lot harder than I realized.*

-----------40th Street Grill, Upper Level----------

<Val>: Here is your work plan and the illustration showing the people who worked with HM to do SOA. I will put it on this memory stick. You'll have to e-mail everything yourself. *He made me insert unidirectional arrows. If he shows this to Doc or to Guzman, it will be the beginning of his suicide, and Gunnar gets a reset.*

<Sharf>: It will also be hand-delivered.

<Val>: Let us review this again to ensure that I have structured everything exactly as you want it.

<Sharf>: That BASE Pie is brilliant. Load it up.

<Val>: Where did you find these?

<Sharf>: You must have discovered that I have excellent sources. *I found it in the pile of papers on the credenza when I was looking for the roles.*

<Val>: *I didn't know Gunnar was paying that much attention.*

<Sharf>: Look, the police made them move Gunnar's car and the stretched Lexus that was in front of it.

<Val>: George is lucky that they didn't give him another ticket.

<Sharf>: Gunnar's car was at the hydrant, not the other one.

<Val>: Let's review.

<Sharf>: This was my idea. I'll show the illustration to the senior people. They'll be happy to see that we're giving them the credit they deserve for helping BASE. I'll show them Ellison's communications framework and explain how it needs to be reinforced. I'll ask them to validate the list of lessons learned, in case their views differ from Marshall's views.

I will not mention that Marshall's thinking processes may be muddled. I won't have to. Gunnar is in there and he can see for himself. The timing was perfect.

I'll explain that after I finish talking to the senior people, I'll need interviews with at least 100 of their middle managers, technologists, and operations people in facilities all over the world. We want to understand where Marshall mangled - substituted their original ideas with his own. *During these interviews, I will learn as much about Daxiao technology as Acton knows.*

<Val>: Are you going to show this to Gunnar before you distribute it? *I hope not. Even he would know enough to stop this.*

<Sharf>: No. I deserve the credit for this, and I want to make sure that I get it. *After Gunnar knows where to look, he could put internal people on it.*

<Val>: We will not emphasize the RandD account. I can't pay you if they shut it down.

<Sharf>: Of course, I won't say a thing *until after they pay me. Then I'll have a foot in the door with accounting and finance too.*

<Val>: Let me make sure I understand the sequence you had planned:

- You start tonight by mailing out the illustration, the numbers, and your work plan.
- You will meet with Mittelman and Dr. Emery-Baldwin tomorrow morning at eight o'clock.
- You'll spend the rest of the day with Piccolo.
- You're on Lorraine Jasper's calendar for Friday morning.
- By the time you meet with Gunnar on Friday afternoon, you'll know more about Daxiao technology than he does.
- I will provide you with a copy of the Roles/Action list from before Maja started making adjustments. Then you can see who actually did what work.
- I may need you to show me how to put that money back where it belongs. I want to retire clean (again).

<Sharf>: *The money goes back after I use to make them replace Acton, either for collusion or confusion. They should know about this. Cane will bow down to me for bringing in technology and accounting work from Daxiao.* Where are you going?

<Val>: There's something wrong. They shouldn't need an ambulance. *I knew this was too good to be true.*

<Sharf>: Didn't you say his kids are accustomed to handling this? You haven't eaten anything.

This will be even better if he dies. "Aging Technology Executive Succumbs to Drug Overdose". I will have a chance to offer condolences to panther Indy and tiger mommy during their period of mourning.

<Val>: Tell Vincent to put it on H's bill. *Then wrap yourself around a tree and wait for your next victim.*

<Sharf>: *Free drinks, free food, and enough information to set me up for life. Indy won't have a chance to thank me for guarding their secret. Nevertheless, this has been a good day.*

------ **West 40th Street during Rush Hour** ------

<Gunnar>: **Look at me.** Why didn't you ride with them?

<Huey>: Val knows Daddy's medical history, and he doesn't want to try to explain this to Mama. Pip and I could probably tell her without being throttled, and I need to be able to hear.

<Gunnar>: When are you going to call your mother?

<Huey>: My batteries are in Daddy's car. I can't read lips on this phone.

<Gunnar>: Let's walk to the corner. You can drive up town and then through the park.

<Huey>: You're more wobbly than I am. Hold on if you want. You don't have to be manly for me.

<Gunnar>: I told you I'm all right. The sidewalk is uneven.

<Huey>: There they are. We'll hop in while the light is red. You are coming with me.

<Gunnar>: *He's moving me around as if I am a twig!*

<Huey>: George, tell James to follow us.

<George>: Are we going to pick up your mother, or should I call Miles?

<Gunnar>: I think we're going to the Hospital for Orthopaedic Surgery.

<Huey>: We're going to the hospital. Go up town and through the park. Hand me Dad's medical kit.

<George>: Nothing in there that would have helped him this time. I checked. Did you hear me?

<Huey>: Here they are. Wait a minute. [...] I'm back online.

<Gunnar>: ***What if I did something that distracted him? It's not my fault. The drawer was opening itself.***

What's in the kit?

<Huey>: Daddy sneaks in Tylanoll when Mama isn't watching. He has her herbal concoctions and sponges to keep the brace from rubbing, plus a supply of batteries for me.

<Gunnar>: Why would he hide that from your mother?

<Huey>: For the same reason that Indy didn't want to call her. Mama is not logical when it comes to Daddy. If he cuts himself shaving, she goes into a frenzy.

<Gunnar>: Give me some Tylanoll, and a bottle of your mother's brew. ***I need something stronger, but this will have to do.***

<George>: How is your father?

<Huey>: He might die.

<Gunnar>: He will not. He was almost - He was in bad shape, but they were able to stabilize him.

<George>: We'll be there as fast as I can manage.

<Gunnar>: Why don't you buy your own batteries?

<Huey>: These units are designed especially for me. The batteries come from the space program. Dan arranged it.

<Gunnar>: What did Piccolo have to do with that wheeled chair?

<Huey>: He designed it, his family built it, and he put in the mechanism.

<Gunnar>: How? He does nothing better than anyone I know.

<Huey>: He's an expert mechanical engineer. He's almost as good at electrical engineering as I am (he taught me my first course).

<Gunnar>: What about computers?

<Huey>: He'll be as good as Daddy is with computers if he keeps going at the rate he's going, although he doesn't seem to think so. He says Daddy is smarter than he is, and it took him 38 years to learn what he does. Dan didn't take a serious interest in business technology until five years ago.

<Gunnar>: Those banks of screens were not for show. ***Marshall can't give ideas to Piccolo fast enough, but Piccolo attended Strafford and MTC. Piccolo knows how to use what he learned. They both had us snookered.***

<Huey>: You've spoken with Daddy. You must know the deal now.

<Gunnar>: Except that I'm not sure what I know.

<Huey>: Daddy and Dan want to make sure you don't have a target. He also wants to make sure you don't reinvent any wheels, unless you do it intentionally. If you helped them and stopped shooting at them, it would be nice. ***I see what Daddy was trying to do.***

<Gunnar>: I did not shoot your father on purpose before, and I was not trying to shoot him this time. I was trying to understand what he does, and he would rather break up the team than tell me.

<Huey>: Daddy hired or saved people were book-smart hard workers. I do too. None of my people would survive in your world, and Daddy's people won't either.

Dan is brilliant and a good talker, but he can't do what Daddy does. Therefore, they were going to work to ensure that the pieces of the team provide maximum benefit to Daxiao after he leaves.

<Gunnar>: What will your father do?

<Huey>: He starts with trying to stay alive.

<Gunnar>: What will Piccolo do?

<Huey>: The same thing he does now. He will play the clown that nobody worries about while the pieces of Daddy's group do the nasty stuff that requires absolute concentration, and you would provide air cover. If it doesn't work, Dan is a full professor on long-term leave. He could teach and give lectures on WFSOA.

<Gunnar>: Why are you telling me and not Mittelman?

<Huey>: We're not eliminating Mittelman. They need him doing what he does, and they need you doing what you do. You are angry, hungry, and accustomed to getting what you want.

Without Daddy's techniques, they are going to need a bully. You were able to see what was happening, so you will be smart enough to see how things will benefit you, as long as you are in control.

<Gunnar>: Does your father read minds as well as lips?

<Huey>: No, he's almost as dumb as I am when it comes to people like Justin, Chiu, and you. Mama and Dan show us how to figure out the hard stuff.

<Gunnar>: *You are as dumb as a stump.* Don't you worry about telling me all this?

<Huey>: I wouldn't tell you anything that would hurt Daddy. It doesn't matter because he's out of the game.

<Gunnar>: He'll be OK. *He could lose that leg, and the lung will be tricky, but he's not going anywhere until he tells me what I need to know.*

<Huey>: You are probably lying, but thanks for helping. How did you know that medical stuff?

<Gunnar>: Didn't you hear what I told Ernest?

<Huey>: No. You weren't looking at me.

<Gunnar>: I'm sorry. I said that I came up through Daxiao's medical equipment unit. A lot of salesmen over there acted like doctors.

<Huey>: Are you one of the medical school dropouts?

<Gunnar>: It's called medical technology training on my résumé.

<Huey>: Why did you drop out?

<Gunnar>: *I'm Dr. Gunnar without a license to practice.* As your father may have mentioned, I'm a control freak. I lost control when two very important people died. I'm better at controlling the living.

<Huey>: I understand. Seeing Daddy as he was made me want to run and hide.

<Gunnar>: *I want to hide too.* Are you going to call your mother now? *I want to give her a chance to thank me for saving your father's life. Maybe she could give me advice about Marshall.*

<Huey>: Maybe I should take the batteries out.

<Gunnar>: Call your mother. I'd like to meet her.

<Huey>: You should pick another day. Val says that when we get to the emergency room, we will have them look at you, but you should stay as far from Mama as you can.

<Gunnar>: I'm generally good with people, when I'm working at it. I believe I can handle your mother. *It is probably a good idea let them look at me. I definitely need something for this headache, something that is non-addictive this time.*

<Huey>: *Just as you handled Indy.* You should rest. You're going to need it.

---------- -----------

<Machi>: Jonas. It's time one of you called. Is your father on the way to the quack?

<Huey>: Yes. He should be there in about [...]

<Gunnar>: Eleven minutes.

<Huey>: Eleven minutes.

<Machi>: Is that Val? He sounds funny.

<Huey>: No Mama, that's somebody else. **Quiet!**

<Machi>: Put your father on.

<Huey>: He's not here. He's in a Fire Department medical unit with Indy and Val, and he has a police escort, and Dr. Church is waiting for them, and he's breathing OK now, and he's going to be all right, except that the thigh is probably broken just like the doctor said it might.

<Machi>: I see. When did this happen?

<Huey>: About 35 minutes ago.

<Machi>: Why didn't you call me 34 minutes ago?

<Huey>: I didn't have batteries, Gunnar was arranging the emergency escort, Indy was helping Ernest with Daddy, and Val came in right behind the ambulance people.

<Machi>: Who did you say arranged the medical escort?

<Huey>: Niklas Gunnar. His people are in Daddy's space now. **Quiet!**

<Machi>: We will discuss details when I see you. Where are you now?

<Huey>: Sixth Avenue and 52nd street. George is moving as fast as he can.

<Machi>: I'll meet you at the hospital. I'll take the Lex.

<Huey>: Call Miles.

<Machi>: That will take too long. It's rush hour. Goodbye.

<Gunnar>: Where is she?

<Huey>: In our main company facilities on Broad Street.

<Gunnar>: *Take notice Gunnar. You have tried to convince everyone that you are a power hitter. Now you are playing outside your league.*

- *You believed you were going to see a hermit, and the hermit hosts intimate little outings with over 800 people.*
- *The hermit could have been bugging and tracking you at least 40 hours per week for the last five years.*
- *You're sitting beside one of the hermit's kids in the customized limousine that he gave to his father (not a company car).*
- *This kid could buy you and sell you 20 or 30 times, and you're thinking about how dumb he is.*
- *Every one of the Marshalls could probably "stupid" you straight into hell, except that the two of his children that you have seen so far could also pick you up and toss you around, as Indy did today to keep you from stabbing anyone with the scissors.*

-----------**Fifth Avenue, Manhattan**----------

<Sharf>: Rennie, I'm coming uptown now. Stay there and wait for me.

<Rennie>: It is 5:35, and I am going home. I'll finish cleaning up your stuff tomorrow. I will begin working for Grayson next week.

<Sharf>: Grayson turned Cane against me.

<Rennie>: We lost Ādaemoa. Grayson wants the team back, and he has work for me.

<Sharf>: I will have work for you and half of Grayson's organization. Who needs Ādaemoa when we can have Daxiao, both SOA and accounting?

<Rennie>: You are hallucinating.

<Sharf>: If I am not hallucinating, you would not want me to be upset with you.

<Rennie>: How long will this take?

<Sharf>: I need you for about two hours. I have all the information, but some of it needs to be reformatted so that it suits my requirements. Find a boilerplate memo while I walk over.

<Rennie>: Where did you find this information?

<Sharf>: That is irrelevant. I have it.

<Rennie>: Where are the people from Daxiao?

<Sharf>: Racing to the hospital with Marshall. They left in an ambulance with a police escort.

<Rennie>: What's wrong with him?

<Sharf>: I think he doesn't react to stress well. He looked like he was in a car wreck. He may also have overdosed on painkillers with a bit of booze tossed in for sweeteners.

<Rennie>: The last part doesn't sound right. Will he be all right?

<Sharf>: Who knows? They didn't invite me to the party.

<Rennie>: Where are they taking him?

<Sharf>: The Hospital for Orthopaedic Surgery.

<Rennie>: Did you check with your contact on the Board?

<Sharf>: He was there. He left with the lumbering nerd.

<Rennie>: Did you see Jonas? How did he look?

<Sharf>: Like a giant sheep dog in designer jeans and glasses. I don't believe I've ever seen that much hair on a man.

Are you going to wait for me?

<Rennie>: Where are you now?

<Sharf>: Five blocks away on foot.

<Rennie>: Hurry up.

-----------**Hospital Emergency Room**----------

<Huey>: How's Daddy? Is he still in pain? I never saw him cry before this.

<Indy>: Pain is the least of our worries. He could die, or if he lives, he could lose his leg. They have two teams of people working on him.

<Huey>: What can we do?

<Indy>: You were supposed to talk to Mama and get her here, and you were supposed to keep him away from her?

<Huey>: I talked to Mama, and I kept him away from her. There's something wrong with him too. He was incoherent part of the time we were on the way here. *She wouldn't care that he was moaning and mumbling about somebody named Amal.*

<Indy>: He looks all right now. Where's Mama?

<Huey>: She's coming up on the train. She said Miles would take too long.

<Indy>: At least she's not jogging. Come.

<Huey>: Don't you think we should stay here?

<Indy>: Let's try to grab her before she enters the building.

---------- ----------

<Huey>: Gunnar said he really wants to meet Mama.

<Indy>: Didn't you warn him?

<Huey>: He thinks that being a master salesman will help him with Mama.

<Indy>: How did she sound?

<Huey>: She sounded like Daddy looks when he gets that look.

<Phillip Miles>: Mr. Jonas, I'm over here. I got here as fast as I could.

<Indy>: Did you bring Mama?

<Miles>: She passed me at the light. She just entered the building.

<Indy>: My idea was a bad idea. I wonder how we missed her.

---------- ----------

<Huey>: We don't have a plan.

<Indy>: We also don't have an elevator. Let's take the stairs.

<Huey>: Slow down. My balance isn't any better than it was yesterday.

<Indy>: I'm sorry. The plan is that you are going to give her one of your big bear hugs. Try not to smother her. Then you will let her comfort while you explain things to her very slowly.

<Huey>: Where are you going to be?

<Indy>: Blocking the door to the treatment room.

<Huey>: Do you hear Mama?

<Indy>: Yes.

<Huey>: I knew we should have stayed upstairs. *I'm still toddling around behind her. I must stop doing that.*

<Indy>: ***Run!***

---------- -----------

<Huey>: Mama! MAMA!

<Machi>: They won't let me to see your father.

<Huey>: The doctors are taking care of him. If you disturb them, you could make it worse.

<Machi>: Then I'll kill them, before I take ownership this entire hospital.

<Huey>: Mama. You can't do that if you're in jail.

<Machi>: Simone. I see you. Stay away from me.

<Indy>: Mama, you don't hit people. Do you want to hurt me too?

<Huey>: Daddy's going to need you. The brats and I need you. You can't take care of us if you're arrested.

<Indy>: Gotcha. Jonas, take that. I should have left it as Ernest suggested.

<Machi>: Turn me loose.

<Indy>: Mama, I know everything you know, and I'm younger and bigger.

<Machi>: Careless fools, all of you!

<Indy>: You made him wait too long.

<Machi>: No! I didn't want to lose him.

<Indy>: Buck up. He could have limped in here a year ago under his own steam, and he'd be all right by now.

<Huey>: Indy! This is the wrong time for that.

Mama, stop doing this, or you won't be here when he wakes up. You hurt two policemen who helped to get Daddy here [...] and Val [...] and Gunnar.

<Machi>: Val is my friend. I wouldn't hurt him.

<Indy>: Look at him! Who did that?

[...] Use some logic. Daddy needs Machi.

<Val>: Nicky. Indy. This is very unladylike.

<Machi>: You really do look funny.

<Val>: I feel funny too.

<Indy>: Mama, it's not that funny. Mama, what's wrong with you?

<Val>: She's hysterical. Indy, let her sit down.

<Indy>: Mama! Machi doesn't laugh like that.

<Machi>: He looks funny too. I did what I've kept your father from doing for five years.

<Gunnar>: Bwoke. *She is a cute little old lady, and* [...] *it feels like the car wreck. What did she do?*

<Machi>: Those were love taps. You broke HM.

<Huey>: I told you she would be upset. Sit before you fall over.

<Police Officer #1>: Lady, you are under arrest for assaulting [...] is she laughing or crying?

<Val>: Leave her alone. Can't you see she's out of it? *It would also be nice if I could see you better than I am seeing now.*

<Police Officer #1>: She is under arrest for assaulting [...]

<Val>: I am a lawyer with 39 years of experience. She has 41 years of experience. My associate and I tripped trying to help with Mr. Marshall who is heavier than the hospital staff realized. Is that right Gunnar?

<Gunnar>: *I'll collect another favor. I need it.* [...]

<Val>: See he's trying to nod.

<Indy>: *He didn't get Mama arrested! There are saints, though I never thought he'd be one of them.*

<Val>: How are you going to explain this to the judge in a courtroom with your peers? A 5'5" senior female (a former ADA who happens to dine with some of the judges) who weighs only 120 pounds injured both of you at the same time with her bare hands?

<Police Officer #1>: She had that big cane.

<Val>: Where? I don't see a cane.

<Police Officer #2>: Gomez. The cane disappeared.

<Police Officer #1>: Where did you put it? I could arrest you for tampering with evidence.

<Huey>: I put it down. I don't know where it went. I've been right here. You can't lose me.

<Police Officer #1>: Look under those chairs or behind the desk.

[...] Look under the radiator and the magazine rack. You can't hide something that big either.

<Huey>: *Thank goodness for gurneys and speedy Linda. It should be in the basement by now. I'll tell Indy to write off that loan.*

<Machi>: Everybody looks deformed.

<Huey>: Nurse, we need you.

<Val>: What do you want?

<Reporter #1>: There seems to be a significant problem here. Tell me what's happening

<Val>: Go away.

<Reporter #1>: Officer [...]

<Police Officer #2>: There was an accident; I can't talk until we fill out a report.

<Indy>: What took you so long? I have the whole story. Come and bring the photographer with you. Jonas is my brother, and the accident victim is my father.

<Reporter #1>: Yes Ma'am.

<Reporter #2>: Where are we going?

<Indy>: Somewhere where we can discuss my father's accident without being disturbed. It's too noisy in there.

<Reporter #1>: That's a good idea.

<Indy>: How did you know that my father had an accident?

<Reporter #1>: I only know that traffic was more jammed than usual around Bryant Park. I arrived just as the cops pulled away.

<Indy>: The ambulance has been here for 45 minutes. Don't you have tracers on them these days?

<Reporter #1>: I'm freelance. I have to find out stuff on my own. All I heard from the people in the building was that this old man who lead the technology unit was very ill. Then this tall guy came along and told us where to find him.

<Indy>: Was it a reliable source? Do you have a name?

<Reporter #1>: His name was Sharf, with an "f".

<Indy>: **Handle the camera.**

<Huey>: **How?**

<Indy>: **Think quickly.** Eew. My phone is vibrating. That means I have to go to Daddy. Come with me.

<Reporter #2>: You're going the wrong way.

<Indy>: I know a short cut.

---------- -----------

<Reporter #1>: What happened?

<Indy>: You must have tripped coming around the corner.

<Reporter #1>: Ouch, my wrist.

<Indy>: I'm so sorry. Let me see.

<Huey>: This one tripped over you.

<Indy>: Find a nurse who is not working on Daddy. I'll sit here beside these nice fellows.

<Huey>: Are you sure that you are all right?

<Indy>: I need my inhaler.

<Huey>: Inhaler? Where do you keep it?

<Indy>: Look until you find it. Hurry!

<Jonas>: I'll be right back. ***Ta-ta hypnosis. They still work.***

---------- ----------

<Val>: Where's Indy.

<Huey>: She's sitting on the floor beside those two reporters, and she's trying to catch her breath because she needs her inhaler. We're going to need another nurse.

<Gunnar>: I'll go [...]

> **Readers**: Gunnar will "sound" funny for a few days of SOA P because "R" and "V" would be painful and difficult to pronounce if a person had several loose teeth and a swollen jaw after close encounters with a titanium-reinforced object.

<Policeman #1>: I'll go. You people are dangerous. ***That kick was a stunner, but I think I'm OK.***

<Nurse #1>: Sit still.

<Val>: What inhaler?

<Gunnar>: She's huht. I haf to go and help heah.

<Nurse #1>: You cannot stand up. The reporters probably need the help.

<Huey>: Barker is right about the reporters needing help. Let him examine you.

<Gunnar>: I haf to see her!

<Nurse #1>: Go ahead.

<Gunnar>: ***I can do this. No, I can't!***

<Nurse #1>: That was very elegant. What do you do for an encore?

<Gunnar>: ***It's more important to stop Sharf before he tightens the noose around both our necks - as soon as the floor stops moving.*** Do it and get it ovah.

<Huey>: ***He was very worried about Indy. I'll mention it to her later.***

<Nurse #1>: Go in there, and put this on. On second thought, I'll help you put this on. Is there anyone that we should contact?

<Gunnar>: No. I mean yes. Call my daughtah. She can bwing me a change uf clothes. ***Kerstin and Len won't mind working a little for this month's condo fees.***

---------- ----------

<Dr. Janice Gaines>: ***There's a scar here already.*** That whack on the head could have messed up something. Where did you get this?

<Gunnar>: I fell against the aahm uf Mahshall's wheelchaiah.

<Gaines>: I mean the one near the back.

<Gunnar>: I was hit by a twuck.

<Gaines>: Patient previously hit by truck. What about the one along your cheekbone? This was a good face job.

<Gunnar>: I was wacing and my caah hit a wall.

<Gaines>: Patient hit by wall. Your arm is a mess, but what happened up here?

<Gunnar>: I went ovah a patch uf ice and hit a twee.

<Gaines>: Got it. Patient previously hit by tree. What happened to your leg?

<Gunnar>: The same wacing accident.

<Gaines>: I'm almost finished. Barker said I should check [...]

<Gunnar>: NO! That's fine.

<Gaines>: Barker, come in here.

---------- ----------

<Huey>: Where's Mama, and what about Daddy?

<Val>: Nicky is behind that curtain resting. I believe she'll be all right.

<Huey>: What about Daddy?

<Val>: No word [...]

<Huey>: You really do look funny. [...] Wait a minute. Nurse, I need help.

<Nurse #2>: Hello Huey. Sorry to see you again so soon.

<Huey>: Me too. Anyway, two fellows down the hall just tripped over my sister. One of them may have injured his wrist, and the other one is acting as dizzy as Gunnar was.

<Nurse #2>: Is Indy OK? It seems like everybody is tripping today.

<Huey>: She's fine. She may have instigated the tripping.

<Nurse #2>: Where are they?

<Huey>: In the hall near the laundry room.

<Nurse #2>: I'll be back in a minute.

<Huey>: What happened with Mama?

<Val>: She ran in, and she insisted that someone should take her to your father.

After she caught her breath, she listened quietly while we explained that your father's leg was bruised again, and he was having a little trouble breathing, but he would be all right. She was holding your father's cane while she listened to us.

Eventually, she asked if your father said anything.

Gunnar tried to make her feel better by telling her that he only said two words and both of them were "Nicky". The "two words" comment let her know that something was very serious. Your father is usually cursing himself for being clumsy.

She said in a very subdued manner, "He needs me. I have to make sure he is all right, especially with all the things he's allergic to". I explained that Indy/Simone had already given the medical staff all the information that we knew about your father, and that Indy would explain what the doctor said as soon as the two of you returned.

She insisted on finding out where your father was. The nurse said he was in surgery, and we should know something in a couple of hours, thereby confirming that it was worse than a bruise and shortness of breath. She started in the direction of the surgical unit.

Gunnar tried to jump in front of her. She induced him to bend over to her level.

[...] Yep, just like that. He may have responded slowly due to the lump on his head. I take that back. She's still a blur. She'd have gotten him, lump, or no lump.

[...] She proceeded to try to try to break the cane on him. I tried to stop her. The police tried to block her from going in there with the doctors. I believe that's when you two came in.

<Huey>: It does appear that the women in our family have a violent streak.

<Indy>: No. I think the people in our family are clumsy. Where's Mama? **Recorder is in dangerous waste. Where is the chip?**

***<Huey>*:** She's resting behind that curtain. **It is in dangerous waste.**

<Indy>: Good. How is Daddy?

<Val>: Still no news.

<Indy>: Did you call Randy and Sandy?

<Huey>: Yes. They are going to hang out with Mike. Ryan will pick Becky up from her doctor's appointment, and then he's taking everyone out to dinner and a movie. Izzy is going along to cheer everybody up.

<Indy>: There is no Izzy. It's good to have an imaginary Ike, but today is the day they might have to start dealing with reality. I never understood why Ryan supports them in their fantasy anyhow. They're 16 years old, for heaven's sake.

<Huey>: Should I tell them to come here instead? We thought it would be better than sitting around smelling antiseptic scrub, and he can get them here in 20 minutes if Pop [...] if necessary. ***You'd never admit that you would rather have Ryan here.***

<Indy>: The first plan sounds like a good plan. Because I keep missing the man, doesn't mean that he doesn't exist.

<Huey>: Mike has seen him too. This Ike-like person is funny to the point of being silly, he has three young children, he's working on his third ex-wife, he is very rich, and he's 10 years younger than Ike would have been if he was still alive. Our kids have seen two of his kids. Do you believe they made up an entire family for him too?

<Indy>: I'm sorry I yelled at you.

<Huey>: Pat will take the first flight he can book, and I left a message for Patty.

<Indy>: Old Sis could use a hug right now.

<Val>: Here's one from me too. Now check on your mother.

<Indy>: I don't believe she'd want to see me.

<Huey>: Yes, she would.

<Indy>: I'll see Mama later. Find me when you hear something about Daddy. **Keep reporters distracted. They will miss the reporting deadline.**

<Val>: You mother would be proud of you.

<Indy>: If she ever speaks to me again.

<Huey>: She will. You have to let her be angry for a while though.

<Nurse #2>: Mrs. Simone Winslow.

<Huey>: That's Indy, except for the Mrs. She's headed for the laundry room.

<Nurse #2>: When she returns, tell her that Mr. Ryan Winslow wants to know if she has time to speak with him.

---------- ----------

<Gunnar>: ***That's the second time they paged Simone Winslow. She is beautiful and strong. Somebody like her could help me to deal with everything!***

<Nurse #1>: You can stop the demo now. The bruise on your thigh will hurt, but that part is working surprisingly well.

<Gunnar>: You stahted it. I said it was all wight. ***Thigh! I can't even sit up to see it. It hurts from my knee to my waist (like the time I was spiked), but thank goodness she missed that.***

<Nurse #1>: You're lucky. If Mrs. Frey had done as much damage here as she did to your arm, we could be considering a gender switch.

<Gunnar>: I wasn't using it to pwotect my head - ***as I do constantly - it protects my heart too.***

<Gaines>: Here is a bit of advice. Barker says Ms. Frey or Marshall or whatever her name is has two black belts, a green one, and special weapons training. The next time you want to tangle with her, consider full body armor, including a reinforced cup. Meanwhile, relax while I order tests.

---------- ----------

<Gunnar>: Wheah aah you taking me?

<Nurse #1>: Didn't you hear the doctor order X-rays? Your skull, your jaw, or your arm could be fractured.

<Gunnar>: Uf coahse I heahed him. I didn't know he meant heah and now.

<Nurse #1>: What better place and time would you imagine? Unless you sign a release, you can't go home without them. ***The doctor is rather obviously a she, in spite of that loose coat and the short hair. We should keep him overnight for observation.***

<Gunnar>: ***I'd better let them look at me. It's after hours. How much damage could Sharf do between now and tomorrow morning?***

Executive Alert!

<Justin Mittelman>: Remind me again why we are having this meeting.

<Doc>: We are meeting the leader of the team that Gunnar hired to figure out how we will keep SOX and Service-Oriented Architecture running after Hamilton Marshall leaves.

<Justin>: Is it time for that already? We just negotiated a contract with Marshall.

<Doc>: He has 21 months left on a three-year contract.

<Justin>: Are you sure. Gunnar acts like he going to leave any day now.

<Doc>: Hand me your keyboard.

<Justin>: You're good at that. Have you been taking Marshall's research challenges?

<Doc>: I was always the fastest one here, including Docente.

Here it is.

<Justin>: Is he asking out of the contract? Do we have a succession plan on file for him? ***I know we don't, but I want you to know that I know that you dropped the ball on this.***

<Doc>: ***Is Gunnar trying to push him out again?*** I didn't hear anything until Monday.

<Justin>: What happened on Monday?

<Doc>: He handed me a tentative staff reassignment plan on Monday. It's a fully loaded Marshall plan. BASE will go away when he leaves.

<Justin>: WHAT? Why? ***What is wrong with that damned fool? Why didn't Piccolo warn me?***

<Doc>: My guess is that he knew Gunnar was coming after him, and he wanted to eliminate the target.

<Justin>: When were you planning on telling me?

<Doc>: Today. I didn't think it was important enough to interrupt the special goodbye festivities that Chiu arranged for you.

<Justin>: ***It was a waste. Van Amberg drank tea and practiced his Chinese with Chiu's assistant. We don't have a clue about why thought he needed to spend three weeks to help them set up planning.*** Let me see it.

<Doc>: Just a minute. Here's the summary.

<Justin>: I sat two feet away from Van Amberg for 24 hours during that flight, and he didn't give me the slightest hint. Why would they play it that way?

I have never understood him, and Piccolo wouldn't tell me whether there was anything to understand. On the other hand, maybe Piccolo doesn't really understand him either.

<Doc>: He says he doesn't have anyone with a tough enough hide to take the abuse that he has taken. He claims that he'd rather have an orderly restructuring that benefits Daxiao than a slow painful death.

<Justin>: That's taking passive a little too far? Gunnar will be confused. ***I'm confused too. Why would he fight so hard to build what he has and then voluntarily destroy it?***

<Doc>: If a game is being played, confusing Gunnar, and maybe you, would be among the desirable objectives. By the way, when did Gunnar become so interested in HM?

<Justin>: When the SOX and CMMI evaluations came in. As the individual who wishes to lead the audit committee while Guzman is trying to keep us from being gobbled up, he says he needs a better understanding of why Marshall is successful. He convinced a lot of other people that they should be confused too.

<Doc>: Why doesn't Guzman explain it to him?

<Justin>: Guzman let Acton explain it to him, and he still acts confused.

<Doc>: He could ask Piccolo.

<Justin>: He's spoken to Piccolo and the explanation was too high-level for him to make sense of it.

<Doc>: He could have asked Marshall.

<Justin>: How would that conversation go? Let's see [...]

Hello H, old buddy. If you felt that I was ignoring you for the last few years, I was. It wasn't personal. I was building a power base, and you seemed to be powerless. Recently, you've been blipping on my radar, and it's time that I found out what you do.

<Doc>: H would look straight through him for a moment, and then he would smile and say OK. Subsequently, he would answer, or cause to have answered, every question in excruciating detail.

<Justin>: There is a middle ground between Piccolo and Marshall, and Gunnar hired someone he believes will find that middle? Gunnar's research will be beneficial to me too. I believe that I have half a dozen people who could replace Marshall, and I want to know what to look for.

<Doc>: I thought I saw your fingerprints in this, and you are very wrong.

<Justin>: Why?

<Doc>: Haven't you been reading the speeches that Maçon writes for you and Armstrong?

<Justin>: Just because I read them doesn't mean I understand them. She highlights where I have to put the emphasis, and I run with it. *My little sister is usually right.*

<Doc>: I will prep you. While you were doing your outward facing job, Piccolo and Marshall, or maybe Marshall and Piccolo, worked with Armstrong to change the way we do business.

<Justin>: You mean they changed the way we do technology.

<Doc>: When were the last two strategy validation sessions?

<Justin>: A month ago and four months ago. Piccolo schedules them every three months, whether we need then or not. What does this have to do with SOA?

<Doc>: The last article that Weldon approved said:

1. We spend $2 billion every year on technology.
2. For Daxiao, that number has been flat for the last three years while our competitors' expenses have increased by 15 - 25%. Our WFSOA Program increases the likelihood that we will spend money on the services that the strategy says we need.
3. With iterative strategy management, it takes Weldon about three (3) months to refocus after a strategy shift. It used to take a year. That saves money.
4. During that nine-month gap, we were wasting money, and it took more work to do the realignment. By the time we made appropriate adjustments, something else had changed.

<Justin>: That sounded impressive, when we approved it, and it sounds impressive now, but it doesn't explain Marshall. Perhaps we actually do need someone to help Marshall explain what he's doing, so that it makes sense - to mortals.

<Doc>: The only mortals that don't understand are you and the ones that Gunnar convinces to have memory lapses.

<Justin>: I really am confused. I believe I know that if real work is involved, Piccolo didn't do it. I know that Weldon has been working on his end game, but I don't know how successful he has been. It's hard to tell where Armstrong drops the ball and Marshall picks it up.

<Doc>: Weldon is still perfecting his opening moves. Marshall might appreciate it if you acknowledged that he's been propping up Armstrong the whole time that Armstrong has been here.

<Justin>: Are you saying that if anything actually was finished, Weldon didn't do it?

<Doc>: I'm saying that if Armstrong is better at finishing, Marshall contributes to his success.

<Justin>: Why haven't I noticed this before?

<Doc>: You ignored Marshall because you (a) screwed him by bringing in Armstrong in the first place and (b) screwed him again by letting Montgomery loose on him five years ago, and (c) screwed him again when you let Armstrong hang the Web Services albatross around his neck. If you acknowledged Marshall's work, you would have to admit that your choices regarding him have been extremely inappropriate.

<Justin>: Since when did you develop such a thing for Marshall that you are willing to question my judgment so openly? I don't know what has your hackles up, but your contract is finished in three months, and I could replace you in about six weeks. I'd make sure I found someone that didn't need the emerald act. *She questions my judgment constantly, and she keeps me out of trouble. I do not usually react that strongly.*

<Doc>: *Since the last 15 or 20 times when he showed me how to save my hide.* The gem is sapphire, not emerald. It's darker, harder, and tough enough to survive in Daxiao. I ran this company for two years before you arrived, I'm the only conscious you have, and a third of your brainpower. You'd last about three months without me.

<Justin>: I'd also find someone who sees the world the way I do. *What am I saying?*

<Doc>: *Free at last!* Give me back the keyboard. I'll give you my resignation, effective in six weeks. I will send you the paper on a few people who might think the way you do. Remember, though, that when you find Mr. See Right, you'll be paying him four times what you pay me. Furthermore, if he is as good as I am, he'd have a clear shot at your job in one year.

<Justin>: *She called my bluff. How do I take it back without admitting that I goofed?* Answer the phone.

<Doc>: What do you want Higgs?

[...] Yes, I have been taking them.

[...] He threatened to fire me.

[...] I just told him that.

[...] It's good to be appreciated, and thanks for the reminder.

<Justin>: *I owe Higgs a raise.* It would be beneficial if we restarted this conversation from a few sentences ago. I'll say, "Why haven't I noticed how much Marshall might have been helping Armstrong?" It is your turn. You will say [...]

<Doc>: Higgs thinks I should apologize, and I will. I'm more upset than I realized about the prospect of not having H around. He is an anchor for a lot more things than you realize. *She says I should keep my mouth shut until I understand how H is doing and what H was doing.*

<Justin>: You still haven't answered my question about Marshall.

<Doc>: You haven't noticed because Armstrong and Marshall both keep it a secret.

<Justin>: I can understand why Armstrong might want to do that, but why would Marshall go along with it?

<Doc>: As both their bosses, you might wish to discuss the matter before an effective team disintegrates.

<Justin>: This is going smoother. Do you have any questions for me?

<Doc>: Yes. My team did not have an opportunity to look into Belvedere as a potential provider of consulting services. Nor did Onesti, for obvious reasons, I suppose. Would you be kind enough to give me some insight as to why you believe they are more suited for this job than Acton is?

<Justin>: We cannot know if they are more suited until we look at them.

<Doc>: How long have you trusted Gunnar?

<Justin>: I never have, but he throws my weight around very effectively. Gunnar scares people. I don't.

<Doc>: He wants your job.

<Justin>: He and about five other people that I could name. Gunnar is the most predictable.

<Doc>: What do you know about Belvedere?

<Justin>: They have a decent reputation. They're small potatoes in comparison to Acton, but occasionally, they dig up something that saves someone money or embarrassment. Not understanding Marshall is starting to be embarrassing.

<Doc>: What do you know about the team that "we" approved, and how do you feel about their first report?

<Justin>: ***Where?***

<Doc>: *Hmmm. That was a real surprise. Maybe I shouldn't have snapped at him.* Look for "Daxiao SOA Etiology - Revelations and Work Plan" in your e-mail. William Sharf sent it to ***E-VER-Y-BO-DY*** *last night.*

<Justin>: He certainly did. Let's see. He wants to do $1,000,000 worth of work in the next four months.

Gunnar said it would cost about half a million. *This is close Marshall's annual compensation package, not half.*

<Doc>: Can you tell if the work plan makes sense for the money that he is requesting? He was not particularly kind to me in his list of suggestions and most of the drawing seems backwards.

<Justin>: It doesn't matter. Whatever they produce will keep Acton on their toes. I'll talk to

Gunnar about why the price moved and why the date switched.

<Marybeth Higgins>: Mr. Mittelman, Mr. Guzman is on his way in. He says we have a problem that needs to be addressed immediately.

<Justin>: Did you tell him I was already in a meeting?

<Higgs>: He says it can't wait. He's coming in now.

<Joe Guzman>: Good morning Dr. Emery-Baldwin. Don't move. I was going to find you next anyhow.

<Doc>: I was going to find you too.

<Joe>: Check your incident reports and tell me how it's related to that garbage from the sniper you and Gunnar brought in from Belvedere.

<Justin>: Both of you fell out of the wrong side of the bed this morning.

<Higgs>: Excuse me again. Mr. Mittelman, perhaps you should look at this morning's incident report. There was quite brouhaha in our midtown site yesterday.

<Joe>: We've got it Higgs. Thank you, and stay close. We will need you to make some quick calls. Click in Monique if you have to step away. Marcella will be tied up.

<Justin>: What do "**WE**" have?

<Joe>: A huge pain in the drain that is directly related to Marshall having pain in a lot of other places.

<Doc>: From what? I talked to him yesterday morning, and he sounded fine. ***Maybe he knew something that we didn't when he filed that plan.***

<Joe>: There was a Level 4 emergency with Fire Department vehicles and a police escort. Marshall was seriously injured, and Gunnar was staggering around and barking out orders.

<Doc>: ***What happened?***

<Justin>: That could have been problematic. Did it hit the news?

<Joe>: There's a report on the Internet, but nothing in the newspaper or on TV or radio.

<Doc>: Even that could be bad for the corporate image. Let's make sure Daxiao is OK.

<Justin>: That's what I'm doing.

Criticality:	Maximum - Level 4 ****
	Fire Department and Police Involvement
All-Tha-News: New York.	
Posted: 11:23 P.M.	
Headline:	Silicone Alley Executives in Freak Accident.
Subheading:	Police injured during rescue efforts.
Daxiao Staff Involved:	Nicholas Gunnar - Hospitalized (Under observation).
	Hamilton Marshall - Hospitalized (Condition Critical).
	Valery Van Amberg - Examined and Released.
Public Image:	Minimal Impact.
Market Impact:	None.
Property Damage:	None.
Security Breach:	None.
Financial Impact:	Possible suit for injury on premises.
	Executive insurance rate adjustment (minimal).
Legal Implications:	Daxiao lawyer involved - further investigation required.
Follow-Up:	Courtesy call(s) highly recommended.
	Employees at the Hospital for Orthopaedic Surgery in New York, New York.

<Joe>: ***Mr. Sensitivity doesn't know she was being sarcastic.***

<Justin>: It's a bad idea to have that many executives in a dangerous place all at the same time.

<Joe>: They were not in usually dangerous places.

<Doc>: That sounds a little more serious than Marshall's knee giving out again. ***This will be a rough ride.***

<Joe>: It definitely was. I spoke to two people last night who say Gunnar may have saved Marshall's life, and two other people who say they saw Marshall smiling and singing before Gunnar showed up and on life support after there were raised voices in Marshall's office. I want to know:

1. Since when does Gunnar visit Marshall?
2. Marshall has been wobbly all his adult life. Why did he almost die the first time Gunnar went calling after the faked apology five years ago?
3. Why is it that Van Amberg looked like he wanted to attack Gunnar?
4. Who attacked Gunnar? He had a lump on his head, and he was moving around like one of those shaky baby toys. How do you call it?

<Justin>: It's a Weeble.

<Joe>: Exactly! Furthermore:

5. Why was the person that you and Gunnar hired sliding these under our windshield wipers this morning? Everything that we haven't already rehashed and resolved is backwards.
6. Why does he want us to pay Belvedere $1 million to rehash what we already resolved and turn around what wasn't backwards until he arrived?
7. Why did you wait so long to fall off the fence? It could appear that a vendetta has gotten out of hand, and you contributed to the problem.

<Doc>: I can answer the first question. Gunnar's people occupy the space that he forced Marshall and Piccolo to give up in New York. You must have approved the move.

H called me yesterday to ensure that he had approval from Armstrong, Gunnar, and me to give Belvedere a copy of our SOA Roles/Responsibility information. Belvedere seemed anxious to have it. Gunnar had not approved it, so perhaps he condescended to discuss the matter face to face on the way to visit his new quarters.

<Justin>: Windshield wiper. ***Dumb is a good idea now.***

<Joe>: That was a figure of speech. Gunnar's goon was standing near the security desk handing these out when I came in. It's a printed version of the thing he sent out last night.

<Justin>: Did you know about this last night?

<Joe>: Of course. Three of our senior people were involved. Security wanted us to be prepared for potential legal problems.

<Justin>: Higgs, call Marshall's office.

<Joe>: Don't bother. None of his people will be there until 8:00 A.M., unless they were there from the night before.

<Justin>: Locate Gunnar. Check the hospital first.

<Joe>: Boyd checked with James. Gunnar has a mild concussion, lumps and bruises, and some loose teeth. He sounds funny. James will pick Gunnar up at the hospital in approximately 45 minutes. He has a dental appointment at 9:30.

<Higgs>: I hate to interrupt again, but this sounds important. Mr. Gunnar's daughter called to say that he may have suffered a concussion, he's badly bruised, and he needs some dental work. He won't be able to make it out here until tomorrow. She would like to [...]

<Justin>: Call Piccolo.

<Joe>: Piccolo was not involved in this.

<Justin>: I pay Piccolo to be involved in everything.

<Higgs>: He's not in his office sir, and he's not picking up his cell.

<Justin>: Call Gunnar's daughter back.

<Higgs>: She's on line 2.

<Kerstin Gunnar>: Hello Mr. Mittelman. Papa told me to leave a message saying stayed at the hospital last night. He has a dental appointment early this morning. He'll fill you in on everything later today.

<Justin>: How bad is it?

<Kerstin>: His jaw and his arm are black and blue, and he has a lump on his head. I've seen him looking almost as bad after a soccer game. He was bloody, but he said most of it wasn't his blood.

<Justin>: You don't seem to be too worried.

<Kerstin>: I am a little, but in comparison to the car crashes, this is nothing. He told me I should go to may classes.

Papa will be all right, but Mr. Marshall almost died. Their whole family is a terrible state.

<Justin>: How long have you known the Marshalls?

<Kerstin>: Since last night when we took Papa a change of clothes.

<Joe>: Is anybody with him?

<Kerstin>: Who is that?

<Justin>: It's one of our co-workers.

<Kerstin>: He told me not to miss school. He says he'll be fine with James. Aunt Margaret can check on him later.

<Joe>: Where's your mother?

<Kerstin>: In Rome where she usually spends this time of year.

<Justin>: What about - is it Vicky?

<Kerstin>: Victoria Thorton. That arrangement was terminated in the spring.

I think he's winding down on Helena already. I haven't seen her in a month.

<Justin>: I see. *Who can keep track?*

<Joe>: Are you all right at home alone?

<Kerstin>: I'm not alone. Len is here with me.

<Joe>: Len who?

<Kerstin>: Len Palatino. We've been married for 8 months.

<Justin>: I knew that. Joe's a little behind the times!

Please tell your father to call me when you see him or hear from him. Thank you for the information, and have a good day at school.

[...] Higgs, call the Hospital for Orthopaedic Surgery in the East 70s in Manhattan. Check on Marshall's status.

<Doc>: I hate to interrupt your Sherlock adventures, but the sniper will be here in 15 minutes. Maybe you should check to see what his targets are, other than me.

<Joe>: He proposes that he can show us how Daxiao can thrive in case Marshall should need to exercises early departure options. Then he proposed actions that could send us back to the Stone Age, and he ended with allusions to surprising revelations that may be of great interest to Daxiao management.

<Justin>: [...] Piccolo, where are you?

<Dan>: I'm in my office.

<Justin>: Why didn't you answer your cell?

<Dan>: I was in the porcelain parlor.

<Justin>: What do you know about Hamilton Marshall?

<Dan>: He's a very tall tanned older gentleman, and he limps. You pretend to listen to him for 30 minutes every three months. If you hear anyone referring to "HM", that's the same person.

<Justin>: *Spare me.* Why didn't you call me and tell me about Marshall?

<Dan>: Why was I supposed to do that? You received the same security alert that I did.

<Justin>: This is different. I pay you to be my eyes and ears.

<Dan>: Marshall fell for the third time this year. He went to the hospital with a bit more fanfare than usual, but there was no significant news coverage. We took care of that.

<Justin>: Tell me what you know about the incident that was not in the news or in the security alert.

<Dan>: Marshall is in critical condition, but he will survive, we hope. He was in surgery 8-1/2 hours out of the last 14. He still needs help breathing.

<Justin>: ***This could be sticky. It will be harder to fake an apology this time.***

<Higgs>: Mr. Mittelman, Mr. Marshall is in critical, but stable condition. I have his wife on the line. Would you like to speak to her?

<Joe>: *Say yes.*

<Justin>: I'm in the middle of a meeting. Give her my regards and send flowers.

<Higgs>: Maybe this once [...]

<Joe>: Say yes, if you plan on sitting in that cushy seat after next year.

<Dan>: Hello Joe, it's good to see that you're on the case. We're going to need a lot of counsel.

<Justin>: Higgs, I changed my mind. Say yes, I'll break for this emergency.

[...] Mrs. Marshall. It's great that we could reach you.

<Machi>: Mittelman, did you sleep well last night?

<Justin>: Yes Mrs. Marshall. I appreciate your concern, especially while your husband is not doing well.

<Machi>: It's Ms. Frey, and I asked because you will not sleep as well tonight.

<Justin>: You sound distraught. I'm sorry about HM.

<Machi>: Skip the "wish him well" script, forget the flowers, and listen carefully.

Hamilton Marshall has contributed significantly to your financial well-being while ignoring how you contributed to situations that negatively affected his well-being. The one last night nearly killed him.

You are rid of the nerdy gimp Weeble™. Feel comfort in knowing that as soon as they remove the breathing tube, we will discuss how to make that official. Start worrying about how that will affect your future and your fortune.

<Justin>: ***What am I supposed to say? How did she know I said that?*** Mrs. Marshall [...] Ms. Frey [...] She hung up.

<Joe>: ***I've never heard Machi sound like that.*** That was probably her deadly sound.

That's why you knew about the shaky toy. When did you call him a nerdy gimp Weeble?

<Doc>: He did it from the day that he met him. ***I'd better keep that resignation in "recent documents".***

<Dan>: Good morning Doc. This is even better.

<Justin>: It was the third time - my first strategy session in Banff. It was un-PC, but it seemed humorous at the time. Who told Marshall what I said? ***I was talking to - I remember now - it was Montgomery and the men that Barca and Ellison replaced.***

<Joe and Doc>: He reads lips.

<Justin>: Why are you telling me this now? Is he deaf?

<Doc>: How many times have I told you, "Shut up, H is looking"?

<Justin>: How many times did I ignore you? You could have been more specific. You just explained that I'm the resident nothing.

<Joe>: ***She gave him his weekly performance appraisal. What would we do without her?***

<Doc>: What was I supposed to do, send you a memo? ***I wanted you to ignore me. Then people would keep talking when they believed he was out of earshot, and he could tell me what they said.***

<Justin>: ***Is he deaf?*** Talk to me Dan.

<Dan>: He is not deaf, but his son is.

<Justin>: *Silicone Huey is deaf!* Why wasn't that in the reports?

<Doc>: Obviously, he compensates well enough that your snoops didn't notice. Most people believe that he is being aloof or absent-minded.

<Dan>: HM learned to read lips because he wanted to understand what his son was going through. Later he discovered that it really aids negotiations.

<Justin>: The ground is starting to feel mushy. What does his wife know about my fortune and my future?

<Dan>: She's talking about how you let Gunnar send Sharf to mess up our gravy train.

<Justin>: What gravy train?

<Higgs>: Mr. Mittelman, your first appointment is here, Mr. William Sharf (with an "f").

<Justin>: Tell him something came up, and we will be able to see him at 8:15, maybe [...]

CHAPTER V - DAXIAO RESPONSE TO PRELIMINARY SOA ASSESSMENT

<Dan>: Take me off the speakerphone.

<Justin>: Would either or both of you like to pick up? I can use the headphone.

<Dan>: It's good to know that someone will be paying attention. *Go easy Dan. You still need Justin, at least until you finish your research.*

<Justin>: *I'm good at paying attention when I must. This seems like a good "must".*

<Dan>:

#1 - Look at Sharf's Etiology hokum. Then search your memory unit and dig out whether Marshall fought for (and suffered political damage) to put those things in place, or whether we gave them to him. Forget who took credit for them in a journal article. I did my share of that.

#2 - Look at the list of recommendations. Only one is worth the electricity Sharf used to run the computer while it was being typed.

<Doc>: I agree. Here is a copy of the response I sent to you, H, and Val (see Table 18 below). I wanted to show it to the people here before I blasted it over the network.

Table 18 - Belvedere Engagement - Taking Daxiao SOA to the Next Level		
Priority	Recommended Areas of Investigation	Doc's Answers to How Would You?
1	Organizational Structure. 1. How would you separate (COSO/COBIT) SOX and SOA functions? Most organizations have separate initiatives. 2. How would you isolate Enterprise Integration and BASE functions? 3. How would you determine how BASE might be split up among the other sectors in case the senior manager departs? 4. Is the organization top-heavy? 5. How would you justify how compliance and SOA competency teams might be in the same sector? 6. How would you explain why technical people might be part of a financial organization? 7. How would you justify the high number of technology people currently involved in the business area (Requirements Management)?	1. Separation is not necessary. Acton and the government approve. 2. Piccolo thinks about Marshall's work, and Piccolo explains it to us. 3. I have Marshall's plan. It may not be a good idea. 4. No. Not given their level of responsibility in the approval processes. 5. At any give time, 80 - 90% of the people are working for either Armstrong or Macedon. 6. Finance is a neutral organization. It keeps people from fighting over service, process, and data ownership. Gunnar has supported the arrangement in the past. 7. They have become highly technical business people.
2	Roles and Responsibilities. 1. How would you reduce the list of roles to a manageable number? 2. How would you re-introduce industry standard role names? 3. How would you improve the effectiveness of hand-offs between the roles?	1. We don't have a problem with the number of roles. It assists with management of access control (security), automated approvals, reviews, and separation of duties. Marshall, Armstrong, Piccolo, and I have defined two complementary techniques for collapsing the roles if necessary. 2. There are no industry standard role names. The role names make sense in Daxiao. 3. That's why Marshall and Maçon want to expand the communications program.

Table 18 - Belvedere Engagement - Taking Daxiao SOA to the Next Level

Priority	Recommended Areas of Investigation	Doc's Answers to How Would You?
3	Training program. 1. How would you justify the typing stipend? 2. How would you justify the usefulness of ISACA training for people who will never be auditors? 3. How would you determine ROI from hundreds training courses? 4. How would you evaluate the usefulness of sales training for people who will never sell anything? 5. How would you justify the need for multiple expensive delivery options for the same information?	1. It's called keyboarding. Keep it. All poor and average performers improve after they receive the stipend, even without additional training in other areas. I have performance data to prove it. 2. Keep it. It is a critical part of our Cultural Change Management program. If more people took it, we'd be better than 70% on resistance reduction measures. 3. We justify the ROI every year when I come in for budget. I'll find the paper and send it to you - again. 4. Keep it. It enhances communications and supports the Cultural Change Management program. 5. It is generally accepted in the training professions that training is more effective when delivered in the styles appropriate to individual preferences.
4	SOA Communications. 1. How would you move BASE communications to the corporate level (and allow corresponding staff reductions? 2. How would you promote a separation between business and technology functions while ensuring appropriate collaboration? 3. How would you focus communications? Senior personnel and a few Board members may be missing critical information. 4. How would you promote use of a universal language? Multilingual efforts may need to be re-evaluated.	1. You would be moving them away from the people they support. The new arrangement would be less effective. 2. We don't want to separate them. The merger of business and technology thinking is a competitive advantage. 3. Gunnar is blocking focused communications. 4. Our cross-border teams are usually happy when they see we are trying to promote mutual understanding. This promotes cultural change management.
5	Partner Consulting. 1. How would you verify that this is effective use of staff time? 2. How would you determine whether outsourcing SOA consulting is an effective option?	1. Business with every partner with whom we have consulted has increased by 10 to 50% during the last year. 2. It would cost Daxiao more and our partners more. This is a bid to get more business for Belvedere.
6	Resistance Management (Cultural Change Management). 1. How would you improve the effectiveness of this program? The average effectiveness hovers about 50%.	It would be more effective if is received more executive support. The only reason SOA works without a mandate is because people trust Marshall.
7	Lessons Learned. 1. How would you verify the content of lessons learned and ensure proper training for future participants?	This is the most beneficial suggestion on his list. I believe you could save more millions of dollars if you followed his advice.
8	Knowledge Center. 1. How would you ensure improved stability? 2. How would you streamline the content to minimize information overload? 3. How would you merge it with Data Management? 4. How would you place more of the research databases under centralized management?	1. Stability has never been a concern. Docente provided high-availability training. They used the Knowledge Cooperative as their working model for the high availability program. I have never known it to be down in the 3-1/2 years that it's been in production. Occasionally, it runs a fraction slower if they add a hot new feature, but they usually resolve it within a few days.

Table 18 - Belvedere Engagement - Taking Daxiao SOA to the Next Level		
Priority	Recommended Areas of Investigation	Doc's Answers to How Would You?
		2. I've never heard anyone complain about overload. Everyone is automatically signed up for a subset of the feeds, depending on their roles. People receive reminders for added subjects if they request them. 3. Knowledge Management didn't work when Travers had it. We changed it to Knowledge Cooperative to camouflage Travers' foray into futility and to acknowledge vendor cooperation. 4. Maja gives Travers control of the critical databases once they are tested. If it's in research, it's not ready for prime time.
9	Planning processes and procedures. 1. How would Daxiao function without the "BASE" planning database? You may be wasting resources to provide a useless product. 2. I propose that experienced planning specialists could function effectively without the database, and Daxiao would save maintenance costs.	1. Planning is easier because we have the ***BASE database.*** 2. The more experienced the planning person, the more likely that person is to use ***BASE.***
10	Funding for Research and Development. 1. How would you development more effective funding options?	That fund allowed us to seize several opportunities that we might have missed. Marshall earns that money in a way. Guidance regarding product improvements shows up in our purchase bottom line. We give the difference to Marshall, and he lends it back when the rest of us need it. The only reason it works is that the vendors trust Marshall.

Table 19 - Daxiao SOA - Financial Implications (BASE Internal Report)		
SOA Component	**Organizational Impact**	**Annual Financial Benefit ($000)**
Corporate Policy **Credit to: Stein**	Compliance with SOX and government regulators. (Significantly less than competition).	-5,000
Roles/Action List ***(Thunk?)*** ***Credit to: Emery-Baldwin***	1. Facilitates process improvement. 2. Facilitates role definition and adjustment. 3. Facilitates skills assessment. 4. Facilitates staff evaluations.	5,000
Automated Process Approvals **Credit to: Jasper**	Decision support, process visibility, effective funding controls.	13,000
Communications Processes **Credit to: Ellison**	1. Facilitate collaboration among business units and between business units and technology. 2. Support merger and acquisition. 3. Support international efforts. **Belvedere Comment:** Claims to save hundreds of millions, however objective measures are impossible.	Unknown
Continuous Process Improvement **Credit to: Barca and Chiu**	Incremental improvements in manufacturing, logistics, and technology development processes.	23,000
Costing Algorithms **Credit to: Jasper**	Facilitates acceptance of SOA.	0
Cultural Change Management	Facilitates acceptance of accelerating environmental change.	Cannot be

Table 19 - Daxiao SOA - Financial Implications (BASE Internal Report)		
Credit to: Emery-Baldwin and Piccolo		measured
Education & Training **Credit to: Docente**	SOA overview, new process training, SOA technology training. **Belvedere Comment:** Includes staff time and course costs.	-34,000
Knowledge Cooperative **Credit to: Travers**	Enables a learning organization. Accelerates collaboration processes and supports common terminology. **Belvedere Comment:** Requires further investigation. Figure may be adjusted in either direction.	70,000
Methodology and Planning **Credit to: Jasper**	Automated cross-organizational planning.	11,000
Partner Consulting **Credit to: Barca**	Facilitates supply chain management. $3 million real income. $18 million savings during fiscal year. $168 million in additional business. **Belvedere Comment:** Larger number may be overstated. To be investigated.	189,000
Program Management Structure **Credit to: Armstrong and Piccolo**	Adapt management skills to business/ technology climate. Increases chances of technology success.	15,000
Requirements Management **Credit to: Macedon**	Building only what we need, on time and accurately.	73,000
Research and Development **Credit to: Li/Piccolo/Gunnar**	Follow-on business from Client/Partner research and development support. **Belvedere Comment:** Could not be validated owing to a system outage. Must be investigated.	200,000
Risk Management **Credit to: Stein**	Spot problems before they get out of control.	42,000
Role-based security **Credit to: Bailey and Forte**	Enables timely and appropriate access to corporate resources.	4,000
Service Management **Credit to: Torres**	Visibility into service execution. Enabled SOA acceptance. **Belvedere Comment:** $15,000,000 initial investment amortized over three years. Ongoing license costs balanced by problem reduction.	0
SOA Governance **Credit to: Piccolo**	Promotes effective use and reuse of IT resources.	23,000
SOA Initiation **Credit to: Armstrong**	Foundation for SOA.	0
SOA Reference Architecture **Credit to: Armstrong**	Consistent technology implementation.	20,000
SOA Reward Structure **Credit to: Executive Staff**	Promotes staff participation and acceptance.	-50,000
Strategy Management **Credit to: Piccolo**	Define, evangelize, tune, and synchronize.	88,000
Tooling and Staff Reduction **Credit to: Armstrong**	Savings on retirements and technology resignations.	50,000
	Total Value to Organization	737,000

<Dan>: I received it, and I agree totally.

<Justin>: *Now I see why Doc is annoyed.*

Gunnar also wants me to support him while he attacks Liz. He will pay for this. I wonder why Dan is so calm.

<Dan>: However, you should not enter a contest for which you are neither anatomically nor politically equipped. Messrs. Mittelman and Guzman should handle this. Let me continue:

#3 - You have been riding on one of the greatest accumulations of power Daxiao has ever seen, and you didn't notice. Marshall, Alex, and I built it for you, and Joe and my team were holding it for you, but you were not ready to take the reins. Gunnar is significantly more attuned to accumulations of power than you are.

#4 - Gunnar has been falling behind his peers on SOA measures that Marshall and I worked with Acton to implement, and that makes him very unhappy.

#5 - Gunnar is willing to destroy what he does not understand or control.

#6 - No person is irreplaceable, but some people are harder to replace than others are. I'm talking about both Marshall and Gunnar.

I will personally crucify Gunnar, but I'll do it later when no one is watching. I have to figure out how to keep him miserable and keep him working - a moneymaking shell. He's probably that already.

Do either of you concur?

<Joe>: I agree with most of what you said.

<Doc>: If I was anatomically equipped, I might be thinking along those lines?

<Dan>: I'm sorry Doc. It was a rough night.

<Justin>: Since you have it figured out already, what do we do next? ***Which "we"?***

<Dan>: Pat Mr. Sharf on the head, tell him he's been a good boy, and run down here. Justin, that means putting one foot in front of the other quickly, no matter how unseemly that may be for a person of your robotic stature. Mr. Guzman, please join us. You could teach him the running trick. When you arrive, I will give you the second installment, while the Doc keeps Sharf occupied. We can't stop them until we find out what Gunnar created while we were not paying attention. I hope all of you have a supply of anti-venom. I will go now and prepare for your much-anticipated arrival.

<Justin>: Doc, can you handle Sharf, given your anatomical shortcomings.

<Doc>: You left yourself wide open, but I will simply say "yes".

<Justin>: I suspect that you will accept Piccolo's invitation, and furthermore that you will join us for our meeting with Mr. Sharf. ***I need breathing room, but I don't expect that you will give me any.***

<Joe>: Of course. The sooner I see how warped this is, the sooner I can decide how to fix it. For starters, you should not have signed that tentative contract without running it past me, even if it is only $500,000. Belvedere may be small, but they have someone who is very good at taking care of Belvedere's interests. Belvedere should have been a Board decision.

<Justin>: I am not a complete fool. Gunnar collected approvals from half the Board. This needed to be done quickly and quietly, or Acton would have blocked it.

<Joe>: This insanity needed to be blocked.

<Justin>: Let me see what Sharf had to say. You've both read this, and I haven't.

<Doc>: Start with the pie (Fig. 15-Daxiao Etiology). It has a lot of slices, but you like pictures.

<Justin>: The first two slices are correct.

History of WFSOA Program - HR Perspective

<Doc>: Not quite. Let me summarize for both of you before Sharf comes in.

1. **SOA Governance:** You sent me as your representative to the first serious working meeting on this topic. You said I had to learn to work with Piccolo. Marshall had an idea that he called a fat clear pipe with carefully spaced input valves and filters. Dan called it adding value and concept veridation. He made up his own word.
2. **Corporate Policy:** The Board approves policy after Stein (who works for Marshall) and Joe's people interpret it for you. Stein is the near-sighted dishrag with the spots on his tie.

<Justin>: Does Stein read lips too? [...] Good.

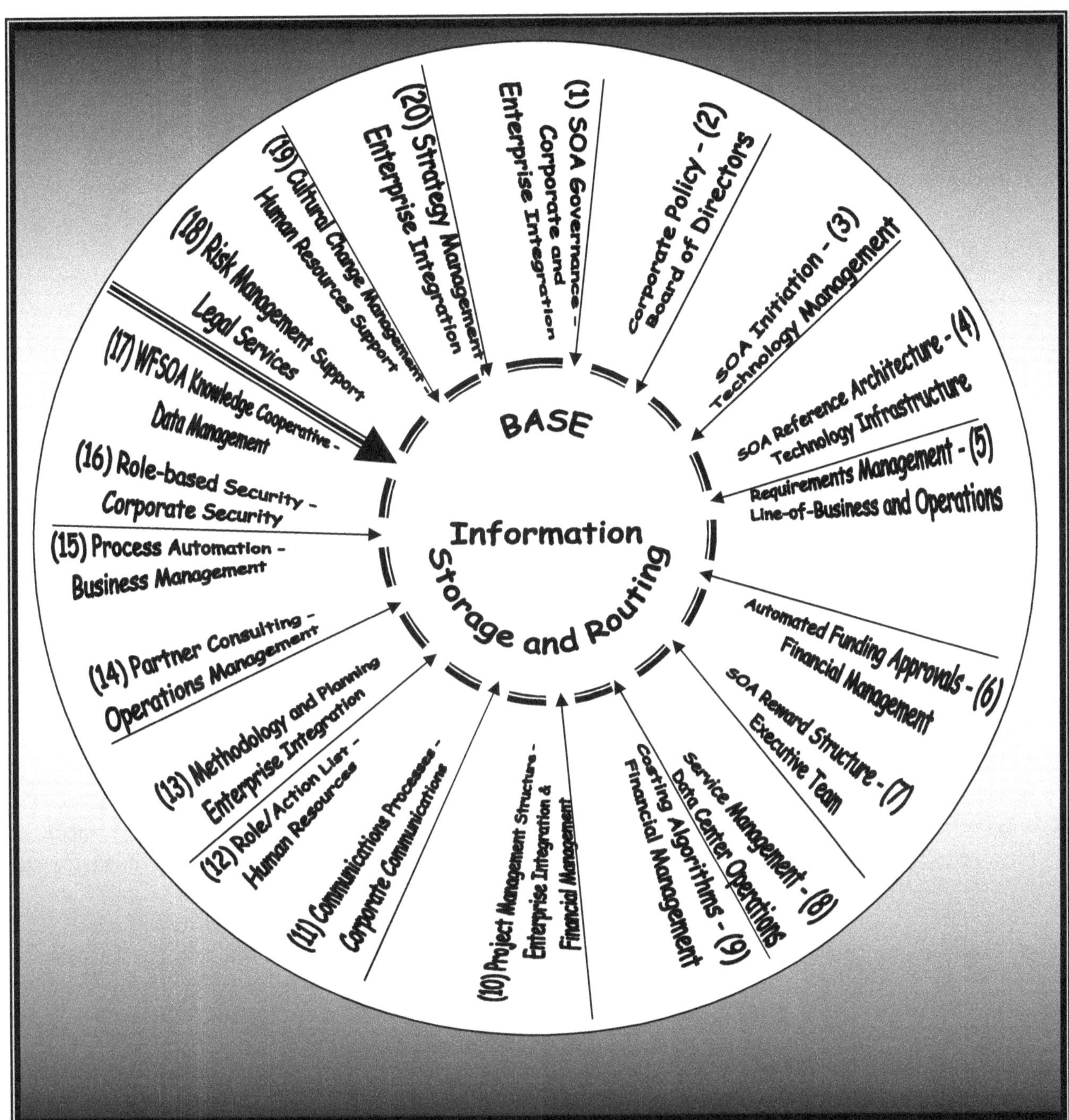

Fig. 15 - Daxiao SOA Etiology (Belvedere Version)

3. **SOA Initiation:** Marshall installed the very first simple Web services (pre-SOA), and Armstrong expanded the number of services (LITTLE SOA) and eventually moved us to the point where we should have been looking at "BIG SOA", except that Armstrong continued to work on a large technology project, not a business/technology project. The third time you (collectively) tried to hang Marshall, he managed to organize the technology spaghetti upon which Armstrong was building business software alphabet soup, and Piccolo turned it into WFSOA. I know what WFSOA is now, because we use common terminology (which is covered under slice 11 of the pie). Marshall kept all Armstrong's "problem people". I was

involved because I had to move all those people around.

4. **Reference Architecture:** That is a model for installing infrastructure platforms or pieces of infrastructure platforms. Marshall's people work with Armstrong's people to ensure that the SOA technology pieces fit with the regular parts.
5. **Requirements Management:** This was part of the big WFSOA shuffle. Alex Macedon wanted to show that he could manage requirements better than either Armstrong or HM, and you wanted to keep an eye on the WFSOA silliness from the inside.
6. **Automated Funding Approvals:** Lorrie fought automation of SOA approvals with everything she had. She wanted paper, even if it did put a 15 - 20% time delay on the smaller projects. She didn't care how clearly we defined the roles or how tightly Forte secured them. Marshall automated and animated the work request documentation, so that people would understand what they were approving and respond more quickly, even when Lorrie insisted that 20 - 50% more people needed to be involved in the automated approvals - she believed that if she overloaded the automated approval requirements, they wouldn't work. Now we receive extremely high marks from COSO and CMMI due to Lorrie's extra authorizations and Marshall's automated processes.
7. **SOA Reward Structure:** That was the first year our profits jumped, and you promoted a small addition to the pool. While middle managers were fighting over a slightly larger pool, few people noticed the disproportionately larger pool for senior management.
8. **Service Management:** This was one of the first Web services fights after Marshall started to discover better containers for the services spaghetti. Torres said his people did not have time to learn new data center management tools and processes because they were still trying to keep up with what they had. Marshall insisted that all of Armstrong's Web services effectiveness would be destroyed if the new products were not used. He was already giving Armstrong the technical credit for WFSOA and this was a very big loose end. Docente and I were caught in the training fights.
9. **Technology Costing Algorithms:** Costing is 50% right. Lorrie validated and revalidated what Van Amberg and Yu (who work for Marshall) and Stein (of stained tie) pulled together. We are almost certain that Marshall or his daughter did the math, but neither one of them will own up to it. Lisse Maçon and my people prepared the executive overview, and I added them to middle management training modules.
10. **Project Management Structure:** Piccolo put more fancy words around Marshall's ideas for putting the best and most flexible project managers with the toughest projects. The business violently opposed losing "their" people and "their" applications, although they continually complain that "their application" people don't deliver what the business wanted. I received the management overview materials from Marshall, not Piccolo. I recommended the matrix management arrangements.
11. **Communications Processes:** This should definitely be a two-way arrow. It's big, but it needs to be bigger. Ellison and Lisse Maçon work well together, especially with innovations for improving international communications. She enforces common terminology, with Ellison's support. It's the best collaboration I've ever seen. They also support our reputation as an innovative trainer in the international arena.

<Justin>: I almost feel a compliment in there somewhere. Let me relish it.

<Joe>: Relish later. Listen now.

12. **Role/Activity *(Thunk)* List:** I thought the action lists were overkill until I used them to show the Board how much work my people accomplished. Now half of your people use it for similar purposes. It supports the next topic.
13. **Methodology and Planning:** Remember how everyone on the Board chuckled and Marshall started to stutter when he said he collected

thousands of plans as part of his hobby. You will also recall how gleeful you were when everyone agreed to drop it on him (after he put his foot in his own mouth) during Goodsand's first tangle with Daxiao. Marshall's planning obsession allowed us to automate technology processes (methodology) and planning.

14. **Partner Consulting:** Marshall's people were involved in that before it had a name. They provided the links between external teams and operations. Gunnar believed they were stepping on his marketing territory, and he pointed out that we were providing free consulting. Marshall agreed to pull back, but important customers were willing to pay for what Marshall did. Van Amberg and Joe accelerated the legal approvals. Marshall let operations take the credit, so that Gunnar would stop shooting at him. Gunnar receives bigger orders from many of the "Partner" organizations, but he is still fighting it. He seems to be willing to shoot himself in the foot.
15. **Process Automation:** Marshall and Macedon adopted concepts from manufacturing and applied them to automation and quality control checkpoints for software development. He lets clients check the quality of their own requirements before they are handed over to development. I provided the training. Of course, Operations took the credit when they started receiving what they asked for.
16. **Role-Based Security:** We all worked on that (HR, Global Security, and BASE), but we formulated the initial ideas based on Marshall's "ridiculous" ***Thunk*** action list.
17. **WFSOA Knowledge Cooperative:** Travers backed away from the Knowledge Center [...]

<Justin>: It's Knowledge Cooperative [...] I know something. What does that have to do with SOA?

<Doc>: It was a Knowledge Center when Travers had it.

At least the size of the arrow is right. The Knowledge Cooperative supports more than 400 different arrangements of data, and it is not overkill (which you would know if you had paid attention when the wiry hyperactive black kid was talking). That is where I keep our training materials.

Maja Johanssen convinced Marshall that we needed this super complicated and extremely stable database to store SOX documentation that became SOA documentation. That became the foundation for most B2E activity (business portals to you, but Marshall calls his the BASE to Employee portal). It is linked to business intelligence applications, and it has links to many of our legal documents.

Travers said the technology that Maja wanted to use was obsolete. Besides, he felt that if he couldn't handle knowledge management, nobody would be able to. He still hasn't forgiven Maja, but he takes credit for providing the database support.

By the way, she's older than Piccolo by a month.

<Joe>: She's also smarter. She's pretty close to Marshall.

<Justin>: How smart is Marshall?

<Doc>: Marshall's raw IQ measurements are in the files we locked after the SOX/purchasing investigation. I'm sure Joe would give you permission to take a peak. The number may be moderately impressive, but you should remember that he has a "wide" IQ and there is no approved technique for measuring width.

18. **Risk Management Support:** Marshall suggested and Piccolo promoted those winking blinking lights that everyone hates when the lights start blinking red. The good news is fewer lights turn red. Joe's staff increased the first couple of years to handle the red, but he's almost back to the pre-WorldCom level. Either way, we can see which way things are moving immediately, and the result is that Daxiao has much better SOX results.
19. **Cultural Change Management:** Marshall gives Piccolo and me credit for it, but Marshall sent me the first list of resistance factors, and he maintains the list. He also coordinates the Grumble program that feeds continuous process improvement, and that is not on this list.

20. **Strategy Management:** As you mentioned earlier, it is almost correct too. Piccolo said we needed it, Marshall said we needed it to be synchronized with SOA, Piccolo's consultant came up with the processes, and Marshall helps them to record, monitor, and update the strategy.

<Justin>: What about the financial implications? That can't be right. That's more than three quarters of a billion dollars.

<Joe>: Marshall presented it all to us, piecemeal. He was afraid to scare people by presenting it all in one place. Don't look so confused. You'd know this if you did more of your sleeping at night.

<Justin>: I don't sleep. I observe quietly.

<Doc>: He's not lying. I've checked. It is a stupid way of trying to trick people into saying things that they shouldn't. I suggest that we check with Lorrie. She would be neutral and more knowledgeable.

<Justin>: Higgs. Find Lorraine Jasper. Tell her it's an emergency.

Now allow me to think deviously.

<Doc>: Don't try to think again. You had two thoughts already today, and both were wrong.

<Justin>: *She's right, but I'll ignore her. You can learn from wrong thoughts if you're willing to listen to the people who know the right answers.*

Sharf was approved by me because of Gunnar's recommendation. He may be brilliant in some perverted way, and he could discover and emphasize 20 critical strategy components within our organization in one day. Nobody ever bothered to organize the information the way Sharf did. He used this information to make it appear that my management team (with emphasis on Armstrong and Piccolo) is thinking creatively and constructively, and that we are very effective risk takers while Marshall is useless. *What do we do if Marshall was making that much of a difference? What would we do if this annoyed him enough to make him leave?* Why are you laughing?

<Joe>: I didn't mean to laugh. It brings up the image that I have of Marshall limping around trying to guess which ledge Armstrong will do push us over next, and then putting nets in place, so we don't crash.

<Doc>: We were approaching a similar image when you joined us. They actually make a good team.

<Justin>: We are in a position where we could be embarrassed if we denied the fact that we are doing the creative and constructive thinking, and taking the risks for the well-being of the company.

<Higgs>: Ms. Jasper is on the line.

<Justin>: What took you so long? Have you checked your e-mail today?

<Lorraine Jasper>: *Two seconds - I'll ignore the first question.* No, I have not checked my e-mail. I'm rushing to prepare for the meeting with the fool that Gunnar wants me to see tomorrow morning.

Now I have a question: When did you agree that Belvedere would be sharing audit responsibilities with Acton?

<Joe>: I'd like to know too. I suspect that half the Board was not aware.

<Lorrie>: Hello Joe, I was about to call you. Something isn't quite in focus.

<Justin>: The other half of us were interested in seeing the kind of talent Belvedere has. Healthy competition is good, and Belvedere is overly optimistic.

<Lorrie>: I know. They left a package under my door this morning. I'm looking at it now.

<Justin>: Then you know what's in the e-mail. Check out those numbers immediately and tell me if they make sense. I will be in Piccolo's office if I'm not here.

<Joe>: He covers a lot of ground.

<Justin>: Gunnar is giving him the inside track to my people. Gunnar has a toothache and a headache that prevented him from rushing in and taking credit for Sharf's handiwork, or he's taking credit with his bunch on the Board even with the toothache. On the other hand, Gunnar may have lost control of his man.

<Doc>: You trusted them enough to push this thing through. He must be your man too.

<Justin>: One can stick by a bad decision, or one can acknowledge a possible error and climb back on the fence where it's safer.

Gunnar wants to pay Sharf $1 million to discover the true geniuses behind Marshall's work. Marshall allowed these geniuses to take credit for his work. Each genius knows how he or she benefits from Marshall's work, but no one necessarily knows how many other people are supported by Marshall. I can't see where this is going (*which has me surprised and annoyed*), but I've never known Gunnar to be as politically subtle as this.

<Joe>: The Gunnar/Sharf duo is very aggressive. You would believe that he knew something that we don't. What might your man and your bunch, which are no longer yours, be plotting?

<Justin>: It will come to me, sooner rather than later. I've been saving neurons for such occasions.

If we were not paying attention, Gunnar might have used Sharf's "discoveries" to put a wedge between Acton and Daxiao. We would want to know why Acton hadn't reported these things.

The half a million dollar (or maybe a million dollar) pittance could have given Belvedere millions of dollars in the long run. Gunnar would control the Audit Committee and the external auditors. They might start finding other things that are not quite true. They create reality very well and Gunnar would control that creativity. There would come a time when he could overwhelm Guzman. *I am in deep trouble. Gunnar tricked me. I am the tricker, not the trickee.*

<Joe>: Not surprisingly, the only person who might successfully oppose this poison pie and aggressive suggestions cannot breathe without assistance at this moment. Both Gunnar and Sharf were on the premises when he almost died from a problem that is usually a painful nuisance.

<Doc>: Perhaps we should all be a bit frightened.

<Higgs>: It's 8:14. May I send Mr. Sharf in now?

<Justin>: Yes, in two minutes. *I may as well discover how big a shovel I will need.*

<Joe>: *The last time it was this bad, the former president had just keeled over where Mittelman is sitting right now.*

---------- ----------

<Justin>: Mr. Sharf. Welcome. I'm Justin Mittelman, this is Dr. Emery-Baldwin, SVP of Human Resources, and that is Mr. Joseph Guzman, our General Counsel.

<Sharf>: I'm delighted to meet you. I've heard and read so much about you - the man in the middle of the greatest electronics turn-around in history.

<Justin>: The press exaggerates.

<Sharf>: Mr. Guzman, I'm equally happy to see you. You have some problems that you should begin to address before they snap up and give you a bloody nose.

I see you have my proposal up on your screen. What do you think of it?

May I sit? I have printed copies for everyone.

<Doc>: *Adonis on stilts. I guess you're not delighted to meet me. That will be a mistake.*

Take my seat. I'll sit over here, *so I can see all of you at once.*

<Joe>: *She's going over there so she can put an arrow in her cross bow. Sharf is about to feel pain.*

<Justin>: I was just explaining to my associates, especially Dr. Emery-Baldwin that I was glad you would be here to give us more insight regarding your proposal.

<Sharf>: Emery, pull up a chair. You're a bit further down my list, but we know that your work is important. My assistant and I will show you how to optimize the training program and save money.

<Doc>: We will talk in a few minutes. They've assigned me the task of being your scheduling secretary. *I will build you a maze that you will never escape, even if I have to leave.*

<Sharf>: Excellent. I was wondering who would handle that tedium.

<Justin>: *Fool! Today is not the day.* Dr. Emery-Baldwin is one of our more talented executives. She possesses a wealth of information that you will find helpful. It would be good for you to keep that in mind.

<Joe>: Calm is good.

<Doc>: Tacky is fine. Everybody pays later.

<Justin>: Where shall we start?

<Sharf>: Let's start with Mr. Gunther. During our initial interview, Mr. Gunther implied that Hamilton Marshall was a genius with techniques for making SOX and SOA work that you needed to understand before Marshall retired.

I'm good at discovering secrets, the best that Belvedere has, so I accepted the challenge. I juggled other important projects, so that I could start at Daxiao a few days earlier. Sometimes the element of surprise creates an environment where clients are more forthcoming with critical information.

It worked perfectly. I was with the old fool less than eight hours before I figured out that he had all of you hoodwinked for years. He's a big nothing, and he hides from you, so you won't know that he is in bad shape.

<Doc>: *He's as crazy in person as he is in writing. I talk to Marshall at least three times per week, at least once from home.*

H would tell me to smile and nod. I will do that while I daydream about 128 days going around the world on the QE2.

I will survive about six weeks without Marshall, just as Justin estimated.

<Joe>: *Marshall is only two years older than I am. I see him as often as he can make time for me.*

<Justin>: You present an interesting set of observations. What else have you discovered? *He's calling one of my EVPs an old fool. How could a world-class salesman make such a poor call on this fool?*

<Sharf>: He may have been a genius, but not any longer. He takes excellent ideas from their owners, glues them together with fancy software, and pretends he's god's gift to Daxiao. That's what the etiology chart covers. I added refinements after I left him yesterday, a little under the weather I might add.

<Doc>: What shape was he in?

<Sharf>: He was gazing at the ceiling. When he looked in my direction, he acted as if I wasn't there.

<Justin>: Are you the one that called the ambulance?

<Sharf>: Did it make the news? *The reporters got the story out.*

<Justin>: It did not, and it should not. Something like this could affect investor confidence, and that would affect our ability to pay you. Do you understand?

<Sharf>: *Gunther didn't mention that he bites. I have to balance sinking Marshall with what I need to make sure Daxiao is happy with me.* I understand completely. How did you find out?

<Joe>: I am among the first to be notified by our security team when events of this nature occur. We seldom have a single occurrence where so many senior people are involved.

<Sharf>: What did they tell you?

<Joe>: That Mr. Marshall was on the way to the hospital, he may not live, and if he lives, he could still have serious problems.

<Sharf>: I didn't know he was in such bad shape, or I wouldn't have left him for his kids to handle. I hear they deal with him and his condition often.

<Joe>: He gazes at the ceiling when he's figuring out how to organize more activities than most of us can load into our brains at once.

<Sharf>: He also does it when he's guzzling booze and overdosing on painkillers, on the premises. There must be something in your bylaws about that. That's why I'm glad you're here Joe.

<Joe>: *We are dealing with a walking time bomb. Machi makes Marshall meditate to deal with the pain.* There certainly is, and we are usually discrete until we have proof.

<Justin>: Who told you that?

<Doc>: *He is a liar. H meditates. Van Amberg is the one who was detoxified after his wife died.*

<Sharf>: I saw if for myself a little before 4:00 o'clock yesterday. They rushed me out, but I saw Gunther going into the building. Gunther can verify what I said.

Meanwhile, I ran uptown and put this together because I wanted your people to see what's really going on, to prepare you to handle Marshall's impending departure, and to show you how I - how

Belvedere could handle the situation immediately. Acton seems to be unaware.

<Doc>: ***I am going to crucify you, for me and for Marshall, and then I will resign.***

<Joe>: Control Taquanda. ***That was pushing it, but "The Original" Taquanda is all right. She didn't throw anything.***

<Justin>: ***He left the man, and he almost died, even if he is addicted to something.*** That certainly merits further investigation.

<Doc>: Is there anything you would like to emphasize?

<Sharf>: Emery, was the cultural change management program his idea or yours?

[...] You don't have to answer. I found the article on the Web. Your description was brilliant.

Barca and Gunther put change management where it is - controlled by the business, although I have misgivings as to whether it should be there. Why wouldn't Marshall keep that for himself? It's a real power base.

<Justin>: ***Marshall recommended Macedon and supports him 200%.***

<Sharf>: My "Pertinent Pie" provides highlights of what I could discover in just one day. I'm sure that I will find dozens of other topics when I have access to the Action List/Roles database. I'm talking about the real one, not the one that he changes to make it appear that his people do more work at review time.

By the way, the action list was also your idea wasn't it, Emery?

<Doc>: ***I remember laughing at HM until he explained it to me. Then I used it to save my hide a few times.*** He was equitable in his allocation of credit for many of our successes.

<Sharf>: He had you fooled. Let me show you SOA participation figures that I stumbled across yesterday. This table indicates that over 50% of your people are somehow participating in SOA. I bet it doesn't show up on your dashboard like that. That's how he keeps the bonus pool for his people.

<Joe>: ***Where is the venom coming from? Dan was right. We need to watch where he bites.***

<Doc>: ***This is exactly how it shows up on the dashboard.***

<Justin>: This is interesting. What do you believe the next steps should be?

<Joe>: ***We should have him declared clinically insane before Machi discovers an inkling of what is happening.***

<Sharf>: You saw my recommendations. If you agree, Emery can schedule me with more of your senior managers. I would like to explain the "Pertinent Pie" to them in person, just as I'm doing with you. After that, they can point me to the people I will use to document the real SOA. Here's the starter list.

<Joe>: ***Everything is documented already.***

<Justin>: ***Higgs checked the process documentation after both Piccolo and Marshall were so adamant that it existed. The workflow diagrams made sense, to her and even to me.***

<Doc>: Where are Marshall's people on your list? They would be the ones who know most about this.

<Sharf>: That would be wasting my valuable time. They are puppets. You should hire typists to do your typing, give Armstrong as many people as he is willing to take back, make Piccolo earn his keep and run the SOA show and maybe compliance, let your data people manage your information, and let the br- head of finance handle procurement.

You're spending a lot of money on low-level communications, and you can't put ROI on it. Cut out the communications multi-lingual mumbo jumbo (teaching your outsourcing teams English would be a good idea). You could release 25% of Marshall's people and save yourself \$10 - \$15 million each year. Emery will save money too when Marshall is no longer around to send her on training wild goose chases.

<Justin>: ***He will not hurt Doc or my baby sister! Doc will take care of Doc, and I will protect Liz.***

<Joe>: ***We are in the Twilight Zone.*** Where is Mr. Gunther? We should hear what he has to say about something as critical as this.

<Sharf>: Physically, I don't know. Intellectually, I made sure he has copies of the report, and I've scheduled a meeting tomorrow afternoon during which I inform him of the criticality of your situation. You might wish to reward him for noticing the problem first, but what he saw was only the tip of the iceberg.

<Joe>: *He refused to acknowledge the iceberg, and now he's trying to blast it before the fresh water arrives at where it needs to be.*

<Justin>: *I have to hurry and see Piccolo.* I really want to thank you for your brilliant insights. By the middle of next week, we will need an outline of how your final report will look. Be more specific about how Daxiao would look if we implemented your recommendations. We have another meeting.

<Sharf>: We need to talk more. If we are going to work closely, we should know each other better. Mr. Guzman, I'd particularly like you to understand the quality of service that Belvedere can provide.

<Joe>: *If they have more people like you, we could change the name from Belvedere to Bellevue. It means the same anyhow. You'd be an extension to their psych ward.*

<Justin>: We were expecting you next week, and we were not expecting the Marshall emergency. We leave you with the best that we have. Dr. Emery-Baldwin - that's two last names, hyphenated - will work with you to schedule those meetings.

<Sharf>: You need my guidance during this emergency.

<Doc>: Mr. Mittelman is our emergency management specialist, Mr. Sharp. He is the reason that Daxiao could do all that turning around. *He should start right in the middle of the multi-lingual mumbo jumbo. Chiu has junior managers in out-of-the way buildings in Asia who are most conservative in their willingness to share.*

<Sharf>: Sharf, with an "f".

<Doc>: *Whatever.* I hear that you are already scheduled with Dr. Piccolo after you leave here and with our CFO tomorrow. Where would you like to focus after that?

<Sharf>: It would be a good idea to talk to Alex Macedon, especially if all SOA work requests pass through his organization. Their processes require clarification.

<Justin>: *It will never happen in this lifetime. It's bad enough that I will owe Doc, Dan, and Lorrie for dealing with you. Macedon charges more and you may not get out alive.*

Macedon is in the middle of critical activities. Doc, put him on the list for next month.

<Sharf>: That will present difficulties. He is central to many things.

<Justin>: He and Valery Van Amberg work hand in glove (*like Frick and Frack*). I dropped Van Amberg off at the heliport, so he could make the meeting with you. Was he on time?

<Sharf>: The other old guy. He made it in time to see Marshall start his meltdown. He may be worth something. I'll let you know.

<Joe>: **Do you want me to stay?**

<Doc>: **To protect him?** This will give Sharp and I an opportunity to know each other better.

Don't forget. You both owe me a lunch, at least. I haven't been to Samuel's lately, and I haven't been to the steak place in Grand Central.

<Justin>: *She's giving us a bargain.*

<Sharf>: This is starting less than optimally. Let's hurry, so I will be on time for Dr. Piccolo.

<Doc>: We will begin by handling security and access requirements for you and your associate.

<Sharf>: Andy and Justin handled that already.

<Doc>: Who's Andy?

<Sharf>: Mr. Gunther.

<Doc>: Anyone who requires continuous access to Daxiao information must pass rigorous security processes administered by Bailey and me. This week's arrangements are temporary. For the level of access that you requested, you also need approval from Valery Van Amberg in Marshall's absence.

<Sharf>: That's a waste of time.

<Doc>: You may be correct. I don't believe that Van Amberg can approve access to everything that you need. Joe may insist on substituting for Marshall when full access is requested.

Joe will approve after he checks with Maja. After last night, Maja wouldn't give him permission to access his own zipper.

Don't worry. The process is fast, but effective. As a SOX expert, I know you will be impressed with the controls that we established. Where are you going?

----------Daniel Piccolo's Office----------

<Dan>: You're both moving under your own steam.

<Justin>: This requires delicate handling. He managed to get to our underbelly in less than a day.

<Dan>: Jay, sit out front and delay Sharf until I give you a call.

<Dr. J. Stanley Johnson>: You just told me to concentrate the strategy presentation.

<Dan>: Concentrate in the reception area. Viola won't be in today.

<Joe>: Humor me while I become paranoid for a while. Justin has one of those conference cameras in his office. I turned it on. If you discovered a way that Mr. Mittelman could see what was happening in his own office that could be a good thing.

<Dan>: Didn't some people get in trouble for doing something like that recently?

<Joe>: My legal opinion is that a person is allowed to see what is happening in his own office. The camera is in plain sight.

<Dan>: Tell Higgs to check on them.

<Joe>: Cut the crap. We left Doc with a mad man.

<Justin>: I didn't know you could do that, but I approve. I don't want one of my executives arrested for mayhem.

<Dan>: That's not ready for prime time. It may never be ready now. **Why scare him?** I can ask security to check on her. We can say that the raccoons are back in the building - or a rat in this case.

<Joe>: Do it.

<Dan>: [...] A guard is on the way.

---------- Back in Mittelman's Office ----------

<Sharf>: I'm going to stop them. This must be resolved immediately.

<Doc>: Justin does not tolerate unnecessary interruptions, especially after he has already taken measures to ensure that you will move through security procedures with the speed that will be commensurate with your importance to Daxiao. Processes that normally take two weeks will take less than two days for you, after you receive security clearance.

<Sharf>: Why would I need that? I'm bonded by Belvedere. I deal with billion-dollar matters all the time.

<Doc>: Financial considerations are among the least of our concerns. We have top-secret contracts with the government and several international organizations - that means B2 clearance or its equivalent in over 15 countries. We have circle of trust arrangements with dozens of partners. We also have to ensure that there are no conflicts of interest.

Therefore, every critical person is cleared when they come on board and certified regularly. You will also receive security training. We can't allow things to slip out the door (or fax or e-mail) accidentally.

<Sharf>: How long will all this take? *Ādaemoa could have put a fly in the ointment, but we won't be working with them. We can say Ādaemoa dropped us because my people wouldn't show them what I faxed from here.*

<Doc>: It seldom takes more than two weeks. The more clearance you need, the longer it takes. You can start with this input screen. Fill in the blanks, we will print it, and you can sign it.

<Sharf>: You're stalling because of what I said about you in my report. You can speed this up, or you can deal with Gunnar and the Board of Directors.

<Doc>: I am following our processes and procedures to the letter. If I didn't, there'd be something in your next report about security loopholes. If that report leaked out, it could affect our business relationships.

<Sharf>: Show me how the processes and procedures work.

The report should have frightened her, but it seems to have made her furious. She could be a major obstacle, and she must be eliminated. Then Daxiao can pay Belvedere to streamline their training program.

<Doc>: Click on the small flow diagram at the top of the form. It shows our security process flow, one of the processes that you said we needed to have documented. It is obviously well documented.

<Sharf>: I see something that any one of my gals could have put together in half an hour. *Speaking of gals, I should send Rennie to talk to her. They could swap training success stories, and Rennie would tell me how to handle her.*

<Doc>: Click on any box, circle, line, or arrow.

<Sharf>: *More overkill.*

<Doc>: Is there anything that your audit experience says that we ***should not*** be doing?

<Sharf>: Not that I can see at an initial glance.

<Doc>: Is there anything missing that your audit experience says we should be doing?

<Higgs>: Dr. Emery-Baldwin. It seems that the raccoons are back in the building. The security guard says the environmental people will arrive soon to check the vents. He wonders if you've heard anything strange.

<Doc>: Tell him everything is all right for the moment, but he can send the environmental people down if he would like. I'm more concerned about rats.

<Sharf>: Forget about animals. You are about to hinder my progress on Board-recommended activities. There must be exceptions.

<Doc>: Type "exceptions" in the search box. How many did you find?

<Sharf>: It says that there are no exceptions?

<Doc>: If I made an exception, could you explain why you forced me to ignore Daxiao's security policy?

<Sharf>: *I wonder why Gunnar never mentioned her.* I was testing you, and you passed. Meanwhile, I see a legitimate branch that allows you to schedule the meetings that I require as soon as the initial form is completed.

<Doc>: *He's fast.* This is why I asked you to fill out the form a few minutes ago.

She that schedules may also un-schedule. Everyone after Lorrie will cancel until you receive clearance. This process has never lost an applicant's data, but Maja will show me how to reroute your information until Joe makes you disappear.

---------- Piccolo's Office Again ----------

<Justin>: Sharf hardly knows Gunnar - he calls him Gunther - and he's trying to displace him.

<Dan>: Sharf may be trying to remove the man in the middle. Gunther is an anglicized version of Gunnar. His wife is Margaret Gunther Sharf. Gunnar gave his brother-in-law the inside track to your underbelly.

<Joe>: This becomes more and more interesting.

<Justin>: A bit of nepotism. Dan and I certainly can't complain about that.

<Dan>: Did you know until that moment?

<Justin>: Of course [...] not. This situation calls for honesty. I did not know about the family relationship.

This is insane. I run a multi-billion dollar business, and I'm getting snookered by a psychotic wannabe who's related to a presidential wannabe, who has lost control of his own pet snake. This entire thing is being precipitated by a power grab for a concentration of power that I could have lost without ever knowing it existed.

However, I am not the one that's slipping. I pay you to act like a snobbish muscle-bound corporate joke while you watch my back. Sharf may be clueless, but you could have made sure he didn't have a clear shot at the net.

<Joe>: I get paid to watch your back too, but you seem determined to back into a mind field.

<Dan>: I was still watching your back, while you forced me to spend time trying to watch my own back! They were coming after me too.

<Justin>: They would have discovered that Liz helps you draw simplified organizational charts. We knew that already.

<Joe>: *It is easier to see what we are trying to achieve since you hired him.*

<Dan>: Gunnar had half the board and our well-informed president supporting him. We had to find out what game they were playing, for your benefit as well as ours. If the lovable klutz hadn't shown up on your corporate image monitor, you would never have given this more than 15 minutes of your time or 11 seconds of thought, *which I know is a lot for you.*

Sharf would have gone around looking stupid. Gunnar would have appeared to be a little foolish for sponsoring another attack on Marshall after being proven 100+ percent wrong the last time.

When Joe and Acton heard of it, they would have arranged for you to talk to Marshall, and you would have ignored him as you usually do. We'd be out half a mil, but Acton would be on their toes, perhaps giving us a little more than usual for the money we pay them. Incidentally, it is not necessarily a bad thing Mr. Guzman.

Finally, if either Sharf or Gunnar proved intractable, we had another tiny point of leverage.

<Joe>: What is the leverage?

<Dan>: Sharf's real reason for showing up early was that he needed information from us to nail down a contract with Ādaemoa.

<Justin>: That must be a conflict. Was Gunnar trying to create more trouble for Marshall?

<Joe>: We are gathered here today because we are trying to figure out what Gunnar is doing.

<Justin>: Both of you mentioned to me that Ādaemoa tried to ramp up the competition, and you said Marshall plugged the leak.

Now we're dealing with industrial espionage. That could affect several government contracts, the ones that Ādaemoa could not land without understanding what we do.

<Dan>: We stopped playing before we gave anything to Ādaemoa that they would know how to use.

On the other hand, we have proof (including video) that Sharf transmitted something to Ādaemoa immediately before he came in the room and attacked Marshall.

<Justin>: It does look bad for Gunnar. ***They trapped Gunnar, not the other way around.***

<Joe>: I will start working on it now. This will be difficult. ***We use the second psychotic fool to eliminate the first one.***

<Dan>: I would like to suggest that we should see whether Gunnar can be salvaged first. You need him hungry and with claws. ***I will figure out how to control the claws.***

<Justin>: ***What is he doing now? I sit on the fence, and he dances on the spikes.*** How upset was Marshall?

<Dan>: He was trying to find a way to turn a negative situation into something positive, as you force him to do often.

<Justin>: I make him earn his keep.

<Dan>: Did you see the numbers in Sharf's report? Maybe Marshall was underpaid.

<Justin>: ***Those numbers certainly have my attention.*** They suggest that I needed Marshall more than I realized, and I probably still need him. Do you have an update on his physical condition?

<Dan>: As of this moment, Marshall is recovering from a collapsed lung and internal bleeding caused by an injured spleen. They had to replace the appliance in his leg under less than optimal conditions. He will be on intravenous antibiotics for a month. His pressure is stabilized. His breathing has improved, and they should be able to take out the breathing tube some time this morning. He's also starting the fourth unit of blood.

<Justin>: ***I asked for gory details, and he gave them to me.***

<Joe>: How do you know stuff that even my people couldn't find out?

<Dan>: I was on the phone with his daughter until 12:15 last night, and Rebecca, his daughter-in-law, gave me an update 10 minutes ago.

<Joe>: What else do you know?

<Dan>: According to Gunnar, who was the only person present for the entire sequence of events, H tripped over an open draw and landed on the corner of his credenza. He broke some ribs that caused the internal injuries. His thighbone detached from the artificial joint that caused other problems.

<Justin>: You should have called me.

<Dan>: Why are you suddenly interested in HM? Until two months ago, you hardly remembered his name.

<Justin>: Until two months ago, he didn't seem to be that important, except that Guzman and Lorrie confirmed that he was good for SOX, and I know we needed to do well with SOX. He became more important when Gunnar explained that I was dealing with a Snuffleupagus and again when Guzman crash-landed in my office a while ago.

<Joe>: What is a Snuffleupagus?

<Dan>: It is a very large slow-moving animal that only one person can see.

<Joe>: That's not quite accurate. The only one that couldn't see Marshall was Justin. Even Gunnar was developing a level of awareness.

<Justin>: I deal with problems. Marshall hides his problems very well.

<Dan>: He hides problems on your carefully formatted dashboards where Liz's user interface specialist added special indicators to accommodate the fact that your optical sensors do not perceive the difference between blue and yellow. You know that Armstrong, Chiu, and Barca made us verify the information three times to guarantee that he was reporting accurately.

<Joe>: *They added the arrows for Mittelman! I never knew he was color-blind.* How did Gunnar show up in time to arrange a police escort for our clumsy Snuffleupagus?

<Dan>: Gunnar says he was in the building to inspect his new offices, and he realized that he could use the opportunity to begin a personal dialog with HM regarding the Belvedere engagement. H asked him to discuss constraints on the information we were allowed to give Sharf, especially since he had not yet received security clearance.

H is truly unlucky. He cut the meeting short with Gunnar because he was rushing to an appointment to get a properly fitted brace that would delay or avoid another joint replacement.

<Joe>: Can Gunnar be troublesome enough to do bodily harm?

<Dan>: Gunnar maintains perfect physical form, primarily for impressing his customers or his customers' female assistants.

He specializes in blackmail, psychological intimidation, and political assassinations.

As far as we can tell, the extent of his physical expression is a twitching pinky right before you discover that you must pursue new career options.

<Justin>: What was in the security report about Ādaemoa? *I should get it erased. This is too close to me.*

<Joe>: Sharf transmitted 60 pages of documents containing our role responsibilities, which is the foundation for our planning processes, and which we believe are providing us with competitive advantages. It was faxed from a machine in Marshall's staff motel to a number associated with Ādaemoa. The video camera showed the back, chest, neck, chin, and nose of a man with sandy blond hair. The eyes and the forehead were cut off, and that tells us that the individual is taller than Marshall is, and [...]

<Justin>: Sharf is taller than Marshall is. Why was Marshall monitoring that spot at that time?

<Joe>: That's the place where vendors work, and our security specialists identified faxes as high-risk areas after that consultant accidentally faxed the material that neutralized our competitive advantages on the WIMP research project.

<Justin>: Even a mild animal may attack when it feels cornered. Could Gunnar have felt that Marshall had him cornered? *I'm feeling trapped now!*

<Dan>: He may have felt cornered, but he did not attack Marshall physically. Jonas, Marshall's son, gives Gunnar a humanity rating of 8, and Jonas's evaluations approach 98% accuracy.

<Justin>: *Here's a chance to detach myself from Gunnar.* Can Jonas be trusted? There is some room between 8 and 10. I hear that he wears Velcro to kick-off banquets because he can't tie his own shoelaces.

<Dan>: If he leans over too far for too long, his balance system goes out of whack, and he falls over.

<Justin>: How do you know that?

<Dan>: I have a different grapevine than you do.

<Justin>: He also spends a lot of time curled up in a knot.

<Dan>: He's evaluating technology that you wouldn't know how to think about and people who can make it work. When he straightens out, he knows how to pick people that have made him and his family filthy rich. It may compensate for not being able to hear.

<Joe>: It is strange that you trust in Jonas's trusting Gunnar.

<Dan>: *I believe Jonas is in his 2% error margin, but I have to watch and see.*

<Justin>: Let us move forward. Do you really believe that Marshall is responsible for the financial benefits that Sharf put on that report?

<Dan>: Some of us believe that he contributes more. Check with Lorrie to make sure.

<Justin>: She's checking now. Why didn't I know?

<Dan>: Every quarter, Marshall stood in front of those charts, and tried not to lose his balance while he told you what he did. You didn't listen. Sometimes you went to sleep.

<Justin>: That deep monotone is boring.

<Dan>: He tries not to stutter while he keeps his balance.

<Justin>: He could have been more assertive.

<Dan>: He decided that overemphasizing the numbers might cause undue alarm. He knew you needed to keep him around to handle the next piles that someone dropped.

<Justin>: If we need him, will he live?

<Dan>: Here's Lorrie now.

<Justin>: Go!

Financial Effects of WFSOA

<Lorrie>: If we are looking at Table 19-Daxiao SOA - Financial Implications (BASE Internal Report), the numbers are somewhat understated, and several items are assigned to the wrong teams.

<Justin>: Doc mentioned that already. Talk to me about the important numbers.

<Lorrie>:

1. **SOX:** Let's start with the $5 million annual expense. People in our bracket with extensive international exposure may spend twice as much. Note: 50% comparative savings.

<Justin>: Since you're starting with the important numbers, just as I requested, why is SOX expense on an SOA list?

<Lorrie>: H has an obsession about making sure that everything does double duty. He uses the information that he must keep updated for SOX as the core for our Knowledge Cooperative, and it is the foundation for Service-Oriented Architecture.

2. **Training**: This is the biggest area of increased spending. Still, that's only about $380 per person each year, and that improves our performance in other areas. Training provides excellent ROI. Doc and I must justify the numbers every year, and I sent copies of the justification numbers to everyone on Sharf's list.
3. **Action Lists:** Talk to the Doc about the action lists. The number on the chart is low.

<Justin>: How low?

<Lorrie>: She told me once that savings on evaluations alone were close to $11 million. I don't know why she wouldn't mention it.

<Justin>: That's impossible.

<Lorrie>: It works for me. Before the action lists, my managers spent about half a day doing a review. Every individual spent about two days either preparing for the review or worrying about it.

Now, everyone who is in the action list (about half of us) can use it to document 50 - 100% of what we did the prior year. It shows whether assignments were delivered on time, in advance, or late, and it documents why assignments may have been late. Everyone spends about half as much time on reviews. At $400 per day per manager and $160 per day for half of the employees, $11,000,000 is the savings that Daxiao realizes.

<Justin>: Add that to the list. *She was so upset about the attack on her training program, that she didn't pay much attention to the numbers.*

<Lorrie>:

4. **Continuous Process Improvement:** Marshall cheats himself on this. He only provides figures for processes for which there were automated baselines. If he added the processes which he automated for Barca that did not start with a baseline, the number could double.
5. **Partner Networks:** Check with Gunnar on the additional sales from Partner Networks. I

propose that Gunnar understated that on purpose. He can't fight the partner consulting and take credit for increased sales to partner organizations simultaneously.

Note: There was no outage in the BASE production system yesterday. Sharf added that to make H look worse. I checked the dashboard, and I checked with Torres. Sharf doesn't know how many of us would drink muddy water before we would make decisions without those dashboards.

6. **Knowledge Cooperative:** That is also low from a corporate-wide perspective. If you paid everyone $20 per hour (which is low), and [...]
   - Everyone saved three hours per week not looking for things (which is also low - when is the last time you had people scrambling for business intelligence reports that Higgs couldn't figure out how to derive from one of Marshall's scorecards or dashboards), and [...]
   - We have 90,000 people.
   - That comes to $270 million each year.
   - Subtract database staff salary, database tools, and chain link storage (ask Maja what it is).
   - Subtract the things that are totally unrelated to SOA (which are fewer as time progresses).

   This number becomes conservative.

<Justin>: How conservative is it?

<Lorrie>: It should be between $50 and $100 million. We'd need an hour to verify which number is closer.

<Justin>: Add $65 million to this list, and put somebody on it. Even Daxiao can't afford to have that much money hiding in the folds.

<Lorrie>: It's not hiding. Somebody took credit for accelerated results who does not report through BASE.

7. **Planning:** This is definitely understated. If you add up the salaries of the 40 people that we no longer need (while doing a better job) at $125K per head, and the two days per month that at least 1600 of your managers no longer waste revising scientific "wild - - - - d" guesses (at $400 per day, and that's low), we're looking at a little more than $20 million.
8. **Project Management:** The $15 million on project management fits into the category with improved planning. My domain people say that may be low when you consider the time saved by Armstrong's managers, Marshall's super managers, and clients. We deliver better products.

<Justin>: How low is that?

<Lorrie>: It's underestimated by at least 50%.

<Justin>: Add $7,000,000.

9. **Research and Development:** The number is less than half of what it could be if Marshall wanted to make a point. He only included sales to clients who became supply chain partners after they had a successful research experience that was supported by BASE technology teams. If you count sales increases from pre-existing clients who went through the lab, the number is tracking toward half a billion this year. Dan's research team, which used to be Gunnar's research team, books another $10 million, but that's not reflected here either. Marshall does 70% of the work, Piccolo does 10%, and Gunnar receives the credit. I will show you where to find this on the Scorecard if you wish to see it.

<Dan>: Make the percentage 20% for me. I keep the dollar figure in front of me at all times. The number is $423 million as of today from companies that we supported last year. Last year's total was over $400 million. Just as Lorrie said, we're tracking toward half a billion. Justin?

<Lorrie>: What's wrong?

<Dan>: Our automaton almost popped an optical sensor. Give him a moment.

<Joe>: *H was right not to let everyone know about this. Mittelman is about to need a physical.*

<Justin>: *If Marshall wasn't damned near dead* [...] *Why am I angry with him? He told us all this, and we ignored him.* Add another $200 million and keep going.

<Lorrie>:

10. **Requirements Management:** More of our projects are coming in on time. Marshall assists Macedon and me with requirements. Macedon and I calculated the cost of a 25% overrun on a third of them and came up with that number.
11. **Risk Management:** Marshall cheated on this one, in a way, but the number is real. He wrote the swap system we use for our commodity components, it was the first thing he put on a scorecard, and he checks on it three or four times an hour if he's in the office. He was the first one to notice when something turned yellow that hadn't been yellow in twenty years. Because he controls purchasing and he's tight with Guzman, they stopped a few things first, and then fought with Chiu and Gunnar. I'm sure there are lots of smaller ones. Trip Joe the next time he whizzes by if you need more information.

<Joe>: That won't be necessary. I'm right here.

<Lorrie>: Huh! Joe knows all this stuff. Why are you yanking my chain?

<Joe>: Keep going. All will become clear at some time in our lifetime, ***though perhaps not in Marshall's.***

<Lorrie>:

12. **Strategy Management:** We calculated the $88 million on Strategy Management in relation to the requests that our people "absolutely had to have" that depended on strategy and policy that had changed, but the requests were still on the work queue. Macedon moves those to an archival work queue once every six months with assistance from Dan, Armstrong, Marshall's competency team, and my domain managers, of course. About 20% of them return in a different form. We made adjustments for that.
13. **Tooling and Staff Reductions:** Would you believe that is understated too? It appears that he only counted the retirees. If 2% of 84,000 people retire each year, and we don't have to replace half of them (a little over 800 people at an annual salary of $50,000 worldwide), then we're saving $40 million. We save about $7 million for the technology people who leave and are not replaced, but he's not counting the non-technology people who leave (not the ones we let go) and are not replaced. We don't let as many people go, because with improved process training, it is easier to move people to where Daxiao needs them. That promotes our reputation as a good employer, and it is invaluable because we lose less company history.

Gunnar prepped him well. Will that be all your graciousness?

<Justin>: What about the approval process? Don't tell me that both you and Doc are having modesty attacks simultaneously.

<Lorrie>: That number is accurate within half a mil. I derived it for them. I'm saving money, and we're saving project time. That means we could add savings to the planning line to, but why bother. We're already over a $1 billion.

<Justin>: I will accept your humble acknowledgement that even you are not 100% correct.

<Lorrie>: Before you go, I should mention something else about Sharf. If he is very tall and almost pretty, I know him.

<Justin>: Yes he is. Stop stalling!

<Lorrie>: I was an undergraduate student with him at Neudorf. The person I knew was almost as good as I am with accounting. He could memorize a three-page balance sheet in two minutes, and he could calculate standard deviations for up to 20 points of information in his head in a split second. He may have been better at it than Marshall was, although it wasn't by much.

<Justin>: ***How much more is there about Marshall that I need to know?*** Finish with Sharf.

<Lorrie>: He bragged about being accepted at Wheaton. ***I never bothered to tell him that I was accepted at "THE B SCHOOL".***

He was the king of the numbers nerds. His idea of a great day was to sit around and analyze theories of economics and finance. We all thought he wanted to stay in the academic community. I guess he went for the money instead.

<Justin>: Thanks. Call me in an hour and we can prepare for that meeting with Sharf.

<Lorrie>: Do you realize that so far neither of you have mentioned that one of our my peers and one of your direct reports nearly died last night immediately before an irrational number cruncher tried to deep six his career?

<Justin>: Guzman has me on a short leash. I was going to mention it when we discussed Sharf.

<Lorrie>: You, Robot, with a missing numeric processor, were going to help Lorraine Sheridan-Jasper prepare for a meeting with a perverted accountant, and you were coincidentally going to mention Marshall. I knew your heart was in the right place. They left it on the assembly bench.

<Justin>: *More insubordination.* Your emotions are showing. EQ is important.

<Lorrie>: I am certain that you must have an international audience to dazzle or a House committee to befuddle. Time management is important. I will handle Sharf.

<Dan>: Please pay attention when the boss and the General Counsel are paying attention. Doc is with him, and we have the security staff checking on them. He may have popped a few gaskets since you knew him.

<Lorrie>: OOOKAAY. Call me when you are ready to "help" me.

<Dan>: You're spending too much time around Van Amberg. We should talk, later.

---------- ----------

<Justin>: How did Sharf manage to come this close to our jugular vein so quickly?

<Dan>: ***H masterminded this, and the only people I know who can beat him occasionally at Master Mind are Jonas and Rebecca.***

He called up, emphasized his close relationship with the Board of Directors, and scheduled with Marshall and me. Marshall checked with you, and you confirmed that you had approved bringing in Belvedere. Liz checked with you, and you told her Gunnar had tricked you into it. Sharf called and rescheduled earlier, collected reams of information from Marshall, expressed some very narrow opinions, made HM angry enough to start stuttering again, and left.

<Justin>: How do you know the last part?

<Dan>: I spoke to Marshall and Van Amberg immediately after Sharf upset HM.

<Justin>: What happened after Sharf upset HM?

<Dan>: This is what I was told.

1. Van Amberg was about to follow HM out of the room to see how he was doing.
2. The network security person, Gary Augen, rushed into the Command Center to give Marshall the FAXtrax report.
3. Gary asked Val to give HM the FAXtrax report when he saw him, because he believed it was important.
4. Val found Marshall in the palace taking a hit of Tylanoll and arranging a brief one-on-one session with Gunnar. HM believed that talking to Gunnar without an intermediary would be more effective.

<Justin>: Why do you talk about Tylanoll as if he was using drugs?

<Dan>: His mate/wife has a very broad definition of drugs. H didn't want her to know that meditation was becoming less effective.

<Justin>: What else does he take? That leg must give him a lot of trouble.

<Dan>: I am not aware of anything else. He's obsessive about keeping a clear head. That's how he survived all these years.

Anyway, I called at about that time to receive an update on what I should expect when I saw Sharf. We were discussing the contents of the morning's meeting summary report when Ernest called to say Sharf was on his way to palace. This is what I saw or heard through the video conferencing hookup.

<Justin>: You gave up the palace.

<Dan>: I did, but Marshall has a deal with the new owner. She really likes Marshall, so we use the palace as often as we like. Let me continue:

1. Val told Sharf that HM wasn't feeling well, and that they should reschedule.
2. Gunnar insisted on seeing HM. He tried to lean around Val and see what was going on.

3. HM became annoyed and looked through Sharf.

<Justin>: I don't understand.

<Dan>: Have you ever seen HM angry?

<Justin>: I've seen him in situations when he should be angry. He smiles, and nods, and looks at you like you aren't there.

<Dan>:

4. Right. I was saying that H looked through him. We are accustomed to that, but I suppose it takes getting used to. Sharf was not amused.
5. Val persuaded him to leave the palace and talk in the hall.
6. Val stuck his head back into the room and explained that HM owed him a favor, because he agreed to spend a few minutes with Sharf while he had "lunch" at the grill.

<Justin>: Sharf causes people to incur debts. Doc is running a tab on me as we speak.

<Dan>: The following is hearsay.

1. Val told Sharf to wait for him at the grill. The security on his laptop had expired, and he wanted to check on the Asia status.
2. During the half hour while Val was checking his security settings and his mail, HM started feeling better because Val saw him limping down the hall and heard him humming.
3. Val was hoping that William would give up and leave, but he didn't.
4. When he arrived at the grill, William was starting on a prime rib.
5. While Val waited for his order, they did the executive boxers' dance.
6. Val was finishing his appetizer when the police showed up.
7. Val had finished the second mouthful of grilled salmon when the medical unit showed up.

<Justin>: Hold it. Why was Van Amberg willing to hang onto my runners get to the meeting with Sharf and then leave when things started to get hot?

<Dan>: *Oh dear, I see a spark of insight. Let me douse it.* I asked him that too, and you answered the question. He knew Gunnar, but he needed to understand more about Sharf. After a light breakfast on the plane (he was hanging onto your runners at lunchtime), he needed something to eat. He felt that Sharf would have been easier on the digestion. One should not tangle with Gunnar on an empty stomach.

<Joe>: That makes sense.

<Dan>: Anyway, Van Amberg ran back when he noticed the fire department ambulance. When he found the crowd, HM was almost dead, and Gunnar was ducking barbs from Marshall's daughter and staggering occasionally himself.

<Justin>: When did Gunnar arrive?

<Dan>: I'm not sure. Do you want me to check?

<Justin>: Yes.

<Dan>: [...] Hello. This is Dr. Daniel Piccolo. I'm with Daxiao in New Jersey, and I use space on the 10th floor in New York.

<Reese>: Yes. I know who you are sir. I've helped you carry in a few things.

<Justin>: *Carrying in is better than carrying out.*

<Dan>: Reese. I'm glad you are there. Were you on duty yesterday?

<Reese>: Unfortunately, yes.

<Dan>: Could you explain to me what happened?

<Reese>: Yes. I filed a very detailed report, but I need information from you first.

<Dan>: What can I do?

<Reese>: I was about to check to see how Mr. Marshall was doing. Twenty people have asked, and I've only been here 10 minutes. He is (was) quite well liked.

<Dan>: He is in critical, but stable condition. We believe that he will survive.

<Reese>: That's better than I imagined. With all those tubes, I was afraid that we would lose him.

<Dan>: Two my co-workers are here, and they are concerned too. May I put you on the speakerphone?

<Reese>: If verify that they have clearance. Mr. Mittelman is very sensitive about such things.

<Dan>: They definitely have clearance. Say hello Mr. Mittelman. *Grace him with your best corporate basso greeting.*

<Justin>: Hello. How's the weather in New York today?

<Reese>: I'm sorry sir. I didn't know he was referring to you? We are experiencing excellent fall weather in New York, although the pollen count is a little high.

<Justin>: How do you know that it is really me?

<Reese>: Your voiceprint matches sir.

<Joe>: Reese, this is Joe. We spoke last night.

<Reese>: Mr. Guzman, I hope I was helpful. Now I can be more precise. I have the log in front of me.

<Dan>: **Why bother? You know this.**

<Joe>: **He wants direct intelligence. I need to confirm.**

<Justin>: *What are they doing? I should have been keeping my eyes open.*

<Reese>: [...] I'm searching for the spot in the log. While I'm searching, how is Mr. Marshall's family? His daughter seemed beside herself with grief, and his son seemed to be in shock after Mr. Van Amberg arrived.

<Dan>: They're both in better shape because their father made it through the night.

<Reese>: I will pass that along. Here is the spot that I was looking for. It began when two police officers came into the building at 16:55 hours. They said they had an emergency call, and that Mr. Marshall was very ill. That was quite peculiar because I had spoken with Mr. Marshall only 45 minutes earlier, and he was fine.

<Dan>: What did you discuss with HM?

<Reese>: He was checking to see if two consultants had left the building.

<Justin>: How did he sound?

<Reese>: He spoke slowly and precisely in the soft low tone that he always uses until he becomes happy.

<Justin>: What happens when he's happy?

<Reese>: He had (I mean has) a wonderful deep voice, and sometimes he laughs so loud that the walls rattle. Sometimes he sings.

<Justin>: *You wouldn't know it to hear him talk.*

<Dan>: Which consultants was he asking about, and had they left?

<Reese>: As I mentioned to Mr. Marshall, the young woman (Renata Vitale) left before the man - at 14:55 hours. She seemed very annoyed. Gary Augen, one of Mr. Marshall's security people, had issued a security watch on the gentleman, Mr. William B. Sharf about 20 minutes earlier, so I was happy to see him leave - he turned in his temporary ID at 15:40. The incongruity was that Mr. Sharf seemed extremely happy, rather like someone looking forward to a luscious adventure.

<Dan>: Luscious is not a word I'd expect from you Reese. Could you be more explicit?

<Reese>: Perhaps like a child who is about to relish a lollypop.

I asked Mr. Marshall if there was a problem. He said that someone was there who wanted to meet the consultants, but he didn't act as if there was a real problem.

<Justin>: Was there a security watch on the woman?

<Reese>: No. It specifically states, William B. Sharf. His logon ID, which we had already canceled, was Goodview1.

<Dan>: What happened with Mr. Marshall?

<Reese>: May I finish with Mr. Sharf first?

<Joe>: Yes. You didn't mention anything else last night.

<Reese>: I wasn't directly involved. While I was trying to finish my part of the report, Henderson was dealing with two reporters. They were being extremely persistent and annoying Henderson. Henderson is not as patient as I am sir, even being delayed as I was.

Henderson ushered them out, and they left with "a tall beautiful gentleman". That is what Henderson wrote. Mr. Sharf is very tall, and his features are flawless except for a small deviation in his nose.

<Justin>: They obviously didn't find much because there was nothing of significance in the news. *Sharf is very dangerous!*

<Joe>: Why didn't you mention the reporters?

<Reese>: Many things had happened, and I was trying to record all of them. Sharf was outside. When Henderson came back inside, I was quite anxious to turn everything over to him, and we had some very tense moments.

<Joe>: About what?

<Reese>: I mentioned that Henderson isn't very patient. I wouldn't want to cause him trouble sir, and he performed each of the procedures correctly after he controlled his temper. He ensured that the appropriate people were notified. He remembered Sharf, and he placed an entry about the reporters in the log.

<Justin>: Why was he upset?

<Reese>: Henderson owes Mr. Marshall for many things, and he arrived just in time to see Mr. Marshall dying [...] I mean almost dead [...] you understand what I mean. It was very unsettling for us all, but it affected Henderson more.

<Dan>: Henderson is only a bit shorter than Marshall is; he's wider than I am, and he puffs up when he's annoyed.

<Reese>: You understand sir. He was cursing and crying simultaneously, and I had to remind him not to break the keyboard.

<Justin>: What could Henderson owe Marshall? Bailey handles physical security.

<Reese>: Mr. Marshall gave him the money to bring his father here from Trinidad, and he directed them to the right medical care. Mr. Henderson, Sr. lived six or seven years longer than he would have otherwise.

<Justin>: *Marshall has an inside track to the security underground. Bailey works for Piccolo. Perhaps I will have difficulty "resolving" the Ādaemoa situation.*

<Joe>: We understand (*at least two of us do*). When did Gunnar arrive?

<Reese>: Do you mean the very authoritative EVP with the nice blue tie?

<Joe>: Yes, the one that you had never seen before.

<Reese>: He arrived 15 minutes before I received the call from Mr. Marshall. That was at [...] 15:55.

<Dan>: Is it time to tell us what happened with Mr. Marshall?

<Reese>: The two officers said that an ambulance would be here immediately to pick up Mr. Marshall. I called upstairs, and they said they would meet us at the freight elevator. I knew this was serious because the family has taken extra precautions to avoid having to call an ambulance. Mr. Jonas had a vehicle specially built for his father.

<Justin>: *When he gave the company car back. Boyd, Oswald, and company became jealous of George the red-nosed driver.*

<Reese>: It was customized so that he can sit comfortably and get in or out without having to bend his leg. The seat swivels, and it makes it easier for him to stand up. The vehicle is stocked with medical supplies, and George was formerly an ambulance drive. Ernest, his administrative assistant, is also a nurse and a weight lifter in case Mr. Marshall needs extra help. Rumor has it that he's a very highly paid consultant.

<Joe>: *He certainly is. I'm glad we don't pay him.*

<Reese>: This is usually sufficient for any problem.

However, it wasn't this time. A rescue unit from the Fire Department arrived in less than four minutes. It is a good thing too, because they have much better equipment than the regular ambulance attendants do. After I performed a proper identity check, we went to the 10th floor. When we arrived, Mr. Marshall was sitting in his fancy wheeled chair that is also his office chair. Ernest, Mr. Marshall's children, and Mr. Gunnar were waiting for us. There was a bit of a crowd too. We all worry about Mr. Marshall and Mr. Gunnar's people still like to gaze at Miss Indy.

<Justin>: Why?

<Reese>: She is stunning until you become accustomed to her. For some people, she is distracting.

<Justin>: *I missed that too.* How did Marshall look?

<Reese>: Terrible. At first, he was staring at nothing and trying to meditate as he did the last two times when his leg gave out. This time he couldn't control his breathing. They had strapped his arm to his body, and the bandage looked appeared to be painfully tight. Though the magic chair has many adjustments and the arms slide out of the way, they still managed to hurt him when they moved him to the gurney. They put an oxygen mask over his nose, and started to look at his leg. Ernest had used some type of cardboard to make a splint, and as soon as the paramedic touched it, he started coughing and crying and a bit of blood sprayed over the inside of the mask. That's when I first realized how serious the situation was.

<Justin>: *Messy!*

<Joe>: You didn't say anything about crying last night.

<Reese>: It was more like sobbing because he couldn't catch his breath, and he was obviously in extreme pain. After they checked his breathing passage and changed the mask, Ernest showed them his credentials and told them to leave the splint alone.

Miss Indy was screaming that they should have given him something for the pain first. Ernest and Mr. Gunnar tried to calm her. She was especially hostile to Mr. Gunnar, calling him names that should not be repeated. She didn't relax until after the rescue team injected Mr. Marshall with something that put him to sleep very quickly.

<Justin>: ***I guess women either love him or hate him, or they hate him after they love him.***

<Reese>: Miss Indy was happy that her father was resting, but Mr. Gunnar and the medical team started looking even more worried, if it is possible.

During that part of the crisis, Mr. Van Amberg arrived. He looked very worried at first, and then he became angry. That's when Ernest, Mr. Gunnar, and the ambulance people found a different kind of medicine. Mr. Guzman, now I can tell you that the name of the medicine was "Naloxone".

<Dan>: ***He wasn't asleep! The paramedics nearly killed him.***

<Joe>: ***Dear God! If Machi finds out, there is nowhere for us to hide.***

<Justin>: ***They look worried. I will have to look up Naloxone.***

<Reese>: They said it would improve his breathing. Then they were in a big hurry to put the apparatus into his throat. It was a device that blocks off an injured lung, so they could force air into the other one. Ernest, Mr. Gunnar, and Mr. Van Amberg were checking every move that they made after that, but I made Ernest find time to explain it to me.

Mr. Gunnar looked anxious and sick himself. He was holding an ice pack over his ear most of the time.

<Dan>: How did Jonas react?

<Reese>: When they were inserting the tube, he was sitting in a corner as far away from his father as possible, rocking and staring at what was happening. Mr. Van Amberg and Miss Indy had to go and get him.

<Justin>: That sounds like what I've heard about him.

<Dan>: He goes to a place where he can see the greatest number of people when he can't hear.

<Reese>: AAH! That explains why they kept waving their hands screaming at him! They were using sign language.

<Justin>: What else happened with Marshall? ***That means Marshall probably knows it too. Maybe Marshall started it!***

<Reese>: After they stabilized Mr. Marshall, Ernest, Mr. Gunnar, and I rode down in the elevator with him. Mr. Van Amberg and Mr. Marshall's children rode down in the regular elevator.

Mr. Van Amberg told Ernest to go back upstairs and contact Mr. Marshall's direct reports. He said they must keep things in working order. Miss Indy and Mr. Van Amberg rode with Mr. Marshall in the ambulance with the police escort. Mr. Gunnar walked away with Mr. Jonas.

That is the end of my section of the report. I was exactly 53 minutes late. Mr. Guzman, you called me a half an hour later. As I said, Henderson is quite efficient when he isn't annoyed.

<Dan>: Thank you. I'll follow-up with you later.

---------- ----------

Now Messrs., we've had our SOA P opera for today. We have 18 minutes to discuss what I'm going to do with Sharf for the next few hours.

<Justin>: We have as much time as we need. Explain the meditation.

<Dan>: We mentioned that he's been sneaking in Tylanoll lately, but the meditation worked for most of 20 years.

People who remember him before he had his knee replaced 20 year ago report that he used to be more volatile. The volatility was related to frustration when he couldn't persuade people to listen to him. He stuttered significantly more than he does now.

When he came back he from the surgery, he was more relaxed, and he spoke better, but very slowly as almost everyone notices. His mate convinced him that he could learn pain control through meditation, which was important because he has allergic reactions to aspirin and a host of other pain reduction medications. Meditation also helps him to concentrate. When he concentrates, he speaks better. He was having trouble yesterday because meditation requires deep breathing.

<Justin>: It's a good thing he wasn't allergic to Naloxone, whatever that was.

<Dan>: I'm guessing that the injection that put him to sleep was a CNS depressant, and the Naloxone was necessary to counter-balance its effects. He's allergic to morphine.

<Joe>: In other words, he wasn't asleep. He may have stopped breathing.

<Justin>: Are you saying that he could have died right there on Daxiao premises? That would have made very bad publicity, and it could have kept Guzman employed for the next 20 years.

<Dan>: *Lorrie is right about him*. I feel your concern. Do you have any other questions?

<Justin>: What do you know about a drinking problem?

<Joe>: There is no drinking problem. The thought of being less than perfect makes him crazy. Alcohol would affect his balance and his limp could easily become a stagger. Therefore, he limits his intake to three ounces of B & B at night when he is at home and ready for bed.

<Justin>: How do you know?

<Joe>: We talk often. We are often engaged when Nicola brings him his toddy.

<Justin>: *I can't find a damned thing to pin on Marshall.*

<Dan>: Are there any more questions?

<Justin>: I'm sure there are, but I don't know what they are yet.

<Dan>: Now, I will ask my question again. What caused your concern about Marshall?

<Justin>: I have a big blank spot when it comes to HM. After the conflict of interest investigation, we knew which toothpaste he used.

<Joe>: *That's when I met him* [...] *and Nicky. I thought I had settled down until I met her, and she's 40 years older than the ones who previously attracted my attention. Daniela doesn't have to worry. Nicky loves Marshall only. I wonder what the Snuffleupagus knows that I don't.*

<Justin>: Then, except for those quarterly reports, he disappeared until his contract came up for review, after which he disappeared again. I don't understand what he does, Gunnar doesn't understand how he does it, and you seldom mention him. You seldom mention him and neither does Joe. Gunnar and I felt that anything that neither one of us knows is potentially dangerous.

<Dan>: You never asked, and I never needed you to nudge him around to anything. I could admit that he's often ahead of me doing things that he doesn't bother to put a name to.

<Joe>: He makes my job easy. I don't have to look over my shoulder when he's behind me doing what he promised he would do.

<Justin>: I'm going around this again. Why didn't I hear about BASE more often?

<Dan>: I answered you already. You are a man of action and a problem solver. Marshall was good at ensuring that you didn't have problems that he caused.

<Justin>: Let us deal with the next confusion. Why did Gunnar go to the hospital with the family?

<Dan>: My crystal ball (this piece of glass) says ask Gunnar. Higgs will be able to find his number, or I can scribble it for you if you don't mind messing up your image by carrying something. *Be*

quite and juggle. You need to look like you are on the fence with him.

<Justin>: Tell your crystal ball to start theorizing.

<Dan>:

1. 0% probability that he was protecting Daxiao's interest (Van Amberg, a lawyer, was there).
2. 10% probability that he was feeling guilty. He has more heart than you do (***which is easy***), but it is offline most of the time.
3. 20% probability that he was merely curious.
4. 90% probability that he wanted to be among the first to know whether HM was out of the picture. A billion dollars, plus or minus $250 million, is a lot of brownie points to be passed around. He wanted to figure out how to jump the line. He wasn't willing to admit that he was already in front of the line because he couldn't admit that Marshall contributed so much to his good fortune.

Van Amberg can give you better numbers. He's on his way out here to help me to keep the viper swaying until you figure out how you are going to deal with our Gunnar goof.

<Justin>: How will you keep him occupied?

<Dan>: The agenda is right in front of you, but it doesn't seem to make sense at this moment.

Daxiao and Belvedere SOX/SOA Information Exchange - Day 2	
WFSOA Theoretical Foundations	30 minutes.
Strategy Management and the Daxiao SOA Maturity Model	1 hour
Break	
Catalog access and security issues (left over from prior session	1 hour
Process Categories and Processes (Discussion)	30 minutes
Break	
Q&A	30 minutes

<Justin>: That's enough to send him into a stupor.

<Dan>: As it is, I'm putting in for hazardous duty pay. How much will Doc squeeze out of the two of you for keeping him busy for only 30 minutes?

<Joe>: The thought is painful.

<Justin>: We should talk after you finish.

<Dan>: I'm going into Manhattan after that.

<Justin>: Cancel any meeting you have. We need you for this.

<Dan>: I'm going to see Marshall.

<Justin>: I missed that.

<Joe>: *Of course, you would.* Sharf will probably mention that Etiology. He's rather proud of it.

<Dan>: I wonder where he found it. ***It is perverted version a preliminary presentation that Liz created for Plan A.***

<Justin>: Find out how much Gunnar told him and how much he figured out himself. Act unconcerned about Marshall. What's one crippled EVP when we have Gunnar and Sharf to take care of us? Give Sharf what he thinks he needs to replace Marshall, but add Piccolo confusion.

<Dan>: Do you have any ideas about Sharf's etiology?

<Justin>: Most of it is backward, except that just enough things are almost correct that people who aren't paying attention might let it slide. We will be paying Belvedere $500,000 to research our own lies.

<Dan>: Additional guidance would be in order. Would you be a little more specific?

History of WFSOA - Presidential Viewpoint

<Justin>: I will give you my entire reading quickly:

1. **SOA Governance:** Marshall provided the ideas, and you added the fancy terminology.
2. **Corporate Policy:** Marshall's people interpret; we pick three things to discuss, and then rubberstamp the rest.
3. **SOA Initiation:** Armstrong did "LITTLE SOA", and you and Marshall were trying to sneak in an entirely new management style under the guise of **"BIG SOA"**.
4. **Reference Architecture:** I don't remember anything about reference architecture coming across my desk. ***What Doc said didn't make sense.***

<Dan>: Marshall's people establish the research environments for the reference architecture, and Weldon's people make it work in the real world, with a few finishing touches from the SOA competency team.

<Justin>:

5. **Requirements Management:** Marshall requested Macedon to teach him a lesson. I went along because I was sick of Alex's bellyaching, and I wanted a man inside.
6. **Automated Approvals:** Lorrie bent my ear about the risks for three months, but Marshall shoved it through after a small but critical project was delayed unnecessarily. She has admitted that it's a good idea more than once since then.
7. **Reward Structure:** Marshall didn't know it, but he came up with another way to keep people fighting over peanuts, leaving more in our executive pots.
8. **Service Management:** Marshall helped us to drop that in, or no one would ever have trusted SOA.
9. **Costing Algorithms:** You couldn't move SOA past the earliest stages without people understanding where their money goes.
10. **SOA Program Management:** You and Marshall cooked that up. Lorrie is building her own CIO organization, which seems a bit out of place.
11. **Communications:** Our shared nepotissa is talented, organized, multi-lingual, and glib. Whatever she touches works. Her programs helped the last international merger. She still has a significant amount of work to finish, and she would be stunted under Gunnar.
12. **Action Lists:** I'm glad we use magnetic media and not trees, but Marshall's dumb idea makes more people happy than it makes unhappy.
13. **Methodology and Planning:** Marshall received a good ribbing when he told us about his planning obsession, but now, with his assistance, more than half of our people produce better plans, even people who are not in technology.
14. **Partner Consulting:** Gunnar is still fighting a process that delivers two-pronged success. That suggests that Gunnar is still trying to prove that he was right about Marshall five years ago.
15. **Process Automation:** Marshall and Macedon work to make that happen, but since operations used process automation first, operations takes the credit.
16. **Role-Based Security:** I know we have many roles because Higgs makes me review the communications survey before she turns it in to someone on Marshall's team. I suspect that the roles are secure because the applications that the Fed worries about have B2 clearance.
17. **Knowledge Cooperative:** That's run by the high-energy kid who is actually older than Dan.

<Dan>: No!

<Joe>: Someone who would know recently mentioned it to him.

<Dan>: Do you know that she's the one responsible for the B2 security rating?

<Justin>: That's another basket with too many eggs in it. For the time being, we have the best business intelligence data in the industry. ***The guys at the club shiver when I hint at their best-kept secrets.***

18. **Risk Management Support:** The dashboards give Guzman what he needs to keep his numbers down while the rest of our numbers increase.
19. **Cultural Change Management:** You and the Doc support Marshall in this area.
20. **Strategy Management:** That's a pain in the rump. Your tweedy egghead makes us pretend that we know what we're doing, and Macedon makes sure we only spend money on what we act as if we know we need, while Marshall reports on what we believe we are doing, every 15 minutes with winking blinking colored lights.

<Dan>: You weren't asleep all those times you looked like you were asleep.

<Justin>: I like to watch how people play when you believe I'm not paying attention.

<Joe>: Doc gave us a summary, and he translated it into his own words.

CHAPTER VI - POLITICAL AND PERSONAL (Part II)

Justin>: It would be easier if we could interest Marshall in staying with us. He could work out his contract from home.

<Dan>: Did you and Liz get DNA tests?

<Joe>: I've often wondered about that myself.

<Justin>: Of course. Why is that relevant now?

<Dan>: Because the thought of being related to you, even by marriage, is almost as scary as spending half a day with Sharf.

<Justin>: You need me the way I am, just as we need Marshall and perhaps Gunnar. Can we convince Marshall to finish what he started? *It took me nine years to admit it, but I just did.*

<Dan>: If you were almost 64 years old, you had raised genius brats who helped you individually accumulate a net worth of $200 million dollars, you'd let yourself get kicked in the teeth for 35 years, seven of which were entirely for ego gratification, and you nearly died as an indirect result of company shenanigans, would you come back?

<Justin>: He's worth twice as much as I am!

<Dan>: *That would be the case if he didn't have a penny.*

<Joe>: I had lost track. He was doing this to have fun, and the fun is over.

<Justin>: All of us get bruised from time to time. The longer you play the more bruises you get.

<Dan>: He knew that. He might believe that this bruising is enough to make him stop playing.

<Justin>: Good for him, but perhaps not optimal for us.

<Joe>: As callous as he sounds, he's making good business sense. I would support him, assuming that Marshall heals adequately. Could there have been damage that is more permanent?

<Dan>: We have to wait until he wakes up to determine whether there was oxygen deprivation.

<Justin>: *There were definitely too many eggs in that basket.* If that turns out to be the case, can Van Amberg take back what we dropped on Marshall while he went on his sentimental journey?

<Dan>: Things are infinitely more complicated than when he left. Van Amberg can keep things running with military precision exactly the way they are for the next 10 years. He can show you how to adapt to changing environments in a very methodical manner. However, creatively is not his strong suit. The good news is that he and Macedon militate well together.

<Justin>: Do you believe we have to worry about losing Van Amberg or Macedon? They are both older than Marshall is?

Can we get Lorrie's head out of the numbers sand long enough to help us?

<Dan>: You've been paying attention!

<Justin>: Doc says I shouldn't think too often, but once I fall into a groove, I do it well.

<Dan>: Lorrie is easiest. She is among the best at doing what she does financially, she is handling the domains adequately, and she would be overloaded if you gave her Marshall's responsibilities too. You need the domains in a neutral spot, and she is the best neutral spot that you have.

Van Amberg is in good physical shape since he cleaned himself up, but he will want to spend time with HM. Marshall saved his life, twice.

Macedon is in equally good shape, he is more emotionally flexible, and he's a lovable bulldozer. Liz winks at him when he calls her little girly.

<Joe>: *It amazes me that Macedon didn't get us sued yet.*

<Justin>: What two times did Marshall save Van Amberg's life? I know about the alcohol poisoning.

<Dan>: Over 40 years ago, Marshall was injured while saving Van Amberg from a sniper attack. That's why Marshall had trouble walking - will have trouble walking.

<Justin>: Does that mean that he has one of those bleeding heart things like Macedon?

<Joe>: *A hero and a scholar* [...] *I'd probably want to rest too.* In the U.S., they call it a Purple Heart, and the answer is yes.

<Justin>: *Hamilton, the hero! This is enough to make you want to throw up. Why! Macedon doesn't affect me that way.*

<Dan>: Let me catch you up on more history. After Van Amberg finished law school, he came to work at Goodsand, and Marshall followed him. Van Amberg took care of some of the good people that Marshall's systems replaced. You know that it was Van Amberg recommended Marshall when he needed time to take care of his wife, which was soon after you sidelined Marshall in favor of Armstrong.

<Justin>: There was a place for everybody.

<Joe>: *They were not necessarily the correct places.*

<Justin>: If Marshall lives, when might he be able to come back and take his place?

<Dan>: You are stuck on that. Perhaps he would believe that he already came back one time too many?

<Justin>: According to Lorrie's assessment of Sharf's report, my persuasive powers and the promotion benefited everyone concerned.

<Dan>: Except Marshall.

<Justin>: *Bull!* If half of anything anyone has told me in the last hour was true, he was running my company, including you.

<Dan>: What?

<Justin>: Remember that I am good when I'm paying attention, and he has my utmost attention. The only one who knew everything that Marshall was doing was Marshall. Not even his wife/lover/girlfriend knew everything. Gunnar's execution was abhorrent, but he had the right idea.

<Joe>: You're as crazy as [...]

<Justin>: It's my turn. Do all of you actually believe that I accidentally remained president for almost 10 years? I let things run when they are running, and I fix them when they break. I pay particular attention when I cause things to break. Some time in the next day or so, we must understand how three of my top ten breaks were related to Marshall.

I want both of you to notice that I admitted making mistakes regarding Marshall. Tell Doc for me.

<Austin Ellison>: [...] This is Ellison. I know Piccolo, Guzman, and Justin are in there. Pick up, or we will be scraping sewage of the boardroom table.

<Justin>: Pick up. *Image is everything.*

<Joe>: Did you find out anything else?

<Justin>: I have explained to you how emotion has no place in what we do.

<Ellison>: I wasn't being emotional. I needed your attention. At this moment there are two reporters sitting in my office who believe they have blackmailed me into checking our printed archives for information on Mr. Marshall. If they try to leave, they will encounter problems with security until we are sure they have the proper mind set. I am offering all of you an opportunity to guide that mindset.

<Joe>: Scary young man.

<Dan>: Father is a diplomat. Babysitters were CIA.

<Justin>: Explain that to me later. I wasn't talking to you Austin. You were effective. What caused this level of concern?

<Ellison>: Two reporters showed up 20 minutes ago and said they had spent the night in the hospital with Indira Marshall. They missed their deadline, but they were still convinced that there was a story. By the way, who is William Sharf, with an "f"?

<Justin>: What do they know about Sharf?

<Ellison>: Sharf pointed them to the right hospital after our security people had turned them away.

<Justin>: Why wasn't there more in the media?

<Dan>: The reporters had accidents too, they lost some of their equipment, Indy had an asthma attack from the excitement, and she had trouble catching her breath.

<Ellison>: It's good to know that somebody else is aware of this. Indy having an asthma attack must be a joy to behold.

<Justin>: It was good for us and bad for her.

[...] What are all of you laughing at?

<Dan>: You will understand the first time you see Indy. Accept our word for it that there was fast thinking and flawless theatrics. Indy was a top-ranked collegiate athlete. I don't believe she has asthma.

<Ellison>: Ignoring her breathing problems, she divided her time between arranging major surgery for her father, checking on her hysterical mother and her withdrawn brother, and making sure the reporters had the best care the emergency facilities could provide. During this time, the reporters found out what a wonderful man her father was. The hospital people confirmed it, especially after he donated money for a step-down ICU. Unfortunately, they missed the deadline for the morning paper.

<Dan>: Why would they drive out here to find a story about a clumsy old man?

<Ellison>: After the hypnosis wore off [...]

<Justin>: You mean the sedatives [...]

<Ellison>: After the hypnosis wore off, it occurred to them that some strange things had occurred.

<Justin>: What hypnosis to you mean?

<Joe>: Ignore him and keep talking. I will explain later.

<Ellison>: The photographer had a blank chip in his camera that has twice the capacity of the original chip. The reporter had a different and significantly better recorder than he started out with, except that there were no notes on it. Both had $500 more than when they started, not counting the $100 that Sharf paid them to follow the story.

<Joe>: Brilliant! They couldn't complain that they had been robbed.

<Ellison>: They had seen Van Amberg with his eye beginning to swell, Gunnar sitting on the floor, two bruised policemen, and Ms. Frey behaving strangely. Yet no one remembered anything.

<Dan>: Funded amnesia. Jonas can be very generous.

<Ellison>: There was no police report of the incident. There was no record at 911. The only things they could find were that Indy's father was in surgery after a bad fall and his family was praying for his survival in an undisclosed location. Indy had disappeared.

<Justin>: How bad is the problem?

<Ellison>: Someone cleaned up so well, that a problem was created. Although they found hundreds of stories about Silicone Huey, they can't find more than two sentences about Marshall, other than 20-year old articles in medical journals that show the inside of his thigh in nauseating detail.

<Joe>: Machi made us lock up everything five years ago.

<Ellison>: What about the last four years. Why do you pay him $500,000+ a year to assist Armstrong, Dan, Doc, Lorrie, Barca, etc.?

<Justin>: What assisting do you mean?

<Ellison>: I've approved at least eight articles this year that said, Executive "Somebody" has discovered, with the assistance of Hamilton Marshall, that [...]

<Justin>: *I've been a blind idiot. Now I don't know what I'm seeing.* What agency employs them?

<Ellison>: They're independent.

<Justin>: Scoop them.

<Ellison>: How shall I do that?

<Justin>: Sap. The title should be something like "Vietnam Defines Boomer Lives".

Hamilton Marshall is a Vietnam veteran who suffered all his adult life from results of an unfortunate injury that he received while risking his life to save a superior officer who later became a good friend.

He is struggling for his life again after all these years because the best of prostheses are not good enough replace what nature intended him to have. He may not live even though two of his closest friends were injured in a mad rush to save his life.

One of those men was the man that Marshall saved originally.

Though he suffered continuously from his terrible injuries he contributed significantly to a little-known electronics company called Daxiao Electronics.

Due to his injuries, he felt that he needed to hide, being a poor maimed victim of an unpopular war.

The injuries did not stop him from raising four wonderful children. He sent them to [...]

<Dan>: U Penn and Strafford, and the babies are at Julliard and the American College in Rome.

<Justin>: He is a humanitarian. He contributed a significant portion of his hard-won earnings to helping others (mention his contribution to the orthopedic hospital).

Mention how he struggles with the pain more than most because several standard painkillers would kill him too. He barely survived near-death experiences due to his special circumstances.

<Ellison>: I have about two thirds of that. Dan [...]

<Justin>: Dan will send you what he has.

Forget about the scoop. Tell them you dug up the Vietnam stuff in the library. Offer to run through it with them. Play up the pain angle and how Marshall hides because he's embarrassed about his deformity. Mention how he walks behind people because he doesn't want anyone to notice him.

<Dan>: He was paying attention!

<Joe>: **He is smarter in emergencies.**

<Justin>: We help him to hide because we really like him and appreciate how hard he tries for us. Tell them if they don't play, we were going to put it out there ourselves.

<Ellison>: What about Sharf and last night's confusing memo?

<Sharf>: Tell them that Sharf is a long-time family acquaintance who always believed Marshall's self-imposed isolation was ridiculous. He wanted Marshall to be proud of himself and the maroon heart.

<Ellison>: Purple Heart - I got it. I'll send each of you the story before they leave. Hasta la bye-bye.

<Justin>: Both of you should stop gaping. I told you I specialize in dealing with things that break.

Speaking of surprising skills, who taught you ASL? *Will he admit that it was Marshall?*

<Dan>: Liz. She knew it when I met her. [...] It was part of her communications training.

<Justin>: What about you?

<Joe>: I learned from Van Amberg. It's useful during tough negotiations.

<Justin>: *Van Amberg probably learned from Marshall. I should have been paying attention.*

How soon Marshall can return if we ensure that he has the best possible medical treatment in the world. I've heard of people with knee replacements being able to walk again in six weeks.

<Dan>: I don't know, and he already has the best medical treatment in the world.

<Justin>: Talk to your crystal ball.

<Dan>: Six weeks is usually people who have bad arthritis. This is more like someone who was crushed in a car wreck. He may be back in the shape he was in yesterday morning in three or four months.

<Justin>: Did Marshall have a plan for what would happen when he finally left?

<Dan>: He hoped you would encourage continued and improved communications and benefit from a long list of lessons he learned the hard way. His team would be split up unless Lorrie or Macedon could handle it. Van Amberg and Yu (his architect) had enough respect that they could have made the transition work without too many hiccups. He figured that if the physical organization disappeared, and a virtual one remained, neither Gunnar nor anyone else would have any obvious targets.

<Justin>: That's exactly what Doc said. He gave her the plan for slicing up his organization earlier this week. Do you think he's bluffing too?

<Joe>: What? Why didn't I know that?

<Justin>: Tilting with takeover windmills has kept you busy.

<Dan>: He may have been bluffing before, but not now. Dying changes your perspective on what's important.

<Joe>: How do you feel about the situation?

<Dan>: I can theorize for Lorrie and Macedon as I theorized for Marshall, although there may be less about which to theorize. I get along with Acton. HM would provide assistance, as a friend, if I needed it.

<Justin>: Is there any benefit, at this late date, to knowing how you two happen to work so well with this invisible giant? Did he save your life too?

<Dan>: In a manner of speaking.

<Joe>: I know this already. We need a sidebar. Stop playing with that glass. As General Counsel, here is my carefully considered advice:

- Cool this down as quickly [...] today if possible.
- Our king has allowed himself to be exposed. He may have also gotten the rooks and the bishops in trouble. We do not want to tangle with their Queen (Nicola Frey).
- Dan will deal with Sharf while I check to see where the pieces are on the board. His level of audacity suggests that he may know something that we don't.
- Alternatively, Sharf may be clinically insane. Fortunately, you are as wide proportionately, as Sharf is tall, so you should be able to take care of yourself. Check your panic button, just in case.
- Stop the fool from talking about booze and pills. As much as I respect (*and love*) Ms. Frey, I would not want to be owned by her. I can understand him being annoyed at Marshall's stare, but I can't imagine myself accusing Marshall of being a drug addict after a 15-second encounter. As a contingency, I will free up some of my best people to deal with being Freyed.
- I will suggest to the Board and to Acton that we should not be too hasty about pushing Gunnar out of the door, if he agrees to participate in our clean-up activities. His ability to be aggressive and supportive of customer needs simultaneously has been as effective for us as Marshall's "*we don't know what in the hell he's doing*" technique.
- Simultaneously, Marshall will leave in a slightly more staid manner and later, assuming that he remains essentially himself.
- Justin, it would be a good thing if you pretended to be a bit more sympathetic. Learn a bit of the supportive part from Gunnar. If you feel the shadow of a sliver of humane concern slipping up on you, give it free reign. We promise not to tell anyone.

Do either of you have any opposing opinions.

<Dan>: What do we do after you check the players on the Board board?

<Joe>: We make sure that Belvedere chains Sharf to a desk in a padded room.

<Justin>: How do you know Marshall's wife?

<Joe>: I come across her work from time to time. She's one of the best technology litigators I have ever seen.

In addition, I attend their spring picnic. We have a lawyer's corner. Van Amberg even tolerates Dan, although he tends to look silly in the clown suit. *If Marshall lives, Nicky and I can still be friends. If he dies, I become her mortal enemy.*

<Dan>: I try to remain consistent. *You have a crush on her, your wife worries, but Marshall thinks it's cute. He's been dealing with the competition for over 40 years.*

<Justin>: I seem to remember reading that she was an assistant district attorney. Isn't there a bit of a gap between criminal law and litigation?

<Dan>: I was in the room on the day when she found out that somebody was trying to steal a patent from a principal in her son's first start-up. Machi may not be as quick as Marshall is, but she is more determined and extraordinarily clever. She slept as little as is humanly possible for the next three months, but her baby kept his patent and everything else after that, whether he needed it or not.

<Justin>: Can anybody be that good?

<Joe>: Yes, they can, especially if they have Marshall backing them up. I will explain later.

If there are no other questions, keep your batteries charged.

---------- ----------

<Justin>: Now you may be straight with me. Begin at the beginning.

<Dan>: What has happened in the last 35 minutes that makes you believe I am not being honest?

<Justin>: Nothing. That's why I believe there's a time bomb ready to explode. What is it that Joe knows already?

<Dan>: His son was the smartest kid I saw the entire time that I was at Strafford. He was limited because he did not hear well. I understood Jonas's isolation. I was a bookish runt in a family where muscle and guile counted. My mother's "runt" brother took pity and helped me scholastically.

Because I sympathized, I may have gone out of my way to discover a way to balance the input from Jonas's two hearing aids so that they stopped giving him a headache. I was not totally altruistic. I may have a patent for that discovery which benefits your little sister and her children.

<Justin>: *The day is full of surprises.* Did you just slip and admit to me that you actually engineered something?

<Dan>: *I'll ignore that.* To repay me, Mr. Marshall agreed to help when I was ready to start my own family. I was Valley elite, but he was Mr. Marshall. He is very impressive when he stands up straight and sticks his chest out. He is also very impressive when he browses through a thesis submission and finds a couple of formulas that were printed incorrectly.

<Justin>: ***Marshall does the "stand up and chest out" act when he attends the quarterly meetings. He wouldn't have to stand up straight to start a flutter in the hearts of some of our Jersey g- women.***

Why would an erudite snob such as you bother with an invisible man like Marshall, even if he has an invisible barrel chest, and his son is smart?

<Dan>: That's Jay calling from the reception area. [...] Hold him 10 minutes, and then send him in.

<Justin>: You were about to explain why you have this fondness for Marshall.

<Dan>: I discovered that the father is as smart as the son is, and he is more effective because he is 70% functional in the real world, while the son only made 50% due to his auditory isolation. He is one of the smartest men I know and collecting smart people is a hobby of mine. ***He also helped me to figure out what I needed to do to lock in your sister.***

<Justin>: How did he survive if he only had 70%?

<Dan>: His life mate is the most formidable woman that I know, as I implied earlier. ***Clara may have been tougher, but she was old by the time I met her.*** She added 20% to his survival repertoire. The remainder he rejects because he considers it to be below him.

<Justin>: ***The key to this is Ms. Frey! I need to meet that mate before I get checked.*** I've been thinking that I could rearrange a few things, and we could fly in to Manhattan together.

<Dan>: Why?

<Justin>: Maybe it would be appropriate for me to visit the family personally. He is, after all, one of my direct reports. I could meet Gunnar at his space in New York.

<Dan>: **No! Not now! Not ever! I forbid you to go anywhere near them!** You're a perverted robot, but Liz loves you. We wouldn't want you injured too.

<Justin>: You dropped your glass, and do not forget that I am still your boss.

<Dan>: Ms. Frey is likely to be near him until they take him off the critical list.

<Justin>: That's logical.

<Dan>: Did you hear what she sounded like a while ago?

<Justin>: Distraught.

<Dan>: A better description is murderous. For the record, she is the accident that happened to Gunnar.

<Justin>: She tried to run him down!

<Dan>: No. It was more of a one-on-one encounter. Though whatever happened was too fast for anyone to see, it was somehow related to Gunnar accidentally falling into Marshall's cane a few times.

<Justin>: She's an old woman - older than Marshall is if I remember. Why didn't Gunnar grab the cane and take it from her?

<Dan>: Reese said he was wobbly already. I don't know why.

<Justin>: Joe mentioned that too.

<Dan>: Second, he was having poor cute little old lady thoughts until she targeted his reproductive capacity, after which he fell into the cane.

<Justin>: Why Gunnar didn't have her arrested?

<Dan>: Describe Gunnar.

<Justin>: He's the typical high-powered sales type - rugged looking, athletic build, 6"2", 195 pounds, ageless (with help).

<Dan>: Ms. Frey is an old lady (65 to be exact), her hair is completely white, she's 5'5" tall, and she weighs 125 pounds in a rain shower.

<Justin>: As I said, he could have defended himself.

<Dan>: In her age and weight category, she is ranked among the top 10 women in martial arts - that's a Marshall pun. She succeeds because she is strong (in her age category), focused, and very fast.

<Justin>: She sounds like one of those walking lethal weapons. Why didn't he press charges?

<Dan>: Because the cane disappeared, Val said he tripped, Ms. Frey was hysterical, and she is chummy with several judges who used to be her co-workers. *There may also be the Indy asthma factor.*

You should be glad he didn't press charges because that would have been harder to hide from the reporters that Sharf sent after us.

<Justin>: I am missing some of this, even while paying attention. Why would she continue to practice at her age?

<Dan>: To stay in shape for [...] Marshall. *You wouldn't believe the real reason if I told you.*

I need to prepare for Sharf, but please listen to these other things that you should know about Nicola Frey:

1. Her nickname is spelled "M-a-c-h-i", not Macky, like Mack the Knife, although recently, the comparison is appropriate. It is short for Machiavella.
2. Nobody hurts anything that belongs to Machi and gets away with it. She will wait 20 or thirty years if she must, but she usually figures out something appropriate in much less time.
3. Gunnar was lucky that she reacted physically this time because he could tell what she's doing.

<Justin>: You are exaggerating.

<Dan>: What is the biggest professional, financial, or personal problem that you have had lately? This is a serious question.

<Justin>: That's none of your business.

<Dan>: You are the brother of my wife. I am looking out for family interests.

<Justin>: There have been none lately.

<Dan>: You could lose a lifetime's worth of accomplishments because you allowed Gunnar and Sharf to hurt Marshall, after you allowed Gunnar and Montgomery to hurt with Marshall before. Machi may know what you did, even if I don't.

[...] Your reaction suggests that you, Robot, have suddenly recalled something from memory.

<Justin>: You'll lose Liz if you let this slip.

<Dan>: Noted.

<Justin>: The last big problem was the time I was audited by the IRS. That was a few months before I hired you. I may have been pushing the limits, and Langstrom, the IRS auditor, was coming after me as if it was personal. I'm sure McBride could have gotten me out of it if he hadn't retired and gone back to the old country. He was late for two hearings and ill for the third one. Meanwhile, McBride's replacement was not sufficiently creative at interpreting the guidelines. That cost me almost $2 million dollars.

<Dan>: It's also a ding on your record the next time someone does a character search. That could be a problem if you wanted to move on or upward.

[...] Jesus, the CEO spot!

<Justin>: It can be explained, although I would rather not have to explain it.

<Dan>: Did that happen before or after the first time you let Gunnar loose on Marshall?

<Justin>: It was the next year [...] NAH! I was selected for a random audit. Nicola Frey's political influence is very local. We checked that.

<Dan>: Perhaps I am exaggerating. I have tried to do a good deed, even though you sent Sharf after me too. *I won't remind you that we have a former international security specialist (a.k.a. hacker) on our staff. I may need Maja. Nor will I mention that someone works for Frey associates who mentioned, only in passing, that he worked with you once.*

<Justin>: Being an alarmist seems very unlike you.

<Dan>: You can't say I didn't try. If you insist on dealing with Machi, I recommend that you should stick your investments under a mattress, update your résumé, clean the skeletons out of your closet, and until she finishes this physical phase, make sure there's room in that bird for Oswald.

<Justin>: The best part of $1 billion is worth a few hours in harm's way.

<Dan>: Take the back stairs. Sharf is out front.

<Justin>: I'm hiding in my own company.

<Dan>: *That should be the least of your worries.*

--------**Waiting Area outside Piccolo's Office**-----

<Rennie>: *We are scheduled to see Dr. Daniel Piccolo, the Corporate Architect, I don't know where Dr. Piccolo's office is located, and Will is not here yet.*

I'm worried that Sharf may be doing something even more stupid than sending out that report last night.

Mr. Cane will be livid. He told me to keep an eye on Sharf, and try to rein him in. How am I supposed to do that while I'm stuck without reins?

I accepted the job with Belvedere because I wanted an opportunity to evaluate the job market from the point of view of boardrooms with a nice salary increase. William gets us kicked out of boardrooms or he makes sure that we never get in. The Daxiao's boardroom is two floors up and on the other end of the building.

Kelvin and I graduated from the same school at the same time, and I had better grades, but he was earning almost twice my salary until I landed this job.

Belvedere is not Big Four, but this was supposed to be a ground-floor opportunity in an area where I am considered an expert, SOA. I earn 85% of my "almost" husband's salary, but I can make it up in bonuses if I figure out how to handle William.

I shouldn't be thinking about my skirt, but I have a weird situation. Admittedly, I only had one skirt (and two suits) when I started at Belvedere. I had taken dress-down a little too far.

Mr. Cane sent me to a fashion consultant and gave me a clothing allowance. We picked two week's worth of clothes, and they cost almost two-month's salary. The problems were (a) the fashion consultant must work with women in the fashion industry, not technology, (b) he would never expect his mother or his sister to wear the outfits he recommended for me (I had to take sitting lessons), and (c) I was only able to charge in one place, Bergman's. He says it's the best I can do without having them made to order.

The William Calamity: He participated in my interviews, but I was given the impression that I would be working for Grayson. Instead, I am Sharf's typing handmaiden in short skirts. This fool:

1. *Often trips himself up before we see a boardroom.*
2. *Makes me spend most of my days trying to stay far enough behind him that I am not sucked into the traps that he builds for himself.*
3. *Knows enough about technology to be dangerous.*
4. *Learned technology during financial audits of small to medium-sized technology organizations.*
5. *Seems to have snapped yesterday evening when he believed he had the senior person in Daxiao's SOA organization caught in a trap.*
6. *Spent two months trying to land a contract with Ādaemoa, risked getting us sued, and walked away humming and singing yesterday evening.*

He made me work until 10 o'clock last night organizing his Day-One report of damning evidence against Mr. Marshall. I asked him to show it to Mr. Gunnar first, but he said he's tired of Gunnar telling him what to do. I thought he had just met Mr. Gunnar. He's hand-delivering copies to Daxiao's executive team now.

Daxiao is building an excellent foundation for an organization-wide Service-Oriented Architecture.

Thus, the report sounds like the ravings of a mad man. William is determined to show that Mr. Marshall is completely incompetent and that Daxiao needs Belvedere and especially Sharf to save them from their plight. There is more to this than William wanting to replace Mr. Marshall.

If I could spend enough time with the BASE people without William's insanity, I could do well for Daxiao and Belvedere.

The librarian is here now. He definitely looks like a librarian or a college professor.

Hello, I'm Renata Vitale, and they sent me here to wait for my associate. We have an appointment to see Dr. Piccolo in a few minutes. Am I in the right place?

<Jay>: Yes, and we are expecting you. Pardon me, but I have to prepare something for your meeting. Coffee or tea and healthy stuff are in the room behind you. Help yourself.

<Rennie>: Thanks. ***We are going to meet in the library. I said that this isn't going well.***

[...] ***Wow, he's faster than Hank.***

[...] ***Here's William, with five minutes to spare.***

---------- ----------

<Sharf>: Rennie, I'm glad you made it. Johnson, I'm William Sharf, and I have an appointment with Dan Piccolo in five minutes. Give us directions, and call to let him know we are on the way.

<Jay>: Wait while I finish this thought. You are where you need to be. Sit - or stand.

<Sharf>: ***He's ignoring me! I will mention this to Piccolo.***

<Jay>: [...] Mr. Sharf is here, and he is very anxious to see you.

[...] I will be ready in less than 20 minutes.

<Sharf>: ***It is time that he paid attention. We have only three minutes.***

<Jay>: He says wait 10 minutes, and then come down. We apologize for the delay. Go through that opening. Walk past the stacks until you come to the double doors. Push one of the panels to enter.

<Sharf>: His office is in the library?

<Jay>: His office is the library.

---------- ----------

<Sharf>: ***Who ever heard of an SVP sitting in a library?*** He must be on the skids.

<Rennie>: ***Maybe not. This is a very nice corporate library.*** How did things go on your rounds?

<Sharf>: Things went well. The ones who were here already were happy to see me so early in the morning. Justin Mittelman, the president, was delighted with my findings. The top lawyer was there to, and he was amazed that I could uncover such unusual things in such a short amount of time.

---------- ----------

<Rennie>: A horseshoe-shaped desk. ***He's fast too.***

<Dan>: Rennie and Will. Come over. What a pleasure to see you. I'm Dr. Daniel Piccolo. Call me Dan.

<Rennie>: ***What a gentle handshake.***

<Sharf>: ***Damn, he's strong. He has the broadest shoulders I ever seen on a runt. He spends too much time in the gym.***

<Dan>: Get comfortable. We must wait until I have at least one backup memory unit. Valery Van Amberg is pulling into the parking lot and Jay will have the presentation ready for us in a moment.

<Sharf>: The gal from Human Resources scheduled the second round with Van Amberg next Wednesday. Whatever we have to discuss can wait until then. ***On second thought, he might be the middle that Gunnar and I need. I was going to call him when I finished with Piccolo. I can pick his brains now and later.***

<Dan>: He obviously didn't think so. He's driving 60 miles to find the closure he felt you needed. The things you and Van Amberg skipped yesterday fit perfectly with what we will be discussing today.

<Sharf>: We will discuss four slices of the SOA pie that I attached to last night's e-mail:

- SOA Governance,
- Strategy Management,
- Methodology and Planning
- Project Management Structure.

Justin, Joe, and the gal from Human Resources approved that pie this morning.

<Dan>: What gal is this?

<Sharf>: The one with the name like a fingernail file. It suits her.

<Dan>: ***The person, after Marshall, who really runs Daxiao. I never saw anyone dig his own grave so quickly.*** You must be referring to Dr. Emery-Baldwin. It is better to have her as a friend.

<Sharf>: ***Only if I decide that Gunnar and I can use her when we take over, and I doubt that.*** Thanks for the advice. I will entertain additional suggestions for today's content if you have other things you believe to be important.

<Dan>: There are ways to synchronize the areas that interest you with an agenda. How does this look?

<Sharf>: I explained to Marshall yesterday that artificially imposed structure limits the discovery process. I prefer to select topics, and as long as we don't wonder too far from those topics, my aims will be served. We take breaks when the timing feels right.

<Dan>: I see what you were trying to do. By noon, we will have this thing back on track.

<Sharf>: We are on track. Everything worked out better than I could have imagined. Did you have an opportunity to study my document?

<Dan>: Yes, and you appear to have been listening to Van Amberg. Thus, I want him here.

<Sharf>: That reflects my view of the situation, not Van Amberg or Marshall's.

<Rennie>: *William is about to get busted.* While we're waiting, how is Mr. Marshall? I hear that he became ill after we left.

<Dan>: Thank you for asking. They didn't have to amputate, but we don't know whether there could be other serious problems.

<Rennie>: What happened?

<Dan>: He tripped over a desk drawer, which you wouldn't believe would be too nasty, except that he tried to catch his balance using his bad leg and his thigh detached from an artificial knee joint. He broke a few ribs on the way to the ground. It's a long way from his chest to a credenza. If it hadn't been for our EVP of Sales and Marketing, he might have died.

<Rennie>: Do you mean Niklas Gunnar, the one who retained us?

<Sharf>: *Marshall was probably drunk and staggering. Gunnar should have stayed out of it.* He's the one. What are they going to do about Marshall's other problems?

<Dan>: They caught the infection before it was out of control. His pressure stabilized and his temperature is dropping.

<Rennie>: That's wonderful. He seems like a nice person, and very knowledgeable too.

<Sharf>: *He's an overrated drug addict. I guess Gunnar didn't confirm my report yet.*

<Dan>: You have a mutual admiration society. He likes you too. *That will enlarge the wedge, even if it is a day late.* While we're waiting, do you have any questions about anything?

<Rennie>: I that a BPM dashboard on the top bank of screens?

<Dan>: Yes. We are proud of it. Someone in Daxiao can see how every process is performing at any location around the clock. We also have CEP (Complex Event Processing) turned on, and that allows us to detect potential problems before they cause difficulties. We can demonstrate later.

<Rennie>: What about the monitors.

<Dan>:

- Terminal #1 is Daxiao's executive scorecard.
- Terminal #2 is the WFSOA dashboard. We use it to monitor the status of work in progress. It's also a window in the executive dashboard, but this has more information.
- Terminal #4 is the Knowledge Cooperative. That should be #1, but protocol is important.
- #5 is the competitor dashboard. I also use it one to keep an eye on international markets. It's a natural pairing I should think.
- Screen #6 allows me to keep abreast of ideas in the theoretical realm.

<Rennie>: These are not temporary quarters, are they?

<Dan>: Of course not. HM and I compete to see who can come up with the cleverest ideas for reuse. I started here by trumping Marshall at his favorite hobby.

<Sharf>: Are you the person who is actually responsible for planning?

<Dan>: It was books! He has as many as I have in this section, but he loses when you count those outside.

<Sharf>: I didn't notice that many. What else does he have in his private conference area?

<Dan>: Ninety percent of what he has at Daxiao is digitized in the Knowledge Cooperative.

I was talking about the books he has at home. One of their corner apartments is their bedroom/library. It is a joy to behold. You should see the sunsets and the view of the Tappan Zee. It's a good reuse idea too. That saves him the trouble of limping too far if he forgets his fact-for-the-day.

<Rennie>: He mentioned that. I set that goal for myself last night.

<Sharf>: *It's a dumb idea. You can be good at a few important things and skip the remainder.*

<Dan>: When I started, the library took up all this space and there was 5% utilization. I digitized 90% too, removed physical copies of out-of-date information, and used 40% of the space for my personal resources and for me. The books on this side of the door are mine. The important ones are repeated out there, but those can be borrowed.

Now I have the most expansive office in the company, even counting Chiu's space. We also reused the reception area. My assistant and the main librarian share the space. Actually, the junior librarian agreed to spend part of her time as my assistant. They had less work to do after the information was digitized. The two women work well together, and I didn't want to break up a good team.

<Sharf>: *Women!* Who's the tweedy person that was ignoring me?

<Dan>: That is the corporate strategist, Double Dr. J. Stanley Johnson.

<Sharf>: I was about to mention how rude he was.

<Rennie>: *He was obviously trying to concentrate, and you were rude to him.* Was Mr. Marshall upset?

<Dan>: No. He came up with a better idea that saved the company even more money.

<Rennie>: What did he do?

<Dan>: He built services that enable grid computing, so we can support our research partners using half the blades that you would expect to use. We saved on real estate, hardware, and software licenses.

<Rennie>: This is more visually impressive.

<Dan>: I know. You should have seen the look on Courier's face when he came down to see me. *Actually, he was on his way to Princeton, and he condescended to drive 23 miles out of his way to see how the loser was doing.*

<Rennie>: Dr. Michele Courier?

<Dan>: Yes! Perhaps you keep up with these things. You'll see more [...]

<Sharf>: When can we start?

<Dan>: Here's Jay. How does it look?

<Jay>: It is customized the way you suggested. Hello, again! I haven't seen either of you in a while.

<Rennie>: I'd like to apologize for our abruptness. Mr. Sharf is a stickler for being on time.

<Sharf>: Why didn't you tell me who you were?

<Jay>: You called me by my name.

<Sharf>: The nameplate said V. Johnson.

<Jay>: That would be Viola Johnson.

<Dan>: *He makes points with everyone.* We can start now.

<Jay>: Wait. Val is getting coffee. Do not laugh when you see him.

<Dan>: **Maja with him?** Of course, I will. You can't buy these things with money.

<Jay>: **Stay late with Indy. Bird will be here soon.**

<Val>: Good morning everybody. Take a good look, chuckle, and get over it.

<Dan>: That's what you get for collaborating with the enemy.

<Sharf>: What enemy?

<Val>: I was standing too close to Niklas Gunnar while Nicola Frey expressed some very strong feelings.

<Dan>: Was it actually that bad?

<Val>: Gunnar is worse off than I am, but he was lucky. He may sound strange for a while, but he could pick himself up off the floor. He was also able to sign himself out of the hospital this morning. *I had more fun than you're having now, even though I could hardly see.*

<Sharf>: What's wrong with Gunnar? *He's been calling me since 7:00 o'clock. So has Mags. Maybe I should have responded.*

<Val>: He received a few bruises while supporting the Marshall family during a very difficult time.

<Sharf>: That's why he wasn't answering his phone! I've been trying to confirm the meeting that we planned for tomorrow.

<Rennie>: *Mr. Marshall, Val, and Mr. Gunnar. This place is dangerous.* How could so many people be injured at once?

<Val>: *She's afraid.* Do not be concerned. This is not usual, and you are not in harm's way. Ms. Nicola Frey was particularly distraught when she believed she would lose her mate of 41 years.

<Sharf>: *She learned that stuff from her mother, not the muscle-bound ball runner.*

<Dan>: Who stopped her? I've worked out with Machi. The only person I know who is faster is Maja?

<Sharf>: *Maja again!*

<Val>: I'm 100% sure that Indy is faster, and Jonas may be as fast for short stretches. I missed some of what happened because my head was ringing. They had to sedate her to keep her from getting arrested.

<Sharf>: *They ruined my career before I really started. Payback is wonderful.*

<Dan>: I forgot. They practice in the morning - *while Liz and I do pull-ups and serve shereal with chocolate milch.*

<Sharf>: *Huey can't even walk straight.* Marshall's son looks more like a drunken sumo wrestler.

<Dan>: *He is one sick puppy.* Jonas Frey-Marshall can do more damage on the floor than I can when I am standing. He has been practicing since he was two. He is the world's only 300-pound sitting ninja. HM was almost as good before his leg started misbehaving again. *That scared the hell out of him.*

<Sharf>: *He wouldn't have to walk straight to cripple me if he knew what I have planned for his father.*

<Dan>: Did Machi apologize when she realized how Gunnar is responsible for saving Marshall's life?

<Val>: I haven't spoken to her, but I'd guess she would say that if HM hadn't been distracted, he wouldn't have tripped. She would blame the distraction on Gunnar and you.

<Sharf>: Me! You know that I left before any of this occurred. *I would love to see him suffering up close.*

<Val>: You were in his presence on the day he was hurt, and you did not keep him from getting hurt.

In fact, she says you've been her least favored list for years. Why would that be?

<Rennie>: *Why is Will turning red again?*

<Sharf>: Maybe she's angry because I won a few contracts that her daughter was bidding for when she was at Acton.

We are wasting time. Where are we going to work? *I'll talk to Gunnar about how to use what we know to keep Marshall's women in check.*

<Dan>: Right here. My desk and my conference table are in the same place. Reuse, reuse. Rennie, there are power and network outlets near your right wrist if you need them.

<Rennie>: *In the rim of the desk.* This certainly beats crawling under the desk.

<Val>: [...] *You shouldn't try to crawl in that outfit.*

<Sharf>: We will compromise on the sequence. Start with your comments on the Etiology, and then we can proceed with your list, but I reserve the right to change direction when it seems appropriate.

<Dan>: Val, I don't believe you were on the mailing list for Will's documents last night. One of them shows how he perceives the Etiology of Daxiao's SOA. I printed a copy for you.

<Val>: This is [...] absolutely [...] unbelievable? It leaves me speechless [...] *I hope I sounded surprised enough.*

<Dan>: As rare as this may be, I was speechless too. Did all of you forget that I existed yesterday? Where would WFSOA be without me?

1. My theoretical syntheses were not mentioned at all. You mention SOA, not WFSOA.
2. You omitted continuous process improvement.
3. I'm only associated with four items out of 20.
4. I should receive credit for my leading contribution to requirements management, automated process approvals, the reward structure, corporate communications, process

automation, the Knowledge Cooperative, and cultural change management?

This should muddy the water.

<Sharf>: I only mentioned the people who appeared to have primary responsibilities.

<Val>: He sticks his fingers in everything. I assumed that Gunnar had told you that.

<Dan>: None of those people could have contributed anything, unless I explained it to them. HM is a man of a few words.

<Val>: When did the price double?

<Sharf>: It doubled when I realized how delicate this situation might be. This could make or break reputations.

<Val>: What did Justin have to say?

<Sharf>: He said my ideas were brilliant and invaluable.

<Val>: Did he say anything about the price?

<Sharf>: It never came up in conversation.

<Dan>: Let's fix the chart first. Once we have it the way I want it, I will convince Justin to pay for the entire thing.

<Val>: Why would he do that?

<Dan>: Maybe he believed Gunnar stumbled onto something that should be shared.

<Sharf>: These are my insights.

<Dan>: WFSOA is my program. I have worked 5 years to pull this together.

<Val>: H worked 35 years and I did too.

<Dan>: It still wouldn't be anything if it hadn't been for me. N'est pas?

<Rennie>: Dr. Piccolo. Mr. Marshall definitely mentioned WFSOA several times. However, Mr. Marshall said that you were the one most qualified to give us the specifics. After William hears your point of view, we can adjust the chart.

<Dan>: Good. Here's the 30-second introduction.

I decide what needs to be glued together to create an effective organizational structure, Jay helps us decide when reconstruction is necessary, HM provides processes to support the structures, Val/Alex make the processes work, and Maja provides the glue.

<Sharf>: Why does Maja pop up all over the place?

<Dan>: She's our alpha geekette, and that's what she does. Geneva recommended her for international security, and she's good at databases. They fit together - most security breaches are aimed at data. In fact, she is popping into the building as we speak. She wanted to clear up some things.

<Val>: She was on vacation.

<Dan>: Didn't you tell Ernest to notify your management team?

<Val>: Yes, but [...]

<Dan>: It was late, so he asked someone named Kenneth Chase to help.

<Val>: **OH NO!**

<Dan>: Don't worry. I had better luck than you did with Machi. She'll be calm when she arrives.

<Val>: How did she get here?

<Jay>: She rented a helicopter, which is probably the one you heard a few minutes ago. Justin's is waiting for Barca.

<Val>: It left, so she wasn't flying it.

I want to know how she got to New York.

<Dan>: She borrowed a Learjet. She has seen H already.

<Val>: Does the owner know the plane was borrowed?

<Dan>: Of course he does. He was happy to fly with her, especially since the borrowing fee was almost twice the corporate rate (short notice and all that).

<Val>: They said only family could see him. Indy made me leave as soon as Ernest showed up.

<Dan>: H's third cousin on his father's side counted as family.

<Sharf>: *I'm not the only one with special relations.*

<Val>: She's not his cousin.

<Dan>: She was last night. Doug Church approved the visit.

<Sharf>: Why are you so stressed out? If you don't want her here, order her to stay away. You're technically two or three levels above her.

<Jay>: He could also drink molten glass. If Maja wants to clear something up, Maja will show us how to clear it up.

<Maja Johanssen>: I hear you talking about me. Good day to everyone.

<Sharf>: Where did you come from?

<Maja>: I lock the doors and I unlock them.

<Dan>: I'm glad you made it. Is Indy OK?

<Maja>: Better. **Now I can talk about thigh replacement.**

<Val>: *What did you just say?*

<Dan>: You mean knee replacement.

<Maja>: **Thigh, hip, and knee. Here to here.**

<Rennie>: **Sounds very serious.**

<Val>: You can't mean that.

<Maja>: **We go through front door and talk.**

<Dan>: **Jay and Rennie, help please.** We have to step outside for a moment. Jay, demonstrate the screens for Rennie.

<Sharf>: What were you doing? Where are you going?

<Rennie>: Communicating. They have to bring Maja up-to-date on what we were discussing.

Meanwhile, I look forward to reviewing all these dashboards?

<Jay>: We also have a few portals that you may find interesting.

<Rennie>: Let's take advantage of Jay. Look, at what he found for us already.

---------- ----------

<Jay>: He could also drink molten glass. If Maja wants to clear something up, Maja will show us how to clear it up.

<Maja Johanssen>: I hear you talking about me. Good day to everyone.

<Sharf>: Where did you come from?

<Maja>: I lock the doors and I unlock them.

<Dan>: I'm glad you made it. Is Indy OK?

<Maja>: Better. **Now I can talk about thigh replacement.**

<Val>: *What did you just say?*

<Dan>: You mean knee replacement.

<Maja>: **Thigh, hip, and knee. Here to here.**

<Rennie>: **Sounds very serious.**

<Val>: You can't mean that.

<Maja>: **We go through front door and talk.**

<Dan>: **Jay and Rennie, help please.** We have to step outside for a moment. Jay, demonstrate the screens for Rennie.

<Sharf>: What were you doing? Where are you going?

<Rennie>: Communicating. They have to bring Maja up-to-date on what we were discussing.

Meanwhile, I look forward to reviewing all these dashboards?

<Jay>: We also have a few portals that you may find interesting.

<Rennie>: Let's take advantage of Jay. Look, at what he found for us already.

<Maja>: *Stänga upp!*

<Dan>: What?

<Val>: She said give her a chance to talk.

<Maja>: Indy feels like you make me feel now, only much worse. She cried for two hours after Machi and Jonas screamed at her.

<Dan>: Will he survive this?

<Maja>: The longer he lives, the more we believe he will live. HM took care of himself very well for the last 18 months. We already have a miracle.

<Val>: I need that chair. We are sorry. Please tell us what happened.

Dan, come back here!

<Dan>: I have to go and see him.

<Maja>: It is not a good idea. He is still not conscious, ***and he looks very bad.***

<Val>: Please tell us how this happened.

<Maja>: HM did not want an artificial limb. Cut too high anyway. Doctors and Ernest tell us that 60/40 success is worse probability. H told Indy and me he was willing to take a chance if odds are only 50/50.

<Val>: Who is "US"?

They told H, Indy, and Machi first. Later they told Becky and me. We don't tell you because you have too much guilt already.

They said that if he lost weight, new thigh odds would be 80/20 success. H lost weight while the thigh became worse, only slower than without weight loss. They measured him during last stay in hospital. They ordered a thighbone. Daxiao health insurance gave money back and so did the government.

He signed a medical proxy with Indy and Machi, with me as the backup. Machi lost her mind when she realized that his condition was very bad. She left Indy to make choices.

<Val>: She's as tough as her mother is.

<Maja>: She needed to be tougher last night. Thigh could not be repaired. Chances were maybe 50/50 if they cut off his leg, and maybe 50/50 if they replaced his thigh. We agreed to do what her father asked.

<Dan>: He was dealing with all that plus Sharf and Gunnar. How did he do it? ***Only Marshall knows everything that is on Marshall's mind.***

<Val>: He had family.

<Dan>: Becky said his odds are back to 60/40. Was she right? ***May I never have to make such a choice?***

<Maja>: Maybe a little better, but not much.

<Val>: Where is Indy now? She must be a wreck.

<Maja>: Indy tries to recover at my place.

[...] Don't call. If she finds sleep, let her rest. She cannot afford sickness now.

<Val>: Where are the other family members?

<Maja>: Jonas apologized, and he gives more blood. Nicky disappeared, and we don't know where she went.

<Val>: We apologize too.

<Dan>: We will finish with Sharf quickly so we can get to New York. Maja, remember that you should behave better than we did the last few minutes.

---------- ----------

<Rennie>: You could have stayed longer? Dr. Johnson has been giving us some unbelievable demonstrations.

<Sharf>: She's right, but not nearly as much as I need to see to do this job correctly.

<Jay>: **H OK?**

<Val>: **We need a miracle.**

<Dan>: It didn't take long to explain how H's people do the work, and I provide the explanations.

<Maja>:

- Jay, here's the strategy research. Catch.
- Val, this is what boxers use when they look like you do. Be careful not to get it in your eye.
- Rennie, we will be able to work together. I keep an extra pair of pants in Dan's cupboard if you believe you'd feel more comfortable.

<Rennie>: ***Oh how I wish*** [...] I'm OK.

<Maja>: Can we look at the etiology circle first? We put this one together in the first place. Sharf made a big mess. He turned everything around backwards from the way it is supposed to be. I sent everybody a copy of the original image.

<Val and Rennie>: ***That's where it came from!***

<Rennie>*: *This is embarrassing.

<Sharf>: I fixed it.

<Dan>: ***He has a big set.***

<Maja>: You and I are going to have problems [...]

<Dan and Val>: AJ! You promised.

<Maja>: I did not promise. You told me what I should remember to do, and I tried to forget what you told me to remember.

But I remember you from ebXML. You work very hard. I am Annika. **Why do you work with a fool?**

<Rennie>: You're that AJ! **He is my biggest mistake. I expected a different boss.**

<Sharf>: It's some kind of sign language! What are you doing? *She's been plotting with them from the time we arrived. Cane will hear about this.*

<Rennie>: It is American Sign Language, and we are communicating.

<Dan>: We must stop keeping secrets. Tell him what you just said.

<Maja>: I asked how she landed a job with Mr. Sharf.

<Rennie>: I said I was hired to work for someone else, but Mr. Sharf uses most of my time.

<Dan>: Now that Mr. Sharf knows our secret, everything should be out in the open. Start with a proper greeting.

<Maja>: Hello Mr. William Sharf. I'm Maja Johanssen. I can't believe that I worked that hard to get you the Roles/Activity Listing, and you left before H could give it to you.

<Dan>: I have copies right here. They'll leave with them today.

<Maja>: You confused many things yesterday. Because I understand everything Dan will say, I can show you how to interpret his complicated thoughts. I will sit here beside you, and we can exchange notes. You do not have to thank me.

<Sharf>: Do you know who I am?

<Maja>: Yes, it is here in this side pocket. Check it for me while I get connected (Fig. 16.1). I know there are gaps, but this was a short notice. I won't show anyone until I fill it in completely. *I was only going to show this to Dan and Val, but he annoyed me.*

> **Readers**: Notice another reason for Sharf's state of mind. He's good with other people's money, but not with his own. He earns twice as much as Maja (see Fig. 16.2), but he has a negative net worth.
>
> **Maja isn't actually that frugal. Half of her net worth is insurance from her deceased husband, and 25% is equity in her apartment.

<Sharf>: How did you [...] *I'm in worse shape than I remembered. If I don't land this assignment, Mags will have to find a job, and I'll never hear the end of it.*

<Dan>: AJ! Please!

<Maja>: He asked. *I have not had so much fun acting dumb in a long while.* The second one is mine. Give it back.

<Sharf>: *I feel like I felt the day I had the meeting with the two Frey-Marshall broads. I see their handiwork in this. The old broad had me tracked before.*

I might as well mention that I'm married to Niklas Gunnar's sister. It's on this sheet anyhow. I'm still the area's most knowledgeable individual in both SOX and SOA.

<Rennie>: *Mr. Cane must have known this. I am miles outside of having inside information about such things.*

<Dan>: Smart knowledgeable people are likely to be associated with smart knowledgeable people. **Maja, do you want me to beg.**

<Maja>: **I feel better now.** Should we stick with the etiology, or should we pick another topic?

<Rennie>: How did you come up with the idea for Daxiao's version of SOA?

<Dan>: I would like to discuss the foundational theories for WFSOA. Then we can return to discussion of the pie.

<Sharf>: That sounds great. *I can hardly talk. Gunnar helped me walk into a trap.*

<Val>: *This is working. Maja put the fear of God in him*

Data Sheet for William Benson Sharf			
Date of Birth:	*January 31, 1962*	Occupation(s):	*CPA, Technology Consultant*
Place of Birth:	*Philadelphia, Pennsylvania*	Education:	*Neudorf* *University of Pennsylvania*
Height:	*6' 6"*	Income:	*$175,000 salary +120,000 bonus*
Weight:	*198 lbs.*	Mortgage:	*$1,173,203.23*
Nationality:	*Mixed Anglo-American and German American*	Net Worth:	*-$157,344*
Parents:	*Dorothy Marian Vernon (deceased)* *William Benson Sharf*	Collar:	*17-1/2*
Spouse:	*Margaret Shirley Gunther Sharf*	Sleeve:	*38*
Address:	*222 Forest Avenue* *Inglewood Heights, New Jersey 07723*	Waist:	*39*
Phone(s):	*201-394-7798 (Home)* *917-262-4831 (Mobile)*	Hobbies:	*None*

Fig. 16.1 - Data Sheet for William Sharf

Data Sheet for Annika Maja Johnson Johanssen. a.k.a. Annika Johanssen, Anne Johnson, Annie Mae Johnson			
Date of Birth:	*June 14, 1964*	Occupation(s):	*Security and Information Analyst*
Place of Birth:	*Stockholm, Sweden*	Education:	*Lund University, Lund, Sweden* *Imperial College, London, England*
Height:	*5'8"*	Income:	*$125,000 salary + 40,000 bonus*
Weight:	*140 lbs.*	Mortgage:	*$119,843.12*
Nationality:	*Mixed Swedish and British*	Net Worth:	*$1,810,243*
Parents:	*Katrina Nicola Swenson.* *Horace David Johnson*	Size:	*Medium*
Spouse:	*Jacob Fredrik Johanssen (deceased)*		
Address:	... *New York, New York*		
Phone(s):	...	Hobbies:	*Flying, hang gliding, rock climbing, martial arts, photography*

Fig. 16.2 - Data Sheet for Maja Johanssen

CHAPTER VII - SOA, WFSOA AND THE CORPORATE ARCHITECT

WFSOA AND MANAGEMENT THEORIES

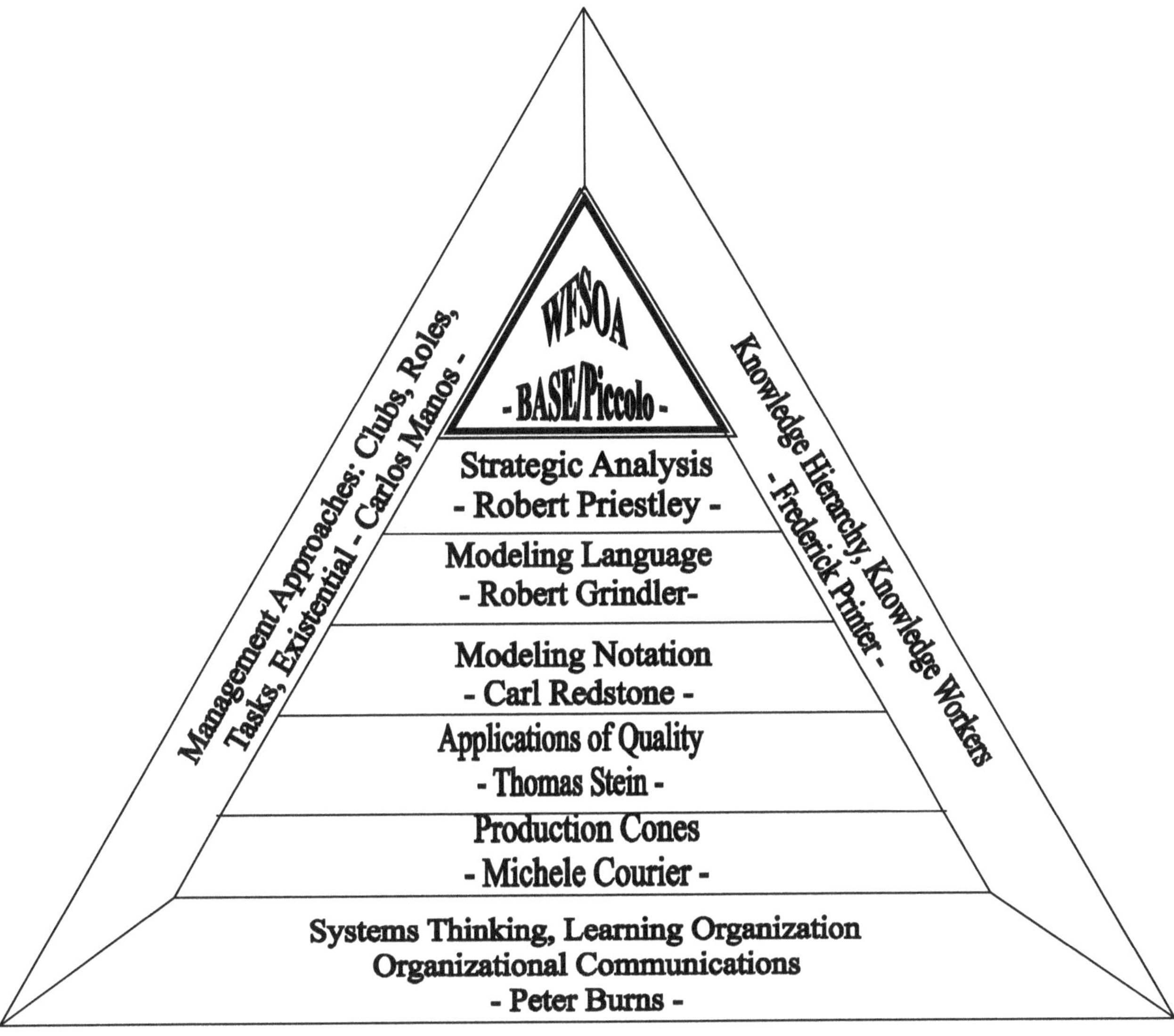

Fig. 17 - WFSOA Theoretical Foundation

Dan>: *This the most concentrated information that I've ever seen. Jay did well.*

Fig. 17 shows how Jay and I merged theories from major management thinkers of the last 50 years into a unified whole that is WFSOA. All those people address a piece of the problem. WFSOA provides empirical proof that they can all work together. Of course, our senior management team added refinements as William pointed out in the Etiology Pie.

<Val>: *H would be smiling and nodding at this point.* Tell them where you fit and where HM fits.

<Rennie>: *Val is smiling and nodding as Mr. Marshall did yesterday.*

<Dan>: We are in the top triangle. My name is there because I provided the guidance. The truth is that I attached names to activities that HM had already initiated.

<Val>: You're doing well. I'm proud of you.

<Dan>: However, if something doesn't have a name, it may as well not exist. I put the communications into the organization, with assistance from Lisse Maçon, of course. Then I took appropriate pieces of the core concepts and formatted them into digestible information. Other managers could suggest improvements after they understood what HM was doing. Is that acceptable Mr. Van Amberg?

> **Readers:** The names in the above table are translations of the names of actual theorists. If you are curious enough, refer the book in the footnote for more information.
>
> (6) Business: The Ultimate Resource, Cambridge, MA: Basic Books, 2006

<Val>: They never gave him time to explain. They kept piling on the work.

<Dan>: I can't do the work, but I have time to explain and the theoretical background. He can do the work, but he doesn't understand what people don't understand. It's a practical merger of skills.

<Sharf>: *He admits to being a windbag, and he's giving credit to Marshall too. Why are they all protecting HM?*

<Dan>: Table 20-WFSOA Theoretical Foundation goes with Fig. 17. The comments show how WFSOA process categories relate to sections of the WFSOA foundational structure.

Table 20 - WFSOA Theoretical Foundation

Theorist	Comments	WFSOA Process Categories
Peter Burns	**Systems Thinking, Learning Organization, Organizational Communications** ♦ Organizations are viewed as dynamic systems where a small change to one part can have a critical effect on another. ♦ Organizations benefit from a positive learning environment.	1. Human Resources Support. ♦ Cultural Change Management. ♦ SOA business and technology training. 2. BASE communications - Highlights relationships between organizational components. 3. SOA Governance. ♦ Program Coordination. ♦ Continuous process improvement.
Michele Courier	**Production Cones** ♦ Products begin as (ideas) slivers of a cone that can barely stand on their own. ♦ The slivers achieve volume and stability as people add appropriate substance **in the correct order**. ♦ If layers are skipped, instability may result. ♦ Some ideas need to be segmented before they can be enhanced.	1. Requirements Coordination - Packaging Requirements. 2. Product Creation - Building and Packaging Products. 3. Environment Management - Execution support for the products.
Carlos Manos	**Management Approaches** ♦ Identified four significant management approaches (club, roles, task, and existential) and the changing nature of organizations. ♦ With WFSOA, Daxiao can benefit from all management types through adjustable roles that exhibit manifestations of each approach.	1. Human Resources Support. ♦ Role definitions and role adjustments. ♦ Techniques for adjusting to changing roles. 2. Project Management - matching individual styles to work requirements.
Frederick Printer	**Knowledge Hierarchy, Knowledge Workers** Identified the steps from information to global knowledge sharing. These include: ♦ Identification of potential knowledge	1. BASE communications - All activities supported by the Knowledge Cooperative. 2. Data Management - Maintains information taxonomies in support of business and

Table 20 - WFSOA Theoretical Foundation

Theorist	Comments	WFSOA Process Categories
	users. ♦ Identification of knowledgeable individuals. ♦ Gathering information from knowledgeable individuals. ♦ Organizing and providing access to knowledge. ♦ Information preservation and integration. ♦ Generation of knowledge (helping people use information for organizational benefit (strategy, policy, and organizational learning). ♦ Creation of knowledge services to address knowledge markets (groups of knowledge users). ♦ Global knowledge integration.	technology.
Robert Priestley	**Strategic Analysis** Strategy mapping, management, and reporting.	Corporate and SOA Governance. 1. SOA evolution. 2. SOA maturity. 3. Iterative strategy and tactics. 4. Dashboards and scorecards.
Carl Redstone	**Modeling Notation** Devised a graphical modeling notation that can be used in system design.	1. Requirements Coordination - Used to model service, process, and application flows. 2. SOA Governance - Techniques for graphically modeling the omission of activities whose preconditions have not been met.
Robert Grindler	**Modeling Language** Created a language for defining processes that interact with each other dynamically. ♦ It supports dynamic addressing of endpoints. ♦ Process activities may be arranged in a sequence, in parallel, in conditional paths, or in loops.	1. Requirements Coordination - Assists definition of process flows. 2. Product Delivery - Supports delivery of services whose physical implementations may be moved without affecting process code. 3. Environment Management - Associated with execution of process management products.
Thomas Stein	**Applications of Quality** ♦ Everything within an organization should be measured at some point. ♦ Measurement improves quality. ♦ Automate as much as possible. ♦ The trade-off between quality measures and production capacity is continually evaluated.	1. Requirements Coordination - Requirements reviews. 2. Data Management - Data quality review and correction. 3. Product Delivery - Software quality reviews. 4. Architecture - Standards enforcement. 5. SOA Governance - Compliance monitoring. 6. Environment Management - Service performance and problem tracking.

<Dan>: Here is the WFSOA emblem again (Fig. 8). Imagine that the WFSOA emblem is sitting on top of the WFSOA triangle of the Theoretical Foundation.

<Rennie>: Logical. All those theories provide a foundation for the practices.

<Dan>: Only if the theories are integrated. The emblem sits on top of the WFSOA triangle only.

<Rennie>: But [...]

<Maja>: Liz and I agree with you Rennie, but she likes him, so we humor him.

<Sharf>: There was no one named Liz or Elizabeth in the materials you distributed yesterday.

<Jay>: Do you remember seeing Lisse Maçon?

<Sharf>: Of course, I remember. She's the gal that does communication overkill and no one listens. She wastes more of Daxiao's money than Emery.

<Maja>: **NEJ!**

<Jay>: ***Dan!*** I have another appointment today. ***Do not make me late!***

<Val>: How would Justin or H handle this?

<Sharf>: Why are all of you so excited?

<Rennie>: I'm very sorry Dr. Piccolo. ***He looks calm, but something went wrong and Sharf didn't see it. That glass must weigh a ton.***

<Val>: ***All-Tha-News: RUNT STUNTS CRACKED NUT.***

It had nothing to do with you. Every one of us has nudged him about this, and he's a little sensitive and a little tired. Aren't you Dan?

<Sharf>: Let's move on. What are you doing with those glass thingies?

<Dan>: ***Where's Machi when you need her?*** I'm trying to collect my thoughts.

[...] What was I saying? I tend to be a little absent minded lately.

[...] I remember now. Each of these theorists contributes, but you have to think of them as a complete - but open - system before WFSOA will work. That transitions to the first theorist in Table 20, Peter Burns. We started at the bottom and went clockwise, and then we started at the bottom again and went to the top.

<Sharf>: ***High-level mumbo-jumbo to match Marshall's detailed over kill.***

<Dan>: Are there any questions?

<Rennie>: ***You packed a degree's worth of information into three pages.*** This is concentrated. I'd like to discuss it with either one of you when you have more time.

<Dan>: Call Val or call me tomorrow, and we will arrange something.

<Sharf>: Do it after you finish your other assignments.

WFSOA - KNOWLEDGE COORDINATOR'S VIEW

<Maja>: It is time to look at the correct (original) Etiology Chart. It is on Screen #3 (See Fig. 18). The differences between that and the one Mr. Sharf sent are:

1. WFSOA replaces SOA on Item #1.
2. BASE does much more than storage and routing (see center circle).
3. All arrows are bi-directional. BASE initiated or collaborated on all those items.
4. Corporate Communications is Item #3. We put it near the top for a good reason. As hard as BASE works on communication, we obviously weren't doing enough of it, or we wouldn't be having this meeting. Notice that the arrow is segmented. Liz isn't happy about it, but she agrees.
5. BASE Planning is #2. All these slices support and are supported by BASE planning.
6. The 20 entries in Liz's pie represent evolving or continuing activities. We omitted SOA Initiation because that happened once we have Continuous Process Improvement (including Lessons Learned) as Item #6.
7. Asterisks beside the item numbers highlight areas where Enterprise Integration supports the indicated team during their collaborations with BASE. I added this to the original image because you expressed curiosity about how much work Dr. Piccolo actually does.

<Sharf>: You can't change my document without my permission.

<Maja>: It was not your document. Liz put it together three weeks ago, and you made bad changes. This corrected version will make you appear less foolish.

<Sharf>: I was hired to find out how Marshall and Piccolo do what they do. Marshall spent six hours trying to redirect me, but I finally figured out that no one can figure out what he does, because he doesn't do anything.

<Dan>: Maja. We must remember that the man is entitled to his opinion! The purpose of advisors is to show different ways of looking at things. You may borrow my paperweights if you like.

<Maja>: *Only if I permanently attach it to his skull.* H worked too hard for his career end in a big mess.

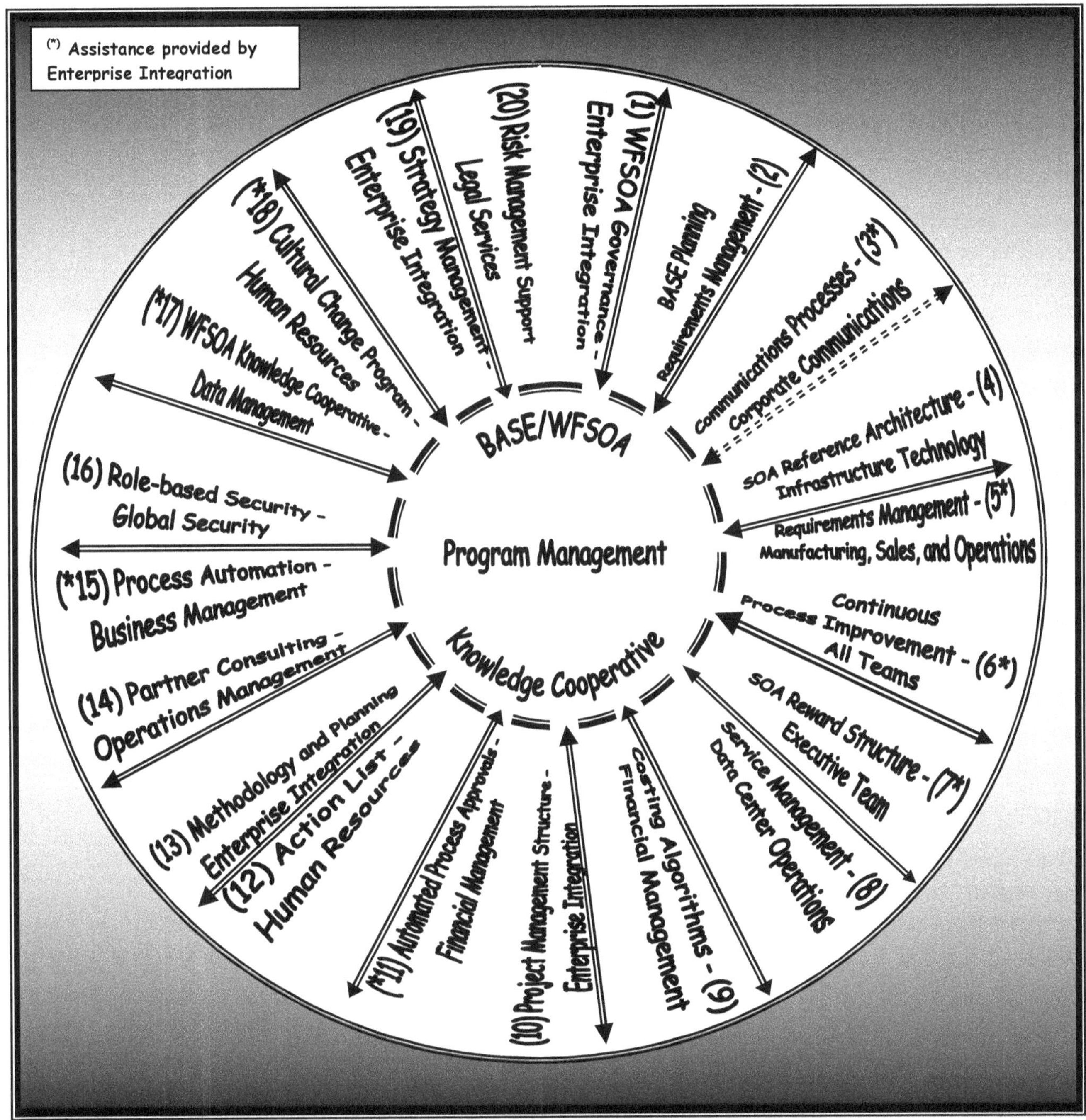

Fig. 18 - Original WFSOA Etiology (Daxiao Version)

<Dan>: We have to acknowledge this problem. If H had found time to explain what he was doing, he may not have had to work as hard as he did. He refused to play by the rules. He didn't even bother to find out what the rules were. He left me to do the hard work while he did what he pleased.

<Sharf>: *It would have been better if I had started with Piccolo.*

<Maja>: You are talking funny, and coming here was a mistake. Jay, I hope you can watch Dan's back better than we did H.

<Dan>: Val did the best he could, and so did you.

<Maja>: I wasted $15,000 of H's family money yesterday, and another $500 today for nothing. *It's a sin to have fun at a time like this, but I hadn't flown anything in almost a year.* At least I can see Lorraine while I'm here. She's needs information for the foolish one too. I will see you at the staff meeting this afternoon.

<Val>: Don't do anything else rash before you talk to me. *Dan is brilliant. The fool is mad at Maja and even more convinced that we are hiding something about H. Gunnar will look really, bad.*

<Maja>: It is good to look at options.

<Sharf>: *She will be the first rat to leave the sinking ship. Good. I won't have to figure out how to get rid of her.*

<Jay>: Does anyone wish to talk about the WFSOA maturity model?

<Dan>: We are not finished with the Etiology. William, what do you believe is the best approach?

<Sharf>: *I will increase my chances of getting paid.* Rennie, add the asterisks to my version. Item #1 will become WFSOA. Dan prefers that. Change Item #3 to "Continuous Process Improvement". The remainder stays as it is.

<Dan>: Then we will see whether additional material supports one view over the other.

<Val>: Dan, I have to prepare for that staff meeting, and then I'll take off early. *I have to give Lorrie a heads-up.*

William, I may see you next Wednesday. I may not.

Good luck Ms. Vitale. Call me if you need me. Here's another one of my cards.

------- **Hallway, Corporate Headquarters** -------

<Sharf>: Where are you going?

<Val>: You are obviously going with the highest bidder. If you hadn't doubled the price, we could have dealt with this and no one would be the wiser. Machi and Indy said I was crazy to trust you, and they were right.

<Sharf>: You didn't answer my question.

<Val>: I'm going to talk to Mittelman, and I will spend a few minutes with Jasper. I do not know how to play this game.

<Sharf>: You are not going to Mittelman, and you are not going to Lorrie. If you try, I will see to it that you spend a few of your golden years in a jail cell.

How does this sound? *"Former Compliance officer Found Non-Compliant", or "Corporate Lawyer Disbarred After 35 Years of Practice".*

<Val>: Thirty-nine years. Gunnar tried that with H, and he failed.

<Sharf>: Gunnar didn't know where to look. I do.

<Val>: It's Machi, Indy, H (if he lives), and me against you. I will take my chances.

Go back and deal with Jeff. I have decided that I will not see you on any Wednesday, not ever.

<Sharf>: Jeff who?

<Val>: Never mind.

<Sharf>: You can't afford to annoy me.

<Val>: Machi handled you before, and she will not be as gentle this time. Take your paw off me. Better yet, take the jacket. It's soiled.

---------- ----------

<Dan>: What are you doing with Val's jacket? *Val and Maja outdid themselves and Maja hadn't even seen the script.*

<Sharf>: He's suicidal.

<Dan>: He's loyal, and naïve. Give me that. I'll send it to him on the next messenger run.

<Sharf>: What do we do now? *I must decide whether I will work with Mittelman or Gunnar.*

<Dan>: You have Justin's attention, and we will use that to maximum advantage. Jay and Rennie are waiting for us.

<Sharf>: With Marshall's people out of the way, there will be fewer things to annoy us.

<Dan>: That's one view of the situation. *With Marshall's people out of the way, things may start going backward for some time.*

<Sharf>: Who's going to pay Belvedere? We need to shut down Marshall's slush fund.

<Dan>: ***He's much too eager and irrational. I'll ignore him and see what happens.*** Money things fix themselves. I told you that Justin will pay you if I tell him to. Recognition does not fix itself. Together, we will publish an empirical work that will move me to the top of every list that is worth being at the top of. We have work to do.

<Sharf>: Did you hear what I said?

<Dan>: ***I don't want you to blurt that out again until it will cause you and Gunnar the most harm.*** We have to put first things first. Piccolo gets his EVP and international recognition first. Marshall and Van Amberg get buried second. ***I hope I'm wrong about the burying part.***

<Sharf>: Only if I help you run this show.

<Dan>: You will receive everything that you are working for, and more.

---------- **Daniel Piccolo's Office**----------

<Rennie>: Do you understand what just happened?

<Jay>: Dan and Val often disagree. Dan is the theorist and Val is the pragmatist. Marshall could make them both feel right at the same time.

<Rennie>: Is Mr. Marshall either as good or as bad as people say he is?

<Jay>: I've never heard anybody say he was bad. He's confusing. His mouth never caught up with his brain. Dan is good at filling in the gaps.

<Rennie>: Is Dr. Piccolo as good or as bad as people say he is?

<Jay>: He is a brilliant academician who tries to make things work in the real world. Most of our peers don't spend as much time creating real things as he does, and that detracts from his theorizing.

Real world people don't respect us because we spend time evaluating what they did or what they plan to do. They believe that keeping track of such things is a waste of time, especially since they feel that many things are better forgotten.

<Rennie>: You could either do something real, or go back and teach.

<Jay>: Teaching is real, and we will teach if we must. For the time being, we're making almost as much money as we could make on the A-circuit of pontificators. I also believe we add value.

<Dan>: Of course, we add value. Daxiao's people no longer trip over themselves accidentally. They trip on purpose.

<Sharf>: What are you two looking at?

<Jay>: How tall are you?

<Sharf>: Six feet and six inches, and I never played basketball.

<Jay>: You're only an inch taller than Marshall is! He never appeared that tall.

<Dan>: That's because he acts short around short people.

Though we are in the middle of a comedy of errors, we will not have any Mutt and Jeff jokes today. We were going to discuss WFSOA maturity. Jay, it's your turn.

<Sharf>: ***The comic strip characters. I'm a joke to Van Amberg. He'll pay for that too.***

MATURITY MODEL, RISK, STRATEGY OPTIONS ©

<Jay>: Most vendors, books, and magazines imply that a suitable SOA strategy should start with simple Web Services (low hanging fruit) and progress until companies are exchanging services with external partners.

For others, the path is from individual services controlled by the technology departments to on-demand processes controlled by the business.

We are convinced that neither of the above captures the essence of what is happening in the real world. After the "test the waters" and "low hanging fruit" Web services, companies may wish to move into deep water quickly, without knowing water depth, temperature, wave height, or underwater risk. Daxiao was among those companies, but Dan and Mr. Marshall helped us to survive our major misadventures.

We started by defining SOA/SOE maturity in a way that agrees with SOA reality within Daxiao. WFSOA recommends that SOA maturity involves positioning along three maturity continua (business, technology, and procedural) with additional positioning determined by two scope parameters (service coverage and process coverage). Then we used the WFSOA maturity model to aid selection of SOA strategy options.

Table 21 demonstrates what a practical classification would be.

Table 21 - WFSOA Maturity Continua and Program Scope				
Description of Maturity Continuum			**Result at Maturity**	**Guided By**
Business maturity: ♦ Limited = Misalignment of business strategy and technology, low technical and SOA governance, no shared knowledge base, and hostile relationships: business/business, business/technology, and technology/technology. ♦ Moderate = Business and data models complete. A cultural change management program is initiated. Common terminology libraries are available for use. ♦ High = Continuous synchronization of business strategy with technology is enabled by high business participation, strong governance structures and a wide information base.			**EA**	**Corporate Governance**
►►Limited►►►	►►Moderate►►	►►►High►►►►		
Technology maturity: ♦ Limited = Simple services on a single server supporting business silos. ♦ Moderate = Core services defined. Application and service refactoring in progress. Enterprise Application Integration expanding. Secured single sign-on works. ♦ High = Composite services and data consolidation or secured and monitored data virtualization services spanning multiple devices and platforms over an enterprise service bus that supports multiple business units.			**SOA**	**IT Governance**
►►Limited►►►	►►Moderate►►	►►►High►►►►		
Service Scope: The proportion of service candidates that are accessible as services				
►►Limited►►►	►►Moderate►►	►►►High►►►►		
Procedural Maturity: ♦ Limited = Manual process control and manual functions. ♦ Moderate = Process automation controlled by technology. Research and development activities funded, including lessons learned from manufacturing process automation. ♦ High = Automated processes with choreographed services supporting business and technology are controlled by clients using externalized business rules.			**SOE**	**SOA Governance**
►►Limited►►►	►►Moderate►►	►►►High►►►►		
Process Scope: The proportion of process candidates that are automated.				
►►Limited►►►	►►Moderate►►	►►►High►►►►		

If three values are assigned to each continuum and each scope in Table 21, Daxiao could be positioned in a five-dimensional WFSOA array with 243 theoretically possible mathematical permutations. Table 22.1 shows practical (and impractical) combinations of maturity factors. The shaded combinations should not occur.

Table 22.1 also shows where units within Daxiao have been rated on these combinations of maturity factors and an average value for all of Daxiao.

Table 22.2 shows practical combinations of service and process scope.

The important points to notice are that:

1. Moderate process maturity requires at least a moderate level of technical maturity.

2. High process maturity requires high business maturity.

<Dan>: Jay, slow down. Let's start improving our communications now. Do either of you have questions?

<Sharf>: Who assesses the maturity levels?

<Dan>: Infrastructure Architecture (technology), Requirements Management (process), and Enterprise Integration (business). Acton verifies the maturity assignments.

<Rennie>: Where does BASE fit?

<Jay>: They maintain the information that is used to support the assessments.

<Sharf>: Do units stay in the same place?

<Jay>: During the four-year period that we've been doing this, some units move one maturity level each year, *except for the Manufacturing and Operations people who stayed in place this year (and Gunnar who moved in the wrong direction this year).*

<Dan>: *Gunnar is going backwards. That's enough to send him after Macedon, Acton and me. It took him two months to prepare his big guns.*

[...] *If H was a naïve as he acts, Sharf would be sitting in his oversized chair in two months and helping Gunnar into Justin's chair.*

[...] *H's chair will be empty anyhow, but we must keep Sharf out of it.*

Table 22.1 WFSOA Practical Combinations of Maturity Factors		
Limited business Maturity	Limited technical maturity	Limited Process Maturity
Limited business Maturity	Limited technical maturity	Moderate Process Maturity
Limited business Maturity	Limited technical maturity	High Process Maturity
Limited business Maturity	Moderate technical maturity	Limited Process Maturity
Limited business Maturity	Moderate technical maturity	Moderate Process Maturity
Limited business Maturity	Moderate technical maturity	High Process Maturity
Limited business Maturity	High technical maturity	Limited Process Maturity
Limited business Maturity	High technical maturity	Moderate Process Maturity
Limited business Maturity	High technical maturity	High Process Maturity
Moderate business Maturity	Limited technical maturity	Limited Process Maturity
Moderate business Maturity	Limited technical maturity	Moderate Process Maturity
Moderate business Maturity	Limited technical maturity	High Process Maturity
Moderate business Maturity	Moderate technical maturity	Limited Process Maturity
Moderate business Maturity ***(Operations)*** ***(Manufacturing)*** ***(Sales & Marketing)***	Moderate technical maturity	Moderate Process Maturity
Moderate business Maturity	Moderate technical maturity	High Process Maturity
Moderate business Maturity	High technical maturity	Limited Process Maturity
Moderate business Maturity ***(Data Center)*** ***(Daxiao - the entire organization)***	High technical maturity	Moderate Process Maturity
Moderate business Maturity	High technical maturity	High Process Maturity
High business Maturity	Limited technical maturity	Limited Process Maturity
High business Maturity	Limited technical maturity	Moderate Process Maturity
High business Maturity	Limited technical maturity	High Process Maturity
High business Maturity	Moderate technical maturity	Limited Process Maturity

Table 22.1 WFSOA Practical Combinations of Maturity Factors		
High business Maturity ***(Human Resources)***	Moderate technical maturity	Moderate Process Maturity
High business Maturity	Moderate technical maturity	High Process Maturity
High business Maturity	High technical maturity	Limited Process Maturity
High business Maturity ***(Data Management)*** ***(Financial Management)*** ***(Infrastructure Architecture)*** ***(Product Delivery)***	High technical maturity	Moderate Process Maturity
High business Maturity ***(BASE sector)*** ***(Enterprise Integration)*** ***(Requirements Management)*** ***(Security Management)*** ***(Research & Development)***	High technical maturity	High Process Maturity

Table 22.2 - Practical Combinations of Service and Process Scope		
Limited Service/Limited Process	Limited Service/Moderate Process	Limited Service/High Process
Moderate Service/Limited Process	Moderate Service/ Moderate Process	Moderate Service/High Process
High Service/Limited Process	High Service/Moderate process	High Service/High Process

<Jay>: Fig. 19.1 illustrates what we believe to be the optimal approach to a service-oriented enterprise. Business maturity facilitates approval of necessary processes for achieving technical maturity. The most critical considerations are data governance and data quality.

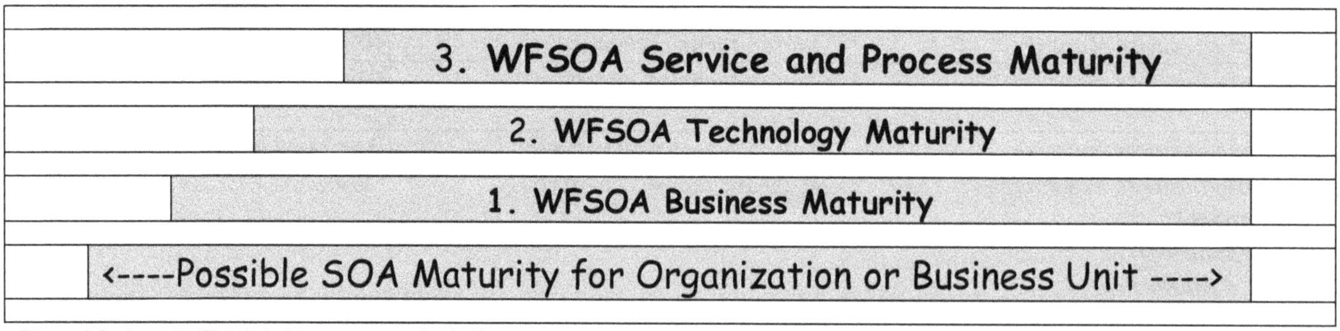

3. WFSOA Service and Process Maturity

2. WFSOA Technology Maturity

1. WFSOA Business Maturity

<----Possible SOA Maturity for Organization or Business Unit ---->

Fig. 19.1 - WFSOA Recommended Maturity Staircase

Of course, that was not how they did it in Daxiao. The notes say that H and Hank explained that Daxiao looked like Fig. 19.2 when Armstrong had his SOA "crash and burn". Business maturity was improving due to SOX and a few BASE stealth projects, but Weldon was running ahead of us.

<Sharf>: You mean Marshall was sneaking things in without telling anyone.

<Jay>: He always tells everyone exactly what he is doing in voluminous detail. He also tells us why. The thing is that he usually builds a little deeper and wider that most of us understand.

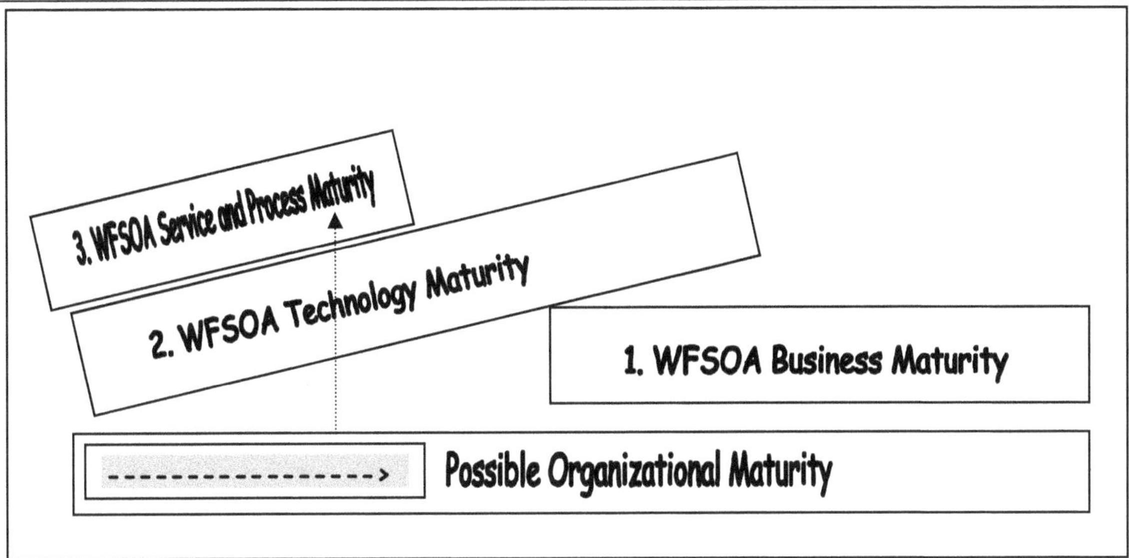

Fig. 19.2 - WFSOA Maturity Limitation before WFSOA

<Sharf>: He's gold plating. How much money does he waste on that? *I caught him in something else!*

<Jay>: Every time somebody, usually Armstrong, tried to prove it, Marshall pointed to a sudden reduction in a problem queue or a surprising number of items on the work backlog that are no longer necessary. We seem to realize three to ten times ROI when he gold plates.

<Sharf>: It is an area of investigation. Daxiao should not depend on Marshall's surprise bags.

<Dan>: Jay, please put it on our list. I will pull the numbers for all those ROI calculations.

Sharf finally said something right. We need to find a pattern to how H's mind works.

<Jay>: Let's return to the maturity discussion. Fig. 19.3 visualizes Daxiao's current maturity. You can see that business maturity is the limiting factor.

<Dan>: *That's not all that Marshal does. His people stand in front of other things that he thinks we need, Weldon figures out what H is "hiding" and takes what he wants, Weldon does the selling and the bungling, while H has the fix ready before he lets Weldon take it in the first place. HM must be doing that on purpose.*

H said I still needed "Research" on my academic résumé. I wonder if he played on my ego to convince me to take Research from Gunnar, so his Competency Team would have more control. That was his way of taking Li back.

He's the most devious one here, or perhaps it's H, Maja, and Machi together.

If he dies, Maja won't tolerate as much of my egotistical oddities as he does. I'll be dried up here in six months and back in an office in a musty academic basement in a year.

<Jay>: Dan. Would you like to join us?

<Dan>: *How did I miss that?*

<Jay>: These illustrations were your idea.

<Dan>: I was still back at the surprise bags. Sharf showed me something else.

<Sharf>: That's my job. Would you be kind enough to share?

<Dan>: In simplest terms, I'd say we have to see how to fit our Research and Partner Network activities into the maturity structure.

<Sharf>: *Not if I can help it.*

<Jay>: They already are. They are covered under "Challenging" projects. That comes later?

<Dan>: "Absent-minded professor" strikes again.

<Sharf>: What challenges are you discussing?

<Jay>: You'll see in a moment.

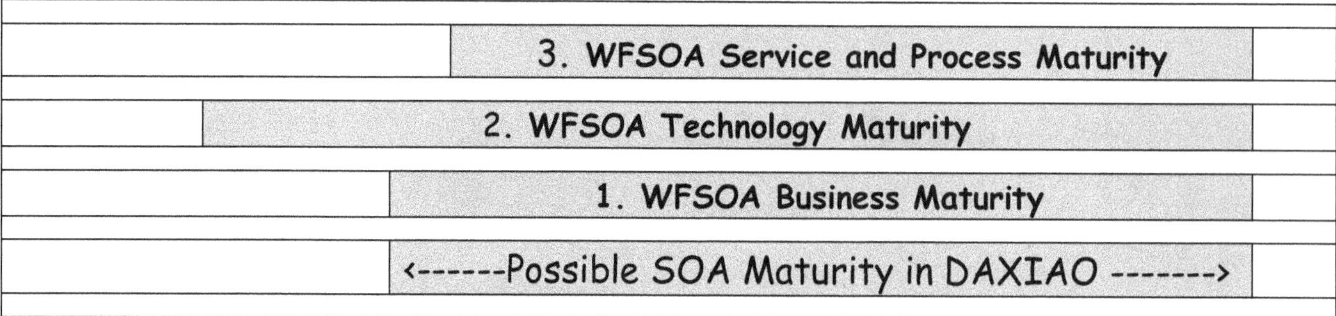

Fig. 19.3 - WFSOA Current Maturity Staircase

<Rennie>: *Something else happened. He flicked Will's nose, so he wouldn't notice.* I'd like to go back to Table 22.1. If the manufacturing people were the process experts, why did they land in the moderate group?

<Jay>: After we learned workflow and process automation from them, the research teams started finding better ideas, and we started running into resistance. The same goes for operations. Job security is a major issue, as we reported in the resistance table. I believe it's in [...]

<Sharf>: Table A.3. How long did it take you to figure out the maturity model?

<Jay>: It's been evolving since Armstrong forced Marshall into SOA. We demonstrated how business glitches can hinder technology in general and WFSOA specifically. The first example was the reorganization that left the first version of SOA without a sponsor. If we pull the technology too far out, it could tilt again.

<Sharf>: Why is Gunnar positioned as he is in Table 22.1?

<Jay>: He is with the bulk of WFSOA Program non-participants, by number. By action:

1. He is the least likely to cooperate with strategy management.
2. He is less likely to allow us to convert his critical applications to services.
3. They avoid our planning processes whenever possible.
4. His people are the least likely to conform to the customer relationship processes that Barca defined. They have their favorites, and they always respond to them first, even if the problem is the positioning of labels on a shipping carton.
5. They use information from the Knowledge Cooperative, but they are not forthcoming with their client lists or marketing techniques.
6. They insist on using mobile devices from vendors that we no longer favor.

Don't bother to run over and tell him this. Acton discussed it with him in detail during an audit committee meeting.

<Sharf>: I wouldn't give Grayson my sales book. *Gunnar sucked me into his problem. That's OK. I got a clear shot at Marshall.*

<Jay>: That whole sales book thing is an unfortunate historical remnant. If he let us know what he was doing, he wouldn't be embarrassed by making a cold call to subsidiary of an organization with which we already have a partner relationship.

<Sharf>: *It would save me the same kind of embarrassment.* If the bulk of your people are only half way into SOA, why was Marshall so sure he would be able to achieve a critical mass before he retired?

<Dan>: H mentioned that 35% of our processing is handled by services. We believe that the existing services could handle between 45% and 55% if more people cooperated.

Furthermore, every team is at least at the middle level of maturity, and a few critical units are near the top.

The endpoint for a business unit occurs when it has achieved a maximum value in three maturity continua and both scope parameters.

<Rennie>: How do you move from five dimensions to two or three?

<Jay>: Look at Tables 23.1 through 23.3 (Strategy Options and SOA Risk). We collapsed practical combinations of business, technical, and process maturity into one cell and then applied practical options for process and service scope.

The business maturity continuum was used to segment the combinations into strategy options.

The result is a set of strategy and risk recommendations. For example, in the WFSOA model, it would be difficult to have moderate or high process coverage if there are a limited or moderate number of services to be incorporated into processes.

Table 23.1 - Strategy Options and SOA Risk at Business Maturity Level 1

Key: BM = Business Maturity
TM = Technical Maturity
PM = Process Maturity

Scope ►►►	Limited Service Coverage Limited Process Coverage	Moderate Service Coverage Limited Process Coverage	Moderate Service Coverage Moderate Process Coverage	High Service Coverage Limited Process Coverage	High Service Coverage Moderate Process Coverage	High Service Coverage High Process Coverage
	Strategy Options - Business Maturity Level 1					
▼ Maturity ▼						
Limited BM Limited TM Limited PM	Safe	Safe	Impractical	Impractical	Impractical	Impractical
Limited BM Moderate TM Limited PM	Safe	Safe	Impractical	Impractical	Impractical	Impractical
Limited BM High TM Limited PM	Safe	Safe	Challenging	Risky	Impractical	Impractical
Limited BM High TM Moderate PM	Safe	Safe	Challenging	Risky	Impractical	Impractical

Readers: ***IMPORTANT NOTE:*** The result **is not** a straight-line continuum. Instead, there are relatively safe strategy options, areas of challenge, areas of risk, and options that are almost doomed to fail. Using these tables, SOA strategy management becomes less of an art - it is a matter of selecting the culturally and financially acceptable alternatives within the practical options.

Table 23.2 - Strategy Options and SOA Risk at Business Maturity Level 2

Scope ►►►	Limited Service Coverage Limited Process Coverage	Moderate Service Coverage Limited Process Coverage	Moderate Service Coverage Moderate Process Coverage	High Service Coverage Limited Process Coverage	High Service Coverage Moderate Process Coverage	High Service Coverage High Process Coverage
	Strategy Options - Business Maturity Level 2					
▼ Maturity ▼						
Moderate BM Limited TM Limited PM	Safe	Safe	Impractical	Impractical	Impractical	Impractical
Moderate BM High TM Limited PM	Safe	Safe	Safe	Challenging	Impractical	Impractical
Moderate BM Moderate TM Limited PM	Safe	Safe	Safe	Challenging	Risky	Impractical
Moderate BM Moderate TM Moderate PM	Safe	Safe	Safe	Safe	Challenging	Impractical
Moderate BM High TM Moderate PM	Safe	Safe	Safe	Safe	Challenging	Risky

Table 23.3 - Strategy Options and SOA Risk at Business Maturity Level 3 & 4

Scope ►►►	Limited Service Coverage Limited Process Coverage	Moderate Service Coverage Limited Process Coverage	Moderate Service Coverage Moderate Process Coverage	High Service Coverage Limited Process Coverage	High Service Coverage Moderate Process Coverage	High Service Coverage High Process Coverage
	Strategy Options - Business Maturity Level 3					
▼ Maturity ▼						
High BM Limited TM Limited PM	Safe	Safe	Challenging	Risky	Impractical	Impractical
High BM Moderate TM Limited PM	Safe	Safe	Challenging	Risky	Impractical	Impractical
High BM Moderate TM Moderate PM	Safe	Safe	Safe	Challenging	Risky	Impractical
High BM High TM Limited PM	Safe	Safe	Safe	Safe	Challenging	Risky
High BM High TM Moderate PM	Safe	Safe	Safe	Safe	Safe	Challenging
High BM High TM High PM	Safe	Safe	Safe	Safe	Safe	Safe (Level 4)

In total, the three tables show:

1. Forty-six (46) safe strategy options - Average performance by Program personnel should deliver specified products within the allotted time and within budget.
2. Eleven (11) challenging strategy options - These options support healthy growth with opportunity for learning by project participants. They must stretch their abilities to achieve the desired results within the allotted time and within budget. There is a small project premium.
3. Eight (8) risky strategy options - There could be significant problems even with superior performance. There is only at 50/50 chance that the project teams will be able to deliver as originally planned. There are large project premiums. Many of them would be treated as research.
4. Twenty-seven (27) would be impractical. They should always be treated as research and development projects.

External Links and SOA Maturity

NOTE: External SOA (links with business partners) is no longer a major determinant in either maturity or coverage. Actually, it never was a determinant in Daxiao. While it is better to have an intermediate level of technical maturity before external links are attempted (excellent security management is paramount), a company may have low business readiness, low process maturity, limited service coverage, and limited process coverage and still have external SOA links.

<Sharf>: How do you explain the ability to build external links without high maturity?

<Dan>: Many of these are green field projects. We're creating new things to eliminate pain points. Therefore:

1. We have more cooperation.
2. Fewer people are worried about losing their jobs.
3. The new technology is fun.
4. It provides major input to our training program and Knowledge Cooperative.
5. We benefit from our partners' lessons learned.
6. There are well-defined industry standards and metadata definitions to support information exchange.

<Rennie>: *I've been trying to explain that to him from the time that I joined Belvedere.*

<Sharf>: Keep going. *Rene tried to hide the "I told you so" look, but I saw it.*

Maturity Model and Feasibility Studies

<Rennie>: I can see how this would be applied to entire business units and to derive an organizational average. Do you use this for individual projects?

<Dan>: Definitely. Macedon's people have a scaled down version that is used in feasibility studies.

<Rennie>: I'll bet it's fascinating. Could you give us a copy?

<Dan>: Ask Macedon whenever you're scheduled to see him, or ask Armstrong.

Security - Again

<Sharf>: Do you have guest passwords for us as Marshall did yesterday? Rennie could find it.

<Dan>: It never occurred to me. People that I meet don't usually ask for passwords. *If Justin has his way, you will never touch another Daxiao keyboard.*

<Sharf>: Can we use one of your terminals?

<Dan>: *Impossible!* Global Security reports to me. I have access to the world. I should not go to the bathroom without shutting everything down, unless Jay is here of course. He knows more about the strategy than I do.

<Sharf>: Where is Bailey? We may as well take care of this.

<Dan>: Bailey is in Mexico.

<Jay>: Let me finish with the maturity model, and then I have to run.

<Sharf>: I have to provide Mittelman with a revised SOA strategy document by the middle of next week, and to do that, Rennie will need access to the Knowledge Center.

<Dan>: Let me call Dr. Emery-Baldwin.

<Sharf>: I spoke to her already.

<Dan>: She can get you through official channels faster than anyone in Daxiao can. Continue Jay.

Challenge and SOA Growth

<Jay>: Most of our people play in the challenge area. So, for example, if Financial Management is High Business, High Technical, and Moderate Process Maturity, they have accepted the challenge of having financial functions converted to services, and they are aiming for High Process coverage. They will succeed because so many of their domain owners were among our best technical managers. They also tend to be conservative, and that supports Lorrie's worldview.

Am I finished?

<Sharf>: I will have questions and suggestions for improvement after I have a chance to review this. Where can I reach you?

<Jay>: Everything's is on my Web site. Look for JSJMANAGEMENT.COM. Here's my card.

<Dan>: Thanks for rescheduling. I'll talk to you later. *He did well, but I don't think he lost Rennie.*

<Rennie>: I can't believe you people have all this information so well structured, and nobody knows about it.

<Dan>: All our people know about it, and half deal with some aspects of it every day. The problem is that Gunnar and Justin were starting to feel left out. William should be able to show us how to straighten this out in no time at all. I can tell that about him.

<Sharf>: I'm sure I can. *Something is wrong, and I can't put my finger on it.*

<Dan>: We will give you the information you need to assist the straightening, but now there are biological necessities. Everything you'll need is near the reception area, including heart healthy snacks.

If you like, the employee cafeteria is on the third floor. Their products are more lethal, and they are open until 11:00 o'clock.

Anyway, we can't proceed until Aaron Forte arrives.

<Rennie>: Who is that?

<Dan>: I am becoming slow in my middle years. The man responsible for technology security is supposed to be here in 13 minutes if he isn't tied up chasing something malicious. He will be discussing role-based accessed. Hank was going to cover that yesterday, and it is crucial to your understanding of WFSOA processes.

He can talk about encryption and XML signatures in ways that would delight the heart, but today he's will discuss UDDI/ebXML catalogs. It would have been more fun if Maja had hung around (she created the data virtualization services), but Rennie can talk to her later.

If you make it back in 20 minutes, we should still have enough time.

<Sharf>: You can't just [...]

<Dan>: Twenty minutes.

CHAPTER VIII - PERSONAL CHECKPOINT

Dan>: Higgs, did Gunnar check in yet?

<Higgs>: You're out of breath.

<Dan>: I was having trouble breathing in my office. What about Gunnar?

<Higgs>: He called and he didn't have much to say. He listened while Justin arranged to meet him at his new location in New York.

<Dan>: I need to borrow a phone.

<Higgs>: Use the conference room.

---------- ----------

<Dan>: Liz, have you heard anything about H?

<Lisse Maçon>: I spoke to Jonas a few minutes ago. They can't remove the breathing tube from his throat.

<Dan>: How could that happen?

<Liz>: His throat closed around it. It happens sometimes.

<Dan>: How's Indy taking that?

<Liz>: Nobody told her yet. Jonas added the straw that broke the camel's back, and now he's trying to carry more of the load himself.

<Dan>: Maja told me about that. What do we do next?

<Liz>: They give HM something to reduce the swelling, and then they try again.

<Dan>: How is H dealing with this?

<Liz>: Jonas says that when he is alert, he is extremely agitated.

<Dan>: How is Machi taking it?

<Liz>: She's still dealing with the femur replacement. She was here and when she left, the building was still standing, but his office is wrecked. Ernest says she did about $10,000 worth of damage, picked up a big yellow envelope and left.

<Dan>: I guess the sedative wore off.

<Liz>: She's awake and deadly. She was quiet, but you could feel a hot breeze when she went by.

<Dan>: Where are the twins?

<Liz>: They may be over Labrador in different planes.

<Dan>: I have less than two hours left on my sentence with Mutt, and then I fly to New York with Justin. I'll meet you at the hospital.

[...] What's that noise?

<Liz>: Octavia threw something at Tomaso. Anita couldn't make it today either.

<Dan>: I see. OK, I'll meet you at the office after I see H.

---------- ----------

<Dan>: Did you catch Maja before she messed something up?

<Val>: Yes. The further she was from Sharf, the calmer she became. You are quite devious. I believe she added to the reality. When are you going to send me my jacket?

<Dan>: I'm flying in with Justin to see H. I'll bring it with me.

<Val>: Justin is coming to see H? Why?

<Dan>: The numbers that Gunnar gave Sharf definitely have Justin's attention. I don't believe he realized that anyone who does not work in sales could make that much of a difference.

<Val>: Did you warn Justin about the health hazards? I'd like to keep using the other eye.

<Dan>: Oswald is coming with us.

<Val>: Did Jay dazzle or baffle?

<Dan>: He dazzled Rennie and baffled Mutt. Sharf is definitely listing to starboard. I can't believe he survived, especially at Belvedere, if he was as uniquely hostile as he appears. We're missing something.

<Val>: Machi and Indy become tense when you mention him, even beyond what he did yesterday. I will talk to them later.

<Dan>: Let's continue this in person. I'll see you around 3:30, I guess.

<Val>: I should be able to make it across town by then.

<Dan>: Wait [...] Machi stormed into H office and retrieved a big yellow envelope.

[...] Confirm for me what it is that she would leave the hospital to retrieve.

<Val>: I'd guess it would be a copy of his contract. The office was closer than the safe in River Glen, although there isn't much left of the office now.

<Dan>: That's what I thought. She told Justin that as soon as the doctors took the tube out of H's throat, they would discuss how H would stop helping him to become richer.

<Val>: We are not surprised.

<Dan>: We are also not ready.

<Val>: You're starting to sound as cold as Justin does.

<Dan>: It's all in the family. Please excuse me.

---------- ----------

<Rennie>: What are you looking for?

<Sharf>: I want to see if there is anything in here about Marshall. Check this for me. Look in the financial section too. Mittelman is very particular about that.

<Rennie>: What is newsworthy about someone tripping over a desk drawer?

<Lillian Simpson>: You are Sharf right?

<Sharf>: Yes. I am William Sharf from Belvedere and this is Renata Vitale my associate.

<Lillian>: ***He looks pretty, not crazy like the Doc says he is.*** I've been researching Mr. Marshall's situation for Mr. Ellison all morning. The most that I can find, fortunately, is an entry on a second-tier news feed. It says that Mr. Marshall had to be rushed to the hospital, he narrowly avoided having his leg amputated, Mr. Van Amberg and Mr. Gunnar were injured in the rush to get him to the hospital (he's not as heavy as he used to be, but he's still big), and two policemen received bruises from undetermined sources. It may be that one of the units smashed into the other trying to rush them through traffic. If that's the case, they were probably too embarrassed to provide details. Two reporters were injured slightly, but were released by 11 o'clock.

<Sharf>: Is that all?

<Lillian>: It has all that schmoozie stuff about how he's sure to recover with the support of beloved family members and friends who will be by his side until he gets back on his feet ***(literally).***

There's one other thing that they thought was unusual, but isn't the least bit surprising to me. It seems that by eleven o'clock last night, he already had "get well" stuff from at least 14 different people. He couldn't have anything in recovery, so the nursing station was swamped until they could clean out a supply shelf and load the flowers into it.

Someone even sent him a case of Twinkies. He was crazy about Twinkies. We used to keep them for him until he started losing weight.

<Rennie>: How much weight did he lose?

<Lillian>: He lost over 90 pounds. He was in the best shape he's been in for years, even with his leg acting up. Nicky said he was as frisky as [...] I'm talking too much.

<Rennie>: I told you he didn't look that big. ***They arrived. Good! If he can't eat them, I hope he appreciates the thought.***

<Lillian>: Why do you look surprised? He was everybody's big brother, substitute father, or rich uncle. I know two families who would have lost their homes if it hadn't been for him. ***I'm one of them.*** I can't tell you how many people still have jobs because of him, even if it is outside of Daxiao.

<Rennie>: William, where are you going?

<Sharf>: I need coffee before the cafeteria closes. ***Why is it that I'm the only one who sees him for what he really is? I'd better call Gunnar after all.***

<Lillian>: The caterers brought down a fresh urn. The chef sent Dr. Piccolo's favorite selection of healthy fruit and unhealthy sweets. You are welcome to serve yourself.

<Sharf>: What chef?

<Lillian>: The one from the executive dining room. It's right above us.

<Sharf>: Save some for me. I need fresh air too.

---------- ----------

<Sharf>: Gunnar, I'm sorry it took so long to get back to you. I tried all your phones last night, but you weren't answering.

<Gunnar>: I left messages this morning. ***I really played this incorrectly.***

<Sharf>: I was out early taking care of things for you while you were playing games with the Marshall clan. Did you see my report?

> **Readers**: Remember that Gunnar's jaw is very swollen, he has stitches in his gum, and he sounds worse than he did yesterday. He sounds so bad, in fact, that we will translate his speech back into normal English orthography.

<Gunnar>: **Reading** now.

<Sharf>: You sound strange. I hear you had a run-in with the old witch.

<Gunnar>: ***Where did you find this?***

<Sharf>: You should be thrilled. While he's down, let's make sure he is out. He was almost running Daxiao, and we will control everything that he controlled. Get me positioned, and I will be able to handle his entire team. After Belvedere takes over from Acton, I will be a partner.

<Gunnar>: What would you do if you had Marshall's job?

<Sharf>: I have almost everything that I need to create an action plan. Half of what they do can be cut, renamed, and reintroduced when you are ready. I need a few more details to understand where to cut.

<Gunnar>: ***What would happen if you annoyed me, I left, and you and your cronies or Sharf forced Dan and Val to do the wrong thing, because you don't know what to do?*** [...] He can see the future!

<Sharf>: You bet I can. I also have proof that Marshall was using Daxiao funds without proper approval. I will talk to Jasper before I let you in on that. We will talk about the drugs and the booze when I see you tomorrow.

<Gunnar>: Slow down. It was ginger! ***If Marshall's family hears about this, they will own Daxiao, and Indy will never speak to me. Indy - where did that come from?***

<Sharf>: You don't really want me to slow down. You'll be sitting in Mittelman's chair in no time if you call someone who can give me access to Daxiao's Knowledge Center. Marshall's people are running from me, and I'm starting to feel strange about Piccolo.

<Gunnar>: Listen!

<Sharf>: I am listening, but make it quick. You sound worse than Marshall looked.

<Gunnar>: ***When did he lose his mind?***

1. Stay with Piccolo. ***I need to know where you are.***
2. Stay away from Lorrie! ***I have to check these numbers with her first. I can't believe Marshall had that much money to give away. He puts a new definition to buying favors.***
3. Go softer on the communications. They have a program that we need to look at.
4. If they start moving their hands, they are [...]

<Sharf>: This is taking too long. I'm about to hand you more than you ever wanted.

<Gunnar>: ***You already handed me more than you could ever imagine.*** On second thought, leave now. We can cut losses.

<Sharf>: ***No.*** I've waited over 20 years for this and nothing will do stop me. ***I will find a way to destroy the Marshall without you, and I will stop catching the scraps from your table too. I will own the table.***

<Gunnar>: What happened 20 years ago?

<Sharf>: The order of things is about to change. I want you moving walls for me, not building them. Make sure you make the right moves when I need you to move.

<Gunnar>: ***I need to talk to Mags before he goes completely over the edge!*** I have to go.

<Sharf>: ***He hung up on me! I'll keep pumping Piccolo for information. Gunnar will be surprised at how much I know when I see him.***

---------- ----------

<Gunnar>: Mags, its Andy. Are you OK?

<Margaret Gunther Sharf>: Why do you ask? You sound funny.

<Gunnar>: Dental work. You talk.

<Mags>: I'm in a good mood today. William was floating on air last night. He says that the assignment you helped him to land will solve our financial problems.

<Gunnar>: *He wouldn't have financial problems if you didn't listen to your mother.* Clay, Teddy?

<Mags>: Both want us to expand their credit card limits - again. I said they need better grades.

<Gunnar>: Take a vacation, on me.

<Mags>: William will do be busy for some time. He says that within a year, we'll be able to travel to wherever we want and stay as long as we want.

<Gunnar>: Come and see me [...] Alone. James will pick you up in 45 minutes.

<Mags>: You sound desperate.

<Gunnar>: Need little sister. Come to Hotel Pietro. Use my account.

<Mags>: *His favorite trysting spot.* I'll call Will.

<Gunnar>: No! Leave now! I'll explain later. Meet you [...] 1:00 o'clock. Pietro [...]

<Mags>: What could be this bad?

<Gunnar>: Answer in New York.

---------- ----------

<Gunnar>: Marcella [...] Gunnar.

<Marcella Haines>: Mr. Gunnar, you do sound bad.

<Gunnar>: Check e-mail.

To: Boardlist@Daxiao.com; JMittelman@Daxiao.com; MHiggins@Daxiao.com; Marcella_Haines@Daxiao.com
From: Niklas_Gunnar@Daxiao.com
CC: VVanAmberg@Daxiao.com; LDawson@Daxiao.com; DPiccolo@Daxiao.com; VJohnson@Daxiao.com; Emery-Baldwin@Daxiao.com ; LJasper@Daxiao.com; WLi004@Daxiao.com
Subj: Status Update - Hamilton Marshall

To follow up on your queries, Mr. Marshall is doing as well as can be expected under the circumstances, and we are hopeful for a good recovery. When I left the hospital this morning, he was in stable condition. He had been taking care of himself and was in excellent physical shape before the accident. His family expresses gratitude for our support.

I am in satisfactory condition. However, I will be speaking with difficulty for a few days due to an unfortunate accident that occurred while assisting Mr. Marshall and his family. The orthodontist says that the damage can be corrected.

Meanwhile, my team is still out there closing sales. I predict that we will continue to exceed quotas.

For the people who called to ask about the communication that they received from the Belvedere consulting team, please note that the candidate selection process is being revisited with senior management at Belvedere. A clarification document will be in their hands by tomorrow afternoon.

I can be reached on Jack Laufer's line in New York today, and I will be in the New Jersey office tomorrow.

Thank you.
Niklas Gunnar, EVP.
Global Sales & Marketing

<Marcella>: How bad is it? I have calls from half a dozen Board members.

<Gunnar>: ***I said check e-mail!*** *I never have to yell. Why did I yell?*

<Marcella>: All right, sir. *He's meaner than ever.*

[...] I read it. Is there anything else you would like me to handle for you?

<Gunnar>: Quick answer. Find my ***Thunk*** password and call me.

<Marcella>: I can give it to you now if you want it.

<Gunnar>: How would you know it?

<Marcella>: Your ***Thunk*** password is your Knowledge Cooperative password, and I have to use it to respond to your "quick answer" questions. *If it wasn't for that, you'd have fired me by now.*

<Gunnar>: Give!

<Marcella>: It's ANGHelena, one word, with the first four letters in uppercase.

<Gunnar>: Why Helena and not Kerstin.

<Marcella>: Your salesmen do it sir. They can explain it better than I can.

<Gunnar>: In case I need more "quick answers", is Higgs your backup today?

<Marcella>: No. She's concentrating on something crucial related to Mr. Marshall. Jack's secretary is my backup today.

<Gunnar>: Find out what they are doing.

<Marcella>: I tried. She said that they are trying to keep us from getting sued and perhaps losing billions. I was hoping you could tell me what's happening. It's strange and lonesome here today.

<Gunnar>: *Freeze out. Marshall is pulling me into the grave with him.* I'll handle everything from here. Things will be normal tomorrow.

---------- **Dan Piccolo's Office** ----------

<Dan>: You found the chef's platter. Where is William?

<Rennie>: He said he needed fresh air.

<Dan>: While we're waiting, meet Aaron Forte. This is Renata Vitale from Belvedere.

<Rennie>: How do you people magically appear?

<Aaron Forte>: I took the secret entrance.

[...] I'm serious. Look behind those racks.

<Rennie>: I'm starting to sound like Will.

<Dan>: Impossible.

<Aaron>: Hello, and welcome aboard. Dan seems to like you. You passed the IQ test and the EQ test. We look forward to working with you.

<Dan>: He means that I said you know how to ask the right questions. I also want to thank you for helping us direct William's attention.

<Rennie>: Do you have any further word about Mr. Marshall or his daughter?

<Dan>: She caved under the pressure of yesterday's decisions, but she should be better after she rests. So will her father.

Meanwhile, Aaron will deliver the remainder of today's presentation. I had to call him on short notice, so I apologize on his behalf for any gaps in his presentation.

<Aaron>: Who says there are going to be gaps? I didn't create this thing, but I made it better. In case there might be something that I forgot, every single item has reams of notes underneath it.

<Dan>: If necessary, you will swallow your pride and call Hank or Maja for reinforcement.

<Aaron>: Speaking of Maja, I saw her running out of the building. She said you'd understand what we said even better if your brain had more oxygen. She said I should find these for you. We can't do anything about the shoes.

<Dan>: Are you trying to get us sued?

<Aaron>: I agree with Maja.

<Dan>: Please excuse us Ms. Vitale. We try to take the edges off, but it takes longer with some people than others. Let me take those.

<Rennie>: First, you have no one who can compete in roughness with my associate? I've never seen him like this. Please accept my apologies on behalf of Mr. Cane.

Second, I prefer those to Bergman, and the size is right. It is also more appropriate to your casual environment. I'll be back.

<Dan>: That hall is shorter. Half way down is a nursery/lounge. Next door to that is a storage room with Express Mail boxes and printed mailing labels that you may use to return the outfit.

---------- ----------

<Aaron>: On first impression, she'll be all right. Who else has seen her?

<Dan>: It was Marshall's idea to pay attention. I'll explain later. Val likes her, but you can't trust his impressions. She's a dead ringer (*that was crass*) for his deceased wife and for his very alive daughter. She passed Hank's assessment, and most important, Maja is sharing wardrobe tips with her.

<Aaron>: How is Mr. Marshall?

<Dan>: He is still alive, and the longer he lives, the more likely it is that he will live. Tune in to Val's status update to receive the most recent information. Let's talk about the talk-about.

<Aaron>: During this conversation you want me to discuss catalog security and role-based access, the four versions of the project catalog (five if you count the archive), catalog support for service, process, and data delivery, registry support for service delivery, and how we use both UDDI and ebXML standards.

You want me to do this in less than two hours with perhaps a 10 - 15 minute break. Later today, I will define the nature of dark matter and dark energy.

<Dan>: Concentrated information is good today. Justin demands it.

Focus on Rennie. She worked on the standards committees for both the repository and the registry.

<Aaron>: Remind me to bow down to her when she comes back. What about this William person?

<Dan>: He's her boss/engagement manager.

1. First, do not mention the word "agenda". He likes serendipity.
2. He's trained as an accountant. He's acknowledged as one of the best in the industry.
3. He is theoretically the person within Belvedere who knows the most about SOX and SOA therefore he is theoretically qualified to audit all HM's responsibilities.
4. He speed-reads, and he has total recall, but he doesn't take time to integrate what he collects, or he is incapable of integrating it. I suspect that he does not work at integrating what he absorbs.
5. On a technical scale of 1 - 10, if H was 9.5 (*is 9.5, I hope*), you are 9.6, Hank is 9.8, and Maja is 9.9, then William is a 4.5.

<Aaron>: Did you just insult me?

<Dan>: You technology types are so sensitive. I figure I'm an 8. What do you think I did?

6. He thinks he's 9.9 when it comes to SOA. He may be at level 7 on LITTLE SOA.
7. With people, Belvedere rates him as a 7, but he's been acting like a -7 for reasons we are not sure about.
8. We are rather sure that he knowingly transmitted information to Ādaemoa five minutes after H and Hank specifically explained the importance of the roles and responsibilities descriptions to him.

<Aaron>: If he's the person that we pulled the video on last night, why are you bothering with him today?

<Dan>: We also want to keep him and Gunnar separated until some other actions take place.

<Aaron>: This seems quite intense.

<Dan>: Let me finish.

9. He's Gunnar's brother-in-law, and something about that which doesn't make sense. Either Gunnar knows something that we don't know, or Gunnar lost control, if he ever had control.

<Aaron>: What about Rennie?

<Dan>: Hank says she's near H in know-how and with natural people skills. We haven't figured out how creative she is yet. She reads sign language, and she speaks Spanish.

<Aaron>: She'll fit.

<Dan>: Let's return to the discussion of William. For the remainder of the day, at least, we believe he has Gunnar's ear and Justin's attention. Therefore, when he utters a Williamism, of which he seems to have an extensive repertoire, nod respectfully, smile while you nod, and keep going.

<Aaron>: Like HM does.

<Dan>: You will do it while you are wondering how often he bangs his head on a rock.

<Rennie>: I thought so. I tried to tell William, but he wouldn't listen. How do I look?

<Dan>: *I was right. There is a BIG wedge.*

<Aaron>: Whoa! You're a quick-change artist.

<Dan>: It would be appropriate for us to say that Maja would approve.

<Sharf>: What did you try to tell me?

<Rennie>: That the chef's selection was wonderful.

<Sharf>: What are you wearing?

<Rennie>: You needed fresh air. I needed to be able to concentrate.

<Sharf>: *This is a little too chummy for my liking.*

<Dan>: Don't worry about her consultant's image. That's somewhat conservative for the ladies out here. Maja uses it to "dress up" when she must.

<Sharf>: Why didn't you mention the executive area upstairs? I noticed that you have a terrace.

<Dan>: I didn't have time to sit with you, and because you're not officially onboard until next week *(I suspect never)*, I needed to avoid any embarrassment.

<Sharf>: *Maybe that makes sense.* Are you Aaron Forte?

<Aaron>: How did you know?

<Sharf>: Dan mentioned that you were coming. I'm William Benson Sharf, and I need access to certain files to accelerate my progress on this assignment. Set us up. We can start with the temporary passwords that Marshall gave us yesterday.

<Dan>: Explain the security process.

<Aaron>: We need EVP approval before we allow that. Nobody requested anything else until you start on Monday.

<Dan>: We could contact Gunnar, Armstrong, or Jasper. However, what they approve today will be ready no earlier than Monday.

<Aaron>: Gunnar and Mr. Mittelman approved a top rank security search week. When you arrive on Monday, we will give you a temporary pass and a temporary password that lasts one week. We will extend it for one week if necessary. If someone requires longer than two weeks for clearance, it probably won't happen.

<Sharf>: Wait a minute. Emery made me fill out the paperwork again!

<Aaron>: Gunnar says you're coming. You tell us you are here. Those events initiate different processes. They provide you with the papers that you sign to give us permission to do a complete background check.

<Dan>: We can't have important information leaking out. If you want, I will show you our security process flow.

<Sharf>: Emery showed me. I was checking to see if I could avoid the processes. This will be a positive check on the security part of my report.

Why do you seem more interested in things leaking out than people breaking in?

<Dan>: At this moment, Bailey, Forte, and Johanssen have a good record at intrusion prevention. The biggest loss we have suffered came from and inside leak. Though we lost several millions of dollars, none of our partners were hurt.

<Aaron>: It may be annoying, but we promised our research partners that we would always perform a double check. That and Marshall's impeccable reputation allow us to maintain our strong partner relationships.

<Dan>: With excellent partner relationships, we make money that we can use to pay Belvedere. *He has to decide whether he wants Daxiao money, or money from the partner contracts that he wants to steal from us.*

<Sharf>: *It won't be impeccable long. I will destroy Marshall and take the contracts.*

CHAPTER IX - SERVICE AND BUSINESS PROCESS MANAGEMENT IN WFSOA

Dan>: You may start on the real reason why you are here.

<Aaron>: Because there are millions of combinations of information that can be derived from the information that Daxiao has provided to Belvedere already, my humble assignment is to discuss one project that pulls together everything that we presented to you in the last 10 hours.

Therefore, I am going to discuss a **business process management project**. Table 24 shows the contents of the work request for process automation, and Table 25 provides a post-implementation review of the project, which is already running successfully in production. This information was printed directly from ReMain. They must have mentioned ReMain yesterday.

AUTOMATING WFSOA PROCESSES - SUMMARIZING ALMOST EVERYTHING

Table 24 - Automating Process Automation - Process Features	
Acceptance criteria	Required
Access	1. Through portlets. 2. Through stand-alone services.
Activity branch and merge	Supported
Activity sequencing	1. Default sequencing available. 2. Controlled modifications to default sequencing supported
Approval of process steps	Automated
Approvers	Validated against access control rules 1. Quality approvers - required. 2. Funding approvers - required. 3. Requirements Management approvers - required.
Business objective and goals	Required
Common terminology	1. Guide usage of common terminology. 2. Support for additions and corrections
Compensating activities	Required for long running services
Configuration	Variable depending on business unit requirements
Data Requirements	Captures input and output requirements for each task
Standards enforced	1. Service naming standards. 2. Process naming standards. 3. Data naming standards. 4. WSDL and B-PEL as implemented by approved vendor product.
Error messages	Enforced
Key performance indicators	1. Required. 2. Formats KPI report.
Links to	1. Access control tables. 2. Business and technical glossaries. 3. Organizational hierarchies. 4. Role descriptions. 5. Service/process catalog. 6. Strategy information. 7. List of support personnel

Logging	Enforced
Manual task definition	Supported
Modeling	1. Incorporates modeling tools (processes, use cases, data). 2. Imports preexisting models. 3. Supports process model simulation.
Multi-lingual support	1. Instructions for use are provided in English, Pinyin (Mandarin Chinese), and Spanish. 2. Requirements are captured in English, Pinyin, or Spanish. 3. Requirements are maintained in the language of capture and translated into to other major languages within one business day.
Notifications to:	1. Architects (multiple roles), data (multiple roles), data center operations, and security (multiple roles) when the scheduled task queues require attention. 2. Human resources when resource gaps occur. 3. Process coordinators if the effort requires process support, new roles, or role changes.
Request for service reuse	1. Notifications generated. 2. Approvals recorded. 3. Impact analyses recorded. 4. Capture requests for reuse of existing services'
Requirements traceability and history	Maintained
Resource assignments	Captured
Rules management	Mandatory links to rules engine.
Security	1. Secure access to project components. 2. Captures security requirements for service/process development. 3. Role-based access to automated requirements capture.
Service catalog	1. Links to UDDI registry for services metadata and discovery. 2. Links to ebXML repository for processes.
Service contract	Connection requirements captured in UDDI and WSDL.
SOAP message formats	Captured in service catalog
Supported roles: default	1. Processes: clients, users, workflow analysts, business analysts (requirements), requirements analyst, process coordinators, process specialist, compliance specialist(s), deployment specialists, security administrator, security specialists, data specialist, data administrators, user support specialist, availability architects, and service managers. 2. Services: clients, users, business analysts (requirements), requirements analyst, developers - SOA, developers - application, compliance specialist(s), deployment specialists, integration specialist, security administrator, security specialists, data specialist, data administrators, user support specialist, availability architects, service managers
Template formats	Four templates are available. 1. For capturing atomic service requests. 2. For capturing composite service requests. 3. For capturing business process requests. 4. For capturing data (only) service requests
Testing Requirements	Mandatory
Tutorial for service/process use	Captured during process creation - required
User definition:	1. Allows assignment by business/technology teams. 2. Allows assignment by business units. 3. Allows assignment by user role. 4. Allows assignment by individual

During this conversation, we will mention:

- How role-based access works.
- The four major project catalogs. The archive will be discussed if we have time.
- How the repository supports service, project, and data delivery.
- How the registry supports service and process delivery.
- How we (actually Maja) combined UDDI and ebXML standards.
- Critical links between the catalog and other Knowledge Cooperative segments.
- How the Roles/Activity list is associated with this project.
- How the catalog supports the communications model.
- Lessons we have learned.

<Sharf>: Hank is the leader of the SOA competency team. You've listed him here as a project manager.

<Aaron>: A person may have multiple roles as you know. He is also among the best business process coordinators that we have.

<Sharf>: Don't you mean technology process coordinator? This looks like a sandbox project for technologist.

<Dan>: We promote the idea that technology processes are also business processes. They are, after all, used by employees of the business.

Please, notice that 60% of the sponsors are not in the technology sector.

<Sharf>: It's beginning to make sense. ***Actually, it doesn't, but I have to humor him until I find out what's wrong with Gunnar.***

<Rennie>: Where does that fit with the maturity model that you showed us earlier?

<Aaron>: BASE, Enterprise Integration, Requirements Management, Security Management, and Research & Development are high in the three maturity factors that we measure. Because that is the case, we are ready to move to high process coverage, and move Daxiao to a service-oriented enterprise.

<Rennie>: You seem to downplay the UDDI registry.

<Dan>: We are talking about the SOA catalog that contains a UDDI compliant registry. It also supports flows for Daxiao's Product Delivery processes (SOA and legacy).

<Sharf>: How long have you had an SOA catalog?

<Dan>: The catalog was approved under the umbrella of MNA (mergers and acquisitions) six years ago. It was originally an ebXML catalog.

WFSOA Process Automation - Post-Implementation Review

Table 25 - Automating Process Automation - Post Mortem Report

Project Name	2008AutomateProcessCreation-01-RES
Business Objective	1. Allow business clients and users direct input to the process creation process. 2. Support process suggestions from "grumble" files. 3. Capture multiple instances of proposed processes as input to collaborative review processes.
Business Problems	1. Creation of new processes takes too long. 2. Adjustments to new processes take too long. 3. Process users feel they do not have enough input to process creation.
Description	Implement a pilot project that will demonstrate when Daxiao is ready to automate the process for creating processes.
Duration - Actual	27 weeks
Duration - Planned	6 months
Effort - Actual	4 person years

Table 25 - Automating Process Automation - Post Mortem Report	
Project Name	**2008AutomateProcessCreation-01-RES**
Effort - Planned	4 person years
Key Performance Indicator	With active participation, we can to move from process conceptualization to implementation within a two-week period.
Lessons Learned	1. **BPEL generation tools**: Were critical to project success. 2. **Graphical representations**: Demonstration of project concepts provided significant assistance to project participants. 3. **Process "sandbox"**: Samples of project artifacts were crucial to project success. They were particularly useful for explaining naming conventions. 4. **Process coordinators**: They find the process creator easier to use than business analysts do. 5. **Requirements analysts**: Must be permanently assigned to support the automated process creator. Otherwise, redundant processes could be created. 6. **Rollout delays**: It is difficult to begin scheduled rollouts. Clients and users do not expect work to be delivered on time. 7. **Technology understanding necessary for Business Users**: Business users will require greater understanding of technical underpinnings before they can create their own automated processes. 8. **Test cases**: Business participants required extensive assistance with the creation and execution of test cases. 9. **Timely process creation**: It is possible to create or modify processes in the designated time frame.
Modifications Requested	1. Communications and user notification tasks should be required for each new process or process change. 2. A feature for requesting modifications to existing service candidates is critical.
Primary Roles	Executives, sponsors, stakeholders, clients, users, business process coordinator, business process specialist, business analysts, and workflow analyst, business testing specialist, security specialist, security administration, project manager, tool specialist, tool administrator, requirements analyst.
Product Creation Team	SOA Competency Team members assigned.
Project Constraints	1. Until further notice, the automated process creator may only be used by units that participated in development. 2. Until further notice, no external partners may use or be parties to automated process creation. 3. Processes must use pre-existing services.
Project Goal	1. Reduce the time required to implement new business processes (includes technology processes) by 10%. 2. Reduce the time required to re-engineer processes by 10%. 3. Reduce re-engineering requirements (in stable business situations) by 20%. 4. Reduce process faults by 20%.
Project Manager	Hank Yu.
Project Risk	High.
Project Sponsors	Emery-Baldwin, Wen Li, Alex Macedon, Hamilton Marshall, Arnold Maurer.
Project Status	Accepted by two teams (Information Logistics and Security Management).
Project Type	New product creation (process).
Results	1. One new business process is being piloted and another will begin its pilot in two weeks. Both were created in two weeks. 2. Three modifications to business processes are in the pilot stage. Each modification required less than a week. 3. Two modifications to technology processes have been accepted already.
Skill Sets	1. Web services analysis, design, development, testing, and deployment. 2. Business process modeling, simulation, development, and deployment.

Table 25 - Automating Process Automation - Post Mortem Report

Project Name	2008AutomateProcessCreation-01-RES
Stakeholders	Senior Management, all Sectors
Standards Knowledge Requirement	WS-Security, WS-BPEL, WS-I, WSDL, XML, SOAP, BPMN, XML Schema, LDAP.
Status	Accepted with defined modifications.
Strategic Area	Business Process Improvement.

<Aaron>: Do you have questions?

<Rennie>: Who performs the post-implementation reviews?

<Aaron>: The project manager conducts the review.

<Rennie>: Who will maintain the process for creating processes?

<Dan>: We have three domain owners who handle WFSOA processes, one for each process domain. This process with be inherited by the Enabling domain owner, eventually.

<Rennie>: Show me the sandbox.

<Aaron>: I'd love to. Here it is [...]

<Sharf>: This is exciting, but we must move on. Rennie can come back later for this.

<Dan>: *That's a good idea. I have to get into New York.* Rennie, Aaron can show you the sandbox on Monday afternoon. That's a good place for you to start.

I agree with William that we should move to the next topic.

Catalogs and Process Flow (CatFiv-e)

<Aaron>: Fig. 20 is a simplified business process flow that shows four affiliated versions of catalogs that support the Product Delivery categories.

The fifth catalog is sitting under the four that you see, and it archives all versions of any service description that was ever saved in or deleted from the four affiliated catalogs. We call the federation CatFiv-e.

<Rennie>: That's funny. Who thinks up all these "punny" names?

<Dan>: H does/did most of them. He and Maja chuckled for 2 days after this one.

<Sharf>: Explain.

<Rennie>: Category 5 was a specification for cable that connected communication devices. Cat-5e is the enhanced version that eliminates signal problems at the endpoints (connection points, actually). Daxiao has five cat-alogs that ensure there is no confusion at the service endpoints during service coupling and decoupling.

I absolutely must figure out a way to keep working with these people, even if I have to quit Belvedere. Then I can get away from Sharf. I like Mr. Cane, but he tricked me.

<Dan and Aaron>: *We should try to keep her around.*

<Aaron>: Fig. 20 also shows how Requirements Coordination and Product Delivery include the traditional methodology steps, except that all the "Requirements Coordination" activities are controlled by the business, not technology.

Note: ReMain tracks work requests and projects, whether they are related to SOA or not, while CatFiv-e tracks the services and processes associated with WFSOA projects. The catalogs are linked to each other as Rennie just explained. They are also linked to ReMain and to the Knowledge Cooperative. The four working catalogs are:

- **Initiation**: This catalog supports assembly of service-related information about work requests, up through detailed analysis and prototyping. Support teams in architecture and data administration may modify entries in this catalog and enter approvals that will allow entries to be promoted to the build catalog. Anything in this catalog that is marked as "reused" was copied from the runtime catalog. It may have the same name, but a different version number.
- **Build**: This catalog supports technology team participants when they are developing or modifying a product. Most of the entries in this catalog should have been promoted from the

Initiation Catalog after necessary approvals have been recorded.

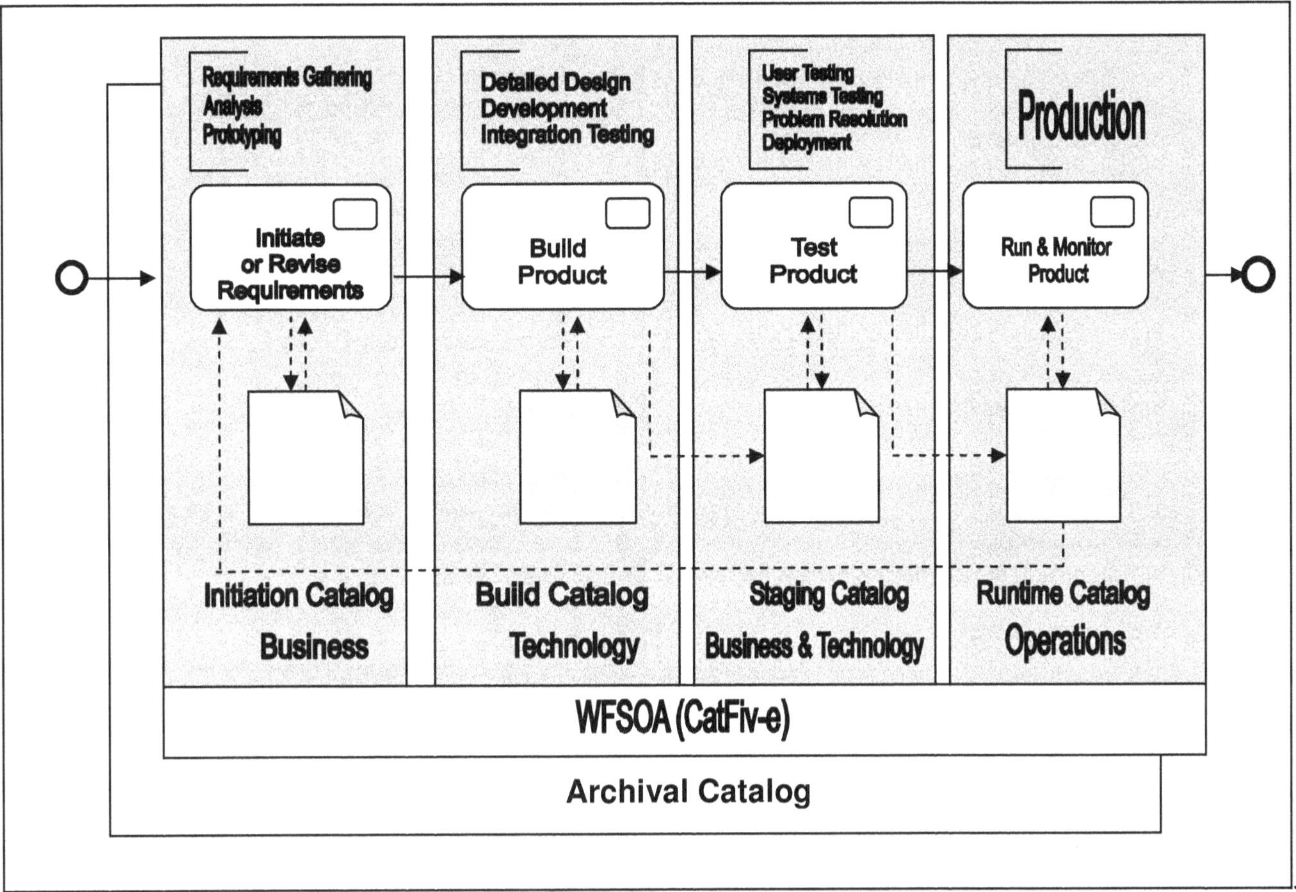

Fig. 20 - **Federated Catalogs and Process Flow for WFSOA (CATFIV-E)**

- **Staging**: This catalog contains entries that are ready for multi-user testing or entries that are ready for production. Services/processes are moved here after most of their components have passed unit tests.
- **Runtime**: This catalog contains information for production ready versions of products. Entries in this catalog would have been promoted from the staging catalog after required approvals have been recorded.

<Rennie>: What information is contained in your catalogs?

<Dan>: Table 26 shows some of the contents of a recent release. Get the most up-to-date information from Maja. She adds information as quickly as the Quality Assurance team can test it.

<Sharf>: Your services must pass QA too? That is wonderful.

<Rennie>: They told us that yesterday.

<Sharf>: They said their requests pass through Requirements Management.

<Aaron>: Once they start in Requirements Management, it takes an act of God to get out without going through QA, which is the most important half of Requirements Management. We pick on Maja's team more than on anyone else. She still has the lowest error rate, and she challenges us to try to catch her.

<Dan>: This is necessary because so many people depend on it. We cannot take a chance on making mistakes. It is also good policy that we adhere to the rules that apply to all Program participants.

Catalog Content

<table>
<tr><th colspan="2">Table 26 - WFSOA Catalog Content (Services and Processes)</th></tr>
<tr><td>1. Identifier (Uniform Resource Identifier (URI) containing a Universally Unique Identifier (UUID)).
2. Name (businessService).
3. Description (tModel).
4. Version number.
----
5. Address (accessPoint - URI for invoking the product).
6. BPEL (Business Process Execution Language - for composite services (processes)) - links.
7. Business entities (businessEntity).
8. Comments and suggestions.
9. Contact Information.
♦ Approvers.
♦ Consumers.
♦ Modifiers (of catalog content).
♦ Owner.
10. Contract information (SLAs).
11. Cost algorithm.
12. Date and time stamps.
13. Dependencies.
14. Category - may include:
♦ Business logic.
♦ Data services.
♦ Lookup services.
♦ Management and control.
♦ Messaging services.
♦ Security services.
♦ Utility (core) services.
15. History (archived).
16. Linkage (assertion) information:
♦ Between publisher and consumer.
♦ Between contracts and services.
♦ Between policies and services.
17. Linkage (outside the catalogs):
♦ Business rules.
♦ To requirements, analysis, and design information in ReMain.
♦ To project plans.</td><td>18. Metrics.
19. Monitoring status.
20. Notification requesters (of changes or additions.
21. Policy (catalog).
22. Policy (compliance requirements).
23. Policy (security requirements).
24. Project identifier.
25. Publisher (businessEntity - sponsor or service domain owner).
26. Related data and graphics.
27. Related processes.
28. Related services and components.
29. Reuse requesters.
30. Sample code for accessing the service.
31. SOAP (message format(s) required to access the service) - link.
32. Software identifier (Service Consumer).
33. Status:
♦ Legacy (candidate).
♦ Legacy (adapted).
♦ New (Creation Phase).
♦ Being Updated.
♦ Production.
34. Terminology.
35. Traceability information (contact information for additions, changes, or deletions).
36. Type:
♦ Atomic.
♦ Composite (service).
♦ Processes.
37. XSLT (transforms documents to and from XML).
36. WSDL (Web Services Description Language) - link.</td></tr>
</table>

<Aaron>: Rennie, I hear that you worked on ebXML and UDDI catalog standards. Maja would really appreciate your input. We added some extensions, but they are outside the registry. We didn't want to risk being out of WS-I compliance.

<Rennie>: Let me look at it.

<Sharf>: Why is everything connected to Maja? One woman cannot possibly manage all the things that you assign to her.

<Rennie>: ***You don't have any trouble assigning all those things to me.***

<Aaron>: She manages very well. She has a team of her own, and she has access to Yu's people, Travers' people, Maurer's people, and Ellison's people. About 200 other people would move half way around the world to work for her. She has ideas, she gives us a sample, and she lets us compete to prove that we are better than she is.

<Dan>: She can explain how she manages in detail when she is less upset about HM, and you engage her in civilized conversation.

<Sharf>: *She's too high-strung for my liking. As soon as I am positioned, she won't have a position.* Perhaps I could let Rennie spend some time with her later in our investigation. I would like to meet her backup.

<Aaron>: Mr. Marshall was her primary backup. Ken Chase is her designated person, though I suspect that anyone on her team is as good as the best person that Travers has. I am her security backup. Five of the data domain owners can handle at least 70% of her job. Plus a lot of her processes are automated.

<Sharf>: She is well backed up. *It won't hurt anything to get rid of her, and I can use her as an example.*

<Rennie>: The catalog access list is next, right?

<Dan>: We divided that information into three parts. You saw how work requests flow from requirements in the work request (Table 24) to the results documented in the post-implementation review (Table 25).

1. Table A.18 describes the actions that a role may perform in CatFiv-e.
2. Tables A.19.1 and A.19.2 show access rights and responsibilities for the WFSOA roles in CatFiv-e.

Note that "search" is not included in the list because every role can read the material in all four catalogs unless there is a block on it for security, compliance, or strategic reasons.

Role Flexibility (Again) and Process Improvement

<Dan>: We have well defined roles, but we require flexibility as part of continuous process improvement. We have found that it is easier to fix something that's well defined, than to fix something floating around in the ether. The catalog access rights must be adjusted to accommodate changing roles.

<Sharf>: Here is a communications challenge. Tell me how you have well defined roles that change frequently.

<Dan>: A better question would be how you could have roles that didn't change in environments that move as quickly as ours do.

<Sharf>: Are you referring to your SOA environment?

<Dan>: I mean our entire business.

<Sharf>: You said SOA allows you to get a better grip on the technology.

<Dan>: Yes. And, because we understand technology better, we understand and plan for changes to the supporting environment. This is a line from Ms. Maçon, but she would say that we are "agile, flexible, and in control", and our changing roles reflect those characteristics.

<Rennie>: Give us an example.

<Dan>: Use the code checker.

<Aaron>: Certainly. Three months ago, we installed a major update to our code-checking tool. It previously handled legacy mainframe languages, and then it added capability for Java and "Visual BC+#".

<Dan>: He means Microsoft languages. He wasn't referring to you.

<Aaron>: Obviously, the tool can't check logic, but it can check any formatting rules that we want to apply. This caused mandatory changes to three roles, and a fourth is changing voluntarily.

1. First, we trained SOA technology specialists on how to place entries in the rules engine for code checking.
2. At the same time, we changed the process for new development to force software through the code analysis tool before check-in. They are finding problems earlier.
3. After two months, we had minimized the amount of visual checking that the technology compliance specialist needed to worry about.
4. Code review sessions are less painful (the religious arguments happen offline), and more business people attend (willingly) because they

can concentrate more on the functional requirements.

<Dan>: The way that change affected catalog access is that business analysts wanted to be able to add their comments to the build catalog. We added that permission two weeks ago.

<Rennie>: Who keeps track of all this?

<Dan>: The process coordinators. Every time we open a change request, they work with us to assess the impact of the change. It is mandatory. I told you that we "eat our own dog food."

<Sharf>: Process coordinators should work with business processes. ***They keep confusing business roles and technology. That has to be split up.***

<Rennie>: There's a technology process coordinator in the roles list.

<Sharf>: They are methodology specialists.

<Dan>: Methodology is process for technologists and business people. The role name includes technology, but it pertains to processes where business must collaborate extensively and intensively with technology.

Do you disagree?

<Sharf>: I have to look at this from a different angle.

<Dan>: ***I wonder if I am actually getting through to him.***

<Rennie>: Let's start with the required approvals.

<Dan>: The next table explains why each approval may be appropriate. The CFO made us put in the promotional approvals. The risk and compliance people insert special approval requirements when there is a high-risk project. They are not always required. We put in the backup approvers to avoid the bottlenecks you accused H of having yesterday.

<Rennie>: ***They keep track of everything.***

WFSOA APPROVAL PROCESS

Minimum Catalog Approvals for Work Promotion

<Sharf>: This is absurd. There must be over 200 approvals on this list.

<Aaron>: This report is extracted from the business rule entries for catalog management. If you would like, I can go down the list, and you can see that there are not as many approval requirements as you would believe when you first look at the table.

<Dan>: Remember 8, 10, 17, and 8 for promotion to development, testing, deployment, and reuse respectively.

Promotion to build catalog (development): The minimum number of approvals for promotion to development is only eight. Refer to **"Approvals"** in Lessons Learned for the list. Processes require one additional approval. Notice that one is the project manager accepting his or her assignment.

Promotion to staging catalog (testing): The minimum number of approvals for promotion to testing is only ten including the additional approval required for processes. The quality management coordinator and service assurance are accepting assignments.

Promotion to runtime catalog (deployment): Notice in Lessons Learned that the number of approvals for deployment is seventeen.

Reuse Approvals

Approval for Reuse (back to initiation): The minimum number of approvals for reuse appears to be the same as for deployment. The number is seventeen. Notice that sponsor approval is required only during the period when a product is not turned over to a domain owner. The burn-in (hardening) period lasts for one or two months. A pre-approval option is available for nine of the roles after a service or process has been hardened. That puts us back to **eight**. I repeat that the list appears under **"Approvals"** in Lessons Learned (Table A.2).

<Rennie>: I would like [...]

<Sharf>: I have to think about this. Why would you show me 200 approvals if the number is really only 43?

<Dan>: I agreed to full disclosure, because I have given the people that you talk to the high-level view, and they say I am glossing over things. If I gave you the list of 8, 10, 17, and 8 without the detail, you would report that something was missing, and that we needed to fill in the blanks.

<Sharf>: We must find a middle ground.

<Aaron>: Perhaps, in your experience, you know of a company that has reached that middle ground.

<Sharf>: I have to pick the one that would be closest to what you need without revealing their internal secrets.

<Rennie>: *He knows that nobody has it so clearly defined.*

<Dan>: We welcome your thoughts. Meanwhile, if you can identify roles that we could eliminate from our minimal lists without incurring the wrath of COBIT, we would really appreciate it.

<Sharf>: How do all those people know what they are approving?

<Dan>: Everything is illustrated, animated, or in a Webinar before it leaves the initiation catalog. The approvers push a button to see the requirement or hear about it.

<Sharf>: What role is responsible for that?

<Dan>: The business analysts, requirements analyst and the software architect work with a user interface specialist from the Communications Team to decide how to animate the models. They look like cartoons with business labels. The clients pay attention.

<Sharf>: They are playing with cartoons! That is ridiculous. *Marshall's communications team is a waste.*

<Aaron>: *Among his many other traits, he is suicidal.*

<Dan>: It's one of our best ideas. It proves that the specifications are clear enough for one of her user interface people to understand, and it gives the clients and the sponsors yet another chance to verify their specifications. *If a bookshelf accidentally fell on him, Machi and Maja would never let me forget it.*

<Rennie>: *He touched a nerve. For a second, Dr. Piccolo looked like Mr. Marshall looked yesterday.*

<Sharf>: *I don't want him angry with me yet.* I was kidding. I'm sure all her processes will make sense after I spend more time with her people.

<Dan>: *Most of the senior people know anyhow. It's time to stop playing this game. I don't want to inflict this fool on Liz. Neither would Justin.* It is time to discuss further improvements to the communications processes. I want to give you ideas about areas where you might focus when you ***are talking to my wife.***

<Sharf>: Who is your wife?

<Dan>: Lisse Maçon Piccolo.

<Sharf>: You could have said something when I confessed about my relationship to Gunther. *I've been trapped. Gunnar must have known this!*

<Dan>: That was the wrong response. You were supposed to say, "Smart knowledgeable people are likely to be associated with smart knowledgeable people." Then we will proceed.

<Rennie>: **That is very, very funny.**

<Dan>: **Thank you.** Where was I?

<Aaron>: At this juncture, you would usually say that the entire company has been introduced to the communications matrix at some level, while the WFSOA registry/repository and ReMain provide input to hundreds of the communication intersections in the matrix. **This is hurting me.**

<Sharf>: *I was going after the Marshalls. Now I have to save myself. I need Gunnar.*

Dan, that's definitely a sign of communications failure. I have been completely honest with you, and you held on to your secret. Daxiao's problem is that no one can trust anyone else.

If she had the problem resolved, you could have saved the Board, Gunnar, and me hours of valuable time.

I hope that worked. What would I be doing if he had talked about Mags the way I did about Maçon/Piccolo?

<Dan>: *He has a wheelbarrow built into his pants legs!* Let me start saving time. This Collaboration Matrix is part of the communications plan that Ellison and Liz are refining. The complete table has over 12,000 intersections.

Readers: I mentioned before that a sample of the collaboration matrix is in Table 17. The entire collaboration matrix is in SOA P (2) where we match major roles and activities to communications. When the two are combined, they significantly improve planning activities.

<Sharf>: This looks like "Big Brother".

<Dan>: The frequency of communication is self-reported at this time. One of the requests on the work queue would allow us to evaluate how the contents of the Knowledge Cooperative (and all its linkages) are used to support each of those collaborations. The advantage of what you are doing is that it will push that request to the highest priority.

<Rennie>: You can't do everything. It's too much.

<Dan>: We'd concentrate on the resistance areas first, and then the high-frequency collaborations.

William, I will again humbly request that you show us where to find examples of organizations that have better practices than we do.

<Rennie>: *No one is dealing with as many issues as they are.*

<Sharf>: I will look at this and get back to you. *I was concentrating on Marshall, and they tricked me. I would not be as composed as he appears to be, and he is not being humble.*

Advantages of Centralized Approval

<Rennie>: Approvals must be time-consuming. *We should move along, the worse he looks, the worse Belvedere and Mr. Cane will look. I can't afford that now.*

<Dan>: We save time in the long run. This is how we verify that projects have the necessary support. We can stop things that could cause problems later. It definitely saves phone messages, e-mail messages, and missed messages. It also reduces the time spent in meetings.

<Rennie>: What about emergencies.

<Dan>: We request the approvals, but we have emergency bypass procedures (accelerated projects) where the SOA librarian, the project initiation manager, and the BASE Program coordinator may get involved if the regular approvers are not available. If we don't have the mandated approvals within a limited period after a change is implemented, we politely suggest to the users that the service is about to be suspended, and we explain why.

<Rennie>: Doesn't that cause trouble?

<Dan>: We would be in more trouble if people believed that the emergency bypass procedure was a way to bypass quality control.

<Rennie>: *This is excellent.* I must spend more time looking at it, but it definitely gives me a feeling for what the important roles do.

Identity Management

<Aaron>: I know that you know we know this; however, I'd like to avoid a report entry such as "Identity management not mentioned".

Within and across the roles, we still work closely with Human Resources to ensure appropriate identity management. We have implemented rigorous business and technical procedures to optimize user provisioning and access management. We provide quick access when it is appropriate and quick removal when it is not, as long as individuals passed our ongoing monitoring processes.

Security provisioning for processes and services includes creating control groups determined by the:

- Role of business users.
- Role of user support personnel.
- Role of BASE participants.
- Role of technology enabling personnel.
- Business entity.
- Business partners.
- Hierarchical position (maintained in collaboration with HR and Business entities).
- Application ownership.
- Service and process ownership (service domain owners).
- Data ownership (data domain owners).

Changes to access rights or access control groups occur when:

- Business entities are created, dissolved, consolidated, or split from existing units.
- Business entities move in the organizational structure.
- Financial approval rights are added or removed.
- Individuals are assigned to new roles.
- Individuals are promoted.
- Individuals resign or are released.
- Individuals are removed from a role group.
- Individuals transfer between business entities.

- New roles are created.
- Role responsibilities change.
- Process approval rights are added for individuals or access groups.
- Process approval rights are removed.
- Rights are transferred after personnel departure.
- Role access privileges are increased or decreased.
- Role names change.
- Service access rights change.
- Individual names change.

Dan knows where to find me when you are ready for the details.

<Rennie>: What do you think William?

<Sharf>: It appears adequate. *This isn't as I felt the day the dean trapped me, but it is close.*

<Aaron>: I am prepared to discuss everything we are doing with the Security Alliance? It is critical to our Partner and Research Networks.

<Sharf>: Bailey is high up on the list of people I will interview. We will handle it then.

<Aaron>: Don't forget to talk to Maja. She is an active participant.

<Sharf>: *If I hear that name one more time* [...]

<Dan>: Thank you for providing assistance on short notice. I'll be in New York after we finish here.

THUNKING SOA - EVERY SOA ACTIVITY (PLUS SOME)

<Dan>: Thunk! That is the *Thunk* extract (Role/Activity list). I can skip the gym today.

> **Readers**: We mentioned earlier that this is the core content of SOA P (2). Refer to Table A.7.1-BASE Procurement Activities for a sample of how the entries will appear.

We created this one specifically for Belvedere. The related FAQs (Table A.20) apply to your extract and the one that we use internally. The differences between the external and internal versions are noted. It contains at least one line item related to everything we have ever done in WFSOA. COSO, COBIT, ERM, CMMI, and ITIL are there too.

Before you ask, yes you may have electronic copies, but remember our intellectual property agreements. This should not be shared.

For the sake of brevity, and I am being serious:

1. We rolled up the activities of deprecated role names. For example, activities that were previously assigned to a methodology specialist appear with the technology process coordinator.
2. If multiple roles with the same name performed the same task, we collapsed them into one line item. For example, each client role has specified non-functional requirements at some time, so there is one line with a role labeled "Client(s)" for that activity.
3. If the same role performed the same activity in several plans, it appears in this extract once.
4. Each individual entry is maintained in the master database.

<Sharf>: Marshall said you used this for planning. How would that work?

<Dan>: You need access to the entire Roles/Activity database for detailed project planning. We have services that allow you to reproduce any plan and planning history that was ever captured in an automated tool. It enables identification of support requirements, task sequences, and expected task durations.

<Sharf>: I will need a minute.

<Rennie>: This list could be valuable in other ways.

<Dan>: We documented several uses for this in Table A.20.

Five critical uses would be:

1. To justify improvements to the validity of your WFSOA etiology chart.
2. To provide a major expansion for the description of roles and responsibilities.
3. To show you exactly how we do what we do, especially if you use it with the list of Activity verbs in Table A.8.
4. To reiterate the high degree of business process automation that we use for technology.
5. As an index into the Knowledge Cooperative. The activity objects are linked to the Knowledge Cooperative Topic List.

<Dan>: This affects our discussion of the etiology chart. It is important that you are perceived as an impartial observer. Do you have any comments?

<Rennie>: ***It appears that Maja's diagram is more accurate than Will's.***

<Sharf>: She could have tampered with it.

<Dan>: Bonuses for 45 -50% of the people in Daxiao are affected by the master from which this is extracted. Remember Table 16.

<Sharf>: I said I need time to review it further!

<Rennie>: Let me know if I understand correctly. You have links between the knowledge portal and about 400 content categories. Then you mapped fields in the Knowledge Cooperative to equivalent fields in information sources outside the Knowledge Cooperative - down to what level do you map?

<Dan>: Down to the field level in hierarchical, relational, and IMS databases. We also index the contents of unstructured data, and we have metadata for about 90% of everything.

<Rennie>: Common terminology and the metadata catalog make it easier for you do the matching.

<Dan>: ***We need Rennie now, especially if we don't have H! With her, we could double the effectiveness of Liz and Maja, even if H comes back.***

<Sharf>: ***This is not relevant to what I need. I'll ask a question anyhow.*** Why can't you achieve 99 or 100%?

***<Rennie>*:** One hundred percent is impossible in a constantly changing and evolving environment.

<Rennie>: Are you doing any work with neural networks?

<Dan>: Not entirely. It has what we call neural services. It tells us what it thinks it learned, and we create the links if they seem appropriate.

<Rennie>: Anything that anybody would ever want to know about WFSOA is in here.

<Dan>: One would need to be as knowledgeable as you are to understand the possibilities.

<Sharf>: ***This is the first time in my life that I have ever been overloaded! It is overkill. They still need a middle ground. They still need me.***

<Dan>: It is time for me to summarize.

<Sharf>: ***Good. I have to find Gunnar. They should have warned me*** [...] ***He did warn me! However, he should have told me they were married.***

<Dan>: The most important thing is tha Hank, Liz, Val and other managers in BASE will continue anything that you started with HM. Macedon will be more involved than ever before. ***I'll have to learn how to salute without actually doing it.***

The things that we owe each other and the next steps are.

<Sharf>: I will handle that:

1. Rennie and I re-evaluate the Etiology diagram.
2. Rennie will provide comments on Cat-Fiv, and clarify how Maja created virtual views combining UDDI and ebXML catalogs.
3. Belvedere will share its "SOA resistance list", as we promised yesterday.
4. I will meet more of your senior, evaluate how they are affected by SOA, and report the results to people designated by Mittelman.
5. Belvedere will send meeting summaries to the same list of people as we did yesterday. I will add Yu, Van Amberg, and Aaron.

<Rennie>: We will ensure that Maja is included.

<Dan>: Don't forget Marshall. Most of what we are talking about exists because of him, with my guidance of course. ***I have to keep him confused.***

<Sharf>: As you wish. Do you mind if I have a word with you before I leave? Rennie, please excuse us.

<Rennie>: ***Please don't let him destroy too much. Please, please, please*** [...]

<Dan>: A few words would be good.

<Sharf>: [...] What's in the box?

<Rennie>: My clothes. I have to send this outfit back to Dr. Piccolo for Maja.

<Sharf>: ***The closeness is all wrong.***

CHAPTER X - POLITICAL AND PERSONAL ADJUSTMENTS

Sharf>: You've worked more closely with Marshall than most of the senior people for the last few years. How much of WFSOA was his idea, and how much was yours? Why haven't you moved him out of the way and taken what you need?

<Dan>: The first question is hard to answer. For the second one, I was waiting for things to reach a critical mass beyond which Daxiao would have to work especially hard to move backward. *Then I complete my life goals that are not related to Daxiao.*

<Sharf>: Since Marshall is out of the picture, how can we work together to achieve your objective?

<Dan>: We have been going in the right direction as you can see, though you are obviously having trouble understanding why. I strongly hope that we have built up enough momentum that we can glide past the point of no return.

<Sharf>: You haven't answered my question.

DULLING A "SHARF"

<Dan>: The first thing we are going to do is break up Marshall's organization, thereby avoiding the slow torture of an agonizing dissolution.

<Sharf>: I definitely have some recommendations in that area.

<Dan>: HM has already filed a plan. Justin, Joe, and Dr. Emery-Baldwin are looking at it now.

<Sharf>: WHEN? You need my input. *They always knew this. Everyone is withholding information.*

<Dan>: Until now, you have spent a great deal of time explaining what is wrong with Marshall. You have not shown us what your approach would be, nor have you shown us how that approach would be better than what we have. We can't afford to slow down while you "***review and get back to us***".

<Sharf>: I promised Justin that I would have what you are requesting within a week. It will be an amalgam of expertise gained working with several large organizations. If I am slow, it is because your people are blocking my access to information.

<Dan>: *You mean small pieces of a few organizations.* No other organization would give you their ***Thunk***, if they had one. We've shown you our innards. What else do you need?

<Sharf>: *I must maintain control of the situation.* We may be able to salvage much of what you have done, except that everything would be simplified.

<Dan>: Everything we have was simpler when we started. We had to grow and take a lot of hits before we got to where we are. **We do not intend to return to the SOA Stone Age.**

<Sharf>: If your people don't understand it, what is the use?

<Dan>: If you and Gunnar don't understand it, why risk Daxiao's competitive advantage until you figure it out? He could personally lose a few million dollars in bonuses over the next few years.

<Sharf>: You've been working on this a few years. I need at least a week to show you how to fix it, *and to figure out how to move some of those bonuses into my pocket.*

<Dan>: That didn't stop you last night.

<Sharf>: That was a start-up ploy that worked. I needed Daxiao's attention, and I have it. There are additional attention-getting items for Jasper. Why did you ignore financial misdoings when I mentioned them earlier?

<Dan>: We each focus on what we understand. Finance is not my strong suit. There's significantly less funny money than there was before SOX, so I'm not sure how much it matters. Jasper and Marshall went after big offenders first. After plugging $100 million leaks multiple times, $10 - 15 million is nothing.

<Sharf>: You still have the fox watching the hen house. If Marshall's daughter figured out how to hide that money, there could be a lot more. They cannot be trusted.

<Dan>: What does Marshall's daughter have to do with this? You seem to know her.

<Sharf>: I'm basing this on rumors. I told you that we had direct confrontations a few times when she was at Acton, and she fights a dirty fight.

<Dan>: Could this be affecting your judgment?

<Sharf>: I am a consummate professional. I am simply providing you with information that you may find useful in your dealings with Marshall or Acton. Acton often mismatches consultants and customers.

<Dan>: I will pass that information along to Joe. Do you have any other concerns?

<Sharf>: How long has Marshall had a substance abuse problem? You need to know that I am aware of this situation. Your people waste energy propping him up.

<Dan>: Why would you mention that? Twinkies are not within the legal definition of substance abuse.

<Sharf>: This is why I may recommend a clean management sweep! You need to understand that I have total recall, and I make decisions according to facts. Too many people at Daxiao adapt their perceptions according to friendships. Fortunately, Justin does not appear to have this problem.

<Dan>: I do now understand what perceptions we are discussing.

<Sharf>: I saw Marshall sitting in your "palace" yesterday completely zonked out. He had bottles of booze lined up and a tray of pills in his hand. He probably fell because he was staggering.

<Dan>: *Juggle something heavy. Striking a consultant would be inappropriate behavior and poor politics. I could reach over and snap his neck while he's sitting down. I could shove this in his mouth. That would ruin all the plans. Our resident robot would say,* "That observation requires verification." I am trying to think of something we can use to validate your perceptions.

<Sharf>: Guzman said something close to that. When do we start?

<Dan>: Let me make a phone call.

[...] Lillian, is Ms. Vitale out there with you?

[...] Good. Would you two come down here and share some brew with us? Bring four bottles. Let her pick.

[...] Humor me. We will use the fine china.

[...] Don't worry about lunch. You can join me upstairs after we finish.

<Sharf>: He keeps a stash out here too! You knew that I was right.

<Dan>: Until they arrive, the most important thing that you need to know is that Marshall nearly died twice, or maybe three times, from doses of morphine that make most people a little groggy. The first time it happened was in a swamp in Southeast Asia. Thus, he is leery of substances that affect the central nervous system. He meditates, and his mate creates herbal concoctions for particular problems.

The strongest thing he will take, and this only began recently, is acetaminophen (Tylanoll to you), and he sneaks that past Machi (Nicola Frey) because he doesn't want her to worry. That would explain the gold pencil case of pills that Ms. Frey believes is his favorite Kristie's auction coup.

He has a drawer full of prescriptions for Perposet that he is proud that he did not fill. For your further enlightenment, acetaminophen is Perposet (an addictive painkiller) without the Oxytoxin the addictive ingredient.

<Sharf>: Van Amberg said that was his secret pain medication.

<Dan>: It is secret from his Ms. Frey.

<Sharf>: Everybody is still trying to cover up.

<Dan>: You are not paying attention. I am trying to save you and your reputation. *I said that with a straight face. I want you to look as ridiculous as possible.*

Three dozen people will testify that they saw him crying from pain yesterday. They will also testify that there was a mad rush to find something called Naloxone after the ambulance team gave him a shot for the pain and his breathing slowed down.

<Sharf>: You are making this up? *He has to be making this up. This could be the second time they tricked me into hurting myself.*

<Dan>: Thank you Lillian. Welcome back Rennie.

<Sharf>: Those are the bottles! **I AM RIGHT!**

<Lillian>: What's the big deal? They're all over the place. Nicky could make a living from her brews.

<Rennie>: We were already sharing one. You should try it. It's good for the nerves and the stomach.

<Dan>: How do you like this version?

<Lillian>: It's relaxing as Nicky said it would be, but I prefer the carrot brew that tastes like carrot cake. That is scheduled for the winter. I lost about eight pounds while I maintained my energy level. Mr. Marshall lost a lot more.

<Dan>: To each his own.

<Sharf>: Tell me about the schedule.

<Dan>: I'll pour while Lillian explains. Scramble them around, and then pick one.

<Lillian>: It's a fun thing with beneficial results for consumers of the brew and for Daxiao. We have been doing for 10 years. The "Home Brew" club cooks up four recipes each year, one for each season. Some years we do only old recipes, and some years Nicky (Mrs. Marshall - Ms. Frey - whatever) comes up with new recipes to deal with whatever is ailing somebody important at the time.

We have members from all over the company. The people who share the brew tend to work together more effectively.

<Sharf>: Who is "We"?

<Lillian>:

1. We have a brew tasting every year at the spring outing, so that means about 1,000 people vote on the next year's selections.
2. Nicky does the recipes.
3. Nicky and I perform the herbal research.
4. H (I mean Mr. Marshall) does the planning.
5. Marshall works with McBride (in Operations) to maintain the flavor calendar. They conduct the flavor survey at the picnic. We may keep favorites for two seasons in a row.
6. One of the employees at the brewery in Farmingdale works with us on the chemistry. A man from the product research group contributes too. They verify the quality of the ingredients.
7. Simone or Indy, depending on whether her mother is around, handles the finances. Melissa, from finance, provides Daxiao's financial guidance.
8. Alex Macedon is responsible for the logistics and scheduling. He works with the brewery people to get the supplies in, and he ensures that the brew is delivered. He's the best we ever had.
9. McBride also maintains the inventory. We store the inventory at the brewery.
10. About 15 of us work with the brewery staff to do the actual brewing. Ernest stood in for Mr. Marshall this year. He and Dr. Piccolo are good with the heavy sacks.

<Dan>: Hidden talents. Talk about the different breweries, the bottles, and the funding.

<Lillian>: We rotate among three of them now. It's rather like timeshares.

The fourth one went out of business. That's where we found all these bottles. They really do conserve the flavor.

The Frey-Marshall Associates Brewery Endowment pays for it now, and we all contribute $0.25 when we drink a bottle. The good doctor owes me $0.75 for this serving.

<Sharf>: How many bottles do you brew?

<Lillian>: It's been increasing. We started with 1,000. This year:

- There were 20,000 bottles in this summer's batch. We need more in hot weather.
- There will be 16,000 bottles of the same thing in the fall. We recycled enough bottles to handle a run.
- There will be 13,000 in the carrot run. I want more, but Mr. Marshall has already lost weight and a lot of people think it's weird.
- There will be 16,000 in the spring. That will be a berry blend.

<Dan>: Remove a cap, pour, and taste your brew.

[...] Let us all toast to the fall brew batch and a speedy recovery for Hamilton Marshall.

<Sharf>: This is flat ginger ale! What's in those?

<Dan>: Pick any bottle you want. We call it ginger tea.

<Sharf>: More ginger ale! Everything here is ginger ale! ***I can't let her ruin me again.***

<Rennie>: Don't you like it?

<Dan>: *That felt s-o-o-o good.* I'm ready for lunch. I must run, but I can squeeze in one of their healthy sandwiches.

<Lillian>: With a chocolate cherry berry sundae. There will be flab on your abs before you know it.

<Dan>: William and Rennie, would you care to join us in the executive dining area?

<Sharf>: NO! We have to return to the office and prepare for a critical meeting tomorrow morning. You will have my first set of suggestions for reorganization as soon as Jasper and I discuss financial matters.

Piccolo just dropped through the netting! I have to regroup.

- ***Justin seems to be impressed with my work.***
- ***Armstrong will be happy to work with me to wipe out all vestiges of Marshall.***
- ***I'm not sure whether the gal in HR matters, but I will neutralize her immediately anyhow.***
- ***I'm sure I will be able to move Jasper to my point of view. I will promise to help her discover the "RandD" fund, and I will promise not to mess with her domains.***
- ***Van Amberg was helpful yesterday. He over reacted to the way I corrected his perceptions, but I will bring him back in line after I talk to Jasper.***
- ***I can bring Gunnar around. I'm betting my future that if he had to choose between Mags and Indy, his sister would win.***

<Rennie>: William. What's wrong with you?

<Sharf>: *Nothing that I can't handle with a little damage control.* You can ride with me back to New York.

<Rennie>: I rented a car. Mr. Cane approved it. I'll see you in the office.

<Sharf>: *She's going over my head too. Everything is going wrong.*

ADJUSTING THE GUNNAR VIEW

------- **Gunnar's Sales Area in New York** -------

Fear of Computers - (SOA Resistance Factor)

<John Laufer>: Vance said you were in here. Let me grab a few things, and we'll meet next door.

<Gunnar>: Wait. Send someone set up *Thunk for me.*

<Laufer>: I can do that. I'll let them start, and I'll be right back.

---------- ----------

<Gunnar>: Were you always this good at this?

<Laufer>: Which this do you mean?

<Gunnar>: You're as good on the keyboard as Marshall is.

<Laufer>: Actually, I may be faster, but he finishes the challenges ahead of me because he knows where Liz and Maja put everything. Higgs and Marcella are still faster, but lately, Armstrong is giving him a run for his money.

<Gunnar>: Why do you waste your time on that? *Sharf and I may agree on that.*

<Laufer>:

1. Since everyone is cutting back on clerical and administrative staff, it's a way to let team members know, especially the older ones, that they don't have an excuse to sit and wait until Vance or Marcella finish with your "Quick Answers". If I can find my own answers, they can too.
2. I learn new things that may be useful to Sales and Marketing, and I let our people know that they should learn too.
3. Knowing where to find everything is very helpful on sales calls. It reduces the number of times we have to say, "I'll get back to you". We close our sales quicker that way.

<Gunnar>: Where did you learn to type?

<Laufer>: It's called keyboarding. When I was at the "B" school, I had a choice of working more hours so that I could afford to pay people to prepare my papers for me, or learning to prepare them myself, and paying people find my errors.

I am better now that I have spent a little while with Docente's training CD.

<Gunnar>: Do you have one here?

<Laufer>: I have several. I keep them around for the 30% of new hires that would benefit from it.

I might even admit that the reason I'm here is that I could get you "Quick Answers" faster than anyone except Liz could. I would not have been able to produce anywhere near the rate that she did if I hadn't learned to find things that she could find.

<Gunnar>: *I am damn uncomfortable with the things that Liz wants to show me on the computer, and I can't tell anyone.*

Mags used to prepare my papers for me. She never lets me forget that.

I suppose I missed the entire Internet wave because I had people to access the information for me.

Maybe Len can do something to earn his keep. I'll have to deal with his arrogance,

How long have you been using ***Thunk***?

<Laufer>: Li showed me how ***Thunk*** worked a few years ago. It's a short route to almost everything. Tell me what you want, and I'll crawl around and find it?

<Gunnar>: What?

<Laufer>: It's a figure of speech. They gave us an internal version of an Internet crawler. If something is not indexed, it will crawl around and find it.

I hope you don't mind me saying this, but Liz and that crazy Swede make one heck of a team. When they give me products to make you look good, we all make money.

[...] *He did mind. I'd better change the topic. That's still a sore spot with him.*

SOA Services for Sales and Marketing

<Gunnar>: Is this where you find information for my sales reports?

<Laufer>: They gave us data mart BI (Business Intelligence) services that retrieve about 70% of what I need from internal sources and another 20% comes from external providers. Some people use it more, and others do less.

We still create spreadsheets when you ask for something more exotic. Then we load them in here, and the next time, they're not exotic. We've stopped going crazy when we have to swap out a desktop that contains the only version of one of your monster pivots.

<Gunnar>: Go back to that matrix. *Marshall showed me that matrix. .*

<Laufer>: That is Liz's experimental sales matrix. It is simple and elegant. We can lock it for our eyes only, or we can share it with selected people.

<Gunnar>: Show me.

<Laufer>: I can see how the entire unit is doing on this one screen (I should say one matrix).

- Our people's names are down the side, and the deals in progress are across the top. We can ensure that the important ones are always on the first screen.
- In the box, we show the deal status.
- The box also has what they call contact state. Yellow (with a question mark) means we're waiting for them, and red (with a splat - asterisk) means we owe them something.
- We can click the box and find names and contact numbers.
- We can click again, and see any reminder notes we put in.

It works on most PDA's, but not ours. They say most of our devices are no longer compliant. I was waiting for the right moment to ask you about that.

<Gunnar>: Is the information correct?

<Laufer>: If we enter it correctly, it comes out right. If we enter it incorrectly, we ping Marcella or Vance, and they fix it for us. See where it says "PING". That will send an instant message, a voice message, or both. It was about 80% accurate when we started two months ago. We are above 90% and improving. We are approaching a point where we really need it. It would be nice if we updated our devices. They'd pay for themselves in two or three weeks.

<Gunnar>: How much?

<Laufer>: Jumpstart makes them using our components, so we're looking at about $283.94 cents a unit. I bought one of my own, and Li pushed the certification. This is how it would look.

<Gunnar>: *Dying octopus.* Let me think. How do you use the Knowledge Center?

<Laufer>: How do you want to use it?

<Gunnar>: Does it give answers to billions of questions?

<Laufer>: Maybe, if you know how to ask. The number was never important to me. You can enter a question in this box using regular English, but you are more likely to find an answer if you use the common terminology drop-down boxes under here. Give me a question, and we'll see if we find an answer.

<Gunnar>: Show sales that BASE affected in any way.

<Laufer>: That would be about 90% of the ones in the U.S., and 60% outside. Please be more specific.

<Gunnar>: How could that be?

<Laufer>: The first thing Macedon requested when he moved over was the creation of logistics services. Those services support almost everything that comes into or goes out of Daxiao. Armstrong's people wrote the services and the mighty Swede ensured that they worked correctly.

<Gunnar>: Who is that?

<Laufer>: Maja Johanssen.

<Gunnar>: What's the last important question you asked?

<Laufer>: Li was excited about how RandD sales were even higher than before. I used it to verify how many sales are related to clients from RandD projects.

<Gunnar>: What was the answer?

<Laufer>: The last two years may have been flukes, but the answer was between $350 million and 400 million. We're on track for half a billion this year.

<Gunnar>: What is the BASE connection?

<Laufer>: BASE maintains the computer labs for Partner Research. The Swede makes sure nobody can steal anything from anybody else. They say she's one of the best in the world. Furthermore, if you sneak past her security walls, she'll find you and shoot you. She's licensed to pack every day, and we believe that she does. She and her husband worked as a team before he died.

<Gunnar>: As a team of what?

<Laufer>: If we knew, she'd have to shoot us.

<Gunnar>: Skip references to injury and death.

<Laufer>: They have special planning and test support services. They have mini-logistics to support their experiments. If the partners build something that works and they decide to manufacture it, either they use our components (orders), or they let Chiu build it for them (more orders). The customers may think our people snake oil salesmen, but they trust Marshall, Macedon, AJ (Maja), and Hank Yu. Marshall and Macedon do the work, and we receive the bonuses.

Here's a "quick answer". As of this instant, sales from companies that completed research projects last year total $423 million. We're tracking toward half a billion as I said. The PDAs would cost about $90,000.

<Gunnar>: Marshall and Liz were taking care of me?

<Laufer>: You'd better believe it.

<Gunnar>: *No kind deed goes unpunished.*

[...] *What if you did something to annoy me, I left, and* [...]

<Laufer>*: *He looked bad, and it just became worse. If you need help, they say Marshall's man Friday is a nurse. He's back from visiting Mr. Marshall already.

<Gunnar>: Buy the PDAs.

<Laufer>: Thanks, and while I have my hand in the till, I would like to talk to the owner about borrowing the conference room next door.

Our status meetings are crowded. This is the biggest space we have, but they have a basketball court next door.

[...] I mean that literally. The conference room has a hoop on one end. The cleaning person says they use foam rubber balls, and Marshall's daughter uses it to wind down.

<Gunnar>: *Indy! I would like to wind down with her. Where did that come from!*

How does she get to use it?

<Laufer>: Probably because of her father. There are also four offices. It appears that no one uses the biggest one. Maybe you could crash over there when you're in the city.

<Gunnar>: How much?

<Laufer>: I decided to mention it to you first. It couldn't be too. Marshall's people are in there often, and Piccolo still acts as if he owns the place. The best part is that Marshall's daughter has been there almost every day since it was finished.

<Gunnar>: What's important about Marshall's daughter?

<Laufer>: That's not related to business, but you would relate. Vance calls it the Jaguar jaunt. They rigged mirrors, and they can see her walk down from the elevator. Yesterday, she received almost as much attention as her father did.

<Gunnar>: Jaguar jaunt or panther pace.

<Laufer>: I saw you paying attention yesterday, but we won't use ANGBabyGirl any time soon. She's for looking, not for touching.

<Gunnar>: You made up the passwords!

<Laufer>: It definitely was not I. I need my job.

Liz started it, and we kept using it. She said you change your "associations" about as often as we have to change passwords. Only people who pull your reports for you would also be likely to know the name of your most recent interest. Thus, it would be easy for us to remember and moderately difficult for outside people to guess.

<Gunnar>: *That's the pot calling the kettle black. Liz "associates" to the level of paternity with everyone, except me.*

I need a quick answer. Why is she Baby Girl?

<Laufer>: I happen to know because I asked this old man (he must be about 70) who she was. I figured he must be almost blind because he barely noticed her one day when she came out of an elevator we were getting on. He said, "Oh, that's Baby Girl". Apparently, he knew Marshall, even before they came to work here. When she was born, Marshall bent somebody's ear at least three times a week about all the wonderful things that his baby girl was learning to do while he was limping between jobs or going to school at night. That included yawning, burping, focusing her eyes, and producing micro-floods when he tried to change her (his fingers were too big for the pins before they discovered Pampers). The most important thing for a long time was laughing. She was a very happy baby. After laughing, it was running. The name stuck.

<Gunnar>: *She's not happy now, and neither am I. Maybe we can work on it together.* Why wouldn't it make a good temporary password?

Type Preferences - an Introduction

<Laufer>: It's not something that I know exactly, even though I really don't believe she is your type. It's more like a request, or perhaps a plea. She's everybody's big sister, literally, or his or her younger sister. I like this space. If you had a problem with her (remembering that your neat split percentage is only about 60%), none of us would ever make it down here from the elevator. Even if you were well, I don't believe you'd want to tangle with her "little" brother.

<Gunnar>: *Marshall mentioned types yesterday, and I never thought about it.* What is my type?

<Laufer>: I was out of place, and I apologize. You are my boss, and I like this job.

<Gunnar>: You've been with me for 13 years. You followed me here.

<Laufer>: I've only seen you close up and personal for four of those years. In that time, I have discovered that you "remove" things that make you uncomfortable. I wish to avoid saying something that would make your pinky twitch more than it's twitching now.

<Gunnar>: You obviously know that I am uncomfortable. Answer the question.

<Laufer>: Can I tell you what the wives usually say after one of your "get to know you" gatherings?

<Gunnar>: "Quick Answer".

<Laufer>: Your associates are all beautiful, though many of them have had intervention. They are often high on the society scale and proportionately lacking in humanity. They tend to prefer rising stars or established individuals. They need companionship, but they tend to be as afraid of commitment as you are. As a result, they are also as flexible in their associations as you are.

That is a synopsis of hundreds of hours of idle gossip. Do I still have a job?

<Gunnar>: ***The commitment part is changing. Lately, I'm running into ones with the ticking clocks. Helena was frightening.***

Good snake oil salesman. I've never heard anyone describe self-centered recycled hypocritical snobs so well.

<Laufer>: Should we worry about a close encounter of the worst kind between you and Marshall, if he survives? We want him to survive, don't we?

<Gunnar>: I definitely want Marshall to survive. One the encounter, we shouldn't play where we eat.

Amal and I played and she's dead. I thought about playing with Liz, and that was a bad idea too.

<Laufer>: Will he survive?

<Gunnar>: I will check when I leave hear.

<Laufer>: Since I still have a job, can we research sharing the conference area?

<Gunnar>: Where would you start?

<Laufer>: I'll contact the owner before I call Lorrie. I stored a link to the lease in KC.

<Gunnar>: Kansas?

<Laufer>: I meant the Knowledge Cooperative.

<Gunnar>: I have to go. Tell me what you found when I return.

<Laufer>: Wait. I have it here. Our landlord is Simone Winslow. Her office is on Broad Street.

[...] That didn't look too good.

<Gunnar>: ***My head is in the beak of a giant Octopus.***

Wait! I'm renting space from Indy. I haven't felt like this since Amal died. The painkiller is wearing off. I need some water.

<Laufer>: Is that aspirin?

<Gunnar>: This scribble is worse than mine is. Can you read it?

<Laufer>: No, but I believe this straight line means one, like o-n-e.

He's been clean since Stephanie left. I hope he doesn't mess up again. I'll have to talk to James.

<Gunnar>: This should hold me until I get the prescriptions filled. I'll be able to read that.

[...] ***All-Tha-News: "Daxiao EVP overdoses on painkillers one day after accusing peer of overdosing on painkillers."***

You do not have to worry [...] about anything.

<Laufer>: I need some fresh air. I'll walk out with you. ***Maybe he should have stayed in the hospital.***

<Gunnar>: No! Yes, that may be a good idea. I will do the walking. You do the standing by, in case [...]

<Laufer>: I understand.

---------- ----------

<Gunnar>: ***Maybe not everybody feels that I'm political poison. Or maybe Laufer is positioning himself in case that chair arm did more damage than I'm willing to admit.***

How did I get to this? Yesterday I was a shark with my choice of meals. Today I'm running from a dying octopus.

I'm forgetting one of the few projects I did with Kerstin. An octopus doesn't live as long as a shark, but it is the most intelligent invertebrate, and in many circumstances, it can overcome a shark of greater mass.

It can also make itself invisible until it is too late for its prey to know what happened, just as Marshall did.

<Laufer>: ***He is one determined fool. I wonder who/whom he is rushing to see. He definitely can't be going on a sales call like that.*** Is that James?

<Gunnar>: I'll be all right from here. I will be back in two hours for a meeting with Mittelman.

<Laufer>: Rest sounds like a better idea.

<Gunnar>: This will help you keep things going. Let Vance put it into the matrix. Share it with ANGHelena and Marcella. Ask Marcella to fix what Vance can't read. Show me how to use it when the information is ready, ***if I'm still here. I was the most successful accidental salesman that ever lived, and it finally caught up with me.***

Call everybody, introduce yourself, and tell them I will be out of commission for at least a week, ***and maybe forever.***

Gooner is a Goner. The Doc and Marshall would like that one.

<Laufer>: Are you sure?

<Gunnar>: It is necessary.

GUNNAR LOSES POSITION

---------- **Hotel Pietro** ----------

<Mags>: This is great, but I'm scared. What happened to you this time?

<Gunnar>: I tripped helping Marshall, and stayed in the hospital last night. It's primarily loose teeth and bruises.

<Mags>: You could stop messing around jump off a high cliff.

[...] I don't really mean that. I suppose it would be ridiculous to ask why you aren't home recovering, and why did you rush me over here.

<Gunnar>: You're here to keep you safe. Will is going crazy.

I'm more worried about you than you are about me. You wouldn't worry at all if you didn't believe you needed my salary to keep the family leeches in the style to which I helped you become accustomed, in spite being only a salesman.

Since Stephanie left, you don't know about the whopping bonuses that Marshall won't be helping me to earn any longer.

<Mags>: Why are you worried about me with Will? You're the one that's acting illogically.

<Gunnar>: How?

<Mags>: William said that you helped save Marshall's life. Why bother if you wanted to move him out?

<Gunnar>: No. I needed to understand him.

<Mags>: What is there to understand? Marshall is an overrated fossil with substance abuse problems.

Meanwhile, Will is fine. He is happier than I've seen him in years.

<Gunnar>: ***Stop that!*** It was Tylanoll and ginger tea! Machi could sue us all. ***I'm yelling again.***

<Mags>: Who is Macky?

<Gunnar>: Not important. Please stop talking about substance abuse, for my sake.

<Mags>: You are actually afraid of something. How could you and Will move this far apart in one day?

<Gunnar>: Will made a mess in one day.

<Mags>: How badly?

<Gunnar>: I'm not exactly sure. Mittelman sounded angry and frightened.

<Mags>: The Robot!

<Gunnar>: You understand.

<Mags>: You sucked William into one of your political whirlpools. You should have told him the rules of the game.

<Gunnar>: He leaped in before I finish talking to him. He started three days early, he didn't tell me, and he trapped both of us.

<Mags>: This was your idea. You are going to get him out without hurting him?

SOA was his chance to earn what he deserves. It would destroy him if he had to go backwards.

<Gunnar>: He refuses to come out, and he won't listen. He hung up on me yesterday.

<Mags>: What exactly did he do?

<Gunnar>: He attacked Marshall [...] faulty premises [...] character assassination [...] tried to take his job.

<Mags>: I didn't realize he was still that upset. This must have something to do with Indira Marshall?

<Gunnar>: ***How do you know Indira Marshall?***

<Mags>: Sit before you fall over, and keep your voice down.

I don't actually know her. Everything I've heard comes from Will.

<Gunnar>: ***TALK*** or we all start job hunting, even you.

<Mags>: If he could slow Marshall down, he could find more business for Belvedere, more commissions for himself, and you would owe him a big favor. All is fair, as you always say.

<Gunnar>: ***Your mother taught me to say that.*** He was too obvious and he attacked too aggressively.

<Mags>: You attacked Marshall without cause, and he almost went to jail because of what you did?

<Gunnar>: It was poor delegation. We lost millions.

<Mags>: How was that different from what William did?

<Gunnar>: I didn't know Marshall. I was following the boss's orders. You are saying William knew Marshall's daughter. Spill! Hurry!

<Mags>: He says that she and her mother hurt his career before he ever started.

<Gunnar>: When?

<Mags>: Almost 21 years ago.

<Gunnar>: That's a long time. How?

<Mags>: She was a female jock who had it in her head that she could major in finance. He was her student adviser. He tried to correct some of her bad practices, and she made trouble for him with the dean.

Her mother had law enforcement connections, and she threatened to have him investigated. He says they are both willing to use flirtation power when they need it.

<Gunnar>: *I must be slipping. Neither one of them tried to flirt with me yesterday.*

<Mags>: He thinks that affected his grant, and that's why he didn't get his PhD. I'm not as upset about it as he is. He earns much more in the business world, though it doesn't have quite the same cachet.

[...] I know - you earn more in the business world too, and we all benefit from your transition. But you were already a doctor, and you walked away. Who ever heard of that?

<Gunnar>: Why would he take a chance on ruining this career for a less profitable career that never happened?

<Mags>: During that incident, her boyfriend and some football thugs attacked Will. They broke his nose and bruised him badly.

<Gunnar>: That was when he fell down the flight of steps.

<Mags>: They made up the story about the flight of stairs and how they found him.

William went along with it because he was afraid. We were both intimidated when they left him with me. The big one was as tall as Will and he had to turn sideways to get through the door.

<Gunnar>: Is it strange to attack someone, and then carry them home?

<Mags>: I [...] don't [...] know. I never thought of that. *Maybe I did, but I tried to make it go away.*

Nevertheless, he hates them as much as he did 21 years ago.

That's why we got married right away. He had to have the surgery before he could get a job and my insurance covered it. If I hadn't been teaching, we would have been in an impossible situation.

Why are you looking like that? You're turning red.

<Gunnar>: *Indy is bigger, stronger, and faster than her mother is, and she can move a 200-pound man against his will. William probably felt the Wrath of Frey.*

<Mags>: Are you going to be all right?

<Gunnar>: I'm woozy from the painkillers. Is there anything else?

<Mags>: Indira's father was targeting William's new practice. I believe he called it Partner Networks.

<Gunnar>: Not on purpose?

<Mags>: Maybe, and maybe not. Nevertheless, William estimates that we lost at least a quarter of a million in bonuses last year because Daxiao underbid him. That was adding insult to injury.

You should have told me!

<Gunnar>: *Marshall helped me bring in almost $200 million in extra sales and a whopping bonus.*

William's bonus loss is my bonus gain. I ended up lending William a third of what he thinks he lost anyhow.

<Mags>: Marshall didn't try to stop him, and I couldn't ruin his chance to learn from the inside what Marshall did to grab all that business. You would have kept quiet too.

<Gunnar>: You're right. Gerthe would insist. *She would not know that it could destroy me, and neither did I.*

[...] This will be delicate, but I have to ask. Was there anything between Will and [...]

<Mags>: Of course not. We were living together. He didn't need to have dealings with her type.

<Gunnar>: What type was that?

<Mags>: I mean "not like us". That Amal woman was not us, and that thing Kerstin married is not us. I've never seen him do anything except eat pizza and stare at that screen.

<Gunnar>: Why would you bring up Amal now?

<Mags>: You and Will were on track for exceptional careers, you were both physically injured, and you both changed careers, within a 12-month period. Mother still hasn't recovered.

At least she helped to save your relationship with Stephanie, and you managed to mess that up too.

<Gunnar>: *Stephanie was her ticket to "proper" society, and I've paid for it my entire adult life.*

Your mother is faking being ill to control us. Daddy worked himself to death trying to please her, she has you making Will crazier than he naturally would be, and if I hadn't listened to her, I might [...]

<Mags>: Where is this coming from? "My" mother wanted the best for both of her children, she taught us to expect the best, and she taught us to go after what we want.

<Gunnar>: I called you to keep you safe from Sharf. Maybe that was a mistake.

<Mags>: I do not need anyone to keep me safe from Will. You are not making sense, and we are on the verge of making a scene.

<Gunnar>: Back up a minute. What did mother do to save my relationship?

<Mags>: She taught Stephanie to fight for you.

<Gunnar>: When did she start?

<Mags>: Before you hurt yourself trying to save that woman.

<Gunnar>: *Kerstin was a consolation baby!*

<Mags>: Sit up! You look like a drunk.

<Gunnar>: I know. Appearances are important.

<Mags>: You and Stephanie wasted 15 years. However, my marriage is still strong and I intend to keep it that way. As tempting as this treat may be, I will be home if William needs me.

<Gunnar>: *That was ironic. I was the gigolo, and she got caught. If the lab hadn't mailed the DNA test results to Mr. & Mrs. Gunnar, I would be raising Prince Whatchacallit's son.*

At least the divorce was neat. She was determined to keep the baby, and one pregnancy balanced approximately 20 affairs. I ended up with Kerstin. Her royalty rating wasn't high enough for Stephanie's new circles. Kerstin turned into a teenage nightmare, but we survived, barely. With parents like us, it's a miracle that she still has an ounce of sanity.

Maybe we were gigolo and gigolette and she left the results where I could find them because she found someone who returned her affection. Maybe she got tired of Gerthe. Maybe Whatchamacallit wouldn't have let me raise his child. There was a strong family resemblance.

<Mags>: Gunnar, you have that dazed look again. What did this lump make you forget?

<Gunnar>: I'm just starting to remember things.

<Mags>: Remember that you have to fix whatever you helped William to break. William must survive and remain in no worse shape than he was when you hooked him into this. Do it quietly. My children cannot be hurt. Am I clear?

<Gunnar>: Exceedingly.

<Mags>: I should go now. Call James.

<Gunnar>: I need James for the rest of the day. *He's all I have. Kerstin doesn't understand Daxiao.*

<Mags>: I'll call a limo, and I will charge it to your account. I can't very well take the bus.

<Gunnar>: Take some cash out of my wallet [...] inside pocket. I may not have an account for long.

<Mags>: *He has to be kidding. We need him.*

Stop kidding, and use some of that to buy yourself a hat with a brim to hide that thing on your head. Your tailor made an assortment of slings after one of your accidents. Find them. They match what you're wearing better than that ugly green thing.

I'll send James aground, and I'll check on you after I find out how Will is doing.

<Gunnar>: *I have to apologize to Indy, I have to avoid whatever revenge her father planned for me, I have to neutralize Sharf, and I have to figure out why Mittelman let me get in trouble the same way twice.*

I have to figure out why I can't get Indy out of my head.

I have to stand up first.

<Doorman/guard>: May I help you sir? *He is not the type of person we wish to have sitting in our lobby.*

<Gunnar>: Yes, you may help me to stand up.

<Doorman/guard>: Mr. Gunnar! I hardly recognized you. What happened?

<Gunnar>: I fell *a very long way.*

<Doorman/guard>: Dr. Montclair is up stairs. Should I call him?

<Gunnar>: That won't be necessary. Let me sit here until James comes around. Then let me hold your arm and walk me to the car.

------- **Hospital for Orthopaedic Surgery** -------

<Gunnar>: Go and move the car. I can walk the rest of the way on my own.

<James Grady>: It didn't seem that way a while ago, and you look worse now. You should use any energy you have to prepare for Mittelman.

<Gunnar>: Take care of the car and come back. I have to do this before I see Mittelman.

---------- ----------

<Nurse #1>: Hello! I remember you from yesterday. Can you tell if I'm a man or a woman?

<Gunnar>: I was confused. Why are you here?

<Nurse #1>: You certainly were confused. I work up here. I hung around yesterday to help Mr. Marshall's family.

I also remembered seeing your collarbone after I got home. Why didn't you mention that you had records here?

<Gunnar>: I did, but later. You said I was confused.

Why would you remember my collarbone?

<Nurse #1>: I remember the parts for which I am responsible. It requires concentration.

<Gunnar>: Marshalls. Where are they?

<Nurse #1>: Mr. Marshall is down the hall. Mrs. Marshall is somewhere else doing something else. She said she'd be back in an hour, which is about 30 minutes from now. Huey and his sister made up, and she went to find food for him.

<Gunnar>: Why were they fighting?

<Nurse #1>: Ask him. He's on the floor over there in the corner.

<Gunnar>: He looks pale. I guess she won the fight. ***I hope she returns soon. I need to see her.***

<Nurse #1>: He gave his father two pints of blood in the last 12 hours because his baby brother was delayed somewhere between here and wherever he be bein'.

<Gunnar>: What?

<Nurse #1>: I'm bad at hip-hop. Anyway, the second pint was pushing the limit, and he forgot to eat.

<Gunnar>: Does he ever sit in chairs?

<Nurse #1>: Not too often. He says he can't fall down if he's already on the floor.

<Gunnar>: Who are the people with him?

<Nurse #1>: The person to his right on the floor is Hank Yu. He works for Mr. Marshall. That's Ryan Winslow on the floor to his left, the younger woman sitting in the chair is his wife, and [...]

<Gunnar>: The rigid proper-looking one beside her is DOCTAH EMEWY-BALDWIN.

<Nurse #1>: That is a great imitation, considering how many stitches you must have in your mouth. She's tough. Be careful.

<Gunnar>: Wasn't Winslow a famous jock at one time? ***He still appears to be in good shape. I would be too if I had stayed away from Marshall.***

<Nurse #1>: He's a sports reporter now. He had to stop playing about three years ago.

<Gunnar>: She is very pregnant. ***GOOD! Scratch Ryan.***

<Nurse #1>: She's going to make it this time. The entire family is more than elated.

<Gunnar>: Why would that be? ***She looks cute and dumb, not gorgeous and in control like Indy. That proves that there is no accounting for taste.***

<Nurse #1>: They worry about miscarriages. With this one they help her lift her spoon and Jonas has been very careful not to shake anything loose.

<Gunnar>: Jonas is married to her?

<Nurse #1>: He's been a big boy for a long time. Mike is almost 15.

<Gunnar>: I thought that she was the second Mrs. Winslow?

<Nurse #1>: Don't be ridiculous. That would drop his chances with Baby Girl from 5% to minus a million percent. He messed around too many times before.

<Gunnar>: He's wearing a ring.

<Nurse #1>: He's worn it for 20 years, and he'll probably die wearing it. He found out the hard way that Frey women are the hottest long-term investment. They are also the 100% genuine article, in comparison to some of his outside experiments.

<Gunnar>: How do you know this?

<Nurse #1>: He will cry on anybody's shoulder that will listen. Mr. Marshall has spent [...] about seven weeks here during the last four years. He cries on my shoulder while he's waiting for an opportunity to bump into Baby Girl, accidentally, of course. Any other time, he has about 90 seconds to do a kid swap. He assures me that what he lost is enough to make five grown men cry.

<Gunnar>: You are enjoying this.

<Nurse #1>: If you knew how he almost destroyed her, you'd understand why. Except for her mother, maybe, she was the #1 type of woman that people like me dream about. Imagine that she (and her mother) only wore knee high stockings when their men were around.

<Gunnar>: What am I missing?

<Nurse #1>: [...] *Slow. I'm still worried about him.* Indy would be in a nunnery if it wasn't for the twins.

<Gunnar>: The mother, still? *I shouldn't act too interested in Indy.*

<Nurse #1>: At least until four years ago when he first started blubbering about it. Mr. Marshall probably has many reasons to want to live.

<Gunnar>: [...] *I am slow today - Now the brief jockey briefs make sense. The investigator was right about the raging fires in Marshall's library. I wonder if it's hereditary.*

Ever-Ready Indy! I must stop this conversation, or I'll embarrass myself right before I collapse.

<Nurse #1>: What's wrong?

<Gunnar>: Medicine is wearing off. Could I see Marshall before the pain gets worse? If he is down here, he must be all right.

<Nurse #1>: He is better than last night, but he has a long way to go. However, you look worse.

<Gunnar>: Can he have visitors?

<Nurse #1>: Two people are down there now. After they come out, promise that you will take 10 minutes or less. Just a minute [...]

Mr. Winslow, I do not know any more than I knew when you were here 15 minutes ago. There have been no codes, so Marshall is the same as he was when you saw him.

<Gunnar>: *Marshall could have a crisis at any minute!*

<Nurse #1>: His daughter went to the family feed trough and watering hole. Because she's not back, I'm guessing that she was too late for lunch and too early for dinner. That means the Samuel is preparing something especially for Jonas.

<Ryan Winslow>: I was coming to say that, having delivered Mrs. Rolly Polly to her Fuzzy Wuzzy, I am going to work. Tell H that I will see him later and tell Mrs. Winslow I will bring our kids to see their grandfather when I finish my broadcast.

<Gunnar>: *Radio voice.*

<Ryan>: Jonas says you're the one that saved my father-in-law's life yesterday, and that you had the unfortunate run-in with Moms. We're sorry. Our women are intense at times.

<Nurse #1>: *He's spraying!*

<Gunnar>: *You left off the "ex-".* Yes, I am Niklas Gunnar, and you are Ryan Winslow. You **were** good.

<Ryan>: *I'd still be good, for my age, if I had listened to Indy.* Before I go, let me say that Indy and I will be forever grateful for what you did for our family.

<Gunnar>: Thank you. I'm sorry I can't shake, or talk much. Perhaps later we can discuss things we may have in common. *There is no "and" between you and Indy. If there was, she'd have told you everything I did, and you would have qualified that statement.*

<Ryan>: What would you propose?

<Gunnar>: *Easy Gunnar. If he sneezes in your direction, you'll fall over.* I was good at soccer once, and I train a little. We may have other areas of mutual interest. I am learning to appreciate HM's contributions more than you'd ever imagine, *especially his contribution of your ex-wife to this world.*

<Ryan>: Perhaps. I will see you tomorrow Barker.

---------- ----------

<Nurse #1>: Impressive for a man in your condition. Ryan is usually his own worse competition.

<Gunnar>: It was stupid too. There is no competition.

<Nurse #1>: I imagine that Indy is not your type, but maybe he's picking up something from Jonas.

<Gunnar>: *Maybe Jonas said something good about me! Thanks to all the Gods. I'm not religious, but Guntur must be putting in a good word for his old man! I'm still not sure about Amal.*

<Nurse #1>: That's the most "we're all one big happy family" bull I've ever heard him try to fake.

<Gunnar>: What is my type?

<Nurse #1>: Give me a minute. [...] I would say Dalton for starters, finishing school, Wellesley or Bryn Mawr with a few courses in Europe, between 5' 9" and 5' 10", 115 lbs. (making her too skinny to actually be statuesque), perfectly blond except in the shower, a little preventive maintenance already, Italian designer clothes this year, memorizes updates to the collection at the Whitney, and can describe the bouquet of 200 different types of wine, a few of which she may appreciate excessively.

<Gunnar>: Like Helena *(and Stephanie, Lauren, Estelle, Boothe, Amanda, Bianca - and my mother except that she really was a blond).* How did you do that?

<Nurse #1>: I've worked and lived here for 23 years. That's my apartment straight out that window. You can see Tiger and her kittens lined up in the window. I've seen the outsides and insides of thousands of men like you and of the Helenas that they prefer. If you ever deviated from your preference, it would be purely experimental.

<Gunnar>: *It started that way with Amal, in a manner of speaking. I wanted to know how she could work harder than I did, but that's not how it ended.* How am I different from Ryan?

<Nurse #1>: Except for the nine or ten years, Ryan wears $1,000 suits from Rochester's, not because he can't afford better, but because that's what he and his team members wore when they could afford their first nice outfits. Your tailor in London or Hong Kong keeps your measurements on file, and sends you fabric samples when he finds something perfect for you. You are currently dressed down in cashmere and silk.

<Gunnar>: *Only since Marshall's work inflated my bonuses.*

<Nurse #1>: Ryan sounds like a Midwestern radio announcer, because he is Midwestern. He probably helped at least two cousins with the down payment on combines. Before Ms. Frey changed your accent, you had a bit of an undertone of European aristocracy.

<Gunnar>: We were painfully middle class, but mother never let us forget the 1/8th royalty part.

<Nurse #1>: Giving further support to what I said about your type preferences.

<Doc>: Hello Gooner. I hate to disturb your conversation, but we need to talk.

Machi whupped him good. You go girl!

<Gunnar>: *I needed an ice water shower, and here she is.* I must see Marshall. Can this wait?

<Doc>: His visitors will be down there a few minutes longer. That gives us time to talk about the itinerary I prepared for Mr. Sharp earlier today.

<Gunnar>: ***Cancel them, immediately!***

<Doc>: *He's screaming. I've never heard Gunnar using anything except his suave salesman voice.*

<Gunnar>: *That really hurt.* I'm sorry I was loud. Sharf is the wrong person. I will explain after I see Marshall.

<Doc>: Let's go. I'll talk while you try to walk.

<Gunnar>: No need to talk. We will select another person. I sent an e-mail.

<Doc>: *That's the fastest backpedaling I've ever seen.* I'll walk with you anyhow. With that wobble, I wouldn't want you to trip over any of H's lifelines.

<Gunnar>: *Give it a break.* I saved him.

<Huey>: Doc, we need you to handle some paperwork for Daddy. If you have time, we could talk about it now.

<Gunnar>: No! *Please wait.*

<Doc>: No what?

<Dr. Rebecca Vincent>: Doc, Jonas needs you.

<Doc>: I'm coming. *There's a Higgs everywhere. These are not erratic hormones. I nearly lost my brother and best friend. We could still lose him. Somebody has to pay.*

Make sure that there are no more accidents.

<Nurse #1>: Weldon's coming out, and with time to spare. *Whew. She was about to clean his clock again, and he can hardly stand up.*

<Weldon Armstrong>: Hello Gunnar. I'll see you later. Hope you're OK.

<Gunnar>: I'm surprised to see you. What's the rush?

<Weldon>: The hospital smells are bothering me. Barker, please tell Joe I'll be outside with Boyd.

<Nurse #1>: *That's strange. He spent days working with Mr. Marshall the last two times he was here.*

<Gunnar>: I'll walk with you. *Joe is the last man on earth that I needed to see right now.*

<Weldon>: You need to sit and rest. We can talk when you feel better, *if you survive this one.*

<Nurse #1>: Jonas is waving Mr. Armstrong.

<Weldon>: Hello Huey, Becky, Doc. Becky, you put the meaning into happy glow. Hank, don't you have a meeting with Wainwright about now?

[...] I understand. I must go.

<Gunnar>: *He knows Marshall's family. Octopus strikes again.*

<Nurse #1>: You were fast too.

<Joe>: I saw what I needed to see. He won't remember us, so please tell him that we were here.

Mr. Gunnar, this is an interesting surprise. We should take advantage of this fortuitous meeting.

<Gunnar>: *I'd rather drive spikes under my toenails.* Good idea.

<Joe>: Did they save your teeth?

<Gunnar>: Yes. Armstrong looks green.

<Joe>: He gets the "Queeze of the Year Award". He turned green when he saw Marshall and his voice started shaking when he saw you.

<Gunnar>: I look bad?

<Joe>: He may have been more concerned about what you planned to do to H until he saw you up close. Fortunately, you look like you fell into a cement mixer. Ms. Frey may have done you a favor.

<Gunnar>: You know about my "accident"?

<Joe>: Everyone here knows. There are several people in the office that would have purchased tickets for the event.

Back to business - why you are here, and why were you in Marshall's office yesterday?

<Gunnar>:

- One - After yesterday, I was worried about him.
- Two - Marshall asked me to stop by since we will be neighbors. He wanted to clear the air.

<Joe>: When the air cleared, you were the last man standing, barely.

<Gunnar>: What do you mean?

<Joe>: That concussion may have clouded your thinking, so I'll give you a hint. A few people have remarked that because Marshall has balance problems, he was trained him in one of the critical martial arts skills. He knew how to take a fall. The first time that his life needed saving (recently) was when you paid a visit.

<Gunnar>: I saved Marshall's life.

<Joe>: My research verifies that you are telling the truth, but Weldon was one of many people who may view things differently.

<Gunnar>: When did Armstrong develop concern about Marshall?

<Joe>: I would estimate that it was 8:30 this morning. He realized that his Daxiao career depended on what the man with the sickle does down the hall. He may not have 18 months to polish up his résumé.

<Gunnar>: How bad is Marshall?

<Joe>: I have no idea what is keeping him alive.

<Gunnar>: I need him. *He can show me how to get everything I need - love, family, friends, respect - not fear.*

<Joe>: What did you just say?

<Nurse #1>: Mr. Marshall is one of the toughest people I have ever seen. Appearances can be deceiving (*I hope*).

<Joe>: I heard you. What kind of act is this?

<Gunnar>: I'm not myself. It must be and unusual reaction to the meds. *Indy is the key to everything!*

<Joe>: Come over here. This will be quick. I can't delay your conversation with Mittelman.

[...] It is still generally agreed that you are valuable to Daxiao. However, the probability of you doing better than OK is tied to Marshall's probability of recovery. Van Amberg can give you some numbers. On second thought, after your performance yesterday, maybe you can calculate your own numbers.

<Gunnar>: That's ridiculous? *I need to sit down.*

<Huey>: Mr. Gunnar. Becky brought me some energy bars. You look like need one.

<Joe>: **Notice jaw.** Go over there with Becky. You should relax and wait for Indy.

<Huey>: **Sorry. He looks very bad.** *Wow! Joe is as upset as I was when I saw Daddy.*

<Joe>: He's right about you being wobbly. Sit. *Jonas does like him. What am I missing?*

<Gunnar>: How many of you do that? I could use it now. *How well does Jonas know Joe?*

<Joe>: What?

<Gunnar>: Lately, I have noticed that many people who know Jonas also know sign language.

<Joe>: Oh, that? I suppose Dan, me, and Marshall's direct reports, especially his procurement people. It aids contract negotiations.

<Gunnar>: *Marshall's been doing that for years, and I didn't notice. What else does he do?*

<Joe>: Settle yourself while he moves out of earshot and eyeshot.

[...] Now pay attention. You know that this situation is a totally unacceptable diversion of company resources.

<Gunnar>: Justin couldn't have said it better.

<Joe>: Therefore, between wobbles, you will use every iota of strength you have left to clean this up quickly, including dealing with the psycho relative that you tried to sneak past me. We have a plan if Marshall lives. It will be tougher if he dies.

<Gunnar>: ***He can't die!*** We need him.

<Joe>: You figured that out all by yourself, did you? If you know that, why did you let Sharf loose on him? *He seems concerned - great acting.*

<Gunnar>: Sharf was strictly a business proposition that got out of hand.

<Joe>: It was expensive too. You wanted us to pay $500,000, of which that whack job would receive at least $50,000, so that you and your boys could have your own private tutorial. It would have been cheaper if you got it from the Doc or from Lisse Maçon. I heard that she worked for you once.

<Gunnar>: *I don't need to be reminded again.* It would keep Acton on their toes. Maybe you need more diligence.

<Joe>: You're good, even if you're ready to collapse. If it was not your vendetta, what is wrong with Sharf?

<Gunnar>: He's a little rough naturally. Ādaemoa was bad judgment.

<Joe>: It was also bad judgment to report that Marshall is an alcoholic drug addict to Mittelman, in front of the Doc and me, after he tried to deep-six his career, before Marshall finishes what Daxiao needed him to do, and right after eight of the top physicians in New York had tried to save his life.

You both worked exceptionally hard to be that [...] Dios mio. Estoy estupefacto.

<Gunnar>: What did you call me?

<Joe>: Ignore that. What I'm about to say is important. If Nicky sues us, we will take it out of your bonuses, should you continue to receive bonuses.

<Gunnar>: *I have to apologize to Amal about Sharf.* I will do whatever you say if you work with me to make this all right.

<Joe>: Contrition, from Gunnar? That's a new act, but here's the deal.

<Gunnar>: ***What are you thinking fool? Indy is a forceful Amazon who looks soft on the outside. Amal was a petite lotus through and through.***

Tough is good. If Amal had been tough like Indy, she might have survived. She may have pushed me in front of the truck, but Guntur would be older than Kerstin. If I had survived, we might have many more Gunturs.

<Joe>: Gunnar! Pay attention. You must:

1. Listen to what Mittelman has to say, and execute to the letter. You will find that he is back on the fence where he works most effectively.
2. Find out what is wrong with Sharf, and tell us. We need wiggle room. We are caught between a Nicola, who is much more dangerous than a cute little old woman with a stick is, and Sharf.
3. There should be a resolution by 5:00 o'clock today.

I must go and work to revise the contract that you tried to sneak past me.

<Gunnar>: We don't need that now.

<Joe>: We need it. That "tentative" agreement that you bullied Shackleton into approving, and that you and Justin signed is the toughest preliminary agreement I have ever seen. Diamonte and Cane really wanted a Belvedere/Daxiao relationship.

We could just pay them the $500,000, but that would set a poor example. If we try to back out without an excellent reason, they could sue us. If we reveal that the reason is related to Sharf attempting character assassination on a man who was barely alive, and Nicola Frey found out, she would make sure that H had nothing to do with us, if he survives. Then she would sue us.

<Huey>: Joe. I can't see what you're saying, but I can tell you're being mean.

<Joe>: ***He's defending him, too.*** Visit HM if you must. After last night's performance, I'd guess that you are not as wimpy as Armstrong is. However, if you even think a wrong thought, his guard nurses could break everything that Nicky didn't, before Jonas and Pipsqueak turn you into mush.

Adios. [...] Doc, are you coming back with us?

<Doc>: Let me adjust the fluid level in my equipment, and I'll be right down.

<Joe>: Piccolo will never live that down.

---------- ----------

<Nurse #1>: They are both very intense.

<Gunnar>: Only when they are awake. Can I see Marshall now?

<Nurse #1>: He's in the suite at the end of the hall on the side with the flowers in the case outside the door. We set the whole area up for him (in return for a $10 million contribution).

The cut flowers will be dead before he sees them, but Ms. Frey took pictures already. She carries a real camera wherever she goes.

<Gunnar>: Can he talk?

<Nurse #1>: With difficulty. The breathing tube was stuck, but they finally got it out.

<Gunnar>: Was he awake?

<Nurse #1>: Part of the time, and you never saw anyone more agitated in your life. Thank goodness for sign language. We're hoping that means there was no brain damage.

<Gunnar>: ***We gave him the injection of Naloxone within 10 minutes, thanks to Van Amberg. If they didn't goof last night, there shouldn't be a problem.*** Why don't we need gowns and caps?

<Nurse #1>: He's in an experimental isolation coffin that we [...]

<Gunnar>: COFFIN! ***If he dies, I'm dead! I lost Amal and Liz. I can't lose Indy. I'm crazier than before!***

<Nurse #1>: [...] Easy. I told Dr. Church that we should call it something else.

<Huey>: I told you we should have called it an incubator.

<Becky>: Pop's too big to be in an incubator. Dan says it's a portable sterile environment. We can use PO and ST, like a post-operative.

<Nurse #1>: ***The bruise on his thigh must be killing him, but he's moving fast.***

---------- ----------

<Frederick Chase>: Stop. I don't remember seeing you before.

<Gunnar>: He's breathing!

<Fred>: Of course. Actually, that's not a given, but he's breathing on his own at this moment.

On the other hand, you are having problems. Who are you?

<Gunnar>: Niklas Gunnar, a co-worker.

<Fred>: You're the one that helped get him here on time. Many people thank you.

<Gunnar>: Don't thank me yet.

[...] It's a giant incubator on an erector set.

<Fred>: It's a post-operative recovery acceleration unit. That won't make a good acronym, but that's what it does. We will use the pistons to shift his body weight so that he won't get decubitus ulcers (bedsores). It's easier to keep the germs out than to keep the people out.

<Gunnar>: Where did it come from?

<Fred>: It's a reject from the space program. Dr. Church had an idea and Dr. Piccolo has these crazy hobbies. We have three in operation, and they seem to work.

<Gunnar>: Piccolo? ***Liz went for green pastures and real companionship. I wonder where he stashes his millions.***

<Fred>: He surprises a lot of people. His silliness hides how much he knows about so many things. He's almost as smart as Mr. Marshall was/is.

<Gunnar>: Can he hear us in there?

<Fred>: Yes. The room has four pick-ups. Therefore, you should try not to wake him up. Wave hello and goodbye, and then leave. I will tell him you were here.

On second thought, plop down here, catch your breath, and then do your waving and leaving.

<Gunnar>: I'm OK.

<Fred>: Except for the shaky knees.

<Gunnar>: Let me catch my breath over there (***right beside one of our terminals, and it is logged in. That's good***).

[...] The wobble is gone. Let me see how he looks.

[...] The Frankenstein Hulk! When did he go from fat to fit?

<Fred>: He lost weight to try to avoid this.

<Gunnar>: Why did they cut him like that? [...] ***From his armpit to his calf! He looks scary even to me.***

<Fred>: You should discuss his condition with his family.

<Gunnar>: That can't be one cut?

<Fred>: No. It stops for about four inches under that pad. Are you trying to fall in there with him?

<Gunnar>: I'm all right. I'm sitting again. See.

<Fred>: You're dealing with it better than most.

<Gunnar>: ***Information source!*** How did most react?

<Fred>: Ernest was first. His contact lenses were bothering him, but he checked all the tubing and the connections. Maja was the calmest. She shook her head and left. His wife started laugh crying (it's the weirdest sound I've ever heard).

<Gunnar>: I remember from yesterday, ***while I was trying not to pass out.***

<Fred>: Huey ran and hid in a closet after he reamed out his sister. Becky had to pull him out of the closet, and Becky is not good at pulling these days. Hank started crying - not just allergies (that was a big surprise). Ryan nearly fell in, just as you did. Mr. Armstrong nearly upchucked, which was less of a surprise, and Mr. Guzman is VERRRY unhappy. Doc was the angriest. She stood there for 10 minutes grinding her teeth. You probably want to avoid her even more than you would want to avoid Ms. Frey.

<Gunnar>: You're late. I saw her already.

How did his daughter react, and why did his son yell at her.

<Fred>: She tried to follow Maja's example until Huey screamed at her for signing the papers. Then she sat where you're sitting and started whimpering. You don't want to be around Huey when he starts screaming. He's louder than his father is, and he can't hear himself.

<Gunnar>: ***My poor wet kitten.*** What papers?

<Fred>: Baby Girl made a death-or-death decision last night, the nature of which you should discover from her family. The doctors showed her how everything would work before she signed the papers. Thus, she was the least surprised, though she was still very upset. I'm talking too much.

<Gunnar>: *I know how to find what I need to know. I have to remember how Laufer does the demonstrations.*

<Fred>: What are you doing? That is private information.

<Gunnar>: I just noticed that this was one of ours.

<Fred>: It doesn't say Daxiao.

<Gunnar>: We sell the insides to other companies. I've always wanted to see how it works in the real world.

I can't really understand doctor talk, but I sell it and his team writes software. There's a Daxiao support number right there.

<Fred>: See fast. I could get in trouble.

<Gunnar>: What happens if I push this button?

<Fred>: You see what moved off the screen. *He's probably lying about the doctor talk, but I want to hear what he has to say.*

<Gunnar>: *Blood loss from punctured lung, ruptured spleen, and a minor artery in his leg. They had to open him up to save his spleen, which he needs to fight potential infection in his leg. They put back as much of his blood as they could. They tapped Jonas, Indy, Richard Marshall, and then Jonas again.*

[...] *They are aggressively dealing with potential infection.*

[...] *No signs of oxygen deprivation and no pneumonia.*

[...] *Extensive bone loss caused the thigh to shatter above the appliance, and they tried to save his leg and thigh by doing a total femur replacement!*

[...] *They could have killed before I found out what I needed to know!*

<Fred>: *That doesn't look good. I will have to watch HM even closer.* Did you find a problem with the program?

<Gunnar>: It is probably working fine, but I wasn't able to put in my contact lenses this morning.

<HM>: Fred?

<Fred>: [...] I'm here.

<HM>: Where's N- Nicky? I made her cry. *Nicky stopped crying.*

<Fred>: She stopped crying. She said she's going to get your freedom package. She'll be [...]

<HM>: ***No, please!*** Need Nicky.

<Fred>: What's wrong?

<HM>: C- Can't leave now.

<Gunnar>: His pressure is spiking. Do something!

<Fred>: Relax, or we can help you relax.

<HM>: Nicky m- mad? No more research!

<Fred>: She's very sad, not mad. You want to be here for her when she returns, don't you?

<HM>: L- let me out! *Jesus, there are spikes in my side and the room is spinning.*

<Fred>: That'll teach you. She nearly killed a few people trying to get to you yesterday. You know she's coming back.

<Gunnar>: *She's his weak point, or his strong point. That's the fastest spike I've ever seen.*

<Fred>: That's Barker calling to find out what's happening. If he has to come down here, you'll be in dreamland for the next 24 hours.

Do you hear me?

<HM>: Tr- trying. *I'm not thinking straight. I have to breathe, even if it hurts like hell.*

[...] *That's better. The freedom package is probably my Daxiao contract.*

[...] *I need my happy thoughts list.*

[...] *Here's a good one. Indy waited for me. I saw her walk on Christmas day. She didn't just walk. She ran for 15 minutes, from her mother to me and then to the Queen, Ike, and Clara. She stopped at Denise once, and she ran around Richard. Nicky was so happy to see her walk finally.*

Nicky was annoyed that she didn't walk during Hanukkah, but Indy always set her own schedule. She waited for me! Prettiest baby girl in the world, and she waited for me to be there. She looked like me when I was her age, including the shiny head. She stayed bald until she was three, just like me. I had a pretty, happy, bald baby girl and her pretty, happy mama.

<Fred>: That's better. Keep doing whatever you're doing.

<HM>: Is Nicky OK?

<Fred>: She's in much better shape than you are. *That is easy.*

<Gunnar>: What did he do?

<Fred>: If we could figure that out, we'd be selling it.

<Gunnar>: Why are you asking about freedom papers? You won't be leaving here any time soon.

<HM>: Ha- Hallucinating?

<Gunnar>: No. Twice in two days.

<HM>: *Why is he still here? I can't let him gloat.* W- Went to hell.

<Gunnar>: Two or three times [...]

<HM>: S- See horn.

<Gunnar>: I see Marshall's mean streak.

<Fred>: He's right. That lump on your head looks like a little horn that is holding up your hat. You should put the hat over the horn, like this.

<HM>: G- Gangster.

<Gunnar>: You look worse.

<HM>: Sound like paint dry and gr- grass grow.

<Gunnar>: *He's OK! Maybe not exactly OK, but better than I thought.* Your friend is mean too. I have loose teeth. I have to choose words.

<HM>: *I wonder what she did. I can't laugh now.* Ch- Choose most of my life.

<Gunnar>: I really do understand now.

<HM>: Hurts now. *I'm too tired to fight now. Let him gloat.*

<Fred>: That means that you should stop trying to talk, and you should leave.

<Gunnar>: *She's not back yet.* I will check on you later.

<HM>: No n- need. You won.

<Gunnar>: *I don't believe you.* He sounds strong.

<Fred>: It's amplified. We don't want to open the unit to hear what the patients are whispering.

<Gunnar>: Marshall! ***Please don't do that.***

<Fred>: He went back to sleep. Check the monitor. *Why is he freaking out like that?*

<Gunnar>: Was that a blip in the bleep?

<Fred>: No. You are the one who is blipping. Did you get an MRI?

<Gunnar>: They have one scheduled for later today.

<Fred>: You should try to rest until then.

<Gunnar>: I will, but I have one more question.

<Fred>: What's the question?

<Gunnar>: Do you know him personally? Everybody else does.

<Fred>: Of course. I've been trying to take care of him for almost 21 years.

<Gunnar>: What did you receive in return?

<Fred>: He gave two of my kids a chance. One has been with him for 10 years, and the other one moved to one of Jonas's start-ups. He took a risk, and now he's rich.

<Gunnar>: *Octopus.* I need one more favor - it will reduce the wobble.

<Fred>: What else?

<Gunnar>: Can I have his Jell-O? *Indy. Please. I'm running out of stall tactics.*

<Fred>: You might as well. He's not swallowing much either.

<Gunnar>: Not hospital Jell-O.

<Fred>: Of course not. It's one of Samuel's gelatin desserts. He will only allow the best for Mr. Marshall. Take the apple mousse too.

<Gunnar>: If he needs to be in there, how do you let him have outside food?

<Fred>: It's not outside food. Samuel sends a chef over here. The patients all eat a little better when Mr. Marshall has a clumsy episode.

---------- ----------

<James>: Why are you sitting on the floor?

<Gunnar>: *Stalling.* Why are you here?

<James>: The nurse said I should check on you.

<Gunnar>: I'm OK. I'm stealing Marshall's food. *Who would imagine that the lummox who isn't a lummox would have gourmet desserts delivered to an entire hospital?*

<James>: Give me your hand.

<Gunnar>: No. Put this on the garbage. I can stand up myself. *It hurts the same way no matter what I do.*

---------- **At the Elevator Banks** ----------

<Church>: Gunnar, I'm glad you came back. Why did you check yourself out before you finished your tests?

<Gunnar>: Go ahead James. I will meet you downstairs in ten minutes.

<Church>: A doctor is the worst patient. I'm certainly glad you didn't lose your touch after all these years.

<Gunnar>: I needed time to figure out what holes Marshall is digging for me, and you risked his life before I could find out what I needed.

<Church>: You are "The Goon"!

<Gunnar>: Some people might refer to me that way.

<Church>: I suggest that you should do Marshall and his family a favor and take what you want at Daxiao. I told Marshall he should have left five years ago, and again when he signed that contract 15 months ago. He'll be better off if he survives, and it won't matter if he doesn't.

<Gunnar>: ***YES, IT WILL!*** You have to help me. I could lose everything! ***I could lose my last chance!***

<Church>: What will you lose? I had a very long night, so my compassion quota for egotistical, sympathy seeking, lechers is very low, even the ones who might possibly be my friend.

<Indy>: Doug. Gunnar! You both look funny. Is Daddy OK?

<Church and Gunnar>: Yes.

<Indy>: Good. You look worse than you did the last time I saw you.

<Gunnar>: *She's talking to me, for the time being.*

<Church>: I was about to ask him to let me look at him. What about you?

<Indy>: I rested while I was donating, and I pieced together a few more hours after I saw your handiwork. I will love you forever.

<Church>: Stop that.

[...] *Indy puts the advantage to being short.*

<Indy>: Sorry, sort of. Thank you too. I have to hurry. Jonas is hungry.

<Gunnar>: *Her lips are soft, and they don't have layers of goop.* Indy, wait.

<Church>: Where do you think you're going?

<Gunnar>: I have to talk to her.

<Church>: About what? How upset you are that she let me try to save her father's leg before you figured out what you needed to try to destroy him the second time. You are Gunnar, the perverse.

<Gunnar>: What do you know about a second time?

<Church>: We should not be having this conversation in the hall? Step in here and relax for a minute.

---------- ----------

<Church>: Why are you so concerned about Marshall?

<Gunnar>: You said something about a second time.

<Church>: I am his doctor and one of his close friends. He needed me and he needed several of my associates when you sent the SOX lynch mob after him.

<Gunnar>: It was a mistake, and all of us apologized profusely, publicly, and privately.

<Church>: For which Marshall and his family paid dearly before the apology.

<Gunnar>: I'm ignoring you. That was the beginning of them becoming filthy rich. The price was small. ***I sound like Gerthe.***

<Church>: He was treated for anxiety attacks, which we originally believed were heart attacks and that was the beginning of his attack of depression. He locked himself in a room for two weeks. Only an unusual family with women like Nicky, Indy, and Becky could have pulled off what they did.

<Gunnar>: ***Those are good reasons for me to want to be in that family and not fighting them, even through Becky doesn't look like she could handle a string of one consecutive thought.***

Marshall was in that room figuring out how to take over the world, and he took over my world.

<Church>: Gunnar, your thinking is irrational and impossible, and I'm talking too much. If he was willing to forgive you, it's none of my business.

<Gunnar>: He didn't forgive me. He was monitoring every move that I made. He allowed me to trap myself.

<Church>: Was that before or after he helped you to earn millions in bonuses?

<Gunnar>: You don't understand. I don't understand.

Why do I care if Indy hates me? There are about eleven other women with strong negative feelings.

I could still have my choice of at least 20 society types. No! I've already spent time with more than 40 of them. I don't want to spend my senior years with another Stephanie or with a Helena, and I don't want to be alone.

<Church>: You are having an attack of paranoia. You should get that MRI, and then get some rest. Gaines thinks you're probably OK, but we should err on the side of caution. I agree with her.

<Gunnar>: You replaced Marshall's very long femur. You wouldn't just happen to have a Marshall-sized femur in the supply closet. Marshall was in bad shape before he tripped. He must have been planning to have this surgery anyhow? He hired a nurse to take care of him if he takes a tumble at work. It took him 33 years to get a company car, and he gave it back because he needed the special SUV. He couldn't get out of a regular stretch. He has furniture built to accommodate his leg.

<Church>: None of this is any of your business.

<Gunnar>: Yes it is. They are going to blame me for the way he looks.

<Church>: That's ridiculous. Indy, Jonas, and Ernest know there was something wrong with the desk drawer.

<Gunnar>: They also know that I tripped over the thing and walked away (*staggered away*).

[...] You're not going to tell me are you?

<Church>: [...] I have to take this call.

[...] I'm on my way. Don't wait for me. Ask Fred how the gloves work.

<Gunnar>: Is that about Marshall? Is he all right?

<Church>: He is better than we expected, but they want me to check him before they let more people see him.

<Gunnar>: I saved you after Ādaemoa. Now you can save me. Talk hypothetically or talk as if we were discussing a study.

<Church>: We are not doing blackmail today. I have to go and work on accumulating some more hugs.

In the meantime, you need immediate intervention. If Gaines prescribed Perposet, stop taking them. Your reaction is not typical, but I've seen it before. If the dentist gave you Hydrocodene, skip that too. Try Marshall's deep breathing. If that doesn't work, let James pick up over-the-counter medication.

<Gunnar>: Does Indira Marshall give private hugs?

<Church>: I doubt it, but I am not the one to ask.

<Gunnar>: You and she seem to have a special relationship that you never mentioned.

<Church>: She and I worked hard to help father avoid [...] that's none of your business.

<Gunnar>: I was thinking of other types of work.

<Church>: Gunnar, not everybody is like you. I am practically over the hill, and Gwen would kill me. Besides, Ryan is probably the only man she has ever loved or will ever love, much to her detriment.

<Gunnar>: I'm not over the hill, even after the ministration of her mother, and Ryan is an inflated, arrogant, bully. He is not the right man for her.

<Church>: Why should I worry about your hills, and when did you become a marriage counselor?

<Gunnar>: Aren't they divorced?

<Church>: That is irrelevant. You have lost any vestiges of sanity you had left.

<Gunnar>: I just recovered my sanity.

<Church>: Convince Daxiao to relieve HM of his responsibilities if you must. In the long run, he will be better off without them.

On the other hand, please stay away from Indy. She may need companionship, but you are the last person on earth that she should consider. Baby Girl is DEFINITELY NOT your type. I never thought I'd say this, but she'd be better off with Ryan.

<Gunnar>: What is my type?

<Church>: A snob that will let you ride according to a calendar schedule.

<Gunnar>: That was self-defense. I couldn't get trapped again.

<Church>: That is exactly why you will stay away from her. Marshalls love for life, and you have never loved anyone except Gunnar, and even that is questionable.

<Gunnar>: I loved my sister - I still do. I loved Amal. *I'd love Indy for life.*

<Church>: Do you mind repeating that?

<Gunnar>: Forget it. I haven't been making sense today.

<Church>: That was more like a rhetorical question. Let me sit and collect my thoughts.

<Gunnar>: Why are you looking at me like that?

<Church>: Was Amal the intern who walked out in front of a truck the last time I ever saw you act as if you cared for someone other than yourself?

<Gunnar>: She slipped on the ice. The truck couldn't stop.

<Church>: Was that the woman where we delivered the baby boy right before she died, but the baby was too immature to survive the injuries he received when the truck hit his mother?

<Gunnar>: *He struggled for two days, but he was too little.* We were going to name him Guntur. It was our private joke. *I've been holding this in for too long. I can't I stop blabbing.*

<Church>: She and her baby were frozen for a month and then the bodies disappeared. You started the fugue around that time.

<Gunnar>: It took me that long to get well enough handle everything. I couldn't stand to look at dead bodies after that.

<Church>: ***Gunnar. We have to get this right. Are you listening to me?***

<Gunnar>: Do I have a choice?

<Church>: The first time I remember hearing Amal's voice, I was a second year intern too, and you were the brilliant first year resident. I was in nap corner in the lounge I heard someone say very forcefully, and I quote, "I don't care what think you did. He is mine, and I will never let him go. Bigamy is not allowed in the United States, and we have been bound together for three years. See this".

<Gunnar>: ***What is he saying? I married Stephanie four months after Amal died.***

<Church>: Anyway, I sat up long enough to see what they looked like, but Amal was blocking my view of the other woman. I could only see the top of a blond head, and she was waving a big envelope at Amal.

<Gunnar>: ***It wasn't real! It must have been*** [...]

<Church>: Let me finish while you think up a lie to explain what happened.

<Gunnar>: [...] ***that stupid engagement certificate that looked like a marriage certificate.***

<Church>: I sat up again after the blond woman left. Amal was rocking and holding her stomach. I hid until she pulled herself together and left the room.

I followed her to see if she was all right. She turned her patients over to me and another intern. She went and wrapped up. I remember her trying to cover her stomach with the scarf. I stood in the door and watched when she left the building.

<Gunnar>: You should have stopped her.

<Church>: She was upset, but she did not intend to hurt herself. She checked the traffic before she crossed Morris Avenue. She was on the island in the middle of the street, holding onto a lamp pole and trying to figure out how to get over the ice when she saw something that made her step in front of that truck.

<Gunnar>: I remember. ***I was late for my shift. Stephanie was pulling on my coat sleeve and saying we had to talk. I couldn't imagine what was important enough that she would actually drive to the Bronx. I pulled away from her when I saw Amal coming across the street.***

<Church>: After the truck skidded to a halt, both of you were laying in the street and both of you were lapsing in and out of consciousness. You lived, in a manner of speaking.

<Gunnar>: Why are you telling me this now?

<Church>: At the time, not knowing of your great ability to love, it was not obvious that there was a connection between you two. We thought you were being heroic. That was probably the most discrete affair that you ever had.

<Gunnar>: ***It wasn't an affair!***

Gerthe wouldn't even speak to Amal, so I didn't tell her about the wedding and Guntur. Amal's parents were upset with her because she broke tradition and had a "love marriage" with a foreigner.

The Chief knew, and two of her friends knew. We had each other, we had Guntur, and we had medicine. We were going to wait for Guntur before we changed all the paperwork.

<Church>: I understand. She was a diversion that gave you a big headache.

<Gunnar>: Ask the Chief.

<Church>: Chief who?

<Gunnar>: He was the head of [...] forget it. You were too far down the totem pole.

<Church>: From where I stand on this totem pole, it seems that you were responsible for the death of a woman and her child. Now you want to destroy a father and his child. You are a sick puppy.

<Gunnar>: ***NO!*** *She was having trouble breathing. I tried to apologize for not getting to her fast enough. She said, "I know you tried."*

Now I remember. You were there. You know I tried. *Her arm was twisted in ways that arms don't bend. I tried to fix it, but I couldn't move the way I wanted it to. She said, "Save Guntur". When I woke up, she was dead and Guntur was dying. He was too little.*

<Church>: If you hadn't confused your relationships, no trying would have been necessary.

<Gunnar>: Nothing will be confused with Indy. I saved her father already. I have time to apologize to the entire family. I would tell her everything. We could be friends.

<Church>: Don't bother to put her on your "occasional friends" list.

This is preventive medicine. I didn't know Amal, but I know and care for Indy. She is not Amal super-sized.

<Gunnar>: I know. *My amazing Amazon would have made it across the street with the baby. My Amazon!*

<Church>: Furthermore, there is no correlation between physical size and emotional resilience. If you did one of your smooth-talking sales numbers and Indy decided, with the same amount of stupidity as Amal, to let you tie her up in knots, and even one strand of hair on her head turned gray before its time, I know eight or nine people who would put out contracts on you, not counting her mother. I am one of those people.

Ryan already did enough damage, and there may have been something wrong before that.

<Gunnar>: Indy is a grown woman, and I am not Ryan. After I tell her the truth, she can make her own choices.

<Church>: Where did this "tell the truth" act come from? You wouldn't tell anyone what time it was, unless it was to your advantage.

<Gunnar>: *I needed all the advantages. I was a fake salesman and a failure as a husband, a father, and a doctor.*

This must be what hyperventilation feels like.

<Church>: Cut the crap. I can tell when someone is pretending. I always believed there was something decent in you somewhere, but I was wrong. You are genuine slime.

If you want to tell someone about how you helped me get rid of Ādaemoa's junk, put it on the public address system. I can take the hit, especially if we keep Marshall alive.

[...] They are calling me again.

Stay away from Marshall and his family. Lenox can treat your sore arm. Consider Bellevue for your head. For the other testing, find a clinic.

<Gunnar>: I understand everything now. *Gerthe sent Stephanie after Amal. Gerthe probably doesn't know that she contributed to the death of her own grandchild. She wouldn't care. They were inconvenient.*

[...] Stephanie wanted to talk to me about Amal. She knew what she did, and she got pregnant to try to replace

Guntur. She stayed around for 15 years, and she knew! Stephanie and Gerthe should rot in hell!

Who made me a judge? I sent Sharf after Indy's father. I'm not sure what Sharf did to Indy 20 years ago. Maybe he's the problem from "before". I lost Indy before I even had a chance.

---------- ----------

<Gunnar>: *I can get up now. I may be the worst father in the world, but I did everything I could to make it up to my baby boy. Guntur Gunnar is well known in Andhra Pradesh. My baby's trust fund has saved the lives of hundreds of other babies.*

Her family almost forgave her "love marriage", even if it was to an outsider. The thought we were in an accident crossing the street together, and she died trying to deliver Guntur. Her ashes are in the Ganges. I buried Guntur with my own hands. I wanted to leave him in the coffin, and he had been dead to long. The priests didn't know how to handle the situation.

I helped her brothers through colleges. I've contributed her dowry 100's of times over for the benefit of the entire community. A notarized copy of our marriage certificate is in a frame between the picture of us in our medical scrubs and her in her red sari. Her picture has flowers around it.

They also believe I'm a crazy American with a spelling problem. Guntur is the name of a city and a district, but is seldom the name of a person. They think the second name is spelled wrong because Gunnar, with an "r", doesn't make sense anywhere in India.

This is worse than before. Remember I lost Amal, plus I'm losing everything I built since Amal died. Whatever happened between Sharf and Indy was almost certainly bad enough to make her hate me, even before I let Montgomery and Sharf loose on her father.

If Kerstin had to choose between Len and me, I'd lose. Turn about is fair play. She was the perfect type of baby, and I went through the motions of being a proper type of father, but part of the love that she needed is buried beside a tree in a field near Amal's home village. I paid to have them plant the tree.

My chances for the top spot are gone.

Maybe I shouldn't hate Stephanie. She thought she loved me, and Gerthe probably put her up to what she did. Neither one of them knew that Amal was carrying Guntur.

Stephanie was the proper type of wife for 15 years. She finally found love, she has two sons by Prince Whatchamacallit, and I am alone.

All my alternate Stephanies and replacement Stephanies mean even less to me than the original, if that is possible. I'm tired of being a self-propelled mannequin with tuxedos that fit properly and special skills, so they can spend less money on "personal trainers".

That's ironic too. Amal and I learned the special skills together from a book that was written at least 1,500 years ago.

Stephanie didn't make Amal suicidal. Church said she wrapped up well, and she was careful crossing the street, until she saw me.

We had a communications problem [............]

<James>: I've been waiting for you for 30 minutes, and you're standing there laughing at the wall.

Get a grip. Oswald says Mittelman is on his way upstairs for their token visit. You are next, and you are nowhere near ready.

<Gunnar>: I still have time to prepare *my resignation.*

<James>: On second thought, we can see whether you should be re-admitted. If Mittelman saw you now, even he would understand that this should be rescheduled.

<Gunnar>: No! I have to stop running.

<James>: From what? You're acting as crazy as you look. You can't even walk.

[...] Don't even think about it. You can't fire me, brother man. Dr. Church told me where to find you, and from the tone of his voice, I'd guess that you goonerized him.

Your Goon Gang's drivers are too busy driving to talk to me, and I imagine that you're receiving the same treatment from their bosses.

Your sister ran out of the hotel as if she had a fire in her exhaust. Madames Frou Frou don't count. Neither does McDonald until he needs you help redirect his wife's suspicions. I'll lay odds that Ticia and I are close to the only friends you have.

<**Gunnar**>: ***Maybe I have Laufer and Jonas. That's irony to the ninth power.*** Bring me back here after I finish with Mittelman. ***You can start with Laufer tomorrow.***

<**James**>: When are you going to explain what is happening with you? You've been hurt worse than this before, but you never acted like this.

<**Gunnar**>: ***I have never hurt like this before.*** If I explained, I would have zero friends.

---------- ----------

<**Machi**>: Fred, I'm sorry to see you again so soon.

<**Fred**>: Mr. Marshall wanted to see you sooner.

<**Machi**>: Barker told me. I did what I needed to do, and now I'm back.

<**Fred**>: The doctor left a few minutes ago. Should I call him back? ***She looks 20 years older than she did two months ago.***

<**Machi**>: No. They took the tube out. I suppose I should be happy about that? ***I can figure out how he's doing without their help.***

<**Fred**>: You should be guardedly elated.

<**Machi**>: That's a quack statement.

<**Fred**>: The head duck and three lesser ducks just had a consultation. They agreed that he is doing somewhat better than they expected, given his circumstances.

<**Machi**>: ***They did this so Church could write some more papers.*** I can't get over how many stitches he has.

<**Fred**>: He'd have lost the leg otherwise Ms. Frey. Dr. Church was not making this up. I saw the images of the operation.

<**Machi**>: Show me.

<**Fred**>: It would be better if you let Dr. Church review it with you and your family simultaneously.

<**Machi**>: Who is paying you? I don't believe it is Dr. Church.

<**Fred**>: Miss Indy.

<**Machi**>: What are the chances that I could make her change her mind?

<**Fred**>: You would lose the best nurse practitioner that they let work with him, or you would become upset again if I showed you the pictures. It wouldn't be good if he woke up again and either one of us was not here. He needs the woman I met 21 years ago.

<**Machi**>: ***I'm backing myself into a corner again.*** Fred, I saw what they did to him 21 years ago. The pictures were in 3 different journals. How much worse could this be?

<**Fred**>: ***You don't want to know.*** Could we compromise?

<**Machi**>: Please forgive me. I know we need you. I promise that I will not make any funny sounds, I will not hit you with anything, I will not fire you, and I will not regurgitate anything.

<**Fred**>: Are you good for your word?

<**Machi**>: What's the compromise?

<**Fred**>: One of the pictures shows his thighbone, the rod that had stopped holding it together and the artificial knee after they had been separated from him.

<**Machi**>: That's a start.

[...] His thigh is in three pieces!

<**Fred**>: The bone was disintegrating near these attachment points. At some time, it was bound to [...]

<**Machi**>: How much did that hurt?

<**Fred**>: It must have been tolerable with the Perposet and whatever other techniques he was using to keep things under control. Dr. Church is still amazed [...]

<**Machi**>: Turn it off. ***He wasn't filling the prescriptions. The pencil case had Tylanoll! Why did I make him suffer so long? That is a dumb question. I'm still a selfish bitch when it comes to HM. No, I'm not. The anesthesia nearly killed him the last time.***

<**Fred**>: Sit, and try not to sob like that. You promised. He worries more about you than about himself.

<**Machi**>: Why were they elated?

<**Fred**>: He is stable. His temperature is 100.2. That has been dropping since the antibiotics started working. His blood oxygen has been at 90% since the tube came out. They want it to be 95%, and they think the oxygen will help. He will sound

hoarse for a while, but that's a local problem. The lung is clearing. The drainage tub in his side will help. The two in his thigh serve the same purpose. His pressure is 140/90 and his pulse is 95. Though both are somewhat higher than we would like, they may be related to the antihistamine, and he must be experiencing severe pain. He can push that button if he wants to. We assured him that there is no morphine and no aspirin, and that there is not enough for him to become addicted. However, he's using about half as much as we would expect. He wants a "clear head".

<Machi>: When will he be able to use his leg?

<Fred>: It depends on him. With the weight loss, he may be able to stand in as little as two months, if you two behave.

<Machi>: Why didn't I know about the antihistamine?

<Fred>: They used it so the throat tube wouldn't irritate him so much.

<Machi>: Will he need more blood? My baby boy should be here soon.

<Fred>: We believe he's finished with that.

WEDDING PLANS FOR HM

<Machi>: ***From this side, he still looks like my Zeus, but the color is all wrong. Bronze is part of the package that I fell in love with. It's ironic. Everyone thought I was crazy then. Now people give themselves skin cancer, so they can look like him.***

<HM>: Nicky! You came back!

<Machi>: Of course, I came back.

<HM>: Are you all right?

<Machi>: Yes. ***He's worried about me.***

<HM>: Please, f- forgive [...]

<Machi>: Be quiet! I'm sorry you suffered so long. Fred. Open this damned thing.

<HM>: ***She's crying again!*** Please st- stop [...]

<Fred>: I shouldn't do that. He's still fighting infection.

<Machi>: He needs me, and I can't touch him!

<HM>: G- Gloves.

<Machi>: What do you want with gloves?

<HM>: For you. Like doctors.

<Machi>: What does he want?

<Fred>: Put these on, sit down, and then put your arms through those holes.

<Machi>: Can I have a few minutes alone with him?

<Fred>: Of course. Tell him to push that button when you're ready to come out of that.

---------- ----------

<Machi>: You have to be calm, or they'll make me leave, do you understand?

<HM>: Yes. But you are not calm.

<Machi>: I was worried about losing you.

<HM>: I'm here. H- Hurts, but I have a clear head.

<Machi>: Please do what you need to survive. You need to stay alive for us. You won't need a clear head for Daxiao. They can't hurt you any more.

<HM>: R- Right man for you. Take c- care of my babies.

<Machi>: ***He's still upset about what Rachel and Joseph said to him over 40 years ago.*** Let's have a wedding.

<HM>: T- testing me? Forty years are real.

<Machi>: I'm talking about a WEDDING WEDDING. The one where we tell everybody, and we stop the research and start on the real thing.

---------- ----------

<Fred>: What's wrong?

<Nurse #1>: His pulse rate zoomed up.

<Fred>: What about his pressure?

<Nurse #1>: It's the same as it was when Gunnar left. Maybe you should check on him anyhow.

<Fred>: It's coming back down. Let's watch and wait.

---------- ---------

<HM>: **Invite Rachel and Joseph?**

<Machi>: We can introduce them to their grandchildren and great grandchildren.

<HM>: **You are scared?**

<Machi>: Trying to grow up, a little.

<HM>: Trick?

<Machi>: Of course there is. You have to be able to stand up for the ceremony.

<HM>: Need cane, maybe f- forever.

<Machi>: A cane is all right. So are crutches. Use two if you need them.

<HM>: **Short List?**

<Machi>: We start as soon as you're ready.

<HM>: F- forty years of fun!

<Machi>: Stop before they come and kick me out. You **are not** ready for that!

<HM>: I'm tired anyhow.

<Machi>: You made your point. *He will be fine!*

<HM>: Tiny point though. We both pun.

<Machi>: Those were double entendres.

<HM>: Still a pun. P- Point for H.

<Machi>: Two points now.

<HM>: [...] L- Laughing hurts.

<Machi>: Never suffer like that for me again. Push that button when you need it.

---------- ---------

<Fred>: Everything blipped again.

<Nurse #1>: Maybe we should get a cardiologist in here. Let's talk to his kids about it.

<Fred>: Give it a few more minutes.

<Indy>: Fred, who's down there with Daddy?

<Nurse #1>: Your mother. While you're here, we were wondering [...]

<Fred>: When are you going to get more rest? You need to take care of yourself too.

---------- ---------

<Indy>: How long was I napping?

<Huey>: About 45 minutes. I left you some food.

<Patrick Frey-Marshall>: Hi Mommy.

<Indy>: *Pipsqueak!*

<Pat>: Stop doing that. I'm over six feet tall.

<Indy>: You also sound like a thunderstorm. I'm sorry. Have you seen Daddy?

<Pat>: Jonas said Machi is with him, he is all right, they don't need my blood any more, and I should wait. Thus, I have been sitting patiently as big brother commanded. When did he start doing that?

<Huey>: It's only been 15 minutes. Daddy is feeling better, and he needs time with Mama. They're not going to call the heart doctor.

<Pat>: What heart doctor do you mean?

<Huey>: Daddy blipped a few times, but now his pressure is down.

<Indy>: Barker, we're going down.

<Nurse #1>: Leave when he gets tired.

---------- ---------

<Indy>: Mama, what are you doing?

<Machi>: I am holding your father's hand.

<Indy>: Daddy, how do you feel?

[...] Don't look at me like that. If you hadn't gone wandering off, you could have had as much private time as you wanted. Look how long you kept Pat waiting.

<HM and Machi>: Hi Pipsqueak!

<Pat>: Hi Pops, Machi. I'm sorry it took so long. I missed the non-stop and waited a few hours at Schiphol, not to mention an extra hour on the Van Wyck.

I'd give you a hug, but [...] what is this thing? ***Pat, be a man and deal with this. I'm almost the same age as the Old Man was when he got popped.***

<Machi>: Piccolo, the mad scientist was at it again. Don't get upset. He looks worse than he is. [...] Pull your pants up.

<Pat>: They are up. I have low pockets. ***The gang up the hill would never let me hear the end it if they saw the Armani everything that I wear over there.***

<Indy>: Stop squeezing. That's the bad hand.

<Pat>: I'm sorry, but it looks like [...]

<HM>: ***I'm scaring another baby.*** Be out soon, and dancing. Feel better already.

<Indy>: Fred calls it a post-operative recovery acceleration unit. Becky calls it a POST environment. It keeps germs out, and all of us can crowd around as we're doing now.

Mama, let's go so he can get some real rest. You're messing with his heart.

<HM>: *She is my heart.*

<Machi>: You already saved his life. I put some things in motion that needed to be in motion, and now it's my turn to keep your father going. I'm not speaking to you anyhow.

<Pat>: What are you two fighting about now?

<Machi>: Ask her, later.

<HM>: Th- Thanks Baby Girl.

<Machi>: Tell her I'm thankful too.

<HM>: *They look exhausted. I am so sorry.* Br- breathing now! G- Good?

<Indy>: Yes. I was so worried. *She's mad because I didn't tell her about Sharf. She'd disown me if he found out about the morphine. I earned that reaming out from Jonas.*

<HM>: Jonas?

<Machi>: He is waiting patiently ***outside*** with Becky.

<HM>: Patty?

<Indy>: On another planet, but she agreed to teleport in. She should be here in about half an hour, if she remembers where the hospital is.

<Pat>: She had to get out of the performances in Paris. Her instructors are not very tolerant. Machi knew, and so did Pops.

<Indy>: She made the cut! Daddy's been tied up lately, so ask your mother why she didn't say something. *She has trouble admitting that the baby Queen is more talented as she was.*

<Machi>: Tell her that I told Jonas, even while they had me drugged.

<HM and Pat>: What drugs?

<Indy>: The ones they gave her, so she could avoid going to jail.

<Machi>: I wanted to see your father and Gunnar stood in the way.

<HM>: *I nearly messed up everything.*

<Pat>: You murked Gooner! Mama got it goin' on.

<Machi>: Please speak English.

<Indy>: Gunnar saved Daddy's life.

<Machi>: She's right. His leg was disintegrating, and [...]

<Pat>: What's happening? *I didn't believe Grandma when she said Machi used to be a drama queen.*

<Indy>: I'll give you the 411 later. *I don't believe I said that.* Tell my mother that she's fogging up the post-operative recovery acceleration unit.

<Machi>: Thanks Pat. I'm all right, really. I cried like this all the time when I was your age. That's a BIG handkerchief.

<Pat>: I have big pockets.

<HM>: I have two legs for wedding.

<Indy>: Did I hear him correctly?

<Machi>: Tell your sister that we are going to have a big wedding when your father can stand up for the ceremony. There will be fifteen hundred invitations.

<Pat>: What are you two saying? Don't you still love each other?

<Indy>: Tell her she hasn't been acting rationally lately. Why would she want to risk a 41-year-old love affair by getting married?

<HM>: M- married. My b- baby girl!

<Indy>: Is he feverish?

<Machi>: He is very tired.

<Indy>: Ask her whether her parents would forbid it again, and whether she'd have the guts tell them where to step off this time.

<Machi>: *I told them to step of the last time. They wanted me to pretend that you were Ike's baby.* Tell her they changed their mind about her father.

<Indy>: Ask her whether it was before or after their chubby non-existent grandson set them up in the Pavilion. *We started earning money just in time to rescue Joe and Rachel after they spent their money spoiling my cousins. Mama's rejected kids help them keep their dignity.*

<Machi>: They believe that David put the money in the trust fund for them. They shouldn't think we forgave them.

<Pat>: *They know where the money comes from. I told them.*

<Indy>: When was it then?

<Machi>: Tell her it was when they had to hide from us at Jonas's high school graduation and your college graduation while they watched Clara and Ike sitting up front and taking turns running outside and watching the twins. Two salutatorians and two beautiful grandchildren in one year generate a lot of nachas, but it's hard to brag about your grandchildren if you were pretending that their parents never existed.

<Pat>: Grandma says Ike let them hold us, but they had to disappear when it was Clara's turn.

<Machi>: They touched our babies!

<HM>: *They were so sorry they missed the first ones.*

<Pat>: Mama, why do you keep doing that? They are very old!

<Machi>: Keep that up, and I will stop talking to you too, after you give me my hug.

<Indy>: How did they know about the graduations? It wasn't front-page news.

<Machi>: Tell her that her uncle David agreed never to mention us to his parents, but he felt proud enough to talk about his nieces and nephews to his uncle, and the word traveled.

<Indy>: Is she talking about the uncle who fired her because she was expecting me?

<Pat>: He was at the graduations too. He says he fired you to keep peace with Grandma, but she relented, and he helped you get a job with a friend after Indy was born. He says that in those days women had to stop working at six months anyhow.

<Machi>: I doubt it. *They wanted me to destroy Indy. They recommended a "hormonal adjustment" specialist to deal with my nausea. Clara went with me to learn about the new nausea treatment. The man was practicing using his middle name, but she recognized him as a "specialist" with a reputation among the military women's network for termination of unplanned nausea.*

I've been crazy since then.

<Pat>: That was so long ago. They were trying to protect their baby girl. They would apologize to you and Indy as many times as you would let them. They already apologized to Pops.

<Machi>: You've been sneaking up to see them again.

<Pat>: I wasn't sneaking. They've practically moved in with Clara. Am I right Pops?

<HM>: **New best friends.**

<Pat>: See!

<Indy>: Daddy, do you know about this?

<HM>: **Yes.**

<Machi>: Please try to understand. They caused harm when we needed help, and they tried to reel us in when it suited their purposes. We were not going to let that happen.

<Pat>: I know I'm too young to understand what happened then. Do you believe I would understand how daddy's leg made you change your mind about getting married?

<Machi>: It is part of a major program transition, and we can't initiate the transition plan until one of us has a wedding. It's better if the wedding includes both of us. Indy can be the Matron of honor, Jonas can be the best man, you can be the ring bearer, and Patty will be the flower child.

<Pat>: I didn't understand what you said.

<Indy>: Patty would be the flower girl!

<HM>: Patty sings.

<Machi>: How could I forget? Patty can hum wedding chants too. *I don't believe I will ever understand either one of my babies.*

<HM>: No! Sing Clara songs. Pat too.

<Indy>: You're right. They'd shake the walls, just like my father.

<HM>: No walls. Rave Hill lawn. Planned.

<Machi>: What plan?

<HM>: Updated. Ready for number.

<Machi>: Where is it?

<HM>: S- secret pocket.

<Machi>: I found the secret pockets. I checked every week to ensure that you didn't sneak in something I couldn't handle. I found the Slim Slacks plan.

<Indy>: *I can't believe the smile on his face.*

<HM>: *I remember the number! The count is 1843!*

<Pat>: You were finished with the diet. You need more calories than that to keep you going.

<Machi>: Pat, bring me your father's backpack. It's on the floor in the closet.

<Pat>: You're finally going to let me touch it.

<Machi>: *You're dangerous without that.* Show your father the pack. Where's the pocket?

[...] H! You are not sleeping. I see you grinning.

<Indy>: Mama, he's tired.

<HM>: Thermos.

<Machi>: There is nothing in there. I always checked that first.

<HM>: Outside.

<Indy>: I remember. It had extra insulation to keep Jonas's milk cold.

[...] I found it!

<Machi>: Let me see that.

<Indy>: Wait.

It has everything that we just mentioned, except that a Matron of honor is usually married.

<Machi>: Tell her she acts more like a widow than any married woman I know.

<Indy>: Tell her I'm ignoring her, and then ask her where she found somebody named Joseph to give her hand in marriage?

<Pat>: You don't know our grandfather's name.

<Indy>: Papa Stacy's name is Adam.

<Machi>: My father's name is Joseph.

<Indy>: Daddy!

<HM>: Begged, cr- cried. Rachel too.

<Machi>: You forgave them after what they tried to do to you?

<HM>: Dying ch- changed things - 20 years ago.

<Machi>: Why didn't you say something before now? I was waiting for you. *It's time for me to hug my father again.*

<HM>: Tried. You ignored me.

<Machi>: **I love you more.** *After I let go of my insanities, I can help Indy. I needed the insanity to keep fighting. Now I need to be sure we have a wonderful wedding - including my parents. Patty can swing from the chandeliers if she wants to.*

<Pat>: Who died?

<Indy>: It was nothing that a lunatic salesman couldn't fix.

I have to go and change.

How can I get my head around this? Those people tried to convince Mama to have a "hormonal adjustment" to avoid ruining her life with Daddy. I had a voluntary procedure after I forgave Ryan the second time, and I caught him hugging a pregnant bimbette two weeks later.

<Pat>: *Now Indy is starting to cry.* I could use a shower too. Pops, I will see you after you get some rest. Mama, are you coming with us?

<Machi>: In a minute. Please wait over there.

<HM>: **Baby Girl needs big hug. Clara help.**

<Machi>: **I Understand. Honeymoon homework First.**

<HM>: **Start with #67. Judge 9:15 and Indy 10:15. Jonas #268 after first big raise.**

<Machi>: **#998 is safe now.**

<HM>: **All my babies!**

<Machi>: *He is all there! I should have thought about praying before. It works.*

<Indy>: *The monitor blipped again.* Daddy, what happened?

<HM>: Going to heaven.

<Indy and Pat>: We'll get help!

<Machi>: Come back here! That was a figure of speech.

---------- ----------

<Fred>: He looks good, but Barker is coming to check on him anyhow. Fire me later, but you have to leave now.

I've never seen anybody so close to being dead who looked so blissful.

<Machi>: It was time to go anyhow. Tell Barker that Hamilton Frey-Marshall is a beautiful living miracle, but get me out of this thing first.

<Indy>: ***Frey-Marshall? Whatever*** [...] ***she looks younger already, and he's still smiling. Mama worked her magic. I certainly wish she had passed the make'em happy gene along to me.***

<Fred>: Thanks for understanding.

---------- ----------

<Machi>: Stop looking at me like that and stop crying. I'll forgive you for everything after I hug my real baby.

<Indy>: I'm confused.

<Machi>: My parents were wrong, and they nearly destroyed us because they wanted the best for me. I was wrong, and I nearly destroyed your father because I wanted to hold on to him as long as possible. I would have, if it wasn't for you.

<Indy>: ***They gave Daddy the morphine because I wanted him to stop crying. He could have died.***

<Machi>: Your father forgave them, and he forgave me. I order you to stop crying. It's time for all of us to start healing.

I'll start with Joseph and Rachel.

<Indy>: Rachel?

<Machi>: [...] Rachel is your grandmother, after whom Jonas and Becky are naming their baby. You can start with your grandparents, and then follow-up with companionship.

<Indy>: Why are you having a companionship attack all of a sudden?

<Machi>: Perhaps it's because I almost lost your father again. My beautiful Baby Girl was not designed to do what you're trying to do.

<Indy>: Maybe, but let's wait until Daddy is feeling better before we start that fight again.

<Machi>: Every moment is precious.

<Pat>: I may be the baby, but I understand that.

<Indy>: Stop doing that. What would my mother have done if she caught somebody that she loved running around on her - many times?

<Machi>: ***It is similar to losing someone to whom I had been betrothed for half of my lifetime. I moved on, quickly.*** It would have depended on how much she loved him at the time.

<Indy>: My mother is avoiding the question.

<Machi>: Quite well, don't you think.

<Pat>: What did my mother say to my father that we couldn't see?

<Machi>: I reminded him of the benefits of companionship.

PRESIDENTIAL IMBALANCES

<Dan>: Hi Indy, Machi, Patrick.

<Indy>: I'm glad to see you. He's at the end of the hall.

<Machi>: My word [...] A real visit, and flowers. You have limited permission. We will talk about his resignation later. Dan, we tired him out already. Don't take too long.

<Indy>: Ask my mother if that is a real person or an android with Dan.

<Machi>: Tell Indy that her father is about to be graced by the presence of Justin Mittelman.

---------- ----------

<Justin>: Are they who I think they are?

He doesn't look like anybody who I know, she looks like her father, and both women are built like wasps, or maybe a wasp and a hornet in a burkini. It's not hiding anything. That's a stunning potato sack.

<Dan>: That is Ms. Snuffleupagus, Baby Girl Snuffleupagus, and Pipsqueak.

<Justin>: Pipsqueak. He's bigger than I am.

<Dan>: He was a preemie with a glass-shattering squeal when Ike gave him that nickname.

<Justin>: I'm surprised that you would refer to someone's size.

<Dan>: To him it's Patrick or Mr. Coffee. Ike gave him the second name too. He stopped squealing after Jonas taught him to use sign language to ask for what he wanted.

<Justin>: It looks like Ms. Frey may have taken a coffee break from Marshall.

<Dan>: *You are losing your mind!* Where is your executive propriety?

<Justin>: Every time I have to deal with Marshall, it makes me crazy.

<Dan>: You'll lose it even more when you see Pat's twin sister.

<Justin>: You were going to introduce us. I'll go and catch them.

<Dan>: How long have you been doing your own chores?

Why would Machi want to talk to somebody who had just accused her of bed hopping?

<Justin>: I have never had to deal with anything like this, and I obviously need coaching or mentoring. Nothing connects with these people. Maybe I could put some pieces together if I met them? At a glance *(or two or three)*, I'd have to say that I really look forward to it.

<Dan>: I couldn't keep you from coming here. However, I can still try to avoid mayhem. There's two of them and only three of us.

<Justin>: There are four if you count the "little one".

<Dan>: They wouldn't need Jonas or Pat, and Oswald couldn't get here in time to save us anyhow.

<Justin>: Let's see Marshall first. Then we will find them. I'm sure Oswald will have no problem keeping both eyes on them.

---------- ----------

<Justin>: It looks like a flower shop.

<Dan>: They are going to need a bigger case for the flowers. Those are huge and elegant. They had to take out a shelf for them. Let's see. [...] They're from you and Grace!

<Justin>: It is likely that Grace and Higgs collaborated on the selection.

<Dan>: This makes it appear that you are the most concerned about his well-being.

<Justin>: Leave it alone. *It looks like the "girls" are in a spin because the graying gimp tripped.*

<Dan>: *That touched something sensitive? Maybe he's not accustomed to doing this much work in one day.* Let's go inside.

<Fred>: Dan, it's good that you made it, and you would be?

<Dan>: This is our boss, Mr. Justin Mittelman.

<Justin>: [...] OOH! He looks like a corpse in a glass coffin.

<Fred>: *He's a very subtle android?* I can see how you made it to the top.

<Dan>: He's asleep. Let's go. *He looks horrible, Justin is going crazy, and I need to go and have it out with Gunnar. I should have been tougher on Sharf this morning.*

<HM>: *Not sl- sleep.* Going to heaven.

<Dan>: Don't talk like that.

<Justin>: *Heaven! I don't have a script for this.* You look [...]

<HM>: Like c- corpse [...]

<Justin>: I am so sorry. You have me a little of balance.

<Dan>: You'll be back on your [...] back in shape in no time.

<HM>: Research finished [...]

<Dan>: No it isn't. You can pull through this.

<HM>: Dan, come close. Please.

[...] Gunnar r- really upset about Liz and BASE. B- Blocking f- fac [...]

<Dan>: Don't worry about that now. We know the plan.

<HM>: Need Maja. Liz will tr- translate.

<Justin>: *He is agitated, and so is Piccolo?* That is nonsense. You will translate when you feel better. We can figure out something that will work for you.

<HM>: [.............] Hurts [....]

<Fred>: The button is right beside your hand. *He pushed it. This is bad!*

[...] You both should leave.

<Dan>: I've heard of laughing oneself to death, but you don't have to prove that it can be done.

<Justin>: What's so funny? *This is weird. That's why you can't let feelings get out of hand.*

<HM>: You [...] replacement W- Weeble, and me napping.

<Justin>: I [...] *what am I supposed to say? Why did I pick on a man with a limp who could read my lips while he was easing my delicate parts in a vise?*

I was complimenting you on your survival skills. You are the toughest man I know. *I may not be lying!* I was not asleep, ever! Doc knows. She will tell you. *He's crying.*

<Fred>: Shut the hell up!

[...] I need help with Marshall.

[...] He laughed, and now he's crying.

[...] No, nothing outside seems to have come apart.

[...] Don't announce a code unless you have people with riot gear. Just get down here!

[...] **Pain is hard to bear, even for him. Doctors say he had 75% chance to live, 50% percent to walk. That may change. Take him away.**

<Alex Macedon>: You missed Little Miss Mama. That's probably the best luck you had all day BOSS?

<Justin>: *Frick and Frack.* How did you two get in?

<Macedon>: I threatened to send Barker to the brig if he didn't let me in.

<Val>: Barker is coming to check on H, but he let us sneak in first.

<Macedon>: *Sh.t. The kid's luck ran out. He didn't cry before! I guess they cut more places this time.*

<Val>: Fred, why is he crying? *It definitely looks worse when you see what they have been describing.*

<Fred>: The senior android did something that tickled his funny bone. People are on their way to ensure that nothing came loose. Before you ask, he had better than even recovery odds until a few seconds ago.

<Val>: Should we send his family back in here?

<Fred>: I was thinking that we should check before we said anything, especially since he hasn't lost consciousness. We do not wish to discover what happens if four Marshalls are angry at once. Everybody was happy before he arrived.

<Justin>: This makes no sense! *I run one of the most sophisticated companies on earth. I deal with heads of state and leaders in industry and academia, but I mess up every time I try to deal with Marshall.*

<Nurse #1>: Make sense of it outside. Leave. NOW!

<Macedon>: The man said get out. This is my problem.

<Justin>: *Why is it his problem?*

<Fred>: You too!

<Nurse #1>: Fred, let him put these on. We have to open the coffin.

<Val>: Dan, let's go. I need your help.

<Dan>: *He called me Dan, and he's asking for help in public and four people heard him, maybe five if you count H!* I'll do what I can.

<Nurse #1>: Go outside and do what you can.

----------- ----------

<Justin>: What was the nurse saying to you?

<Dan>: He said H could still die and to get you the hell away from him. *I can't believe he figured out how to hurt HM again.*

<Justin>: Aren't you going to say something sarcastic?

<Dan>: I'm open to suggestions.

<Justin>: Val?

<Val>: He's not going to make it this time. You finally got rid of him.

<Justin>: I was trying to keep him.

[...] I order you to say something - either one of you.

[...] This has me upset too.

<Dan>: I'll tell H's family that he should not have upset you or gotten you off balance. He always got the politics wrong. There, I said something. Did it make you feel better?

<Justin>: No.

<Val>: When we get around that corner, we will all look cheerful, and I am going to talk to his family.

<Justin>: Why?

<Val>: Did you notice that those three people came around that corner is a very sedate manner, and then they started running? Did you hear what Fred said about the riot gear?

<Justin>: We'll look cheerful.

[...] Where are you going?

<Dan>: I have to find the hospital gift shop. I need something for my allergies. Please stay away from them and good luck with Gunnar.

I didn't mean the part about the luck.

---------- ----------

<Dan>: I expected that you would be gone by now.

<Justin>: *Hoping. I may be earning my entire bonus today. I have to stay on board until I know where this is going.*

You went the wrong way. I wanted to show you this hospital guide in case you came back through here. It appears that your allergies cleared up by themselves.

<Dan>: They do that sometimes.

<Justin>: I also figured that in case you couldn't control your allergies, I could stay around and give Van Amberg some executive support. He's over there with them trying to be cheery.

<Dan>: *He's also trying to prevent mayhem. Jonas could sit on Oswald while Pat disassembled the android. Val, Alex, and I could force ourselves to remain neutral.*

<Gerome Oswald>: If I went over there, I could share some of the hugs?

<Dan>: Only if you let the older woman beat you with a stick first.

<Oswald>: Where do they keep the canes?

<Justin>: Oswald. Curb your enthusiasm. Dan, would you care to rest your allergies.

<Dan>: That's OK. What are they so happy about?

<Justin>: Macedon! What happened down there?

<Macedon>: The view of East River is great from that window. Let's have a look.

<Justin>: Why are you whistling?

<Macedon>: I do that sometimes. I'm surprised that you never noticed.

<Val>: *Marshall is all right!*

<Justin>: Please tell me what happened.

<Macedon>: The situation is under control. They used a portable "look-it" thing that we sold them, and they didn't see any internal bleeding. Church used some type of glue to keep him from bleeding out in addition to the sutures that hold things together. Everything worked.

He used the maximum dose of the painkiller, and they gave him a mild sedative. That will reduce the blips in his pulse rate. He seems to be having a lot of those lately.

<Justin>: That is excellent! I meant that. I wasn't reading a script.

<Dan>: I have to sit down.

<Macedon>: Please walk over here with me BOSS.

<Justin>: What is it Alex? We are not keeping secrets from Dan or Val.

<Macedon>: I have a recommendation for you, and it doesn't apply to them.

---------- ----------

<Macedon>: Let me show you one of my favorite hobby toys. It's plastic, and the pieces go together like this.

<Justin>: Is it real?

<Macedon>: Yes. Since I retired, I feel naked without it. However, I am willing to share.

<Justin>: What are you saying?

<Macedon>: The next time you want to f.ck up, borrow this from me. Go some place where you won't frighten people, take off the safety like this, put it in your mouth, and press on this. You won't feel a thing, and they can fix it so you'll be a damned good-looking android for the showing.

<Justin>: You're crazy! You're fired!

<Macedon>: With Marshall in the shape he's in, you just f.cked up again. I will insert this component clip. It is even more unique. It looks like a comb on an x-ray machine. Let me explain the process again.

---------- ----------

<Justin>: He doesn't need a comb. He's bald.

<Dan>: What's wrong with Justin? He sounds hysterical.

<Macedon>: Didn't he ever tell you about his heart murmur? In cases of severe stress, the blood goes in the wrong direction, and it causes him to get dumb. Due to Marshall's condition, he is suffering from severe dumbness, and he forgot that I am hair challenged.

<Dan>: Does Liz know about this?

<Macedon>: If she doesn't, you shouldn't worry her, especially not now. I noticed more bread rising in the oven.

<Dan>: You are observant. After this, we're getting out of the baking business.

<Macedon>: Notice how quickly he recovers. Is everything all right BOSS?

<Dan>: Why do you call him BOSS?

<Macedon>: He won't let me call him SIR.

<Justin>: I should be dealing with this better. I'll take care of everything, so I won't need to use your suggestion.

<Dan>: What was that?

<Macedon>: I told him he could save us all a lot of trouble if he went somewhere and blew his brains out. Maybe I added to his stress. I'm sorry BOSS.

<Dan>: Maybe we shouldn't be kidding like that now.

<Justin>: ***He wasn't kidding, and Oswald was useless. He was over there gawking at Marshall's gene expression. He waited until now to look in my direction.***

Van Amberg and the willowy one managed to tear away from the hug fest. I suppose that I should act cheerful. ***A Nordic queen! I must have passed out. I didn't see her come in.***

<Macedon>: It would reduce stress.

<Patricia Frey-Marshall>: Hello Dan. Hello Mr. Macedon.

<Macedon>: Hello, little Queen. Ray and Dave send their regards. ***If they still had betrothals, I'd be parked on Nicky's doorstep to get that one hooked up with one of my boys.***

<Dan>: How are the performances going?

<Patty>: Quite well until this unfortunate occurrence. My instructor must substitute for me, and she is not amused. Would you be kind enough to introduce us?

<Dan>: Patricia Frey-Marshall, meet Justin Mittelman, the president of Daxiao. Mr. Mittelman, this is HM's younger daughter.

<Justin>: I'm delighted to meet you. What performances will you miss? ***My voice is shaking.***

<Patty>: Our class was invited to study with the quadrilles in Paris. We are learning, even at that level. It is not nearly as tedious as I thought it would be.

<Justin>: ***She's a child, but she is hypnotic.*** I actually know enough about dance to be impressed. My wife only misses a ballet company performance when it conflicts with Verdi.

<Patty>: I understand. My mother goes through phases where she is equally intense.

Mr. Mittelman, I would like to impose upon you for about 90 seconds. I wish to place my hand beside your neck for 45 seconds and over your heart for 45 seconds. It will be beneficial to you and to me. My hands are immaculate, see.

<Justin>: ***I can't collapse again!***

<Dan>: You wanted to meet the Marshalls. This is a good place to start.

<Justin>: Go right ahead. [...] ***This is the second longest 90 seconds of my life.***

<Patty>: Dan, you have a pen and note pad. [...] Thank you.

[...] Mr. Mittelman, this may be incorrect. I am not as accurate as Jonas is, but I am quicker. Please consider this.

<Justin>: ***Angry, conflicted, confused, and frightened.***

I am not angry! I should never let anyone get that close to me.

<Dan>: ***Look serious Dan.*** Mr. Mittelman, are you all right?

<Macedon>: ***I didn't have to go up the middle. I should have waited for Little Queen Missy. She had as much effect as I did, and there is no collateral damage.***

<Val>: *She zapped him. She's tougher than her mother is, but so was the Queen. He deserved more than that.*

<Patty>: He is trying to organize many incongruities, and I believe he will manage, especially because he is more aware than he was before. Meanwhile, Mr. Barker is signaling to me. My father is ready to hear me sing.

<Val>: *Thank god, he's all right.*

<Dan>: That seat looks good. I'm more tired than I realized.

<Val>: We can go downstairs and talk. I need a drink.

<Macedon>: That would be a faulty maneuver.

<Justin>: Let us all share a few restful moments while Oswald goes to get the car. *I have to understand what just happened.* ***Oswald!***

<Oswald>: What was she doing?

<Justin>: Don't try to think. Get the car and wait.

[...] Watch the chair! No more tripping is allowed.

---------- ----------

<Justin>: Are all three of them that powerful?

<Val>: In different ways. We are convinced that Queen-2 was born to replace Kabiri.

<Macedon>: That is for damned sure.

<Justin>: How does he know, and who is Kabiri?

<Val>: Patty is a dance-trim version of Marshall's mother. She has the emotional strength and wisdom of her grandmother and her parents' physical strength. She also takes downloads from Clara as often as she can. The aura is extra. She was hypnotic like that in an incubator.

<Justin>: ***That's the twin!*** *Why am I screaming?*

<Macedon>: Marshall created his own personal Rainbow Coalition. He makes me believe in miracles.

<Dan>: *Justin must be leaking fluid, and Macedon just used three days of his un-PC allotment.* We're getting off track.

<Justin>: *I'm screaming because I'm in the middle of the Marshall Camp, I never knew he had a camp, and I need everybody in his camp.*

I'm still tougher than they are. I can handle this, as soon as I clear up a few things:

1. *When did Macedon get so tight with Marshall that he would threaten his job and me? Macedon was supposed to be my man on the inside.*
2. *When did the clown start crying, and why would he cry over Marshall?*
3. *Where can I find Clara? They nodded reverentially when Val mentioned her name.*
4. *How do I convince all of them to help me to get Marshall back, assuming that he lives, until we can finish hearing what he has to say? We should start listening to what he has to say first.*

<Val>: While Mr. Mittelman deals with his incongruities, what did they say about H?

<Macedon>: They glued him and stitched him so nothing came loose. At this moment, he is feeling no pain.

<Dan>: You asked for help before. What happened at the BASE meeting this afternoon?

<Val>: Less than 50% effective. Too many people saw how bad H looked yesterday.

- "Critical, but stable" upsets them.
- Hank didn't bother to attend, and that was bad, even if the excuse was he came here instead.
- My sunglasses did not have a positive effect.
- Mrs. Piccolo's positive rumor campaign has 50 - 60% probability of effectiveness, unless we figure out how to put some body paint on H.
- They'll need a lot of hand holding while we do the transitions. This won't work if we lose 40 or 50 people. We couldn't afford to replace them, even if they existed.
- **Sizzler**: This is from Doc. Twenty percent of the staff is eligible for early retirement, and they are financially well off enough to handle it. H and Machi have been giving them savings tips for 30 or 35 years. Doc is considering too, also because of Marshall's financial guidance. She says she mentioned it to you this morning.

<Justin>: *I need Doc as much as I need Marshall. If he wasn't dying, I'd consider becoming less constrained and using a cane on him.* There will be no transitions and no early retirements. I will come and talk to the BASE team tomorrow afternoon.

<Macedon>: What page was that on?

<Dan>: Close your mouth and catch your breath. Then say, "Thank you. The staff will appreciate your concern and your assurances during this difficult time."

<Val>: Thanks. What time?

<Justin>: Make it 2:00 P.M. Then the ones who need to take off early can start their weekends early.

<Dan>: The last part is definitely not in the script book.

<Justin>: *Macedon is giving me a thumbs-up. I may survive this physically and financially.*

For most of a $1 billion, I will improvise. We have 20 minutes to spend with the rest of his family. *I really need to speak with Ms. Frey.*

<Val>: NO! I mean please wait. They're celebrating the fact there'll be a wedding as soon as H can walk again. Let them have these few minutes.

<Macedon>: *What wedding? He was talking about heaven and doing life flashbacks. The last time I saw him like this, he got worse before he got better.*

<Justin>: Why does that make Frick and Frack so glum?

<Macedon>: You are right BOSS. I was dwelling on the negative, and that is usually not beneficial. Marshall is full of surprises.

<Dan>: The wedding sounds like a very positive idea. If Machi accepted his proposal after all this time, she must be very frightened. Sorry, a negative dwelling slipped in.

<Val>: She proposed to him. I just said she would marry him, when he can walk again. Machi always has an angle, but I don't think it's going to work this time.

<Justin>: *She is scary. I have to finish that conversation with Piccolo.* I must meet them soon.

<Dan>: You waited 10 years. 10 days won't hurt.

<Justin>: In that time, he could be out of that thing and strong and enough to sign his resignation, *or he could be dead, and she'll be coming after us with a vengeance.* I saw the yellow envelop on the nurse's desk.

<Val>: What is the probability that upsetting them now will keep that from happening?

<Justin>: Who says I'm a slow learner? I'll wave as we walk out. I could use a few extra minutes with Gunnar anyhow. As this may affect your well-being, you are all welcome to join us at West 40th Street.

<Val>: I'm too old for this.

<Dan>: Say, "I'm glad that you felt it would be appropriate to include us. There is much that needs to be done since HM will not be available for some time. Perhaps Dan and I could improve our ability to work together. The palace is more comfortable than the barracks that I call a studio anyhow."

I will get the opportunity to deal with Gunnar personally.

<Val>: You talk as if he's coming back.

<Dan>: Mr. Mittelman and Mr. Guzman seem to be leaning in that direction.

<Val>: H and his family would lean strongly in the other direction, especially with Gunnar's henchman around.

<Macedon>: Thank you BOSS. I really look forward to seeing Mr. Gunnar. I want to thank him for saving Marshall's life.

Simultaneously, I may be able to show the henchman a few rope handling tricks.

<Val>: *The way he tied up the sniper that hurt H. That would be a wonderful sight to see.*

<Dan>: The henchman is already trying to unscramble his brains. Maja, Val, and I spoke with him this morning.

<Justin>: Joe is also working on the situation.

<Macedon>: *Maybe I should start succession planning. I didn't actually threaten to shoot him myself. It is true that without Marshall and me, he may as well shoot himself. Armstrong is too anxious to please. He would never get a proper handle on the new requirements process.*

<Justin>: As far as Mr. Marshall is concerned, I know that after an appropriate period for mental and physical recuperation, accompanied by henchman removal, we can demonstrate to Marshall and his family how many people all over Daxiao would benefit from a more orderly departure.

<Val>: *You want another $13,000,000 bonus.* What would you do if you were in Marshall's position?

<**Macedon**>: ***I'd show the bastards how I was still the toughest bastard in the valley or on the mountain.***

<**Justin**>: I would heal first. While I was healing, I would notice how my unfortunate accident (*and Sharf's insanity*) directed people's attention toward my life's work, and they saw things that they didn't notice before. I could be amused that several articles in prestigious magazines and journals touted my miraculous accomplishments. These things are more important to him than money or leisure, wouldn't you both agree?

<**Val**>: I believe H would start worrying that people would really start gunning for him, pun intended.

<**Justin**>: ***The mention of guns is suddenly making me nervous.*** I know that the artillery specialist is backpedaling from the henchman as quickly as he can. He sent an e-mail indicating that Belvedere's recommendation for this assignment requires re-evaluation.

<**Dan**>: I saw Gunnar's memo. It is an excellent example of what happens when you cross him.

<**Val**>: I'm not seeing as well as I would like. ***Plan C is working, but what a price to pay! All we have to do is keep them thinking that Sharf came up with those numbers.***

<**Justin**>: If I was riding on Gunnar's coattails, I might realize that his execution is faulty. He lacks subtlety, especially when it comes to Marshall. ***I do too.*** I might seek other avenues for self-aggrandizement, at least for the moment. What would you say Dan?

<**Dan**>: I am selfish, as everybody knows. Marshall has been good for my family and me.

<**Justin**>: ***That would include my family and me.*** Two of us agree. What about you Frick?

<**Macedon**>: I already said too much today. ***It sounds like the damned fool won again, and he doesn't know it. Marshall could have been one of the best logistics people we ever had.***

<**Justin**>: Frack?

<**Val**>: ***We won't let him come back, but I need to see what they intend to do.*** All things may be considered.

------ **Daxiao BASE Office, New York** ------

<**Justin**>: This is quite presentable. The landlord has made several improvements recently. I haven't been here since they opened the command center.

<**Dan**>: Gunnar's people are at the far end of the hall. Their area has been fixed up best of all.

<**Justin**>: Where's Marshall's office? We can meet there. ***Gunnar should come to me.***

<**Dan**>: It's the third door in the other direction, but the command center is much larger, and we can still borrow space in what used to be my office.

<**Val**>: Please consider a space other than H's office. Nicky re-arranged some things earlier today.

<**Justin**>: Why didn't his assistant put things back?

<**Val**>: He tried already. It's still not a good idea.

<**Justin**>: I will decide.

---------- ----------

<**Ernest**>: I don't believe I know you.

<**Val**>: This is Justin Mittelman, ***THE Justin Mittelman***. He'd like to use Mr. Marshall's office.

<**Ernest**>: It's quite small for a person of your stature. Perhaps you would like to use the command center.

<**Justin**>: I know it's small. This is where I started. It would be like a homecoming.

[...] Who did this?

<**Ernest**>: Ms. Frey paid us a visit.

<**Macedon**>: ***Whew! That little lady has a temper. I wonder why I didn't notice it all these years.***

<**Justin**>: Why are you smiling?

<**Macedon**>: It's a personal joke. ***I have to get myself under control. Stoical is better.***

<**Justin**>: I don't see anything humorous. Does she walk around with a sledgehammer?

<**Ernest**>: I believe it was a tire iron.

<**Justin**>: Why didn't you stop her? This is company property.

<**Ernest**>: Look at Mr. Van Amberg sir and wait until you see Mr. Gunnar. We do not want to be around Ms. Frey when she is swinging blunt objects.

<Val>: This is not company property. It was specially built for HM as a gift from his son. The antique furniture that facilities found for him has been in storage for several years.

<Justin>: We don't pay for antiques.

<Dan>: It was new when Raycroft bought it.

<Justin>: Goodsand bought out Raycroft 30 years ago! Oh! [...] He could have insisted on better.

<Dan>: Other battles needed to be fought.

<Justin>: *What battles is he talking about?* What are all these things?

<Val>: She created that neat pile with all his training and educational certificates.

[...] Before you ask the question, the answer is, yes. H completed all those courses and more.

These are his trophies and awards. She put them on the floor where you see them, and then she totaled everything else.

<Ernest>: She took the family photo and the baby pictures, but she left the staff picnic photos. I guess they were too big to fit in H's backpack.

I'm trying to sort out the remainder, but you can see I have a way to go. The phones have been unbelievably busy, as you might imagine.

<Justin>: How many people is that?

<Ernest>: There are about 800 people in the big picture. This year 1,432 showed up.

<Justin>: He only has 400 employees. Did he fly people in from China and Mexico, along with their parents and grandparents?

<Ernest>: Only 47 agreed to come.

<Justin>: Did I pay for all this?

<Ernest>: You paid half the annual entertainment allotment for 410 people, which came to $8,200.

<Justin>: That would pay for a frank, a box of juice for each kid, and a bottle of beer or soda for the adults.

<Ernest>: Jonas's picnic endowment paid the other $30,000. Many of his former and prospective clients are in there, along with the Frey-Marshall staff. They can write it off.

<Val>: *It's a great way for our nerds to meet Jonas's nerds.*

<Dan>: *I don't remember whether Forester was there for the photo session, but I need to get his attention off this.*

<Justin>: That's Higgs. What's she doing there?

<Ernest>: We invited her when we invited you. Furthermore, I believe she was Mr. Marshall's first secretary many years ago.

<Justin>: *More history. Marshall is like a seine.* Doc and Jay are looking very chummy. What am I missing?

<Val>: Jay's daughter is married to Doc's son. Notice the two young people standing beside them. They met at the picnic two years ago.

<Justin>: *Here's Tomaso* and *Octavia. There's a lot to be learned from this photo. Perhaps I should have condescended to attend.* Whose children are those?

<Ernest>: Those are Ms. Maçon's children. They were there along with about 200 others. We had special staff entertain them, plus Dr. Piccolo did his clown act.

<Justin>: *He was babysitting again.* Lillian?

<Ernest>: She's part of the brew committee.

<Justin>: *I'll find out what that is from Lillian.*

<Val>: Mr. Mittelman, this is fascinating, but when are we going to see Mr. Gunnar. I have annotated versions that you can examine in detail at your leisure.

<Dan>: *That was good. Thank you, thank you.*

<Justin>: Send it to me when you return to your office. What happened here and here?

<Ernest>: Because he tripped over the drawer and broke his ribs on the credenza, they received her special attention. Mr. Marshall's replacement would have to redo the décor anyhow. The desk is too tall for anyone except Jonas or the auditor who was in here yesterday.

<Val>: Where's the gold pencil case? That must be worth a few thousand dollars.

<Justin>: *Grace is obsessed with Kristie's, and I think it's a waste of time.*

<Ernest>: Would you like to take it to him?

<Val>: That would be good.

<Ernest>: [...] It's gone, along with some other papers! Somebody was in the safe. I'll call security.

<Dan>: Don't worry. We know where it went.

<Ernest>: Where? [...] OH!

<Justin>: What's this pile?

<Ernest>: Those are unfilled prescriptions for painkillers. He was very proud of those.

<Macedon>: ***He's still tough. Maybe he can pull through this.***

<Justin>: ***Perposet and Cozaar. I'll tell Higgs to research them for me.*** How could one tiny woman do this? How did she sneak in a tire iron?

<Ernest>: She came in with one of his computer cases. She said she wanted to pick up some of his things. When I heard the noise, I peeked in, and then I backed out. I heard her crying a long time after she stopped hitting things. She left it [...] there, and carried out his backpack. There was a big yellow envelope sticking out of the side pocket.

<Justin>: Why would she leave a Tume wheely and take his patched Amy/Navy discard?

<Dan>: Machi doesn't cry. She did the robot thing better than Justin. ***She wouldn't want it tossed out before she checked what he may have left in there, not that they'll ever be able to use them again.***

<Val>: She was capable of extreme emotion before she met HM ***(before her family punished her for having his baby).*** She worried that she had lost him yesterday, and the switch flipped back to on.

<Justin>: What about the backpack?

<Val>: ***He's paying attention.*** Over the years, H developed a passionate attachment to it. He used it when he needed both hands for crutches or canes.

<Justin>: What's in here?

<Macedon>: Good. She didn't break those. Hand me one, and give me one for Val.

<Dan>: I'll take one too. Ernest there's one left.

<Ernest>: There are more down the hall. Mr. Mittelman might want to try that one.

<Justin>: Are all of you a bunch of drunks?

<Val>: No. I'm the only one. This is Machi's quarterly mixture. It has ginger and chamomile.

<Macedon>: It's good for the nerves and for the stomach. Appropriate, don't you think.

<Ernest>: I'll find a cup. The ones in here didn't survive.

<Dan>: Take a slurp. We promise we won't tell anyone.

<Justin>: It is excellent ginger tea.

<Macedon>: That was a proper response. You receive Machi points if you like her concoctions.

<Justin>: I agree that we cannot meet here. The command center is impersonal. Show me your palace.

<Dan>: It is no longer mine, thanks to Gunnar, and you know that.

<Justin>: Viola says you continue to have meetings there.

<Dan>: The new owner lets me use it occasionally.

<Justin>: Is it being used now?

<Ernest>: I don't think so. Everyone is [...]

<Justin>: We'll use it. Call Mr. Gunnar and tell him to meet us in Dan's former office.

----------- ----------

<Justin>: What is this space now?

<Dan>: It's a conference room, offices with a reception area, and a lounge/rest section. I suggest the first office after the conference space.

<Justin>: This was Piccolo's palace! How did you convince Lorrie to approve this? It's better than what I have, but so is "our" library.

<Dan>: I didn't, and she didn't. The new owner commissioned renovations.

<Justin>: How is it that you are still able to use it?

<Gunnar>: Simone Winslow. Piccolo knows details.

<Justin>: Gunnar! What did she do? ***He looks like he fell out of a window.***

<Macedon>: ***She kicked his ass. Stoical is better. I'll sit over here in the corner and try to disappear.***

<Gunnar>: Braces are holding in the loose teeth. The contusions on my arm are not good, but it's not broken.

<Dan>: *Maybe I don't have to do any pounding or strangling. Machi is good!*

<Justin>: Dan, who is Simone Winslow?

<Dan>: Due to Gunnar's space-saving campaign, Marshall and I had to give up space, and the landlord found a buyer for the space quickly. That allowed Daxiao to break the lease without a penalty.

Before the new users could use the space for its intended purpose (start-up electronics firms) Gunnar realized that he needed space in town, and it occurred to him that this would be a good location.

<Justin>: I felt the same as he did.

<Dan>: Daxiao rented everything, excluding this area, from Simone Winslow, and Gunnar pays a minute premium to cover the cost of redecorating the Daxiao space and the hallway. Still, for the money, we didn't have to pay for breaking the lease, Daxiao will be in the same position financially for the next five years, and Gunnar has a better, but slightly smaller, space than Marshall had.

<Justin>: That's a very nice real estate story, but who is Simone Winslow?

<Macedon>: *Baby Girl pulled this off! I always knew she was as smart as her daddy was! Remember stoical.*

<Dan>: Indira Simone Frey-Marshall Winslow is Baby Girl Snuffleupagus, but not the baby girl.

<Val and Gunnar>: What is a Snuffleupagus?

<Dan>: A giant friend that no one ever sees. Didn't either of you watch TV with your daughters?

<Justin>: Forget that. Are you saying that Marshall's daughter is my landlord?

<Dan>: *Gunnar's hurting, but he still needs to be watched.* Marshall's family is your landlord. However, it doesn't include this area. The Frey-Marshalls kept this, and they let me use it occasionally.

<Justin>: There must be something wrong with this picture?

<Val>: I found out yesterday. You can check with Joe, but my money is on Frey, Esq.

<Dan>: Gunnar made Piccolo and Marshall dump it. Frey-Marshall bought it. Gunnar insisted on leasing it back, and the rate is below the market for the quality he is receiving. What could be wrong?

<Gunnar>: Don't stop. Tell him about decorators. You talk faster.

<Dan>: Gaetano. Those are my mother's brothers and my cousins. They let my father and his sons join. *Which means your sister has a piece of the action.*

<Justin>: How much did you have to do with this?

<Gunnar>: Designer and master craftsman?

<Dan>: There was no misappropriation of funds or overspending. Frey-Marshall paid for the materials, and the labor was free. That's why the premium was so low. In return, my family uses it to showcase their commercial decoration abilities.

Now you are going to check the records to see who worked on the library. You will find that Tomaso, my uncle, did the work for exactly 15% less than the standard rate. He has fewer display opportunities, but he is upgrading libraries for three major companies in our area.

<Macedon>: *Fine maneuvering. I'm starting to appreciate the runt.*

<Gunnar>: *More money! Liz went for the whole package, minus the height of course.*

<Justin>: *He may not need the job at Daxiao either.* You actually work? Can this be legal?

<Dan>: 110%. After the SOX gauntlet, Machi made sure of it. She has moves that make Skattin Ark blush.

<Justin>: When did you have time?

<Dan>: You give me weekends and evenings off. My place is only 17 blocks from here.

<Justin>: Who figured out the finances?

<Dan>: HM was (I mean is) a mathematical genius, but he is extremely cautious when it comes to financial risk.

<Justin>: That's the second time I've heard that today. How many people knew that?

<Val>: Acton, Armstrong, Dan, Doc, Higgs, Joe, Ernest, Lorrie, Macedon, Stein, every vendor [...]

<Justin>: STOP, I'm sorry I asked. *I'm sorry I had to ask at this late date.*

<Dan>: Indy has all her father's aptitude, and she can identify acceptable risk. She makes pennies grow into money trees. The two of them would be written up in entrepreneurial magazines if Daddy didn't nix it.

<Gunnar>: *Sharf lied to Mags about that too. Why didn't Marshall report Sharf before he got here?* Do you mind if I sit?

<Val>: *He should have stayed at the hospital. He looks much worse that he did yesterday.*

<Dan>: This particular tree will allow Marshall's grandchildren to live on the rental for the space next door alone. Frey Associates will have a space to meet with clients who don't want the downtown hassle. They write off the redecoration against any new Baby Huey adventure.

<Justin>: What downtown hassle?

<Dan>: For the time being, they use the money they earn here to pay the rent on the space at Broad Street. It is a very acceptable tech haven.

<Gunnar>: We underestimated everybody.

<Justin>: *I have a very large tiger by the tail.* Would you gentlemen mind waiting outside while Mr. Gunnar and I have a talk?

<Dan>: I strongly suggest that you use the office next door if you want more privacy. This space has conference pick-ups.

<Val>: Call my office (Ext. 3752) when you're ready.

<Macedon>: Can I borrow him for two minutes? There will be no suggestions.

<Justin>: Two minutes.

GUNNAR'S INQUISITION

<Gunnar>: Save your breath. I don't need your help. I'm about to go down there and hand in my resignation.

<Macedon>: Don't be hasty. I always need a decent general standing in front of me, especially if he is willing to learn from his mistakes.

<Gunnar>: This general made two very bad mistakes on the same battlefield.

<Macedon>: Marshall had you outnumbered and outgunned this time. There was no way you were going to win with the equipment you were using.

<Gunnar>: He did set me up.

<Macedon>: You set yourself up. Set-up is spelled S-h-a-r-f. Still, you took care of him when he took a hit, and that was good. Hundreds of people appreciate what you did.

Now hang on to me, and I'll walk you down there.

<Gunnar>: *What was that all about?* I'm OK. I look and sound worse than I feel. *I can't show weakness. I AM GUNNAR.*

<Macedon>: *He's a tough one too. Marshall was right. He will be useful if we can convince him that being useful to us is a good idea.*

---------- ----------

<Justin>: The first one may be bugged too. The second one is locked. The one on the end is big, but it's full of boxes. We'll have to use this one.

<Gunnar>: *This one smells like Indy. This is Indy's office. Those are her kids, and there's another Guntur montage.*

<Justin>: *He looks dazed.* Gunnar?

<Gunnar>: Concerned about me. *This will be the toughest sell of my life. I hope the mousse holds up.*

<Justin>: As much as I would be about anyone who caused financial or political risk without any indication of acceptable return. What did Macedon want?

<Gunnar>: He said Marshall had me outgunned, he thanked me for helping Marshall, and he said I should learn from my mistakes.

<Justin>: I agree. You goofed the same way again.

<Gunnar>: What do you mean, again? *I want to see how he's going to spin this.*

<Justin>: Gunnar. Five years ago, I wanted you to find out what Marshall was doing before we took action. I wanted the same thing this time.

<Gunnar>: It is more obvious now than it was then. Armstrong didn't like the Weeble, and Armstrong was your right-hand man in those days.

You knew Montgomery. It would have happened differently if you had let me know that he hated Marshall more than you do?

<Justin>: ***Who says I hate Marshall?*** I never hated Marshall. I didn't understand Marshall, and that event practically ensured that I never would.

<Gunnar>: You were his boss for four years before I arrived. You could have paid attention when he tried to tell you things.

<Justin>: ***I had labeled him as a big nothing, with emphasis on the big. He was fat, but the women still loved him.*** It was your "learn the ropes" assignment. You were supposed to handle it, not drop it on Montgomery.

<Gunnar>: How did I get it wrong this time?

<Justin>: You were supposed to find a seasoned C-level consultant, experienced in both SOX and this new thing, who could provide an objective evaluation of Marshall's Program and recommend what we would have to do if he retired in 21 months.

<Gunnar>: ***It's coming fast. I can skip the probing.***

<Justin>: Instead, you brought in your crazed brother-in-law.

You'd slide on the brother-in-law part if it wasn't for the fact that you hastened Marshall's departure, his people intend to break up the team (which could have us running in place technically for a couple of years), you made sure Sharf got zingers in on Lisse Maçon, and the Doc, and Marshall's paramour would own a significant part of Daxiao if she heard what Sharf is saying about Marshall's drug un-problem and his booze un-problem. You can no longer use the "I'm new here excuse."

What do you have to say for yourself?

<Gunnar>: Your assessment of the situation seems accurate.

<Justin>: ***That's a twist. He's not fighting.*** Would you be kind enough to explain why you selected Sharf if you knew how he felt about Marshall?

<Gunnar>: I didn't know how he felt about Marshall until yesterday.

<Justin>: What did you find out yesterday?

<Gunnar>: That Marshall's Partner Networks have been competing directly with Sharf's SOA consulting teams and winning. He feels that he may have lost hundreds of thousands in bonuses.

<Justin>: I understand - I think. Sharf hates Partner Networks because he's losing money, and you hate Partner Networks because they help you earn money. How do you think he feels about the RandD follow-up business?

<Gunnar>: I'm not sure.

Marshall is making me look bad by making me look good. What if you annoyed me, and I [...]

<Justin>: While we're on the subject, explain Ādaemoa. We have evidence that he was feeding information directly to one of our dirtiest competitors using our transmission equipment. It would look bad for both of us if that became general knowledge. Marshall made sure too many people saw Sharf's chin, so we can't make it go away. You fight beneficial relationships, and support dangerous ones.

<Gunnar>: ***It's time to try the "help me out" routine.*** I'm sure I could argue to refine a point or two, but I know I'm in trouble *(so are you)*, close to the worse professional situation I have had in my life. Everything is out in the open. Tell me what I need to do to clean up this problem.

<Justin>: I doubt that everything is out. The man is much too venomous when it comes to Marshall. What else are you hiding?

<Gunnar>: You already have enough to hang me. Why extend the torture?

<Justin>: ***He's right. I'm enjoying this too much.*** Answer quickly:

1. Will it benefit us (Mittelman, Gunnar, or Daxiao) to have a better understanding of what Marshall does?
2. Can we figure out how Marshall does what he does without Marshall (alive or dead)?
3. How long will it take?
4. How much does Piccolo know?

<Gunnar>: Marshall has to live!

<Justin>: I don't need your prognosis. Answer what I asked.

<Gunnar>:

1. Yes, **Yes**, **YES**.
2. Yes.
3. Two years, standing in place. You called that.
4. About sixty percent. He's smart, but he needs more time to catch up.

<Justin>: How long have you known how powerful Marshall was?

<Gunnar>: Five years ago, I had to leave him alone before I figured it out. What I know now, I just figured out during the last two months.

<Justin>: What did you figure out?

<Gunnar>: Marshall plays family games better than the "Godfather" does.

Armstrong, Chiu, and I replace people and there is no resistance. They go underground. They show up later in Compliance, Partner Network companies, Operations, Logistics, Macedon's teams, Lorrie's team, even my team.

He has relationships with 20% of low- to mid-level managers in U.S., Canada, Ireland, and even Geneva. They are excellent workers and poor players. Mexico owes him and favors were starting in Asia. That's why Van Amberg spent three weeks over there.

<Justin>: Why didn't you tell me?

<Gunnar>: I needed to verify the size of the monster before I could recommend how to dismantle it, especially since you believed Marshall was here because he blackmailed you to get the title.

<Justin>: Gunnar. I obviously have more people convinced of my stupidity than Piccolo has convinced of his innocuousness. You didn't want to cut the worm apart! You wanted to own it, but you needed to figure out how to control Marshall! Is that why you hid those numbers from me?

<Gunnar>: I noticed the numbers when you did. Sharf really is a numbers genius, maybe as good as Marshall or his daughter. I repeat. You managed him for the last nine years. Why didn't you know?

<Justin>: ***I have to go into a quiet corner and figure out why I didn't know. Now I must push back on Gunnar.*** I was letting him accomplish things that significantly increased your annual income and mine, while simultaneously directing attention away from the reality that our incomes were growing with disproportionate speed. You entirely overlooked that you earned last year what I earned the first year you were here.

<Gunnar>: ***I found the way out!*** You entirely missed that one little tripping could cause us to stop those earnings. ***GOOOOAL for Gunnar!***

<Justin>: ***If I had a temper, I would be losing it at this moment.*** Let us try another approach. Where do you believe Piccolo fits in all this? Is he in front of Marshall or behind him?

<Gunnar>: He is Escher on steroids. He doesn't scare anybody. He's almost a perfect player.

<Justin>: You can't tell which way he's going either, but you didn't answer the question. Can he replace Marshall?

<Gunnar>: I told you before. He needs support of Marshall-type people.

<Justin>: Do we have anyone that we can grow into a Marshall?

<Gunnar>: I don't know. Sharf was supposed to clarify our options. ***If he doesn't mention Macedon or Jasper, I won't.***

<Justin>: ***You wouldn't tell me if you knew.*** Let's talk about when the price doubled.

<Gunnar>: It didn't double. Sharf was throwing out bait to see how strongly we will resist. I do that often, especially when we add new features. He knew Marshall was almost dead before he sent the tainted tart.

<Justin>: Is he under your control or not?

<Gunnar>: Any answer I give will be equally bad.

<Justin>: ***He's good on his feet, even when he looks almost comatose.*** I almost forgot. Something strange happened when I saw Marshall a little while ago.

<Gunnar>: Is he still OK?

<Justin>: He was worse when I left his room than when I arrived, but he's OK. I stayed in the waiting room for 30 minutes afterward, and I wasn't chased out by a mob with contaminated syringes. ***Am I worried about him, or am I worried about their reaction to what I did to him?***

<Gunnar>: You can't let him die! Let me check.

<Justin>: ***What is this all about?*** Gunnar, calm down. They used some kind of super glue to hold him together. If it unglues, Piccolo, Van Amberg, Higgs, Ernest, and Marcella know we're here.

Now let me return to my original thought. Piccolo was there with me.

<Gunnar>: Go on.

<Justin>: I'm trying to figure this out myself.

<Gunnar>: What?

<Justin>: When I left, he was still in an oxygen-enriched environment. He's stuttering again because he can't control his breathing, and it sounds like his throat hurts when he talks. However, he's not particularly feverish. If he killed any brain cells yesterday, he had massive backup capacity.

Whatever he has left is functioning rather well because he doesn't push the pain button, although he may be putting extra stress on his heart.

He thinks that he is dying.

<Gunnar>: I saw him. He's hurting enough to feel like he's dying, but I don't think he will.

<Justin>: That means that any words he is likely to say will be carefully chosen.

<Gunnar>: All his life. I don't see your point.

<Justin>: He thought he was whispering. He didn't know, or he had forgotten, that the coffin (I should have said environmental control device) amplifies the patient's voice. Seven out of approximately 28 words he said to Piccolo were, "Gunnar really angry about Liz. Blocking facts." I'm guessing at the last word, because Piccolo cut him off. Why would that be important to a man who is wrestling the grim reaper and who thinks he's doing his last professional turnover after 35 years on a job?

<Gunnar>: Lisse Maçon made bad professional and personal choices, and I'll wager that she complains to you and Marshall that I keep her from performing as well as she could by not supporting her silliness. ***We both know that you started her problems.***

<Justin>: I believe he was trying to say that you are keeping Daxiao from doing as well as it could. Gunnar can fire whomever he wants, but nobody walks away from Gunnar.

I have let you play your games for years, even hanging a long-time acquaintance of mine out to dry. However, your crazy in-law showed us that you were willing to shoot a goose that enhances our ability to lay golden eggs (between half a billion and a billion dollars worth each year), which you knew about. Marshall was putting over $2,000,000 per year into your pocket in addition to your salary. Such a lack of personal control is totally unacceptable.

<Gunnar>: You are a hypocritical fool. You lacked personal control when you got Liz pregnant, and you bribed Piccolo into taking her off your hands by giving him a job here. That's why you let him play his silly games. The little girl doesn't look much like you now, but you should tell Mrs. Piccolo to hide the baby pictures. She was the consummate professional salesperson, and now she is wasting time writing notes for Marshall and pumping out babies for Piccolo.

Do you know that she's pregnant again? Of course you do. There's obviously something still going on between the three of you. Are you and Piccolo going to share the third one?

Why did I do that?

<Justin>: ***There it is!*** Our raving lunatic for today is [...]

<Gunnar>: I am not raving! Liz isn't one of the new breed of unmarried mothers after all. It's a matter of public record that she married Piccolo immediately before he started working here. The little girl was born seven months after they were married. Liz may have helped Viola find a job here, but Johnson actually helps Papa Piccolo watch their brats, except that the gene pool might be a little mixed on the first one. What does your "save the unfortunate children of the world" wife think about your personal control? She must know by now.

If my snooping was unreliable, Marshall built the gallows, and I hung myself. He's deadly even when he's dying.

Here's the resignation.

<Justin>: Stay with us. As Piccolo might say, "we may have just found a crux."

<Gunnar>: Do you admit it? *He looks like a confused puppy, but he's not upset. I didn't do that right?*

<Justin>: *This is only the third time since I could talk that I have been at a loss for words. The first two times were with Macedon and the Witch-2.*

- *Marshall was right to think that something related to the Liz and Gunnar was blocking his Snuffleupagus program.*
- *Piccolo looked like someone hit him in the forehead with a board when Marshall mentioned the blocking.*
- *Gunnar noticed that Octavia looks like her uncle and her grandfather, but if I was her father, why would a gigolo that schedules his affairs by the calendar quarter be upset about it? Such things are known to happen, and the handling is neat, given the close quarters. My father kept his separated by 11,000 miles.*
- *Why did he take the trouble to look up Liz's marital status?*
- *He could have tried to use this to squeeze more money out of me for the last four years. Why would he wait to try and blackmail me now? Dumb question. He was saving the best for rough times.*
- *Liz helped Laufer transition her clients while he handled his own, so neither Gunnar nor Daxiao lost money.*
- *Lassiter and Clarkson wear shorter blue skirts and less material in their little black dresses than Liz did. They miss the exotic undertone, but they compensate with worldly sophistication. We're not missing sales because of that.*
- *Huang handles far eastern sales differently from Liz, but his net volume is the same.*
- *To my knowledge, Gunnar does not play where he eats. He feasts in the upper echelons.*

<Gunnar>: Say something.

<Justin>: Wait while I try to evaluate how Ms. Maçon's life choices may have flipped you into an emotional state similar to the one I saw from Sharf this morning.

1. You have not lost money because of her.
2. You have not lost stature because of her.
3. You have been married, and have had at least 18 official affairs during the time that I have known you, three of which overlapped with your marriage.

Why would you so vehemently begrudge an associate having similar options, even if I was involved in the affair? Certainly, you are not a person with double standards.

<Gunnar>: My associates are always free to do as they please, as long as they are discrete.

<Justin>: She is discrete. This sounds like an affair gone awry. If I asked Higgs to check the deep vines, would she find anything that Dan might consider interesting?

<Gunnar>: No. Liz is not my type. *Neither was Amal, and neither is Indy. Why am I thinking like this?*

<Justin>: I understand what you mean. My mother was very concerned about types. My aunts and sisters still are. My father pretended to understand the benefits of type matching.

He waited until Mother died to acknowledge Liz. This means that though the part about Octavia looking like me is correct, I am not her father. I am her uncle.

I will further say that you are now realizing the benefits of personal control, because if you were on this side of the desk, you would have reached across and pounded me to death with your twitchy pinky.

<Gunnar>: You were taking care of your little sister.

Breathe slowly Gunnar! I have a few million in the bank, aside from Guntur's trust fund. If I sell the house in Baskin Bridge, I'll have even more. I can go to Andhra Pradesh and work in the clinic they set up in Guntur's name. Kerstin and Len can live on what they make. Mags just chose William over me. Gerthe can rot in hell.

No, I can't leave Indy. I must apologize to Indy.

<Justin>: She did her job well. Isn't that the reason that "we" are so upset? You said she was a consummate salesperson.

<Gunnar>: She gave it up to take a job for which she has no prior experience.

<Justin>: Is it true that effective sales require effective communications?

<Gunnar>: You can't change like that.

<Justin>: Were you not reviewer of medical publications before you started selling medical equipment? You took the reverse path.

<Gunnar>: ***What do you know about that?***

<Justin>: Everyone is reviewed carefully before a major promotion. Your résumé says medical technology training, but Stephanie filled Grace in on the details. I know that you enrolled in Albert Medical School; you dropped out before you finished your residency, but you were already Dr. Andrew Nicholas Gunther. You were hit by a truck, and you had a concussion that shook something loose. The lump you received yesterday must have moved the clock back.

You became the medical reviewer named A. Niklas Gunnar while you were in a fugue. You took back your birth name, which your parents had gone through the trouble to anglicize.

<Gunnar>: ***My mother made my father do it. She wanted to be an American snob and Swedish royalty all at the same time.***

<Justin>: That is why you are so good in medical sales. I suppose you went on a reverse fugue last night. The Marshall's could sue you for practicing without a license, but I doubt that they will, considering the circumstances.

<Gunnar>: You are very thorough. ***I was not having a fugue. I couldn't even stand to see a picture of a corpse in the books I was editing. When I went into sales I expected to be a miserable failure, and Stephanie would leave for someone who was her type. She would have, but she "accidentally" missed a few pills while she was helping me heal. And then she waited 15 years to leave me for someone who was her type.***

She killed Amal! No, Amal killed Amal. She should have stayed put and let me explain. I killed Amal. I should have ended the engagement, once and for all, but I let is string out because of the connections, as Gerthe suggested. Thanks to Stephanie, I have been a miserable success for the last 20 years.

<Justin>: Gunnar, I know that salesmen are supposed to have a variety of emotions at their disposal, but this one does not seem appropriate. You didn't even laugh first.

<Gunnar>: How is laughing related to my allergies acting up?

<Justin>: The autumn pollen is affecting many people lately. Grab a few tissues. I don't suppose the owner would mind.

In spite of all this pollen, we have to finish clearing up the air clearing before we clarify the original issue.

Contrary to corporate legend, I do carry a few things. Here is the picture of my kids holding Octavia and Tomaso at Disney World recently. That man is my father, and you can see the resemblance. Notice that Grace and I are both in the picture. This may prove that Grace understands the connection between Liz and me. You will also notice that Liz and Piccolo are not in the picture. We calculate that this is when the most recent pumping up occurred. We will share a moment of silence while you digest all that.

<Gunnar>: How long are you going to sit like that?

<Justin>: This pregnant pause ***(Marshall makes everybody pun)*** gives you the opportunity to blurt out something that explains the prior blurting out. We can afford another two minutes.

<Gunnar>: If we both listened to Ms. Piccolo né Maçon, we would only know what Marshall/Piccolo or Piccolo/Marshall wanted us to know. Nothing is the way it seems. You just proved that.

<Justin>: However, she provided a middle ground between Marshall and Piccolo. You told me that you couldn't find one.

<Gunnar>: It's time for another fugue. ***Then I can stop worrying about what Marshall did to get even with me.***

<Justin>: We are not ready for that yet. Before the blurting out, I agreed with Guzman and several other people that the situation, including you, could be salvaged, though it will be easier if Marshall lives. The blurting out was beneficial because it lead us to the root cause of the problem.

<Gunnar>: You love that common terminology crap.

<Justin>: I'm communicating.

<Gunnar>: What was the root cause?

<Justin>: Liz transferred soon after your divorce from Stephanie. You had decided that you would have an exotic experiment as your first seasonal accoutrement after your divorce, the exotic experiment was ready to settle down with someone more stable, and being Gunnar, the magnificent, you are not accustomed to being the rejectee, especially by someone who isn't your "type". If you decided to condescend, Liz was supposed to be thankful.

<Gunnar>: *It wouldn't have been an exotic experiment. I was free to get married to a real human.*

<Justin>: Unfortunately, such things are part of business reality. Your cost/benefit ratio is still positive, but you will have to work to make up for the difference if we lose Marshall. I'm offering you an opportunity to try.

Hidden SOA Inhibitor

<Gunnar>: You have to work harder too. He was handling things that were your responsibility. You have never been a leader when it comes to Marshall's SOA or whatever he calls it.

<Justin>: I am not the topic of this conversation. However, you now understand why I found it necessary to be neutral toward Liz's messages, just as I now understand your negative inclinations.

<Gunnar>: You have never been neutral when it comes to Marshall. You never picked on SOA, but you picked on him. Your nastiness affects other people's responses to him, and that affects his ability to achieve goals that are helping you to earn at least five times as much as I do. ***Why is that?***

<Justin>: It's perverted, but that's how we bond. *I don't know why I'm nasty. He's injured, but he's still very Gunnar.*

<Gunnar>: *I'm onto something. How far can I take this?* There was no bonding between you and Marshall. What did he do that would explain why you call him a nerdy gimp Weeble on a good day?

Why else would I completely ignore somebody who was that powerful, especially since I knew how much we needed him before?

<Justin>: *I have to get him off this track. I'll confuse him with honesty.* I have to confess that you may be correct. I've already been lectured about that today by both the Doc and Guzman. Ms. Frey started the discussion at 7:45 this morning. Marshall has always known [...]

<Justin and Gunnar>: [...] Because he can read lips.

<Justin>: I'm probably annoyed because he [...] I am not sure why I am annoyed. I will be examining my circuits to discover probable causes.

Until today, I considered Marshall as a relatively cheap nerdy prop for nerdy Armstrong.

However, $750 million is a lot of smoke and mirrors, and that's with you dragging them down, and with me not promoting them. Let us dwell upon that for a moment.

<Gunnar>: I have other information, which requires dwelling, if you believe I should stay; I want you to understand how deeply we are in this together.

<Justin>: Let me hear it.

<Gunnar>: Marshall told me that I shouldn't upset him because he could leave when we still need him.

<Justin>: Why did you upset him anyhow?

<Gunnar>: He was already upset when he said that. He discovered my connection with Montgomery immediately after he returned, and maybe he knew more about where you fit than I ever will.

<Justin>: How? *Piccolo was trying to warn me.*

<Gunnar>: He has an underground network, access to every security video, and he reads lips.

<Justin>: You waited until now to tell me! They could have been laying traps that would be tripped faster if something happened to him.

<Gunnar>: I found out immediately before the tripping. That was a good reason for me to try to save his life, don't you think.

What are you doing?

<Justin>: *The b.stard has me surrounded.*

It's time for me to do something to keep from springing those traps.

[...] This is Justin. How is Marshall doing?

CHAPTER XI - EXTREMELY PERSONAL - PASSION FOR SURVIVAL

**** Stop ****
Gratuitous Passion (Planning)
starts here
**** Skip to ****
WFSOA Success Planning
If you believe this is
irrelevant

Dan>: I vote for "Live". Van Amberg and Macedon would too, except that Van Amberg insists that H will want to live as far away from Daxiao as possible.

> **Readers:** I promised you about 320 pages ago that this SOA P opera would have passion. I'm finally getting around to it.
>
> Passion affects the course of events in business technology environments, even with a robotic president, just as it does in many other places.
>
> Furthermore, I promise it this will help you to remember common terminology and concepts related to WFSOA.

<Justin>: Upon what do you base your recommendation? Why does Macedon sound like that? ***I knew he had popped a gasket.***

<Dan>: Jonas called. Doctors from the VA came and checked HM again, and he passed again. He'll be off the oxygen soon. His pressure is down to 135/85. It was lower when Queen-2 was singing to him. His temperature is down to 99.9.

The most important thing is that the doctors ordered them to stop the visitors so he could rest, and he started dreaming about his ***honeymoon.*** Lattimore had to adjust his tubing twice. Jonas sounds ecstatic, his mother is looking coy, Pipsqueak is amazed at the "Old Man", Van Amberg is smiling, but both his eyes took a turn for the worse. My allergies have cleared up completely. We also have a chortling Macedon.

<Justin>: Who is Lattimore?

<Dan>: He's the second-shift private duty nurse.

<Justin>: I missed something.

<Dan>: As a robot naturally would.

<Justin>: Wait! Are you saying what I think you're saying?

[...] How can that be for someone who was dying? ***And I helped push the situation.***

<Gunnar>: He can't die. ***I can figure out something for him.*** Send my pink slip to the hospital. I'll see you later. ***The apple mousse ran out.***

<Justin>: Sit Gunnar. ***You're having trouble standing up anyhow. I'll have to make sure he takes a complete physical. He's not acting like Gunnar.***

<Gunnar>: Doug Church is good, but maybe I know some people that could help him with Marshall.

<Justin>: He's getting what he needs. After I finish reviewing our options, you can do the same.

[...] Talk to me Dan.

<Dan>: I thought he was dying because he said his research was finished. Val and Alex thought so too until we compared notes. The outstanding nature of his dream is related to a 41-year-long planning and research project.

<Justin>: Planning and research in a situation like this seem highly illogical.

<Gunnar>: What are they saying?

<Justin>: Nothing that makes sense. When they clarify it for me, I'll explain it to you.

<Dan>: You should hear it from Val. He knew H at the time of the original research structuring. His explanation would also sound more appropriate. I keep thinking about minks on tranquilizers.

<Val>: A proper explanation would not be appropriate to this environment. You have a business to run, and I need some rest. "Live" is the correct vote.

<Justin>: To ensure that I have all the information that I need to make a correct decision, at least once when it comes to Marshall, I order you to elaborate.

<Macedon>: I can't order any more, but I would request forcefully if I thought I could get away with it. You folks have been holding out on me, and I helped to save his equipment.

<Val>: His wife helped him to have a good life, against all odds, and she will continue to do so. He dreams about her.

<Justin>: Macedon. What equipment did you help him to save? For that matter, why did they let you stay in the room with him today?

<Val>: **Hide the handle. He's a master twister.**

<Macedon>: BOSS, you know more than anyone else does how upset I am about Marshall. They let me stay because I have the biggest mouth, and they wanted me in there with HM rather than outside blabbing to the Marshall clan.

<Justin>: Guzman is sitting on two memos with decidedly different tones. The first will create the ***BEST POSSIBLE ENVIRONMENT*** for Marshall to finish whatever needs finishing. The other shows how Belvedere may extend Acton's capabilities in case of his untimely demise.

<Gunnar>: ***NO DEMISE!***

<Justin>: Gunnar is about to fry a few circuits. If you keep this up, I will have two executives completely out of commission.

Before I commit to either recommendation, I must complete my own research, especially since my preliminary investigation suggests the "Die" option. Having a wonderful wife is not a sufficient explanation.

<Val>: It is the explanation. I said he was dreaming about his honeymoon.

<Justin>: Would you make a billion-dollar decision based on what you just told me?

<Val>: Mr. Mittelman, Hamilton Marshall is unusually strong. He could bench-press 300 pounds when he came out of rehab 41 years ago, and he stayed strong, even after he put on weight. He had a little high blood pressure until he lost 90 pounds recently. Other than that, he was never physically ill. That special strength and encouragement from his lifetime partner are what helped him to survive yesterday, and to dream today.

<Justin>: One billion dollars per year and lifetimes worth of work.

<Val>: This is blackmail.

<Justin>: This is focused persuasion. ***I will finally discover what gives the Weeble his wobble resistance.***

<Val>: Why would you vote for "Die"? Is that wishful thinking?

<Justin>: ***He thinks I have something against Marshall too.*** I checked with two acquaintances who are doctors, and they say that it is likely that Marshall had something called a total femur replacement.

<Val>: Maja confirmed that after you left earlier.

<Justin>: They say that with a punctured lung and other internal injuries, an operation of that nature would have been done only if he was in extremis. The alternative was amputation, which he also may not have survived, physically or emotionally.

<Macedon>: You're probably right about the extremis, and he definitely has some loose screws around the idea of amputation.

<Justin>: They said that it is highly likely that he is still in extremis, and that somebody was inflating his chances to keep Ms. Frey from losing it again.

<Val>: Now we know it is less extreme.

<Gunnar>: He's tired and hurting, but he is really in good shape. If they control the infection, he should be all right. ***Indy won't associate me with her father's death, even if it wasn't my fault.***

<Macedon>: When is he going to tell us how he knows this stuff?

<Justin>: He sells medical equipment and he's a trained medical technician.

<Gunnar>: *Thank you.*

<Justin>: Without considering Gunnar's expertise, these unusual wedding plans seem very unlikely.

<Gunnar>: *He's already married!*

<Val>: Do you find that the Blue Light thing is useful?

<Justin>: Of course I do. It keeps my hands free. Can you hear me?

Confusing Personal Communications

<Val>: Machi reminded HM of historical planning and research activities that he started before he was involved in technology. This unusual planning continued, probably until yesterday morning.

<Dan>: We are talking about requirements apart from her requirement that he should be able to stand up at his wedding. She wants standing up after the wedding.

> **Readers:** This is crucial. Notice that Justin is using one set of words and having two conversations, on purpose.
>
> In the real world of business technology, this happens **frequently and accidentally.**

<Val>: Fred (the nurse that kicked you out) saw unexplained blips on the monitor while Nicky was in the room. Lattimore saw upstanding indications that were visible without the monitor while H mumbled about family planning. Jonas helped Lattimore connect the dots and called.

<Justin>: Explain the nature of these plans.

<Macedon>: **I'll say please.**

<Val>: Before I met HM, he affected the opposite gender as Sharf might have, except that Marshall was bronze and handsome, not pale and pretty.

<Macedon>: You're damned right he did.

<Val>: Ignore Alex.

Marshall also had unrealized giftedness in an area that might be appreciated by the opposite gender. Nicky calls him her Zeus on a leash. Even with his injuries, if he had the inclination he might exceed Gunnar in an area where Gunnar has an outstanding reputation, and I am not talking about sales.

<Macedon>: Who says it was unrealized? His unit set up a little realizing to celebrate surviving boot camp. The ladies on the base started lining up after that. After he hooked up with Denise, he had to fight them off.

<Dan>: ***Jonas had the same happy problem.***

<Justin>: How do you know this?

<Macedon>: **What can it hurt now?**

<Val>: **Go ahead.**

<Macedon>: I was his commanding officer.

<Justin>: That was Van Amberg.

<Macedon>: Nope.

<Justin>: You knew Marshall when I hired you!

<Gunnar>: ***The giant octopus was in his best form.***

<Macedon>: I had offers from five different companies. I figured I would have an inside track if I came here, and I owed the kid a favor, though he's definitely not a kid any longer. It was not your robotic silver tongue.

<Justin>: Now I understand the comb. You tricked me, both of you - all of you.

<Gunnar>: What does a comb have to do with this?

<Macedon>: Stop bellyaching. We helped you quadruple your income while we were tricking you.

<Justin>: Dan?

<Dan>: I just found out one minute ago. You told me that Marshall is the only one who knows everything that Marshall does.

<Val>: *He certainly is.* I'll proceed.

Mrs. Frey-Marshall assumed long-term ownership of Mr. Realized after he received injuries that came within an inch of permanently eliminating his ability to realize. The injuries actually did affect his abilities, psychologically, for more than a year.

<Macedon>: She is one powerful little mama. I was almost sure he was going to have to switch roles.

<Justin>: Explain the exceedingly large results that I saw today. There are obvious signs of his contribution.

<Gunnar>: Several of the pie slices were wrong, and so are the numbers on that table. They tricked us into making money.

<Val>: His partner helped him to him to refocus his initial potential using highly structured plans and implementations. Special research sessions produced the original output.

Today she promised him that the research was over, and they could start the serious work. They will concentrate on 41 years of best practices and lessons learned. The planning modules are in a fireproof safe to prevent spontaneous combustion. He has reasons to live that you could never imagine.

<Dan>: Some of those best practices would explain how the muscle-bound arrogant clown became your brother-in-law.

<Justin>: Grace and I wonder how the clown switches roles.

<Dan>: It is two aspects of the same individual. One helped me to become a father relatively late in life, and the clown helps me to be a funny father.

<Val>: The late in life part applies to me too. Pauline is #268 after eight years of childless marriage. Jonas was the original #268.

<Dan>: Tommy is a 268 too! Octavia is #67 and Indy is the original #67. Those are great numbers for start-up projects. It makes you want to run out and sign long-term contracts.

<Macedon>: **Attention!** This is about as obvious as a snow fox in a blizzard.

<Justin>: Alex and I still agree on something. The numbers appear to be irrelevant.

<Gunnar>: They may be bragging about Marshall's numbers, but they are relevant. My man checked.

<Val>: **You must stop this.**

<Dan>: It is confusing. We will hang up, and you can call Guzman. "Live" is the correct message.

<Macedon>: I don't know what in hell they are talking about, but I agree to "Live".

Give me details later.

<Justin>: Not until you clarify those numbers.

<Val>: You said that the information was irrelevant.

<Justin>: Guzman said I should take long enough to ensure that I get the details right. Why doesn't Marshall stay over when he falls over? ***I'll spread the curiosity around.***

<Dan>: Details. Who hit you over the head?

<Val>: *When you push him over.* We told you. He has natural talent, an impressive research assistant, and enough strength to keep dreaming about life with his research assistant in the worst possible circumstances.

<Gunnar>: His friend/mate helps him find ways to get him through whatever he needs to go through.

<Justin>: What do you know about this?

<Gunnar>: He needs his Nicky.

<Macedon>: He didn't pronounce that correctly.

<Val>: Shut up!

<Gunnar>: He almost had a stroke today, literally, because she wasn't there when he woke up. He was screaming, actually whispering loudly, about her and a research project. We always knew she was propping him up.

<Val>: Listen to Gunnar. We are finished.

<Justin>: We are not finished. You'll have what you want when I have what I want.

<Dan>: Admit that you're just plain curious.

<Macedon>: **I am curious too.**

<Val>: What if what you and Piccolo want is not what H wants?

<Justin>: Do you want to remove his options before he has a chance to decide?

<Macedon>: Let HM say no if he wishes. He worked too hard and he nearly died to get the options.

<Justin>: *They already convinced me to say "Live". I'll start the "Die" backup plan after tomorrow's "Live" announcement. Meanwhile, I am more curious than they think.*

<Val>: If you approved a "Die" memo, you'd be shooting yourself in the foot.

<Justin>: That provides further proof of how dumb I continue to be when it comes to a person who affects 30% of my bottom line. Are we hesitating because of something illegal?

<Macedon>: *I have some other suggestions.*

<Val>: The illegal tact is likely to make me want to withhold information. Didn't you learn your lesson five years ago?

<Gunnar>: Leave the man alone. We hurt him enough already.

<Justin>: *Gunnar is acting humane! He definitely needs to have that lump checked. I may have to find another "bad boy", and it won't be Macedon.* I already have your opinion.

<Dan>: We need help while HM is flat on his back. The research plans are awesome and they buy time. Machi is proud of the man and the plans.

<Macedon>: I agree. You are outnumbered.

<Justin>: I know you're waving your hands around.

<Dan>: I'll give him the version that I know.

This is hilarious. Alex was right about the pronunciation. Your career depends on Nicky's [...]

<Val>: To keep this common terminology from getting too common, I will keep this as formal as possible. It will take me longer to phrase things properly.

This information is provided on a "need to know" basis, and Gunnar needs to know less than you do.

<Dan>: *It would also give him an inferiority complex.*

<Justin>: I'm waiting with bated breath. *I want to see what Grace sees. What does Grace have to do with this?*

<Val>: *You may be breathing differently when I finish.*

> **Readers:** This is your final warning. Proceed only if you are as curious as Justin and Alex are.
>
> The passion is interspersed with technology and planning concepts.

<Val>: H and Alex were among the muscle-headed marines they assigned to help us with the logistics of building a base further into the boondocks.

The first time I noticed H, he was on top of me. He begged me not to move, and then he lost consciousness. He wanted some unfriendly people with rifles to believe we were dead. He was bleeding enough for both of us.

<Justin>: *I may have to include a halo with Marshall's next bonus, if he's not in line for his own halo.*

That's it! I'll woo him and his family with a halo.

<Val>: A minute earlier, Alex and I had been sitting on a log at the edge of a clearing and discussing whether that particular clearing was the place for the new base.

H was guarding us. When he noticed movement in the brush on the other side of the clearing, he pushed us out of the way. In the process, his thigh was shattered near the knee and broken in the middle. A third projectile missed bone and exited near the most painful place you could imagine.

<Macedon>: Pushed. He hit me so hard that I landed four feet into the bush. That was good. I was able to pull my men together and convince the unfriendly people to stop shooting at us. I came back and held Marshall's crotch together while Val and Flannery dealt with splits and a tourniquet.

It was my first command, and I didn't have the logistics right. After that, I promised I would become the best that there was, and I did. Still, I lost two men, and would have ruined Marshall's life if it hadn't been for Little Miss Mama.

<Val>: There was no direct contact with that painful place, but scarring produced extreme physical and mental discomfort. The doctors were more concerned about the shattering and splintering. They promised him that the near miss had probably missed important internal tubing. Plus, there was a backup unit on the other side of his body.

<Macedon>: I wasn't so sure. The exit wound was a big hole.

<Justin>: *I'm starting to feel off balance again.* Get to the point.

<Dan>: He's describing what Marshall survived then, and what he could survive now.

<Justin>: Probably turned out to be all right.

<Gunnar>: Don't trust probably. Call the VA.

<Justin>: Macedon called last night. They check Marshall already - he's as all right as he might possibly be.

<Val>: H didn't like "probably". The uncertainty became an obsession after multiple embarrassments lead to termination of his relationship with Denise. We know now that he tried "prematurely", but he didn't know then.

<Justin>: Appropriate maturity can facilitate project success and manage risk.

<Gunnar>: I'm not sure I agree with the SOA maturity assessment, but tell Piccolo we can look at it again.

If there was something useful in what the runt was saying, I may have blocked it. For Indy, I will be cooperative. Why can't I get her out of my head?

<Val>: He was especially worried about how "probably" might affect his creative abilities.

He needed to show that he could be a better father than his own had been (that wouldn't have been too hard).

He started sleeping in the medical library at the VA hospital.

He studied artificial joints, and he realized that nothing that he could use was anywhere near being perfected. He studied muscle control. He learned what there was to learn about pain management at the time. He learned that it was possible to apply pressure and dull some nerve endings, while he simultaneously learned surprising techniques for stimulating other nerve endings.

He learned how to build strength and agility in the good leg to compensate for the injured one.

He did as much research as he could on his injury. He traced the projectile though his own body and determined that the reproductive stream "probably" would still function, but internal swelling may have produced temporary blockage. The projectile entered his thigh while he was in mid-jump and came out higher up than it went in.

He learned about conversion reactions and stuttering, hopefully increasing his ability to talk to another engagement partner if he found.

He didn't want to leave a mess in the library, because he didn't want to lose his research privileges. He didn't need a ladder to reach books, but putting them back required two hands. He fell a few times, and ended up with bruises shaped like metal shelving in addition to his original injuries.

PLANNING FOR PASSION

<Justin>: What does this have to do with planning?

<Val>: Everything. The head librarian recommended the planning.

She was impressed by his determination; she took pity on him, and agreed to advise him.

<Macedon>: Everybody needs a Clara.

<Justin>: Hands on experience?

<Macedon>: You are incorrect and inappropriate. Clara is a retired army officer, a retired nurse, and a veteran of WW II. At the time, she was already almost old enough to be his grandmother. Now she's 96 years old.

<Justin>: *Since when does Macedon worry about being inappropriate? Still, I don't want any more suggestions. He could claim temporary insanity associated with that post-trauma stupidity.*

I apologize. We know that my condition is aggravating my usual level of retardation today. What was the true nature of that contribution?

<Gunnar>: *What condition?*

<Val>: Clara received permission to help H if he agreed to treat his efforts as a controlled research project. Her special red-tape scissors got the research approved. Marshall's extraordinarily high IQ scores sharpened the scissors.

He had to create detailed plans that could be used to rehabilitate other veterans with similar problems.

Clara found the publications he needed and put them back on the shelves.

She made him deal with the appearance of his scars by paying for his first official vacation outside the country (from her own savings). He had to spend time on Paradise Island in gaudy swim trunks and bring back a picture of himself on the beach in full gaudiness.

<Dan>: I saw those. With his physique, hardly anybody noticed the scars.

<Val>: Clara introduced him to veterans with similar problems. From them, H learned coping techniques that allowed functionality without increasing pain levels. Guys would talk to him when they wouldn't talk uninjured medical personnel.

Clara insisted that he should consider the feminine aspects research and planning, from intellectual and physical points of view. She taught him the benefits of patience and being gentle for himself and for his partners.

<Justin>: He seems to have accumulated an extensive list of lessons learned.

<Gunnar>: The lessons learned list that he showed me yesterday had over 150 items on it.

<Justin>: Thank you Gunnar. That is good to know. ***It is truly good to know. Liz never mentioned that.*** Val, please continue.

Finding Stakeholders

<Val>: After almost a year, Clara felt that he had healed enough and learned enough to enroll in one of the limited number of clinics that dealt with probability problems at the time.

He needed to bring his own wife or a surrogate, but no one was available. His older brother had married Denise, and H was afraid to start looking again.

<Justin>: Why would you do that to someone with such obvious difficulties? ***Why did I do what I did?***

<Gunnar>: ***Because you told me to do it the first time, and you supported me the second time. Don't try to act as if you are blameless.***

<Val>: It was an extreme case of sibling rivalry, and Richard didn't mind stomping a man when he was down, similar to another very tall slim person of our recent acquaintance.

H was so depressed that he didn't object when the engagement was announced.

<Macedon>: Don't feel bad for the boy. H won the mate/friendship lottery. Denise was a decent catch intellectually and physically, but Nicky had both of those areas covered. She also makes lemonade while Denise complains about whether the rind is bruised. That was the attitude that contributed to his "premature" failures.

<Val>: Before he met Nicky, things became worse. Clara had to support him during episodes of depression after fee for service disasters. She found a service weapon in his backpack. He said it was for protection, but he would never have been able to reach it a mugger attacked.

<Justin>: ***All-Tha-News: Daxiao executive's suicide attributed to health and professional problems. Things can get worse now too.***

<Dan>: Now I see! Machi had to make sure he didn't slide down that path again. Nicky/Machi always has two or three angles.

<Val>: At the time, Clara reminded him that he was only 22 (he sounded as if he was 70 and miserable). She encouraged him to continue the intellectual planning exercise for the benefit of other veterans. She encouraged him to continue home study to increase his ability to control research variables.

She assured him that he would find the proper research situation if he kept trying. She encouraged him to go back to school, even with his mobility problems - there were no online courses in those days.

She was right about helping people. Thousands of veterans and their mates have benefited from that research. Clara's boss took the research from him and Clara (and Nicky) and ran with it after Indy was born.

<Macedon>: ***I heard about his plans through the VA, but I thought they were an academic exercise.***

<Justin>: ***Enhanced halo for a stud Weeble. I could be jealous, if I allowed such an emotion.*** I noticed that you still managed to skip the details.

<Val>: You sleep when we provide details.

<Dan>: He doesn't really, but it is not relevant now.

<Macedon>: When I saw him again, it was two years later, and Little Miss Mama had made Baby Girl for him. She was the spitting image of her daddy. That's when I started believing in miracles. I was shipped out again before he explained how the miracle happened.

<Val>: He wouldn't have told you anyhow. He was ashamed that he wasn't like "normal" people.

<Justin>: I will stay awake for $750,000,000 million dollars.

<Val>: **You want more research time.**

<Dan>: **You get extra time for 2,500 people you and H stashed outside of BASE.**

<Macedon>: **I need time too. My people became Marshall's people after today's suggestion.**

<Justin>: I can't see you, but I feel the breeze.

<Val>: The day that he met Nicky, he had just come from the VA hospital with his new government-issued canes with the arm clamps. His backpack contained neatly typed plans that he had verified medically and academically in the VA library. He still uses the same backpack to store plans that haven't been implemented yet. That's why Machi took it today.

Planning Format (Personal)

Each plan had entry criteria, work breakdown structures with dependencies, estimates of duration, and expected results. He had a section where he could summarize the actual results.

<Justin>: Post-implementation review.

<Val>: He had little hope of anything except solo implementations.

<Justin>: That's enough background. When did the synchronization of research efforts begin?

<Val>: I suspect that it began on the first day.

<Dan>: ***Suspect. They almost set fire to the Village before they ever touched each other.***

<Justin>: Why would a sophisticated research partner enter into such a relationship if a major component had software and hardware limitations, especially a partner who must have had many input options? ***She still does. Guzman's eyes glaze when he mentions her.***

<Gunnar>: That is absurd. Li says we have the most robust research environments.

<Dan>: **Ike is dead. Telling can't hurt.**

<Val>: She was 24 years old, and her software gateway was still in place. After a five-year engagement, she had recently found her engagement partner "in the closet" with his male boss. The engagement had caused her to avoid other input options.

<Justin>: Major adjustments must have been necessary.

<Val>: It caused only slight modifications in the original relationship. They called off the engagement and ultimately maintained a wonderful brother/sister relationship.

<Justin>: Where might one find the former engagement partner?

<Gunnar>: Look in the Knowledge Center.

<Val>: Forget the focused persuasion. He's permanently located six feet under in a spot off the Jacky Robinson Highway. The next answer is "Yes, his early demise was related to his lifestyle."

<Justin>: Keep going with the research?

<Gunnar>: ***This is getting confusing.***

<Val>: Nicky first saw Marshall a week after her surprising discovery. She was worried that there was something wrong with her that caused Ike's alternative experiences.

While thinking about what to do next, she remembered talking to Paula about HM's research. Paula was her apartment mate during law school, and Paula was my fiancée. I never had a thought that I didn't share with Paula.

[...] Tell me again why I should finish this story.

<Justin>: Something about the research situation gave him new life.

<Val>: *I guess you're right.*

We felt that the day they met was a very good day. Nicky had dropped by my place in the Village to bring us our first wedding present. We had eloped to the same spot on Paradise Island where H had to wear his gaudy trunks. We were going to celebrate because Nicky had just passed the bar exam, and we were going to celebrate H's greater mobility.

Nicky acted subdued. We thought she was practicing modesty after passing the bar exam at the earliest possible opportunity. Paula had used her study time to help me to get into law school.

Marshall was very quiet. He never knew when his stuttering would kick in. He took only a sip of Champaign because he was afraid of what it would do to his balance. ***That has always been the case. That's why Machi's brew never has alcohol. Sharf was lying.***

<Justin>: I know about the brew. That statement was not necessary.

<Val>: He tried to be cheerful for me, but he was having such a rough time that we skipped discussion of the wedding that Nicky was supposed to have soon after she passed the bar.

Except that one leg didn't bend, he still looked like an oversized model for a Marine poster from the neck to the hip.

From the neck up, the mane of curly hair and the beard reminded Nicky of statues of Zeus.

<Macedon>: He was one of the best-looking mutts we had. They used him in our promotional literature. Boys in all colors, shapes, and sizes signed up because they wanted to look like him.

<Val>: We saw Nicky noticing how H's muscles moved under his turtleneck sweater when he placed a Scrabble tile on the board, but we didn't think much of it. Nicky likes shoulders. Ike was no slouch either.

Nicky was impressive in a turtleneck too, but he believed that she wasn't his type.

[...] What did I say that was so hilarious? You almost sounded like H.

<Gunnar>: Robots don't laugh. ***I don't remember ever hearing more than an executive chuckle from him.***

<Justin>: Today's ironies are enough to affect even an android. What do you believe Marshall would have preferred?

<Gunnar>: He would have preferred anybody but Sharf. He wanted me to get him out of here.

<Val>: He admitted to me that he was looking for a Clara, only 35 years younger. He wanted someone who wasn't a "princess" or a society snob. He wanted someone who was less petite and fragile looking. He weighed almost twice as much as she did, and none of it was fat. He wanted someone who would help him over rough spots, not help to create them.

<Justin>: Performance and stability without bells and whistles and low cost of ownership.

<Dan>: Liz says you've been keeping up with the terminology. I'm impressed [...] sorry Val.

<Val>: However, there were many social barriers, even to a research situation. Paula and I liked him, which is the only thing that gave him limited acceptability.

He was of mixed ancestry, a college dropout, and a veteran of an unpopular war. The government was paying for his education. His major source of income was disability payments, and he lived at home with his mother. He had no social status that she could see.

Nicky was a lawyer from a well-to-do Northchester family with strong social connections. She had ethnic and religious purity, and she was not yet "liberated".

She had turned down an opportunity at Julliard because her parents decided that she should be the lawyer and her brother would be the doctor. She still danced as a hobby, while he couldn't walk five steps without falling over unless he had help.

However, she was worried about whether she was a "real" woman, especially since Paula had already hooked and married me. Her logic was that if she could get satisfactory input from a man who experienced some level of pain most of the time, couldn't take painkillers, and couldn't bend his leg more than 20 degrees, then there was nothing wrong with her.

During intense Scrabble games, each one of us almost beat him once. Machi was/is an intellectual snob. She wanted to know how someone like H could beat all of us. H earned his first Nicky points beyond the points for shoulders and his Zeus appearance.

<Dan>: Be careful how you pronounce her name. [...] Ouch!

<Val>: Our gathering ended when an unexpected rain/sleet/snow storm arrived. Queen Kabiri Marshall called to make sure that her baby boy was safe, and to remind him that he should head home. He had to walk five slippery blocks to reach the train. He wasn't good with crowds, and she didn't trust him in the dark in bad weather, even if he did have his new canes.

<Justin>: The same royalty that we discussed this morning?

<Val>: Yes. She was the world's toughest mathematics teacher to River Glen high school students, but she was The Queen to everyone else.

Marshall collected more Nicky points. He wasn't a social reject. In River Glen, he was Ms. Marshall's baby boy, even if he was from a "broken home". He was also from a home that insisted on education.

<Justin>: What type of name is that?

<Val>: It's an East Indian name. I'm surprised that you don't have that in the dossier.

<Justin>: You could correct any oversights now?

<Val>: The Queen was part Indo-Trinidadian and part Trinidadian mixture. His father is part Anglo-American and part Indo-Trinidadian.

<Justin>: They have Marshall's picture in the dictionary beside each human subtype.

Maybe he's not beside Hottentots.

Gunnar is right. I am nasty to him and he never did a damned thing to me, I don't think.

<Gunnar>: TYPES, Types, and more types!

<Macedon>: Papa Stacy provided the Zeus looks and realization tendencies. Eleven half brothers and sisters found HM after The Queen died.

<Justin>: What naming conventions are we using?

<Val>: Marshall uses his mother's name. Stacy stopped helping her when she refused to share his giftedness. She raised her two "baby boys" without his assistance, and there was no way that Stacy would get credit for the work that Marshall did.

She developed the attitude that "caaan't is unacceptable". She had no tolerance for weakness or failure. In the process, she became The Queen in action as well as appearance. Imagine Queen-2 weighing 250 pounds.

<Justin>: Marshall's drivers have been his mother, Queen Kabiri, who said he'd better succeed or else, Clara who taught him the importance of research and planning and encouraged him to be gentle, patient, persistent and resourceful, and Ms. Frey who taught him to expect things he never imagined, and then showed him how to him to achieve those impossible things.

<Gunnar>: ***Marshall's mother was Kabiri! That's what we were going to name Guntur if he was a girl.***

<Val>: What's the point?

<Justin>: If the part about almost dying wasn't a little extreme, I'd say they planned this.

<Val>: Don't be ridiculous. **I never knew Justin was smart like this.**

<Dan>: Who could possibly predict that far into the future? **It is only when he pays attention.**

<Justin>: Let me think about this.

<Val>: **Help. We need a diversion.**

<Gunnar>: Long beautiful hair. ***Gunnar, keep your mouth shut before he comes after you again.***

<Val>: **That's a diversion.** *What did Gunnar say?*

<Justin>: He's mumbling about beautiful hair.

<Gunnar>: ***He thinks I'm babbling. Good.***

<Val>: Later - we are in a hurry - ask Gunnar how he knew the meaning of the Queen's Telugu name.

<Justin>: ***I'm doing two year's worth of work today.*** Where could one find Marshall's mother now?

<Val>: She's in Woodlawn Cemetery in the Bronx. She worked hard to take care of everyone else, but she didn't have advice about taking care of herself. She had a stroke the day after she retired.

She held on long enough to make sure H was all right after his knee replacement, she held on to see her last set of grandchildren when she found out Nicky was pregnant again, and she held on another three weeks to make sure Nicky and Pat would be all right. She died in her sleep the night after she first held the new babies.

<Macedon>: I was there the last day, and so was Val. She showed them how to make Pipsqueak comfortable, she downloaded a copy of herself into Queen-2, and she stopped communicating.

<Justin>: That sounds like sorcery or witchcraft.

<Gunnar>: This doesn't sound like you.

<Val>: You saw Queen-2. What do you think?

<Justin>: I suppose thoughts about dying early could be going through Marshall's head.

<Gunnar>: ***NO!*** He joked about dying and going to hell because the knot looked like a horn. He kidded me about my slow speech too.

<Justin>: I didn't know he had a sense of humor.

[...] I know I'm late, but I'm learning.

<Val>: Remember that you diverted me.

<Justin>: It was necessary for an adequate understanding of the topic. Continue.

<Val>: Nicky left when H left at about 3:30 P.M. on Wednesday, the day before Thanksgiving.

They agreed to enter into the research and planning relationship with each other. They continued for 40 years. They separated the heavenly plans from the ordinary plans. There are now approximately 1,800 plans in total and over 300 on the heavenly lust - list.

After letting the world know that they are not, and have not been, flouting tradition, they will stop the research project. For their honeymoon, which will last for an undetermined period, they will concentrate on variations of the top 300.

You now know everything that there is to know.

<Justin>: Repeat those numbers, and tell me how such large numbers are possible.

<Gunnar>: Why don't you talk to Lorrie?

<Val>: It's easy when you think about it. He started out with a little more than thirty plans. She added several the first evening.

They each agreed to come up with two plans per month. They have been together for almost 480 months. After covering the exploits mythical Roman, Greek, Norse, and Indian characters, they both sneak peeks at romance novels in their favorite bookstores.

They add random plans when something memorable occurs outside the normal procedure. About half the plans were recorded after the fact.

They omitted several while she was having babies, when he is having work done on his knee, and when his mother was ill.

Now call Joe.

<Gunnar>: What are you saying to him? His gyros are spinning, but his processors just overloaded.

<Justin>: I'm processing very well, thank you, except that I'm having trouble filling in some gaps.

<Gunnar>: While you're processing, I would feel better if I adjusted my fluid levels.

<Val>: Tell him to turn left when he leaves the office. The one in the lounge area is closer.

<Gunnar>: [...] Thank you. ***Take it slow Gunnar. Walk straight, even if that bruise makes you want to crawl. You can't crawl. Your arm won't hold you up. I can also take those last two pills. No! I will take ONE, as it says on the envelope. Indy would think I'm a wimp in comparison to her father, even if I take only one.***

<Justin>: Hurry this up while he's gone.

<Val>: I'm finished.

<Justin>: Val, when I go through the trouble to think seriously, you have to humor me.

<Val>: What else do you expect me to tell you? I was never in the lab when the research occurred.

<Justin>: You should know that I have taken technology management courses, including all the overviews that Docente and Liz prepare. All the serious courses include a cartoon of a flow diagram with a box that says, "**AND THEN A MIRACLE OCCURS**".

You just explained that a passionate romantic **MIRACLE** occurred that allowed HM to transition from a tall muscular nobody with possible reproductive issues to a world-conquering Snuffleupagus. He was aided by a brilliant beautiful woman, who was not his type, and the children that he wasn't sure he could have.

Furthermore, you are saying that he's forty years older and his injuries are more extensive, but another **MIRACLE** will save our fortunes and our futures, to use Ms. Frey's turn of phrase.

<Macedon>: Justin just used up his allocation of logic for this week, and he made sense.

<Dan>: **Give him something based on the research summaries.**

<Val>: **I never saw any research summaries. That would be too personal anyhow.**

<Justin>: Helle-e-ew.

<Macedon>: Hang on. They're trying to resolve a communications gap.

<Val>: **Did you ever see notes?**

<Dan>: **Yes, but only for about half of the ones on the short list.**

<Macedon>: **We need time!** BOSS, they are going to collaborate and communicate for the next few minutes. Most of it will be hearsay, but they will do the best that they can. Val, you can start.

<Val>: *Who promoted you?* [...] *Forget it.*

It is hearsay that H lent Nicky his jacket and followed her home to retrieve it after she slipped in snow-covered ice water on the way to their respective destinations.

The slipping may not have been accidental, given Nicky's perfect balance and training.

When he arrived at her apartment, he was wet and cold. She took his clothes to the laundry room to dry, and he tried to look stately in his skivvies and a sheet toga. While they waited, she casually mentioned his research and how good he must have felt to be helping so many people.

He was upset and embarrassed that this Northchester princess knew the extent of his inadequacies. He offered to kill me and he was coming to get me, but he forgot to clamp on his canes. He tripped over the sheet and landed in a pile of her laundry. The knot in the toga came loose. Sight of the packaging enhanced her belief in the research idea.

<Macedon>: He made a lot of my boys jealous.

<Val>: That is when Nicky became Machi. She didn't try to help him up. She grabbed the canes, sat across from him, and promised that she would return the canes after he listened to her.

He practiced pain control and tried to cover up again while she explained her problem - she worried that something was wrong with her, and she had never been injured.

She still liked Ike, but she had caught him with someone else, her parents had suggested that she should forgive Ike because he was a man, and he probably did what he did to protect her until their wedding night. She explained that she had tried to get around Ike's protective tendencies, to no avail, before she caught him. She omitted the extra surprise factor.

She was wearing her ring because Ike had begged her to do it, and her parents ordered her not to do anything hasty because Ike was still a good catch. He was the cantor's son, he had a decent career, - accounting was acceptable - he had a house for them already, a nice new car, and he wasn't bad looking either. However, she still had the gateway.

Between stutters, he accused her of slumming because she was angry with Ike. He had no degree, no career, and no money - he had to take the train because a cab ride to River Glen would have used his travel allowance for the month. To make matters worse, Nicky was holding on to his clothes, and his canes.

She explained that she wanted a structured professional approach to her problem, and his was the only one she had ever heard about.

He gave her the stare that The Queen mastered to control spoiled River Glen kids who saw no need for either algebra or trigonometry.

<Val>: Nicky returned his canes and ran to the laundry room to retrieve his clothes.

<Justin>: ***He was as stupid as many of us believed he was, or Van Amberg is lying. Wait!***

[...] They've been together for 41 years, so he didn't turn down the offer after all. When did he change his mind?

<Val>: Everything I am saying is hearsay.

<Justin>: Hurry and let me hear you say it.

<Val>: It was the bikinis in the laundry.

In order to stand up, he had to dig out of the pile of her laundry. It included some of the first bikini underwear - she really wanted to entice Ike. He was curious because the parts of Nicky's bikini sets appeared to belong to two different women. Paula was always a little jealous about that.

<Macedon>: Maria is still very jealous about that.

<Val>: While he evaluated the laundry, he realized that he might have passed up a wonderful opportunity, especially since the performance issue seemed less an issue. It fact, he couldn't make it go away.

They agreed that he had a stunned look and a crooked smile on his face and a pile of towels on his lap when Nicky returned. She tossed his clothes at the crooked smile, ran into the bathroom, and started her hysterical laugh cry.

I heard it yesterday when she felt that she was going to lose him.

<Justin>: Did he follow her and show proof that he had reconsidered her offer?

<Val>: He remembered Clara's lessons about patience. He let things settle, he dressed, and he waited for her to calm down. Then he yelled out to her that he was scared and embarrassed. She admitted that she was too.

More embarrassing moments occurred while they agreed that they were not each other's type, but they would consider the research with each other found a more suitable partner could be found.

They also agreed that he would not kill me, but they would keep the research to themselves.

The next thing that I am certain about is that at eight o'clock the next morning the Queen and her perfectly maintained 20-year-old car were at the corner of 8th and University Place waiting for her baby. Everything was melting, but she wasn't taking any chances.

<Justin>: You skipped.

<Val>: I have to explain how Nicky discovered that H was miles from being a loser, even at his lowest point. After I tell what I know, Dan can elaborate on the synchronization details. OK?

<Justin>: OK, ***I guess.***

<Val>: The Queen invited Nicky to come to Thanksgiving dinner with their family and Clara when H called to explain why he couldn't make it home (the weather and the ice water).

Richard was coming with H's former fiancée and the Queen was trying to level the deck for her baby.

Nicky didn't want to deal with her parents or Ike, so she agreed to Thanksgiving in River Glen with a friend of Paula's, not Northchester. Ike convinced Nicky's parents that it was a good idea to let the situation settle. He didn't know what to do next either.

<Justin>: The Queen must have been curious about the new friendship.

<Val>: They explained that H was working on a research project that had significant implications, and Nicky had volunteered to give him legal advice, pro bono, while his clothes dried. She showed the paper that proved she had just passed the bar.

They had spent the evening reviewing his plans, and collecting her thoughts on how the research should go. It would be quiet around school over the weekend, and they were looking forward to starting the in-depth research the next day.

<Justin>: Did the Queen believe that nothing had happened?

<Val>: The Queen had never known her baby to lie, and Nicky was wearing a huge engagement ring, so she let it go.

Clara heard H was humming a song she had taught him, and she knew about the cooling off period. She was extraordinarily amused and happy that her advice was about to produce outstanding results, especially if Nicky was willing to risk the ring.

<Justin>: What song, and what cooling off period.

<Val>: Clara said something about a rough mountain.

<Dan>: You mean "I'm Coming Up". *You should listen to what he's saying when he sings.*

<Val>: Denise grilled Nicky for details about how long she had been engaged, to whom, what he did [taxes], where was he [working on a serious tax situation], how big was the diamond [2.5 carats], and how much it must have cost Ike [she couldn't guess].

She wanted to understand whether H had a glimmer of a chance with Nicky. It was starting to occur to her that she may have passed on the wrong option. Not all tall handsome men are created equal.

Richard reminded everybody about embarrassing experiences H had when he was growing up, and it backfired. It gave The Queen an excuse to show family photo albums.

Some women have images of how her first born should look and H's baby pictures exactly matched Nick's image - points for H. She also saw shots of him shaved and suited up for his graduation, singing in the church choir, and in his uniform guarding stuff. Nicky was attracted to both the wrapped and unwrapped versions of the product.

Nicky was impressed because the Queen had bookcases (hand finished by The Queen and her "babies") on every wall, and they were filled with books on every conceivable topic. The Queen explained that she took library discards and patched them with clear tape. She also backtracked from every moving van that came into the complex. She had read most of the books and forced her sons to read them too.

Nicky chose books at random and tested H and Richard. They both did unbelievably well, but H knew something about more things than both Ricky and Nicky did. H was really piling on points.

In an attempt to make Princess Denise and Princess Nicola understand that they were in proper company, The Queen set the table perfectly with only slightly scratched real china, slightly mismatched crystal, shiny silver-plated flatware from an estate sale, and blazingly white hand washed linen. Clara helped. She had been to enough military banquets to know how things worked. The Queen had taught her "babies" good manners and they tried to impress the princesses. Nicky was impressed - H earned more points.

[...] ***You wanted details. Listen or we can stop.***

[...] The point that you may gather from this that he had a very proper upbringing. The Queen wanted to make sure that her boys didn't accidentally shut any doors on themselves.

Machi truly enjoyed her first Trinidadian/Indian/Soul Food meal. Machi scribbled the menu and she still has it - turkey, beef roti, curry shrimp, fried chicken, potato salad, mango chutney (not cranberry sauce), potato salad, collard greens, corn on the bob, tossed salad, and homemade rolls.

Things went well until The Queen realized that she didn't remember the etiquette for getting the tasty morsels off a Southern-Fried chicken breast - one of Clara's contributions to the meal.

Nicky noticed. She commented that she had never such tasted such good chicken, picked up her chicken thigh with both hands, and started looking for the good parts. Denise wrinkled up her nose.

[...] The point to be made from this is that Nicky has always done what it takes to resolve a problem, while Denise worried about the proper way to deal with a problem.

Clara noticed what happened and started laughing, which made The Queen and HM start laughing. Nicola heard the female and male versions of the Marshall laugh simultaneously. She wanted to hear the laugh again.

They played more games of Scrabble, and The Queen and H split the games, even though Richard and Denise were both graduate students at Teacher's College and Nicky was a lawyer.

<Dan>: Now it's my turn.

During the ride back to the Village in a car service vehicle, Nicky began to think that she may have fallen love (she felt differently than she felt about Ike, even before the surprise).

<Justin>: ***The first sight foolishness - strong affection is sufficient. Then you can have an orderly relationship.***

Clara made HM use strict medical terminology in his plans. She wanted her boss (the doctor that took the program from them) to see that the planning had medical merit.

The plans are written in the best Latin that he can manage. He writes using what he learned from a compact Latin dictionary that his mother made him memorize.

Cicero would not approve and some of the results are hilarious, but it works. Take the raw definitions out of Chambers', and you're in business.

<Justin>: ***He's a Latin lover, literally.***

<Val>: How would you know when something written in Latin was hilarious?

<Dan>: I was the designated priest in my circle of friends and family until I had to decide whether to attend Strafford, Caltech, or the seminary.

<Justin>: ***The almost priest married the ex-nun.***

<Val>: Now I'm confused.

<Dan>: Nevertheless, the appearance of the plans earned Nicky points and removed some of her final inhibitions. Her younger brother was in medical school, and she saw that the "big nothing" knew almost as much about medicine as David knew.

<Dan>: H agreed that he would record the results of his research and the dates (in Latin). Machi agreed to the notes as long as he promised to omit the name and address of the research partner.

<Justin>: Val knew what happened that night.

<Dan>: Clara and the VA doctors saw the notes that H and Machi recorded until Indy was three months old (Indy was the prototype output of the research).

I saw notes for the original short-list of plans. No one has seen any notes since they went into the safe 18 years ago. Thus, I am the only one qualified to satisfy your voyeuristic tendencies.

<Justin>: If you met HM later, how do you know him better than Val does?

<Dan>: Let me keep talking while I don't have to worry about your responses in front of Gunnar.

<Justin>: Keep talking.

H had research initiation Plans #1 through #5 in his backpack.

Machi realized that you needed to agree on several things before you initiated anything. Thus, Plan #0 was created and signed before the other plans were initiated.

She wrote it and it was a legally binding document. It still is. It specified:

1. Research termination procedures.
   - Either one could stop the research any time they wished.
   - They could stop the research if they got married - Neither of them remembers why marriage was a consideration so early in the relationship.
2. Risk management. She stopped on the way home that Thanksgiving evening and upgraded her supply.
3. Processing constraints, which that allowed minimal stress on either set of equipment, considering her gateway and the location of his injury.
4. Maintenance of a short list of good plans, if there were any.
5. No partner redundancy.
6. A waiting period, Plan #5, to give her time to think about Ike and the ring.

<Justin>: It was a Program plan (covering the entire initiative).

<Val>: They agreed to stop the research today, because they are going to let everybody know they are married to each other. Now they will start the real thing, age-, health-, and experience-adjusted versions of their most successful implementations.

<Justin>: He wasn't really talking about dying. He was talking about research heaven. How could you forget something like that?

<Macedon>: I want to know too.

<Dan>: I never heard him connect research and heaven. I only know about the sloppy Latin.

<Val>: When was he talking about heaven?

<Macedon>: I was in there trying to ensure that he stayed glued together and you were outside trying to prevent a riot.

<Dan>: It was in the first few words that he said to Justin and me. [...] Let me finish with the plans.

Plan #1 required that they get to know each other (***mental knowledge***). They spent two hours trying to cover 22 years of his life and 24 years of hers. H became solemn when he came to the Denise part. She lost it when she told him about Ike's surprise. They hugged for the first time.

<Justin>: Loose coupling.

<Dan>: Plan #2 required that they both contribute to the planning. Together they created plans with themes related to classical literature. Nicky's Zeus plans could have melted the snow.

<Justin>: Stakeholder participation. If you don't have it, the project could slow down later.

<Macedon>: It is rather like the situation we are dealing with currently, don't you think.

<Dan>: Plan #3 is iterative. They translated the Latin into terms they both understood. Translation often improves the probability that tight coupling will occur.

<Justin>: Common terminology.

<Val>: 99% probability. Paula used to [...] keep going.

<Dan>: Plan #4 was a feasibility study that required developing familiarity with the research apparatus. University Place would have shown up on infrared satellites' if any had existed.

<Justin>: Would you be talking about test strips?

<Dan>: The term is test scripts, but your slip of the tongue was accurate. Machi modeled her laundry, which caused Marshall to iterate his prior laundry performance. The prototype demonstration was encouraging to both of research participants.

Val told you everything that happened during the waiting period.

<Justin>: How stupid do you think I am?

<Dan>: The notes say he used his only risk management equipment in a demonstration of application techniques during Plan #4. The pack that she had carried in her purse for five years seemed unsafe, and they did not provide adequate software coverage.

<Val>: That's too much information. He could overload one of his peripheral devices.

<Dan>: Don't be ridiculous. Robots don't overload.

<Macedon>: *That's my boy H.* This might be getting a little too personal, even for me.

<Justin>: My peripherals are just fine.

<Dan>: They started a three-day planning marathon that Friday afternoon. We'd be here until tomorrow morning if you wanted to know those details. It was a week before they caught up with the notes. His total, though not totally objective recall made that possible.

<Val>: When Paula saw Nicky the next Monday, she wasn't wearing the rock. She said something was loose, and Ike would have to take care of it.

<Justin>: The marathon details are irrelevant. ***There's no need to put extra stress on the peripheral control mechanisms.***

However, I am now more confused that before. If he's from an educated family, extremely smart, and he spent his youth in River Glen, why did he drop out of college? He could have saved himself the trouble of getting shot.

<Val>: He was Richard's baby brother, he was shy, and he was arrogant.

<Justin>: I understand the part about being shy, but not the other two things.

<Val>: He was shy in high school, so he lost points that students receive for class participation. Though he scored well on his SATs, he barely made the top 5 percentile in grades. He worked after school to help make ends meet after his older brother was accepted at White. Thus, there were no extra-curricula activities. He occasionally took naps in class [...] Justin.

<Justin>: Don't start.

<Val>: He won a partial scholarship to a good school and that required taking out significant loans. His mother was already stretched beyond her limits with Richard, and his father still refused to help. By then, he had nine other kids. He was proud of H, but he suggested that H could transfer to the city university after his first year. Richard only had a year to go before he finished at White.

Because his brother was attending an Ivy League school, H did not want to attend a city or a state school. He was determined to graduate from a good school without putting more strain on his mother. He was going to show Richard and The Queen that he was the better son and the tougher son.

His arrogance nearly killed him.

He was sucked in by the military promise to pay for his education just before the situation in Asia escalated. He tested well intellectually and physically, so a Marine recruiter promised him the world, including a cushy assignment on their logistics team.

<Justin>: How did he pass the physical if he stuttered?

<Val>: He was shy. The stutter came after he was hurt. It's called a conversion reaction.

<Val>: How did you see the plans with the implementation details?

<Dan>: We don't have time for that now.

<Justin>: I need to know why my brother-in-law knows intimate details about the Snuffleupagus and his life-long friend does not.

<Val>: If Justin can make the time, I'd like to hear too.

<Dan>: I paid attention to a giant baby-faced giant who brought his own chair to the lecture hall and sat exactly at the spot below the lectern where I pretended that all my students sat.

<Justin, Val, and Macedon>: Why?

<Dan>: He was trying to read my lips.

<Val>: He had two hearing aids. His father and Ike paid a fortune for them.

<Dan>: They weren't adjusted for large spaces. He had to turn the volume down, and try to pick up what he missed by looking straight at me. As I said earlier today, I fixed the problem.

<Val>: You were sneaking in work even then!

<Justin>: How does that relate to the plans?

<Dan>: Jonas was an unusually popular near-sighted deaf introvert. He was too absorbed in his studies to chase women, but after a couple of them seduced the ultra-geek freshman, Chubby Zeus had to chase them away if he needed to study.

<Macedon>: Like his papa.

<Dan>: They would drop by and bring him pizza, Bolt, and special favors. He didn't know he was practicing variable reinforcement, but it worked.

On the other hand, I was 25 years old and bad at "planning". I weighed 123 pounds, and I needed LASIXX before it was a generally accepted procedure. I had flunked my geek seduction. I thank you Alex for trying not to laugh.

When one of his special friends dropped by in the middle of a doping experiment, I asked Jonas how he did what he did. He said his parents taught him.

[...] I spoke incorrectly. He said he learned from his parents.

He was four when he realized that something about the Latin book and the papers in the original wooden file/nightstand made his parents very happy. At the age of six, he was trying to find out what was in the Latin dictionary that was funny.

By the time he was nine, they had left the drawer unlocked often enough that he had read a few of the plans (without the notes). He could translate them, but they seemed like dry medical notes.

After H explained why it was natural for him to require frequent unexpected changes of pajamas, the plans started to make sense. Jonas substituted them for the secret magazines that his classmates wouldn't share.

The Queen assured Nicky that the unexpected frequency was to be expected for Papa Stacy's grandson or H's son. Nicky understood.

By the time Jonas started college, he had absorbed close to a thousand plans without bothering to mention them to anyone. He went to college with extra laundry money, lectures on risk management, and a stock of risk management supplies, just in case something came up while he was awake.

[...] Was that a double entendre or a pun?

H discovered that Jonas knew about the plans after Jonas "borrowed" the originals of the short list and gave them to me as a thank you present, or maybe it was a pity present.

<Dan>: It was more interesting than you might imagine. There were no all-in-ones in those days and Jonas would have had to go through extra trouble to make copies. He didn't bother because they were in a separate section, there was scribbling all over them, and he believed that they were discards.

I met H when he hobbled onto a plane and flew to California to meet me and retrieve the originals.

<Val>: I remember that trip. He was very annoyed, and he wouldn't say why.

<Macedon>: *Jonas found the midget! Jonas is very good at picking the right people.*

<Dan>: H was embarrassed, but he was happy that his son had found a friend. He pitied me too, and took over where my uncle, the runt priest, left off.

<Val>: *He's an adopted son! The conflicts were for the benefit of Mittelman! How did I miss that?*

<Justin>: *That explains why he forgot to mention things about H.* What was Ms. Frey's reaction?

<Dan>: It is not possible for Jonas to do anything wrong in her eyesight. She was amused at Jonas's ballooning talents, and she gave him extra advice on how to avoid being associated with unexpected ballooning situations.

She was happy that I had taken good care of the plans and had not passed them around. However, she took precautions and bought a safe.

<Val>: What happened with Becky?

<Dan>: Becky got around Machi's advice because she was smart enough to study with Jonas, intelligent enough to explain the limited number of things he didn't understand about both electronics and planning, and talented enough to convince him that a monopoly was good.

<Val>: It's my turn again.

Nicky went to work at her uncle's law firm after a couple of weeks while H found a job as a technical writer/typist to supplement the disability checks. Being newly-weds, we paid little attention to them until three months later. Paula moved in with me officially and H moved in with Nicky.

They said it was a mutually beneficial financial relationship. It saved almost enough commuting time for him to work at his part-time job.

Five months later, we noticed that the planning was yielding explosive results.

We thought the explosion was initiated at the first research window, but Nicky assured us that the results had been installed after two months of detailed investigation. Indy verified the timing. She was born on Halloween, eleven months after her parents.

<Justin>: Were there unplanned events.

<Dan>: You'd better believe it. Most plans were documented after the fact. The most outstanding example produced Queen-2 and Mr. Coffee.

<Val>: **He's heard enough.**

<Dan>: He's going to ask anyhow.

[...] They were practicing Plan #4 after Marshall's original knee replacement. She thought she was old enough to stop worrying about risk management, and he didn't think he had healed enough. They were both wrong. They wrote it up as Plan #998.

<Val>: How would Grace react if she knew how persistent you are being with this topic?

<Justin>: *Grace would consider discrete contributions to his research efforts, even though he's not her type.*

Because Grace is discrete, they don't know that my marriage to the almost perfect (slightly chubby) society wife is a marriage of convenience. I got the connections and she got someone who didn't want her for her family's money.

The rules were that she keeps morning after pills, I keep risk management supplies, nothing should be long-term, and we don't discuss it.

She broke the long-term rule. She's had a crush on Hamilton since that first strategy off-site in Banff.

- *Hamilton, how wonderful it is to meet you. I am certain that I have heard your name before.*
- *Hamilton, I have heard so many wonderful things about you.*
- *Hamilton, I'll get you a fork. She doesn't get her own forks.*

- ***Hamilton, have you really been with Goodsand that long?***
- ***Hamilton, you will help Justin do well, won't you?***
- ***Hamilton, what a wonderful laugh you have. Don't try to hide it. Goodsand is much too rigid, and it is going to get worse. (She didn't know I was listening).***
- ***Hamilton, the pictures are in the office, but you are here. You should always carry pictures of your kids. Even Justin does that.***
- ***Hamilton, you live in River Glen. We had a wonderful fundraiser at Rave Hill.***
- ***Hamilton, you're Presbyterian too. Do you attend the quaint little landmark church that we have in River Glen?***

<Val>: You're quiet. Does this mean that we are finished?

<Gunnar>: I made it back.

<Justin>: You look a little better than when you left. What did you do?

<Gunnar>: They have very soft sofas and a snack machine back there. Occasionally someone will come by who will help you off the sofa.

Meanwhile, you look worse than when I left. Has Ms. Frey been here?

<Justin>: I'm pursuing the issue of Marshall's physical stamina, while I am personally about to crash.

<Dan>: He lost 90 pounds in the last 18 months. Ernest helped him find machines that exercised other muscle groups to compensate for his bad leg. He was in great shape and extraordinarily agile.

<Justin>: He must have had some shortcomings.

<Val>: Nicky hinted to Paula that there were hardly ever any shortcomings.

Aside from love, another "L" word applied. The frequency of the plug-ins extended his software capability, and after the first Friday, Nicky never intend to let her Zeus loose.

<Justin>: What's wrong with them?

<Val>: I got them both. Let me enjoy it for a moment.

<Justin>: Is there extraneous partnering activity?

<Gunnar>: He does a little to initiate a partner relationship, but he has clear guidelines about where to draw the line. I checked that.

<Val>: Forget using focused persuasion on H. He receives even offers now than before, especially since he has beaucoup bucks. However, we are 99% certain that he never got loose.

<Dan>: Val's rating is probably accurate. He still has his critical system components and Machi has not done any jail time. She is a serious believer in research silos.

They discuss hot external proposals with each other. I love the plans where they each pretend to step out on each other with each other.

<Justin>: ***That still leaves 1% for Grace and his 1% appears to be major input. She is accustomed to getting what she wants in her mild-mannered aristocratic way, and she is extraordinarily discrete.***

DAMN, this is THE ULTIMATE CRUX! I HAVE BEEN JEALOUS for the last nine years. That is why I keep gnawing on this bone, and I kept letting people trip him up. I shouldn't be thinking about tripping.

I'VE WANTED TO GET RID OF HM and I've been ignoring how I feel. Maybe I love Grace!

<Gunnar>: Justin went somewhere else.

<Val and Dan>: When?

<Justin>: I'm still here, but even robots need to organize their memory cores occasionally. Finish, but don't skip anything.

<Val>: When she was five months pregnant, her parents disowned her, and they forced her uncle fire her. At the end of the spring semester, H dropped out again and started working at his second job.

<Justin>: Wouldn't clarification of the partner preferences have solved the misunderstanding?

<Gunnar>: Ādaemoa wanted us show them how to eat our lunch.

<Val>: They are both very loyal. She promised she wouldn't tell, because she still liked Ike as a friend. H kept the secret because Ike's preferences helped him get Nicky.

Ike came back when she almost had a miscarriage. He said he owed them for keeping his secret, and he wanted to make it up to Nicky for losing her family.

Picture the three of them out strolling together that fall. H managed to look like a giant peacock, even on his two canes. Ike propped Nicky up when she was almost too pregnant to walk.

<Val>: Clara retired after Indy was born, and she and the Queen argued over the proper care and tending of Baby Girl. Nicky went back to work, and that allowed H to quit his second job and attend night classes.

He finished two years of full-time requirements in three years at night and Saturday mornings, and he graduated with honors, summa cum laude the same year I finished my law degree.

I came to work here, and I helped him get hired as a techno-gopher, the best decision I ever made.

A year after he started working here, Jonas was born. Professionally he was still a techno-gopher.

The twins came 19 years later. That was the year after the knee replacement, and the year that his mother died. Professionally he was a junior VP.

He made SVP in four years and that is where he stayed until after the sabbatical. We don't know whether the speed of promotions was his new self-control, greater mobility, less pain, or prejudices against the handicapped when he needed two canes.

<Dan>: The personal research and planning kept going and going. Jonas says Machi found two plans in his backpack this morning, plus he had a plan for his wedding wrapped around the thermos bottle.

Because he literally gets enjoyment from planning, planning became an obsession for him. Professionally, he is more thorough than he is personally - he doesn't need the "cigarette breaks".

<Val>: He never smoked either.

<Macedon>: Yes he did, until he moved back in with The Queen. He wanted his own place, so he put his cigarette money in the bank.

<Justin>: *Structured Stud Weeble! With Gunnar coming up his tail pipe, he was still planning.* How did Val hear about the plans if they were a secret?

<Gunnar>: The planning process was already in place when he came to work for H.

<Val>: After eight years of childless marriage, Paula asked Nicky for advice. They didn't know as much about fertility as they do now.

H was enjoying the planning, but he worried that he wasn't like "normal" people. Nicky convinced him that he was super-normal. She also suggested that he owed us, because they wouldn't have been together if I hadn't blabbed to Paula.

A week later, Nicky handed us a brown envelope with copies vanilla versions of the first 450 plans.

They gave me a super pack three years ago when they decided I should try to start over again after Paula. Whenever I'm ready, I'll probably try #1673.

<Dan>: That's how we got the last project in the oven. Make sure you're in shape first. You could start over and end up all at the same time.

<Macedon>: Maria and I are doing OK, but a little improvement wouldn't hurt. I'll take a copy of anything any of you have. Maria is a teacher. She can figure out the common terminology.

<Justin>: ***I don't have time for this.***

<Val>: You perpetuated the situation.

Now I am stopping it. I have independently evaluated the situation, and I believe that the research approach will generate sufficient stimulus to keep things going.

We'll go with "Live". I will now call Joe and give him instructions.

I could use some focused persuasion on Macedon and get a copy of whatever he receives. Even if he was upset, he had no right to get me off balance.

Grace and I could redo our Plan #0. Maybe we could step out on each other with each other.

<Gunnar>: *Justin is acting a little strange, but it seems that the odds are a little more in my favor, for everything?* It's about time. What took you so and why are you sweating? It's not hot in here.

<Justin>: I needed to understand what would so strongly influence his ability to survive this trauma.

<Gunnar>: What did you find?

<Justin>: *Let me squelch this.* Gunnar I'm trying to save the $1 billion that we nearly lost and the livelihoods of thousands of people. Research into SOA improvements is a critical part of that. The research needs to be planned. It's worth an hour and a little sweat.

You are worried about the Audit Committee.

<Gunnar>: *When my head feels better, I'll think about why he is trying to intimidate "The Intimidator".*

Now, I'm worried about getting my life back.

I could do that with Indy? We would be unstoppable. She could help me with the politics as her mother helps her father. Her father and I could help each other.

I could develop real self-confidence. Then I wouldn't need to be "The Intimidator".

She'd be the only one on my calendar - I wouldn't have a calendar. She could forget about that other fool.

There would be no dark shrouds and lots of knee-highs. She's young enough to have one more baby, maybe two. Her mother was older when she had Marshall's twins.

No! She would never consider that.

Yes! I would show her how I could be a good father like my father tried to be to Mags and me. Machi could handle Gerthe if there was a problem.

However, I must have a civil conversation with her first, and I must apologize for Sharf!

---------- ----------

<Justin>: Gunnar, we will start working on communications immediately. Listen.

[...] Melissa, tell her she's wasting company time, and to do the transfer NOW!

[...] This is ***Justin Mittelman!***

<Lorrie>: I'm here, and stop screaming. Robots don't scream.

<Justin>: I told Melissa that you should send the money to Belvedere. Buzz me twice when it's done.

<Lorrie>: I already hit the button. I'll see you in the morning.

<Gunnar>: Why are you doing that?

<Justin>: Pay attention and let me communicate.

---------- ----------

<Justin>: [...] Joe?

<Joe>: I guess Gunnar put up a strong defense.

<Justin>: He did. We'll discuss appropriate details later. For the moment, read me the "Live" e-mail.

<Joe>: Jonas must have called over there too. Doc says the improvement in H's vital signs is almost miraculous.

<Justin>: I must feel lucky because you won't have to fight with Mrs. Frey-Marshall, but unlucky since you won't inherit the long-term research program.

<Joe>: Piccolo is effective in research. Why would you associate that with me?

<Justin>: Right - wrong man. Read the e-mail.

Dan is a family insider and the Joe is a fringe player. Marshall knows how to protect his turf, better than anyone understood except Gunnar.

[...] That sounds OK, but make it sweeter. Add something about all his achievements to date. Make sure it is obvious that we are helping Van Amberg finish what Marshall started. Make him St. Marshall of the Daxiao business and technology collaboration. Lorrie sent the money already.

[...] That was fast. How did you do that so quickly?

<Joe>: We knew how good he was. The last one was written first, and then we weakened it. It's you and Gooner's goons who were missing the point.

<Justin>: Send the message! Tell Doc what we decided. That should put her in a better mood.

<Doc>: He needed someone who was fast on the keyboard and leak proof. Have a good evening. .

<Justin>: *I am definitely surrounded!*

CHAPTER XII - WFSOA SUCCESS PLANNING

<Gunnar>: What was in the note?

PERSONAL RECOVERY OF AN SOA NEAR FAILURE

<Justin>: When we call them back in here, we will confirm to them that:

1. Since we have no choice but to use Belvedere's services, we can use them to show us how to interpret the exquisitely documented middle that we still don't understand.
2. We are going to create $500,000 worth of work for Belvedere. We will say that Sharf directed us toward what we needed to investigate. His method was backhanded, but effective.
3. We sent Sharf/Belvedere a down payment of $250,000 using Marshall's RandD account. Lorrie entered the transfer already.

<Gunnar>: ***WHY?*** I could have told him not to show up on Monday.

<Justin>: Sharf will not to show up on Monday, but we still have to pay Belvedere. After you rushed me to sign the indication of interest, we would have to come up good reasons for backing out. What reasons do you propose?

<Gunnar>: We could mention a personality conflict or extreme aggressiveness.

<Justin>: You knew he was aggressive when you selected him. What personality conflict would you mention? Marshall will be out on disability.

<Gunnar>: You already have a plan. Keep going. ***I bet it's a Marshall plan.***

<Justin>:

4. We will deliver exciting WFSOA/Belvedere news at the meeting that Sharf has with Jasper tomorrow. All my direct reports (or a high-level representative) will be there.
5. A WFSOA policy statement will promote re-invigoration of the Program with a mandate this time. Though we backed into SOA, we were able to achieve significant financial benefit and we expect to achieve significantly more.
6. WFSOA will no longer be a grass roots effort (we build a visible network that works better than Marshall's hidden links).
7. We show that we are finally paying attention to everything that Marshall and Liz were saying.
8. We report that Van Amberg, Piccolo, and Macedon will temporarily fill in for Marshall (we will emphasize the temporary nature of their roles).
9. We will show our managers the "WFSOA Resistance List" and how it is draining our resources. Belvedere's first assignment will be to work with Doc and see how we can minimize areas of resistance without Sharf. She nearly quit due to his preliminary report.

<Gunnar>: Keep piling it on.

<Justin>: I am making you aware of the gravity of the situation that **we** precipitated.

You will never know the real reason why I let you pull "WE" into this the second time.

> **Readers: This summarizes the initial premises and explains the purpose for the "Passion" discussion.**
>
> 1. Two senior managers had to resolve PERSONAL JEALOUSIES before they stopped sabotaging the WFSOA Program, overtly or covertly.
> 2. A positive PERSONAL relationship for the EVP of Sales and Marketing may produce a disproportionately large benefit for the WFSOA Program.

10. Belvedere will focus on the Communications Plan. It was working, but it needs to work even better if WFSOA is to take us to new levels of

agility and flexibility, or whatever the buzzwords are.

11. Belvedere will work with at least mid-level representatives of each role and learn how they actually communicate and how to improve it. We will no longer give the surveys to our summer interns.
12. Belvedere will look at the list of lessons learned, expand them, and give them a critical place in the Knowledge Cooperative. Docente will create an online training session for lessons learned, and we expect that every mid-level manager and up will complete the course. It will become an item on their performance reviews. You fit into that category, and you have a head start of Chiu and Barca.
13. Going forward, every object in the ***Thunk*** roles/activities list will be mapped to a communications cell. Acton will help Macedon, Van Amberg, and Armstrong with that. Belvedere won't have time to do a good job for the money we're paying them.
14. We must do something about the "reams" of information that we gave to Sharf. We want our managers to know at least as much as Belvedere will know if they pay attention to the information that we forced Marshall to give them. I will have Doc create yet another executive training program. This time you will support it and participate. **Note**: Belvedere will pay attention. Cane is quite shrewd.
15. Planning will take on new importance. *It will certainly never be the same for me again.* Everyone will contribute to planning for the re-invigoration. After Marshall risked looking foolish to let us know almost everything that anyone has ever done related to WFSOA business services and processes, we have finally realized how it provides the foundation for his "planning" miracle.
16. We want clearly defined business roles and role flexibility simultaneously. We will focus on techniques for rapidly adjusting business roles to market reality. As the head of sales and marketing, you will give your 100% support.
17. Partner Networks is making us all rich, and we are going to use it to get richer. We can't measure how much you benefited from the good will. RandD follow-up business is good for you too. You agree.
18. Sharing information through the Knowledge Cooperative is good. You will share.
19. Macedon and Piccolo's ideas for requirements management are brilliant. Sharf helped us to see that, and you see it better than ever before.
20. Process automation and continuous process improvement are good. You will use the automation that Weldon (really Marshall) provided already, and you will contribute to future efforts. It gives you more time to apply your own unique sales techniques.
21. I will come back tomorrow and as often as possible to keep them from cutting up the worm or to keep the worm from splitting up until we understand whether and how such a split will benefit Daxiao.
22. We start listening harder to Acton, Piccolo, Van Amberg, Macedon, and Marshall should he choose to speak to us again.

Sharf goes away, after having done a wonderful job. It is more effective to have less expensive consultants for the mundane repetitive work required to complete this assignment. Marshall likes Sharf's assistant, so he may talk to her.

<Gunnar>: How does the management team feel about this?

<Justin>: There are few surprises here - Armstrong (neutral), Barca (neutral), Chiu (in favor), Emery-Baldwin (neutral), Jasper (in favor), Macedon (neutral), Piccolo (in favor), Van Amberg (neutral), Guzman (in favor - no surprise there) and Acton (opposed). I will lean slightly in the direction of being in favor, so that's about as close to a quorum as I'm likely to get. *I flipped a few of those around. You figure out the politics.*

Note: Acton is opposed only because they don't want Belvedere swimming in their pool. However, they like the idea of strengthening WFSOA.

Do you have any objections that you are willing to share with me at this point?

<Gunnar>: No. *He didn't drop the other shoe.*

<Justin>: Between you and me:

1. We have to head off any mention of substance abuse. I will start the meeting with a discussion of Marshall's medical status and how he's suffering more than he must because he won't push the pain button.
2. I'll make a joke about the brew that Marshall's wife/girlfriend makes. You're nodding, so you know about it too.
3. Who would ever trust you again if they believed your brutality contributed to Marshall's condition? Therefore, don't bother trying to look good for tomorrow's meeting. You need to look like a victim of this unfortunate accident. Fake it if you have to. *You won't have to.* That shoulder sling may be the latest in super jock accessories, but didn't they give you one of those ugly blue/green ones at the hospital. It shows better. *Even I can see it.*
4. Joe will take it back responsibility for the Audit Committee while you "heal" physically and politically, and catch up on the sales you may have missed due to your unfortunate mishap.
5. Chiu, Barca, and Marshall have people who can help Joe with the takeover fights. Chiu will work with Joe more directly.

You no longer have Chiu in your pocket. Chiu wants to know how Joe can help him get my job since you messed up again.

6. Think about how to handle potential fallout with Sharf. Should he squawk, remind him that he will receive an immediate bonus from this assignment, even though he bungled it.
7. If he doesn't listen, mention how much trouble we could make for him and Belvedere with the FAXTrax and the video. You might ruminate over that a bit for yourself.
8. If (when) Marshall tries to resign, we ignore him until we have a better handle on his underground.
9. Finally, Gunnar lied about his connection to you on the security report. After he finished with tomorrow's meeting, he will never set foot on Daxiao property again. I might wonder whether you told him to do that, but we will not push the point at this time.

<Gunnar>: We are going to let my brother-in-law walk away with $50,000 for two day's work, even though he messed up everything.

<Justin>: That is how it must appear. However, I do not believe that will be the end of it. Sharf put Belvedere's reputation on the line along with yours and mine. You can tell that this made Diamonte and Cane extremely agitated.

<Gunnar>: Something is not right. Marshall will be furious. *Indy will be furious. I am furious. He ruined my career, and he will pay.*

<Justin>: When did you become squeamish about a little injustice? Your sister should sing praises to you. Marshall will have his new leg, and even more ego satisfaction than the last time you helped us mess up. Let's get out of here.

In case I don't have time after we speak with Frick and Frack and Piccolo, I order you to go back to the hospital and finish getting whatever you need tested. To ensure that you don't forget, you can ride with Oswald and me. *You took out my top money saver, you had better keep earning.*

<Gunnar>: That may be a good idea if you have the bird on the east side. It's been a long day for James. *Why is he concerned about me?*

<Justin>: The bird is parked. I have a dinner date with Mrs. Mittelman after we visit the hospital and give our regards to the Marshalls. *Sooner is better, no matter what Piccolo says.* Grace loves Samuel's and our place in New York is half way between there and the hospital.

<Gunnar>: Thanks for the offer. I can use a little sympathy from Grace. I'm not getting any from you.

It's funny that you mentioned Samuel's restaurant. Marshall's clan loves it so much that one of his chefs works with the hospital dietician whenever Marshall is hospitalized. Samuel personally cooked a special meal for Marshalls' son today.

<Justin>: *Marshall's favorite place to eat is Grace's favorite place. It is five blocks away from Kristie's, which he loves, and a building with a very discrete entrance and a private elevator to our penthouse. I wonder if the odds of such a coincidence are about 1%.*

<Gunnar>: You have that strange look again.

CHAPTER XIII - PERSONAL - EXPLANATION OF SHARFNESS

Indy>: What are you doing in here?

<Justin>: Val and Dan said there were empty rooms down here.

<Gunnar>: *Amazing jeans! Amazing Indy.*

<Indy>: I saw you earlier. You're Mittelman, is that correct?

<Justin>: You look different - *Still in black, and definitely a hornet.*

<Indy>: Never mind that. *This is what I could find at Mama's place. She hides my business outfits.*

<Justin>: Yes, I am Justin Mittelman. I came by to wish your father well and let him know that he will be missed, but he should take as much time as he needs to heal before he returns.

<Indy>: Then you did something that could have made him take longer to heal.

<Gunnar>: ***What did you do? Why?***

<Justin>: *Why is he so manic? This is more than worry about Marshall's booby traps. Maybe those boobies have him trapped.* Apologies are in order. I made him laugh, though I definitely was not trying to be funny.

<Indy>: Laugh! What could you possibly say that he would find funny enough to cause himself pain?

<Justin>: You'd have to be there.

<Indy>: Are you all as sadistic as Sharky? *I should have stopped him when I had the chance.*

<Justin>: To whom are you referring?

<Indy>: William Benson Sharf. Who else preyed on my family, twice? *Andy looks like I slapped him.*

[...] You're excused, sort of. Daddy is alive because of you, *and Mama already made adjustments.*

<Justin>: How do you know Sharf?

<Indy>: He tried to ruin my grade point average in college, and we competed for the same clients a few times when I was at Acton. Didn't one of you bother to check this out before you brought him onboard?

<Gunnar>: No, and I am so sorry. I would never [...]

<Justin>: Many of our avenues were closed. *I didn't bother to mention apologies, because I didn't believe he would know how to fake it.*

<Gunnar>: *I hurt the women that I love, Amal, maybe Liz, and now you.*

<Indy>: What's wrong with you?

<Justin>: His allergies are acting up more and more lately. I tried to persuade him to see my allergist, but he's too manly to admit that he has a problem. *She affects him as her mother does her father, and she is "not his type".*

However, "Andy" had just mentioned the possible conflict of interest between your father's staff and Mr. Sharf's consulting objectives. I suspect that he was about to provide me with additional information when you walked in.

<Indy>: You looked like you were about to leave.

<Justin>: Let's try another angle. Please accept the second apology. Mr. Sharf ran ahead of us and apparently had his own agenda. He wasn't even supposed to have started until Monday. We will make sure that he does not start on Monday or at any future time.

<Indy>: That is closing the barn door after the horse is out.

<Gunnar>: We didn't hurt your father. He tripped. His thigh was disintegrating. That femur had to be made to measure.

<Indy>: The leg had to be fixed, but you both helped Sharf do something that was worse than the tripping.

<Gunnar>: I wanted to find out what your father did, and Sharf twisted it to his own purposes.

<Indy>: Why didn't you listen to Liz? She was screaming from the rooftops.

<Gunnar>: I couldn't hear her.

<Indy>: *Gunnar looks like a sick puppy.* Mittelman, what caused your deafness, especially you?

<Justin>: *I have to turn this around.* Miss, Ms., or Mrs. Winslow, we acknowledge that Sharf's behavior was abominable. However, it is more and more obvious that the behavior may have been triggered by something that happened in your prior interactions. You and your father withheld information, and the situation may have gotten out of hand. I have always found that secrets have a way of coming back to bite us, as this one obviously did.

<Gunnar>: *He doesn't know he's being suicidal! He didn't see her tossing me around yesterday!*

<Indy>: Justin, dear boy, you will exchange places with me. I need something out of that drawer.

<Gunnar>: *Her mother was calm like when she was listening to Van Amberg and me.*

<Justin>: *Boy! I was never a boy, even when I was a boy.*

<Indy>: Sit for a moment.

<Justin>: *What did she do? I wasn't planning on moving from there or sitting here, and definitely not in her side chair. The hierarchy is backwards.*

<Gunnar>: *Justin is lighter than I am by 30 pounds. He's easier to move.*

<Justin>: [...] *Cotton swabs! She's cleaning her ears.* You are wasting my valuable time. I'm sure it's nothing we can't clear up quickly if you cooperate.

<Gunnar>: ***Leave her alone, for both our sakes!***

<Justin>: We must discover what she may have done to provoke him.

<Indy>: It was necessary for me to ensure that I was not having a hearing problem too. I have extra swabs if you think they may help. They contain Jonas's special medication.

<Justin>: I'm fine. *Ear to mouth with an angry hornet!*

<Indy>: That is good, because I want you to hear with absolute clarity.

You are a f.cking idiot android, and almost as big a bully as Sharf! You are sitting in my chair, in my office, on my property, trying to bamboozle a woman that was trained by Nicola Frey.

You have been serving my father crap since you got here, and you have the balls to suggest that something I did to defend myself against that slaughterhouse offal justified him sabotaging whatever you left of my father's dignity.

You must be wearing a muffler, because I didn't hear anything clang when you walked.

<Justin>: *I was trying to get him away from the woman I need, even more than Higgs or Doc.*

I don't believe in love, so when did I fall in love with Grace!

<Gunnar>: *I am very weak. I should try to stand up while she's not paying attention.*

<Indy>: Understand well that due to this sabotage, my Daddy won't be wasting his time trying to prove that he is as good as the rest of you fools, which was truly a waste because he was always at least twice as good. Without his broad shoulders, Goodsand would have been Quicksand.

<Justin>: *I didn't play that right. I'll let her wind down, and then try another angle.*

<Indy>: Nevertheless, I will be tolerant. Let me escort you out of the area. Andy, please join us.

<Justin>: *I moved again, and I wasn't planning to move.*

[...] *This is what it feels like to be shoulder-to-shoulder with an angry hornet. Her ribs feel like a steel cage.*

Maybe that was the wrong script.

<Indy>: Who says idiot androids can't learn?

<Justin>: [...] *This is starting to hurt. It hurts more when I try to reach her.* Gunnar, do something!

<Gunnar>: Indy! He's a fwagile andwoid. Not tough like me. Look!

<Indy>: *Take a deep breath Indy. Meditation is good sometimes. It may be related to something that I did when I was upset, as I am now.* Get the hell out.

<Gunnar>: He didn't mean to make it worse. We are sorry.

<Justin>: *We certainly are sorry.* You dislocated my shoulder.

<Indy>: No, I wanted you to avoid making painful navigational errors on your way out. If your sight is as bad as your hearing, you could bang those things into something, and then you would sue us.

<Gunnar>: *I love that woman! That was a slip.*

<Justin>: That is remarkable. My sight improved, and I found a better script.

<Indy>: *I see why Mama snapped.* ***You are a persistent f.cking idiot android.***

<Justin>: *Maybe it was all the time she spent with all those jocks, female and male. Maybe she spent too much time around Macedon.*

<Indy>: *Slow down Baby Girl. Take deep breaths. I must remember Clara. My mind is what matters.*

<Justin>: *I messed up with another Marshall. However, they have a sense of humor, and she's not sliced from stem to stern.* Please listen and that is not how asthmatics breathe. The room might be yours, but we can share the air.

<Gunnar>: *He has a death wish.*

No [...] She's laughing. She's about to become hysterical as her mother did yesterday!

Indy, are you all right? *Her hand is strong, but it's been broken, and it didn't heal right.*

I'm wobbling again. I'm about to become the local Weeble.

<Justin>: *She sounds like her father.* Can't any of you Marshall's take a joke without crying? That is what happened to your father.

<Gunnar>: Try this. I used all your tissues.

<Indy>: *Dental gauze. Mama is good at murking.*

Say what you have to say and leave. You are messing with my business schedule. *Forester is coming to rush the Lambert deal with Bateman. Sharf will never know what hit him!*

<Justin>: You will like this script better?

There's a madman loose, and you may understand why he would want to hurt your family. We don't.

We were not trying to hurt any of you. *Marshall had "Little Miss Mama" and a piece of Grace.*

Sharf has too many jokers in his deck, and I found out too late.

Because of your father's work, we made and saved large sums of money. We didn't know because he kept giving the credit to everyone else.

It was a way to ensure support for some of his more threatening ideas, especially since the Program received less support than it warranted. I don't want to discontinue what your father started. We need him. A lifetime of groundwork could be wasted. Many wheels would be re-invented.

I'll say it another way. I didn't know that Sharf was a cracked crock and Gunnar failed to mention that they were related, which is silly because many of the people in Daxiao are related to somebody in Daxiao, even me.

Furthermore, nepotism is not necessarily bad. The Frey-Marshalls have turned it into high art.

I won't offend your family by offering money because we know either one of you could buy and sell most of us. The only title higher than your father's is mine.

<Gunnar>: *There is the CEO spot. That would be ironic.*

<Justin>: I believe it's important to him to receive the credit he deserves. I was trying to figure out a way to make that happen without having the likes of "Andy" tripping him up again (please pardon the reference to tripping), at least until a cleaner transition is arranged. I know your father can't sit in his oversized closet forever.

I heard that Sharf is almost as smart as you are, but I didn't know that he was listing to starboard.

<Indy>: Who cares half a jot about a clean transition?

<Justin>: Your father put over 38 years of his life into this company, and it would be nice if he left with a big retirement party where everyone knew how they benefited from his work (*polish up the halo*). If he wasn't such a Snuffleupagus, and you know I am right about that, we wouldn't be going through this.

<Indy>: That sounded almost 90% sincere. I wish Jonas was here to hear it.

<Gunnar>: *I have been underestimating Mittelman.*

<Justin>: Trust your own senses. *Whew! I just earned this year's bonus.*

She nearly missed the chair!

<Gunnar>: ***Indy, please be careful!***

<Indy>: I am tired, very tired.

You nearly fell too. Sit and rest, or they may have to wheel us both out today.

<Gunnar>: *She noticed! She is worried about me too.*

<Justin>: I know I am risking something dear, but I am still convinced that something about the current situation is related to something about which you have information, and I do not. This is not appropriate for an android, but my curiosity is about to overcome my will to keep functioning. How long have you known Sharf?

<Indy>: Mama and I didn't even mention it to Daddy until last week. He had too many physical and professional issues when I tangled with Sharf. That was over 21 years ago.

<Justin>: Since elementary school?

<Indy>: No! I told you he messed with my college grades. I was a junior in college. Before you try to do the calculation, I will be 40 in two weeks. I have the gray hairs to prove it. Look.

<Justin>: *I've never heard a woman increase her age, but WOW. She is in unbelievable shape.* You tell your age. Could you share the rest of the story?

<Indy>: It's not a secret. It simply didn't come up in any conversations that you heard. I talk about it to young women that I mentor. *He's trying to find out how much Andy messed up, and Andy is forgetting to breathe.*

<Justin>: Pretend that you are mentoring Andrea and Justina. Ignore Andrea's beard. Her right arm isn't working well today.

<Indy>: The short version is that Daddy wasn't earning a lot of money when I applied to college and Mama had just left the DA's office. Nevertheless, they were making $1,000 a year too much for me to qualify for most financial aid. I had excellent grades, but so did everyone who was admitted to the school. Therefore, I went to B-school on a basketball scholarship. Some people said I was going to basketball school. I was determined to show that I could handle books and balls.

<Justin>: *Keep a straight face self. There's a lot at stake.*

<Indy>: I maintained a 4.0 average in finance, and I turned down the offer to be the team captain during my junior year because I couldn't afford to mess anything up.

That year, I took a course where Sharf was a teaching assistant, and that year I started making mistakes on weekly quizzes that didn't make sense. Someone seemed to be changing every answer that I corrected before I submitted a quiz. I complained to Sharf, and he said that I could have been changing the answers and confusing myself. He suggested that I was trying to handle too much, but he was willing to tutor me through my "problems".

I didn't believe I had any problems. He would show me his profile and pontificate about topics that were in no way related to the course I was taking. Furthermore, the tutoring often overlapped with my athletic requirements. I needed A's because I wanted to attend graduate school and Daddy and Machi were trying to save money in case Jonas was accepted at Strafford.

<Justin>: Why couldn't he get a basketball scholarship?

<Indy>: Jonas is the smartest one in the family, and he is big and strong, but he has limited physical endurance, and he's absent-minded, near-sighted, and deaf. An athletic scholarship was not an option for him.

Daddy was working on a major system installation when we had the family powwow. Mama told me to write the answers in ink. That is difficult when you're working with formulas and calculations. Uncle Ike came up with the second idea.

<Justin>: You don't have an Uncle Ike. One is Richard and your mother's brother is David.

<Indy>: Uncle Ike was Mama's oldest boyfriend. Oh dear, I meant hoodie (which is what Randy and Sandy would say) [...] childhood sweetheart [...] oldest best friend. Oh, forget it. My grandparents liked Ike, and Mama liked Daddy. Given his preferences, Uncle Ike was willing to settle for being our pseudo-uncle and godfather.

<Justin>: What happened to him?

<Indy>: His final significant other didn't get along with Mama.

<Justin>: Where is he now?

<Indy>: Dead. His significant other also had AIDS.

<Justin>: I'm sorry about that, and I'm sorry I interrupted you. Please keep going. *That wraps Van Amberg's revelation in a neat package.*

<Indy>: Anyway, Uncle Ike was an accountant, so he understood my dilemma. He found carbon copy paper that was light on one side. He showed me how to trim the edges, so the sheets would fit between the test sheet and the "evidence" sheet without being noticed. He also bought mechanical pencils with tough lead. I used them to keep a copy of the answers I submitted. Two more tests came back before the mid-term with 8 and 11 points shaved off, and I could prove it. It made the difference between an "A" and a "B."

Mama came to my final tutoring session with the evidence. She explained her legal connections and threatened Sharf with either criminal or civil charges if he persisted. She also suggested that he should correct the grades for the "problems" for which we had evidence.

She promised that she would not make him pay for prior misunderstandings if he made fewer mistakes going forward. If you're interested, I kept the tests and the carbon copies. I use them when I mentor.

<Justin>: Given his Sharfness, he could have figured out ways to cause more trouble.

<Indy>: If you know him, you're not going to believe anything I tell you. Why should I bother?

<Justin>: I've only known him since 8:16 this morning. He is not a person that one forgets.

<Gunnar>: He didn't know Sharf. This was my mistake. I've tried to make it up to you and your family, and I will continue to do so.

<Indy>: *What's with the nice guy act?* You are Anderssen Niklas Gunnar, right?

<Justin>: He is confusing me too. Please continue.

<Indy>: He may have behaved because of the big man in the dark suit with the gun bulge and sunglasses. Ike sent him along to protect us.

Mama introduced him as Lieutenant Masters. She didn't lie too much. He had been a sergeant before he retired from the force, and he was a part-time actor and health guru. Ike paid him $300 for six hours work. It was good pay in those days.

<Justin>: Why didn't you go to the dean?

<Indy>: We decided against going to the dean after we spoke to Uncle Richard and Aunt Denise about a hypothetical situation. They were both college professors and both seemed amused that one of Daddy's brats had finally hit a wall. They told us that an important part of the educational experience was to give the instructor what was requested.

Mama and I disagreed with that recommendation, and we were sure that Ryan would not have approved either.

However, Sharf was a Main Line pretender who spent a lot of time with the dean, while I was the daughter of a Bronx mutt, and I spent a lot of time trying to get a rubber ball through a metal hoop.

<Justin>: Where was your father while all this was happening?

<Indy>: Grandma had just had her stroke, and Daddy was spending as much time with her as he could while he was being evaluated by doctors to determine whether he should have (a) a wonderful new experimental appliance or (b) a wonderful new artificial leg and thigh. He was simultaneously doing something unreasonable at Goodsand. We really needed him to keep his job in those days.

<Justin>: *Now we need him infinitely more than he needs us.*

<Gunnar>: Why didn't your father tell us about Sharf?

<Indy>: We figured that if you knew, you didn't care, and if you didn't know, you wouldn't believe Sharf would do what he did. You're sitting there now trying not to believe me.

<Justin>: *I certainly am. I worked with Gunnar to accelerate the agreement.*

<Indy>: For us, he was a relatively known quantity, and we could use him to find a hint of what you were planning. Daddy, Dan, Alex, Acton, and even Armstrong have spoiled Daxiao with the quality of the work they deliver. They would let Sharf be himself, he would appear to be extremely incompetent and occasionally very stupid, and then he would move along to the next victim.

<Gunnar>: Are you and Jonas always so straightforward?

<Indy>: Only when the information won't hurt anything. Daxiao can't hurt Daddy any more.

<Justin>: We never intended to hurt him in the first place. *She's getting that look again!*

<Gunnar>: Why did your father give them so much information?

<Indy>: In order to use the material to best advantage, you need access to Maja's "keep track of everything" database. After Ādaemoa, they could ensure that Sharf never got close to it. Furthermore, they realized that only Sharf's assistant would know how to use the material and the database, and Sharf was blocking her.

<Justin>: When did they tell you this?

<Indy>: Val had the meeting notes in his briefcase when he came to the hospital. I read them while I was giving blood.

<Justin>: How did you do that? *Nothing stops them! I'm getting that mushy feeling again.*

<Indy>: It was very difficult. Situations like this send me into the doldrums. If it wasn't for Clara's "control you mind" mantra, I'd be sitting in a windowless room with the lights out. I may do that later anyhow, *now that Maja and I have provided Mama with the information she needs to take care of Sharf.*

<Gunnar>: *She inherited Marshall's morbidity.*

<Justin>: Things make more sense. However, is there something you're not saying because Sharf's brother-in-law is in the room?

<Indy>: You like being on the edge don't you?

<Justin>: I usually stay safely in the middle, but for $750,000,000, I will take a risk, or a few.

<Indy>: The answer is "absolutely not". He was pretty, and he was one of the only people, outside the basketball team, that was tall enough for me. Still, he was not my type.

<Justin>: What was your type?

<Indy>: In those days, I liked the athletic type with nice shoulders. I would still like the athletic type with nice shoulders, if I was interested in those things. When I had a choice of being Ryan Winslow's fiancée or William Sharf's experiment on the dark side, I chose Ryan. *Ryan was the wrong choice too.*

<Justin>: What's wrong now?

<Indy>: I tend to get hoarse when I'm tired. It's been a LONG 24 hours.

<Justin>: *Dry throat syndrome is going around too.*

<Indy>: To finish the answer, Sharf ever touched me except when he threatened me.

<Gunnar>: What threat!

<Justin>: *He's going to have a stroke.* She was going to tell us, but if you'd rather stop, I will understand. *I'm not sure I want to hear this.*

<Indy>: I'm almost done. One night early the next semester, Sharf accosted me on the way to dinner after basketball practice. He said Mama and me went back on our word and talked to the dean after he "gave" me the grade that I wanted. He accused us of ruining his academic career.

I reminded him that he was hurting my career first. He said that I must have been cheating. I told him he was crazy and tried to walk away. He grabbed my arm and told me he was not finished with me, and that I wasn't going anywhere until I told him what I said to the dean.

I was frightened and confused. I assured him than I had not said anything to the dean.

<Gunnar>: *She's about to start crying.* You don't have to finish this.

<Indy>: If you know what happened, and you don't do anything, that will also valuable information.

<Justin>: We already dealt with Sharf. After tomorrow morning, he will never be allowed near Daxiao or your father. Please pass that along to your parents, after you tell us what happened. *I need to know, and I really don't want to know.*

<Indy>: He called me a lying witch, with a "b". I had never seen anyone who was larger than I am who looked that angry up close, until I saw Jonas today, of course. Sharf grabbed both of my shoulders and started snarling at me. I remember hearing him say that I would tell him what he wanted to know, or he would shake it out of me.

<Justin>: Is it fair to say that you did not stroll across the campus with him as you just did with me? ***I wonder if Sharf has children.***

<Indy>: I don't know what I did. The next thing I remember is seeing him on the ground, with his feet up on a bench, and his hands over his face. He called me a "witch" again, and he said I was finished. He repeated that several times.

I was frightened. I didn't know the penalty for injuring a student assistant, but I was sure that I was in deep trouble. I sprinted to the place where I was supposed to meet Ryan.

<Justin>: You can breathe now Gunnar. She left him on the ground. ***I have to look serious. I cannot laugh. The robot can handle this.***

<Gunnar>: How many people saw this?

<Indy>: Apparently, nobody. The Palestra is somewhat out of the way, and Sharf selected a very isolated spot. Ryan and Greg found him sitting on the ground near the bench.

<Justin>: You skipped something.

<Indy>: When I got to Nesmith's (the food was cheap and plentiful), Ryan was there with Greg Peterson, Lee Southers, and their girlfriends. I tried to explain how Sharf had tripped over the bench while he was shaking me. I am sure that I mentioned how Sharf threatened to get me kicked out of school.

Ryan told Lee to stay with us, and he and Greg went to discuss the matter with Sharf.

<Gunnar>: Was that "the Greg Peterson"?

<Justin>: Who is Greg Peterson?

<Gunnar>: He was big as Jonas without fat, and he could run the length of a football field in less time than it's taking me to say this.

<Indy>: They didn't hurt him though. They offered to take him to the infirmary, but he insisted that he wanted to go home. They cleaned him up as much as they could, and they walked with him, making sure that they took him back along a route where people could see them. They wanted people to remember that they were helping him.

Along the way, Sharf realized that he must have tripped on a loose stone in the flight of steps coming from the upper campus to the lower campus. It was dusk, and the area was unfamiliar to him.

Greg may have mentioned that there were looser stones and steeper steps anywhere Sharf was likely to find himself, especially if he followed through on his promise to get me expelled.

When they came back to Nesmith's, Greg promised that Sharf wouldn't bother me again, and he didn't.

<Gunnar>: You're the flight of stairs! [...............]

<Justin>: Gunnar, when Indy's father laughed like that he hurt himself, and he almost got me killed.

<Indy>: Don't lie. Daddy was in a drugged stupor before anybody mentioned what you did.

<Justin>: ***You underestimate Macedon and his comb.***

<Gunnar>: It hurts, but it's worth it. He had a broken nose, lawn marks on his face, a bruised kidney, and a sore rump. He looked worse than I do now. I know it's hard to believe.

<Indy>: I thought he had a bloody nose.

<Justin>: I suppose his ego was somewhat more fragile than Mr. Gunnar's or mine for that matter. ***A time bomb was set.***

<Indy>: It was not my fault! He started the problem both times.

<Gunnar>: I understand.

<Justin>: You obviously weren't hurt.

<Indy>: I had trouble holding my glass and my silverware (plastic ware) all during the meal. We though it was nerves at first. When it started swelling, they put ice on it and wrapped it in an ace bandage (football medicine). The girls had to help me undress that night and help me dress the next morning. During practice the next day, I fell so I would have an excuse to go to the infirmary.

<Gunnar>: [...] Now you're laughing?

<Justin>: No. I'm being hysterical. ***I walked in front of a moving train.***

<Indy>: They found that I had a fractured 5th right metacarpal (my hand was broken), and they put on a temporary cast. I had trouble handling BASKETBALLS for almost four weeks, but we made the finals. Daddy and Grandma came in wheelchairs, but they saw me play.

<Gunnar>: The bone is crooked. You never gave it enough time to heal.

<Indy>: Is it that obvious?

<Gunnar>: Only if you're paying attention.

<Justin>: *He's almost unconscious, and he's paying more attention to her than I've seen him pay to any of his quarterly misses.*

<Justin>: How did your family react?

<Indy>: I didn't tell them. That occurred four days before Daddy was scheduled to have his first knee replacement, and they were both trying to make sure that The Queen would be comfortable with 24-hour nursing care while Mama spent time with Daddy. Until this morning, Mama thought I ran into the stands and hurt my hand.

<Gunnar>: *My Amazon Panther.*

<Justin>: I confess that I know most of what I need to know, and we are about to move along to things that I want to know. How did you learn how to handle Sharf and to make me move when I wasn't planning on moving?

<Gunnar>: *I want to know too.*

<Indy>: Mama took martial arts training - she believed it was necessary for protection from angry defendants. She took me to practice with her after Jonas was born. Jonas had to wait until he was four because of his balance problems. Mama said the lessons were cheaper than paying a babysitter, even through she wasn't paying a babysitter. We had fun together, and it gave Queen Kabiri and Clara a break.

<Justin>: Who is Queen Kabiri? Val said your baby sister was Queen-2. *I may as well verify this part.*

<Indy>: *Gunnar is holding his breath again. I wonder what's wrong now.* I have ten minutes to answer any more questions. Then you will leave, right?

<Justin>: We promise.

Clara St. John is easy - maybe not. If it hadn't been for Clara, there wouldn't be any Frey-Marshalls.

People thought she was our Nanny, but she is more like St. Clara. She was a nurse, a captain in the Army, and one of the head librarians at the VA hospital in the mid-sixties. She lost her husband during WW II, and her only son in Cambodia. We became her alternate family.

She supported Daddy through serious physical and emotional problems after he was injured the first time, and after he had his knee replaced.

She also compensated for the absence of Rachel Frey (my mother's mother), after Mama and Rachel had the disagreement over whether Daddy was the right choice for me. *It sticks in my throat when I try to call Rachel grandmother.*

Kabira Marshall was my real grandmother. We believed Papa Stacy nicknamed her The Queen because she looked like a Nordic queen (the gene pool was really scrambled), and she was accustomed to getting what she wanted, even if she had to get it for herself. After she died, Papa Stacy assured us that her family was Telugu royalty, and so was his family until they lost a disagreement with the British Raj. Keep that in mind the next time you are dealing with Prince Marshall, or Princess Indy, for that matter.

<Justin>: Where is Telugu? *I could know that. Grace is always talking about the states in India, but it wasn't related to any problem I had to solve, so I ignored her.*

<Indy>: Two of my great, great grandparents were born in a place called Guntur in Andhra Pradesh on the east coast of India. That's G-U-N-T-U-R. Over 80% of the people in that state speak Telugu. My relatives were forced to immigrate to Trinidad where they performed less than royal work on the sugar cane plantations.

That's where The Queen and Papa Stacy were born, but you probably know that already.

<Gunnar>: Are you sure? *Her baby brother looked like Guntur, and it is not my imagination!*

<Indy>: As sure as you can be with any genealogical research. Mama had an acquaintance that performed research for W.A.R. They met at a ballet performance.

She asked Mama to show her how to trace the Holocaust links, which she had just discovered among her Park Avenue connections. Mama had a reputation in the DA's office for doing thorough background checks, long before there were genealogy databases on the Internet. In return, this woman had an inside track on Indian genealogy. She did charity work in India.

<Justin>: How long ago was this? My wife is a W.A.R. Maybe these women know each other. *Grace Nelson did genealogical work for the W.A.R. That's how she discovered that one of her great grandfathers was Jewish.*

<Indy>: I have to calculate [...] We Papa Stacy after The Queen died, which is three weeks after the twins were born, and Queen-2 is 19 now. It was some time during the next year. I don't remember hearing the woman's name, but if you and Mama ever have a civilized conversation, you can ask her.

<Gunnar>: *That sounds like grace. She has been working with Indian girl orphans for 25 years.*

<Justin>: *It was Grace! Nicky/Machi was the woman with the beautiful mismatched twins that she mentioned, repeatedly. Grace had heard Marshall's name before!* What does Kabiri mean?

<Indy>: Something about long hair. It was a joke because Grandma was bald when she was born. Daddy and I started out bald too. Now he has almost as much hair as Jonas when he lets it grow. *Gunnar looks stunned.*

Ike used to call Daddy Mama's Fuzzy Wuzzy.

<Justin>: *I will find out what Gunnar knows about India and Telugu hair later.*

<Gunnar>: *That's why Ryan calls Jonas a fuzzy wuzzy.*

<Justin>: We used five minutes, and I don't know about the martial arts.

<Indy>: There's not much to say except that we kept doing it, and we added weight training when that became popular. Mama said it built her self-confidence. She made me continue because I matured early, and Jonas learned to use his eyes as partial compensation for his balance problem. It also partially compensated for his tendency to overeat. When I left for college, I knew everything that Mama knew. I was also in much better physical shape than I am now.

<Justin and Gunnar>: *Better shape. That cannot be possible.*

<Justin>: Can your brothers do what you do?

<Indy>: Jonas is as strong as daddy, and he has a longer reach than we do, but his weight and the balance problems affect his performance. The good news is that bullies only tended to pick on him once.

Pip never took formal training in anything, but he and his friends do things that require extreme physical fitness. Some of their dance routines are unbelievable. He could hang with Maja before he went away to school. I mean he could hang off the side of Washington Mountain.

<Justin>: *This is making me forget to breathe. Val saved my life.*

<Gunnar>: *Huey could have broken me in two yesterday.*

<Justin>: I have one last question. Squeeze in as much information as you can into the next three minutes.

If you didn't so to the dean, do you know who did?

<Indy>: Sharf blabbed on himself.

<Justin>: How do you know that? *Sharf is a genuine gold-plated moron.*

<Indy>: The only two times I ever saw the dean were at receptions for honors graduates, and both times he was utterly gracious yet equally determined to avoid more than a two-sentence conversation with me.

Evan, one of my project mates in another class, mentioned that he was having a problem similar to my problem. He was upset because his father had promised him a fancy new sports car if he maintained a 4 point average any semester while he was in school and his own condo the second time. He was already a junior, and he had blown half of his semesters. I told him about the carbon paper trick, he tried it, and found irregularities on two tests.

Evan was "Main Line", and his uncle, who had established a large endowment fund, knew the dean. The grading issue was discussed over lunch somewhere, with enough emphasis that the dean was willing to follow up.

The dean mentioned the topic to Will, without names, and asked how they could research the complaint about unusual grading. Sharf immediately assumed that I had filed the complaint. Evan say he blurted out "surely you don't believe anything those witches (with a "b") say". That's when the dean realized that his friend's nephew may not have been the only one with the problem and that his friend's nephew wasn't being lazy and trying to use family connections to compensate for the deficit.

When the dean asked Sharf what they should do about the situation, Sharf's response was to kick me out and let the legal department deal with the consequences. He accused me of being involved in a cheating ring, and that the carbon paper was used to pass the answers around. How else could anyone who spent that much time at sports possibly be that good academically?

The dean figured out that I was William's "cheater", but he had also heard positive reports from other members of the faculty, including two women. The dean promised to consider William's suggestions, and he asked William to keep quiet until he could gather evidence that was more substantial. Apparently, that happened the day of the evening that Sharf accosted me.

After further research, they found one more person who had inherited the carbon paper trick and four seniors who had no proof, but were willing to share their feelings about Sharf's grading practices. Two of them suggested that while some grades fell mysteriously, some others rose mysteriously.

William was allowed to leave quietly.

<Justin>: Do you have any idea why Sharf did what you claim?

<Indy>: Yesterday or 20 years ago?

<Justin>: Start twenty years ago, and then work forward.

<Indy>: Mama said he was sexist and a racist.

Ryan said Sharky thought I was beautiful, he wanted to be alone in a room with me, and he created a situation that would make that happen. People used to think that I was attractive.

<Justin>: *She's being sarcastic.*

<Gunnar>: *You are incredible now. I'll go with Ryan's theory.*

<Indy>: Ike said he was guarding the top of the heap. Mama and Ike may have been right, but I believe it related to money and a twisted Robin Hood ethic. The grants graduate studies were available without consideration of family incomes. He was helping members of his fan club, and hurting everyone else. I wasn't Main Line or Germantown for that matter, and I was not one of his fans.

<Justin>: Have you seen him since then?

<Indy>: When I was at Acton, we competed for the same customer once.

He won because he could tell that I was expecting, and he made sure the client found out. Even though it was a three-month assignment, and I was only three months pregnant, I lost the bid. The clients wanted someone who would see the project through and handle any follow-up issues. It worked out for the best. The twins weighed 7 and 6-1/2 pounds when they were born. I stopped working after 5-1/2 months, and I threw up until after they were born.

<Gunnar>: *I bet she was able to nurse both of them.*

<Indy>: OK. Time's up. If you need urine samples and a cheek swab, we can arrange something tomorrow. Leave.

<Justin>: What's wrong now?

<Indy>: I have an interview. You may borrow the first office (that's Dan's space), or use the conference area.

<Justin>: Will you talk to your parents for us?

<Indy>: Don't push your luck. Your timing is bad.

<Justin>: Slipped script again [...] let's go "Andy".

<Gunnar>: *I'm trying, and it's getting harder and harder.*

<Indy>: You appear to be really run down. You don't have a fever, but the lump looks ugly. You should rest.

<Gunnar>: I will, as soon as I finish those follow-up tests. I had to come and take my licking first.

<Justin>: *What is he up to?*

<Indy>: Thanks again for helping with Daddy. Ernest said he might be in worse shape, or dead, if you hadn't gotten him the right kind of help in time, here and at the hospital. I also apologize for Mama. I've never seen her as she was yesterday.

<Gunnar>: Thanks, but I will believe your mother's apology when I hear it from her. *She touched my forehead. Now the challenge is to figure out what I can do so that she will touch me again without nine people wanting me dead.*

<Indy>: Maybe I was pushing it a bit. Mama can carry a grudge.

<Gunnar>: Did they call anyone to fix the drawer?

<Indy>: There was nothing wrong with the drawer. After Mama did more damage to it than she did to you, Ernest went to clean up and he found a plastic folder that had fallen behind the drawer. The harder we tried to close it, the more likely it was to push itself open.

<Gunnar>: What did your mother do?

<Justin>: I can explain later. The woman needs her office, and we need to speak to ***OUR TEAM***.

<Gunnar>: I can't leave now.

<Justin>: We have information that clarifies Mr. Sharf's unusual behavior. What else do you need?

<Gunnar>: I have eaten a gelatin dessert and apple mousse from your father's lunch tray in the last 28 hours, and I swallowed a few more pills than the doctor recommended. If I try to move now, something dramatic could happen. Do you have any soft energy food?

<Justin>: *He's stalling, or maybe not. He was having trouble standing up a while ago.* I'll call Oswald.

<Indy>: There must be something behind the door marked "fredo" in the conference room. Even better, I keep Mama's carrot brew around. I could use one too. Open the panel beside your shoulder.

[...] I'm sorry. Lean to the side, and I'll get it for you.

<Justin>: *That was a very long lean. Sometimes it is good to be a Robot.*

<Gunnar>: *She should have men standing in line* [...] *Gunnar, she's not worth dying for, or maybe she is.*

<Justin>: I'll take a ginger tea if you have one.

<Indy>: Of course. *This is cutting it close.*

---------- ----------

<Gunnar>: [...] It worked. Pardon the drooling

[...] I know we have to go.

<Helena Styles>: Andy. Laufer said he saw you coming in here! You can't imagine how glad I am to see that you're all right - mostly.

[...] I'm sorry. What did I do?

<Gunnar>: *Why did you have to find me now?* I'm very sore.

<Helena>: You look [...]

<Gunnar>: Let me guess. I look like somebody beat me with a stick. How did you find out?

<Helena>: Your mother called and said you had been injured. I promised I'd check on you for her. How bad is this?

Now you will have to stay put while I figure out how to extend our situation.

<Gunnar>: I am probably OK, but I need more tests. *Damn you Gerthe. I may need to get married again and settle down, but not with her.*

<Indy>: *She is Boston Brahmin, Park Avenue, or Main Line - Why am I not surprised?* It is crowded in here.

<Helena>: Yes it is. Please excuse us. I'd like to speak to Andy in private.

<Justin>: Andy, would you step into the conference room when you are finished here.

<Helena>: I'm sorry that we haven't met. You are [...]

<Gunnar>: A work associate.

<Justin>: I am Justin Mittelman.

<Helena>: Mr. Mittelman, I'm Helena Styles, and I've heard so many wonderful things about you. I see you're taking care of Andy. This is smaller than his office across the river, but more than acceptable for New York quarters. The appointments are quite elegant. Everything is fine except for the bottles and [...]

<Indy>: I'm glad you like it. Bye, bye.

<Helena>: [...] her. She is not right for you, Gunnar. She dresses much too severely and she is much too brusque. She would not be good for sales. My agency can have someone appropriate for you by tomorrow at noon.

<Gunnar>: Where are your manners? *She ruined everything!*

<Helena>: Who would dare to speak to me of manners?

<Indy>: I would be more concerned about your departure, Madame Madame. Your lucky number is seven. One [...]

<Justin>: *I recognize that look. I'll stand near the door and watch how she does that arm/wrist lock thing.*

[...] *I changed my mind. He kept her from breaking my arm, and I don't think Ms. Styles would help us keep anything quiet.* Ms. Styles, this is not Gunnar's office. We borrowed the space from Ms. Frey-Marshall, and our allotted time has run out.

<Gunnar>: ***She's my landlord Helena. Apologize NOW!***

<Indy>: *It took him long enough.* [...] five, six, s-

<Justin>: Indy! ***Fragile!***

[...] *The Marshall laugh becomes music to my ears.*

<Helena>: *Why are they yelling and why is she roaring like that? New money can be so crude.*

I will not apologize. Gunnar, whatever you have in those bottles is affecting your mental processes. You shouldn't be drinking in your condition. You have my permission to call when you recover.

<Gunnar>: Indy [...] *Indy made me disappear again.*

<Indy>: One, two [...]

<Clarence Forester>: What was that? Hello Indy.

[...] Mr. Mittelman!

<Justin>: *That accountant lost my IRS appeal.* What are you doing here?

<Indy>: You're early. Could you be trying to make a good impression, and you're not even hired yet? What do you have in your hands? *Thank goodness that he's wearing a suit.*

<Forester>: *I've been hired for almost five years!* Your brother told me to bring these papers to you. He says your mother wants to concentrate on getting Lambert to the bank and that will almost guarantee success with the other issue.

<Gunnar>: Who are you?

<Indy>: **Flirt. Now!**

<Forester>: *Not hired yet? Flirt? What is she doing?* I'm the person who wants an opportunity to work more closely with Indy, I mean Ms. Frey-Marshall. I'm also good at accounting. *Lord, please don't let this get back to Phyllis.*

<Indy>: He's also good for the ego.

<Justin>: In a situation like this, you are still interviewing?

<Indy>: Daddy says you should arrange for things to keep going, even if you are hit by a truck.

How do you two know each other? *Mama made sure we found a place for him after you convinced his company to let him go. There was no way he was going to win your case if he had to tangle with Langstrom.*

<Justin>: He did some work for me once. He's definitely a straight shooter, and good with keeping confidences. We can discuss him later if you wish.

Forester, I will call you. We can discuss old times. *How much will I have to pay him to keep his mouth shut?*

<Indy>: [...] three, four, [...]

<Forester>: I'm sorry, but we were not introduced.

<Indy>: That's Gunnar. He helped us with Daddy last night. They were leaving.

<Forester>: Hello. I'm Clarence Forester.

[...] Sorry about your arm. We'll shake some other time, right boss?

<Indy>: You're still consulting for Jonas. We'll see how this goes.

<Justin>: Come along Andy. Let the woman do her work.

<Forester>: I'm sorry about your father. If you need a shoulder to cry on, mine are [...]

<Indy>: Shut the door. We have a lot to cover.

<Forester>: It will be my pleasure. **They went in meeting room. Big one is in bad shape.**

<Indy>: **That was very close!** *Damn Helena!*

<Forester>: **Bad timing. Did I do all right?**

<Indy>: **Machi would approve.**

---------- ----------

<Gunnar>: What happened? You lost your cool again and your artificial tan.

<Justin>: How could you notice? Randy "Andy" is thunderstruck.

<Gunnar>: That is not true. I like snobbier, dumber, weaker, and needier like Helena. They are easier to handle.

<Justin>: That is a practical answer. Even so, it doesn't matter. Until "your type" walked in, she seemed willing to tolerate you in spite of what WE gave done to her father. However, she treats you like a kid, and your association with Ms. Styles moved you into the negative points range.

<Gunnar>: You're the "Boy". She treats you like a buffoon.

<Justin>: A buffoon that touched a sore spot. Let's speak to the natives.

<Dan>: If you are referring to me, I haven't been the least bit buffoonish recently. Justin is the buffoon of the day. We have the memo. Why are we still waiting?

<Justin>: We should still spend a few minutes on the script. Everything must go perfectly tomorrow morning.

<Gunnar>: ***She's laughing again, and that sounds like a real one.***

<Dan>: I didn't know Indy was down there.

<Justin>: She is interviewing someone named Forester. It seems to be going very well.

<Dan>: ***Busted. No, he thinks she's interviewing.*** Today!

<Justin>: It seemed strange to me too.

<Dan>: His contract must be up, and she didn't want to lose him. Jonas says he's not particularly brilliant, but he's very persistent, like their mother. That is about the highest compliment he can give.

<Gunnar>: ***I can be persistent too.***

<Justin>: ***He must have changed since he bungled the case for me. On the other hand, Langstrom was very persistent too, and he'd been going it longer. You'd think it was personal.***

Maybe she's interested in something other than his brilliance.

<Dan>: I doubt it. I don't believe he's her type, but maybe she doesn't have a type anymore. Forester practices being arrogant and he's bulked up a little, but he has to go a bit before he catches Ryan.

<Justin>: ***A ray of hope. Gunnar will be back in the gym by the beginning of the week, contusions and all.***

He'll also need a satellite office on this floor so that he can work more closely with Marshall's people (person is more like it). Ms. Styles could be replaced by Ms. Frump.

<Dan>: [...] She is calling now.

[...] Indy, we were discussing you. We heard you laughing. That's good.

[...] I'm in the conference room with Justin and Gunnar.

[...] We know. Val and Macedon are as happy as you and your family, and I'm close behind.

[...] If you kept extra batteries, you'd have known before we did. How is your interview going?

[...] He should be able to handle the tax area very nicely. If you decide to keep him around, tell him I said congratulations.

[...] I talked to him at the picnic. Let me go. Mittelman was about to fill us in on some more good news.

[...] I believe that he was being honest. You should see today's correspondence.

[...] We will move slowly, and we will see whether things work out.

<Justin and Gunnar>: What happened?

<Dan>: She heard the good news about her father, and she picked up a man to handle their company taxes, so she'll have more time to work on financing.

She thinks you and Gunnar were almost sincere when you apologized for Sharf and this entire fiasco. We have to wait and see how her parents will respond.

[...] Could we speculate later? Val is ready to fall over, even with Macedon propping him up. Also, I promised to let Ms. Maçon's kids play in the conference room while she works on a "new" Communications Program.

<Justin>: Mrs. Piccolo's marital status is now in the open dear silly brother-in-law.

[...] The alternative was for Gunnar to keep believing that I am Octavia's father. She looked a lot more like my father and me when she was a baby.

<Dan>: You never saw Octavia when she was a baby, and why did you care? ***That was today's dumb question.***

<Justin>: Gunnar is willing to use serious blackmail to avoid a sticky situation. He probably knows how often you and Marshall jaywalk.

<Gunnar>: Marshall doesn't jaywalk. He never knows if his leg would give out.

<Justin>: As I was saying [...]

<Dan>: I'm sure we have a few things that Gunnar would not want us to share. Can we call it a draw? ***I'll put him through a shredder when no one is looking. Machi will provide guidance.***

<Justin>: It's better than a draw. We feel certain that Mr. Gunnar will pay closer attention to Mrs. Piccolo's communications, and he will support Marshall's complete program in the future.

<Gunnar>: ***I'll type Liz's speeches if I can use them to buy time with Indy. I have to learn to type first.***

<Dan>: ***Sure! And I'm going to grow eight more inches.*** Let's call the other natives.

CHAPTER XIV - RAISING CANE FOR WFSOA

----------Isaiah Cane's Office at Belvedere----------

Isaiah Cane>: Nicola, is that you under there? Why do you need a cloak in October, and those dark glasses?

BURYING KAHN

<Machi>: Who are you, and why are you on your knees?

<Izzy>: You know who I am. My voice didn't change. Close the door.

<Machi>: Dear God! You are alive. I have three of you back in one day!

<Izzy>: What three?

<Machi>: H is coming back to me again, he forgave my father, and I have you back.

<Izzy>: How can you be so certain about H?

<Machi>: I feel it, deep within.

<Izzy>: *You checked the pilot light already. I wonder how you managed that.* It's time that you and your father made up, and I'm Izzy, not Ike.

<Machi>: Where is Ike Kahn?

<Izzy>: I'm in here, but it is well hidden I hope.

<Machi>: Everything is insane. You were my oldest friend, and you are no longer you. What happened after I left?

<Izzy>: Are you going to cry right here, right now? You gave that up.

<Machi>: I don't have to worry about any more miscarriages.

<Izzy>: Does that mean you need your brutal shrink again? I can do that, in spite of the fact that you deserted me.

<Machi>: You ran out on me first.

<Izzy>: I came back when you needed me.

<Machi>: I tried, but you were "dead" already.

<Izzy>: I know. But, both leavings turned out for the best. You have your Zeus mutt, the four wunderkinds, and the plans in the combustion-proof safe. I have this and many things that came with it.

<Machi>: I needed a favor too, but it's too late for that. I may settle for a hug, as soon as I decide whether your new features need to be updated. Many special people owe me favors.

<Izzy>: I apologize for everything, absolutely everything. Now can I get off these old knees, which you may remember are technically a few years older than yours?

<Machi>: How much apologizing do you need to do?

<Izzy>: I'm sorry about what Sharf tried to do to H. He was supposed to get our foot in the door that Acton kept shutting on us. He was also a way to ease back into my family. Sharf was a serious mistake on my part, and I swear I will make it up to every Frey-Marshall, even the one who isn't born yet. I still love all of you as much as I love my life.

<Machi>: That's why I'm not sure it's you. Why would you send Sharf anywhere near us when you know what he tried to do to Simone all those years ago?

<Izzy>: What did he do to Simone? When? We can go and splay him now.

<Machi>: Did you have a lobotomy when they were reconstructing your jaw?

<Izzy>: I haven't seen you so angry since the teaching assistant tinkered with Simone's grades.

<Machi>: What do you suppose that we are discussing? The person you just apologized for is the person that wanted Simone to perform extra tasks for her grades.

<Izzy>: How could Billy Bastard Sharky be the same person as William Benson Sharf?

<Machi>: You remember!

<Izzy>: ***How was I supposed to know that they were the same person?*** Neither one of you ever told me his real name. You also never mentioned that he was a lanky giant.

<Machi>: Let me think.

[...] There was a lot of depersonalization, and his height was normal to me. I was the midget in the bunch.

Get up.

<Izzy>: Give me a minute. They fixed the face, but they can't fix the arthritis without a new knee. H and I will have more in common.

<Machi>: Like Deborah?

<Izzy>: Like Devora. Mother hated "Deborah". H started his knee research again after my mother had her knee fixed. I know many other things if you are willing to listen.

<Machi>: Go ahead.

<Izzy>: The first time I saw you, you were one month old, and I was three years old. I thought your parents had brought my sister a pretty, new doll, except that you moved on your own, and you could cry more ways than her old doll. You also knew how to turn milk yellow, instantly. I wanted you for myself.

My doll was my best friend until 14 years ago, not counting the five-month glitch after we broke our engagement, and you were trying to corral Zeus.

We were engaged on your 19th birthday, the day after I passed my CPA exam. The ring was exactly 2.5 carats. I stayed with my parents for a year after I graduated so I could afford to pay for it.

Five years after the engagement, on the day you received the notice that you had passed the bar exam and the day of the evening when we were supposed to establish a wedding date, you came by our house to pick up swatches of the silk material we had chosen for the brides maids gowns.

Rather than disturb my self-expression, you left the ring and the ombre silk fabric swatches in one of the crystal goblets we had chosen for the bridal registry. Langstrom found them during an intermission.

You were not willing to be as tolerant as Langstrom's wife was, but you let me convince you to wear the ring until we could create an acceptable reason to break up.

You and Zeus created the reason. He named her Indira. Your parents, not knowing what we knew, wanted us to (a) pretend that we had eloped, or (b) correct your hormonal imbalance.

You refused, they disowned you, and you both came close to losing your minds (H more so than you) after you nearly lost Simone anyhow. Clara and I had to reach in and yank you both out by your hair.

You refuse to accept that Joseph and Rachel were trying to protect their daughter from a fate they believed was horrible - life with an impoverished, undereducated, handicapped nobody who was the wrong religion and was riding the color bar.

Now, not counting Huey and Becky, Zeus is doing five times as well as Joseph's import business did on a good day. Why does he still torture himself?

[...] ***What's wrong with you?***

<Machi>: He's still trying to impress me. I nearly killed him.

<Izzy>: Stop that. You sound like you did when we broke up, and the water will ruin the color transitions in the ombre silk. That would be totally unacceptable.

I got you! You almost smiled.

<Machi>: H delayed the operation because of me. He suffered so much. The scar is four feet long this time.

<Izzy>: *Guzman said it was gruesome.*

I'll make this lighter. We call HM's "Baby Girl" Simone because I sat with you and listened to Nina Simone when you were so pregnant that you needed help to get out of a chair. H was trying to handle two jobs on two canes.

I nearly dropped Simone the first time she let out a Marshall laugh. He was tied up at work. He didn't hear it until two weeks later.

Jonas got his name because he grew in the belly of our favorite whale (you were bigger with him than with Simone). He weighed almost 10 pounds. He was

Fuzzy Wuzzy, Jr. because he had a mat of blond hair from the beginning and peach fuzz all over.

You almost died carrying the twins. You were too short and too old to carry 11-1/2 pounds of babies. You were flat on your back for the last month, and they had to take them early anyhow. You let them tie your tubes while they were in there.

As much as Marshall worried about being sterile, he had a vasectomy to be double certain. He was feeling friskier with his new knee (I never understood how that was possible), he didn't want to lose you, and he never wanted to do what your parents suggested to correct your original "planning" glitch.

<Machi>: That was not a glitch. We moved the plan two years ahead on purpose.

<Izzy>: *He always sent your logic out the window.* Pipsqueak weighed a little less than five pounds, but he had the loudest squeal any of us had ever heard. They say his voice is as deep as H's now, but I never heard that version. You sent him to Andover after he had the run-ins with your friends at the station house.

The ex-A.D.A.'s son was trying to prove that he was your average every-day multi-lingual freak, so he could hang with his friends. That happened at the same time that they almost sent Zeus to jail.

Don't look so surprised. I kept track.

The tiny queen was completely healthy, except that you worried that she was deaf like Jonas, or she had a speech problem like Pipsqueak. She was quiet, intense, and methodical. She could conduct sign language conversations by the time she was a year old. You were both elated when she started singing the gospel songs that Clara taught her, but she never bothered to talk to anyone except Clara until she was four.

<Machi>: That's enough. You might have stopped with the vasectomy part. H was too upset to tell anyone else.

Open the third and fourth buttons on your shirt and remove the sock on your left foot.

<Izzy>: The scar from the gall bladder surgery is still here - see -, and so is the raspberry birthmark on my heel.

[...] there it is.

<Machi>: Talk to me about Sharky.

<Izzy>: Do you know Niklas Gunnar?

<Machi>: Gunnar is one of the reasons I was almost arrested yesterday, and why I need my shrink.

<Izzy>: Are you the unfortunate accident that happened to Gunnar?

<Machi>: I was in the vicinity when he tripped and injured himself a few times.

<Izzy>: I see. Are you still ranked?

<Machi>: Third among seniors and much further down for women, but I didn't play fair. H's cane was available for a brief period before my chubby Fuzzy Wuzzy made it disappear. Val and two policemen fell into it too.

<Izzy>: Since when does one attack H's anchorman?

<Machi>: Val was an accident. He miscalculated the arc on a moving object. Why am I explaining? You're the culprit. Tell me what you did.

<Izzy>: Gunnar called Diamonte, the owner, and Paul passed the call to me. Gunnar said he would soon be in charge of Daxiao's Audit committee, and he wanted to investigate options for keeping Acton on their toes.

Mallory had died two months earlier, and I leaped at the opportunity, especially since I would have an opportunity to tickle your Titan. With Mallory gone, there was no one to remind me of how insane I was to get involved with you again.

<Machi>: Who is Mallory?

<Izzy>: He guided the creation of Izzy.

<Machi>: *He must have really been angry with us.* You guilted H and me for nine years. After you explain Sharky, explain how you went from dead Isaac Kahn to live Isaiah Cane, at least for the next few minutes.

<Izzy>: Only if you will tell me why my best friend deserted me after 50 years. I have a letter in my safe that I have been trying to understand for 14 years. It says, "I will always love you, and that is why it will be better for all concerned if we part ways. You will always be in my heart if not in my life". Did H make you do that?

<Machi>: Why would H do that?

<Izzy>: I asked you first.

<Machi>: It was Jerry. He really, really didn't like me. He said I was a selfish "person" who was using you to fill in the gaps that H couldn't or wouldn't fill. He said that H was only good for filling one gap.

<Izzy>: Jerry could be crude.

<Machi>: He begged me to give you a chance to have a full life. He said I never gave H a chance to be a real father to his first two kids, and they were grown already. He said we had time for Patrick and Patricia.

After that, we smothered the babies with too much attention, and they rebelled.

[...] Why are you acting so surprised?

<Izzy>: If he wasn't dead, he would be.

<Machi>: You've hit a violent patch too. What are you talking about and what are you taking?

<Izzy>: Anxiety medicine.

<Machi>: Still hooked after all these years. What happened with Jerry?

<Izzy>: I finally understand what happened. I was asking him to commit, and you were supposed to fight for your original, while hanging on to your red-hot back up. Then he would have had an excuse to do what he intended to do anyhow. He cleaned out my accounts and our house - half of it is still yours - and he went off to die in luxury.

<Machi>: I was using you. We were using you.

<Izzy>: Maybe, but you gave as much as you got. I had a family. H and I liked each other. If I wasn't like me, he wouldn't have had you. I was the older brother that he wished Richard was, and he was a sibling who wasn't ashamed of me. You remember how and Lea and Abe avoided me.

<Machi>: They liked you.

<Izzy>: It was more important to be in Abe's will. Now they're taking care of him, and they won't get a cent unless my estate gives them have my half of our house.

<Machi>: I didn't know you and Jerry had separated. Are you [...] all right?

<Izzy>: Yes. Jerry saved my life by leaving. Maybe I shouldn't want to kill him.

[...] Let's talk about my grandchildren.

<Machi>: I'm not finished. After I heard about Jerry, I asked Langstrom about you. He said that you had succumbed to a painful bout with Karposi's sarcoma, which explained why you disappeared two years before you died. We've been putting flowers on your grave and donating to your favorite charity for the last nine years.

<Izzy>: It was part of the transition. Mallory's lawyer made sure that Langstrom, my family, and a few of Jerry's acquaintances found out about my premature departure. It was close enough to Jerry, that nobody asked any questions.

<Machi>: I retrieved your photographic equipment from your father after Devora died. He was afraid to touch it. He still believes that I destroyed your life by running off with H the first time and that I killed you by moving out of the way to let you have a life with Jerry.

<Izzy>: *They couldn't accept that* [...]

Could I have the equipment back? I can still use the Mamya.

<Machi>: You are definitely Ike.

<Izzy>: I'm Izzy.

<Machi>: Your father was also annoyed that Simone and Jonas got the proceeds of your life insurance policy. We didn't know anything about an insurance policy.

<Izzy>: He'll touch my money, but he wouldn't touch me. The proceeds from our house are in trust for him, but he's still greedy. By the way, the house is worth $2.5 million now.

<Machi>: I know. I checked on that when I checked on the insurance policy.

Forget about then. How long have you been here? When did you do the alphabet swap?

<Izzy>: The alphabet swap was part of the transition too. Ike Kahn the IRS auditor became Izzy Cane the senior tax advisor in an effectively executed real life second life strategy. Mallory suggested it, and it worked.

<Machi>: Who is Mallory and why would you agree to his recommendations?

<Izzy>: Mallory is the person who gave me tax work after Jerry left, which is four months after you and Marshall became unavailable, and I stopped forcing Val to make excuses for you.

Losing all the important people in my life, 10 if you count babies and grandchildren, depressed me so much that I lost my job at the IRS. Even Langstrom couldn't protect me.

I was so desperate, not to mention lonely, that I almost sold the ring to get money to pay taxes on the house. Mallory loaned me the money after he knew me for only a month.

Here's the ring.

[...] It's all right to touch it. Your hands are a little less smooth, but it should still fit.

<Machi>: Now I understand why you would want to hurt us, but I was trying to do the right thing for you. You really liked Jerry, I thought you were finally about to settle into a stable relationship, and I didn't want to do anything to hurt the relationship.

<Izzy>: ***I DID NOT want to hurt you.*** Jerry was right about me needing a good relationship, but it was with Mallory. Together, we made the external adjustments that positioned me to be here. He'd done it himself.

<Machi>: How did you become Belvedere snob material? It's a long way from Simms to hand-tailored worsted with a touch of silk, I would guess. You were always obsessed with silk.

<Izzy>: If you spend 27 years helping the government collect taxes where they might not have, you're well positioned to give advice on how to avoid unnecessary taxes, especially if you contributed significantly to code revisions.

Mallory hired me after a year, and he took me under his wing after the second. Maybe I should say we flew off together.

He was tired as I am now, and he wanted stability. Written beneath his wing was advice on how to make life transitions and sophisticated options for acting upon life's preferences.

<Machi>: You definitely did a lot of adjustments. How did you manage without anyone noticing?

<Izzy>: I was one of the first telecommuters while the physical adjustments were happening.

People burn out quickly doing taxes, so by the end of the 5th year, nobody was with Mallory who remembered how I looked when I started.

Other than you, H, Langstrom, and the Van Ambergs, most of my friends were usually the friends of my friends. Jerry took his with him.

<Machi>: Was the slicing and dicing necessary?

<Izzy>: It was an optional, but beneficial, part of the transition. More people listen to financial advice delivered by an ageless international finance wizard with square jaws than will listen to an old tax accountant with a weak chin.

Handsome Cane enhanced Mallory's reputation by helping people limit their exposure to the code that ordinary Kahn write.

<Machi>: When did you and Mallory part ways?

<Izzy>: Two months ago when he died [...]

<Machi>: From?

<Izzy>: Being old. He was 84, but he appeared to be an artificial 65.

<Machi>: How was he related to Belvedere?

<Izzy>: When he was ready to retire, Acton acquired his company. Acton already had a huge tax division. I was finally hitting my stride, and I could have handled the politics, but I didn't want to take a chance on running into Simone.

Belvedere needed more strength in the tax area, and Mallory made them an offer they didn't refuse. They bought my unit, and Mallory "lent" me the money from the sale so that I could become a partner. I brought over good people and Belvedere gave me a few hot shots, including Sharky [...] Sharf.

I was almost as good as H at making average people look good, and good people really shine. As a result, 20% of Belvedere belongs to me.

<Machi>: I've missed a lot, and I am sorry I couldn't share it with you. Why did you wait until now?

<Izzy>: Whenever I considered breaking the silence, Mallory reminded me of how miserable I was when he hired me. He was helping me up and over. You helped me down and out. I decided to stay in touch without touching.

<Machi>: What do you mean?

<Izzy>: I told you I kept track of things.

- Today Randy wore one of his father's football parkas to school - he's tall enough (like his mother), but not quite broad enough.
- Ryan spoils both of his kids because he's afraid to do anything that would make them stop wanting to see him.
- Sandy looks a lot like her grandmother, except that she is almost six inches taller. When she stopped growing, she was an inch shorter than Mr. Coffee was, and he was elated.
- Mr. Coffee grew another inch for good measure, but he's still two inches shorter than Queen-2.
- O'Malley and I helped Pipsqueak's juvenile problems disappear. O'Malley still remembers that you made sure some of the really bad folks remained guests of the state.
- Though Queen-2 didn't need my help, I was able to promote her singing and dancing abilities to Girard. He still remembers you.
- Randy and Sandy are doing much better than their mother who hasn't recovered from being blond-sided by their father.

<Machi>: Where do you get all this?

<Izzy>: I watch and I listen. The condo that I own on Greenwich St. is cramped, but I can tell you what time Randy and Sandy get to school at least two days a week. They don't remember me.

<Machi>: They would remember you if you looked like yourself. I showed them pictures.

<Izzy>: Where did Simone find a "Black Potato Sacks "R" Us" outlet?

<Machi>: You haven't been paying perfect attention. Two thirds of them are either dark gray or dark blue. She has them custom tailored.

<Izzy>: I helped her out of her worries about being a freak. When did she slip backwards?

<Machi>: Ryan messed with her head. She lost the love of her life several times and a modeling career after she went through the trouble trying to look as perfect as the bimbos that he kept marching in front of her.

<Izzy>: Why would she bother? She finally put on the weight that goes with her height.

<Machi>: She needed to show the world that she was not an overweight, overgrown freak, as Ryan called her when he was trying to justify his bimbette adventures.

<Izzy>: She's as crazy as you are.

<Machi>: We know, but Ryan had been the sole arbiter of her self-image for all of her adult life. It was hard for her to take back control.

<Izzy>: It's just as well. Models require more than stunning beauty to do well, as Pipsqueak is proving.

<Machi>: Simone had more than stunning beauty. She and your Merle were making inroads with top-of-the-line travel companies, in her spare time, until a Ryan bimbette tried to convince him to take a South Pacific cruise to celebrate his divorce.

<Izzy>: You mean my friend Merle. Pure friendships are possible.

<Machi>: Mia culpa. Anyway, the bimbette showed Ryan a very tasteful Merle brochure with Simone bareback and getting a massage (from Merle), Simone apparently dressed only in her hair in a wood-paneled suite (with Merle), Simone having a romantic dinner and drinking Dom grape juice (with

Merle), Simone on a secluded beach wearing a bikini that Merle designed especially for Simone (with Merle), Simone dancing in the moonlight in a very diaphanous dress (with Merle), and Simone and the twins walking along a beach (with Merle).

<Izzy>: They would make a gorgeous family. I hear that Merle chose the handsome gray-haired route. He must look as handsome as H.

<Machi>: He's close.

<Izzy>: They probably sold a lot of cruises. Why did she stop?

<Machi>: Ryan accused her of inappropriate activities, and of exposing the twins to the wrong environments? When she suggested that he should learn how to do some very painful contortions with himself, he threatened to sue for custody of Randy and Sandy.

<Izzy>: That leads back to "Black Potato Sacks "R" Us". *I messed that up too.*

I got the impression that she wasn't doing well because she is too muscular and her body proportions were wrong. She wears at least a size 12/10 on most days.

<Machi>: The sizes are right, but the impression is wrong. Who told you that?

<Izzy>: Around the time that H got in trouble a few years ago, I began hanging around with Ryan. It was a way to keep tabs on you up close, and being a sports insider improves my masculine image. Ryan and I cry over beer after his broadcasts.

When I say he cries in his beer, I mean it. We both lost Frey women.

<Machi>: You're dealing with another fool who hurt my baby. He gave Simone away three times.

<Izzy>: This isn't going to be pretty, is it?

<Machi>: She gave him two chances to come in from the cold, she caught him in action after the first return, and holding the stomach of bubble bimba the second time.

<Izzy>: *He didn't mention that she gave him two chances.* Ryan was not the father of the bimbette's baby. He proved that.

<Machi>: He could have been. Bubble bimba and Ryan participated in the most memorable of the endurance videos that the investigator produced.

<Izzy>: *Poor Baby Girl.* She didn't have to go into mourning to keep the kids if she had details regarding his adventures.

<Machi>: This isn't mourning. She had a Simone tantrum, and that is worse than a Machi tantrum when she realized that Ryan was tacking on the custody fight to prolong the divorce process. She has already wasted the last 3-1/2 years of her life.

<Izzy>: It must have been horrible. What else did she do to him?

<Machi>: You mean what else is she doing?

He tortured her for five years, and she will torture him for five years and one month. It is coincidental that his five years of torture will end three months after Randy and Sandy go off to college, and he won't be able to threaten her with a custody battle, even one that he couldn't win after the evidence that our investigators found.

<Izzy>: Are you talking about the ones that had the military-grade infrared telephoto equipment? How many agencies have that kind of equipment?

<Machi>: H has an employee who knows people that would do what it took to keep us from losing our grandchildren.

<Izzy>: What is she still doing to him?

<Machi>: If he cries in his beer, literally, I'm surprised that he hasn't told you what is happening, unless he doesn't know what is happening.

<Izzy>: She seems to be doing absolutely nothing.

<Machi>: That's the tantrum. The next time you sneak a peak at Simone, notice that every one of her black/blue/gray potato sacks is cut to provide maximum emphasis on everything that she is covering so expertly. The hoods frame her face perfectly. She wears perfect non-make up. Merle taught her how to do that, and she was one of his best students.

She keeps sit-down exercise kits in both offices because she is determined that every ounce of fat will be exactly where it will have maximum effect, even if it is only for 90 seconds four time a month when Ryan delivers the kids.

He doesn't have to pick them up, but he makes sure that he brings them home late at night when Simone should be ready for bed. She has the sexiest coverall black pajamas that were ever specially designed for a woman.

She makes sure that he gets at least 30 seconds of the enhanced panther pace in the black pajamas.

Ryan always loved hair, and he found out later that a blond with even a third as much hair as Simone probably isn't a true blond. Meanwhile, Simone let her hair grow again. It reaches the bend in her knee when she lets it down. Strands of hair with glistening white streaks stray perfectly [...]

<Izzy>: He told me this part. She loops it around her neck with enough left over to reach her belly button, which often peeks out between the top and the bottom of the black pajamas. There is just enough to remind him of what he lost. It drives him crazy.

<Machi>: There's more. She encourages the kids to carry containers of their favorite foods when they visit their father. Ryan loved the Indo-Trinidadian Soul Food that The Queen and Clara taught Simone to cook.

<Izzy>: When does she have time to cook?

<Machi>: She doesn't. We invested $2,000,000 when Samuel wanted to upgrade, and now he always has someone around who knows how to prepare a meal exactly as Simone would. In a pinch, Samuel will prepare a few courses himself. The restaurant press raves about his creativity, which is actually Simone's creativity, we are making money, and she is working on every one of his senses.

<Izzy>: *Tantalus!* It's the worst torture imaginable. I believe the psychological term for it is variable reinforcement.

He won't marry one of the bimbettes, or even Jacky, even though the kids say Jacky is all right.

<Machi>: Maybe if he understood what she's doing, he'd finish what he started (three times), and she can move on with her life.

<Izzy>: I'll summarize, using Ryan's words. Where will he look to find a stunningly beautiful freak (like the one he always loved) that is a brilliant professional multi-millionaire, and can play in both opera/art/dance circles and in sports circles? She knows her way around the kitchen (even if it's not her own), and has access to your planning safe.

It appears that the bimbettes tend to exhaust their creativity in about a month and their endurance runs out soon after that.

<Machi>: Except for a few dollars extra dollars, she hasn't changed - maybe she lost 20 pounds. Why did he hurt her the way he did?

<Izzy>: He was hurting. He knew he was coming apart. He needed what the bimbettes offered. They still idolized the image of Ryan Winslow or his money.

<Machi>: What was she supposed to do while he was being idolized?

<Izzy>: He listened to the wrong locker room wisdom. He honestly believed that she would stay at home and wait for him as many sports wives do, especially if he could make her feel insecure.

<Machi>: I suppose that he decided to use another tactic when he saw the cruise brochure.

<Izzy>: She's still at home, even though it's not his home, so he holds on to the stupid idea.

<Machi>: After three strikes, you're out. That's a sportsman-like way of describing the situation.

<Izzy>: He figures that as long as the kids like him, he can get another time at bat. H helps recently by getting himself hospitalized frequently. Then he tries to be the world's most supportive ex-son-in-law.

<Machi>: How often do you notice that he's holding on to his fantasies?

<Izzy>: We could start at yesterday and work backward. We skipped the beer and I spent the evening with Ryan, my grandchildren, and the replacement whale. Becky is giving you a run for the money.

I heard blow-by-blow updates from Jonas while you were getting your beauty rest, except that he failed to mention your blows on Gunnar.

<Machi>: [...] *I don't believe it!* You were the old jock that Ryan brought along, and the imaginary Ike that only Ryan and the kids can see!

<Izzy>: It works. They think I'm as crazy as Simone and Jonas once did. I'm going to miss them.

<Machi>: Don't stop until we work out what needs working out. It appears that Simone already extracted her revenge. She'll be unstuck in 21 months, we hope.

<Izzy>: Thank you.

<Machi>: *He's trying not to cry. He still loves us, so why would he send Sharf after us.* Can we return to Sharf and Gunnar?

<Izzy>: Gunnar asked for the best people I had. I suggested Grayson. He's a good accountant with exceptional technical credentials. Sharf is an exceptional accountant with lukewarm technical credentials, but he got SOA on his résumé first. Somehow, Sharf bubbled to the top of Gunnar's list.

<Machi>: Might that be because Sharf is Gunnar's brother-in-law?

<Izzy>: OOH!

[...] I slipped on that too. Maybe I was too anxious. Why didn't you mention it when you called?

<Machi>: I believed I should at least exchange a few platitudes while I tried to figure out where your head was and how badly you wanted to get even with us, if you were the same person.

<Izzy>: I would never [...]

<Machi>: I needed to be convinced.

<Izzy>: I worked with him for almost nine years to smooth the "sharfness". Until yesterday, I thought he was worth the effort. He plays adequately, with tutoring.

<Machi>: I was right to be leery of you. I still don't understand why you deal with the two people that hurt Simone the most, even before Sharky tried to destroy H?

<Izzy>: Simone is hurting herself to punish Ryan, just as you do with your parents. I told you I didn't know about Sharf.

<Machi>: You may be right about Simone and Ryan. She should move on and let him move on.

<Izzy>: *I think they still love each other, but I wouldn't dare to say that now.* I know I'm right about your parents too. They apologized and begged for forgiveness. Mine never did.

<Machi>: Have you been hanging around with Pat?

<Izzy>: Ryan goes to see Clara every time he gets an inkling that Simone might show up, and you can't see Clara without seeing Ray and Joe. Clara makes them hide when Simone actually shows up. Ryan says they've papered their walls with pictures of your kid(s) - notice the plural - and the grandchildren, especially Simone, Pat, and Randy.

<Machi>: The brownest ones! You're lying.

<Izzy>: The prettiest ones. Your parents don't claim to be on the vanguard of cultural enlightenment, but they know pretty grandchildren when they see them.

<Machi>: What would have happened if they had been as plain as David's kids were?

<Izzy>: They weren't, so we will never know. They love their grandchildren and their great grandchildren, all of them. They loved you too much. That's how this all started.

<Machi>: You can stop preaching. H forgave them. Now Simone is the only holdout.

<Izzy>: That is reasonable. Simone won't understand Rachel until Sandy or Randy must make tough choices, if they ever have to make such choices.

<Machi>: Bite your tongue.

<Izzy>: Let's change the topic. Does Simone know that Sharky - Sharf - works for me?

<Machi>: She knows that he works for Isaiah Cane. After we saw a picture of Sharf and Sharf's boss, H said he remembered seeing you, but he didn't know where. Simone was in the middle of a tiff with Sandy, so she didn't pay much attention after she gagged at the sight of Sharf.

<Izzy>: But you recognized me?

<Machi>: There were enough hints that I decided to do further research.

You have a moderately impressive monument, which is two sections over from your family's plot, but there was no funeral exactly a year before the monument was placed. I found an obituary, but as I mentioned before, I couldn't find a copy of your death certificate.

However, the real give-away was the bottom half of that picture of Palisades that you took on our balcony. Trees are blocking part of the view now, but I still remembered. That's what I came to see.

<Izzy>: You helped me blow it up. It's still a great conversation piece.

<Machi>: Why doesn't Ryan know?

<Izzy>: I never give him a reason to come here. He may have seen Ike twice, and both times, I was hanging out with the ladies and goo- gooing the grandchildren.

Fast forward a few years, 70 stitches, liposuction, and a physical trainer, and I'm another sports hanger-on who can afford to run with his crowd. By the way, I approve of the way he handles the kids. He's a fool, but he is a good father.

<Machi>: You are right about the fool part. Simone was doing what she saw me doing all her life - showing him how to work within the limits of his injuries, and he kept flashing the bimbettes in her face.

<Izzy>: The bimbettes thought he was "whole". He didn't want to be a crip like her father.

<Machi>: Is that what he calls H?

<Izzy>: Only until he had the last parts lashed back together. That's when H became "our father". He says that with reverence.

<Machi>: You're still defending Ryan.

<Izzy>: [...] I'm saying that, at this moment, she has 100% of nothing, while he can have 100% of a lot of things that he doesn't want. Happiness is a-wasting.

<Machi>: H and I agree about wasting time, and we told her.

<Izzy>: Thanks for saying that. For a moment, I worried that we were about to bury Izzy.

<Machi>: *We still have time. I love you, but I love H more.* How would you defend Sharf?

<Izzy>: I told you that I stopped defending Sharf when the Sharky traits appeared.

<Machi>: What about Gunnar?

<Izzy>: I believe he wanted to position himself to take over whatever H left. He didn't know what there was to take over, and he didn't feel that he could stroll into H's office and ask him. At the same time, he was scared that H was smothering him with a clear odorless gas called SOA.

<Machi>: What about five years ago when Gunnar tried to send H to jail. Gunnar initiated the collection of the incriminating evidence.

<Izzy>: Are you talking about when H had time for himself for the first time in 33 years (other than medical leave), and you used that free time to boost Huey into the exosphere?

<Machi>: We thought H was going to have a heart attack.

<Izzy>: H was 100 pounds overweight. He could have had a heart attack anyhow.

<Machi>: Now you're defending Gunnar.

<Izzy>: Gunnar told me that he cleaned up everything after he found out that an employee he inherited had a vendetta going against H.

<Machi>: He was supposed to handle the details, and he farmed it out instead.

<Izzy>: Did he know H then?

<Machi>: No. He was taking cues from Mittelman.

<Izzy>: Langstrom took Mittelman to the cleaners.

<Machi>: Langstrom knows you're alive.

<Izzy>: No. The case was all over the tax circuits. Because of that discovery, Langstrom was promoted to one of the top spots in the region.

<Machi>: Back to Gunnar.

<Izzy>: I doubt that he would waste time on someone about whom he knew nothing, unless there was identifiable return. At the time, the return was to curry favor with Mittelman. If you're going after anyone, it should be Mittelman.

<Machi>: I sent the anonymous tip that contributed to Langstrom's discovery of Mittelman's financial shenanigans. The $2,000,000 that Mittelman paid in back taxes is relatively unimportant. The sweet part is that he will be challenged any time he has to pass another financial evaluation. I am rather convinced that he passes on the CEO spot because of that.

<Izzy>: I trained you too well. What about Gunnar.

<Machi>: I will leave Gunnar near the bottom of the list for the time being - again. ***I was working on something extra special for Gunnar five years ago, but then Maja told me about the divorce, his rehab, and his problems with his daughter. I planned to wait until he got better, but H started doing so well that I decided to skip it.***

Meanwhile, he saved H's life, and yesterday may end up being in H's best interest. The thighbone was disintegrating.

<Izzy>: If you know that, why did you Machify Gunnar?

<Machi>: I thought H was dying, and I wanted to see him. Gunnar was blocking my access.

<Izzy>: Jonas seems to like him. That annoyed the heck out of Ryan.

<Machi>: I know, and Fuzzy Wuzzy 2 knows how to pick people who are right for Frey and Marshall.

I don't know why he likes Gunnar, but the only fun thoughts I've had all day included images of Gunnar tangling with Ryan. Ryan has been fighting ghosts that he can't see since Merle.

<Izzy>: Gunnar is not Simone's type.

<Machi>: Who would be Simone's type?

Jonas says the chemistry is there. A little discrete research and planning would be good for her. She doesn't have to circulate it in a brochure.

Saving H's life more than compensates for giving him anxiety attacks five years ago. We got his EVP because of that, and everybody backed off far enough for my Zeus to take over the company. They are fools.

She could keep an eye on him for her father and have some fun while she got back into the game. H won't be there, but she can make sure Gunnar doesn't destroy too many things.

She would know that he was going to move on eventually. Nothing he did would surprise her.

What am I saying? She'd stop talking to me, forever!

<Izzy>: I hadn't thought about that a lot.

<Machi>: Does Sharky know about Ike?

<Izzy>: Impossible. [...] Sharf's attractiveness causes him to receive attention from quarters that make him feel uncomfortable. He developed a phobia that borders on hatred. If he had any inkling about me, he'd have requested a transfer the first month I was here.

<Machi>: What does he believe he knows about you? My investigators say you have three babies. What do their mothers know that I didn't?

<Izzy>: My people believe I find them on business trips while I'm drunk. In reality, I know people who provide prenatal counseling to women who consider early termination and then change their minds.

Thus, I helped three young women out of difficulties that I didn't cause, in exchange for hastily arranged marriages.

<Machi>: You use them during their time of desperation.

<Izzy>: I offered business proposals and only 30% of them accepted.

Three were as disgusted as you look right now. I don't know how well they fared.

Three of the fathers changed their minds at the prospect of having their babies named Cane. None of them ran into the parental opposition that H did.

One tried to make it on her own. Eventually, she let me hire her to run my unit for me. Her office is near the door that you tried to sneak through.

<Machi>: She must know that you are Ike.

<Izzy>: Both she and Paul Diamonte understand that I had a special relationship with Dennis Mallory. Paul's only requirement is that I don't mix business and pleasure.

<Machi>: Your wives must cost you a fortune.

<Izzy>: Mallory taught me well. My pre-nups are written like consulting contracts, complete with DNA tests, and termination dates.

<Machi>: Why would anyone take a chance on this?

<Izzy>: They leave with pampered very loved munchkins, like the ones you had, one degree more than they had when I adopted them, if they have the inclination, a designer wardrobe (even the one that was built like Kabiri), a cultural upgrade, a few connections that they would not have had otherwise, trust funds (for Dennis, Haley, and Ronald), and young enough to have that full life that Jerry tricked you with.

Because I'm older than their fathers are, they tend to play around, and I catch them somewhere close to the termination date. The last one caught me with another woman. After a tearful encounter, we have uncontested divorces, and they move on to relationships with someone closer to their age.

Mallory died soon after the last tearful divorce.

<Machi>: Why did you go to such extremes?

<Izzy>: It fills in the gaps that you left when you took my children. It works for everyone, and I'm still friendly with everyone. This is my family photo. This is Dennis Cane (he's six). Haley Wooley on the left is eight (she was adopted by her mother's new husband). Ronald Cane is three.

That's Janice's daughter, Melissa. Janice runs the place for me. She's almost as good as Doc is.

<Machi>: Mr. and Mrs. Wooley rent our house.

<Izzy>: H would say that's an example of reuse. She's my first wife, and that's her second husband.

<Machi>: I'm not sure I like it.

<Izzy>: Fait accompli. Is there anything else I should know about Sharky?

<Machi>: He and Simone had a run-in when she was at Acton, and she was pregnant. It wasn't too bad because she was so busy rerouting her meals that she was in no shape to be on customer premises.

<Izzy>: That was during the blue whale pregnancy. She called him the pretty anaconda that time. What else?

<Machi>: It's not Simone. Sharf competed with H's people last year, but we didn't find out until this week.

<Izzy>: Daxiao didn't need to make a profit on their consulting, but we did. I tried to guide him away from those projects, but he was unusually persistent. Now I know why.

<Machi>: Why did you let him keep trying if you knew he wasn't likely to win against H?

<Izzy>: Competing with H was excellent training. My people learned by losing to him.

RAISING A TITANIC

<Machi>: With all these mistaken identities, Sharf really hurt us this time. Yesterday, he turned my baby Titan's career into the Titanic.

<Izzy>: Nonsense. Daxiao will mandate SOA implementation and expand the WFSOA Program. I will work to cover a few of Zeus's political bases while they test the new super glue. Mittelman says he may need three or four months before he goes back to work.

<Machi>: Why would H go back? Where is Ike?

<Izzy>: Izzy and Paul Diamonte, my boss, have been on the phone at least 3-1/2 hours today with either Justin Mittelman or Joe Guzman. They really want to fix this. We received this from Mittelman 18 minutes before you arrived. (See e-mail on the next page).

<Izzy>: I may have goofed with Sharf, but I helped you and HM in the long run.

<Machi>: *That is Plan A!*

That creates another problem. How much of a bonus will Sharf receive?

<Izzy>: He'll probably receive the usual amount, but perhaps a little more.

<Machi>: If you do that, you will delay a reward that I have prepared for him. If you are giving him cash advances, stop. If you are not giving him cash advances, don't start.

From: JMittelman@Daxiao.com
To: IsaiahCane@Belvedere.org; PaulDiamonte@Belvedere.org; HMarshall@Daxiao.com; JGuzman@Daxiao.com; Niklas_Gunnar@Daxiao.com
CC: Emery-Baldwin@Daxiao.com; VVanAmberg@Daxiao.com; DPiccolo@Daxiao.com; HYu@Daxiao.com; AEllison02@Daxiao.com; LMaçon@Daxiao.com; MJohanssen@Daxiao.com; AMacedon@Daxiao.com; WArmstrong@Daxiao.com; LJasper@Daxiao.com; MHiggins@Daxiao.com; LDawson@Daxiao.com; Marcella_Haines@Daxiao.com; JSampson@Daxiao.com; ROnesti@Daxiao.com; OReed@Daxiao.com; HStein@Daxiao.com; Timothy-Lazlow@Acton.org; Boardlist@Daxiao.com; RenataVitale@Belvedere.org; DesmondGrayson@Belvedere.org; WilliamSharf@Belvedere.org
Subj: WFSOA Mandate and Belvedere SOA Engagement

Mr. Cane.

This confirms that have we have signed the contract with Belvedere, as amended by Daxiao and Belvedere today.

Contract Summary:

Belvedere will provide management consulting to Daxiao for the fixed fee of $500,000. The work will begin officially on October 22 of this year and will be completed within six months. Belvedere will supply 400 person-days of consulting in addition to the four (4) days already provided. Belvedere will assume responsibility for all travel expenses.

Belvedere will supply an engagement manager with hands-on expertise in Service-Oriented Architecture. He or she will work with Daxiao to continue the global implementation of the already successful WFSOA Program that has been guided since its inception by Mr. Hamilton Marshall with assistance from Valery Van Amberg, Dr. Daniel Piccolo, Alex Macedon, and Weldon Armstrong. An official announcement of this joint effort will occur on Friday, October 19th at 8:00 A.M. in the boardroom at our Daxiao site in Far Hills, New Jersey.

The engagement manager will report to Valery Van Amberg, SVP, and Director of SOA Program Management, with a matrix relationship to Dr. Daniel Piccolo, our Corporate Architect. They will work on critical initiatives already identified by Hamilton Marshall, EVP of BASE (Business Achievement through Service Excellence).

The Belvedere engagement manager will be assisted by:

1. Belvedere advisors with expertise in interpersonal skills to assist Dr. T. Emery-Baldwin, SVP of Human Resources, with expansion of the WFSOA Cultural Change Management (resistance identification and mitigation).
2. Belvedere advisors with expertise in interpersonal communications skills to assist Corporate Communications in expanding the already effective WFSOA communications initiative. These people will work closely with the staff of Lisse Maçon, SVP of BASE communications and with Maja Johanssen. Every intersection in the BASE communications plan will be matched to information in the Knowledge Cooperative.
3. Belvedere advisors familiar with both SOA technology and the electronics industry to assist Requirements Management with clarification and promulgation of historical and continuing "WFSOA Lessons Learned". These people will work with Alexander Macedon, SVP - Information Logistics.

We would like to express our appreciation to Belvedere's employees, Mr. William Sharf and Renata Vitale, for their extraordinarily rapid recognition of Mr. Hamilton's insightful suggestions for Program improvement and expansion.

Due to Belvedere's exceptional performance, we have agreed to provide an immediate down payment of $250,000 against the total value of the contract. Our EVP of finance is arranging the transaction this afternoon. Expect a funds transfer drawn against our Research and Development account later today.

We look forward to a mutually rewarding relationship.

Justin Mittelman, President
Daxiao Electronics
999-888-9999, Ext. 1000

<Izzy>: What have you cooked up?

<Machi>: One of the banks with significant interests in three of Jonas's start-ups is associated with the mortgage company that holds Sharf's jumbo. We have a fourth company in the pipeline Sharf started missing mortgage payments after both of his sons started college, but the mortgage company has been lenient. Simone could convince them to become less lenient.

<Izzy>: With the market the way it is, he'd barely break even if he tried to sell the house. That would rearrange his entire life.

He has two children.

<Machi>: One is a year older than Indy was when Sharf tried to victimize her and the other is a year younger. Sharf could have messed up Indy's chances to go to graduate school or Jonas's chance to go to Strafford.

<Izzy>: Will you regret doing this later? William didn't actually hurt either Simone or H.

<Machi>: The legal term for what he did is intent. If someone aims a gun at your heart and fires it, should he walk away free because you had someone to pull you out of the way?

He thought she was helpless, and he could have affected her ability to earn her livelihood. How many girls on college basketball teams have us to back them up? Don't mention Ryan. There was no guarantee that he would get a professional contract, that he would marry her, or that he would guarantee the well-being of his children after he messed up.

Sharf wanted H to leave in disgrace after 38 years during which he actually worked about 60 years. How many people have Val, Macedon, Piccolo, and Maja to back them up?

Therefore, I have ***intent to even the score***, and I would like to ensure that you do not pull him out of the way.

Ike would have thought of something more devious and painful in this circumstance. I learned a lot from him.

<Izzy>: *I want my family, and I want to live.* I'm certain that I am more devious than I was then. However, when did you have time to start this?

<Machi>: I started as soon as I came to my senses, Tacky read me a copy of Sharf's pertinent memo, and Simone explained to Maja what happened after our initial intervention with Sharf.

<Izzy>: You never said anything about anything after Masters went down there with you.

<Machi>: Simone didn't say anything until this morning.

<Izzy>: What, and why?

<Machi>: Sharf accused her of going to the dean after all, he attacked her (he grabbed her and started shaking her) - and she broke her hand and his nose while she was trying to get away from him.

He threatened to get her kicked out of school for attacking him, and Ryan threaten to push him down a flight of steps. Nobody said anything.

It gets worse - this happened after The Queen had her stroke and four days before H had his knee fixed. You may remember that H almost didn't make it through that either.

<Izzy>: We agreed that she wouldn't go to the dean.

<Machi>: She didn't. The summary is that Sharf picked on people with more clout than Simone had, Simone showed them the carbon paper trick, they went to the dean, and Sharf lost an opportunity to get a PhD.

<Izzy>: Baby Girl made a mess.

<Machi>: You're blaming her too! That's why she was afraid to tell anyone. Now I have to go and apologize.

<Izzy>: She made a mess by not telling anyone that something happened that would make him so vindictive.

<Machi>: She thought all he had was a bloody nose. That happened to her teammates all the time.

Simone was given the impression that he left school to start making big money in the real world. She had less of a clue because the dean and the faculty kept everything quiet while they lamented the loss of such a brilliant academician to the business world - no grading scandal.

She found out about the broken nose and the expulsion from her carbon paper caper buddy this morning.

<Izzy>: How did she find this buddy after all these years?

<Machi>: You may have heard of Steve Doering. Sharf picked on his nephew (Evan Hovland) two years after Doering provided a major endowment to the business school. We arrange start-up financing through them.

<Izzy>: [...] This is double embarrassment for me too. Sharf really knows how to pick 'em.

<Machi>: What do you mean? ***Give me those pills!***

<Izzy>: [...] Doering's company stopped doing business with me; even through he knew how good I was, soon after I came to Belvedere. Doering smirked whenever I mentioned how brilliant Sharf was. He's probably been redirecting other business. Easton wouldn't even let me come down there to recruit.

<Machi>: He's bites the hand that feeds him, as Easton commented this morning.

<Izzy>: I will take care of things, just like old times.

<Machi>: Take as much time as you need - *starting now.* I was thinking that you shouldn't fire him. We'd rather keep him where you can watch him, but keep him away from us. You could also [...]

<Izzy>: *She's about to give me a Marshall plan.* Those are good ideas for starters. Trust the part of Izzy who wants his original family back.

<Machi>: *That sounded like Ike.*

<Izzy>: On a different note, who is Maja? Who is so significant that Simone would talk to her and not you? Daxiao approved the substitute engagement manager because Maja likes her.

<Machi>: She's an unbelievable person who adopted us after her husband was killed. She is loyal, she is stronger than Simone or me, she may be as smart as H, and she is better than I am at discovering things that people want to keep hidden.

<Izzy>: I'll believe her when I see her. She must have wings.

<Machi>: Not exactly, but she did hijack an airplane last night (practically) so she could help Simone while I was hiding behind my insanity.

<Izzy>: Are you going to sue Daxiao?

<Machi>: We'll do more damage to Daxiao if we keep him at home. A lifetime of work could dwindle to nothing, but we will have him.

<Izzy>: Stop that. You can cry about HM and his health, but stop babbling about his career.

<Machi>: You still don't understand how much this last Program meant to H.

<Izzy>: Look at me when I say this.

Sharf's report was so ridiculous that people at Daxiao started paying attention to what HM has been sneaking past them.

Everything will be out in the open, and Marshall will receive credit for his work. Sharf almost did you a favor. Marshall could not have done a better job if he had personally planned every detail.

<Machi>: ***He did plan most of it. I didn't think of it that way. He could have died, but he won!***

<Izzy>: I will send my best associate to handle the assignment. I doubt that even H has anybody who is as good as she is.

<Machi>: You haven't met Maja. There's also Hank. H found "HIS" and "HERS" replacements for himself.

<Izzy>: This associate knows how to deal with people and politics.

<Machi>: I'll believe her when I see her, especially since you are forgetting how to deal with people yourself. Is there something else that I should know about Mr. Sharf's special status?

<Izzy>: Mallory and I had the best senior relationship possible. [...] OK, maybe you and H had (will have) the best senior relationship, but we had a good one. I never took a chance on hurting him. I even avoided you when I knew you were looking.

<Machi>: *I think I believe him.* Who will handle the assignment?

<Izzy>: My magic associate (soon to be engagement manager). Her name is Renata Vitale.

<Machi>: *Ms. TWINKIES!*

<Izzy>: She's good, but I could ask Grayson to recommend someone else!

<Machi>: I was kidding, sort of. She sent H a case of his favorite poison with the get well card.

<Izzy>: *They should outlast the flowers and H.*

---------- ----------

Can we talk about the many favors I need from you after you forgive me?

<Machi>: I have nothing to give.

<Izzy>: I need a shoulder to cry on, like the old days. I'm too old for another wedding plan, but I'm even better with Pampers and Huggies. I can help Becky with Rachel.

<Machi>: H will need both shoulders.

<Izzy>: I have two. Can we rotate? If I come to the hospital, the three of us can work out a crying schedule.

<Machi>: Give me time to prep him, so he won't think he died.

<Izzy>: I have Sharf matters to attend. I'll meet you at the Hospital in about an hour. You might even re-introduce me to my kids. Ryan will be very surprised.

<Machi>: We should start with H and me. If things go well, we will expand the circle. Anybody important should know by the time we invite you to our wedding.

<Izzy>: It's about time!

<Machi>: You were helping him with the plan, weren't you?

<Izzy>: H never wanted to waste a good plan. What happened to it?

<Machi>: He kept it up-to-date, and he showed it to me today.

<Izzy>: Can I cry now?

<Machi>: If we hugged each other right now, would you stop crying?

<Izzy>: It used to work before.

<Machi>: I also have a little secret for you, and I don't care if you let it slip to Joe and Ray. I'll whisper it in your ear.

<Izzy>: What?

<Machi>: H and I got married on the morning of the day that we started working on Simone. He has been Hamilton Frey-Marshall for almost 41 years, and I am Nicola Frey-Marshall.

<Izzy>: **WHAT!** ***I need the pills.***

<Machi>: You would have let it slip to Mama. It would have ruined my profligate image.

<Izzy>: **WHY?** She begged for your forgiveness, profligate and all.

[...] ***Grayson!***

<Desmond Grayson>: *Janice told me to check on him. That looked exciting.* I'm sorry. I should have knocked.

I'll leave this here. I highlighted the parts that I feel we can use right away.

<Izzy>: Come back here. I want to introduce you to one of my dearest friends.

<Grayson>: *That didn't sound too friendly*. What's wrong with your foot?

<Izzy>: The plantar fasciitis is acting up and I can't find my shoehorn. *I'll hold the tie in place.*

<Grayson>: I never knew you had whatever that is.

I've heard of men with foot fetishes, but not women. Why are they both smiling?

<Izzy>: The foot is a recent condition. Meanwhile, I must introduce you. Rennie and you will be working with her husband's team at Daxiao.

<Grayson>: You're Mrs. Marshall!

It's great to meet you. Rennie can't stop gushing about the great team your husband built. Tell your husband when he's better that I have ideas about how he can expand the ***Thunk*** database so that it will work in more parts of an organization. I have at least 10 things that we can add to the "lessons learned", and I really want to discuss in more detail how he handled items 14, 17, and 53 on the resistance list. I know technology should be less important, but I'd like to know if he's dealt with [...]

<Izzy>: This is Ms. Nicola Frey - Mrs. Nicola Frey-Marshall, and he is Desmond Grayson. Now go.

She has to visit her very sick husband, and I have to talk to Sharf about the Daxiao transition.

<Grayson>: That also means that you are one of the senior partners at Frey Associates. My nephew worked with Jonas Frey last summer, and he says [...] All right, I'm leaving, but [...]

<Izzy>: I promise that we will sit together with Rennie after the official turnover of responsibility.

<Grayson>: **YES!** I'll be next door.

<Izzy>: Desmond, we need a favor. You are going to discover that I was hugging a friend that I have known for six [...] fifty-five years, and that Marshall really does know me. We're such good friends that it could look like blatant nepotism.

Mention the hug to Marshall when you see him, but with everyone else, I will trust you to be as discrete as you believed you needed to be before I introduced you.

<Grayson>: Absolutely!

SINKING A SHARK

------William Sharf's Office at Belvedere------

<Mags>: William, please call me when you hear this message. I talked to Gunnar, and he will fix whatever the Daxiao problem turns out to be. He shouldn't have tricked you into dealing with those witches again. I love you.

<Evan Hovland>: Sharf. I am Evan Hovland, and I am calling to follow up on an e-mail that you should not delete. The topic is Wheaton, Carbon Paper, and Steve Doering.

You may be giving credit where it is not due.

I will back in the country in two weeks. At that time, we should discuss my uncle's financial interests in the school and his relationship with Dr. Easton. I will contact you.

<Sharf>: *What is that about?*

[...] ***The e-mail repeats the phone message. I thought Easton, Marshall, and I are the only people who knew about the carbon paper.***

When Easton told me I had to leave Wheaton, he said, "You can appeal, but the evidence is incontrovertible. Why would you bite the hand that feeds you?" He thought I had something going on with the b.itch.

[...] ***Doering is one of those lucky investment managers.***

[...] ***It will take me a while to remember Evan. I don't have to remember. The name isn't that usual.***

[...] ***This looks interesting. Evan Hovland, Wheaton, Class of '88, EVP of Bateman Enterprises, is a scion of the well-known Doering family of financial wizards. Since joining Bateman, he has pulled their far-flung group of subsidiaries into*** [...]

<Rennie>: This will take only a minute. I revised the WFSOA Etiology pie, and I have Belvedere's SOA resistance list. Grayson and I found a few items that Daxiao missed.

<Sharf>: Leave them. I have to think.

<Rennie>: While you're thinking, tell me what else I need for tomorrow. I would rather not be here late today.

<Sharf>: **Go away**!

Hovland graduated the year after I left. He could have been one of my students and he could have been taking classes with Marshall.

<Rennie>: We have to do this. Tell me what you need, and then I can think while you're thinking. ***I was right to upgrade my résumé. This is so-o-o bad.***

<Sharf>: *I'll ignore her.*

I remember now! Hovland was the arrogant swaggering little b.stard. He complained about his grades, but he never came for tutoring.

Hovland didn't need grades. His family was loaded. His family had just given the business school its third largest endowment. Doering was the hand that was feeding me!

NO!

I still hate the b.tch. Maybe she didn't go to the dean, but she helped Hovland.

She had other ways to get what she wanted, but she wouldn't let me touch her. I put my hand on her shoulder and the next thing I remember, I was sitting on the bench between her musclemen. I didn't even know they were there.

I never should have thought about touching her. If it wasn't for Mags, I don't know where I would be now.

<Rennie>: No what? If I leave now, you'll have to use what Grayson and I put together.

<Izzy>: Rennie, I'm glad I caught you and William together. We have news for both of you. Let me speak to William while you go and talk to Paul. You, William, and I will sit together in a few minutes.

<Rennie>: Paul who?

<Izzy>: Paul Diamonte. He's waiting for you in the boardroom.

<Rennie>: *Now I'm in trouble because I couldn't control that fool. I wonder if Kelvin will support me while I get my teacher's certification. At least I'm dressed to leave.*

<Izzy>: That's a different look, but quite elegant. She's finding her own style.

<Sharf>: A woman named Maja at Daxiao loaned them to her. She was dressed too formally for their New Jersey location.

<Izzy>: I can't believe our good luck.

<Sharf>: What are you saying? I missed Ādaemoa, and I have to work harder at Daxiao. The geezer I started with may not be around.

<Izzy>: I have told you often that you should always speak kindly of customers. *That geezer is younger than I am by almost five years.*

<Sharf>: I know. It has been two long days. I suppose Paul is going to tell her that she will start working for Grayson.

<Izzy>: He's going to show her this. It's the latest e-mail that I received from Daxiao. You have pulled off something that no one in Belvedere has managed in 15 years. We have a foothold in Daxiao!

I checked with Finance, and we received the transfer. Because you pulled this off, your bonus will include 20% of this contract, and you bought yourself time to continue growing SOA. The partners have agreed to let you work on SOA for another year, as long as you agree to allocate at least 75% of your time to "Special Accounts". You're still the best money snoop that we have. The rest of the time, you will continue to supervise the two SOA teams that you have in client locations. It will be easier to bring in more work like this after we show Daxiao how good we are.

<Sharf>: *What the f.ck is going on?* I don't know what to say.

<Izzy>: You should be as excited as I am.

<Sharf>: I am, but you've increased the accounting part to 75%, and both the teams that I have at client locations will be finished within the next two months.

<Izzy>: Grayson can handle SOA sales and marketing, but he can't help with major accounting problems. You're still the best we have for that, *if you don't count me*.

<Sharf>: But I brought this in. *I don't know how.*

<Izzy>: And you did a great job.

<Sharf>: We weren't working with Research and Development. I should investigate this financial glitch. I was going to talk to their gal; I mean the head of their Finance Department tomorrow morning. That's where I can add the value. *Piccolo ignored me, but I still have teeth.*

<Izzy>: Mittelman says it's their most widely known "secret". They use it for emergency funds. It pays for everything from "blades", whatever they are, to language translation consultants. It is so well known that it's in a note in their SEC 10 K report. I'm surprised that you didn't memorize it as you normally would.

<Sharf>: That was part of my homework for this weekend. What's the hurry?

<Izzy>: They are in a big hurry to show Hamilton Marshall how much they appreciate the work he has been doing. He is very ill, and they are hoping that this will cheer him up. You showed them how he affects more than 25% of their bottom line.

<Sharf>: *He won't even fall over when he's dying.* They want me to report to Van Amberg?

<Izzy>: Of course not. Vitale will handle the messy details.

<Sharf>: Good. I can interpret what she finds for Mittelman or Gunther.

I had some great ideas about how I could streamline Daxiao's SOA Program. Marshall and Piccolo (his mouthpiece) are doing it wrong. What I outlined last night was only the tip of the iceberg.

<Izzy>: You can pass them along to Rennie or to Grayson. Rennie will interpret.

<Sharf>: She's not senior enough. SOA is about business and organizational structures.

<Izzy>: She's senior enough as of approximately [...] I'd say three minutes ago. By now, Paul should have informed her that:

1. She earned a promotion after finishing the most grueling initiation period we could imagine, and she did a great job. Several customers and potential customers have commented on her skills, and Daxiao was very impressed with her knowledge.
2. As of [...] one minute ago, she reports directly to me, and she is the engagement manager at Daxiao. ***I have to keep Rennie safe and sane, and that means nowhere near you.***
3. Paul and I will mentor her through the business parts of her assignment, and Grayson will mentor her on the technical parts, although that mentoring will probably work more in the opposite direction. She's naturally good with people, but we can't take a chance on her making any mistakes.
4. She will receive the raise we promised her after her initiation period.
5. The office beside Grayson that we left empty will be ready for her by the end of next week.

I won't mention the $50,000 check that she has in her hands at this moment. She'll be deciding how she will gloat to Hugh about the $100,000 bonus that she will earn for this assignment.

<Sharf>: I don't know what to say. Give me a minute to arrange my thoughts. ***I'm trapped in a tar pit, but I'm not sure who did it. Marshall's too dumb. Gunnar and Piccolo warned me that I should keep my mouth shut. Van Amberg told me the truth, and Rennie kept warning me that things were not as they seemed.***

<Izzy>: You don't have to say anything. Come to my office for the official turnover to Rennie.

<Sharf>: ***They're stripping me down.*** I will need at least one dedicated technology associate.

<Izzy>: I'm ahead of you. While you are working on these two special accounting situations, we can groom someone, or we can hire someone. In two months, we may even be able to find you another Rennie. She says there are a few of Grayson's people that she can bring up to speed quickly.

<Sharf>: What will I do when I need a team of people?

<Izzy>: We are going to build an SOA Competency Team like the one they have at Daxiao. We will expand it until at least half of Grayson's people have SOA training. Rennie agreed to outline a training program. The information in Daxiao's role descriptions, and the education and communications charts will be invaluable.

<Sharf>: When did you have these conversations with Rennie? ***I can't explain this to Mags until I figure it out myself?***

<Izzy>: Yesterday afternoon while you were still working your magic at Daxiao.

You look like you need some rest. Relax tomorrow afternoon and a couple of days next week. You've earned it.

<Sharf>: Mr. Gunnar chose me.

<Izzy>: Mr. Gunnar has experienced medical and professional difficulties. While he recovers, Valery Van Amberg, Dr. Daniel Piccolo and their staffs believe that Ms. Vitale is a better fit for this assignment.

It is also important for me to mention that the approach that you used at Daxiao was extraordinarily unique. It got the results that we needed. However, I would recommend extreme caution in the future. It could have backfired on Belvedere, and it would backfire on you.

<Sharf>: It worked. You can't do this to me.

<Izzy>: What are you doing?

<Sharf>: I'm calling Paul. You're both making a terrible mistake.

<Izzy>: Put the phone down. Because of Rennie, Daxiao is giving us a chance fix the biggest mistake Daxiao may have ever made.

<Sharf>: What does she have that I don't, except for the obvious? You're between wives. *Maybe I shouldn't have said that.*

<Izzy>: Let's start with something that Rennie doesn't have.

Geezer and gal were never part of her vocabulary. That positions her more effectively with Van Amberg, the head of something that they call Requirements Management, Maja Johanssen (I think that's right), Lorraine Jasper (the "gal" in finance who happens to be one of the toughest women in our field, *not counting Simone*), and Tacky. *I just slipped. How would I know that?*

<Sharf>: Who is Tacky?

<Izzy>: Guzman says they called her Tacky before she became Doc. I believe you referred to her as the gal from HR.

<Sharf>: Gal and geezer mean nothing. Talent counts.

<Izzy>: First, they both indicate a lack of respect, and second Daxiao doesn't need accounting talent. They need SOA talent.

<Sharf>: They also need management talent.

<Izzy>: How many SOA projects have you managed in the last two years?

<Sharf>: Fourteen.

<Izzy>: How big were they?

<Sharf>: Mostly small, but the two I'm about to finish are medium sized.

<Izzy>: How were your ratings?

<Sharf>: They started out low, but the ones this year are eights and nines.

<Izzy>: The ones that you did since Rennie arrived.

<Sharf>: That's why I need her.

<Izzy>: Did you notice that Acton reported on 83 at our last industry conference, 17 of which were in collaboration with Daxiao. I spoke with the "geezer" named Larson whose name is on that e-mail and he admits that someone named Hamilton Marshall (also on that e-mail) provides significant input to what they do, and that in return, they gave Daxiao the benefit of what they learned on the other 64 projects. How will you improve on that?

<Sharf>: I made Daxiao give us the contents of their Knowledge Center.

[...] Why are you shaking your head?

<Izzy>: Suppose you gave someone the outline of an ISACA training program. Would that make them a top-tier auditor?

<Sharf>: Rennie can make sense of it.

<Izzy>: Why would Daxiao pay your rates if Rennie does not need anyone to make sense of SOA?

<Sharf>: She was undercutting me the whole time at Daxiao. She talks to them with her hands.

<Izzy>: *She was pleasantly surprised when she discovered that I could too, even if I'm rusty.*

Are you saying is that they can't slip anything by her, but they could slip things past you.

<Sharf>: I protected your back for nine years, and you're turning on me.

<Izzy>: I'm letting you work where you can excel, and I gave you a chance to learn something new. So far, your new skills are average. We cannot afford to have anyone at Daxiao who is average.

What would you say if we put someone who had two years of accounting experience on small business accounts between you and the most valuable accounting customer that we found to date?

<Sharf>: I would be loyal to the people who have been loyal to me. Rennie wouldn't be the first person who made a superior look good, and she won't be the last.

<Izzy>: She can only make you look good if you stand out of the way and let her do her job.

<Sharf>: She's slow and weak. The people at Daxiao will walk all over her. You need someone who can take charge - someone who can put the fear of god into them.

<Izzy>: *Paul was right. I have to deal with him head on.* You are not going to let me do this the easy way, and I do not wish to keep Rennie waiting.

<Sharf>: Easy!

<Izzy>: We have to resolve many issues, but these are the top four:

1. In nine years, you have not learned to adjust your style to customer preferences. Your prior statement just proved that.

   As far as I can discern, Hamilton Marshall fears losing Nicola Frey-Marshall, his wife of more than forty years, and nothing else.

   He no longer fears losing his job, and that has them very worried. He wields the "fear of god", not the other way around.

<Sharf>: If he leaves, I can make more money for Belvedere.

2. I have a copy of the fax that you sent to our people at Ādaemoa yesterday. At the top of the first sheet is an intellectual property notice.

   We will talk later about why you faxed the information to that location in the first place. That was unacceptable sloppiness. Rennie is our roles expert and she was in the room with you when you received the list.

   Bernie had the sense to check with Grayson before she delivered it to Ādaemoa. Grayson told her no, and Ādaemoa booted us out. That is a good thing, or we would not have the Daxiao contract.

<Sharf>: Certainly, Daxiao would allow one mistake.

<Izzy>:

3. You made two others. The next mistake is that you paid reporters to follow Hamilton Marshall to the hospital. When they couldn't get a story there, they showed up in New Jersey this morning and tried to blackmail their head of communications into giving them a story on Marshall. Mittelman is pathologically afraid of negative publicity. Why did you do that?

<Sharf>: I didn't know about Mittelman's aversion. Besides, as you said, they didn't find anything.

<Izzy>: *Machi was right. I've lost my people sense when it came to Sharf and to Ryan. I owe more than I can think of ways to pay.*

4. The final mistake, and the most important, is that you will never pass Daxiao's security process. After tomorrow's meeting, where you will be monitored carefully, you will never be allowed in any Daxiao facility.

<Sharf>: Doc doesn't like me.

<Izzy>: Anderson Nicholas Gunther, né Gunnar, is your brother-in-law. You've been slipping and calling him Gunther since I've been in the room. Yet on the form you completed this morning, you indicated that you had no direct associations with anyone in Daxiao.

Gunnar was about to be in a position to affect their audit, security, and financial policies, and you have known him at least for the duration of your marriage, which is 21 years.

<Sharf>: I was following Gunnar's orders.

<Izzy>: Though he says that he intended to carry you around and introduce you tomorrow, this irregularity is related to his political difficulties.

<Sharf>: Everyone over there is related to some one or connected to someone.

<Izzy>: As far as they know, none of them lied about it on security documents. People who do that are released immediately, or they are never hired in the first place.

Furthermore, I suggest that you should not say anything else, lest you create more difficulties for yourself than you have already. You will:

- Come back into my office with me and congratulate Rennie on her promotion. Don't pretend that any of this was your idea.
- Go home tonight and be thankful that my way of being loyal is to give you a chance to overcome the damage that you could have done to Belvedere's reputation, and earn more of a bonus than most people's annual salary.
- Show up tomorrow, sit quietly, and acknowledge whoever congratulates you for going out on a limb to show Marshall's importance Daxiao.
- Leave before any gals and geezers slip out.
- Then take the time off that I suggested.
- While you're out, think about how I can find someone who is nearly as good as you are to

backfill while you're playing with SOA. Indira Simone Frey-Marshall Winslow's name keeps popping up on my radar. I thought it would be a nice reciprocal relationship, on a purely professional basis, of course. *I want to see what fiction he will make up about Simone. This could be an even stronger noose.*

Come with me.

[...] That's Niklas Gunnar.

<Sharf>: He can wait. *I have to get my thoughts together, and I can't do it with Cane hovering over me.*

<Izzy>: They told me that he would be calling. Pick it up and put him on the speakerphone.

<Sharf>: Hello, Mr. Gunnar. I'm glad you returned my call. My boss and I were discussing the good news. He insists on joining our conversation.

<Gunnar>: Go wight ahead.

[...] Hello Mistah Cane. I'm sowwy that I sound funny. I left a message with Janice alweady. I wanted to thank you pehsonally foah sending us such a gweat team, and foah giving my bwother-in-law a chance to show what he can do.

Readers: Gunnar's speech is getting worse. He is extremely uncomfortable.

<Sharf>: *Gunnar just did a 180. That means I'm hung out to dry! No, I'm not. I'm getting $90,000.*

<Izzy>: *It seems that Gunnar is a bit more amenable to change than Sharf is.*

Save your breath. I should be thanking you and Daxiao for many things.

I'll need William for work in his accounting specialty by the end of next week, but I'm sure Ms. Vitale will provide you with the high quality boutique service that you will learn to expect from Belvedere.

<Gunnar>: I was also calling to ensure that both of your people would be at the official kick-off tomorrow morning.

<Izzy>: I wouldn't dare to let them miss something that important. Moreover, know that Ms. Vitale will have access to our finest resources, including direct input from Paul, Desmond Grayson, me.

<Sharf>: *I have to act as if I'm cooperating?*

Grayson is among our best technical people, and Mr. Cane really needs me to handle these accounting issues. It's another couple of hair-raisers. I'll explain what I can the next time Mags and I treat you to dinner. Express my appreciation to Daxiao for the advanced payment.

<Gunnar>: *It sounds like he knows that someone worked overtime to save his (our) hides.*

<Izzy>: *Good recovery. I did train him well.* How is your associate, the one who was seriously injured?

<Gunnar>: Mr. Marshall is in bad shape, but he is strong, and he has a wonderful and supportive family. *He was dying to make a point - I'm punning like HM.*

They are hoping that he will be better than normal and ready to come back to us in no time. Because of William, we see how much we have always needed what Marshall does.

<Sharf>: *Now I see why he's good at sales. He's the best actor I've ever heard, even with a cracked jaw.*

<Izzy>: I was planning to visit Mr. Marshall at the hospital when he is able to hand it. Would it be too obvious that I was promoting Belvedere?

<Gunnar>: I'm not sure of the protocol. Perhaps when he's off the critical list, both his mate and his children may welcome a friendly gesture. However, they are still taking precautions to avoid infection, the doctors from the Veteran's Administration feel that he needs his rest, and the family is emotionally fragile. You can't take a chance on agitating Marshall, even accidentally.

<Izzy>: What does the Veteran's Administration have to do with this?

<Gunnar>: He's a marine hero who was injured in the process of saving several people's lives. Those injuries contributed to his current condition.

<Izzy>: This sounds extremely serious. How well do you know the Marshalls?

<Gunnar>: I'm just getting to know them, and they are truly unique individuals. The meeting with Mama Marshall is not something I'm likely to forget soon.

<Izzy>: You'll have to tell me about it.

<Gunnar>: When you get to the hospital, you will hear about it. I was a not an objective witness.

I will say that Ms. Frey is willing to kill for the man she loves, I didn't listen to her son's advice, and you hear the results. ***I think I'm jealous of Marshall.***

<Izzy>: Just between us guys, as the connoisseur that I've heard that you are, would you say that his women are nearly as attractive as rumors suggest?

<Sharf>: What about the fashion plate that we saw going into your office a while ago? Janice said the outfit cost at least two weeks' salary. ***I don't need to hear anything about Indira. Besides, you're old enough to be Indy's father, in spite of the plastic surgery.***

<Izzy>: ***The disguise worked.*** William is shaking his head and turning red. Don't say anything to embarrass an old married man.

<Gunnar>: I will try to be politically correct.

I haven't seen the youngest daughter, but I know she's closer to our daughter's ages than to ours.

Rated on natural appearance, his wife rates 11 out of 10 for her age bracket.

The older daughter is twice as old as the younger one, and [...]

One might try to describe her over the phone, but I it would be very hard to be politically correct.

<Izzy>: ***Let's see if there are any fish in this pond.*** Is she suitable for your rotation or for mine?

<Gunnar>: ***Neither, not now!*** She's still working out some issues. Let's talk in person when I can talk. ***Helena already did enough damage and I don't want to have to deal with both you and Forester.***

<Izzy>: ***Excellent response. I'll check again as soon as we "accidentally run into each other".*** I appreciate your discretion. I sometimes step out of bounds.

<Sharf>: I ran into the daughter when she was at Acton. Her skills were overrated, and she was pregnant. A pregnant Amazon is a very unusual sight.

<Izzy>: ***She looked almost as good as Nicky did when she was carrying Simone (except for Nicky's problem month).***

<Gunnar>: She definitely looks better now. ***I'd love to see her carrying a Frey-Marshall-Gunnar. That would be an incredible baby. I need help!***

<Izzy>: ***They both have mixed feelings about her, and their reactions are diametrically opposite.*** I'm sorry for the diversion. You sound as tired as William looks. You both need to refresh for tomorrow's meeting.

<Indy>: Gunnar. You're still here!

<Gunnar>: Excuse me a moment please.

[...] I'm sorry; did I hang up on you?

<Izzy>: No, we're still here.

<Indy>: Who's that? ***It sounds like Ike. I'm more tired than I realized.***

<Izzy>: ***That was too close. Nicky says I have to wait until the timing is right***

<Gunnar>: I had to call Belvedere to ensure that their people would make the meeting with your father's team tomorrow morning. Van Amberg said it was all right.

<Indy>: It's not a problem. Forester is still here too.

<Gunnar>: He's working late already!

<Indy>: He is finishing a few things in Mama's office. He really wants this job. ***He will ensure that Sharky loses his teeth faster than they can grow back. That also got a rise out of you.***

<Gunnar>: ***I bet he does.*** I'm surprised that you're speaking to me, given the Helena confusion.

<Indy>: It happens. Besides, I just received such wonderful news about Daddy that I would hug you if it wouldn't hurt you.

<Gunnar>: I'm happy for you, ***and for me.*** What was the news?

<Indy>: Daddy was getting ready for [...]

Mama and Daddy are going to get married, and that seems to have affected his ability to stand up already.

<Gunnar>: It's too early. I don't understand.

<Izzy>: ***The pilot light - H is still H.***

<Indy>: I have to hurry. If you see Jonas, talk to him. ***It's all over the hospital, but I can't think of a delicate way to mention the topic to Randy Andy.***

I'm on my way to the hospital. You can ride with us if you're going back to get those tests. George started later today than James did.

<Gunnar>: Thanks, but Justin already offered. They are waiting for me downstairs. Maybe I'll see you there.

<Indy>: If I have time, I'll check on you. Bye.

<Gunnar>: *They forgave me. Amal and Guntur forgave me!*

<Sharf>: Who was that? *I want to know what he has to say about the Amazon b.itch.*

<Izzy>: ***I was worried about Gunnar using Indy, but that sounded like the purr that her mother tried to use on me. Maybe she's about to give Ryan a dose of his own medicine.***

<Gunnar>: That was Mr. Marshall's daughter. She offered me a ride to the hospital, but Mr. Mittelman is already waiting for me downstairs.

She also said she heard great news about her father. I'll tell you both when I find out what it is.

You knew who she was, and I will make sure you regret the day she ever walked into a room with you.

<Sharf>: ***Meanwhile, she put Hovland on my tail. What would he do? He can't make a stink. It would still reflect badly on his alma mater. He can tell Cane that I tried to mess with his grades. That's a stupid thing to do after 20 years.***

We can get this back on track. I was good for Cane and he was good for me. I'll try a little male bonding.

<Izzy>: ***Gunnar is not too anxious. That's good.*** Take care of yourself, and I wish you the best evening possible, given the circumstances.

It's an amazing new beginning for everybody.

<Gunnar>: It certainly is. ***I still smell the lotus.***

<Izzy>: You handled that well.

<Sharf>: I have to take a short walk. I'll meet you in your office in five minutes.

I have to think:

- ***I'm more valuable to Izzy than I was to the dean, even if he is angry with me now.***
- ***I have to decide how to deal with Hovland, or if I want to deal with Hovland. I need to make that part of my life go away.***
- ***WFSOA will slow down, even if Marshall recovers. That will limit the ways they compete with me. I'm in conflict with myself. If he was useless, they can keep going without him.***
- ***Rennie will find out the truth when she starts digging. Maybe I will offer her the original $10,000. I need to be among the first to know the details of Daxiao's sleight of hand.***
- ***I can tell Mags that this was a big win for me and for Belvedere. Cane will verify what I am saying, and I'll be able to show the $90,000 bonus for three days work to prove it. That is not bad.***

This is going to take time. Meanwhile, I don't want that broad anywhere around Cane. After the intelligence report I create for her, he won't let her sharpen our pencils.

---------- **Isaiah Cane's Office** ----------

<Izzy>: ***The meeting with Rennie went well. She promised to work twice as hard, now that she's happy. I think we gave her enough perks that she'll turn down Daxiao's offer at the end of this contract. She was the concession we had to make to compensate for Sharf's Ādaemoa silliness. The idea of having Paul deliver the information in the boardroom was a nice touch. It is good that I remembered her boardroom comments during her first interview.***

I'm glad that Machi agreed to let me handle Sharky my way. We will start by applying his bonus against the overly generous cash advances that Paul's finance department is about to notice. Maybe I did have a soft spot for him. Otherwise, Grayson would be responsible for SOA.

After he gets angry with me for tightening the purse strings, we will leave something around for him to steal.

After he has tied a very strong noose for himself, he will discover that I'm the reason Indy chose accounting in the first place.

I will let him discover that I am the one that rushed Nicky to the hospital for the delivery of both Indy and Jonas. I was standing beside Marshall the first time he held his miracle Baby Girl, and he cried on my shoulder, literally, when Nicky almost died from carrying the twins.

By then, Nicky should have a few other critical situations ready for him.

A DISCRETE MAYBE

--------- ***Limo Riding to the Hospital*** ----------

<Indy>: ***I have control of two problems, in a manner of speaking, and one to go.***

Clara confirmed that Daddy forgave my grandparents and that it might be a good idea to speak to them. I did. They were sitting beside her in the sunroom.

Mama is speaking to me again. She forgave me for not mentioning my run-in with Sharf. Now she's asleep in a chair in the room with Daddy. For $10 million, she gets special privileges, even if they are worried about infection. The POST seems to be handling that.

The final problem is Mama's companionship prattle. She can't imagine life without Daddy, and she doesn't understand how the daughter of Nicky and Zeus could manage being alone for so long.

The answer is that I am afraid of everything associated with relationships. However, being alone is getting harder, and it will be worse after the kids leave.

Maybe they won't leave. Now I'm being silly.

Ryan is beginning to look tempting again, but I can't give him a chance to hurt the oversized freak again.

I'm sure that Ryan changed his mind about Miss Freak. He tried to scare away a prospect, even if I never considered him as a prospect until I saw Helena's reaction? Barker says Gunnar stood up to Ryan, even though he was almost doubled over with pain.

Mama admitted that perhaps Gunnar saved Daddy's life. I know he did. The ambulance team gave Daddy the morphine because I was screaming like a banshee.

He didn't have Mama arrested. She hurt him, but she didn't hurt his ego. I know he has a huge ego, but it's not around this. I have to think about that.

Jonas reminded me that if Gunnar hadn't done what he did five years ago, we wouldn't be doing so well now. Becky's father was getting tired of paying for Jonas's absent-mindedness.

Jonas also says Gunnar does mean things, but he's not mean. He's miserable, lonely, and scared.

I understand lonely and scared, but I don't know why he would feel that way. How could he be lonely with all the sophisticated women he has?

I'm betting that Gunnar is worried about Daddy, mainly because he realized that Daxiao may start losing money without him. However, he seemed concerned about what Sharf did to me. He was too sick to be acting. Even I can tell that.

He's handsome enough (actually he's very handsome), and he seems to be gentle when he is not trying to control everything. He also has a reputation for being "masterful".

I'm curious. Mama always said I was missing something because Ryan didn't believe in the planning. He wanted to be his own manly self.

If I start with no expectations of fidelity, I can't be disappointed. Gunnar could be a discrete warm-up for a new me. He could explain how his lady friends avoid having their heads and hearts tied up in knots.

I'm not his type, but I have a feeling that he wouldn't turn down a few quick hits. I'd take a refresher course from Mama's safe, and show him a few things that might surprise Ms. Styles.

EPILOG

Gunnar>: *Medical Note: I had a moderately serious concussion, and I needed at least a week of rest.*

There was no difference in the 21-year-old fracture in my skull or the 10-year-old fracture in my jaw. The lump is still tender, but most of the swelling is gone, and so is most of the headache. It fits under my Ferrari baseball cap very nicely. Nothing feels numb like the last time, and my vision was never blurry.

My teeth stayed put, and I can pronounce both "R" and "V". The deep bruises on my upper arm and upper thigh will heal with time. Both are now ugly green with yellow centers, but I can shave myself, slowly, dress slowly, and walk slowly.

The first thing I did when I arrived at the meeting last Friday was to apologize to Piccolo and Liz. That was difficult, physically and emotionally. I only had five minutes, and I don't know whether they accepted the apology. They looked at each other, and Liz said, "You must act as if you mean it."

Then they started working different sides of the room. They actually are a cute pair of midgets.

I would like to pair with ***Indy****.*

They reported that Marshall had made it through the night in great shape for a man who had stopped breathing twice the day before - they left off the part about how he had stopped breathing. He was the happiest man anyone had ever seen in a coffin. His temperature was holding at 99.5. His lung was clearing, and the pain medication allowed him to breathe more deeply. He was a little groggy, but his oxygen level was up to 95%.

I felt happy for Indy and for myself. It meant that I still had career choices, and maybe ***Indy*** *options.*

A MANDATE FOR WFSOA - SOA IS UNSTUCK

Piccolo had convinced Macedon and Van Amberg to work most of the night before the meeting. They outlined what we will do in WFSOA until Marshall's return. They acted as if Marshall's return was an absolute certainty.

Piccolo is surprising everybody. He knows how to work hard. He is a difficult taskmaster, but he makes people laugh so they forget that they are working 12 or 13 hours a day.

It is now official. All business processing and processes in the future will be evaluated as candidates for SOA. Technology processes will be updated to conform to WFSOA, where they make sense. SOA and WFSOA don't apply to everything, but Piccolo estimates that if we continue to move in the direction that he and Marshall set, we should be able to realize an additional $150 million in savings each year for the next four years. Mittelman smiled and nodded. He stayed awake.

Most of the people who attended the meeting didn't have an inkling of how important it was to their financial and political well-being before the meeting started.

After the meeting, we felt that Daxiao would be all right.

Liz played a video showing examples of the benefits that Daxiao received from WFSOA. It had been in KC for two months. Then she showed Sharf's money list. A few figures had been added and others updated so that the total came to more than $1 billion.

That got everyone's attention. They realized why Justin had fallen of the fence in the direction of a WFSOA mandate!

SOA is very important to my well-being. Someone in that room may tell ***Indy*** *how I am supportive of her father's program.*

I showed a perfect combination of authority, contrition, and willingness to cooperate, as reported by Mittelman. I nodded a lot and said very little. My jaw was in worse shape than it had been the day before.

The replacement engagement manager from Belvedere seems to be competent. Marshall's people like her. I can't tell whether Johanssen and Yu are as good as everybody says, but Armstrong was raving about them. He wants to inherit them, even though he once gave Yu away. I think Piccolo has first refusal rights on both of them.

William accepted credit, very graciously, for ensuring that the Program gets the attention it deserves. He stayed as far from me as it was possible while remaining in the same room. He rushed out immediately after the meeting.

Laufer assured everyone that we were ahead of our prior year's sales goal while he plied me with lukewarm black coffee and lukewarm water to wash it down.

Justin conceded that the sling, which exactly matched the plaid in my dress-down jacket, was a nice touch. James helped me to get dressed, as he did after I skied into the tree.

PERSONAL PLANNING - GUNNAR IS UNSTUCK

James drove me to my place in New Jersey after the meeting. I needed information that I had stored in the safe and I needed to sulk privately. I felt truly morbid. Fortunately, Helena does not like the country.

**** STOP ****
If you do not wish read about Gunnar, Indy, and more personal PLANNING

**** SKIP ****
to the Appendix and peruse the tables.

Bye!

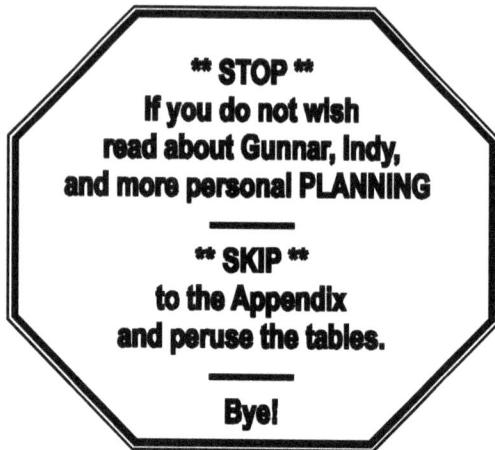

Marcella called a cleaning service - and they had half of the first floor ready by the time I arrived. She arranged for a visiting nurse, she ordered tons of soft food, and she arranged for a local eatery to bring me two meals a day.

I need Marcella as much as I need James. Marshall doesn't need her. He has everybody else.

I still had two of the four bottles of carrot brew that Van Amberg lifted for me from the carrot underground. James opened both of them for me before he left.

I daydreamed about sharing the carrot brew with **Indy**. *I felt less morbid.*

Mags called and thanked me for helping William get the bonus. I doubt that she believed I would be here alone. I assured her that Marcella had taken care of everything.

James came by Saturday through Thursday, even though I gave him the week off.

Kerstin and Len came by on Saturday and spent the night. Maybe she does love me in her own special way, just as I loved her in my own special way.

I acted comatose when Gerthe called.

---------- ----------

Mittelman called on Monday and every day this week. He calls exactly when the visiting nurse is about to leave. He seems more concerned now than when I totaled my car. He's probably following Guzman's orders.

Stein delivered the quarterly update for BASE at Tuesday's board meeting (Van Amberg needed R&R too), and Laufer reported for me. His demonstrated our "new" old customer contact matrix and how it was tied to the customer relationship management system by one of a new SOA service. Laufer said that Piccolo smiled a lot.

Ms. Frey gave me permission to spend time with HM yesterday. She didn't exactly thank me for saving Marshall's life, and she didn't exactly apologize for running up my dental bill. She only said, "We're even now, don't mess it up".

By Wednesday, I felt that I was ready to ask William some questions. He was back in the office but he was busy with an accounting customer.

Mags called on Thursday to ensure that the doctor was healing himself at my normal accelerated speed and to determine whether I was in serious trouble at Daxiao. I explained that I would probably survive both, but it would be harder to come back from the Daxiao situation. She apologized for leaving me in the hotel lobby a week earlier and offered to come and check on me.

She also offered to bring Gerthe - my mother was worried about me too. I thanked her for both offers, and declined. I was doing well enough that the visiting nurse had given me permission to return to a reduced work schedule next week. All I needed was rest.

That level of niceness is usually associated with a loan request, except they already had the money from the Daxiao bonus, I thought.

An hour later, William called and said that his kids needed my financial assistance again. He had received his bonus, but he had to give it back immediately. Diamonte was changing the policy on advances against bonus and William owed Belvedere $110,000 for this year. It was tuition time, and his salary wouldn't cover everything (tuition, mortgage, rent, cars, etc.).

I reminded him that Mags and his kids were already running a $350,000 tab, I had just paid Kerstin's tuition, I hadn't received a bonus for this year, and his shenanigans would probably affect my bonus.

He became annoyed and proceeded to explain that the bonus policy change was probably related to the fact that I hadn't explained Daxiao's security policy.

I reminded him that I asked him to leave Daxiao and meet me at my place while I could still speak clearly, and before he sent the e-mail to all the wrong people. He said that his battery was dying and he couldn't hear me.

I reminded him that I told him that I had not finished explaining things to him before the battery died. He didn't answer when I asked why he didn't call me back on a landline, given that he understood my level of concern.

Then I reminded him that I called him and Mags starting at 6:30 on Thursday morning - before he lied on the security application [he had left home already, and his battery was still dead]. He didn't try to explain when his battery got recharged - he was able to call me at mid-morning.

He started sputtering when I explained how we were going to walk around Daxiao last Friday and introduce him as a top-tier advisor who happened to be my brother-in-law.

I decided to wait until I saw him in person to ask what he did to **Indy**. *I am non-violent, but I was considering how I could do physical harm.*

---------- ----------

I drove myself to New York yesterday. I took the new SUV because I would have trouble climbing into it and out of the sports car.

I was praying that I would run into **Indy**. *I was feeling spry at the thought of that.*

Barker told me what it was that **Indy** *was embarrassed to explain. He regularly dreams about going to "Machi Heaven", and everyone on the floor jokes about it. Barker says there are many things that Marshall can teach most men, if he likes them.*

I wanted to learn lessons for **Indy**.

Marshall's hair and beard are growing, and he is starting to look like tan Zeus in custom-made gowns.

I confirmed that Ms. Frey is built like a smaller version of Indy - I suppose it's the other way around. The silver vixen is much prettier than she was when she was loosening my teeth, even though she had been sleeping in the chair beside Marshall for a week. She has the most beautiful gray hair that I have ever seen.

As she left, I confirmed that **Indy**'*s pace is hereditary. Marshall is sick, but he noticed too. My noticing must have been properly respectful because he smiled and his chest inflated, pain or no pain. HM is a lucky man.*

Marshall's baby montage was hanging below the TV monitor. Ms. Frey had rearranged the pictures and added one. Rachel was born Tuesday morning, totally healthy, and she can hear, but she weighs "only 8-1/2 lbs". Becky will have to exercise for months to take off the weight she gained while no one would let her do anything.

Rachel is newborn baby cute, and she looks a little like both of her parents. With her thick mat of dark hair, and she's already Fuzzy Wuzzy 3. Guntur/Patrick is still the prettiest.

I had started thinking about babies too, and Marshall's pictures kept going around in my mind. Patrick made me feel morbid, but **Indy** *made me smile. She was beautiful and bald, and she appeared to be letting out a Marshall roar.*

Marshall says that his primary goal in life is to hold his newest grandchild. There is probably a correlation between Rachel's birth on Tuesday and Marshall coming out of the coffin on Wednesday. He's survived for nine days. Now his chances are 95% to live and 70% to walk again with one or two canes. I wonder if they found the one that Ms. Frey used on me.

After Rachel, his goal is to get well enough to stand up at his wedding. I believe that will be sooner rather than later. He can move the leg a little already, although the pain is excruciating. He cut back on the amount of pain medicine again.

He is tough, but weak. He had enough energy to spend 30 minutes with me. We completed a third of the meeting that we were scheduled to have on Tuesday. HM still wants his people to do well with WFSOA.

Jonas wasn't lying. The family decided that I would be "forceful" enough to ensure that WFSOA succeeds after Marshall leaves, if he leaves, if I practice listening to Liz, spent more time as Dr. Jekyll, and reserved Hyde for special situations. Speaking of doctors, Marshall thanked me for rediscovering my medical skills.

He ended our meeting because he wanted to save energy to spend time with his children, especially Pat who would be heading back to school.

I would almost definitely see **Indy**.

Leaving Marshall's room, my heart almost stopped. I saw a living breathing Guntur. His name is Patrick Marshall, but he looks like a combination of the best features of Amal's three brothers.

I tripped over an EKG unit, and when I tried to stand up, I was staggering again. I was embarrassed when Guntur/Patrick walked with me back to the waiting room and **Indy** *and his twin sister were there.*

He left me explaining how this was my first day out in a week, and I had probably over extended myself. At first I was having trouble talking because I was stunned by the younger blond one (an extended version of Kerstin) and overwhelmed by the sight of **Indy**.

We agreed I should not try to drive back to New Jersey during Friday afternoon traffic, even if the car was automatic, and the dizziness had gone away. Indy had sold their place in Upper Saddle Run, and she thought she had an idea of where my place might be.

She explained that Laufer had permission to use her conference room. My people are third in line behind Frey Associates and the Marshall/Piccolo amalgam. I could not use the big office. That would be shared by Ms. Frey, Dr. Vincent-Frey-Marshall, and tiny Rachel Frey-Marshall.

I had to be careful not to choke. "Cute Dumb" Rolly Polly Becky can also buy and sell Justin several times. I'm not even in the running. Dr. Vincent owns 25% of Frey-Marshall Associates and 50% of Vincent Partners. She received her PhD from Strafford the same year that Jonas received his Masters, which was the same year that their first child was born. Her father provided the start-up money and the first patents for Frey-Marshall Associates. Marshall males have a way with powerful women.

Patty is hypnotic in ways that I don't understand. She said that she is a mystic, and she wanted to put her hand beside my neck and over my heart. I didn't know what to make of it. Patty sat on her feet with her hands across her stomach, just like your every-day 6 ft. 3 in. blond Buddhist monk. Indy gave me a sort of "take it or leave it" shrug.

Now I know how a deer in a spotlight feels. I was tempted to utter a very assertive "perhaps later", when I got the hunch that there would be no later if I didn't do it now.

I nodded, and went into my "preparing for a cold call trance" while she unfolded herself. That was the second longest 90 seconds of my life. The longest was from the time I saw Amal step on the ice slick until I crawled over to see whether she was still breathing.

Patty looked at Indy and said, "We could have listened to Jonas. Then she sat and folded herself up again.

I am Gunnar the Intimidator, and I was afraid to ask someone younger than my daughter is what she meant.

I was running through the things that you could tell about a person through a stethoscope, when "Guntur" traded places with his sisters.

He watched me watch **Indy** *pacing while his twin sister glided. They were both wearing dancer's tights and T-shirts. Indy's was dark gray and it looked like it was tailored to fit her - who would tailor a T-shirt?*

I could hardly resist the urge to grab Patrick (not Guntur) and hug him while he explained that (a) Jonas at home with Rebecca and Rachel (b) he was flying back to Rome after he saw his new niece, and (c) two different designers paid him to walk around the east side and around Rome in suits like the $5,000 outfit which he was wearing. He has a strange accent.

He also said that he would kill me if I hurt his father again, or if I hurt Indy the first time. He sounded like the men on Kerry's Rap albums, but I knew what he meant.

He associated me with **Indy***! I was happy. He thought I had lost my mind.*

I explained in my most commanding fatherly voice that everything that happened with his father was an accident, I saw the business and financial benefit of avoiding such accidents in the future, and I had no clue as to what he meant about Indy.

I mentioned that he would have to get in line with the other people that were wasting their threats, especially since I hadn't seen or heard from **Indy** *after she and her children stopped to see me while I was waiting for the results of the MRI.*

Sandy seemed curious. She stood behind everyone and watched. Randy seemed to be neutral. He even helped me to get dressed.

He said, speaking English again, with a different accent, "my brother, there are men who gaze at Indy, and there are men who see Indy". He didn't have Jonas's extra sense, but he surmised that I was trying to do both. He said, "surmised".

My heart started acting up again, but I know how to dissemble with the best of them, at least after I have a warning. We sat and stared at the ceiling until his sisters finished their visit.

I daydreamed that I felt my baby kicking in **Indy***'s womb. A second later, Indy and I were playing basketball with him or her. I was old and winded, but I was happier than I had ever been in my life.*

Before they left, I grabbed Patrick (not Guntur) and gave him the biggest hug I could manage with my bruised arm. He felt like a pile of rocks. He was bemused, Patricia was amused, and Indy was confused.

I looked over Patrick's shoulder, and I thought I saw Izzy Cane coming out of the elevator. Whoever it was thought better of it and went back the way he came.

Indy thanked me for showing interest in her father's program. When she shook my hand, she did something that exploded in my head and further down. She said I'd probably see her around.

Indy! Indy! Indy!

Patrick still appeared to be a little dazed when he walked away with his sisters.

I was dazed too. I sat for 15 minutes waiting for the world to solidify.

During that time, Church came by handed me my package of papers, and apologized for being hard on me. He also gave me the results of my blood work. He ran every possible test. He thought I was doing my quarterly checkup. I didn't explain that I wanted to be sure that I am safe for **Indy** *and my babies. I am.*

He said Marshall was doing well, and he was sure Gwen would want us to get together and have dinner soon.

A hundred-pound weight lifted from my chest. I would have at least one less person wanting to kill me.

I had to run and do some shopping.

---------- ----------

One Degree of Separation: I went to my place in New York after I finished shopping. Helena came by to check on me, and to admit that she may have overreacted to the obvious chemistry between Simone and me. She didn't go so far as to apologize. She had verified that Simone Winslow was my landlord.

She was close to the last person on earth that I wanted to see. The last person was Gerthe.

We went to Samuel's for dinner - they have good soft food and an excellent wine list - for Helena. I caught myself tapping the linen with my pinky.

I wished that I was eating with **Indy***!*

The wine chef was explaining the 4-page wine-menu when the Mittelmans, Isaiah Cane, and Ms. Frey came in. Justin and Grace invited us to join them.

I felt as if I had been caught with another woman by my mother-in-law. It amused me that I never worried about Stephanie's mother catching me.

The situation would have been strained if we joined them, and more strained if we didn't. I decided to use it as an information-gathering opportunity. I could catch up on a week of politics and Ms. Frey might mention **Indy**.

Grace Nelson was the W.A.R. member who helped Nicola Frey research the family tree of Kabiri Marshall and Adam Stacy, during the same year that she married a middle management corporate nomad and relocated to Singapore. She had never seen Hamilton Marshall before Banff, but she had heard and written his name. It was in the papers that Grace stored when they moved to Japan.

Nicola had introduced Grace to Samuel's when they swapped genealogy secrets on at least four different occasions. Samuel's was new then and it was the most luxurious inexpensive place that a struggling ex-A.D.A with four children (two with special problems), and a struggling husband could afford.

I had seen Cane at the hospital. He wanted to see how Marshall looked outside of the coffin. I didn't ask why he turned and went in the other direction when he saw me hugging Patrick, and he didn't mention it.

When he returned, Grace and Justin were visiting the Frey-Marshalls for the third time since HM was injured. Mittelman delivered a positive Belvedere status report, and Cane offered to take them to dinner to celebrate.

Marshall assured Ms. Frey that he would be all right while she had a nice sit-down meal with her old acquaintance, especially someone who had found evidence that he was a disenfranchised prince Weeble.

The android cringed and Ms. Frey smirked when Grace retold the story and asked why "Hamilton" would refer to himself as a Weeble. Marshall is mean. Ms. Frey changed the topic.

Of course, they never met at Samuel's place. The Frey-Marshalls used the special entrance and sat in a booth with curtains that could be closed. Ironically, the Mittelmans sometimes used the same booth, but on different days.

I thanked Ms. Frey for allowing me to see her husband, congratulated her on having four wonderful children, and made special comments on Patrick's good looks, his style consciousness, and the $5,000 suit. I didn't dare to mention Indy, and neither did Ms. Frey.

Ms. Frey explained how much Patrick looked like pictures of his great-great grandparents in the Asian line. I managed to look surprised and interested.

Then she mentioned how people spent as much time gazing at Patrick as they did their own babies when he was in the in the hospital nursery.

Cane mentioned that Pipsqueak was beautiful, but the squeal got people's attention. Ms. Frey frowned at Cane's comment. I spent a few seconds wondering how Cane would know anything about Marshall's baby. Maybe he asked, just as I had.

Grace commented that she had seen Patrick once, and he was even more beautiful than his pictures. She also acknowledged that his squeal was ultra-sonic, but it was probably because the "poor little fellow" was so uncomfortable.

Ms. Frey assured Grace that the holes in Patrick's diaphragm, his heart, and his palate had healed perfectly. The scars were invisible. His speech therapist had noticed that he had a gift for languages, and he spoke many.

I could not avoid thinking about Guntur (not Patrick). I know the difference. While I tried to maintain a neutral expression, Ms. Frey apologized for boring us with talk of her "little man", and she changed the topic to [...] *Grace and her wonderful children.*

The last time they had eaten at Samuel's, Ms. Frey had four children and Grace had none. Now Grace and Justin's children were 15, 12, and 9. One wants to be a dancer as Ms. Frey was (almost), and as Queen-2 will be. One wants to be "something medical", and the youngest wants to be a BOSS like his father. Justin showed the picture of the Mittelman kids and their cousins in Florida.

Helena commented on how much Octavia looked like her uncle and her grandfather. Ms. Frey was not surprised at the connection.

Justin focused on every second of the exchange between Grace and Ms. Frey when Grace brought up the topic of "Hamilton".

- *I can't believe how good Hamilton looks, and he almost died just a week ago. [That's his Zeus look. Wait until his hair gets a little longer.]*
- *The women at Daxiao adore Hamilton. He is such a gentleman. Higgs and Doc would kill for him. [He has that affect on people].*
- *Hamilton's puns are so silly, that sometimes they are hilarious. [Most of the time we think they are silly and embarrassing - Love HM, love his puns.]*
- *How did you keep Hamilton all these years? [It took ongoing planning and working through hard situations, but it was big fun].*

Grace commented about how she had also heard about Hamilton's life-saving plans. Her sample plan, #998, had been effective three times, and she had waited 18 years for the next installment.

They laughed like long-lost sisters.

Cane acted as if they were talking about the weather.

Helena was confused.

The android grinned in a very human-like way and his eyes glazed over when Ms. Frey passed an envelope under the table.

Ms. Frey commented that they were excluding half the table. They moved on before I had time to ask what #998 meant.

Helena wanted to know whether Isaiah Cane had children. That let loose a gusher. He raved about his three beautiful children (by three ex-wives) and how he still had wonderful relationships with all of the children and all of the wives. He showed us the miniature photo album with all the children and all the wives. He commented on how he was old when he started and lamented how he had trouble changing his wondering ways. He is currently between relationships. Helena leaned just slightly in his direction. I was more delighted than upset.

My turn was next. I explained how I lost my first wife and child in a horrible accident. Only Helena was surprised. Everyone offered condolences.

I explained that I had time to heal, and my beautiful daughter by my second marriage helped. I didn't mention that she was a consolation gift from Stephanie. I also mentioned the son-in-law who was almost like my son; although I didn't understand his geek speak most of the time - I wanted that to get back to Jonas.

Helena explained how she had a life plan that required waiting until about now to start a family. If she started soon, she could squeeze in two by the time she was 40. She had already found a designer who did pre-natal miracles for women who were willing to watch what they ate. She leaned back in my direction. I leaned away. I wanted ***Indy*** *to have strapping babies for me. This was becoming a nightmare.*

Ms. Frey is wicked in addition to her violent tendencies. She looked at me, smiled ever so slightly, and asked whether I was the lucky father.

Helena saved me. She explained that she was finally beginning to understand the phrase, "more slippery than a greased pig". She commented that the thought caused me to break out in sweat - I was sweating. She leaned back in Cane's direction slightly.

Ms. Frey smiled. So did Cane. I thought I saw him do one of the signing things, very subtly with his elbows leaning on the table - maybe not. My paranoia was slipping out. It was time to change topics again.

Wrong Styles: Helena managed to use Patrick and the suit comment to steer the conversation to fashion. She wanted to discuss trends for women over 40. She wondered if Grace or Ms. Frey could provide inexpensive recommendations for her older employees.

That lasted three minutes or less. Grace believed in classic styles, which were ageless. Ms. Frey bought whatever Bergman's had for mature women. Helena believed that Bergman's was a decent alternative for a woman who didn't have her own designer, especially if you waited for the sales.

Ms. Frey looked at the table. I could see her refusing to have the look that she had when she was hitting me with the stick. Cane commented on the excellent quality of the china and the table linen. I tried to disappear.

Then Helena started the "business flirt" with Mittelman and Cane. She saw a chance to increase her temporary job placements, and she wasn't going to pass it up.

Mittelman bragged that Daxiao was holding the line on headcount and handling 10% more business each year because of the wonderful work that Marshall was doing with WFSOA and the automation of process automation. He explained to Helena that the statement was not redundant.

He spoke as if Marshall would show up on Monday and roll out his next set of processes. The android was so smooth that Ms. Frey almost choked on her gassy water.

Cane seems to be making inroads with Ms. Frey. He's the one that patted her back and made sure she was all right after the misdirected liquid.

I wouldn't be Gunnar if I hadn't watched for signs of something other than business. There was, but it was more like the relationship between Mags and me, without the hostility. I'll think about that later to.

Cane determined that Helena's recruiters emphasized typing more than skills and promised to call her the next time he needed front-office assistance.

The Samuel's Experience: The meal was excellent. Samuel has chefs that prepare customized dishes for his (ultra rich) Asian clients. We all agreed (except for Helena) that we would try a sampler of the Asian dishes, several of which they were willing to prepare especially for the chewing challenged.

The apple mousse was in that category. It wasn't actually mouse. What he served in the restaurant was a significantly more "vigorous" version of the one I had tasted at the hospital. It contained apple chutney, it tasted like a dish that Amal had prepared a couple of times, and it wasn't my imagination. I managed not to get stuck in my post-Amal Hyde persona.

Helena chose a small salad, and an even smaller salmon filet, because she always watched what she ate. I wondered whether she was trying to annoy Grace who definitely has a designer to create classic outfits for her zaftig proportions.

Grace smiled and raised one eyebrow at least an inch above the other. I suppose all the women who are her "type" know how to do that.

Ms. Frey looked at the table.

For the remainder of the meal, I sat and tried to remember every topic that Ms. Frey discussed. Any hobby that she had was about to become my hobby.

Justin was paying attention too. He was trying to find something that she wanted enough that she would convince Marshall to return to Daxiao. As far as I could tell, she wanted HM, her children, and her grandchildren, and she already had them. Becky counted as a daughter, by Ryan was not on the list. Good!

The service was excellent. I was beginning to believe that the staff was reading our minds until I noticed that Ms. Frey was manipulating buttons on a small square pad that appeared to be a coaster. Nothing was printed, but you could feel the symbols.

We were discussing the relative merits of the experimental techno-coaster when Helena noticed the ring that Ms. Frey was wearing. I asked how HM had managed to find something that perfect during the past nine days. She said H got a special deal from a very special long-time friend. She mentioned that it was an excellent example of reuse, and she changed the topic.

-------- ---------

We left without paying. A Bentley, with a driver, a Porsche (Helena's), and Cane's Roadster were waiting for us at the curb. There must be a transportation button on the coaster.

Changing Styles: Helena was a little surprised when Justin and Grace decided to walk to their New York apartment while the driver (Miles) held the door for Ms. Frey.

I was thanking Ms. Frey for the excellent dining experience and was about to ask how she liked her car when she pointed at Helena leaning against Cane and a parking attendant.

Her four-inch designer heels and her weak ankle (from a skiing mishap) had hampered her ability to negotiate the curb.

It was the wine list. I have been getting more "high" to go with my "class" recently.

Nevertheless, Gerthe likes Helena's ticking clock. She promotes the image of how we can be one big happy family and she would help us with the kids if we had any. She means she would give a nanny hell while I redid the house to accommodate her senior mobility issues. Never! She and Stephanie killed Amal and Guntur. This is one case where Marshall's pain is my painful gain. I finally understand what happened. That is morbid!

Anyway, the parking attendant verified that only Helena's pride and the shoe had been injured (no lawsuits), handed me the keys, and raced off to assist the next patron.

Helena lamented the workmanship on the heel, while I explained to Cane that I could not drive Helena's car. I would be slow with the shift and even slower with the clutch. He tried not to smile while I looked for words to describe the clutch problem.

Helena rescued me again. She explained, as only an excessive user of fine wine lists can explain, how we came to Samuel's because this old broad had rammed a stick into my "seminal area", and I offered to feed her because I couldn't - the seminal area wasn't functioning properly".

We decided that it would be a good idea to leave Helena's car at the restaurant. We rode to her place with me sitting beside Miles while Helena congratulated Ms. Frey on having four children and still keeping everything tight enough to hook a sweet daddy who could pay for the Bentley and for Miles.

Apparently, Helena had forgotten I was in the car, and I wanted to leap out of the car.

Ms. Frey finally apologized for doing more damage than she realized while Miles and I extracted Helena from the back seat.

I did not try to hide the limp. It had been a long day. Thus, Miles helped me carry Helena upstairs and place her and her disheveled designer togs between the satin sheets. Miles is built like George who is built like Ernest and Fred. Marshall must have needed a lot of help lately.

They dropped me off at Kerstin's place (which is really my place that we converted to two apartments again). It was on the way to River Glen. Ms. Frey hated sleeping without her Fuzzy Wuzzy, but she needed real rest.

I needed rest too - I slept 10 solid hours. I couldn't have taken an overdose of medicine, because I only had one pill with me.

When I awoke, the message on my nightstand under the key and the friendship aquamarine bauble said:

> Andy,
>
> My ankle is OK and I was able to drive the car with little difficulty.
>
> I stopped by because I was worried about you. You didn't answer either of your phones.
>
> You may be happy to learn that your bruise affects nothing when you are asleep.
>
> I thought you had reconsidered my proposal from yesterday, except that I am not your **Baby Girl, and I** do not know any passwords.
>
> **Styles** [...]

The leftover baubles make great gifts for the household assistants.

My neat break-up percentage improved.

---------- ----------

I went to my New York office this morning. Laufer moved two of his junior people into a supply closet that didn't have supplies yet. This made room for me in a smaller space, but it had a window facing the rooftops on 39th Street. Marcella ordered furniture upgrades and panoramic pictures so that people would know that it was the boss's New York office.

The former occupants were the creative young men who had rigged the Indy jaunt mirrors to a video camera, and they hadn't had time to move it.

I turned in on to see how it worked. Piccolo came in with Liz and the terror tots. So did Van Amberg and about 10 more of Marshall's people.

Indy also came to work. She waved at Liz and Van Amberg, and then she paced the length of the hallway. My morbidity disappeared.

Hank Yu left a "fully loaded" laptop on my tiny executive desk, and I determined that the instructions for updating the security didn't make sense. Daxiao pulled some strings to get me a high-speed line in New Jersey, but I wouldn't have known how to use anyhow. Len says he will come out and show me how it works tomorrow. He also wants to talk to me about getting a job working for Jonas.

Octopus network - I decided to stop fighting it. If Marshall was serious about his option #2, maybe he'll let me use the network.

I checked the messages that Marcella and Laufer said I should handle and spent time on Marshall's material. My SOA sight is improving rapidly.

I also spent time learning to use the executive dashboards. I can still see a lot when I'm looking, even when I have other things on my mind.

As near as I could determine, I was sitting thirty feet away from ***Indy*** *on the other side of 12 inches of masonry. I couldn't think of a single excuse for going around the wall, especially since I wasn't supposed to know that she was there.*

By noon, people were leaving for lunch, or simply leaving. I figured she must be getting hungry too. I decided to sit in my car in front of the building and wave at her when she went to get something to eat. I might even convince her to eat with me, and I could discuss how I enjoyed having dinner with her mother. I planned to mention how Helena and I realized that our short-lived relationship had died.

Thus, I was standing in front of the building cursing at my SUV 90 minutes ago. I couldn't open the door with either the key or the remote, and it sounded strange. As I expressed my annoyance with the manufacturer, I noticed ***Indy*** *staring at me. Sometimes I'm lucky.*

She wanted to know why I was trying to get into her car. We checked the plates and realized that she was right. I also checked the warm-up suit she was wearing. It was dark blue, with a subtle velvety sheen, not black as it appeared in the camera. I managed a very laid-back nod of appreciation.

Before I became too upset about my missing car, she suggested that perhaps I should try the identical vehicle that was setting on the other side of the street behind one of Vincent's delivery trucks. I did, and it was mine. I was too embarrassed to ask her to lunch. Where did the suave Gunnar go?

She watched as I pulled out of the parking spot without scraping the delivery truck and barely avoided being sideswiped by the taxi that was racing to stand at the red light at 5th Avenue.

However, I drove to the corner in a very executive authoritative manner. When I turned the corner, she was waving at me very enthusiastically, so I waved back.

I received an enthusiastic wave from ***Indy****.*

I needed James, but I made it home without running into anything.

I felt like taking a nap sitting in the garage, but I needed to move the case of carrot brew that the deliveryman left beside the basketball net, just as Macedon promised. He said I really owed him for the brew. He only has eight cases to last until they start the winter batch. He promised to tell Little Miss Mama how much I like her concoction.

I dragged it inside and took a few bottles upstairs where I planned to alternate between that and lukewarm coffee.

I was down to my new Marshall-type briefs when I realized I had to get my meals out of the bin before they spoiled. James found the brief briefs for me. Marshall has reason to be vain, but he is also smart. They do not irritate the bruise like the regular ones. James also picked up a few for himself. He said he needed to exercise more and sit less, but Ticia likes them anyhow. She said he still had potential.

I imagined modeling my potential for ***Indy****.*

For the first time in my life, I worried about whether my potential was too old. No! Marshall is off the voltmeter, and he's 13 years older than I am.

I put on lounge pants, and the bending still got my attention. The nearest neighbors are almost a block away, but I didn't want to take another chance on trying to grab the towel with one good arm as I tried to do a week earlier.

Someone was coming up my driveway. I thought I was hallucinating this time. It was ***Indy!***

The sheen is magnetic when she paces.

She opened the cargo area and took out a computer case and an attaché case, my attaché case - the one Chiu bought for me in Hong Kong!

<Indy>: Hi. I'm sorry to disturb you, but you left these on the roof rack of ***MY*** truck. Your wallet and your cell phone were in the attaché case. So is the information my father tired himself out trying to explain to you. You hadn't tossed it, so I figured you might use it. There are also church materials. You don't seem like a religious man, but tomorrow is Sunday.

<Gunnar>: *I'm about to get religion.*

<Indy>: You saw me jumping and waving like a fool when you turned the corner? Didn't you notice that you didn't have these?

<Gunnar>: No. *Will I ever stop making a fool of myself with this woman?*

<Indy>: The way you started out, I figured I'd catch you before you got to Route 80.

<Gunnar>: *I never noticed that she has that much hair. It's like her mother and her father's hair all on one head. The gray streaks are brilliant in the sun light.*

<Indy>: [...] You shouldn't drive like that in your condition. You shouldn't drive the like that in any condition. The greenness of that bruise means your arm hurts less, but it must still be slowing your reflexes. *Randy was right. He is as buff as Ryan is.*

<Gunnar>: *She was worried about me.*

<Indy>: [...] I'll set these inside, let me use your facilities, and I'll be on my way. *I had to rush. He was at the elevator before I noticed him on the security monitor.*

[...] If I interrupted something, I'll leave these here, and I will find facilities on the way home.

I am no good at this, and this is embarrassing.

<Gunnar>: No! NO!

<Indy>: No, what?

<Gunnar>: There.

<Indy>: Are you going to move?

<Gunnar>: Yes. *I'm dreaming that I'm here alone with Indy! I smell the lotus. I don't remember having a dream with smells?*

<Indy>: You can come in too. It's chilly out there.

<Gunnar>: I have food. There. *Why can't I think of something sophisticated to say? Why can't I think of a good sales line? Why can't I think of something suave or executive-like? Why can't I think of anything?*

<Indy>: I'll come back and help you in a minute.

A Dull Lunch Offer

<Gunnar>: *She's fast. I guess she doesn't fix her face. I barely had time to find my executive robe.*

<Indy>: *It was a good coincidence, and I tried to take advantage of it. The place is empty, and half of his furniture is covered. We could be very discrete out here, except that Mama said some things were not working.*

I'm unlucky with men. Maybe I'm lucky to be unlucky with Gunnar. I should stick with the devil I know.

You have the food in already. Good. Have a good weekend, and feel better.

<Gunnar>: Wait, please. I appreciate the fact that you took the trouble to bring these to me.

I have enough pâté, puree, and soft flat bread for two. We can chase it with your mother's carrot brew. Would you care to join me?

That wasn't sophisticated, but my mouth is working again.

<Indy>: *He's offering me my mother's carrot juice.*

<Gunnar>: Don't look at me like that. I promise to behave. Covering up takes longer now. If you hold the robe for me, I'll do it faster.

<Indy>: I can do that. *He has more scars than Daddy does, and he's too young or too old to have been in any wars.*

[...] I'll even help you tie it. Hand me that end of the belt. *He's solid. I wonder if* [...]

<Gunnar>: Thank you. We'll have to eat in the kitchen. Everything in the dining room is still covered. *I'm in control now. I will behave appropriately.*

<Indy>: I'll grab a couple of these. Which way do we go? *No candlelight and wine. I'm definitely not his type.*

---------- ----------

<Indy>: Where is everything?

<Gunnar>: James brought me this plastic stuff. My wife - I mean my ex-wife - took most of the utensils. I don't know how to cook.

<Indy>: It's not a problem. It looks like the restaurant sent everything you need.

<Gunnar>: *Her hair looks like a shawl. I'd love to see what that body suit looks like.* It's warmer in here than it is outside. Would I be too forward if I offered to hang up that warm-up jacket for you?

<Indy>: You could ask, but I can't get if off. My hair is caught in the zipper. I'm afraid to ask you for scissors. *There's my punishment for trying to be sultry. It never got caught in the buttons of my pajamas.*

<Gunnar>: I wouldn't ask me for scissors either, even if I knew where to find them.

<Indy>: I'm not that hot. Eat.

Delivering on a Promise

This has Indian seasoning.

<Gunnar>: Don't you like Indian food? Your mother likes the food they serve at Samuel's place. My **ex**-girlfriend liked the wine too.

[...] I know Ms. Frey told you what happened and Helena is my ex-girlfriend now. Go ahead and laugh.

<Indy>: *I bet Mama used Piccolo's techno-coaster to get extra refills for Helena.* I'll just smile a little.

<Gunnar>: This is decent, but the food in Samuel's was some of the best I've ever tasted. It was even better than the dishes that my first wife used to prepare for me.

<Indy>: How many wives have you had?

<Gunnar>: Just two. First, it was Amal, and then Stephanie.

<Indy>: Were you and Amal really married?

<Gunnar>: Definitely [...]

<Indy>: Where are you going?

<Gunnar>: I need to show you some things. I can prove I'm not lying.

<Indy>: Come back here.

---------- ----------

<Gunnar>: Here's a copy of the marriage license. It is real. You can look it up. Here's a copy of the paperwork we were going to file as soon as Guntur was born. This is a copy of Guntur's birth certificate, and this is when I married Stephanie.

<Indy>: Why are you showing me this?

A Very Exciting Life Offer

<Gunnar>: I want to start over [...] with you.

<Indy>: Whoa. I can't compete with a ghost. *I'm talking too much.*

<Gunnar>: You thought about me too!

<Indy>: I thought about how the Amal situation could have made you crazy, even if she wasn't your wife.

<Gunnar>: When?

<Indy>: We wanted to find out how you knew so much about medicine and what friend died that made you stop practicing. You mentioned saving someone when you hit your head. We should have done more checking. I am so sorry.

<Gunnar>: Thank you.

<Indy>: But now I need to unthink. I am not Amal reconstituted. Nor am I Stephanie, Boothe, Helena or any of the other few dozen that lasted longer than one night. *Why did I say that? I wanted a few quick hits myself.*

<Gunnar>: I'll never do that again. They were my protection until I found you.

<Indy>: Mr. Swah-vay. The cat had your tongue, but you're back on your game now.

<Gunnar>: You didn't notice this.

<Indy>: I was looking, not snooping. You seem to have a supply.

<Gunnar>: That's a trinket.

This shows how I feel about you compared to how I felt about Helena.

This is almost as clear as your mother's is, and it's bigger. It's blue for hope, it's from Guntur like the Hope Diamond, and we'll make sure that we have no bad luck. *I got her attention!*

[...] It's real. Here's the certificate of authenticity. I needed a wide band for all your names. It says Indira Simone Frey-Marshall-Gunnar, not Helena. See for yourself.

That's silver, and this is platinum.

<Indy>: *Marriage!* I've got to go.

<Gunnar>: ***NO, please.*** I need help [...]

<Indy>: With what?

<Gunnar>: I'm jealous of your father.

<Indy>: Who would be jealous of the nerdy gimp Weeble?

<Gunnar>: Justin called him that. I said he was a terrible salesman, and he speaks slowly. Justin is jealous of your father too.

I figured it out! I've been looking straight at it for five years, and I missed it. Grace looks at Marshall (even when he was overweight) as Joe looks at Ms. Frey.

I can use that. No, I can't. It would look as if I was accusing my father-in-law of having an affair.

<Indy>: **You are as insane as they say you are!**

<Gunnar>: Anyone who met your mother and your family would be jealous. I want what your father has. I don't have anybody who would kill for me. *Stephanie didn't intend to, I don't think.*

<Indy>: Why would go to these extremes to make sure you keep the inside track on Daddy? You must be in big trouble at Daxiao.

<Gunnar>: You father is going to be all right. That means I'll be all right, if I cooperate with Piccolo, Liz, and Macedon.

This is separate. People have been threatening to kill me if I hurt you. This way you and all of them will know that I'm serious, especially about the marriage part.

<Indy>: *What people?* When did this insanity hit.

<Gunnar>: The first time I saw you walk, the first time I smelled you, when I landed on you, when I saw you handle Justin, especially when I saw you beside Helena, when Forester walked in, and when you let your son help me get dressed.

Hey! She sent Ryan away and spent time with me!

<Indy>: *He sounds sincere, but I can never tell.* There's nothing between Forester and me. I was angry.

<Gunnar>: I know. This is not an Indy wave. It means, "flirt". You wanted me to be jealous, and it worked.

<Indy>: How much of that do you know?

<Gunnar>: Ticia (James's wife) picked up a book and a DVD for me.

I know this too. I saw your father and your mother do it yesterday, but this is for you. It means, **"I love you"**, right?

<Indy>: It means [...] I don't know what it means. This is too fast.

<Gunnar>: It took your parents four hours, and they were an unlikely pair too. I've known you for nine days.

<Indy>: Who told you that?

<Gunnar>: Barker mentioned the dreams that you were embarrassed to tell me about, and he was about to tell me what gave your father the will to live - then he had to run to another patient.

I've been dead for 21 years. You could bring me back.

<Indy>: That was a good one too.

<Gunnar>: That's almost a proposal.

<Indy>: What about Liz?

<Gunnar>: I never touched Liz, I apologized for strenuously ignoring her, and I'll memorize all 9,700,000 links in KC as soon as my son-in-law shows me how to logon from here. I have a typing CD. Here it is.

<Indy>: You must have loved Liz if you carried a grudge for that long.

<Gunnar>: I liked her. She wasn't the first woman that turned me down, but she was the first one that kept generating projects for mutual acquaintances while she would not give me the time of day. I thought Justin was Octavia's father.

[...] Go ahead and laugh. You have to admit that I work hard at everything that I do, even being stupid.

Mittelman explained it to me - so much for Gunnar, the super snoop.

<Indy>: *The ring is distracting. The track lights really make it shine.*

<Gunnar>: That was the most amazing thing that they had at the Exchange. It's amazing like you.

<Indy>: Stop that.

This could be Sharf's idea of Dangerous Liaisons. He scares Mama and me. He's the only one that ever got to us twice.

<Gunnar>: I'll let him know that I will kill him if he sneezes in the same room with you.

<Indy>: He hurt us and he was rewarded for it. ***I was starting to slip. This will bring me to my senses.***

<Gunnar>: ***She's getting that mad "Frey" look again.*** I told Mittelman you would say that.

[...] ***Listen,*** please.

<Indy>: Make it good.

<Gunnar>: Cane and Diamonte slipped some things into the preliminary agreement that would force Daxiao to pay Belvedere anyhow.

On the Daxiao side, Mittelman and Guzman wanted Sharf to stop blabbing about your father's substance abuse problems - I know you know about that because he blurted it out in front of Doc.

Speaking of substance abuse, you saw all the scars. The shrink says I was punishing myself for Amal and Guntur. When Daxiao thought I was on a cruise in the South Pacific after Stephanie left, I was getting clean and sober. These are reminder bottles from before. I almost started again last week, but your fathered embarrassed me. If he can survive on less painkillers (or none), I can too.

<Indy>: Don't change the topic. Sharf is still getting rewarded for acting on evil intentions.

<Gunnar>: He'll never see a cent of that money. Diamonte and Cane are so angry with him that they changed the bonus advance policy.

Sharf mentioned it on Thursday when he called to ask for another loan, for the kids this time - it's always for Mags or the kids. I verified the policy change with Cane yesterday.

<Indy>: How much are you going to lend him?

<Gunnar>: ***She's a little calmer. She almost smiled.*** He would get nothing, unless you gave me permission. That means that you have to forgive him. He still believes that he was stealing from the rich to give to the poor, in both cases.

<Indy>: We were poor.

<Gunnar>: You were never poor if you had Nicky and Marshall. You also had you.

<Indy>: That's another good Gunnar line. Now I understand your success factors.

<Gunnar>: He hurt you and he nearly destroyed my second career. It's not what I always dreamed about, but it pays the bills very well, with significant help from your father.

<Indy>: What about your sister and her kids? ***I would not dare to try to come between him and his family. I wasn't even good enough to stand between Ryan and the bimbettes.***

<Gunnar>: Her husband and her kids come before me. Last Thursday, a couple of hours before I saw you, Mags took $200 out of my wallet and used it to rush home in proper style to be with her poor William, after I brought her to New York to protect her from his wave of insanity.

She left me sitting in a chair in the lobby of Hotel Pietro. I looked so bad that the doorman was about to toss me out.

That reminded me that my wife and my kids should come first.

<Indy>: You don't have a wife, and you only have one kid.

<Gunnar>: I'll have your kids too ***(even the ones you haven't had yet).*** I'm not Ryan, but I think they appreciate the fact that I saved their grandfather's life. Am I correct?

<Indy>: Randy says you're all right. He's looking forward to the soccer tips. That's something Ryan refuses to do.

They both acknowledge that their father has special friends; ***he's much more discrete now***. However, they are accustomed to me being 100% theirs.

<Gunnar>: ***They discussed it!***

Kerstin would share me; ***she always has.***

<Indy>: Let's go back to the original topic. What are they asking for?

<Gunnar>: It doesn't matter. The everlasting font has run dry.

[...] I am serious. My wife-to-be would need to know that Maggie/William Sharf and Gertrude Gunnar have already borrowed over $500,000 from me. They have repaid about $10,000. I have the loan notes, but I think of it as a gift fund.

<Indy>: How did you let them do that?

<Gunnar>: They made me feel guilty that I was a lowly salesman and not an esteemed doctor. I tried to prove that selling was a valid occupation by piling my money on the table for them.

<Indy>: How will they manage? I bet you'll change your mind after you stop being angry.

<Gunnar>: They will manage by working smart and financial planning.

His kids live in luxury off-campus studios and they both drive Ferraris. They could move into campus housing, and they could sell the cars and pay this year's tuition. Both their parents could trade down too.

They could get loans and work-study as I did. Scholarships are probably not an option. They chide Kerstin for studying and having a part-time job when her father is "rolling in dough".

Mags can go back to work. It's time for her stop running the afternoon social circuit in Inglewood.

They could move from Inglewood to Inwood where Stephanie and I lived after I left medical school. Then he could get by with zero car payments.

<Indy>: You spent time thinking about this.

<Gunnar>: I know how to be poor. For the first five years, I sent more than half of my income to Amal's family. Stephanie worked to make up the difference. ***Now I know why Stephanie never complained about my "investment" losses.***

For five years Mags, Gerthe, and William reminded me of what a failure I was. Stephanie had to work and Mags stopped after Teddy was born.

<Indy>: He'll be angry with me. I bet the ring would pay for a year's tuition. ***If I play along with the wife thing, Sharf will have to sweat the finances until Mama lowers the big boom.***

<Gunnar>: Mags has a big ring to, but it's not nearly as perfect. They celebrated the 25th year of knowing each other last spring. I'm sure I managed to contribute to that.

<Indy>: This is still not making sense.

<Gunnar>: You like me, at least a little, or you wouldn't be here.

<Indy>: I was curious, but was frightened, even before I knew you were married to Amal.

<Gunnar>: She released me after 21 years.

[...] That's not right. She released me 21 years ago, and I just remembered last week. I'm finally healing.

She is the reason I saved your father's life. I will be right for you. I can show you.

<Indy>: ***He probably didn't show this to Helena.*** What do you expect us to do now?

<Gunnar>: I could use a friendly hug, but your hair is sort of in the way. Isn't it uncomfortable like that?

<Indy>: Maybe we could start with a hug, and yes, the hair is uncomfortable. Give me the Swiss Army knife that you had in the case. I'll use one of those pointy things to get the hair loose. If all else fails, I'll cut of this section. It's time for a trim anyhow.

<Gunnar>: **NO!** I mean no please. Never hurt even one of your many strands of hair because of me.

<Indy>: Did Amal have hair like mine?

<Gunnar>: It was black, and it was pretty, but it was not like yours. Amal was Amal, and you are you.

<Indy>: I heard that you prefer blonds.

<Gunnar>: Only half of them were natural blonds anyhow. If they were blond, they reminded me of Stephanie and Gerthe. That was protection.

<Indy>: ***Sweet, and smooth.*** OK. We can pry the zipper apart. It's a birthday present from Pat, but I can take it back and let them replace the zipper.

<Gunnar>: We'll be very gentle and we can save everything, all the time, and forever.

<Indy>: ***He's selling again.*** If there are no more surprises in the attaché case, we can move it. Take your phone. That should save you some steps.

---------- ----------

<Gunnar>: Let me help with that. You can't see around those anyhow.

I will not let my hands shake. Surgeons need steady hands. I have been with many beautiful women. I am sophisticated and 50 years old - not 14.

OK, so I can't keep my hands from shaking. I can blame it on the bruise. No. I can blame it on the contact lenses.

Give me that back. My eyeglass case is in there.

<Indy>: They make you look [...] intelligent.

<Gunnar>: I am intelligent - I like to keep people confused. Your father does a better job of that than I do.

<Indy>: That's only for people who don't know him.

<Gunnar>: I figured that out, the hard way.

[...] Why do you smell like lotus?

<Indy>: *His hands are shaking. If he's pretending, he gets Nicky points for the act.* This was grandma's only personal luxury. Don't you like it?

<Gunnar>: Yes. It is very nice. *It's making me drunk.*

There! Your hair is loose. Let's try the zipper.

<Indy>: It works. We did it! *He really is gentle.*

<Gunnar>: What are you going to do with the hair?

<Indy>: I'm going to tie it in three knots like this. Then it looks short.

<Gunnar>: *Kabiri! That's the most fascinating hair knotting I have ever seen.* Can we have the friendly hug now?

<Indy>: Yes. *His shoulders feel good.*

<Gunnar>: *I'll be very gentlemanly, but I have surgeon's fingers. She feels just like I thought she would feel.*

Marshall should be ready for that wedding in about four months with crutches and five months with canes. Maybe we can make it a double ceremony. Next year this time, she could have a beautiful round profile when she knots her hair.

Maybe we could elope and announce the marriage and baby Frey-Marshall-Gunnar at Marshall's wedding.

We have to pick boy names and girl names for Little Frey-Marshall-Gunnar.

<Indy>: Gunnar. Why are you staring at me like that? *They don't usually stare at my belly button.*

<Gunnar>: I have a navel fetish. Are you an inny or an outy?

<Indy>: I'm an inny.

<Gunnar>: Could I see?

[...] I'm not being forward. People with middles like yours often want to show it.

<Indy>: I don't. The twins pushed the elasticity limit. *Ryan made fun of my tan zebra stripes.*

[...] Why are you smiling?

<Gunnar>: Let's see if the ring fits.

<Indy>: It's beautiful, and it fits. How did you do that? *He's also very sensual.*

<Gunnar>: I felt your hand.

[...] Why are you taking it off?

<Indy>: I'm terrible at relationships, and I don't believe in love at first sight, *except maybe Mama and Daddy.*

If I don't wear it, I won't be embarrassed next month when you get over whatever it is that you think you are feeling, and I have to give it back.

<Gunnar>: *That means we will be doing something this month!*

I figured you'd say something like that. That's why I bought this. We can be as discrete as you like, *until you let me tell the world. Maybe I'll be Niklas Frey-Marshall-Gunnar. Won't that be a kicker?*

Wear it around your neck until you trust me.

<Indy>: *It's delicate and heavy. I like that.*

<Gunnar>: You can tuck it down in there. I won't even peek. No one will know except you and me. *She didn't pull away. Sometimes technique is good.*

<Indy>: I'll keep it on while we talk about what's happening. Maybe we could kiss too. It would be a little friendship kiss.

[...] *That was* [...] *he's good.*

<Gunnar>: That was very friendly. *They forgave me. Amal and Guntur forgave me!*

Planning Delay

<Indy>: Let's talk about how Mama and Daddy plan, and we will see if it's right for us. Plan #0 is all about agreement. It's a program plan for a relationship.

<Gunnar>: I agree! Your parents have been together for 40 years.

<Indy>: Wait. We have to agree.

[...] Is that someone coming up the driveway?

<Gunnar>: *How can anyone be as unlucky as I am?* We can start practicing discretion now, unless you want me to start singing about you now.

<Indy>: We should finish planning first.

<Gunnar>: Run upstairs. Take your jacket.

<Indy>: Who is it?

<Gunnar>: That's my sister's car, Sharf's wife.

<Indy>: My car's out front.

<Gunnar>: She'll think it's mine. I did.

<Indy>: What are you doing?

<Gunnar>: Go. I'll be right up. Take this too.

---------- ----------

<Gunnar>: Indy, where are you?

<Indy>: I'm over here.

<Gunnar>: What are you doing in the dressing closet?

<Indy>: The bedrooms would have been a little unsubtle, if you had to let her in.

<Gunnar>: It was not just Mags. Gerthe and William came too. I forgot that William said he wanted to talk to me this weekend about the loan and the dangerous Marshall broads.

I suppose that they decided that if they did a sneak attacked, in force, while I was still weak, they could find some loose change.

<Indy>: You're going to leave your mother outside.

<Gunnar>: Where she belongs. You'll meet her after we finish planning and after your mother agrees to protect you from her.

<Indy>: She can't be that bad.

<Gunnar>: She's worse than Sharf. I have to protect you from my family.

<Indy>: Who's going to protect us from you?

<Gunnar>: [...] You will. I will never do anything that will make me lose you.

<Indy>: That's almost blackmail.

<Gunnar>: It's a commitment.

<Indy>: *Oh, how I wish I could believe him.* What are you doing?

<Gunnar>: I'm squeezing into the closet with you.

<Indy>: It's and a big closet.

<Gunnar>: That was poor planning.

<Indy>: Your phone is ringing.

<Gunnar>: I took the phone out of here, and the lump affected my hearing.

[...] I'm sorry. That was a bad joke.

<Indy>: Why do we need your attaché case?

<Gunnar>: You never know if contains something that we might need.

<Indy>: The phone in your pocket is buzzing now.

<Gunnar>: We'll ignore it.

<Indy>: I feel it again. Answer it. You don't want them breaking down doors to check on you.

<Gunnar>: [...] Who is this? ***What is she doing?***

<Indy>: ***The BROAD will help him maintain his financial resolve, at least for the next few hours.***

[...] ***He was holding out on Helena - maybe for me. It was a significant withholding too. This has potential!***

[...] ***When Ryan brings the kids tomorrow, I'll be wearing khaki slacks and a workmen's shirt.***

<Mags>: Why didn't you answer before?

<Gunnar>: When? What day is this? ***Please don't stop!***

<Mags>: It's Saturday.

<Gunnar>: I thought it would be Sunday by now.

I can't talk now. I probably wouldn't remember what you said anyhow.

<Mags>: You sound funny again, but different. Are you sure that you are all right?

<Gunnar>: I'm a little light-headed, but generally, I feel better than I've felt in the last 21 years. Let me finish doing what I need to heal.

<Mags>: When can we see you?

<Gunnar>: Len and Kerstin will be here on Sunday, if you insist. I told you I'm fine.

<Mags>: We'll see you tomorrow. Bye.

<Indy>: What happened?

<Gunnar>: There's a security camera in my office - two doors down - we'll move quietly.

<Indy>: ***Why is he lugging around that attaché case?***

---------- ----------

<Sharf>: What happened?

<Mags>: He sounds as if we woke him up from deep sleep. He said he needs to rest, and we can come back tomorrow while Kerstin is here.

<Sharf>: I need to talk to him without Kerstin.

<Mags>: We should wait. We don't want him angry or annoyed. ***After the way I left him last week, I'm surprised that he is willing to see me at all.***

<Sharf>: When did he get New York plates? Insurance is cheaper in New Jersey.

<Mags>: He's been talking about selling this place. You said his people moved into the building with Marshall. Maybe he's serious.

<Gerthe Gunther>: You should pray that he doesn't sell it. This is big, empty, and paid for.

<Mags>: You're the one that wants to be the mistress of this manor. Don't mess with what we need. Your turn will come.

<Sharf>: Mags is right. We have to talk to about the political mess that he created for me.

<Mags>: He can't fix anything between now and tomorrow.

<Gerthe>: I have the combination. I should talk to him while we're here. He's messing up another wonderful chance.

<Mags>: Helena and Baby Girl can wait. He's here, and not in the Pietro, so nothing is likely to happen that won't wait until tomorrow.

<Gerthe>: It doesn't work anyhow. Something is wrong.

<Mags>: Mama. People are supposed to change their combinations regularly. We'll ask him for the current numbers tomorrow.

[...] William, what are you doing?

<Sharf>: I agree with your mother. I'm checking to see what I can see.

<Gerthe>: [...] What do you see?

<Sharf>: He has piles of supplies stacked in the kitchen, he left a plate and a bottle of ginger tea on the counter, and it appears that he was living in the library. Everything else is covered. ***There was also a bottle of that brew. He's trying to grab the brew committee life preserver. The old witch runs the brew committee!***

<Mags>: He also has a security service. He would be upset if they called him to tell him we were prowling around his house.

<Gerthe>: We're family. It's our duty to take care of him. Call him back and tell him that we are here and we are worried about him.

<Mags>: Last week changed him. I can hear it in his voice. We should let things settle.

<Gerthe>: That's why we should check. Maybe this Baby Girl is poisoning his mind against us.

<Sharf>: Mags is right. He's more likely to say no when he is tired and irritable. ***I need more time to think about this. If he's angry, and he's in cahoots with the brew bunch, the situation is dangerous.***

What did I do to deserve this?

---------- ----------

<Indy>: They left?

<Gunnar>: They'll be back tomorrow with Kerstin and Len.

<Indy>: Don't they have a key?

<Gunnar>: They had the combination, but I just changed it. The new number is 10-31-10-26.

<Indy>: The first one is my birthday. What's the second one?

<Gunnar>: Today, the day we started planning.

<Indy>: Your family will want to know the new combination. Maybe you can change it back for tomorrow.

<Gunnar>: I'll do that. The old one was 04-18-20-03. That's the day I started working for Daxiao.

I have a key for the place in New York, but I'd rather change the lock and clean out some unnecessary junk first. You can have that on Tuesday, and you can meet Kerstin. She mastered discretion for both her parents.

Let me sneak this in while I'm talking about Kerstin. Both she and her husband have computer smarts. Len told me he wants to work for Jonas when he was here last weekend.

I'm trying to take advantage of you already.

<Indy>: It's not up to me. He would have to pass a Jonas screening.

Help me put the ring, on and we can continue discussing our planning requirements.

He picked me over them, at least once! I may live to regret this, but what can he do that Ryan didn't do?

---------- ---------

<Indy>: *This is wrong. I have to be honest with him.*

Gunnar. We shouldn't skip ahead. I was angry with your family, and I was testing you. We should go back to Plan #0.

<Gunnar>: I'm glad they made you want to test me. We should keep testing until I pass. *This is all original equipment. A surgeon can tell.*

<Indy>: Gunnar. We have to learn to communicate. [...] Gunnar. Did you hear me?

<Gunnar>: *I don't want her upset. I am a mature sophisticated gentleman. I can wait, even if it kills me.* What does Plan #0 say?

<Indy>: It has many parts. The first is that we must be kind to each other and take care of each other for the duration of the research.

<Gunnar>: I know how to do that. We can start with these. *Until we get married.* What else?

<Indy>: *The magic attaché case. I should have known.* We should be honest with each other. That's what I'm trying to do now.

<Gunnar>: You are the 43rd project, and you will be the last. I want to marry you, and I want to stop using these as soon as we get married.

<Indy>: My navel. *Somebody for me when the kids leave and when Gunnar leaves! He (or she) could grow up with Rachel. I wanted Ryan's baby, but* [...]

<Gunnar>: Yes. *She didn't bat an eyelash! She almost smiled again.*

<Indy>: We'd have to do a full system check, including a virus scan. Forty-three is a dangerous number.

<Gunnar>: I did that already. The labs tested everything that could be tested last week. This would be a trusted signature.

<Indy>: Why would you go to Church?

<Gunnar>: He was my doctor before he was your father's doctor. He was the first one on the scene when Amal [...]

Seven years later, he fixed my shin, and after that, his team fixed my shoulder.

<Indy>: Mama will destroy him.

<Gunnar>: She shouldn't do that while your father needs him. He is very conscious of patient privacy. I found out we had the same doctor last week when Jonas dialed his number. He found out I knew your father when I was trying to find out why he risked your father life to do the femur replacement.

I was afraid of the traps you father had set for me if he died. I still am.

I'm being as honest as I know how to be, and that look is about to Frey my brains. Please don't make me go away either.

<Indy>: *My brain feels as if it's in a blender and the rest of me* [...] *He was being careful for me.* I will try to be open minded.

<Gunnar>: He didn't complete this round of tests until after he threatened to kill me and until after I showed him all the papers that I just showed you.

Yesterday, he gave me a week to tell you everything. That's why I was planning on sitting in front of the building on 40th street and waiting for you to come out. If you hadn't, I'd have scheduled three or four meetings in your conference room next week, and I had meetings scheduled with your father.

<Indy>: Did you leave the stuff on top of my car on purpose?

<Gunnar>: It was a great idea, but it was an accident. You make me lose control, and I was embarrassed.

<Indy>: I think I'm glad.

<Gunnar>: How do you feel about me? Remember, I'm fragile.

<Indy>: I am lonely, and I need to take my life back. The idea of research with you is growing on me. I'm still afraid of you, but I figured you couldn't hurt me because I knew what to expect. You would teach me how to be like you and your calendar mates, and you would be an expert teacher.

<Gunnar>: You don't want to be like the old Gunnar. We can work on the new Gunnar together.

<Indy>: Let me finish.

You are #2 and two halves. I started with a boy in high school, but I changed my mind during Plan #5. I found out that he had a bet with his buddies about the freak.

<Gunnar>: What is Plan #5?

<Indy>: That's the part where we give ourselves 24 hours to think about the program before we start working on detailed projects.

<Gunnar>: Take as long as you need. ***I am 50, not 14.***

<Indy>: Merle was the other half. We gave the impression that we were having an affair while he was my modeling partner. He designed bikinis for me, and he put make-up on my stretch marks.

He has alternate preferences, and an exclusive partner. He is more careful than Ike was.

<Gunnar>: Lucky Merle. He has the best of both worlds.

<Indy>: Ryan had an exclusive on me from the time I was a freshman in college until 4-1/2 years ago.

<Gunnar>: Four and a half years is a long time for a beautiful woman who should be in the prime of her life. Do you still love Ryan?

<Indy>: I definitely **do not** [...] **know**. There is a heap of anger and pain between us, but he got to be a habit. It's been 22 years.

Do you still love Amal?

<Gunnar>: I love her memory, but after 21 years, I think I'm ready to move back to the world of the living.

Maybe it's time for both of us.

<Indy>: You're not moving very far.

<Gunnar>: You hair is the same color as her hair was and you have an Indian name (plus a French name, a Jewish name, and an Anglo-Saxon name). You might as well tack on something Swedish.

Amal was the size of your mother, very brown, and very meek.

You are bronze like your father, and I doubt that anyone ever used meek in the same chapter as Indira.

Her eyes were dark brown and your eyes - they're always changing - I need to investigate more closely.

[...] They're hazel! You could have told me before I did all that investigating.

<Indy>: I wanted to see whether yours were bluish-gray or grayish-blue, but I couldn't tell with your eyes closed.

<Gunnar>: We have to try that again.

<Indy>: Gunnar! The most important part for you is that you can change research partners or stop the research at any time, as long you let me know. Frey women are not inclined to share.

<Gunnar>: That part is unnecessary. What was the plan that you stopped?

<Indy>: That was #1673. I really wanted to get your attention.

<Gunnar>: ***You still have it.*** That's a large number. How is that possible? I can't even imagine a number that high. No wonder your father is dreaming.

<Indy>: It's almost a lifetime of continuous process improvement.

However, we have to go back to Plan #1. That's the one where we get to know each other even better, starting with our feelings about Ryan and Amal and your navel obsession.

If we do this right, maybe I can keep the potential for longer than a month or two.

Gunnar Family Plans

<Mags>: You're wearing your glasses. Is your vision messed up again?

<Gunnar>: No. My hand is still a little shaky. That doesn't work with contact lenses. ***Indy likes them.***

<Mags>: You look different, other than the glasses.

<Gunnar>: How do I look different?

<Kerstin>: Papa, Len has your computer working. He says you should come and change the password.

<Gunnar>: I'm coming right now.

<Mags>: Andy, we weren't finished.

<Gunnar>: With what?

<Mags>: You look [...] content. I haven't seen you like this since before - you know.

<Gunnar>: I lost two thousand pounds. I'm glad you noticed.

I have to go and change that password. I also have to let Len laugh at how dumb I am.

<Len Palatino>: Gunnar, they ran some awesome cable out here, and this thing has one heck of a modem. I brought it to you.

[...] Look right here. You have to change the default password before you can connect to Daxiao.

You also have to update the security on a regular basis. I can show you that too.

<Gunnar>: Take it slowly. I have to get it right.

<Mags>: Don't you have Marcella and Laufer to handle that for you? *I have to find out what changed.*

<Gunnar>: Please go down stairs. Len and I will be finished in [...]

<Len>: Ten - make it 30 minutes.

<Gunnar>: We will be down in about an hour. He is going to show me what I need to do to catch up on five years of work and to get my career back on track. I don't plan on sleeping in the office. *I don't plan on sleeping at home either - I'll have a 41-year backlog, and then I'll have the baby formula, one set or two.*

<Mags>: You don't like computers.

<Gunnar>: They are growing on me.

The TV in the library works. Kerry, show William where I put the remote, and ***WAIT*** for me.

Mags please help her take the covers off the dining room furniture. In about an hour, I'll be getting a food delivery from this great restaurant in New York. I hope you like Indian Food [...] *and kosher food, and soul food.*

<Mags>: How do you get a New York restaurant to deliver all the way out here?

<Gunnar>: This was arranged by someone who helped to train the chef. *There was a lot of other stuff that I didn't know about Indy.*

<Mags>: I needed to talk to you alone.

<Gunnar>: We are all going to talk together.

<Mags>: But [...]

<Gunnar>: Downstairs [...] together [...] in an hour.

---------- ----------

<Gunnar>: How did you like it?

<Len>: It was a nice change from spaghetti and pizza.

<Mags>: It was decent and not too spicy. The apple thing was good.

<Gerthe>: You didn't even taste the wine. Those two bottles must have cost at least $1,000 and the selection was perfect for the meal.

<Gunnar>: I'm trying to stay on the wagon.

<Sharf>: Where did you get the beer bottles?

<Gunnar>: I'm sure I mentioned Alex Macedon. He sent me an entire case. It's a way for me to connect to the SOA underground. The carrot juice is also healthy. It kept me going when I couldn't chew.

<Sharf>: How much did you pay them to bring that entire set up and wait around until we finished?

<Gunnar>: I don't know yet.

<Gerthe>: It was a waste of money. You could have let me cook, and saved that money for something else.

<Gunnar>: I don't have any pots out here.

<Mags>: Kids, we need to talk to your father alone.

<Gunnar>: I would say nothing to you that they couldn't hear. They've been taking care of the old man.

<Len>: Speaking of taking care. I made it to the hardware store in time yesterday. The handyman helped me install the new lock, Kerry has a key, the concierge has a key, and here are three for you. You're all set.

<Gerthe>: Did you get one for us?

<Gunnar>: Later. I need these.

<Gerthe>: Is the extra for Baby Girl?

<Gunnar>: Yes. How do you know?

<Mags>: Helena called Mother. She was very upset.

<Gunnar>: She left the old key and me.

<Gerthe>: You didn't give her much choice. Who is Baby Girl?

<Gunnar>: I can't tell you until she gives me permission to tell you.

<Gerthe>: Why would she want to keep it a secret?

<Gunnar>: She wants to talk discuss it with her brother, and we have to pass a few critical planning milestones.

<Mags>: Do you know who she is?

<Kerstin>: I don't know who she is, but this one is serious. He proposed to her already.

We worked six hours last night cleaning out leftover stuff - you know what I mean. Today the maid's staff is doing a major cleaning and sanitizing job. He's paying $1,000 extra for them to work over the weekend.

<Mags>: When did you arrange this? You were asleep.

<Gunnar>: After we hung up, it was impossible for me to sleep. I worked on plans instead.

<Gerthe>: I told you.

<Gunnar>: What did you tell her?

<Sharf>: Did you find yourself another high-class gold digger?

<Kerstin>: Definitely not this one.

<Mags>: What do you know about her?

<Kerstin>: Can I tell them now?

<Gunnar>: You might as well. *I wish I had a camera. I want to replay this.*

<Kerstin>: I have to get my bag.

[...] Uncle William. What do you think about this?

[...] It's not bad for one night's work.

<Mags>: What is it?

<Sharf>: It's an irrevocable trust.

<Gerthe>: Fool! You gave her all our money after one [...]

<Mags>: Our money!

<Gunnar>: *This is excellent. It feels like I skipped to #1673.*

<Sharf>: This is for Kerstin.

<Gunnar>: That wasn't one night's work. Kerstin has been a good daughter all her life (almost), in spite of her crazy parents.

<Kerstin>: It was with the concierge when we came out this morning. I was supposed to sign it and send one copy back? Is it real?

<Sharf>: Yes. But, where did you find a notary this morning?

<Len>: Our building has a full service concierge service 24 x 7. Mr. Hoffman handled it for us.

<Mags>: *She's ecstatic and William looks ill?*

<Kerstin>: It is just so-o-o amazing. Whoever Baby Girl is, she didn't want me to worry that she would take all of Papa's money.

She told him to set up this trust. Once the money goes in, I'm the only one who can get it out. Even I can't get it out all at once, right Uncle William?

<Sharf>: Yes.

<Kerstin>: It has $2 million, and I get enough every year to pay for my part of the condo and money for graduate school if I want it. Len can also trade in his clunker.

<Len>: My clunker is smooth and I'm keeping is as long as my father can keep it running.

<Sharf>: *He won't help us with car payments while that fool insists on driving a 15-year-old used car.*

<Kerstin>: The most important part is - maestro please [...]

<Gunnar>: I am going to be a grandfather.

<Kerstin>: It's as if he knew. This comes just in time for Tina Palatino.

<Gerthe>: You just got married. *That's why she's wearing that ugly Pay-Mart blousy thing.*

<Kerstin>: I was born [...]

<Gerthe>: That was different. Your parents had been close for over three years. *All the money will go to her children!*

<Kerstin>: Len and I have been close for [...] years.

<Gunnar>: I'm broke, she's happy and secure, and my grandchildren will be taken care of. ***She gets half, Guntur gets half, and I keep the bonus money that you know nothing about for a little Frey-Marshall-Gunnar or two.***

<Len>: I told Papa that if Baby Girl doesn't work out, we can use the money from the trust to help him.

<Kerstin>: Soon, we should be doing well enough that we can use the interest for Tina's education and childcare, and still have money for Papa if he needs it. It's time that somebody took care of him, don't you think.

<Marge>: How do you manage?

<Kerstin>: Len is excellent with networks and security, and I do games. I'm good with the female characters.

<Mags>: This will interfere with school.

<Kerstin>: The doctor says she should be here a little after spring break. Len and his mother will help me while I study for finals. If something happens, I can delay the finals. I only have three courses next semester anyhow.

<Gerthe>: You're going to pass on a career too.

<Kerstin>: Of course not. I already have a part-time job. I can keep working part-time for the first year, and then I can start full time. I earn $35 an hour already.

<Len>: We made almost a $100K last year.

<Gerthe>: Aren't you worried about what this woman is like? She used your father's money to buy you.

<Mags>: ***My mother is jealous of her granddaughter, the Gerthe/Stephanie pawn.***

<Kerstin>: I don't think I'm worried. Why would you say it like that?

<Gunnar>: Why shouldn't my child, my grandchild, and my future wife be as important to me as Mags' family is to her?

<Mags>: I knew it. You're mad about last week. I thought William needed me.

<Sharf>: I did need you.

<Kerstin>: What did you do?

<Mags>: I left him in the lobby of the Pietro last Thursday, and I ran home to be with William, using carfare that he gave me.

<Sharf>: What were you doing in New York?

<Mags>: He was worried about me.

<Gerthe>: ***She's the one that messed up something.***

<Gunnar>: ***She understands perfectly.*** I got her into the city, and I had to get her home. Your wife and your daughter helped me to set my priorities.

<Mags>: Can you forgive me? ***Now I'll have to work. Clay and Teddy will have to do something too.***

They don't know how to do anything!

<Gerthe>: Of course, he forgives you. A woman has to take care of her man.

<Gunnar>: And a man has to take care of his woman. That was an excellent lesson learned.

<Gerthe>: We don't know if she's right for you.

<Len>: You mean like me?

<Kerstin>: You are right for me. You make me giggle and she makes him giggle.

<Gerthe>: Andrew does not giggle.

<Kerstin>: He does now.

<Mags>: Have you spoken to her?

<Kerstin>: Not directly. I'm certain that she was listening in when her accountant talked me through the papers this morning. When I got here, she was having an x-rated conversation with Papa. He wants her to have a baby for him.

<Gerthe>: ***Another Baby!*** [...] ***ahead of me.***

<Kerstin>: She's not pregnant yet. They were talking about babies and #998, whatever that is.

<Gunnar>: You shouldn't have tried to sneak up on me like that. You nearly scared me to death.

Keep pouring it on. The looks on Gerthe's face and on William's face are exquisite. This is better than sex - well maybe not. With Indy, it's not even better than preliminary planning, but they are still sights to behold.

<Kerstin>: I wanted to give you a surprise hug.

<Gerthe>: How did you get in? ***I have time to talk sense into him.***

<Kerstin>: I used the combination, as usual.

<Gunnar>: *Indy is brilliant. She even left her car in my garage, just in case. I want to giggle now.*

<Gerthe>: Do you think you love this woman?

<Gunnar>: I haven't had a lot of practice, but it has a high probability.

<Gerthe>: When did you have time? You just broke up with Helena yesterday morning.

<Gunnar>: Helena probably mentioned that Baby Girl was on my mind before then.

<Gerthe>: I have not approved this woman.

<Gunnar>: She is a brilliant corporate executive, beautiful enough to be a model, ivy league educated, cultured, and her family is filthy rich. She also cooks and sews.

<Gerthe>: There is no one in the circuit with those qualifications who is free at this time. No one in the circuit ever needed to cook or sew.

<Gunnar>: She has her own circuit.

<Gerthe>: *She will be hard to control.* I would be helping you with the baby. You would want us to get along.

<Gunnar>: *She doesn't miss a beat.* Mother, I am 50 years old, and you definitely did not let anyone approve of your boyfriends after Father died. I believe you were 48 when he passed. I can make my own mistakes as easily as you did.

<Kerstin>: Papa, I just thought of something. If she gets pregnant soon, we can share a Nanny and Len's mother can help with your's too.

Then we won't be a burden on Grandma as I was. You were sick then, and you're even older now, right Grandma.

<Gerthe>: Modern medicine is wonderful. I'm in better shape now than I was then.

<Mags>: *Andy was right. She just developed a sudden case of wellness.*

<Sharf>: Where did you meet this br- woman?

<Gunnar>: It was a chance encounter. I fell into it, in a manner of speaking.

<Sharf>: Does this Babe know that you're in trouble professionally?

<Gunnar>: Yes. Her entire family is willing to help me get through it, if I behave.

<Sharf>: How bad is it at Daxiao, really?

<Gunnar>: How bad is it at Belvedere?

<Sharf>: You got me in a pile of trouble.

<Gunnar>: We got each other in a pile of trouble. I had to go to the back of the line. Guzman is taking back the Audit Committee. For a few moments, my resignation was on the table, literally.

<Sharf>: You have to fix what you did.

<Gunnar>: How? A good word from me would be poison for you. *It would make me lose Indy, and that's never going to happen.*

<Sharf>: You still owe me. You owe us. I was trying to help you run Daxiao.

<Gunnar>: I understand (*you will never admit that you are a raving sociopath*), and I'm prepared to pay you immediately. Look at these.

This proves that there are no hard feelings, in spite of last week.

Mother, these are for you.

<Mags>: William, where are you going?

<Sharf>: It's time for us to get home.

<Mags>: Now what?

---------- ----------

<Gunnar>: Baby Girl makes me feel generous. Those are notes for the $350,000 in loans that you've received from me already. It would be half a million if I charged interest.

They're canceled. I canceled your's too Mother.

That's almost three years of William's bonus and three year's of Mother's pension payments. It will be five years before Kerry collects that much money from the trust. It's also the total amount of the contract between Belvedere and Daxiao.

Now I can start a new life with my new wife and no baggage. You start fresh too.

<Gerthe>: We are grateful.

<Gunnar>: *You are livid, and you don't know why.*

I was insane to try to tangle with the Marshall clan. Indy figured this out in the middle of Plan #1 while we were sneaking in parts of #4. I even get a tax write-off - I lent most of the money to Sharf's dummy corporation.

Denouement - Finally

<Gerthe>: I lost him again. This woman is evil.

<Sharf>: Can't you take a guess at who might fit that description?

<Gerthe>: I do not have a clue.

<Mags>: *I do. He was screaming about her the day I left him sitting in the hotel lobby.*

How could she be evil? She locked his money up for Stephanie's daughter, and she convinced him to cancel half a million in debt for us. To top it off, she sent us a meal that could have cost a few thousand dollars.

<Gerthe>: She's probably the one that convinced him to relocate his office to New York. He'll probably sell the house, as you said yesterday.

<Mags>: If he can hang on to his job, he would probably give it to Kerry, especially if she has more children. Baby Girl probably wouldn't want to live in Stephanie's house with Stephanie's aura.

<Gerthe>: *I did not approve Len and that's a problem. I'll have trouble convincing her that she should let me move in with them. She still has time to find someone more acceptable. I have to see what I can do.*

<Sharf>: It looks like Kerry is getting everything, and we'll never get anything else from him.

<Mags>: What does he have to give? He'll be living on his paycheck, if he manages to keep it.

<Sharf>: He must have more stashed somewhere. Daxiao gives good bonuses. Marshall's Partner Networks were helping them bring in a bundle. Some of that should have been in my pocket.

<Mags>: Some of it is in your pocket. We took large "***gifts***" from him since he has been at Daxiao.

<Sharf>: It didn't hurt him. He still paid for a condo, a house, and stashed $2 million for Kerstin.

<Mags>: That was easier after he stopped racing and crashing cars. Now he only has two.

<Sharf>: He has three if you count the company car. He hardly needs to drive his own. His Ferrari has 8,000 miles on it and its three years old. It's probably paid for too.

<Mags>: Are you saying that Andy is in trouble and we are in trouble, but we want him to give us lumps of his income so that our sons can stay in college, but his daughter goes to college and she works while she is growing a family.

Why would he do that? All we ever gave him was an inferiority complex.

<Gerthe>: *That's how we control him.*

<Sharf>: *She's having another moralistic attack. I wonder what brought this on.* Our sons didn't inherit my numbers sense or your language sense. They need time to study.

<Mags>: They never studied. Their grades are horrible. You and Gerthe put the entitlement stuff in their heads and they believed it.

Gerthe and William think alike! That's why she thought he was the right man for me. She had me on her hook too.

<Gerthe>: They are entitled, and so are you.

Besides, you helped him when he was in school. You were typing for both Andy and William.

<Mags>: That was over 20 years ago.

<Gerthe>: You helped both of them get through school.

<Mags>: How much more should he pay for that?

<Gerthe>: *As much as we can get. If I can't live in the house, I want to go to the Pavilion, or something just as good. That's where my friends are moving.*

<Sharf>: Enough to help me get on my feet with the new consulting practice. Marshall won't be taking any more business from me. Cane will cut the accounting back to 25% after he calms down.

<Mags>: No, he won't.

<Sharf>: What are you saying?

<Mags>: I talked to Mr. Cane. After he was kind enough to explain the new bonus policy to me, he explained that your strength is accounting, not technology consulting. The situation at Daxiao almost got them sued by the company with which they are most interested in doing business.

<Sharf>: ***You're on their side!***

<Gerthe>: William, do not scream at Mags. She's upset too. Can't you hear it in her voice? *She sounds*

like her father used to sound when he was scolding me. I can't lose Mags too.

<Gerthe>: What are we going to do?

<Mags>: My husband, the brilliant accountant, is going to heal himself. He will stop getting us further into debt so he can brag at the club.

I go back to work. I will help him out of this mess as I helped him 20 years ago. Maybe Helena will find me a placement through her agency. Even if I am over 40, my English is excellent, I know how to type, and I still fit into my moderately worn classic attire.

<Gerthe>: My daughter shouldn't have to work. That's what men do.

<Mags>: Daddy went back to work too soon after his heart attack and he died.

<Gerthe>: He had weak genes. That's why you have to be careful with your health.

<Mags>: But he set you up for life. You are going to start using the money that he left you, the part that's in the bank, not just the pension.

<Gerthe>: That was for Teddy, Clay, [...] and Kerstin. ***How did she find out about that?***

<Sharf>: Kerstin won't need it now.

<Mags>: She is still Gerthe's granddaughter, even though she was a pawn in Gerthe's and Stephanie's game with Andy.

<William>: ***This is how she sounded when I had to leave school.***

<Gerthe>: He needed Stephanie to help him get positioned properly.

<Mags>: I will stop creating society events where you can sit around and play the matriarch.

<Mags>: While we are discussing 20 years ago, William will explain, again, the situation at Wheaton. ***I can't hold this any longer.***

You'll be hearing from Hovland in a few days.

<Sharf>: How do you know about that?

<Gerthe>: Excellent! I've heard of Hovland and Doering. You would do well with them.

<Mags>: I received a special package from them.

<Sharf>: You shouldn't have opened anything from Hovland!

<Mags>: It was addressed to me, and I didn't know who Hovland was until I opened it. It contains samples and a note from Dr. Easton. He retired, but Hovland found him for this situation.

<Sharf>: You should have said something. The dean was in Hovland's pocket.

<Mags>: Is it possible that Hovland showed those samples to the dean, and not Indira Marshall?

<Sharf>: Damn! I heard it in his voice last week. ***The Babe is the Marshall broad! She put Hovland and Andy up to this.***

<Gerthe>: Calm down - both of you, and tell me about these Marshalls. I've never heard of them.

<Mags>: You will.

<Sharf>: I can explain [...]

<Mags>: ***Watch where you're going! Don't kill yourself before I get around to it.***

---------- ----------

<Laufer>: Did Gunnar make it in today?

<Marcella>: There's a man in Gunnar's office, but he's not acting like Gunnar. He's humming.

He even looks different. He's letting his hair grow, and I never knew he needed glasses. They make him look intellectual.

<Laufer>: What happened yesterday?

<Marcella>: First, he was up late Sunday night because his sister, his mother, and his brother-in-law were in a car accident. His brother-in-law totaled a new car, but those safety ratings and airbags worked this time.

He said everybody walked away from it. However, he had to drive them home from the hospital

<Laufer>: I guess they're lucky.

<Marcella>: I don't think so. Afterward, he spent hours giving tips for future health and well-being.

<Laufer>: How? Gunnar knows all the things that you should do if you want to have an accident.

<Marcella>: I know.

Anyway, yesterday morning, he went to New York to take more tests. He volunteered for one of those long-term research projects, he started the preliminary requirements last week, and he wanted to deliver samples as quickly as possible.

<Laufer>: Did he pass the test?

<Marcella>: He says he's almost certain that he did well, but if he didn't pass, he will be allowed repeat the test until they get the expected results.

However, the important thing is that he's hooked up now, and he can work at home in either New York or New Jersey. He spoke to Lisse Maçon and Macedon for an hour, he did his own research, and he spent the rest of the afternoon calming down people in Marshall's Partner network.

<Laufer>: Are you sure that he was talking to Liz and Macedon?

<Marcella>: I had to patch them into a three-way conversation.

<Laufer>: Are you sure that he was helping with Partner Networks?

<Marcella>: He sent me copies of four follow-up messages and I Fed-Exed four letters of confirmation. I'm sure.

<Laufer>: What else is unusual?

<Marcella>: When I got here, he had turned on his own computer, he checked the sales matrix, he fixed four things that we entered wrong, and he did not tap his pinky at me. He's slow, but he's persistent.

The kicker is that he thanked me profusely for helping him last week, and he sent the note requesting a raise and a promotion to the Doc already. I have a copy.

<Laufer>: Congratulations. That was past due.

<Marcella>: Here's a heads-up. When you meet him today, be serious about SOA Lessons Learned and common terminology. He's in there circling things.

<Laufer>: He mentioned it last week, but thanks.

The real reason I called is that I need to know his new password.

<Marcella>: I almost forgot. He changed it himself. He said we should replace the whole thing with RATIO998NOVUSVITAE (all uppercase).

<Laufer>: *My Latin is rusty. I'll have to check to see what that means.* The Swede would approve. That's a very strong password.

APPENDIX

Table A.1.1 - Corporate Sector Teams and Roles - Support for COBIT and COSO		
Team and Roles	**Responsibility for Control Group, Component, or Objective**	**Level of Responsibility**
Corporate Sector Managers		
♦ Architect - corporate	Compliance with applicable laws and regulations (ERM)	Primary
	Information and Communication (COSO)	Primary
	Objective Setting (COSO)	Secondary
	Obtain Independent Assurance	Secondary
	Provide for Independent Audit	Secondary
♦ Board of Directors	Control Activities (COSO)	Primary
	Information and Communication (COSO)	Primary
	Objective Setting (COSO)	Secondary
	Obtain Independent Assurance	Secondary
	Define IT Strategic Plan	Primary
♦ Executive - corporate	Define Strategic IT Plan	Secondary
	Manage Human Resources	Secondary
	Objective Setting (COSO)	Primary
♦ Sponsor - corporate	Manage IT Investment	Secondary
Corporate Communications		
♦ Communications specialist - corporate	Communicate Management Aims and Direction	Primary
	Information and Communication (COSO)	Primary
Global Security		
♦ Security specialist - corporate	Compliance with applicable laws and regulations (ERM)	Secondary
	Ensure Systems Security	Primary
	Internal Environment (COSO)	Primary
	Risk Response (COSO)	Primary
♦ Security specialist - technology	Define Information Architecture	Secondary
Enterprise Integration		
♦ Business Analyst - corporate	Define Strategic IT Plan	Secondary
	Ensure Systems Security	Secondary
	Identify Automated Solutions	Secondary
♦ Strategist - corporate	Define Strategic IT Plan	Secondary
	Conformity to the organization's strategy (ERM)	Primary
	Objective Setting (COSO)	Secondary
Financial Management		
♦ Domain owner - data	Manage Data	Primary
	Manage Problems and Incidents	Secondary
	Define Information Architecture	Secondary
♦ Domain owner - service	Acquire and Maintain Application Software	Secondary
♦ Financial specialist - corporate	Reliability of financial reporting (ERM)	Primary
	Manage IT Investment	Secondary
	Reliability of financial reporting (ERM)	Secondary
Human Resources		
♦ Personnel specialist	Manage Human Resources	Primary
♦ Training specialist	Educate and Train Users	Primary
Legal Services		

♦ Corporate lawyer	Assess Internal Control Adequacy	Secondary
	Assess Risks	Secondary
	Compliance with applicable laws and regulations (ERM)	Primary
	Control Activities (COSO)	Primary
	Ensure Compliance with External Requirements	Primary
	Event Identification (COSO)	Secondary
	Monitor Processes	Secondary
	Monitoring (COSO)	Secondary
	Obtain Independent Assurance	Secondary
	Provide for Independent Audit	Secondary
	Risk Assessment (COSO)	Secondary
	Risk Response (COSO)	Primary

Table A.1.2 - Business Sector Teams and Roles - Support for COBIT and COSO

Team and Roles	Responsibility for Control Group, Component, or Objective	Level of Responsibility
All Teams		
♦ All Roles	Event Identification (COSO)	Secondary
Business Clients		
♦ Client - business operations	Control Activities (COSO)	Secondary
	Define and Manage Service Levels	Secondary
♦ Client - manufacturing	Define and Manage Service Levels	Primary
♦ Client - sales and marketing	Define and Manage Service Levels	Secondary
Business Sector Managers		
♦ Executive - manufacturing	Define Strategic IT Plan	Secondary
	Manage Human Resources	Secondary
	Objective Setting (COSO)	Secondary
	Risk Response (COSO)	Secondary
♦ Executive - operations	Define Strategic IT Plan	Secondary
	effectiveness and efficiency of operations (ERM)	Primary
	Manage Human Resources	Secondary
	Objective Setting (COSO)	Secondary
	Risk Response (COSO)	Secondary
♦ Executive - sales and marketing	Define Strategic IT Plan	Secondary
	Manage Human Resources	Secondary
	Objective Setting (COSO)	Secondary
	Risk Response (COSO)	Secondary
♦ Sponsor - business operations	Manage IT Investment	Secondary
♦ Sponsor - manufacturing	Manage IT Investment	Secondary
♦ Sponsor - sales and marketing	Manage IT Investment	Secondary
Quality Assurance		
♦ Quality management coordinator	Manage Problems and Incidents	Secondary
	Manage Quality	Primary
Process Management		
♦ Process coordinator - business	Develop and Maintain Procedures	Primary
♦ Workflow analyst	Develop and Maintain Procedures	Secondary
Requirements Management		
♦ Business analyst - client team	Acquire and Maintain Application Software	Secondary
	Define Information Architecture	Secondary

	Manage Change	Secondary
♦ Project initiation manager	Acquire and Maintain Application Software	Primary
	Identify Automated Solutions	Primary
	Manage Changes	Primary
♦ Requirements analyst	Acquire and Maintain Application Software	Secondary
	Manage Changes	Secondary

Table A.1.3 - BASE (Governance) Sector Teams and Roles - Support for COBIT and COSO

Team and Roles	Responsibility for Control Group, Component, or Objective	Level of Responsibility
Compliance Management		
♦ Compliance specialist - business	Assess Internal Control Adequacy	Primary
	Assess Risks	Secondary
	Ensure Compliance with External Requirements	Primary
	Event Identification (COSO)	Primary
	Monitor Processes	Primary
	Obtain Independent Assurance	Primary
	Provide for Independent Audit	Primary
	Compliance with applicable laws and regulations (ERM)	Secondary
	Control Activities (COSO)	Secondary
	Monitoring (COSO)	Primary
	Risk Assessment (COSO)	Secondary
♦ Compliance specialist - technology	Assess Risks	Secondary
	Monitor Processes	Secondary
	Control Activities (COSO)	Secondary
	Monitoring (COSO)	Secondary
♦ Process coordinator - technology	Develop and Maintain Procedures	Secondary
	Manage Quality	Secondary
♦ Risk analyst - business	Assess Risks	Primary
	Risk Assessment (COSO)	Primary
♦ Risk analyst - technology	Assess Risks	Secondary
Governance Sector Managers		
♦ Executive - SOA	Communicate Management Aims and Direction	Secondary
	Define IT Organization and Relationships	Secondary
	Define Strategic IT Plan	Secondary
	Conformity to the organization's strategy (ERM)	Secondary
	Manage Human Resources	Secondary
	Manage IT Investment	Secondary
	Objective Setting (COSO)	Secondary
	Risk Response (COSO)	Secondary
SOA Implementation		
♦ Project Manager - SOA	Manage Projects	Secondary
	Manage IT Investment	Secondary
	Manage Problems and Incidents	Secondary
SOA Communications		
♦ Communications specialist - BASE	Communicate Management Aims and Direction	Secondary
	Information and Communication (COSO)	Secondary
♦ User interface specialist	Acquire and Maintain Application Software	Secondary
SOA Competency		

Table A.1.3 - BASE (Governance) Sector Teams and Roles - Support for COBIT and COSO		
Team and Roles	**Responsibility for Control Group, Component, or Objective**	**Level of Responsibility**
♦ Architect - SOA	Define IT Organization and Relationships	Secondary
	Determine Technological Direction	Primary
	Identify Automated Solutions	Secondary
	Manage Performance and Capacity	Secondary
SOA Library Management		
♦ Knowledge consolidator	Communicate Management Aims and Direction	Secondary
♦ SOA librarian	Manage Changes	Secondary
SOA Program Management		
♦ BASE Program coordinator	Assess Internal Control Adequacy	Secondary
	Manage Changes	Secondary
♦ Business analyst - Extranet	Define IT Organization and Relationships	Secondary
♦ Business analyst - Governance	Acquire and Maintain Application Software	Secondary
♦ Financial specialist - BASE	Identify and Allocate Costs	Primary
♦ Planning specialist	Manage Projects	Secondary
Vendor Management		
♦ Procurement specialist	Acquire and Maintain Application Software	Secondary
	Identify Automated Solutions	Secondary

Table A.1.4 - Technology Sector Teams and Roles - Support for COBIT and COSO		
Team and Roles	**Responsibility for Control Group, Component, or Objective**	**Level of Responsibility**
Business Technology		
♦ Architect - software	Acquire and Maintain Application Software	Secondary
♦ Developer - application	Acquire and Maintain Application Software	Secondary
♦ Developer - legacy adaptation	Acquire and Maintain Application Software	Secondary
♦ Developer - process	Develop and Maintain Procedures	Secondary
♦ Developer - SOA	Acquire and Maintain Application Software	Secondary
♦ Team leader	Acquire and Maintain Application Software	Secondary
Data Center		
♦ Architect - Availability	Define and Manage Service Levels	Secondary
	Ensure Continuous Service	Primary
	Manage Performance and Capacity	Primary
♦ Service assurance	Identify and Allocate Costs	Secondary
	Manage Problems and Incidents	Secondary
Data Management		
♦ Data specialist	Acquire and Maintain Application Software	Secondary
	Define Information Architecture	Primary
	Manage Data	Secondary
♦ Data administrator	Acquire and Maintain Application Software	Secondary

Table A.1.4 - Technology Sector Teams and Roles - Support for COBIT and COSO		
	Define Information Architecture	Secondary
	Ensure Systems Security	Secondary
	Manage Data	Secondary
♦ Developer - database	Acquire and Maintain Application Software	Secondary
Infrastructure Technology		
♦ Architect - enterprise technology	Determine Technological Direction	Secondary
	Ensure Continuous Service	Secondary
	Define Strategic IT Plan	Secondary
	Objective Setting (COSO)	Secondary
	Risk Response (COSO)	Secondary
♦ Architect - infrastructure	Acquire and Maintain Technology Infrastructure	Primary
	Identify Automated Solutions	Secondary
	Install and Accredit Systems	Primary
	Manage Configuration	Primary
	Manage Performance and Capacity	Secondary
	Risk Response (COSO)	Secondary
♦ Architect - network	Acquire and Maintain Technology Infrastructure	Secondary
	Identify Automated Solutions	Secondary
	Manage Performance and Capacity	Secondary
♦ Asset librarian	Manage Configuration	Secondary
♦ Deployment specialist	Manage Configuration	Secondary
	Manage Problems and Incidents	Secondary
♦ Integration specialist	Manage Configuration	Secondary
	Manage Problems and Incidents	Secondary
♦ Network services specialist	Manage Third-Party Services	Secondary
	Install and Accredit Systems	Secondary
	Manage Configuration	Secondary
♦ Tool administrator	Acquire and Maintain Technology Infrastructure	Secondary
	Install and Accredit Systems	Secondary
Technology Sector Managers		
♦ Executive - technology	Define IT Organization and Relationships	Primary
	Define Strategic IT Plan	Secondary
	effectiveness and efficiency of operations (ERM)	Secondary
	Internal Environment (COSO)	Secondary
	Manage Facilities	Primary
	Manage Human Resources	Secondary
	Manage Operations	Primary
	Objective Setting (COSO)	Secondary
	Risk Response (COSO)	Secondary
♦ Sponsor - technology	Manage IT Investment	Primary
♦ Project manager - infrastructure	Determine Technological Direction	Secondary
	Manage Changes	Secondary
	Manage Facilities	Secondary
	Manage IT Investment	Secondary
	Manage Operations	Primary
	Manage Problems and Incidents	Secondary
	Manage Projects	Secondary
	Manage Third-Party Services	Primary
Project manager - business technology	Acquire and Maintain Application Software	Secondary

Table A.1.4 - Technology Sector Teams and Roles - Support for COBIT and COSO		
	Manage IT Investment	Secondary
	Manage Problems and Incidents	Secondary
	Manage Projects	Primary
	Manage Third-Party Services	Secondary
User Support		
♦ Help desk	Assist and Advise Customers	Secondary
	Manage Problems and Incidents	Secondary
♦ Security administrator	Ensure Systems Security	Secondary
♦ User support specialist	Acquire and Maintain Application Software	Secondary
	Assist and Advise Customers	Primary
	Manage Problems and Incidents	Primary

Table A.2 - Lessons Learned

Accelerated rate of change, as required to support Daxiao's evolving SOA, met resistance across the organization, even though Daxiao believed it was a change-tolerant organization.

Recommended Solution:

1. Define the risk of stagnation for the individual and for the organization.
2. Institute a risk mitigation program.
3. Provide training, and personal mentoring.

Acceptance criteria must be defined in Requirements Management before the application is turned over to the product creation teams (developers). Modifications to acceptance criteria should go through a change management process that may result in changes to costs or delivery schedules.

Adherence to internal technology standards and policy by Program participants, especially those hired by the technology executive, was believed to be a waste of time.

Recommended Solution:

1. Demonstrate benefits of consistent standards (even if they are not perfect).
2. Demonstrate the cost of non-compliance.
3. Listen to suggestions for improvements to standards.
4. Monitor and report problems related to non-compliance.
5. Recognize compliance and penalize problems caused by non-compliance.

Agile development required supervision by SOA (highly experienced project managers) and equally talented team leaders. If not, services created using agile techniques often had to be refactored to improve reusability.

Alignment problems between business requirements and available technology justified pursuit of SOA. Daxiao started with less than 50% alignment between business units and applications. Daxiao had to:

1. Demonstrate extra costs associated with running unaligned applications.
2. Identify and prioritize units that needed alignment.
3. Provide cost estimates for aligning products using traditional, EAI, and SOA techniques.
4. Reset to organizational or process boundaries.

Refer to the alignment example in Figs. 6.1 - 6.3, 7.1 and 7.2.

Amnesia projects - attempts to hide failed projects - caused problems in Daxiao because valuable Lessons Learned were lost. Daxiao instituted failed/canceled project reviews so that we could benefit from our failures.

Anomalous product purchases often did not work as expected, conform to standards, or fit into reference architecture.

Recommended Solution:

1. Bring products under procurement management quickly.
2. Centralize funding.
3. Help the accepted procurement process occur as quickly as the incorrect ones.
4. Penalize vendors who go around the normal processes.
5. Report negative technical and financial consequences of anomalous purchases.

Another wild goose technology chase was the business units' original perception of SOA. They believed it was another money-wasting technical fad.

Recommended Solution:

1. Define the risks of staying in place.

Table A.2 - Lessons Learned
2. Provide examples (storytelling) to demonstrate the benefits of SOA. 3. Show that SOA is more business than technology.
Anti-patterns are as important as patterns. Maintaining a catalog of things that people do wrong is as important as lists of best practices. Daxiao capture anti-patterns from failed, failing, or troubled projects, and from industry literature.
Application retirement was resisted by both business and technology. They wanted "their own systems" even when they are obviously redundant or problematic. **Recommended Solution:** 1. Define and publish objective guidelines for retirement recommendations. 2. Define cost of running redundant processing. 3. Define costs for running replacement processes. 4. Demonstrate performance and availability of the new product. 5. Demonstrate that replacement software performs correctly and provides equivalent or better functionality than the product to be retired. 6. Make migration to the new service as transparent as possible. 7. Provide technology professionals with alternate challenges.
Approvals for SOA catalog: 1. Backup approvers had to be assigned to avoid bottlenecks. 2. Compliance and financial specialists or requirements and risk analysts may demand approvals from additional roles for more difficult or risky projects. 3. Senior stakeholders may request review and approval rights for specific work efforts. 4. Though there are more than 100 active roles, the minimum number of approvals required for project delivery or service reuse is very small. They are: **Approval for promotion to development:** 1. Client or visionary (at least one). 2. Process coordinator - business. 3. Process coordinator - technology. 4. Project initiation manager. 5. Project manager (accepting responsibility for the project). 6. Requirements analyst. 7. Security specialist - technology. 8. Sponsor (at least one). **Approval for deployment:** 1. Architect - Availability. 2. Asset librarian.

Table A.2 - Lessons Learned
3. Client or visionary (at least one). 4. Compliance specialist - business. 5. Compliance specialist - technology. 6. Deployment specialist. 7. Process coordinator - business. 8. Process coordinator - technology. 9. Project initiation manager. 10. Quality management coordinator. 11. Risk analyst - business. 12. Risk analyst - technology. 13. Security specialist - technology. 14. Service assurance. 15. SOA librarian. 16. Sponsor - business operations. 17. User - business operations. **Promotion to development:** 1. Architect - Availability. 2. Client or visionary (at least one). 3. Process coordinator - business. 4. Process coordinator - technology. 5. Project initiation manager. 6. Quality management coordinator (acknowledging turnover to testing). 7. Security specialist - technology. 8. Service assurance (agreeing to support testing). 9. SOA librarian. 10. Sponsor (at least one). **Approval for Reuse:** 1. Architect - Availability. 2. Architect - SOA (Pre-approval is an option). 3. Asset librarian. 4. Data administrator (Pre-approval is an option). 5. Data specialist (Pre-approval is an option). 6. Domain owner - data (Pre-approval is an option). 7. Domain owner - service (Pre-approval is an option). 8. Planning specialist. 9. Process coordinator - business (Pre-approval is an option). 10. Requirements analyst (Pre-approval is an option). 11. Risk analyst - business (Pre-approval is an option). 12. Risk analyst - technology (Pre-approval is an option). 13. Security administrator. 14. Security specialist - technology. 15. SOA librarian. 16. Sponsor - (only if product was not turned over to a domain owner). 17. Sponsor (before turnover to a domain owner).
Assumptions management allowed reduction of project costs by reducing rework. Daxiao had to:

Table A.2 - Lessons Learned
1. Develop costing algorithms for unverified assumptions. 2. Establish assumptions life cycle management processes and procedures. 3. Evaluate and verifying assumptions as early as possible.
Attribution, sharing credit for SOA successes, improves the likelihood of SOA support.
Auditability must be built into service design. Standards mandated logging and useful error messages.
Automated approvals resistance lead to improved processes that eventually accelerated project approvals. **Recommended Solution**: 1. Demonstrate that automated approvals can accelerate migration through review and funding processes. 2. Demonstrate that the approval process can be monitored and secured. 3. Showed that automated processes can increase the likelihood of proper funding reviews.
Automation of methodology steps promotes Program success when used to improve or replace manual processes. Automated processes may assist: 1. Adherence to service delivery processes and procedures. 2. Cross-border development teams. 3. Software compliance evaluation. 4. Testing.
BASE Support (SOA Governance) provides the policies, processes, and monitoring required for evolution to a full SOA. It includes: 1. Automation of approval processes. 2. Blending the flexibility of service orientation with the control of traditional IT architectures. 3. Coordination of service requirements across organizational boundaries working with the Requirements Management Team. 4. Definition of and visibility into costing algorithms. 5. Definition of roles and responsibilities associated with service and process creation and use. 6. Distribution of decision-making and approval rights within the organization. 7. Ensuring collaboration between business and IT on service creation. 8. Ensuring service compliance to company policy, SOA recommendations, industry rules, and government, and international regulations. 9. Ensuring that services support company strategy. 10. Facilitation of Program collaboration (provision of facilitators and collaboration tools) 11. Identifying and managing the potential impact of

Table A.2 - Lessons Learned
service and process changes. 12. Knowledge Cooperative that minimizes the time required to research information for work requests and projects. 13. Management of exceptions to processes. 14. Managing service life cycle. 15. Managing service quality, reliability, interdependence, and reusability. 16. Promoting incremental adaptation with a focus on lessons learned in each project to improve subsequent projects. 17. Promoting trust by ensuring quality and predictability. 18. Promotion of common terminology. 19. Research and promotion of an SOA reference Architecture. 20. Reuse of Program artifacts beyond software (plans, lessons learned, etc.). 21. Standardization and automation of SOA development processes. 22. Standardization of processes and minimization of process exceptions. 23. Standardization of systems and system-management tools. 24. Support and guidance of service management and monitoring. 25. Support for cultural change management.
Best practices maintenance: Best practices evolve. They must be regularly evaluated and updated. We had to: 1. Ensure that Program participants are notified of new, updated, or deprecated practices. 2. Evaluate internal best practices against evolving industry expectation. 3. Maintain best practices for vendor products. 4. Review every project for possible best practices.
Business creation of processes is only practical when a unit has reached high levels of business, technology, and process maturity. Technology had valid concerns about the effects that processes created by business teams could have on the operating environment. Some business analysts and clients do not like the idea of becoming "programmers". **Recommended Solution:** 1. Carefully monitor pilot activities and ensure that they are successful by providing adequate input from supporting roles. 2. Enforce rules life cycle for business-created processes. 3. Permit experimentation in research environments. 4. Start with simpler processes. 5. Update and carefully manage catalog access and

Table A.2 - Lessons Learned
approval rights.
Business learning technology concepts: Business team participants felt that they do not have time to learn about technology, that learning technology was below them, or were afraid that they could not learn technology. **Recommended Solution:** 1. Demonstrate how "simple problems" are often not simple. 2. Provide simple animations of technology concepts. 3. Show how understanding technology simplifies the requirements process (it limits the number of people who ask for the impossible) and facilitates problem prevention.
Business modeling is a major foundation project for the WFSOA evolution. The Daxiao model includes: 1. Business events and related responses. 2. Processes and related guidelines. 3. Business policies and justification. 4. Key performance indicators.
Business Process Management (BPM) was necessary to achieve the process coverage required in the SOA maturity model. It provides procedures and tools that support analysis, definition (modeling), execution, monitoring and administration, and coordination of end-to-end business processes. It is used for enterprise-level modeling or project-level modeling. It includes: 1. Models of the current state of the enterprise and the intended future state(s). 2. Workflow, functional, organizational and data resource views for linking business strategy to IT development. 3. Guidelines for continuous process improvement. 4. Business process re-engineering when major process adjustments are necessary.
Business response services must be created to respond to business situations that are not yet addressed in either strategic or tactical plans. They through normal Product Delivery processes with the following additional steps: 1. Justification for the service will be included in the next strategy management cycle. 2. They must be approved by the senior executive in the affected area and the corporate architect.
Business rules externalization assists service reuse, agility, and business flexibility. However, developers resisted the extra work necessary to synchronize development efforts with a rules engine. Business units initially resisted the schedule delays required to implement rules management. **Recommended Solution:** 1. Automate the business rules maintenance process.

Table A.2 - Lessons Learned
2. Define a business rule life cycle. 3. Established a business rules governance board that includes corporate business analysts and subject matter experts. 4. Mandate separation of business rules from programming. 5. Purchased a simple fast rules processing engine that supports capture, revision, and tracking of business rules out side processing software. 6. Show business and technology how external rules can reduce programmer involvement in rules maintenance. 7. Train developers and business analysts to use the business rules engine.
Business rules for technology: Daxiao learned to treat technology standards as business rules and externalized them during (methodology) process automation.
Business rules mining is a continuing process. Daxiao: 1. Mandated rules mining for legacy service wrapping projects. 2. Mandated rules mining for very legacy application maintenance activity. 3. Provided software to assist with rules mining.
Capture of tacit knowledge - Refer to "Sharing Knowledge".
Catalog of Record: Daxiao: 1. Created an SOA catalog of record and lock it well. 2. Created federated catalogs to support the service development life cycle. 3. Defined approval and promotion processes.
Centralized funding of work requests saved money, but business unit resisted changes to the way they controlled funding and timing of work requests. **Recommended Solution:** 1. Show that high priority requirements are handled in a timelier manner and always by the best people available. 2. Show them how this facilitates service reuse.
Change Advisory Boards (CAB): Daxiao required two: 1. The business CAB includes executives and Board members who collaborate on input to Strategy Management Processes and procedures. They also work with Human Resources Support to ensure the success of cultural change management activities. 2. The technology CAB includes people who collaborate with the Requirements Management Team. With input from clients, users, technology, and governance teams, they may prioritize requests, recommend allocation of implementation resources, and assist user liaison during the change life cycle.

Table A.2 - Lessons Learned
CICS: This transaction manager is not going away in Daxiao, even if an SOA standard (probably standards) is approved, tested, and implemented that is as effective as CICS transaction management and back-out. Daxiao benefits from existing capabilities by wrapping successful transactions (with appropriate refactoring) to provide effective services.
COBOL is not going away in Daxiao. Daxiao decided to: 1. Wrap legacy COBOL applications as services. 2. Retain, train, or hiring experienced staff. 3. Cross-train staff in other languages and rotate them into COBOL project teams.
Common terminology promotes SOA consistency and reuse. However, people in all roles felt more comfortable with historically familiar terms. **Recommended Solution:** 1. Build cross-references to link corporate terminology and proprietary products, legacy terminology and Service-Oriented Architecture, and native language and cross-border interests. 2. Build user interface services that maintained user preferences. 3. Check for real-time use of non-common terminology. 4. Demonstrate how confusion can occur when multiple names are used for the same entity or concept. 5. Encourage business units to use similar terminology among internal teams, across business entities, and between business entities and their partners, using industry-approved terminology when it is possible. 6. Ensure identical names and value domains for identical data items. 7. Identify and define acronyms. 8. Mandate documentation of business, technology, and role-based vocabulary and semantics. 9. Support alternate labeling for core definitions and build a cross reference to aliases. 10. Synchronize common terminology with metadata. 11. Track and record new terms and usages. 12. Updates terminology when: ♦ New policies and standards are promulgated. ♦ New corporate products were created. ♦ Terminology refinements became available.
Communications processes are critical to Program success. They keep Program participants aware of the Program and ensure that they have timely access to necessary information. The BASE communications specialist: 1. Captured relevant content from ad hoc communications. 2. Created and maintained Program a communications plan that defined when, how, to whom, and what information would normally flow among BASE Program or project participants. 3. Defined processes for evangelizing the Program. 4. Ensured the creation of a communications plan for every project. 5. Established processes for rapid access to subject matter experts when appropriate. 6. Identified communications gaps. 7. Identified conflicts in communications. 8. Monitored perceived communication frequency between all combinations of roles. 9. Promoted common terminology. 10. Recommended guidelines for ensuring that Program participants have "just-enough-information" for their roles and responsibilities without being overloaded.
Competition among teams proved a good way to get SOA buy-in. Financial and recognition incentives were given for quality product delivery and shortened time-to-market.
Computer Comfort Level and SOA: People who are 45 years or older may still feel uncomfortable with computers even if they use the internet. Several important Daxiao's managers fell into this category. They always had assistants, who could find the information for them, so they were less than enthusiastic about using processes that provided information more quickly, but required facility with computers outside of simple e-mail. **Recommended Solution:** 1. Consider voice recognition. 2. Created services that provided the most critical managerial information in succinct formats. 3. Make everything short and simple. 4. Minimize the clicks required to get to relevant information. 5. Provide notification options for people who do not wish bells, blings, or blinking colors. 6. Provide simple interfaces that require minimal input. 7. Provide simple short animations. 8. Provide simple written instructions in pocket-sized formats. 9. Understand that senior management often thinks differently than regular staff. Adjust interfaces and content.
Continuous process improvement was necessary for the success of the WFSOA Program. No one knew enough to do everything right the first time. However, people on operations and technology teams resisted change content or the increasing frequency of changes.

Table A.2 - Lessons Learned
Recommended Solution: 1. Encourage submission of recommendations for improvements to business and technology processes. 2. Establish and support the process coordination roles. 3. Explain how changing environments necessitate process changes. 4. Explain process benefits in training activities. 5. Explain that process elimination or integration may be required. 6. Identify reasons for resistance and learn from valid resistance. 7. Reassign people who pose serious project risks. 8. Recognize rapid adoption of process changes. 9. Report lessons learned from process changes. 10. Track metrics.
Core services: A critical mass of services, identified with guidance from the business community, must be installed and stabilized before promoting conformance to SOA
Corporate Architecture is a critical foundation component for WFSOA success, applying architectural techniques to a human organization. **Note:** Daxiao uses this term to avoid confusion with the technical function that is performed by the enterprise architect. It provides a blueprint of the organizational structure, including relationships among (people) management systems, information (application) systems, and computer systems (hardware and operating systems). The blueprint includes: 1. Business and technology inefficiencies. 2. Business processes, overlaps, and gaps. 3. Business/technology alignment strategy, implementation, and problems. 4. Corporate Architecture must be iterative, as it is impossible to fill in all the details of the blueprint while the organization is changing. 5. Interactions between business entities. 6. Interactions between humans and systems. 7. Major stakeholders. 8. Organizational goals. 9. Recommendations for renovation and continuous process improvements through "as-is" and "to-be" scenarios. 10. ROI on technology investments. 11. Techniques that facilitate rapid change to maintain business and technology advantages.
Costing algorithms are critical for WFSOA success. Business units resisted support for shared until they understood the pricing.

Table A.2 - Lessons Learned
Recommended Solution: 1. Implement metering to of resource utilization. 2. Plan for early implementation of an updated cost structure. 3. Provide business with visibility into costing algorithms and provide training to promote understanding. 4. Provide dashboards that demonstrate resource utilization.
Critical mass: SOA Program benefits accrue geometrically after a critical mass of services is available. It: 1. Helps to deliver within schedule and budget. 2. Helps to reduce functional defects 3. Reduces development time for new applications.
Cross-border projects - Business units resist using products created outside geographic boundaries. **Recommended Solution:** 1. Demonstrate benefits of sharing technology and processes. 2. Demonstrate how all COTS products are often created by external (cross-border developers). 3. Promote understanding of cultural differences. 4. Promote understanding of technology differences across geographic boundaries. 5. Provide language-specific user interfaces. 6. Support creation of cross-border teams. 7. Translate standards and procedures.
Cross training is essential for Program success. 1. Developers and architects who are familiar with multiple platforms and languages have fewer interface errors. 2. Technology savvy business analysts are as import as business savvy developers.
Cultural change management may be more important than technical success to WFSOA. The corporate architect and BASE executive had to: 1. Assess corporate culture. 2. Customize the Program for individual business sectors and units. 3. Establish a continuing training and mentoring. 4. Establish a flexible process for role creation, modification, and assignment. 5. Implement policy changes (internal and partner-related). 6. Implement targeted organizational restructuring (primarily domain management, requirements management, and the SOA competency team). 7. Provide automated processes to support the cultural change. 8. Work with Human Resources to establish a formal program.

Table A.2 - Lessons Learned
Culture of innovation - Historically successful teams resist changing what works. **Recommended Solution:** 1. Provide examples of what happens to companies that do not innovate. 2. Provide training in cultural change.
Customer self-service - Refer to "Business creation of automated processes".
Dashboard & scorecards promote SOA visibility and success. Use copiously.
Data consolidation and reuse was resisted by business system owners who did not wish to lose control of "their" data. **Recommended Solution:** 1. Demonstrate the continuing problems with data synchronization. 2. Demonstrate the long-term financial benefits of data sharing. 3. Ensure active participation of business data owners in consolidation projects. 4. Facilitate the process of migrating users to consolidated data sources. 5. Recognize sharing. 6. Understand that it may be necessary to spend money to save money by ensuring that the results of consolation perform well and adequately address multiple user requirements.
Data governance and quality emerged as critical adjuncts to SOA governance. Daxiao: 1. Created data services to access unified databases. 2. Created metadata for consolidated data sources. 3. Defined data governance processes and procedures. 4. Defined data taxonomy. 5. Defined the cost benefits of improved data quality. 6. Defined the cost benefits of managed data. 7. Demonstrated benefits of data quality to SOA success. 8. Established a data governance committee. 9. Established the data domain owner role at the corporate level. 10. Initiated consolidation plans (minimize the number one-off databases).
Data services were required to support a common data terminology, metadata management, query processing, data caching, or data transformation, and loose coupling between data sources and users. They included: 1. Data capture. 2. Data enhancement. 3. Data standardization. 4. Data validation. 5. Data virtualization.

Table A.2 - Lessons Learned
6. Data warehouse/mart access. 7. Master database management. 8. Reference data management.
Deployment processes should be outlined during the design phase and tuned during testing.
Design patterns (SOA) provided program participants with repeatable ways for delivering quality software. 1. Compliance teams monitored their use. 2. Program participants were trained in the use of design patterns.
Development methodologies for SOA still evolving. **Daxiao** customized methodology approaches project requirements. The technology process coordinator (methodology specialist) defined processes and procedures for selecting an approach suitable to the project. Approaches included: 1. Agile database 2. Agile modeling 3. DSDM 4. MDD 5. OpenUP 6. RAD 7. RUP 8. Scrum 9. Waterfall (traditional) 10. Combinations of the above.
Development process automation: Technologists resisted automation because they believed they know a better way. **Recommended Solution:** 1. Balance innovation with consistent product delivery. ♦ Monitor exceptions as possible research opportunities. ♦ Identify problems associated with process exceptions. 2. Bring exceptions under control during testing. 3. Invite recommendations for process improvement. 4. Show how automation has advantages for learning new technology. 5. Show how automation has advantages for methodology compliance.
Domains (service and data) were resisted by owners of business systems who did not wish to lose control of "their" data and their applications. **Recommended Solution:** 1. Explain that the corporation owns the data and the services/processes. 2. Explain that neutral domains are required to support shared services and service reuse. 3. Match data and service domain owners with the business areas they previously supported as often

Table A.2 - Lessons Learned
as possible.
Duplicated functionality may be justified by special business situations, especially after mergers and acquisitions (when 70 - 90% is duplicated). Duplication often remains long after the original justification no longer exists.
Dynamic service discovery was impractical at the beginning of SOA. Daxiao evolved toward dynamic discovery as it gathered experience with SOA.
Early adopters - Achieve benefits, but may also pay a penalty later. They often have to make changes to catch up with standards that were not available at Program initiation. Daxiao used a standards management process to minimize this risk.
Early test team involvement - Business and technology teams do not understand the benefits of having QA involvement when there is nothing to test. **Recommended Solution:** 1. Deliver initial test cases and test along with the requirements document. 2. Demonstrate that involvement of the test team in the requirements gathering process contributes to clarification of requirements. 3. Demonstrate that testing specialists can avoid problems because they have seen so many of them. 4. Ensure that no requirements are allowed where the client cannot define testing requirements. 5. Use test cases to facilitate the requirements process.
Elimination of "Requirements by Handshake": Business and technical teams wished to continue doing business as usual, even though "handshake" requirements often caused problems. **Recommended Solution:** 1. Assign business analysts to collect formal requirements. 2. Demonstrate how this promotes scope creep. 3. Demonstrate the problems that result from inadequate requirements, even for "small changes". 4. Provide a business rules engines that allows business units to make process control changes for themselves. 5. Provide business or technical writers to complete documentation. 6. Streamline accepted change management processes.
Emergency fixes were used by clients and technical teams to avoid Requirements Management. Emergency changes often cause additional problems. **Recommended Solution:** 1. Assign extra costs to emergency changes. 2. Create an emergency change follow-up process that

Table A.2 - Lessons Learned
takes longer and more is more expensive than for regular work requests. 3. Maximize rewards for groups that submit the fewest emergency changes. 4. Provide a business rules product and processes that allow clients to control their own parameter changes. 5. Provide emergency test teams. 6. Provide internal clients with visibility into the prioritization process (emergencies may delay regularly scheduled work). 7. Rigorously define "emergency" a significant loss of money, payment of fines, or significant loss of customers or partners.
Enterprise service bus is important but it cannot be the only coordination point in the infrastructure.
Environment management (data center management) was initially the MOST critical requirement for SOA success. Otherwise, SOA would have been a failure before it ever really started. Appropriate monitoring tools and training were required at the beginning of Web services implementation.
Environment robustness for test environments improves chances of on-time delivery. 1. Build the test environment along with the development environment. 2. Build the test environment as similar to the production environment as possible. 3. Synchronize infrastructure hardware and software across environments
Error reduction program accelerated SOA acceptance.
Evolutionary SOA: Executives resist funding a program where they cannot see the endpoint. **Recommended Solution:** 1. Address pain points while building the foundation structures. 2. Explain that business units' SOA evolution may be different because unit starts at different points. 3. Explain that SOA requires evolution in the business areas as well as in the technology areas. 4. Explain that there is no "Big Bang" approach to SOA (either the business or technology aspects). It is achieved through structured evolutionary processes. 5. Explain the benefits of having a strong Program base (See alignment example in Fig. 6.1 through 6.3, 7.1, and 7.2). 6. Use information from pre-existing efforts (e.g., Sarbanes-Oxley) to accelerate evolutionary phases.
Executive leadership is necessary to ensure across-the-board SOA success.
External (partner) SOA is often easier than internal

Table A.2 - Lessons Learned
SOA because it is green field (it does not carry the cultural and political baggage of pre-existing applications).
Facilitation training should be provided to the maximum number of people. Technologists stop getting in their own way.
Fault tolerance is more critical in SOA because failure of shared services affects a wider business population. It should be: 1. Built into infrastructure architecture. 2. Considered early in the requirements process. 3. Supported by virtualization efforts.
Fear of making mistakes: Because problem reporting schemes penalize operations and development teams for making mistakes, individuals, or entire groups may resist participation in new activities. **Recommended Solution:** Treat mistakes as a learning activity in new activities.
Fear of not being the best - Refer to "Ongoing Learning"
Feedback loops must be closed to achieve maximum results as a learning organization
Floating project managers and teams: Business teams are accustomed to having "their technology people", and they will strongly resist giving up the best ones. Daxiao needs to move project managers to handle the most critical SOA initiatives. **Recommended Solution:** 1. Explain that people who are comfortable with "floating" will provide the maximum benefit for Daxiao in the long run. 2. Explain that the domain owners are equally good managers. 3. Explain that the idea of floating project managers and teams is not new. Demonstrate successes of the "consulting" model. 4. Explain that there are only twenty floating managers and an equally small number of floating teams. 5. Explain the different characteristics of maintenance teams and new product teams. 6. Externalize project knowledge so that multiple managers and developers can deal with system issues. 7. Support socialization between business and multiple technology participants.
Foundation projects were required to support the WFSOA evolution. These continuing projects include: 1. Refactoring frequently used legacy functions into services, and transfer of ownership to service domain owners. 2. Clean up, merger, and transfer of ownership for

Table A.2 - Lessons Learned
data resources and transfer of ownership to data domain owners. 3. Ongoing SOA education and training. 4. Building Knowledge Cooperative resources. 5. Conducting SOA research and technology evaluations.
Governance as facilitation - governance cannot be an obstacle. SOA governance should: 1. Automate as many new tasks as possible. 2. Explain benefits of performing tasks differently. 3. Provide assistance with performing new tasks. 4. Provide easy ways to perform tasks that were never necessary before.
Governance authority - both technology and business teams resist taking orders from the compliance organization. This is a historical problem was exacerbated when WFSOA began to gain traction. **Recommended Solution:** 1. Demonstrate accelerated product creation. 2. Make governance decisions as objective as possible. 3. Make governance processes as transparent as possible.
Governance spending: Business and technology units try to control BASE by limiting budget allocations. **Recommended Solution:** 1. Demonstrate ROI. 2. Matrix BASE competency and project management team members to organizations who need their skills. 3. Tie BASE functions to existing initiatives such as general compliance and SOX.
Granularity of services: Discovery of the proper level requires trial and error. 1. Fine-grained services are easier to create and test. 2. Functions containing multiple fine-grained services will take longer to execute than a single coarse-grained service. 3. Granularity recommendations should be reviewed regularly.
Grid computing promises optimum use of computing resources for SOA service performance and fault tolerance. Grid computing is a Research and Development effort at Daxiao.
Grumble files are important sources of feedback for continuous process improvement in Daxiao. BASE team members: 1. Respond to suggestions through a feedback loop. 2. Support multiple input sources. 3. Treat all staff contributions as potentially valid.
If it works, don't fix it: After original pain points are eliminated, business units did not see the benefits of changing products that work.

Table A.2 - Lessons Learned

Recommended Solution:

1. Accept that some areas may not require SOA.
2. Define change objectives and change goals and how they fit into the overall strategy.
3. Demonstrate competitive disadvantages of staying in place.
4. Demonstrate the benefit of delivering services from the best-functioning systems to the entire organization.
5. Illustrate the narrowing gap between the company and competitors.
6. Recognize acceptance of change
7. Recommend participation in the cultural change management program.

Industry terminology: Incorporation of industry terminology into common terminology facilitates communication with partners.

Infrastructure/staff trade-offs rules should be evaluated constantly.

Infrastructure: SOA requires significant infrastructure modifications. Refer to the vendor product list in Table A.7.2.

Integration process and schedule must be defined during the design phase.

ISACA certification improves SOA management performance for business and technology managers.

Key performance indicators should be defined during the requirements phase. They must be easily measured.

Keyboarding: Automation of previously manual processes requires that more people become familiar with data input techniques.

1. If there are two people with equal knowledge, the person who is comfortable with a keyboard will deliver better results.
2. Similarly, a person in senior management can wait 10 minutes while her admin person pulls the information that supports a dashboard entry, or she can spend 30 seconds and retrieve the information herself.

Knowledge Cooperative - a centralized information capture and distribution tool is essential to SOA success. However, people in multiple roles resisted mandated updates of critical project components.

Recommended Solution:

1. Acknowledge people who consistently provide expected Knowledge Cooperative input.
2. Demonstrate problems that occur when documentation is incomplete.
3. Establish and evangelize formal processes and procedures for management of WFSOA (and corporate) information.
4. Evaluated and recommended external information sources.
5. Give lower research priority to people or teams who do not provide timely input.
6. Identify and maintain relationships with knowledge domain experts (subject matter experts).
7. Make information capture easy.
8. Provide subscription and notification features.
9. Require scheduled input from specific Program participants/roles.

Learning Styles: Daxiao accepts the theory that people benefit differentially from varying styles of information input. They include:

1. Seeing activities performed.
2. Hearing descriptions of activities.
3. Practicing activities.
4. Reading about activities.

When it is possible, BASE provides the same training materials using at least two delivery formats. Participants have the option of choosing the one(s) that fit(s) their needs

Life cycle management: Completion of lifecycles and retirement of outdated versions of artifacts from the list below saves processing and staff resources. Daxiao maintains life cycles for:

1. Access rights.
2. Activities (Thunk Database).
3. Applications.
4. Approval authority.
5. Architecture.
6. Asset Management (physical components).
7. Assumptions.
8. Best practices.
9. Business rules.
10. Catalogs.
11. Communications.
12. Costing algorithms.
13. Data (databases and files).
14. Data value domains.
15. Data models and schema.
16. Failed Projects.
17. Hardware.
18. Infrastructure and Architecture.
19. International variations (of all life cycles).
20. Issues.
21. Knowledge Management.
22. Lessons Learned.
23. Localization artifacts.
24. Methodology (processes for technology).
25. Models (all types).
26. Partner relationships.
27. Planning.
28. Policy (business and technology).

Table A.2 - Lessons Learned
29. Processes (business and technology). 30. Procurement. 31. Projects. 32. Regulations. 33. Problems and Incidents. 34. Emergency Changes. 35. Research and development. 36. Risks. 37. Roles. 38. Rules Management. 39. Security. 40. Service level agreements. 41. Services. 42. Software development. 43. Standards (business and technology). 44. Strategy. 45. Terminology. 46. Testing and testing artifacts. 47. Training content. 48. Vendor products. 49. Versions. 50. Work requests (project requests),
Localization is supported by extraction of international requirements from service logic and adding to a rules engine.
Logging is essential for success of service success. It is used for: 1. Error detection. 2. Input to costing algorithms 3. Security and processing audits.
Loss of a dedicated technology team - Refer to "Floating Project Managers and Teams".
Loss of dedicated databases - Refer to "Data Consolidation and Reuse".
Loss of dedicated processes meets resistance from business units. **Recommended Solution:** 1. Ensure system performance on shared processes. 2. Recognize sharing. 3. Show the financial benefits of process sharing. 4. Support business rules management that allows individual units to control processing parameters.
Manufacturing focus facilitates acceptance of service modularization.
Mash-ups are used by developers and business units to avoid SOA processes that they perceive as restrictive. **Recommended Solution:** 1. Acknowledge the potential the benefits and adopt beneficial features. 2. Document risks and lessons learned associated with mash-ups. 3. Explain the risks associated with using data and

Table A.2 - Lessons Learned
processing that are neither controlled by nor validated by Daxiao teams. 4. Monitor usage. 5. Refactor mash-ups wherever appropriate (adapt to standards). 6. Stabilize mash-ups wherever appropriate. 7. Treat mash-ups as R&D or prototypes
Maturity level assessment and monitoring for SOA (across the organization and within business units) facilitates SOA planning. Daxiao reports average SOA maturity for Daxiao and for individual business units and technology units.
Meeting notes and follow-up are essential for confirmation of meeting results. SOA Programs participants always have two people taking notes, one with a business focus and the other with a technical focus. The facilitator (if one is available) or the team leader synchronizes the results.
Methodology formalization is essential for dealing with the complicated work requirements of SOA. At least 25% of technologists believe they have a better way of doing things while clients believe that some process steps are a waste of time. **Recommended Solution:** 1. Accelerate correction of identified methodology problems. 2. Demonstrate savings realized by minimizing unnecessary experimentation. 3. Demonstrate that formalization produces consistent results. 4. Demonstrate that structured research into methodology improvements is constantly in progress and invite participation. 5. Demonstrate the problems associated with process inconsistencies. 6. Ensure visibility into process creation processes. 7. Explain the benefits of consistency for applying process changes. 8. Explain the benefits of consistency for new hires and rotating teams and managers. 9. Identify problems associated with process inconsistencies. 10. Provide training in the use of processes. 11. Recognize compliance and penalize problems caused by non-compliance. 12. Respond to recommendations for improvements and reward improvement recommendations that are accepted.
Modeling facilitates business understanding of SOA requirements. The more difficult the business processes, the more essential it is to model them. It also helps to define service interfaces. Daxiao:

Table A.2 - Lessons Learned
1. Included modeling tools in automated methodology processes. 2. Models processes whether they will be automated or not.
Naming conventions are significantly more important to SOA. However, clients and technology teams feel that adherence to naming conventions wastes time. Daxiao requires adherence to naming conventions for: 1. Application artifacts (including legacy components) 2. Business process management artifacts 3. Business products 4. Business rules 5. Changes to work requests 6. Configuration items (infrastructure software) 7. Data and data artifacts 8. Error messages and codes 9. Incidents and problems 10. Metadata 11. Models 12. Namespaces 13. Network nodes 14. Process artifacts 15. Projects 16. Requirements 17. Security policy 18. Service artifacts 19. Service level agreements 20. Some Knowledge Cooperative content 21. Testing artifacts 22. Use cases 23. Vendor software components 24. Web content 25. Work product libraries 26. Work requests 27. Workflow rules 28. WSDL 29. XML schema and content. **Recommended Solution:** 1. Explain reasons for and benefits of naming conventions. 2. Perform compliance checks and reject improperly named items early. 3. Provide automated support for naming of artifacts and name verification.
New/updated vendor products met resistance from many Program participants. **Recommended Solution:** 1. Define features and benefits (and shortcomings if necessary) of new products. 2. Identify recommended product features. 3. Provide timely notification product changes. 4. Provide training for new products as necessary

Table A.2 - Lessons Learned
5. Request assistance with product evaluation from technology and business participants.
No immediate benefits - Refer to "Evolutionary Nature of SOA".
Note: The recommendations are in alphabetical order, not in time sequence.
Ongoing learning is frightening, especially to people who were not successful in school and do not want to repeat the experience. Some wish to avoid being less than the best in a new arena while others fear the change that comes with new learning. **Recommended Solution:** 1. Customize training and education to learning styles. 2. Explain the disadvantages of being the best in areas that are no longer perceived as important. 3. Explain the benefits of being among the first in a new skill area. 4. Make learning accessible. 5. Provide transitional support. 6. Provide personal mentoring in cultural change. 7. Provide personal mentoring critical subjects. 8. Recognize learning.
Organizational restructuring supported SOA evolution, but there was resistance. **Recommended Solution:** 1. Deal with rumors, positive or negative. 2. Define how a restructuring will support the business strategy. 3. Define new or updated roles and responsibilities and job titles before a restructuring is announced. 4. Expect that adjustments will be required and prepared to deal with them. 5. Identify known alignment issues before restructuring. 6. Identify problems after restructuring and plan on how to deal with them. 7. Identify strong people who are likely to support restructuring or likely to resist it. 8. Minimize the time between official announcement and implementation. 9. Perform a risk/benefit analysis before approving restructuring. 10. Plan everything, and prepare to adjust the plan. 11. Provide counseling and mentoring as required.
Ownership management was addressed early in the Program by establishing roles for data and service domain owners.
Pain points: Reduction promotes SOA success. BASE and Requirements Managements: 1. Accelerated SOA maturity in the affected areas. 2. Automated that which changed most often. 3. Externalize business rules, giving business units

Table A.2 - Lessons Learned
control over processing requirements 4. Fixed what was broken first. 5. Identified business processes with high maintenance and operational costs as ideal candidates for SOA. 6. Identified error-prone processes as ideal candidates for SOA.
Plan for success: Be prepared to ensure performance and scalability for very successful services.
Planning in SOA is more critical than with prior trends because SOA enables linkages among business units and processing components that could not exist before. To address these issues, Daxiao: 1. Automates most planning processes. 2. Defines and maintains lists of roles associated with planning activities. 3. Established and actively maintains the ***Thunk*** database of planning roles, activities, and history. 4. Maintains a centralized pool of project development resources. 5. Maintains historical information regarding resource utilization for "typical" activities. 6. Mandates retention of planning history. 7. Promotes definition and use of common (planning) terminology. 8. Promotes the use of planning software. 9. Provides subject matter experts to support planning activities. 10. Requires formal plans for all funding approval. 11. Supports automated approval of plan activities.
Platform preferences: At least 60% of developers had "religious" preferences for a given platform that resulted in resistance to reuse of services on other platforms. **Recommended Solution:** 1. Train people on multiple platforms. 2. Explain the pros and cons of each platform. 3. Reward successful delivery on alternate platforms.
Policy governance and life cycle are necessary for SOA success. It was necessary to define: 1. How policy compliance is monitored. 2. Penalties for non-compliance. 3. Procedures for policy notification. 4. Techniques for evaluation of policy effectiveness. 5. Who can make SOA policy, who can approve it, and who enforces it?
Post-implementation reviews enabled SOA Program improvement. They are performed for both successful and problem projects. Failed projects taught the most valuable lessons.
Prioritization: 1. Guidelines for SOA prioritization were clearly

Table A.2 - Lessons Learned
defined. 2. New services allowed clients to view and manage their own priorities. 3. Synchronization between work priorities and corporate strategy was mandatory. 4. Visibility into prioritization processes promoted SOA acceptance.
Problems with historical success - Refer to "If it works, don't fix it".
Process changes - Refer to "Continuous Process improvement".
Process coordinator - business: This permanent role assignment increases the probability that new services and processes will be implemented effectively.
Project difficulty: This risk estimate must be assigned to every project. The requirements analyst assigns a number between one and four to each factor. A high total indicates higher difficulty. Factors related to project difficulty are: 1. Assumptions associated with project. 2. Cross (business) unit requirements. 3. Cross-platform requirements. 4. Degree of client agreement. 5. Degree of client participation. 6. Development support requirements. 7. Device mix. 8. International requirements. 9. Knowledge level of client team(s). 10. New data requirements. 11. New technology requirements. 12. Number of project functions. 13. Outstanding issues associated with project. 14. Security requirements. 15. Similarity to existing processes. 16. Skill level of technology team(s). 17. Stakeholder characteristics. 18. Testing support requirements. 19. User mix.
Project initiation team was originally staffed with people who had prior relationships with the business units to ease transition to new requirements gathering processes.
Project size should be as small as possible. Consider: 1. Maximum project duration of two years. 2. Maximum project resources of 50 person-years. Iterate as often as necessary.
Proprietary products cannot be eliminated, but reliance should be reduced. Procurement: 1. Looks for SOA standards-based upgrades to proprietary products. 2. Monitors and retires non-compliant products when it is possible

Table A.2 - Lessons Learned
Prototypes contribute to implementation success. Project participants: 1. Prototype as often as possible. 2. Set expectations. It's a long way from a prototype to full implementation. 3. Simulate and analyze before software architecture recommendations
Quality costs and lack of quality costs more. It could destroy an SOA Program. After comparing the cost for quality testing with the cost for corrective maintenance, it was agreed that extensive testing is cheaper.
Rebel guidance is required to capture the best ideas from Program visionaries while simultaneously maintain appropriate consistency. Daxiao: 1. Provides a research and development environment where "Rebels" can experiment with new techniques without affecting standard processes. 2. Invites "Rebels" to share their ideas. 3. Updates existing processes with input from "Rebels". 4. Monitors the results of experimentation.
ReMain (Request Maintenance): Daxiao had to build this utility (a combination of proprietary and vendor products) to capture and manage work requests that affect technology, BASE sector personnel, or the business. It provides links to infrastructure and SOA management products (the SOA catalog, infrastructure asset and configuration libraries, and procurement databases). It is the recommended tool for managing: 1. Indications of intention to retire data collections. 2. Indications of intention to retire infrastructure components. 3. Indications of intention to retire services, processes, and business applications. 4. Requests for modification to infrastructure components. 5. Requests for modifications to data collections. 6. Requests for modifications to services, processes, and business applications. 7. Requests for new data collections. 8. Requests for new infrastructure components. 9. Requests for new services, processes, and business applications. 10. Tracing requests to sources and sending notification when sources are modified (departures, organizational restructuring, etc.)
Requirements Problems: The requirements management team had to address to major problems: 1. **Clients versus Users** - They had to ensure that clients delivering work requirements gathered

Table A.2 - Lessons Learned
input from users of the delivered product. 2. **Clients versus Clients** - They had to ensure that clients across business units learned to communicate more clearly and frequently with each other using common terminology.
Requirements upgrade: Significant upgrades are treated as canceled + new projects. The Requirements Management Team: 1. Documents reasons for significant upgrades (they may be caused by external factors). 2. Highlights costs associated with canceled/renewed projects. 3. Links canceled and new projects.
Research environments facilitate SOA adaptation by allowing: 1. Hands-on evaluation of new products by business and technology participants. 2. Modeling and prototyping of services and processes.
Resistance is inevitable. A structured program for handling resistance contributes to SOA success.
Resistance to BASE (SOA) governance was strong among Technology sector employees. **Recommended Solution:** 1. De-emphasize the governance and emphasize assistance. 2. Encourage technology teams to accept credit for successes. 3. Explain the advantages of a peer relationship for governance.
Resistance to knowledge sharing was strong among people who believed that knowledge hoarding would provide job security in rapidly changing environments. **Recommended Solution:** 1. Assign a Workflow analyst to "shadow" resistant employees. 2. Capture shared knowledge in the Knowledge Cooperative for future use. 3. Establish and recognize mentoring relationships. 4. Explain that knowledge sharing is essential for SOA Program success. 5. Monitor and report delayed responses to information requests. 6. Recognize contributions to modeling of business and data processes. 7. Recognize timely and complete responses to requests for information.
Resistance to role assignments revisions: Continuous process improvement required frequent creation or updates of roles. Change-averse people resisted. **Recommended Solution:** 1. Explain that process changes are necessary to keep

Table A.2 - Lessons Learned
pace with changing business and industry environments. 2. Explain the alternatives to accepting new or changed roles. 3. Provide training and mentoring where necessary. 4. Recognize acquisition of additional skills.
Resistance to sharing services and processes: Clients and developers of services and processes do not wish to give up control of "their" products. **Recommended Solution:** 1. Explain the business benefits of sharing. 2. Explain the financial benefits of sharing. 3. Recognize sharing
Resource availability - a centralized view of SOA resource availability facilitates project scheduling.
Reuse Enablement: Ease of evaluating, obtaining, installing, and using existing services is critical for SOA success.
Reverse engineering software is a good investment for critical service candidates
Review processes are more critical to SOA, but encounter the same resistance as with prior technologies. Insecure participants are afraid of all reviews (requirements, design, code, compliance, etc.) while experts in their respective roles may see reviews as waste of time. **Recommended Solution:** 1. Automate as much of the review process as possible. 2. Ensure consistent review guidelines. 3. Explain the advantages of finding potential problems before software goes into testing. 4. Show expert role incumbents how they also learn from the review process. 5. Treat reviews as learning experiences (for reviewers and the people being reviewed). 6. Use facilitators for reviews. 7. Use trusted reviewers and let them work with product owners before review meetings.
Rewards for SOA participation contribute to Program success.
Risk assessment for SOA must be formalized and rigorous. Risk processes: 1. Identify, categorize, prioritize, and price risks. 2. Charge for risk factors. 3. Monitor project and Program risk.
Roles and responsibilities: Clear, but flexible, definition is critical to SOA success. It: 1. Facilitates automation of the approval process. 2. Facilitates security management (role-based security). 3. Facilitates team selection and team interaction.

Table A.2 - Lessons Learned
4. Reduces redundant effort. 5. Supports identification of skill requirements and gaps.
Roles for business processes should be reviewed or refined during the requirements phase for new or changed processes.
Rotation of skilled managers benefits the overall SOA Program.
Sales training improves SOA collaboration and facilitation skills.
Scope creep - Clients continue to request changes to work requests after they have been promoted to development: **Recommended Solution:** 1. Create processes to manage scope creep. 2. Explain the costs associated with changes to in-flight projects. 3. Introduce shorter delivery cycles and project iterations. 4. Show the financial advantages of adding changes at iteration points.
Security administration should plan early for authorization of support roles and testing participants to avoid project delays.
Security management: Both business and technology viewed security as a set of locked gates that slowed their ability to access what they need. **Recommended Solution:** 1. Define a generic security-provisioning model for work requests and projects. 2. Demonstrate that early involvement of security ensures better long-term results. 3. Demonstrate that SOA security must be more rigorous due to XML and plaintext transmission. 4. Demonstrate the costs of late involvement of security specialists. 5. Submit initial security test cases and test scripts along with the requirements document.
Selling services - Refer to "Service mart".
Service catalog aids Governance - it is not governance:
Service catalog management: WFSOA cannot succeed without it. Daxiao: 1. Maintains five federated catalogs (single image with fault tolerant hardware and software) 2. Defined processes for access and updates, approvals, and promotions. 3. Associated clearly defined roles for each catalog process. 4. Synchronizes features of a UDDI registry with an ebXML repository. 5. Uses the catalog to support a service mart (promotion of service reuse).

Table A.2 - Lessons Learned
Service categories should be defined early in SOA evolution and reviewed regularly.
Service domains - Refer to "Domains for processes and data"
Service level agreements should be: 1. Assessed during testing. 2. Associated with a grievance process. 3. Defined during requirements gathering. 4. Modeled after satisfactory existing agreements. 5. Monitored regularly in production.
Service management processes must be available early to facilitate SOA evolution. Daxiao: 1. Created the role of availability architect to improve service management capabilities. 2. Modeled service management. 3. Purchased products with dashboard capability. 4. Purchased service management software after the first controlled pilot services went into production. 5. Upgraded software as the Program evolved from **LITTLE SOA** to **"BIG SOA"**.
Service mart promoted reuse of services. A web-based service mart. 1. Provided animated documentation for potential service uses. 2. Provided user-friendly access to service discovery and requests for reuse.
Service platform irrelevance: If the service, security, and the service bus work, SOA reduces concern about the platform where the service executes.
Sharing data - Refer to "Data Consolidation".
Six Sigma concepts promote SOA evolution and success, however the experimentation required for SOA evolution seldom allows attainment of Six Sigma.
Small SOA projects are easier to control
SOA and risk is unavoidable with SOA. It must be monitored and controlled.
SOA approaches: Daxiao had to evaluate and implement portions of each of the following approaches with different business units: 1. Data-Driven - Integration of data and provision of data access services across the organization. 2. Legacy Transformation - Perform legacy transformation and componentization for embedded functions to extract services from embedded processing. 3. Legacy Wrapping - Discover existing functionality in legacy systems and expose to clients, partners, and a service ecosystem. 4. Message-Driven System - integration through messaging (SOI), and elimination of proprietary protocols. 5. Model-Driven Architecture (MDA) - Tool based

Table A.2 - Lessons Learned
approach supporting the definition of models that can generate code to build services. 6. Process driven - Start with business processes and work way down to services required to support those processes then to the business logic required to build the services.
SOA assessment on a continuing basis is necessary to determine progress against the Program plan and to determine whether the plan should be changed. It includes: 1. Examination of existing business strategy. 2. Examination of planned business strategy. 3. Examination of process readiness. 4. Examination of technology sophistication. 5. Examination of cultural readiness. 6. Identification of relevant assets. 7. Development of a technology gap analysis (what's needed for SOA).
SOA competency team is critical to the success of SOA technology implementations. This center of excellence is staffed with cross-trained architects, business analysts, and developers. Team members: 1. Are expert in at least two areas of SOA specialty. 2. Are fully knowledgeable in business concepts. 3. Are trained in facilitation and sales techniques. 4. Recommend tools for service creation. 5. Forester business/technology feedback loops. 6. Provide pathways for communication among business and technology teams. 7. Publish design principles, guidelines, best practices, patterns, and templates. 8. Rotate into and out of SOA project teams. 9. Support continuing architectural research.
SOA difficulty: SOA is the most complicated implementation that has ever been attempted in IT. It requires: 1. Better planning and risk management. 2. Extensive business/technology collaboration. 3. Greater business-to-business crosses training. 4. Greater technology-to-technology crosses training. 5. Greater visibility into processes and status.
SOA evolution: SOA does not spring up full-grown. The company had to: 1. Create Program plans for start-up, implementation, and expansion. 2. Revise Program plans depending upon project successes or failures
SOA exceptions: Expect some business areas to insist on exceptions to SOA process. They should be monitored and budgets should be provided for eventual SOA alignment.
SOA fit - SOA provides benefits when:

Table A.2 - Lessons Learned

1. The organization or unit is changing constantly (new business processes, markets, products, or acquisitions).
2. The organization or unit is tolerant of change.
3. The technical architecture needs to be integrated.

SOA funding: SOA Program improvements were funded by reduced application maintenance costs.

SOA Governance - See "BASE Support".

SOA learning: Establishing and maintaining SOA learning loops facilitates knowledge transfer.

SOA maturity variations: Different parts of the organization are at different SOA maturity levels. Assessment results are used to determine unit by unit SOA strategy

SOA misfit: SOA may not be required when the organization or unit does not require constant change and there is limited interaction with external units.

SOA piggyback: SOA success may be facilitated through synchronization with other initiatives (SOX, CMMI, ITIL, and Six Sigma).

SOA security must be more rigorous because information is transmitted in plain text: Daxiao:

1. Incorporated security standards (WS-S and SAML).
2. Installed rigorous identify management systems.
3. Installed security gateways to accelerate processing (encryption/decryption, digital signature processing, etc.).
4. Worked with the Liberty Alliance.

SOA validation - Refer to "SOA Assessment".

Specifications resistance -.

1. Some clients were accustomed to letting technology figure out requirement details either because (a) technology did not fully involve them in the specification process, or (b) because the clients were accustomed to "tossing incomplete requirements over the wall".
2. Clients complained about the quality of project deliverables, even after "tossing requirements over the wall".

Recommended Solution:

1. Assign additional costs to issues, assumptions, and missing content.
2. Assign business or technical writers for critical projects.
3. Automated support for requirements gathering and provide templates and samples to facilitate capture.
4. Define minimum and recommended documentation requirements (overkill is as bad as no documentation).
5. Demonstrate how to reuse portions of similar requirements documents.
6. Enable assisted (facilitated) requirements gathering sessions.
7. Enforce common terminology to promote clarity.
8. Ensure that clients become more involved than before WFSOA.
9. Provide support from competency team members.
10. Reject requests with unclear specifications when it is possible.
11. Train Program participants in the use of ReMain (work request documentation product) and provide process mentors and prompts to assist requirements input.
12. Train Program participants in the use of the Knowledge Cooperative to assist requirements research.
13. Use test cases to clarify specifications.

Staff reductions from successful projects: Initial Program successes and related savings (staff displacements) caused strong resistance in advanced stages of the program.

Recommended Solution:

1. Assist with new job assignments and train staff in new roles.
2. Share benefits with displaced employees.
3. Show financial benefits to firm.

Stakeholder identification - Understanding who needs to participate in Program and project activities is critical. Project managers and project initiation managers had to:

1. Apply resistance mitigation techniques.
2. Identify negative stakeholders who could sabotage a project.
3. Identify relevant stakeholders early with assistance from client teams.
4. Identify resistance reasons and resistance techniques.
5. Over-involve stakeholders and let them bow out.

Standards Management is essential. Tables A.6.1 through A.6.5 list standards that may affect SOA implementation in Daxiao. Program participants had to:

1. Helped drive acceptance of standards that supported pre-existing Daxiao implementations.
2. Managed standards gaps.
3. Supported vendors who implemented desired standards.
4. Worked to consolidate conflicting standards.

Strategy alignment and management scheduled on a quarterly basis was initially resisted by Executive Team and Board members. They thought it was a waste of time or an intrusion on their management prerogatives.

Recommended Solution:

Table A.2 - Lessons Learned
1. Calculate savings for an actively managed strategic plan. 2. Demonstrate how interim strategy adjustments accommodate market changes. 3. Demonstrate how interim strategy adjustments reduce strategic conflicts. 4. Embark on parallel or conflicting strategy components with foreknowledge. 5. Ensures that work requests either fit into the existing strategy, or collect approvals from people who will subsequently synchronize the strategy with the work request. 6. Evaluate the work backlog, and update or delete as necessary. 7. Evangelize strategy and tactics (or changes) along with their justification 8. Provide formal strategy education for executives. 9. Provide real-time business intelligence to enable appropriate strategy decisions. 10. Report the cost of existing applications that are not aligned with strategy - modify or sunset as appropriate. 11. Report the cost of work in progress that is not aligned with strategy - cancel or modify as appropriate. 12. Track cost of "critical" projects that are outside strategy bounds.
Subject matter experts are major contributors to project success. Daxiao: 1. Captured input on frequently asked questions and saved it in the Knowledge Cooperative. 2. Designated knowledgeable individuals as resources and allocated time for project and Program support. 3. Identified critical areas of expertise.
Technology resistance to SOA is stronger than in previous technology changes. They resisted losing control of their applications and the need to understand unfamiliar platforms. **Recommended Solution:** 1. Provide training and education on the business benefits of SOA and service reuse. 2. Provide training and mentoring on the technical pros and cons of all platform implementations. 3. Provide training and mentoring on the business benefits of executing services on a chosen platform. 4. Recognize flexibility.
Test case sources: Multiple sources are required to guarantee full test coverage. Requirements, analysis, and design documents, security requirements, and service level agreements (SLAs) provided input to test cases, test scripts, and test suits.
Test data preparation must start during requirements gathering. It used full databases if possible and included data privacy transformations.
Test types and responsibility are divided between business and technology tests as follows:

Business Has Primary Responsibility
Acceptance - Evaluation of system functionality by the actual users.
Alpha - Evaluation of system functionality by internal groups using real-world data and environments. This test is coordinated with technology test participants.
Beta - Evaluation of system functionality by external groups using real-world data and environments.
Black box - Evaluation of a product according to requirements or design specifications.
Component - Evaluation of a portion of a product.
Function - Validating software support of client requirements.
Parallel - Feeding identical data into old and new or revised functionality to ensure the results are the same.
Pilot - Software evaluation in the production environment with limited users and close supervision.
Structural - See "White Box" test.
Usability - Evaluates ease of use and aesthetics of a product. This includes user interface, help systems, user documentation, and training materials.
White box - Software evaluation that requires an understanding the details of its design, logic, and data.
Technology Has Primary Responsibility
Alpha - Evaluation of system functionality by internal groups using real-world data and environments.
Benchmark - Compares performance of a new or updated product with a reference system. Identifies inconsistencies and areas for improvement.
Configuration - Evaluates system performance using variable system configurations.
Contention - Evaluation of product performance in a shared resource environment.
Deployment - Evaluates performance and stability of newly deployed software before it is made available to the user.
Fuzz - Generation of inappropriate service input to identify security vulnerabilities.
Integration - Evaluation of the interfaces between the components of a product.

Table A.2 - Lessons Learned
Integrity - Evaluates a system's technical quality and resistance to failure.
Interoperability - Ensuring that Web service components interact according to standards (WS-I Basic Profile).
Load - Compares system performance under normal and peak loads.
Platform - Evaluation of software performance on different hardware, system software, and network configurations.
Regression - Rerunning portions of test scenarios to ensure changes or corrections have not introduced additional errors.
Sanity - See "Smoke test".
Security - Ensuring that system components may be accessed only by their intended users.
Smoke - Evaluation (usually automated) of a proposed release to ensure it is stable enough to withstand the planned set of tests.
Stress - Evaluation of how the system performs under abnormal conditions.
System - Evaluation of overall system responses.
Volume - Ensuring that project components can handle extreme data access requirements.
Testing skills: SOA testing requires expanded skill sets and different tools than traditional applications. This budget increment that was offset by reduced maintenance costs.
***Thunk* database**: In Daxiao, this database of planning history supports planning processes and continuous process improvement. It is useful for: 1. Demonstrating when work requests are unrealistic. 2. Justifying changes to roles and responsibilities. 3. Providing supporting details for cost estimates.
Training delivery styles: Understanding and accommodating different learning styles facilitated knowledge delivery.
Transition planning is critical to successful service, or process implementation and upgrade, though it may be a significant increment to SOA budgets. It requires 1. Appropriate training. 2. Definition of new roles, role change requirements, and role deletions.
Troubled projects were recovered when compliance teams learned early signs of problems and recommended appropriate intervention.
Uneven SOA implementation is related to different degrees of initial SOA readiness or acceptance. Continuous monitoring is necessary to determine when organizations are ready for SOA. The most successful units were often the slowest to implement SOA (why

Table A.2 - Lessons Learned
fix if it isn't broken).
Unreasonable delivery dates - Contribute to project failure. Project initiation managers can minimize this problem by: 1. Ensuring the creation and maintenance of a project plan. 2. Explaining plan content and dependencies to clients. 3. Negotiating reasonable dates
Updated vendor products - Refer to "New vendor products"
Vendor knowledge capture is a valuable source of training. Successful vendor knowledge capture required: 1. Capturing what vendors learned while working in-house. 2. Re-evaluating vendor information after product and industry changes. 3. Writing requirements for knowledge transfer into contracts.
Vendor supported resistance was a problem initially. Established vendors tried to end run the procurement process by supporting resistance to new vendor's products. **Recommended Solution:** Estimate the cost of resistance and deduct from future contracts, if there are any.
Version control is a top priority and must be considered as part of service interface design. Once a service interface is published, it must be honored until the version is formally deprecated and retired.
Virtual teams work, but collocation during critical points in the project is beneficial. Daxiao: 1. Budgeted for collocation expenses. 2. Conducted multiple team building activities. 3. Promoted use of common terminology. 4. Provided improved collaboration tools. 5. Provided training in the management of virtual teams. 6. Provisioned team motels.
WFSOA funding was supported by SOA savings.

Table A.3 - Resistance Factors and Effectiveness of Mitigation Program		
Key for Success Rating: 1 = There continues to be major resistance. 2 = Progress has been made, but major effort is still necessary. 3 = The Program is achieving moderate success. 4 = The Program is achieving excellent success. 5 = This is not a problem at this time, but will continue to be monitored		
Resistance Factor	**Comment and Discussion**	**Success Rating**
1. Accelerated rate of change	Restricted by the change tolerance of individual participants	3
2. Anomalous product purchases	CMMI's acquisition methodology and Daxiao purchase processes are almost identical. The speed of the current processes, facilitated by automated approvals and supported by the skilled testing and implementation teams, makes circumvention almost pointless. However, there are still occasional issues with international units.	4
3. Another wild-goose technology chase	The units that have adopted SOA, totally, or partially, seem to be satisfied. Half of the units that haven't adopted it have successful applications in place, and they don't want to tinker with things that work. The other 25% say they don't have time to do anything new because they have to deal with existing problems and keep the business running. They also tend to have low SOA maturity. BASE analysts have performed SOA risk analyses and ranked the second 25% from low to higher probability of success. They are waiting for executive approval to begin working in each of these areas.	3
4. Application elimination	Forty-five percent of the applications that are candidates for retirement and for which alternate applications, or services, or available are still running with small contingents of users. The approach in of these areas is to wait until they have a major problem, and then perform a migration rather than a correction. A stronger SOA mandate would accelerate the migrations.	3
5. Asset library updates	Success in this area has been attributed to process improvements that support automated updates of asset libraries. The outlying areas run software products that are not easily integrated into automated processes. Asset teams perform manual synchronization according to a schedule determined by application criticality to the firm.	4
6. Audits - SOA	SOA audits have been extremely successful for teams working in the program. The success factor can be increased only when all teams are using SOA.	4
7. Automated approvals	They are fast and traceable. Savings are channeled back into the research budgets of the business units. Everybody benefits.	5
8. Business creation of automated processes	This is in its initial stages and must be limited to teams with high maturity. Yet, few teams are sufficiently mature. Two initial implementations have been successful.	2
9. Business learning basic technology concepts	After overview courses, the business does not keep up with technology changes.	3
10. Business ownership of change management process	Technology finally appreciates the benefits of this arrangement. They can provide input without taking the blame for incomplete requirements. Some business teams realize they have to do more up front work. They complain that they need more training. However, they are also beginning to realize measurable results.	4
11. Business rules	Teams using SOA, or converting to SOA adhere to business rules processes. Legacy teams tend to stick with the old way (rules embedded in code).	3

Table A.3 - Resistance Factors and Effectiveness of Mitigation Program		
12. Capture of tacit knowledge	Some of the most difficult people leave rather than share information.	3
13. Centralized funding of work requests	Give backs for money saved on processing funding requests promoted acceptance.	4
14. Common terminology	The global availability of the Knowledge Cooperation, assignment, and maintenance of aliases, and a concerted effort by the BASE communications team is helping to make this a success.	4
15. Computer Comfort Level and use of Services	At the beginning of SOA it was estimated, 60% of the managers who were VP or above were comfortable with computers. The number is now estimated to be 80%. The remaining 20% tends to include senior managers who often have staff who can find information for them. They use automated services and processes only when the services provide critical information, which changes frequently. This rating is not likely to change.	3
16. Continuous process improvement	Process automation and extensive training have contributed to success. It benefits because process activities do not have to be services. They can be legacy functions.	4
17. Corporate architecture	From a functional point of view, Enterprise Integration is achieving its objectives - understanding business direction and helping to ensure that business unit efforts are synchronized. In the middle of a continuing series of wins for the company, business leaders continue to resist intrusion of the "academic overkill".	3
18. Costing algorithms	Business units have better visibility into the costing structure than ever before. Slightly better understanding of technology allows them to understand what they are paying for, and they are learning ways to reduce their own costs.	4
19. Cross-border projects	Several successful projects (assisted by multi-lingual support) guarantee that this strategy will continue.	4
20. Culture of innovation	This is developing into a Catch-22. As more teams achieve and exceed financial goals, it is more difficult to persuade them to move to the next level of innovation. It represents a continual challenge for the corporate architect and his research team.	3
21. Data consolidation	Ninety percent of the data consolidation projects have been successful. The units who resist consolidations continue to highlight the consolidations that caused problems. This continues to be a major area of conflict.	3
22. Data domains	Their performance is excellent, and their performance is appreciated by the people who have migrated to WFSOA. Passive resistance from the Data Management team in slowing progress.	3
23. Development process automation	By pulling the "Rebels" into R&D, or onto the SOA competency team, mainstream technology participants are reaping major benefits from process automation.	4
24. Early security involvement	To date, there have been no SOA security breaches. There are also fewer access delays because security teams understand product delivery requirements from the beginning.	4
25. Early test team involvement	The lower success in this factor may be related to staffing issues on the Quality Assurance Team. When there is a resource shortage, the quality management coordinator will focus on projects that are nearing their deadlines rather than projects that are just starting. The solution may be to provide more in-depth QA training to business analysts and clients. This is a high priority item for the heads of Requirements Management and BASE Program coordination.	2
26. Elimination of "requirements by handshake"	The people who always did the handshakes continue to try it and legacy project managers continue to accommodate their "friends" in the business until they are caught. That is, they deliver something that their "friend" didn't really	3

Table A.3 - Resistance Factors and Effectiveness of Mitigation Program		
	want, and the "friend" complains about technology performance. Enough managers have been burned by this process that this rating may move to "4" in the next review cycle.	
27. Emergency fixes	Most of the teams who have tried to end run the process (and are caught) learn from the experience, including how to use ReMain, and the do not repeat their attempts. However, it appears that most teams (business or technology) outside WFSOA will try at least once.	3
28. Enforcement of standards and policy	Automated tools for checking compliance and process automation have contributed to progress in this area.	4
29. Evolutionary nature of SOA	We believe that this is the best rating that can be achieved without an SOA mandate, or a critical mass of fully involved participants. Only 35% of processing actually uses Service-Oriented Architecture at this time.	3
30. Fear of making mistakes	Overcoming this factor requires overcoming basic human nature. Training has moved it from a low "3" to a high "3", but it is probably going to remain a "3".	3
31. Fear of not being the best	This is another complicated situation. The more success we have in areas that previously performed poorly, the stronger the good teams want to hold on to what they have. Otherwise, they have to start SOA behind their competitors. This is at the top of the issues queue for the corporate architect.	3
32. Floating project managers and teams	The SOA project teams have achieved over 80% success in the last three years (on time and within budget), and 90% within the last year. Unfortunately, there are only 20 managers and teams working at any given time. This will be as good as it gets.	4
33. Governance authority	De-emphasizing the word "governance" has achieved moderate success. A clearer mandate for SOA would accelerate acceptance.	3
34. Governance spending	There is only moderate resistance to the BASE budget because it is the smallest of any sector, and the processes other areas significantly improve earnings. BASE also promotes providing research funding for other areas.	4
35. If it works, don't fix it	This is closely related to "Fear of not being the best" above. Few of the areas that entertain this philosophy will move until the surrounding environment (internal and external) forces them to change. For example, if the company decides to discontinue business in a given niche or to expand in a way that the existing technology will not support these entrenched areas will have to change.	2
36. Job rotation	This continues to be resisted by people who are change-averse and well accepted by people who are not. We strive to maintain it at this level.	3
37. Keyboarding	Input error rates are down and documentation quality has improved. Both are attributed to improved keyboarding skills.	4
38. Knowledge Cooperative	Access and contribution rates are up. Structured relationships with subject matter experts assist with keeping the information current. Knowledge Cooperative competitions raised awareness of the system's features.	4
39. Long-term projects	As they fail, new planning processes are implemented that promote short to medium-term projects with iterations.	3
40. Loss of dedicated services and processes	Rewarding areas whose processes and services become popular has helped in the technology area. Providing business rules software that allows business units to control performance of their individual processes also helps.	3
41. Loss of dedicated technology team	This value was close to "3", but it had to be rounded down. Business units are still relatively unhappy about losing their dedicated teams. The next phase of the Program will be to show them that they have dedicated (but shared) domain owners. The savings from shared resources justify keeping the services domains in place	2
42. Mash-ups	This continues to be a major resistance technique. Technology often has to wait until the mash-ups fail before re-engineering or refactoring can occur.	2

Table A.3 - Resistance Factors and Effectiveness of Mitigation Program		
43. Methodology formalization	Getting the "rebels" and innovative technology team members to participate in the methodology formalization has greatly facilitated the processes. Automation of the methodology and providing training and mentoring also contributed to its success.	4
44. Naming conventions	They are effective within WFSOA projects, but problems occur at the boundaries between new Web services and adapted legacy services.	3
45. New/updated vendor products	People who crave new things rush in. People who are change averse take their time. Education and mentoring help these people. Due to basic human nature, this rating may never be "4", but fewer people are putting up extreme resistance. After a few vendors were penalized for supporting resistance to replacement products, it became easier for procurement to make the decisions they believe are correct the company.	3
46. Ongoing learning	Over 70% of technology participants appreciate it. It gives them more options. Many technology managers do not like it, especially the ones who have lost good people. Business teams are beginning to offer greater resistance. For the time being, management hopes that a modest increase in business's reward structure, linked with advanced training options, will be beneficial.	3
47. Organizational restructuring	The most obvious restructuring in Daxiao involved creation of the Requirements Management and Domain Management Organizations. The people whose jobs and reporting structure were affected by this change expressed the least resistance. The teams who were supported by the new organizations and the related processes strongly resist the perception of loss of control, and are still fighting "OUR" data, services, processes, business analysts, etc. They want "MY" everything back. The less obvious restructurings are happening more frequently, and they are happening across the organization. ♦ Process automation increases productivity and reduces staffing requirements. Daxiao tries to handle this through attrition and transfers, but the few job losses increase the fear levels. ♦ Process documentation and monitoring support continuous process improvements, and these in their turn, accelerate organizational restructuring. This is good for Daxiao, but frightening for people accustomed to doing thing the same way for years at a time. Greater visibility into strategy management and alignment requirements and extensive training in project management and planning allows people to understand why things are happening, but this is still an uphill struggle against human nature.	3
48. Planning history	Automated support for the planning process has contributed to success in this resistance area. The challenge is to learn other effective ways to interpret planning history. Both planning specialists and SOA financial specialists are working on a highly prioritized project to address this issue.	4
49. Planning processes	This has been viewed as a surprising success. The ***Thunk*** (roles/activity) database is viewed has a primary source of lessons learned, both for project management and for project planning. The promotion and acceptance of iterative planning and "Just enough planning" have also proven to be beneficial. Senior management and the Board are evaluating whether these processes will be mandated outside WFSOA.	4
50. Platform preferences	While a few people resigned when they were asked to work on legacy adaptation, many of the mainframe people who missed the client/server bandwagon have used this as an opportunity to expand into Web services while maintaining their historical skills. The net result has been positive.	4
51. Procurement -	The process is saving the company money and improving vendor relations, but	3

Table A.3 - Resistance Factors and Effectiveness of Mitigation Program		
centralized	managers in the technology and business units still complain about the loss of control. The technology executive is leading the resistance. This is currently a stalemate.	
52. Quality measures	Business and technology teams admit that quality measures are more consistent, but still complain about the length of time allocated to testing.	3
53. Review processes	These are still perceived as painful by almost half of participants. This represents improvement. Two years previously, they were perceived as painful by all participants. Technology management believes that the processes are working and will continue the reviews.	3
54. Role assignments and role revisions	Though the number of roles appears excessive, it is now easier for people to understand what is required of them and when. Less confusion occurs when roles change. The role-related processes help the security team to manage access to company resources. Both CMMI and the external auditors believe the processes contribute to WFSOA success. The process is continually monitored to figure out if there are opportunities for process improvement.	4
55. Scope creep	In reality, project clocks have always been reset when there was major scope creep. The difference is that the client takes more of the blame for the changes. This encourages them to allow prioritization of their "Better Ideas".	4
56. Sharing knowledge	This is another area of continuous struggle. As improved processes eliminate jobs or force job reassignments, several people tried to hold on tighter to what they know.	3
57. Sharing services and processes	The processes and procedures within WFSOA make sharing and reuse easy. As SOA is not yet a company mandate, there are still teams who try to develop and maintain their own services. If they run into problems (it is better to say "when they run into problems") that they cannot resolve, they are brought into the WFSOA fold, and BASE team members work to convert eligible services for corporate-wide use.	3
58. SOA re-organization	High ratings from both CMMI and PCAOB have helped senior management to view the BASE organization as a success. Both organizations point to improvement in on-time project delivery, thorough but rapid procurement processes, and zero security breaches over a two-year period as reasons for their favorable recommendations. The business and technology teams are happy that competency team members always seem to make time for them. The Knowledge Cooperative has become "can't live without it". The SOA architecture team is perceived as brilliant within the company and among industry peers. The Partner Networks and Research programs contribute revenue to the bottom line. The BASE management team is working to maintain its position while gathering a critical mass that will ensure the success of WFSOA.	4
59. Specifications	Clients are beginning to realize that they often don't know how to say what they want. The Requirements Management team is helping them to do a better job, but there is room for improvement.	3
60. Staff reductions from successful projects	This value is going in the reverse direction. The more savings we achieve, the more entrenched the surviving units become. Rewarding flexibility was more effecting at the beginning of the Program than it is now.	3
61. Strategy alignment and management	The strategy management processes are helping the company to save money and to make money. However, senior managers view them as intrusions on their management prerogatives. The rating is not likely to change.	3
62. Technology learning business	The technology teams have embraced online training. They like the reward structure, and they realize that it enables deliver of better products. The training will continue in its present format.	4
63. Technology resistance	This rating is improving slowly. The mainframe people are happy for an	3

Table A.3 - Resistance Factors and Effectiveness of Mitigation Program

	opportunity to learn "the other stuff", and the Web and client/server people are surprised at how smart some of the mainframe people are. Most teams still resist giving up control of "their components", but enough people are starting to move into the service domains with "their components" that the anxiety level is holding steady and occasionally being reduced.	
64. Vendor knowledge sharing	This has improved since exclusion of major vendors for lack of cooperation. We expect that this value will remain as it is due to some vendor's internal policies about intellectual property.	4
65. Vendor supported resistance	Exclusion of major vendors from significant contracts encouraged co-operation from all the other vendors.	5
66. Virtual teams	Collaboration products and processes have facilitated performance of virtual teams. This technique still allows negative participants to hide. The Human Resources area is working with the communications and technology team managers to reach the final level of improvement.	4

Table A.4 - WFSOA Methodology (Evolutionary Stages and Process Groups)

Key: c = Corporate
d = Data
s = Service-Oriented Architecture
t = Technology

Evolutionary Stage #1 - Start-up Activities

Business Strategy Definition and Maintenance	2002 - **Present**
1. Define Strategy Maintenance Process	Governance (c)
2. Assess organization change tolerance	Governance (c)
3. Outline Services Strategy within the business strategy	Governance (c, t)
4. Outline Technology Strategy within the business strategy	Governance (c, t)
5. Document and maintain corporate and business unit strategy	Governance (c)
6. Align business units with business strategy	Governance (c)
Information and Documentation	1997 - **Present**
1. Define common terminology	Governance (c, t), SOA Communications
2. Synchronize terminology across business units	Governance (c, t), SOA Communications
3. Cross reference common terminology to local usage	Governance (c), SOA Communications
4. Enhance security administration functions	Architecture
5. Roll out Knowledge Cooperative functionality across the organization	Governance (c), Human Resources Support, SOA Communications
Business Model	1997 - **Present**
1. Identify business processes and relationships	Governance (c)
2. Cross reference business processes to business strategy	Governance (c, t)
3. Cross reference business systems to business processes	Governance (c, t)
4. Identify corporate, industry, and government rules & regulations	Governance (c, t)
5. Cross reference business processes to rules and regulations	Governance (c, t)
6. Document business systems	Architecture, Governance (c)
7. Cross reference business systems to business processes	Architecture, Governance (c)
8. Document business system components	Architecture, Governance (c, t)
9. Cross reference business system components to business processes	Architecture, Governance (c, t)
Data Model	1997 - **Present**

Table A.4 - WFSOA Methodology (Evolutionary Stages and Process Groups)	
1. Model business data	Data Management, Governance (c, d)
2. Cross reference business data to business systems	Data Management, Governance (c, d)
3. Cross reference data to system components	Data Management, Governance (d)
Web Services Initiation	1997 - 2003
1. Implement pilot Web services investigation	Product Creation
2. Justify further SOA	
3. Capture lessons learned	Governance (c)
4. Establish Research Environment	Architecture, Governance (c)
5. Establish Training Program	Governance (c), Human Resources Support
Evolution Stage #2 - Service Oriented Architecture Foundation	
SOA Strategy	2003 - **Present**
1. Formulate and refine SOA vision	Governance (c, s, t)
2. Define and refine BASE objectives and goals	Governance (c, s, t)
3. Define and refine BASE service/process architecture	Governance (c, s, t)
4. Define and refine infrastructure evolution to support process, data, and management evolution	Governance (d, t, s)
5. Define and refine data platform evolution to support SOA process evolution	Governance (c, d, t, s)
SOA Preparation	2002 - 2003
1. Recommend SOA Security Policy	Governance (c, s, t)
2. Formulate BASE vision	Governance (c, s, t)
3. Define infrastructure baseline	Governance (t)
4. Define data baseline	Governance (d, t)
5. Initiate the SOA governance functions (service and data)	Governance (s)
6. Establish a BASE communications program	SOA Communications
7. Link BASE communications and Knowledge Cooperative	SOA Communications
8. Establish standards coordination process	Governance (s)
9. Establish SOA product purchase guidelines	Governance (s)
10. Establish service/process management and monitoring	Environment Management, Governance (s)
11. Integrate service catalog into Knowledge Cooperative	Architecture, Governance (s)
12. Design a cultural change management program (resistance mitigation)	Governance (c, s, t), Human Resources Support, SOA Communications
13. Recommend reuse policies	Architecture, Governance (s, t)
14. Prioritize processing components	Architecture, Governance (c)
15. Identify redundant system components	Architecture
16. Prioritize data components	Data Management, Governance (c, d)
17. Identify redundant data components	Data Management, Governance (d)
18. Begin SOA Education	Human Resources Support
Define Service/Process Model	2003
1. Recommend service categories	Architecture, Governance (c)
2. Identify and categorize existing services	Architecture, Governance (t)
3. Recommend core services	Architecture, Governance (s, t)
4. Prioritize proposed services within categories	Architecture, Governance (c, s)
5. Recommend candidates for wrapping and reuse	Architecture, Governance (s, t)
6. Establish rules engine and processes	Architecture, Governance (s, t)
7. Begin implementation of service model	Architecture, Governance (s, t), Product Creation
Define Data Model	2002 - 2003
1. Refine data categories	Architecture, Governance (c)
2. Identify and categorize existing data	Architecture, Governance (d, t)

Table A.4 - WFSOA Methodology (Evolutionary Stages and Process Groups)

3. Recommend core data	Architecture, Governance (d, t)
4. Prioritize data within categories	Architecture, Governance (c, d)
5. Recommend candidates for consolidation	Architecture, Governance (s, d)
6. Recommend candidates for clean up	Architecture, Governance (s, d)
7. Recommend candidates for elimination	Architecture, Governance (s, d)
Evolution Stage #3 - SOA Implementation	
SOA Strategy Evolution	
1. Adjust BASE vision	Governance (c, s, t)
2. Refine BASE objectives and goals	Governance (c, s, t)
3. Implement organizational change management	Governance (c)
4. Evolve infrastructure to support BASE evolution	Governance (t)
5. Evolve data to support BASE evolution	Governance (d, t)
Organizational Evolution	2003 - 2004
1. Establish SOA as a business process optimization initiative	Governance (c, s)
2. Define SOA roles and responsibilities	Governance (c, s, t), Human Resources Support
3. Establish SOA organizational structure (across four major sectors)	Governance (c, s, t), Human Resources Support
4. Establish a resistance mitigation program (cultural change management)	Communications, Governance, Human Resources Support
5. Clarify SOA security requirements	Architecture, Governance (c, s, t)
6. Channel all change requests through Requirements Coordination	Governance (c, s), Requirements Coordination
7. Ensure all changes conform to strategy	Governance (c, s), Requirements Coordination
Technical evolution	2003 - **Ongoing**
1. Coordinate all technical activities	Project Management
2. Automate SOA methodology (for business and technology)	Architecture, Governance (s), Requirements Coordination
1. Expand service/process execution platform (super-size it)	Architecture, Governance (s, t)
2. Expand service/process management and monitoring	Architecture, Environment Management
3. Expand service/process research environment	Architecture, Governance (s, t)
4. Consolidate, clean, and deploy frequently accessed data	Architecture, Data Management
Implement Service/Process Model	2003 - **Ongoing**
1. Create service "marketing" and reuse processes	Governance (c, s), SOA Communications
2. Continue to build and deploy prioritized services/processes	Architecture, Governance (c, s, t), Product Creation
3. Evaluate all system change requests as possible services	Requirements Coordination
4. Evaluate all process change requests for possible process automation	Requirements Coordination
5. Deliver service/product artifacts	Product Creation
6. Prioritize candidate systems for re-engineering	Requirements coordination
7. Convert candidate systems to run in a service-oriented environment	Governance (s), Product Creation
8. Schedule remaining systems for conversion to service platform	Architecture, Governance (s, t)
Implement Data Model	2003 - **Ongoing**
1. Create data "marketing" and reuse processes	Data Management, Governance (c, d)
2. Synchronize data improvement projects with prioritized services and processes	Architecture, Governance (d, t)
Evolutionary Stage #4 - Client-Controlled Process Maintenance	

Table A.4 - WFSOA Methodology (Evolutionary Stages and Process Groups)

Client development and maintenance of composite services (processes)	2006 - **Ongoing**
1. Research client-controlled process automation	Architecture, Governance (c, s, t), Requirements Coordination
2. Define policies and methodology for client creation and modification of composite services	Architecture, Governance (c, s, t), Requirements Coordination,
3. Pilot client-controlled process automation	Architecture, Governance (c, s, t), Requirements Coordination
4. Ensure synchronization of processes with business strategy	Governance, Requirements Coordination
5. Refine roles and responsibilities for client-controlled process automation	Architecture, Governance (c, s, t), Requirements Coordination, Human Resources Support,
6. Automate methodology for client-controlled process automation	Governance, Architecture
7. Refine processes for client-controlled process automation	Architecture, Governance (c, s, t), Requirements Coordination
8. Promote client-controlled process automation	Governance (c, s, t), Requirements Coordination
Evolutionary Stage #5 - Future Features	
Hypothetical	2009 **and beyond**
1. Self-evaluating processes	Governance (c, s, t), Requirements Coordination
2. Self-adjusting processes	Governance (c, s, t), Requirements Coordination

---

Table A.5 - SOA P Notes and Glossary

Accelerated projects - An emergency change in Daxiao technology. Projects are allowed to bypass Program methodology steps to address emergencies. The skipped steps are flagged and backfilled after the correction is implemented.

Acceptance test - Conducted by or on behalf of designated approvers to determine whether a product addresses functional and non-functional requirements and is ready for deployment.

ACL - Access Control List /= definition of the permissions that users, groups, processes, services, or devices have for system resources.

Activity -

1. Part of the work breakdown structure for a work request (while still with the business) or a project plan (after turnover to technology). It has expected and actual duration, resource requirements and cost, and it may have prerequisites, co-requisites, and dependencies.
2. One of the segments in a workflow process that has input and output work products (or artifacts).

Activity dictionary - See "Thunk".

Adapter - Middleware that allows traditional application or vendor product components to function as services.

Agile development - Methodology for creating software to accommodate rapidly changing business environments. It requires use of industry best practices, teamwork, customer involvement, thorough testing, collocation of business and technology participants, and frequent creation of small deliverables.

Agile enterprise - A major objective of SOA /= organization with the ability to thrive in complex, frequently changing business environments.

Alignment-Synchronization of technology offerings with business needs.

Analysis - Phase in the creation of a business solution (after requirements gathering and before design). It includes:

1. Understanding and modeling customer needs and constraints.

Table A.5 - SOA P Notes and Glossary

2. Examination of documents, files, environmental components, or staff input.
3. Determination of process, data, flow, and security requirements.

Anomalous business system - Application installed in a legacy environment after official kick-off of SOA, but before the Program is fully implemented. They were originally used to avoid the "strictures" and "structures" of SOA. They continue to be used to address emergency requirements.

Anomalous practice -

1. A way of performing tasks required in WFSOA that are not recommended, but may deliver acceptable results.
2. Some are promoted to best practices, while others are monitored and disparaged.

Anti-patterns catalog - Listings of things that companies or individuals do to endanger technology projects. Daxiao recommends that managers review the list in preparation for each new project.

Application -

1. BASE definition /= set of legacy artifacts that serves a specific function for a set of users.
2. Group of computer programs that support a specific use. They may be in-house developed or purchased from vendors (COTS). Services may use application components.
3. Files that have to be installed (executable files, configuration files, and scripts) before software can run.

Contrast with "system" /= combination of applications, services, automated and manual processes that support a business requirement.

Application endpoint - Name of the work product that ultimately provides the service requested in SOAP messages.

Application modeling - Specification of requirements in a graphic modeling tool

Approval Role Clusters -

Client(s)	Approval is required from the client group(s) that entered the request. Multiple client areas may participate in the same request.
Data Domain Owner	Approval from a data domain owner may replace sponsor approval for data only projects.
Service Domain Owner	Approval from a service domain owner will replace sponsor approval after a service or process is turned over to a domain owner.
Visionary	A visionary approval may substitute for a client approval with the same restrictions that apply to clients.

Architecture -

1. Principals and guidelines used to control acquiring, building, modifying, and connecting enterprise resources (hardware, system software, application software, data, communications, development techniques, and modeling tools).
2. Design of a system, including hardware, devices that may connect to it, the software that may run on it, allowable software interactions, access methods, network protocols, and the expected system capacity.
3. The structure of and relationships among components of an organization, business unit, or system. It includes standards and guidelines for creation and maintenance of the organization, business unit, or system.

Articulated knowledge - Description by role incumbents of how they do their work, including the transfer of tacit knowledge. This is provided by several role incumbents in **Table A.**16 where they discuss their views of their roles and responsibilities.

Artifact -

1. Digital information /= usually has a creator, an owner, relationships with other artifacts, and can be accessed or manipulated.
2. Software or hardware components.
3. Work product /= result of a defined set of activities.

Asset - Working solution supporting business or technology processing requirements. It may directly support a business function or provide support to other assets that provide the business functionality.

Asset management - Procedures that track hardware, software, and network assets through their life cycles.

Audit -

1. Measurement of compliance to a standard that reports the degree of compliance and measures that may be taken to become more compliant.
2. Formal inspection and verification.

Authentication - Use of passwords, tokens, digital certificates, or biometrics to verify identity before granting

Table A.5 - SOA P Notes and Glossary
access to a system, or entry into a facility.
Autonomation - The ability to stop a production line if a defect is discovered. The concept is applied during Requirements Management in WFSOA. If requirements are not complete and validated, extra risk factors and related costs are applied before a project is promoted to development. If the client accepts the added cost and risk, the project is allowed to proceed and is tightly monitored.
Autonomic computing - One of the goals of Daxiao SOA Maturity Level #5. In this environment, self-managing software will control the functions of services with minimal input from administrators.
Availability management - Formalized processes and procedures that monitor and guarantee the availability of services and application components within defined cost constraints.
Backfill - Completion of project documentation requirements for "accelerated projects".
Backward scheduling - Establishing project milestones according to when the completed project is due. The Daxiao planning process attempts to avoid backward scheduling as it has been proven to fail 80 to 90% of the time.
Balanced Scorecard - Strategic management concept that aligns business strategy with business activities and manages performance against goals. It tracks financial, customer, internal efficiency, and learning/innovation indicators. The WFSOA Program measures success on these indicators where business and technology meet.
BAM - Business Activity Monitoring /= processes and procedures that provide visibility into key performance indicators (KPIs), usually through dashboards that provide ideas for business process improvement.
BASE - Business Achievement through Service Excellence /= motto for Daxiao's compliance organization. It was assumed by Daxiao's SOA governance organization after encountering significant resistance from the senior management team to The idea of being "governed" by a peer. The idea of having SOA foundation activities as a "base" for sustainable technology innovation was more acceptable. BASE teams include: 1. Compliance Management. 2. SOA communications. 3. SOA Competency. 4. SOA Implementation. 5. SOA Library Management. 6. SOA Program Management. 7. Vendor Management.
Basic Profile - Web Services Interoperability (WS-I) basic profile
Benchmark - 1. A measure of performance or results against a generally accepted standard. 2. A record of the state of an environment or and environmental component at a point in time.
Best practices - Application development guidelines for procedure that have been proven to work.
Beta - Product tests performed by users in their own facilities under normal operating conditions before full release.
BI - Business Intelligence: 1. Knowledge and information (historical, current, and projected) that allows the organization to make informed decisions regarding SOA. 2. Automated processes that analyzes information about customers, suppliers, products, services, and competitors to discover SOA trends and patterns.
Blade server - A rack-mounted chassis that provides shared network and power sources for modularized processing units (blades).
Bottom-up analysis-analysis that starts with software that is running in production and works backwards to user requirements.
BPM - Business Process Management /= Procedures and tools that support analysis, definition (modeling), execution, monitoring and administration, and coordination of end-to-end business processes.
BPMN - Business Process Modeling Notation /= proposed standard (OMG) for a graphical notation to capture and display business processes within a workflow. Its four primary elements are flow objects, connection objects, swim lanes, and artifacts.
BPMS - Business Rules Management System /= Foundation product for "on-demand" processing. 1. It gives business process coordinators and business analysts the ability to control business logic with limited intervention from IT departments. 2. It provides runtime engines, management, and monitoring of business rules.

Table A.5 - SOA P Notes and Glossary
Bus - Pathway linking system components.
Business architecture - A subset of corporate architecture that describes how the organization achieves its business objectives. It contains: 1. A hierarchy from major processes down to successively smaller component processes. 2. Links to roles and people responsible for process execution and links to technology that supports the processes.
Business case - Rationale for undertaking an activity or the justification for an expenditure
Business function - A set of related business activities/tasks that are designed to provide specific products and services. In Daxiao, these include research, manufacturing, sales, financial management, etc.
Business model - Description of how a company makes money. It includes:
Business plan - A statement of strategy, which is translated into tactical plans for achieving the desired results.
Business Process Execution Language - See "BPEL".
Business Process Reengineering - See "BPR".
Business profile - Description of a company's ebXML capabilities, constraints, and its supported business scenarios
Business rule - 1. Policy that can be applied using business software. 2. Declaration of an auditable policy or condition. 3. Regulation or practice for a business. 4. Requirement or constraint used to guide processes.
Business rules engine - Software that runs outside of business processing routines, evaluates events according to rules, and initiates actions according to the results of the evaluation. Clients may use a rules engine to control processing logic flows.
Business Technology Team - people responsible for creating/maintaining business software. They may also install, customize, and monitor COTS products.
CAB - Change Advisory Board
Capabilities-based Lookup - Service discovery operation where the target of the search is described in terms of required operations and characteristics.
Capacity management - Activities that ensure processing resources match business demands.
Cat-5e - extension for the Category-5 networking cable specification.
Catalog - service registry, service repository, or a combination of the two as is the case in Daxiao.
CatFiv-e - The five versions of related catalogs that support Daxiao service and process creation. They are initiation, build, staging, runtime, and archive.
CEFACT - Center for Trade Facilitation and Electronic Business, a United Nations organization whose activities are monitored in Daxiao.
Champion - An individual who promotes a person, concept, or a product by persuading others of its benefits.
Change history - Documentation of all the changes implemented or requested for a configuration item.
Change management - Processes and procedures that minimize the impact of change-related incidents upon service expectations and service quality. It assumes the existence of the SOA version of a change advisory board (CAB) with representatives from client organizations, the governance teams, and the architecture teams. It includes: 1. A structure for creating, modifying, or acquiring hardware, communications equipment and software, system software, security software, services, processes, application software, and data. 2. Naming conventions, version control, retention of prior versions, and the ability to roll back to prior versions. 3. Tracking, notification, synchronization, and documentation. 4. A change model for affecting different change categories.
Change request - Artifact for formally tracking a proposed modification to a work product or group of work products. It describes a problem, the proposed solution, system impact, cost, and origin of the request. It also contains tracking information from request inception to completion or cancellation. Change requests are a subset of work requests. All information is captured and tracked in Daxiao's ReMain (Request Maintenance) system. Daxiao maintains separate processes for: 1. Changes to production products. 2. Changes to work in development by technology teams. 3. Changes to work in progress by business teams (experimental on-demand process automation).

Table A.5 - SOA P Notes and Glossary
4. Changes to work in Requirements Management (before it is turned over to a technology team).
Choreography - Definition of the sequence and conditions under which information is exchanged within or among business processes. There is no central controller (equate to a dance performance).
CIO - In Daxiao, this title refers to the Coordinator of Information Optimization, the senior data/service domain owner reporting to the CFO.
CISA - Certified Information Systems Auditor /= individual who has passed the exam administered by ISACA (Information System Audit and Control Association).
Client - 1. A computer that is used directly by a user of computing resources. 2. A role assumed by a system component while making a request to another system entity.
CMMI - Capability Maturity Model (Integration)/= process developed by the Software Engineering Institute (SEI) in 1986 to improve delivery of software technologies. Within CMM, organizations are assigned to one of five competence levels: 1. Level 1 - Ad hoc with no development methodology and few, if any, controls are in place. 2. Level 2 - Repeatable processes and procedures have been defined well enough to forecast project results with reasonable accuracy. 3. Level 3 - Defined the development processes have been fully implemented, and are measurable. The organization can predict the effect of implementing changes. 4. Level 4 - Managed each implementation as part of an overall planned architecture. 5. Level 5 - Optimized the highest level where the development organization can focus on improving the processes rather than executing them. Effective implementation of SOA and IT governance improved Daxiao's capability level. CMMI defines more process areas and best practices.
COBIT - An open standard for IT control and security practices published by the IT Governance Institute (ITGI) and the Information Systems Audit and Control Association (ISACA) an in 1990. Version 4.0, published in 2006, included 300+ control objectives divided into 34 control groups along with performance management recommendations, a list of critical success factors, and a maturity model.
COINS - Coordinator of Information Services /= title assumed by the EVP responsible for WFSOA governance.
Collaboration - sharing of knowledge to achieve common organizational goals.
Collaboration software - Product that allows program/project participants to work together on project information shared across a network. It may include e-mail, videoconferencing, and instant messaging.
Common terminology - definitions agreed upon across business and technology units that assure the adequacy of communications, facilitate data management, and accelerate product creation.
Competitive advantage - Innovative services and processes that allow Daxiao to provide quality to is customers.
Competitive intelligence - Evaluating the practices of external organizations and determining whether they can be used to model internal processes and procedures.
Complex event processing - Identification of important patterns among critical business events in real time that provides an information foundation for proactive maintenance and business intelligence.
Compliance audit - Ensuring conformance to internal policy and standards or external guidelines
Component - An artifact that will contribute to a finished product, but is not the finished product itself. Note that a component to a process developer may be a finished product for a service developer.
Composite application - Functionality that appears as a single application to the user, but contains components from independently created applications. Synonyms are business process and composite service.
Composite service - 1. Collections of services that provide business solutions. 2. An alternative designation for a process.
Configuration - 1. Parameter settings for system components. 2. Processing assets that are being used (in any environment), and their relationships to each other the environments where they run.
Conformance -

Table A.5 - SOA P Notes and Glossary
1. Adherence to applicable standards, regulatory requirements, or laws. 2. A measure of the degree of adherence to standards, regulatory requirements, etc.
Consensus - Situation where group members support an action or process, even if all do not fully agree with it.
Constraint - A restriction that affects how a product may be delivered. The classic constraints are scope, time, and money. Examples are: 1. Technology constraints (a) it doesn't work that way, (b) we never used it that way (c) we don't have the software to do that, (d) we don't have the hardware or network capacity to do that (e) we're committed to that software (f) we committed to that hardware (g) our standards require that. 2. Standards constraints (industry standards). 3. Regulatory constraints -- we will be fined if we don't do it that way. 4. Industry constraints -- all companies do it that way. 5. Legal constraints (we will get sued if we don't do it that way). 6. Operational constraints (a) It must be available to ______ (b) It must be available between _____ and _____. 7. Organizational constraints (policy statements). 8. Staffing constraints. 9. Skills constraints. 10. Data constraints (a) we don't have the data to do that (b) data quality won't allow that. 11. Knowledge constraints (a) we don't know why they did it, (b) we can't figure out how they did it, (c) we're not sure what it does.
Construction - Three related process categories in WFSOA are Requirements Management, Process Creation, and Project Management.
Continuous process improvement - The use of feedback loops to provide guidance for implementation of best practices in business and technical processes.
Co-opetition - A combination of cooperation and competition that provides the possibility for rivals to benefit from each other's activities. An example would be group purchases where members leverage buying power to gain reduced pricing.
Core process - A capability that is central to a company's competitive strategy.
Core team - A group of technologists who stay together during multiple Daxiao projects. The core will usually consist of a team leader, a software architect, a lead programmer and one or more junior programmers.
Corporate Architecture - Application of architectural techniques to a human organization.
Corporate governance - The system of internal controls designed to safeguard the organization's assets.
Corporate memory - Practices and intellectual capital that influence an organization's behavior.
COSO - 1. Committee of Sponsoring Organizations /= organization working to create standardized guidelines for implementing internal business controls. 2. Process categories recommended for SOX through PCAOB.
Costing algorithms - Processes and procedures for distributing the costs of creating and running services and processes equitably among clients (internal), partners (external) and customers.
COTS - Commercial off-the-shelf/= business software purchased from an external provider.
Coupling - Dependency between elements that collaborate to provide a service.
Coverage - An indication of how much code in a business system has been tested.
CPI - See "Continuous process improvement".
Critical success factor - An element that must be present for an organization to achieve its mission.
CRUD - Create, read, update, or delete data.
Cultural Change Management - Changes necessary to ensure successful SOA implementation.
Dashboard - 1. Consolidated view of the results from business and technology activities to assist trend analysis and decision-making. 2. Tool that summarizes Key Performance Indicators (KPIs)/metrics of a company.
Data flow diagram - Illustration of the movement of data between processes.
Data hygiene - Condition of data in a database. Clean data has few errors, redundancies, or omissions.
Data Management -

Table A.5 - SOA P Notes and Glossary
1. The organization responsible for managing data placement, database performance, backup and recovery, collection, quality assurance, integrity, maintenance, access, archival, and disposal. 2. WFSOA Support Process Category /= Processes and procedures for analysis, design, implementation, and maintenance of Daxiao's data as a critical resource.
Data redundancy - In Daxiao, this term is pejorative. It refers to incomplete, changed, or one-off copies of data that exist after the original reasons for their creation are no longer valid.
Data replication - Creation and synchronization, usually to facilitate enhanced performance or to provide a hot back up in case of emergencies.
Data sanitation - Modifications to data required to comply with security constraints.
Data synchronization - Ensuring that multiple instances of the same data object remain identical.
Deming, W. Edward - Statistician credited with improving production in the United States during WW II, for assisting the Japanese recovery after WW II, and for helping to turn around the American automobile industry.
Deployment - Part of the last phase of Product Creation where the system is delivered to users. It involves: 1. Distribution to the appropriate locations. 2. Installation (preparing software to run in a given environment). 3. Ensuring that the software runs as expected. 4. Preparing users and support personnel for new systems and systems changes.
Deprecated - Indication that an artifact, command, or statement is considered obsolete and may be deleted in future releases of a product.
Design - Definition of a solution to problems identified in a requirements document and clarified in an analysis document.
Design review - Formal, documented, systematic examination of design recommendations.
Design template - Consistent format in ReMain for capturing and reviewing product specifications.
Development methodologies - Techniques for delivering business technology that define deliverables expected at the end of predefined phases.
Digital signature - Component of a public key infrastructure (specified in ISO 9796) that represents a handwritten signature and may be used to prove identity and ensure data integrity.
Discipline - Collection of related activities or knowledge requirements.
Discovery service - Software that matches service requirements with available services.
Domain - 1. A definable business area or scope. 2. A subnet of a local area network (LAN) that controls resources and security. 3. Highest subdivision of the Internet.
Domain modeling - Capturing a subset of the complete business model
ebXML - Joint effort by CEFACT and OASIS that recommends a framework for consistent use of XML in B2B applications. It is intended to be a successor to EDI for the Internet. It provides descriptors for modeling business processes and their software components. It contains a dictionary of common business objects. It supports: 1. Registry federation. 2. Metadata replication. 3. XACML and SAML security. 4. Extensible service interfaces. 5. Definition of service request/response types. 6. HTTP binding to registry services. 7. Registry content management (validation and life cycle).
EDI - Electronic Data Interchange /= older format for electronic communication of business transactions between companies (B2B). ebXML supports transition to Web Services for data interchange.
Enterprise service bus - ESB /= Middleware between SOA services that removes direct connection dependencies and supports security, reliability, and interoperability. It should include: 1. A rules engine. 2. A standardized security model. 3. Adapters for incorporating existing applications into the bus.

Table A.5 - SOA P Notes and Glossary
4. Data transformation between sending and receiving applications. 5. distributed deployment with centralized management and administration. 6. Exception handling. 7. Instrumentation for service monitoring. 8. Logging and audit support. 9. Message mediation (rules-based message rerouting and transformation). 10. Message queuing. 11. Message schema validation. 12. Service prioritization. 13. Support for asynchronous processing.
ERM - Enterprise Risk Management /= framework added to COSO in 2004 to improve and consolidate organizational objective setting, event detection, assessment, response, control, monitoring, and reporting of risk.
ESB - See "Enterprise service bus".
ESM - Enterprise Service Management /= software that includes: 1. Application management /= ensuring the availability of service-related application components. 2. Event management /= monitoring, logging, and reporting usual and unusual system events. 3. Load balancing. 4. Metering and billing. 5. Monitoring of networks, disk arrays, servers, databases, and transaction processing systems. 6. Service level management /= tracking and reporting service performance against pre-established requirements.
Estimation (top-down) - Using duration and cost figures from similar activities in prior projects. This is a major feature of Daxiao planning and is supported by the ***Thunk*** database.
Executive Dashboard - Scorecard /= Cross-functional metrics that indicate an organization's overall health.
External audit - Periodic examinations of the books of an organization to ensure they have been properly maintained, are accurate, and comply with established accounting standards.
Extra cost factor - Additional costs attached to base project estimates if critical requirements are not provided before a development team is assigned.
Extra risk factor - Additional risk factor assigned to a project if critical requirements are not provided before a development team is assigned.
Extranet - Secured Internet connections between an organization and its external partners.
Facilitation - helping groups or individuals find a solution, or reach a consensus without dictating a result.
Feasibility study - A study performed by the Project Initiation manager before a request for funding to ascertain the likelihood of success. It evaluates financial, technical, scheduling, organizational, cultural, and legal considerations. It includes an analysis of alternative solutions and a recommendation on the best alternative.
Financial Management - Daxiao organization responsible for budgeting, accounting, and chargeback requirements.
Findings - The output of audit and/or review functions that contain: 1. Status information. 2. Opportunities for enhancement. 3. Problems with recommended solutions.
First mover advantage - Benefits received by being the first to enter the market with a new product or service.
First mover disadvantage - Costs incurred to correct service delivery processes after industry standards evolve and industry best practices evolve.
Five nines - 99.999% availability. This is Daxiao's technology goal. They are currently at 99.99.
Forward engineering - Transforming a design model into code.
Functional Requirement - Description of how a user will interact with a system or how a system fulfills a business function.
Gatekeeper - A person who influences policy by controlling information flow.
Governance, SOA - WFSOA Process Category. These are the processes for implementing, directing, and controlling the SOA. It inherits some of the functions of IT governance. Refer to the Governance section in **Table A.**10 - Processes in the Enabling Domain for the list of currently enabled processes.
Granularity - Degree of modularity of a business system, service, or process. High granularity supports ease of

Table A.5 - SOA P Notes and Glossary
maintenance, but may increase processing time.
Green field project - Program or project started without legacy system constraints. Easier to implement, but often results in additional application silos.
Grid Computing - Software that allows companies to access all their computing resources, on demand, without regard to the location of the physical hardware.
Guidance - 1. Activity details added to methodologies or processes. 2. Guidelines for performing process steps.
Guide - An indexing term that refers to a level in a hierarchy that can be used to group related concepts.
Harvest - Create reusable assets from existing system functions.
History - The trail of changes made to an asset.
HTML - Hypertext Markup Language. The original language for Internet documents.
HTTP - Hypertext Transfer Protocol. The Internet protocol used to fetch hypertext objects from remote hosts.
HTTPS - Secure Hypertext Transfer Protocol /= extensions to HTTP that provides security services for browser-based Internet applications.
Human Resources Support - Process category responsible for personnel policies and training to support WFSOA.
IETF - Internet Engineering Task Force /= standards body that defined Internet operating protocols such as TCP/IP, DNS, HTTP, SMTP, etc. Proposals are submitted to the IETF in the form of RFCs (Request for Comment). See **Table A**.6.1 for a list of standards tracked in Daxiao.
Impact analysis - 1. Evaluation of the cost of failure of a system or business process. 2. Identification of the effect that a new system or system change will have on its users and the processing environment.
IMS XML - IBM's hierarchical database product (introduced in the 1970s), which is being repurposed with Release 9.0 to handle native XML hierarchical schema.
Indexing service - Software that alphabetizes terms in the Knowledge Cooperative.
Infrastructure Architecture - Blueprint for integrating delivery of hardware, operating systems, database management, communications, and development functions.
Infrastructure Technology Team - The group of people responsible for maintaining infrastructure, networks, and access to processing resources.
Initiation - Processes that establish minimum requirements for the official start of a project.
Instrumentation - Adding management and monitoring components into software used by Environment Management tools to ensure applications meet quality of service requirements.
Integration - Bringing together independently developed work products to form a testable piece of software.
Intellectual property - Information assets that are protected by law.
Interoperability Testing - Ensuring that Web service components interact according to Web services standards (WS-I Basic Profile).
Intranet - Private network for an organization using Internet protocols such as TCP/IP.
ISACA ® - Information Systems Audit and Control Association ® /= leading association of professionals in information systems (IS) audit, control, security and governance.
ISO - International Standards Organization (derived from the Greek word meaning "equal") /= group of standards organizations from 148 countries with headquarters in Geneva, Switzerland. Refer to the list in Appendix A.6.2 for the subset of standards being tracked in Daxiao.
Iteration - An instance of a process cycle in software and system development. Methodologies are said to be iterative if they focus on short cycles that provide feedback needed to refine the overall project plan. Thus the results of one iteration affect the goals of the next. Different methodologies define iterations of varying length and complexity.
ITIL - Information Technology Infrastructure Library /= is a customizable framework for defining skills and best practices for delivering computing services. Developed by the Office of Government Commerce (OGC) in the United Kingdom, it is covered by ISO 20000. Concepts were applied to Daxiao Data Center service requirements and provided input to business technology service management.
Kaplan, Robert - Management theorist who (along with David Norton) promotes the idea of the Balanced Scorecard.

Table A.5 - SOA P Notes and Glossary
KC - See "Knowledge Cooperative".
Knowledge audit - Evaluation of internal and external knowledge sources to determine information quality, information gaps and overlaps, ease of access, and frequency of use.
Knowledge Cooperative - KC /= vehicle for capture, formatting, and exchange of all BASE information. A list of the major information categories may be derived by sorting on the "LINK" verb in the Roles/Activity table in SOA P (2).
Knowledge Management - Formalized management (capture, storage, analysis, organization, and sharing) of the organization's intellectual assets.
Knowledge management - underground - Knowledge management techniques implemented within higher-level processes and without wide promotion. This technique was used extensively in Daxiao.
Knowledge management chain - Data (facts), information (context), knowledge (how to use information), wisdom (when to use information).
Knowledge mapping - Determining the location of knowledge assets, relationships between the assets, the processes for knowledge flow, and knowledge flow problems (too little, too much, or misdirected flows) within Daxiao.
Learning organization - A company such as Daxiao that has advanced techniques for creating, gathering, interpreting, updating, and retaining knowledge, and subsequently modifying behavior because of newly gained knowledge.
Legacy Application - Originally applied to mainframe applications, it now refers to anything in production when new functionality is requested.
Libraries, life cycle - Systems in Daxiao have some or all the following: 1. Archival - Retired or sunset versions of work products. 2. Deployment - Ready for production. 3. Development - Work in progress. 4. Historical - Prior versions of work products. 5. Integration - Integrated components. 6. Production - Supporting active business requirements. 7. Research and Development. 8. Staging - Work ready for integration. 9. Testing - Integrated code for differing levels of testing.
Localization - Identifying and supporting culture-specific requirements in a business system.
Logistics - The science (and art) of managing the flow of goods, energy, information, products, services, and people.
Low hanging fruit - The objectives that are easiest to achieve.
Management Services - Network services that centrally administer and manage tasks such as license tracking, security auditing, asset management, address management, software distribution, traffic monitoring, load balancing, and hardware diagnosis.
Markup language - Language syntax that uses tags to define content and style.
Marshaling - Packaging and sending XML across processing boundaries via serialization and deserialization.
Mash-up - Web site or application that delivers content from more than one source where the sources are often not controlled by the organization using the application.
Master data management - Control of critical information, which is essential for the successful operation of Daxiao. This function is handled by the data Governance organization.
Maturity Levels - SOA - 1. Level 1 - Startup activities include training the developers, preparing the corporate culture for SOA, developing SOA skills, exploring new technologies and standards, and delivering targeted Web services (pilot) to demonstrate possibilities of the approach. 2. Level 2 - Integration of major system functions into services using standardized messaging. This is called Service Oriented Integration (SOI). 3. Level 3 - An architected solution capable of supporting service delivery to all business functions. 4. Level 4 - Flexible services that support on-demand adjustment to market conditions. 5. Level 5 - Adjustment of the business model to take advantage of available services along with self-management and adjustment of services.
Maturity Model - Recommended practices that describe progressively more effective ways to implement an organization's goals. The organization may move from non-repeatable processes performed by people in organizational sub-units to practices that are standardized across the organization.

Table A.5 - SOA P Notes and Glossary

Mayo, Elton - Management theorist who proposed that the process of measuring often corresponds to positive results in whatever is being measured.

McKinsey 7-S Model - A framework for evaluating requirements for moving from strategy formulation to strategy implementation.

Metadata - Data about data. Metadata used to describe services in business terms is usually contained in a UDDI registry. A file record layout is metadata about the file.

Metadata service - Provides XML descriptions of business services that enable discovery and usage. Includes:
1. Business information /= service function, line of business, e.g.
2. Technical information /= transport type, authentication requirements, interfaces.
3. Governance information /= policies and service dependencies.

Methodology - See "Development methodology"

Middleware - Software that performs conversion, translation, consolidation, and integration on behalf of business applications. It includes products for:
1. Database management - Provides an interface between a query and data on multiple databases on different platforms and/or different locations.
2. Messaging - Software that allows applications on different platforms to communicate with each other asynchronously by storing service requests in a queue until the necessary resources become available.
3. Networking - managing connections and routing. May be part of an ESB.
4. Security - Software (optionally hardware or firmware) that provides common means for allowing users access to network resources.
5. Transaction processing - handles queries to multiple databases and ensures all are updated properly, or rolled back (compensation) if the transaction does not complete successfully.
6. XML - makes SQL database queries and formats the results into XML.

Milestone, major - Point in a Program or project where stakeholders assess project progress against plans, and make "go/no-go" decisions.

Model -
1. A description of a system from a single perspective.
2. Abstraction describing a problem domain or recommending a problem solution.

- or -

1. Capture abstract information and present it the form of diagrams or illustrations.
2. Create a sketch or mockup.

Model-Driven Architecture - MDA /= architecture recommendation from OMG that supports generation of code structures from an abstract model.

Non-Functional Requirements - NFR /= a quality of a product that does not affect what it does. They may include:

1. Availability	14. Manageability
2. Cultural and political requirements	15. Message transformation
3. Data handling requirements	16. Metering and billing
4. Disaster recovery	17. Monitoring and reporting
5. Error reporting	18. Operational/scheduling requirements
6. Fail over	19. Performance requirements
7. International processing requirements	20. Reliability
8. Interoperability	21. Routing
9. Legal requirements	22. Scalability
10. Load balancing	23. Security requirements
11. Logging	24. Transactional Integrity
12. Look and feel	25. Usability requirements and user interface design
13. Maintainability and portability	

OASIS - Organization for the Advancement of Structured Information Standards /= Web services standards consortium. Refer to the list in **Table A**.6.3 for the list of standards tracked in Daxiao.

Offshore development - Outsourcing application development to Daxiao subsidiaries in Canada, Ireland, or China.

Table A.5 - SOA P Notes and Glossary
OMG - Object Management Group /= open membership consortium that sets standards in object-oriented programming and systems modeling. See **Table A**.6.4 for OMG standards monitored in WFSOA.
On-demand - Services and processes, available in the final stage of SOA maturity where clients can quickly create or adjust to deal with customer demand, market opportunity, or external challenges. Dependency on technology is reduced, but not eliminated.
Ontology - The relationship between objects in a domain.
Orchestration - Definition of the flow between service components including events and triggers where there is a central controller (equate to an orchestra with a conductor).
Organizational learning - Processes for capturing knowledge from experience and through research activities.
Organizational memory - Tacit or captured understanding of processes, procedures, traditions, and values shared by members of an organization.
Organizational readiness - A measure of the existence of adequate management structure, personnel acceptance and skills, and technical capabilities necessary for SOA implementation.
Ownership - A critical issue for SOA implementation /= Daxiao handles ownership of shared data and application components by transferring them to the Financial Services organization where they are owned by the entire organization.
Parser - Program that splits XML it into elements and attributes
Patterns - recognized techniques for implementing business and infrastructure techniques.
PCAOB - Public Company Accounting Oversight Board /= organization created by the Sarbanes Oxley law to guide auditors in maintaining SOX compliance.
PERT - Program Evaluation Review Technique /= project management tool used in Daxiao to schedule, organize, and coordinate project tasks. It is a chart with numbered milestones, definition, and duration of the events between the milestones, and arrows indicating dependencies among major milestones.
Phase - 1. A stage of a project or subproject whose activities produce similar deliverables. 2. The time between major milestones in a development process. 3. Activities that achieve major project milestones.
Plaintext - Human-readable message that is input to an encryption algorithm to produce ciphertext.
Plan - List of actions performed to achieve a specified objective. It includes: 1. Identification of activities (and optionally tasks), sequences, and timing. 2. Identification of activity dependencies (within and outside the project). 3. Identification of inputs and outputs. 4. Identification of necessary resources. 5. Assignment of responsibility and authority.
Planning template - Reusable sets of activities and tasks for standard work products. The project manager will modify the templates as realities dictate.
Platform - The operating system, programming language, hardware, software, and security used to run a business system.
PMBOK - Project Management Book of Knowledge /= guidelines from the Project Management Institute.
PMI - Project Management Institute /= leading project management professional organization.
Porter, Michael - Management theorist who promotes the concept of the value chain.
Post mortem - Evaluation and reporting of significant project events after both successful completion and project failure. Both positive and negative events must be reported to assist future projects.
Prioritization factors - Daxiao priorities are: 1. Problems negatively affecting external clients. 2. Problems causing loss of revenue. 3. Addressing competitive threats. 4. Revenue generation. 5. Cost savings. 6. Client needs and preferences (pain points).
Procedure - Documented steps for achieving a result.

Table A.5 - SOA P Notes and Glossary
Process - Systematic series of related activities designed to achieve a predefined measurable business objective. A set of services and (optionally) manual tasks that is orchestrated or choreographed to address a business objective.
Process Category, WFSOA - One of the nine sets of related processes that move Daxiao toward mature service-oriented architecture, leading to a service-oriented enterprise (SOE). The three groups of three are: Enabling Process Categories are: 1. Governance. 2. SOA Communications. 3. Personnel Support. Creation Process Categories are: 1. Requirements Coordination (Includes Project Initiation Phase). 2. Product Creation (Includes traditional methodology phases). 3. Project Management. Supporting Process Categories are: 1. Architecture. 2. Data Management. 3. Environment Management (Includes Production Implementation).
Process Domain - One of the three groupings off process categories in WFSOA. They are: 1. Enabling Domain - Governance, SOA Communications, and Human Resources Support. 2. Delivery Domain - Requirements Coordination, Product Creation, and Project Management. 3. Support Domain - Architecture, Data Management, and Environment Management.
Process Management - The team responsible for specification, planning, design, creation, implementation, and maintenance of Daxiao's processes.
Production - Processes included in Environment Management. They include all activities after deployments that are required to keep project output running properly.
Program - Coordinated set of projects that collectively advance the organization toward BASE goals. The foundation for BASE was laid during the SOX and ITIL implementations.
Project - Collection of activities with start and end dates that are intended to create or improve a product or service. Within Daxiao, the Requirements Management team decides how and when work requests become projects for the product creation teams.
Project Charter - Project initiation document. It contains the initial project description and includes formal authorization and funding approval.
Project glossary - List of terms (business and technology) related to a specific project. The project glossary may be extracted from common terminology lists. In the reverse direction, contents of the project glossary may be used to update common terminology lists.
Project History - Includes project Plans, planning history, and specification changes.
Protocol - Format and procedures for information exchange.
Prototype - Simulations of a proposed service or process that promote refinement of business requirements by giving clients a preview of what they will receive. They identify areas of risk, give developers an opportunity to exercise new technology, and help project managers and planners to understand the activities involved in creation of work products. They may include: 1. Whiteboard or paper mock-ups. 2. Sample applications created using rapid development and testing techniques during the analysis and design project phase.
Provisioning - Planning, set up, configuring, and establishing rights to hardware, software, and networks.
Public Company Accounting Oversight Board - See "PCAOB".
Publish - Place information in a registry and notify subscribers that it is available.
QoS - Quality of service /= measurement of product conformance to the contract between a user and a service provider.
Quality Assurance - According to IEEE Standard 610, all actions necessary to provide adequate confidence in product quality including evaluation of the process used to develop the product.
Refactor - Improve the quality of a work product without altering its functionality. Applies to systems and data.

Table A.5 - SOA P Notes and Glossary

Reference Architecture - Technical blueprint of a recommendation for how software, hardware, and network components should be organized.

Reference List -

1. Business, the Ultimate Resource, Basic Books, Cambridge, Massachusetts, 2006.
2. Free Online Dictionary of Computing - http://foldoc.org/.
3. Friedman, Alan, Computer Desktop Encyclopedia ©, The Computer Language Company Inc., Version 20.1, 2007.
4. ISO/IEC Overview - http://www.iso.org/iso/home.htm.
5. OASIS Standards - http//www.oasis-open.org/specs/index.php.
6. Object Management Group standards-http//www.omg.org/.
7. RFC (Request for Comment) List from the IETF (Internet Engineering Task Force) with status and disposition http//www.rfc-editor.org/.
8. Technical Reports and Publications of the World Wide Web - http//www.w3.org/TR/

Registry - Database of information about available services and a mechanism for advertising services. A registry contains pointers to service artifacts, and not the artifacts themselves.

Registry, federated - Federation allows multiple registries to behave as one logical registry. Daxiao maintains four registries that are treated as one (initiation, build, staging, and runtime).

Rejection recommendations - Suggestions filed with a project rejection that suggest whether a project can be revived. They include:

1. Improve quality of existing deliverables.
2. Eliminate assumptions.
3. Secure adequate funding.
4. Improve technology.
5. Improve staff skills.
6. Resolve business conflicts.
7. Reduce project scope.

11. **ReMain** - Request Maintenance /= Daxiao utility used to capture and manage work requests that affect technology, BASE sector personnel, or the business.

Repository - A database containing information about system components as well as the components themselves.

Requirements Coordination Process Category - Within Daxiao, processes in this group replace the isolated initiation and requirements phases in traditional life cycle methodologies. It includes a set of centralized functions managed by the Requirements Management Team that supports the WFSOA strategy.

Requirements Management - The Daxiao team that is responsible for collecting, validating, synchronizing, and packaging work requests before they are delivered to a technology team for development.

Resistance Points - Risk posed to the Program or project by negative stakeholders (people or organizations who perceive disadvantages if the proposed Program or project is successful). Resistance points are tracked as part of Program or project risk.

Resource - Infrastructure, staff, or funds required to deliver business technology to clients.

Responsibility - Obligations associated with a role.

Retirement - Removal of system components from production.

Reusable artifacts -

1. Animations.
2. Documentation.
3. Plans.
4. Services - the more granular they are, the more likely they are to be reused.
5. Work request documentation.

Reverse engineering - Converting undocumented code into a processing model

ROI - Return on Investment /= Monetary benefits derived from spending money to create, update, or maintain a system.

Role- Related activities expected to be performed by Program participant.

1. A role may be the same as a job title, but often not the case.
2. A single individual may perform multiple roles.
3. Multiple people may perform the same role.

Table A.5 - SOA P Notes and Glossary

4. An actor, person, or system that participates in a use case ("actor performs activity").

Table A.13.1 contains the list of roles that are applicable in BASE in the winter of 2007.

Role-based access control - Access management model where the software matches the individual or resource requesting access with the role(s) assigned to the users and the access rights allowed for each role.

Rolling wave planning - technique where short-term activities have more detailed tasks and more rigorous schedules than those that are further into the future.

Rules engine - Software that supports recording, tracking, and revision of business processes.

SaaS - Software as a Service /= model of software delivery where a software company provides maintenance, daily operational support, and user support for the software provided to their clients.

Sandbox - Daxiao's internal research platform where SOA technology specialists and architects can experiment with new technology or test problem solutions.

Sarbanes Oxley Act and SOA - SOX /= Government regulation passed in 2002 that defines the types of corporate financial records that must be kept and for how long, and provides penalties for abuse and falsification of data. SOX created the Public Company Accounting Oversight Board (PCAOB) to guide auditors in maintaining SOX compliance and PCAOB recommended COBIT guidelines to control IT-related aspects of compliance.

Note: Because COBIT guidelines and SOA best practices are almost identical, each practice provides benefits for the other within Daxiao.

Scalability - The ability to adjust processing capacity (up or down) in correspondence to business requirements.

Scope creep - Uncontrolled changes in a project's requirements. The Requirements Management Team ensures that all changes to project scope that take longer than a day are documented.

Scorecard - Executive level reports covering business processes and trends.

Security considerations -

1. Authorization	♦ Non-repudiation
2. Confidentiality	♦ Privacy
3. Cryptography	♦ Session Management
4. Federation	♦ Trust
5. Integrity	♦ User Authentication
6. Message Authentication	♦ User Identity

Segregation of Duties (Security) - SOX requirement that IT roles, responsibilities, and accountabilities for information security be segregated, defined, and documented.

SEI - Software Engineering Institute /= federally funded research and development center at Carnegie Mellon devoted to discovering techniques for improving the quality of delivered software.

Semantic gap - The difference between what can be expressed in a language (human or technical) and the real world. E.g., English does not allow adequate distinctions between the different qualities of desert sand or arctic snow.

Semantics - Study of the meaning of words.

Senge, Peter - Management theorist who promotes the concept of the learning organization.

Service architecture - Software and related hardware that manage loose coupling between service components, and between the services and the service consumers.

Service catalog management - Best practices, processes and procedures for creation and maintenance of a registry or repository of Program services and processes.

Service categories - Service categories defined in Daxiao are:

1. Atomic services - granular services that can be composed into higher-level services.
2. Business services - services the include business processing logic.
3. Data access services - CRUD, transformation, and virtualization.
4. Interaction services - provide the interfaces between people and business software.
5. Networking services -enable optimal network performance.
6. Partner services - enable connection with external organizations.
7. Policy enforcement services - intermediaries between service providers and service consumers. Enforces security, message size, and proof of origin.
8. Policy validation services - ensures integrity of XML schema.
9. Process (composite) services -automate and orchestrate business processes.

Table A.5 - SOA P Notes and Glossary

10. Utility services - services such as logging and security that support other automated services.
11. WSM (Web services management) - monitoring, security, logging, and SLA.

Service composition - Combining granular services into more complex services.

Service Consumer - Business software that sends service request messages and subsequently consumes service response messages.

Service Contract - Agreement between a service provider and a service consumer.
It defines the functions that the service exposes to consumers.

1. Generic contracts are stored with the service description and are reusable. This may be customized to accommodate specific user/provider relationships.
2. In a SOAP-based system, the contract is expressed as a set of WSDL messages that the service will consume or produce as output.
3. Documentation describing the real-world meaning of the input and output parameters, either within the WSDL or in a separate document, shows developers how to use the service correctly.

Service Delivery Environment - Must support:

1. Accessing local and remote services.
2. Assembly of higher level services from component services.
3. Creation of processes using services and business rules.
4. Data transformation.
5. Error detection and resolution.
6. Multiple forms of human interaction.
7. Service definition independent of implementation.
8. Service deployment.
9. Service development.
10. Service discovery.
11. Service hosting.
12. Service management and monitoring.
13. Simulating, testing, and debugging services.
14. Synchronous, asynchronous, and conversational services.

Service development methodology - Layer on top of existing methodologies that takes advantage of their best features and deals with added complexity.

1. It may require a combination of methodologies.
2. It may not provide savings initially, but creates products that are reusable and provide savings in the long run.

Service Domain - Related automation products to which a common management policy is applied.

Service level agreement - SLA /= parameters dictated by service users regarding expectations about service/process performance, availability, and resiliency.

Service orientation - The architecture required to deliver services and the enterprise commitment to using services for addressing business processes. To be successful, an SOA must:

1. Centralize the definition of services to prevent gaps and overlap between service offerings.
2. Review each service definition for completeness and compliance with applicable regulations and organizational policies.
3. Define a means for service discovery.
4. Define a means for the establishment of SLAs between provider and consumer.
5. Define patterns and best practices for the implementation of services.

Service owner - An organization that provides a collection of services.

Service Provider - Publisher of service descriptions to one or more service registries and recipients of service invocations from service requestors.

Service Taxonomy - Description of the relationships between services.

Service Transition - Controlling migration from deprecated services to their replacements.

Service-Oriented Architecture (SOA) - Provides business structure and technology frameworks that align information requesters and information providers with business strategy. If SOA works properly, it will allow organizations to remedy countless problems that were created with existing technology. It will also allow organizations to earn or save money (millions to billions of dollars).

Table A.5 - SOA P Notes and Glossary
Service-Oriented Enterprise - SOE /= final stage in SOA maturity where the business is supported entirely by services and processes under control of the business organization with assistance and guidance from technology. In this environment, business teams may create their own services and processes (on-demand services).
Services versus processes - The following concepts are included in the Daxiao definitions: 1. Processes are controlled by process management software. 2. Processes may include services and other processes. 3. Processes may include automated and manual activities. 4. Processes may include only manual activities. - or - 1. Services executive in a service execution environment. 2. Services may include other services. 3. Services do not include manual activities. 4. Services do not include processes.
Shadowing - Harvesting tacit knowledge by observing the practices of Program participants during their work-related activities.
Silo - Processes and systems that are written for and used by a specific organizational entity (often a subset of possible users).
Six Sigma - 3.4 defects per million opportunities to make a mistake (99.9997% error-free). Other levels are: 1. Five Sigma = 230 defects per million (99.8% error-free). 2. Four Sigma = 6,200 defects per million opportunities (99.4% error-free). 3. Three Sigma = approximately 67,000 defects per million opportunities (93% error-free). 4. Two Sigma = approximately 309,000 defects per million (69% error-free).
SLA - See "Service level agreement".
SOA - BASE definitions - 1. Service-Oriented Architecture is a business strategy that allows finer definition of business requirements and successively better alignment of technical support with business requirements. 2. Service-Oriented Architecture is the technical framework, supported by industry standards, that supports modularized computing functions as services for easier alignment with business requirements. It also includes policies and practices to ensure the quality of provided services. 3. SOA. ♦ Changes the relationships between people, applications, and data. ♦ Drives centralization. ♦ Requires centralization. ♦ Promotes elimination of application silos. ♦ Promotes elimination data silos.
SOA - Business definition - Service-Oriented Architecture is a cross-organizational management strategy for aligning business and technology (BIG SOA).
SOA - Technology definition - Service-Oriented Architecture supports coupled and interoperable services or processes and definition of a process for integrating these interoperable components. It includes mechanisms for describing services, advertising, discovering services, and communicating with services.
SOA Assessment - Analysis to support an organization's SOA planning.
SOA Benefits - 1. Control of service composition by business community. 2. Decommissioning outdated functionality (applications, services). 3. Elimination of redundant services. 4. Increased asset reuse. 5. Increased business agility. 6. Reduced integration expense by using standards-based communications for inter-application integration. 7. Reduction in duplication of effort. 8. Support for policy compliance. 9. Support for regulatory compliance.
SOA Best Practices -

Table A.5 - SOA P Notes and Glossary
1. Loosely coupled services. 2. Separation of interfaces from the implementation. 3. Connecting interfaces to a service bus. 4. Opaque services. 5. Assumption that arbitrary consumers will use the service.
SOA catalog - The combination of a UDDI registry and an ebXML catalog which is used to hold information about Daxiao services, processes, applications, and systems.
SOA Competency Center - BASE Team /= permanent centralized area of expertise that supports implementation, enhancement and maintenance of SOA business services and processes.
SOA compliance policy - Governance policy describing the internal and industry standards that should be followed when creating services.
SOA Governance - Management of the processes and systems required for evolution to a full SOA.
SOA methodology issues - Differences that arise from the need balance speed and agility in WFSOA with the need for accuracy to ensure SOA acceptance.
SOA reference architecture - Infrastructure services necessary to support the organization's SOA.
SOAP - No longer an acronym as of version 1.2, it formerly meant Simple Object Access Protocol. It is a messaging specification for an XML-based protocol from the W3C that supports exchange of information among applications running on different operating systems, different technologies, and written in different languages.
SOE - See "Service-Oriented Enterprise"
SOX - See "Sarbanes-Oxley Act".
Sponsor - The most important client of who can lobby for budget, and appeal, approve, or modify project deadlines.
Stakeholder - Person or organization that may affect or be affected by Program or project implementation success. The effects may be either positive or negative. Daxiao promotes positive stakeholder participation and tries to mitigate the actions of negative stakeholders through its advisory counsel.
Standard - 1. Recommendation for performing similar tasks the same way across business and technology processes. BASE is concerned with standards in software development, process development, procurement, databases, infrastructure architecture, programming languages, and manufacturing. 2. Formal requirements developed to prescribe consistent approaches to development.
Standards Gap Management - Implemented when an approved standard does not exist. It includes: 1. Developing interim services to address standards gaps. 2. Recommending a standard. 3. Reviewing standards candidates. 4. Reviewing vendor directions. 5. Reviewing vendor relations with standards committees.
Start-up - The subset of Governance processes that laid the foundation for successful SOA implementation in Daxiao. Several of the processes were created and continue to be maintained for Sarbanes-Oxley conformance (SOX).
Storytelling - The use of stories to share knowledge and facilitate learning. They may be used to describe complicated issues, explain events, communicate lessons learned, or bring about cultural change. That is the technique used for this book.
Strategic plan - Documentation of an organization's objectives and goals.
Strong Naming - Artifact name that includes a simple text name, its version number, date, and optional "business" information.
Subscription - Standing request to inform a subscriber of changes to the entity in a subscription.
Sunset - Retirement of system components.
Swim lane - A grouping of activities performed by the same actor on an activity diagram.
System development life cycle - SDLC /= set of activities starting with requirements capture and proceeding through system implementation and maintenance.
System vs. Application - A system is a broader category that includes everything necessary to support a business objective. It may include legacy applications or components, services (SOA or non-SOA), and processes (automated or manual). →Contrast with "application" a group of related processing components that address the requirements of a limited set

Table A.5 - SOA P Notes and Glossary
of users.
Tacit knowledge - The knowledge that people carry in their heads. It may include skills, experiences, insight, intuition, and judgment. Daxiao requirements management, knowledge consolidation, and communications processes aim to capture and share as much tacit knowledge as possible.
Tactic - Short-term action sequence that is a subset of an overall business strategy.
Task - The result of decomposition of plan activities.
Taxonomy - Hierarchical structure used to categorized information or knowledge.
Template - Online form for information collection with input edit and output formatting capabilities.
Test plan - Description of testing strategy and tactics.
Test script - Instructions on how test cases are to be executed.
Test suite - Collection of logically related test cases.
Testing strategy - Approaches to testing that emphasize particular test areas (i.e., user interface, service interoperability, etc.).
Thesaurus - Index of terms used classify the content of the Knowledge Cooperative.
TOGAF - The Open Group Architectural /= method and supporting tools for developing a corporate architecture.
Tool mentor - A description of how a tool may be used to perform a process activity.
Traceability matrix - A diagram showing the source of system requirements.
UDDI - Universal Description, Discovery and Integration /= standard for a repository that allows storing, discovering, and retrieving Web services metadata. A UDDI registry is a Web service that supports other services. Private registries are maintained by individual organizations and occasionally shared with business partners. Version 3 is the current standard (released in February of 2005). It supports: 1. Custody transfer. 2. Digital signatures on UDDI messages. 3. Improved access security. 4. Inquiry. 5. Multiple registry nodes. 6. Publication. 7. Replication. 8. Subscription listener. 9. Subscription. 10. UDDI policy. 11. User-defined keys and UUID keys. 12. Value set data. 13. Value set validation.
UML used in ReMain - The subset of UML diagrams used in Daxiao to support Product Delivery (Requirements through production). They are: 1. Activity Diagram /= used to model activity flow and data flow. 2. Class Diagram /= depiction of components, processing functions, and relationships. 3. Collaboration Diagram /= shows the message flows between the components in a software system. 4. Component Diagram /= shows the structural relationship between autonomous software and data components in a system. 5. Deployment Diagram /= depiction of a run-time configuration. 6. Sequence Diagram /= shows the interactions between objects and their sequences. 7. State Machine Diagram /= model of the states of an object and the events that cause state changes. 8. Use Case Diagram /= shows the relationships between actors and activities within a system.
Unified Modeling Language - See "UML".
Universal Description, Discovery and Integration - See "UDDI".
Valid XML - XML that is well formed and conforms to constraints imposed by a document type definition (DTD) or an XML Schema Definition (XSD).
Value chain - A sequence of activities that provides value to a user.
Version control - 1. Procedures and tools to manage versions of program deliverables, according to dates, change indicators, or

Table A.5 - SOA P Notes and Glossary

specialized numbering schemes.
2. Maintaining the ability to identify and track multiple copies of a work product.

W3C - World Wide Web Consortium /= founded in 1994 by Timothy Berners-Lee to develop Web standards. The W3C has more than 500 Member organizations worldwide. The U.S. component is hosted at MIT.

SOA assumptions -
1. Most required business functionality is already embedded in existing systems.
2. It is more effective to use existing functions that work than to create new ones.

Web services -
1. Business software that processes and exchanges information using Internet-based communications, usually SOAP (without the space). The pieces may be anywhere in the world as long as the information requesters (consumers) know where to find the information providers. The consumers must also be approved to receive information from the providers.
2. Platform-independent software components that can be described using service description language (WSDL), published to a registry of services (UDDI), discovered through a SOAP-based query (at runtime or design time), invoked over a network, and composed with other services.

Well-formed - XML document that meets XML syntax requirements as specified in the XML standard. DTDs and schemas may add additional requirements to the document.

Well-formed SOA - See "WFSOA".

Well-formed XML - Syntactically correct document that:
1. Supports Unicode encoding (UTF-8 or UTF-16, and optionally UTF-32).
2. Has only one root element.
3. Has all elements defined by start and end tags.
4. Contains properly nested tags.
5. Contains properly labeled tags.

WFSOA© - Well-Formed Service Oriented Architecture /= description the methodology described in this set of publications that promotes evolution of an SOA that supports organizational objectives and helps to achieve organizational goals. It also defines a supporting organizational structure and a set of roles and responsibilities. The "Well-formed" concept is borrowed from XML, meaning that it is syntactically correct. The degree of success within an organization decides whether Well-formed SOA is also valid SOA for Daxiao.

Work product - Result of a BASE project. It could be a single service, a set of services, a process, a group of processes, or it may be traditional programs, components, objects, or applications.

Work request - Artifact for formally tracking a proposed addition, modification, or deletion of a work product or group of work products while it is still in the Requirements Management area. Change requests are subsets of work requests.
1. It describes a problem, the proposed solution, system impact, cost, and origin of the request.
2. It also contains tracking information from request inception to completion or cancellation.
3. All information is captured and tracked in Daxiao's ReMain (Request Maintenance) system.
4. A single work request may become a single project.
5. A single work request may be split into multiple projects.
6. Work requests may be merged to form a single project.

XML - eXtensible Markup Language /= general-purpose markup language developed by the W3C for defining, transmitting, validating, and interpreting data/information

XML database - Storage for XML documents. It may be an XML-enabled version of a relational or object-oriented database, or it may be a native XML database.

XML element - Structure in an XML document defined by a start and end tag.

XML Namespace - Technique for uniquely identifying XML elements and attributes that have the same name by using a URL prefix in front of the "local name".

XML Parser - Software that reads the tags in an XML document and passes data to a business system.

XML signature - XML syntax and processing rules for validating the identity of the sender of an XML message and ensuring that the data was not modified during transmission.

Zachman Framework - A structured technique for defining an enterprise's architecture. In Daxiao, it is referred to as corporate architecture to distinguish it from the technology function performed by the enterprise architect. It

Table A.5 - SOA P Notes and Glossary
uses a grid formatted around six queries (What - data, How - functions, Where - network location, Who - organization, When - schedule, and Why - strategy) asked across rows of five stakeholder groups (Planner, Owner, Designer, Builder and Subcontractor) to provide a view of the enterprise.

Table A.5.1 - Dublin Core Tags	
Abstract	A summary of the content of an information source
Access rights	Information regarding the security status of an information source
Accrual method	The method by which items are added to a collection of information sources
Accrual periodicity	The frequency which items are added to a collection
Accrual policy	Rules governing the addition of items to a collection
Alternative	A substitute title for an information source
Audience	The class of entity expected to access the information source
Available	Date when an information source became available
Bibliographic citation	Reference data for the information source
Collection	An aggregation of information sources
Conforms to	Standard associated with the information source
Contributor	Entity responsible for contributing an information source.
Coverage	Time period or geographical location where the information source is applicable.
Created	Data of creation of the information source
Creator	Person, organization, or service responsible for creating the information source
Data accepted	Date when an information source was approved for formal publication
Data submitted	Data when an information source is delivered for review
Date	The date or time associated with an event in the information source life cycle.
Date copyrighted	Date on a statement of copyright
Description	May include an abstract, a table of contents, a graphical representation, or a text.
Education level	Prerequisites or co requisites for understanding the information source
Extent	Coverage or duration of the information source
Format	Physical medium or recording format, size, and duration
Has format	Description of a related source with similar intellectual content
Has part	The referenced information is divided into parts
Has version	Version, edition, or adaptation of an information source.
Identifier	Unambiguous reference to the information source. May be a UUID.
Instructional method	Process used to convert the information source to knowledge
Is part of	The referenced information source is part of another source
Is format of	Description of a pre-existing source with similar intellectual content
Is referenced by	External source that points to this information
Is replaced by	Described source is superseded by another
Is required by	Name of a source that needs the described source for completion
Is version of	Name of source of the described information source is a version
Issued	Formal date of publication of the information source
Language	Code as specified in IETF RFC 3066.
License	Legal document giving official permission to use the information source
Mediator	An intermediate between an information source an its ultimate audience
Medium	Physical carrier of the resource
Modified	Data on which the information source was modified
Provenance	Information regarding changes in ownership or custody of an information source.
Publisher	Person, organization, or service responsible for making the information source available.
References	Name of a resource that referenced or cited by the described information source
Relation	A reference to a related information source
Replaces	Name of a resource which is superseded by the described source

Requires	The name of a resource required by the described information source
Rights	A link to information (usually intellectual property rights) for a information source
Rights Holder	A person or organization owning or managing rights over a information source
Source	An information source used as input to the topic information
Spatial	Geographic location of an information source
Subject	Consists of keywords, key phrases, or classification codes
Title	The name associated with the information source
Type	The nature of information source. Valid Dublin Core types are (a) collection, (b) dataset - lists, tables, and databases (c) Event, (d) image, (e) interactive source, (f) moving image, (g) physical object, (h) service, (i) software, (j) sound, (k) still image, (l) and text

Table A.6.1 - IETF Standards Tracked in BASE (As of Spring 2008)

Standard	Description	RFC
FTP	File Transfer Protocol	959
IP	Internet Protocol	791
SMTP	Simple Mail Transfer Protocol	821
TCP	Transmission Control Protocol	793
Draft. Standard		
HTTP	Hypertext Transfer Protocol -- HTTP/1.1	2616
DHCP	Dynamic Host Configuration Protocol	2131
MIME	Multipurpose Internet Mail Extensions (MIME)	2045 - 2049
Proposed Standards		
BEEP	The Blocks Extensible Exchange Protocol Core	3080
(LDAP)	Lightweight Directory Access Protocol	4511

Table A.6.2 - ISO/IEC Standards Tracked in BASE (As of Spring 2008)

Number: Year or Parts	Description	Acronym
ISO/IEC 10116:2006	Modes of operation for an n-bit block cipher	
ISO/IEC 10118 (all parts)	Hash-functions	
ISO/IEC 11179 (all parts)	Metadata registries	MDR
ISO/IEC 11770 (all parts)	Key management	
ISO/IEC 13335-1:2004	Concepts and models for information and communications technology security management	
ISO/IEC 13888 (all parts)	Non-repudiation	
ISO/IEC 14143 (all parts)	Software measurement -- Functional size measurement	
ISO/IEC 14496 (part 1 and 3)	Intellectual Property Management and Protection extensions	IPMP
ISO/IEC 14598 (all parts)	Software product evaluation	
ISO/IEC 14764:2006	Software Life Cycle Processes -- Maintenance	
ISO/IEC 14888 (all parts)	Digital signatures with appendix	
ISO 15000-1:2004	ebXML Collaborative Partner Profile Agreement	ebXML
ISO 15000-2:2004	ebXML Messaging Service Specification	ebXML

ISO 15000-3:2004	ebXML Registry Information Model	ebXML
ISO 15000-4:2004.	ebXML Registry Services Specification	ebXML
ISO/TS 15000-5:2005	ebXML Core Components Technical Specification, Version 2.01(ebCCTS)	ebXML
ISO/IEC 15289:2006	Purpose and content of systems and software life cycle information items	
ISO/IEC 15408 (all parts)	Evaluation criteria for IT security	
ISO/IEC 15459 (all parts)	Unique identifiers	
ISO/IEC 15476 (all parts)	CASE Data Interchange Format	CDIF
ISO/IEC 15504 (all parts)	Process assessment	
ISO/IEC 15940:2006	Software Engineering Environment Services	
ISO/IEC 15946 (all parts)	Cryptographic techniques using elliptic curves	
ISO/IEC 16085:2006	Life cycle processes -- Risk management	
ISO/IEC 17799:2005	Code of practice for information security management	
ISO/IEC 18014 (2 parts)	Time-stamping services	
ISO/IEC 18019:2004	Design and preparation of user documentation for application software	
ISO/IEC 18028 (all parts)	IT network security	
ISO/IEC 18033 (all parts)	Encryption algorithms	
ISO/IEC 18045:2005	Methodology for IT security evaluation	
ISO/IEC 19011:2002	Quality management systems auditing and guidelines for evaluating the competence of auditors.	
ISO/IEC 19501:2005	Open distributed processing -- Unified Modeling Language Version 1.4.2	UML
ISO/IEC 19502:2005	Meta Object Facility	MOF
ISO/IEC 19503:2005	XML Metadata Interchange	XMI
ISO/IEC 19763-1:2007 (2 parts)	Metamodel framework for interoperability	MFI
ISO/IEC 19770-1:2006	Software asset management	
ISO/IEC 20000-1:2005	Techniques for benchmarking IT service management.	
ISO/IEC 20000-2:2005	Auditing of service management processes.	
ISO/IEC 21827:2002	Systems Security Engineering -- Capability Maturity Model (SSE-CMM®)	
ISO/IEC 22537:2006	ECMAScript for XML specification	ECMAScript
ISO/IEC 23026:2006	Recommended Practice for the Internet -- Web Site Engineering, Web Site Management, and Web Site Life Cycle	
ISO/IEC 2382 (all parts)	Information technology vocabularies	
ISO/IEC 24744:2007	Metamodel for development methodologies	
ISO/IEC 25000:2005	Software product Quality Requirements and Evaluation -- Guide	SQuaRE
ISO/IEC 25001:2007	Software product Quality Requirements and Evaluation -- Planning and management	SQuaRE
ISO/IEC 25020:2007	Software product Quality Requirements and Evaluation -- Measurement reference model and guide	SQuaRE
ISO/IEC 25051:2006	Requirements for quality of Commercial Off-The-Shelf (COTS) software product and instructions for testing	SQuaRE
ISO/IEC 25062:2006	Common Industry Format (CIF) for usability test reports	SQuaRE
ISO/IEC 27000:2005	Glossary of terms used in the ISO 27000-series of information security standards	
ISO/IEC 27001:2005	Information security management systems requirements	
ISO/IEC 27006:2007	Requirements for audit and certification of information security management systems	
ISO/IEC 7064:2003	Check character systems	

ISO/IEC 9000:2005	Fundamentals of quality management systems in the ISO 9000 family of standards.	
ISO/IEC 9001:2000	Requirements for a quality management system. It combines 9001, 9002, and 9003 from earlier standard.	
ISO/IEC 9126 (all parts)	Product quality	
ISO/IEC 9796 (parts 2 and 3)	Digital signature schemes giving message recovery	
ISO/IEC 9797 (2 parts)	Message authentication codes	MACs
ISO/IEC 9798 (all parts)	Entity authentication	
ISO/IEC TR 13335 (all parts)	Management of IT Security	
ISO/IEC TR 14516:2002	Use and management of Trusted Third Party services	
ISO/IEC TR 15443 (2 parts)	Security assurance framework	
ISO/IEC TR 15452:2000	Specification of data value domains	
ISO/IEC TR 15947:2002	IT intrusion detection framework	
ISO/IEC TR 18044:2004	Information security incident management	
ISO/IEC TR 19791:2006	Security assessment of operational systems	
ISO/IEC TR 20943 (2 parts)	Procedures for achieving metadata registry content consistency	
ISO/IEC TR 9294:2005	Management of software documentation	
ISO/TS 15000-1:2004	Electronic business eXtensible Markup Language (ebXML) -- Collaboration-protocol profile and agreement specification	ebCPP
ISO/TS 15000-2:2004	Electronic business eXtensible Markup Language (ebXML) -- Part 2: Message service specification	ebMS
ISO/TS 15000-3:2004	Electronic business eXtensible Markup Language (ebXML) Registry information model specification	ebRIM
ISO/TS 15000-4:2004	Electronic business eXtensible Markup Language (ebXML) -- Registry services specification	ebRS
ISO/TS 15000-5:2005	Electronic Business Extensible Markup Language (ebXML) -- Core Components Technical Specification, Version 2.01	ebCCTS
ISO/TS 16668:2000	Basic Semantics Register	BSR

Table A.6.3 - OASIS Standards Tracked in BASE (As of Spring 2008)

Description	Acronym	Approval Date
Business Centric Methodology Specification v1.0	BCM	2006/04
Darwin Information Typing Architecture v1.1	DITA	2007/08
Digital Signature Services v1.0		2007/04
DocBook v4.5		2006/10
ebXML Collaborative Partner Profile Agreement v2	CPPA	2002/11
ebXML Messaging Services v3.0		2007/10
ebXML Registry Information Model v3.0	RIM	2005/05
ebXML Registry Services Specification v3.0	RS	2005/05
ebXML v2.0.4	ebXML	2006/12
Extensible Access Control Markup Language v2.0	XACML	2005/02
Reference Model for Service Oriented Architecture v1.0		2006/10
Security Assertion Markup Language v2.0	SAML	2005/03
Service Provisioning Markup Language v2.0	SPML	2006/04
Universal Business Language v2.0	UBL	2006/12
Universal Description, Discovery and Integration v3.0.2	UDDI	2005/02
Web Computer Graphics Metafile v2.0 - ISO standard issued jointly with the W3C	WebCGM	2007/01
Web Services Business Process Execution Language 2.0	WS-BPEL	2007/04
Web Services Distributed Management v1.1	WSDM	2006/08

Web Services for Remote Portlets	WSRP	2003/08
Web Services Notification v1.3. 1. Web Services Base Notification v1.3. 2. Web Services Brokered Notification v1.3. 3. Web Services Topics v1.	WSN	2006/10
Web Services Resource Framework v1.2	WSRF	2006/04
Web Services Security v1.1	WSS	2006/02
Web Services Transaction v1.1 - Includes: 1. WS-Coordination. 2. WS-AtomicTransaction. 3. WS-BusinessActivity		2007/03
WSDM Management of Web Services v1.0	WSDM-MOWS	2005/03
WSDM Management Using Web Services v1.0	WSDM-MUWS	2005/03
WS-Reliability v1.1		2004/11
WS-ReliableMessaging 1.1		2007/06
WS-SecureConversation v1.3		2007/03
WS-SecurityPolicy v1.2		2007/07
WS-Trust v1.3		2007/03
XML Catalogs		2005/10
XML Localization Interchange File Format v1.2	XLIFF	2008/02

Table A.6.4 - OMG Standards Tracked in BASE (As of Spring 2008)

Available Specifications	Acronym	Approval date
C IDL Language Mapping (Version 1.0)		1999/07
C++ IDL Language Mapping (Version 1.1)		2003/06
COBOL IDL Language Mapping (Version 1.0)		1999/07
Data Distribution Services (Version 1.2)	DDS	2007/01
IDL to Java Language Mapping (Version 1.2)		2002/08
Java to IDL Language Mapping (Version 1.3)		2003/09
Meta-Object Facility Core (Version 2.0)	MOF™	2006/01
Negotiation Facility (Version 1.0)		2002/03
Object Constraint Language (Version 2.0)	OCL	2006/05
PL/1 IDL Language Mapping (Version 1.0)		2002/09
Reusable Asset Specification (Version 2.2)	RAS	2005/11
Software Process Engineering Metamodel (Version 1.1)	SPEM	2005/01
UML Diagram Interchange (Version 1.0)		2006/04
UML Profile for Schedulability, Performance and Time (Version 1.1)		2005/01
Unified Modeling Language - Infrastructure (Version 2.(Version 1.1)	UML™	2007/02
Workflow Management Facility (Version 1.2)	WMF	2000/05
WSDL/SOAP-CORBA Interworking (Version 1.0)		2004/04
XML IDL Language Mapping (Version 1.1)		2003/04
XML Metadata Interchange (Version 2.1)	XMI®	2005/09
Adopted (in Finalization)		**Adoption Date**
Business Motivation Model (Version 1.0)	BMM	2006/08
Business Process Maturity Model	BPMM	2007/07
Business Process Modeling Notation (Version 1.0)	BPMN	2006/11
DDS Interoperability (Version 1.0)		2006/08
Knowledge Discovery Metamodel (Version 1.0)	KDM	2007/03
MOF 2 Versioning and Development Life cycle (Version 1.0)		2006/06
MOF Model to Text Transformation Language (Version 1.0)		2006/11

MOF Query / Views / Transformations (Version 1.0)		2005/11
Ontology Definition Metamodel (Version 1.0)	ODM	2006/10
Semantics of Business Vocabulary and Business Rules (Version 1.0)	SBVR	2006/08
WSDL to C++ Language Mapping (Version (Version 1.0)		2006/08

Table A.6.5 - W3C Standards Tracked in BASE (As of Spring 2008)		
Standard	**Acronym**	**Publication Date**
Canonical XML Version 1.0	XML	2001/03
Character Model for the World Wide Web 1.0: Fundamentals		2005/02
Document Object Model (DOM) Level 3 Core Specification	DOM	2004/04
Extensible Markup Language (XML) 1.0 (Fourth Edition)		Rev. 2006/08
Extensible Markup Language (XML) 1.1 (Second Edition)	XML	2006/08
Extensible Stylesheet Language (XSL) Version 1.1	XSL	2006/12
HTML 4.01		1999/12
Namespaces in XML 1.1 (Second Edition)		2006/08
Web Ontology Language Semantics and Abstract Syntax	OWL	2004/02
Resource Description Framework Concepts and Abstract Syntax	RDF	2004/02
Semantic Annotations for WSDL and XML schema		2007/08
SOAP Message Transmission Optimization Mechanism (MTOM)		2005/01
SOAP Version 1.2	SOAP	2003/06
Synchronized Multimedia Integration Language 2.0	SMIL	2001/08
Web Services Addressing 1.0 - Core		2006/05
Web Services Description Language (WSDL) 1.1 (W3C Note - never approved by W3C)	WSDL	2001/03
Web Services Description Language (WSDL) 2.0	WSDL	2007/06
WebCGM (Web Computer Graphics Metafile) - ISO standard issued jointly with OASIS.	WebCGM	2007/01
Web Services Policy	WS-Policy	2007/09
XHTML ™ 1.0 (Revised)	XHTML	2002/08
XML Encryption Syntax and Processing		2002/12
XML Key Management Specification (XKMS 2.0)		2005/06
XML Path Language (XPath) 2.0		2007/01
XML Schema (Second edition)		Rev. 2004/10
XML-Signature Syntax and Processing		2002/02
XPointer		2003/03
XQuery 1.0: An XML Query Language		2007/01
XSL Transformations (XSLT) Version 2.0	XSLT	2007/01

Table A.7.1 - BASE Procurement Activities		
Requirements gathering		
Tool administrator	Document	Necessary and optional product functions and features
Tool administrator	Compare	Requirements to existing products (earlier versions, different vendors, or in-house developed)
Tool administrator	Identify	Vendor assumptions for product creation
Tool administrator	Identify	Current product users and locations
Tool administrator	Link	Product requirement to strategic or tactical plan
Client(s)	Identify	Product users (number and concurrence)

Table A.7.1 - BASE Procurement Activities		
Tool administrator	Identify	Product to be replaced (if any)
Tool administrator	Identify	Products with overlapping functionality (if any)
Process coordinator(s)	Identify	Existing (manual or automated) procedures will be affected by the product
Process coordinator(s)	Identify	New processes required for product use
Process coordinator(s)	Identify	Process elimination enable by this product
Client(s)	Estimate	Duration of product use
Tool administrator	Determine	Internal usage requirements
Tool administrator	Determine	International variations
Tool administrator	Determine	Availability of international support
Procurement specialist	Deliver	Make-or-buy recommendation
Planning		
Procurement specialist	Assign	Procurement priority
Planning specialist	Create	Procurement plan and product schedule
Planning specialist	Identify	Product evaluation participants
Production selection		
Procurement specialist	Perform	Vendor evaluations
Procurement specialist	Determine	Vendor maturity
Procurement specialist	Select	Vendor candidates
Tool administrator	Select	Product candidates
Procurement specialist	Submit	Requests for information (RFI)
Sponsor(s)	Approve	Preliminary funding agreement from
Support requirements risk considerations		
Tool administrator	Identify	Hardware upgrade dependencies
Architect - availability	Identify	Software upgrade dependencies (related products)
Architect - infrastructure	Identify	Hardware elimination opportunities
Tool administrator	Identify	Customization requirements
Tool administrator	Identify	Customization skill requirements and sources (vendor, internal, consultants)
Architect - SOA	Identify	Supported Web/SOA standards (and versions)
Tool administrator	Determine	Product maturity
Tool administrator	Determine	The vendor upgrade schedule
Tool administrator	Determine	Upgrade planning requirements
Tool administrator	Identify	Required DBMS or file structures
Data specialist	Identify	Data translation or transformation requirements
Tool administrator	Identify	Known outstanding problems
Tool administrator	Determine	Operating system(s) supported by the product
Tool administrator	Determine	Requirements for integration and implementation
Procurement specialist	Determine	Product support options
Training specialist	Determine	Training requirements and providers
Financial specialist - BASE	Verify	Annual maintenance cost?
Financial specialist	Estimate	The total cost of implementation
Financial specialist	Estimated	Expected ROI
Sponsor(s)	Evaluate	Make-or-buy recommendation
Acquisition		
Tool administrator	Schedule	Internal technical support for product installation
Tool administrator	Schedule	Testing support for product evaluation
Tool administrator	Ensure	Facilities support for hardware products
Tool administrator	Acquire	Product (bring it in house)
Tool administrator	Understand	Special library requirements
Tool administrator	Understand	Product defaults

Table A.7.1 - BASE Procurement Activities		
Tool administrator	Install	Product
Security administrator	Authorize	Product evaluators
Evaluation		
Tool administrator	Review	Product documentation
Testing specialist - technology	Secure	Vendor's test cases
Testing specialist - technology	Create	Test cases, scripts and plans
Testing specialist - technology	Test	Product
Testing specialist - technology	Identify	Product defects
Tool administrator	Evaluate	Products against requirements
Tool administrator	Evaluate	Products against stated capabilities
Tool administrator	Identify	Conformance to relevant standards
Tool administrator	Review	Proprietary components
Tool administrator	Evaluate	Ease of use features
Tool administrator	Develop	Prototypes, if appropriate
Tool administrator	Verify	Interoperability with associated products
Tool administrator	Document	Product limitations
Tool administrator	Document	Product benefits
Tool administrator	Secure	Functional approval from product users
Tool administrator	Acquire	Fixes from vendor
Tool administrator	Recommend	Product purchase
Purchase		
Procurement specialist	Issue	Request for quotation (RFQ)
Procurement specialist	Negotiate	Support agreements
Procurement specialist	Negotiate	Training agreements
Procurement specialist	Negotiate	Licensing agreements
Procurement specialist	Publish	Purchase recommendation (finish contract)
Procurement specialist	Collect	Signatures for purchase approval (final contract)
Sponsors	Fund	Product purchase
Procurement specialist	Place	Orders for products or services
Roll out		
Tool administrator	Create	Roll out plan
Tool administrator	Integrate	The product into the environment
Tool administrator	Add	Documentation to Knowledge Cooperative
Communications specialist - BASE	Notify	Users of availability
Tool administrator	Schedule	The implementation
Security administrator	Authorize	Users
Training specialist	Train	Users
Data administrator	Migrate	Content from replaced product
Process coordinator(s)	Migrate	User from replaced products
Tool administrator	Perform	Post-implementation
Tool administrator	Monitor	Product performance
Tool administrator	Retire	Obsolete products

Table A.7.2 - Daxiao Procurement Product List

Key: "E" - product required enhancement to support SOX and/or SOA.
"N" - products were acquired specifically for Service-Oriented Architecture.
Blank - no change required.

Product	Key
Adapters for packaged products	N
Archival services	
Asset management software	E
Authentication software (security)	E
Automated documentation software	E
Automated standards verification software	N
Batch testing harness	E
BPEL process designer and debugger	N
Business Activity Monitoring (BAM) software	N
Business intelligence services	E
Business intelligence software	E
Business process management software	N
Business rules management software	N
Certification agency services	E
Code coverage software	E
Code generation tools - SOA	N
Collaboration and social networking products	E
Complex event processing software	N
Compliance monitoring and evaluation software	E
Content management software	E
Cross-platform integration software	E
Data aggregation software	E
Data graphing software	
Data mart and warehouse software	E
Data quality assessment product	E
Data translation tools - platform specific	E
Database middleware (hierarchical, relational, XML)	E
Debugging tools	E
Design tools	E
Development software - services and processes	N
Document management software	E
Dynamic report generation software	E
E-book library	E
Enterprise service bus	E
ERP applications	E
ETL (extract, translation, load) software	E
Event notification software	E
Expert systems software	E
External data services	E
Financial tracking software	E
Firewalls (XML)	E
Grid processing software	N
Hardware for BASE and technology teams	E
Human language translation software	E
Impact analysis software	E
Indexing software	E
Infrastructure hardware - all environments and	E

Product	Key
Legacy adaptation (wrapper) software	N
Library management software	E
Management reporting products (scorecards, dashboards, etc)	E
Messaging middleware	E
Metadata repository	N
Modeling software - business events	E
Modeling software - data	E
Modeling software - service and process	N
Monitoring products	E
Network products (servers, routers, bridges, gateways)	E
Notification software (alerts and events)	E
Online courses	E
Outsourcing services	E
Planning software	E
Policy management software	N
Problem tracking software	E
Process animation software	N
Process management software (server and console)	N
Process server software	N
Process virtualization software	N
Project specific software	E&N
Prototyping tools	E
Records management software	E
Release management software	E
Requirements tracking software	E
Reverse engineering software	E
SaaS products	N
Security gateway products	E
Security products (administration, monitoring, appliances, middleware, modeling)	E
Server hardware (applications, services, and processes)	E
Service management and monitoring products	N
SOA integration support software	N
SOA performance upgrade products (intelligent routers, hubs, gateways, network appliances, and switches)	E
SOA registry/catalog software	N
SOAP engine	N
Software quality evaluation software	E
Software re-engineering products	E
Test automation and management products	E
Test defect tracking software	E
Training vendor services	E
Transaction middleware	E

platforms	
Infrastructure software - all environments and platforms	E
Infrastructure management tools	E
Integrated development software (including SOA extensions)	E
Integration tools	E
Knowledge broker services	E
Knowledge-based software	E
Learning management system	E
UML roundtrip modeling software	N
Unit testing software (e.g., XUnit)	E
User hardware	E
Vendor consulting services	E
Web content for project implementation	
WSDL inspection product	N
WS-I validation product	N
XML appliances	N
XML gateway products	N
XML tools (schema development, parsers, editors, accelerators, validation products, shredders, etc.)	N

Table A.8 - List of Planning Verbs
See SOA P (2) for definitions of how they are used in WFSOA planning

Accept	Consume	Forecast	Package	Route
Access	Contribute	Format	Perform	Schedule
Achieve	Contribute to	Freeze	Pilot	Search
Acknowledge	Control	Fund	Plan	Secure
Acquire	Convert	Generate	Populate	Select
Add	Coordinate	Guide	Postpone	Send
Adhere to	Correct	Handle	Prepare	Separate
Adjust	Create	Highlight	Prevent	Sequence
Administer	Customize	Hire	Prioritize	Serialize
Advertise	Debug	Identify	Procure	Shadow
Advise (on)	Decompose	Implement	Produce	Share
Align	Decrypt	Import	Promote	Shred
Allocate	Define	Incorporate	Propagate	Sign
Analyze	Delegate	Increase	Propose	Simulate
Animate	Delete	Index	Prototype	Specify
Annotate	Deliver	Initiate	Provide	Split
Approve	Demonstrate	Install	Provision	Standardize
Archive	De-normalize	Institutionalize	Publish	Submit
Assemble	Deploy	Instrument	Realign	Subscribe to
Assess	Describe	Integrate	Reassign	Support
Assign	Design	Interpret	Rebuild	Synchronize
Assist with	Designate	Interview	Recommend	Syndicate
Attach	Determine	Inventory	Record	Synthesize
Audit	Develop	Investigate	Recover	Test
Authorize	Diagram	Join	Reduce	Trace
Automate	Digitize	Justify	Refactor	Track
Back up	Discover	Link	Reference	Train
Balance	Distribute	Link to	Refine	Transfer
Benchmark	Document	Load	Register	Transform
Build	Educate	Locate	Reject	Translate
Calculate	Eliminate	Lock	Remove	Tune
Cancel	Enable	Maintain	Rename	Understand
Capture	Encourage	Manage	Replace	Unit test
Catalog	Enforce	Mandate	Report	Unlock
Categorize	Engage	Map	Reproduce	Update
Champion	Ensure	Mentor	Request	Upgrade
Check in	Escalate	Merge	Research	Use
Check out	Establish	Migrate	Resolve	Validate
Clarify	Estimate	Mirror	Respond to	Verify
Classify	Evaluate	Mitigate	Restore	Wrap
Cleanse	Execute	Model	Retain	Write
Close	Export	Modify	Retest	
Collaborate	Extend	Monitor	Retire	
Collect	Extract	Name	Reuse	
Communicate	Facilitate	Negotiate	Reverse engineer	
Compare	Finalize	Normalize	Review	
Complete	Follow-up	Notify	Revise	
Conduct	Forecast	Optimize	Reward	
Configure	Format	Orchestrate	Rotate	

Table A.9 - *Thunk* Roles/Activity Information Relationships		
Information Type	**Relationship**	**Affected Information/ Comment**
Access Control List	Secures	Artifacts
Access Control List	Secures	Knowledge Cooperative
Action Items	Added to	Action List: These action items are discovered while parsing additions and updates to Knowledge Cooperative information sources. The items are reviewed by the knowledge consolidator, personnel, and the manager of the team to which a suggested role is assigned. These action list entries will contain: ♦ Action - recommended. ♦ Action comments. ♦ Action object - recommended. ♦ Date added. ♦ Role - recommended. ♦ Source - Knowledge Cooperative Data Collection. ♦ Team
Action items	Linked to	Roles: A related set of action items define the expected work performed by a person who has accepted a BASE role.
Action items	Validated against	Common Terminology: Automated validation occurs before the approval process. Further manual validation may be required.
Action list	Edited against	Common terminology
Action list	Facilitates	Performance reviews: The action list provides an excellent skills inventory. When the Action List is sorted by Actor, role, and date, this would show, among other things: ♦ Action items associated with an individual. ♦ Activities completed (on time). ♦ Activities in progress. ♦ Artifacts an individual has produced or maintained. ♦ Business areas an individual has worked with. ♦ Effort an individual contributes to plan. ♦ Projects with which a person was associated. ♦ Roles an individual has assumed. ♦ Teams an individual has worked on. ♦ Technologies with which an individual has demonstrated familiarity
Action List	Refines	Roles: ♦ Actions may be added to roles if they appear on the action list frequently enough that they need to be assigned. ♦ Actions may be removed from roles if they are part of a role description by are never performed by individuals in a specific role. ♦ Actions may be moved from one role to another, depending upon information found in the Action List.
Action list	Suggests	Training content: When a person is assigned to a new role, their skill sets are compared to the actions performed by that role in the action list. If there is a gap, people are scheduled for the appropriate training.
Action List	Suggests	Activities:

Table A.9 - *Thunk* Roles/Activity Information Relationships		
Information Type	**Relationship**	**Affected Information/ Comment**
	entries for	Planners or project managers may use action lists to discover applicable items that may have been overlooked.
Action List	Validated against	Common terminology
Activities	Loaded into	Action List: A single combination of role/action verb/action object may produce multiple entries in the Action List: Each will be associated with the same UUID. For example: ♦ There will be one entry for each resource (combination of actor and role) associated with a planned action. ♦ If a plan includes a higher level of detail, there may be one entry for each artifact acted upon by a resource. ♦ The same resource may perform the same work (e.g. maintenance) on the same artifact in different plans. Both entries will appear in the action list. ♦ A planned action may appear in an action list with the resource fields containing "unknown" for the actor, and /or "undefined" in the role field. When the resources or roles are assigned, new entries are added to the action list. ----------------------------------- Data elements [(1)] : Action items contain: ♦ Identifier (UUID) - required ♦ Action verb - required ♦ Actor information ♦ Date (item creation) - required ♦ Link to plan location (most recent version) ♦ Object of action - required ♦ Role - required [(3)] ♦ Source - required [(2)] ----------------------------------- ♦ Action comments ♦ Artifact (work product) ♦ Business area ♦ Date (action ended) ♦ Date (action started) ♦ Date (planned start) ♦ Date (planned end) ♦ Date (plan) ♦ Plan activity sequence ♦ Plan comments ♦ Activity comments ♦ Plan name ♦ Plan preparer(s) ♦ Project identifier ♦ Resources estimated ♦ Work contribution by actor ♦ Technology(s) ♦ Team ♦ BASE governance stage ♦ WFSOA process group ♦ WFSOA Project stage -------------------------------- [(1)] Action items may be sorted or extracted depending upon the content of all data

Table A.9 - *Thunk* Roles/Activity Information Relationships		
Information Type	**Relationship**	**Affected Information/ Comment**
		elements. (2) Sources: 1. Pre-merger plans (Planning History). 2. Working plans. 3. Knowledge Cooperative documentation (suggestions reviewed before addition to action list). (3) The value in the role field may be "unassigned"
Activity	Produces	Artifacts
Actors	Accept	Roles
Actors	Associated with	Resource: All resources have a role value. "Unassigned" is the default.
Actors	Contained in	Access control list: Specific privileges may be assigned to individuals, if allowed by corporate policy and approved by information owners
Actors	Members of	Control Groups - Examples of groups are: 1. Budget approvers. 2. All members of a team. 3. Requirements approvers. 4. All the people in a department. 5. By definition, all members in a specific role are in a control group
Actors	Responsible for	Artifacts: The person who creates an artifact automatically receives access to the artifact
Artifacts	Documented in	Knowledge Cooperative
Budget allocations	Require	Plans: An approved plan must be filed with finance administration before funds are allocated.
Groups	Contained in	Access Control List
Knowledge Cooperative	Suggests	Action Items: This includes items that may not yet be included in a technology project plan or the SOA Program plan. It also includes action items outside technology and SOA that affect the Program and Program participants. Examples are: 1. Tasks required to work with newly purchased products (provides input to initial plans using the product). 2. Training plan. 3. BASE communications plan. 4. Cultural change management plan. 5. Strategic plans.
Knowledge Cooperative	Updates	Common Terminology
Performance Reviews	Add to	Action Lists. Unscheduled action items are added to umbrella projects in the action list during the performance process.
Planning History	Highlights	Best Practices: ♦ Plans are assigned an effectiveness rating. ♦ Formats of successful plans are documented and used as planning mentors. ♦ Contents of successful plans are used as input to continuous process improvement

Table A.9 - *Thunk* Roles/Activity Information Relationships		
Information Type	**Relationship**	**Affected Information/ Comment**
Planning History	Loaded into	Action List: Pre-merger plans are parsed and formatted to create entries in the action list. They contain all the data available from historical sources. The minimum data elements are: ♦ Action object. ♦ Action verb. ♦ Date (of entry creation). ♦ Plan identifier. ♦ Source - Pre-merger plans. ♦ Link to scanned image of plan
Planning History	Provides input to	Plans: ♦ Copies of existing plans may be imported and used as the foundation for new plans. ♦ Portions (branches) of existing plans may be imported into new plans. ♦ Portions of multiple plans may be merged into a single plan. ♦ Resource utilization from existing plans assist work estimation
Plans	Justify	Budget allocations
Plans	Organize	Activities: ♦ Activities may contain multiple tasks. ♦ Plans define activity sequences, and dependencies. ♦ Actions may be either tasks or activities
Plans	Saved in	Planning History: ♦ Planning history includes pre-merger plans in multiple formats (Memos (scanned), faxes, spreadsheets, text documents, and output of planning software. ♦ Post-merger plans must be in spreadsheet format or the output of planning software. ♦ Planning history includes copies of each approved plan. ♦ Planning history includes copies of each approved plan update. ♦ Planning history includes plans for successful and unsuccessful projects
Plans	Synchronized with	Strategy: No plan is approved that cannot be related to the business strategy
Plans	Track	Activities
Resource	Allocated to	Activity
Roles	Assigned to	Actors
Roles	Associated with	Resource
Roles	Associated with	Resource
Roles	Contained in	Access control list: A default of privileges are associated with each role in the access control list
Strategy	Supported by	Plans
Training Content	Adds to	Action List
Training Content	Updates	Common Terminology

Table A.10 - Processes in the Enabling Domain	
Communications Process Category	
Process Identifier	**Role Responsible for Maintaining the Process**
Common terminology research and maintenance	Communications specialist - BASE
Facilitation	Communications specialist - BASE
International character sets	Communications specialist - corporate
Knowledge Cooperative (information gathering, evaluation, synthesis, delivery, and archiving)	Knowledge consolidator
Multi-language communications (including international character sets)	Communications specialist - BASE
Process transparency	Communications specialist - BASE
Program communications (BASE)	Communications specialist - BASE
Role interactions (collaboration)	Communications specialist - BASE
Unstructured data (a subset of Knowledge Cooperative processes)	Knowledge consolidator
User interface management	User interface specialist
Vendor knowledge capture	Knowledge consolidator
Web content management	User interface specialist
Governance Process Category	
Process Identifier	**Role Responsible for Maintaining the Process**
Anomalous project integration	Compliance specialist - business
Approval/rejection of product delivery phases	Financial specialist - corporate
Approvals - procurement	Financial specialist - corporate
Asset life cycle	Asset librarian
Audit coordination	BASE Program coordinator
Audits - business unit, SOA Program, project, software, IT	Compliance specialists (business and technology)
Audits - corporate	Corporate lawyer
Authentication (subset of security management)	Security specialist - technology
Automated approvals (funding)	Financial specialist - corporate
Automated approvals (project gateways)	BASE Program coordinator
Automated software compliance checking	Compliance specialist - technology
BASE Program Synchronization (SOA, SOX, CMMI, ITIL)	Executive - BASE
Business compliance	Compliance specialist - business
Business modeling	Business analyst - corporate
Business process management and automation	Business analyst - corporate
Business rules management	Business analyst - corporate
Catalog management	SOA librarian
Continuous process improvement (including "Grumble Files" and "Rebel Guidance")	Executive - BASE
Contract management	Procurement specialist
Cross-boarder development	Process coordinator - technology
Development and maintenance of legacy applications	Process coordinator - technology
Development and maintenance of processes	Process coordinator - technology
Development and maintenance of services	Process coordinator - technology
Emergency change management	Compliance specialist - technology
Enterprise governance	Board of Directors
Error handling	Compliance specialist - technology
Exception handling - Process	Process coordinator - business

Table A.10 - Processes in the Enabling Domain

Exception handling - BASE	BASE Program coordinator
Failed project analysis	BASE Program coordinator
Federated identify	Security specialist - corporate
Financial management	Financial specialist - corporate
Governance coordination (Corporate, SOA, IT, Data)	Architect - corporate
International compliance	Compliance specialist - business
IT governance	Executive - technology
Lessons Learned and Best Practices	Architect - SOA
License management (subset of procurement)	Procurement specialist
Life cycle management	**Executive - BASE**
Naming and versioning	Compliance specialist - technology
Organizational structure (supporting SOA)	Architect - Corporate
Ownership of business assets	Financial specialist - corporate
Partner networks (includes supply chain management)	Business analyst - Extranet
Partner research support	Research scientist
Policy management - business (internal and regulatory)	Compliance specialist - business
Policy management - services	SOA librarian
Policy management - technology	Compliance specialist - technology
Procurement	Procurement specialist
Project recovery	Compliance specialist - business
Project turnover	Compliance specialist - business
Redundancy Management and Monitoring	Project initiation manager
Reuse of services	Domain owner - services
Reuse of data	Domain owner - data
Retirement of data	Domain owner - data
Retirement of software (services, processes, applications)	Process coordinator - technology
Risk management	Risk analysts (business and technology)
Risk response	Risk analyst - business
Roles and Responsibilities	Personnel specialist
Security audit	Security specialist - technology
Service audit	Compliance specialist - technology
Service level management	Architect - corporate
Service life cycle	Process coordinator - technology
SOA governance	Executive - BASE
SOA Program Evolution and Planning	Executive - BASE
SOA Program Methodology (WFSOA)	Executive - BASE
SOA security management	Security specialist - tech
Software re-engineering	Process coordinator - technology
Standards Coordination (Industry)	Architect - SOA
Strategy management and alignment	Strategist - corporate
Vendor management (subset of procurement)	Procurement specialist
Vendor selection (subset of procurement)	Procurement specialist
Wireless security (subset of security management)	Security specialist - technology
Work queue management (business and technology)	Process coordinator - business
Human Resources Support Process Category	
Process Identifier	**Role Responsible for Maintaining the Process**
Cultural change management (includes resistance mitigation)	Personnel specialist
Mentoring support	Personnel specialist
New employee orientation	Personnel specialist

Table A.10 - Processes in the Enabling Domain	
Resistance management	Personnel specialist
Role definitions, updates, and assignments	Personnel specialist
Skills tracking	Training specialist
Subject matter expert support	Personnel specialist
Training	Training specialist

Table A.11 - Processes in the Product Delivery Domain	
Requirements Coordination Process Category	
Process Identifier	**Role Responsible for Maintaining the Process**
Analysis	Project initiation manager
Assumptions management	Project initiation manager
Change Advisory Board - business/technology	Project initiation manager
Defect tracking	Quality management coordinator
Location-specific adjustments	Process coordinator - business
Mash-up integration	Project initiation manager
Project early termination	Project initiation manager
Project initiation	Project initiation manager
Project modification (during product creation)	Project initiation manager
Project scheduling (and rescheduling)	Project initiation manager
Requirements analysis	Requirements analyst
Requirements gathering	Project initiation manager
Work requirements modification (during Requirements coordination)	Project initiation manager
Project Management Process Category	
Process Identifier	**Role Responsible for Maintaining the Process**
Project planning (including "just enough planning")	Planning specialist
Project management	BASE Program coordinator
Team building	Project manager - SOA
Project control and monitoring	Project manager - SOA
Project resource management	Project manager - SOA
Project communications	Project manager - SOA
Project modification (during product creation)	Project initiation manager
Product Creation Process Category	
Process Identifier	**Role Responsible for Maintaining the Process**
Agile development	Process coordinator - tech
Business process coordination	Process coordinator - business
Coordination of business processes	Process coordinator - business
Coordination of technology processes	Process coordinator - technology
Creating reusable legacy components (adaptation)	Architect - SOA
Debugging applications	Process coordinator - technology
Debugging processes	Process coordinator - business
Debugging services	Process coordinator - technology
Design	Process coordinator - technology
Development of applications	Process coordinator - technology
Maintenance of business technology products (applications, data, services, processes)	Process coordinator - technology
On-demand services	Architect - SOA
Partner development	Architect - SOA

Production turnover	Deployment specialist
Quality management	Quality management coordinator
Rapid application development	Process coordinator - technology
Refactoring legacy components (subset of maintenance)	Process coordinator - technology
Refactoring processes (subset of maintenance)	Architect - SOA
Refactoring services (subset of maintenance)	Process coordinator - technology
ReMain support for all phases	Process coordinator - technology
Requirements traceability	Project initiation manager
Software integration	Integration specialist
Software re-engineering	Process coordinator - technology
Source code control (part of software integration)	Integration specialist
Waterfall development	Process coordinator - technology

Table A.12 - Processes in the Support Domain	
Architecture Process Category	
Process Identifier	**Role Responsible for Maintaining the Process**
Availability management	Architect - availability
Business continuity management	Architect - availability
Capacity management	Architect - availability
Data protection	Security specialist - corporate
Enterprise Application Integration	Architect - infrastructure
Fail over (infrastructure)	Architect - availability
Fail over (project-specific)	Architect - availability
High availability	Architect - availability
Infrastructure management	Architect - infrastructure
Infrastructure modifications for SOA evolution	Architect - SOA
Management of vendor artifacts	Tool administrator
Middleware management	Architect - infrastructure
Network management	Network services specialist
Partner research support	Architect - SOA
Partner security	Security specialist - technology
Performance management	Architect - availability
Platform variations and synchronization	Architect - infrastructure
Release management and deployment	Deployment specialist
Rollback - business software	Architect - infrastructure
Rollback - infrastructure software	Architect - infrastructure
SaaS/SOA integration	Architect - SOA
Vendor product/tool management	Tool administrator
Data Management Process Category	
Process Identifier	**Role Responsible for Maintaining the Process**
Backup and recovery of data	Data administrator
Data consolidation	Domain owner - data
Data governance	Data specialist
Data modeling	Data specialist
Data quality management	Domain owner - data
Data refactoring	Domain owner - data
Data sharing	Domain owner - data
Database and file management	Domain specialist - data

Table A.12 - Processes in the Support Domain	
Metadata management	Data specialist
Refactoring data (subset of data management)	Domain owner - data
Semantic web	Data specialist
Sensitive data management	Domain specialist - data
XML data management	Data specialist
Environment Management Process Category	
Process Identifier	**Role Responsible for Maintaining the Process**
Data center operations	Project manager - infrastructure technology
Metrics management	Architect - availability
Problem and incident management - all phases	User support specialist
Retirement of applications	Deployment specialist
Service management	Project manager - infrastructure technology
SLA grievance resolution (subset of service level management)	Architect - availability
User support	User support specialist

Table A.13.1 - WFSOA Roles, Teams, Process Categories, and Sectors ©

Key: WFSOA Process Grid:

Degree of Role Involvement

1. ***Arial Black: Actively involved***
2. Papyrus: Moderately involved
3. Kartika: Limited Involvement

Process Categories:

A = Architecture
C = Communications
D = Data Management
DV = Product Creation
E = Environment Management
G = Governance
H = Human Resources Support
P = Project Management
R = Requirements Coordination

Role Name	Team	Sector
Architect - availability	Data Center G / H / C / R / P / DV / ***A*** / D / ***E***	Technology
Architect - corporate	Corporate Sector Management ***G*** / H / C / R / P / DV / A / ***D*** / E	Corporate
Architect - enterprise technology	Infrastructure technology ***G*** / H / C / R / P / DV / ***A*** / D / E	Technology
Architect - infrastructure	Infrastructure technology ***G*** / H / C / R / P / DV / ***A*** / D / ***E***	Technology
Architect - Network	Infrastructure technology ***G*** / H / ***C*** / R / P / DV / ***A*** / D / ***E***	Technology
Architect - SOA	SOA Competency ***G*** / H / C / ***R*** / ***P*** / ***DV*** / ***A*** / ***D*** / ***E***	Base
Architect - software	Business Technology Management G / H / C / ***R*** / P / ***DV*** / ***A*** / ***D*** / E	Technology
Asset librarian	Infrastructure technology G / H / C / ***R*** / P / DV / ***A*** / D / ***E***	Technology
BASE Program coordinator	SOA Program Management ***G*** / ***H*** / ***C*** / R / ***P*** / DV / A / D / E	Base
Board of Directors	Corporate Sector Management	Corporate

Table A.13.1 - WFSOA Roles, Teams, Process Categories, and Sectors ©		
	G / H / C / R / P / DV / A / D / E	
Business analyst - BASE	SOA Competency G / H / C / R / P / DV / A / D / E	Base
Business analyst - client team	Requirements Management G / H / C / R / P / DV / A / D / E	Business
Business analyst - corporate	Enterprise Integration G / H / C / R / P / DV / A / D / E	Corporate
Business analyst - Extranet	SOA competency G / H / C / R / P / DV / A / D / E	Base
Client - BASE	Any team within sector G / H / C / R / P / DV / A / D / E	Base
Client - business operations	Any team within sector G / H / C / R / P / DV / A / D / E	Business
Client - corporate	Any team within sector G / H / C / R / P / DV / A / D / E	Corporate
Client - manufacturing	Any team within sector G / H / C / R / P / DV / A / D / E	Business
Client - partner	May work with any team in operations sector or with the Extranet business analyst G / H / C / R / P / DV / A / D / E	Business
Client - sales and marketing	Any team within sector G / H / C / R / P / DV / A / D / E	Business
Client - technology	Any team within sector G / H / C / R / P / DV / A / D / E	Technology
Communications specialist - BASE	SOA Communications G / H / C / R / P / DV / A / D / E	Base
Communications specialist - Corporate	Corporate Communications G / H / C / R / P / DV / A / D / E	Corporate
Compliance specialist - business	Compliance Management G / H / C / R / P / DV / A / D / E	Base
Compliance specialist - technology	Compliance Management G / H / C / R / P / DV / A / D / E	Base
Corporate lawyer	Legal Services G / H / C / R / P / DV / A / D / E	Corporate
Data administrator	Data Management G / H / C / R / P / DV / A / D / E	Technology
Data specialist	Data Management G / H / C / R / P / DV / A / D / E	Technology
Deployment specialist	Infrastructure technology G / H / C / R / P / DV / A / D / E	Technology
Developer - application	Business Technology Management G / H / C / R / P / DV / A / D / E	Technology
Developer - database	Data Management G / H / C / R / P / DV / A / D / E	Technology
Developer - legacy adaptation	Business Technology Management G / H / C / R / P / DV / A / D / E	Technology
Developer - process	Process Management G / H / C / R / P / DV / A / D / E	Business

Table A.13.1 - WFSOA Roles, Teams, Process Categories, and Sectors ©

Role	Team / Process Categories	Sector
Developer - SOA	Business Technology Management G / H / C / R / P / **DV** / **A** / **D** / E	Technology
Domain owner - data	Financial Management **G** / H / **C** / **R** / **P** / DV / **A** / **D** / **E**	Corporate
Domain owner - service	Financial Management **G** / H / C / **R** / **P** / DV / **A** / **D** / **E**	Corporate
Executive - BASE	BASE Management **G** / **H** / **C** / R / P / DV / A / **D** / E	Base
Executive - corporate	Corporate Sector Management **G** / **H** / **C** / R / P / DV / A / D / E	Corporate
Executive - manufacturing	Business Sector Management **G** / **H** / **C** / R / P / DV / A / D / E	Business
Executive - operations	Business Sector Management **G** / **H** / **C** / R / P / DV / A / D / E	Business
Executive - sales and marketing	Business Sector Management **G** / **H** / **C** / R / P / DV / A / D / E	Business
Executive - technology	Technology Sector Management **G** / H / C / R / **P** / **DV** / **A** / **D** / **E**	Technology
Facilitator	SOA Communications G / H / **C** / **R** / P / DV / A / D / E	Base
Financial specialist - BASE	SOA Program Management **G** / H / C / R / P / DV / A / D / E	Base
Financial specialist - corporate	Financial Management **G** / **H** / **C** / R / **P** / **DV** / A / D / E	Corporate
Help desk	User Support G / H / **C** / R / P / DV / A / D / **E**	Technology
Integration specialist	Infrastructure Technology G / H / **C** / R / P / **DV** / **A** / **D** / **E**	Technology
Knowledge consolidator	SOA Library Management **G** / **H** / **C** / **R** / **P** / **DV** / **A** / **D** / **E**	Base
Network services specialist	Infrastructure Technology G / H / C / R / P / DV / **A** / D / **E**	Technology
Personnel specialist	Human Resources **G** / **H** / **C** / R / P / DV / A / D / E	Corporate
Planning specialist	Requirements Management G / H / **C** / **R** / P / DV / A / D / E	Business
Process coordinator - business	Process Management **G** / **H** / **C** / **R** / P / DV / A / **D** / **E**	Business
Process coordinator - technology	Compliance Management **G** / H / C / **R** / **P** / **DV** / **A** / **D** / **E**	Base
Procurement specialist	Vendor Management **G** / **H** / **C** / R / P / DV / A / D / E	Base
Project initiation manager	Requirements Management **G** / **H** / **C** / **R** / **P** / **DV** / A / **D** / **E**	Business
Project manager - business technology	Technology Sector Management G / H / C / R / **P** / **DV** / A / D / E	Technology
Project manager - infrastructure technology	Technology Sector Management G / H / C / R / **P** / **DV** / **A** / **D** / **E**	Technology

Table A.13.1 - WFSOA Roles, Teams, Process Categories, and Sectors ©		
Project manager - SOA	SOA Implementation G/H/C/R/P/DV/A/D/E	Base
Quality management coordinator	Quality Assurance G/H/C/R/P/DV/A/D/E	Business
Requirements analyst	Requirements Management G/H/C/R/P/DV/A/D/E	Business
Research scientist	Research & Development G/H/C/R/P/DV/A/D/E	Corporate
Risk analyst - business	Compliance Management G/H/C/R/P/DV/A/D/E	Base
Risk analyst - technology	Compliance Management G/H/C/R/P/DV/A/D/E	Base
Security administrator	User Support G/H/C/R/P/DV/A/D/E	Technology
Security specialist - corporate	Global Security G/H/C/R/P/DV/A/D/E	Corporate
Security specialist - technology	Global Security G/H/C/R/P/DV/A/D/E	Corporate
Service assurance	Data Center G/H/C/R/P/DV/A/D/E	Technology
SOA librarian	SOA Library Management G/H/C/R/P/DV/A/D/E	Base
SOA technology specialist	SOA Competency G/H/C/R/P/DV/A/D/E	Base
Sponsor - BASE	BASE Management G/H/C/R/P/DV/A/D/E	Base
Sponsor - business operations	Business Sector Management G/H/C/R/P/DV/A/D/E	Business
Sponsor - corporate	Corporate Sector Management G/H/C/R/P/DV/A/D/E	Corporate
Sponsor - manufacturing	Business Sector Management G/H/C/R/P/DV/A/D/E	Business
Sponsor - sales and marketing	Business Sector Management G/H/C/R/P/DV/A/D/E	Business
Sponsor - technology	Technology Sector Management G/H/C/R/P/DV/A/D/E	Technology
Stakeholder - BASE	Any team within sector G/H/C/R/P/DV/A/D/E	BASE
Stakeholder - business operations	Any team within sector G/H/C/R/P/DV/A/D/E	Business
Stakeholder - corporate	Any team within sector G/H/C/R/P/DV/A/D/E	Corporate
Stakeholder - manufacturing	Any team within sector G/H/C/R/P/DV/A/D/E	Business
Stakeholder - sales and marketing	Any team within sector G/H/C/R/P/DV/A/D/E	Business
Stakeholders - technology	Any team within sector G/H/C/R/P/DV/A/D/E	Technology

Table A.13.1 - WFSOA Roles, Teams, Process Categories, and Sectors ©		
Strategist - corporate	Enterprise Integration G / H / C / R / P / DV / A / D / E	Corporate
Subject matter expert - BASE	Any team within sector G / H / C / R / P / DV / A / D / E	BASE
Subject matter expert - business operations	Any team within sector G / H / C / R / P / DV / A / D / E	Corporate
Subject matter expert - corporate	Any team within sector G / H / C / R / P / DV / A / D / E	Business
Subject matter expert - manufacturing	Any team within sector G / H / C / R / P / DV / A / D / E	Business
Subject matter expert - sales and marketing	Any team within sector G / H / C / R / P / DV / A / D / E	Business
Subject matter expert - technology	Any team within sector G / H / C / R / P / DV / A / D / E	Technology
Team leader	Business Technology G / H / C / R / P / DV / A / D / E	Technology
Testing specialist - business	Quality Assurance G / H / C / R / P / DV / A / D / E	Business
Testing specialist - technology	SOA Competency G / H / C / R / P / DV / A / D / E	BASE
Tool administrator	Infrastructure Technology G / H / C / R / P / DV / A / D / E	Technology
Tool specialist	Business Technology G / H / C / R / P / DV / A / D / E	Technology
Training specialist	Human Resources G / H / C / R / P / DV / A / D / E	Corporate
User - BASE	Any team within sector G / H / C / R / P / DV / A / D / E	BASE
User - business operations	Any team within sector G / H / C / R / P / DV / A / D / E	Business
User - corporate	Any team within sector G / H / C / R / P / DV / A / D / E	Corporate
User - manufacturing	Any team within sector G / H / C / R / P / DV / A / D / E	Business
User - partner	May work with any team in operations sector or with the Extranet business analyst G / H / C / R / P / DV / A / D / E	Business
User - sales and marketing	Any team within sector G / H / C / R / P / DV / A / D / E	Business
User - technology	Any team within sector G / H / C / R / P / DV / A / D / E	Technology
User interface specialist	SOA Communications G / H / C / R / P / DV / A / D / E	BASE
User support specialist	User Support G / H / C / R / P / DV / A / D / E	Technology
Visionary - BASE	Any team within sector G / H / C / R / P / DV / A / D / E	BASE

Table A.13.1 - WFSOA Roles, Teams, Process Categories, and Sectors ©		
Visionary - business operations	Any team within sector G / H / C / R / P / DV / A / D / E	Business
Visionary - corporate	Any team within sector G / H / C / R / P / DV / A / D / E	Corporate
Visionary - manufacturing	Any team within sector G / H / C / R / P / DV / A / D / E	Business
Visionary - sales and marketing	Any team within sector G / H / C / R / P / DV / A / D / E	Business
Visionary - technology	Any team within sector G / H / C / R / P / DV / A / D / E	Technology
Workflow analyst	Process Management G / H / C / R / P / DV / A / D / E	Business
Writer - business (BASE)	SOA Communications G / H / C / R / P / DV / A / D / E	BASE
Writer - corporate	Corporate Communications G / H / C / R / P / DV / A / D / E	Corporate
Writer - requirements	Requirements Management G / H / C / R / P / DV / A / D / E	Business
Writer - technology (BASE)	SOA Communications G / H / C / R / P / DV / A / D / E	BASE

Table A.13.2 - WFSOA Alternate and Deprecated Role Names	
Alternate Role Name	Daxiao Role Name(s)
1. Account manager	Business analyst - Extranet
2. Application design specialist	Architect - software
3. Application development manager	Project manager - business technology
4. Application manager	Project manager - business technology
5. Application project manager	Project manager - business technology
6. Application support	User support specialist
7. Architecture manager	Project manager - infrastructure technology
8. Arrow shooter	Jargon. Visionary
9. Art director	User interface specialist
10. Budget analyst	Financial specialist - BASE
11. Build manager	Integration specialist
12. Business architect	Architect - corporate
13. Business expert	Subject matter expert(s)
14. Business intelligence manager	Domain owner - data
15. Business process manager	Process coordinator - business
16. Business process modeler	Business Analyst(s) or Developer - process
17. Business project manager	Business analyst - client team or business analyst - Extranet
18. Business rules manager	Business analyst - corporate or Process coordinator - business
19. Call center manager	Project manager - infrastructure technology
20. Capacity planning	Architect - availability
21. Catalog manager	SOA librarian
22. Change advisory board (CAB) manager	Project initiation manager
23. Change control analyst	Requirements analyst
24. Change control manager	Project initiation manager
25. Change management	Project initiation manager

Table A.13.2 - WFSOA Alternate and Deprecated Role Names	
Alternate Role Name	**Daxiao Role Name(s)**
26. Change review specialist	Requirements analyst
27. Chief architect	Architect - enterprise technology
28. Chief knowledge officer	Knowledge consolidator
29. Chief security officer	Security specialist - corporate
30. Client liaison	Process coordinator - business
31. Compliance analyst	Business analyst - BASE
32. Computer operator	Service assurance
33. Configuration librarian	Asset librarian
34. Configuration manager	Architect - infrastructure or Tool administrator
35. Content management specialist	Knowledge consolidator
36. Customer	Client - BASE, Client - business, Client - corporate, Client - partner, Client - technology, User - BASE, User - business, User - corporate, User - partner or User - technology
37. Customer service representative	Help Desk
38. Data analyst	Data specialist
39. Data center manager	Project manager - infrastructure technology
40. Data manager	Domain owner - data
41. Data owner	Domain owner - data
42. Data warehouse specialist	Domain owner - data
43. Database administrator	Data administrator
44. Database analyst	Data specialist
45. Database programmer	Developer - database
46. Desktop publisher	Writer - business (BASE), Writer - corporate, or Writer - requirements
47. Development manager	Project manager - business technology
48. Documentation specialist	Writer - technical (BASE)
49. Domain specialist	Domain owner - service
50. E-commerce specialist	business analyst - Extranet
51. Embedded systems engineer	Developer - application
52. Emerging technology project manager	Architect - SOA
53. ERP specialist	Developer - application
54. Executive - line-of-business	Executive - manufacturing , Executive - operations, or Executive - sales and marketing
55. External customer	Client - partner
56. Graphic designer	User interface specialist
57. Human resources manager	Personnel specialist
58. Information architect	Knowledge consolidator
59. Instructional designer	Training specialist
60. Intellectual property manager	Knowledge consolidator
61. Internal auditor	Compliance specialist - business or Compliance specialist - technology
62. Interoperability tester	Testing specialist - technology
63. IT governance	Executive - technology
64. IT manager	Executive - technology
65. Legacy adaptation specialist	Developer - legacy adaptation
66. Localization engineer	Deployment specialist
67. Media librarian	Asset librarian
68. Methodology specialist	Process Coordinator - technology
69. Middleware specialist	Architect - infrastructure or Tool administrator
70. MIS Manager	Domain owner - data
71. Multimedia specialist	User interface specialist
72. Network architect	Network services specialist
73. Network engineer	Network services specialist

Table A.13.2 - WFSOA Alternate and Deprecated Role Names	
Alternate Role Name	Daxiao Role Name(s)
74. Network manager	Network services specialist
75. Operator	Service assurance
76. Performance engineer	Architect - availability
77. Performance management	Architect - availability
78. Problem administrator	Domain owners(s), Project manager(s) or User support specialist
79. Problem management	Architect - availability or User support specialist
80. Process analyst	Workflow analyst
81. Process manager	Process coordinator - business
82. Process modeler	Workflow analyst
83. Process owner	Process coordinator - business
84. Process specialist	Developer - process
85. Product manager	Project manager - business technology, Project manager - infrastructure technology or Tool administrator
86. Production support	User support specialist
87. Program accountant	Financial specialist - BASE
88. Programmer	Developer - application
89. Programmer analyst	Team leader
90. Programming manager	Team leader
91. Project administrator	Financial specialist - BASE or Planning specialist
92. Project leader	Team leader
93. Purchasing manager	Procurement specialist
94. Quality assurance manager	Quality management coordinator
95. Quality management coordinator	Quality management coordinator
96. Release manager	Deployment specialist or Integration specialist
97. Research and development architect	Architect - SOA
98. Research client	client - partner
99. Reuse coordinator	Business analyst - BASE, Requirements analyst or SOA librarian
100. Roll-out manager	Deployment specialist
101. Service contract manager	Architect - availability
102. Service developer	Developer - SOA
103. Service librarian	SOA librarian
104. Service manager	Domain owner - service or Service assurance
105. Service monitoring	Architect - availability
106. SOA competency team	SOA technology specialist
107. SOA development manager	Project manager - SOA
108. SOA executive	Executive - BASE
109. SOA governance	Executive - BASE
110. SOA program manager	BASE Program coordinator
111. SOA security expert	Security specialist - technology
112. SOA strategist	Executive - BASE
113. SOAP programmer	Developer - SOA
114. Software analyst	Architect - software
115. Strategy manager	Strategist - Corporate
116. Systems administrator	Security administrator or Service assurance
117. Systems analyst	Architect - software
118. Systems architect	Architect - infrastructure or Tool administrator
119. Systems manager	Architect - infrastructure
120. Technology expert	Subject matter expert(s)
121. Technology process manager	Process Coordinator - technology
122. Testing architect	Quality management coordinator
123. Testing coordinator	Quality management coordinator
124. Toolsmith	Tool specialist

Table A.13.2 - WFSOA Alternate and Deprecated Role Names

Alternate Role Name	Daxiao Role Name(s)
125. Training coordinator	Training specialist
126. UDDI catalog administrator	SOA librarian
127. User liaison	Process coordinator - business
128. Vendor product manager	Tool administrator
129. Vendor relationship management	Procurement specialist
130. Web designer	User interface specialist
131. Web developer	Developer - application
132. Webmaster	Developer - application or Project manager - infrastructure technology
133. WSDL expert	Developer - SOA
134. WS-I specialist	Testing specialist - technology
135. XML programmer	Database developer or SOA developer

Table A.14.1 - Determination of Unique BASE Roles

Total Roles on Roles List			114
Role Category	**Reason for Reduction**	**Remove**	**Leaving**
Business analyst	Collapse three business analyst roles (client team, Extranet, and BASE) into one, remembering that they require different breath breaths of knowledge	2	112
Client	Collapse six internal client roles into one. ♦ They were broken out to emphasize which areas are actually involved in a project. ♦ The client - partner is treated separately	5	107
Communication specialist	Collapse two communications roles into one	1	106
Executive	Collapse six executive roles into one.	5	101
Financial specialist	Collapse two financial specialist roles into one, remembering that one has a wider scope of responsibility than the other does.	1	100
Security specialist	Collapse two security specialist roles into one, remembering that one has a wider scope of responsibility than the other does.	1	99
Sponsor	Collapse six sponsor roles into one. These are senior level clients, whose approval is necessary before funds may be allocated for a project.	5	94
Stakeholder	Collapse six stakeholder roles into one.	5	89
Subject matter expert	Collapse six subject matter expert roles into one. ♦ This allows us to track "expert" information sources. ♦ A person with his role often has a few others	5	84
User	Collapse six internal user roles into one. ♦ They are broken out so that User Support will have an indication of the type of support a person needs when he or she contacts the call center. The user - partner role is treated separately.	5	79
Visionary	Subtract six (6) visionaries. Those are clients with advanced ideas. ♦ Their projects my involve research or support competitive differential projects. ♦ Their projects will be more challenging. ♦ Their projects may provide input to methodology enhancements (continuous process improvement).	6	73
Writer	Collapse business, corporate, and requirements writer roles into one. They are similar, though they require different breaths of knowledge.	2	71
	Total	43	71

Table A.14.2 - BASE Clusters of Similar Roles	
Role Clusters (Grouped According to Overlapping Skill Requirements)	
Architect - corporate	<-- Strategist - corporate
Architect - infrastructure	<-- Architect - availability
Architect - SOA	<-- Architect - enterprise technology
Business analyst - client team	<-- Workflow analyst
Communication specialist - corporate	<-- Communication specialist - BASE
Compliance specialist(s)	<-- Process coordinator-technology and risk analyst(s)
Developer - SOA	<-- Developer(s) - legacy adaptation and process
Domain owner - data	<-- Data administrator and data specialist
Executive - BASE	<-- BASE Program coordinator
Executive(s)	<-- Sponsor(s)
Financial specialist - BASE	<-- Planning specialist
Help desk	<-- User support specialist
Integration specialist	<-- Deployment specialist
Project initiation manager	<-- Process coordinator-business and requirements analyst
Project manager - SOA	<-- Domain owner - service
Quality management coordinator	<-- Testing specialist - business
SOA technology specialist	<-- Developer-SOA and tool specialist
Software architect	<-- Team leader and user interface specialist
Visionary	<-- Research scientist
Writer - corporate	<-- Writer business (BASE) and requirements

Table A.15.1 - BASE Educational Disciplines and Education/Training Options	
Key:[b] = Bundled with other courses [c] = In-class training or seminar available [f] = FAQs, samples, or snippets available	[m] = Mentoring is available (Who Knows?) [s] = Self-directed training available [v] = From product vendor (often on-line)
Architecture Discipline [f], [m]	1. Development platforms [c], [s], [v] 2. Enterprise Application Integration (EAI) [c], [s], [v] 3. Enterprise resource planning (ERP) [c], [s], [v] 4. Internal technology standards [c], [s] 5. Localization requirements [c], [s] 6. Networking middleware [c], [s], [v] 7. Platform specific architecture variants [c], [s], [v] 8. Reference architectures (SOA and traditional) [c], [s] 9. Research and development environments 10. Service and process categories [b] 11. Software as a Service (SaaS) [s], [v] 12. Software deployment techniques [c], [s], [v] 13. Software integration techniques [c], [s], [v] 14. Storage devices [b] 15. Third party services [s], [v] 16. Virtualization and grid computing [s], [v]
Audit and Compliance Discipline [f], [m]	1. Auditing IT service management [c], [s] 2. Auditing Quality Management [c], [s] 3. COBIT and COSO [c], [s] 4. Compliance management processes [c], [s] 5. GAAP - Generally Accepted Accounting Principles [s] 6. ISACA Audit certification [c], [s] 7. Overview of audit practices [s]
Catalog Management	1. UDDI (Universal Description, Discovery, and Integration) [c], [s], [v]

Table A.15.1 - BASE Educational Disciplines and Education/Training Options	
Discipline [f], [m]	2. ebXML - Registry Services Specification [s], [v] 3. Daxiao integrated catalog [c], [s] 4. Metadata registries [s] 5. RAS - Reusable Asset Specification [b]
Common Terminology [f]	Business, technology, industry, Internet (Required for all Program participants) [s]
Communications (BASE) Discipline [f], [m]	1. Accelerated information capture [s] **2. Common terminology (required for all Program participants) [s]** 3. Communication style preferences [b] 4. Consensus building [b] 5. Corporate communications [c], [s] 6. Documentation practices [c], [s], [v] 7. DocBook Standard [s] 8. Facilitation [c], [s] 9. Human interface requirements [c], [s], [v] 10. Human performance engineering [c], [s] 11. Information delivery devices [c], [s], [v] 12. Interpersonal communication skills [c], [s] 13. Management of software documentation [b] 14. Negotiation [b] 15. Public speaking [c], [s] 16. Sales overview and basic principles [c], [s]
Corporate Architecture Discipline [f], [m]	1. BCM - Business Centric Methodology [s] 2. BMM - Business Motivation Model [s] 3. Enterprise architecture frameworks (DoDAF, FEAF, TOGAF, Zachman) [c], [s] 4. Industrial psychology [s] 5. Management science [s] 6. Strategy management [c], [s]
Corporate Management Discipline [f], [m]	1. Business intelligence [c], [s], [v] 2. Business objectives and goals [c], [s] 3. Business unit strategy [c], [s] 4. Corporate governance 5. Corporate policy management 6. Corporate strategy [c], [s] 7. Organizational structure [s]
Data Discipline [f], [m]	1. Data modeling [c], [s], [v] 2. Data value domains [s] 3. Data warehouses and data marts [c], [s], [v] 4. Database management and middleware (hierarchical, relational, or XML native databases) [c], [s], [v] 5. ebXML - eXtensible Business Markup Language [c], [s] 6. ETL - Extract, translation, load [b] 7. File structures (platform specific) [b] 8. Information architecture [c], [s] 9. Information security models [c], [s] 10. Ontology Definition Metamodel [c], [s] 11. Physical database design [c], [s], [v] 12. Principles of database security [c], [s] 13. ReMain - Requirements management software (in-house) [c], [s] 14. Schema modeling [c], [s], [v] 15. SQL [b] 16. Unique identifiers [b] 17. XML - eXtensible Mark-up Language [c], [s]

Table A.15.1 - BASE Educational Disciplines and Education/Training Options	
	18. XQuery [b] 19. XSD - XML Schema Definition [c], [s], [v]
Governance Discipline [f], [m]	1. Data Governance [c], [s] 2. Enterprise governance 3. IT Governance [s] 4. SOA Governance [c], [s]
Human Resources Discipline [f], [m]	1. Building relationships [b] 2. Career planning and talent management 3. Certified professional in Learning and Performance (CPLP) 4. Coaching [c], [s] 5. Cognitive styles [c], [s] 6. Continuing education guidance 7. Contracts - consulting 8. Corporate learning academy [s] 9. E-learning instructional design 10. Facilitating Organizational Change [c], [s] 11. Human Performance Improvement (HPI) 12. Industrial psychology [s] 13. Managing Organizational Knowledge 14. Managing the Learning Organization 15. Personnel evaluations [c], [s] 16. Personnel provisioning processes [s] 17. Position descriptions [s] 18. Recruiting practices 19. Roles and responsibilities [s] 20. Service procurement processes 21. Skills assessment [c], [s] 22. Test Design and Delivery
International Discipline [f], [m]	1. Linguistic training [c], [s] 2. International policy [c], [s] 3. Cross-cultural differences [c], [s] 4. International security requirements [c], [s], [v] 5. Cross-border vendor product differences [v]
Knowledge Management Discipline [f], [m]	1. Collaboration products [s], [v] 2. Content Management systems [s], [v] 3. Darwin Information Typing Architecture (DITA) 4. Knowledge Discovery Metamodel 5. Knowledge management overview [c], [s] 6. Knowledge map overview and search techniques [c], [s] 7. Monitoring knowledge flows 8. Vendor knowledge capture 9. Managing Organizational Knowledge [s]
Legacy Development Discipline [f], [m]	1. C^{++} or C# [c], [s], [v] 2. COBOL [s] 3. CORBA [c], [s] 4. Development tools - legacy application [s] 5. DHTML - Dynamic Hypertext Mark-up Language [b] 6. DOM - document object model [c], [s] 7. HTML - Hypertext Mark-up Language [c], [s] 8. Human interface guidelines [s] 9. IDL - Interface Definition Language Mappings 10. Java [c], [s]

Table A.15.1 - BASE Educational Disciplines and Education/Training Options	
	11. ReMain - Requirements management software (in-house) [c], [s] 12. Transaction management [c], [s], [v] 13. Visual Basic [c], [s] 14. Wrapper application software [s], [v] 15. XHTML - eXtensible Hypertext Mark-up Language [b]
Management Discipline [f], [m]	1. Creating and Managing a Virtual Team [c] 2. Financial management concepts and procedures [c] 3. Lessons learned in SOA Program [c - new], [s] 4. Managing the learning organization [c], [s] 5. Planning processes and tools [c], [s] 6. PMI Certification [c], [s] 7. Project development metrics [b] 8. Resistance to SOA processes and structures [c - new], [s] 9. ReMain - Requirements management software (in-house) [c], [s] 10. Roles and responsibilities (BASE participants) [s] 11. SOA Program management challenges - (SOA overview course) [s] 12. SOA project management fundamentals [c], [s]
Methodology Discipline [f], [m]	1. Agile methods [c], [s] 2. Capability Maturity Model (CMMI) © [c], [s], [v] 3. CASE Data Interchange Format [b] 4. Metamodel for development methodologies [b] 5. Overview of development methodologies [c], [s] 6. Rational Unified Process © [c], [s], [v] 7. ReMain - Requirements management software (in-house) [c], [s] 8. SDLC - System Development Life cycle Management [c], [s], [v] 9. Service life cycle management [c], [s], [v] 10. Software measurement [b]
Policy/Rules Discipline [f], [m]	1. Rules Management processes and software [c], [s], [v] 2. Business policy life cycle and management [c], [s] 3. Government policy life cycle and management [b] 4. IT policy life cycle management [c], [s] 5. Industry policy life cycle and management [b] 6. International policy life cycle and management [b] 7. Partner business policy awareness [b] 8. Policy overviews [c], [s] 9. Service and process policy life cycle and management [c], [s]
Process Management, (Business and Technology) [f], [m]	1. BPEL - Business Process Execution Language (WS-BPEL, BPEL4WS) [c], [s], [v] 2. BPEL processing servers [c], [s], [v] 3. BPML - Business Process Modeling Language [b] 4. BPMN - Business Process Modeling Notation [b] 5. BPMN - Business Process Modeling Overview [s], [v] 6. Development tools - processes [s], [v] 7. ebXML - eXtensible Business Markup Language [c], [s] 8. ebXML - Collaborative Partner Profile Agreement (CPPA) [b] 9. Internal business processes [c], [s] 10. Internal business/technology processes [c], [s] 11. Internal technology processes [c], [s] 12. Partner business processes 13. Process modeling and assessment [c], [s], [v] 14. Process life cycle management [c], [s] 15. ReMain - Requirements management software (in-house) [c], [s] 16. Semantics for processes and business rules [b], [s]

Table A.15.1 - BASE Educational Disciplines and Education/Training Options	
	17. SPEM - Software Process Engineering Metamodel [c], [s] 18. Supply chain management [c], [s] 19. UML - Unified Modeling Language [c], [s], [v] 20. WMF - Workflow Management Facility [c], [s]
Processing Reliability Discipline [f], [m]	1. Capacity planning [c], [s], [v] 2. Performance management [c], [s], [v] 3. Problem and incident management [c], [s], [v] 4. Backup and (disaster) recovery [c], [s], [v] 5. High availability [c], [s], [v] 6. Benchmarking IT Service Management [b] 7. WS-DM (Web Services Distributed Management) [c], [s], [v]
Procurement Discipline [f], [m]	1. Asset life cycle management [s] 2. Contract management 3. Open source software [c], [s] 4. Vendor management 5. Procurement life cycle management [s] 6. Product evaluation processes [s] 7. Roles and responsibilities [s] 8. Vendor product information base (See **Table A**.7.2) [c], [s], [v] 9. RFI specification 10. RFP specification 11. Vendor knowledge capture [c], [s], [v]
Quality Management Discipline [f], [m]	1. Information Technology Infrastructure Library (ITIL) [c], [s] 2. Quality Management - ISO 9000X Family [c], [s] 3. Six Sigma [c], [s] 4. Software product evaluation [c], [s] 5. Software Quality Requirements including COTS [c], [s] 6. Testing automation products [c], [s], [v] 7. Testing methodology and test types [c], [s], [v] 8. XUnit [b]
Risk Management Discipline [f], [m]	1. Business risk management [c], [s] 2. Life cycle processes - risk management [c], [s] 3. Security risk management [c], [s], [v] 4. Technology risk management (including SOA) [c], [s], [v]
Scripting Languages - General Purpose [f]	1. Perl [c], [s] 2. Tcl [s]
Scripting Languages - OS [f], [m]	1. Bash [b] 2. cmd.exe [b] 3. JCL [s]
Scripting Languages - Web [f], [m]	1. AJAX [s] 2. ASP - Active Server Pages [s], [v] 3. CGI - Common Gateway Interface [b], [s], [v] 4. DHTML - Dynamic HTML [b] 5. JavaScript (ECMAScript or E4X) [c], [s], [v] 6. JSP - Java Server Pages [s], [v] 7. PHP - Personal Home Page [c], [s] 8. VBScript [s]
Security Management Discipline [f], [m]	1. Biometrics [c], [s] 2. Certification examinations (multiple) [c], [s] 3. Code of practice for Security Management - ISO 17799:2005 [b] 4. Digital signatures [b] 5. Encryption algorithms [b]

Table A.15.1 - BASE Educational Disciplines and Education/Training Options	
	6. Entity authentication [b] 7. Hacker techniques [c] 8. Information security models and incident management [c], [s], [v] 9. Internal security policy and standards [c], [s] 10. International security requirements [c], [s] 11. Intrusion detection [s], [v] 12. IT intrusion detection products and techniques [c], [s], [v] 13. IT network security [c], [s], [v] 14. IT Security Audit [c], [s] 15. LDAP - Lightweight Directory Access Protocol [b] 16. Message authentication codes [b] 17. Non-repudiation [b] 18. Physical security [c], [s], [v] 19. Principles of database security [c], [s], [v] 20. SAML (Security Assertion Markup Language) [c], [s] 21. Security assessment of operational systems [c], [s] 22. Security best practices [c], [s] 23. Security management and monitoring products [c], [s], [v] 24. Security overview (authentication, authorization, integrity) [c], [s], [v] 25. Security standards (domestic and international) with emphasis on Web Services Security (WS-S) and WS-Trust [c], [s], [v] 26. SPML - Service Provisioning Markup Language [b] 27. Systems Security Engineering (CMMI) [c], [s], [v] 28. Time stamping services [b] 29. XACML - eXtensible Access control Markup Language [b] 30. XKMS - XML Key Management Specification [b] 31. XML encryption [b] 32. XML signature [b]
Service Management Discipline [f], [m]	1. A+ Certification [c], [s] 2. Asset management [c], [s], [v] 3. Benchmarking IT Service Management [c], [s], [v] 4. Incident management and escalation procedures [c], [s], [v] 5. Information Technology Infrastructure Library (ITIL) [c], [s] 6. Service Level Agreements [c], [s], [v] 7. Service Policy [c], [s], [v] 8. WS-DM (Web Services Distributed Management) [c], [s], [v]
SOA Discipline [f], [m]	1. Data in a Service-Oriented Architecture environment [c], [s] 2. Lessons learned in SOA Program [c], [s] 3. Managing in a Service-Oriented Architecture environment [c], [s], [v] 4. Process management overview [c], [s], [v] 5. Resistance to SOA processes and structures [c], [s] 6. REST versus SOA [b] 7. Reusability concepts [c], [s], [v] 8. Semantic Web [s] 9. SOA architecture concepts (service and process delivery) [c], [s] 10. SOA cultural change management (Required for managers) [c], [s] 11. SOA market impact and ROI potential [b] 12. SOA maturity concepts and organizational impact [b] 13. SOA strategy [c], [s] 14. Web Services overview [c], [s]
SOA Platform Discipline [f], [m]	1. Platform interoperability successes and issues [c], [s], [v] 2. Legacy integration products [c], [s], [v]

Table A.15.1 - BASE Educational Disciplines and Education/Training Options	
	3. Development tools - platform specific [c], [s], [v] 4. SOA appliances [c], [s], [v]
SOA Standards Discipline [f], [m]	1. IETF standards 2. ISO/IEC standards 3. OASIS standards 4. OMG standards 5. SOA standards 6. SOAP [c], [s] 7. Standards Organizations [b] 8. UDDI - Universal Description, Discovery, and Integration [c], [s], [v] 9. W3C standards 10. WebCGM - Web Computer Graphics Metafile [b] 11. WS-Addressing [b] 12. WSDL - Web Services Description Language [c], [s], [v] 13. WS-I - Web Services Interoperability [c], [s] 14. WSN - Web Services Notification [b] 15. WS-Reliability [b] 16. WSRF - Web Services Resource Framework [b] 17. WSRP - Web Services for Remote Portlets [b] 18. WSS - Web Services Security [b] 19. WS-SecureConversation [b] 20. WS-Trust [b] 21. XML (eXtensible Markup Language) [c], [s]
Tools/Software Discipline [f], [m]	1. Role specific tool training [c], [s], [v] 2. Overviews for critical tool categories
Training Discipline [f], [m]	1. Training design 2. Training environments 3. Training products [v] 4. Online/web training products [v] 5. Learning management systems [v] 6. Training vendors 7. User learning preferences [s] 8. Validation of training materials 9. Training product life cycle
Transmission Protocols Discipline [f], [m]	1. FTP - File Transfer Protocol [b] 2. HTTP - Hypertext Transfer Protocol [c], [s] 3. SMTP - Simple Mail Transfer Protocol [b] 4. TCP/IP - Transmission Control Protocol/ Internet Protocol [c], [s] 5. WAP - Wireless Access Protocol [c], [s]
Web Development Discipline [f], [m]	1. Browsers [c], [s] 2. CSS - Cascading Style Sheets (for HTML) [c], [s] 3. Development requirements for reusability [c], [s] 4. HTML, DHTML, and XHTML [c], [s], [v] 5. Human Interface Guidelines [c], [s] 6. Multimedia [c], [s], [v] 7. Portals [c], [s], [v] 8. ReMain - Requirements management software (in-house) [c], [s] 9. RSS - Really Simple Syndication [c], [s], [v] 10. SMIL - Synchronized Multimedia Integration Language [c], [s], [v] 11. SOA Development methodologies [c], [s] 12. State management [b] 13. SVG - Scalable Vector Graphics [s]

Table A.15.1 - BASE Educational Disciplines and Education/Training Options	
	14. Transaction management [c], [s], [v] 15. Web development tools [c], [s], [v] 16. Web Services & Internet best practices [c], [s] 17. WML - Wireless Mark-up Language [c], [s], [v] 18. WSDL - Web Services Description Language [c], [s] 19. XForms - Forms for XHTML [b] 20. XLink - XML to non-XML Linkage [b] 21. XML (eXtensible Markup Language) [c], [s] 22. XML Gateways [c], [s], [v] 23. XML Infoset - XML Information Set [b] 24. XML Namespaces in XML 1.1 (Second Edition) [b] 25. XML Schema [c], [s] 26. XML tools (including parsers and shredders) [c], [s] 27. XPath (XML Path Language) [b] 28. Xpointer [b] 29. XSL - XML Stylesheet Language (CSS for XML) [c], [s] 30. XSL-FO - Extensible Stylesheet Language Formatting Objects [b] 31. XSLT (XML Stylesheet Language Transformation) [b]
Web Services Best Practices [f], [m]	1. Service development best practices [c], [s] 2. Infrastructure best practices [c], [s]
XML Discipline [f], [m]	1. OWL - Web Ontology Language [c], [s] 2. RDF - (Web) Resource Description Language [c], [s], [v] 3. UBL - Universal Business Language [c], [s] 4. XMI - XML Metadata Interchange [b] 5. XML - eXtensible Mark-up Language [c], [s] 6. XML appliance(s) [c], [s], [v] 7. XML Vocabulary(s) - industry specific [c], [s] 8. XSL - XML Stylesheet Language [c], [s]

Table A.15.2.1 - Mandatory, Recommended, and Optional Disciplines for Role Incumbents (Part 1)

Key: M = Must have (without knowledge or experience in this area, the incumbent will fail)
R = Recommend for best performance in role
E = Enabling (Knowledge in this area supports improved performance by some individuals)

Disciplines and Training Options ➥ Roles ↓	Architecture	Audit and Compliance	Catalog Management	Common Terminology	Communications (SOA)	Corporate Architecture	Corporate Management	Data	Governance	Human Resources	International	Knowledge Management
Architect - availability	M	R	E	M	R	-	-	R	E	-	R	R
Architect - corporate	E	M	R	M	M	M	M	R	R	E	R	M
Architect - enterprise technology	M	M	E	M	R	E	-	R	R	E	M	M
Architect - infrastructure	M	R	E	M	E	E	-	E	-	-	R	R
Architect - network	M	R	R	M	E	E	-	E	E	-	M	E
Architect - SOA	M	M	M	M	R	R	R	R	M	E	R	R
Architect - software	M	E	M	M	R	E	M	R	R	E	E	M
Asset librarian	R	E	R	M	E	-	-	R	-	-	M	M
BASE Program coordinator	R	M	R	M	M	M	M	R	M	M	M	M
Board of Directors	-	R	-	M	R	M	M	E	R	E	R	R
Business analyst - BASE	R	R	R	M	M	E	R	R	R	-	R	M

Table A.15.2.1 - Mandatory, Recommended, and Optional Disciplines for Role Incumbents (Part 1)												
Business analyst - client team	E	E	R	M	R	E	R	R	R	E	R	R
Business analyst - corporate	E	E	E	M	E	M	R	R	R	R	R	M
Business analyst - Extranet	M	R	R	M	M	R	R	R	R	E	R	M
Client - BASE	E	E	E	M	E	R	R	R	R	E	R	R
Client - business operations	E	E	E	M	E	R	R	R	E	E	R	E
Client - corporate	E	E	E	M	E	M	R	R	E	E	R	M
Client - manufacturing	E	E	E	M	E	R	R	R	E	E	M	E
Client - partner	E	E	E	M	E	-	E	E	-	-	E	E
Client - sales and marketing, technology	E	E	E	M	E	E	R	R	E	E	M	E
Communications specialist - BASE	E	R	R	M	M	R	M	E	R	E	M	M
Communications specialist - Corporate	-	E	-	M	M	R	M	-	R	R	M	M
Compliance specialist - business	R	M	R	M	R	R	M	R	M	R	M	M
Compliance specialist - technology	M	M	R	M	E	R	R	M	M	E	M	M
Corporate lawyer	-	M	E	M	R	M	M	E	E	M	R	R
Data administrator	M	R	R	M	E	-	-	M	R	-	M	R
Data specialist	M	M	M	M	R	E	-	M	R	-	M	M
Deployment specialist	M	R	M	M	R	E	-	R	R	-	M	R
Developer - application	R	E	E	M	E	E	-	R	E	-	E	R
Developer - database	R	E	R	M	E	-	-	M	E	-	R	M
Developer - legacy adaptation	M	E	R	M	E	E	-	M	E	-	R	M
Developer - process	R	M	M	M	R	E	E	E	E	E	R	M
Developer - SOA	M	M	M	M	R	R	E	M	M	-	R	M
Domain owner - data	M	M	M	M	R	R	R	M	R	E	R	M
Domain owner - service	M	M	M	M	R	R	R	R	R	R	R	M
Executive - BASE	R	M	R	M	M	M	M	R	M	R	M	M
Executive - corporate	-	R	E	M	R	M	M	-	R	M	E	R
Executive - technology	R	M	E	M	E	R	R	E	M	M	R	M
Executive(s) - business operations, manufacturing, sales and marketing	-	R	E	M	R	E	R	-	E	E	E	R
Facilitator	E	E	-	M	M	E	R	E	M	E	R	M
Financial specialist - BASE	E	M	E	M	E	R	M	E	M	E	R	M
Financial specialist - corporate	E	M	-	M	R	M	M	R	R	M	R	M
Help desk	E	-	R	M	M	E	-	-	-	-	M	M
Integration specialist	M	R	R	M	E	E	-	R	-	-	M	R
Knowledge Consolidator	R	M	M	M	R	M	R	M	M	E	M	M
Network services specialist	M	E	E	M	E	-	-	R	-	-	R	R
Personnel specialist	-	M	-	M	R	M	M	E	M	M	M	R
Planning specialist	R	R	R	M	R	E	E	E	R	E	R	M
Process coordinator - business	E	R	R	M	M	R	R	E	R	M	R	R
Process coordinator - technology	M	R	R	M	R	E	E	R	R	-	R	R
Procurement specialist	R	M	E	M	R	E	R	E	E	-	R	R
Project initiation manager	E	M	E	M	R	R	R	E	M	E	R	R

Table A.15.2.1 - Mandatory, Recommended, and Optional Disciplines for Role Incumbents (Part 1)												
Project manager - business technology	R	R	E	M	R	E	E	R	R	R	E	E
Project manager - infrastructure technology	M	E	E	M	E	E	E	R	R	R	E	E
Project manager - SOA	R	R	R	M	M	R	R	M	M	M	R	R
Quality management coordinator	R	M	E	M	R	E	E	R	E	E	R	R
Requirements analyst	R	M	E	M	R	M	M	R	R	E	R	R
Research scientist	R	R	E	M	R	M	M	R	R	E	M	M
Risk analyst - business	E	M	E	M	R	R	M	R	R	E	R	R
Risk analyst - technology	M	M	R	M	R	R	R	M	R	E	R	R
Security administrator	M	M	R	M	E	-	E	R	E	E	R	M
Security specialist - corporate	R	R	E	M	R	M	M	E	R	R	R	R
Security specialist - technology	M	M	R	M	E	E	R	R	R	E	R	M
Service assurance	R	E	E	M	E	-	-	E	E	-	E	E
SOA librarian	E	R	M	M	R	R	R	R	M	-	E	R
SOA technology specialist	M	R	M	M	R	R	E	R	R	-	R	M
Sponsor - BASE	M	R	R	M	R	M	M	M	M	M	M	R
Sponsor - technology	R	R	E	M	R	R	M	R	R	R	R	R
Sponsor(s) - business operations, corporate, manufacturing, sales and marketing	-	R	E	M	-	R	M	R	R	R	R	R
Stakeholder - BASE	R	R	E	M	E	R	M	R	M	E	E	M
Stakeholder - technology	R	R	E	M	R	E	R	E	E	E	E	R
Stakeholder(s) - business operations, corporate, manufacturing, sales and marketing	E	E	E	M	E	E	R	E	E	E	E	R
Strategist - corporate	E	M	-	M	R	M	M	R	M	R	M	R
Subject matter expert - BASE	R	M	R	M	R	R	R	R	R	E	R	M
Subject matter expert - business operations	-	E	E	M	R	E	R	E	R	-	R	R
Subject matter expert - corporate, manufacturing, sales and marketing, technology	-	-	-	M	R	E	R	E	R	-	R	R
Team leader	R	E	R	M	R	E	R	R	R	R	R	R
Testing specialist - business	E	R	R	M	R	R	R	R	E	E	E	R
Testing specialist - technology	M	R	M	M	R	E	E	R	E	-	E	R
Tool administrator	M	R	R	M	R	E	E	E	E	E	R	R
Tool specialist	M	R	E	M	E	-	-	R	E	-	R	R
Training specialist	-	R	E	M	M	R	R	E	R	M	R	R
User - BASE	E	E	E	M	E	R	E	R	R	-	R	R
User - business operations, corporate, manufacturing, sales and marketing	E	E	E	M	E	E	E	E	E	-	E	E

Table A.15.2.1 - Mandatory, Recommended, and Optional Disciplines for Role Incumbents (Part 1)

User - partner	-	-	E	M	E	-	-	E	-	-	E	E
User - technology	R	E	E	M	E	-	-	E	E	-	E	E
User interface specialist	E	R	R	M	R	E	E	R	E	R	M	M
User support specialist	R	E	E	M	R	E	-	R	E	E	R	M
Visionary - BASE	M	R	E	M	E	E	R	R	R	E	R	R
Visionary - business operations, manufacturing, sales and marketing	E	E	E	M	E	-	R	R	E	-	E	E
Visionary - corporate	E	E	E	M	E	M	R	R	E	E	E	E
Visionary - technology	M	R	E	M	E	E	-	R	E	-	E	E
Workflow analyst	E	E	E	M	R	E	E	E	E	E	E	R
Writer - business (BASE)	E	E	E	M	M	R	R	E	E	-	R	R
Writer - corporate	-	R	-	M	M	R	R	-	-	-	R	M
Writer - requirements	E	E	E	M	M	R	R	E	E	-	R	M
Writer - technology (BASE)	R	E	E	M	M	R	R	E	E	-	R	M

Table A.15.2.2 - Mandatory, Recommended, and Optional Disciplines for Role Incumbents (Part 2)

Key: M = Must have (without knowledge or experience in this area, the incumbent will fail)
R = Recommend for best performance in role
E = Enabling (Knowledge in this area supports improved performance by some individuals)

Disciplines and Training Options → Roles ↓	Legacy Development	Management	Methodology	Policy/Business Rules	Process Management	Processing Reliability	Procurement	Quality Management	Risk Management	Scripting Languages - General Purpose	Scripting Languages - OS	Scripting Languages - Web
Architect - availability	E	-	-	R	R	M	E	M	R	E	R	R
Architect - corporate	-	E	-	M	R	-	E	R	M	-	-	-
Architect - enterprise technology	R	M	M	R	R	M	R	M	M	R	R	E
Architect - infrastructure	E	E	R	E	R	M	E	R	R	E	R	E
Architect - network	E	E	R	E	R	M	E	R	R	R	R	M
Architect - SOA	R	R	M	R	R	R	E	M	M	E	E	E
Architect - software	R	-	M	M	E	R	-	R	R	E	E	E
Asset librarian	E	-	R	E	E	-	M	-	E	-	-	-
BASE Program coordinator	-	M	M	M	M	M	M	M	M	-	-	-
Board of Directors	-	-	-	R	-	E	E	R	M	-	-	-
Business analyst(s) - BASE, client, corporate	E	E	R	R	R	R	E	R	R	-	-	-
Business analyst - Extranet	E	E	R	M	M	M	E	M	M	-	-	-
Client - BASE	R	E	R	R	E	E	E	M	R	-	-	-
Communications specialist - BASE	-	-	E	E	R	E	E	R	R	-	-	-
Client(s) - business operations, corporate, manufacturing, partner, sales and marketing, technology	-	-	E	R	E	E	E	M	R	-	-	-
Communications specialist - Corporate	-	-	-	E	E	E	-	E	R	-	-	-
Compliance specialist -	-	R	R	M	M	M	R	M	M	-	-	-

Table A.15.2.2 - Mandatory, Recommended, and Optional Disciplines for Role Incumbents (Part 2)												
business												
Compliance specialist - technology	M	R	M	M	M	M	R	M	M	R	R	R
Corporate lawyer	-	-	-	M	E	-	M	E	M	-	-	-
Data administrator	R	-	R	R	R	M	E	M	R	R	R	R
Data specialist	R	-	R	R	R	R	E	M	R	E	E	E
Deployment specialist	R	-	R	R	R	R	E	M	M	M	M	M
Developer - application	M	-	R	R	E	R	-	M	E	E	E	M
Developer - database	R	-	R	R	E	R	-	M	E	R	R	E
Developer - legacy adaptation	M	-	R	R	E	R	-	M	E	R	R	E
Developer - process	-	-	R	M	M	R	-	M	R	R	E	R
Developer - SOA	R	-	R	M	E	R	-	M	E	M	M	M
Domain owner - data	E	R	R	M	R	M	E	M	M	E	E	E
Domain owner - service	R	R	R	M	R	M	E	M	M	-	-	-
Executive - BASE	E	M	-	R	E	R	R	R	M	-	-	-
Executive - technology	E	M	R	R	R	M	M	M	M	E	E	E
Executive - corporate, manufacturing, operations, sales and marketing	-	M	-	R	E	R	R	R	M	-	-	-
Facilitator	-	E	E	E	E	E	E	R	R	-	-	-
Financial specialist - BASE	-	E	R	R	R	R	M	E	M	-	-	-
Financial specialist - corporate	-	E	E	R	R	R	M	R	M	-	-	-
Help desk	-	-	-	R	E	M	E	R	R	-	-	-
Integration specialist	E	-	M	R	R	R	E	M	R	R	R	R
Knowledge Consolidator	E	E	M	M	M	M	R	M	M	E	E	E
Network services specialist	-	-	E	E	E	M	-	E	M	R	R	R
Personnel specialist	-	R	E	R	M	E	R	R	M	-	-	-
Process coordinator - business	-	R	R	M	M	R	R	M	M	-	-	-
Process coordinator - technology	M	-	M	M	M	M	E	M	M	E	E	E
Planning specialist	E	R	M	R	R	R	E	R	M	-	-	-
Procurement specialist	-	-	-	M	M	R	M	R	R	-	-	-
Project initiation manager	E	M	R	R	R	R	R	M	M	-	-	-
Project manager - business technology	R	M	M	R	R	R	E	M	M	-	-	-
Project manager - infrastructure technology	E	M	M	R	R	R	E	M	M	E	E	E
Project manager - SOA	M	M	M	R	M	M	E	M	M	E	E	R
Quality management coordinator	E	M	M	R	R	R	E	M	M	E	E	E
Requirements analyst	E	E	M	M	M	R	E	M	M	-	-	-
Research scientist	E	E	R	R	R	R	M	M	M	E	-	E
Risk analyst - business	-	E	M	M	M	R	E	M	M	-	-	-
Risk analyst - technology	R	-	M	M	M	M	M	M	M	R	R	R
Security administrator	E	-	R	R	R	R	E	M	M	R	R	R
Security specialist - corporate	-	E	R	M	R	M	R	R	M	-	-	-
Security specialist - technology	E	E	R	R	R	M	R	R	M	R	R	R

Table A.15.2.2 - Mandatory, Recommended, and Optional Disciplines for Role Incumbents (Part 2)

Service assurance	E	-	E	R	R	M	-	R	M	R	R	R
SOA librarian	E	-	R	R	R	R	-	R	R	R	E	R
SOA technology specialist	E	-	M	R	R	R	E	M	R	M	M	M
Sponsor - BASE	E	R	R	M	M	M	M	M	M	E	E	E
Sponsor(s) - business operations, corporate, manufacturing, sales and marketing	-	R	E	R	R	R	M	R	M	-	-	-
Sponsor - technology	E	R	R	R	R	R	M	R	M	E	E	E
Stakeholder - BASE	E	E	R	R	R	R	R	M	M	E	E	E
Stakeholder(s) - business operations, corporate, manufacturing, sales and marketing	-	-	R	R	R	R	E	R	M	-	-	-
Stakeholder - technology	E	-	R	R	R	R	R	M	M	E	E	E
Strategist - corporate	-	E	E	M	M	E	E	M	M	-	-	-
Subject matter expert - BASE	R	-	R	M	M	R	E	M	M	E	E	E
Subject matter expert (s) - business operations, corporate, manufacturing, sales and marketing	-	-	-	M	M	R	E	R	M	-	-	-
Subject matter expert - technology	R	-	R	M	M	E	E	R	M	E	E	E
Team leader	M	E	M	R	R	R	-	M	R	R	R	R
Testing specialist - business	E	-	R	M	M	R	-	M	R	E	E	E
Testing specialist - technology	R	-	M	R	R	M	-	M	M	M	M	M
Tool administrator	E	-	-	E	R	M	M	R	R	E	E	E
Tool specialist	M	-	R	R	E	R	R	M	R	M	M	M
Training specialist	-	E	E	E	E	E	M	E	R	-	-	-
User - BASE	R	-	R	R	R	E	E	M	M	E	E	E
User(s) - business operations, corporate, manufacturing, partner, sales and marketing	-	-	-	R	E	E	-	R	R	-	-	-
User - technology	-	-	E	R	R	R	-	R	R	R	R	R
User interface specialist	R	-	E	R	R	R	-	M	M	R	R	M
User support specialist	-	-	E	R	R	R	E	M	M	E	E	E
Visionary - BASE	R	-	R	R	R	R	E	M	M	E	E	E
Visionary - technology	R	-	R	R	E	E	E	R	R	E	E	E
Visionaries - business operations, corporate, manufacturing, sales and marketing	-	-	E	R	E	E	E	R	R	-	-	-
Workflow analyst	-	-	R	R	M	E	-	M	R	R	R	R
Writer - technology (BASE)	E	-	-	-	R	-	-	R	R	-	-	-
Writer(s) - business (BASE), corporate, requirements	-	-	-	-	R	-	-	R	R	-	-	-

Table A.15.2.3 - Mandatory, Recommended, and Optional Disciplines for Role Incumbents (Part 3)

Key: M = Must have (without knowledge or experience in this area, the incumbent will fail)
R = Recommend for best performance in role
E = Enabling (Knowledge in this area supports improved performance by some individuals)

Disciplines and Training Options ➥ / Roles ⬇	Security Management	Service Management	SOA Concepts	SOA Platform	SOA Standards	Tools/Software	Training	Transmission Protocols	Web Development	Web Services Best Practices	XML
Architect - availability	R	M	R	R	E	R	-	M	R	R	E
Architect - corporate	-	-	M	E	R	-	R	-	-	R	-
Architect - enterprise technology	M	R	M	M	M	M	R	M	R	R	R
Architect - infrastructure	R	E	R	M	R	R	-	M	R	R	E
Architect - network	M	R	R	M	M	R	-	M	R	M	R
Architect - SOA	R	R	M	M	M	M	E	M	M	M	M
Architect - software	R	E	R	R	R	R	-	R	R	M	M
Asset librarian	E	-	E	E	R	M	-	E	E	E	R
BASE Program coordinator	M	R	M	E	M	R	R	E	E	M	E
Board of Directors	-	-	R	-	-	-	-	-	-	E	-
Business analyst - BASE	R	E	M	M	M	E	E	E	E	R	E
Business analyst - client team	R	-	R	R	R	E	-	E	-	E	E
Business analyst - corporate	M	E	R	R	E	E	E	E	-	R	E
Business analyst - Extranet	M	R	M	M	M	R	E	E	E	R	E
Client(s) - All	R	E	R	E	E	E	E	-	E	R	-
Communications specialist - BASE	E	E	M	E	R	E	E	-	-	R	E
Communications specialist - Corporate	R	E	R	-	E	-	-	-	-	R	-
Compliance specialist - business	R	R	R	E	R	R	-	E	E	R	E
Compliance specialist - technology	M	R	M	M	M	R	-	M	M	M	M
Corporate lawyer	R	E	R	-	E	-	-	-	-	E	-
Data administrator	M	R	M	M	R	M	-	R	R	M	M
Data specialist	M	R	M	M	R	M	-	R	E	M	M
Deployment specialist	M	R	M	M	M	M	R	M	R	M	R
Developer - application	R	E	R	R	E	R	-	R	E	E	R
Developer - database	M	R	M	M	R	R	-	R	R	M	M
Developer - legacy adaptation	M	R	M	M	M	R	-	M	M	M	M
Developer - process	M	R	M	M	M	M	-	R	M	M	M
Developer - SOA	M	R	M	M	M	M	-	R	M	M	M
Domain owner(s) - data, service	M	R	M	M	R	R	E	E	R	M	M
Executive - BASE	R	E	R	R	M	E	R	R	R	R	R
Executive - technology	M	M	R	R	R	E	E	E	R	R	R
Executive(s) - business operations, corporate, manufacturing, sales and marketing	R	E	R	-	E	-	-	R	-	R	-
Facilitator	-	-	R	E	E	E	R	-	E	R	E

Table A.15.2.3 - Mandatory, Recommended, and Optional Disciplines for Role Incumbents (Part 3)

Financial specialist - BASE	E	E	R	E	E	E	E	-	-	R	-
Financial specialist - corporate	R	R	M	-	R	-	E	-	-	E	-
Help desk	M	R	R	E	E	E	E	E	E	R	E
Integration specialist	M	E	M	M	R	M	E	R	M	M	M
Knowledge Consolidator	M	R	M	M	M	R	R	R	M	M	M
Network services specialist	M	R	R	M	R	R	-	M	R	M	E
Personnel specialist	R	-	R	E	-	R	M	-	E	R	-
Planning specialist	R	R	M	R	R	R	R	E	E	M	E
Process coordinator - business	M	M	M	E	R	R	M	E	E	M	E
Process coordinator - technology	M	R	M	M	M	M	M	M	R	M	R
Procurement specialist	E	E	R	R	M	M	R	E	-	R	E
Project initiation manager	M	M	M	E	R	R	R	E	-	M	E
Project manager - business technology	M	M	R	E	E	R	R	E	E	M	E
Project manager - infrastructure technology	M	M	M	M	M	M	E	M	E	M	E
Project manager - SOA	M	M	M	M	M	R	R	R	R	M	R
Quality management coordinator	M	R	M	R	R	M	E	R	E	M	R
Requirements analyst	R	R	R	R	M	R	E	E	R	M	E
Research scientist	R	R	R	E	R	R	E	R	E	E	R
Risk analyst - business	M	R	M	R	R	E	R	E	E	M	R
Risk analyst - technology	M	R	M	M	M	M	R	M	M	M	M
Security administrator	M	R	M	M	M	M	R	M	E	M	E
Security specialist - corporate	M	R	R	E	R	R	E	M	E	M	E
Security specialist - technology	M	R	M	R	M	M	R	M	R	M	R
Service assurance	M	M	R	M	R	E	-	M	E	R	E
SOA librarian	M	R	M	M	M	M	E	E	R	M	M
SOA technology specialist	M	R	M	M	M	M	R	M	M	M	M
Sponsor - BASE	M	M	R	R	R	M	R	R	R	M	R
Sponsor - technology	M	M	M	M	R	M	R	R	M	M	R
Sponsor(s) - business operations, corporate, manufacturing, sales and marketing	R	R	R	E	R	E	R	-	-	R	E
Stakeholder - BASE	M	M	R	E	R	E	-	E	E	R	R
Stakeholder - technology	M	M	R	E	R	E	-	E	E	R	R
Stakeholder(s) - business operations, corporate, manufacturing, sales and marketing	R	R	R	E	R	E	-	-	-	R	-
Strategist - corporate	M	R	M	E	R	E	R	-	-	R	E
Subject matter expert - BASE	M	M	M	M	M	R	E	R	R	R	R
Subject matter expert - technology	R	E	R	E	R	E	E	R	R	R	R
Subject matter expert(s) - business operations, corporate, manufacturing, sales and marketing	R	E	R	E	R	E	-	-	R	R	-

Table A.15.2.3 - Mandatory, Recommended, and Optional Disciplines for Role Incumbents (Part 3)											
Team leader	M	R	M	M	M	M	R	R	M	M	R
Testing specialist - business	R	R	M	R	R	R	E	E	E	M	E
Testing specialist - technology	M	R	M	M	M	M	E	M	R	M	R
Tool administrator	M	E	R	M	M	M	R	E	E	R	E
Tool specialist	M	E	R	M	R	R	-	M	M	M	M
Training specialist	R	E	R	R	R	M	M	-	E	E	E
User - technology	M	E	R	E	R	R	-	R	E	R	R
User interface specialist	M	E	M	M	R	M	M	E	M	M	R
User support specialist	M	R	R	R	R	R	M	R	E	R	E
User(s) - BASE, business operations, corporate, manufacturing, partner, sales and marketing	M	E	R	E	E	E	-	E	E	R	E
Writer(s) - business (BASE), corporate, requirements, technology (BASE)	E	E	E	-	E	E	-	-	-	E	E

Table A.16 - Comments from Role Incumbents

Architect - availability (Incumbent: Ward Hooper): Data Center Team, Technology

I received the offer to transfer to Data Center Operations directly from Weldon Armstrong. I didn't know he knew my name, even though I was among the best infrastructure architect that they had. Wright (my original manager) didn't like me, and the few people who knew my name heard it in relation to serious problems. I was the one that figured out how to resolve systems "challenges" after Wright had bent over a little too far while attempting to impress Armstrong. After I solved a problem, Wright earned points for fixing something that didn't need to be a problem in the first place.

I had nightmares of filling in for service operators who ran outside to get their nicotine fixes. I started looking for another job immediately. Then Armstrong produced a 10% raise, the senior manager in the data center recommended me for management training, and Hamilton Marshall called me to New York for an old-fashioned "sit down".

This was often after I had yelled and screamed to try to keep them from doing something in the stupidest way possible. For example, after they installed the Service Bus things were better for the first month, but by the end of the third month, things were worse than before. They put too many services on it before they understood how it works.

HM was actually the one that had done the recommending. He explained that this was one of the most important jobs envisioned for support of Service-Oriented Architecture. It would be my job (and the job of my team) to find things before they happened. The first thing I needed to do was enroll in communications training and facilitation.

I would have my own team, starting with three more of Armstrong's people (I could only have junior people), three new hires, and three of the best people from the data center that I would be expected to train.

Now I know even more about the technology and much more about the business than I knew before. I provide input to architecture decisions, and they listen, sometimes (more often than they did before). They say I am doing a great job. I have a junior VP title. That means that a few more people may be willing to listen to me.

Architect - corporate: (Incumbent: Daniel Piccolo): Enterprise Integration Team, Corporate
Title: SVP of Enterprise Integration reporting to the president. Member of the Board of Directors

I am the corporate (business) architect, not the technical "enterprise architect".

I have my job due to Sarbanes Oxley (SOX). Most organizations hate it, but I love it. The earliest recommendation for a corporate-wide business architecture came from John Zachman in 1987 (the Zachman Framework), followed by others, including

TOGAF, and DoDAF. Business architecture was having limited success until 2002 when the collapse of major corporations caused legislative intervention that resulted in SOX. For almost five years, I have been adopting the best features of all these frameworks for Daxiao. CMMI, ITIL, and foundation structures for Six Sigma are included in my mega-framework.

I monitor and/or coordinate business strategy, business cycles, organizational structure, business processes, localization (where do we do what we do), and information architecture (what data do we need to do what we do).

I view Service-Oriented Architecture (SOA) as a subset of corporate architecture. Daxiao has a Well-Formed Service-Oriented Architecture (WFSOA). It facilitates the connection between business process definition and supporting technology. Using SOX guidelines (COSO, COBIT, and ERM), my teams work with BASE (SOA) governance and Requirements Management to provide centralized oversight of management systems, information systems, and computer systems.

My (our) teams recommend structured processes that support business architecture and business decision making. In reality, Hamilton Marshall's people recommend the processes, and I translate what he's doing so that senior management will listen to us, even if they don't support us. Our job is extremely challenging because a few of my peers are proud of their ability to make the right decisions according to "gut feel", not structured decision making.

Marshall lets me have a disproportionate amount of the credit. He's happy for the opportunity to implement lessons learned during a 40-year career.

For me personally this job is one huge academic experiment. It includes several management theories proposed by my academic colleagues. If I (we) manage to get a critical mass of people to use our hodgepodge (Zachman/DoDAF/TOGAF/SOX/ SOA/CMMI/ITIL/Six Sigma) Program, it will be one of the greatest academic/professional coups ever. We need another two years, but I'm trying to squeeze everything in before Marshall retires in 21 months, if he retires. I'll be back on the A Circuit. Actually, I never was on the A Circuit, but this will give me a shot.

Fortunately, the president of the Daxiao supports me. Earnings have increased every year that I have been here, and having me around gives him credence in the academic community. That allows us to attract research brainpower and research money, which fattens his annual bonus. He probably doesn't understand exactly what I (we) are doing, which is good. He would be frightened by us if he understood.

Architect - enterprise technology (Incumbent: Wayne Wright): Infrastructure Technology Team, Technology

The Foundations for Everything: My people do what they have always done, except that SOA adds significantly more complications. We work to define and enforce internal technology standards, including Web services. We maintain the hardware, systems software, tools, and networks for the existing environment (in seven countries if you count the servers in Geneva) while implementing environments to support the SOA evolution. SOA requires more middleware and more tools - we installed and maintain the services catalog, enterprise content management, configuration and asset databases, management and reporting tools (scorecards and dashboards), and middleware (databases, transaction, messaging, and security).

We enable procurement by supporting test installations of new and updated products. If a product is approved, we ensure seamless integration with the target environments. At least two of my people have expert-level expertise in most products, if you count Yu's people as part of my team.

Eighty percent of them reported me before Marshall blackmailed us into transferring them. Ninety percent of them have assignments with my team on any given day.

The SOA architect comes up with new ideas (so do we) and builds SOA architecture prototypes (SOA reference architecture), but we make it work in the real world. We provide environments for development, testing, deployment, production, research, and disaster recovery.

Disaster Recovery: We have tested processes that allow disaster recovery to take over the research machines in case of a problem. We no longer allow production overflow to the on research machines.

Research Environments: We control about 50% of the research capacity while the BASE architect handles the remainder. The research environments are constantly changing. We use ours for to evaluate new vendor software, software upgrades, and prototypes for analysis and design of business applications. The SOA people support new product research (for marketing and manufacturing), and work with external customers and standards organizations. That aids both business intelligence (BI) and technology intelligence.

Service Domains and Grid Computing: Since the corporate sector assumed control of several important service applications and databases (they are no longer in user silos), Yu and I share control of the associated processing power. We experiment with virtualization (processing and data) and grid computing.

Advisory Function: Even though they moved a few of our good managers into Requirements Management (I advised them not to pass up the promotions and pay increases), we still provide input to feasibility studies and impact analyses. We participate in requirements, analysis, and design, testing, deployment, and post-implementation reviews, and we identify potential problems with service reuse.

Requirements that obviously cannot be supported by the technology are eliminated before they pass the analysis stage. We show the software architects how to design services that fit into the service model, while providing recommendations for SOA (WFSOA) best practices during product evaluations and development support.

We conduct continuing assessment of infrastructure and show the availability architect ways to improve performance, capacity, and availability while ensuring that infrastructure components are updated appropriately.

In short, we make everything related to infrastructure and architecture happen.

Architect - network: (Incumbent: Guy Porter): Infrastructure Technology Team, Technology Sector

I don't know whether SOA made my job easier or harder. It definitely gave my career a boost, soon after I almost didn't have a career at Goodsand. I am really looking forward to the day when I can move from under the enterprise architect and report directly to the head of technology. My day will come.

My problem is that Wright would rather split a vein than let that happen, especially since I handle most of his SOA-related requirements - 70% percent of our servers (I count the mainframe as a server) around the world are connected to the enterprise service bus (ESB), whether they execute services or not. The availability architect and I are prepared for any reuse surprise successes.

Armstrong learned the hard way after 9/11 that conserving on networks and bandwidth is not necessarily the best idea. Wright was going to blame the inadequacies on me after our fail over site failed. It was in the shadow of the telephone company building downtown. Hamilton Marshall saved me by pulling me away from Armstrong for the duration of the crisis.

He borrowed some of his son's toys and used it to route traffic away from the downtown hub. His leg worked a lot better then, and we personally set up the microwave units that moved the data from midtown to transmitters in Jersey City and then to the routers in Far Hills. That made me a hero. I will never be able to repay him for that one. We were both unhappy that HM didn't have a budget for me at the time while Wright figured out how to squeeze out a decent bonus for me, in spite of what we had to spend to stay ahead of the pack after 9/11.

Now we have backups for our backups. I can hardly believe the size of the pipes they let me have - landline, mobile, satellite, and we keep microwave for short distances. The research and compliance people enjoy taking out portions of the backbone and checking to see how quickly they can send multi-megabit images to Taiwan or Geneva.

I keep quiet, keep transmitting, and humor Maja Johanssen and the head of research (Li).

Architect - SOA: Incumbent: Hank Yu, SOA Competency Team, BASE

Research and Development Support: I supported all technology research for Daxiao before the merger with Goodsand. In Goodsand/Daxiao, I handle Service-Oriented Architecture and partner research. They are larger and more complicated than all my previous work responsibilities. In these assignments, I get to handle a big wax ball (infrastructure, networking, and data). Because the partners change, and the related platforms also change, I get experience with more platform flavors than I would ever have seen previously. It gives my competency team and me a technical advantage over the infrastructure team. My boss says I shouldn't tell people if they do not notice. That is how I will be able to keep it. This allows me to be a better SOA architect to remain a secret "enterprise architect".

Service Model: My architects and the SOA Competency team defined the service model for the BASE SOA Program and refine it as SOA evolves. We provided standards for naming services with the model. The compliance specialists coordinate with technology process coordinators (the new name for methodology specialist) to ensure the processes and procedures comply with the service model.

Standards Management: I'm trying to manage five major standards organizations. You read correctly. That is my ego voyage. I cannot manage entirely. I worry only about parts that affect Goodsand/Daxiao. We guide the most important standards from all five organizations to minimize "first mover" disadvantages. We try to make them catch us. Staff members join standards teams that might affect us. Our excellent communications team assists them with writing standards. We urge vendors to join committees that we cannot join. Together we push committees in the direction we wanted to go. We also work with the committees to test the standards that we want. It is easier for us than most organizations due to the dozens of research platforms (mentioned above) and dozens of "rebels" that wish to do new things.

Architect - Software: Incumbent: Adrian Sturgis, Business Technology Team, Technology

I was a Microsoft chauvinist for the first 10 years of my career, and I held out a lot longer than Armstrong (he brought me over from our start-up that was finished). I am developing a moderate tolerance for Java, but only after the introduction of C# provided veiled hints that Visual C++ may not have been perfect.

In the middle of detailed analysis for one of the earlier official SOA projects, I realized that I could no longer avoid the mainframe. The client from the logistics area in Mexico wanted to verify that the components he shipped were accurately reflected in the Global Inventory Master Database at the time they were received. The preliminary analysis document showed that:

1. The Global Master Inventory Database ran on a mainframe in Ireland.
2. The master contained enough information to support the query. They had added a few data elements since the last time I saw it, including localization data items that existed in an MS SQL database in Mexico.
3. Inventory updates were batched and shipped to the Mexico every 30 minutes. Batches were applied whenever server capacity was available.
4. Similar data existed in New Jersey, Ireland, Mexico, and Taiwan, except that the Mexico extract was missing three of the fields required for the query.

During the feasibility study, we:

1. Prototyped a query that would access the inventory extract and the localization database in Mexico.
2. Entered a request to have the three extra pieces of data added to the Mexico extract.
3. Requested an estimate of what it would take to synchronize updates of the master and extract databases.

In the meeting that I scheduled to discuss database synchronization, the DB2 DBA said we didn't need the extract for this request because the mainframe could support Web services. They had proven that service consumer software running on an HP server in Mexico could access a service provider on a z/OS server in Ireland - we could read the data directly from the mainframe. Documentation for all the work they had done, including wrapping the existing CICS transaction, was in the Knowledge Cooperative.

The SOA architect was nodding, and the manager of the requirements team was nodding too. This would be another step toward reducing extraneous databases (he meant the hundreds of excellent databases that had been pulled from the mainframe and cleaned up to meet real user needs).

They suggested that I should redo the prototype using the mainframe service. I asked about capacity and performance. They said that database handled over 450,000 queries and 57,000 updates every day. It was available 24x7, and had 15 minutes of scheduled downtime in the last 9 months. 20,000 added queries wouldn't hurt it.

I remember feeling as if I was sinking into quicksand. I tried as hard as I could to show that the software wouldn't work or that the documentation was wrong. I couldn't, and it wasn't, at least not much. They fixed every documentation quirk in less than an hour, even a few that we reported at 2:00 A.M. Some of the SOA competency people are crazier than we are. They are still making Armstrong regret that he dumped them, even if it means learning JCL.

When I asked about costs, they said Mexico would have to run 80,000 queries every day for 24 months to equal the cost for the project that would have implemented real-time updates and added the additional data fields. The average end-to-end response time is 2 seconds slower, but it is also more consistent. It doesn't slow down for batch updates.

I have to admit that though I wouldn't design anything new to run on the mainframe, reusing what already exists may be an acceptable option.

Asset librarian: (Incumbent: Brian Luce): Infrastructure Technology Team, Technology

My nickname for myself used to be Sissy. That is not a reference to a lifestyle preference, but an allusion to the Greek character that was always pushing a big rock up a hill. No matter how hard I worked, I was always behind somebody. No matter how nicely I asked people to let me know what they were doing, about a third of them ignored me. These people raised a ruckus when they needed an asset from another organization, and that organization's teams had taken the liberty of ignoring me too.

I tried to transfer back to development, but they bribed me with a promotion and more people. They say that what I do is critical since SOX. I worried that my development skills will become obsolete. They say that it is important to have development experience to do the job well. To avoid becoming rusty, I am allowed to attend programming classes for every "new language", language upgrade, or development product that comes out. Lately, almost everything that I study has links to (or from) XML.

Extra Strong Arms for the Job: I have more assistance when I wish to "encourage" people to deliver new or upgraded assets to the asset library. First, I ask nicely. Then the knowledge consolidator reminds them nicely. Then the security people lock them out of their own libraries - Maja's people can make that happen. The knowledge/compliance strongmen (and women) have been known to make unscheduled visits to the work areas of especially recalcitrant teams and leave with their hard drives. The rule is that if Goodsand/Daxiao pays you to create it, then Goodsand/Daxiao owns it. These teams lose control of "their" assets and typically find their bonuses reduced. One raid usually generates at least five freely given "asset revelations". Many people leave after a raid. The SOA architect and his people have proven that they can reverse-engineer most of these "secreted" systems with less trouble than it takes to deal with the personalities.

We believe that the number of "overlooked" systems is significantly smaller than it was four years ago.

BASE Program coordinator
(Incumbent: Valery Van Amberg)
SOA Program Management Team, BASE

The first question that you might ask is, "How do I feel about working for Hamilton Marshall?" The answer is that I feel the same as I always felt. The difference is that I work for Marshall officially. I spend every waking moment trying to make him look as good as he did me for over thirty years while everybody believed I was mentoring him.

I wouldn't have survived nearly as long without him and his wife/friend/lover/career advisor, Nicola Frey. Nicky was Paula's best friend for most of their adult life.

The next question is why I retired and came back. The answer is that without the structure that doing this job imposes, I would probably be dead from alcohol poisoning. I retired to spend a few golden years with Paula, but she died five years earlier than we had hoped. She tripped and fell on a new variety of rose bushes, scraped her leg in multiple places, and died from an infection because the chemotherapy (for multiple myeloma) had weakened her immune system.

When she died, I didn't have anything to do that didn't remind me of her. Pauline (our daughter) had recently opened her own law firm, but I couldn't practice because that reminded me of Paula - she was a lawyer before I was. I sold the golf clubs, the archery equipment, and the boat within two months. The prize winning rose garden (with greenhouse), and the house were gone in another two months. Two weeks after the closing on the house, my "Baby Girl" and Marshall checked me into a detoxification center.

Now I have a closet on the upper west side. Some might call it a studio. I attend AA meetings, and I spend more nights in Piccolo's palace (an executive lounge) than I do in the closet.

Do I want my job back? Not on your life. Stein is as good as I was, and he has 20 twenty more years for further improvement. It is an example of transition planning that worked. He may even learn how to dress, but I believe it is his way of rebelling.

Recommending Marshall to replace me was also a good idea. There was a glitch because he wasn't a lawyer, but Nicky was, and the assignment was supposed to be temporary anyhow.

I am responsible for coordination of everything that our four super whizzes conjure up. I'm talking about Marshall, Maja, Yu, and Dan Piccolo, though I hate to admit it anything about Piccolo. I have no idea how he uses 90% of the same words that I assign to one of Marshall's ideas, spins the last 10%, acts stupid, and convinces at least 50% of the people to accept what he says. He is the president's brother-in-law, but few people know that and Mittelman appears to remain scrupulously neutral about Piccolo's amazing ideas that originally were Marshall's (or Nicky's) ideas. Below is a table listing the things that I do and their probability of success.

BASE Responsibilities and Success Probability

Description of Responsibilities	Short-Term	Long-term
Ensuring smooth interactions among the BASE teams. If there appeared to be a crack in the BASE façade, Armstrong or Chiu would destroy us within three months	98%	98%
Ensuring smooth merger of the SOX, CMMI, ITIL, and SOA initiatives. We call it whatever it needs to be called, depending upon the audience.	90%	98%
Monitoring and reporting sector spending on the merged initiatives.	99%	99%
Synchronizing Service-Oriented Architecture with corporate architecture and corporate strategy.	90%	95%
Synchronizing BASE activities with the EIGHT committees that oversee what we do. We hit a snag because Gunnar wants to become head of the audit committee. Joe says it's a good way to teach Gunnar the importance of compliance. I am not so sure.	95%	Not Known
Synchronizing data consolidation efforts. Macedon can usually prevent construction of new databases that	40%	75%

we don't need, but removing existing redundancy is more difficult. Convincing two junior operations managers in Taiwan to give up the Sybase database that 17 of their people have been using for the last 11 years is a significantly more difficult, even if all 54,243 records have been loaded into the inventory master for three years now.		
Synchronizing internal development with partner consulting and research projects. Hank and I work together.	99%	99%
Monitoring SOA (WFSOA) progress against plans and ensuring input to dashboards and scorecards.	99%	99%
Assisting with transition of work requests from project initiation to business technology teams. This includes: ♦ Providing financial specialists to work with Macedon's planning specialists on refining project estimates. ♦ Working with Doc to maintain the matrix of skills and staff availability. ♦ Working with Reed to free up super managers for the hot projects. ♦ Working with Hank to provide competency team support as necessary. ♦ Working with Hank and Armstrong to coordinate offshore (in-house) development (Ireland and Taiwan)	90%	95%
Ensuring that core services recommended by BASE business analysts are properly prioritized and implemented by the best people that we have	80%	98%
Ensuring that Marshall's process automation recommendations and process improvements pass through the work queue in the shortest possible time. That is somewhat easy because we built ReMain, the request maintenance product	90%	95%

I know that I forgot something, but it's not because my brain is pickled. I'm among the oldest of the managers who are SVP or above, and this job is tough. In a few years, Stein, Piccolo, or Macedon may be able to handle it. Forget Macedon. He's a year older than I am.

Business analyst - Extranet (Incumbent: Pamela Lincoln): SOA Program Management Team, BASE

I was one of our EDI casualties, and now I'm glad I was. Every time I show Daxiao how to make or save money with a partner link, I earn a hefty bonus. I try to do at least two each year. Now my husband can spend time with our kids.

I can't imagine having more fun at one job or working harder at a job. I have to know a little about everything within Daxiao and a great deal about many things such as networking and security. I have to understand how internal platforms work (or don't) and learn quickly how partner platforms work (or don't). I have to understand minute details of company strategy to reduce the number of times I have to tell a partner, "I'll get back to you on that."

Every time we are successful with a partner linkage or update, jobs are changed or eliminated on both sides. I have to discover and highlight areas of resistance within Daxiao and outside.

I have two problems. Extranet analysts often find themselves competing with independent and vendor consultants for lucrative B2B contracts. We have an advantage because we don't have to make a profit on the consulting, even though we are beginning to generate a revenue stream. The second problem is that the head of Sales and Marketing thinks we are stepping on his toes while we are trying to do a better job for the head of the Operations unit. Everybody benefits from what we do, but he fights us every time he can.

I must run. The Board agreed to let me try to set up links between our team in Mexico, manufacturing in Taiwan, and a new partner on mainland China. Lisse Maçon and Joe Guzman will be helping us. Wish me luck.

Client - business operations: (Incumbent: Clyde Hastings)

Requirements Gathering: I just came from a requirements meeting for my new database update application. They agreed to give me everything that I needed, and a few things I didn't know I needed. It took us four hours to do a week's worth of work. I still feel as if I should be complaining that I lost something, but I haven't figured out how to say it. I'll let my boss run it past Barca first.

This was supposed to be an extension of work that my technology people did for me a year ago. They built a special query database for the product distribution people in Brussels. They needed to see the parts inventory by 8:00 A.M. CET (Central European Time). That time is six hours ahead of us and usually at the beginning of our first backup cycle. Last year we created an extract file after of the first batch update cycle of the night, run a language translator to create descriptions in German, French, and Italian, and loaded everything into the EURO database that sits on a computer in Ireland. That time is five hours ahead of us. They were able to do queries as early as midnight, which is 0600 hours their time. It was better than they had before. The next request is to be able to place (inventory) reservations against the database extract. I was not looking forward to the fight with the database people.

Organizational Changes - To confuse matters, I called the project manager who did the work for me last year. He told me he had given up his dedicated team, and he was working as a project initiation manager (PIM). He no longer builds anything. He helps other people decide what to build. He was still there for me. I would be his third client in his new role. I had no idea how someone with no staff was going to do anything for me, but I figured it couldn't hurt to spend a couple of hours with him. Maybe he could teach me the new ropes.

Initiating Requirements - A week ago, I sent him an e-mail that outlined my suggestions for enhancing the database. He sent me an e-mail explaining the new procedures, but I didn't really read it because I was organizing the documentation I believed we would need for the database fight. He suggested that he and I should get a half hour head start before the rest of the team showed up.

Collaboration Setup - My assistant and I met him and an SOA specialist in the collaboration center. It was actually the old video conference room, with new equipment. There was space for six "monitor" people on one side of the table, eight real people on our side of the table. The name I had suggested for the new project was scrolling across each of the screens, and there was a documentation package beside each keyboard.

The facilitator reminded me of all the people I have ever forgotten, but he had a "just right" handshake, and a deep voice with a bit of an accent. He sat down beside me. The business analyst was a tiny perky woman that used to be my "answer" person when they set up a new procedure. The SOA specialist said he was an internal consultant, and he would be helping us take notes for today. My contact was wearing a silly button that said, "A PIM is a friend". He handed me a card that suggested, "Know your local PIM" with his new title. They promoted him for this!

We went over the agenda while we waited for people to show up or check in. He explained that we would fill out the requirements template, create assumptions and issues lists, and match it to the business strategy. He assured me that I wouldn't have a problem on the last part. If we made enough progress in one session, we could put the work request on a queue for risk analysis, prioritization, and funding request notification. This wasn't an actual funding request. A requirements analyst had to complete a real feasibility study (including risk analysis) before the real funding request occurred. He promised to show me how to look at the queue at the end of the session.

I commented that we seemed to have too many analysts analyzing things. He explained that the job of the business analyst is to capture what the areas want, while the requirements analyst ensures that the requirements provide maximum benefit for the business. They also ensure that we don't build more duplicates for software and data that we have already.

Return on Investment - The facilitator put the agenda on the screen, and we started working. The man in Brussels started out by demanding that his people should have real-time access to inventory in the EURO database. He explained how much they contributed to the bottom line last year, how the database helped, and how much more there would have been if they had problems with 8 big orders due to inventory mix-ups.

I suggested that we could apply the same update programs that we use on the core data could add one more step that would synchronize our data and theirs. Everybody nodded. I was beginning to feel like I was in the twilight zone.

Requirement Details - Then the business analyst started working on the requirements template. The facilitator did something so that all of us could see her list of questions and the responses she was entering as we talked. There were 50 questions. Fortunately, 35 were filled in already. I told you I did my homework. She had changed the wording on a few of them, but her adjustments were more accurate. The product people corrected three of the answers and added to five others. Nobody raised an eyebrow when the clients requested four added languages and emphasized their need for product images.

Testing Requirements - The testing specialist was very cheery and supportive, but he slowed down the process. Every time we reviewed a requirement, he asked how you would test it. If nobody could explain how the requirement would be tested, he asked us to change the requirement. We adjusted 10 requirements during the session. There were five "must haves" that the people in Europe couldn't explain how to test. All these went on a list of issues. One was labeled "Highly Significant" (the one about security compliance in Europe), one was moderate, and three were low.

User Interface: This was not what I expected. I thought her job was to understand how we wanted the screens to look (which it was). Her additional job was to make sure that the U.S. people understood what the people in Brussels meant (not what they said), and vice versa. There was a French version of the template that she updated as soon as the business analyst finished typing.

Strategy Synchronization: Two hours and 15 minutes later (including one 20-minute break), we were almost through with the requirements, except for one last question. Where does this fit in the Strategy? My friend the PIM pulled up our sector strategy and the strategy document for the people in Europe. Everybody nodded. This seemed too easy. I asked directly, "So the strategy says it's all right to allow them to start updating the EURO database?" The answer was a very carefully delivered "NO". We were finally returning to normal.

Feasibility Discussion: The data analyst put his recommendation up on the screen. H proposed that we could find what we need in the main database. In the last six months, they had eliminated 80% of the nightly batch cycle. Everything happens in real time, and they take incremental backups (only the things that change). The database is available at all times. When I asked about the translations, the software architect explained that the people in Europe have improved translation software (Software as a Service - SaaS) that handles vocabulary for all their units. It does adequate translations into and out of all the Schengen languages. (I'll have to look that up). He can design a composite service that reads our master, translates into whatever language is associated with the user profile and deliver that data along with the images they requested. They can capture updates in real time and place them in the database of record. Development and testing should cost about $250,000. To add update capability, database synchronization, images, and language translation for the EURO database would cost $550,000 plus continuing database maintenance, which would be about $20,000 each year. The product team nodded. They had seen services running on the database of record, they liked it, they looked forward to saving €225,000, and they were willing to give up "their own" database after the technology team (people that I didn't know) proved that they could deliver.

Funding: Everyone agreed that we had enough information to post this project request to the prioritization and approval queue. My friend requested $100,000 for analysis and design, $100,000 for development and testing, and $50,000 for deployment. I commented that it seemed we would be spending too much on analysis and design because we already knew what we were going to do, but the SOA person said they like to spend more time up front.

My other service worked across Europe, but we needed to test working across the Atlantic. We agreed to schedule the next meeting after we gathered input from the requirements analyst. The requirements analyst promised he would be finished in two days! He had been paying attention to the work request from the time I sent my e-mail, but he had to incorporate today's adjustments.

Pricing Issues and Assumptions: Every issue was prefixed with money symbols ($€) on the requirements screens and on the documents that we carried away. The PIM explained that the $250,000 estimate was derived before the requirements session depending upon their understanding of the issues. We had cleared up some issues, but added others.

- High significance costs $20,000 per issue.
- Medium significance costs $10,000 per issue.
- Low significance cost $2,000 per issue.

I asked them how they knew what increment to assign. They said they had looked at hundreds of previous plans and price overruns to come up with these numbers. However, due to limited experience with SOA, the numbers were still being tuned. He showed me that these were conservative estimates, supported by some of our prior experiences. Then he added a bit of incentive. The quicker we finished answering the outstanding questionings, eliminated the issues list, and cleared out the assumptions the lower the final price tag would be.

Approval Notifications: The facilitator hit a "communications" button and e-mails when out. My boss and the product team's boss received the approval request, the feasibility study, and a URL if they wanted to look up the details. A planning specialist was on the distribution list. The approval request had a "review by" date. Everyone in the session received meeting minutes with the requirements, the feasibility study, approval request, assumptions, and issues list attached. My friend the PIM would review the work priorities, talk to the approvers, and agree upon tentative delivery dates.

I am in my office trying to understand what happened. My PIM said I could call him any time, even if I was only thinking about the possibility of having a question. I'll start by reading the BASE Program information that they provided and signing up for the BASE education that my boss recommended during my last review.

Communications specialist - BASE:
(Incumbent: Lisse Maçon): BASE Communications

Team

Transition from Sales: For the first 5 years of my career, I was a fundraiser, for the next five, I worked in sales, and for the last four, I have been in communications. They used to say I could sell snow to Eskimos, but I actually sold embedded software to senior managers. I'm able to figure out what people need to hear and give them what they want to ease their purchase fears. If a product was good, I could sell more of it than anyone else could. I wanted to leave to start a family, but Daxiao offered me an opportunity to put together a communications program for BASE. I'm still at it four years later.

I had heard of SOA before I received the offer because it was beginning to pop up on customer calls. However, Daxiao committed to it sooner (almost). I evangelize the ideas to our internal people to make it happen. Fortunately, I know most of them. They're the ones Gunnar taught me to scream at when one of my customers weren't satisfied. This is certainly a switch.

Common terminology: We had to expend more effort on the corporate dictionary than I expected. I discovered on my first sales call how my customers and I were using different words to mean the same things. On the second sales call, I realized that my customers didn't always agree on their own terminology. Soon I had to take an assistant with me to take notes.

I didn't realize that we had the same problem inside Daxiao/Goodsand. We all worked for a hardware manufacturing company. A few weeks ago, the technology people admitted that they had assigned two people to talk to me, the ones that could translate "sales speak". I'd been skimming over the top of the technology terminology canopy for five years. I only peeked underneath when I was dealing with a particularly intense customer.

The knowledge consolidator helped me realize how big the problem was when she showed me the list of 84 areas she believed we should include in common terminology. Ellison made them whittle it down to 61. As soon as they finished interviewing the first line of business units, they asked me to expand the list again, adding one entry for each of the top-producing product areas.

Communications specialist - corporate: (Incumbent: Austin Ellison): Corporate Communications

I am the newest and youngest of Justin Mittelman's direct reports. Father and I agree that this is an excellent opportunity. Time that my family spent following him around with the diplomatic corps will do pay off.

I am also able to justify majoring in linguistics. He worried that I would end up teaching lemurs or other primate species how to communicate with humans. In reality, I was helping speech-impaired orphans from Southeast Asia learn to communicate with their caregivers when I met Grace Mittelman. She's a softhearted Park Avenue snob who thinks she can fix most of the problems of the world by issuing commands, gently, and giving away the interest on her father's money. In all fairness, there are two to three hundred pampered ex-orphan girls chattering on cell phones in McMansions who wouldn't be alive if it wasn't for her intervention.

Back to me [...] with an understanding of international diplomacy (listening to Mother and Father discuss tricky situations), speaking fluently in six languages, writing accurately in four, and a PhD dissertation on "The Limiting Effects of Pinyin Romanization on the Understanding of Ming Literary Tradition", I went from a low five-figure income to over $200,000 in one month.

To shorten a long story, Mrs. Mittelman was quite pleasantly surprised when she discovered that I was the scion of one of her prep school buddies. Having the right genes, in addition to a good golf swing and familiarity with the names of yacht parts, were beneficial when funding for my research/humanitarian experiment dried up. Father was ecstatic. He spoke to Grace, Grace spoke to Justin, and Justin ordered Lisse Maçon to show me the ropes. I quickly came to think of her as a big sister, though she's petite (5'4" and about 110 lbs.).

Now my specialty is saying very little, and using exactly the right number of words in the correct register while offending no one. My mother says that puts me in a good position to take over Mittelman's job if he manages to hang on for a few more years. Mittelman says I'm good at what I do. I have a good working relationship with Lisse Maçon and Mittelman accepts her opinion. Joe Guzman obviously approves of what I do in Latin America. It is good that Father's diplomatic connections have gotten us out of a few difficult situations. He kept our foot in the door while Van Amberg worked on improving his register. Military precision often needs to be camouflaged.

Liz shows me the ropes, and I pretend that her communications programs are my communications programs and promote them with everyone. She doesn't seem to worry whether this is fair. She says the ends justify the means. I also work with her on common terminology (corporate-wide and not merely computer-related as it was when I started). The cross-cultural semantics issues would be worthy of several papers if I still worried about such things. I also support translation of business and computer technology terms between

English, Spanish, and Chinese and occasionally French for a few people in Canada, Brussels, and Geneva. I am finally learning computer terminology - starting in Chinese and then translating into English.

I also talk to the head of Sales and Marketing, (Andy) Niklas Gunnar. My job is to tell him what Mr. Marshall thinks he needs to know about SOA while pretending that (a) they are my ideas, or (b) it is one of Liz's silly ideas, and I need to run it by him to get his input. Niklas Gunnar ignores Liz, Mr. Marshall, and me, but he ignores her most. I'll take time to figure out why that might be after I put all my anchors in the water.

Justin said that one of my anchors should be to try to figure out Mr. Marshall - he says the first problem is that I still call him Mr. Marshall. I call him Mr. Marshall because I have seldom actually spoken to him. We exchange very precise e-mails, or we talk through Liz. I had been here two months before I saw him in person at his "Sector Picnic".

I felt like an Episcopalian on a pilgrimage to Mecca. I was trying to make the best of it (prolonging my purely academic evaluation of Indira Marshall's body language) and wondering why my "working the crowd skills" were slipping when Joe Guzman sat down beside me. We joked about how it takes a while for some people to get accustomed to Indy's height, and how it was a good idea that my fiancée hadn't come along with me. Then we started discussing the most recent Spanish translation collaboration.

It is during that conversation that the picnic photographer stopped by to talk to us. Nicola Frey appeared to be a 45-year-old woman wearing a silver wig and a black designer tankini. She apologized for being wet, but "one needs a dip before a difficult photo shoot". I kept looking for the subliminal arrows in her cover-up that highlighted everything that was supposed to be covered. She didn't work at Daxiao, but she was an old friend of Mr. Marshall. After she left, I mentioned to Joe that I had this skin crawling feeling that someone had hypnotized me and plugged electrodes into my brain. He said, "Someone did, and you didn't flunk". Then I commented that careful empirical observation revealed that the photographer and Indy had the same unique body proportions and body language, although the younger woman was almost a foot taller than the older. Joe explained that those were inheritable traits, and that the hair color reflected Ms. Frey's real age. That is when I pulled something in my neck.

The good news is that my communications skills improved instantaneously. Mr. Marshall reminded me that his nickname was HM. He commented within hearing distance of several people that he liked my work, and Alex Macedon let me stand near Mr. Marshall in the official picnic photo.

Extraneous comment: Joe Guzman has as much trouble adjusting to Nicola Frey's absence of height as I did dealing with her daughter's height. Joe's wife was at the picnic. She was not amused.

Compliance specialist - technology:
(Incumbent: Hugo Stein):
Compliance Management Team, BASE

They let me keep Valery Van Amberg's job, even after he came back. They said it had changed enough that he would have to learn it all over again anyhow. Furthermore, the SEC auditors said I was doing a good job, and Marshall takes care of people who take care of him.

I held everything together when they made Marshall take that sabbatical. While Marshall was out, Montgomery and his buddies slipped some things past me, and that caused major problems for Daxiao, but vindicated Marshall and his purchasing über processes.

Marshall came back, took the promotion they promised him, and pulled me up with him. I do the reserved arms-length audits, and Van Amberg audits how well we all work together.

In some respects, the job is easier. Since SOX, I have significantly more enforcement capability. In other respects, it is much more difficult. I am responsible for the effectiveness of over 180 BASE processes and for oversight of hundreds of others across the company. The time and effort I saved by automating existing processes is taken up trying to make the processes "transparent" or struggling with the international implications of everything. Sixty percent of my people work outside the United States now.

Concerning international law, my biggest challenge is keeping up with Guzman, literally. I learned to hear and move more quickly. Fortunately, I am able to absorb the written word almost as fast as Marshall is. It's easy to know what Guzman is referring to, even while I am slower at figuring out why. The biggest problem is I have to wait until the regulations are translated into English. Even after intensive training, I can only hear English and German.

Both of the compliance teams and the methodology specialists (technology process coordinators) report to me. It's not nearly as bad as I thought. It's easier with Maja's Knowledge Cooperative (with SOX clout for maintaining it) and Liz's common terminology. The international parts of the common terminology are tricky too, but the kid in corporate communications (Ellison) is a lot more helpful than I believed he could possibly me.

Developer - application: (Incumbent: Eric Cooke):

Business Technology Team, Technology

I'm a C# programmer, and I don't believe I like SOA. That may be because they are forcing me to learn how to use services that run on the mainframe, rather than rewriting them in a language that makes sense. If this keeps up, they'll be forcing me to learn COBOL or CICS.

It may also be because the compliance people are using SOA (or SOX, depending on the day) to force me to adhere to development standards that I feel are a waste of time. Not only am I forced to add comments to every piece of new software that I write, I have to add comments to code that I maintain. Recently, I have more and more maintenance assignments.

They are also strict about naming conventions for classes, namespaces, functions, and variable names. Variable names are further restricted because they have a metadata glossary that recommends names for commonly used variables. I don't know why anyone should be concerned about whether I use accNum as I always have or accIdentifier as the data team recommended in the last application that I worked on. The data specialist says that accIdentifier is generic and is used for accounts that may have alphabetic and numeric characters, while accNum would be expected to contain only numeric values. I told them that this seems arbitrary, and they agreed, but these are the new rules. They believe that if everyone is consistent, it will be easier for everyone to use the data virtualization services. I don't need data virtualization services, at least not yet.

The supreme insult is that they added software to the check-in process that verifies whether I adhere to standards that they believe are important. It places exception flags on my work when I avoid rules that I don't like. I found a way around the check-in process, but the integration specialist runs the automatic checker again before she builds any code into a team application. The worst problem occurred when she called me at 4:00 A.M. to tell me that I was holding up a major project prototype. The next day my project manager called my team leader and me. He showed us a blinking "green" light beside the project that I was working on. He said we were still OK, but the blinking meant that we were a day late for our first complete build, and my code was the problem.

I asked which was more important, code that worked or code that met compliance's silly standards. He said the teams that managed to do both would have "bonus" advantages over the teams who didn't.

I modified the code to conform to standards, and then immediately started looking for an organization where standards are not as important. It took me only two days to schedule my first interview with an onshore company that does offshore SOA development for a company in England. When I asked the interview team how important standards and documentation were in their organization, they smiled and congratulated me for being aware of the importance of consistency in an organization such as theirs. They said a few their competitors went out of business because they delivered sloppy products.

That means that for the time being, I adhere to their silly standards. We are expecting our second child in three months and were hoping that she would be able to stay at home with the kids for at least a year.

Developer - legacy adaptation:
(Incumbent: Helen Lee):
Business Technology Team, Technology

When I heard about the job as a legacy adaptation specialist, I felt sorry for the poor slobs that would be pulled into doing that job. Visions of the mainframe danced in my head. Then I noticed that they would only accept applications from the people with the highest performance ratings, and that they were going to pay successful applications about 15% more than I was making.

I decided that I might consider the five-letter word that began with "C". I was accepted for the job, but I haven't touched a COBOL program yet. They give mainframe legacy adaptation assignments to mainframe developers, whether they work on Java programs that run on Linux or COBOL programs that run on z/OS.

I convert functions written in C++ into services. You can't imagine how surprised I was when I learned that these were considered legacy applications too. Some of them run on Sun and others run on Windows. Some were Web applications already, but they didn't have interfaces that allowed discovery through a UDDI catalog.

This job keeps me extremely busy. The BASE business analyst and the corporate business analyst worked together to identify core functions that needed to be converted to services. After the SOA competency team evaluated the feasibility of doing the conversions, the business teams voted on their priority. We started at the top and worked our way down the list.

Over 80% of the core functions are available as services now. Sometimes the services work, but they are not accepted because the data is not in good shape. Data clean up requires more time than "legacy" adaptation, so we have to wait. I'm sitting on two services for this reason, one where they are cleaning the data and leaving the database design in place, and another where they are merging two existing databases.

When the list is finished, I look forward to moving to a service domain team, and if I am luckier, they may let me move to the SOA competency team. I believe I made the right career move.

Domain owner - data: (Incumbent: Raymond Morgan): Financial Management, Corporate

My former boss, Dennis Travers, is very conservative. He has always been one of the best when it comes to keeping things stable. He did well working for Marshall before Armstrong arrived. That also means that during Armstrong's early "rip it and fix it" period, Travers was walking a very thin line. Travers' mantra was and is that a tall building needs a deep strong foundation. He ended up being Armstrong's strongest person during 9/11. He and Wright (Armstrong's yes man) have established a workable relationship while he keeps the door open to Marshall. Though I like Marshall, it always seemed that maintaining a relationship with him was a real waste of political energy. That is, until the people in Europe sent us Maja Johanssen to beef up our security, and she refused to work with anyone except Marshall.

I can be almost as careful as Travers can, but I like to be careful about new things. The idea of loading and tweaking the same data structure year after year would drive me to distraction. The idea of using new technology to make order out of things that everybody says cannot be ordered brings me ecstasy. Running around trying to keep up with that crazy woman technically is like dying and going to heaven. If I tried to keep up with her physically, I would die and end up somewhere else. Her main hobby is rock climbing. This year she's training for an iron woman competition. She says she intends to return to skydiving next year.

Getting to work with Maja required careful handling of the fallout from one of Travers' only professional failures. Due to his conservative approach to everything, he did not do well at Knowledge Management. Because he had never failed at anything else, and the entire KM industry was going into the dumpster, Travers asserted that Knowledge Management couldn't be done, at least not in a company as complicated as Daxiao.

Maja told Marshall that she could do it in her spare time, as long as he promised she would not be in trouble for "unauthorized discovery". She doesn't steal anything. She uses her specialized skills to help people remember where they may have misplaced information that is vital to the success of important endeavors. That translated into ensuring that every desktop was online, ensuring that no laptop could access Daxiao information if the laptop was not properly secured and backed up, hacking into information caches that people kept for job security, or physically accessing certain hard-to-find information.

After she completed the first five of six things that Travers said couldn't be done, I convinced Travers and then Armstrong to let me keep an eye on her. Maja agreed that I was subtle enough and crazy enough to play the "man in the middle".

Metadata catalog: The first important thing that I did in this job was to define the metadata for ReMain (Request Maintenance, the change documentation and management system). They wanted one system to capture requirements for each of the sectors and locations. We completed the first version four years ago.

Data services requirements: Next, we built data services to access the ReMain database.

There came a time when being in the middle left me hardly any room to breath. That is how I became the first data domain owner reporting to the CFO. My domain covers technology metadata and databases. There is always something new to do. This is sweet.

Domain owner - service: (Incumbent: Megan Denaro): Financial Management - Corporate

I'm responsible for financial services. That is, I am responsible for the software services that may be used to calculate anything related to money. Fortunately, my primary user is also my boss, Lorraine Jasper. Other areas use the services, including the technology people who need them to calculate return on investment, the strategy management team, and the sales team.

The services for which I am responsible come from varying locations (mainframe financial support applications, client/server applications, and ERP components). They wrapped them and gave them to me. Some of the services were rewritten as services to replace important older, but problematic functions.

I still have many challenges. One occurred when they found a slightly different variation of one of my calculations written in a version of Excel that is no longer supported and sitting on the desktop of a new marketing analyst. He complained that his machine was running too slowly, he was falling behind in his work, and he needed more memory. The machine was eight years old, he was running Windows 98, and there were no more memory slots.

The head of Sales and Marketing always blames me when his people have problems after not adhering to corporate policy recommendations. He says that as long as they are recommendations, we should have processes in place to deal with people who don't like the recommendations.

We persuaded our boss, the CFO, to support a policy that said:

1. We would stop supporting calculations that ran on unsupported vendor software after a given date (no exceptions).
2. All client teams have three months to provide examples of critical calculations that required conversion and a subject matter expert to explain input fields and expected results (no exceptions after the three-month period).
3. If someone outside technology, BASE, or Finance produced the calculation, and there was no one who could explain it, then we couldn't reproduce it.
4. We would not reproduce rounding errors.
5. Our people would provide documented replacement calculations in the form of services in no less than three months after an approved conversion request.
6. We would show them how to verify the accuracy of the results returned by our services. We keep the mathematical geniuses around for that.

In the interim, we would:

1. Give them Option A (import unsupported software into a new machine with a new operating system and hope it works) or Option B (use replacement services supported by industry-standard calculations).
2. Allow interface specialists to show them how to build their own calculation portals by dropping in documented calculation services.

We hear that Gunnar is not happy. He and his people are still reacting vociferously to the demise of individual machines. Lorrie believes she has every legitimate calculation covered by three sets of industry-standard calculation packages. He and Lorrie started a dangerous game of "chicken" and Mittelman will have to broker a compromise. Meanwhile, Gunnar is trying to fight in an area where Lorrie is an acknowledged expert.

Executive - technology:
(Incumbent: Weldon Armstrong): Management Team, Technology

Ensuring high quality information systems for Daxiao is like racing a formula 18-wheeler (with amphibian capabilities) carrying ultra-wide trailers across sand dunes. The environment keeps shifting, the destinations move, the contents shift, and I'm driving a vehicle that originally didn't tolerate sand or water as well.

I was hired to improve the design of the Goodsand "technology vehicle". Goodsand became Daxiao after the last merger. Marshall and some other people (who didn't survive my arrival) had built and adequate off-road vehicle, but the company president recognized the need for something more advanced. The Web was coming and Goodsand was not ready. I have delivered what I was hired to do.

The obvious question is, "Why bother with land vehicles when I could fly to my destination much faster". The answer is that I tried, as Mittelman recommended, when I first came onboard. During those days, I could reach wrong destinations quickly, and I could crash equally quickly. There were a few problems:

1. Flight plans were inaccurate or incomplete.
2. Flights often reached the wrong destinations before flight plans could be corrected.
3. Planes and helicopters are much more expensive over shorter distances.
4. The ground crews at the start and end destinations were not properly trained.
5. The fastest planes required long and well-maintained runways, which limited the places you could land.
6. Rebuilding the runways for constantly changing destinations was extremely difficult and expensive.
7. In hostile environments, aircraft were easier to see, and therefore, easier to shoot down.
8. Airplanes and helicopters require special fuel (talent) that was not readily available, and was extraordinarily expensive.
9. Stealth planes (anomalous projects) don't carry cargo well.
10. The instrumentation was changing more quickly than we could train the pilots. There were unavoidable crashes.
11. The planes and the helicopters had too many pilots. While they were trying to resolve different interpretations of the directions, additional crashes occurred.

On the other hand:

1. Overturned tractors may be righted, the drivers often survive, and the trailer contents may be recovered. On the other hand, aerial crashes tend to be harder to recover and more newsworthy (and thus harder on the reputation).
2. 18-wheelers, even with wide loads, can get closer to their destinations than aircraft. Products that are flown to one location usually have to be delivered to their ultimate destinations by surface transportation.

I recommended that a combination of surface and air transportation provided the best solutions, and I persuaded everyone that we needed to back up and get better at surface transportation.

I assigned Marshall the task of improving the seals (standards, guidelines, processes, and procedures) to prevent sand and salt water from affecting critical moving parts or cargo contents. More than once, I could see the destination, but stray particles of sand made it past the seals he had originally installed and delayed the delivery of critical projects. I wasn't sure he could fix the seals, but I have been pleasantly surprised.

Marshall also stores the fuel reserve that I delivered to his care. These are expert technologists that I transferred to his organization, originally to ensure they would be as close as possible to the sources of any changes to (or new) standards, policies, procedures, etc. Now, I encourage collaboration between the expatriates and my technology residents for a mutually beneficial exchange of problem resolution techniques. To continue the idiom, I allow them to be assigned to "pit crews" for my racing (project) teams.

Daniel Piccolo does a good job of mapping the terrain for me (he keeps the strategy information current). I already had an IT strategy organization that was synchronized with the corporate strategy. The problem is that the corporate strategy needed more attention. There were two consecutive years where the company made 90o degree turns, and I ended up having to cancel major initiatives when they were six to nine months later than they should have been. I soon realized that a person in Piccolo's role would be valuable. It was beneficial to have an associate who could launch and maintain the communications satellites while I did the driving.

Alexander Macedon ensures that I have better flight plans, and he maintains my satellite reception. He monitors the map changes and informs me when the terrain is changing, in real time, rather than six months later. He also lets me know which destinations I need to visit, and which ones I need to remove from my itinerary.

Daxiao's "ultra (project delivery) trailer" is extraordinarily expensive. The budget is 100 times the budget for my entire .COM organization; however, I work to ensure that the budget remains flat while we remain abreast of or ahead of the industry.

Facilitator: (Incumbent: He Wei): BASE Communications

Austin Ellison, Daxiao's head of corporate communications, recommended me for the job in SOA (BASE) communications. I am stationed in Taiwan. I speak Mandarin Chinese (my first language), Mexican Spanish, and American English (the last two with about equal facility). I speak with a Chinese accent, unlike Hank who sounds like a Brit.

Everyone on Lisse Maçon's team speaks at least two languages and some are fluent in as many as four languages. The head of corporate communications is fluent in six.

Everyone in communications had prior experience in business management, technology management, or sales before they went to work with Ms. Maçon. I was a database manager before they wooed me into this job with the promise of more money (which they delivered) and an opportunity to work with Maja Johanssen to keep my database credentials up do date. I had to sign a three-year contract.

I spent four months in facilitation boot camp before they let me facilitate anything. That included:

1. Three weeks each of diplomatic training in both Taiwan (my parents grew up near Beijing on the mainland) and in Mexico.
2. Three weeks in Ireland attending meetings that were facilitated by people who had completed their training and moved back into their organizations.
3. A course where I learned to dress up or down, to accommodate the styles of the people I was facilitating. In Taiwan, I tend to dress up.
4. After I understood the cultural differences, they made me learn about the high-level political arena, and our niche products.
5. Introductory sales training (two more weeks).

They made me take a technology overview course that I originally thought would be a wasted week. It consisted, primarily of video sequences that Hank Yu put together. I learned the similarities and differences between "C" languages and Java, and between the object oriented languages and COBOL. I was taught how to perform similar tasks on Unix/Linux, Windows, and z/OS (mainframe). I learned how to load databases using Oracle (my area of specialty), MSSQL, DB2, and an old mainframe database system called IMS. The important point of the training seemed to be that technology platforms are much less important than I thought. You can do almost anything on almost any platform if you are good. You can create problems on almost any platform if you are bad.

On the other hand, Maja is a bit fanatical about IMS. This 40-year-old product provides a hierarchical structure that almost perfectly supports XML (the language of SOA). In fact, Maja is fanatical about everything that she believes is important. Ooops. I'm wandering. That is not good for a facilitator.

Finally, I spent a month working with the two major collaboration products in BASE (the Knowledge Cooperative and ReMain). Both were cobbled together from vendor products by Maja and Mr. Marshall (both MAD, MAD database nuts). The indexes on the information (they call it the thesaurus), take up more space than the information. The indexes are all loaded in IMS. They borrowed search algorithms from Internet search engines and tacked on a few that Maja invented. I'm sorry. It is hard for a database person not to worship the Goddess Maja.

The significance of the Knowledge Cooperative and ReMain for me as a facilitator is that I don't have to remember all the things I was taught in the first three months. In fact, between these two products, few people have to remember anything, except where to look for what they want. The good news is that:

1. We argue less about what happened in a prior review session. Writers enter the information into templates and distribute it while I'm summarizing the session.
2. We have fewer inter-language misunderstandings. Input from critical sessions is translated into the native language of the participants overnight.
3. We argue less about business policy. On a good day, I will find the answer to 80% of our questions in three minutes or less.
4. We don't argue about whom we should contact for answers to the other 20%. We can pull up the list of SMEs and find the answers to about half of that 20% while the session is still in progress.

The hardest thing that I had to learn, and the part that I am still working on, is how to be neutral. My job is to facilitate, not to lead. Leadership is the job of the people who request our services.

For example, Ms. Maçon reminds us to listen to what Maja has to say, but ignore "religious" attachments to anything. She says that whatever we believe about Daxiao will change in the next few weeks, months, or years anyhow.

Financial specialist - corporate:
Incumbent: Lorraine Jasper, CFO):
Financial Management Team, Corporate

Financial management: The finance part of my job would be much more difficult if we didn't have SOX. If you give me a set of rules, I can follow the hell out of them. I have SEC and PCAOB evaluations to prove it. With SOX, I could justify enforcing policy that I recommended earlier when everybody believed I was being difficult.

Compliance and Purchase: I am fortunate to have Marshall for compliance and purchasing. I gave him a hard time when he tried to put in automated approvals, but he made it possible to have the best of all worlds - more people reviewing requests, more quickly, and with greater traceability. I knew that the senior managers used to sign blank forms back when I required paper, but I couldn't figure a way around it. With digital signatures, they have to update their credentials often enough that we know someone is paying attention at least every three months, even if it is their admin person.

Domain Management: In addition to finance, my people are responsible for thirty percent of the processing and data in Daxiao. I never thought that I would ever find myself on the technology side of the business, but I'm in up to my hips in this challenge, and I don't plan on giving anybody a reason to take it away.

They created domain owner roles and gave them to me after Macedon and Marshall became good at helping Armstrong deliver popular services. Business units wanted their own service silos. Funding fights and service reuse conflicts were taking longer to resolve than it took to create the services in the first place.

- If business unit X1 paid for service development and unit B2 wanted to use it, X1 wanted B2 to give them part of the development cost.
- If unit J4 wanted to use the service, X1 wanted them to pay too, but B2 wanted some of the money.

Ironically, business units were using Marshall's Thunk system to prove how much they spent to create and maintain the services.

This was in addition to cost-per-use algorithms. I was feeling that it would have been easier to balance the national budget. It was limiting reuse.

Piccolo ran the cost-benefit analysis on the time it was taking finance people to agree on the funding algorithms. Piccolo also calculated how long it was taking service owners to resolve service level issues with service re-users.

That's when he stood on his head in the middle of the boardroom table to demonstrate how silly the existing premises were. We were asking people to stand on their heads to deliver the results of their painfully developed and costly services to teams with which they had years of adversarial history.

Gunnar, who seems to detest Piccolo and participated in the most protracted reuse fight, said, "now that you've made a fool of yourself again, I suppose the solution is to let you or Marshall control all the services".

Dan flipped over backward, landed in his seat, and said, "Definitely not. I don't know how to work that hard, and it's too much extra work for Marshall. He's just digging out from under the last challenge we gave him. I was thinking that Daxiao should own the services, and they should be controlled by the person who would benefit most from eliminating the financial fights." I nearly choked on my tea, to good effect.

They had run the idea past Justin, Joe, and Acton first. I suspect that it was Marshall's idea, but he sat and scanned everybody while Piccolo ran over to the white board and drew a diagram as if he was pulling it out of his head for the first time. He "guessed" at how much money we wasted each year to move development money around ($3,342,000). Piccolo isn't good at finance, so he asked Board members to help him put together a list of money transfers:

1. I transferred money to Macedon, Armstrong, Marshall, and the business units for requirements and analysis.
2. I transferred money to Armstrong for infrastructure.
3. When units approve development, testing, or deployment of requested services, I transferred money to Armstrong.
4. If they want to purchase equipment or vendor software, they transferred money to Marshall.
5. If a project runs over budget, I transferred more money to Armstrong.
6. If a project made it to production, I transferred money to Armstrong to operate it.
7. If an application or service required a change, I transferred money to Macedon and then to Armstrong.
8. If the project produced a reusable service, I started transferring the development and procurement money between the business units.

He then put up another calculation to show how much business time had been spent fighting reuse. He estimated only eight full-time equivalents over the period of a year, but the number was still $670,000 (more or less).

He suggested that as an alternative that we should give Macedon the Requirements budget, Armstrong the Development budget, and split the maintenance between Armstrong for traditional applications and me for services and processes, and then bill for usage on anything that is delivered. The more a service is used, the lower the per use price.

I asked where I would get the people to do the service maintenance, and he said they would be the people who were maintaining the services, which was true at the time. My heart was pounding until Piccolo gave me the sign that said, "HM knows".

Justin told everybody that he wanted us to vote on the proposal within a week. Everybody who was opposed had to recommend a different solution that would save at least $4,012,000. Any person who registered opposition had to provide reasonable justification for their numbers.

Resistance: Gunnar's response was, "That means that everything I do will have to pass through Macedon's organization." Barca's predecessor responded, "Like the rest of us".

Justin asked whether Macedon had failed to deliver on any promises. Gunnar complained that the problem was getting Macedon to make any promises. He makes you spend too much time explaining what you want, and sometimes you don't know what you want.

Then Piccolo suggested, just off the top of his head, of course, that maybe everybody could have their own individual Research and Development slush money, and that we could use the people that Armstrong placed on "permanent" loan with Marshall to show people how to refine their ideas before they went to Macedon. It would be a giant prototyping fund.

Chiu wanted to know how much slush. Justin almost fell off the fence. He suggested that the slush might be a percentage of their current budgets, and that it could grow or shrink depending upon their year-over-year contribution to the company. Gunnar wanted to know where we would find the slush. Justin said we could start with $4,012,000, more or less.

Piccolo explained to the managers that they were not actually losing their technology allocations, and the benefit was that they would no longer have to skimp with Macedon. He also said that if the new process didn't work, we could look for another way to eliminate the technology silos (SOA and otherwise), and they had no choice but to eliminate the silos that were costing Daxiao $500 million each year in a $2 billion budget. I had helped Piccolo and Guzman arrive at that number. He reported that we were working on an algorithm to allocate wasted resources to the respective units. He admitted that it was a form of blackmail, but he was fighting to get bonus increases for all of us out of the $500,000,000 that could be saved. That was a sweet touch.

Gunnar becomes furious when he is losing control. You could also tell that he was carrying almost 50% of the room with him. He decided not to fight the $500 million number. He insisted that Piccolo and I should first prove whether the $4,012,000 was a valid number. With Marshall's Thunk file, that was a no-brainer.

After the meeting, I started screaming at Joe for not telling me what he had in mind. They let me scream before they let Gunnar pound on the desk. Gunnar's assignment was to explain how the new scheme could decrease the quality of the service he was receiving since he continually asserted that it was already abominable. Later they explained that my surprised reaction helped prove that I was not trying to take over anything.

I'm sorry to report that Gunnar fired the person from marketing who was not able to put together a better proposal than Piccolo/Marshall. I'm happy to report that Van Amberg hired him, and he's doing a good job for BASE.

Now that the process is working and there is always at least $15 million worth of slush, Gunnar takes credit for helping me to work out the details of my proposal. He simply wanted to be sure that all the bases were covered before making such an unusual organizational change.

Help desk: (Incumbent: Marjory Hilfen):
User Support Team, Technology

By the time they had implemented only 20 services, a third of our open tickets were somehow related to services. We needed to know how to support services that span traditional business systems, and sometimes parts of the services run in different physical locations. The application developers were not doing anything wrong on purpose. They told us they were adding these new Web applications to our servers, and they told us they linked to functions on other servers, but we didn't understand what it meant until the problems started rolling in.

The first time I was involved was the time when they changed the document server out in Nebraska. A valued customer was sitting with the head of Sales & Marketing trying to work out a contract for a new product. He wanted to see who had signed the prior contract. Mr. Gunnar's assistant queried the new service that had been running quite well for over a month and nothing happened. She called us, and we couldn't find anything wrong in New Jersey. I called the help desk in Nebraska, and they said they didn't see a problem. They had installed this new bigger server because the service was very popular. The sales area called the operations area in Nebraska directly to request a fax of the documents. He was informed that the only person who did faxes wasn't in yet. When it's 8:30 A.M. in New Jersey, it is 7:30 out there. The "FAX" team had been reduced, so there was no one on the swing shift who knew how to run the new application.

I called the development team and the database team, and we all verified that neither the code nor the databases had been changed. Then the developer remembered that she had hard-coded the address of the image server into her point-to-point query. The new server had a different name, and it was on a different segment of their network. They had changed all their batch scripts to point to the new address, but it hadn't occurred to them to tell the developer. The top salesman had to humor the customer for an extra hour. He was embarrassed, and he becomes very angry when he's embarrassed. People are fired or relocated when Mr. Gunnar is angry, even if it's not their fault.

Now we have software that can trace service execution across the network. The developers agreed to create better error messages. "Service Failure" is not a good message. Even if there had been a good message, the logging process was turned off. Our people log everything now.

Knowledge consolidator:
(Incumbent: Maja Johanssen):
SOA Library Management Team, BASE

When Daxiao decided they were ready for Level 2 of the BASE evolution, they gave me a dream job for the person that loves data. BASE needed someone who loves risk that was also obsessed with accuracy. I still work with security, but now I report to the SOA communication specialist, and I am guided by the BASE manager and the SOA Architect.

Without my team and the data structures that we have created, the SOA Program would have a very difficult time. Even with perfect strategy management, automated methodology processes, and appropriate standards, all those things are not very useful if Program participants do not know where to find them, and they do not know about the supporting materials.

When I started, Mr. Marshall had already digitized almost 60% of the documentation for legacy systems and manual business processes. He used it for the century rollover and later for SOX compliance. The people on his compliance team knew where to find the information, and they knew how to use it. Other Daxiao people received information depending upon whom they knew. You needed to know who remembered where everything was filed and who had time to show you how to find what you needed.

I created a proprietary structure that would capture and provide access to all the data that the Program would need forever. It serves as the backbone for the communications management processes, business strategy, business operations, and technology. It is a database of databases, and a database about databases.

We have to ensure that Program participants provide us with the information that the Program requires so that it will be there when other people need it. That is why we call it the Knowledge Cooperative. Getting people to provide information to support our processes and procedures is not as hard as it could be because we have a BASE communications specialist (my boss). We still need to encourage people sometimes. The same people who are in a hurry to use what we provide to them often claim they don't have time to contribute the information store.

Now we have commercial enterprise content management (ECM) software to capture and distribute the information. With it I can capture, manage, store, preserve, and deliver structured and unstructured content related to SOA processes. It supports e-mail and instant messaging in decision-making processes. It provides audit trails, check-in and checkout functions, version control, and algorithms for content destruction. It minimized information loss, gaps, and redundancies. It supports knowledge sharing, personalization and standardization, workflow management, and archiving. There are filtering, routing, and notification features supported by corporate hierarchy and role structures. Personalized distribution will avoid information overload. Collaboration extensions allow simultaneous information processing, white boards, and video conferencing. It links to other applications such as asset management and configuration management files.

Now I concentrate on providing virtualization services for the things the content management product still cannot handle.

Planning specialist: (Incumbent: Anita Strauss): Requirements Management Team, Business

Project Planning: You have to know more to plan SOA projects, but we are using automation to make the planning easier. I must learn from the people who actually do the work so that we may improve planning accuracy as the Program progresses. Each project has at least four official plans, one when the project initiation manager lets business analysts proceed with analysis, one in the middle of analysis after they review the prototypes, one at the end of design, and one after the sponsor has approved test results. If they discover that they need to add more features (we try to avoid that), or the work is stalled for any of several reasons, we redo the plan. We document reasons for everything.

Project Initiation Plan: A skeleton plan, funded through the end of analysis, may be generated automatically. The business analyst proposes what type of Web services will be created and the automated process inserts activities, dependencies, deliverables, and durations that we usually associate with that type of development. We did 30 pilot projects before the "BIG SOA" Program became official, and they captured detailed metrics. These provided durations that are plugged into the plans. It's actually good for the developer because these are "learning metrics" when tasks took longer. Early in the design phase, the team leader and the project manager fine-tune roles, responsibilities, and dates.

Project budget multipliers: Hamilton Marshall comes up with some strange ideas, but this is one of the smartest. He makes them pay extra for every item on the Assumptions list and the risk/issues lists. Some items add as little as 2% to the budget, but some may add as much as 10%. Examples of 10% multipliers would be unclear specification of user roles, conflicting process requirements, or unclear security requirements. When clients complain, he explains that if they eliminate the assumptions, they eliminate the cost increments. He assigns monetary value to the increments by examining planning history for delayed and failed projects. Clients are usually willing to expend $10,000 worth of effort to save $200,000 on a $2,000,000 project.

Mr. Armstrong didn't agree with the extra charge initially (he disagreed with Mr. Macedon as a matter of principle). The boss is usually accommodating. We removed the multipliers. Two out of 12 projects were delivered close to the original estimates, but the clients were not happy with the results. Six of the twelve projects where we removed the multiplier came in over time and over budget by almost exactly the amount that we had suggested in the multiplier. Three ran over their budgets by double the amount that we had suggested. One was canceled before it was delivered. Mr. Armstrong began supporting the budget increments.

Automated notifications: There are automated routines that notify the support teams of support requirements and time frames. There are also reminders to the project managers that they should follow up in person.

Deliverables tracking: The process people were clever with this too. They know the names and locations of the artifact libraries. As soon as an approval is registered, it checks to see if there is an entry where the deliverable should be. If a deliverable exists, the process marks the task as completed. If something is missing, it sends another notification. If there are more activities and deliverables than originally defined, they must be entered into the plan.

Process coordinator - business (Incumbent: Evangeline Fuhrer) Requirements Management Team, Business

I want things to be the way that they were before SOA [...] I'm making a bad joke. What I really wish is that Mr. Barca and Mr. Chiu would allocate more people so that we could implement new processes and process improvements.

It is embarrassing to have external customers or internal clients complaining about problems for which we have solutions, but where the operations managers do not have time to do perform the acceptance tests.

In the old days, they would allocate a few days to a beta test of software that was already two or three months late. They would find a few showstoppers and send everyone back to the drawing board for three or four additional months. During that time, they would train people or prepare for the staffing adjustments (hiring, role creation, role revision, or job transition) required for the new process.

Since SOA:

1. Half of the functions required for a new process are already in the catalog.
2. The technology teams deliver new or updated services close to when they promised (and occasionally earlier), and the services work as specified.
3. The SOA competency team sends people to my process developers when additional expertise is required. We can deliver what we promised.
4. The communications team creates documentation along with the process developers (in two or three languages if necessary).
5. The training people prepare training materials wile the processes are being tested.
6. Security administration is prepared to authorize appropriate access.

Then, unless there is a critical new initiative, we wait until there are enough problems or enough embarrassment with the old process to generate a crisis. My boss, Alex Macedon says this is how things have to work until we have a better cultural change management program in place. Actually, the cultural change management program is rather robust, but there has never been an SOA mandate that forces operations managers to participate in the program.

For the time being, I am able to appear to produce miracles about once every two months. This is troublesome, but not nearly as hair-raising as it was in the days when we had crises without solutions already in hand.

Process coordinator - technology:
(Incumbent: Lane Schwimmer):
Compliance Management Team, BASE

Who does what, and in what order? I've spent 17 years of my life trying to figure that out. For the record, I don't really have to be an expert in the entire list of things on the methodology discipline list (Table A.15.1), but someone on my team is. Before I became an SOA Technology process coordinator, I was a SOX compliance specialist who specialized in technology processes. Before that, I was a client server developer, good enough that they wanted me to "bottle" what I did.

I was half way through implementing a Daxiao version of a unified process when they hired in the new CTO (CIO in most places). He decided the process wasn't agile enough to support his winking blinking flashy Web implementations.

He hired a group of agile consultants. It was impossible to integrate what they produced into the existing architecture platform.

Whereas they spent a lot of time with clients, and they tested to perfection in their testing environments, none of them seemed to understand that you shouldn't attach long-running database queries to databases that were tuned to give two-second response time for CICS queries. They also missed the concept of deadly embrace. The production databases started locking up. There were also a few security breaches.

When they asked me why I didn't tell them, I explained that I had. Then they asked why I hadn't more forcefully. They hired another team to extract Web query databases, and they gave me three months to "find other opportunities". Mr. Marshall had recently started working on something called SOX, and he said someone who understood good object oriented methods and bad agile methods would benefit his organization. Soon after I transferred, he had to take a leave of absence. I started reporting to Henry Yu instead.

They sent me to training in Web programming, XML, and agile methodologies. After I came back, Hank told me to figure out how to automate the Unified Process that I had been working on in addition to the agile processes. I had to add steps that ensured that the agile teams talked to infrastructure, database, testing, and security teams in the beginning of project planning, or action plan creation if the project is very small.

Process Automation: I created two processes (parts were manual, but as much as I could manage was automated), devised naming standards, provided documentation (it was all online with pretty pictures), tested them to the best of my ability and left them while I worked on other SOX projects that Mr. Marshall wanted when he came back from his leave.

After three months, six of us took courses in advanced XML, SOAP, and WSDL. The boss said he had a feeling something was about to happen. When we came back from training, five of us, with Hank working part time, updated my semi-automated processes to include SOAP and WSDL. Maja Johanssen was one of the five. She designed databases and content recognition software that we used to link the parts of the methodology together. She wrote access routines that could interface with a Web Services registry, planning software, asset inventory, work queues, and with project development libraries. Her theory was that any valid piece of information should only be entered once. She helped us pull it off, even though she had to sleep in Piccolo's palace for an entire month. Then Mr. Marshall did everything possible to break the automation that we had put together. He succeeded seven times. After three more months, the methodologies were almost HM proof.

By that time, the agile consultants were gone and some of my ex-coworkers were trying to clean up what the consultants had broken, with limited success. When Stein conducted technology audits, he knew where he was likely to find problems (he twisted my arm and forced me to tell all their secrets). He would then offer our semi-automated processes to help them remain agile while improving their effectiveness. They were forced to ignore Stein too. They didn't have time for his methodology silliness, even if we called it agile.

After four more months, the Agile Web project had over 100 services that worked from a technical point of view in the test environment running against a subset of the new extracted database. The DBA was working out a way to synchronize the two databases in real time. Meanwhile, they had new users who didn't know whether they agreed with the original specifications that had never been written anywhere except in the code. The project was nine months late, $10,000,000 over budget, and everyone that they could think of to blame was somewhere else doing something else.

I'm not sure how they pulled it off, but they managed to blame the boss (Mr. Marshall) for not telling them what they were doing fast enough, just as they had blamed me. It couldn't have been his fault. He had been on the unexplained leave of absence when they let the "agile" consultants leave and gave the project to internal people.

His penalty for not telling them fast enough was that he had six months to turn the project around. The people who had been ordered to ignore us became our team members.

Fortunately, most of the people were very talented (Armstrong wanted only the best for his pet project). The problem is that they were misguided. A few left the company (they went to work for the not-so-agile agile firm).

Mr. Marshall already had a complete plan hidden somewhere. He must have because it took him only two days to deliver it. He said the company had to do things his way until something was delivered, or else [...] some people say that he was looking for a reason to sue us.

He made them do unusual re-organizations. For example, the primary change management functions became the responsibility of the business units. They had absolute control of requirements, and they had total visibility into the requirements process (using my semi-automation and Maja's database), then they couldn't complain if the requirements were wrong. He also selected two of the best of the good people (they say he hired them), and they worked with me to make the automated processes even better.

That happened four years ago. After many iterations and controlled improvements, most of my methodology processes are fully automated. The process developer does most of the actual work. We use the same BPEL engine that the business people use.

I'm almost afraid to admit it, but I can honestly say that I am having fun.

Procurement specialist
(Incumbent: Rafael Onesti):
Vendor Management Team, BASE

Vendors trying to pay me compliments, as they often do, tell me that I am one of the most "impactful" people in Daxiao.

Right! I respond by saying that I have the least amount of discretionary power of any SVP in Daxiao. I am not allowed to authorize any purchase without having at least two other approvals first.

Nobody has been caught doing anything wrong since upper management tried to invent things that Hamilton Marshall was doing wrong five years ago. The first thing he did after he came back was to automate the 20% of the purchase processes that were not automated, including the automated approval processes. The technology people believed he fought for automated approvals to speed up the development processes, but Lorrie and I know that he wanted to automate himself out of harm's way. Everything we accomplish shows up on a dashboard that everyone in finance, legal, and on the internal Board can see.

There's a rumor that he had a heart attack and almost died because of what they did to him. I don't understand exactly why he came back, and he will not discuss it. When people ask me why I would take a job that almost killed Marshall, I say that I'm younger than he was, I'm in better shape than he was, the price was right (without mentioning the 20% raise that Marshall showed me how to negotiate), and that the automation provides a shield from the types of accusations they made against him. Any hypothetical wrongdoing may be proven or disproved in less than 30 minutes.

The next question is what I needed to do to qualify for the job. The answer is that it is good that I am a lawyer, and it is good that I had Macedon's original job (logistics) before Mittelman booted me into legal to make room for his wife's brother-in-law's cousin. It is also good that I impressed Marshall while I was in logistics and Guzman for the year that I worked for him.

Coordinating purchases is actually a subset of logistics and deals with most of the complications. With me doing what I do here, they were able to let Macedon play at Requirements Management.

Project Initiation Manager:
(Incumbent: Alexander Macedon):
Requirements Management Team, Business

On this detail, I am responsible for ensuring that client requests for technology support are completed to a level that can be accurately implemented. I also help the business decide whether the request should be implemented. Then I (my testing people) run around to the other side of development and make sure the technology people delivered what was requested. It's rather like hitting a ball, and then running to catch it.

Since I joined Daxiao, I realize that it is easier to move the equivalent of a mid-sized city half way around the world than it is to roll out some of these services. If someone ordered me to get an aircraft carrier across the Indian Ocean in a certain number of days, we would agree that we were talking about a large floating object that carried machines that fly. If you pointed it in the right direction and put in enough plutonium, it arrived within 12 hours of the designated time. You couldn't lose it, even if it went straight down. The satellite network guaranteed that. The enemy (a competitor) could sink it, but it was not likely that it would sink itself. It wouldn't turn into an (empty) supertanker or a diesel powered submarine before it reached its destination.

For the first four years at Daxiao, I could also get the contents of 20 cargo containers with a manifest containing 170 different widgets to the right place on 10 assembly lines in four different countries, and I was seldom off by more than two days. Now my projects come in on time about 55.8% of the time, and I usually need somebody from BASE to maintain that 55.8%. But, I will not be outdone. If there is a way to make this thing work, I will find it.

I accepted the assignment to prove a point. After spending so much time picking on Armstrong especially, and on Marshall to a lesser degree, although I like the boy, I couldn't refuse the opportunity to show them how to do a better job. Armstrong would promise me a stealth bomber and deliver a puddle hopper, for the same cost and three months late. Marshall would deliver exactly what I requested, usually on time, but I always felt that he was inflating the requirements.

After Marshall gave me what I asked for, he would also give me what I needed. He wasn't a kid anymore, and he knew his business. He'd make me put in another project request if he felt I had been particularly nasty. I was particularly nasty more than I'd care to admit. Marshall was doing this for fun, and I made his job less than fun. He returned the favor.

I figured out that we are dealing with things that you can't actually see, requested by people who don't know what they want, and delivered by people who were making the same sounds, but speaking different languages. Before Marshall started his Roles/Activity database, the business people usually didn't have a clue regarding what their technology teams did.

The corporate architect, Dan Piccolo, nails down the strategy for at least two weeks each quarter, and he convinces senior managers to agree (hypothetically) to consistent SOA work prioritization guidelines. Piccolo acts silly, but he is one of the most structured people that I know, even more than Van Amberg is. Piccolo will make you laugh while you to tie all the laces on all your shoes, although you may not know why you should. Van Amberg will try to explain why you should tie your shoes, including probabilities of problems if you don't tie them.

Marshall has less patience for silliness. He will tie your shoelaces more quickly than you can see, but if you annoy him, he will let you tie your shoes together and try to run. He will also let you leave them untied and try to run. He said he ruined his career trying to prevent scraped knees and elbows. Now he specializes in bandages and reconstructive surgery.
Ironically, many people started to request "Marshall Plans" (structured shoe securing). If he assists you with creation of a plan, you may not like the dates, but you can bet your bonus on it, which most of us do. If you change one of his plans, you're on your own. The part about paying extra money for assumptions used to annoy me. I quickly realized that it was a stroke of genius.

Shoelaces were not as important to Armstrong, although recently he is better at his job. He may never be as good as Marshall is, but he delivers on time twice as often as he once did. Most importantly, he no longer tries to help his (theoretical) buddies make end runs around me. Ninety percent of the time when he tried, his (theoretical) buddies attacked him when he failed to deliver. It took him almost a year before he figured that he could stop dropping live grenades into his own shorts. If he wasn't a friend of Mittelman's, and he didn't have Marshall to clean up his messes, he would have been gone long ago.

Project manager - business technology:
(Incumbent: Bruce Sneller):
Business Technology Team, Technology

I'm still getting accustomed to the new name for my role. I'm still officially in the technology sector, but they managed to stick "business" in the middle to emphasize that my goal is to support the business.

The job is easier now. I'm not supposed to accept requests from the business people until they pass requirements and analysis reviews. Work is reviewed again after my people complete design. We lose brownie points (I mean SOA points) if we do not code what the business approves. If the business wants significant changes after we start working, they reset the clock. That is good.

I delivered one of the first official Web services projects. We had to link the customer database to the image processing system that handled legal documents. The project was small, but intense. We didn't have to hide the project as we did in the beginning. In fact, someone was watching our every move. We had a high-level vendor consultant and a technical writer following everyone around.

We sat with the business analyst for three hours. We experimented with screen layouts while the consultant did business event modeling. The client mentioned that they had freed him up for the next two months to work with us on this. The senior managers were having an SOA challenge, but he didn't know the details.

The client gave us a customer number and password for the test database and a folder number and password for the images database out in Nebraska. After my technical people had what they needed, they left, but the consultant sat with the client for another hour discussing Web services concepts. I was worried that he would get too many silly ideas.

Our team had the prototype running in two days. They hard-coded the customer and folder numbers into the data access routines, and they hard-coded the passwords into the user interface code. We knew where the test customer data was, and the architect found the test images database in less than a day. The client/user loved the prototype until he tried to put in a customer number that was different from the one he gave us. That was where the reality started.

The consultant saved us. He explained that this was merely a proof-of-concept. We proved that we could make Web queries to databases in different applications on different technology platforms that were 1500 miles apart.

Then the client had to answer or find the answers for 50 standard questions in the requirements gathering template on the enhanced ReMain (requirements tracking) system. There were other templates for analysis, design, development, and testing. We had to create and archive four different versions of the project plan, document and automate the original manual retrieval processes, and agree that testing, security, and data quality requirements should be established as close to the beginning as possible. They emphasized that security is much more rigorous when services span platforms.

After 14 weeks, the service actually was ready for production.

Beginning next week, we will work with the project managers from the other pilot teams to formalize a sequence of Product Creation steps for future SOA projects.

Project manager - SOA: (Incumbent: Olivia Reed): SOA Implementation Team, BASE

SOA project processes: I delivered two of the first five services. Then they cut back on all my legacy assignments and asked me to work with the SOA team to put together three SOA plans (short-term (very), medium-term (short actually), and long-term (medium according to the old time lines). I spent another month working with the technology process coordinator (methodology person) to explain the activities we performed to create reusable services. For the last three months, I've been working with a process developer to plug steps into ReMain. ReMain supports automation of development from requirements through deployment. They also trained me in what they call soft skills; I had to become more expert in handling people.

SOA project planning: They said there would be a planning change. They told me to work with Hank Yu, representatives from three different vendors, two other SOA project managers-to-be, a security specialist, a testing specialist, three database administrators, and the head of enterprise architecture to create a master SOA project plan.

We worked together in facilitated sessions four hours a day for a month. They gave us homework.

This plan is huge. It contains every SOA-related project activity that any of us could think of at the time. It also contains items from HM's roles/activity (Thunk) database. It will become the base for future planning.

It sounds insane, but Dr. Piccolo had one of his friends perform a resource utilization study. They decided that an experienced planner could cut the master plan down to a short-term plan in two days to a week. On the other hand, if the client pushed for a short-term plan that left out critical steps, a one-month project could be delayed by a month or two. He said it is easier to take steps out that you don't need than to add steps that you forgot. At the time, 65% of our projects were at least a month late.

SOA project kick-off: They finally gave me another real Web Services project. I was lucky enough to have seven of my old team back. I'm not happy because the team goes back to the Team Pool as soon as we finish a project. The SOA Program coordinator calls it Velcro® management. I'm supposed to hold everything together when it needs to be together, and release everything quickly when we are finished. I have to be strong yet flexible. I call it loosely coupled management for loosely coupled services. We have to work well together, and then break the session after we deliver the (service) messages.

The planning specialist sent us a preliminary project plan. I thought it was humorous. It was a stripped down version of the SOA master plan that we had just completed.

We met with the clients and the project initiation manager in a two-hour meeting: It was the official project turnover and the first design session. The analysis has been done already.

Role assignment: The first day I was back with my team, we reviewed the list of roles the methodology people said we were expected to assume. This wasn't as difficult for us as it might have been for other teams because I had helped the methodology team define the roles according to the way we worked together. We voted three times until we agreed on a primary and backups for the team leader, software architect, regular application developer, SOA developer, integration, and deployment roles. I had to enter the names and roles into a project template.

Tools: At the first meeting, we agreed on the tools we were going to use. Two of the products needed updates. I sent a request to the procurement specialist and notified the process developer. We added the UDDI/ebXML catalog to our list. That didn't exist when we started. I sent the list of roles and tools to security administration to ensure that we had the necessary authorizations.

Quality management coordinator:
(Incumbent: Aine O'hara):
Quality Assurance Team, Business
Title: The senior person in this role is the VP and Director of Quality Assurance reporting to the SVP of Information Logistics.

When people ask me why I don't use the title "quality assurance manager", I respond that I do not assure quality. My specialty is exactly as the title says. I coordinate the activities of the teams that assure quality. I am concerned about four primary areas. They are:

1. Business requirements verification.
2. Technology performance with a subsidiary specification related to WS-I (Web services interoperability).
3. Data quality verification.
4. Security requirements verification.

My job was tough before, and now SOA requires that I do almost twice as many things. Fortunately, I have more sophisticated testing products and more assistance in the form of testing process automation. They also remind me how lucky I am to be at Daxiao because most other companies are 15 months to two years behind us in SOA testing sophistication.

I remind them that those other companies don't have Niklas Gunnar who refuses to allocate time for testing, and then try to get me fired when something blows up. They remind me that the other companies tend to have their own Gunnars, but they do not necessarily have Alex Macedon (my current boss), Valery Van Amberg (my former boss), and Hamilton Marshall to guide me through Gunnar attacks.

They also remind me of the number of my processes that have been automated, especially the Testing Requirements Analyzer, software that generates a matrix indicating which types of tests should be performed depending of the scope and importance of the change being implemented. The matrix also estimates the amount of time that will be required for testing and the associated cost.

The tool can evaluate requirements in seven or eight dimensions, while I feel as if I can only handle only three. Before HM's people built the matrix, I could guess with about 90% accuracy, but often I could not explain why I worried about problems that no one else could see. The business clients and the technology people often accused me of inflating the estimates. With the new processes, I give both areas a computer-generated list that recommends from 2 to 20+ test types along with testing sequences. Then they can tell me which tests they do not wish me to coordinate.

The compliance teams are automatically notified when they request elimination of tests that have historically found problems. They follow-up when they believe something important may be omitted. During the first six months that the test coordination matrix was in place, problems occurred in 60% of the areas that would have been covered by the eliminated tests. The problems were 2 to ten times more expensive than the costs of performing the recommend tests.

Mr. Marshall says we have to do it this way. If you spend extra money and problems do not occur, you are accused of wasting money. If you do not spend the money, and major problems occur, you are perceived as adding value for a while. Then the cycle repeats itself. Fortunately, documented maintenance costs and problem costs associated with major problems are helping to reduce the time we spend in the "skip unnecessary testing" doldrums.

Requirements Analyst:
(Incumbent - Eduardo Ricco)
Requirements Management

What I do now is not exactly on the cutting edge of philosophical thought, but it pays about five times as much as I made as a teaching assistant when I was working on my PhD. Sometimes, one must make sacrifices.

The title of my role confuses people. I do not help the business people decide what they think they want initially. That would drive me crazy. I know what they need most of the time, but they never listen. It takes them two or three weeks to wiggle their way around to what I can figure out in about 15 minutes. I usually join the first hour or so of a requirements gathering session, write suggestions for the business analyst, and then leave. There are about 200 of business analysts, and 10 requirements analysts, so that's usually all the time that I can spare.

My job is to analyze requirements that the business analysts deliver to me. My tasks include:

1. Verifying that the requirements are clear and reasonably complete. If they are not, I work with business analysts to clarify them. Sometimes, if basic information is missing, I fill in the blanks and notify the business analyst and the client of what I have done. Few people complain. Requests that I can neither clarify nor complete are rejected.
2. Making sure that the requirement doesn't duplicate or overlap something that:
   - Is already running in production.
   - Somebody is working on.
   - We rejected already.
   - Already exists in the work backlog. The business analysts try to do this, but they have trouble translating what their users say to the terminology used to record existing requirements. The common terminology list helps, but keeping track of the 5 alternate terms for the same concept sometimes gives even me a headache. If requirements overlap, they must have a meeting or two or three until they reach a consensus. When that is not possible, requirements go into a suspended work queue.
3. Ensuring that work requests conform to business strategy. Sometimes the strategy evaluation gets fuzzy, either because a business unit forced Jay to include a fuzzy strategy statement. If I can't "defuzz it", I tack a fuzzy specification premium to the project price. Then they must either clear up the strategy statement or adjust the specification. Several of the fuzzy ones go onto the suspended work queue.
4. Checking to see whether the request agrees all the policy policies (<- that is not a typo). If there is a conflict, I pull groups together to resolve the conflicts. If conflicts cannot be resolved, I reject the request.
5. Evaluating the issues list (including risks and assumptions lists). It took me a while to convince clients and analysts that every assumption posed a risk to something, but they finally got the message. I tack on a premium percentage based on recommendations from Marshall's assumptions price list. He's usually right. He doesn't appear to be that smart, but I used to have trouble thinking my way around him. I don't bother much any more. If Marshall says we should do something a certain way, it's usually worth a try. Every now and then, I actually learn something from him. Even better, on a few occasions I have taught him a thing or two. That's when I really feel great.

Lately, almost 70% of the requirements get past these initial gateways. Then the serious work begins:

1. I pay particular attention to the security requirements. That's the area that's most important, and the area that they know the least about.
2. I look at the data requirements. The analysts are better at that now, but they often leave out the quality requirements. If they do, I try to slip something in that will provide a slight improvement over what they already have. Maja helps me with this. She can scan formatted text record layouts with up to 100 characters per line and find a 1-byte data error in 1000 records in two minutes. There's no stopping her when she has a data validation tool.
3. I look at service level agreements. I make sure they have one that is practical and achievable without costing the company too much money or causing us too much embarrassment. If they put something in that's ridiculous, I put a price tag on it. When I explain the cost components (actually when the Project Implementation Manager does the explaining), they usually back down.
4. I assign a project difficulty rating that will later be reviewed by the software architect.

Finally, I package the successful requests into a bundle, recommend a priority, and pass them back to a project initiation manager.

Research scientist: (Incumbent: Wen Li): Research & Development team, corporate

I feel like a ping-pong ball. First, I transferred to the compliance team and moved to America from my job with Mr. Chiu in manufacturing. It was a friendly transfer. Mr. Chiu wanted someone to help him understand how the Americans worked, Mr. Marshall wanted someone who could audit the processes in China, and I wanted a chance to be near my family in America.

Mr. Gunnar decided he wanted a research unit in sales and marketing, he had made friends with Mr. Chiu, and Mr. Chiu recommended me. I transferred to Mr. Gunnar, but I was not happy. Mr. Gunnar was erratic and difficult in comparison to Mr. Marshall who was demanding but very supportive. Mr. Marshall continued to support me in every way that he could, even after I went to work for Mr. Gunnar. He assigned Hank Yu to assist me. This included writing special utility and security software to support my research clients.

That did not make sense because Mr. Gunnar seems to have very negative feelings toward Mr. Marshall. On the other hand, Mr. Marshall deals with many things in ways that would only make sense in my culture. He confused Mr. Gunnar with kindness.

Six months ago, Mr. Gunnar made Mr. Chiu unhappy by moving his requests down on my priority list. Mr. Chiu complained to Mr. Mittelman and soon Dr. Piccolo could make an argument that Research and Development should belong to Dr. Piccolo. He has degrees from three very important schools in the United States, and two of them perform important technology research.

I have a larger staff, and I have time to support Mr. Gunnar, Mr. Chiu, and Mr. Marshall in return for the assistance that I still receive from Hank Yu.

Security administrator: (Incumbent: I. C. Gates): User Support Team, Technology

Today I started working on the security hierarchy for a service registry and catalog. They expect me to use this new database to control each programming project. There are four versions that required Daxiao-created services to keep them synchronized. There are only 50 services in it now, but they're treating it like Fort Knox.

The database team is confused because the infrastructure people gave them blade servers to build this thing on. The blades are in three different buildings in two different states. There are complicated fail over and backup processes. They started running production level backup and recovery jobs when the product had only been in-house for a week. It's sitting behind three firewalls, but everyone inside Daxiao and our alliance partners will be able to browse through it. Fewer people will be able to change it.

They gave us a list of over 100 roles and an access control matrix along with the list of roles. It looks complicated, but is still simpler than setting up rights for each individual user.

I believe they are over doing it, but the security specialist, the SOA architect, and Maja want it. Maja tends to get what she wants. They have enough computing power and big enough pipes that the logging doesn't slow anything down.

The catalog has more logging features than any product I've ever seen. They don't want me to turn any of the logging. As of this moment, there are 36 fields associated with every catalog entry. I have to secure every field individually. They want me to log who changes a field and especially who changes the metadata describing field contents.

It was tedious, but it runs. They'll decide that it is excessive eventually, but for the time being, this is what they want to pay me to do.

Service assurance: (Incumbent: Allen Forbes): Data Center Team, technology

I like my new job title, new tools for the job, and I like the facts that there is always an availability architect, a deployment specialist, and a network architect within 20 feet of us at all times. We track processes as they jump from a UNIX box to the mainframe and then to a Windows Server. I know how to pretend to be in Ireland or China when I must. We have information bouncing off satellites and running on underground cables, and I can trace that too.

The new software helps us keep this supertanker on course. Supertanker may not be the proper allusion. Daxiao is more like a jumbo jet with rotors. Sometimes we have to fly straight up or sideways to get where they need us to be.

We don't have as many operators as before, but we make more money because we know more. Everybody has certifications in at least two areas, thanks to Dr. Piccolo and Mr. Armstrong. I am certified in Tivoli (IBM) and HP Operations management.

I was in the bunch of people who used to believe Dr. Piccolo was a snob. He may be a snob, but not the way you would think. He favors people who accumulate skills and knowledge. The people that took advantage of the training he promoted, even if it was off shift, are doing well. With the training, I understand the Mainixowsco (Mainframe, UNIX, Windows, and Cisco) dashboards that Ward Hooper helped design.

Mr. Marshall used to help us get as much training as he could, but he didn't have much of a budget before the silly midget arrived. In those days, the lazy people could always move to the back of the training line. Mr. Marshall finally has money. He used some of it to expand the Knowledge Cooperative which we use to replay and reinforce the formal training that Dr. Piccolo encourages management to make available to us.

For the record, the people who voluntarily moved themselves to the back of the training line don't work here anymore. As SOA progressed, some of them simply did not know enough to handle their jobs.

Stakeholder: (Incumbent: Shen Chiu): Manufacturing

I am responsible for Global Manufacturing, but I am speaking as a stakeholder with feelings of conflict.

I do not like SOA. We expected that our superior production would position me to take over the merged company by now, but we have lost our advantage. SOA is helping all the units to become as efficient as my people were before the merger. The new SOA processes are more efficient. My people have to work to catch up with them. That is good for Daxiao earnings, but it is bad for my career ambitions.

Hank Yu, Wen Li, and He Wei are helping them to succeed. They were on the fringes in the original Daxiao, but now they are helping the new one to do well. My technology people (Armstrong's people for the last four years), leap at the opportunity to work with the newest technology. I have welcomed them to the inner circles, but I do not believe that they understood what I was saying.

It is another mental conflict that I do not personally dislike Marshall. He is probably one of the few people in Goodsand who can teach me anything.

He makes sure that my people receive the best training in the world so they can be reassigned when manual jobs are eliminated. They really appreciate the online courses that are presented in Chinese.

Marshall worries me, because I do not understand him. I wonder what is on his mind when he studies us without saying anything. He is much too quiet. We cannot find his weaknesses. He may be better at hiding things than we are, even while he pretends to share everything he does in three languages. Gunnar agrees.

I hate SOA communications. We are losing control of my company due to a tainted Vietnamese woman whose first language is French.

Gunnar shares my dislike for this woman, and we have limited her effectiveness. I will be sure to award Gunnar when I am in control again. I already owed him when he helped me to save face after Ling's ill-timed greediness.

We expected to be able to hide behind language and cultural barriers. There will always be barriers, but Maçon is helping people to see over them. Managers at Goodsand offended us many times in the beginning. I depended upon those offenses to keep our group isolated and strong. The offenses have decreased significantly. She sends people to school to learn our culture. They emphasize things that should not be done that would offend us.

Marshall says that if you understand a language, you understand the culture. Everyone on their team has taken elementary courses in Chinese. They use people who are retired from the U.S. Diplomatic corps for the training. Every manager on the SOA BASE team has extensive exposure to our language. Van Amberg will never speak proper Chinese because he cannot get the tones right, but I believe that he understands most of what we are saying. Marshall has a speech difficulty, even in English, but he understands better than Van Amberg does. Both can read and write the simplified symbols. Some of my people like them because they really work hard to understand. It limits our ability to keep the old ways in place.

Jin, new second in command after Ling's departure, sometimes reminds me that we would be a subsidiary of our most hated internal competitor, and I would not be here if we had not accepted the offer from Goodsand. He is right, but I wonder how Marshall is beginning to affect his thoughts and the thoughts of my other managers.

Marshall will retire soon, and then I will have my plans in order, unless Jin figures out a way to replace me before Marshall departs.

Strategist - corporate (Incumbent: J. Stanley Johnson) Enterprise Integration

When Dan Piccolo asked me to run his strategy management team at Daxiao, I thought it was a joke. He had actually taken a job as an employee in his brother-in-law's company.

I declined, primarily because it was a no-win situation. Managers in Daxiao did what they wanted to do, when and if they wanted to do something, and Mittelman had built a comfortable platform on the fence.

Furthermore, I would be helping Dan implement something called SOA, rather than merely thinking about the possible organizational consequences implied by SOA. Dan's habit of actually sneaking in work, even with his bare hands, is often frightening. He says it helps to anchor his thoughts, so that future thoughts have more validity.

I changed my mind after I met Hamilton Marshall and Alex Macedon. They agreed with my assessment of Daxiao, but they proposed that we could work together to show the organization when their gunslingers were doing more harm than good.

Marshall had ideas for dashboards that could illustrate the complete strategy and strategy alignment in real time. It would also show when organizations deviated from strategy and why. He also suggested that we should have more frequent strategy assessments and evaluations. This would allow gunslingers to become visionaries, who would be "ahead" of the strategy for no more than three months.

Macedon suggested that if I turned strategy into a competition with rewards, more of our senior managers might be willing to cooperate. Then he ordered me to use the opportunity for an up-close evaluation of several of my pet theories while receiving a reliable income stream. He issues orders without being aware that he is doing it.

I don't like taking orders, and I was spoiled by the freedom associated with the academic environment, but the idea of a handsome steady income stream was attractive. I accepted a 15-month consulting assignment, which has been extended three times.

For our first strategy session, we were locked up in a conference center in the Rockies without cell phones or access to e-mail during the day. Only the facilitators had access to computers, and they were used to retrieve information about Daxiao that could be used to help define the existing strategy. That was the shortest strategy session up to that time.

The first topic that I introduced was SOA and the fact that we felt it would be a strategy component that could reduce technology redundancy and provide competitive advantages. I realized that all the managers were either afraid to try SOA and fail, or they were afraid of what would happen if they don't try. They wished to avoid problems that the CTO barely survived.

There was a general feeling of "here we go again", even after the hour-long introductory session. Gunnar took a nap during the SOA overview session, but Mittelman did not. That was an indication that everyone should at least act as if he or she would consider SOA. It also indicated that Mittelman needed to talk to Gunnar, who is usually hyper-attentive. He doesn't want to miss a single shrug or eye blink that could have political implications.

We separated the participants into teams for breakout sessions, and asked each team to return with ideas for SOA implementations that would solve major competitive problems. The team that came back with the best ideas for SOA implementations would get priority status on the company helicopter (behind Mittelman) for a month. No one was allowed to vote for his or her ideas.

In Session #2, we distributed the prior year's business strategy and told them to update it. We asked for two plans, one tactical (for a year or less), and one for the next two years. By the end of the year, we would try for the five-year plan.

We had to get into a strategy groove first. Dan had convinced the head of finance to calculate the expense associated with one year's strategy alignment problems. We used that to show how much money could be saved if strategy was updated every three months (without benefit of the off-site).

Just as in past sessions, the managers realized that their top priorities were stepping on each other's territories. That year's facilitator helped them through their traditional conflicts faster than usual. Dr. Baldwin is a no-nonsense woman who actually ran the company for six months from her administrative chair before her prior boss died. She runs the personnel department now. She was privy to information (including business unit "secrets") that everyone in the room wondered how she had discovered. She also helped them to identify the gaps that were not being addressed. After the items were prioritized, Dan promised to send a corporate analyst to each business unit to work on the details of the strategy synchronization among the business units.

After the session, I asked Dan why Dr. Baldwin wasn't the corporate strategist. Dan replied that Mittelman needed Dr. Emery-Baldwin for tougher assignments. I wanted to spend more time with that person.

During Session #3 on the second day, the managers had to tie strategic goals to strategy enablers, and 75% of the enablers were tied to technology. Mid-level managers from technology architecture and development teams with a couple of Acton consultants were in the joint session, but they were not allowed to say anything, even after the senior managers began to point-out their stickiest technology problems. They listened, typed, and produced worksheets that we used to prioritize the problems. The #1 problem was relationships with vertical partners and supply-chain management. That is one of my favorite research areas.

Then, with Mittelman's permission, we tricked them. Every business unit had to volunteer two or three their most AVERAGE people to work in a new business/technology unit that would handle sticky problems, based on the priority list. That was the beginning of **Requirements Management**. Macedon insisted that he needed special assistance from the compliance organization to ensure that his new team did not create compliance problems, especially when dealing with external clients. That was the beginning of **Partner Networks**.

In Session #4, the head of corporate communications demonstrated a working prototype of the dashboards that would be available for strategy monitoring. It already showed the strategy items defined in Session #2, business units responsible for the strategy items, major business and technology projects their relationships to strategy items, and associated expenses.

That required 90 minutes of the session, 30 minutes of which the managers spent trying to break the prototype. There were suggestions for improvement, but it didn't break (Marshall, Maçon, and Maja are good!). That is what nailed the new strategy process.

Thus, the managers believed us when we showed them that we had several long-running expensive projects that did not have obvious ties to the strategy.

The breakout for Session #4 was to look at each strategy item and determine whether:

1. The communications specialist (with help from Maja Johanssen) had properly aligned the projects.
2. The communications specialist has incorrectly identified unaligned projects.
3. The strategy needed to be updated.
4. The unaligned projects should be canceled, suspended, or merged with other projects.

For this, we gave them back their cell phones and computers. They were also assigned dedicated specialists from corporate finance and dedicated business analysts.

The objective of Session #5 on the third day was to adjust the strategy based on information discovered during the breakout section of Session #4. Managers came back and reported:

1. The project is aligned correctly.
2. The project should be moved to a different strategy item.
3. The project should be moved to multiple strategy items.
4. The project should be killed (with approximate impact -staff and budget - and timetables).
5. **They didn't know enough about the project to make a decision.** Ten projects that had already cost the company at least $1 million fell into this category. Dan promised to assign a corporate analyst to work with the responsible manager on each of these projects.

This time, we were linked to the information systems at Daxiao, and Ellison's people were updating the dashboard every 15 minutes. We left with revision #2 of the strategies, and scheduled a half-day teleconference a week later to finalize the strategies.

Subject matter expert:
(Incumbent: Jesus Gonzalez, Esq.):
Compliance Team, BASE

If I hear one more comment about going to talk to Jesus, I swear I will hurt somebody (intellectually, not physically). I'm really a pacifist. I specialize in international law, with a specialty in trade and commerce.

I am expected to allocate at least 10% of my time to being a subject matter expert (SME), at least for the next four months. Joe Guzman and Hugo Stein both try to adjust my workload so that I can accommodate this requirement. They say that someone has to put the brakes on (or at least guide) the slick services and processes that Hank, Maja, Macedon, and Maurer create so quickly.

The result is that my fellow SMEs or I must attend design reviews for any services that are built to accommodate cross-border requirements. Lately, there are many of those. My bosses believe that 400 hours or less over a one-year period may save millions of dollars in litigation fees or penalties. Joe is usually right and Marshall has a better track record than Joe does. Thus, I am half of the legal SME team.

I have to answer questions such as when do you legally transfer inventory from a warehouse in China to a warehouse in Mexico, especially if the inventory is parked in a container ship off the Canary Islands because there is a hurricane brewing in the Atlantic ocean. I suppose things could be worse.

Tool administrator: (Incumbent: Randall Smythe):
Infrastructure Technology Team, Technology

I'm settling into my new assignment. Before this, I was an infrastructure architect. They made me a Project Manager for SOA tools and middleware products. I do nothing other than SOA, even though I work on the Technology side, not BASE. I worked with the procurement people since the last reorganization, but I never imagined it could become a full-time job. After I sat and listed all the things we have to do, I realized that it is a big job, and it is important.

Tool problems: Many of the vendors bundled several categories in tools into one package. We have to match the tools to the standards. We have overlapping everything. A few of the tools need to be updated. Contract terms and licenses have to be reviewed. When clients went around the procurement processes, tools were seldom integrated into the infrastructure or with other. Some of the tools were used once and abandoned. There are better products that could replace some of the older tools - older is 18 months old these days.

Tool administrator Objectives: We have to select an optimal tool in each category, depending upon conformance to standards, product quality, user preference, or ease of use. Then we have to integrate them into the infrastructure and with each other. The hardest part, which is also the fun part, is that we have to automate the development cycle (I mean product delivery cycle) from end to end. The teams will be able to choose among development tools, depending upon the types of services they are developing. If they choose to deviate from the process, that will raise exception flags, and they will have to document what they are doing and how. If their way turns out to be a better way, the process team modifies the procedures so that everyone benefits from process improvements.

They were thinking about moving me into procurement, but the team manager convinced them that I needed to stay closer to the people who can help me make this work. I have my own development team, and they loaned me a process developer to show us how to automate what we do.

Tool specialist: (Incumbent: Lloyd Howe): Business Technology Team, Technology

Not all tool specialists are experts with the latest PERL parser. I have been a COBOL batch programmer for 27 years, and you would be amazed at the things I can do with COBOL. I sometimes write two or three "quick and dirty" programs a day to help analysts discover something they need to know for impact or feasibility studies. I also maintain some of the stickiest and most ancient programs in critical mainframe systems. They are eliminating my job. First, they made me refactor the code for the input edit program that I inherited from Marian when she retired six years ago. I must ensure that the program does the same thing that it always did, only more effectively.

When I complained that I didn't have time due to the number of requests I received from my clients, they made me stop taking requests from clients. I had to deliver the requests that I already had to a new group called Requirements Management.

They gave me a process for doing the refactoring and a plan that made absolutely no sense.
They wanted me to spend three weeks reformatting the program (with fancy new reformatting software).
I had two weeks to define the metadata for the fields I was editing (with assistance from a data specialist).
I had to change the names of the fields to long business names. For example, ACCT1 became PARTNER_ACCOUNT_NUM and ACCNOIN became INTERNAL_ACCOUNT_NUM.
After I changed the names, I had a week to put the "if, then, else" parts of the program into a rules engine (with assistance from a business analyst).
They gave me six weeks to test it! The same business analyst that put the rules in the rules engine also built test cases and test scripts and stored them in the automated testing software. The testing showed that the program executed in 6 minutes with the rules engine and 4 minutes without it. They bumped up the priority, so that it would run in the same amount of time as it did before.

This seemed like too much effort to fix a program that only edited 20,000 records each night. Meanwhile, no one was handling my work requests. When I mentioned that to the business analyst, she told me that once the new version of my program is installed, we wouldn't have to change the program as often. She said that 15 of the change requests on my old work queue could have been completed in 5 minutes with an hour of testing using new testing processes. Furthermore, they had discovered that three out of the 20 requests that I delivered to Requirements Management conflicted with other requests on the same queue. That wasn't a surprise. I always waited to see whether the sales people or the finance people had more clout before I implemented one of the conflicting changes.
Now they have a rules engine, and the rules can be reviewed by a rules committee without having to involve developers in business turf conflicts. The rules engine also allows different rules for different units if that is appropriate.

We tested the thing, put it back into production, and it worked. I'm good at what I do, even if it is "only batch". But, I was worried because the rules engine had taken away 90% of my work.

The very next day, Josh came to me and explained that my next job was to turn the editing program into a Web service that could be used by everybody. He gave me the batch legacy adaptation process, another plan, the curriculum for the three courses they wanted me to take, and the list of people who would support me. I am a BATCH MAINFRAME PROGRAMMER. I felt sure that somebody somewhere was trying to make me leave.

Hamilton Marshall is a real big shot now, but he made time to see me. He explained that if I do this right, I'd prove that I was ready for a new role, legacy adaptation specialist, and that would ensure my job for as many years as I want it. He also explained that I had always been smart enough to do what needed to be done, but that I was overly afraid of change.

Marshall is the only executive in the company that I have never caught lying. He must, but I have never caught him. I have no choice but to trust him. Yesterday, I enrolled in the SOA overview course, the first training that I've taken since they replaced our "green screens" with PCs.

User: (Incumbent: Richard Testa):
Sales and Marketing Team, Business

I don't like the new automated process for handling my sales input. It takes away my wiggle room, and I'm becoming a data entry clerk. I used to be able to scribble the basic information on a form, let the clerical people figure out the details, and let them take the heat if anything went wrong. If they didn't have the right attitude, I was usually able to get them moved to where they wouldn't annoy me. I learned from Gunnar.

Now I have to enter everything myself. They set it up so that little typing is required. They have windows that open up to show you customer identification information, part numbers (showing exact inventory on hand and location), and available delivery dates. After you approve the information that you entered, the order confirmation goes to the customer immediately. If they are waiting for the order, they may approve it immediately. User support people are available 24 hours to provide order entry assistance. The entire process takes about 20 minutes if I follow the procedures and two days over a two-week period when I don't.

I simply do not like the idea of being my own clerk. I complained that all this data entry was taking away from my sales time. The process coordinator showed me how it provided me with more sales time. I no longer needed to spend time proving who made a mistake on an entry, explaining why the parts they ordered were delayed, or they were the wrong parts (the clerk spoke to a customer that thought she was talking about last week's order).

Furthermore, there are no more clerical people to fire. If I wanted help, I could enter the sales information into a formatted e-mail and ship it to Bangalore where a clerk would enter it for me. I tried it a few times, there were problems, and it took me two days to locate the exact clerk who could demonstrate that I had typed the wrong quantity in the e-mail for 2 of the 17 parts.

I said she should have used her business judgment. Her supervisor explained that she was one of 300 people who entered information for 54 different companies in 14 industries. Understanding the business was not written into the contract. She had orders to enter what we told her to enter.

I can't dump on the secretary either. Since they installed calendar software, I share my secretary with three kids (two young men and a woman) who don't mind entering their own orders. The secretary ignores me when I asked her to do mine. I bribed her a few times, but she stopped the first time that I screamed at her, as Gunnar would. The other three salespeople like her, so I had to back off.

I am only able to give her hand-written forms when the system is down. The system was down a day and a half after 9/11 and slowed down for 19 minutes during the last northeast power failure. Armstrong is determined not to have to fight Gunnar again. Gunnar is not sympathetic. He still has Marcella and the rest of us to dump his problems on.

Table A.17 - Belvedere Topics-Exhibits, Tables, and Follow-up Contacts	
Topic	**Information Presented**
Sarbanes-Oxley (General)	Fig. 2.1-Daxiao Organizational Structure (Sectors, Teams, and Staffing) Fig. 2.2-BASE view of Daxiao Organizational Hierarchy Table 4-Comparison of Critical Requirements for SOX and SOA Table 5-Daxiao Teams and SOX Responsibility Table A.1.1-Corporate Sector Teams and Roles-Support for COBIT and COSO Table A.1.2-Business Sector Teams and Roles-Support for COBIT and COSO Table A.1.3-Governance (BASE) Sector Teams and Roles-Support for COBIT and COSO Table A.1.4-Technology Sector Teams and Roles-Support for COBIT and COSO Comments: Though we provided a wealth of information there was limited discussion. The assumption is that the subject is well understood, and that we provided the appropriate high-level overview, as we tend to do on this topic. We were encouraged to move quickly to Service-Oriented Architecture, which is less well understood For additional information contact: Hugo Stein
Areas for improvement	Table A.3-Resistance Factors- effectiveness of Mitigation Program Comments: We assume you mean Service-Oriented Architecture. Opportunities for SOX improvement are decreasing quickly All items on the resistance list with effectiveness ratings of 3 or less are being addressed For additional information, contact individuals of your choice on the Managers' contact list.
Business continuity planning	For additional information, contact: 1. Leonard Torres 2. Wayne Wright 3. Hank Yu
Business process evaluation	Table 26-Automating Process Automation-Process Features Table 27- Automating Process Automation-Post-Implementation Review Summary Table A.10-Processes in the Enabling Domain Table A.11-Processes in the Product Delivery Domain Table A.12-Processes in the Support Domain Comments: Topic also discussed under communications, specifically the "Grumble" Process For additional information, contact: 1. Alex Macedon 2. Peter Barca
Business system acquisition	Table A.7.1-BASE Procurement Activities Table A.7.2-Daxiao Procurement Product list For additional information, contact: 1. Lorraine Jasper 2. Rafael Onesti
Business system development[1]	Table 12-The Only Plan (Business Systems Planning, Management, and Communications) Table 15-BASE (Governance) Role Participation In WFSOA Process Categories Table 16.1-Sequence of Role Participation in BASE Work Request and Project Phases Table 16.2-Discussion of Roles, BASE Work Request, and Project Phases

Table A.17 - Belvedere Topics-Exhibits, Tables, and Follow-up Contacts	
	For additional information, contact: 1. Alex Macedon 2. Arnold Maurer 3. Aine O'Hara 4. Olivia Reid 5. Denise Travers
Communications structure	Fig. 9-Side View of WFSOA Emblem with Knowledge Cooperative Data Flows Table 10-Common Terminology Jargon Lists Table 18-Extract of Collaboration Matrix Table A.5-SOA Personal Notes and Glossary Table A.5.1-Dublin Core Tags Comments: Knowledge Cooperative usage statistics to be provided For additional information, contact: 1. Austin Ellison 2. Maja Johanssen 3. Lisse Maçon
Critical success factors	Table 7-SOA Critical Requirements Table 8-WFSOA Objectives and Goals Table A.2-Lessons Learned Table A.3-Resistance Factors- effectiveness of Mitigation Program Comments: Marshall version of the factors delivered. This included elimination of resistance factors, organizational change management, management support, effective marketing of services and ease of information capture For additional information, contact: 1. Hamilton Marshall 2. Dr. Daniel Piccolo 3. Valery Van Amberg
Management structure	Fig. 2.1-Daxiao Organizational Structure (Sectors, Teams, and Staffing) Fig. 2.2-BASE View of Daxiao Organizational Hierarchy Fig. 3.1-Daxiao Layers of Governance Fig. 3.2-SOA Governance Relationships and Functions Fig. 3.3-SOA (BASE) Governance Components Table 1-BASE (Governance) Management Structure Table 2-BASE Teams and Managers Table 3-Daxiao Committees Affecting BASE Comments: Project management discussion limited due to time constraints dictated by examiners For additional information, contact: 1. Hamilton Marshall 2. Dr. Daniel Piccolo
WFSOA Program Methodology	Fig. 8-Emblem for the Well-Formed Service-Oriented Architecture Methodology Fig. 10-Daxiao Process Groupings until 2003 (pre-SOA) Table 9-Daxiao SOA Maturity Self-Evaluation-Belvedere Format Table A.4-WFSOA Methodology: Evolutionary Stages and Process Groups

Table A.17 - Belvedere Topics-Exhibits, Tables, and Follow-up Contacts	
	Comments: Standard exhibits provided. Discussion limited due to time constraints imposed by examination team. Should be revisited For additional information, contact: 1. Alex Macedon 2. Aine O'Hara 3. Hugo Stein 4. Hank Yu
Organizational structure	Fig. 2.1-Daxiao Organizational Structure (Sectors, Teams, and Staffing) Fig. 2.2-BASE View of Daxiao Organizational Hierarchy Fig. 3.1-Daxiao Layers of Governance Fig. 3.2-SOA Governance Relationships and Functions Fig. 3.3-SOA (BASE) Governance Components Table A.16-Daxiao WFSOA-Related Roles and Responsibilities Comments: 1. Detailed structure to be provided by Human Resources 2. Organizational headcount to be provided by Human Resources. Please note that the relationship between headcount and role is not valid outside of BASE For additional information, contact: 1. Dr. Emery-Baldwin 2. Austin Ellison 3. Hamilton Marshall 4. Dr. Daniel Piccolo
Planning processes	Fig. 11-BASE Planning, Roles, and Activities (***Thunk***) Information Relationships Table 12-The Only Plan (Business Systems Planning, Management, and Communications) Table 13-Users of ***Thunk*** Activity List Table A.8-Planning Verbs List Table A.9-***Thunk*** Roles/Activity Information Relationships Table A.20-***Thunk*** FAQs-WFSOA Role/Activity Cross Reference For additional information, contact: 1. Maja Johanssen 2. J. Stanley Johnson 3. Hamilton Marshall 4. Valery Van Amberg
Policies	Table A.3-Resistance Factors- effectiveness of Mitigation Program Table A.2-Lessons Learned For additional information, contact: 1. Lorraine Jasper 2. Hamilton Marshall 3. Daniel Piccolo or Hugo Stein 4. Leonard Torres 5. Valery Van Amberg 6. Wayne Wright
Risk	Comments: To be discussed as part of strategy on Day 2

Table A.17 - Belvedere Topics-Exhibits, Tables, and Follow-up Contacts	
management	For additional information, contact: 1. Vincent Bailey 2. Aaron Forte 3. Hugo Stein
Roles & responsibility [1]	Fig. 11-BASE Planning, Roles, and Activities (*Thunk*) Information Relationships Fig. 12-Architectures and Scopes within Daxiao Fig. 13-Daxiao WFSOA-Related Teams and Roles Fig. 14-Roles within Process Domains and Process Categories Table 14-BASE Teams and Headcount Table 15-BASE (Governance) Role Participation In WFSOA Process Categories Table 16.1-Sequence of Role Participation in BASE Work Request and Project Phases Table 16.2-Discussion of Roles, BASE Work Request, and Project Phases Table A.1.1 Corporate Sector Teams and Roles-Support for COBIT and COSO Table A.1.2-Business Sector Teams and Roles-Support for COBIT and COSO Table A.1.3-Governance (BASE) Sector Teams and Roles-Support for COBIT and COSO Table A.1.4-Technology Sector Teams and Roles-Support for COBIT and COSO Table A.13.1-BASE WFSOA© Roles, Teams, and Sectors Table A.13.2-Alternate and Deprecated Role Names Table A.14.1-Determination of Unique BASE roles Table A.14.2-BASE Clusters of Similar Roles Table A.15.1-BASE Disciplines and Education/Training Options Table A.15.2.1-Mandatory, Recommended, and Optional Disciplines for Role Incumbents (Part 1) Table A.15.2.2-Mandatory, Recommended, and Optional Disciplines for Role Incumbents (Part 2) Table A.16-Daxiao WFSOA-Related Roles and Responsibilities Table A.20-***Thunk*** FAQs-WFSOA Role/Activity Cross Reference Comments: 1. Number of roles deemed excessive. Relationship to role-based access control mentioned 2. Examiner may request long descriptions. Will check with Audit Committee before request is submitted For additional information, contact: Dr. Emery-Baldwin
Security and Information Asset Protection [1]	For additional information, contact: 1. Vincent Bailey 2. Aaron Forte
Standards	Table A.6.1-IETF Standards Tracked in BASE Table A.6.2-ISO Standards Tracked in BASE ISO/IEC standards in BASE Table A.6.3-OASIS Standards Tracked in BASE Table A.6.4-OMG Standards Tracked in BASE Table A.6.5-W3C Standards Tracked in BASE Table A.6.6-Standards Approval Processes For additional information, contact: 1. Hugo Stein 2. Wayne Wright 3. Hank Yu
Strategy	Fig. 4-Before BASE-A Plane with Many Engines Fig. 5-After SOA: BASE Airplane

Table A.17 - Belvedere Topics-Exhibits, Tables, and Follow-up Contacts	
	Fig. 6.1-Business and application alignment Fig. 6.2-Client and operations shift to accommodate market changes Fig. 6.3-Application changes required before SOA Fig. 7.1-Services before market change with SOA Fig. 7.2-Services after market change with SOA Table 25.1-Strategy Options and SOA Risk at Business Maturity Level 1 Table 25.2-Strategy Options and SOA Risk at Business Maturity Level 2 Table 25.3-Strategy Options and SOA Risk at Business Maturity Level 3 Table A.4-WFSOA Methodology: Evolutionary Stages and Process Groups Table A.2-Lessons Learned Table A.3-Resistance Factors- effectiveness of Mitigation Program Table 7-SOA Critical Requirements Table 8-WFSOA Objectives and Goals Comments: 1. Rated at the highest stage of maturity on Belvedere maturity assessment 2. SOA evolutionary strategy discussed 3. Enterprise Integration maturity model and SOA strategy scheduled for later this week 4. For additional information, contact: 1. J. Stanley Johnson 2. Hamilton Marshall 3. Daniel Piccolo
Succession planning	Comments: Valery Van Amberg recommended as transitional manager For additional information, contact: 1. Hamilton Marshall 2. Dr. Daniel Piccolo 3. Valery Van Amberg
Technical infrastructure	Table A.7.1-BASE Procurement Activities Table A.7.2-Daxiao Procurement Product list For additional information, contact: 1. Wayne Wright 2. Hank Yu
Miscellaneous	Send ROI calculation for SME participation. Send information on Daxiao participation in JCP. Send information on Daxiao participation in the OSI.

Table A.18 - Catalog Permissions Summary	
Code	**Discussion, Notes, and Constraints**
A	Role incumbent has reviewed and accepted the entry. This is treated as a comment.
Ab	Role incumbent may serve as **backup** approver in place of a client or sponsor.
Ap	Role incumbent (associated with product ID) must grant approval for promotion to a subsequent catalog. **Note:** Role may **explicitly deny** approval (they must provide explanations and suggest remedial actions).
Ar	Role incumbent must approve reuse. **Pre-approval.** 1. Products that have passed rigorous testing and review by the availability architect may be pre-approved. Pre-approval is encouraged. 2. When an assertion is published against a pre-approved serviced, role incumbent is notified of the intended reuse. **Note:** Role may **explicitly deny** approval (they must provide explanations and suggest remedial actions).
As	1. A risk analyst, requirements analyst, or compliance specialist has identified exceptional risk associated with this product. 2. Role incumbent (associated with product ID) is required to provide **special** approval. Promotion to a subsequent catalog or reuse cannot occur without this approval. **Note:** Role may **explicitly deny** approval (they must provide explanations and suggest remedial actions).
C	1. Role incumbent may create catalog entry for a service, process, service contract, policy, or assertion. 2. Assertions: 1. An assertion indicates intention to consume an entry in one of the catalogs. 2. Matching assertions and policy are promoted with product entries. 3. Policies: This may indicate a security, business, or technology policy. **Constraints:** 1. Software ensures that it is impossible to create a duplicate entry (with the same name or version number) as an entry that exists in any of the other three catalogs. 2. Creation of service or process entries in the build, staging, and production catalogs is discouraged. Entries should have been promoted from the initiation catalog.
Cr	Role incumbent has responsibility for creating the entry in the indicated version of the catalog
M	1. Role incumbent may modify a catalog entry before it is promoted. 2. A rules engine decides which information each role may modify (includes adding or changing links to related artifacts, supporting material, or service users). 3. All modifications are **logged and archived.**
P	Role incumbent may perform one of the three actions indicated below. 1. **Publish**: Make entry available for potential process or service consumers. 2. **Deprecate**: Discourage use by potential consumers. 3. **Unpublish**: Disallow access by potential consumers. **Notes**: 1. Unpublish is not allowed after promotion to a subsequent catalog. 2. Unpublish is not allowed as long as there are active consumers of the service.
Pb	Role incumbent may serve as a **backup** publisher in case the intended publisher is not available.
Pr	Role incumbent is usually responsible for publishing the entry in the indicated version of the catalog. **Notes:** 1. The requirements analyst is responsible for publishing (1) Initiate catalog entries. 2. Developer(s) are responsible for publishing (2) Build catalog entries. 3. The integration specialist is responsible for publishing (3) Stage catalog entries. 4. The deployment specialist is responsible for publishing production (run) catalog entries.
R	Role incumbent may remove an entry long as it has not been promoted to a subsequent catalog. Entries that are removed are saved in the archival catalog.
Rb	Role incumbent may serve as a backup for the SOA librarian in case of an emergency.
Rr	Role incumbent (usually the SOA librarian) is responsible for deleting catalog entries. They have access to all versions of the catalog. Deleted entries are preserved in the archival catalog.

Table A.18 - Catalog Permissions Summary	
Code	**Discussion, Notes, and Constraints**
	Note: All links to users or other catalog entries must be removed first.
R	Role incumbent may remove an entry as long as it has not been promoted to a subsequent catalog.

Table A.19.1 - WFSOA Catalog Access Rights and Responsibilities - Part I										
Role	**(1) Initiation Catalog**					**(2) Build Catalog**				
Architect - availability	C	M	P	As	R	C	M	P	Ap	R
Architect - SOA	C	M	P	As	R	C	M	P	As	R
Architect - software	C	M	-	-	R	C	M	P	-	-
Architect(s) - enterprise, infrastructure, network	C	M	-	As	R	C	M	P	As	-
Asset librarian	C	M	-	-	Rb	C	M		-	Rb
BASE Program coordinator	-	-	-	Ab	-	-	-	-	Ab	-
Business analyst - client team	Cr	M	P	As	R	-	M	-	As	-
Business analyst(s) - BASE, Extranet	Cr	M	P	As	R	C	M	-	As	-
Client(s) - all	-	M	-	Ap	-	-	M	-	Ap	-
Communication specialist - BASE	-	M	-	-	-	-	M	-	-	-
Compliance specialist(s) - business, technology	-	M	-	As	Rb	-	M	-	As	Rb
Corporate lawyer	-	M	-	-	-	-	M	-	-	-
Data administrator	C	M	P	As	R	-	M	P	As	-
Data specialist	C	M	P	As	R	-	M	Pb	As	-
Deployment specialist	-	-	-	-	-	-	-	P	As	-
Developer - application	-	M	-	-	-	-	M	P	-	-
Developer(s) - database, legacy adaptation, process, SOA	C	M	P	-	R	-	M	Pr	-	-
Domain owner(s) - data, service	C	M	P	As	R	-	M	Pb	As	-
Executive(s) - All	-	-	-	Ab	-	-	-	-	Ab	-
Help desk	-	M	-	-	-	-	M	-	-	-
Integration specialist	-	-	-	-	-	C	-	P	-	-
Knowledge Consolidator	C	M	P	Ab	Rb	C	M	P	Ab	Rb
Planning specialist	-	M	-	As	-	-	M	-	As	-
Process coordinator(s) - business, technology	C	M	P	Ap	R	C	M	Pb	Ap	-
Procurement specialist	-	M	-	-	-	-	M	-	-	-
Project initiation manager	-	M	-	Ap	-	-	M	Pb	Ap	-
Project manager(s) - business and infrastructure technology	-	M	-	Ap	-	-	M	Pb	-	-
Project manager - SOA	C	M	P	Ap	R	C	M	Pb	-	-
Quality management coordinator	-	M	-	As	-	-	M	-	Ap	-
Requirements analyst	C	M	Pr	Ap	R	-	M	-	As	-
Research scientist	C	M	P	As	R	C	M	P	As	R
Risk analyst - technology	-	M	-	As	Rb	-	M	-	As	Rb
Security administrator	C	M	P	Ab	R	C	M	P	Ab	R
Security specialist - technology	C	M	P	Ap	R	C	M	P	Ap	R
Service assurance	-	M	-	-	-	-	M	-	Ap	-
SOA librarian	C	M	P	As	Rr	C	M	P	Ap	Rr
SOA technology specialist	C	M	P	As	R	C	M	Pb	-	-

Table A.19.1 - WFSOA Catalog Access Rights and Responsibilities - Part I										
Sponsor(s) - All	-	M	-	Ap	-	-	M	-	Ap	-
Stakeholder(s) - All	-	M	-	As	-	-	M	-	As	-
Team leader	C	M	P	Ab	R	C	M	Pb	-	-
Testing specialist - business	-	M	-	As		-	M	P	As	
Testing specialist - technology	C	M	P	As	R	C	M	P	As	-
Tool administrator	C	M	P	Ab	R	C	M	P	Ab	-
Tool specialist	C	M	P	-	R	C	M	Pr	-	-
Training specialist	-	-	-	-	-	-	-	P	-	-
User Interface specialist	C	M	P	As	R	C	M	Pr	-	-
User support specialist	-	M	-	-	-	-	M	-	-	-
User(s) - All	-	M	-	As	-	-	M	-	As	-
Visionaries - All	C	M	-	Ap	R	-	M	-	Ap	-
Workflow analyst	C	M	P	As	R	C	M	-	-	-
Writer(s) - business and technology (BASE), requirements	C	M	-	-	-	-	M	-	-	-

Table A.19.2 - WFSOA Catalog Access Rights and Responsibilities - Part II										
Role	(3) Stage Catalog					Production (Runtime) Catalog				
Architect - availability	C	M	P	Ap	R	C	M	P	Ar	-
Architect - enterprise technology, infrastructure, network	C	M	P	As	-	C	M	P	As	-
Architect - SOA	C	M	P	As	R	C	M	P	Ar	R
Asset librarian	-	-	-	Ap	Rb	-	-	-	Ar	-
Business analyst(s) - BASE, Extranet	C	M	-	As	-	-	-	-	As	-
Business analyst - client team	-	M	-	As	-	-	-	-	As	-
Client(s) - All	-	M	-	Ap	-	-	-	-	As	-
Communication specialist - BASE	-	M	-	-	-	-	-	-	-	-
Compliance specialist - business and technology	-	M	-	Ap	Rb	-	M	-	As	Rb
Corporate lawyer	-	M	-	-	-	-	M	-	-	-
Data administrator	-	M	P	As	-	-	M	P	Ar	-
Data specialist	-	M	Pb	As	-	-	M	Pb	Ar	-
Deployment specialist	C	M	P	Ap	-	C	M	Pr	-	-
Developer - application	-	M	P	-	-	-	M	-	-	-
Developer(s) - database, legacy adaptation, process, SOA	-	M	P	-	-	-	M	P	-	-
Domain owner - data	-	M	Pb	As	-	-	M	Pb	Ar	-
Domain owner - service	-	M	Pb	As	-	-	M	Pb	Ar	-
Executives - All	-	-	-	Ab	-	-	-	-	Ab	-
Integration specialist	C	M	Pr	-	-	C	M	P	-	-
Knowledge Consolidator	C	M	P	Ab	Rb	C	M	P	Ab	Rb
Planning specialist	-	-	-	As	-	-	-	-	Ar	-
Process coordinator - business	C	M	Pb	Ap	-	-	M	-	Ar	-
Process coordinator - technology	C	M	Pb	AP	-	-	M	Pb	-	-
Project initiation manager	-	M	Pb	Ap	-	-	M	Pb	-	-
Project manager(s) - business and infrastructure technology	-	M	-	-	-	-	M	-	-	-
Project manager - SOA	-	M	-	-	-	-	M	-	-	-
Quality management coordinator	-	M	-	Ap	-	-	M	-	-	-

Table A.19.2 - WFSOA Catalog Access Rights and Responsibilities - Part II										
Role	**(3) Stage Catalog**					**Production (Runtime) Catalog**				
Research scientist	C	M	P	As	R	C	M	P	Ar	R
Requirements analyst [(3)]	-	M	-	As	-	-	M	-	Ar	-
Risk analyst(s) - business, technology	-	M	-	Ap	Rb	-	M	-	Ar	Rb
Security administrator	C	M	P	Ab	R	C	M	P	Ar	Rb
Security specialist - technology	C	M	P	Ap	R	C	M	P	Ar	Rb
Service assurance	-	M	-	Ap	-	-	M	-	-	-
SOA librarian	C	M	P	Ap	Rr	C	M	P	Ar	Rr
BASE Program coordinator	-	-	-	Ab	-	-	-	-	Ab	-
SOA technology specialist	C	M	P	-	-	-	M	P	-	-
Sponsor(s) - All	-	M	-	Ap	-	-	M	-	Ar	-
Stakeholder - business operations	-	M	-	As	-	-	M	-	As	-
Stakeholder(s) - BASE, corporate, manufacturing, sales and marketing, technology	-	M	-	As	-	-	-	-	As	-
Subject matter expert(s) - All	-	M	-	-	-	-	-	-	-	-
Team leader	-	M	Pb	-	-	-	M	P	-	-
Testing specialist - business	-	M	P	A	-	-	M	P	-	-
Testing specialist - technology	C	M	P	A	-	C	M	P	-	-
Tool administrator		M	-	-	-	C	M	-	-	-
Tool specialist	C	M	P	-	-	C	M	P	-	-
Training specialist	-	M	-	-	-	-	M	-	-	-
User(s) - All	-	M	-	Ap	-	-	-	-	-	-
User Interface specialist	-	M	P	-	-	-	M	P	-	-
User support specialist	-	M	-	-	-	-	-	-	-	-
Visionaries - All	-	M	-	Ap	-	-	-	-	As	-
Workflow analyst	-	M	-	-	-	-	-	-	-	-
Writer(s) - business and technology (BASE), corporate, requirements	-	M	-	-	-	-	-	-	-	-

Table A.20 - Thunk FAQs - WFSOA Role/Activity Cross Reference	
Question	**Responses**
What are the acronyms and abbreviations that appear frequently in this extract?	1. KC /= Knowledge Cooperative (Daxiao's centralized information source). 2. ReMain /= Daxiao's work request maintenance system. 3. SOA /= Service-Oriented Architecture. 4. WFSOA /= Well-Formed Service-Oriented Architecture. 5. XML /= eXtensible Markup Language
How would you summarize uses for the *Thunk* extract?	1. It provides a history with at least 70% of the IT activities performed in Goodsand, everything related to COSO and COBIT, 90 - 95% of the business/technology collaborative activities completed since the Daxiao merger. About 3% of the entries originated with Raycroft. 2. For internal users, it provides a moderate level of detail about how we do what we do. It provides links to the details. 3. For external technical user, it provides an excellent summary of how we do what we do. 4. It helps to determine which processes are associated with each role. 5. BASE communications uses it as one of the indexes for the Knowledge Cooperative. 6. Security uses this as input to verify the Access Control List. 7. It helps clients to understand the range of tasks that technology areas must

Table A.20 - Thunk FAQs - WFSOA Role/Activity Cross Reference	
	perform before a project is completed. 8. It shows clients understand what is expected of them. 9. Incumbents can compare their usual activities to what other individuals with the same role have done. 10. Incumbents may use it to get an idea of what they might need to improve their performance. 11. Incumbents may decide whether they wish to exchange roles. 12. Rotation candidates can begin to learn what may be expected of them in new roles. 13. We identify role overlaps and determine when the overlaps may be beneficial for the organization. Reasonable backup is a good thing.
Where does ***Thunk*** content come from?	1. Automated project planning tools. 2. E-mails. 3. Historical planning documents provided by the BASE executive. 4. Manual approval documents. 5. Manually created project plans. 6. Process documentation. 7. Skill assessments. 8. SOX communications. 9. Status reports (for non-planned activities). 10. Training materials. 11. Vendor product installation guides.
Who uses this extract?	Individuals performing than 25 roles (approximately 6,500 people) use the extract frequently. Approximately 39,000 more use it with intermediate or casual frequency.
How can the extracted information be used to assist planning?	The online version of the list can be used to locate all plans that contain either an activity, role, or object (component)
Are all these entries at the same planning level?	No. Some plans are more detailed than others are. Some information did not come from official plans. We use what we find. We believe that reading through the extra line items is less wasteful than omitting a task that may cause project problems.
How is this list used in performance reviews?	Program participants who have started new roles use the list to identify critical few objectives for performance evaluation purposes.
Some of the role names seem unusual. Where did they come from?	Daxiao executives, process coordinators, and architects agree on the role names. The "unusual" names are generally related to expanded scope for additional roles. **Table A**.13.2 maps traditional role names to current WFSOA roles names. **Table A**.16 provides a high-level description of the responsibilities associated with each role.
If a project plan contains an old role name, how is it related to ***Thunk*** activities?	BASE and Human Resources Support maintain business rules tables that support translation from traditional role names to WFSOA role names.
If a project plan contains a non-standard activity verb, how is it related activities allowed in ***Thunk***?	Human Resources Support and BASE communications maintain business rules supporting translation between verbs. An extract of the rules table is presented in **Table A**.8 - List of Planning Verbs.
How many items are in the ***Thunk*** database and how many are in this extract?	Approximately 800,000 as of late 2007 in the full database, and there are approximately 9,000 in this short extract.
How do you achieve almost. 90 - 1 compression?	1. (**New in this version**) If multiple roles with similar functions have reported performing an activity, the role is shown as "Role(s)". See **Table A**.16 for the roles that may be combined in this extract. For example, if both the business writers and technical writers assist with creation of user documentation, the entry in the extracted table will appear as:

<table>
<tr><th colspan="2">Table A.20 - Thunk FAQs - WFSOA Role/Activity Cross Reference</th></tr>
<tr><td></td><td>
<table>
<tr><td>Client(s)</td><td>Review</td><td>Requirements</td></tr>
<tr><td>Risk analyst(s)</td><td>Review</td><td>Feasibility study</td></tr>
<tr><td>Writer(s)</td><td>Assist with</td><td>User documentation</td></tr>
</table>
2. Further compression is achieved by merging related subtasks into one activity. For example, "Enforce" is defined in WFSOA to mean:
♦ Ensure that Program staff understands processes, procedures, and guidelines.
♦ Verify that processes, procedures, and standards are being used.
♦ Reject work that does not conform to processes, procedures, and guidelines.
♦ Define corrective actions.
♦ Where necessary, identify compliance deadlines.
Thus, whenever a role appears with the "Enforce" activity in the condensed table, any or all the related subtasks have an entry in the Roles/Activity/Planning master database. Refer to Table A.8-List of Planning Verbs for the list of actions.
3. Activities for deprecated roles are collapsed under the active role name. For example, all tasks formerly associated a with methodology specialist have been collapsed under process coordinator - technology.
4. If the same combination of Role/Activity/Object has appeared in multiple project plans, it will appear in Thunk only once.
</td></tr>
<tr><td>Some activities appear to be repeated using slightly different verbs or object names. WHY?</td><td>We are still moving toward use of common terminology. These items may have been extracted from historical plans on from manual input where the parser could not identify the common terminology requirement. We try not to discard anything.</td></tr>
<tr><td>Some activities appear to be repeated by different roles. WHY?</td><td>This is one of the major benefits of the Thunk extract. See comment #13 in the second FAQ.</td></tr>
<tr><td>Why would more than one role perform identical activities on an object?</td><td>This is one of the major benefits of the Thunk extract. See comment #13 in the second FAQ.</td></tr>
</table>

INDEX

A

B

C

D

E

F

G

H

I

O

P

Q

R

S

T

U

V

W

X

Z

www.ingramcontent.com/pod-product-compliance
Lightning Source LLC
Chambersburg PA
CBHW082118210326
41599CB00031B/5799

9780615201573